AMERICAN CONSTITUTIONAL LAW: STRUCTURE AND RECONSTRUCTION

CASES, NOTES, AND PROBLEMS

Second Edition

By

Charles A. Shanor
Professor of Law
Emory University

AMERICAN CASEBOOK SERIES®

THOMSON
＊ ™
WEST

Mat #40165338

American Casebook Series and West Group are trademarks registered in the U.S. Patent and Trademark Office.

COPYRIGHT © 2001 By WEST GROUP
© 2003 By West, a Thomson business
      610 Opperman Drive
      P.O. Box 64526
      St. Paul, MN 55164–0526
      1–800–328–9352

ISBN 0–314–14900-7

TEXT IS PRINTED ON 10% POST CONSUMER RECYCLED PAPER

To Susan

*

Whose love and support
Made this book possible

*

Preface

AMERICAN CONSTITUTIONAL LAW: STRUCTURE AND RECONSTRUCTION
(SECOND EDITION)

———————

The first edition of this book began years ago with the arrival of the latest edition of the constitutional law casebook I had been using. Already bloated, it had just become 300 pages worse, but I found no better casebook on the market. So I began assembling my own materials.

Editing and organizing the core cases, I tried not to shred them to snippets, hide them among cites to marginal cases, bury them under references to academic commentators, or order them eccentrically. My priority was to let the Justices speak who authored the opinions, concurrences, and dissents. Terse notes provided context and perspective, and problems encouraged students to apply the cases in sophisticated and innovative ways—much as they would be required to do as lawyers. Finally, I added transitional materials, a couple of longer notes, quotes to open each chapter, and images adding a touch of humor, human interest, or perspective.

The second edition retains the philosophy that animated the first edition. It takes account of major additions to the field and an appendix deals with constitutional issues in the War on Terrorism. The second edition has grown only marginally, however; I have edited some cases a bit more tightly and have deleted materials that have been superseded.

Despite my efforts, some students will complain that the material is difficult. All I can say is that I hope the result—a deeper understanding of and ability to work within the fundamental legal framework of the Constitution of the United States of America—is worth the effort.

I thank Emory Law School for funding research assistants over the years, editions, and supplements. These students include Athanasios Agelakopoulos, Gene Hayes, John Flippen, Chris Fritsch, Alisa Hutoron, Shane Keith, Susan Lin, Dan Lipner, Thomas Mondelli, Steve Paolini, Helen Silver, and Emily Wessman. I appreciate the confidence and suggestions of colleagues, here and elsewhere, who have used this book.

This second edition would not have been possible without the diligent professionalism of Rhonda Heermans, who made the manuscript camera-ready with unfailing good humor. All errors, either of substance or style, are mine alone.

CHARLES A. SHANOR

Atlanta, GA.
October 22, 2003

Summary of Contents

Table of Contents

—————

Table of Cases

The principal cases are in bold type. Cases cited or discussed in the text are roman type. References are to pages. Cases cited in principal cases and within other quoted materials are not included nor are cases included that are referred to without full citation.

The Constitution of the United States

Preamble

We the People of the United States, in Order to form a more perfect Union, establish Justice, insure domestic Tranquility, provide for the common defence, promote the general Welfare, and secure the Blessings of Liberty to ourselves and our Posterity, do ordain and establish this Constitution for the United States of America.

Article I

Section 1. All legislative Powers herein granted shall be vested in a Congress of the United States, which shall consist of a Senate and House of Representatives.

Section 2. [1] The House of Representatives shall be composed of Members chosen every second Year by the People of the several States, and the Electors in each State shall have the Qualifications requisite for Electors of the most numerous Branch of the State Legislature.

[2] No Person shall be a Representative who shall not have attained to the Age of twenty five Years, and been seven Years a Citizen of the United States, and who shall not, when elected, be an Inhabitant of that State in which he shall be chosen.

[3] [Representatives and direct Taxes shall be apportioned among the several States which may be included within this Union, according to their respective Numbers, which shall be determined by adding to the whole Number of free Persons, including those bound to Service for a Term of Years, and excluding Indians not taxed, three fifths of all other Persons.] The actual Enumeration shall be made within three Years after the first Meeting of the Congress of the United States, and within every subsequent Term of ten Years, in such Manner as they shall by Law direct. The Number of Representatives shall not exceed one for every thirty Thousand, but each State shall have at Least one Representative; and until such enumeration shall be made, the State of New Hampshire shall be entitled to chuse three, Massachusetts eight, Rhode Island and Providence Plantations one, Connecticut five, New York six, New Jersey four, Pennsylvania eight, Delaware one, Maryland six, Virginia ten, North Carolina five, South Carolina five, and Georgia three.

> **The clause of this paragraph inclosed in brackets was amended, as to the mode of apportionment of representatives among the several states, by the Fourteenth Amendment, § 2, and as to taxes on incomes without apportionment, by the Sixteenth Amendment.**

[4] When vacancies happen in the Representation from any State, the Executive Authority thereof shall issue Writs of Election to fill such Vacancies.

[5] The House of Representatives shall chuse their Speaker and other Officers; and shall have the sole Power of Impeachment.

Section 3. [1] [The Senate of the United States shall be composed of two Senators from each State, chosen by the Legislature thereof, for six Years; and each Senator shall have one Vote.]

This paragraph and the clause of following paragraph inclosed in brackets were superseded by the Seventeenth Amendment.

[2] Immediately after they shall be assembled in Consequence of the first Election, they shall be divided as equally as may be into three Classes. The Seats of the Senators of the first Class shall be vacated at the Expiration of the Second Year, of the second Class at the Expiration of the fourth Year, and of the third Class at the Expiration of the sixth Year, so that one third may be chosen every second Year; [and if Vacancies happen by Resignation, or otherwise, during the Recess of the Legislature of any State, the Executive thereof may make temporary Appointments until the next Meeting of the Legislature, which shall then fill such Vacancies.]

See note to preceding paragraph.

[3] No Person shall be a Senator who shall not have attained to the Age of thirty Years, and been nine Years a Citizen of the United States, and who shall not, when elected, be an Inhabitant of that State for which he shall be chosen.

[4] The Vice President of the United States shall be President of the Senate, but shall have no Vote, unless they be equally divided.

[5] The Senate shall chuse their other Officers, and also a President pro tempore, in the Absence of the Vice President, or when he shall exercise the Office of President of the United States.

[6] The Senate shall have the sole Power to try all Impeachments. When sitting for that Purpose, they shall be on Oath or Affirmation. When the President of the United States is tried, the Chief Justice shall preside: And no Person shall be convicted without the Concurrence of two thirds of the Members present.

[7] Judgment in Cases of Impeachment shall not extend further than to removal from Office, and disqualification to hold and enjoy any Office of honor, Trust, or Profit under the United States: but the Party convicted shall nevertheless be liable and subject to Indictment, Trial, Judgment, and Punishment, according to Law.

Section 4. [1] The Times, Places and Manner of holding Elections for Senators and Representatives, shall be prescribed in each State by the Legislature thereof; but the Congress may at any time by Law make or alter such Regulations, except as to the Places of chusing Senators.

[2] The Congress shall assemble at least once in every Year, and such Meeting shall be on the first Monday in December, unless they shall by Law appoint a different Day.

Section 5. [1] Each House shall be the Judge of the Elections, Returns, and Qualifications of its own Members, and a Majority of each shall constitute a Quorum to do Business; but a smaller Number may adjourn from day to day, and may be authorized to compel the Attendance of absent Members, in such Manner, and under such Penalties as each House may provide.

[2] Each House may determine the Rules of its Proceedings, punish its Members for disorderly Behaviour, and, with the Concurrence of two thirds, expel a Member.

[3] Each House shall keep a Journal of its Proceedings, and from time to time publish the same, excepting such Parts as may in their Judgment require Secrecy; and the Yeas and Nays of the Members of either House on any question shall, at the Desire of one fifth of those Present, be entered on the Journal.

[4] Neither House, during the Session of Congress, shall, without the Consent of the other, adjourn for more than three days, nor to any other Place than that in which the two Houses shall be sitting.

Section 6. [1] The Senators and Representatives shall receive a Compensation for their Services, to be ascertained by Law, and paid out of the Treasury of the United States. They shall in all Cases, except Treason, Felony and Breach of the Peace, be privileged from Arrest during their Attendance at the Session of their respective Houses, and in going to and returning from the same; and for any Speech or Debate in either House, they shall not be questioned in any other Place.

[2] No Senator or Representative shall, during the Time for which he was elected, be appointed to any civil Office under the Authority of the United States, which shall have been created, or the Emoluments whereof shall have been increased during such time; and no Person holding any Office under the United States, shall be a Member of either House during his Continuance in Office.

Section 7. [1] All Bills for raising Revenue shall originate in the House of Representatives; but the Senate may propose or concur with Amendments as on other Bills.

[2] Every Bill which shall have passed the House of Representatives and the Senate, shall, before it become a Law, be presented to the President of the United States; If he approve he shall sign it, but if not he shall return it, with his Objections to the House in which it shall have originated, who shall enter the Objections at large on their Journal, and proceed to reconsider it. If after such Reconsideration two thirds of that House shall agree to pass the Bill, it shall be sent together with the Objections, to the other House, by which it shall likewise be reconsidered, and if approved by two thirds of that House, it shall become a Law. But in all such Cases the Votes of both Houses shall be determined by Yeas and Nays, and the Names of the Persons voting for and against the Bill shall be entered on the Journal of each House respectively. If any Bill shall not be returned by the President within ten Days (Sundays excepted) after it shall have been presented to him, the Same shall be a Law, in like Manner as if he had signed it, unless the Congress by their Adjournment prevent its Return in which Case it shall not be a Law.

[3] Every Order, Resolution, or Vote, to Which the Concurrence of the Senate and House of Representatives may be necessary (except on a question of Adjournment) shall be presented to the President of the United States; and before the Same shall take Effect, shall be approved by him, or being disapproved by him, shall be repassed by two thirds of the Senate and House of Representatives, according to the Rules and Limitations prescribed in the Case of a Bill.

Section 8. [1] The Congress shall have Power to lay and collect Taxes, Duties, Imposts and Excises, to pay the Debts and provide for the common Defence and general Welfare of the United States; but all Duties, Imposts and Excises shall be uniform throughout the United States;

[2] To borrow money on the credit of the United States;

[3] To regulate Commerce with foreign Nations, and among the several States, and with the Indian Tribes;

[4] To establish an uniform Rule of Naturalization, and uniform Laws on the subject of Bankruptcies throughout the United States;

[5] To coin Money, regulate the Value thereof, and of foreign Coin, and fix the Standard of Weights and Measures;

[6] To provide for the Punishment of counterfeiting the Securities and current Coin of the United States;

[7] To Establish Post Offices and Post Roads;

[8] To promote the Progress of Science and useful Arts, by securing for limited Times to Authors and Inventors the exclusive Right to their respective Writings and Discoveries;

[9] To constitute Tribunals inferior to the supreme Court;

[10] To define and punish Piracies and Felonies committed on the high Seas, and Offenses against the Law of Nations;

[11] To declare War, grant Letters of Marque and Reprisal, and make Rules concerning Captures on Land and Water;

[12] To raise and support Armies, but no Appropriation of Money to that Use shall be for a longer Term than two Years;

[13] To provide and maintain a Navy;

[14] To make Rules for the Government and Regulation of the land and naval Forces;

[15] To provide for calling forth the Militia to execute the Laws of the Union, suppress Insurrections and repel Invasions;

[16] To provide for organizing, arming, and disciplining, the Militia, and for governing such Part of them as may be employed in the Service of the United States, reserving to the States respectively, the Appointment of the Officers, and the Authority of training the Militia according to the discipline prescribed by Congress;

[17]   To exercise exclusive Legislation in all Cases whatsoever, over such District (not exceeding ten Miles square) as may, by Cession of particular States and the Acceptance of Congress, become the Seat of the Government of the United States, and to exercise like Authority over all Places purchased by the Consent of the Legislature of the State in which the Same shall be, for the Erection of Forts, Magazines, Arsenals, dock-Yards, and other needful Buildings;—And

[18]   To make all Laws which shall be necessary and proper for carrying into Execution the foregoing Powers, and all other Powers vested by this Constitution in the Government of the United States, or in any Department or Officer thereof.

Section 9. [1] The Migration or Importation of Such Persons as any of the States now existing shall think proper to admit, shall not be prohibited by the Congress prior to the Year one thousand eight hundred and eight, but a Tax or duty may be imposed on such Importation, not exceeding ten dollars for each Person.

[2]   The privilege of the Writ of Habeas Corpus shall not be suspended, unless when in Cases of Rebellion or Invasion the public Safety may require it.

[3]   No Bill of Attainder or ex post facto Law shall be passed.

[4]   No Capitation, or other direct, Tax shall be laid, unless in Proportion to the Census or Enumeration herein before directed to be taken.

[5]   No Tax or Duty shall be laid on Articles exported from any State.

[6]   No Preference shall be given by any Regulation of Commerce or Revenue to the Ports of one State over those of another: nor shall Vessels bound to, or from, one State be obliged to enter, clear, or pay Duties in another.

[7]   No money shall be drawn from the Treasury, but in Consequence of Appropriations made by Law; and a regular Statement and Account of the Receipts and Expenditures of all public Money shall be published from time to time.

[8]   No Title of Nobility shall be granted by the United States: And no Person holding any Office of Profit or Trust under them, shall, without the Consent of the Congress, accept of any present, Emolument, Office, or Title, of any kind whatever, from any King, Prince, or foreign State.

Section 10. [1] No State shall enter into any Treaty, Alliance, or Confederation; grant Letters of Marque and Reprisal; coin Money; emit Bills of Credit; make any Thing but gold and silver Coin a Tender in Payment of Debts; pass any Bill of Attainder, ex post facto Law, or Law impairing the Obligation of Contracts, or grant any Title of Nobility.

[2]   No State shall, without the Consent of the Congress, lay any Imposts or Duties on Imports or Exports, except what may be absolutely necessary for executing it's inspection Laws: and the net Produce of all Duties and Imposts, laid by any State on Imports or Exports, shall be for the Use of the Treasury of the United States; and all such Laws shall be subject to the Revision and Controul of the Congress.

[3]   No State shall, without the Consent of Congress, lay any Duty of Tonnage, keep Troops, or Ships of War in time of Peace, enter into any Agreement or Compact with another State, or with a foreign Power or engage in War, unless actually invaded, or in such imminent Danger as will not admit of delay.

Article II

Section 1. [1] The executive Power shall be vested in a President of the United States of America. He shall hold his Office during the Term of four Years, and, together with the Vice President, chosen for the same Term, be elected, as follows:

[2]   Each State shall appoint, in such Manner as the Legislature thereof may direct, a Number of Electors, equal to the whole Number of Senators and Representatives to which the State may be entitled in the Congress; but no Senator or Representative, or Person holding an Office of Trust or Profit under the United States, shall be appointed an Elector.

[3]   [The Electors shall meet in their respective States, and vote by Ballot for two Persons, of whom one at least shall not be an Inhabitant of the same State with themselves. And they shall make a List of all the Persons voted for, and of the Number of Votes for each; which List they shall sign and certify, and transmit sealed to the Seat of the Government of the United States, directed to the President of the Senate. The President of the Senate shall, in the Presence of the Senate and House of Representatives, open all the Certificates, and the Votes shall then be counted. The Person having the greatest Number of Votes shall be the President, if such Number be a Majority of the whole Number of Electors appointed; and if there be more than one who have such Majority, and have an equal Number of Votes, then the House of Representatives shall immediately chuse by Ballot one of them for President; and if no Person have a Majority, then from the five highest on the List the said House shall in like Manner chuse the President. But in chusing the President, the Votes shall be taken by States, the Representation from each State having one Vote; A quorum for this Purpose shall consist of a Member or Members from two thirds of the States, and a Majority of all the States shall be necessary to a Choice. In every Case, after the Choice of the President, the Person having the greater Number of Votes of the Electors shall be the Vice President. But if there should remain two or more who have equal Votes, the Senate shall chuse from them by Ballot the Vice President.]

This paragraph, inclosed in brackets, was superseded by the Twelfth Amendment.

[4]   The Congress may determine the Time of chusing the Electors, and the Day on which they shall give their Votes; which Day shall be the same throughout the United States.

[5]   No person except a natural born Citizen, or a Citizen of the United States, at the time of the Adoption of this Constitution, shall be eligible to the Office of President; neither shall any Person be eligible to that Office who shall

not have attained to the Age of thirty five Years, and been fourteen Years a Resident within the United States.

[6] In case of the removal of the President from Office, or of his Death, Resignation or Inability to discharge the Powers and Duties of the said Office, the Same shall devolve on the Vice President and the Congress may by Law provide for the Case of Removal, Death, Resignation or Inability, both of the President and Vice President, declaring what Officer shall then act as President, and such Officer shall act accordingly, until the Disability be removed, or a President shall be elected.

[7] The President shall, at stated Times, receive for his Services, a Compensation, which shall neither be increased nor diminished during the Period for which he shall have been elected, and he shall not receive within that Period any other Emolument from the United States, or any of them.

[8] Before he enter on the Execution of his Office, he shall take the following Oath or Affirmation: "I do solemnly swear (or affirm) that I will faithfully execute the Office of President of the United States, and will to the best of my Ability, preserve, protect and defend the Constitution of the United States."

Section 2. [1] The President shall be Commander in Chief of the Army and Navy of the United States, and of the militia of the several States, when called into the actual Service of the United States; he may require the Opinion, in writing, of the principal Officer in each of the Executive Departments, upon any Subject relating to the Duties of their respective Offices and he shall have Power to grant Reprieves and Pardons for Offenses against the United States, except in Cases of Impeachment.

[2] He shall have Power, by and with the Advice and Consent of the Senate, to make Treaties, provided two thirds of the Senators present concur; and he shall nominate, and by and with the Advice and Consent of the Senate, shall appoint Ambassadors, other public Ministers and Consuls, Judges of the supreme Court, and all other Officers of the United States, whose Appointments are not herein otherwise provided for, and which shall be established by Law; but the Congress may by Law vest the Appointment of such inferior Officers, as they think proper, in the President alone, in the Courts of Law, or in the Heads of Departments.

[3] The President shall have Power to fill up all Vacancies that may happen during the Recess of the Senate, by granting Commissions which shall expire at the End of their next Session.

Section 3. He shall from time to time give to the Congress Information of the State of the Union, and recommend to their Consideration such Measures as he shall judge necessary and expedient; he may, on extraordinary Occasions, convene both Houses, or either of them, and in Case of Disagreement between them, with Respect to the Time of Adjournment, he may adjourn them to such Time as he shall think proper; he shall receive Ambassadors and other public Ministers; he shall take Care that the Laws be faithfully executed, and shall Commission all the Officers of the United States.

Section 4. The President, Vice President and all civil Officers of the United States, shall be removed from Office on Impeachment for, and Conviction of, Treason, Bribery, or other high Crimes and Misdemeanors.

Article III

Section 1. The judicial Power of the United States, shall be vested in one supreme Court, and in such inferior Courts as the Congress may from time to time ordain and establish. The Judges, both of the supreme and inferior Courts, shall hold their Offices during good Behaviour, and shall, at stated Times, receive for their Services a Compensation, which shall not be diminished during their Continuance in Office.

Section 2. [1] The judicial Power shall extend to all Cases, in Law and Equity, arising under this Constitution, the Laws of the United States, and Treaties made, or which shall be made, under their Authority;—to all Cases affecting Ambassadors, other public Ministers and Consuls;—to all Cases of admiralty and maritime Jurisdiction;—to Controversies to which the United States shall be a Party;—to Controversies between two or more States;—between a State and Citizens of another State;—between Citizens of different States;—between Citizens of the same State claiming Lands under the Grants of different States, and between a State, or the Citizens thereof, and foreign States, Citizens or Subjects.

[2] In all Cases affecting Ambassadors, other public Ministers and Consuls, and those in which a State shall be a Party, the supreme Court shall have original Jurisdiction. In all the other Cases before mentioned, the supreme Court shall have appellate Jurisdiction, both as to Law and Fact, with such Exceptions, and under such Regulations as the Congress shall make.

[3] The trial of all Crimes, except in Cases of Impeachment, shall be by Jury; and such Trial shall be held in the State where the said Crimes shall have been committed; but when not committed within any State, the Trial shall be at such Place or Places as the Congress may by Law have directed.

Section 3. [1] Treason against the United States, shall consist only in levying War against them, or, in adhering to their Enemies, giving them Aid and Comfort. No Person shall be convicted of Treason unless on the Testimony of two Witnesses to the same overt Act, or on Confession in open Court.

[2] The Congress shall have Power to declare the Punishment of Treason, but no Attainder of Treason shall work Corruption of Blood, or Forfeiture except during the Life of the Person attainted.

Article IV

Section 1. Full Faith and Credit shall be given in each State to the public Acts, Records, and judicial Proceedings of every other State. And the Congress may by general Laws prescribe the Manner in which such Acts, Records and Proceedings shall be proved, and the Effect thereof.

Section 2. [1] The Citizens of each State shall be entitled to all Privileges and Immunities of Citizens in the several States.

[2] A Person charged in any State with Treason, Felony, or other Crime, who shall flee from Justice, and be found in another State, shall on demand of the executive Authority of the State from which he fled, be delivered up, to be removed to the State having Jurisdiction of the Crime.

[3] No Person held to Service or Labour in one State, under the Laws thereof, escaping into another, shall, in Consequence of any Law or Regulation therein, be discharged from such Service or Labour, but shall be delivered up on Claim of the Party to whom such Service or Labour may be due.

Section 3. [1] New States may be admitted by the Congress into this Union; but no new State shall be formed or erected within the Jurisdiction of any other State; nor any State be formed by the Junction of two or more States, or Parts of States, without the Consent of the Legislatures of the States concerned as well as of the Congress.

[2] The Congress shall have Power to dispose of and make all needful Rules and Regulations respecting the Territory or other Property belonging to the United States; and nothing in this Constitution shall be so construed as to Prejudice any Claims of the United States, or of any particular State.

Section 4. The United States shall guarantee to every State in this Union a Republican Form of Government, and shall protect each of them against Invasion; and on Application of the Legislature, or of the Executive (when the Legislature cannot be convened) against domestic Violence.

Article V

The Congress, whenever two thirds of both Houses shall deem it necessary, shall propose Amendments to this Constitution, or, on the Application of the Legislatures of two thirds of the several States, shall call a Convention for proposing Amendments, which, in either Case, shall be valid to all Intents and Purposes, as part of this Constitution, when ratified by the Legislatures of three fourths of the several States, or by Conventions in three fourths thereof, as the one or the other Mode of Ratification may be proposed by the Congress; Provided that no Amendment which may be made prior to the Year One thousand eight hundred and eight shall in any Manner affect the first and fourth Clauses in the Ninth Section of the first Article; and that no State, without its Consent, shall be deprived of its equal Suffrage in the Senate.

Article VI

[1] All Debts contracted and Engagements entered into, before the Adoption of this Constitution, shall be as valid against the United States under this Constitution, as under the Confederation.

[2] This Constitution, and the Laws of the United States which shall be made in Pursuance thereof; and all Treaties made, or which shall be made, under the Authority of the United States, shall be the supreme Law of the Land; and the Judges in every State shall be bound thereby, any Thing in the Constitution or Laws of any State to the Contrary notwithstanding.

[3]   The Senators and Representatives before mentioned, and the Members of the several State Legislatures, and all executive and judicial Officers, both of the United States and of the several States, shall be bound by Oath or Affirmation, to support this Constitution; but no religious Test shall ever be required as a Qualification to any Office or public Trust under the United States.

Article VII

The Ratification of the Conventions of nine States shall be sufficient for the Establishment of this Constitution between the States so ratifying the Same.

DONE in Convention by the Unanimous Consent of the States present the Seventeenth Day of September in the Year of Our Lord one thousand seven hundred and Eighty seven and of the Independence of the United States of America the Twelfth. IN WITNESS whereof We have hereunto subscribed our Names,

Go. WASHINGTON—
Presidt.
and deputy from Virginia

[Signatures of Delegates Omitted]

Amendment I [1791]

Congress shall make no law respecting an establishment of religion, or prohibiting the free exercise thereof; or abridging the freedom of speech, or of the press; or the right of the people peaceably to assemble, and to petition the Government for a redress of grievances.

Amendment II [1791]

A well regulated Militia, being necessary to the security of a free State, the right of the people to keep and bear Arms, shall not be infringed.

Amendment III [1791]

No Soldier shall, in time of peace be quartered in any house, without the consent of the Owner, nor in time of war, but in a manner to be prescribed by law.

Amendment IV [1791]

The right of the people to be secure in their persons, houses, papers, and effects, against unreasonable searches and seizures, shall not be violated, and no Warrants shall issue, but upon probable cause, supported by Oath or affirmation, and particularly describing the place to be searched, and the persons or things to be seized.

Amendment V [1791]

No person shall be held to answer for a capital, or otherwise infamous crime, unless on a presentment or indictment of a Grand Jury, except in cases arising in the land or naval forces, or in the Militia, when in actual service in time of War or public danger; nor shall any person be subject for the same offence to be twice put in jeopardy of life or limb; nor shall be compelled in any criminal case to be a witness against himself, nor be deprived of life, liberty, or property, without due process of law; nor shall private property be taken for public use, without just compensation.

Amendment VI [1791]

In all criminal prosecutions, the accused shall enjoy the right to a speedy and public trial, by an impartial jury of the State and district wherein the crime shall have been committed, which district shall have been previously ascertained by law, and to be informed of the nature and cause of the accusation; to be confronted with the witnesses against him; to have compulsory process for obtaining witnesses in his favor, and to have the Assistance of Counsel for his defence.

Amendment VII [1791]

In Suits at common law, where the value in controversy shall exceed twenty dollars, the right of trial by jury shall be preserved, and no fact tried by jury, shall be otherwise re-examined in any Court of the United States, than according to the rules of the common law.

Amendment VIII [1791]

Excessive bail shall not be required, nor excessive fines imposed, nor cruel and unusual punishments inflicted.

Amendment IX [1791]

The enumeration in the Constitution, of certain rights, shall not be construed to deny or disparage others retained by the people.

Amendment X [1791]

The powers not delegated to the United States by the Constitution, nor prohibited by it to the States, are reserved to the States respectively, or to the people.

Amendment XI [1798]

The Judicial power of the United States shall not be construed to extend to any suit in law or equity, commenced or prosecuted against one of the United States by Citizens of another State, or by Citizens or Subjects of any Foreign State.

Amendment XII [1804]

The Electors shall meet in their respective states and vote by ballot for President and Vice-President, one of whom, at least, shall not be an inhabitant of the same state with themselves; they shall name in their ballots the person voted for as President, and in distinct ballots the person voted for as Vice-President, and they shall make distinct lists of all persons voted for as President, and of all persons voted for as Vice-President, and of the number of votes for each, which lists they shall sign and certify, and transmit sealed to the seat of the government of the United States, directed to the President of the Senate;—The President of the Senate shall, in the presence of the Senate and House of Representatives, open all the certificates and the votes shall then be counted;—The person having the greatest number of votes for President, shall be the President, if such number be a majority of the whole number of Electors appointed; and if no person have such majority, then from the persons having the highest numbers not exceeding three on the list of those voted for as President, the House of Representatives shall choose immediately, by ballot, the President. But in choosing the President, the votes shall be taken by states, the representation from each state having one vote; a quorum for this purpose shall consist of a member or members from two-thirds of the states, and a majority of all the states shall be necessary to a choice. And if the House of Representatives shall not choose a President whenever the right of choice shall devolve upon them before the fourth day of March next following, then the Vice-President shall act as President, as in the case of the death or other constitutional disability of the President.—The person having the greatest number of votes as Vice-President, shall be the Vice-President, if such number be a majority of the whole number of Electors appointed, and if no person have a majority, then from the two highest numbers on the list, the Senate shall choose the Vice-President; a quorum for the purpose shall consist of two-thirds of the whole number of Senators, and a majority of the whole number shall be necessary to a choice. But no person constitutionally ineligible to the office of President shall be eligible to that of Vice-President of the United States.

Amendment XIII [1865]

Section 1. Neither slavery nor involuntary servitude, except as a punishment for crime whereof the party shall have been duly convicted, shall exist within the United States, or any place subject to their jurisdiction.

Section 2. Congress shall have power to enforce this article by appropriate legislation.

Amendment XIV [1868]

Section 1. All persons born or naturalized in the United States, and subject to the jurisdiction thereof, are citizens of the United States and of the State wherein they reside. No State shall make or enforce any law which shall abridge the privileges or immunities of citizens of the United States; nor shall any State deprive any person of life, liberty, or property, without due process of

Amendment XVII [1913]

[1]   The Senate of the United States shall be composed of two Senators from each State, elected by the people thereof, for six years; and each Senator shall have one vote. The electors in each State shall have the qualifications requisite for electors of the most numerous branch of the State legislatures.

[2]   When vacancies happen in the representation of any State in the Senate, the executive authority of such State shall issue writs of election to fill such vacancies: *Provided, that the legislature of any State may empower the executive thereof to make temporary appointments until the people fill the vacancies by election as the legislature may direct.*

[3]   This amendment shall not be so construed as to affect the election or term of any Senator chosen before it becomes valid as part of the Constitution.

Amendment XVIII [1919]

Section 1.   After one year from the ratification of this article the manufacture, sale, or transportation of intoxicating liquors within, the importation thereof into, or the exportation thereof from the United States and all territory subject to the jurisdiction thereof for beverage purposes is hereby prohibited.

Section 2.   The Congress and the several States shall have concurrent power to enforce this article by appropriate legislation.

Section 3.   This article shall be inoperative unless it shall have been ratified as an amendment to the Constitution by the legislatures of the several States, as provided in the Constitution, within seven years from the date of the submission hereof to the States by the Congress.

Amendment XIX [1920]

[1]   The right of citizens of the United States to vote shall not be denied or abridged by the United States or by any State on account of sex.

[2]   Congress shall have power to enforce this article by appropriate legislation.

Amendment XX [1933]

Section 1.   The terms of the President and Vice President shall end at noon on the 20th day of January, and the terms of Senators and Representatives at noon on the 3d day of January, of the years in which such terms would have ended if this article had not been ratified; and the terms of their successors shall then begin.

Section 2.   The Congress shall assemble at least once in every year, and such meeting shall begin at noon on the 3d day of January, unless they shall by law appoint a different day.

Section 3.   If, at the time fixed for the beginning of the term of the President, the President elect shall have died, the Vice President elect shall become President.   If the President shall not have been chosen before the time law; nor deny to any person within its jurisdiction the equal protection of the laws.

Section 2. Representatives shall be apportioned among the several States according to their respective numbers, counting the whole number of persons in each State, excluding Indians not taxed. But when the right to vote at any election for the choice of electors for President and Vice President of the United States, Representatives in Congress, the Executive and Judicial officers of a State, or the members of the Legislature thereof, is denied to any of the male inhabitants of such State, being twenty-one years of age, and citizens of the United States, or in any way abridged, except for participation in rebellion, or other crime, the basis of representation therein shall be reduced in the proportion which the number of such male citizens shall bear to the whole number of male citizens twenty-one years of age in such State.

Section 3. No person shall be a Senator or Representative in Congress, or elector of President and Vice President, or hold any office, civil or military, under the United States, or under any State, who having previously taken an oath, as a member of Congress, or as an officer of the United States, or as a member of any State legislature, or as an executive or judicial officer of any State, to support the Constitution of the United States, shall have engaged in insurrection or rebellion against the same, or given aid or comfort to the enemies thereof. But Congress may by a vote of two-thirds of each House, remove such disability.

Section 4. The validity of the public debt of the United States, authorized by law, including debts incurred for payment of pensions and bounties for services in suppressing insurrection or rebellion, shall not be questioned. But neither the United States nor any State shall assume or pay any debt or obligation incurred in aid of insurrection or rebellion against the United States, or any claim for the loss or emancipation of any slave; but all such debts, obligations and claims shall be held illegal and void.

Section 5. The Congress shall have power to enforce, by appropriate legislation, the provisions of this article.

Amendment XV [1870]

Section 1. The right of citizens of the United States to vote shall not be denied or abridged by the United States or by any State on account of race, color, or previous condition of servitude.

Section 2. The Congress shall have power to enforce this article by appropriate legislation.

Amendment XVI [1913]

The Congress shall have power to lay and collect taxes on incomes, from whatever source derived, without apportionment among the several States, and without regard to any census or enumeration.

fixed for the beginning of his term, or if the President elect shall have failed to qualify, then the Vice President elect shall act as President until a President shall have qualified; and the Congress may by law provide for the case wherein neither a President elect nor a Vice President elect shall have qualified, declaring who shall then act as President, or the manner in which one who is to act shall be selected, and such person shall act accordingly until a President or Vice President shall have qualified.

Section 4. The Congress may by law provide for the case of the death of any of the persons from whom the House of Representatives may choose a President whenever the right of choice shall have devolved upon them, and for the case of the death of any of the persons from whom the Senate may choose a Vice President whenever the right of choice shall have devolved upon them.

Section 5. Sections 1 and 2 shall take effect on the 15th day of October following the ratification of this article.

Section 6. This article shall be inoperative unless it shall have been ratified as an amendment to the Constitution by the legislatures of three-fourths of the several States within seven years from the date of its submission.

Amendment XXI [1933]

Section 1. The eighteenth article of amendment to the Constitution of the United States is hereby repealed.

Section 2. The transportation or importation into any State, Territory, or possession of the United States for delivery or use therein of intoxicating liquors, in violation of the laws thereof, is hereby prohibited.

Section 3. This article shall be inoperative unless it shall have been ratified as an amendment to the Constitution by conventions in the several States, as provided in the Constitution, within seven years from the date of the submission hereof to the States by the Congress.

Amendment XXII [1951]

Section 1. No person shall be elected to the office of the President more than twice, and no person who has held the office of President, or acted as President, for more than two years of a term to which some other person was elected President shall be elected to the office of President more than once. But this Article shall not apply to any person holding the office of President when this Article was proposed by the Congress, and shall not prevent any person who may be holding the office of President, or acting as President, during the term within which this Article becomes operative from holding the office of President or acting as President during the remainder of such term.

Section 2. This article shall be inoperative unless it shall have been ratified as an amendment to the Constitution by the legislatures of three-fourths of the several States within seven years from the date of its submission to the States by the Congress.

Amendment XXIII [1961]

Section 1. The District constituting the seat of Government of the United States shall appoint in such manner as the Congress may direct:

A number of electors of President and Vice President equal to the whole number of Senators and Representatives in Congress to which the District would be entitled if it were a State, but in no event more than the least populous state; they shall be in addition to those appointed by the states, but they shall be considered, for the purposes of the election of President and Vice President, to be electors appointed by a state; and they shall meet in the District and perform such duties as provided by the twelfth article of amendment.

Section 2. The Congress shall have power to enforce this article by appropriate legislation.

Amendment XXIV [1964]

Section 1. The right of citizens of the United States to vote in any primary or other election for President or Vice President, for electors for President or Vice President, or for Senator or Representative in Congress, shall not be denied or abridged by the United States or any State by reason of failure to pay any poll tax or other tax.

Section 2. The Congress shall have power to enforce this article by appropriate legislation.

Amendment XXV [1967]

Section 1. In the case of the removal of the President from office or of his death or resignation, the Vice President shall become President.

Section 2. Whenever there is a vacancy in the office of the Vice President, the President shall nominate a Vice President who shall take office upon confirmation by a majority vote of both Houses of Congress.

Section 3. Whenever the President transmits to the President pro tempore of the Senate and the Speaker of the House of Representatives his written declaration that he is unable to discharge the powers and duties of his office, and until he transmits to them a written declaration to the contrary, such powers and duties shall be discharged by the Vice President as Acting President.

Section 4. Whenever the Vice President and a majority of either the principal officers of the executive departments or of such other body as Congress may by law provide, transmit to the President pro tempore of the Senate and the Speaker of the House of Representatives, their written declaration that the President is unable to discharge the powers and duties of his office, the Vice President shall immediately assume the powers and duties of the office as Acting President.

Thereafter, when the President transmits to the President pro tempore of the Senate and the Speaker of the House of Representatives his written declaration that no inability exists, he shall resume the powers and duties of his office unless the Vice President and a majority of either the principal officers of the executive department or of such other body as Congress may by law provide, transmit within four days to the President pro tempore of the Senate and the Speaker of the House of Representatives their written declaration that the President is unable to discharge the powers and duties of his office. Thereupon Congress shall decide the issue, assembling within forty-eight hours for that purpose if not in session. If the Congress, within twenty-one days after receipt of the latter written declaration, or, if Congress is not in session, within twenty-one days after Congress is required to assemble, determines by two-thirds vote of both Houses that the President is unable to discharge the powers and duties of his office, the Vice President shall continue to discharge the same as Acting President; otherwise, the President shall resume the powers and duties of his office.

Amendment XXVI [1971]

Section 1. The right of citizens of the United States, who are eighteen years of age or older, to vote shall not be denied or abridged by the United States or by any State on account of age.

Section 2. The Congress shall have power to enforce this article by appropriate legislation.

Amendment XXVII [1992]

No law, varying the compensation for the services of the Senators and Representatives, shall take effect, until an election of Representatives shall have intervened.

*

AMERICAN CONSTITUTIONAL LAW: STRUCTURE AND RECONSTRUCTION

CASES, NOTES, AND PROBLEMS

Second Edition

I

INTRODUCTION

A. A BRIEF OUTLINE OF THE CONSTITUTION'S TEXT

JUSTICE FELIX FRANKFURTER once advised a law clerk for JUSTICE HUGO BLACK that "The problem with your judge is that he thinks you can understand the Constitution by reading it." NOT reading the Constitution, however, is even worse.

Supporters of political positions and citizens who believe they have been treated unfairly frequently support their positions with references to the Constitution. If they oppose a governmental action, saying it is "unconstitutional" appears to add weight and legitimacy to their arguments. Refutations arguing that challenged actions are "constitutional" may neutralize such claims and deflect attention from the action's lack of wisdom. Often, neither side's claims are checked against the document itself, despite its brevity.

READ the Constitution. While it is not a particularly exciting exercise, the text will provide you with a critical starting point for making constitutional arguments.

The Constitution is divided into Articles, sections, and clauses. You might outline the Constitution's articles and sections as follows:

Preamble: General Purposes of the Constitution

Article I: Congress

§ 1: Vests legislative powers in the Senate and House.

§ 2: House of Representatives: members chosen every two years; prescribes qualifications for members; requires census for apportionment; gives House power to initiate Impeachments.

§ 3: Senate: members have six year terms; prescribes qualifications; Senate gets power to try Impeachments.

§ 4: Provides for Senate and House elections.

§ 5: Notes independence of each house's rules, requires journals by each.

§ 6: Members and Senators paid by US Treasury; receive certain privileges; can hold no other office.

§ 7: Bills passed by Congress go to President; Congress overrides veto by 2/3 vote.

§ 8: Enumerates Congress' powers: tax, spend, regulate commerce, coin money, create inferior federal courts, declare war, etc.; make "Necessary & Proper" laws to carry out these powers.

§ 9: Restricts powers of Congress: no ex post facto laws or bills of attainder, certain taxes barred, no titles of nobility.

§ 10: Restricts state powers: can't make treaties, coin money, tax exports (unless necessary for inspection laws), keep troops, or engage in war.

Article II: President

§ 1: Establishes President and Vice President, length of terms, electors and election, and qualifications; provides for removal, compensation, and oath of office.

§ 2: President's powers: be Commander-in-Chief, grant pardons, make treaties, appoint officers, fill Senate vacancies.

§ 3: President's duties: State of the Union Address, convene Congress, receive Ambassadors, commission officers; "take Care that the Laws be faithfully executed."

§ 4: Sets impeachment standard.

Article III: Judiciary

§ 1: Vests the judicial power of the US in Supreme Court and inferior courts Congress creates; hold office during good behavior.

§ 2: Establishes jurisdiction of the Federal Courts, cases in which the Supreme Court has original and appellate jurisdiction, and provides jury trials for crimes.

§ 3: Establishes the crime of and punishment for treason.

Article IV: State Relations

§ 1: Provides for Full Faith & Credit among states.

§ 2: Confers Privileges & Immunities among state citizens, provides for extradition and fugitive slaves.

§ 3: Sets rules for addition of new states and grants power for governing territories.

§ 4: US guarantees states "a Republican Form of Government" and protects them from invasion.

Article V: Amendments to the Constitution: sets procedures for amending the Constitution.

Article VI: Constitution's Effects

§ 1: Pre-existing debts are good against the US.

§ 2: Supremacy of the Constitution, laws "made in pursuance thereof," and treaties.

§ 3: Government officials bound by oath to support the Constitution; no religious test for office.

Article VII: Ratification of the Constitution: sets rule for ratification by states.

The Amendments

There are 27 Amendments to the Constitution. The first ten, the Bill of Rights, were adopted in 1791, shortly after the Constitution was ratified; several important Amendments (13, 14, and 15) were adopted following the Civil War; the latest Amendment was ratified in 1992.

The text does not answer many questions neatly. Some items that seem clear may in fact be less so upon reflection. For example, the Constitution requires that the President be at least 35 years old. Is the relevant date the nomination, the election, or the swearing-in? If the President dies and the Vice President is not 35 at the time of the President's death, can the Vice President assume office? If not the Vice President, who? Do the 12th and 25th Amendments answer these questions?

The Constitution also contains a number of provisions that, even on cursory consideration, are ambiguous. Most of this course is devoted to such provisions, including the provisions of the original Constitution that allocate powers to the legislative, executive, and judicial branches of government, those that coordinate Federal and State governmental powers, and those that require "due process of law" and "equal protection of the laws."

Preliminary Exercises

1. **Ambiguity.** Find examples in the Constitution of (a) maddeningly vague language, (b) modifiers like "exclusive" which may imply non-exclusivity elsewhere, and (c) different uses of the same word or phrase in different parts of the document. What benefits and disadvantages do you see to such ambiguities in the Constitution?

2. **Basic Political Science.** Where in the document do you find "checks and balances," "separation of powers," "federalism," and "individual rights," terms that are widely used in discussions of the Constitution? What do these terms mean to you, based on your reading of the document and your college political science background (if any)?

3. **Democracy.** The United States is often referred to as a democracy. Does the Constitution support this popular view?

4. **Political Hot–Button Issues.** How does the Constitution deal with military issues? Slavery and other racial issues? Crime and punishment?

B. A BRIEF HISTORY OF THE CONSTITUTION
AND ITS INTERPRETATION

I–1. "The Signing of the Constitution" by Thomas P. Rossiter. Independence National Historical Park.

The Declaration of Independence identified a number of ideals the American colonists believed to be "self-evident" and listed a number of specific grievances against England and King George III.   The first agreement uniting the states, the 1777 Articles of Confederation, provided for a Congress having various powers, including the authority to conduct foreign affairs. READ the Articles of Confederation, reproduced as Appendix A at the end of this book.

Independence was achieved following a war led by General George Washington, whose personal begging, borrowing, and pleading held the colonies together during military hostilities. Following the end of the war in 1781, the states reverted to semiautonomous status: trade barriers were erected among them, and local uprisings (like Shay's Rebellion) disrupted public order. Many decried the demise of the "civic virtue" which had carried the colonies through the war; others concluded that structural changes were needed in the framework of the central government if the states were to progress economically and attain prominence among the nations of the world.

In the summer of 1787, a "Constitutional Convention" comprised of delegates from each state met in Philadelphia to discuss how to reform the Articles of Confederation.   George Washington chaired the Convention. James Madison played a formative role and took extensive notes. Though chartered to reform the Articles, the Convention proposed an entirely new constitutional structure.   Indeed, the work of the Convention and the subsequent ratification of the Constitution might be called "unconfederational."

Much debate at the Convention centered on how much to strengthen the central government relative to the state governments. Creation of a bicameral legislature was the "Great Compromise" of the Convention; each state would be represented equally in the Senate (pleasing the small states), while state population would determine representation in the House (pleasing the large states).

Because of concerns about how Congress' legislative power would be wielded, Article I was drafted to give specific limited powers to Congress and to preclude Congress from doing certain things that the English Parliament had done. Article I also imposed some limits on state power. Debate about executive power focused more on whether to have a unitary or divided executive branch, rather than on the exact powers of the presidency. The result was Article II, granting "all executive power" to a President designated "Commander-in-Chief" and directed to "take care" to enforce the law. The creation of a Supreme Court was discussed in technical terms; attention focused upon what "Cases and Controversies" could be heard by that court and by "such inferior courts as the Congress may from time to time ordain and establish." Though delegates at the Convention disagreed vehemently about slavery, the word was not mentioned in the Constitution. Several provisions elliptically alluded to this southern institution, but the tensions between the North and the South over slavery were left unresolved.

The Constitution of the United States was submitted to the states for ratification on September 17, 1787. During the following months, it was hotly debated within the individual states. Supporters of the Constitution were called Federalists; opponents were called Antifederalists. The arguments of Federalists Madison, Hamilton, and Jay, explaining the Constitution and urging its adoption, originally appeared in newspaper articles that were later collected as The Federalist Papers. Although produced for advocacy rather than pure description, The Federalist Papers remain a frequently-used source of information for discerning the "original intent" of the Constitution's framers.

One of the most serious criticisms made of the Constitution by the Antifederalists was the absence of a bill of rights, for most state constitutions at that time guaranteed citizens certain rights and freedoms. The Constitution received the last required state ratification in mid–1788, but was not put into operation until early 1789. Two large states, New York and Massachusetts, ratified the Constitution, but called for adoption of a bill of rights in their ratification resolutions. Rhode Island ratified the Constitution in 1790 only after being threatened by the other states with isolation and trade sanctions.

George Washington was inaugurated as the first President of the United States on April 30, 1789. John Jay became the first Chief Justice of the United States Supreme Court (1789–95). The First Congress passed legislation establishing the new government, including the Judiciary Act of 1789.

James Madison introduced a Bill of Rights in Congress on June 8, 1789, as a series of amendments to the Constitution. READ excerpts of his speech introducing the Bill of Rights, reproduced as Appendix B. These twelve amendments, with some modifications, were adopted by Congress and sent to the states for ratification under one of the procedures set up in Article V (passage by 2/3 of each house of Congress and ratification by 3/4 of the state legislatures). Ten of these twelve provisions received the necessary ratifications in 1791.[1] In general, the Bill of Rights limited the national government's power.[2]

After adoption of the Bill of Rights, the text of the Constitution remained virtually unchanged until after the Civil War.[3] The functioning Constitution did change, however, mainly as a result of active interpretation by the Supreme Court.[4] Under CHIEF JUSTICE JOHN MARSHALL's leadership from 1801 to 1835, the Supreme Court established its authority to invalidate federal laws as unconstitutional and to review state law for conformity to federal law. *See Marbury v. Madison* (p. 17) and *Martin v. Hunter's Lessee* (p. 31). Additionally, the Marshall Court rendered several decisions that expansively interpreted the powers of Congress. *See McCulloch v. Maryland* (p. 211) and *Gibbons v. Ogden* (p. 225). Finally, the Marshall Court limited the powers of the states, primarily by using the contracts clause of Article I, § 10 to invalidate state infringements on contractual expectations, rather than by applying the Bill of Rights to the States. *Barron v. Mayor and City Council of Baltimore*, 32 U.S. (7 Pet.) 243 (1833). CHIEF JUSTICE MARSHALL greatly enhanced the stature of the Supreme Court, writing over 1,000 opinions himself, most of them for a unanimous Court.

From 1836 to 1864, the Court was led by CHIEF JUSTICE ROGER TANEY. The Taney Court did not reverse the precedents of the Marshall Court, but it did emphasize states' rights and limits on national powers in cases the Marshall Court might have decided differently. More importantly, the Taney Court became known for the worst decision in the history of the Supreme Court. In *Dred Scott v. Sandford* (p. 472), the Court held that a slave was not a "citizen" entitled to invoke judicial processes, and that a federal statute compromising slavery matters (the Missouri Compromise) was unconstitutional. Rather than "settling" the slavery issue, as Taney had planned, the decision inflamed the abolitionists, removed the issue of slavery from processes of political compromise, and helped precipitate the Civil War.

Following the Civil War, three new amendments were added to the Constitution. These amendments abolished slavery, established citizenship rights for the former slaves, required the states to provide certain privileges and immunities, equal protection of the laws, and due process of law, granted

---

[1] An eleventh, prohibiting certain congressional pay raises, was ratified nearly 200 years later as the Twenty–Seventh Amendment.

[2] Most of the Bill of Rights provisions have been applied to the states as requirements of Fourteenth Amendment due process during the Twentieth Century. See infra p. 555.

[3] The Eleventh Amendment (1795) restricted suits against states in federal court, in reaction to the Court's decision in *Chisholm v. Georgia*, 2 U.S. (2 Dall.) 419 (1793). The Twelfth Amendment (1804) changed the Electoral College system to avoid problems that had arisen in the election of 1800.

[4] The other branches of government also placed glosses on the Constitution. For example, President Thomas Jefferson doubled the size of the United States by purchasing Louisiana from France, even though the Constitution did not expressly authorize presidential purchase of territory.

the former slaves the right to vote, and gave Congress the power to enforce these rights.   These amendments, but most importantly the Fourteenth Amendment, ratified under duress by the southern states,[5] transformed the relationship between the United States and the states into a more nationalistic mold.

During the last quarter of the nineteenth century and the first third of the twentieth century, the Constitution was amended through a number of "Progressive Era" amendments and interpreted in a number of "Regressive Era" decisions by the Supreme Court.   The Sixteenth, Seventeenth and Nineteenth Amendments empowered Congress to "lay and collect taxes on incomes," provided for direct popular election of Senators, and granted the right to vote to women.[6] The Court's interpretations narrowed the reach of the Fourteenth Amendment, eviscerated the Privileges or Immunities Clause, constrained the scope of the Thirteenth and Fourteenth Amendment powers of Congress, and construed the Equal Protection Clause to permit apartheid ("separate but equal"). *See The Slaughter House Cases* (p. 490), *The Civil Rights Cases* (p. 272), and *Plessy v. Ferguson* (p.664). Subsequently, the Court transformed the Due Process Clause of the Fourteenth Amendment into a tool for protecting property interests.   For example, it invalidated state legislation that guaranteed minimum standards of employment. *See Lochner v. New York* (p. 534).

During the Great Depression, the Court's view of the Constitution conflicted with that of President Franklin D. Roosevelt, who was elected with large majorities in 1932 and 1936.   Court decisions in 1935 and 1936 invalidated New Deal legislation, such as the Railroad Retirement Act, the National Industrial Recovery Act, and the Agricultural Adjustment Act. *See, e.g., Schechter Poultry Corp. v. United States* (p. 170). Infuriated, President Roosevelt referred to the Justices as "nine old men." In February 1937, he proposed a plan to prevent "hardening of the judicial arteries" by appointment of a new Justice for each Justice who had not resigned or retired within six months after reaching age seventy, thus allowing for an expansion of the Court from nine to as many as fifteen Justices. In March and April, 1937, the Court reversed earlier restrictions on state labor legislation and upheld the National Labor Relations Act. *See West Coast Hotel v. Parrish* (p. 543), *NLRB v. Jones & Laughlin Steel Corp.*, 301 U.S. 1 (1937). The Senate Judiciary Committee forcefully rejected the Roosevelt "court-packing" plan in June 1937.

---

[5] The unusual process by which the Fourteenth Amendment was adopted is extensively surveyed by Bruce Ackerman in WE THE PEOPLE: TRANSFORMATIONS (1998), at 99–252. In a nutshell, the story is one of dubious conformity to the requirements of Article V. The text of the Fourteenth Amendment received a 2/3 vote from a Congress that had excluded representatives from the southern states (Democrats who would have blocked passage). State ratification followed dissolution of the governments of the southern states, establishment of military rule pursuant to the Reconstruction Acts of 1867, and creation of new state governments. Readmission to the United States was predicated on their legislatures ratifying the Fourteenth Amendment.

[6] The Eighteenth Amendment, prohibiting the "manufacture, sale, or transportation" of alcohol, was repealed fifteen years later by the Twenty–First Amendment.

From 1937 to 1941, President Roosevelt appointed many new Justices to the Court to replace those who had died or retired. Without any explicit amendment of the Constitution, these appointees (Hugo Black, Stanley Reed, Felix Frankfurter, William O. Douglas, Frank Murphy, James Byrnes, and Robert Jackson) transformed constitutional law. The Court stopped reviewing economic legislation, whether state or federal, hence facilitating a broader construction of congressional power in the federal system. *See Wickard v. Filburn* (p. 235). It also began to consider civil liberties issues in terms of broader theories of political power, *United States v. Carolene Products* (p. 663), though this development occasionally seemed in tension with granting broad authority to the federal government. *See Korematsu v. United States* (p. 677). When the Court perceived tension between the political branches of the federal government, it was willing to reexamine basic precepts of constitutional theory. *See Youngstown Sheet & Tube v. Sawyer* (p. 114).

In 1953, President Eisenhower appointed former California Governor Earl Warren as Chief Justice. Warren's mission on the Court was equal justice. Under Warren's leadership, the Court reversed *Plessy v. Ferguson* in *Brown v. Board of Education* (p. 669), expanded constitutional protections accorded criminal defendants, reevaluated political fairness (*Baker v. Carr*, p. 58), enhanced First Amendment protections (speech, press, and religion), and created a right of privacy (*Griswold v. Connecticut*, p. 559).

Earl Warren's successor, Warren Burger, was appointed by President Nixon in 1969 to lead a counter-revolution of the Warren Court's jurisprudence, especially in the criminal procedure area. The counter-revolution never came. Though the Burger Court sometimes refused to extend Warren Court decisions, it seldom took a position flatly at odds with its predecessor. Indeed, the right of privacy established in *Griswold* was extended in *Roe v. Wade* (p. 569). The Burger Court expansively interpreted Title VII to encompass disparate impact theory, though it declined to apply that theory to racial matters under the equal protection clause. *See Washington v. Davis* (p.687). One of the most far-reaching decisions of the Burger Court invalidated over 200 federal statutes containing "legislative vetoes." *See INS v. Chadha* (p. 170).

When Warren Burger resigned in 1986, President Reagan selected Associate Justice William Rehnquist as Chief Justice. This elevation has been followed, to date, with five appointments by Republican Presidents Ronald Reagan and George Bush from 1985 through 1992 (Sandra Day O'Connor, Antonin Scalia, Anthony Kennedy, David Souter, and Clarence Thomas) and two appointments by Democratic President Clinton (Ruth Bader Ginsberg and Stephen Breyer). The Rehnquist Court has moved in some new directions not predicted fifteen years ago. Federalism issues, for the first time since the New Deal, have assumed prominence as the Court has sometimes restricted the reach of federal legislation. *See generally* Chapter V. New life has been breathed into the Privileges or Immunities Clause (*Saenz v. Roe*, p. 500), *Roe v. Wade* was reaffirmed but reinterpreted (cases beginning at p. 578), privacy protections were extended to homosexuals

(*Lawrence v. Texas*, p. 628), affirmative action was reexamined (cases beginning at p. 703), and equal protection principles were applied, controversially, in the 2000 presidential election (*Bush v. Gore*, p. 789).

As the United States enters the twenty–first century, each term of court brings new decisions in which the Court reshapes previous interpretations of the Constitution.

I–2. Current Supreme Court. Photograph by Richard Strauss, Smithsonian Institution, Courtesy the Supreme Court of the United States.

More Preliminary Exercises

1. **Articles and Constitution.** Find at least three ways in which the Constitution differs from its predecessor, the Articles of Confederation (reproduced as Appendix A).

2. **Madison's Proposal and Bill of Rights.** Find at least three ways in which the first ten amendments to the Constitution differ from James Madison's proposal (reproduced as Appendix B).

3. **Significance of Differences.** Are the Articles and Madison's proposal relevant to interpreting the Constitution? Construct an argument concerning the meaning of a provision in the Constitution from different language in the Articles and in Madison's proposal.

C. CONSTITUTIONAL PRINCIPLES

Support (indeed reverence) for the Constitution is a defining characteristic of the increasingly diverse people of the United States. Yet most Americans have not read the Constitution as recently or as carefully as you. Nor have they read even the short systematic history of the Constitution's interpretation that you have just finished. What does it mean for an American citizen to say that he or she is "attached to the principles" (even if not the text or history) of the United States Constitution? The following case shows the importance of that attachment as well as its ambiguity.

SCHNEIDERMAN v. UNITED STATES
320 U.S. 118, 63 S.Ct. 1333, 87 L.Ed. 1796 (1943).

Mr. JUSTICE MURPHY delivered the opinion of the Court.

*** Petitioner came to this country from Russia in 1907 or 1908 when he was approximately three. In 1922, at the age of sixteen, he became a charter member of the Young Workers (now Communist) League in Los Angeles and remained a member until 1929 or 1930. *** [E]arly in 1925 he became a member of the Workers Party, the predecessor of the Communist Party of the United States. That membership has continued to the present. His petition for naturalization was filed on January 18, 1927, and his certificate of citizenship was issued on June 10, 1927 *** From 1922 to about 1925 he was 'educational director' of the League. *** His first executive position with the Party came in 1930 when he was made an organizational secretary first in California, then in Connecticut and later in Minnesota where he was the Communist Party candidate for governor in 1932. Since 1934 he has been a member of the Party's National Committee. *** When petitioner was naturalized in 1927, the applicable statutes did not proscribe Communist beliefs or affiliation as such. They did *** forbid the naturalization of disbelievers in organized government or members of organizations teaching such disbelief. Polygamists and advocates of political assassination were also barred. *** Applicants for citizenship were required to take an oath to support the Constitution, to bear true faith and allegiance to the same and the laws of the United States, and to renounce all allegiance to any foreign prince, potentate, state or sovereignty. And, it was to 'be made to appear to the satisfaction of the court' of naturalization that immediately preceding the application, the applicant 'has resided continuously within the United States five years at least, *** and that during that time he has behaved as a man of good moral character, attached to the principles of the Constitution of the United States, and well disposed to the good order and happiness of the same.' Whether petitioner satisfied this last requirement is the crucial issue in this case.

*** The claim that petitioner was not in fact attached to the Constitution and well disposed to the good order and happiness of the United States at the time of his naturalization and for the previous five year period is twofold: First, that he believed in such sweeping changes in the Constitution that he simply could not be attached to it; Second, that he believed in and advocated the overthrow by force and violence of the Government, Constitution and laws of the United States.

In support of its position that petitioner was not in fact attached to the principles of the Constitution because of his membership in the League and the Party, the Government has directed our attention first to petitioner's testimony that he subscribed to the principles of those organizations, and then to certain alleged Party principles and statements by Party Leaders which are said to be fundamentally at variance with the principles of the Constitution. *** Said to be among those Communist principles in 1927 are: the abolition of private property without compensation; the erection of a new proletarian state upon the ruins of the old bourgeois state; the creation of a dictatorship of the proletariat; [and the] denial of political rights to others than members of the Party or of the proletariat. *** Those principles and views are not generally accepted—in fact they are distasteful to most of us—and they call for considerable change in our present form of government and society. ***

The constitutional fathers, fresh from a revolution, did not forge a political strait-jacket for the generations to come. Instead they wrote Article V and the First Amendment, guaranteeing freedom of thought, soon followed. Article V contains procedural provisions for constitutional change by amendment without any present limitation whatsoever except that no State may be deprived of equal representation in the Senate without its consent. This provision and the many important and far-reaching changes made in the Constitution since 1787 refute the idea that attachment to any particular provision or provisions is essential, or that one who advocates radical changes is necessarily not attached to the Constitution. As JUSTICE HOLMES said, 'Surely it cannot show lack of attachment to the principles of the Constitution that (one) thinks that it can be improved.' Criticism of, and the sincerity of desires to improve the Constitution should not be judged by conformity to prevailing thought because, 'if there is any principle of the Constitution that more imperatively calls for attachment than any other it is the principle of free thought—not free thought for those who agree with us but freedom for the thought that we hate.' *** The Government agrees that an alien 'may think that the laws and the Constitution should be amended in some or many respects' and still be attached to the principles of the Constitution within the meaning of the statute. Without discussing the nature and extent of those permissible changes, the Government insists that an alien must believe in and sincerely adhere to the 'general political philosophy' of the Constitution. Petitioner is said to be opposed to that 'political philosophy'. ***

With regard to the constitutional changes he desired petitioner testified that he believed in the nationalization of the means of production and exchange with compensation, and the preservation and utilization of our 'democratic structure *** as far as possible for the advantage of the working classes.' *** None of this is necessarily incompatible with the 'general political philosophy' of the Constitution as outlined above by the Government. It is true that the Fifth Amendment protects private property, even against taking for public use without compensation. But throughout our history many sincere people whose attachment to the general constitutional scheme cannot be doubted have, for various and even divergent reasons, urged differing degrees of governmental ownership *** either with or without compensation. And something once regarded as a species of private property was abolished without compensating the owners when the institution of slavery was forbidden. Can it be said that the author of the Emancipation Proclamation and the supporters of the Thirteenth Amendment were not attached to the Constitution? ***

The concept of the dictatorship of the proletariat *** may be taken to describe a state in which the workers or the masses, rather than the bourgeoisie or capitalists are the dominant class. *** There are only meager indications of the form the 'dictatorship' would take in this country. It does not appear that it would necessarily mean the end of representative government or the federal system. *** The 1928 platform of the Communist Party of the United States, *** advocated the abolition of the Senate, [and] of the Supreme Court, and of the veto power of the President.*** These would indeed be significant changes in our present government structure—changes which it is safe to say are not desired by the majority of the people in this country—but whatever our personal views, as judges we cannot say that a person who advocates their adoption through peaceful and constitutional means is not in fact attached to the Constitution— *** and it is conceivable that 'ordered liberty' could be maintained without [those institutions]. The Senate has not gone free of criticism and *** unicameral legislature is not unknown in the country. It is true that this Court has played a large part in the unfolding of the constitutional plan (sometimes too much so in the opinion of some observers), but we would be arrogant indeed if we presumed that a government of laws, with protection for minority groups, would be impossible without it. ***

If any provisions of the Constitution can be singled out as requiring unqualified attachment, they are the guaranties of the Bill of Rights and especially that of freedom of thought contained in the First Amendment. We do not reach, however the question whether petitioner was attached to the principles of the Constitution if he believed in denying political and civil rights to persons not members of the Party or of the so-called proletariat, for on the basis of the record before us it has not been clearly shown that such denial was a principle of the organizations to which petitioner belonged. *** The party's 1928 platform demanded the unrestricted right to organize, to strike and to picket and the unrestricted right of free speech, free press and free assemblage for the working class. ***

*** [T]he Government asserts that the organizations with which petitioner was actively affiliated advised, advocated and taught the overthrow of the Government, Constitution and laws of the United States by force and violence. *** Apart from his membership in the League and the Party, the record is barren of any conduct or statement on petitioner's part which indicates in the slightest that he believed in and advocated the employment of force and violence, instead of peaceful persuasion, as a means of attaining political ends. To find that he so believed and advocated it is necessary, therefore, to find that such was a principle of the organizations to which he belonged and then impute that principle to him on the basis of his activity in those organizations and his statement that he subscribed to their principles. The Government frankly concedes that 'it is normally true *** that it is unsound to impute to an organization the views expressed in the writings of all its members, or to impute such writings to each member ***.' But the Government contends, however, that it is proper to impute to petitioner certain excerpts from the documents *** because those documents were official publications carefully supervised by the Party, *** and because petitioner was not a mere 'rank and file or accidental member of the Party', but 'an intelligent and educated individual' who 'became a leader of these organizations as an intellectual revolutionary.' ***

With commendable candor the Government admits the presence of sharply conflicting views on the issue of force and violence as a Party principle. *** [W]e would deny our experience as men if we did not recognize that official party programs are unfortunately often opportunistic devices as much honored in the breach as in the observance. On the basis of the present record we cannot say that the Communist Party is so different in this respect that its principles stand forth with perfect clarity, and especially is this so with relation to the crucial issue of advocacy of force and violence, upon which the Government admits the evidence is sharply conflicting. *** [A] court in a denaturalization proceeding *** is not justified in canceling a certificate of citizenship by imputing the reprehensible interpretation to a member of the organization in the absence of overt acts indicating that such was his interpretation. So uncertain a chain of proof does not add up to the requisite 'clear, unequivocal, and convincing' evidence for setting aside a naturalization decree. Were the law otherwise, valuable rights would rest upon a slender reed, and the security of the status of our naturalized citizens might depend in considerable degree upon the political temper of majority thought and the stresses of the times. Those are consequences foreign to the best traditions of this nation, and the characteristics of our institutions. ***

Mr. JUSTICE DOUGLAS, concurring. [omitted]

Mr. JUSTICE RUTLEDGE, concurring.

*** Immediately we are concerned with only one man, William Schneiderman. Actually, though indirectly, the decision affects millions. If, seventeen years after a federal court adjudged him entitled to be a citizen, that judgment can be nullified and he can be stripped of this most precious right, by nothing more than reexamination upon the merits of the very facts the judgment established, no naturalized person's citizenship is or can be secure. *** If this is the law and the right the naturalized citizen acquires, his admission creates nothing more than citizenship in attenuated, if not suspended, animation. He acquires but prima facie status, if that. Until the Government moves to cancel his certificate and he knows the outcome, he cannot know whether he is in or out. And when that is done, nothing forbids repeating the harrowing process again and again, unless the weariness of the courts should lead them finally to speak res judicata.

No citizen with such a threat hanging over his head could be free. *** For whatever he might say or whatever any such organization might advocate could be hauled forth at any time to show 'continuity' of belief from the day of his admission, or 'concealment' at that time. Such a citizen would not be admitted to liberty. His best course would be silence or hypocrisy. This is not citizenship. *** It may be doubted that the framers of the Constitution intended to create two classes of citizens, one free and independent, one haltered with a lifetime string tied to its status. *** If every fact in issue going to the right to be a citizen, can be reexamined, upon the same or different proof, years or decades later; and if this can be done de novo, as if no judgment had been entered, whether with respect to the burden of proof required to reach a different decision or otherwise, what does the judgment determine? What does it settle with finality? If review is had and the admission is affirmed, what fact is adjudicated, if next day any or all involved can be redecided to the contrary? ***

Mr. CHIEF JUSTICE STONE, dissenting.

*** [A]t the time of petitioner's naturalization, the statutes of the United States excluded from admission into this country 'aliens who believe in, advise, advocate, or teach, or who are members of or affiliated with any organization, association, society, or group, that believes in, advises, advocates, or teaches: (1) the overthrow by force or violence of the Government of the United States *** '. The statutes also barred admission to the United States of 'aliens who *** knowingly cause to be circulated, distributed, printed, published, or displayed *** any written or printed matter *** advising, advocating, or teaching: (1) the overthrow by force or violence of the Government of the United States *** '. *** The evidence makes it clear beyond all reasonable doubt that petitioner, up to the time of his naturalization, was an alien who knowingly circulated or distributed, or caused to be circulated or distributed, printed matter advocating the overthrow of the Government by force or violence. *** [T]he trial court was justified in finding that petitioner, in 1927, was not and had not been attached to the principles of the Constitution. *** I shall assume that there are such principles and that among them are at least the principle of constitutional protection of civil rights and of life, liberty and property, the principle of representative government, and the principle that constitutional laws are not to be broken down by planned disobedience. I assume also that all the principles of the Constitution are hostile to dictatorship and minority rule; and that it is a principle of our Constitution that change in the organization of our government is to be effected by the orderly procedures ordained by the Constitution and not by force or fraud. ***

Perusal of the record can leave no doubt of petitioner's unqualified loyalty to the Communist Party. *** There is abundant documentary evidence of the character already described to support the court's finding that the Communist Party organizations, of which petitioner was a member, diligently circulated printed matter which advocated the overthrow of the Government of the United States by force and violence, and that petitioner aided in that circulation and advocacy. *** It would be little short of preposterous to assert that vigorous aid knowingly given by a pledged Party member in disseminating the Party teachings, *** is compatible with attachment to the principles of the Constitution. *** It would be difficult also to find as a fact that petitioner behaved as a man attached to the principles of the Constitution. The trial judge found that he did not. *** Yet the Court's opinion seems to tell us that the trier of fact must not examine petitioner's gospel to find out what kind of man he was, or even what his gospel was; that the trier of fact could not 'impute' to petitioner any genuine attachment to the doctrines of these organizations whose teachings he so assiduously spread. It might as well be said that it is impossible to infer that a man is attached to the principles of a religious movement from the fact that he conducts its prayer meetings, or, to take a more sinister example, that it could not be inferred that a man is a Nazi and consequently not attached to constitutional principles who, for more than five years, had diligently circulated the doctrines of Mein Kampf. *** A man can be known by the ideas he spreads as well as by the company he keeps. And when one does not challenge the proof that he has given his life to spreading a particular class of well-defined ideas, it is convincing evidence that his attachment is to them rather than their opposites. ***

Mr. JUSTICE ROBERTS and Mr. JUSTICE FRANKFURTER join in this dissent.

Mr. JUSTICE JACKSON. I do not participate in this decision.

Notes

1. **Constitutional Attachment.** May Congress make membership in the Nazi Party, al Qaeda, or the Ku Klux Klan a basis for citizenship revocation? Is your attachment (assuming you are attached) based on substantive principles or procedure?

2. **Priorities.** Abraham Lincoln wrote that "There is something back of [the Constitution and the Union] entwining itself more closely about the human heart. That something is the principle of 'liberty to all'—the principle that clears the path for all—gives hope to all—and, by consequence, enterprise and industry to all." Lincoln went on to refer to the Declaration of Independence as an "apple of gold" and to say that "the Union and the Constitution are the picture of silver subsequently framed around it. The picture was made, not to conceal or destroy the apple; but to adorn, and preserve it." When and how might Lincoln's biblically-based analogy be important?

3. **Supreme Court Decision-making.** *Schneiderman* was "one of the decade's most ideologically divisive cases." JUSTICE FRANKFURTER sent a note to JUSTICE MURPHY suggesting this headnote to his draft opinion:

> The American Constitution ain't got no principles. The Communist Party don't stand for nothin'. The Soopreme Court don't mean nuthin'. Nuthin' means nuthin', and ter Hell with the U.S.A. so long as a guy is attached to the principles of the U.S.S.R.

At a later conference on the case, Frankfurter explained that his strong feelings came from his own experience as a naturalized citizen, saying "It is well known that a convert is more zealous than one born to the faith." Would most naturalized Americans react similarly?

4. **War and Constitutional Law.** Several cases in this book are widely cited as evidence that "during war, the law is silent." Is *Schneiderman*, decided during World War II, consistent with this maxim?

5. **Citizenship and the Constitution.** Under the Constitution, how does a citizen of the United States differ from a resident alien? Does citizenship by naturalization differ materially, even after *Schneiderman*, from birthright citizenship?

D. OVERVIEW OF THIS BOOK

The United States Constitution has significance far beyond its interpretation by the United States Supreme Court: governmental officials are confronted almost daily by the grants and limits upon their power embodied in the Constitution; citizens are regularly affected in their dealings with government officials by the Constitution's grants of rights; political discourse is often shaped by constitutional interpretations; other nations have used the Constitution as a model.

This set of materials, however, primarily concerns the "Constitutional Law" articulated by the Supreme Court. Is this focus appropriate? I think so, for two reasons.

First, these materials are designed for use primarily by law students, who will be building constitutional arguments for clients or advising governmental officials primarily from judicial opinions. Second, the Supreme Court's stock in trade—written opinions providing reasoned justifications for decisions reached—provides appropriate material from which to develop a sophisticated understanding of constitutional law.

In organizing these materials, I have chosen a traditional structure. Chapter II examines the sources of and limits upon the Supreme Court's power to interpret the United States Constitution. Chapter III presents the Court's interpretations of the Constitution's distribution of national powers between Congress and the President. Chapter IV focuses on the constitutional framework of Congress' powers. Chapter V investigates the limits federalism imposes on Congress and the states. Chapter VI looks at the Supreme Court's role in invalidating state burdens on interstate commerce and at the Article IV privileges and immunities of citizens. Chapter VII sets out the genesis of the post-Civil War amendments and the Court's construction of the privileges or immunities clause of the Fourteenth Amendment. Chapter VIII examines both procedural and substantive applications of the due process clause of that amendment. Chapter IX explores the theory and practice of "equal protection of the laws" under the Fourteenth Amendment. Finally, Chapter X, using the concept of state action, reviews the interface between governmental power and individual rights under the Constitution.

A few words are in order about how this book differs from other basic constitutional law casebooks. Most importantly, its theory is that less is more. Neither voluminous collateral case citations nor extensive references to scholarly works facilitate the learning of constitutional law. Rather, they get in the way. I have tried to keep two goals firmly in mind: teaching students how to read constitutional law cases and providing practice in applying these cases to new circumstances. Another difference, as the subtitle indicates, is that this book focuses on the structure of the Constitution and its reconstruction, both by amendment and by judicial interpretation. My book does not cover the First Amendment, just as earlier constitutional law casebooks excised the constitutional law aspects of criminal procedure. The First Amendment and criminal procedure are for other courses, other books.

II

JUDICIAL POWER TO ENFORCE THE CONSTITUTION

"It is emphatically the province and duty of the judicial department to say what the law is. Those who apply the rule to particular cases, must of necessity expound and interpret that rule. *** So if a law be in opposition to the constitution; if both the law and the constitution apply to a particular case, so that the court must either decide that case conformably to the law, disregarding the constitution; or conformably to the constitution, disregarding the law; the court must determine which of these conflicting rules governs the case. *** If then the courts are to regard the constitution; and the constitution is superior to any ordinary act of the legislature; the constitution, and not such ordinary act, must govern the case to which they both apply."

—CHIEF JUSTICE JOHN MARSHALL in
Marbury v. Madison (1803)

The power of the federal judiciary and ultimately the Supreme Court to invalidate federal and state legislation is an awesome power. Parts A and B of this chapter consider the scope of the Supreme Court's power to interpret the Constitution. Part C looks at the tools Supreme Court justices use to interpret the Constitution. Part D examines various limits to the Court's exercise of the power of interpretation.

A. INVALIDATION OF FEDERAL LAWS

As you read the following case, credited with establishing the power of judicial review, focus on the logic and ramifications of the decision. How are the issues in the opinion organized? Was the outcome as inevitable as CHIEF JUSTICE MARSHALL's opinion makes it seem?

MARBURY v. MADISON
5 U.S. (1 Cranch) 137, 2 L.Ed. 60 (1803).

At the December term, 1801, William Marbury *** moved the court for a rule to James Madison, secretary of state of the United States, to show cause why a mandamus should not issue commanding him to cause to be delivered to them respectively their several commissions as justices of the peace in the district of Columbia. This motion was supported by affidavits of the following facts; that notice of this motion had been given to Mr. Madison; that Mr. Adams, the late president of the United States, nominated the applicants to the senate for their advice and consent to be appointed justices of the peace of the district of Columbia; that the senate advised and consented to the appointments; that commissions in due form were signed by the said president appointing them justices, &c. and that the seal of the United States was in due form affixed to the said commissions by the secretary of state; that the applicants have requested Mr. Madison to deliver them their said commissions, who has not complied with that request; and that their said commissions are withheld from them; that the applicants have made application to Mr. Madison as secretary of state of the United States at his office, for information whether the commissions were signed and sealed as aforesaid; that explicit and satisfactory information has not been given in answer to that inquiry, either by the secretary of state or any officer in the department of state; that application has been made to the secretary of the Senate for a certificate of the nomination of the applicants, and of the advice and consent of the senate, who has declined giving such a certificate; whereupon a rule was laid to show cause on the 4th day of this term. This rule [was] duly served *** [and the questions argued by the counsel for the relators were,]

1. Whether the supreme court can award the writ of mandamus in any case.

2. Whether it will lie to a secretary of state in any case whatever.

3. Whether in the present case the court may award a mandamus to James Madison, secretary of state. ***

MR. CHIEF JUSTICE MARSHALL delivered the opinion of the court.

At the last term on the affidavits then read and filed with the clerk, a rule was granted in this case, requiring the secretary of state to show cause why a mandamus should not issue, directing him to deliver to William Marbury his commission as a justice of the peace for the county of Washington, in the district of Columbia.

No cause has been shown, and the present motion is for a mandamus. The peculiar delicacy of this case, the novelty of some of its circumstances, and the real difficulty attending the points which occur in it, require a complete exposition of the principles, on which the opinion to be given by the court, is founded.

These principles have been, on the side of the applicant, very ably argued at the bar. In rendering the opinion of the court, there will be some departure in form, though not in substance, from the points stated in that argument.

In the order in which the court has viewed this subject, the following questions have been considered and decided.

1st.   Has the applicant a right to the commission he demands?

2ndly. If he has a right, and that right has been violated, do the laws of his country afford him a remedy?

3rdly. If they do afford him a remedy, is it a mandamus issuing from this court?

The first object of inquiry is,

1st. Has the applicant a right to the commission he demands?

His right originates in an act of congress passed in February 1801, concerning the district of Columbia.

After dividing the district into two counties, the 11th section of this law, enacts "that there shall be appointed in and for each of the said counties, such number of discreet persons to be justices of the peace as the president of the United States shall, from time to time, think expedient, to continue in office for five years.["]

It appears from the affidavits, that in compliance with this law, a commission for William Marbury as a justice of peace for the county of Washington, was signed by John Adams, then president of the United States; after which the seal of the United States was affixed to it; but the commission has never reached the person for whom it was made out.

In order to determine whether he is entitled to this commission, it becomes necessary to inquire whether he has been appointed to the office. For if he has been appointed, the law continues him in office for five years, and he is entitled to the possession of those evidences of office, which, being completed, became his property. ***

[The Court then considered whether Marbury had been appointed.]

The appointment being the sole act of the President, must be completely evidenced, when it is shown that he has done every thing to be performed by him. ***

The last act to be done by the President, is the signature of the commission. He has then acted on the advice and consent of the senate to his own nomination. The time for deliberation has then passed. He has decided. His judgment, on the advice and consent of the senate concurring with his nomination, has been made, and the officer is appointed. This appointment is evidenced by an open, unequivocal act; and being the last act required from the person making it, necessarily excludes the idea of its being, so far as it respects the appointment, an inchoate and incomplete transaction.

Some point of time must be taken when the power of the executive over an officer, not removable at his will, must cease. That point of time must be when the constitutional power of appointment has been exercised. And this power has been exercised when the last act, required from the person possessing the power, has been performed. This last act is the signature of the commission. *** The commission being signed, the subsequent duty of the secretary of state is prescribed by law, and not to be guided by the will of the President. He is to affix the seal of the United States to the commission, and is to record it. *** [His] is a ministerial act which the law enjoins on a particular officer for a particular purpose. ***

It is therefore decidedly the opinion of the court, that when a commission has been signed by the President, the appointment is made; and that the commission is complete, when the seal of the United States has been affixed to it by the secretary of state.

Where an officer is removable at the will of the executive, the circumstance which completes his appointment is of no concern; because the act is at any time revocable; and the commission may be arrested, if still in the office. But when the officer is not removable at the will of the executive, the appointment is not revocable, and cannot be annulled. It has conferred legal rights which cannot be resumed. *** Mr. Marbury, then, since his commission was signed by the President, and sealed by the secretary of state, was appointed; and as the law creating the office, gave the officer a right to hold for five years, independent of the executive, the appointment was not revocable; but vested in the officer legal rights, which are protected by the laws of his country.

To withhold the commission, therefore, is an act deemed by the court not warranted by law, but violative of a vested legal right.

This brings us to the second inquiry; which is, 2ndly. If he has a right, and that right has been violated, do the laws of his country afford him a remedy?

The very essence of civil liberty certainly consists in the right of every individual to claim the protection of the laws, whenever he receives an injury. One of the first duties of government is to afford that protection. In Great Britain the king himself is sued in the respectful form of a petition, and he never fails to comply with the judgment of his court. ***

The government of the United States has been emphatically termed a government of laws, and not of men. It will certainly cease to deserve this high appellation, if the laws furnish no remedy for the violation of a vested legal right. If this obloquy is to be cast on the jurisprudence of our country, it must arise from the peculiar character of the case.

It behooves us then to inquire whether there be in its composition any ingredient which shall exempt it from legal investigation, or exclude the injured party from legal redress. ***

Is it in the nature of the transaction? Is the act of delivering or withholding a commission to be considered as a mere political act, belonging to the executive department alone, for the performance of which entire confidence is placed by our constitution in the supreme executive; and for any misconduct respecting which, the injured individual has no remedy. That there may be such cases is not to be questioned; but that every act of duty, to be performed in any of the great departments of government, constitutes such a case, is not to be admitted. ***

It follows then that the question, whether the legality of an act of the head of a department be examinable in a court of justice or not, must always depend on the nature of that act. If some acts be examinable, and others not, there must be some rule of law to guide the court in the exercise of its jurisdiction. In some instances there may be difficulty in applying the rule to particular cases; but there cannot, it is believed, be much difficulty in laying down the rule.

By the constitution of the United States, the President is invested with certain important political powers, in the exercise of which he is to use his own discretion, and is accountable only to his country in his political character, and to his own conscience. To aid him in the performance of these duties, he is authorized to appoint certain officers, who act by his authority and in conformity with his orders. In such cases, their acts are his acts; and whatever opinion may be entertained of the manner in which executive discretion may be used, still there exists, and can exist, no power to control that discretion. The subjects are political. They respect the nation, not individual rights, and being entrusted to the executive, the decision of the executive is conclusive. The application of this remark will be perceived by adverting to the act of congress for establishing the department of foreign affairs. This officer, as his duties were prescribed by that act, is to conform precisely to the will of the President. He is the mere organ by whom that will is communicated. The acts of such an officer, as an officer, can never be examinable by the courts. But when the legislature proceeds to impose on that officer other duties; when he is directed peremptorily to perform certain acts; when the rights of individuals are dependent on the performance of those acts; he is so far the officer of the law; is amenable to the laws for his conduct; and cannot at his discretion sport away the vested rights of others.

The conclusion from this reasoning is, that where the heads of departments are the political or confidential agents of the executive, merely to execute the will of the President, or rather to act in cases in which the executive possesses a constitutional or legal discretion, nothing can be more perfectly clear than that their acts are only politically examinable. But where a specific duty is assigned by law, and individual rights depend upon the performance of that duty, it seems equally clear that the individual who considers himself injured, has a right to resort to the laws of his country for a remedy.

If this be the rule, let us inquire how it applies to the case under the consideration of the court. ***

The question whether a right has vested or not, is, in its nature, judicial, and must be tried by the judicial authority. If, for example, Mr. Marbury had taken the oaths of a magistrate, and proceeded to act as one; in consequence of which a suit had been instituted against him, in which his defence had depended on his being a magistrate; the validity of his appointment must have been determined by judicial authority. So, if he conceives that, by virtue of his appointment, he has a legal right, either to the commission which has been made out for him or to a copy of that commission, it is equally a question examinable in a court, and the decision of the court upon it must depend on the opinion entertained of his appointment. That question has been discussed, and the opinion is, that the latest point of time which can be taken as that at which the appointment was complete, and evidenced, was when, after the signature of the president, the seal of the United States was affixed to the commission.

It is then the opinion of the court,

1st. That by signing the commission of Mr. Marbury, the president of the United States appointed him a justice of peace, for the county of Washington in the district of Columbia; and that the seal of the United States, affixed thereto by the secretary of state, is conclusive testimony of the verity of the signature, and of the completion of the appointment; and that the appointment conferred on him a legal right to the office for the space of five years. 2ndly. That, having this legal title to the office, he has a consequent right to the commission; a refusal to deliver which, is a plain violation of that right, for which the laws of his country afford him a remedy.

It remains to be inquired whether 3rdly. is entitled to the remedy for which he applies. This depends on, 1st The nature of the writ applied for, and, 2ndly The power of this court.

1. The nature of the writ. ***

[T]o render the mandamus a proper remedy, the officer to whom it is to be directed, must be one to whom, on legal principles, such writ may be directed; and the person applying for it must be without any other specific and legal remedy.

1st. With respect to the officer to whom it would be directed. The intimate political relation, subsisting between the president of the United States and the heads of departments, necessarily renders any legal investigation of the acts of one of those high officers peculiarly irksome, as well as delicate; and excites some hesitation with respect to the propriety of entering into such investigation. Impressions are often received without much reflection or examination, and it is not wonderful that in such a case as this, the assertion, by an individual, of his legal claims in a court of justice; to which claims it is the duty of that court to attend; should at first view be considered by some, as an attempt to intrude into the cabinet, and to intermeddle with the prerogatives of the executive.

It is scarcely necessary for the court to disclaim all pretensions to such a jurisdiction. An extravagance, so absurd and excessive, could not have been entertained for a moment. The province of the court is, solely, to decide on the rights of individuals, not to inquire how the executive, or executive officers, perform duties in which they have a discretion. Questions, in their nature political, or which are, by the constitution and laws, submitted to the executive, can never be made in this court.

But, if this be not such a question; if so far from being an intrusion into the secrets of the cabinet, it respects a paper, which, according to law, is upon record, and to a copy of which the law gives a right, on the payment of ten cents; if it be no intermeddling with a subject, over which the executive can be considered as having exercised any control; what is there in the exalted station of the officer, which shall bar a citizen from asserting, in a court of justice, his legal rights, or shall forbid a court to listen to the claim; or to issue a mandamus, directing the performance of a duty, not depending on executive discretion, but on particular acts of congress and the general principles of law? ***

It is not by the office of the person to whom the writ is directed, but the nature of the thing to be done that the propriety or impropriety of issuing a mandamus, is to be determined. Where the head of a department acts in a case, in which executive discretion is to be exercised; in which he is the mere organ of executive will; it is again repeated, that any application to a court to control, in any respect, his conduct, would be rejected without hesitation. But where he is directed by law to do a certain act affecting the absolute rights of individuals, in the performance of which he is not placed under the particular direction of the President, and the performance of which; the President cannot lawfully forbid, and therefore is never presumed to have forbidden; as for example, to record a commission, or a patent for land, which has received all the legal solemnities; or to give a copy of such record; in such cases, it is not perceived on what ground the courts of the country are further excused from the duty of giving judgment, that right to be done to an injured individual, than if the same services were to be performed by a person not the head of a department. ***

This, then, is a plain case of a mandamus, either to deliver the commission, or a copy of it from the record; and it only remains to be inquired,

Whether it can issue from this court.

The act to establish the judicial courts of the United States authorizes the supreme court "to issue writs of mandamus, in cases warranted by the principles and usages of law, to any courts appointed, or persons holding office, under the authority of the United States."*

The secretary of state, being a person holding an office under the authority of the United States, is precisely within the letter of the description; and if this court is not authorized to issue a writ of mandamus to such an officer, it must be because the law is unconstitutional, and therefore absolutely incapable of conferring the authority, and assigning the duties which its words purport to confer and assign.

---

* Section 13 of the Judiciary Act of 1789 provides:

That the Supreme Court shall have the exclusive jurisdiction of all controversies of a civil nature, where a state is a party, except between a state and its citizens; and except also between a state and citizens of other states, or aliens, in which latter case it shall have original but not exclusive jurisdiction. And shall have exclusively all such jurisdiction of suits or proceedings against ambassadors, or other public ministers, or their domestics, or domestic servants, as a court of law can have or exercise consistently with the law of nations; and original, but not exclusive jurisdiction of all suits brought by ambassadors, or other public ministers, or in which a consul, or vice consul, shall be a party. And the trial of issues of fact in the Supreme Court, in all actions at law against citizens of the United States, shall be by jury. The Supreme Court shall also have appellate jurisdiction from the circuit courts and courts of the several states, in the cases herein after specially provided for; and shall have power to issue writs of prohibition to the district courts, when proceeding as courts of admiralty and maritime jurisdiction, and writs of mandamus, in cases warranted by the principles and usages of law, to any courts appointed, or persons holding office, under the authority of the United States.

The constitution vests the whole judicial power of the United States in one supreme court, and such inferior courts as congress shall, from time to time, ordain and establish. This power is expressly extended to all cases arising under the laws of the United States; and consequently, in some form, may be exercised over the present case; because the right claimed is given by a law of the United States.

In the distribution of this power it is declared that "the supreme court shall have original jurisdiction in all cases affecting ambassadors, other public ministers and consuls, and those in which a state shall be a party. In all other cases, the supreme court shall have appellate jurisdiction."

It has been insisted, at the bar, that as the original grant of jurisdiction, to the supreme and inferior courts, is general, and the clause, assigning original jurisdiction to the supreme court, contains no negative or restrictive words; the power remains to the legislature, to assign original jurisdiction to that court in other cases than those specified in the article which has been recited; provided those cases belong to the judicial power of the United States.

If it had been intended to leave it in the discretion of the legislature to apportion the judicial power between the supreme and inferior courts according to the will of that body, it would certainly have been useless to have proceeded further than to have defined the judicial power, and the tribunals in which it should be vested. The subsequent part of the section is mere surplusage, is entirely without meaning, if such is to be the construction. If congress remains at liberty to give this court appellate jurisdiction, where the constitution has declared their jurisdiction shall be original; and original jurisdiction where the constitution has declared it shall be appellate; the distribution of jurisdiction, made in the constitution, is form without substance.

Affirmative words are often, in their operation, negative of other objects than those affirmed; and in this case, a negative or exclusive sense must be given to them or they have no operation at all.

It cannot be presumed that any clause in the constitution is intended to be without effect; and therefore such construction is inadmissible, unless the words require it. ***

When an instrument organizing fundamentally a judicial system, divides it into one supreme, and so many inferior courts as the legislature may ordain and establish; then enumerates its powers, and proceeds so far to distribute them, as to define the jurisdiction of the supreme court by declaring the cases in which it shall take original jurisdiction, and that in others it shall take appellate jurisdiction; the plain import of the words seems to be, that in one class of cases its jurisdiction is original, and not appellate; in the other it is appellate, and not original. If any other construction would render the clause inoperative, that is an additional reason for rejecting such other construction, and for adhering to the obvious meaning.

To enable this court then to issue a mandamus, it must be shown to be an exercise of appellate jurisdiction, or to be necessary to enable them to exercise appellate jurisdiction.

It has been stated at the bar that the appellate jurisdiction may be exercised in a variety of forms, and that if it be the will of the legislature that a mandamus should be used for that purpose, that will must be obeyed. This is true, yet the jurisdiction must be appellate, not original.

It is the essential criterion of appellate jurisdiction, that it revises and corrects the proceedings in a cause already instituted, and does not create that case. Although, therefore, a mandamus may be directed to courts, yet to issue such a writ to an officer for the delivery of a paper, is in effect the same as to sustain an original action for that paper, and therefore seems not to belong to appellate, but to original jurisdiction. Neither is it necessary in such a case as this, to enable the court to exercise its appellate jurisdiction.

The authority, therefore, given to the supreme court, by the act establishing the judicial courts of the United States, to issue writs of mandamus to public officers, appears not to be warranted by the constitution; and it becomes necessary to inquire whether a jurisdiction, so conferred, can be exercised.

The question, whether an act, repugnant to the constitution, can become the law of the land, is a question deeply interesting to the United States; but, happily, not of an intricacy proportioned to its interest. It seems only necessary to recognize certain principles, supposed to have been long and well established, to decide it.

That the people have an original right to establish, for their future government, such principles as, in their opinion, shall most conduce to their own happiness, is the basis on which the whole American fabric has been erected. The exercise of this original right is a very great exertion; nor can it, nor ought it to be frequently repeated. The principles, therefore, so established, are deemed fundamental. And as the authority, from which they proceed, is supreme, and can seldom act, they are designed to be permanent.

This original and supreme will organizes the government, and assigns, to different departments, their respective powers. It may either stop here; or establish certain limits not to be transcended by those departments.

The government of the United States is of the latter description. The powers of the legislature are defined, and limited; and that those limits may not be mistaken, or forgotten, the constitution is written. To what purpose are powers limited, and to what purpose is that limitation committed to writing, if these limits may, at any time, be passed by those intended to be restrained? The distinction, between a government with limited and unlimited powers, is abolished, if those limits do not confine the persons on whom they are imposed, and if acts prohibited and acts allowed, are of equal obligation. It is a proposition too plain to be contested, that the constitution controls any legislative act repugnant to it; or, that the legislature may alter the constitution by an ordinary act.

Between these alternatives there is no middle ground. The constitution is either a superior, paramount law, unchangeable by ordinary means, or it is on a level with ordinary legislative acts, and like other acts, is alterable when the legislature shall please to alter it.

If the former part of the alternative be true, then a legislative act contrary to the constitution is not law: if the latter part be true, then written constitutions are absurd attempts, on the part of the people, to limit a power, in its own nature illimitable.

Certainly all those who have framed written constitutions contemplate them as forming the fundamental and paramount law of the nation, and consequently the theory of every such government must be, that an act of the legislature, repugnant to the constitution, is void.

This theory is essentially attached to a written constitution, and is consequently to be considered, by this court, as one of the fundamental principles of our society. It is not therefore to be lost sight of in the further consideration of this subject.

If an act of the legislature, repugnant to the constitution, is void, does it, notwithstanding its invalidity, bind the courts and oblige them to give it effect? Or, in other words, though it be not law, does it constitute a rule as operative as if it was a law? This would be to overthrow in fact what was established in theory; and would seem, at first view, an absurdity too gross to be insisted on. It shall, however, receive a more attentive consideration.

It is emphatically the province and duty of the judicial department to say what the law is. Those who apply the rule to particular cases, must of necessity expound and interpret that rule. If two laws conflict with each other, the courts must decide on the operation of each.

So if a law be in opposition to the constitution; if both the law and the constitution apply to a particular case, so that the court must either decide that case conformably to the law, disregarding the constitution; or conformably to the constitution, disregarding the law; the court must determine which of these conflicting rules governs the case. This is of the very essence of judicial duty.

If then the courts are to regard the constitution; and the constitution is superior to any ordinary act of the legislature; the constitution, and not such ordinary act, must govern the case to which they both apply.

Those then who controvert the principle that the constitution is to be considered, in court, as a paramount law, are reduced to the necessity of maintaining that courts must close their eyes on the constitution, and see only the law.

This doctrine would subvert the very foundation of all written constitutions. It would declare that an act, which, according to the principles and theory of our government, is entirely void; is yet, in practice, completely obligatory. It would declare, that if the legislature shall do what is expressly forbidden, such act, notwithstanding the express prohibition, is in reality effectual. It would be giving to the legislature a practical and real omnipotence, with the same breath which professes to restrict their powers within narrow limits. It is prescribing limits, and declaring that those limits may be passed at pleasure.

That it thus reduces to nothing what we have deemed the greatest improvement on political institutions—a written constitution—would of itself be sufficient, in America, where written constitutions have been viewed with so much reverence, for rejecting the construction. But the peculiar expressions of the constitution of the United States furnish additional arguments in favour of its rejection.

The judicial power of the United States is extended to all cases arising under the constitution. Could it be the intention of those who gave this power, to say that, in using it, the constitution should not be looked into? That a case arising under the constitution should be decided without examining the instrument under which it arises?

This is too extravagant to be maintained.

In some cases then, the constitution must be looked into by the judges. And if they can open it at all, what part of it are they forbidden to read, or to obey?

There are many other parts of the constitution which serve to illustrate this subject.

It is declared that "no tax or duty shall be laid on articles exported from any state." Suppose a duty on the export of cotton, of tobacco, or of flour; and a suit instituted to recover it. Ought judgment to be rendered in such a case? ought the judges to close their eyes on the constitution, and only see the law.

The constitution declares that "no bill of attainder or *ex post facto* law shall be passed."

If, however, such a bill should be passed and a person should be prosecuted under it; must the court condemn to death those victims whom the constitution endeavours to preserve?

"No person," says the constitution, "shall be convicted of treason unless on the testimony of two witnesses to the same overt act, or on confession in open court."

Here the language of the constitution is addressed especially to the courts. It prescribes, directly for them, a rule of evidence not to be departed from. If the legislature should change that rule, and declare *one* witness, or a confession *out of* court, sufficient for conviction, must the constitutional principle yield to the legislative act?

From these, and many other selections which might be made, it is apparent, that the framers of the constitution contemplated that instrument, as a rule for the government *of courts*, as well as of the legislature.

Why otherwise does it direct the judges to take an oath to support it? This oath certainly applies, in an especial manner, to their conduct in their official character. How immoral to impose it on them, if they were to be used as the instruments, and the knowing instruments, for violating what they swear to support?

The oath of office, too, imposed by the legislature, is completely demonstrative of the legislative opinion on this subject. It is in these words, "I do solemnly swear that I will administer justice without respect to persons, and do equal right to the poor and to the rich; and that I will faithfully and impartially discharge all the duties incumbent on ***, according to the best of my abilities and understanding, agreeably to the constitution and laws of the United States."

Why does a judge swear to discharge his duties agreeably to the constitution of the United States, if that constitution forms no rule for his government? If it is closed upon him, and cannot be inspected by him?

If such be the real state of things, this is worse than solemn mockery. To prescribe, or to take this oath, becomes equally a crime.

It is also not entirely unworthy of observation, that in declaring what shall be the *supreme* law of the land, the *constitution* itself is first mentioned; and not the laws of the United States generally, but those only which shall be made in *pursuance* of the constitution, have that rank.

Thus, the particular phraseology of the constitution of the United States confirms and strengthens the principle, supposed to be essential to all written constitutions, that a law repugnant to the constitution is void; and that *courts*, as well as other departments, are bound by that instrument. ***

Notes

1. **History and Politics.** CHIEF JUSTICE MARSHALL's opinion was written in politically turbulent times. Marshall, as Acting Secretary of State for Federalist President John Adams, had signed the commissions of Marbury and other justices of the peace whose positions had been created by the Federalist Congress in the last few days before Republican Thomas Jefferson took office on March 4, 1801. In this context, it is hardly surprising that President Jefferson refused to deliver the commissions and claimed that they were void. The Republican Congress subsequently repealed other "midnight legislation" enacted by the Federalists, but left the justice of the peace appointments intact. The Republican Congress also abolished the 1801 and 1802 terms of the Supreme Court, so as to avoid having the Court (headed by Federalist Marshall) resolve the constitutionality of its legislation. *Marbury* was decided at the next term of Court, in 1803.

2. **Preliminary Matters.** Consider these separate components of the Court's opinion.

   · Why is the commission complete upon signing rather than delivery?

   · CHIEF JUSTICE MARSHALL discusses cases "in which the executive professes a constitutional or legal discretion" and which are "only politically examinable." What cases fall within this category?

- How can one distinguish political matters from cases involving individual rights?

- Why is mandamus appropriate rather than money damages?

- Do you agree with CHIEF JUSTICE MARSHALL's presentation of the issues concerning the merits of the case before he considers the issue of whether the Supreme Court has jurisdiction? Consider, in light of the very brief history in Note 1, why he ordered the issues as he did.

- When you read the language of §13 of the Judiciary Act and the language of Article III, are you convinced that the Supreme Court has no jurisdiction over this case? Can you read §13 so that it would be constitutional?

- Did Marbury's lawyer make a dumb error by filing his writ of mandamus in the Supreme Court rather than a state (or lower federal) court?

3. **Reasons for Judicial Review.** Are you convinced that judicial review of acts of Congress is logically compelled? Which of the following rationales for the power of the Supreme Court to declare acts of Congress unconstitutional do you find convincing: oath of office, judicial role, Supremacy Clause, All Writs provision, written constitution?

4. **Other Reasons for Judicial Review.** What other factors would convince you that judicial review is part of the constitutional framework?

- The intent of the Framers? *See, e.g.* Federalist No. 78 ("No legislative act, therefore, contrary to the Constitution, can be valid ***. The courts were designed to be an intermediate body between the people and the legislature, in order, among other things, to keep the latter within the limits assigned to their authority. A constitution is, in fact, and must be regarded by the judges, as a fundamental law. It therefore belongs to them to ascertain its meaning ***.").

- Subsequent practice over the last 200 years?

- Necessity? Consider the alternative of having no judicial review.

5. **The "Countermajoritarian Difficulty."** "We the People" select our President, our Senators, and our Representatives. We never vote on Supreme Court Justices or other federal judges. This is profoundly undemocratic. Why should unelected judges be allowed to overturn the will of the people? Are your concerns lessened because the President nominates judges and the Senate confirms these nominations? When may a judge be removed from office? Would you be less concerned about undemocratic judicial power if the judicial function were relatively mechanical? Does the fact that there are other nonmajoritarian components of the Constitution (e.g. supermajoritarian requirements) alleviate the "countermajoritarian difficulty"?

6. **Thoughts on Applying the Constitution.**

- "The government of the United States has been emphatically termed a government of laws, and not of men." CHIEF JUSTICE MARSHALL in *Marbury.*

- "[W]hoever hath an absolute authority to interpret any written or spoken laws, it is he who is truly the Law-giver to all intents and purposes, and not the person who first wrote or spake them." Gray, NATURE AND SOURCES OF THE LAW (2d ed. 1924) (Bishop Hoadly).

• "We are not supreme because we are infallible, we are supreme because we are final." JUSTICE ROBERT A. JACKSON.

7.   **Executive and Legislative Interpretation of the Constitution.** What role, if any, do the other branches of government have in interpreting the Constitution? Thomas Jefferson's view was that "nothing in the Constitution has given [the Court] a right to decide for the Executive" whether a law is unconstitutional and that "the Executive, believing the law to be unconstitutional, was bound to remit the execution of it ***." Andrew Jackson considered it "as much the duty of the House of Representatives, of the Senate, and of the President to decide upon the constitutionality of any bill or resolution which may be presented to them for passage or approval as it is of the supreme judges when it may be brought before them for judicial decision." Conversely, Franklin Roosevelt sent New Deal legislation to Congress which would not pass muster under recent (and, in Roosevelt's view, regressive) decisions of the Supreme Court, saying "no one is in a position to give assurance that the proposed legislation will withstand constitutional tests *** [but I] hope your committee will not permit doubts as to constitutionality, however reasonable, to block the suggested legislation."

8.   **Conflict Concerning Constitutional Interpretation.** A more troubling issue is that of disagreements between the judiciary and the other branches over constitutional issues.   Must the other branches follow the Supreme Court's interpretations, or do the Court's decisions only bind the parties and provide guidance for litigants who follow?   Abraham Lincoln, speaking about the Supreme Court's *Dred Scott* decision, said: "[We] propose resisting it and to have it reversed if we can, and a new judicial rule established upon this subject." Further, Lincoln opined that "if the policy of the Government upon vital questions affecting the whole people is to be irrevocably fixed by decisions of the Supreme Court, *** the people will have ceased to be their own rulers." The most sweeping challenge by a President to the Supreme Court's authority was that attributed to Andrew Jackson concerning *Worcester v. Georgia*, 31 U.S. (6 Pet.) 515 (1832), in which the Marshall Court held Georgia had no legislative authority over Cherokee Nation lands: "John Marshall has made his decision. Now let him enforce it."

9.   **The Court's View of its Power.** Perhaps not surprisingly, the Court's view of its power is: "[*Marbury*] declared the basic principle that the federal judiciary is supreme in the exposition of the law of the Constitution." *Cooper v. Aaron*, 358 U.S. 1 (1958).   The Court's statement was made in response to claims by Governor Faubus and other Arkansas officials that they were not "bound" by *Brown v. Board of Education*, 347 U.S. 483 (1954). More recently, in response to the argument that a federal statute overturned the requirement established in *Miranda v. Arizona*, 384 U.S. 436 (1966), that police inform suspects of their constitutional rights, CHIEF JUSTICE REHNQUIST wrote: "Congress retains the ultimate authority to modify or set aside any judicially created rules of evidence and procedure that are not required by the Constitution. But Congress may not legislatively supercede our decisions interpreting and applying the Constitution." *Dickerson v. United States*, 530 U.S. 428 (2000).   Seven members of the Court agreed that *Miranda* "announced a constitutional rule" and that there was "no justification for overruling" it.   JUSTICE SCALIA, dissenting for himself and

JUSTICE THOMAS, claimed that "[W]hat [*Dickerson*] will stand for, whether the JUSTICES can bring themselves to say it or not, is the power of the Supreme Court to write a prophylactic, extraconstitutional Constitution, binding on Congress and the States. *** This is not the system that was established by the Framers, or that would be established by any sane supporter of government by the people."

10. **Constitutional Amendments.** Many Supreme Court interpretations of the Constitution have been unpopular. A few have been reversed through the amendment process. *See* Amendments 11, 13, 14, 16, 19, and 26. Should the difficulty of the amendment process set forth in Article V affect the Supreme Court's willingness to reinterpret the Constitution to bring it in line with modern conditions? What role, if any, should the Supreme Court have in determining the constitutionality of amendments overturning its decisions?

B. INVALIDATION OF STATE LAWS

The power of the federal courts to invalidate state laws and to nullify actions of state and local officials as unconstitutional is discussed in the following case. Are the sources of this authority the same as or different from those used in *Marbury*? Is the power exercised in this case more or less controversial than that exercised in *Marbury*?

MARTIN v. HUNTER'S LESSEE
14 U.S. (1 Wheat.) 304, 4 L.Ed. 97 (1816).

[The Court of Appeals of Virginia refused to obey an earlier decision of the Supreme Court reversing the Virginia court's holding that land escheated under Virginia law was not affected by a 1794 treaty confirming British land titles. The basis for its refusal was that "the appellate power of the supreme court of the United States does not extend to this court under a sound construction of the constitution of the United States; that so much of the 25th section of the act of congress, to establish the judicial courts of the United States, as extends the appellate jurisdiction of the supreme court to this court, is not in pursuance of the constitution of the United States."

The underlying dispute was a classic case of disputed titles to property. Lord Fairfax, when he died in 1781, devised the Northern Neck of Virginia, claimed through charters and grants from Kings Charles II and James II (affirmed by the Virginia Assembly in 1736) to Denny Fairfax, an English subject and resident. The claim of the plaintiff came from a 1789 Virginia statute: "[T]he patents or grants of land from the crown of England, under the former government, shall be, and are hereby declared null and void; and that all lands thereby respectively granted shall be held in absolute and unconditional property, to all intents and purposes whatsoever, in the same manner with the lands hereafter granted by the commonwealth, by virtue of this act." On April 30, 1789, the Governor of Virginia conveyed the land to David Hunter, who leased it to the plaintiff, who sued to eject Denny Fairfax. In 1783, the United States and Great Britain signed a treaty of peace and in 1794 entered into a treaty of amity, commerce, and navigation.]

STORY, J., delivered the opinion of the court.

*** The constitution of the United States was ordained and established, not by the states in their sovereign capacities, but emphatically, as the preamble of the constitution declares, by "the people of the United States." There can be no doubt that it was competent to the people to invest the general government with all the powers which they might deem proper and necessary; to extend or restrain these powers according to their own good pleasure, and to give them a paramount and supreme authority. As little doubt can there be, that the people had a right to prohibit to the states the exercise of any powers which were, in their judgment, incompatible with the objects of the general compact; to make the powers of the state governments, in given cases, subordinate to those of the nation, or to reserve to themselves those sovereign authorities which they might not choose to delegate to either. The constitution was not, therefore, necessarily carved out of existing state sovereignties, nor a surrender of powers already existing in state institutions, for the powers of the states depend upon their own constitutions; and the people of every state had the right to modify and restrain them, according to their own views of the policy or principle. On the other hand, it is perfectly clear that the sovereign powers vested in the state governments, by their respective constitutions, remained unaltered and unimpaired, except so far as they were granted to the government of the United States. ***

With these principles in view, principles in respect to which no difference of opinion ought to be indulged, let us now proceed to the interpretation of the constitution, so far as regards the great points in controversy.

The third article of the constitution is that which must principally attract our attention. *** The appellate power is not limited by the terms of the third article to any particular courts. The words are, "the judicial power (which includes appellate power) shall extend *to all cases*," &c., and "in all other cases before mentioned the supreme court shall have appellate jurisdiction." It is the *case*, then, and not *the court*, that gives the jurisdiction. If the judicial power extends to the case, it will be in vain to search in the letter of the constitution for any qualification as to the tribunal where it depends. It is incumbent, then, upon those who assert such a qualification to show its existence by necessary implication. If the text be clear and distinct, no restriction upon its plain and obvious import ought to be admitted, unless the inference be irresistible.

If the constitution meant to limit the appellate jurisdiction to cases pending in the courts of the United States, it would necessarily follow that the jurisdiction of these courts would, in all the cases enumerated in the constitution, be exclusive of state tribunals. How otherwise could the jurisdiction extend to *all* cases arising under the constitution, laws, and treaties of the United States, or to *all* cases of admiralty and maritime jurisdiction? If some of these cases might be entertained by state tribunals, and no appellate jurisdiction as to them should exist, then the appellate power would not extend to *all*, but to *some*, cases. If state tribunals might exercise concurrent jurisdiction over all or some of the other classes of cases in the constitution without control, then the appellate jurisdiction of the United States might, as to such cases, have no real existence, contrary to the manifest intent of the constitution. Under such circumstances, to give effect to the judicial power, it must be construed to be exclusive; and this not only when the *casus foederis* should arise directly, but when it should arise, incidentally, in cases pending in state courts. This construction would abridge the jurisdiction of such court far more than has been ever contemplated in any act of congress.

*** [I]t is plain that the framers of the constitution did contemplate that cases within the judicial cognizance of the United States not only might but would arise in the state courts, in the exercise of their ordinary jurisdiction. With this view the sixth article declares, that "this constitution, and the laws of the United States which shall be made in pursuance thereof, and all treaties made, or which shall be made, under the authority of the United States, shall be the supreme law of the land, and the judges in every state shall be bound thereby, any thing in the constitution or laws of any state to the contrary notwithstanding." It is obvious that this obligation is imperative upon the state judges in their official, and not merely in their private, capacities. From the very nature of their judicial duties they would be called upon to pronounce the law applicable to the case in judgment. They were not to decide merely according to the laws or constitution of the state, but according to the constitution, laws and treaties of the United States—"the supreme law of the land."

A moment's consideration will show us the necessity and propriety of this provision in cases where the jurisdiction of the state courts is unquestionable. Suppose a contract for the payment of money is made between citizens of the same state, and performance thereof is sought in the courts of that state; no person can doubt that the jurisdiction completely and exclusively attaches, in the first instance, to such courts. Suppose at the trial the defendant sets up in his defence a tender under a state law, making paper money a good tender, or a state law, impairing the obligation of such contract, which law, if binding, would defeat the suit. The constitution of the United States has declared that no state shall make any thing but gold or silver coin a tender in payment of debts, or pass a law impairing the obligation of contracts. If congress shall not have passed a law providing for the removal of such a suit to the courts of the United States, must not the state court proceed to hear and determine it? Can a mere plea in defence be of itself a bar to further proceedings, so as to prohibit an inquiry into its truth or legal propriety, when no other tribunal exists to whom judicial cognizance of such cases is confided? Suppose an indictment for a crime in a state court, and the defendant should allege in his defence that the crime was created by an *ex post facto* act of the state, must not the state court, in the exercise of a jurisdiction which has already rightfully attached, have a right to pronounce on the validity and sufficiency of the defence? It would be extremely difficult, upon any legal principles, to give a negative answer to these inquiries. Innumerable instances of the same sort might be stated, in illustration of the position; and unless the state courts could sustain jurisdiction in such cases, this clause of the sixth article would be without meaning or effect, and public mischiefs, of a most enormous magnitude, would inevitably ensue.

It must, therefore, be conceded that the constitution not only contemplated, but meant to provide for cases within the scope of the judicial power of the United States, which might yet depend before state tribunals. It was foreseen that in the exercise of their ordinary jurisdiction, state courts would incidentally take cognizance of cases arising under the constitution, the laws, and treaties of the United States. Yet to all these cases the judicial power, by the very terms of the constitution, is to extend. It cannot extend by original jurisdiction if that was already rightfully and exclusively attached in the state courts, which (as has been already shown) may occur; it must, therefore, extend by appellate jurisdiction, or not at all. It would seem to follow that the appellate power of the United States must, in such cases, extend to state tribunals; and if in such cases, there is no reason why it should not equally attach upon all others within the purview of the constitution.

It has been argued that such an appellate jurisdiction over state courts is inconsistent with the genius of our governments, and the spirit of the constitution. That the latter was never designed to act upon state sovereignties, but only upon the people, and that if the power exists, it will materially impair the sovereignty of the states, and the independence of their courts. We cannot yield to the force of this reasoning; it assumes principles which we cannot admit, and draws conclusions to which we do not yield our assent.

It is a mistake that the constitution was not designed to operate upon states, in their corporate capacities. It is crowded with provisions which restrain or annul the sovereignty of the states in some of the highest branches of their prerogatives. The tenth section of the first article contains a long list of disabilities and prohibitions imposed upon the states. Surely, when such essential portions of state sovereignty are taken away, or prohibited to be exercised, it cannot be correctly asserted that the constitution does not act upon the states. The language of the constitution is also imperative upon the states as to the performance of many duties. It is imperative upon the state legislatures to make laws prescribing the time, places, and manner of holding elections for senators and representatives, and for electors of president and vice-president. And in these, as well as some other cases, congress have a right to revise, amend, or supercede the laws which may be passed by state legislatures. When, therefore, the states are stripped of some of the highest attributes of sovereignty, and the same are given to the United States; when the legislatures of the states are, in some respects, under the control of congress, and in every case are, under the constitution, bound by the paramount authority of the United States; it is certainly difficult to support the argument that the appellate power over the decisions of state courts is contrary to the genius of our institutions. The courts of the United States can, without question, revise the proceedings of the executive and legislative authorities of the states, and if they are found to be contrary to the constitution, may declare them to be of no legal validity. Surely the exercise of the same right over judicial tribunals is not a higher or more dangerous act of sovereign power.

Nor can such a right be deemed to impair the independence of state judges. It is assuming the very ground in controversy to assert that they possess an absolute independence of the United States. In respect to the powers granted to the United States, they are not independent; they are expressly bound to obedience by the letter of the constitution; and if they should unintentionally transcend their authority, or misconstrue the constitution, there is no more reason for giving their judgments an absolute and irresistible force, than for giving it to the acts of the other co-ordinate departments of state sovereignty.

The argument urged from the possibility of the abuse of the revising power, is equally unsatisfactory. It is always a doubtful course, to argue against the use or existence of a power, from the possibility of its abuse. It is still more difficult, by such an argument, to ingraft upon a general power a restriction which is not to be found in the terms in which it is given. From the very nature of things, the absolute right of decision, in the last resort, must rest somewhere—wherever it may be vested it is susceptible of abuse. In all questions of jurisdiction the inferior, or appellate court, must pronounce the final judgment; and common sense, as well as legal reasoning, has conferred it upon the latter. ***

It is further argued, that no great public mischief can result from a construction which shall limit the appellate power of the United States to cases in their own courts: first, because state judges are bound by an oath to support the constitution of the United States, and must be presumed to be men of learning and integrity; and, secondly, because congress must have an unquestionable right to remove all cases within the scope of the judicial power from the state courts to the courts of the United States, at any time before final judgment, though not after final judgment. As to the first reason—admitting that the judges of the state courts are, and always will be, of as much learning, integrity, and wisdom, as those of the courts of the United States, (which we very cheerfully admit,) it does not aid the argument. It is manifest that the constitution has proceeded upon a theory of its own, and given or withheld powers according to the judgment of the American people, by whom it was adopted. We can only construe its powers, and cannot inquire into the policy or principles which induced the grant of them. The constitution has presumed (whether rightly or wrongly we do not inquire) that state attachments, state prejudices, state jealousies, and state interests, might some times obstruct, or control, or be supposed to obstruct or control, the regular administration of justice. Hence, in controversies between states; between citizens of different states; between citizens claiming grants under different states; between a state and its citizens, or foreigners, and between citizens and foreigners, it enables the parties, under the authority of congress, to have the controversies heard, tried, and determined before the national tribunals. No other reason than that which has been stated can be assigned, why some, at least, of those cases should not have been left to the cognizance of the state courts. In respect to the other enumerated cases—the cases arising under the constitution, laws, and treaties of the United States, cases affecting ambassadors and other public ministers, and cases of admiralty and maritime jurisdiction—reasons of a higher and more extensive nature, touching the safety, peace, and sovereignty of the nation, might well justify a grant of exclusive jurisdiction.

This is not all. A motive of another kind, perfectly compatible with the most sincere respect for state tribunals, might induce the grant of appellate power over their decisions. That motive is the importance, and even necessity of *uniformity* of decisions throughout the whole United States, upon all subjects within the purview of the constitution. Judges of equal learning and integrity, in different states, might differently interpret a statute, or a treaty of the United States, or even the constitution itself: If there were no revising authority to control these jarring and discordant judgments, and harmonize them into uniformity, the laws, the treaties, and the constitution of the United States would be different in different states, and might, perhaps, never have precisely the same construction, obligation, or efficacy, in any two states. The public mischiefs that would attend such a state of things would be truly deplorable; and it cannot be believed that they could have escaped the enlightened convention which formed the constitution. What, indeed, might then have been only prophecy, has now become fact; and the appellate jurisdiction must continue to be the only adequate remedy for such evils.

There is an additional consideration, which is entitled to great weight. The constitution of the United States was designed for the common and equal benefit of all the people of the United States. The judicial power was granted for the same benign and salutary purposes. It was not to be exercised exclusively for the benefit of parties who might be plaintiffs, and would elect the national forum, but also for the protection of defendants who might be entitled to try their rights, or assert their privileges, before the same forum. Yet, if the construction contended for be correct, it will follow, that as the plaintiff may always elect the state court, the defendant may be deprived of all the security which the constitution intended in aid of his rights. Such a state of things can, in no respect, be considered as giving equal rights. ***

On the whole, the court are of opinion, that the appellate power of the United States does extend to cases pending in the state courts; and that the 25th section of the judiciary act, which authorizes the exercise of this jurisdiction in the specified cases, by a writ of error, is supported by the letter and spirit of the constitution. We find no clause in that instrument which limits this power; and we dare not interpose a limitation where the people have not been disposed to create one. ***

Notes

1. **Text of § 25 of the Judiciary Act of 1789:**

    That a final judgment or decree in any suit, in the highest court of law or equity of a State in which a decision in the suit could be had, where is drawn in question the validity of a treaty or statute of, or an authority exercised under the United States, and the decision is against their validity; or where is drawn in question the validity of a statute of, or an authority exercised under any State on the ground of their being repugnant to the constitution, treaties or laws of the United States, and the decision is in favour of their validity, or where is drawn in question the construction of any clause of the constitution, or of a treaty, or statute of, or commission held under the United States, and the decision is against the title, right, privilege or exemption specially set up or claimed by either party, under such clause of the said constitution, treaty, statute or commission, may be re-examined and reversed or affirmed in the Supreme Court of the United States upon a writ of error. [But] no other error shall be assigned or regarded as a ground of reversal in any such case as aforesaid, than such as appears on the face of the record, and immediately respects the before mentioned questions of validity or construction of the said constitution, treaties, statutes, commissions, or authorities in dispute.

What policy choices do you see embedded in this legislation? Is the scope of this grant of authority sufficient for modern America? Compare the text of § 25 of the Judiciary Act of 1789 with its current form, codified in 28 U.S.C. § 1257:

Final judgments or decrees rendered by the highest court of a State in which a decision could be had, may be reviewed by the Supreme Court by writ of certiorari where the validity of a treaty or statute of the United States is drawn in question or where the validity of a statute of any State is drawn in question on the ground of its being repugnant to the Constitution, treaties, or laws of the United States, or where any title, right, privilege, or immunity is specially set up or claimed under the Constitution or the treaties or statutes of, or any commission held or authority exercised under, the United States.

2. *Martin* and Federalism. Does *Martin* threaten the independence of state government? Does it square with the Tenth Amendment? Do you find the outcome of the case consistent with your notions of federalism? One way of reading *Martin* would be to say that the Court found substantive power to flow to the federal authority because of the Supremacy Clause and the Court's location at the apex of the federal and state judicial systems. Another way of viewing the case is that the Court left tremendous responsibility and discretion concerning enforcement of substantive law, at least in the first instance, in the hands of decentralized state courts. If Hunter's Lessee had prevailed over Martin, might not Congress have responded by centralizing enforcement of federal rights in federal courts?

3. Policy. "I do not think the United States would come to an end if we lost our power to declare an Act of Congress void. I do think the Union would be imperiled if we could not make that declaration as to the laws of the several states." OLIVER W. HOLMES, JR., COLLECTED LEGAL PAPERS 295–96 (1920).

4. Bird's Eye View of the Court's Exercise of its Authority. Before John Marshall (1789–1801), the Supreme Court did not invalidate any federal or state laws. Under Marshall (1801–1835), it overturned only one federal statute (in *Marbury*) and invalidated 18 state laws. The Taney Court (1836–1864) overturned only one act of Congress (in *Dred Scott*) and 21 state laws. Contrast the Warren Court (1953–1969), which overturned 25 acts of Congress and 150 state laws, and the Burger Court (1969–1986), which invalidated 34 federal and 192 state laws (counting *Chadha* as one federal law rather than the 212 actually affected). The Rehnquist Court's pace of constitutional invalidations to date is more comparable to the Warren and Burger courts than to the Marshall and Taney courts. Does

this prove: (a) that the Court has become more aggressive in expanding the reach of the Constitution, or (b) that Congress and the states are sloppier in writing laws (and write more of them)?

5.   **Discretionary Review by the Supreme Court.** The Supreme Court currently receives more than 7,000 petitions to review cases each year. The Court grants plenary review (with oral arguments) in less than 100 cases per Term. Rule 10 of the Rules of the Supreme Court stipulates that "review on a writ of certiorari is not a matter of right, but of judicial discretion." Four of the nine Justices must agree for the Court to hear a case (grant the writ of certiorari). The reasons for granting review are (1) to resolve conflicting rulings (among the circuit courts, among state courts of last resort, between a circuit court and a state court of last resort, or between a state court or lower federal court and the Supreme Court) and (2) to decide questions of substantial public importance. If you are a lawyer who believes a ruling against your client was wrong, what do you tell her about taking her case to the Supreme Court? Is review more or less likely to be granted if the ruling was the first appellate ruling on a particular statutory or constitutional issue? Assume you are a law clerk for a Justice who thinks an issue is important but your Justice likely would be in the minority on the merits of the case. Should you urge the Justice to vote against granting review?

6.   **Questions and Problems.**

(a) Could Congress constitutionally abolish the federal courts other than the Supreme Court? What do you think of JUSTICE STORY's statement that "the whole judicial power of the United States should be, at all times, vested, either in an original or appellate form, in some courts created under its authority"?

(b) A District Court Judge, upon issuing a preliminary injunction against implementation of a state constitutional provision passed by a voter referendum, said that "the issue is not whether one judge can thwart the will of the people; rather, the issue is whether the challenged enactment complies with our Constitution and the Bill of Rights." Do you agree? Should federal judges treat state referenda any differently than state judicial opinions (the facts of *Martin*)?

(c) Suppose that a federal judge rules a state statute unconstitutional and enjoins the local officials who were parties to that litigation from enforcing the statute. Subsequently, in a state court action involving different parties, a state court judge rules that the statute is not unconstitutional and may be enforced by the local officials involved in the second suit. Should the federal or state court interpretation prevail? How should our judicial system deal with this unseemly divergence of interpretations?

C. SOURCES AND METHODS
OF JUDICIAL DECISIONS

1.   INTRODUCTION TO INTERPRETIVE ISSUES

Marbury, *Martin*, and innumerable subsequent cases confirm the judiciary's *power* to void federal statutes and state laws as unconstitutional. The justifications for allowing unelected judges to wield such power in a democracy have been addressed through the notes accompanying the principal cases. The *substance* of the judiciary's exercise of this power in connection with separation of federal powers, federalism's allocation of power between the federal and state governments, and the protection of individual rights is the focus of the remainder of this book.

First, however, it is worthwhile to assess the *interpretive techniques* used by Supreme Court justices and other interpreters of the Constitution. Examining how judges go about saying what the Constitution means is critical to understanding the difficulty of their task and to becoming better constitutional law advocates.

There are many schools of constitutional interpretation. Scholars sometimes discuss textualist, original intent, natural law, and philosophically-based modes of constitutional interpretation. Those who reject rigid borders around constitutional interpretation techniques are often called pragmatists; others who think all these interpretive modes are mere window-dressing for personal preferences have been called realists. These schools of interpretive techniques operate within a legal system in which precedent may constrain justices from interpreting the Constitution the way they would interpret it if a prior decision did not exist.

Textualism. Hugo Black was sometimes viewed as a textualist, especially in connection with his reading of the First Amendment. Black was fond of saying "No law means NO LAW" in broadly upholding freedom of speech and religion. Such literal reading of the words of the Constitution may be supplemented by structural textualism, in which the meaning of particular words may be clarified by examining their relationship to other provisions of the text. *See McCulloch v. Maryland*, 17 U.S. (4 Wheat.) 316 (1819), infra p. 211. One member of the present Supreme Court, JUSTICE ANTONIN SCALIA, is a self-professed textualist. Antonin Scalia, A MATTER OF INTERPRETATION: FEDERAL COURTS AND THE LAW (Princeton University Press 1997).

Obviously, since we have a written Constitution, few justices will ever admit to deciding cases contrary to the text of the Constitution. The problem is that, as we saw in the introductory exercises, many textual provisions are ambiguous. Perhaps because the Constitution was drafted hastily in the summer of 1787, the framers included deliberate ambiguities to be resolved later, or it may be that the facts of a modern case do not fit neatly into the textual framework of the Constitution.

Originalism. To resolve textual ambiguity, justices and scholars often examine the original intention of the framers of the Constitution. The primary benefit of ferreting out the original intention of the framers is that the judicial decision-making becomes less subjective. The justice's role is merely to implement the desire of the drafters and ratifiers of the Constitution. A good example of a case in which the majority and dissenters both draw extensively upon such materials is *U.S. Term Limits v. Thornton*, infra p.370.

One disadvantage of originalism is that the historical materials are often incomplete or indeterminate. There were no tape recorders present at the Constitutional Convention, and the notes of those who were there sometimes reveal opposing interpretations by the note-takers of what went on during the deliberations.

The Federalist Papers, frequently used as a source of original intent, were written by supporters of the Constitution after the Convention. They were never meant to serve as an objective reading of the document, but rather to advocate its ratification. One might well imagine James Madison, John Jay, and Alexander Hamilton skirting the edges of difficult topics and sugar coating the most controversial components of the Constitution in order to improve its chances of ratification!

Natural Law. A second problem with originalism is that later generations of Americans might not wish to accord power over present-day decisions to the intentions of those who drafted the Constitution more than 200 years ago. James Madison and others present at the Constitutional Convention avoided making their notes of the deliberations available after adoption of the Constitution in part to avoid prejudicing those who would be implementing and interpreting the Constitution.

An early discussion of the proper role of text and intent of the founders as the touchstones of constitutional interpretation occurs in *Calder v. Bull*, 3 U.S. (3 Dall.) 386 (1798). The opinion of JUSTICE CHASE contains the following discussion of natural law and constitutional law:

"I cannot subscribe to the omnipotence of a State Legislature, or that it is absolute and without control; although its authority should not be expressly restrained by the Constitution, or fundamental law, of the State. The people of the United States erected their Constitutions, or forms of government, to establish justice, to promote the general welfare, to secure the blessings of liberty; and to protect their persons and property from violence. The purposes for which men enter into society will determine the nature and terms of the social compact; and as they are the foundation of the legislative power, they will decide what are the proper objects of it: The nature, and ends of legislative power will limit the exercise of it. This fundamental principle flows from the very nature of our free Republican governments, that no man should be compelled to do what the laws do not require; nor to refrain from acts which the laws permit. There are acts which the Federal, or State, Legislature cannot do, without exceeding their authority. There are certain vital principles in our free Republican governments, which will determine and over-rule an apparent and flagrant abuse of legislative power; as to authorize manifest injustice by positive law; or to take away that security for personal liberty, or private property, for the protection whereof of the government was established. An ACT of the Legislature (for I cannot call it a law) contrary to the great first principles of the social compact, cannot be considered a rightful exercise of legislative authority. The obligation of a law in governments established on express compact, and on republican principles, must be determined by the nature of the power, on which it is founded. A few instances will suffice to explain what I mean. A law that punished a citizen for an innocent action, or, in other words, for an act, which, when done, was in violation of no existing law; a law that destroys, or impairs, the lawful private contracts of citizens; a law that makes a man a Judge in his own cause; or a law that takes property from A and gives it to B: It is against all reason and justice, for a people to entrust a Legislature with SUCH powers; and, therefore, it cannot be presumed that they have done it. The genius, the nature, and the spirit, of our State Governments, amount to a prohibition of such acts of legislation; and the general principles of law and reason forbid them. The Legislature may enjoin, permit, forbid, and punish; they may declare new crimes; and establish rules of conduct for all its citizens in future cases; they may command what is right, and prohibit what is wrong; but they cannot change innocence into guilt; or punish innocence as a crime; or violate the right of an antecedent lawful private contract; or the right of private property. To maintain that our Federal, or State, Legislature possesses such powers, if they had not been expressly restrained; would, in my opinion, be a political heresy, altogether inadmissible in our free republican governments."

JUSTICE IREDELL concurred in the decision, but objected to the discussion of natural law in a political system organized under a written constitution. He wrote:

"If, then, a government, composed of Legislative, Executive and Judicial departments, were established, by a Constitution, which imposed no limits on the legislative power, the consequence would inevitably be, that whatever the legislative power chose to enact, would be lawfully enacted, and the judicial power could never interpose to pronounce it void. It is true, that some speculative jurists have held, that a legislative act against natural justice must, in itself, be void; but I cannot think that, under such a government, any Court of Justice would possess a power to declare it so. Sir William Blackstone, having put the strong case of an act of Parliament, which should authorize a man to try his own cause, explicitly adds, that even in that case, 'there is no court that has power to defeat the intent of the Legislature, when couched in such evident and express words, as leave no doubt whether it was the intent of the Legislature, or no.

In order, therefore, to guard against so great an evil, it has been the policy of all the American states, which have, individually, framed their state constitutions since the revolution, and of the people of the United States, when they framed the Federal Constitution, to define with precision the objects of the legislative power, and to restrain its exercise within marked and settled boundaries. If any act of Congress, or of the Legislature of a state, violates those constitutional provisions, it is unquestionably void; though, I admit, that as the authority to declare it void is of a delicate and awful nature, the Court will never resort to that authority, but in a clear and urgent case. If, on the other hand, the Legislature of the Union, or the Legislature of any member of the Union, shall pass a law, within the general scope of their constitutional power, the Court cannot pronounce it to be void, merely because it is, in their judgment, contrary to the principles of natural justice. The ideas of natural justice are regulated by no fixed standard: the ablest and the purest men have differed upon the subject; and all that the Court could properly say, in such an event, would be, that the Legislature (possessed of an equal right of opinion) had passed an act which, in the opinion of the judges, was inconsistent with the abstract principles of natural justice. There are then but two lights, in which the subject can be viewed: 1st. If the Legislature pursue the authority delegated to them, their acts are valid. 2nd. If they transgress the boundaries of that authority, their acts are invalid. In the former case, they exercise the discretion vested in them by the people, to whom alone they are responsible for the faithful discharge of their trust: but in the latter case, they violate a fundamental law, which must be our guide, whenever we are called upon as judges to determine the validity of a legislative act."

Natural law was mainly honored in the breach during the early years of the republic. Slavery and the conquest of the Native American population are particularly poignant examples. Take, for example, *The Antelope*, 23 U.S. (10 Wheat.) 66 (1825). The narrow issue was whether federal law prohibiting the slave trade required forfeiture of slaves whom the owners said were bound for Brazil or Cuba, when the slaves were found in United States waters only because pirates had seized the ship and brought it into U.S. waters. CHIEF JUSTICE MARSHALL argued it was irrelevant that the slave trade was "contrary to the law of nature" and "[t]hat every man has a natural right to the fruits of his own labor"; the slaves were returned to their Spanish and Portuguese owners. Marshall noted that the case was one in which "the sacred rights of liberty and of property come in conflict with each other." As for the American Indians, Marshall said, "Conquest gives a title which the Courts of the conqueror cannot deny *** [however] opposed to natural right, and to the usages of civilized nations ***." *Johnson and Graham's Lessee v. William M'Intosh*, 21 U.S. 543 (1823).

In modern times, pure natural law has not been brought directly into constitutional decision-making. However, many Supreme Court justices have undoubtedly interpreted vague constitutional text in accordance with their own notions of justice. The Warren Court (1953–69) is generally viewed as marking the high point of judicial rejection of textualism and originalism in favor of philosophical interpretivism or framing a "living constitution." For example, JUSTICE WILLIAM O. DOUGLAS sometimes spoke of "penumbras" of words in the constitution to expansively protect particular philosophical values. *See Griswold v. Connecticut*, infra p. XXX. JUSTICE WILLIAM BRENNAN, another central figure on the Warren Court, sometimes read constitutional provisions broadly in an effort to make them more philosophically coherent, reading the text expansively to encompass situations he thought analogous to those explicitly covered by the text. *See Craig v. Boren,* infra p. 740; *Plyer v. Doe,* infra p. 779.

Pragmatism. One favorite strategy of constitutional law scholars is to show how a judge who belongs to a particular school of interpretation has acted inconsistently with the canons of that school in a particular case. Thus, a textualist judge is found to be result-oriented when the judge does not pay close attention to a particular textual provision about which he or she is unenthusiastic. The pragmatist school of interpretation rejects the very notion of a preferred technique for reading the Constitution. Pragmatists utilize components of various schools of constitutional interpretation to reach decisions. A pragmatist uses textual leanings, historical glosses, and philosophical arguments to argue for a particular reading of the Constitution. The pragmatist argues that this flexibility, on balance, provides a better mechanism to reach decisions than any one technique affords.

"Do you ever have one of those days when every-thing seems unconstitutional?"

II–1. "Do you ever have one of those days when everything seems unconstitutional?" © The New Yorker Collection 1974 Joseph Mirachi from cartoonbank.com. All Rights reserved.

Precedent. Supreme Court justices use the foregoing interpretive techniques within a framework of precedent. The Supreme Court almost never overturns a previous decision concerning statutory construction. If the Court was "wrong" in determining what Congress intended, Congress can simply pass a statute amending the interpreted legislation to overturn the Supreme Court's construction. The Court has been more willing to overturn its decisions construing the Constitution, in large part because the Article V supermajoritarian amendment processes are so difficult.

Precedent may, however, save a decision once made that the Court might not adopt today were it writing on a clean slate. In 1966, the Supreme Court held that the police must provide warnings to suspects of their constitutional rights to remain silent, have a lawyer, and so forth. This decision, *Miranda v. Arizona*, 384 U.S. 436 (1966), had many critics, including several members of the current Court. Nevertheless, in *Dickerson v. United States*, 120 S.Ct. 2326 (2000), the Court refused to overturn *Miranda*. CHIEF JUSTICE REHNQUIST wrote:

"Whether or not we would agree with *Miranda's* reasoning and its resulting rule, were we addressing the issue in the first instance, the principles of *stare decisis* weigh heavily against overruling it now. While '"stare decisis is not an inexorable command," 'particularly when we are interpreting the Constitution, *Agostini v. Felton*, 521 U.S. 203 (1997), 'even in constitutional cases, the doctrine carries such persuasive force that we have always required a departure from precedent to be supported by some 'special justification'.'"

The following excerpts from *Planned Parenthood v. Casey*, 505 U.S. 833 (1992), contain an extended discussion of the Court's use (or lack of use) of precedent in interpreting the Constitution. As you read them, try to articulate which side of the debate appeals to you most and why. What conclusions do you draw about precedent and your opportunities to use the Constitution for clients when you become a lawyer?

JUSTICE O'CONNOR, joined in this portion of the opinion by JUSTICES KENNEDY and SOUTER, wrote:

"[In] this case we may enquire whether [*Roe v. Wade's*] central rule [protecting a woman's liberty interest in aborting a fetus] has been found unworkable; whether the rule's limitation on state power could be removed without serious inequity to those who have relied upon it or significant damage to the stability of the society governed by it; whether the law's growth in the intervening years has left *Roe's* central rule a doctrinal anachronism discounted by society; and whether *Roe's* premises of fact have so far changed in the ensuing two decades as to render its central holding somehow irrelevant or unjustifiable in dealing with the issue it addressed.

Although *Roe* has engendered opposition, it has in no sense proven 'unworkable,' *see Garcia v. San Antonio Metropolitan Transit Authority*, 469 U.S. 528, 546 (1985), representing as it does a simple limitation beyond which a state law is unenforceable. While *Roe* has, of course, required judicial assessment of state laws affecting the exercise of the choice guaranteed against government infringement, and although the need for such review will remain as a consequence of today's decision, the required determinations fall within judicial competence.

The inquiry into reliance counts the cost of a rule's repudiation as it would fall on those who have relied reasonably on the rule's continued application. *** For two decades of economic and social developments, people have organized intimate relationships and made choices that define their views of themselves and their places in society, in reliance on the availability of abortion in the event that contraception should fail. ***

No evolution of legal principle has left *Roe*'s doctrinal footings weaker than they were in 1973. No development of constitutional law since the case was decided has implicitly or explicitly left *Roe* behind as a mere survivor of obsolete constitutional thinking. ***

[While] time has overtaken some of *Roe*'s factual assumptions, *** the divergences from the factual premises of 1973 have no bearing on the validity of *Roe*'s central holding, that viability marks the earliest point at which the State's interest in fetal life is constitutionally adequate to justify a legislative ban on nontherapeutic abortions. ***

The sum of the precedential enquiry to this point shows *Roe*'s underpinnings unweakened in any way affecting its central holding. While it has engendered disapproval, it has not been unworkable. *** Within the bounds of normal stare decisis analysis, then, and subject to the considerations on which it customarily turns, the stronger argument is for affirming *Roe*'s central holding, with whatever degree of personal reluctance any of us may have, not for overruling it.

In a less significant case, stare decisis analysis could, and would, stop at the point we have reached. But the sustained and widespread debate *Roe* has provoked calls for some comparison between that case and others of comparable dimension that have responded to national controversies ***.

The first example is that line of cases identified with *Lochner v. New York*, which imposed substantive limitations on legislation limiting economic autonomy in favor of health and welfare regulation ***. Fourteen years later, *West Coast Hotel Co. v. Parrish* signaled the demise of *Lochner* ***. In the meantime, the Depression had come and, with it, the lesson that seemed unmistakable to most people by 1937, that the interpretation of contractual freedom *** rested on fundamentally false factual assumptions about the capacity of a relatively unregulated market to satisfy minimal levels of human welfare. *** The facts upon which the earlier case had premised a constitutional resolution of social controversy had proven to be untrue, and history's demonstration of their untruth not only justified but required the new choice of constitutional principle that *West Coast Hotel* announced. ***

The second comparison that 20th century history invites is with the cases employing the separate-but-equal rule for applying the Fourteenth Amendment's equal protection guarantee. They began with *Plessy v. Ferguson*, 163 U.S. 537 (1896), holding that legislatively mandated racial segregation in public transportation works no denial of equal protection, rejecting the argument that racial separation enforced by the legal machinery of American society treats the black race as inferior. *** The Court in [*Brown v. Board*] addressed these facts of life by observing that whatever may have been the understanding in *Plessy*'s time of the power of segregation to stigmatize those who were segregated with a "badge of inferiority," it was clear by 1954 that legally sanctioned segregation had just such an effect, to the point that racially separate public educational facilities were deemed inherently unequal. ***

West Coast Hotel and *Brown* each rested on facts, or an understanding of facts, changed from those which furnished the claimed justifications for the earlier constitutional resolutions. Each case was comprehensible as the Court's response to facts that the country could understand, or had come to understand already, but which the Court of an earlier day, as its own declarations disclosed, had not been able to perceive. As the decisions were thus comprehensible they were also defensible, not merely as the victories of one doctrinal school over another by dint of numbers (victories though they were), but as applications of constitutional principle to facts as they had not been seen by the Court before. In constitutional adjudication as elsewhere in life, changed circumstances may impose new obligations, and the thoughtful part of the Nation could accept each decision to overrule a prior case as a response to the Court's constitutional duty.

Because the cases before us present no such occasion it could be seen as no such response. *** To overrule prior law for no other reason than that would run counter to the view repeated in our cases, that a decision to overrule should rest on some special reason over and above the belief that a prior case was wrongly decided. ***

The underlying substance of [the Court's] legitimacy is of course the warrant for the Court's decisions in the Constitution and the lesser sources of legal principle on which the Court draws. That substance is expressed in the Court's opinions, and our contemporary understanding is such that a decision without principled justification would be no judicial act at all. *** The Court must take care to speak and act in ways that allow people to accept its decisions on the terms the Court claims for them, as grounded truly in principle, not as compromises with social and political pressures having, as such, no bearing on the principled choices that the Court is obliged to make. ***

The need for principled action to be perceived as such is implicated to some degree whenever this, or any other appellate court, overrules a prior case. *** In two circumstances, however, the Court would almost certainly fail to receive the benefit of the doubt in overruling prior cases. There is, first, a point beyond which frequent overruling would overtax the country's belief in the Court's good faith. Despite the variety of reasons that may inform and justify a decision to overrule, we cannot forget that such a decision is usually perceived (and perceived correctly) as, at the least, a statement that a prior decision was wrong. That first circumstance can be described as hypothetical; the second is to the point here and now. Where, in the performance of its judicial duties, the Court decides a case in such a way as to resolve the sort of intensely divisive controversy reflected in *Roe* and those rare, comparable cases, its decision has a dimension that the resolution of the normal case does not carry. It is the dimension present whenever the Court's interpretation of the Constitution calls the contending sides of a national controversy to end their national division by accepting a common mandate rooted in the Constitution.

The Court is not asked to do this very often, having thus addressed the Nation only twice in our lifetime, in the decisions of *Brown* and *Roe*. But when the Court does act in this way, its decision requires an equally rare precedential force to counter the inevitable efforts to overturn it and to thwart its implementation. *** [To] overrule under fire in the absence of the most compelling reason to reexamine a watershed decision would subvert the Court's legitimacy beyond any serious question. *** A decision to overrule *Roe*'s essential holding under the existing circumstances would address error, if error there was, at the cost of both profound and unnecessary damage to the Court's legitimacy, and to the Nation's commitment to the rule of law. It is therefore imperative to adhere to the essence of *Roe*'s original decision, and we do so today."

CHIEF JUSTICE REHNQUIST, joined by JUSTICES WHITE, SCALIA, and THOMAS in dissent, wrote on this point as follows:

"The joint opinion of JUSTICES O'CONNOR, KENNEDY, and SOUTER cannot bring itself to say that *Roe* was correct as an original matter, but the authors are of the view that 'the immediate question is not the soundness of *Roe*'s resolution of the issue, but the precedential force that must be accorded to its holding.' Instead of claiming that *Roe* was correct as a matter of original constitutional interpretation, the opinion therefore contains an elaborate discussion of stare decisis. This discussion of the principle of stare decisis appears to be almost entirely dicta, because the joint opinion does not apply that principle in dealing with *Roe*. *Roe* decided that a woman had a fundamental right to an abortion. The joint opinion rejects that view. *Roe* decided that abortion regulations were to be subjected to 'strict scrutiny' and could be justified only in the light of 'compelling state interests.' The joint opinion rejects that view. *Roe* analyzed abortion regulation under a rigid trimester framework, a framework which has guided this Court's decision making for 19 years. The joint opinion rejects that framework. ***

In our view, authentic principles of stare decisis do not require that any portion of the reasoning in *Roe* be kept intact. *** Erroneous decisions in such constitutional cases are uniquely durable, because correction through legislative action, save for constitutional amendment, is impossible. It is therefore our duty to reconsider constitutional interpretations that 'depar[t] from a proper understanding' of the Constitution. ***

The joint opinion discusses several stare decisis factors which, it asserts, point toward retaining a portion of *Roe*. Two of these factors are that the main 'factual underpinning' of *Roe* has remained the same, and that its doctrinal foundation is no weaker now than it was in 1973. Of course, what might be called the basic facts which gave rise to *Roe* have remained the same— women become pregnant, there is a point somewhere, depending on medical technology, where a fetus becomes viable, and women give birth to children. But this is only to say that the same facts which gave rise to *Roe* will continue to give rise to similar cases. It is not a reason, in and of itself, why those cases must be decided in the same incorrect manner as was the first case to deal with the question. ***

The joint opinion also points to the reliance interests involved in this context in its effort to explain why precedent must be followed for precedent's sake. Certainly it is true that where reliance is truly at issue, as in the case of judicial decisions that have formed the basis for private decisions, '[c]onsiderations in favor of stare decisis are at their acme.' But, as the joint opinion apparently agrees, any traditional notion of reliance is not applicable here. ***

In the end, having failed to put forth any evidence to prove any true reliance, the joint opinion's argument is based solely on generalized assertions about the national psyche, on a belief that the people of this country have grown accustomed to the *Roe* decision over the last 19 years and have 'ordered their thinking and living around' it. *** However, the simple fact that a generation or more had grown used to these major decisions [such as *Lochner* and *Plessy*] did not prevent the Court from correcting its errors in those cases, nor should it prevent us from correctly interpreting the Constitution here.

Apparently realizing that conventional stare decisis principles do not support its position, the joint opinion advances a belief that retaining a portion of *Roe* is necessary to protect the 'legitimacy' of this Court. Because the Court must take care to render decisions 'grounded truly in principle,' and not simply as political and social compromises, the joint opinion properly declares it to be this Court's duty to ignore the public criticism and protest that may arise as a result of a decision. ***

The joint opinion picks out and discusses two prior Court rulings that it believes are of the 'intensely divisive' variety, and concludes that they are of comparable dimension to *Roe*. It appears to us very odd indeed that the joint opinion chooses as benchmarks two cases in which the Court chose not to adhere to erroneous constitutional precedent, but instead enhanced its stature by acknowledging and correcting its error, apparently in violation of the joint opinion's 'legitimacy' principle. *** [T]he opinion contends that the Court was entitled to overrule *Plessy* and *Lochner* in those cases, despite the existence of opposition to the original decisions, only because both the Nation and the Court had learned new lessons in the interim. This is at best a feebly supported, post hoc rationalization for those decisions. ***

The joint opinion *** agrees that the Court acted properly in rejecting the doctrine of 'separate but equal' in *Brown*. In fact, the opinion lauds *Brown* in comparing it to *Roe*. This is strange, in that under the opinion's 'legitimacy' principle the Court would seemingly have been forced to adhere to its erroneous decision in *Plessy* because of its 'intensely divisive' character. To us, adherence to *Roe* today under the guise of 'legitimacy' would seem to resemble more closely adherence to *Plessy* on the same ground. Fortunately, the Court did not choose that option in *Brown*, and instead frankly repudiated *Plessy*. *** The Court in *Brown* simply recognized, as JUSTICE HARLAN had recognized beforehand, that the Fourteenth Amendment does not permit racial segregation. The rule of *Brown* is not tied to popular opinion about the evils of segregation; it is a judgment that the Equal Protection Clause does not permit racial segregation, no matter whether the public might come to believe that it is beneficial. On that ground it stands, and on that ground alone the Court was justified in properly concluding that the *Plessy* Court had erred ***

The end result of the joint opinion's paeans of praise for legitimacy is the enunciation of a brand new standard for evaluating state regulation of a woman's right to abortion—the 'undue burden' standard. *** In evaluating abortion regulations under that standard, judges will have to decide whether they place a 'substantial obstacle' in the path of a woman seeking an abortion. In that this standard is based even more on a judge's subjective determinations than was the trimester framework, the standard will do nothing to prevent 'judges from roaming at large in the constitutional field' guided only by their personal views. ***"

Finally, JUSTICE SCALIA, joined by CHIEF JUSTICE REHNQUIST and JUSTICES WHITE and THOMAS, wrote as follows in response to JUSTICE O'CONNOR'S opinion:

> "'Liberty finds no refuge in a jurisprudence of doubt.'

One might have feared to encounter this august and sonorous phrase in an opinion defending the real *Roe v. Wade*, rather than the revised version fabricated today by the authors of the joint opinion. The shortcomings of *Roe* did not include lack of clarity ***. But to come across this phrase in the joint opinion—which calls upon federal district judges to apply an 'undue burden' standard as doubtful in application as it is unprincipled in origin—is really more than one should have to bear.

> '*While we appreciate the weight of the arguments *** that Roe should be overruled, the reservations any of us may have in reaffirming the central holding of Roe are outweighed by the explication of individual liberty we have given combined with the force of stare decisis.*'

The Court's reliance upon stare decisis can best be described as contrived. It insists upon the necessity of adhering not to all of *Roe*, but only to what it calls the 'central holding.' It seems to me that stare decisis ought to be applied even to the doctrine of stare decisis, and I confess never to have heard of this new, keep-what-you-want-and-throw-away-the-rest version. *** I am certainly not in a good position to dispute that the Court has saved the 'central holding' of *Roe*, since to do that effectively I would have to know what the Court has saved, which in turn would require me to understand (as I do not) what the 'undue burden' test means. ***

> '*[The American people's] belief in themselves as *** a people [who aspire to live according to the rule of law] is not readily separable from their understanding of the Court invested with the authority to decide their constitutional cases and speak before all others for their constitutional ideals. If the Court's legitimacy should be undermined, then, so would the country be in its very ability to see itself through its constitutional ideals.*'

The Imperial Judiciary lives. It is instructive to compare this Nietzschean vision of us unelected, life-tenured judges—leading a Volk who will be 'tested by following,' and whose very 'belief in themselves' is mystically bound up in their 'understanding' of a Court that 'speak[s] before all others for their constitutional ideals'—with the somewhat more modest role envisioned for these lawyers by the Founders. 'The judiciary *** has *** no direction either of the strength or of the wealth of the society, and can take no active resolution whatever. It may truly be said to have neither Force nor Will, but merely judgment. *** 'The Federalist No. 78. ***

What makes all this relevant to the bothersome application of 'political pressure' against the Court are the twin facts that the American people love democracy and the American people are not fools. As long as this Court thought (and the people thought) that we Justices were doing essentially lawyers' work up here— reading text and discerning our society's traditional understanding of that text—the public pretty much left us alone. Texts and traditions are facts to study, not convictions to demonstrate about. *** "

Notes

1. **Subjectivity.** Why should there be different rules of precedent for "blockbuster cases" and "ordinary constitutional cases"? How should the Justices determine which cases fit in which category? Wasn't the Court's overruling of *Swift v. Tyson*, 41 U.S. 1 (1842), in *Erie Ry. v. Tompkins*, 304 U.S. 64 (1938), as important as the decisions cited by the Court? If not, why not?

2. **Relationship of Methodologies.** Should the Court be more willing to review an earlier decision when that decision was not faithful to the text of the Constitution? To the historical meaning of the provision? To modern necessities?

3. **The Politics of Judicial Appointments.** Potential Supreme Court appointments have been important issues in virtually all recent Presidential elections. For example, Presidential Candidate Richard Nixon promised that, as President, he would appoint "strict constructionists" to the Court. As a Senator of the opposite party and ideology of the President, how would you go about exploring a nominee's interpretive approaches and possible substantive decisions?

4. **Precedent and the Judicial Function.** Eighth Circuit Rule 28A(i) ("Unpublished opinions are not precedent and parties generally should not cite them") was held unconstitutional because "[t]he judicial power of the United States is limited by the doctrine of precedent." *Anastasoff v. United States*, 223 F.3d 898 (2000), vacated 235 F.3d 1054 (2000). "[M]odern judicial scholars tend to justify the authority of precedents on equitable or prudential grounds," said the Court, unlike eighteenth-century scholars and the Founders. For example, Hamilton in Federalist No. 78 concluded that "to avoid an arbitrary discretion in the courts, it is indispensable that they should be bound down by strict rules and precedents, which serve to define and point out their duty in every particular case that comes before them." Precedent was viewed as a touchstone of the distinction between the judicial and the legislative power ("the judge's duty to follow precedent derives from the nature of the judicial power itself"). Madison even thought (overly optimistically, at least to this date) that the development of constitutional precedents would accrete until "[the Constitution's] meaning on all great points shall have been settled by precedent"! In light of the foregoing, is overruling of precedents unconstitutional? Are appellate court decisions not to

hear cases, to summarily affirm lower court decisions without opinion, and not to publish decisions unconstitutional?

2. PROBLEM: INTERPRETING THE SECOND AMENDMENT

Discuss whether a hypothetical federal statute—"It shall be a felony for anyone to own a handgun without having a handgun license"—violates the Second Amendment to the Constitution. Handgun control is the subject of much contemporary debate, with advocates of handgun control arguing that licensing will reduce crime. Opponents generally say that only outlaws will have unlicensed guns while law-abiding citizens will have their freedom limited unnecessarily. As a matter of constitutional law, how should the Supreme Court rule on a Second Amendment challenge to the hypothetical statute? Incorporate the following materials into the fabric of your argument:

a. Text of the Second Amendment and Related Contemporaneous Provisions.

1. *Second Amendment. A well regulated Militia, being necessary to the security of a free State, the right of the people to bear Arms, shall not be infringed.*

2. *English Bill of Rights. That the subject which are protestants may have arms for their defence suitable to their conditions and as allowed by law.* (1689)

3. *Massachusetts. The people have a right to keep and to bear arms for the common defence.* (1780)

4. *Virginia. That a well regulated militia, composed of the body of the people, trained to arms, is the proper, natural, and safe defense of a free state; that standing armies, in time of peace, should be avoided as dangerous to liberty; and that in all cases the military should be under strict subordination to, and governed by, the civil power.* (1776)

5. *Pennsylvania. The right of the citizens to bear arms in defence of themselves and the State shall not be questioned.* (1790)

b. Calls for the Second Amendment from State Ratification Conventions.

Five ratifying states sent demands for a Bill of Rights, all of which included a right to keep and bear arms. New Hampshire submitted text saying *"Congress shall never disarm any Citizen unless such are or have been in Actual Rebellion."* The Virginia, North Carolina, and Rhode Island provisions were nearly identical. Virginia's read: "*That the people shall have a right to keep and bear arms; that a well regulated Militia composed of the body of the people trained to arms is the proper, natural and safe defence of a free State. That standing armies in time of peace are dangerous to liberty, and therefore ought to be avoided, as far as the circumstances and protection of the Community will admit; and that in all cases the military should be under strict subordination to and governed by the Civil power.*" New York's suggestion was similar to Virginia's, but New York added a proviso saying *"the militia shall not be subject to Martial Law."* The Rhode Island provision said *"the body of the people capable of bearing arms"* rather than *"the body of the people trained to arms."*

c. The "Right of the People" provisions in the First, Fourth, Ninth, and Tenth Amendments. [Review the Constitution.]

d. Supreme Court Precedent.

In *United States v. Cruikshank,* 92 U.S. 542 (1876), the Supreme Court said, "The second amendment declares that it shall not be infringed; but this *** means no more than that it shall not be infringed by Congress. This is one of the amendments that has no other effect than to restrict the powers of the national government, leaving the people to look for their protection against any violation by their fellow-citizens of the rights it recognizes, to what is called *** the 'powers which relate to merely municipal legislation *** not surrendered or restrained' by the Constitution of the United States."

United States v. Miller, 307 U.S. 174 (1939), in an opinion of JUSTICE MCREYNOLDS excerpted below, contains the only sustained discussion of the meaning of the Second Amendment:

"An indictment in the District Court Western District Arkansas, charged that Jack Miller and Frank Layton did unlawfully, knowingly, wilfully, and feloniously transport in interstate commerce from the town of Claremore in the State of Oklahoma to the town of Siloam Springs in the State of Arkansas a certain firearm, to-wit, a double barrel 12–gauge Stevens shotgun having a barrel less than 18 inches in length, bearing identification number 76230, said defendants, at the time of so transporting said firearm in interstate commerce as aforesaid, not having registered said firearm as required by *** the 'National Firearms Act' approved June 26, 1934 ***. The District Court held that *** the Act violates the Second Amendment. It accordingly *** quashed the indictment. The cause is here by direct appeal. ***

In the absence of any evidence tending to show that possession or use of a 'shotgun having a barrel of less than eighteen inches in length' at this time has some reasonable relationship to the preservation or efficiency of a well regulated militia, we cannot say that the Second Amendment guarantees the right to keep and bear such an instrument. Certainly it is not within judicial notice that this weapon is any part of the ordinary military equipment or that its use could contribute to the common defense.

The Constitution as originally adopted granted to the Congress power—'To provide for calling forth the Militia to execute the Laws of the Union, suppress Insurrections and repel Invasions; To provide for organizing, arming, and disciplining, the Militia, and for governing such Part of them as may be employed in the

Service of the United States, reserving to the States respectively, the Appointment of the Officers, and the Authority of training the Militia according to the discipline prescribed by Congress.' U.S.C.A. Const. art. 1, § 8. With obvious purpose to assure the continuation and render possible the effectiveness of such forces the declaration and guarantee of the Second Amendment were made. It must be interpreted and applied with that end in view.

The Militia which the States were expected to maintain and train is set in contrast with Troops which they were forbidden to keep without the consent of Congress. The sentiment of the time strongly disfavored standing armies; the common view was that adequate defense of country and laws could be secured through the Militia—civilians primarily, soldiers on occasion.

The signification attributed to the term Militia appears from the debates in the Convention, the history and legislation of Colonies and States, and the writings of approved commentators. These show plainly enough that the Militia comprised all males physically capable of acting in concert for the common defense. 'A body of citizens enrolled for military discipline.' And further, that ordinarily when called for service these men were expected to appear bearing arms supplied by themselves and of the kind in common use at the time. ***

Most if not all of the States have adopted provisions touching the right to keep and bear arms. Differences in the language employed in these have naturally led to somewhat variant conclusions concerning the scope of the right guaranteed. But none of them seem to afford any material support for the challenged ruling of the court below.

We are unable to accept the conclusion of the court below and the challenged judgment must be reversed. The cause will be remanded for further proceedings."

e. Commentators' Observations.

1. "A standard move of those legal analysts who wish to limit the Second Amendment's force is to focus on its 'preamble' as setting out a restrictive purpose. [Some assert] that [the] purpose was to allow the states to keep their militias and to protect against the possibility that the new national government will use its power to establish a powerful standing army and eliminate the state militias. This *** reading quickly disposes of any notion that there is an 'individual' right to keep and bear arms. The right, if such it be, is only a state's right." Levinson, *The Embarrassing Second Amendment,* 99 YALE L.J. 637 (1989).

2. "[T]he Second Amendment adheres to the guarantee of the right of the people to keep and bear arms as the predicate for the other provision to which it speaks, i.e., the provision respecting the militia *** [I]t looks to an ultimate reliance on the common citizen who has a right to keep and bear

arms *** as an essential source of security of a free state. *** [The Amendment] embraces that right [of the people to bear arms] and indeed it erects the very scaffolding of a free state upon that guarantee. It derives its definition of a well-regulated militia in just this way for a 'free State': The militia to be well-regulated is a militia to be drawn from *** people with a right to keep and bear arms." Van Alstyne, *The Second Amendment and the Personal Right to Arms*, 43 DUKE L.J. 1236 (1994).

3. "The amendment speaks of a right of 'the people' collectively rather than a right of 'persons' individually. And it uses a distinctly military phrase: 'bear arms.' *** A modern translation of the amendment might thus be: 'An armed and militarily trained citizenry being conducive to freedom, the right of the electorate to organize itself militarily shall not be infringed.' *** The Framers envisioned Minutemen bearing guns, not Daniel Boone gunning bears." Amar, *Second thoughts: What the right to bear arms really means*, THE NEW REPUBLIC, July 12, 1999, pp. 24–27.

f. The Government's Position

In *United States v. Emerson*, 270 F.3d 203 (5th Cir. 2001), the Fifth Circuit upheld a statute prohibiting persons under domestic restraining orders from possessing firearms, but stated that the Second Amendment "protects the right of *individuals*, including those not then actually a member of any militia or engaged in active military service or training, to privately possess and bear their own firearms ***." However, said the Court, this individual right to bear arms does not preclude States from setting reasonable restrictions to prevent unfit persons from possessing firearms or restricting possession of firearms particularly suited for criminal use.

The Department of Justice endorsed this position on the meaning of the Second Amendment. *See* Memorandum From the Attorney General To All United States Attorneys; Re: United States v. Emerson, Nov. 9, 2001. In two petitions for writs of certiorari to the United States Supreme Court, the Solicitor General reiterated the individual rights view of the amendment's meaning. *Emerson v. United States*, 2001 U.S. Briefs 8780, 19-20 (May 2002) and *Haney v. United States*, 2001 U.S. Briefs 8272, 5 (May 2002). The Supreme Court denied certiorari in both cases.

D. LIMITS ON THE JUDICIAL POWER

Parts A and B of this chapter demonstrated the broad expanse of the Supreme Court's power to interpret the Constitution. Part C explored the substantial flexibility Supreme Court justices exercise in interpreting the Constitution. Thus, at this point, the student of constitutional law might reasonably perceive that the Supreme Court has limitless authority to impose its view of the Constitution on the whole of American society, displacing democracy with a judicial dictatorship.

This view would be quite perverse, however, for two reasons. First, as explored earlier, the Court has only the power of judgment, and cannot impress its decisions on society against the will of elected officials and the people. Second, as explored below, Congress, the Court, and a constitutional provision, the Eleventh Amendment, each impose limits on the exercise of federal judicial power.

1. CONGRESSIONAL LIMITS

Article III, § 1, states that "The judicial Power of the United States, shall be vested in one supreme court, and in such inferior Courts as the Congress may from time to time ordain and establish." The next section gives the Supreme Court "appellate Jurisdiction, both as to Law and Fact, with such Exceptions, and under such Regulations as the Congress shall make." Do these clauses give such broad authority to Congress that it can abolish the lower federal courts? Can Congress simply exclude from appellate jurisdiction particular types of cases or particular questions which it does not want the Court to hear? Can Congress reverse a judicial decision of which it does not approve? The cases in this section provide a framework for evaluating how far Congress can go in controlling the Article III judicial power.

a. *Limits on Habeas Corpus*

Some factual background is helpful to reading the first of these cases, *Ex Parte McCardle*. The writ of habeas corpus, guaranteed by Article I, § 9, of the Constitution, was implemented in § 14 of the Judiciary Act of 1789, which allowed the federal courts, including the Supreme Court, to issue the writ to free only those held "in custody, under or by colour of the authority of the United States." In the aftermath of the Civil War, Congress perceived this authorization of the writ to be too narrow because state prisoners could not obtain federal habeas corpus relief. For example, a freed former slave held under color of state law in violation of the rights recently granted under the Thirteenth Amendment would have been dependent on southern state courts to obtain release.

In February of 1867, the Reconstruction Congress passed an act which for the first time provided federal courts with the power "to grant writs of habeas corpus in all cases where any person may be restrained of his or her liberty in violation of the Constitution or of any treaty or law of the United States." Less than a month after passing this legislation, Congress adopted the Military Reconstruction Act, which divided the South into districts subject to military command. On November 12, 1867, McCardle, an unreconstructed white southerner who edited the *Vicksburg Times*, was arrested by Major General Alvin Gillem and held for trial for the nonmilitary offenses of disturbing the peace, inciting to insurrection and disorder, libel, and impeding reconstruction.

McCardle filed a petition for habeas corpus under the 1867 Act. His petition was denied by the federal circuit court and he appealed to the Supreme Court. McCardle claimed that suspension of his right to a jury trial under martial law was unconstitutional, that application of the Reconstruction Act to his editorials violated the First Amendment, and that the Reconstruction Act's placement of ten states under military jurisdiction was unconstitutional. The Supreme Court denied a motion by the United States to dismiss McCardle's appeal. Oral arguments on the merits were concluded on March 9, 1868. Three days later, the House and Senate, fearing the Supreme Court would hold the Reconstruction Act unconstitutional in its ruling on McCardle's appeal, passed legislation, which was vetoed by President Andrew Johnson on March 25, but quickly overridden by the Senate and the House. This new legislation stated, "That so much of the [1867 Act] as authorizes an appeal from the judgment of the circuit court to the Supreme Court of the United States, or the exercise of any such jurisdiction by said Supreme Court on appeals which have been or may hereafter be taken, be, and the same is, hereby repealed."

EX PARTE McCARDLE
74 U.S. (7 Wall.) 506, 19 L.Ed. 264 (1869).

The CHIEF JUSTICE delivered the opinion of the court.

The first question necessarily is that of jurisdiction; for, if the act of March, 1868, takes away the jurisdiction defined by the act of February, 1867, it is useless, if not improper, to enter into any discussion of other questions.

It is quite true, as was argued by the counsel for the petitioner, that the appellate jurisdiction of this court is not derived from acts of Congress. It is, strictly speaking, conferred by the Constitution. But it is conferred "with such exceptions and under such regulations as Congress shall make."

It is unnecessary to consider whether, if Congress had made no exceptions and no regulations, this court might not have exercised general appellate jurisdiction under rules prescribed by itself. For among the earliest acts of the first Congress, at its first session, was the act of September 24th, 1789, to establish the judicial courts of the United States. That act provided for the organization of this court, and prescribed regulations for the exercise of its jurisdiction.

The source of that jurisdiction, and the limitations of it by the Constitution and by statute, have been on several occasions subjects of consideration here. In the case of *Durousseau v. The United States*, particularly, the whole matter was carefully examined, and the court held, that while "the appellate powers of this court are not given by the judicial act, but are given by the Constitution," they are, nevertheless, "limited and regulated by that act, and by such other acts as have been passed on the subject." The court said, further, that the judicial act was an exercise of the power given by the Constitution to Congress "of making exceptions to the appellate jurisdiction of the Supreme Court." "They have described affirmatively," said the court, "its jurisdiction, and this affirmative description has been understood to imply a negation of the exercise of such appellate power as is not comprehended within it."

The principle that the affirmation of appellate jurisdiction implies the negation of all such jurisdiction not affirmed having been thus established, it was an almost necessary consequence that acts of Congress, providing for the exercise of jurisdiction, should come to be spoken of as acts granting jurisdiction, and not as acts making exceptions to the constitutional grant of it.

The exception to appellate jurisdiction in the case before us, however, is not an inference from the affirmation of other appellate jurisdiction. It is made in terms. The provision of the act of 1867, affirming the appellate jurisdiction of this court in cases of habeas corpus is expressly repealed. It is hardly possible to imagine a plainer instance of positive exception.

We are not at liberty to inquire into the motives of the legislature. We can only examine into its power under the Constitution; and the power to make exceptions to the appellate jurisdiction of this court is given by express words.

What, then, is the effect of the repealing act upon the case before us? We cannot doubt as to this. Without jurisdiction the court cannot proceed at all in any cause. Jurisdiction is power to declare the law, and when it ceases to exist, the only function remaining to the court is that of announcing the fact and dismissing the cause. And this is not less clear upon authority than upon principle.

Several cases were cited by the counsel for the petitioner in support of the position that jurisdiction of this case is not affected by the repealing act. But none of them, in our judgment, afford any support to it. They are all cases of the exercise of judicial power by the legislature, or of legislative interference with courts in the exercising of continuing jurisdiction.

On the other hand, the general rule, supported by the best elementary writers, is, that "when an act of the legislature is repealed, it must be considered, except as to transactions past and closed, as if it never existed." And the effect of repealing acts upon suits under acts repealed, has been determined by the adjudications of this court. The subject was fully considered in *Norris v. Crecker*, and more recently in *Insurance Company v. Ritchie*. In both of these cases it was held that no judgment could be rendered in a suit after the repeal of the act under which it was brought and prosecuted.

It is quite clear, therefore, that this court cannot proceed to pronounce judgment in this case, for it has no longer jurisdiction of the appeal; and judicial duty is not less fitly performed by declining ungranted jurisdiction than in exercising firmly that which the Constitution and the laws confer.

Counsel seem to have supposed, if effect be given to the repealing act in question, that the whole appellate power of the court, in cases of habeas corpus, is denied. But this is an error. The act of 1868 does not except from that jurisdiction any cases but appeals from Circuit Courts under the act of 1867. It does not affect the jurisdiction which was previously exercised.

The appeal of the petitioner in this case must be

DISMISSED FOR WANT OF JURISDICTION.

Notes

1. **Text.** Are there any textual limits to Congress' power to grant or deny the reach of federal court jurisdiction? To Supreme Court jurisdiction? To the availability of habeas corpus?

2. **Holding.** Did the Court hold (a) that Congress' power to regulate federal court jurisdiction (including access to the Supreme Court) is plenary or (b) that Congress' withdrawal of its power by repeal of the Act of 1867 was permissible only because there was another avenue for Supreme Court review? Which holding is more consistent with *Marbury*? What would you do after the Supreme Court's decision if you were McCardle's lawyer?

3. **Update on *McCardle*.** In *Felker v. Turpin*, 519 U.S. 989 (1996), the Court considered the constitutionality of the Antiterrorism and Effective Death Penalty Act of 1996, which placed severe limits on second and subsequent habeas petitions and permitted such petitions only after a special appellate panel granted a motion for leave to file the petition. Following *McCardle*, the Court unanimously held that Congress had not infringed on the judicial power to hear cases on an "original" writ of habeas corpus and that the limits on second and later writs did not unconstitutionally cause "suspension of the writ."

4. **Meaning of Suspension of the Writ.** The next case presents a more detailed picture of how the Writ of Habeas Corpus operates and an unresolved issue concerning what the Constitution means in prohibiting the suspension of that writ.

INS v. ST. CYR
533 U.S. 289, 121 S.Ct. 2271, 150 L.Ed.2d 347 (2001).

JUSTICE STEVENS delivered the opinion of the Court.

Both the Antiterrorism and Effective Death Penalty Act of 1996 (AEDPA) *** and the Illegal Immigration Reform and Immigrant Responsibility Act of 1996 (IIRIRA) *** contain comprehensive amendments to the Immigration and Nationality Act (INA). ***

The first question we must consider is whether the District Court retains jurisdiction under the general habeas corpus statute, 28 U.S.C. § 2241, to entertain St. Cyr's challenge. His application for a writ raises a pure question of law. He does not dispute any of the facts that establish his deportability or the conclusion that he is deportable. Nor does he contend that he would have any right to have an unfavorable exercise of the Attorney General's discretion reviewed in a judicial forum. Rather, he contests the Attorney General's conclusion that, as a matter of statutory interpretation, he is not eligible for discretionary relief. *** A construction of the amendments at issue that would entirely preclude review of a pure question of law by any court would give rise to substantial constitutional questions. Article I, § 9, cl. 2, of the Constitution provides: "The Privilege of the Writ of Habeas Corpus shall not be suspended, unless when in Cases of Rebellion or Invasion the public Safety may require it." Because of that Clause, some "judicial intervention in deportation cases" is unquestionably "required by the Constitution." *Heikkila v. Barber*, 345 U.S. 229, 235 (1953).

Unlike the provisions of AEDPA that we construed in *Felker v. Turpin*,

518 U.S. 651 (1996), this case involves an alien subject to a federal removal order rather than a person confined pursuant to a state-court conviction. Accordingly, regardless of whether the protection of the Suspension Clause encompasses all cases covered by the 1867 Amendment extending the protection of the writ to state prisoners, or by subsequent legal developments, at the absolute minimum, the Suspension Clause protects the writ "as it existed in 1789."

At its historical core, the writ of habeas corpus has served as a means of reviewing the legality of executive detention, and it is in that context that its protections have been strongest. *** In sum, even assuming that the Suspension Clause protects only the writ as it existed in 1789, there is substantial evidence to support the proposition that pure questions of law like the one raised by the respondent in this case could have been answered in 1789 by a common law judge with power to issue the writ of habeas corpus. It necessarily follows that a serious Suspension Clause issue would be presented if we were to accept the INS's submission that the 1996 statutes have withdrawn that power from federal judges and provided no adequate substitute for its exercise. The necessity of resolving such a serious and difficult constitutional issue—and the desirability of avoiding that necessity—simply reinforce the reasons for requiring a clear and unambiguous statement of constitutional intent.

Moreover, to conclude that the writ is no longer available in this context would represent a departure from historical practice in immigration law. *** The actual text of § 401(e), unlike its title, merely repeals a subsection of the 1961 statute amending the judicial review provisions of the 1952 Immigration and Nationality Act. Neither the title nor the text makes any mention of 28 U.S.C. § 2241.

The term "judicial review" or "jurisdiction to review" is the focus of each of these three provisions. In the immigration context, "judicial review" and "habeas corpus" have historically distinct meanings. In *Heikkila*, the Court concluded that the finality provisions at issue "preclud[ed] judicial review" to the maximum extent possible under the Constitution, and thus concluded that the APA was inapplicable. Nevertheless, the Court reaffirmed the right to habeas corpus. Noting that the limited role played by the courts in habeas corpus proceedings was far narrower than the judicial review authorized by the APA, the Court concluded that "it is the scope of inquiry on habeas corpus that differentiates" habeas review from "judicial review." Both §§ 1252(a)(1) and (a)(2)(C) speak of "judicial review"—that is, full, nonhabeas review. Neither explicitly mentions habeas, or 28 U.S.C. § 2241. Accordingly, neither provision speaks with sufficient clarity to bar jurisdiction pursuant to the general habeas statute.

If it were clear that the question of law could be answered in another judicial forum, it might be permissible to accept the INS' reading of § 1252. But the absence of such a forum, coupled with the lack of a clear, unambiguous, and express statement of congressional intent to preclude judicial consideration on habeas of such an important question of law, strongly counsels against adopting a construction that would raise serious constitutional questions. Accordingly, we conclude that habeas jurisdiction under § 2241 was not repealed by AEDPA and IIRIRA. ***

JUSTICE O'CONNOR, dissenting.

*** I do not join Part II [of JUSTICE SCALIA's dissenting opinion] because I believe that, assuming, arguendo, that the Suspension Clause guarantees some minimum extent of habeas review, the right asserted by the alien in this case falls outside the scope of that review for the reasons explained by JUSTICE SCALIA in Part II-B of his dissenting opinion. The question whether the Suspension Clause assures habeas jurisdiction in this particular case properly is resolved on this ground alone, and there is no need to say more.

JUSTICE SCALIA, with whom THE CHIEF JUSTICE and JUSTICE THOMAS join, and with whom JUSTICE O'CONNOR joins as to Parts I and III, dissenting

*** In the remainder of this opinion I address the question the Court should have addressed: Whether these provisions of IIRIRA are unconstitutional.

A straightforward reading of this text [of the Suspension Clause] discloses that it does not guarantee any content to (or even the existence of) the writ of habeas corpus, but merely provides that the writ shall not (except in case of rebellion or invasion) be suspended. Indeed, that was precisely the objection expressed by four of the state ratifying conventions–that the Constitution failed affirmatively to guarantee a right to habeas corpus.

To "suspend" the writ was not to fail to enact it, much less to refuse to accord it particular content. This was a distinct abuse of majority power, and one that had manifested itself often in the Framers' experience: temporarily but entirely eliminating the "Privilege of the Writ" for a certain geographic area or areas, or for a certain class or classes of individuals. *** In the present case, of course, Congress has not temporarily withheld operation of the writ, but has permanently altered its content. That is, to be sure, an act subject to majoritarian abuse, as is Congress's framing (or its determination not to frame) a habeas statute in the first place. But that is not the majoritarian abuse against which the Suspension Clause was directed. It is no more irrational to guard against the common and well known "suspension" abuse, without guaranteeing any particular habeas right that enjoys immunity from suspension, than it is, in the Equal Protection Clause, to guard against unequal application of the laws, without guaranteeing any particular law which enjoys that protection. And it is no more acceptable for this Court to write a habeas law, in order that the Suspension Clause might have some effect, than it would be for this Court to write other laws, in order that the Equal Protection Clause might have some effect.

The Court cites many cases, which it says establish that it is a "serious and difficult constitutional issue," whether the Suspension Clause prohibits the elimination of habeas jurisdiction effected by IIRIRA. Every one of those cases, however, pertains not to the meaning of the Suspension Clause, but to the content of the habeas corpus provision of the United States Code, which is quite a different matter. The closest the Court can come is a statement in one of those cases to the effect that the Immigration Act of 1917 "had the effect of precluding judicial intervention in deportation cases except insofar as it was required by the Constitution." *Heikkila*. That statement (1) was pure dictum, since the Court went on to hold that the judicial review of petitioner's deportation order was unavailable; (2) does not specify to what extent judicial review was "required by the Constitution," which could (as far as the Court's holding was concerned) be zero; and, most important of all, (3) does not refer to the Suspension Clause, so could well have had in mind the due process limitations upon the procedures for determining deportability that our later cases establish, see Part III, infra.

There is, however, another Supreme Court dictum that is unquestionably on point—an unusually authoritative one at that, since it was written by CHIEF JUSTICE MARSHALL in 1807. It supports precisely the interpretation of the Suspension Clause I have set forth above. In *Ex parte Bollman*, 4 Cranch 75, one of the cases arising out of the Burr conspiracy, the issue presented was whether the Supreme Court had the power to issue a writ of habeas corpus for the release of two prisoners held for trial under warrant of the Circuit Court of the District of Columbia. Counsel for the detainees asserted not only statutory authority for issuance of the writ, but inherent power. The Court would have nothing to do with that *** In the ensuing discussion of the Judiciary Act of 1789, the opinion specifically addresses the Suspension Clause *** pointing out that without legislated habeas jurisdiction the Suspension Clause would have no effect.

"It may be worthy of remark, that this act was passed by the first congress of the United States, sitting under a constitution which had declared 'that the privilege of the writ of habeas corpus should not be suspended, unless when, in cases of rebellion or invasion, the public safety might require it. Acting under the immediate influence of this injunction, they must have felt, with peculiar force, the obligation of providing efficient means by which this great constitutional privilege should receive life and activity; for if the means be not in existence, the privilege itself would be lost, although no law for its suspension should be enacted. Under the impression of this obligation, they give to all the courts the power of awarding writs of habeas corpus."[5]

There is no more reason for us to believe, than there was for the Marshall Court to believe, that the Suspension Clause means anything other than what it says.

Even if one were to assume that the Suspension Clause, despite its text and the Marshall Court's understanding, guarantees some constitutional

---

[5] *** If, as the Court concedes, "the writ could not be suspended," within the meaning of the Suspension Clause until Congress affirmatively provided for habeas by statute, then surely Congress may subsequently alter what it had initially provided for, lest the Clause become a one-way ratchet. The Court's position that a permanent repeal of habeas jurisdiction is unthinkable (and hence a violation of the Suspension Clause) is simply incompatible with its (and Marshall's) belief that a failure to confer habeas jurisdiction is not unthinkable.

minimum of habeas relief, that minimum would assuredly not embrace the rarified right asserted here: the right to judicial compulsion of the exercise of Executive discretion (which may be exercised favorably or unfavorably) regarding a prisoner's release. If one reads the Suspension Clause as a guarantee of habeas relief, the obvious question presented is: What habeas relief? There are only two alternatives, the first of which is too absurd to be seriously entertained. It could be contended that Congress "suspends" the writ whenever it eliminates any prior ground for the writ that it adopted. *** The Suspension Clause, in other words, would be a one-way ratchet that enshrines in the Constitution every grant of habeas jurisdiction. ***

The other alternative is that the Suspension Clause guarantees the common-law right of habeas corpus, as it was understood when the Constitution was ratified. There is no doubt whatever that this did not include the right to obtain discretionary release. *** An exhaustive search of cases antedating the Suspension Clause discloses few instances in which courts even discussed the concept of executive discretion; and on the rare occasions when they did, they simply confirmed what seems obvious from the paucity of such discussions—namely, that courts understood executive discretion as lying entirely beyond the judicial ken. That is precisely what one would expect, since even the executive's evaluation of the facts—a duty that was a good deal more than discretionary—was not subject to review on habeas. *** In sum, there is no authority whatever for the proposition that, at the time the Suspension Clause was ratified—or, for that matter, even for a century and a half thereafter—habeas corpus relief was available to compel the Executive's allegedly wrongful refusal to exercise discretion. ***

Notes

1. **Suspension Clause Discussion dicta?** Albeit in dictum, majority opinion clearly states that the Suspension Clause protects the writ of habeas corpus, at least as the writ existed at the time the original thirteen States ratified the Constitution. Given the historic purpose and modern-day function of the writ of habeas corpus, as well as the effect that outright repeal of the writ would have on the ability of Article III courts to review executive detention of individuals, does this indicate the Supreme Court will not cede authority to decide pure questions of law, regardless of the context in which those questions are raised?

2. **Suspension Clause substantive content.** The majority opinion reads the clause as a self-enforcing constitutional provision not needing enabling legislation. JUSTICE SCALIA expresses his doubts, based upon information gleaned from the text of, and history surrounding, the Suspension Clause. If JUSTICE SCALIA'S history is correct, how might a more substantial majority opinion analyze the constitutional issue?

3. **Suspension of Habeas.** Concurring in *Demore v. Kim*, 123 S. Ct. 1708 (2003), JUSTICE O'CONNOR concluded that "the writ was generally not available [until at least 1952] to aliens to challenge their detention while removal proceedings were ongoing." *St. Cyr* held that the Suspension Clause protected at a minimum the writ as it existed in 1789, she said, but "I need not conclusively decide the thorny

question whether [the statute concerning detention pending deportation hearing] violates the Suspension Clause."

4. **Questions.** Congress on a number of occasions has threatened to restrict judicial jurisdiction to avoid having its statutory policy choices challenged in the courts. Generally, Congress has not followed through on these threats and the Supreme Court has not been forced to consider such efforts. Which, if any, of the following hypothetical federal laws would be constitutional?

(a) "Notwithstanding any other provision of law, the United States District Courts shall not have jurisdiction over any case that challenges the constitutionality of any state or federal law relating to school busing."

(b) "The Supreme Court shall not have jurisdiction to review any case arising out of any State statute which relates to voluntary prayers in a public school or public building; nor shall its jurisdiction extend to any case relating to placement by any State official of the Ten Commandments in a public place or building."

(c) "No court in the United States shall have jurisdiction to review any claim that the federal statutory prohibition on abortions is unconstitutional."

b. Reversal of Judicial Decisions

MILLER v. FRENCH
530 U.S. 327, 120 S.Ct. 2246, 147 L.Ed.2d 326 (2000).

JUSTICE O'CONNOR delivered the opinion of the Court.

The Prison Litigation Reform Act of 1995 (PLRA) establishes standards for the entry and termination of prospective relief in civil actions challenging prison conditions. If prospective relief under an existing injunction does not satisfy these standards, a defendant or intervenor is entitled to "immediate termination" of that relief. And under the PLRA's "automatic stay" provision, a motion to terminate prospective relief "shall operate as a stay" of that relief during the period beginning 30 days after the filing of the motion (extendable to up to 90 days for "good cause") and ending when the court rules on the motion. The superintendent of the Pendleton Correctional Facility, which is currently operating under an ongoing injunction to remedy violations of the Eighth Amendment regarding conditions of confinement, filed a motion to terminate prospective relief under the PLRA. Respondent prisoners moved to enjoin the operation of the automatic stay provision of § 3626(e)(2), arguing that it is unconstitutional. *** We must decide whether a district court may enjoin the operation of the PLRA's automatic stay provision and, if not, whether that provision violates separation of powers principles.

I

This litigation began in 1975, when four inmates at what is now the Pendleton Correctional Facility brought a class action on behalf of all persons who were, or would be, confined at the facility against the predecessors in office of petitioners (hereinafter State). After a trial, the District Court found that living conditions at the prison violated both state and federal law, including the Eighth Amendment's prohibition against cruel and unusual punishment, and the court issued an injunction to correct those violations. While the State's appeal was pending, this Court decided *Pennhurst State School and Hospital v. Halderman*, 465 U.S. 89 (1984), which held that the Eleventh Amendment deprives federal courts of jurisdiction over claims for injunctive relief against state officials based on state law. Accordingly, the Court of Appeals for the Seventh Circuit remanded the action to the District Court for reconsideration. On remand, the District Court concluded that most of the state law violations also ran afoul of the Eighth Amendment, and it issued an amended remedial order to address those constitutional violations. The order also accounted for improvements in living conditions at the Pendleton facility that had occurred in the interim.

The Court of Appeals affirmed the amended remedial order as to those aspects governing overcrowding and doublecelling, the use of mechanical restraints, staffing, and the quality of food and medical services, but it vacated those portions pertaining to exercise and recreation, protective custody, and fire and occupational safety standards. This ongoing injunctive relief has remained in effect ever since, with the last modification occurring in October 1988, when the parties resolved by joint stipulation the remaining issues related to fire and occupational safety standards.

In 1996, Congress enacted the PLRA. As relevant here, the PLRA establishes standards for the entry and termination of prospective relief in civil actions challenging conditions at prison facilities. Specifically, a court "shall not grant or approve any prospective relief unless the court finds that such relief is narrowly drawn, extends no further than necessary to correct the violation of a Federal right, and is the least intrusive means necessary to correct the violation of the Federal right." The same criteria apply to existing injunctions, and a defendant or intervenor may move to terminate prospective relief that does not meet this standard. In particular, § 3626(b)(2) provides:

> "In any civil action with respect to prison conditions, a defendant or intervener shall be entitled to the immediate termination of any prospective relief if the relief was approved or granted in the absence of a finding by the court that the relief is narrowly drawn, extends no further than necessary to correct the violation of the Federal right, and is the least intrusive means necessary to correct the violation of the Federal right."

A court may not terminate prospective relief, however, if it "makes written findings based on the record that prospective relief remains necessary to correct a current and ongoing violation of the Federal right, extends no further than necessary to correct the violation of the Federal right, and that the prospective relief is narrowly drawn and the least intrusive means necessary to correct the violation." The PLRA also requires courts to rule "promptly" on motions to terminate prospective relief, with mandamus available to remedy a court's failure to do so.

Finally, the provision at issue here, § 3626(e)(2), dictates that, in certain circumstances, prospective relief shall be stayed pending resolution of a motion to terminate. Specifically, subsection (e)(2), entitled "Automatic Stay," states:

> "Any motion to modify or terminate prospective relief made under subsection (b) shall operate as a stay during the period—

> "(A)(i) beginning on the 30th day after such motion is filed ***; and

> "(B) ending on the date the court enters a final order ruling on the motion."

As one of several 1997 amendments to the PLRA, Congress permitted courts to postpone the entry of the automatic stay for not more than 60 days for "good cause," which cannot include general congestion of the court's docket.

On June 5, 1997, the State filed a motion under § 3626(b) to terminate the prospective relief governing the conditions of confinement at the Pendleton Correctional Facility. In response, the prisoner class moved for a temporary restraining order or preliminary injunction to enjoin the operation of the automatic stay, arguing that § 3626(e)(2) is unconstitutional as both a violation of the Due Process Clause of the Fifth Amendment and separation of powers principles. *** [The Court of Appeals decided PLRA violated the separation of powers, but did not reach the due process claim. The Supreme Court likewise did not address the due process claim, but remanded for "further proceedings consistent with this opinion."]

II

We address the statutory question first. Both the State and the prisoner class agree, as did the majority and dissenting judges below, that § 3626(e)(2) precludes a district court from exercising its equitable powers to enjoin the automatic stay. *** Like the Court of Appeals, we find that § 3626(e)(2) is unambiguous, and accordingly, we cannot adopt JUSTICE BREYER's "more flexible interpretation" of the statute. Any construction that preserved courts' equitable discretion to enjoin the automatic stay would effectively convert the PLRA's mandatory stay into a discretionary one. Because this would be plainly contrary to Congress' intent in enacting the stay provision, we must confront the constitutional issue.

III

The Constitution enumerates and separates the powers of the three branches of Government in Articles I, II, and III, and it is this "very structure" of the Constitution that exemplifies the concept of separation of powers. While the boundaries between the three branches are not "'hermetically' sealed," the Constitution prohibits one branch from encroaching on the central prerogatives of another. The powers of the Judicial Branch are set forth in Article III, § 1, which states that the "judicial Power of the United States shall be vested in one supreme Court and in such inferior Courts as Congress may from time to time ordain and establish," and provides that these federal courts shall be staffed by judges who hold office during good behavior, and whose compensation shall not be diminished during tenure in office. As we explained in *Plaut v. Spendthrift Farm, Inc.*, 514 U.S., at 218–219, Article III "gives the Federal Judiciary the power, not merely to rule on cases, but to decide them, subject to review only by superior courts in the Article III hierarchy."

Respondent prisoners contend that § 3626(e)(2) encroaches on the central prerogatives of the Judiciary and thereby violates the separation of powers doctrine. It does this, the prisoners assert, by legislatively suspending a final judgment of an Article III court in violation of *Plaut* and *Hayburn's Case*, 2 Dall. 409 (1792). According to the prisoners, the remedial order governing living conditions at the Pendleton Correctional Facility is a final judgment of an Article III court, and § 3626(e)(2) constitutes an impermissible usurpation of judicial power because it commands the district court to suspend prospective relief under that order, albeit temporarily. ***

Hayburn's Case arose out of a 1792 statute that authorized pensions for veterans of the Revolutionary War. The statute provided that the circuit courts were to review the applications and determine the appropriate amount of the pension, but that the Secretary of War had the discretion either to adopt or reject the courts' findings. Although this Court did not reach the constitutional issue in *Hayburn's Case*, the opinions of five Justices, sitting on Circuit Courts, were reported, and we have since recognized that the case "stands for the principle that Congress cannot vest review of the decisions of Article III courts in officials of the Executive Branch." *Plaut*. As we recognized in *Plaut*, such an effort by a coequal branch to "annul a final judgment" is " 'an assumption of Judicial power' and therefore forbidden."

Unlike the situation in *Hayburn's Case*, § 3626(e)(2) does not involve the direct review of a judicial decision by officials of the Legislative or Executive Branches. Nonetheless, the prisoners suggest that § 3626(e)(2) falls within *Hayburn's* prohibition against an indirect legislative "suspension" or reopening of a final judgment, such as that addressed in *Plaut*. In *Plaut*, we held that a federal statute that required federal courts to reopen final judgments that had been entered before the statute's enactment was unconstitutional on separation of powers grounds. The plaintiffs had brought a civil securities fraud action seeking money damages. While that action was pending, we ruled in *Lampf, Pleva, Lipkind, Prupis & Petigrow v. Gilbertson*, 501 U.S. 350 (1991), that such suits must be commenced within one year after the discovery of the facts constituting the violation and within three years after such violation. In light of this intervening decision, the *Plaut* plaintiffs' suit was untimely, and the District Court accordingly dismissed the action as time barred. After the judgment dismissing the case had become final, Congress enacted a statute providing for the reinstatement of those actions, including the *Plaut* plaintiffs', that had been dismissed under *Lampf* but that would have been timely under the previously applicable statute of limitations.

We concluded that this retroactive command that federal courts reopen final judgments exceeded Congress' authority. The decision of an inferior court within the Article III hierarchy is not the final word of the department (unless the time for appeal has expired), and "[i]t is the obligation of the last court in the hierarchy that rules on the case to give effect to Congress's latest enactment, even when that has the effect of overturning the judgment of an inferior court, since each court, at every level, must 'decide according to existing laws.' " But once a judicial decision achieves finality, it "becomes the last word of the judicial department." And because Article III "gives the Federal Judiciary the power, not merely to rule on cases, but to decide them, subject to review only by superior courts in the Article III hierarchy," the "judicial Power is one to render dispositive judgments," and Congress cannot retroactively command Article III courts to reopen final judgments.

Plaut, however, was careful to distinguish the situation before the Court in that case—legislation that attempted to reopen the dismissal of a suit seeking money damages—from legislation that "altered the prospective effect of injunctions entered by Article III courts." We emphasized that "nothing in our holding today calls ... into question" Congress' authority to alter the prospective effect of previously entered injunctions. Prospective relief under a continuing, executory decree remains subject to alteration due to changes in the underlying law. This conclusion follows from our decisions in *Pennsylvania v. Wheeling & Belmont Bridge Co.*, 13 How. 518 (1852) (*Wheeling Bridge I*) and *Pennsylvania v. Wheeling & Belmont Bridge Co.*, 18 How. 421 (1856) (*Wheeling Bridge II*).

In *Wheeling Bridge I*, we held that a bridge across the Ohio River, because it was too low, unlawfully "obstruct[ed] the navigation of the Ohio," and ordered that the bridge be raised or permanently removed. Shortly thereafter, Congress enacted legislation declaring the bridge to be "lawful structur[e]," establishing the bridge as a "'post-roa[d] for the passage of the mails of the United States,'" and declaring that the Wheeling and Belmont Bridge Company was authorized to maintain the bridge at its then-current site and elevation. *Wheeling Bridge II*. After the bridge was destroyed in a storm, Pennsylvania sued to enjoin the bridge's reconstruction, arguing that the statute legalizing the bridge was unconstitutional because it effectively annulled the Court's decision in *Wheeling Bridge I*. We rejected that argument, concluding that the decree in *Wheeling Bridge I* provided for ongoing relief by "directing the abatement of the obstruction" which enjoined the defendants' from any continuance or reconstruction of the obstruction. Because the intervening statute altered the underlying law such that the bridge was no longer an unlawful obstruction, we held that it was "quite plain the decree of the court cannot be enforced." *Wheeling Bridge II*. The Court explained that had *Wheeling Bridge I* awarded money damages in an action at law, then that judgment would be final, and Congress' later action could not have affected plaintiff's right to those damages. But because the decree entered in *Wheeling Bridge I* provided for prospective relief—a continuing injunction against the continuation or reconstruction of the bridge—the ongoing validity of the injunctive relief depended on "whether or not [the bridge] interferes with the right of navigation." When Congress altered the underlying law such that the bridge was no longer an unlawful obstruction, the injunction against the maintenance of the bridge was not enforceable.

Applied here, the principles of *Wheeling Bridge II* demonstrate that the automatic stay *** does not unconstitutionally "suspend" or reopen a judgment of an Article III court. [It] does not by itself "tell judges when, how, or what to do." Instead, [it] merely reflects the change implemented by § 3626(b), which does the "heavy lifting" in the statutory scheme by establishing new standards for prospective relief. Section 3626 prohibits the continuation of prospective relief that was "approved or granted in the absence of a finding by the court that the relief is narrowly drawn, extends no further than necessary to correct the violation of the Federal right, and is the least intrusive means to correct the violation," or in the absence of "findings based on the record that prospective relief remains necessary to correct a current and ongoing violation of a Federal right, extends no further than necessary to correct the violation of the Federal right, and that the prospective relief is narrowly drawn and the least intrusive means necessary to correct the violation." Accordingly, if prospective relief under an existing decree had been granted or approved absent such findings, then that prospective relief must cease, unless and until the court makes findings on the record that such relief remains necessary to correct an ongoing violation and is narrowly tailored. The PLRA's automatic stay provision *** requir[es] the court to stay any prospective relief that, due to the change in the underlying standard, is no longer enforceable, i.e., prospective relief that is not supported by the findings specified ***.

By establishing new standards for the enforcement of prospective relief in § 3626(b), Congress has altered the relevant underlying law. The PLRA has restricted courts' authority to issue and enforce prospective relief concerning prison conditions, requiring that such relief be supported by findings and precisely tailored to what is needed to remedy the violation of a federal right. We note that the constitutionality of § 3626(b) is not challenged here; we assume, without deciding, that the new standards it pronounces are effective. As *Plaut* and *Wheeling Bridge II* instruct, when Congress changes the law underlying a judgment awarding prospective relief, that relief is no longer enforceable to the extent it is inconsistent with the new law. Although the remedial injunction here is a "final judgment" for purposes of appeal, it is not the "last word of the judicial department." *Plaut*. The provision of prospective relief is subject to the continuing supervisory jurisdiction of the court, and therefore may be altered according to subsequent changes in the law. See *Rufo v. Inmates of Suffolk County Jail*, 502 U.S. 367 (1992). Prospective relief must be "modified if, as it later turns out, one or more of the obligations placed upon the parties has become impermissible under federal law."

The entry of the automatic stay under § 3626(e)(2) helps to implement the change in the law caused by §§ 3626(b)(2) and (3). If the prospective relief under the existing decree is not supported by the findings required ***, and the court has not made the findings required ***, then prospective relief is no longer enforceable and must be stayed. The entry of the stay does not reopen or "suspend" the previous judgment, nor does it divest the court of authority to decide the merits of the termination motion. Rather, the stay merely reflects the changed legal circumstances—that prospective relief under the existing decree is no longer enforceable, and remains unenforceable unless and until the court makes the findings required ***.

For the same reasons, § 3626(e)(2) does not violate the separation of powers principle articulated in *United States v. Klein*, 13 Wall. 128 (1872). In that case, *Klein*, the executor of the estate of a Confederate sympathizer, sought to recover the value of property seized by the United States during the Civil War, which by statute was recoverable if Klein could demonstrate that the decedent had not given aid or comfort to the rebellion. In *United States v. Padelford*, 9 Wall. 531 (1870), we held that a Presidential pardon satisfied the burden of proving that no such aid or comfort had been given. While Klein's case was pending, Congress enacted a statute providing that a pardon would instead be taken as proof that the pardoned individual had in fact aided the enemy, and if the claimant offered proof of a pardon the court must dismiss the case for lack of jurisdiction. *Klein*. We concluded that the statute was unconstitutional because it purported to "prescribe rules of decision to the Judicial Department of the government in cases pending before it."

Here, the prisoners argue that Congress has similarly prescribed a rule of decision because, for the period of time until the district court makes a final decision on the merits of the motion to terminate prospective relief, § 3626(e)(2) mandates a particular outcome: the termination of prospective relief. As we noted in *Plaut*, however, "[w]hatever the precise scope of *Klein*, later decisions have made clear that its prohibition does not take hold when Congress 'amend[s] applicable law.'" The prisoners concede this point but contend that, because § 3626(e)(2) does not itself amend the legal standard, *Klein* is still applicable. As we have explained, however, § 3626(e)(2) must be read not in isolation, but in the context of § 3626 as a whole. Section 3626(e)(2) operates in conjunction with the new standards for the continuation of prospective relief; if the new standards *** are not met, then the stay "shall operate" unless and until the court makes the findings required ***. Rather than prescribing a rule of decision, § 3626(e)(2) simply imposes the consequences of the court's application of the new legal standard.

Finally, the prisoners assert that, even if § 3626(e)(2) does not fall within the recognized prohibitions of *Hayburn's Case*, *Plaut*, or *Klein*, it still offends the principles of separation of powers because it places a deadline on judicial decisionmaking, thereby interfering with core judicial functions. Congress' imposition of a time limit in § 3626(e)(2), however, does not in itself offend the structural concerns underlying the Constitution's separation of powers. For example, if the PLRA granted courts 10 years to determine whether they could make the required findings, then certainly the PLRA would raise no apprehensions that Congress had encroached on the core function of the Judiciary to decide "cases and controversies properly before them." Respondents' concern with the time limit, then, must be its relative brevity. But whether the time is so short that it deprives litigants of a meaningful opportunity to be heard is a due process question, an issue that is not before us. We leave open, therefore, the question whether this time limit, particularly in a complex case, may implicate due process concerns.

In contrast to due process, which principally serves to protect the personal rights of litigants to a full and fair hearing, separation of powers principles are primarily addressed to the structural concerns of protecting the role of the independent Judiciary within the constitutional design. In this action, we have no occasion to decide whether there could be a time constraint on judicial action that was so severe that it implicated these structural separation of powers concerns. The PLRA does not deprive courts of their adjudicatory role, but merely provides a new legal standard for relief and encourages courts to apply that standard promptly.

Through the PLRA, Congress clearly intended to make operation of the automatic stay mandatory, precluding courts from exercising their equitable powers to enjoin the stay. And we conclude that this provision does not violate separation of powers principles. ***

JUSTICE SOUTER, with whom JUSTICE GINSBURG joins, concurring in part and dissenting in part.

I agree that 18 U.S.C. § 3626(e)(2) is unambiguous and join Parts I and II of the majority opinion. I also agree that applying the automatic stay may raise the due process issue, of whether a plaintiff has a fair chance to preserve an existing judgment that was valid when entered. But I believe that applying the statute may also raise a serious separation-of-powers issue if the time it allows turns out to be inadequate for a court to determine whether the new prerequisite to relief is satisfied in a particular case. I thus do not join Part III of the Court's opinion and on remand would require proceedings consistent with this one. I respectfully dissent from the terms of the Court's disposition.

A prospective remedial order may rest on at least three different legal premises: the underlying right meant to be secured; the rules of procedure for obtaining relief, defining requisites of pleading, notice, and so on; and, in some cases, rules lying between the other two, such as those defining a required level of certainty before some remedy may be ordered, or the permissible scope of relief. At issue here are rules of the last variety.

Congress has the authority to change rules of this sort by imposing new conditions precedent for the continuing enforcement of existing, prospective remedial orders and requiring courts to apply the new rules to those orders. Cf. *Plaut v. Spendthrift Farm, Inc.* If its legislation gives courts adequate time to determine the applicability of a new rule to an old order and to take the action necessary to apply it or to vacate the order, there seems little basis for claiming that Congress has crossed the constitutional line to interfere with the performance of any judicial function. But if determining whether a new rule applies requires time (say, for new factfinding) and if the statute provides insufficient time for a court to make that determination before the statute invalidates an extant remedial order, the application of the statute raises a serious question whether Congress has in practical terms assumed the judicial function. In such a case, the prospective order suddenly turns unenforceable not because a court has made a judgment to terminate it due to changed law or fact, but because no one can tell in the time allowed whether the new rule requires modification of the old order. One way to view this result is to see the Congress as mandating modification of an order that may turn out to be perfectly enforceable under the new rule, depending on judicial factfinding. If the facts are taken this way, the new statute might well be treated as usurping the judicial function of determining the applicability of a general rule in particular factual circumstances.[3] Cf. *United States v. Klein.*

Whether this constitutional issue arises on the facts of this action, however, is something we cannot yet tell ***. If the District Court determined both that it lacked adequate time to make the requisite findings in the period before the automatic stay would become effective, and that applying the stay would violate the separation of powers, the question would then be properly presented.

JUSTICE BREYER, with whom JUSTICE STEVENS joins, dissenting. [on statutory construction grounds]

Notes

1. **Legislative Alternatives.** Usually, if the Supreme Court rules an act of Congress unconstitutional, the legislators simply go back to the drawing board and rewrite the problematic part to comport with the Court's decision. But *Plaut*, discussed in *Miller*, involved judgments finalized before Congress acted. Moreover, Congress prospectively adopted, rather than repudiating, the statutes of limitations periods held appropriate in the Court's earlier decisions. What was going on in Congress to produce this response to the Supreme Court?

2. **Lesser Judicial Review for Prisoners?** *Ex Parte McCardle*, *Miller v. French*, and *Felker v. Turpin* all upheld limitations on judicial review in prisoner cases. Does the Court just not want to hear prisoners' allegations of unfairness and mistreatment? In *Lauf v. Shinner*, 303 U.S. 323 (1938), the Court upheld the Norris–LaGuardia Act's preclusion of federal court injunctions in labor disputes. The statute was designed to keep conservative judges from stopping strikes by workers and their unions. While the Court had held other New Deal statutes unconstitutional, it accepted this restriction on federal court jurisdiction.

3. **Problem.** In *Employment Division v. Smith*, 494 U.S. 872 (1990), the Supreme Court said that "generally applicable, religion neutral laws that have the effect of burdening a particular religious practice need not be justified by a compelling governmental interest" under the Free Exercise clause of the First Amendment. The Court found that religion-neutral laws need only be "rational," and that the

---

[3] The constitutional question inherent in these possible circumstances does not seem to be squarely addressed by any of our cases. Congress did not engage in discretionary review of a particular judicial judgment, cf. *Plaut* (characterizing *Hayburn's Case*), or try to modify a final, non-prospective judgment. Nor would a stay result from the judicial application of a change in the underlying law, cf. [*Wheeling Bridge II*]; *Plaut* (characterizing *Klein*). Instead, if the time is insufficient for a court to make a judicial determination about the applicability of the new rules, the stay would result from the inability of the Judicial Branch to exercise the judicial power of determining whether the new rules applied at all. Cf. *Marbury v. Madison* ("It is emphatically the province and duty of the judicial department to say what the law is").

plaintiff, a member of the Native American Church, was not protected from discharge for "work-related misconduct" when he engaged in sacramental use of the drug peyote. In response to the decision, Congress passed the Religious Freedom Restoration Act (RFRA), which provides in part that "Government may substantially burden a person's exercise of religion only if it demonstrates that application of the burden to the person (1) is in furtherance of a compelling governmental interest and (2) is the least restrictive means of furthering that compelling governmental interest." RFRA requires the courts to apply the compelling interest test in all instances, even though before *Smith* the Supreme Court had not rigorously applied a compelling interest test. Argue from the cases you have read thus far whether RFRA is constitutional. The Court's decision in *City of Boerne v. Flores*, infra p. 289, decided on other grounds, won't help you at all.

4. **Another Problem.** Assume that Congress, following extensive hearings, concludes that the Supreme Court is overworked and that this has affected the quality of its decisions. To solve this problem, Congress passes legislation dividing the Supreme Court into two divisions. The current Supreme Court becomes the Federal Division, with review authority over all appeals from decisions of federal courts. The legislation provides that appeals from state court decisions will be reviewed by the Supreme Court–State Division (nine Justices, each appointed for life-tenured positions in the same manner that the Justices of the Supreme Court–Federal Division were appointed). Is this legislation constitutional?

2. THE "CASE OR CONTROVERSY" LIMIT

One might assume that the Supreme Court would not limit its own power to decide matters brought to it. Such an assumption would be quite erroneous. The Supreme Court has with great frequency found the exercise of the federal judicial power to be outside its power to decide "Cases" and "Controversies" under Article III. When the Court finds a matter to be "nonjusticiable" under Article III, the suit is thrown out of the federal court system altogether. Whether it might be brought in state court is a matter of state law outside the scope of this course.

Justiciability encompasses a range of different problems that fall generally within the following broad "hornbook" categories:

• **Advisory Opinions.** The Court early on responded negatively to President Washington's request for an opinion concerning various legal issues arising from the United States' neutrality in a war between France and England. The Justices declined the invitation to render advice on the grounds that the three branches were "in certain respects checks upon each other; that they were judges of "a court in the last resort; and that extrajudicial decisions of questions did not square with the Article II power of the President to call on the heads of executive departments for opinions. What advantages/disadvantages do you see to advisory opinions?

• **Standing.** This component of justiciability focuses on whether the plaintiff is a proper party to bring a legal action. This issue occurs in a remarkably large number of cases involving attempts to enforce modern statutes and will be explored in *Laidlaw*, the next case.

•   **Ripeness.** A controversy is not ripe if it is premature; the Court views it as inadequately developed factually. Further actions, such as by a federal agency adopting a particular rule that harms (or fails to harm) particular individuals, may make a case ripe that previously was not ripe.

•   **Mootness.** A case that has become irrelevant because the dispute between the parties has ended is said to be moot. An otherwise moot case may be adjudicated, however, if there is a continuing controversy concerning damages from no longer continuing conduct or if, in the Court's words, the controversy is one "capable of repetition, yet evading review." Some aspects of mootness are discussed in *Laidlaw*.

•   **Political Questions.** When the Constitution entrusts a discretionary decision to Congress or the President, rather than to the Court, the decision is said to be a political question. When you read *Baker v. Carr* later in this section, think about whether the formulation of the test for what is a political question squares with the political question discussion in *Marbury*.

The Supreme Court has stated on numerous occasions that the justiciability doctrines "define with respect to the Judicial Branch the idea of separation of powers on which the Federal Government is founded" and that these doctrines demonstrate "concern about the proper—and properly limited—role of the courts in a democratic society." *Allen v. Wright*, 468 U.S. 737, 750 (1984). Nevertheless, both the Court and commentators acknowledge that justiciability is "more than an intuition but less than a rigorous and explicit theory." *Id.* Most of the discussion about justiciability ultimately comes back to whether the Court (1) is overusing justiciability doctrines to avoid deciding cases it would rather avoid (because of the controversial nature of the substantive question, the difficulty of the issue, or the poor quality of the factual setting or advocacy in the case presented) or (2) is ignoring justiciability considerations to decide matters best left to another forum (one of the political branches of the government).

As you read the following materials, consider why the Court would limit exercise of the judicial power. Is the Court seeking to obtain the best possible advocacy in cases heard by the federal courts? Is it trying to stake out the judicial power in principled ways that differentiate its power from the legislative and executive powers set forth in Articles I and II of the Constitution? Is it attempting to avoid issues which might arouse criticism?

a. *Standing and Mootness*

FRIENDS OF THE EARTH v. LAIDLAW ENVIRONMENTAL SERVICES, INC.
528 U.S. 167, 120 S.Ct. 693, 145 L.Ed.2d 610 (2000).

JUSTICE GINSBURG delivered the opinion of the Court.

This case presents an important question concerning the operation of the citizen-suit provisions of the Clean Water Act. Congress authorized the federal district courts to entertain Clean Water Act suits initiated by "a person or persons having an interest which is or may be adversely affected." 33 U.S.C. §§ 1365(a), (g). To impel future compliance with the Act, a district court may prescribe injunctive relief in such a suit; additionally or alternatively, the court may impose civil penalties payable to the United States Treasury. In the Clean Water Act citizen suit now before us, the District Court determined that injunctive relief was inappropriate because the defendant, after the institution of the litigation, achieved substantial compliance with the terms of its discharge permit. The court did, however, assess a civil penalty of $405,800. *** The Court of Appeals vacated the District Court's order. The case became moot, the appellate court declared, once the defendant fully complied with the terms of its permit and the plaintiff failed to appeal the denial of equitable relief. "[C]ivil penalties payable to the government," the Court of Appeals stated, "would not redress any injury Plaintiffs have suffered." ***

I

In 1972, Congress enacted the Clean Water Act (Act), also known as the Federal Water Pollution Control Act. *** Under § 505(a) of the Act, a suit to enforce any limitation in a [pollution] permit may be brought by any "citizen," defined as "a person or persons having an interest which is or may be adversely affected." Sixty days before initiating a citizen suit, however, the would-be plaintiff must give notice of the alleged violation to the EPA, the State in which the alleged violation occurred, and the alleged violator. "[T]he purpose of notice to the alleged violator is to give it an opportunity to bring itself into complete compliance with the Act and thus *** render unnecessary a citizen suit." Accordingly, we have held that citizens lack statutory standing under § 505(a) to sue for violations that have ceased by the time the complaint is filed. The Act also bars a citizen from suing if the EPA or the State has already commenced, and is "diligently prosecuting," an enforcement action.

The Act authorizes district courts in citizen-suit proceedings to enter injunctions and to assess civil penalties, which are payable to the United States Treasury. In determining the amount of any civil penalty, the district court must take into account "the seriousness of the violation or violations, the economic benefit (if any) resulting from the violation, any history of such violations, any good-faith efforts to comply with the applicable requirements, the economic impact of the penalty on the violator, and such other matters as justice may require." ***

In 1986, defendant-respondent Laidlaw Environmental Services (TOC), Inc., bought a hazardous waste incinerator facility in Roebuck, South Carolina, that included a wastewater treatment plant. *** Once it received its permit, Laidlaw began to discharge various pollutants into the waterway; repeatedly, Laidlaw's discharges exceeded the limits set by the permit. ***

On April 10, 1992, plaintiff-petitioners Friends of the Earth (FOE) and Citizens Local Environmental Action Network, Inc. (CLEAN) (referred to collectively in this opinion, together with later joined plaintiff-petitioner

Sierra Club, as "FOE") took the preliminary step necessary to the institution of litigation. They sent a letter to Laidlaw notifying the company of their intention to file a citizen suit against it under the Act after the expiration of the requisite 60–day notice period ***. Laidlaw's lawyer then contacted [the State to file suit barring] FOE's proposed citizen suit ***. On June 9, 1992, the last day before FOE's 60–day notice period expired, [the State] and Laidlaw reached a settlement requiring Laidlaw to pay $100,000 in civil penalties and to make "every effort" to comply with its permit obligations.

On June 12, 1992, FOE filed this citizen suit against Laidlaw ***, alleging noncompliance with the permit and seeking declaratory and injunctive relief and an award of civil penalties. Laidlaw moved for summary judgment on the ground that FOE had failed to present evidence demonstrating injury in fact, and therefore lacked Article III standing to bring the lawsuit. In opposition to this motion, FOE submitted affidavits and deposition testimony from members of the plaintiff organizations. *** After examining this evidence, the District Court denied Laidlaw's summary judgment motion, finding—albeit "by the very slimmest of margins"—that FOE had standing to bring the suit. ***

On January 22, 1997, the District Court issued its judgment. It found that Laidlaw had gained a total economic benefit of $1,092,581 as a result of its extended period of noncompliance with the mercury discharge limit in its permit. The court concluded, however, that a civil penalty of $405,800 was adequate. *** The court declined to grant FOE's request for injunctive relief, stating that an injunction was inappropriate because "Laidlaw has been in substantial compliance with all parameters in its NPDES [National Pollutant Discharge Elimination System] permit since at least August 1992."

*** The Court of Appeals assumed without deciding that FOE initially had standing to bring the action, but went on to hold that the case had become moot *** because "the only remedy currently available to [FOE]— civil penalties payable to the government—would not redress any injury [FOE has] suffered." *** According to Laidlaw, after the Court of Appeals issued its decision but before this Court granted certiorari, the entire incinerator facility in Roebuck was permanently closed, dismantled, and put up for sale, and all discharges from the facility permanently ceased. ***

II

The Constitution's case-or-controversy limitation on federal judicial authority, Art. III, § 2, underpins both our standing and our mootness jurisprudence, but the two inquiries differ in respects critical to the proper resolution of this case, so we address them separately. *** In *Lujan v. Defenders of Wildlife*, 504 U.S. 555, 560–561 (1992), we held that, to satisfy Article III's standing requirements, a plaintiff must show (1) it has suffered an "injury in fact" that is (a) concrete and particularized and (b) actual or imminent, not conjectural or hypothetical; (2) the injury is fairly traceable to the challenged action of the defendant; and (3) it is likely, as opposed to merely speculative, that the injury will be redressed by a favorable decision. An association has standing to bring suit on behalf of its members when its members would otherwise have standing to sue in their own right, the interests at stake are germane to the organization's purpose, and neither the claim asserted nor the relief requested requires the participation of individual members in the lawsuit. *Hunt v. Washington State Apple Advertising Comm'n*, 432 U.S. 333, 343 (1977).

Laidlaw contends first that FOE lacked standing from the outset even to seek injunctive relief, because the plaintiff organizations failed to show that any of their members had sustained or faced the threat of any "injury in fact" from Laidlaw's activities. In support of this contention Laidlaw points to the District Court's finding, made in the course of setting the penalty amount, that there had been "no demonstrated proof of harm to the environment" from Laidlaw's mercury discharge violations.

The relevant showing for purposes of Article III standing, however, is not injury to the environment but injury to the plaintiff. *** Focusing properly on injury to the plaintiff, the District Court found that FOE had demonstrated sufficient injury to establish standing. For example, FOE member Kenneth Lee Curtis averred in affidavits that he lived a half-mile from Laidlaw's facility; that he occasionally drove over the North Tyger River, and that it looked and smelled polluted; and that he would like to fish, camp, swim, and picnic in and near the river between 3 and 15 miles downstream from the facility, as he did when he was a teenager, but would not do so because he was concerned that the water was polluted by Laidlaw's discharges. Curtis reaffirmed these statements in extensive deposition testimony. *** Other members presented evidence to similar effect. ***

These sworn statements, as the District Court determined, adequately documented injury in fact. We have held that environmental plaintiffs adequately allege injury in fact when they aver that they use the affected area and are persons "for whom the aesthetic and recreational values of the area will be lessened" by the challenged activity. *Sierra Club v. Morton*, 405 U.S. 727, 735 (1972). See also *Defenders of Wildlife*, 504 U.S., at 562–563 ("Of course, the desire to use or observe an animal species, even for purely esthetic purposes, is undeniably a cognizable interest for purposes of standing.").

Our decision in *Lujan v. National Wildlife Federation*, 497 U.S. 871 (1990), is not to the contrary. *** We held that the plaintiff could not survive the summary judgment motion merely by offering "averments which state only that one of [the organization's] members uses unspecified portions of an immense tract of territory, on some portions of which mining activity has occurred or probably will occur by virtue of the governmental action." *** Nor can the affiants' conditional statements—that they would use the nearby North Tyger River for recreation if Laidlaw were not discharging pollutants into it—be equated with the speculative " 'some day' intentions" to visit endangered species halfway around the world that we held insufficient to show injury in fact in *Defenders of Wildlife*.

Los Angeles v. Lyons, 461 U.S. 95 (1983), relied on by the dissent, does not weigh against standing in this case. In *Lyons*, we held that a plaintiff lacked standing to seek an injunction against the enforcement of a police chokehold policy because he could not credibly allege that he faced a realistic threat from the policy. *** Here, in contrast, it is undisputed that Laidlaw's unlawful conduct—discharging pollutants in excess of permit limits—was occurring at the time the complaint was filed. ***

Laidlaw argues next that even if FOE had standing to seek injunctive relief, it lacked standing to seek civil penalties. Here the asserted defect is not injury but redressability. Civil penalties offer no redress to private plaintiffs, Laidlaw argues, because they are paid to the government, and therefore a citizen plaintiff can never have standing to seek them.

Laidlaw is right to insist that a plaintiff must demonstrate standing separately for each form of relief sought. But it is wrong to maintain that citizen plaintiffs facing ongoing violations never have standing to seek civil penalties.

We have recognized on numerous occasions that "all civil penalties have some deterrent effect." More specifically, Congress has found that civil penalties in Clean Water Act cases do more than promote immediate compliance by limiting the defendant's economic incentive to delay its attainment of permit limits; they also deter future violations. This congressional determination warrants judicial attention and respect. *** To the extent that they encourage defendants to discontinue current violations and deter them from committing future ones, they afford redress to citizen plaintiffs who are injured or threatened with injury as a consequence of ongoing unlawful conduct.

The dissent argues that it is the availability rather than the imposition of civil penalties that deters any particular polluter from continuing to pollute. This argument misses the mark in two ways. First, it overlooks the interdependence of the availability and the imposition; a threat has no deterrent value unless it is credible that it will be carried out. Second, it is reasonable for Congress to conclude that an actual award of civil penalties does in fact bring with it a significant quantum of deterrence over and above what is achieved by the mere prospect of such penalties. A would-be polluter may or may not be dissuaded by the existence of a remedy on the books, but a defendant once hit in its pocketbook will surely think twice before polluting again.

We recognize that there may be a point at which the deterrent effect of a claim for civil penalties becomes so insubstantial or so remote that it cannot support citizen standing. The fact that this vanishing point is not easy to ascertain does not detract from the deterrent power of such penalties in the ordinary case. *** In this case we need not explore the outer limits of the principle that civil penalties provide sufficient deterrence to support redressability. Here, the civil penalties sought by FOE carried with them a deterrent effect that made it likely, as opposed to merely speculative, that the penalties would redress FOE's injuries by abating current violations and preventing future ones ***. [*Steel Co. v. Citizens for a Better Environment,* 523 U.S. 83 (1998)] did not reach the issue of standing to seek penalties for violations that are ongoing at the time of the complaint and that could continue into the future if undeterred.

Satisfied that FOE had standing under Article III to bring this action, we turn to the question of mootness.

The only conceivable basis for a finding of mootness in this case is Laidlaw's voluntary conduct—either its achievement by August 1992 of substantial compliance with its permit or its more recent shutdown of the Roebuck facility. It is well settled that "a defendant's voluntary cessation of a challenged practice does not deprive a federal court of its power to determine the legality of the practice." "[I]f it did, the courts would be compelled to leave '[t]he defendant *** free to return to his old ways.'" In accordance with this principle, the standard we have announced for determining whether a case has been mooted by the defendant's voluntary conduct is stringent: "A case might become moot if subsequent events made it absolutely clear that the allegedly wrongful behavior could not reasonably be expected to recur." The "heavy burden of persua[ding]" the court that the challenged conduct cannot reasonably be expected to start up again lies with the party asserting mootness.

The Court of Appeals justified its mootness disposition by reference to *Steel Co.*, which held that citizen plaintiffs lack standing to seek civil penalties for wholly past violations. In relying on *Steel Co.*, the Court of Appeals confused mootness with standing. The confusion is understandable, given this Court's repeated statements that the doctrine of mootness can be described as "the doctrine of standing set in a time frame: The requisite personal interest that must exist at the commencement of the litigation (standing) must continue throughout its existence (mootness)." *Arizonans for Official English*, 520 U.S., at 68.

*** [T]here are circumstances in which the prospect that a defendant will engage in (or resume) harmful conduct may be too speculative to support standing, but not too speculative to overcome mootness. Furthermore, if mootness were simply "standing set in a time frame," the exception to mootness that arises when the defendant's allegedly unlawful activity is "capable of repetition, yet evading review" could not exist. *** Standing admits of no similar exception; if a plaintiff lacks standing at the time the action commences, the fact that the dispute is capable of repetition yet evading review will not entitle the complainant to a federal judicial forum. ***

Standing doctrine functions to ensure, among other things, that the scarce resources of the federal courts are devoted to those disputes in which the parties have a concrete stake. In contrast, by the time mootness is an issue, the case has been brought and litigated, often (as here) for years. To abandon the case at an advanced stage may prove more wasteful than frugal. This argument from sunk costs [to the judicial system, not the litigants] does not license courts to retain jurisdiction over cases in which one or both of the parties plainly lacks a continuing interest, as when the parties have settled or a plaintiff pursuing a nonsurviving claim has died. *** The effect of both

Laidlaw's compliance and the facility closure on the prospect of future violations is a disputed factual matter. *** These issues have not been aired in the lower courts; they remain open for consideration on remand. ***

JUSTICE STEVENS, concurring. [omitted]

JUSTICE KENNEDY, concurring.

Difficult and fundamental questions are raised when we ask whether exactions of public fines by private litigants, and the delegation of Executive power which might be inferable from the authorization, are permissible in view of the responsibilities committed to the Executive by Article II of the Constitution of the United States. *** In my view these matters are best reserved for a later case. ***

JUSTICE SCALIA, with whom JUSTICE THOMAS joins, dissenting.

The Court begins its analysis by finding injury in fact on the basis of vague affidavits that are undermined by the District Court's express finding that Laidlaw's discharges caused no demonstrable harm to the environment. It then proceeds to marry private wrong with public remedy in a union that violates traditional principles of federal standing—thereby permitting law enforcement to be placed in the hands of private individuals. Finally, the Court suggests that to avoid mootness one needs even less of a stake in the outcome than the Court's watered-down requirements for initial standing. I dissent from all of this.

I

Plaintiffs, as the parties invoking federal jurisdiction, have the burden of proof and persuasion as to the existence of standing. *Lujan v. Defenders of Wildlife*, 504 U.S. 555, 561 (1992) (hereinafter *Lujan*). The plaintiffs in this case fell far short of carrying their burden of demonstrating injury in fact. The Court cites affiants' testimony asserting that their enjoyment of the North Tyger River has been diminished due to "concern" that the water was polluted, and that they "believed" that Laidlaw's mercury exceedances had reduced the value of their homes. These averments alone cannot carry the plaintiffs' burden of demonstrating that they have suffered a "concrete and particularized" injury. General allegations of injury may suffice at the pleading stage, but at summary judgment plaintiffs must set forth "specific facts" to support their claims. And where, as here, the case has proceeded to judgment, those specific facts must be "supported adequately by the evidence adduced at trial." In this case, the affidavits themselves are woefully short on "specific facts," and the vague allegations of injury they do make are undermined by the evidence adduced at trial.

Typically, an environmental plaintiff claiming injury due to discharges in violation of the Clean Water Act argues that the discharges harm the environment, and that the harm to the environment injures him. This route to injury is barred in the present case, however, since the District Court concluded after considering all the evidence that there had been "no demonstrated proof of harm to the environment," that the "permit violations at issue in this citizen suit did not result in any health risk or environmental harm," that "[a]ll available data *** fail to show that Laidlaw's actual discharges have resulted in harm to the North Tyger River," and that "the overall quality of the river exceeds levels necessary to support *** recreation in and on the water."

The Court finds these conclusions unproblematic for standing, because "[t]he relevant showing for purposes of Article III standing *** is not injury to the environment but injury to the plaintiff." This statement is correct, as far as it goes. We have certainly held that a demonstration of harm to the environment is not enough to satisfy the injury-in-fact requirement unless the plaintiff can demonstrate how he personally was harmed. In the normal course, however, a lack of demonstrable harm to the environment will translate, as it plainly does here, into a lack of demonstrable harm to citizen plaintiffs. While it is perhaps possible that a plaintiff could be harmed even though the environment was not, such a plaintiff would have the burden of articulating and demonstrating the nature of that injury. Ongoing "concerns" about the environment are not enough, for "[i]t is the reality of the threat of repeated injury that is relevant to the standing inquiry, not the plaintiff's subjective apprehensions," *Los Angeles v. Lyons*, 461 U.S. 95, 107, n. 8 (1983). At the very least, in the present case, one would expect to see evidence supporting the affidavits' bald assertions regarding decreasing recreational usage and declining home values, as well as evidence for the improbable proposition that Laidlaw's violations, even though harmless to the environment, are somehow responsible for these effects. *** These affiants have established nothing but "subjective apprehensions." *** By accepting plaintiffs' vague, contradictory, and unsubstantiated allegations of "concern" about the environment as adequate to prove injury in fact, and accepting them even in the face of a finding that the environment was not demonstrably harmed, the Court makes the injury-in-fact requirement a sham. If there are permit violations, and a member of a plaintiff environmental organization lives near the offending plant, it would be difficult not to satisfy today's lenient standard.

II

The Court's treatment of the redressability requirement—which would have been unnecessary if it resolved the injury-in-fact question correctly—is equally cavalier. As discussed above, petitioners allege ongoing injury consisting of diminished enjoyment of the affected waterways and decreased property values. They allege that these injuries are caused by Laidlaw's continuing permit violations. But the remedy petitioners seek is neither recompense for their injuries nor an injunction against future violations. Instead, the remedy is a statutorily specified "penalty" for past violations, payable entirely to the United States Treasury. Only last Term, we held that such penalties do not redress any injury a citizen plaintiff has suffered from past violations. *Steel Co. v. Citizens for a Better Environment.* The Court nonetheless finds the redressability requirement satisfied here, distinguishing *Steel Co.* on the ground that in this case the petitioners allege ongoing violations; payment of the penalties, it says, will remedy petitioners' injury by deterring future violations by Laidlaw. It holds that a penalty payable to the public "remedies" a threatened private harm, and suffices to sustain a private suit.

That holding has no precedent in our jurisprudence, and takes this Court beyond the "cases and controversies" that Article III of the Constitution has entrusted to its resolution. Even if it were appropriate, moreover, to allow Article III's remediation requirement to be satisfied by the indirect private consequences of a public penalty, those consequences are entirely too speculative in the present case. The new standing law that the Court makes—like all expansions of standing beyond the traditional constitutional limits—has grave implications for democratic governance. I shall discuss these three points in turn.

In *Linda R.S. v. Richard D.*, 410 U.S. 614 (1973), the plaintiff, mother of an illegitimate child, sought, on behalf of herself, her child, and all others similarly situated, an injunction against discriminatory application of *** [a statute making it] a misdemeanor for "any parent" to refuse to support his or her minor children under 18 years of age, [although] it was enforced only against married parents. That refusal, the plaintiff contended, deprived her and her child of the equal protection of the law by denying them the deterrent effect of the statute upon the father's failure to fulfill his support obligation. The Court held that there was no Article III standing. *** There was no "logical nexus" between nonenforcement of the statute and Linda R. S.'s failure to receive support payments because "[t]he prospect that prosecution will *** result in payment of support" was "speculative" ***. The principle that "in American jurisprudence *** a private citizen lacks a judicially cognizable interest in the prosecution or nonprosecution of another" applies no less to prosecution for civil penalties payable to the State than to prosecution for criminal penalties owing to the State.

The Court's opinion reads as though the only purpose and effect of the redressability requirement is to assure that the plaintiff receive some of the benefit of the relief that a court orders. That is not so. If it were, a federal tort plaintiff fearing repetition of the injury could ask for tort damages to be paid, not only to himself but to other victims as well, on the theory that those damages would have at least some deterrent effect beneficial to him. Such a suit is preposterous because the "remediation" that is the traditional business of Anglo–American courts is relief specifically tailored to the plaintiff's injury, and not any sort of relief that has some incidental benefit to the plaintiff. *** Thus, relief against prospective harm is traditionally afforded by way of an injunction, the scope of which is limited by the scope of the threatened injury. In seeking to overturn that tradition by giving an individual plaintiff the power to invoke a public remedy, Congress has done precisely what we have said it cannot do: convert an "undifferentiated public interest" into an "individual right" vindicable in the courts. *** A claim of particularized future injury has today been made the vehicle for pursuing generalized penalties for past violations, and a threshold showing of injury in fact has become a lever that will move the world.

As I have just discussed, it is my view that a plaintiff's desire to benefit from the deterrent effect of a public penalty for past conduct can never suffice to establish a case or controversy of the sort known to our law. Such deterrent effect is, so to speak, "speculative as a matter of law." Even if that were not so, however, the deterrent effect in the present case would surely be speculative as a matter of fact. *** As a general matter, polluters as a class are deterred from violating discharge limits by the availability of civil penalties. However, none of the cases the Court cites focused on the deterrent effect of a single imposition of penalties on a particular lawbreaker. Even less did they focus on the question whether that particularized deterrent effect (if any) was enough to redress the injury of a citizen plaintiff in the sense required by Article III. They all involved penalties pursued by the government, not by citizens.

If the Court had undertaken the necessary inquiry into whether significant deterrence of the plaintiffs' feared injury was "likely," it would have had to reason something like this: Strictly speaking, no polluter is deterred by a penalty for past pollution; he is deterred by the fear of a penalty for future pollution. That fear will be virtually nonexistent if the prospective polluter knows that all emissions violators are given a free pass; it will be substantial under an emissions program such as the federal scheme here, which is regularly and notoriously enforced; it will be even higher when a prospective polluter subject to such a regularly enforced program has, as here, been the object of public charges of pollution and a suit for injunction; and it will surely be near the top of the graph when, as here, the prospective polluter has already been subjected to state penalties for the past pollution. The deterrence on which the plaintiffs must rely for standing in the present case is the marginal increase in Laidlaw's fear of future penalties that will be achieved by adding federal penalties for Laidlaw's past conduct.

I cannot say for certain that this marginal increase is zero; but I can say for certain that it is entirely speculative whether it will make the difference between these plaintiffs' suffering injury in the future and these plaintiffs' going unharmed. In fact, the assertion that it will "likely" do so is entirely farfetched. *** In sum, if this case is, as the Court suggests, within the central core of "deterrence" standing, it is impossible to imagine what the "outer limits" could possibly be. The Court's expressed reluctance to define those "outer limits" serves only to disguise the fact that it has promulgated a revolutionary new doctrine of standing that will permit the entire body of public civil penalties to be handed over to enforcement by private interests.

Article II of the Constitution commits it to the President to "take Care that the Laws be faithfully executed," Art. II, § 3, and provides specific methods by which all persons exercising significant executive power are to be appointed, Art. II, § 2. As JUSTICE KENNEDY's concurrence correctly observes, the question of the conformity of this legislation with Article II has not been argued—and I, like the Court, do not address it. But Article III, no less than Article II, has consequences for the structure of our government, and it is worth noting the changes in that structure which today's decision allows.

By permitting citizens to pursue civil penalties payable to the Federal Treasury, the Act does not provide a mechanism for individual relief in any traditional sense, but turns over to private citizens the function of enforcing the law. A Clean Water Act plaintiff pursuing civil penalties acts as a self-appointed mini-EPA. Where, as is often the case, the plaintiff is a national association, it has significant discretion in choosing enforcement targets. Once the association is aware of a reported violation, it need not look long for an injured member, at least under the theory of injury the Court applies today. And once the target is chosen, the suit goes forward without meaningful public control. The availability of civil penalties vastly disproportionate to the individual injury gives citizen plaintiffs massive bargaining power—which is often used to achieve settlements requiring the defendant to support environmental projects of the plaintiffs' choosing. Thus is a public fine diverted to a private interest.

To be sure, the EPA may foreclose the citizen suit by itself bringing suit. This allows public authorities to avoid private enforcement only by accepting private direction as to when enforcement should be undertaken—which is no less constitutionally bizarre. Elected officials are entirely deprived of their discretion to decide that a given violation should not be the object of suit at all, or that the enforcement decision should be postponed. *** This is the predictable and inevitable consequence of the Court's allowing the use of public remedies for private wrongs.

III

Finally, I offer a few comments regarding the Court's discussion of whether FOE's claims became moot by reason of Laidlaw's substantial compliance with the permit limits. I do not disagree with the conclusion that the Court reaches. *** Laidlaw's claimed compliance is squarely within the bounds of our "voluntary cessation" doctrine, which is the basis for the remand. *** Nonetheless, I am troubled by the Court's too-hasty retreat from our characterization of mootness as "the doctrine of standing set in a time frame." We have repeatedly recognized that what is required for litigation to continue is essentially identical to what is required for litigation to begin: There must be a justiciable case or controversy as required by Article III. *** Because the requirement of a continuing case or controversy derives from the Constitution, it may not be ignored when inconvenient, or, as the Court suggests, to save "sunk costs."

It is true that mootness has some added wrinkles that standing lacks. One is the "voluntary cessation" doctrine to which the Court refers. But it is inaccurate to regard this as a reduction of the basic requirement for standing that obtained at the beginning of the suit. A genuine controversy must exist at both stages. And just as the initial suit could be brought (by way of suit for declaratory judgment) before the defendant actually violated the plaintiff's alleged rights, so also the initial suit can be continued even though the defendant has stopped violating the plaintiff's alleged rights. The "voluntary cessation" doctrine is nothing more than an evidentiary presumption that the controversy reflected by the violation of alleged rights continues to exist. Similarly, the fact that we do not find cases moot when the challenged conduct is "capable of repetition, yet evading review" does not demonstrate that the requirements for mootness and for standing differ. "Where the conduct has ceased for the time being but there is a demonstrated probability that it will recur, a real-life controversy between parties with a personal stake in the outcome continues to exist."

Part of the confusion in the Court's discussion is engendered by the fact that it compares standing, on the one hand, with mootness based on voluntary cessation, on the other hand. The required showing that it is "absolutely clear" that the conduct "could not reasonably be expected to recur" is not the threshold showing required for mootness, but the heightened showing required in a particular category of cases where we have sensibly concluded that there is reason to be skeptical that cessation of violation means cessation of live controversy. For claims of mootness based on changes in circumstances other than voluntary cessation, the showing we have required is less taxing, and the inquiry is indeed properly characterized as one of " 'standing set in a time frame.' " ***

By uncritically accepting vague claims of injury, the Court has turned the Article III requirement of injury in fact into a "mere pleading requirement," *Lujan*, 504 U.S., at 561; and by approving the novel theory that public penalties can redress anticipated private wrongs, it has come close to "mak[ing] the redressability requirement vanish," *Steel Co.*, supra, at 107. The undesirable and unconstitutional consequence of today's decision is to place the immense power of suing to enforce the public laws in private hands. I respectfully dissent.

Notes

1. **Some Basic Points.**

  • What are the Constitution's commands about standing? About citizen suits as an alternative to federal prosecution?

  • Is standing now, as JUSTICE SCALIA charges in his *Laidlaw* dissent, merely a matter of pleading?

  • What is Congress' role on issues of standing?

  • How does mootness differ from standing?

  • What are the political or policy results of these doctrines? Should they affect the Court's assessment of standing and mootness issues?

2. *Lujan and Laidlaw*. *Lujan v. Defenders of Wildlife*, 504 U.S. 555 (1992), held that plaintiffs who might at some future date visit endangered species halfway around the globe did not have standing to seek enforcement of the Endangered Species Act. JUSTICE SCALIA wrote the majority opinion, which held that absence of definite plans to visit those remote locations, demonstrated for instance by obtaining a ticket to travel there, doomed the plaintiffs' standing. The Court also rejected the plaintiffs' claims that they suffered a "procedural injury"; a plaintiff cannot force the Executive Branch to follow statutory procedures absent a specific interest in the outcome of such procedures. Finally, the opinion discussed whether an injury was "redressable" since agencies that might have funded projects endangering

portions of overseas projects. The redressability portion of the opinion lacked a majority rationale. Are the distinctions between *Lujan* and *Laidlaw* principled?

3. **Standing of Bounty Hunters.** Qui tam actions are suits in which individuals file suit to recover money allegedly owed to the government. Typically, the incentive for the private suit is that the plaintiff who prevails gets a percentage of the recovery. In *Vermont Agency of Natural Resources v. United States ex rel. Stevens*, 529 U.S. 765 (2000), the Court considered whether a person who commenced an action under the False Claims Act to recover money defrauded from the United States had Article III standing to commence such a suit. In unanimously upholding the plaintiff's standing, the Court said:

> "There is no doubt, of course, that as to this portion of the recovery—the bounty he will receive if the suit is successful—a qui tam relator has a 'concrete private interest in the outcome of [the] suit.' But the same might be said of someone who has placed a wager upon the outcome. An interest unrelated to injury in fact is insufficient to give a plaintiff standing. The interest must consist of obtaining compensation for, or preventing, the violation of a legally protected right. A qui tam relator has suffered no such invasion— indeed, the 'right' he seeks to vindicate does not even fully materialize until the litigation is completed and the relator prevails. This is not to suggest that Congress cannot define new legal rights, which in turn will confer standing to vindicate an injury caused to the claimant. As we have held in another context, however, an interest that is merely a 'byproduct' of the suit itself cannot give rise to a cognizable injury in fact for Article III standing purposes.

> We believe, however, that adequate basis for the relator's suit for his bounty is to be found in the doctrine that the assignee of a claim has standing to assert the injury in fact suffered by the assignor. The FCA can reasonably be regarded as effecting a partial assignment of the Government's damages claim. Although we have never expressly recognized 'representational standing' on the part of assignees, we have routinely entertained their suits—and also suits by subrogees, who have been described as 'equitable assign[ees].' We conclude, therefore, that the United States' injury in fact suffices to confer standing on respondent Stevens.

> We are confirmed in this conclusion by the long tradition of qui tam actions in England and the American Colonies. That history is particularly relevant to the constitutional standing inquiry since, as we have said elsewhere, Article III's restriction of the judicial power to 'Cases' and 'Controversies' is properly understood to mean 'cases and controversies of the sort traditionally amenable to, and resolved by, the judicial process.'

> Qui tam actions appear to have originated around the end of the 13th century, when private individuals who had suffered injury began bringing actions in the royal courts on both their own and the Crown's behalf. *** Qui tam actions appear to have been as prevalent in America as in England, at least in the period immediately before and after the framing of the Constitution. *** Moreover, immediately after the framing, the First Congress enacted a considerable number

of informer statutes. Like their English counterparts, some of them provided both a bounty and an express cause of action; others provided a bounty only. *** When combined with the theoretical justification for relator standing discussed earlier, [this history] leaves no room for doubt that a qui tam relator under the FCA has Article III standing."

4. **"Procedural Injury" and Standing.** In *Federal Election Commission v. Akins*, 524 U.S. 11 (1998), [the Supreme Court held] that a group of voters satisfied constitutional standing requirements to challenge the FEC's decision not to bring an enforcement action. The voters' inability to obtain information they claim the Federal Election Commission Act requires the defendant to make public meets the genuine "injury in fact" requirement that helps assure that the court will adjudicate "[a] concrete, living contest between adversaries." Congress has the constitutional power to vindicate this harm in federal courts even though the harm at issue is widely shared. The informational injury here, directly related to voting, the most basic of political rights, is sufficiently concrete. The voters also satisfied the remaining two constitutional standing requirements: the harm asserted is "fairly traceable" to the FEC's decision not to issue its complaint, and the courts in this case can "redress" that injury.

5. **Problems.**

(a) A good friend of yours is concerned that she and others may develop skin cancer because of the "ozone hole" in the atmosphere and inadequate steps taken by the United States to ban the production of substances responsible for creating the hole. Your friend, who has unlimited financial resources to pursue the issue in court and a passionate commitment to this environmental issue, asks you whether there are any barriers (other than the usual expert testimony to prove probable skin damage) to her successful prosecution of such a suit. Advise her about justiciability issues.

(b) Suppose a state legislature adopted a variant of the Confederate Flag as the state flag. Who, if anyone, would have standing to object to this decision?

(c) A contractor's association, most of whose members are nonminority contractors, files a suit claiming that an ordinance requiring that 10% of the money spent on city contracts be "set aside" for minority business enterprises violates the Equal Protection Clause of the Fourteenth Amendment. Would the association have to show (1) that some of its members' bids for work were rejected because of the set aside, (2) that some of its members would have bid for such work but were deterred because of the set aside program, or (3) nothing beyond the fact that the program placed its nonminority members on an unequal footing in the bidding process? *See Northeastern Florida Chapter of Associated General Contractors v. Jacksonville*, 508 U.S. 656 (1993). If the city later changes its setaside program to permit nonminority businesses to qualify for the 10% "set asides," would the association lose its standing? Or would the case be moot? What is the difference, if any? *See Adarand Constructors, Inc. v. Slater*, 528 U.S. 216 (2000).

(d) After the Line Item Veto Act became effective, but before it was actually used by the President to veto specific items for which Congress had appropriated money, several Members of Congress who had voted against the Act brought suit against the Secretary of the Treasury challenging its constitutionality. The Act contained a provision saying "[a]ny Member of Congress or any individual adversely affected by [this Act] may bring an action *** on the ground that any provision *** violates the Constitution." How should the courts rule on the plaintiffs' standing? *See Raines v. Byrd*, 521 U.S. 811 (1997). Would Members of the House or Senators have standing to challenge legislation which called for sampling rather than actual counting of persons in the decennial census? *See Department of Commerce v. United States House of Representatives*, 525 U.S. 316 (1999); *see also Utah v. Evans*, 536 U.S. 452 (2002) (Utah has standing to challenge allocation of representative to North Carolina through "imputation" by the Census Bureau and the Secretary of Commerce; a court could order the Secretary to "recalculate the numbers and to recertify the official census result").

b. *Political Questions*

BAKER v. CARR
369 U.S. 186, 82 S.Ct. 691, 7 L.Ed.2d 663 (1962).

MR. JUSTICE BRENNAN delivered the opinion of the Court.

[T]ennessee's standard for allocating legislative representation among her counties is the total number of qualified voters resident in the respective counties, subject only to minor qualifications. *** Between 1901 and 1961, Tennessee has experienced substantial growth and redistribution of her population. *** The relative standings of the counties in terms of qualified voters have changed significantly. It is primarily the continued application of the 1901 Apportionment Act to this shifted and enlarged voting population which gives rise to the present controversy. *** [T]he complaint alleges that the 1901 statute, even as of the time of its passage, "made no apportionment of Representatives and Senators in accordance with the constitutional formula ***, but instead arbitrarily and capriciously apportioned representatives in the Senate and House without reference *** to any logical or reasonable formula whatever." It is further alleged that "because of the population changes since 1900, and the failure of the Legislature to reapportion itself since 1901," the 1901 statute became "unconstitutional and obsolete." Appellants also argue that, because of the composition of the legislature effected by the 1901 Apportionment Act, redress in the form of a state constitutional amendment to change the entire mechanism for reapportioning, or any other change short of that, is difficult or impossible ***. [T]hey seek a declaration that the 1901 statute is unconstitutional [under the equal protection clause of the Fourteenth Amendment] and an injunction restraining the appellees from acting to conduct any further elections under it. They also pray that unless and until the General Assembly enacts a valid reapportionment, the District Court should either decree a reapportionment by mathematical application of the Tennessee constitutional formulae to the most recent Federal Census figures, or direct the appellees to conduct legislative elections, primary and general, at large. They also pray for such other and further relief as may be appropriate.

[The Court first determined that it had subject matter jurisdiction and that plaintiffs had standing.]

*** We hold that this challenge to an apportionment presents no nonjusticiable "political question." *** Of course the mere fact that the suit seeks protection of a political right does not mean it presents a political question. Such an objection "is little more than a play upon words." *** Rather, it is argued that apportionment cases, whatever the actual wording of the complaint, can involve no federal constitutional right except one resting on the guaranty of a republican form of government, and that complaints based on that clause have been held to present political questions which are nonjusticiable.

We hold that the claim pleaded here neither rests upon nor implicates the Guaranty Clause and that its justiciability is therefore not foreclosed by our decisions of cases involving that clause. *** To show why we reject the argument based on the Guaranty Clause, we must examine the authorities under it. But because there appears to be some uncertainty as to why those cases did present political questions, and specifically as to whether this apportionment case is like those cases, we deem it necessary first to consider the contours of the "political question" doctrine.

Our discussion *** requires review of a number of political question cases, in order to expose the attributes of the doctrine—attributes which, in various settings, diverge, combine, appear, and disappear in seeming disorderliness. ***

We have said that "In determining whether a question falls within (the political question) category, the appropriateness under our system of government of attributing finality to the action of the political departments and also the lack of satisfactory criteria for a judicial determination are dominant considerations." *** The nonjusticiability of a political question is primarily a function of the separation of powers. Much confusion results from the capacity of the "political question" label to obscure the need for case-by-case inquiry. Deciding whether a matter has in any measure been committed by the Constitution to another branch of government, or whether the action of that branch exceeds whatever authority has been committed, is itself a delicate exercise in constitutional interpretation, and is a responsibility of this Court as ultimate interpreter of the Constitution. ***

Foreign relations: There are sweeping statements to the effect that all questions touching foreign relations are political questions. Not only does resolution of such issues frequently turn on standards that defy judicial application, or involve the exercise of a discretion demonstrably committed to the executive or legislature; but many such questions uniquely demand single-voiced statement of the Government's views. Yet it is error to suppose that every case or controversy which touches foreign relations lies beyond judicial cognizance. Our cases in this field seem invariably to show a discriminating analysis of the particular question posed, in terms of the history of its management by the political branches, of its susceptibility to judicial handling in the light of its nature and posture in the specific case, and of the possible consequences of judicial action. ***

Dates of duration of hostilities: Though it has been stated broadly that "the power which declared the necessity is the power to declare its cessation, and what the cessation requires," *** here too analysis reveals isolable reasons for the presence of political questions, underlying this Court's refusal to review the political departments' determination of when or whether a war has ended. Dominant is the need for finality in the political determination, for emergency's nature demands "A prompt and unhesitating obedience." *** Further, clearly definable criteria for decision may be available. In such case the political question barrier falls away: "(A) Court is not at liberty to shut its eyes to an obvious mistake, when the validity of the law depends upon the truth of what is declared. *** (It can) inquire whether the exigency still existed upon which the continued operation of the law depended." ***

Validity of enactments: In *Coleman v. Miller*, supra, this Court held that the questions of how long a proposed amendment to the Federal Constitution remained open to ratification, and what effect a prior rejection had on a subsequent ratification, were committed to congressional resolution and involved criteria of decision that necessarily escaped the judicial grasp. Similar considerations apply to the enacting process: "The respect due to coequal and independent departments," and the need for finality and certainty about the status of a statute contribute to judicial reluctance to inquire whether, as passed, it complied with all requisite formalities. *** But it is not true that courts will never delve into a legislature's records upon such a quest: If the enrolled statute lacks an effective date, a court will not hesitate to seek it in the legislative journals in order to preserve the enactment. The political question doctrine, a tool for maintenance of governmental order, will not be so applied as to promote only disorder.

*** It is apparent that several formulations which vary slightly according to the settings in which the questions arise may describe a political question, although each has one or more elements which identify it as essentially a function of the separation of powers. Prominent on the surface of any case held to involve a political question is found a textually demonstrable constitutional commitment of the issue to a coordinate political department; or a lack of judicially discoverable and manageable standards for resolving it; or the impossibility of deciding without an initial policy determination of a kind clearly for nonjudicial discretion; or the impossibility of a court's undertaking independent resolution without expressing lack of the respect due coordinate branches of government; or an unusual need for unquestioning adherence to a political decision already made; or the potentiality of embarrassment from multifarious pronouncements by various departments on one question.

Unless one of these formulations is inextricable from the case at bar, there should be no dismissal for non-justiciability on the ground of a political question's presence. The doctrine of which we treat is one of "political questions," not one of "political cases." The courts cannot reject as 'no law suit' a bona fide controversy as to whether some action denominated "political" exceeds constitutional authority. The cases we have reviewed show the necessity for discriminating inquiry into the precise facts and posture of the particular case, and the impossibility of resolution by any semantic cataloguing.

But it is argued that this case shares the characteristics of decisions that constitute a category not yet considered, cases concerning the Constitution's guaranty, in Art. IV, § 4, of a republican form of government ***. [G]uaranty Clause claims involve those elements which define a "political question," and for that reason and no other, they are nonjusticiable. In particular, we shall discover that the nonjusticiability of such claims has nothing to do with their touching upon matters of state governmental organization.

*** *Luther v. Borden*, 7 How. 1, though in form simply an action for damages for trespass was, as Daniel Webster said in opening the argument for the defense, "an unusual case." The defendants, admitting an otherwise tortious breaking and entering, sought to justify their action on the ground that they were agents of the established lawful government of Rhode Island, which State was then under martial law to defend itself from active insurrection; that the plaintiff was engaged in that insurrection; and that they entered under orders to arrest the plaintiff. The case arose "out of the unfortunate political differences which agitated the people of Rhode Island in 1841 and 1842," 7 How., at 34, and which had resulted in a situation wherein two groups laid competing claims to recognition as the lawful government. The plaintiff's right to recover depended upon which of the two groups was entitled to such recognition; but the lower court's refusal to receive evidence or hear argument on that issue, its charge to the jury that the earlier established or "charter" government was lawful, and the verdict for the defendants, were affirmed upon appeal to this Court.

CHIEF JUSTICE TANEY's opinion for the Court reasoned as follows:

(1) If a court were to hold the defendants' acts unjustified because the charter government had no legal existence during the period in question, it would follow that all of that government's actions—laws enacted, taxes collected, salaries paid, accounts settled, sentences passed—were of no effect; and that "the officers who carried their decisions into operation (were) answerable as trespassers, if not in some cases as criminals." There was, of course, no room for application of any doctrine of de facto status to uphold prior acts of an officer not authorized de jure, for such would have defeated the plaintiff's very action. A decision for the plaintiff would inevitably have produced some significant measure of chaos, a consequence to be avoided if it could be done without abnegation of the judicial duty to uphold the Constitution.

(2) No state court had recognized as a judicial responsibility settlement of the issue of the locus of state governmental authority. Indeed, the courts of Rhode Island had in several cases held that "it rested with the political power to decide whether the charter government had been displaced or not," and that that department had acknowledged no change.

(3) Since "(t)he question relates, altogether, to the constitution and laws of (the) *** State," the courts of the United States had to follow the state courts' decisions unless there was a federal constitutional ground for overturning them.

(4) No provision of the Constitution could be or had been invoked for this purpose except Art. IV, § 4, the Guaranty Clause. Having already noted the absence of standards whereby the choice between governments could be made by a court acting independently, CHIEF JUSTICE TANEY now found further textual and practical reasons for concluding that, if any department of the United States was empowered by the Guaranty Clause to resolve the issue, it was not the judiciary: "Under this article of the Constitution it rests with Congress to decide what government is the established one in a State. *** [And further,] [a]fter the President has acted and called out the militia, is a Circuit Court of the United States authorized to inquire whether his decision was right? *** If the judicial power extends so far, the guarantee contained in the Constitution *** is a guarantee of anarchy, and not of order."

Clearly, several factors were thought by the Court in *Luther* to make the question there "political": the commitment to the other branches of the decision as to which is the lawful state government; the unambiguous action by the President, in recognizing the charter government as the lawful authority; the need for finality in the executive's decision; and the lack of criteria by which a court could determine which form of government was republican.

But the only significance that *Luther* could have for our immediate purposes is in its holding that the Guaranty Clause is not a repository of judicially manageable standards which a court could utilize independently in order to identify a State's lawful government. The Court has since refused to resort to the Guaranty Clause—which alone had been invoked for the purpose—as the source of a constitutional standard for invalidating state action. ***

We come, finally, to the ultimate inquiry whether our precedents as to what constitutes a nonjusticiable "political question" bring the case before us under the umbrella of that doctrine. A natural beginning is to note whether any of the common characteristics which we have been able to identify and label descriptively are present. We find none: The question here is the consistency of state action with the Federal Constitution. We have no question decided, or to be decided, by a political branch of government coequal with this Court. Nor do we risk embarrassment of our government abroad, or grave disturbance at home if we take issue with Tennessee as to the constitutionality of her action here challenged. Nor need the appellants, in order to succeed in this action, ask the Court to enter upon policy determinations for which judicially manageable standards are lacking. Judicial standards under the Equal Protection Clause are well developed and familiar, and it has been open to courts since the enactment of the

Fourteenth Amendment to determine, if on the particular facts they must, that a discrimination reflects no policy, but simply arbitrary and capricious action.

This case does, in one sense, involve the allocation of political power within a State, and the appellants might conceivably have added a claim under the Guaranty Clause. Of course, as we have seen, any reliance on that clause would be futile. But because any reliance on the Guaranty Clause could not have succeeded it does not follow that appellants may not be heard on the equal protection claim which in fact they tender. True, it must be clear that the Fourteenth Amendment claim is not so enmeshed with those political question elements which render Guaranty Clause claims nonjusticiable as actually to present a political question itself. But we have found that not to be the case here. *** The right asserted is within the reach of judicial protection under the Fourteenth Amendment. ***

Separate concurrences of MR. JUSTICE DOUGLAS, MR. JUSTICE CLARK, and MR. JUSTICE STEWART are omitted.

MR. JUSTICE FRANKFURTER, whom MR. JUSTICE HARLAN joins, dissenting.

The Court today reverses a uniform course of decision established by a dozen cases, including one by which the very claim now sustained was unanimously rejected only five years ago. The impressive body of rulings thus cast aside reflected the equally uniform course of our political history regarding the relationship between population and legislative representation—a wholly different matter from denial of the franchise to individuals because of race, color, religion or sex. *** Disregard of inherent limits in the effective exercise of the Court's "Judicial Power" not only presages the futility of judicial intervention in the essentially political conflict of forces by which the relation between population and representation has time out of mind been and now is determined. It may well impair the Court's position as the ultimate organ of "the supreme Law of the Land" in that vast range of legal problems, often strongly entangled in popular feeling, on which this Court must pronounce. The Court's authority—possessed of neither the purse nor the sword—ultimately rests on sustained public confidence in its moral sanction. Such feeling must be nourished by the Court's complete detachment, in fact and in appearance, from political entanglements and by abstention from injecting itself into the clash of political forces in political settlements.

A hypothetical claim resting on abstract assumptions is now for the first time made the basis for affording illusory relief for a particular evil even though it foreshadows deeper and more pervasive difficulties in consequence. The claim is hypothetical and the assumptions are abstract because the Court does not vouchsafe the lower courts—state and federal—guidelines for formulating specific, definite, wholly unprecedented remedies for the inevitable litigations that today's umbrageous disposition is bound to stimulate in connection with politically motivated reapportionments in so many States. In such a setting, to promulgate jurisdiction in the abstract is meaningless. It is as devoid of reality as "a brooding omnipresence in the sky," for it conveys no intimation what relief, if any, a District Court is capable of affording that would not invite legislatures to play ducks and drakes with the judiciary. *** To charge courts with the task of accommodating the incommensurable factors of policy that underlie these mathematical puzzles is to attribute, however flatteringly, omnicompetence to judges. The Framers of the Constitution persistently rejected a proposal that embodied this assumption and Thomas Jefferson never entertained it. ***

[F]rom its earliest opinions this Court has consistently recognized a class of controversies which do not lend themselves to judicial standards and judicial remedies. ***

1. The cases concerning war or foreign affairs, for example, are usually explained by the necessity of the country's speaking with one voice in such matters. While this concern alone undoubtedly accounts for many of the decisions, others do not fit the pattern. It would hardly embarrass the conduct of war were this Court to determine, in connection with private transactions between litigants, the date upon which war is to be deemed terminated. But the Court has refused to do so. *** A controlling factor in such cases is that, decision respecting these kinds of complex matters of policy being traditionally committed not to courts but to the political agencies of government for determination by criteria of political expediency, there exists no standard ascertainable by settled judicial experience or process by reference to which a political decision affecting the question at issue between the parties can be judged. Where the question arises in the course of a litigation involving primarily the adjudication of other issues between the litigants, the Court accepts as a basis for adjudication the political departments' decision of it. But where its determination is the sole function to be served by the exercise of the judicial power, the Court will not entertain the action. ***

2. The Court has been particularly unwilling to intervene in matters concerning the structure and organization of the political institutions of the States. The abstention from judicial entry into such areas has been greater even than that which marks the Court's ordinary approach to issues of state power challenged under broad federal guarantees. *** Where, however, state law has made particular federal questions determinative of relations within the structure of state government, not in challenge of it, the Court has resolved such narrow, legally defined questions in proper proceedings. *** In such instances there is no conflict between state policy and the exercise of federal judicial power. ***

3. The cases involving Negro disfranchisement are no exception to the principle of avoiding federal judicial intervention into matters of state government in the absence of an explicit and clear constitutional imperative. For here the controlling command of Supreme Law is plain and unequivocal. An end of discrimination against the Negro was the compelling motive of the Civil War Amendments. ***

4. The Court has refused to exercise its jurisdiction to pass on "abstract questions of political power, of sovereignty, of government." *** The "political question" doctrine, in this aspect, reflects the policies underlying the requirement of "standing": that the litigant who would challenge official action must claim infringement of an interest particular and personal to himself, as distinguished from a cause of dissatisfaction with the general frame and functioning of government—a complaint that the political institutions are awry. *** What renders cases of this kind non-justiciable is not necessarily the nature of the parties to them, for the Court has resolved other issues between similar parties; nor is it the nature of the legal question involved, for the same type of question has been adjudicated when presented in other forms of controversy. The crux of the matter is that courts are not fit instruments of decision where what is essentially at stake is the composition of those large contests of policy traditionally fought out in non-judicial forums, by which governments and the actions of governments are made and unmade. ***

5. The influence of these converging considerations—the caution not to undertake decision where standards meet for judicial judgment are lacking, the reluctance to interfere with matters of state government in the absence of an unquestionable and effectively enforceable mandate, the unwillingness to make courts arbiters of the broad issues of political organization historically committed to other institutions and for whose adjustment the judicial process is ill adapted—has been decisive of the settled line of cases, reaching back more than a century, which holds that Art. IV, § 4, of the Constitution, guaranteeing to the States "a Republican Form of Government," is not enforceable through the courts. ***

The present case involves all of the elements that have made the Guarantee Clause cases non-justiciable. It is, in effect, a Guarantee Clause claim masquerading under a different label. But it cannot make the case more fit for judicial action that appellants invoke the Fourteenth Amendment rather than Art. IV, § 4, where, in fact, the gist of their complaint is the same—unless it can be found that the Fourteenth Amendment speaks with greater particularity to their situation. We have been admonished to avoid "the tyranny of labels." *** Art. IV, § 4, is not committed by express constitutional terms to Congress. It is the nature of the controversies arising under it, nothing else, which has made it judicially unenforceable. Of course, if a controversy falls within judicial power, it depends "on how he (the plaintiff) casts his action," *** whether he brings himself within a jurisdictional statute. But where judicial competence is wanting, it cannot be created by invoking one clause of the Constitution rather than another.

*** [Appellants] invoke the right to vote and to have their votes counted. But they are permitted to vote and their votes are counted. They go to the polls, they cast their ballots, they send their representatives to the state councils. Their complaint is simply that the representatives are not sufficiently numerous or powerful—in short, that Tennessee has adopted a basis of representation with which they are dissatisfied. Talk of "debasement" or "dilution" is circular talk. One cannot speak of "debasement" or "dilution" of the value of a vote until there is first defined a standard of reference as to what a vote should be worth. What is actually asked of the Court in this case is to choose among competing bases of representation—ultimately, really, among competing theories of political philosophy—in order to establish an appropriate frame of government for the State of Tennessee and thereby for all the States of the Union. ***

Dissenting opinion of MR. JUSTICE HARLAN, whom MR. JUSTICE FRANKFURTER joins. [omitted]

Notes

1. **The Factors.** Generations of law students have memorized and mechanically applied the six factors listed in *Baker v. Carr*: (1) a constitutional commitment of the issue to another political branch, (2) a lack of judicially discoverable and manageable standards, (3) the impossibility of deciding the question without an initial policy determination, (4) the impossibility of a court's undertaking resolution without expressing lack of respect for other political branches, (5) an "unusual need for unquestioning adherence to a political decision already made," and (6) the potential for "embarrassment from multifarious pronouncements by the various departments on one question." The case itself concludes that only one factor—"judicially manageable standards"—was relevant because state officials were involved, not a coequal branch of the federal government. Because "manageable standards" issues exist in many cases, not just those labeled political questions, isn't this very different from CHIEF JUSTICE MARSHALL's notions of political questions? Consider the other *Baker* factors. Isn't *any* exercise of judicial power against a coequal branch in some sense a decision which "upsets a political decision already made," demonstrates a "lack of respect," and holds "the potentiality for embarrassment"? Finally, given what you know of the Constitution's text, the notion of a "textually demonstrable commitment of the issue to a coordinate political department" could potentially sweep out from judicial review all matters contained in Articles I and II. Isn't the real issue whether, given the text, structure, and history of the Constitution, a particular question should be left to a final, nonreviewable decision by a political branch of government?

2. **Reapportionment Reconsidered.** There is nothing unmanageable about a "one person, one vote" standard, is there? Is there a manageability problem if the issue is gerrymandered districts whose overall populations are equal? Should the Supreme Court play different roles in racial gerrymandering, political gerrymandering, and geographical gerrymandering cases?

3. **Reapportionment and Standing.** Do blacks in a majority-white electoral district have standing to challenge the parameters of the district in which they live? Do whites in a majority-black district have standing to challenge the parameters of the district in which they live? *See* Ely, *Standing to Challenge Pro-minority Gerrymanders*, 111 HARV. L. REV. 576 (1997) (yes; not because of "segregation" or any "expressive harm"; rather, "filler people" are an "identifiable class separated out for disadvantage.")

4. **Application of the Political Question Doctrine.** Since *Baker*, only two (of fourteen) Supreme Court cases discussing the political question doctrine have concluded that there was a political question. *Gilligan v. Morgan*, 413 U.S. 1

(1973), dismissed a complaint that Kent State student protesters had been killed because of negligent training of the National Guard on the ground that military training is left by the Constitution entirely to the elected branches of government. *Nixon v. United States*, 506 U.S. 224 (1993), held that it was a political question whether the Senate had violated its Article I impeachment power by convicting a federal judge based on a fact-finding report by a Senate committee.

(a) Does *Gilligan* bar a claim of negligent actions by military personnel that cause civilian deaths?

(b) *Nixon* focused on the language concerning impeachment trials ("The Senate shall have the sole Power to try all Impeachments."). Would *Nixon* come out differently if the Senate had tossed a coin ("heads you're guilty, tails you're innocent")?

(c) Think about the constitutional provisions involved in these cases. Are there any other candidates in Articles I and II for "overcoming the strong but rebuttable presumption of judicial review" established by *Marbury*? Consider Presidential nominations and conduct of foreign affairs, Congress' power to control the militia and to declare war, the President's veto of a bill, Senate action on appointments, and treaty-making and ratification.

(d) Assume that a high government official who was impeached and removed from office on grounds of adultery seeks reinstatement, asserting that adultery is not a high crime or misdemeanor under Art. II, § 4. Does the official's suit present a nonjusticiable political question?

5. **The Guarantee Clause Reconsidered.** What does the Guarantee Clause mean? Some scholars argue that state constitutional referenda are unconstitutional on the theory that the clause calls for a "republican form of government" rather than direct democracy in the states. Try to formulate arguments on this issue. Should *Luther* bar a suit challenging a state referendum on this ground? Or was *Luther* more limited to its facts, a case in which the Supreme Court was being asked to invalidate an entire state government seven years after the challenging faction had collapsed? See JUSTICE O'CONNOR's opinion in *New York v. United States*, 505 U.S. 144, 184 (1992), in which she argues that the "limited holding" of *Luther* has undergone a "sweeping metamorphosis" into the notion that the Guarantee Clause is in all circumstances off limits to judicial interpretation. *See* Mayton, "Direct Democracy, Federalism, & the Guarantee Clause," 2 GREEN BAG 2d 269 (1999).

6. **Justiciability Choices.** On August 2, 1990, Iraq invaded Kuwait. President Bush immediately sent troops to the Persian Gulf. The United States took other steps, including participation in a blockade of Iraq, which was approved by the United Nations Security Council. On November 8, President Bush increased the number of Persian Gulf troops to 230,000 to provide "an adequate offensive military option" against Iraq. Congress was not asked for and did not take action "to declare war" on Iraq under Art. 1, § 8, cl. 11 of the Constitution. Several Members of Congress filed suit to enjoin the President from going to war without a Congressional declaration of war. Is this suit justiciable? *See Ange v. Bush*, 752 F.Supp. 509 (D.D.C. 1990), *Dellums v. Bush*, 752 F.Supp. 1141 (D.D.C. 1990). Congress later passed a resolution authorizing use of military action against Iraq but never formally declared war.

3. THE ELEVENTH AMENDMENT LIMIT

SEMINOLE TRIBE OF FLORIDA v. FLORIDA
517 U.S. 44, 116 S.Ct. 1114, 134 L.Ed.2d 252 (1996).

CHIEF JUSTICE REHNQUIST delivered the opinion of the Court.

The Indian Gaming Regulatory Act provides that an Indian tribe may conduct certain gaming activities only in conformance with a valid compact between the tribe and the State in which the gaming activities are located. The Act, passed by Congress under the Indian Commerce Clause, U.S. Const., Art. I, § 8, cl. 3, imposes upon the States a duty to negotiate in good faith with an Indian tribe toward the formation of a compact, and authorizes a tribe to bring suit in federal court against a State in order to compel performance of that duty. We hold that notwithstanding Congress' clear intent to abrogate the States' sovereign immunity, the Indian Commerce Clause does not grant Congress that power, and therefore cannot grant jurisdiction over a State that does not consent to be sued. ***

I

Congress passed the Indian Gaming Regulatory Act in 1988 in order to provide a statutory basis for the operation and regulation of gaming by Indian tribes. *** The Act provides that class III gaming [slot machines, casino games, banking card games, dog racing, and lotteries] is lawful only where it is: (1) authorized by an ordinance or resolution that (a) is adopted by the governing body of the Indian tribe, (b) satisfies certain statutorily prescribed requirements, and (c) is approved by the National Indian Gaming Commission; (2) located in a State that permits such gaming for any purpose by any person, organization, or entity; and (3) "conducted in conformance with a Tribal–State compact entered into by the Indian tribe and the State under paragraph (3) that is in effect."

The "paragraph (3)" to which the last prerequisite refers describes the permissible scope of a Tribal–State compact and provides that the compact is effective "only when notice of approval by the Secretary [of the Interior] of such compact has been published by the Secretary in the Federal Register." More significant for our purposes, however, is that [the Act] describes the process by which a State and an Indian tribe begin negotiations toward a Tribal–State compact: "(A) Any Indian tribe having jurisdiction over the Indian lands upon which a class III gaming activity is being conducted, or is to be conducted, shall request the State in which such lands are located to enter into negotiations for the purpose of entering into a Tribal–State compact governing the conduct of gaming activities. Upon receiving such a request, the State shall negotiate with the Indian tribe in good faith to enter into such a compact."

The State's obligation to "negotiate with the Indian tribe in good faith," is made judicially enforceable. *** If the district court concludes that the State has failed to negotiate in good faith toward the formation of a Tribal–State compact, then it "shall order the State and Indian tribe to conclude such a compact within a 60–day period." If no compact has been concluded 60 days after the court's order, then "the Indian tribe and the State shall each submit to a mediator appointed by the court a proposed compact that represents their last best offer for a compact." If the State does not consent, then the Act provides that the mediator "shall notify the Secretary [of the Interior]" and that the Secretary "shall prescribe *** procedures *** under which class III gaming may be conducted on the Indian lands over which the Indian tribe has jurisdiction."

In September 1991, the Seminole Tribe of Indians, petitioner, sued the State of Florida and its Governor, Lawton Chiles, respondents. Invoking jurisdiction under [the Act], petitioner alleged that respondents had "refused to enter into any negotiation for inclusion of [certain gaming activities] in a tribal-state compact," thereby violating the "requirement of good faith negotiation" ***.

The Court of Appeals for the Eleventh Circuit [held] that the Eleventh Amendment barred petitioner's suit against respondents. ***

The Eleventh Amendment provides: "The Judicial power of the United States shall not be construed to extend to any suit in law or equity, commenced or prosecuted against one of the United States by Citizens of another State, or by Citizens or Subjects of any Foreign State." Although the text of the Amendment would appear to restrict only the Article III diversity jurisdiction of the federal courts, "we have understood the Eleventh Amendment to stand not so much for what it says, but for the presupposition *** which it confirms." *Blatchford v. Native Village of Noatak*, 501 U.S. 775 (1991). That presupposition has two parts: first, that each State is a sovereign entity in our federal system; and second, that "[i]t is inherent in the nature of 'face right' directions sovereignty not to be amenable to the suit of an individual without its consent." For over a century we have reaffirmed that federal jurisdiction over suits against unconsenting States "was not contemplated by the Constitution when establishing the judicial power of the United States."

Here, petitioner has sued the State of Florida and it is undisputed that Florida has not consented to the suit. ***

II

Petitioner argues that Congress through the Act abrogated the States' immunity from suit. In order to determine whether Congress has abrogated the States' sovereign immunity, we ask two questions: first, whether Congress has "unequivocally expresse[d] its intent to abrogate the immunity," *Green v. Mansour*, 474 U.S. 64, 68 (1985); and second, whether Congress has acted "pursuant to a valid exercise of power."

Congress' intent to abrogate the States' immunity from suit must be obvious from "a clear legislative statement." *** In *Atascadero State Hospital v. Scanlon*, 473 U.S. 234 (1985), we held that "[a] general authorization for suit in federal court is not the kind of unequivocal statutory language sufficient to abrogate the Eleventh Amendment." Rather, as we said in *Dellmuth v. Muth*, 491 U.S. 223 (1989), "To temper Congress' acknowledged powers of abrogation with due concern for the Eleventh Amendment's role as an essential component of our constitutional structure, we have applied a simple but stringent test: 'Congress may abrogate the States' constitutionally secured immunity from suit in federal court only by making its intention unmistakably clear in the language of the statute.'" Here, *** Congress has in the Act provided an "unmistakably clear" statement of its intent to abrogate. *** [The Act refers] to the "State" in a context that makes it clear that the State is the defendant to the suit brought by an Indian tribe. In sum, we think that the numerous references to the "State" in the text of [the Indian Gaming Act] make it indubitable that Congress intended through the Act to abrogate the States' sovereign immunity from suit.

Having concluded that Congress clearly intended to abrogate the States' sovereign immunity, we turn now to consider whether the Act was passed "pursuant to a valid exercise of power." *** [Our] inquiry into whether Congress has the power to abrogate unilaterally the States' immunity from suit is narrowly focused on one question: Was the Act in question passed pursuant to a constitutional provision granting Congress the power to abrogate? Previously, in conducting that inquiry, we have found authority to abrogate under only two provisions of the Constitution. In *Fitzpatrick*, we recognized that the Fourteenth Amendment, by expanding federal power at the expense of state autonomy, had fundamentally altered the balance of state and federal power struck by the Constitution. We noted that § 1 of the Fourteenth Amendment contained prohibitions expressly directed at the States and that § 5 of the Amendment expressly provided that "The Congress shall have the power to enforce, by appropriate legislation, the provisions of this article." We held that through the Fourteenth Amendment, federal power extended to intrude upon the province of the Eleventh Amendment and therefore that § 5 of the Fourteenth Amendment allowed Congress to abrogate the immunity from suit guaranteed by that Amendment.

In only one other case has congressional abrogation of the States' Eleventh Amendment immunity been upheld. In *Pennsylvania v. Union Gas Co.*, 491 U.S 1 (1989), a plurality of the Court found that the Interstate Commerce Clause, Art. I, § 8, cl. 3, granted Congress the power to abrogate state sovereign immunity, stating that the power to regulate interstate commerce would be "incomplete without the authority to render States liable in damages." *** Following the rationale of the *Union Gas* plurality, our inquiry is limited to determining whether the Indian Commerce Clause, like the Interstate Commerce Clause, is a grant of authority to the Federal Government at the expense of the States. The answer to that question is obvious. If anything, the Indian Commerce Clause accomplishes a greater transfer of power from the States to the Federal Government than does the Interstate Commerce Clause. *** We agree with the petitioner that the plurality opinion in *Union Gas* allows no principled distinction in favor of the States to be drawn between the Indian Commerce Clause and the Interstate Commerce Clause.

*** Generally, the principle of *stare decisis*, and the interests that it serves, viz., "the evenhanded, predictable, and consistent development of legal principles, *** reliance on judicial decisions, and *** the actual and perceived integrity of the judicial process," *Payne v. Tennessee*, 501 U.S. 808, 827 (1991), counsel strongly against reconsideration of our precedent. Nevertheless, we always have treated *stare decisis* as a "principle of policy," and not as an "inexorable command." Our willingness to reconsider our earlier decisions has been "particularly true in constitutional cases, because in such cases 'correction through legislative action is practically impossible.'"

The Court in *Union Gas* reached a result without an expressed rationale agreed upon by a majority of the Court. JUSTICE BRENNAN's opinion received the support of only three other Justices. Of the other five, JUSTICE WHITE, who provided the fifth vote for the result, wrote separately in order to indicate his disagreement with the majority's rationale, and four Justices joined together in a dissent that rejected the plurality's rationale. Since it was issued, *Union Gas* has created confusion among the lower courts that have sought to understand and apply the deeply fractured decision. *** It was well established in 1989 when *Union Gas* was decided that the Eleventh Amendment stood for the constitutional principle that state sovereign immunity limited the federal courts' jurisdiction under Article III. *** And our [more recent] decisions had been equally clear that the Eleventh Amendment reflects "the fundamental principle of sovereign immunity [that] limits the grant of judicial authority in Article III." As the dissent in *Union Gas* recognized, the plurality's conclusion—that Congress could under Article I expand the scope of the federal courts' jurisdiction under Article III— "contradict[ed] our unvarying approach to Article III as setting forth the exclusive catalog of permissible federal court jurisdiction."

Never before the decision in *Union Gas* had we suggested that the bounds of Article III could be expanded by Congress operating pursuant to any constitutional provision other than the Fourteenth Amendment. Indeed, it had seemed fundamental that Congress could not expand the jurisdiction of the federal courts beyond the bounds of Article III. *Marbury v. Madison*, 1 Cranch 137 (1803).

The plurality's extended reliance upon our decision [in *Fitzpatrick*] that Congress could under the Fourteenth Amendment abrogate the States' sovereign immunity was also, we believe, misplaced. *Fitzpatrick* was based upon a rationale wholly inapplicable to the Interstate Commerce Clause, viz., that the Fourteenth Amendment, adopted well after the adoption of the Eleventh Amendment and the ratification of the Constitution, operated to alter the pre-existing balance between state and federal power achieved by Article III and the Eleventh Amendment. As the dissent in *Union Gas* made clear, *Fitzpatrick* cannot be read to justify "limitation of the principle embodied in the Eleventh Amendment through appeal to antecedent provisions of the Constitution." *Union Gas*, 491 U.S., at 42 (SCALIA, J., dissenting).

In the five years since it was decided, *Union Gas* has proven to be a solitary departure from established law. Reconsidering the decision in *Union Gas*, we conclude that none of the policies underlying *stare decisis* require our continuing adherence to its holding. The decision has, since its issuance, been of questionable precedential value, largely because a majority of the Court expressly disagreed with the rationale of the plurality. The case involved the interpretation of the Constitution and therefore may be altered only by constitutional amendment or revision by this Court. Finally, both the result in *Union Gas* and the plurality's rationale depart from our established understanding of the Eleventh Amendment and undermine the accepted function of Article III. We feel bound to conclude that *Union Gas* was wrongly decided and that it should be, and now is, overruled. ***

In overruling *Union Gas* today, we reconfirm that the background principle of state sovereign immunity embodied in the Eleventh Amendment is not so ephemeral as to dissipate when the subject of the suit is an area, like the regulation of Indian commerce, that is under the exclusive control of the Federal Government. Even when the Constitution vests in Congress complete law-making authority over a particular area, the Eleventh Amendment prevents congressional authorization of suits by private parties against unconsenting States. The Eleventh Amendment restricts the judicial power under Article III, and Article I cannot be used to circumvent the constitutional limitations placed upon federal jurisdiction. Petitioner's suit against the State of Florida must be dismissed for a lack of jurisdiction. ***

JUSTICE STEVENS, dissenting.

This case is about power—the power of the Congress of the United States to create a private federal cause of action against a State, or its Governor, for the violation of a federal right. In *Chisholm v. Georgia*, 2 Dall. 419 (1793), the entire Court—including JUSTICE IREDELL whose dissent provided the blueprint for the Eleventh Amendment—assumed that Congress had such power. Nevertheless, in a sharp break with the past, today the Court holds that with the narrow and illogical exception of statutes enacted pursuant to the Enforcement Clause of the Fourteenth Amendment, Congress has no such power.

The importance of the majority's decision to overrule the Court's holding in *Pennsylvania v. Union Gas Co.* cannot be overstated. The majority's opinion does not simply preclude Congress from establishing the rather curious statutory scheme under which Indian tribes may seek the aid of a federal court to secure a State's good faith negotiations over gaming regulations. Rather, it prevents Congress from providing a federal forum for a broad range of actions against States, from those sounding in copyright and patent law, to those concerning bankruptcy, environmental law, and the regulation of our vast national economy.

There may be room for debate over whether, in light of the Eleventh Amendment, Congress has the power to ensure that such a cause of action may be enforced in federal court by a citizen of another State or a foreign citizen. There can be no serious debate, however, over whether Congress has the power to ensure that such a cause of action may be brought by a citizen of the State being sued. Congress' authority in that regard is clear. ***

For the purpose of deciding this case, I can readily assume that JUSTICE IREDELL's dissent in *Chisholm v. Georgia* correctly stated the law that should govern our decision today. *** In concluding that the federal courts could not entertain Chisholm's action against the State of Georgia, JUSTICE IREDELL relied on the text of the Judiciary Act of 1789, not the State's assertion that Article III did not extend the judicial power to suits against unconsenting States. Justice Iredell argued that, under Article III, federal courts possessed only such jurisdiction as Congress had provided, and that the Judiciary Act expressly limited federal-court jurisdiction to that which could be exercised in accordance with "the principles and usages of law." He reasoned that the inclusion of this phrase constituted a command to the federal courts to construe their jurisdiction in light of the prevailing common law, a background legal regime which he believed incorporated the doctrine of sovereign immunity. Because JUSTICE IREDELL believed that the expansive text of Article III did not prevent Congress from imposing this common-law limitation on federal-court jurisdiction, he concluded that judges had no authority to entertain a suit against an unconsenting State. ***

The precise holding in *Chisholm* is difficult to state because each of the Justices in the majority wrote his own opinion. They seem to have held, however, not that the Judiciary Act of 1789 precluded the defense of sovereign immunity, but that Article III of the Constitution itself required the Supreme Court to entertain original actions against unconsenting States. I agree with JUSTICE IREDELL that such a construction of Article III is incorrect; that Article should not then have been construed, and should not now be construed, to prevent Congress from granting States a sovereign immunity defense in such cases. That reading of Article III, however, explains why the majority's holding in *Chisholm* could not have been reversed by a simple statutory amendment adopting JUSTICE IREDELL's interpretation of the Judiciary Act of 1789. There is a special irony in the fact that the error committed by the *Chisholm* majority was its decision that this Court, rather than Congress, should define the scope of the sovereign immunity defense. That, of course, is precisely the same error the Court commits today. ***

JUSTICE SOUTER, with whom JUSTICE GINSBURG and JUSTICE BREYER join, dissenting.

In holding the State of Florida immune to suit under the Indian Gaming Regulatory Act, the Court today holds for the first time since the founding of the Republic that Congress has no authority to subject a State to the jurisdiction of a federal court at the behest of an individual asserting a federal right. Although the Court invokes the Eleventh Amendment as authority for this proposition, the only sense in which that amendment might be claimed as pertinent here was tolerantly phrased by JUSTICE STEVENS in his concurring opinion in *Pennsylvania v. Union Gas*, 491 U.S. 1, 23 (1989) (STEVENS, J.., concurring). There, he explained how it has come about that we have two Eleventh Amendments, the one ratified in 1795, the other (so-called) invented by the Court nearly a century later in *Hans v. Louisiana*, 134 U.S. 1 (1890). JUSTICE STEVENS saw in that second Eleventh Amendment no bar to the exercise of congressional authority under the Commerce Clause in providing for suits on a federal question by individuals against a State ***.

His position, of course, was also the holding in *Union Gas*, which the Court now overrules and repudiates. ***

I

It is useful to separate three questions: (1) whether the States enjoyed sovereign immunity if sued in their own courts in the period prior to ratification of the National Constitution; (2) if so, whether after ratification the States were entitled to claim some such immunity when sued in a federal court exercising jurisdiction either because the suit was between a State and a non-state litigant who was not its citizen, or because the issue in the case raised a federal question; and (3) whether any state sovereign immunity recognized in federal court may be abrogated by Congress.

The answer to the first question is not clear, although some of the Framers assumed that States did enjoy immunity in their own courts. The second question was not debated at the time of ratification; there was no unanimity, but in due course the Court in *Chisholm v. Georgia*, 2 Dall. 419 (1793), answered that a state defendant enjoyed no such immunity. As to federal question jurisdiction, state sovereign immunity seems not to have been debated prior to ratification, the silence probably showing a general understanding at the time that the States would have no immunity in such cases. *** The Court's answer today to the third question is [at] odds with the Founders' view that common law *** was always subject to legislative amendment. In ignoring the reasons for this pervasive understanding at the time of the ratification, and in holding that a nontextual common-law rule limits a clear grant of congressional power under Article I, the Court follows a course that has brought it to grief before in our history, and promises to do so again.

The doctrine of sovereign immunity comprises two distinct rules, which are not always separately recognized. The one rule holds that the King or the Crown, as the font of law, is not bound by the law's provisions; the other provides that the King or Crown, as the font of justice, is not subject to suit in its own courts. The one rule limits the reach of substantive law; the other, the jurisdiction of the courts. We are concerned here only with the latter rule, which took its common-law form in the high middle ages. "At least as early as the thirteenth century, during the reign of Henry III (1216–1272), it was recognized that the king could not be sued in his own courts." *** [T]he 1787 Constitution might have addressed state sovereign immunity by eliminating whatever sovereign immunity the States previously had, as to any matter subject to federal law or jurisdiction; by recognizing an analogue to the old immunity in the new context of federal jurisdiction, but subject to abrogation as to any matter within that jurisdiction; or by enshrining a doctrine of inviolable state sovereign immunity in the text, thereby giving it constitutional protection in the new federal jurisdiction. The 1787 draft in fact said nothing on the subject, and it was this very silence that occasioned some, though apparently not widespread, dispute among the Framers and others over whether ratification of the Constitution would preclude a State sued in federal court from asserting sovereign immunity as it could have done on any matter of nonfederal law litigated in its own courts. As it has come down to us, the discussion gave no attention to congressional power under the proposed Article I but focused entirely on the limits of the judicial power provided in Article III ***.

The argument among the Framers and their friends about sovereign immunity in federal citizen-state diversity cases, in any event, was short lived and ended when this Court, in *Chisholm v. Georgia*, 2 Dall. 419 (1793), chose between the constitutional alternatives of abrogation and recognition of the immunity enjoyed at common law. *** The case settled, by implication, any question there could possibly have been about recognizing state sovereign immunity in actions depending on the federal question (or "arising under") head of jurisdiction as well. *** The Eleventh Amendment, of course, repudiated *Chisholm* and clearly divested federal courts of some jurisdiction as to cases against state parties ***. There are two plausible readings of this provision's text. Under the first, it simply repeals the Citizen–State Diversity Clauses of Article III for all cases in which the State appears as a defendant. Under the second, it strips the federal courts of jurisdiction in any case in which a state defendant is sued by a citizen not its own, even if jurisdiction might otherwise rest on the existence of a federal question in the suit.

The history and structure of the Eleventh Amendment convincingly show that it reaches only to suits subject to federal jurisdiction exclusively under the Citizen–State Diversity Clauses. In precisely tracking the language in Article III providing for citizen-state diversity jurisdiction, the text of the Amendment does, after all, suggest to common sense that only the Diversity Clauses are being addressed. If the Framers had meant the Amendment to bar federal question suits as well, they could not only have made their intentions clearer very easily, but could simply have adopted the first post-*Chisholm* proposal, introduced in the House of Representatives by Theodore Sedgwick of Massachusetts on instructions from the Legislature of that Commonwealth. Its provisions would have had exactly that expansive effect:

> "[N]o state shall be liable to be made a party defendant, in any of the judicial courts, established, or which shall be established under the authority of the United States, at the suit of any person or persons, whether a citizen or citizens, or a foreigner or foreigners, or of any body politic or corporate, whether within or without the United States."

Gazette of the United States 303 (Feb. 20, 1793). ***

Congress took no action on Sedgwick's proposal ***.

In sum, reading the Eleventh Amendment solely as a limit on citizen-state diversity jurisdiction has the virtue of coherence with this Court's practice, with the views of John Marshall, with the history of the Amendment's drafting, and with its allusive language. Today's majority does not appear to disagree, at least insofar as the constitutional text is concerned; the Court concedes, after all, that "the text of the Amendment would appear to restrict only the Article III diversity jurisdiction of the federal courts." ***

We must therefore look elsewhere for the source of that immunity by which the Court says their suit is barred from a federal court.

II

The obvious place to look elsewhere, of course, is *Hans v. Louisiana*, 134 U.S. 1 (1890), and *Hans* was indeed a leap in the direction of today's holding, even though it does not take the Court all the way. The [Court] in that case answered only [the] question whether the Constitution, without more, permits a State to plead sovereign immunity to bar the exercise of federal question jurisdiction. Although the Court invoked a principle of sovereign immunity to cure what it took to be the Eleventh Amendment's anomaly of barring only those state suits brought by noncitizen plaintiffs, the *Hans* Court had no occasion to consider whether Congress could abrogate that background immunity by statute.

*** Taking *Hans* only as far as its holding, its vulnerability is apparent. The Court rested its opinion on avoiding the supposed anomaly of recognizing jurisdiction to entertain a citizen's federal question suit, but not one brought by a noncitizen. There was, however, no such anomaly at all. As already explained, federal question cases are not touched by the Eleventh Amendment, which leaves a State open to federal question suits by citizens and noncitizens alike. If *Hans* had been from Massachusetts the Eleventh Amendment would not have barred his action against Louisiana. ***

Although there was thus no anomaly to be cured by *Hans*, the case certainly created its own anomaly in leaving federal courts entirely without jurisdiction to enforce paramount federal law at the behest of a citizen against a State that broke it. It destroyed the congruence of the judicial power under Article III with the substantive guarantees of the Constitution, and with the provisions of statutes passed by Congress in the exercise of its power under Article I: when a State injured an individual in violation of federal law no federal forum could provide direct relief. *** The majority does not dispute the point that [the *Hans* Court] had no occasion to decide whether Congress could abrogate a State's immunity from federal question suits. *** The exact rationale to which the majority refers, unfortunately, is not easy to discern. Indeed, as I have noted, JUSTICE BRADLEY's opinion in *Hans* conceded that Hans might successfully have pursued his claim "if there were no other reason or ground [other than the Amendment itself] for abating his suit." The *Hans* Court, rather, held the suit barred by a nonconstitutional common-law immunity.

*** If it is indeed true that private suits against States [are] not permitted under Article III *** then it is hard to see how a State's sovereign immunity may be waived any more than it may be abrogated by Congress. After all, consent of a party is in all other instances wholly insufficient to create subject-matter jurisdiction where it would not otherwise exist. *** [If] consent to suit in state court is not sufficient to show consent in federal court, then Article III would hardly permit this Court to exercise appellate jurisdiction over issues of federal law arising in lawsuits brought against the States in their own courts. ***

III

Three critical errors in *Hans* weigh against constitutionalizing its holding as the majority does today. The first we have already seen: the *Hans* Court misread the Eleventh Amendment. It also misunderstood the conditions under which common-law doctrines were received or rejected at the time of the Founding, and it fundamentally mistook the very nature of sovereignty in the young Republic that was supposed to entail a State's immunity to federal question jurisdiction in a federal court. ***

[JUSTICE SOUTER opined that the debates over reception of English common law in the Colonies suggested States would not be immune from the type of suit at issue in this case.]

*** [The] Court's attempt to convert isolated statements by the Framers into answers to questions not before them is fundamentally misguided. The Court's difficulty is far more fundamental however, than inconsistency with a particular quotation, for the Court's position runs afoul of the general theory of sovereignty that gave shape to the Framers' enterprise. An [inquiry] into the development of that concept demonstrates that American political thought had so revolutionized the concept of sovereignty itself that calling for the immunity of a State as against the jurisdiction of the national courts would have been sheer illogic. *** While there is no need here to calculate exactly how close the American States came to sovereignty in the classic sense prior to ratification of the Constitution, it is clear that the act of ratification affected their sovereignty in a way different from any previous political event in America or anywhere else. For the adoption of the Constitution made them members of a novel federal system that sought to balance the States' exercise of some sovereign prerogatives delegated from their own people with the principle of a limited but centralizing federal supremacy.

*** Given the Framers' general concern with curbing abuses by state governments, it would be amazing if the scheme of delegated powers embodied in the Constitution had left the National Government powerless to render the States judicially accountable for violations of federal rights. And of course the Framers did not understand the scheme to leave the government powerless. In The Federalist No. 80, Hamilton observed that "[n]o man of sense will believe that such prohibitions [running against the states] would be scrupulously regarded, without some effectual power in the government to restrain or correct the infractions of them," and that "an authority in the federal courts, to over-rule such as might be in manifest contravention of the articles of union" was the Convention's preferred remedy. By speaking in the plural of an authority in the federal "courts," Hamilton made it clear that he envisioned more than this Court's exercise of appellate jurisdiction to review federal questions decided by state courts. Nor is it plausible that he was thinking merely of suits brought against States by the National Government itself, which The Federalist's authors did not describe in the paternalistic terms that would pass without an eyebrow raised today. Hamilton's power of the Government to restrain violations of citizens' rights was a power to be exercised by the federal courts at the citizens' behest.

*** [I]t is equally understandable that questions seem not to have been raised about state sovereign immunity in federal question cases. The very idea of a federal question depended on the rejection of the simple concept of sovereignty from which the immunity doctrine had developed; under the English common law, the question of immunity in a system of layered sovereignty simply could not have arisen. The Framers' principal objectives in rejecting English theories of unitary sovereignty, moreover, would have been impeded if a new concept of sovereign immunity had taken its place in federal question cases, and would have been substantially thwarted if that new immunity had been held to be untouchable by any congressional effort to abrogate it. *** The considerations expressed so far, based on text, *Chisholm*, caution in common-law reception, and sovereignty theory, have pointed both to the mistakes inherent in *Hans* and, even more strongly, to the error of today's holding. ***

V

*** In being ready to hold that the [federal] relationship may still be altered, not by the Court but by Congress, I would tread the course laid out elsewhere in our cases. The Court has repeatedly stated its assumption that insofar as the relative positions of States and Nation may be affected consistently with the Tenth Amendment, they would not be modified without deliberately expressed intent. The plain statement rule, which "assures that the legislature has in fact faced, and intended to bring into issue, the critical matters involved in the judicial decision," is particularly appropriate in light of our primary reliance on "[t]he effectiveness of the federal political process in preserving the States' interests." Hence, we have required such a plain statement when Congress pre-empts the historic powers of the States, imposes a condition on the grant of federal moneys, or seeks to regulate a State's ability to determine the qualifications of its own officials.

When judging legislation passed under unmistakable Article I powers, no further restriction could be required. Nor does the Court explain why more could be demanded. In the past, we have assumed that a plain statement requirement is sufficient to protect the States from undue federal encroachments upon their traditional immunity from suit. It is hard to contend that this rule has set the bar too low, for (except in *Union Gas*) we have never found the requirement to be met outside the context of laws passed under § 5 of the Fourteenth Amendment. The exception I would recognize today proves the rule, moreover, because the federal abrogation of state immunity comes as part of a regulatory scheme which is itself designed to invest the States with regulatory powers that Congress need not extend to them. This fact suggests to me that the political safeguards of federalism are working, that a plain statement rule is an adequate check on congressional overreaching, and that today's abandonment of that approach is wholly unwarranted. *** Because neither text, precedent, nor history supports the majority's abdication of our responsibility to exercise the jurisdiction entrusted to us in Article III, I would reverse the judgment of the Court of Appeals.

Notes

1. *Seminole Tribe* **and the Eleventh Amendment.** Now that you have read both the case and the amendment carefully, consider these questions.

(a) Does the Eleventh Amendment have any effect on a suit by a citizen of Florida against the State of Florida in the Federal District Court for the Northern District of Florida?

(b) Is the Seminole Tribe a citizen of Florida? Of any state? Does this matter?

(c) Can plaintiffs circumvent the Eleventh Amendment by filing suit against state officials rather than the State itself? Why didn't the plaintiffs merely restyle their complaint in *Seminole Tribe* to name the Governor as defendant?

(d) Does the Eleventh Amendment bar suit against a city or county in federal court?

(e) Couldn't the tribe simply have filed suit in state court against the State of Florida to avoid Eleventh Amendment problems?

(f) What does the Eleventh Amendment have to do with sovereign immunity? Do you see any reason to be skeptical of "sovereign immunity," a concept developed in Europe before the American Revolution, in light of our Constitution and its values?

(g) If the Court had not barred the suit and the Seminole Tribe had proceeded to judgment, what judicial relief could be granted? Would this make any judgment an advisory opinion?

(h) Can you construct an argument for Florida based on the Tenth Amendment?

2. **Problems.**
(a) Mary Doe, who attends Western State University, sues the University for failure to provide equal athletic programs and facilities for women in accordance with the requirements of Title IX of the Civil Rights Act of 1964. What factors would you consider in advising her whether she is foreclosed from suit in federal court under *Seminole Tribe*?

(b) Metrodata, Inc. developed and patented computer software subsequently used by Eastern State without obtaining a license from Metrodata. Metrodata asks you whether it can get around the Eleventh Amendment and sue the state in federal court. Advise Metrodata.

3. **State waiver of Eleventh Amendment immunity.** If a State voluntarily removes a suit from state court to federal court, does the State waive its Eleventh Amendment immunity? In *Lapides v. Board of Regents of University System of Georgia*, 535 U.S. 613 (2002), JUSTICE BREYER wrote for a unanimous court:

"It would seem anomalous and inconsistent for a State both (1) to invoke federal jurisdiction *** contending that the 'Judicial power of the United States' extends to the case at hand, and (2) to claim Eleventh Amendment immunity *** denying that the 'Judicial power of the United States' extends to the case at hand. And a Constitution that permitted States to follow their litigation interests by freely asserting both claims in the same case could generate seriously unfair results. *** And the Court has made clear in general that 'where a State *voluntarily* becomes a party to a cause and submits its rights for judicial determination, it will be bound thereby and cannot escape the result of its own voluntary act by invoking the prohibitions of the Eleventh Amendment.' (emphasis added)."

4. **Exception to Eleventh Amendment immunity.** In *Verizon Maryland v. Public Service Commission of Maryland*, 535 U.S. 635 (2002), the Court allowed a claim for prospective injunctive and declaratory relief against a state commission based on its violation of the Constitution, citing *Ex Parte Young*, 209 U.S. 123 (1908).

III

THE DISTRIBUTION OF
NATIONAL POWERS

"The powers delegated by this Constitution are appropriated to the departments to which they are respectively distributed: so that the Legislative Department shall never exercise powers vested in the Executive or Judicial, nor the Executive exercise powers vested in the Legislative or Judicial, nor the Judicial exercise the powers vested in the Legislative or Executive Departments."

> —James Madison
> Introducing Bill of Rights,
> June 8, 1789

This chapter examines the horizontal relationship between the powers of Congress (set forth primarily in Article I) and the powers of the President (generally outlined in Article II). Political scientists often refer to the relationship between the political branches of the federal government in terms of "separation of powers" and "checks and balances." These words hide important differences in meaning and emphasis: separation of powers suggests noninvolvement of branches that do not possess a specified power, while checks and balances signifies division and dispersion of a specified power between the branches. The purposes behind separation of powers and checks and balances generally identified by courts and commentators are (1) prevention of tyranny and (2) efficiency of administration. Most authorities lay heavy emphasis on the former.

- **Prevention of Tyranny.** Federalist No. 47 stressed that the "accumulation of all powers, legislative, executive, and judiciary, in the same hands *** [is] the very definition of tyranny." Such concentration, which had been common in England's administration of the North American colonies, was a substantial reason for the American Revolution. Separation of powers facilitates the rule of law since different entities make, administer, and apply the law. During the early years of the United States, the greatest fear was of overreaching legislative power; in recent decades, the focus has often been on the growth of executive power. Only occasionally, as with the *Brown* and *Roe* decisions, does the public seem concerned about overreaching judicial power. The checks and balances, as well as the separation of powers, in the Constitution have also been viewed as tools for

111

limiting the size and power of the federal government, since a broad consensus is required to change the status quo.

• **Efficiency.** The three-part federal structure was originally seen as a move towards efficiency, a repudiation of the congressional hegemony created under the Articles of Confederation. In particular, the framers sought to establish a strong executive to conduct foreign affairs and military matters more effectively at the federal level. Ironically, a modern complaint is that separation of powers creates inefficiency in the operation of the federal government.

Academic commentary stresses two dominant modes of analyzing separation of powers issues under the Constitution.

• **Formalism** demands adherence by each branch to the powers granted that branch. Congress can make laws only if it follows specified procedures, but may not enforce the laws it makes. Conversely, the President enforces laws but may not make them.

• **Functionalism** commands fidelity to the purposes of the distribution of powers. For the functionalist, the Constitution's distribution of powers is violated only if one branch of the federal government aggrandizes its power at the expense of another branch.

In a nutshell, the formalist takes separation of powers as a command of the Constitution's text and structure; the functionalist views such separation as a component of fulfilling the Constitution's goals.

There are problems with this dichotomy, both theoretical and practical. Theoretically, there is a lack of clarity or definition to the formalist distinction between making, executing, and adjudicating; there is a lack of understanding in the functionalist approach as to precisely how separation of powers facilitates the goals discussed above. Moreover, it is not altogether clear that this dichotomy is coherent: the cases use it sparingly, and both schools share concerns over both separating functions and avoiding power imbalances among the three branches of the federal government. Practically, the dichotomy leads to different results, not merely at the margins, but with respect to core aspects of whether operations of the federal government are constitutional.

Federal agencies pose a classic example of diverging formalist and functionalist results. The Constitution does not mention, even generically, agencies like the FTC, FAA, EEOC, NLRB, and EPA. Created by Congress, these agencies generally are subject to varying levels of Presidential control, but they are not "departments" of the Executive Branch (such as the Department of Justice, the State Department, and the Department of Defense). Furthermore, these agencies frequently combine rulemaking (lawmaking), prosecution of violators (law execution), and claim resolution (adjudication).

A pure formalist would conclude that such agencies are unconstitutional: the Constitution does not permit a "fourth branch" of the federal government, much less a fourth branch that combines Article I, II, and III powers. The formalist responds to the complaint "This is how the federal government has done business for nearly a century," with the response that authorization of fourth branch agencies requires constitutional amendment.   The functionalist, on the other hand, argues that these agencies are creative tools for delivering federal goods, services, and regulations that are not clearly prohibited by the Constitution. Some functionalists argue that the Constitution only mandates separation of powers at the apex of the federal government: the President, the Congress, and the Supreme Court. Separation of powers restrictions do not apply to such agencies, they argue: broad rules crafted by Congress as well as congressional oversight and budgetary controls, varying degrees of Presidential control over personnel, and judicial review, although restrained, provide ample controls over exercise of governmental power by such agencies.

The cases below demonstrate that the Supreme Court's decisions concerning the distribution of federal powers take place within a wide variety of contexts and contain differing mixes of formal and functional components. As you will see, the cases in this chapter include the President's authority to initiate policy, both domestic and foreign; the President's ability to "veto" parts of legislation; Presidential privileges, including confidentiality and immunity from suit; the roles of Congress and the President (and even the courts) in appointing and removing federal officials; "legislative veto" by Congress or parts of Congress.

The following case is widely perceived to be the Supreme Court's most important decision concerning the relationship between executive and legislative powers. Part B of this Chapter examines executive powers, both in domestic and foreign affairs contexts, and explores executive privileges. Part C deals with the powers of Congress relative to the President, again in the contexts of foreign and domestic affairs. The powers of Congress as they relate to state power are reserved for Chapters IV and V.

A. THE FRAMEWORK

Harry Truman's popularity plummeted between the start of the Korean War and early 1952. At that time, Truman believed a union-management dispute between the steel mills and the Steelworkers' Union threatened the nation's ability to press forward in Korea. Truman, however, refused to use the injunctive powers granted to him under the Taft–Hartley Act (which Congress had passed over his veto) to halt a proposed strike, because he perceived that management intransigence, not union recalcitrance, caused the steel crisis. On April 9, 1952, he seized the steel mills and designated management to keep them operating for the United States. Management feared the President would try to solve the labor-management dispute by unilaterally raising wages.

President Truman was promptly sued by Youngstown Sheet & Tube Company, which argued that his action was unconstitutional. The Court's decision to grant certiorari was made only hours before a planned announcement that the parties, under the pressure of Truman's seizure of the mills, had reached a settlement. When the parties learned of the Court's action, bargaining ceased: management perceived that it had nothing to lose by awaiting a Supreme Court decision. After the Court's ruling (only two months after the seizure of the mills), the union struck for fifty-three days; neither a steel shortage nor any noticeable impact on the war effort materialized.

In light of this brief history, do you think the Court was too hasty? Was the Administration's position, described by the justices, excessive? Incidentally, Truman's memoirs show him to be unrepentant: "[We cannot] separate the economic facts from the problems of defense and security. [The President,] who is Commander in Chief and who represents the interests of all the people, must be able to act at all times to meet any sudden threat to the national security." 2 H.S. TRUMAN, MEMOIRS: YEARS OF TRIAL AND HOPE 478 (1956).

YOUNGSTOWN SHEET & TUBE CO. v. SAWYER
343 U.S. 579, 72 S.Ct. 863, 96 L.Ed. 1153 (1952).

MR. JUSTICE BLACK delivered the opinion of the Court.

We are asked to decide whether the President was acting within his constitutional power when he issued an order directing the Secretary of Commerce to take possession of and operate most of the Nation's steel mills. The mill owners argue that the President's order amounts to lawmaking, a legislative function which the Constitution has expressly confided to the Congress and not to the President. The Government's position is that the order was made on findings of the President that his action was necessary to avert a national catastrophe which would inevitably result from a stoppage of steel production, and that in meeting this grave emergency the President was acting within the aggregate of his constitutional powers as the Nation's Chief Executive and the Commander in Chief of the Armed Forces of the United States. The issue emerges here from the following series of events:

In the latter part of 1951, a dispute arose between the steel companies and their employees over terms and conditions that should be included in new collective bargaining agreements. Long-continued conferences failed to resolve the dispute. On December 18, 1951, the employees' representative, United Steelworkers of America, C.I.O., gave notice of an intention to strike when the existing bargaining agreements expired on December 31. The Federal Mediation and Conciliation Service then intervened in an effort to get labor and management to agree. This failing, the President on December 22, 1951, referred the dispute to the Federal Wage Stabilization Board to investigate and make recommendations for fair and equitable terms of settlement. This Board's report resulted in no settlement. On April 4, 1952, the Union gave notice of a nation-wide strike called to begin at 12:01 a.m. April 9. The indispensability of steel as a component of substantially all weapons and other war materials led the President to believe that the proposed work stoppage would immediately jeopardize our national defense and that governmental seizure of the steel mills was necessary in order to assure the continued availability of steel. Reciting these considerations for his action, the President, a few hours before the strike was to begin, issued Executive Order 10340. The order directed the Secretary of Commerce to take possession of most of the steel mills and keep them running. The Secretary immediately issued his own possessory orders, calling upon the presidents of the various seized companies to serve as operational managers for the United States. They were directed to carry on their activities in accordance with regulations and directions of the Secretary. The next morning the President sent a message to Congress reporting his action. Twelve days later he sent a second message. Congress has taken no action.

Obeying the Secretary's orders under protest, the companies brought proceedings against him in the District Court. Their complaints charged that the seizure was not authorized by an act of Congress or by any constitutional provisions. *** Holding against the Government on all points, the District Court on April 30 issued a preliminary injunction restraining the Secretary from "continuing the seizure and possession of the plant *** and from acting under the purported authority of Executive Order No. 10340." On the same day the Court of Appeals stayed the District Court's injunction. Deeming it best that the issues raised be promptly decided by this Court, we granted certiorari.

III–1. "We're Waiting to Hear from the Principal" by Silvey Jackson Ray/The Kansas City Star, 1952.

The President's power, if any, to issue the order must stem either from an act of Congress or from the Constitution itself. There is no statute that expressly authorizes the President to take possession of property as he did here. Nor is there any act of Congress to which our attention has been directed from which such a power can fairly be implied. Indeed, we do not understand the Government to rely on statutory authorization for this seizure. There are two statutes which do authorize the President to take both personal and real property under certain conditions. However, the Government admits that these conditions were not met and that the President's order was not rooted in either of the statutes. The Government refers to the seizure provisions of one of these statutes (§ 201(b) of the Defense Production Act) as "much too cumbersome, involved, and time-consuming for the crisis which was at hand."

Moreover, the use of the seizure technique to solve labor disputes in order to prevent work stoppages was not only unauthorized by any congressional enactment; prior to this controversy, Congress had refused to adopt that method of settling labor disputes. When the Taft–Hartley Act was under consideration in 1947, Congress rejected an amendment which would have authorized such governmental seizures in cases of emergency. ***

It is clear that if the President had authority to issue the order he did, it must be found in some provisions of the Constitution. And it is not claimed that express constitutional language grants this power to the President. The contention is that presidential power should be implied from the aggregate of his powers under the Constitution. Particular reliance is placed on provisions in Article II which say that "the executive Power shall be vested in a President *** "; that "he shall take Care that the Laws be faithfully executed"; and that he "shall be Commander in Chief of the Army and Navy of the United States."

The order cannot properly be sustained as an exercise of the President's military power as Commander in Chief of the Armed Forces. The Government attempts to do so by citing a number of cases upholding broad powers in military commanders engaged in day-to-day fighting in a theater of war. Such cases need not concern us here. Even though "theater of war" be an expanding concept, we cannot with faithfulness to our constitutional system hold that the Commander in Chief of the Armed Forces has the ultimate power as such to take possession of private property in order to keep labor disputes from stopping production. This is a job for the Nation's lawmakers, not for its military authorities.

Nor can the seizure order be sustained because of the several constitutional provisions that grant executive power to the President. In the framework of our Constitution, the President's power to see that the laws are faithfully executed refutes the idea that he is to be a lawmaker. The Constitution limits his functions in the lawmaking process to the recommending of laws he thinks wise and the vetoing of laws he thinks bad. And the Constitution is neither silent nor equivocal about who shall make laws which the President is to execute. The first section of the first article says that "All legislative Powers herein granted shall be vested in a Congress of the United States ***." After granting many powers to the Congress, Article I goes on to provide that Congress may "make all Laws which shall be necessary and proper for carrying into Execution the foregoing Powers and all other Powers vested by this Constitution in the Government of the United States, or in any Department or Officer thereof."

The President's order does not direct that a congressional policy be executed in a manner prescribed by Congress—it directs that a presidential policy be executed in a manner prescribed by the President. The preamble of the order itself, like that of many statutes, sets out reasons why the President believes certain policies should be adopted, proclaims these policies as rules of conduct to be followed, and again, like a statute, authorizes a government official to promulgate additional rules and regulations consistent with the policy proclaimed and needed to carry that policy into execution. The power of Congress to adopt such public policies as those proclaimed by the order is beyond question. It can authorize the taking of private property for public use. It can makes laws regulating the relationships between employers and employees, prescribing rules designed to settle labor disputes, and fixing wages and working conditions in certain fields of our economy. The Constitution did not subject this law-making power of Congress to presidential or military supervision or control.

It is said that other Presidents without congressional authority have taken possession of private business enterprises in order to settle labor disputes. But even if this be true, Congress has not thereby lost its exclusive constitutional authority to make laws necessary and proper to carry out the powers vested by the Constitution "in the Government of the United States, or in any Department or Officer thereof."

The Founders of this Nation entrusted the lawmaking power to the Congress alone in both good and bad times. It would do no good to recall the historical events, the fears of power and the hopes for freedom that lay behind their choice. Such a review would but confirm our holding that this seizure order cannot stand. ***

MR. J USTICE JACKSON, concurring in the judgment and opinion of the court.

*** A judge, like an executive adviser, may be surprised at the poverty of really useful and unambiguous authority applicable to concrete problems of executive power as they actually present themselves. Just what our forefathers did envision, or would have envisioned had they foreseen modern conditions, must be divined from materials almost as enigmatic as the dreams Joseph was called upon to interpret for Pharaoh. A century and a half of partisan debate and scholarly speculation yields no net result but only supplies more or less apt quotations from respected sources on each side of any question. They largely cancel each other. And court decisions are indecisive because of the judicial practice of dealing with the largest questions in the most narrow way.

The actual art of governing under our Constitution does not and cannot conform to judicial definitions of the power of any of its branches based on isolated clauses or even single Articles torn from context. While the Constitution diffuses power the better to secure liberty, it also contemplates that practice will integrate the dispersed powers into a workable government. It enjoins upon its branches separateness but interdependence, autonomy but reciprocity. Presidential powers are not fixed but fluctuate, depending upon their disjunction or conjunction with those of Congress. We may well begin by a somewhat over-simplified grouping of practical situations in which a President may doubt, or others may challenge, his powers, and by distinguishing roughly the legal consequences of this factor of relativity.

1. When the President acts pursuant to an express or implied authorization of Congress, his authority is at its maximum, for it includes all that he possesses in his own right plus all that Congress can delegate. In these circumstances, and in these only, may he be said (for what it may be worth), to personify the federal sovereignty. If his act is held unconstitutional under these circumstances, it usually means that the Federal Government as an undivided whole lacks power. A seizure executed by the President pursuant to an Act of Congress would be supported by the strongest of presumptions and the widest latitude of judicial interpretation, and the burden of persuasion would rest heavily upon any who might attack it.

2. When the President acts in absence of either a congressional grant or denial of authority, he can only rely upon his own independent powers, but there is a zone of twilight in which he and Congress may have concurrent authority, or in which its distribution is uncertain. Therefore, congressional inertia, indifference or quiescence may sometimes, at least as a practical matter, enable, if not invite, measures on independent presidential responsibility. In this area, any actual test of power is likely to depend on the imperatives of events and contemporary imponderables rather than on abstract theories of law.

3. When the President takes measures incompatible with the expressed or implied will of Congress, his power is at its lowest ebb, for then he can rely only upon his own constitutional powers minus any constitutional powers of Congress over the matter. Courts can sustain exclusive Presidential control in such a case only by disabling the Congress from acting upon the subject. Presidential claim to a power at once so conclusive and preclusive must be scrutinized with caution, for what is at stake is the equilibrium established by our constitutional system.

Into which of these classifications does this executive seizure of the steel industry fit? It is eliminated from the first by admission, for it is conceded that no congressional authorization exists for this seizure. ***

Can it then be defended under flexible tests available to the second category? It seems clearly eliminated from that class because Congress has not left seizure of private property an open field but has covered it by three statutory policies inconsistent with this seizure.

*** This leaves the current seizure to be justified only by the severe tests under the third grouping, where it can be supported only by any remainder of executive power after subtraction of such powers as Congress may have over the subject. In short, we can sustain the President only by holding that seizure of such strike-bound industries is within his domain and beyond control by Congress. ***

The Solicitor General seeks the power of seizure in three clauses of the Executive Article, the first reading, "The executive Power shall be vested in a President of the United States of America." Lest I be thought to exaggerate, I quote the interpretation which his brief puts upon it: "In our view, this clause constitutes a grant of all the executive powers of which the Government is capable." If that be true, it is difficult to see why the forefathers bothered to add several specific items, including some trifling ones.

The example of such unlimited executive power that must have most impressed the forefathers was the prerogative exercised by George III, and the description of its evils in the Declaration of Independence leads me to doubt that they were creating their new Executive in his image. Continental European examples were no more appealing. And if we seek instruction from our own times, we can match it only from the executive powers in those governments we disparagingly describe as totalitarian. I cannot accept the view that this clause is a grant in bulk of all conceivable executive power but regard it as an allocation to the presidential office of the generic powers thereafter stated.

The clause on which the Government next relies is that "The President shall be Commander in Chief ***." But just what authority goes with the name has plagued Presidential advisers who would not waive or narrow it by nonassertion yet cannot say where it begins or ends. It undoubtedly puts the Nation's armed forces under Presidential command. Hence, this loose appellation is sometimes advanced as support for any Presidential action, internal or external, involving use of force, the idea being that it vests power to do anything, anywhere, that can be done with an army or navy.

That seems to be the logic of an argument tendered at our bar—that the President having, on his own responsibility, sent American troops abroad derives from that act "affirmative power" to seize the means of producing a supply of steel for them. ***

I cannot foresee all that it might entail if the Court should endorse this argument. Nothing in our Constitution is plainer than that declaration of a war is entrusted only to Congress. Of course, a state of war may in fact exist without a formal declaration. But no doctrine that the Court could promulgate would seem to me more sinister and alarming than that a President whose conduct of foreign affairs is so largely uncontrolled, and often even is unknown, can vastly enlarge his mastery over the internal affairs of the country by his own commitment of the Nation's armed forces to some foreign venture. I do not, however, find it necessary or appropriate to consider the legal status of the Korean enterprise to discountenance argument based on it.

Assuming that we are in a war de facto, whether it is or is not a war de jure, does that empower the Commander-in-Chief to seize industries he thinks necessary to supply our army? The Constitution expressly places in Congress power "to raise and support Armies" and "to provide and maintain a

Navy." This certainly lays upon Congress primary responsibility for supplying the armed forces. Congress alone controls the raising of revenues and their appropriation and may determine in what manner and by what means they shall be spent for military and naval procurement. ***

There are indications that the Constitution did not contemplate that the title Commander-in-Chief of the Army and Navy will constitute him also Commander-in-Chief of the country, its industries and its inhabitants. He has no monopoly of "war powers," whatever they are. ***

The third clause in which the Solicitor General finds seizure powers is that "he shall take Care that the Laws be faithfully executed ***." That authority must be matched against words of the Fifth Amendment that "No person shall be *** deprived of life, liberty, or property, without due process of law ***." One gives a governmental authority that reaches so far as there is law, the other gives a private right that authority shall go no farther. These signify about all there is of the principle that ours is a government of laws, not of men, and that we submit ourselves to rulers only if under rules.

The Solicitor General lastly grounds support of the seizure upon nebulous, inherent powers never expressly granted but said to have accrued to the office from the customs and claims of preceding administrations. The plea is for a resulting power to deal with a crisis or an emergency according to the necessities of the case, the unarticulated assumption being that necessity knows no law. ***

The vagueness and generality of the clauses that set forth presidential powers afford a plausible basis for pressures within and without an administration for presidential action beyond that supported by those whose responsibility it is to defend his actions in court. The claim of inherent and unrestricted presidential powers has long been a persuasive dialectical weapon in political controversy. While it is not surprising that counsel should grasp support from such unadjudicated claims of power, a judge cannot accept self-serving press statements of the attorney for one of the interested parties as authority in answering a constitutional question, even if the advocate was himself. But prudence has counseled that actual reliance on such nebulous claims stop short of provoking a judicial test. ***

The appeal, however, that we declare the existence of inherent powers ex necessitate to meet an emergency asks us to do what many think would be wise, although it is something the forefathers omitted. They knew what emergencies were, knew the pressures they engender for authoritative action, knew, too, how they afford a ready pretext for usurpation. We may also suspect that they suspected that emergency powers would tend to kindle emergencies. Aside from suspension of the privilege of the writ of habeas corpus in time of rebellion or invasion, when the public safety may require it, they made no express provision for exercise of extraordinary authority because of a crisis. I do not think we rightfully may so amend their work, and, if we could, I am not convinced it would be wise to do so, although many modern nations have forthrightly recognized that war and economic crises may upset the normal balance between liberty and authority. Their experience with emergency powers may not be irrelevant to the argument here that we should say that the Executive, of his own volition, can invest himself with undefined emergency powers. ***

In view of the ease, expedition and safety with which Congress can grant and has granted large emergency powers, certainly ample to embrace this crisis, I am quite unimpressed with the argument that we should affirm possession of them without statute. Such power either has no beginning or it has no end. If it exists, it need submit to no legal restraint. I am not alarmed that it would plunge us straightway into dictatorship, but it is at least a step in that wrong direction.

As to whether there is imperative necessity for such powers, it is relevant to note the gap that exists between the President's paper powers and his real powers. The Constitution does not disclose the measure of the actual controls wielded by the modern presidential office. That instrument must be understood as an Eighteenth–Century sketch of a government hoped for, not as a blueprint of the Government that is. Vast accretions of federal power, eroded from that reserved by the States, have magnified the scope of presidential activity. Subtle shifts take place in the centers of real power that do not show on the face of the Constitution.

Executive power has the advantage of concentration in a single head in those choice the whole Nation has a part, making him the focus of public hopes and expectations. ***

The essence of our free Government is "leave to live by no man's leave, underneath the law"—to be governed by those impersonal forces which we call law. Our Government is fashioned to fulfill this concept so far as humanly possible. The Executive, except for recommendation and veto, has no legislative power. The executive action we have here originates in the individual will of the President and represents an exercise of authority without law. No one, perhaps not even the President, knows the limits of the power he may seek to exert in this instance and the parties affected cannot learn the limit of their rights. We do not know today what powers over labor or property would be claimed to flow from Government possession if we should legalize it, what rights to compensation would be claimed or recognized, or on what contingency it would end. With all its defects, delays and inconveniences, men have discovered no technique for long preserving free government except that the Executive be under the law, and that the law be made by parliamentary deliberations.

Such institutions may be destined to pass away. But it is the duty of the Court to be last, not first, to give them up.

[Separate concurrences of MR. JUSTICE BURTON, and MR. JUSTICE CLARK, are omitted.]

MR. JUSTICE DOUGLAS, concurring.

[The] legislative nature of the action taken by the President seems to me to be clear. *** The President might seize and the Congress by subsequent action might ratify the seizure. But until and unless Congress acted, no condemnation would be lawful. The branch of government that has the power to pay compensation for a seizure is the only one able to authorize a seizure or make lawful one that the President had effected. That seems to me to be the necessary result of the condemnation provision in the Fifth Amendment. It squares with the theory of checks and balances expounded by Mr. JUSTICE BLACK in the opinion of the Court in which I join. *** If we sanctioned the present exercise of power by the President, we would be expanding Article II of the Constitution and rewriting it to suit the political conveniences of the present emergency. *** We pay a price for our system of checks and balances, for the distribution of power among the three branches of government. It is a price that today may seem exorbitant to many. Today a kindly President uses the seizure power to effect a wage increase and to keep the steel furnaces in production. Yet tomorrow another President might use the same power to prevent a wage increase, to curb trade unionists, to regiment labor as oppressively as industry thinks it has been regimented by this seizure.

MR. JUSTICE FRANKFURTER, concurring.

*** Not so long ago it was fashionable to find our system of checks and balances obstructive to effective government. It was easy to ridicule that system as outmoded—too easy. The experience through which the world has passed in our own day has made vivid the realization that the Framers of our Constitution were not inexperienced doctrinaires. These long-headed statesmen had no illusion that our people enjoyed biological or psychological or sociological immunities from the hazards of concentrated power. It is absurd to see a dictator in a representative product of the sturdy democratic traditions of the Mississippi Valley. The accretion of dangerous power does not come in a day. It does come, however slowly, from the generative force of unchecked disregard of the restrictions that fence in even the most disinterested assertion of authority.

*** Marshall's admonition [in *McCulloch v. Maryland*] that "it is a constitution we are expounding" is especially relevant when the Court is required to give legal sanctions to an underlying principle of the Constitution—that of separation of powers. *** We must therefore put to one side consideration of what powers the President would have had if there had been no legislation whatever bearing on the authority asserted by the seizure, or if the seizure had been only for a short, explicitly temporary period, to be terminated automatically unless Congressional approval were given. ***

The question before the Court comes in this setting. Congress has frequently—at least 16 times since 1916—specifically provided for executive seizure of production, transportation, communications, or storage facilities. In every case it has qualified this grant of power with limitations and safeguards. This body of enactments *** demonstrates that Congress deemed seizure so drastic a power as to require that it be carefully circumscribed whenever the President was vested with this extraordinary authority. ***

In any event, nothing can be plainer than that Congress made a conscious choice of policy in a field full of perplexity and peculiarly within legislative responsibility for choice. In formulating legislation for dealing with industrial conflicts, Congress could not more clearly and emphatically have withheld authority than it did in [the Taft–Hartley Act of] 1947. ***

It cannot be contended that the President would have had power to issue this order had Congress explicitly negated such authority in formal legislation. Congress has expressed its will to withhold this power from the President as though it had said so in so many words. ***

Apart from his vast share of responsibility for the conduct of our foreign relations, the embracing function of the President is that "he shall take Care that the Laws be faithfully executed ***." Art. II, § 3. The nature of that authority has for me been comprehensively indicated by MR. JUSTICE HOLMES. "The duty of the President to see that the laws be executed is a duty that does not go beyond the laws or require him to achieve more than Congress sees fit to leave within his power." *Myers v. United States*, 272 U.S. 52, 177. The powers of the President are not as particularized as are those of Congress. But unenumerated powers do not mean undefined powers. The separation of powers built into our Constitution gives essential content to undefined provisions in the frame of our government.

To be sure, the content of the three authorities of government is not to be derived from an abstract analysis. The areas are partly interacting, not wholly disjointed. The Constitution is a framework for government. Therefore the way the framework has consistently operated fairly establishes that it has operated according to its true nature. Deeply embedded traditional ways of conducting government cannot supplant the Constitution or legislation, but they give meaning to the words of a text or supply them. It is an inadmissibly narrow conception of American constitutional law to confine it to the words of the Constitution and to disregard the gloss which life has written upon them. In short, a systematic, unbroken, executive practice, long pursued to the knowledge of the Congress and never before questioned, engaged in by Presidents who have also sworn to uphold the Constitution, making as it were such exercise of power part of the structure of our government, may be treated as a gloss on "executive Power" vested in the President by § 1 of Art. II. ***

Down to the World War II period *** the record is barren of instances comparable to the one before us. *** In this case, reliance on the powers that flow from declared war has been commendably disclaimed by the Solicitor General. Thus the list of executive assertions of the power of seizure in circumstances comparable to the present reduces to three in the six-month period from June to December of 1941. *** Without passing on their validity, as we are not called upon to do, it suffices to say that these three isolated instances do not add up, either in number, scope, duration or contemporaneous legal justification, to the [necessary] kind of executive construction of the Constitution. Nor do they come to us sanctioned by long-continued acquiescence of Congress giving decisive weight to a construction by the Executive of its powers. *** No doubt a government with distributed authority, subject to be challenged in the courts of law, at least long enough to consider and adjudicate the challenge, labors under restrictions from which other governments are free. It has not been our tradition to envy such governments. In any event our government was designed to have such restrictions.

MR. CHIEF JUSTICE VINSON, with whom MR. JUSTICE REED and MR. JUSTICE MINTON join, dissenting.

The President of the United States directed the Secretary of Commerce to take temporary possession of the Nation's steel mills during the existing emergency because "a work stoppage would immediately jeopardize and imperil our national defense and the defense of those joined with us in resisting aggression, and would add to the continuing danger of our soldiers, sailors and airmen engaged in combat in the field."

*** In passing upon the question of Presidential powers in this case, we must first consider the context in which those powers were exercised. *** The President has the duty to execute *** legislative programs. Their successful execution depends upon continued production of steel and stabilized prices for steel. Accordingly, when the collective bargaining agreements between the Nation's steel producers and their employees, represented by the United Steel Workers, were due to expire on December 31, 1951, and a strike shutting down the entire basic steel industry was threatened, the President acted to avert a complete shutdown of steel production.

*** One is not here called upon even to consider the possibility of executive seizure of a farm, a corner grocery store or even a single industrial plant. Such considerations arise only when one ignores the central fact of this case—that the Nation's entire basic steel production would have shut down completely if there had been no Government seizure. Even ignoring for the moment whatever confidential information the President may possess as "the Nation's organ for foreign affairs," the uncontroverted affidavits in this record amply support the finding that "a work stoppage would immediately jeopardize and imperil our national defense."

Plaintiffs do not remotely suggest any basis for rejecting the President's finding that any stoppage of steel production would immediately place the Nation in peril. Under [Plaintiff's] view, the President is left powerless at the very moment when the need for action may be most pressing and when no one, other than he, is immediately capable of action. Under this view, he is left powerless because a power not expressly given to Congress is nevertheless found to rest exclusively with Congress.

*** [However, the] whole of the "executive Power" is vested in the President. *** This comprehensive grant of the executive power to a single person was bestowed soon after the country had thrown the yoke of monarchy. Only by instilling initiative and vigor in all of the three departments of Government, declared Madison, could tyranny in any form be avoided. Hamilton added: "Energy in the Executive is a leading character in the definition of good government. It is essential to the protection of the community against foreign attack; it is not less essential to the steady administration of the laws; to the protection of property against those irregular and highhanded combinations which sometimes interrupt the ordinary course of justice; to the security of liberty against the enterprises and assaults of ambition, of faction, and of anarchy." It is thus apparent that the Presidency was deliberately fashioned as an office of power and independence. Of course, the Framers created no autocrat capable of arrogating any power unto himself at any time. But neither did they create an automaton impotent to exercise the powers of Government at a time when the survival of the Republic itself may be at stake.

In passing upon the grave constitutional question presented in this case, we must never forget, as CHIEF JUSTICE MARSHALL admonished, that the Constitution is "intended to endure for ages to come, and consequently, to be adapted to the various crises of human affairs," and that "(i)ts means are adequate to its ends." Cases do arise presenting questions which could not have been foreseen by the Framers. In such cases, the Constitution has been treated as a living document adaptable to new situations. But we are not called upon today to expand the Constitution to meet a new situation. For, in this case, we need only look to history and time-honored principles of constitutional law—principles that have been applied consistently by all branches of the Government throughout our history. It is those who assert the invalidity of the Executive Order who seek to amend the Constitution in this case.

A review of executive action demonstrates that our Presidents have on many occasions exhibited the leadership contemplated by the Framers when they made the President Commander in Chief, and imposed upon him the trust to "take Care that the Laws be faithfully executed." With or without explicit statutory authorization, Presidents have at such times dealt with national emergencies by acting promptly and resolutely to enforce legislative programs, at least to save those programs until Congress could act. Congress and the courts have responded to such executive initiative with consistent approval.

Our first President displayed at once the leadership contemplated by the Framers. When the national revenue laws were openly flouted in some sections of Pennsylvania, President Washington, without waiting for a call from the state government, summoned the militia and took decisive steps to secure the faithful execution of the laws. When international disputes engendered by the French revolution threatened to involve this country in war, and while congressional policy remained uncertain, Washington issued his Proclamation of Neutrality. Hamilton, whose defense of the Proclamation has endured the test of time, invoked the argument that the Executive has the duty to do that which will preserve peace until Congress acts and, in addition, pointed to the need for keeping the Nation informed of the requirements of existing laws and treaties as part of the faithful execution of the laws. ***

In an action furnishing a most apt precedent for this case, President Lincoln without statutory authority directed the seizure of rail and telegraph lines leading to Washington. *** In his autobiography, President [Theodore] Roosevelt expounded the "Stewardship Theory" of Presidential power, stating that "the executive is subject only to the people, and, under the Constitution, bound to serve the people affirmatively in cases where the Constitution does not explicitly forbid him to render the service." *** During World War I, President Wilson established a War Labor Board without awaiting specific direction by Congress. *** [Twenty years later,] the President [FDR] directed seizure of the Nation's coal mines to remove an obstruction to the effective prosecution of the war. *** The procedures adopted by President Roosevelt closely resembled the methods employed by President Wilson. A National War Labor Board, like its predecessor of World War I, was created by Executive Order to deal effectively and fairly with disputes affecting defense production. Seizures were considered necessary, upon disobedience of War Labor Board orders, to assure that the mobilization effort remained a "going concern," and to enforce the economic stabilization program. ***

This is but a cursory summary of executive leadership. But it amply demonstrates that Presidents have taken prompt action to enforce the laws and protect the country whether or not Congress happened to provide in advance for the particular method of execution. At the minimum, the executive actions reviewed herein sustain the action of the President in this case. And many of the cited examples of Presidential practice go far beyond the extent of power necessary to sustain the President's order to seize the steel mills. The fact that temporary executive seizures of industrial plants to meet an emergency have not been directly tested in this Court furnishes not the slightest suggestion that such actions have been illegal. Rather, the fact that Congress and the courts have consistently recognized and given their support to such executive action indicates that such a power of seizure has been accepted throughout our history.

History bears out the genius of the Founding Fathers, who created a Government subject to law but not left subject to inertia when vigor and initiative are required. *** Much of the argument in this case has been directed at straw men. We do not now have before us the case of a President acting solely on the basis of his own notions of the public welfare. Nor is there any question of unlimited executive power in this case. The President himself closed the door to any such claim when he sent his Message to Congress stating his purpose to abide by any action of Congress, whether approving or disapproving his seizure action. Here, the President immediately made sure that Congress was fully informed of the temporary action he had taken only to preserve the legislative programs from destruction until Congress could act.

The absence of a specific statute authorizing seizure of the steel mills as a mode of executing the laws—both the military procurement program and the anti-inflation program—has not until today been thought to prevent the President from executing the laws. Unlike an administrative commission confined to the enforcement of the statute under which it was created, or the head to a department when administering a particular statute, the President is a constitutional officer charged with taking care that a "mass of legislation" be executed. Flexibility as to mode of execution to meet critical situations is a matter of practical necessity.

*** The broad executive power granted by Article II to an officer on duty 365 days a year cannot, it is said, be invoked to avert disaster. Instead, the President must confine himself to sending a message to Congress recommending action. Under this messenger-boy concept of the Office, the President cannot even act to preserve legislative programs from destruction so that Congress will have something left to act upon. There is no judicial finding that the executive action was unwarranted because there was in fact no basis for the President's finding of the existence of an emergency for, under this view, the gravity of the emergency and the immediacy of the threatened disaster are considered irrelevant as a matter of law. *** Faced with the duty of executing the defense programs which Congress had enacted and the disastrous effects that any stoppage in steel production would have on those programs, the President acted to preserve those programs by seizing the steel mills. There is no question that the possession was other than temporary in character and subject to congressional direction—either approving, disapproving or regulating the manner in which the mills were to be administered and returned to the owners. The President immediately informed Congress of his action and clearly stated his intention to abide by the legislative will. No basis for claims of arbitrary action, unlimited powers or dictatorial usurpation of congressional power appears from the facts of this case. On the contrary, judicial, legislative and executive precedents throughout our history demonstrate that in this case the President acted in full conformity with his duties under the Constitution. ***

Notes

1. **Constitutional Theory.** There is no majority rationale in *Youngstown*. Each of the opinions adopts a very different methodology for assessing the constitutionality of the seizure of the mills.

   (a) Under JUSTICE BLACK's formalist approach, does the President's power depend at all on whether Congress has or has not acted? Does JUSTICE DOUGLAS solve this problem?

   (b) Under JUSTICE JACKSON's functionalist approach, how does the Court decide which zone fits any particular action of the President?

   (c) What do you think of the uses of history by JUSTICE FRANKFURTER and the dissenters?

   (d) Do you agree with the Court that, whatever the substantive outcome of the case, this is a proper decision for the Supreme Court to be making? Why or why not?

2. **Fluctuating Powers Approach.** JUSTICE JACKSON's concurrence breaks the actions of the President into three categories: (1) Where the President acts in accord with the express or implied authorization of Congress, (2) Where the President acts in the absence of any Congressional declaration on the matter, and (3) Where the President acts in direct contradiction to the express or implied will of Congress. The President's powers fluctuate with each category, being the greatest in the first category and the least in the third category. Although Jackson wrote only for himself in his concurrence, his approach appears to be the one accepted by today's Court, *see Dames & Moore v. Regan*, infra, p. 143.

JUSTICE REHNQUIST, author of the Court's opinion in *Dames & Moore*, was JUSTICE JACKSON's clerk at the time *Youngstown* was decided.

B. EXECUTIVE POWER, PRIVILEGE, AND IMMUNITY

1. EXECUTIVE POWER

The *Youngstown* framework is theoretically applicable to the entire range of authority problems that might arise between the Executive and Legislative branches of the federal government. In fact, as the following cases demonstrate, other factors besides this framework may play important roles in the outcomes of specific separation of powers cases. One important consideration seems to be whether the context is that of domestic or foreign affairs.

a. *Domestic Affairs*

CLINTON v. CITY OF NEW YORK
524 U.S. 417, 118 S.Ct. 2091, 141 L.Ed.2d 393 (1998).

JUSTICE STEVENS delivered the opinion of the Court.

The Line Item Veto Act (Act) was enacted in April 1996 and became effective on January 1, 1997. The following day, six Members of Congress who had voted against the Act brought suit in the District Court for the District of Columbia challenging its constitutionality. *** [T]he District Court entered an order holding that the Act is unconstitutional. *** We determined, however, that the Members of Congress did not have standing to sue because they had not "alleged a sufficiently concrete injury to have established Article III standing," *Raines v. Byrd*, 117 S.Ct. 2312, 2322 (1997); thus, *** we remanded the case to the District Court with instructions to dismiss the complaint for lack of jurisdiction.

Less than two months after our decision in that case, the President exercised his authority to cancel one provision in the Balanced Budget Act of 1997, and two provisions in the Taxpayer Relief Act of 1997. Appellees, claiming that they had been injured by two of those cancellations, filed these cases in the District Court. That Court again held the statute invalid ***. We now hold that these appellees have standing to challenge the constitutionality of the Act and, reaching the merits, we agree that the cancellation procedures set forth in the Act violate the Presentment Clause, Art. I, § 7, cl. 2, of the Constitution.

I

We begin by reviewing the canceled items that are at issue in these cases.

Section 4722(c) of the Balanced Budget Act. Title XIX of the Social Security Act authorizes the Federal Government to transfer huge sums of money to the States to help finance medical care for the indigent. In 1991, Congress directed that those federal subsidies be reduced by the amount of certain taxes levied by the States on health care providers. In 1994, the Department of Health and Human Services (HHS) notified the State of New

York that 15 of its taxes were covered by the 1991 Act, and that as of June 30, 1994, the statute therefore required New York to return $955 million to the United States. The notice advised the State that it could apply for a waiver on certain statutory grounds. New York did request a waiver for those tax programs, as well as for a number of others, but HHS has not formally acted on any of those waiver requests. New York has estimated that the amount at issue for the period from October 1992 through March 1997 is as high as $2.6 billion.

Because HHS had not taken any action on the waiver requests, New York turned to Congress for relief. On August 5, 1997, Congress enacted a law that resolved the issue in New York's favor. Section 4722(c) of the Balanced Budget Act of 1997 identifies the disputed taxes and provides that they "are deemed to be permissible health care related taxes and in compliance with the requirements" of the relevant provisions of the 1991 statute.

On August 11, 1997, the President sent identical notices to the Senate and to the House of Representatives canceling "one item of new direct spending," specifying § 4722(c) as that item, and stating that he had determined that "this cancellation will reduce the Federal budget deficit." He explained that § 4722(c) would have permitted New York "to continue relying upon impermissible provider taxes to finance its Medicaid program" and that "[t]his preferential treatment would have increased Medicaid costs, would have treated New York differently from all other States, and would have established a costly precedent for other States to request comparable treatment."

Section 968 of the Taxpayer Relief Act. A person who realizes a profit from the sale of securities is generally subject to a capital gains tax. Under existing law, however, an ordinary business corporation can acquire a corporation, including a food processing or refining company, in a merger or stock-for-stock transaction in which no gain is recognized to the seller; the seller's tax payment, therefore, is deferred. If, however, the purchaser is a farmers' cooperative, the parties cannot structure such a transaction because the stock of the cooperative may be held only by its members; thus, a seller dealing with a farmers' cooperative cannot obtain the benefits of tax deferral.

In § 968 of the Taxpayer Relief Act of 1997, Congress amended § 1042 of the Internal Revenue Code to permit owners of certain food refiners and processors to defer the recognition of gain if they sell their stock to eligible farmers' cooperatives. The purpose of the amendment, as repeatedly explained by its sponsors, was "to facilitate the transfer of refiners and processors to farmers' cooperatives." The amendment to § 1042 was one of the 79 "limited tax benefits" authorized by the Taxpayer Relief Act of 1997 and specifically identified in Title XVII of that Act as "subject to [the] line item veto."

On the same date that he canceled the "item of new direct spending" involving New York's health care programs, the President also canceled this limited tax benefit. In his explanation of that action, the President endorsed the objective of encouraging "value-added farming through the purchase by farmers' cooperatives of refiners or processors of agricultural goods," but concluded that the provision lacked safeguards and also "failed to target its benefits to small-and-medium-size cooperatives."

II

Appellees filed two separate actions against the President[9] and other federal officials challenging these two cancellations. The plaintiffs in the first case are the City of New York, two hospital associations, one hospital, and two unions representing health care employees. The plaintiffs in the second are a farmers' cooperative consisting of about 30 potato growers in Idaho and an individual farmer who is a member and officer of the cooperative. The District Court consolidated the two cases and determined that at least one of the plaintiffs in each had standing under Article III of the Constitution. *** On the merits, the District Court held that the cancellations did not conform to the constitutionally mandated procedures for the enactment or repeal of laws in two respects. First, the laws that resulted after the cancellations "were different from those consented to by both Houses of Congress.[11] Moreover, the President violated Article I 'when he unilaterally canceled provisions of duly enacted statutes.'" As a separate basis for its decision, the District Court also held that the Act "impermissibly disrupts the balance of powers among the three branches of government."

III

[The Court determined that the Appellees had standing to sue the President for use of the Line Item Veto and that the Court had authority to review the cases in an expedited manner.]

IV

The Line Item Veto Act gives the President the power to "cancel in whole" three types of provisions that have been signed into law: "(1) any dollar amount of discretionary budget authority; (2) any item of new direct spending; or (3) any limited tax benefit." 2 U.S.C. § 691(a). It is undisputed that the New York case involves an "item of new direct spending" and that the Snake River case involves a "limited tax benefit" as those terms are defined in the Act. It is also undisputed that each of those provisions had been signed into law pursuant to Article I, § 7 of the Constitution before it was canceled.

---

[9] In both actions, the plaintiffs sought a declaratory judgment that the Line Item Veto Act is unconstitutional and that the particular cancellation was invalid; neither set of plaintiffs sought injunctive relief against the President.

[11] As the District Court explained: "These laws reflected the best judgment of both Houses. The laws that resulted after the President's line item veto were different from those consented to by both Houses of Congress. There is no way of knowing whether these laws, in their truncated form, would have received the requisite support from both the House and the Senate. Because the laws that emerged after the Line Item Veto are not the same laws that proceeded through the legislative process, as required, the resulting laws are not valid."

The Act requires the President to adhere to precise procedures whenever he exercises his cancellation authority. In identifying items for cancellation he must consider the legislative history, the purposes, and other relevant information about the item. He must determine, with respect to each cancellation, that it will "(i) reduce the Federal budget deficit; (ii) not impair any essential Government functions; and (iii) not harm the national interest." Moreover, he must transmit a special message to Congress notifying it of each cancellation within five calendar days (excluding Sundays) after the enactment of the canceled provision. It is undisputed that the President meticulously followed these procedures in these cases.

A cancellation takes effect upon receipt by Congress of the special message from the President. If, however, a "disapproval bill" pertaining to a special message is enacted into law, the cancellations set forth in that message become "null and void." The Act sets forth a detailed expedited procedure for the consideration of a "disapproval bill," but no such bill was passed for either of the cancellations involved in these cases. ***

The effect of a cancellation is plainly stated in § 691e, which defines the principal terms used in the Act. With respect to both an item of new direct spending and a limited tax benefit, the cancellation prevents the item "from having legal force or effect." Thus, under the plain text of the statute, the two actions of the President that are challenged in these cases prevented one section of the Balanced Budget Act of 1997 and one section of the Taxpayer Relief Act of 1997 "from having legal force or effect." The remaining provisions of those statutes, with the exception of the second canceled item in the latter, continue to have the same force and effect as they had when signed into law.

In both legal and practical effect, the President has amended two Acts of Congress by repealing a portion of each. [R]epeal of statutes, no less than enactment, must conform with Art. I. *INS v. Chadha*, 462 U.S. 919, 954 (1983). There is no provision in the Constitution that authorizes the President to enact, to amend, or to repeal statutes. Both Article I and Article II assign responsibilities to the President that directly relate to the lawmaking process, but neither addresses the issue presented by these cases. The President *** may initiate and influence legislative proposals. Moreover, after a bill has passed both Houses of Congress, but "before it become[s] a Law," it must be presented to the President. If he approves it, "he shall sign it, but if not he shall return it, with his Objections to that House in which it shall have originated, who shall enter the Objections at large on their Journal, and proceed to reconsider it." Art. I, § 7, cl. 2. His "return" of a bill, which is usually described as a "veto," is subject to being overridden by a two-thirds vote in each House.

There are important differences between the President's "return" of a bill pursuant to Article I, § 7, and the exercise of the President's cancellation authority pursuant to the Line Item Veto Act. The constitutional return takes place before the bill becomes law; the statutory cancellation occurs after the bill becomes law. The constitutional return is of the entire bill; the statutory cancellation is of only a part. Although the Constitution expressly authorizes the President to play a role in the process of enacting statutes, it is silent on the subject of unilateral Presidential action that either repeals or amends parts of duly enacted statutes.

There are powerful reasons for construing constitutional silence on this profoundly important issue as equivalent to an express prohibition. The procedures governing the enactment of statutes set forth in the text of Article I were the product of the great debates and compromises that produced the Constitution itself. Familiar historical materials provide abundant support for the conclusion that the power to enact statutes may only "be exercised in accord with a single, finely wrought and exhaustively considered, procedure." *Chadha*, 462 U.S., at 951. Our first President understood the text of the Presentment Clause as requiring that he either "approve all the parts of a Bill, or reject it in toto." What has emerged in these cases from the President's exercise of his statutory cancellation powers, however, are truncated versions of two bills that passed both Houses of Congress. They are not the product of the "finely wrought" procedure that the Framers designed.

At oral argument, the Government suggested that the cancellations at issue in these cases do not effect a "repeal" of the canceled items because under the special "lockbox" provisions of the Act,[31] a canceled item "retain[s] real, legal budgetary effect" insofar as it prevents Congress and the President from spending the savings that result from the cancellation. The text of the Act expressly provides, however, that a cancellation prevents a direct spending or tax benefit provision "from having legal force or effect." That a canceled item may have "real, legal budgetary effect" as a result of the lockbox procedure does not change the fact that by canceling the items at issue in these cases, the President made them entirely inoperative as to appellees. Section 968 of the Taxpayer Relief Act no longer provides a tax benefit, and § 4722(c) of the Balanced Budget Act of 1997 no longer relieves New York of its contingent liability. Such significant changes do not lose their character simply because the canceled provisions may have some continuing financial effect on the Government. The cancellation of one section of a statute may be the functional equivalent of a partial repeal even if a portion of the section is not canceled.

V

The Government advances two related arguments to support its position that despite the unambiguous provisions of the Act, cancellations do not amend or repeal properly enacted statutes in violation of the Presentment Clause. First, relying primarily on *Field v. Clark*, 143 U.S. 649, the Government contends that the cancellations were merely exercises of discretionary authority granted to the President by the Balanced Budget Act and the Taxpayer Relief Act read in light of the previously enacted Line Item Veto Act. Second, the Government submits that the substance of the authority to cancel tax and spending items "is, in practical effect, no more

---

[31] The lockbox procedure ensures that savings resulting from cancellations are used to reduce the deficit, rather than to offset deficit increases arising from other laws. ***

and no less than the power to 'decline to spend' specified sums of money, or to 'decline to implement' specified tax measures." Neither argument is persuasive.

In *Field v. Clark*, the Court upheld the constitutionality of the Tariff Act of 1890. That statute contained a "free list" of almost 300 specific articles that were exempted from import duties "unless otherwise specially provided for in this act." Section 3 was a special provision that directed the President to suspend that exemption for sugar, molasses, coffee, tea, and hides "whenever, and so often" as he should be satisfied that any country producing and exporting those products imposed duties on the agricultural products of the United States that he deemed to be "reciprocally unequal and unreasonable ***." The section then specified the duties to be imposed on those products during any such suspension. The Court provided this explanation for its conclusion that § 3 had not delegated legislative power to the President:

> Nothing involving the expediency or the just operation of such legislation was left to the determination of the President. *** [W]hen he ascertained the fact that duties and exactions, reciprocally unequal and unreasonable, were imposed upon the agricultural or other products of the United States by a country producing and exporting sugar, molasses, coffee, tea or hides, it became his duty to issue a proclamation declaring the suspension, as to that country, which Congress had determined should occur. He had no discretion in the premises except in respect to the duration of the suspension so ordered. But that related only to the enforcement of the policy established by Congress. As the suspension was absolutely required when the President ascertained the existence of a particular fact, it cannot be said that in ascertaining that fact and in issuing his proclamation, in obedience to the legislative will, he exercised the function of making laws. *** It was a part of the law itself as it left the hands of Congress that the provisions, full and complete in themselves, permitting the free introduction of sugars, molasses, coffee, tea and hides, from particular countries, should be suspended, in a given contingency, and that in case of such suspensions certain duties should be imposed.

This passage identifies three critical differences between the power to suspend the exemption from import duties and the power to cancel portions of a duly enacted statute. First, the exercise of the suspension power was contingent upon a condition that did not exist when the Tariff Act was passed: the imposition of "reciprocally unequal and unreasonable" import duties by other countries. In contrast, the exercise of the cancellation power within five days after the enactment of the Balanced Budget and Tax Reform Acts necessarily was based on the same conditions that Congress evaluated when it passed those statutes. Second, under the Tariff Act, when the President determined that the contingency had arisen, he had a duty to suspend; in contrast, while it is true that the President was required by the Act to make three determinations before he canceled a provision, those determinations did not qualify his discretion to cancel or not to cancel. Finally, whenever the President suspended an exemption under the Tariff Act, he was executing the policy that Congress had embodied in the statute. In contrast, whenever the President cancels an item of new direct spending or a limited tax benefit he is rejecting the policy judgment made by Congress and relying on his own policy judgment. Thus, the conclusion in *Field v. Clark* that the suspensions mandated by the Tariff Act were not exercises of legislative power does not undermine our opinion that cancellations pursuant to the Line Item Veto Act are the functional equivalent of partial repeals of Acts of Congress that fail to satisfy Article I, § 7.

The Government's reliance upon other tariff and import statutes, discussed in *Field*, that contain provisions similar to the one challenged in *Field* is unavailing for the same reasons. ***

The statutes [cited by the government] all relate to foreign trade, and this Court has recognized that in the foreign affairs arena, the President has "a degree of discretion and freedom from statutory restriction which would not be admissible were domestic affairs alone involved." *United States v. Curtiss–Wright Export Corp.*, 299 U.S. 304, 320 (1936). *** More important, when enacting the statutes discussed in *Field*, Congress itself made the decision to suspend or repeal the particular provisions at issue upon the occurrence of particular events subsequent to enactment, and it left only the determination of whether such events occurred up to the President. The Line Item Veto Act authorizes the President himself to effect the repeal of laws, for his own policy reasons, without observing the procedures set out in Article I, § 7. The fact that Congress intended such a result is of no moment. *** Congress cannot alter the procedures set out in Article I, § 7, without amending the Constitution.

Neither are we persuaded by the Government's contention that the President's authority to cancel new direct spending and tax benefit items is no greater than his traditional authority to decline to spend appropriated funds. The Government has reviewed in some detail the series of statutes in which Congress has given the Executive broad discretion over the expenditure of appropriated funds. For example, the First Congress appropriated "sum[s] not exceeding" specified amounts to be spent on various Government operations. In those statutes, as in later years, the President was given wide discretion with respect to both the amounts to be spent and how the money would be allocated among different functions. It is argued that the Line Item Veto Act merely confers comparable discretionary authority over the expenditure of appropriated funds. The critical difference between this statute and all of its predecessors, however, is that unlike any of them, this Act gives the President the unilateral power to change the text of duly enacted statutes. None of the Act's predecessors could even arguably have been construed to authorize such a change.

VI

Although they are implicit in what we have already written, the profound importance of these cases makes it appropriate to emphasize three points.

First, we express no opinion about the wisdom of the procedures authorized by the Line Item Veto Act. Many members of both major political parties who have served in the Legislative and the Executive Branches have long advocated the enactment of such procedures for the purpose of "ensur[ing] greater fiscal accountability in Washington." ***

Second, although appellees challenge the validity of the Act on alternative grounds, the only issue we address concerns the "finely wrought" procedure commanded by the Constitution. *Chadha*. *** [W]e find it unnecessary to consider the District Court's alternative holding that the Act "impermissibly disrupts the balance of powers among the three branches of government."

Third, our decision rests on the narrow ground that the procedures authorized by the Line Item Veto Act are not authorized by the Constitution. The Balanced Budget Act of 1997 is a 500–page document that became "Public Law 105–33" after three procedural steps were taken: (1) a bill containing its exact text was approved by a majority of the Members of the House of Representatives; (2) the Senate approved precisely the same text; and (3) that text was signed into law by the President. The Constitution explicitly requires that each of those three steps be taken before a bill may "become a law." Art. I, § 7. If one paragraph of that text had been omitted at any one of those three stages, Public Law 105–33 would not have been validly enacted. If the Line Item Veto Act were valid, it would authorize the President to create a different law—one whose text was not voted on by either House of Congress or presented to the President for signature. Something that might be known as "Public Law 105–33 as modified by the President" may or may not be desirable, but it is surely not a document that may "become a law" pursuant to the procedures designed by the Framers of Article I, § 7, of the Constitution. ***

JUSTICE KENNEDY, concurring.

*** I write to respond to my colleague JUSTICE BREYER, who observes that the statute does not threaten the liberties of individual citizens, a point on which I disagree. The argument is related to his earlier suggestion that our role is lessened here because the two political branches are adjusting their own powers between themselves. To say the political branches have a somewhat free hand to reallocate their own authority would seem to require acceptance of two premises: first, that the public good demands it, and second, that liberty is not at risk. The former premise is inadmissible. The Constitution's structure requires a stability which transcends the convenience of the moment. The latter premise, too, is flawed. Liberty is always at stake when one or more of the branches seek to transgress the separation of powers. ***

In recent years, perhaps, we have come to think of liberty as defined by that word in the Fifth and Fourteenth Amendments and as illuminated by the other provisions of the Bill of Rights. The conception of liberty embraced by the Framers was not so confined. They used the principles of separation of powers and federalism to secure liberty in the fundamental political sense of the term, quite in addition to the idea of freedom from intrusive governmental acts. The idea and the promise were that when the people delegate some degree of control to a remote central authority, one branch of government ought not possess the power to shape their destiny without a sufficient check from the other two.

It follows that if a citizen who is taxed has the measure of the tax or the decision to spend determined by the Executive alone, without adequate control by the citizen's Representatives in Congress, liberty is threatened. Money is the instrument of policy and policy affects the lives of citizens. The individual loses liberty in a real sense if that instrument is not subject to traditional constitutional constraints.

The principal object of the statute, it is true, was not to enhance the President's power to reward one group and punish another, to help one set of taxpayers and hurt another, to favor one State and ignore another. Yet these are its undeniable effects. The law establishes a new mechanism which gives the President the sole ability to hurt a group that is a visible target, in order to disfavor the group or to extract further concessions from Congress. The law is the functional equivalent of a line item veto and enhances the President's powers beyond what the Framers would have endorsed.

It is no answer, of course, to say that Congress surrendered its authority by its own hand; nor does it suffice to point out that a new statute, signed by the President or enacted over his veto, could restore to Congress the power it now seeks to relinquish. That a congressional cession of power is voluntary does not make it innocuous. The Constitution is a compact enduring for more than our time, and one Congress cannot yield up its own powers, much less those of other Congresses to follow. Abdication of responsibility is not part of the constitutional design.

Separation of powers helps to ensure the ability of each branch to be vigorous in asserting its proper authority. In this respect the device operates on a horizontal axis to secure a proper balance of legislative, executive, and judicial authority. Separation of powers operates on a vertical axis as well, between each branch and the citizens in whose interest powers must be exercised. The citizen has a vital interest in the regularity of the exercise of governmental power. If this point was not clear before *Chadha*, it should have been so afterwards. Though *Chadha* involved the deportation of a person, while the case before us involves the expenditure of money or the grant of a tax exemption, this circumstance does not mean that the vertical operation of the separation of powers is irrelevant here. By increasing the power of the President beyond what the Framers envisioned, the statute compromises the political liberty of our citizens, liberty which the separation of powers seeks to secure.

The Constitution is not bereft of controls over improvident spending. Federalism is one safeguard, for political accountability is easier to enforce within the States than nationwide. The other principal mechanism, of course, is control of the political branches by an informed and responsible electorate.

JUSTICE SCALIA, with whom JUSTICE O'CONNOR joins, and with whom JUSTICE BREYER joins as to Part III, concurring in part and dissenting in part.

Today the Court acknowledges the "'overriding and time-honored concern about keeping the Judiciary's power within its proper constitutional sphere.'" *** In my view, the Snake River appellees lack standing to challenge the President's cancellation of the "limited tax benefit," and the constitutionality of that action should not be addressed. I think the New York appellees have standing to challenge the President's cancellation of an "item of new direct spending"; but unlike the Court I find the President's cancellation of spending items to be entirely in accord with the Constitution. ***

III

*** The Presentment Clause requires, in relevant part, that "[e]very Bill which shall have passed the House of Representatives and the Senate, shall, before it becomes a Law, be presented to the President of the United States; If he approve he shall sign it, but if not he shall return it," U.S. Const., Art. I, § 7, cl. 2. There is no question that enactment of the Balanced Budget Act complied with these requirements: the House and Senate passed the bill, and the President signed it into law. It was only after the requirements of the Presentment Clause had been satisfied that the President exercised his authority under the Line Item Veto Act to cancel the spending item. Thus, the Court's problem with the Act is not that it authorizes the President to veto parts of a bill and sign others into law, but rather that it authorizes him to "cancel"—prevent from "having legal force or effect"—certain parts of duly enacted statutes.

Article I, § 7 of the Constitution obviously prevents the President from cancelling a law that Congress has not authorized him to cancel. Such action cannot possibly be considered part of his execution of the law, and if it is legislative action, as the Court observes, "'repeal of statutes, no less than enactment, must conform with Art. I.'" But that is not this case. It was certainly arguable, as an original matter, that Art. I, § 7 also prevents the President from cancelling a law which itself authorizes the President to cancel it. But as the Court acknowledges, that argument has long since been made and rejected. In 1809, Congress passed a law authorizing the President to cancel trade restrictions against Great Britain and France if either revoked edicts directed at the United States. *** The Tariff Act of 1890 authorized the President to "suspend, by proclamation to that effect" certain of its provisions if he determined that other countries were imposing "reciprocally unequal and unreasonable" duties. This Court upheld the constitutionality of that Act in *Field v. Clark*, 143 U.S. 649 (1892), reciting the history since 1798 of statutes conferring upon the President the power to, inter alia, "discontinue the prohibitions and restraints hereby enacted and declared," "suspend the operation of the aforesaid act," and "declare the provisions of this act to be inoperative."

As much as the Court goes on about Art. I, § 7, therefore, that provision does not demand the result the Court reaches. It no more categorically prohibits the Executive reduction of congressional dispositions in the course of implementing statutes that authorize such reduction, than it categorically prohibits the Executive augmentation of congressional dispositions in the course of implementing statutes that authorize such augmentation—generally known as substantive rulemaking. There are, to be sure, limits upon the former just as there are limits upon the latter—and I am prepared to acknowledge that the limits upon the former may be much more severe. Those limits are established, however, not by some categorical prohibition of Art. I, § 7, which our cases conclusively disprove, but by what has come to be known as the doctrine of unconstitutional delegation of legislative authority: When authorized Executive reduction or augmentation is allowed to go too far, it usurps the nondelegable function of Congress and violates the separation of powers.

It is this doctrine, and not the Presentment Clause, that was discussed in the *Field* opinion, and it is this doctrine, and not the Presentment Clause, that is the issue presented by the statute before us here. That is why the Court is correct to distinguish prior authorizations of Executive cancellation, such as the one involved in *Field*, on the ground that they were contingent upon an Executive finding of fact, and on the ground that they related to the field of foreign affairs, an area where the President has a special "degree of discretion and freedom." These distinctions have nothing to do with whether the details of Art. I, § 7 have been complied with, but everything to do with whether the authorizations went too far by transferring to the Executive a degree of political, lawmaking power that our traditions demand be retained by the Legislative Branch.

I turn, then, to the crux of the matter: whether Congress's authorizing the President to cancel an item of spending gives him a power that our history and traditions show must reside exclusively in the Legislative Branch. ***

Insofar as the degree of political, "lawmaking" power conferred upon the Executive is concerned, there is not a dime's worth of difference between Congress's authorizing the President to cancel a spending item, and Congress's authorizing money to be spent on a particular item at the President's discretion. And the latter has been done since the Founding of the Nation. From 1789–1791, the First Congress made lump-sum appropriations for the entire Government—"sum[s] not exceeding" specified amounts for broad purposes. From a very early date Congress also made permissive individual appropriations, leaving the decision whether to spend the money to the President's unfettered discretion. *** The constitutionality of such appropriations has never seriously been questioned. Rather, "[t]hat Congress has wide discretion in the matter of prescribing details of expenditures for which it appropriates must, of course, be plain. Appropriations and other acts of Congress are replete with instances of general appropriations of large amounts, to be allotted and expended as directed by designated government agencies."

Certain Presidents have claimed Executive authority to withhold appropriated funds even absent an express conferral of discretion to do so. In

1876, for example, President Grant reported to Congress that he would not spend money appropriated for certain harbor and river improvements, because "[u]nder no circumstances [would he] allow expenditures upon works not clearly national," and in his view, the appropriations were for "works of purely private or local interest, in no sense national." President Franklin D. Roosevelt impounded funds appropriated for a flood control reservoir and levee in Oklahoma. President Truman ordered the impoundment of hundreds of millions of dollars that had been appropriated for military aircraft. President Nixon, the Mahatma Ghandi of all impounders, asserted at a press conference in 1973 that his "constitutional right" to impound appropriated funds was "absolutely clear." Our decision two years later in *Train v. City of New York*, 420 U.S. 35 (1975), proved him wrong, but it implicitly confirmed that Congress may confer discretion upon the executive to withhold appropriated funds, even funds appropriated for a specific purpose. The statute at issue in *Train* authorized spending "not to exceed" specified sums for certain projects, and directed that such "[s]ums authorized to be appropriated *** shall be allotted" by the Administrator of the Environmental Protection Agency. Upon enactment of this statute, the President directed the Administrator to allot no more than a certain part of the amount authorized. This Court held, as a matter of statutory interpretation, that the statute did not grant the Executive discretion to withhold the funds, but required allotment of the full amount authorized.

The short of the matter is this: Had the Line Item Veto Act authorized the President to "decline to spend" any item of spending contained in the Balanced Budget Act of 1997, there is not the slightest doubt that authorization would have been constitutional. What the Line Item Veto Act does instead—authorizing the President to "cancel" an item of spending—is technically different. But the technical difference does not relate to the technicalities of the Presentment Clause, which have been fully complied with; and the doctrine of unconstitutional delegation, which is at issue here, is preeminently not a doctrine of technicalities. The title of the Line Item Veto Act, which was perhaps designed to simplify for public comprehension, or perhaps merely to comply with the terms of a campaign pledge, has succeeded in faking out the Supreme Court. The President's action it authorizes in fact is not a line-item veto and thus does not offend Art. I, § 7; and insofar as the substance of that action is concerned, it is no different from what Congress has permitted the President to do since the formation of the Union. ***

Notes

1. **Congress' Options.** Is there any way Congress can respond effectively to this decision? (a) Consider the option of a constitutional amendment. Other than the difficulty of passage, how might you word such an amendment if you favored giving the President line-item veto authority? (b) Is there any way to accomplish the same goal through legislation? Consider the feasibility and desirability of Congress defining "to cancel" as meaning "to decline to spend or enforce." (c) Could Congress overcome the Court's decision through legislation establishing more explicit standards the President could use in declining to spend or in

canceling a tax benefit? (d) Why not simply separately enroll each provision of an omnibus spending or tax bill?

2. **Significance of the Line Item Veto Power.** Given how minor the provisions were that President Clinton "vetoed," are you skeptical that anything significant would ever be accomplished through a "line item veto"? Some political analysts think the real significance of the President's power might be that he would never have to use it, except in symbolic situations.

3. **Problem.** On March 8, 1995, President Clinton issued Executive Order No. 12,954, which declared that it was the policy of the United States in procuring goods and services to cease contracting with companies that permanently replaced lawfully striking workers. In *Chamber of Commerce v. Reich*, 74 F.3d 1322 (D.C. Cir. 1996) the Circuit Court of Appeals held that this order was preempted by the National Labor Relations Act, which, nearly fifty years earlier, had been interpreted by the Supreme Court as allowing companies permanently to replace lawful strikers. Most government contractor companies are also subject to the National Labor Relations Act. The preemption rationale of the Court of Appeals was developed by analogy from the doctrine of the preemptive supremacy of federal law over state law. See infra at pp. 388-407. You are an advisor to President Clinton. Do you advise him to appeal this loss to the Supreme Court?

4. **Presidential Orders.** Was President Lincoln's Emancipation Proclamation legislative? Aren't all Executive Orders legislative?

b. Foreign Affairs

Is the separation of powers balance between the President and Congress different when "foreign affairs" are involved? The next two cases, one decided before and one after *Youngstown*, help to answer this question.

UNITED STATES v. CURTISS–WRIGHT
299 U.S. 304, 57 S.Ct. 216, 81 L.Ed. 255 (1936).

MR. JUSTICE SUTHERLAND delivered the opinion of the Court.

On January 27, 1936, an indictment was returned in the court below, the first count of which charges that appellees, beginning with the 29th day of May, 1934, conspired to sell in the United States certain arms of war, namely, fifteen machine guns, to Bolivia, a country then engaged in armed conflict in the Chaco, in violation of the Joint Resolution of Congress approved May 28, 1934, and the provisions of a proclamation issued on the same day by the President of the United States pursuant to authority conferred by section 1 of the resolution. *** The Joint Resolution [states]:

Resolved by the Senate and House of Representatives of the United States of America in Congress assembled, That if the President finds that the prohibition of the sale of arms and munitions of war in the United States to those countries now engaged in armed conflict in the Chaco may contribute to the reestablishment of peace between those countries, and *** he makes proclamation to that effect, it shall be unlawful to sell *** any arms or munitions of war in any place in the United States to the countries now engaged in that armed conflict, or to any person, company, or association acting in the interest of either country, until otherwise ordered by the President or by Congress.

*** Whether, if the Joint Resolution had related solely to internal affairs, it would be open to the challenge that it constituted an unlawful delegation of legislative power to the Executive, we find it unnecessary to determine. The whole aim of the resolution is to affect a situation entirely external to the United States, and falling within the category of foreign affairs. The determination which we are called to make, therefore, is whether the Joint Resolution, as applied to that situation, is vulnerable to attack under the rule that forbids a delegation of the lawmaking power. In other words, assuming (but not deciding) that the challenged delegation, if it were confined to internal affairs, would be invalid, may it nevertheless be sustained on the ground that its exclusive aim is to afford a remedy for a hurtful condition within foreign territory?

It will contribute to the elucidation of the question if we first consider the differences between the powers of the federal government in respect of foreign or external affairs and those in respect of domestic or internal affairs. That there are differences between them, and that these differences are fundamental, may not be doubted.

The two classes of powers are different, both in respect of their origin and their nature. The broad statement that the federal government can exercise no powers except those specifically enumerated in the Constitution, and such implied powers as are necessary and proper to carry into effect the enumerated powers, is categorically true only in respect of our internal affairs. In that field, the primary purpose of the Constitution was to carve from the general mass of legislative powers then possessed by the states such portions as it was thought desirable to vest in the federal government, leaving those not included in the enumeration still in the states. That this doctrine applies only to powers which the states had is self-evident. And since the states severally never possessed international powers, such powers could not have been carved from the mass of state powers but obviously were transmitted to the United States from some other source. ***

As a result of the separation from Great Britain by the colonies, acting as a unit, the powers of external sovereignty passed from the Crown not to the colonies severally, but to the colonies in their collective and corporate capacity as the United States of America. *** Rulers come and go; governments end and forms of government change; but sovereignty survives. A political society cannot endure without a supreme will somewhere. Sovereignty is never held in suspense. When, therefore, the external sovereignty of Great Britain in respect of the colonies ceased, it immediately passed to the Union.

*** It results that the investment of the federal government with the powers of external sovereignty did not depend upon the affirmative grants of the Constitution. The powers to declare and wage war, to conclude peace, to make treaties, to maintain diplomatic relations with other sovereignties, if they had never been mentioned in the Constitution, would have vested in the federal government as necessary concomitants of nationality. *** Not only, as we have shown, is the federal power over external affairs in origin and essential character different from that over internal affairs, but participation in the exercise of the power is significantly limited. In this vast external realm, with its important, complicated, delicate and manifold problems, the President alone has the power to speak or listen as a representative of the nation. He makes treaties with the advice and consent of the Senate; but he alone negotiates. Into the field of negotiation the Senate cannot intrude; and Congress itself is powerless to invade it. As Marshall said in his great argument of March 7, 1800, in the House of Representatives, 'The President is the sole organ of the nation in its external relations, and its sole representative with foreign nations.'

*** It is important to bear in mind that we are here dealing not alone with an authority vested in the President by an exertion of legislative power, but with such an authority plus the very delicate, plenary and exclusive power of the President as the sole organ of the federal government in the field of international relations—a power which does not require as a basis for its exercise an act of Congress, but which, of course, like every other governmental power, must be exercised in subordination to the applicable provisions of the Constitution. It is quite apparent that if, in the maintenance of our international relations, embarrassment—perhaps serious embarrassment—is to be avoided and success for our aims achieved, congressional legislation which is to be made effective through negotiation and inquiry within the international field must often accord to the President a degree of discretion and freedom from statutory restriction which would not be admissible were domestic affairs alone involved. Moreover, he, not Congress, has the better opportunity of knowing the conditions which prevail in foreign countries, and especially is this true in time of war. He has his confidential sources of information. He has his agents in the form of diplomatic, consular and other officials. Secrecy in respect of information gathered by them may be highly necessary, and the premature disclosure of it productive of harmful results.

*** In the light of the foregoing observations, it is evident that this court should not be in haste to apply a general rule which will have the effect of condemning legislation like that under review as constituting an unlawful delegation of legislative power. The principles which justify such legislation find overwhelming support in the unbroken legislative practice which has prevailed almost from the inception of the national government to the present day. *** Practically every volume of the United States Statutes contains one or more acts or joint resolutions of Congress authorizing action by the President in respect of subjects affecting foreign relations, which either leave the exercise of the power to his unrestricted judgment, or provide a standard far more general than that which has always been considered requisite with regard to domestic affairs. ***

MR. JUSTICE MCREYNOLDS does not agree. He is of opinion that the court below reached the right conclusion and its judgment ought to be affirmed.

MR. JUSTICE STONE took no part in the consideration or decision of this case.

Notes

1. **Implied Presidential Powers.** Could this case have been decided without reference to the Constitution? Doesn't the Court's starting point seem diametrically opposite that of *Youngstown* and other cases involving constitutional allocation of domestic affairs powers? Were the broad pronouncements about Presidential power necessary to the decision? As an interesting aside, Justice Department lawyers, representing the President, have been known to refer to the case informally as "*Curtiss-Wright*, so I'm right."

2. **Preconstitutional Powers.** Why does the Court say the President is "the sole organ of the federal government in the field of international relations"? Is the text clear on this? Is historical practice clear? Are you comfortable with the Court's assessment of preconstitutional powers? Has such an analysis shown up anywhere else in the cases you have read to date?

3. **Functionalism.** What preconceptions about the type of foreign policies the United States should have are implicit in the Court's analysis?

DAMES & MOORE v. REGAN
453 U.S. 654, 101 S.Ct. 2972, 69 L.Ed.2d 918 (1981).

JUSTICE REHNQUIST delivered the opinion of the Court.

*** On November 4, 1979, the American Embassy in Tehran was seized and our diplomatic personnel were captured and held hostage. In response to that crisis, President Carter, acting pursuant to the International Emergency Economic Powers Act (hereinafter IEEPA), declared a national emergency on November 14, 1979, and blocked the removal or transfer of "all property and interests in property of the Government of Iran, its instrumentalities and controlled entities and the Central Bank of Iran which are or become subject to the jurisdiction of the United States. *** " On November 15, 1979, the Treasury Department's Office of Foreign Assets Control issued a regulation providing that "[u]nless licensed or authorized *** any attachment, judgment, decree, lien, execution, garnishment, or other judicial process is null and void with respect to any property in which on or since [November 14, 1979,] there existed an interest of Iran." The regulations also made clear that any licenses or authorizations granted could be "amended, modified, or revoked at any time." ***

On December 19, 1979, petitioner Dames & Moore filed suit in the United States District Court for the Central District of California against the Government of Iran, the Atomic Energy Organization of Iran, and a number of Iranian banks. In its complaint, petitioner alleged that its wholly owned subsidiary, Dames & Moore International, S. R. L., was a party to a written contract with the Atomic Energy Organization, and that the subsidiary's entire interest in the contract had been assigned to petitioner. Under the contract, the subsidiary was to conduct site studies for a proposed nuclear power plant in Iran. As provided in the terms of the contract, the Atomic

Energy Organization terminated the agreement for its own convenience on June 30, 1979. Petitioner contended, however, that it was owed $3,436,694.30 plus interest for services performed under the contract prior to the date of termination. The District Court issued orders of attachment directed against property of the defendants, and the property of certain Iranian banks was then attached to secure any judgment that might be entered against them.

On January 20, 1981, the Americans held hostage were released by Iran pursuant to an [Executive] Agreement entered into the day before ***. The Agreement stated that "[i]t is the purpose of [the United States and Iran] *** to terminate all litigation as between the Government of each party and the nationals of the other, and to bring about the settlement and termination of all such claims through binding arbitration." In furtherance of this goal, the Agreement called for the establishment of an Iran–United States Claims Tribunal which would arbitrate any claims not settled within six months. Awards of the Claims Tribunal are to be "final and binding" and "enforceable *** in the courts of any nation in accordance with its laws." Under the Agreement, the United States is obligated "to terminate all legal proceedings in United States courts involving claims of United States persons and institutions against Iran and its state enterprises, to nullify all attachments and judgments obtained therein, to prohibit all further litigation based on such claims, and to bring about the termination of such claims through binding arbitration." In addition, the United States must "act to bring about the transfer" by July 19, 1981, of all Iranian assets held in this country by American banks. One billion dollars of these assets will be deposited in a security account in the Bank of England, to the account of the Algerian Central Bank, and used to satisfy awards rendered against Iran by the Claims Tribunal.

On January 19, 1981, President Carter issued a series of Executive Orders implementing the terms of the agreement. *** On February 24, 1981, President Reagan issued an Executive Order in which he "ratified" the January 19th Executive Orders. Moreover, he "suspended" all "claims which may be presented to the *** Tribunal" and provided that such claims "shall have no legal effect in any action now pending in any court of the United States." *Ibid.* The suspension of any particular claim terminates if the Claims Tribunal determines that it has no jurisdiction over that claim; claims are discharged for all purposes when the Claims Tribunal either awards some recovery and that amount is paid, or determines that no recovery is due. ***

[The lower courts upheld the Executive Orders.]

The parties and the lower courts, confronted with the instant questions, have all agreed that much relevant analysis is contained in *Youngstown Sheet & Tube Co. v. Sawyer*, 343 U.S. 579 (1952). *** Although we have in the past found and do today find JUSTICE JACKSON's classification of executive actions into three general categories analytically useful, we should be mindful of JUSTICE HOLMES' admonition *** that "[t]he great ordinances of the Constitution do not establish and divide fields of black and white." JUSTICE JACKSON himself recognized that his three categories represented "a somewhat over-simplified grouping," and it is doubtless the case that executive action in any particular instance falls, not neatly in one of three pigeonholes, but rather at some point along a spectrum running from explicit congressional authorization to explicit congressional prohibition. This is particularly true as respects cases such as the one before us, involving responses to international crises the nature of which Congress can hardly have been expected to anticipate in any detail.

*** The Government *** has principally relied on § 203 of the IEEPA as authorization for these actions. Section 1702(a)(1) provides in part: " *** [T]he President may, under such regulations as he may prescribe, by means of instructions, licenses, or otherwise, investigate, regulate, direct and compel, nullify, void, prevent or prohibit, any acquisition, holding, withholding, use, transfer, withdrawal, transportation, importation or exportation of, or dealing in, or exercising any right, power, or privilege with respect to, or transactions involving, any property in which any foreign country or a national thereof has any interest; by any person, or with respect to any property, subject to the jurisdiction of the United States."

The Government contends that the acts of "nullifying" the attachments and ordering the "transfer" of the frozen assets are specifically authorized by the plain language of the above statute. ***

Because the President's action in nullifying the attachments and ordering the transfer of the assets was taken pursuant to specific congressional authorization, it is "supported by the strongest of presumptions and the widest latitude of judicial interpretation, and the burden of persuasion would rest heavily upon any who might attack it." *Youngstown*, 343 U.S., at 637 (JACKSON, J., concurring). Under the circumstances of this case, we cannot say that petitioner has sustained that heavy burden. A contrary ruling would mean that the Federal Government as a whole lacked the power exercised by the President, and that we are not prepared to say.

Although we have concluded that the IEEPA constitutes specific congressional authorization to the President to nullify the attachments and order the transfer of Iranian assets, there remains the question of the President's authority to suspend claims pending in American courts. Such claims have, of course, an existence apart from the attachments which accompanied them. In terminating these claims through Executive Order No. 12294 the President purported to act under authority of both the IEEPA and 22 U.S.C. § 1732, the so-called "Hostage Act."

*** [We conclude] that neither the IEEPA nor the Hostage Act constitutes specific authorization of the President's action suspending claims[.] [H]owever, [this] is not to say that these statutory provisions are entirely irrelevant to the question of the validity of the President's action. We think both statutes highly relevant in the looser sense of indicating congressional acceptance of a broad scope for executive action in circumstances such as those presented in this case. *** [T]he IEEPA delegates broad authority to the President to act in times of national emergency with respect to property of a foreign country. The Hostage Act similarly indicates congressional willingness that the President have broad discretion when responding to the hostile acts of foreign sovereigns.

*** [W]e cannot ignore the general tenor of Congress' legislation in this area in trying to determine whether the President is acting alone or at least with the acceptance of Congress. As we have noted, Congress cannot anticipate and legislate with regard to every possible action the President may find it necessary to take or every possible situation in which he might act. Such failure of Congress specifically to delegate authority does not, "especially *** in the areas of foreign policy and national security," imply "congressional disapproval" of action taken by the Executive. On the contrary, the enactment of legislation closely related to the question of the President's authority in a particular case which evinces legislative intent to accord the President broad discretion may be considered to "invite" "measures on independent presidential responsibility," *Youngstown*, 343 U.S., at 637 (JACKSON, J., concurring). At least this is so where there is no contrary indication of legislative intent and when, as here, there is a history of congressional acquiescence in conduct of the sort engaged in by the President. It is to that history which we now turn.

Not infrequently in affairs between nations, outstanding claims by nationals of one country against the government of another country are "sources of friction" between the two sovereigns. To resolve these difficulties, nations have often entered into agreements settling the claims of their respective nationals. *** Under such agreements, the President has agreed to renounce or extinguish claims of United States nationals against foreign governments in return for lump-sum payments or the establishment of arbitration procedures. ***

Crucial to our decision today is the conclusion that Congress has implicitly approved the practice of claim settlement by executive agreement. This is best demonstrated by Congress' enactment of the International Claims Settlement Act of 1949[.] *** Over the years Congress has frequently amended the International Claims Settlement Act to provide for particular problems arising out of settlement agreements, thus demonstrating Congress' continuing acceptance of the President's claim settlement authority.

*** In light of all of the foregoing—the inferences to be drawn from the character of the legislation Congress has enacted in the area, such as the IEEPA and the Hostage Act, and from the history of acquiescence in executive claims settlement—we conclude that the President was authorized to suspend pending claims. As JUSTICE FRANKFURTER pointed out in *Youngstown*, 343 U.S., at 610–611, "a systematic, unbroken, executive practice, long pursued to the knowledge of the Congress and never before questioned *** may be treated as a gloss on 'Executive Power' vested in the President by s 1 of Art. II." Past practice does not, by itself, create power, but "long-continued practice, known to and acquiesced in by Congress, would raise a presumption that the [action] had been [taken] in pursuance of its consent. *** " Such practice is present here and such a presumption is also appropriate. In light of the fact that Congress may be considered to have consented to the President's action in suspending claims, we cannot say that action exceeded the President's powers.

Our conclusion is buttressed by the fact that the means chosen by the President to settle the claims of American nationals provided an alternative forum, the Claims Tribunal, which is capable of providing meaningful relief. *** Just as importantly, Congress has not disapproved of the action taken here. Though Congress has held hearings on the Iranian Agreement itself, Congress has not enacted legislation, or even passed a resolution, indicating its displeasure with the Agreement. Quite the contrary, the relevant Senate Committee has stated that the establishment of the Tribunal is "of vital importance to the United States." We are thus clearly not confronted with a situation in which Congress has in some way resisted the exercise of Presidential authority.

Finally, we re-emphasize the narrowness of our decision. We do not decide that the President possesses plenary power to settle claims, even as against foreign governmental entities. As the Court of Appeals for the First Circuit stressed, "[t]he sheer magnitude of such a power, considered against the background of the diversity and complexity of modern international trade, cautions against any broader construction of authority than is necessary." But where, as here, the settlement of claims has been determined to be a necessary incident to the resolution of a major foreign policy dispute between our country and another, and where, as here, we can conclude that Congress acquiesced in the President's action, we are not prepared to say that the President lacks the power to settle such claims. ***

JUSTICE STEVENS, concurring in part. [omitted]

JUSTICE POWELL, concurring and dissenting in part. [omitted]

Notes

1. **Political Necessity.** The Court's decision has been criticized as pure politics (a "political decision politically made") and for its shoddy methodology ("crisis atmosphere *** Court should have demanded more specific legislative approval for the president's far-reaching measures"). Do you agree?

2. **Comparisons.**

(a) Does *Dames & Moore* reject JUSTICE BLACK's methodology in *Youngstown*? Is there anything in the Constitution's text that gives the President inherent foreign affairs (but not domestic affairs) powers?

(b) Do you agree that *Dames & Moore*, "[By] finding legislative 'approval' when Congress had given none, *** inverted the *Steel Seizure* holding— which construed statutory nonapproval of the president's act to mean legislative disapproval—[and] condoned legislative inactivity at a time that demanded interbranch dialogue and bipartisan consensus"? Harold Koh, THE NATIONAL SECURITY CONSTITUTION: SHARING POWER AFTER THE IRAN–CONTRA AFFAIR 139–140 (1990).

(c) Why did the Court characterize President Truman's seizure of the steel mills as "domestic" and President Carter's Executive Agreement establishing the Iran–United States Claims Tribunal as "foreign affairs"? Is the line between the two capable of principled judicial delineation?

(d) How did President Carter manage to avoid going to the Senate for its "Advice and Consent" under Article II, § 2, cl. 2 concerning the Claims Tribunal Agreement?

2. EXECUTIVE PRIVILEGE AND IMMUNITY

Powers enable the President to engage in particular tasks, whereas privileges and immunities shield the President from inquiries concerning whether particular actions taken were lawful or not. In the Presidential Powers cases above, the Supreme Court, at least arguably, was a truly neutral referee between the President and Congress. Can the same be said of the following cases in which the Court is evaluating the President's claims not to be reached by judicial processes?

UNITED STATES v. NIXON
418 U.S. 683, 94 S.Ct. 3090, 41 L.Ed.2d 1039 (1974).

MR. CHIEF JUSTICE BURGER delivered the opinion of the Court.

This litigation presents for review the denial of a motion, filed in the District Court on behalf of the President of the United States, in the case of *United States v. Mitchell et al.*, to quash a third-party subpoena duces tecum issued by the United States District Court for the District of Columbia, pursuant to Fed.Rule Crim.Proc. 17(c). The subpoena directed the President to produce certain tape recordings and documents relating to his conversations with aides and advisers. The court rejected the President's claims of absolute executive privilege, of lack of jurisdiction, and of failure to satisfy the requirements of Rule 17(c). The President appealed to the Court of Appeals. We granted both the United States' petition for certiorari before judgment and also the President's cross-petition for certiorari before judgment, because of the public importance of the issues presented and the need for their prompt resolution.

On March 1, 1974, a grand jury of the United States District Court for the District of Columbia returned an indictment charging seven named individuals[3] with various offenses, including conspiracy to defraud the United States and to obstruct justice. Although he was not designated as such in the indictment, the grand jury named the President, among others, as an unindicted coconspirator. On April 18, 1974, upon motion of the Special Prosecutor, a subpoena duces tecum was issued pursuant to Rule 17(c) to the President by the United States District Court. The subpoena required the production, in advance of the September 9 trial date, of certain tapes, memoranda, papers, transcripts or other writings relating to certain precisely identified meetings between the President and others. On April 30, the

---

[3] The seven defendants were John N. Mitchell, H. R. Haldeman, John D. Ehrlichman, Charles W. Colson, Robert C. Mardian, Kenneth W. Parkinson, and Gordon Strachan. Each had occupied either a position of responsibility on the White House staff or the Committee for the Re-election of the President. Colson entered a guilty plea on another charge and is no longer a defendant.

President publicly released edited transcripts of 43 conversations; portions of 20 conversations subject to subpoena in the present case were included. On May 1, 1974, the President's counsel, filed a 'special appearance' and a motion to quash the subpoena under Rule 17(c). This motion was accompanied by a formal claim of privilege. ***

On May 20, 1974, the District Court denied the motion to quash and the motions to expunge and for protective orders. It further ordered 'the President or any subordinate officer, official, or employee with custody or control of the documents or objects subpoenaed,' to deliver to the District Court, on or before May 31, 1974, the originals of all subpoenaed items. The District Court rejected *** the contention that the Judiciary was without authority to review an assertion of executive privilege by the President, *** [holding] that the judiciary, not the President, was the final arbiter of a claim of executive privilege.

[The President sought review and the Supreme Court granted certiorari before judgment.]

*** In the District Court, the President's counsel argued that the court lacked jurisdiction to issue the subpoena because the matter was an intra-branch dispute between a subordinate and superior officer of the Executive Branch and hence not subject to judicial resolution. *** Since the Executive Branch has exclusive authority and absolute discretion to decide whether to prosecute a case, it is contended that a President's decision is final in determining what evidence is to be used in a given criminal case.

*** Under the authority of Art. II, s 2, Congress has vested in the Attorney General the power to conduct the criminal litigation of the United States Government. It has also vested in him the power to appoint subordinate officers to assist him in the discharge of his duties. Acting pursuant to those statutes, the Attorney General has delegated the authority to represent the United States in these particular matters to a Special Prosecutor with unique authority and tenure. The regulation gives the Special Prosecutor explicit power to contest the invocation of executive privilege in the process of seeking evidence deemed relevant to the performance of these specially delegated duties.

*** [I]t is theoretically possible for the Attorney General to amend or revoke the regulation defining the Special Prosecutor's authority. But he has not done so. So long as this regulation remains in force the Executive Branch is bound by it, and indeed the United States as the sovereign composed of the three branches is bound to respect and to enforce it. Moreover, the delegation of authority to the Special Prosecutor in this case is not an ordinary delegation by the Attorney General to a subordinate officer: with the authorization of the President, the Acting Attorney General provided in the regulation that the Special Prosecutor was not to be removed without the 'consensus' of eight designated leaders of Congress.

*** In light of the uniqueness of the setting in which the conflict arises, the fact that both parties are officers of the Executive Branch cannot be viewed as a barrier to justiciability. It would be inconsistent with the applicable law and regulation, and the unique facts of this case to conclude other than that the Special Prosecutor has standing to bring this action and that a justiciable controversy is presented for decision.

*** Having determined that the requirements of [Fed. R. Civ. Pro.] Rule 17(c) were satisfied, we turn to the claim that the subpoena should be quashed because it demands 'confidential conversations between a President and his close advisors that it would be inconsistent with the public interest to produce.' The first contention is a broad claim that the separation of powers doctrine precludes judicial review of a President's claim of privilege. The second contention is that if he does not prevail on the claim of absolute privilege, the court should hold as a matter of constitutional law that the privilege prevails over the subpoena duces tecum.

In the performance of assigned constitutional duties, each branch of the Government must initially interpret the Constitution, and the interpretation of its powers by any branch is due great respect from the others. The President's counsel reads the Constitution as providing an absolute privilege of confidentiality for all Presidential communications. Many decisions of this Court, however, have unequivocally reaffirmed the holding of *Marbury v. Madison*, 1 Cranch 137 (1803), that '(i)t is emphatically the province and duty of the judicial department to say what the law is.'

No holding of the Court has defined the scope of judicial power specifically relating to the enforcement of a subpoena for confidential Presidential communications for use in a criminal prosecution, but other exercises of power by the Executive Branch and the Legislative Branch have been found invalid as in conflict with the Constitution. *Powell v. McCormack*, 395 U.S. 486 (1969); *Youngstown Sheet & Tube Co. v. Sawyer*, 343 U.S. 579 (1952). In a series of cases, the Court interpreted the explicit immunity conferred by express provisions of the Constitution on Members of the House and Senate by the Speech or Debate Clause, U.S.Const. Art. I, § 6. Since this Court has consistently exercised the power to construe and delineate claims arising under express powers, it must follow that the Court has authority to interpret claims with respect to powers alleged to derive from enumerated powers.

Our system of government 'requires that federal courts on occasion interpret the Constitution in a manner at variance with the construction given the document by another branch.' *Powell v. McCormack*, supra. Notwithstanding the deference each branch must accord the others, the 'judicial Power of the United States' vested in the federal courts by Art. III, § 1, of the Constitution can no more be shared with the Executive Branch than the Chief Executive, for example, can share with the Judiciary the veto power, or the Congress share with the Judiciary the power to override a Presidential veto. Any other conclusion would be contrary to the basic concept of separation of powers and the checks and balances that flow from the scheme of a tripartite government. The Federalist, No. 47. We therefore reaffirm that it is the province and duty of this Court 'to say what the law is' with respect to the claim of privilege presented in this case.

In support of his claim of absolute privilege, the President's counsel urges *** the valid need for protection of communications between high Government officials and those who advise and assist them in the performance of their manifold duties; the importance of this confidentiality is too plain to require further discussion. *** Whatever the nature of the privilege of confidentiality of Presidential communications in the exercise of Art. II powers, the privilege can be said to derive from the supremacy of each branch within its own assigned area of constitutional duties. Certain powers and privileges flow from the nature of enumerated powers; the protection of the confidentiality of Presidential communications has similar constitutional underpinnings.

The second ground asserted by the President's counsel in support of the claim of absolute privilege rests on the doctrine of separation of powers. Here it is argued that the independence of the Executive Branch within its own sphere, *Humphrey's Executor v. United States*, 295 U.S. 602 (1935), insulates a President from a judicial subpoena in an ongoing criminal prosecution, and thereby protects confidential Presidential communications.

However, neither the doctrine of separation of powers, nor the need for confidentiality of high-level communications, without more, can sustain an absolute, unqualified Presidential privilege of immunity from judicial process under all circumstances. The President's need for complete candor and objectivity from advisers calls for great deference from the courts. However, when the privilege depends solely on the broad, undifferentiated claim of public interest in the confidentiality of such conversations, a confrontation with other values arises. Absent a claim of need to protect military, diplomatic, or sensitive national security secrets, we find it difficult to accept the argument that even the very important interest in confidentiality of Presidential communications is significantly diminished by production of such material for in camera inspection with all the protection that a district court will be obliged to provide.

The impediment that an absolute, unqualified privilege would place in the way of the primary constitutional duty of the Judicial Branch to do justice in criminal prosecutions would plainly conflict with the function of the courts under Art. III. In designing the structure of our Government and dividing and allocating the sovereign power among three co-equal branches, the Framers of the Constitution sought to provide a comprehensive system, but the separate powers were not intended to operate with absolute independence.

*** The expectation of a President to the confidentiality of his conversations and correspondence, like the claim of confidentiality of judicial deliberations, for example, has all the values to which we accord deference for the privacy of all citizens and, added to those values, is the necessity for protection of the public interest in candid, objective, and even blunt or harsh opinions in Presidential decisionmaking. *** The privilege is fundamental to the operation of Government and inextricably rooted in the separation of powers under the Constitution. ***

III–2. "Coming Down to the Tape" Lepelley/ © *The Christian Science Monitor.*

But this presumptive privilege must be considered in light of our historic commitment to the rule of law. This is nowhere more profoundly manifest than in our view that 'the twofold aim (of criminal justice) is that guilt shall not escape or innocence suffer.' *Berger v. United States*, 295 U.S., at 88. We have elected to employ an adversary system of criminal justice in which the parties contest all issues before a court of law. The need to develop all relevant facts in the adversary system is both fundamental and comprehensive. *** To ensure that justice is done, it is imperative to the function of courts that compulsory process be available for the production of evidence needed either by the prosecution or by the defense.

Only recently the Court restated the ancient proposition of law, albeit in the context of a grand jury inquiry rather than a trial, that 'the public *** has a right to every man's evidence,' except for those persons protected by a constitutional, common-law, or statutory privilege. The [evidentiary] privileges referred to by the Court are designed to protect weighty and legitimate competing interests. Thus, the Fifth Amendment to the Constitution provides that no man 'shall be compelled in any criminal case to be a witness against himself.' And, generally, an attorney or a priest may not be required to disclose what has been revealed in professional confidence. These and other interests are recognized in law by privileges against forced disclosure, established in the Constitution, by statute, or at common law. Whatever their origins, these exceptions to the demand for every man's evidence are not lightly created nor expansively construed, for they are in derogation of the search for truth.

In this case the President challenges a subpoena served on him as a third party requiring the production of materials for use in a criminal prosecution; he does so on the claim that he has a privilege against disclosure of confidential communications. He does not place his claim of privilege on the ground they are military or diplomatic secrets. As to these areas of Art. II duties the courts have traditionally shown the utmost deference to Presidential responsibilities. *** No case of the Court, however, has extended this high degree of deference to a President's generalized interest in confidentiality. Nowhere in the Constitution, as we have noted earlier, is there any explicit reference to a privilege of confidentiality, yet to the extent this interest relates to the effective discharge of a President's powers, it is constitutionally based.

The right to the production of all evidence at a criminal trial similarly has constitutional dimensions. The Sixth Amendment explicitly confers upon every defendant in a criminal trial the right 'to be confronted with the witnesses against him' and 'to have compulsory process for obtaining witnesses in his favor. Moreover, the Fifth Amendment also guarantees that no person shall be deprived of liberty without due process of law. It is the manifest duty of the courts to vindicate those guarantees, and to accomplish that it is essential that all relevant and admissible evidence be produced.

In this case we must weigh the importance of the general privilege of confidentiality of Presidential communications in performance of the President's responsibilities against the inroads of such a privilege on the fair administration of criminal justice. The interest in preserving confidentiality is weighty indeed and entitled to great respect. However, we cannot conclude that advisers will be moved to temper the candor of their remarks by the infrequent occasions of disclosure because of the possibility that such conversations will be called for in the context of a criminal prosecution.

On the other hand, the allowance of the privilege to withhold evidence that is demonstrably relevant in a criminal trial would cut deeply into the guarantee of due process of law and gravely impair the basic function of the courts. A President's acknowledged need for confidentiality in the communications of his office is general in nature, whereas the constitutional need for production of relevant evidence in a criminal proceeding is specific and central to the fair adjudication of a particular criminal case in the administration of justice. Without access to specific facts a criminal prosecution may be totally frustrated. The President's broad interest in confidentiality of communications will not be vitiated by disclosure of a limited number of conversations preliminarily shown to have some bearing on the pending criminal cases.

*** If a President concludes that compliance with a subpoena would be injurious to the public interest he may properly, as was done here, invoke a claim of privilege on the return of the subpoena. Upon receiving a claim of privilege from the Chief Executive, it became the further duty of the District

Court to treat the subpoenaed material as presumptively privileged and to require the Special Prosecutor to demonstrate that the Presidential material was 'essential to the justice of the (pending criminal) case.' *United States v. Burr*, 25 Fed.Cas., at 192. Here the District Court treated the material as presumptively privileged, proceeded to find that the Special Prosecutor had made a sufficient showing to rebut the presumption, and ordered an in camera examination of the subpoenaed material. On the basis of our examination of the record we are unable to conclude that the District Court erred in ordering the inspection. Accordingly we affirm the order of the District Court that subpoenaed materials be transmitted to that court. We now turn to the important question of the District Court's responsibilities in conducting the in camera examination of Presidential materials or communications delivered under the compulsion of the subpoena duces tecum.

*** Statements that meet the test of admissibility and relevance must be isolated; all other material must be excised. At this stage the District Court is not limited to representations of the Special Prosecutor as to the evidence sought by the subpoena; the material will be available to the District Court. It is elementary that in camera inspection of evidence is always a procedure calling for scrupulous protection against any release or publication of material not found by the court, at that stage, probably admissible in evidence and relevant to the issues of the trial for which it is sought. That being true of an ordinary situation, it is obvious that the District Court has a very heavy responsibility to see to it that Presidential conversations, which are either not relevant or not admissible, are accorded that high degree of respect due the President of the United States. MR. CHIEF JUSTICE MARSHALL, sitting as a trial judge in the *Burr* case, supra, was extraordinarily careful to point out that '(i)n no case of this kind would a court be required to proceed against the president as against an ordinary individual.' Marshall's statement cannot be read to mean in any sense that a President is above the law, but relates to the singularly unique role under Art. II of a President's communications and activities, related to the performance of duties under that Article. Moreover, a President's communications and activities encompass a vastly wider range of sensitive material than would be true of any 'ordinary individual.' It is therefore necessary in the public interest to afford Presidential confidentiality the greatest protection consistent with the fair administration of justice. The need for confidentiality even as to idle conversations with associates in which casual reference might be made concerning political leaders within the country or foreign statesmen is too obvious to call for further treatment. We have no doubt that the District Judge will at all times accord to Presidential records that high degree of deference suggested in *United States v. Burr*, and will discharge his responsibility to see to it that until released to the Special Prosecutor no in camera material is revealed to anyone. This burden applies with even greater force to excised material; once the decision is made to excise, the material is restored to its privileged status and should be returned under seal to its lawful custodian.

Since this matter came before the Court during the pendency of a criminal prosecution, and on representations that time is of the essence, the mandate shall issue forthwith.

Affirmed.

MR. JUSTICE REHNQUIST took no part in the consideration or decision of this case.

Notes

1. **Political Question.** Was the Court's conclusion that the issue posed was not a "political question" consistent with the use of that term in *Marbury*? Its use in *Baker v. Carr*?

2. **Judicial Trial and Congressional Impeachment.** At the time this case was pending, the House was considering three Articles of Impeachment against President Nixon: Article I concerned obstruction of justice; Article II dealt with violating citizens' rights through misuse of the IRS, FBI, and CIA; and Article III involved failure to respond to congressional subpoenas. Within five days after the Court's decision in *United States v. Nixon*, the House Judiciary Committee adopted each of the three Articles of Impeachment; within seven days, President Nixon decided to make transcripts of the Watergate tapes available. Three days after that, President Nixon resigned. The House, presumably thinking the issue moot, dropped further impeachment proceedings. Should the Court have deferred to the impeachment process? If Nixon had been impeached, rather than resigning, would the issue of whether the President committed "high Crimes and Misdemeanors" have been judicially reviewable?

3. **Constitutional Theory of Immunity and Privilege.**

    (a) Legislative immunity is provided in the "Speech or Debate" Clause of Art. I, § 6, cl. 1 (House and Senate members "shall not be questioned in any other Place"). Why didn't the Court find that, in the absence of a comparable provision, the President has no executive privilege? Ironically, was the decision that the President was entitled to some privileged communications a victory?

    (b) Even if their communications enjoy only a qualified privilege, Presidents enjoy absolute immunity from civil suits based on performance of official functions. *See Clinton v. Jones*, infra. If Presidential privileges and immunities are a function of separation of powers principles, do they extend to presidential aides? *See Harlow v. Fitzgerald*, 457 U.S. 800 (1982) (privilege is the President's, but Presidential aides have qualified immunity).

    (c) Was it predictable that the Court would balance the "generalized" interests of the President adversely when faced by the "specific" needs of the criminal justice system? Is this simply institutional myopia by the judiciary? Some commentators have speculated that the balance might have been different if the counterweight to immunity had been an investigation by Congress.

    (d) If you had represented Nixon, would an argument that the tapes contained materials affecting national security interests have been helpful? What should the judiciary do in the face of such a claim?

4.   **Followup.** President Nixon lost yet another Supreme Court case when the Court held in *Nixon v. Administrator of General Services*, 433 U.S. 425 (1977), that a statute directing the Administrator to take custody of Nixon's presidential papers and tape recordings, sort them for archival purposes, and return only those which were personal in nature did not violate separation of powers principles. The Court noted that Presidents Ford and Carter supported the statute and that the materials remained in the Executive Branch.

CLINTON v. JONES
520 U.S. 681, 117 S.Ct. 1636, 137 L.Ed.2d 945 (1997).

JUSTICE STEVENS delivered the opinion of the Court.

This case raises a constitutional and a prudential question concerning the Office of the President of the United States. Respondent, a private citizen, seeks to recover damages from the current occupant of that office based on actions allegedly taken before his term began. The President submits that in all but the most exceptional cases the Constitution requires federal courts to defer such litigation until his term ends and that, in any event, respect for the office warrants such a stay. Despite the force of the arguments supporting the President's submissions, we conclude that they must be rejected.

I

Petitioner, William Jefferson Clinton, was elected to the Presidency in 1992, and re-elected in 1996. His term of office expires on January 20, 2001. In 1991 he was the Governor of the State of Arkansas. Respondent, Paula Corbin Jones, is a resident of California. In 1991 she lived in Arkansas, and was an employee of the Arkansas Industrial Development Commission.

On May 6, 1994, she commenced this action in the United States District Court for the Eastern District of Arkansas by filing a complaint naming petitioner and Danny Ferguson, a former Arkansas State Police officer, as defendants. *** As the case comes to us, we are required to assume the truth of the detailed—but as yet untested—factual allegations in the complaint.

Those allegations principally describe events that are said to have occurred on the afternoon of May 8, 1991, during an official conference held at the Excelsior Hotel in Little Rock, Arkansas. The Governor delivered a speech at the conference; respondent—working as a state employee—staffed the registration desk. She alleges that Ferguson persuaded her to leave her desk and to visit the Governor in a business suite at the hotel, where he made "abhorrent" sexual advances that she vehemently rejected ***. [I]t is perfectly clear that the alleged misconduct of petitioner was unrelated to any of his official duties as President of the United States and, indeed, occurred before he was elected to that office. ***

IV

Petitioner's principal submission—that "in all but the most exceptional cases" the Constitution affords the President temporary immunity from civil damages litigation arising out of events that occurred before he took office— cannot be sustained on the basis of precedent.

Only three sitting Presidents have been defendants in civil litigation involving their actions prior to taking office. Complaints against Theodore Roosevelt and Harry Truman had been dismissed before they took office; the dismissals were affirmed after their respective inaugurations. Two companion cases arising out of an automobile accident were filed against John F. Kennedy in 1960 during the Presidential campaign. After taking office, he unsuccessfully argued that his status as Commander in Chief gave him a right to a stay under the Soldiers' and Sailors' Civil Relief Act of 1940, 50 U.S.C.App. §§ 501–525. The motion for a stay was denied by the District Court, and the matter was settled out of court. Thus, none of those cases sheds any light on the constitutional issue before us.

The principal rationale for affording certain public servants immunity from suits for money damages arising out of their official acts is inapplicable to unofficial conduct. In cases involving prosecutors, legislators, and judges we have repeatedly explained that the immunity serves the public interest in enabling such officials to perform their designated functions effectively without fear that a particular decision may give rise to personal liability. We explained in *Ferri v. Ackerman*, 444 U.S. 193 (1979):

"As public servants, the prosecutor and the judge represent the interest of society as a whole. The conduct of their official duties may adversely affect a wide variety of different individuals, each of whom may be a potential source of future controversy. The societal interest in providing such public officials with the maximum ability to deal fearlessly and impartially with the public at large has long been recognized as an acceptable justification for official immunity. The point of immunity for such officials is to forestall an atmosphere of intimidation that would conflict with their resolve to perform their designated functions in a principled fashion."

That rationale provided the principal basis for our holding that a former President of the United States was "entitled to absolute immunity from damages liability predicated on his official acts." Our central concern was to avoid rendering the President "unduly cautious in the discharge of his official duties."[19]

_____

[19] Petitioner draws our attention to dicta in [*Nixon v.*] *Fitzgerald* which he suggests are helpful to his cause. We noted there that "[b]ecause of the singular importance of the President's duties, diversion of his energies by concern with private lawsuits would raise unique risks to the effective functioning of government," and suggested further that "[c]ognizance of *** personal vulnerability frequently could distract a President from his public duties." Petitioner argues that in this aspect the Court's concern was parallel to the issue he suggests is of great importance in this case, the possibility that a sitting President might be distracted by the need to participate in litigation during the pendency of his office. In context, however, it is clear that our dominant concern was with the diversion of the President's attention during the decisionmaking process caused by needless worry as to the possibility of damages actions stemming from any particular

This reasoning provides no support for an immunity for unofficial conduct. As we explained in [*Nixon v.*] *Fitzgerald*, [457 U.S. 731 (1982),] "the sphere of protected action must be related closely to the immunity's justifying purposes." Because of the President's broad responsibilities, we recognized in that case an immunity from damages claims arising out of official acts extending to the "outer perimeter of his authority." But we have never suggested that the President, or any other official, has an immunity that extends beyond the scope of any action taken in an official capacity.

Moreover, when defining the scope of an immunity for acts clearly taken within an official capacity, we have applied a functional approach. *** Hence, for example, a judge's absolute immunity does not extend to actions performed in a purely administrative capacity. As our opinions have made clear, immunities are grounded in "the nature of the function performed, not the identity of the actor who performed it." Petitioner's effort to construct an immunity from suit for unofficial acts grounded purely in the identity of his office is unsupported by precedent.

V

We are also unpersuaded by the evidence from the historical record to which petitioner has called our attention. He points to a comment by Thomas Jefferson protesting the subpoena duces tecum CHIEF JUSTICE MARSHALL directed to him in the Burr trial,[20] a statement in the diaries kept by Senator William Maclay of the first Senate debates, in which then Vice–President John Adams and Senator Oliver Ellsworth are recorded as having said that "the President personally [is] not *** subject to any process whatever," lest it be "put *** in the power of a common Justice to exercise any Authority over him and Stop the Whole Machine of Government," and to a quotation from JUSTICE STORY's Commentaries on the Constitution. None of these sources sheds much light on the question at hand.[23]

Respondent, in turn, has called our attention to conflicting historical evidence. Speaking in favor of the Constitution's adoption at the Pennsylvania Convention, James Wilson—who had participated in the Philadelphia Convention at which the document was drafted—explained that, although the President "is placed [on] high," "not a single privilege is annexed to his character; far from being above the laws, he is amenable to

---

official decision. Moreover, *Fitzgerald* did not present the issue raised in this case because that decision involved claims against a former President.

[20] In Jefferson's view, the subpoena jeopardized the separation of powers by subjecting the Executive Branch to judicial command.

[23] Jefferson's argument provides little support for respondent's position. As we explain later, the prerogative Jefferson claimed was denied him by the Chief Justice in the very decision Jefferson was protesting, and this Court has subsequently reaffirmed that holding. *See United States v. Nixon* *** [In his constitutional law treatise, JUSTICE] STORY said only that "an official inviolability," *** was necessary to preserve the President's ability to perform the functions of the office; he did not specify the dimensions of the necessary immunity. While we have held that an immunity from suits grounded on official acts is necessary to serve this purpose, *** it does not follow that the broad immunity from all civil damages suits that petitioner seeks is also necessary.

them in his private character as a citizen, and in his public character by impeachment." This description is consistent with both the doctrine of presidential immunity as set forth in *Fitzgerald*, and rejection of the immunity claim in this case. With respect to acts taken in his "public character"—that is official acts—the President may be disciplined principally by impeachment, not by private lawsuits for damages. But he is otherwise subject to the laws for his purely private acts.

In the end, *** we reach the same conclusion about these historical materials that JUSTICE JACKSON described when confronted with an issue concerning the dimensions of the President's power. "Just what our forefathers did envision, or would have envisioned had they foreseen modern conditions, must be divined from materials almost as enigmatic as the dreams Joseph was called upon to interpret for Pharoah. A century and a half of partisan debate and scholarly speculation yields no net result but only supplies more or less apt quotations from respected sources on each side. *** They largely cancel each other." *Youngstown.*

VI

Petitioner's strongest argument supporting his immunity claim is based on the text and structure of the Constitution. He does not contend that the occupant of the Office of the President is "above the law," in the sense that his conduct is entirely immune from judicial scrutiny.[24] The President argues merely for a postponement of the judicial proceedings that will determine whether he violated any law. His argument is grounded in the character of the office that was created by Article II of the Constitution, and relies on separation of powers principles that have structured our constitutional arrangement since the founding.

As a starting premise, petitioner contends that he occupies a unique office with powers and responsibilities so vast and important that the public interest demands that he devote his undivided time and attention to his public duties. *** We have no dispute with the initial premise of the argument. Former presidents, from George Washington to George Bush, have consistently endorsed petitioner's characterization of the office. *** As JUSTICE JACKSON has pointed out, the Presidency concentrates executive authority "in a single head in whose choice the whole Nation has a part, making him the focus of public hopes and expectations. In drama, magnitude and finality his decisions so far overshadow any others that almost alone he fills the public eye and ear." *Youngstown Sheet & Tube Co. v. Sawyer*, 343 U.S., at 653 (JACKSON, J., concurring). We have, in short, long recognized the

---

[24] For that reason, the argument does not place any reliance on the English ancestry that informs our common-law jurisprudence; he does not claim the prerogatives of the monarchs who asserted that "[t]he King can do no wrong." See 1 W. Blackstone, Commentaries. Although we have adopted the related doctrine of sovereign immunity, the common-law fiction that "[t]he king *** is not only incapable of *doing* wrong, but even of *thinking* wrong," was rejected at the birth of the Republic.

"unique position in the constitutional scheme" that this office occupies.[29] Thus, while we suspect that even in our modern era there remains some truth to CHIEF JUSTICE MARSHALL's suggestion that the duties of the Presidency are not entirely "unremitting," *United States v. Burr*, 25 F.Cas. 30, 34 (C.C.Va.1807), we accept the initial premise of the Executive's argument.

It does not follow, however, that separation of powers principles would be violated by allowing this action to proceed. The doctrine of separation of powers is concerned with the allocation of official power among the three co-equal branches of our Government. The Framers "built into the tripartite Federal Government *** a self-executing safeguard against the encroachment or aggrandizement of one branch at the expense of the other." *Buckley v. Valeo*, 424 U.S., at 122. Thus, for example, the Congress may not exercise the judicial power to revise final judgments, *Plaut v. Spendthrift Farm, Inc.*, or the executive power to manage an airport, *see Metropolitan Washington Airports Authority v. Citizens for Abatement of Aircraft Noise, Inc.*, 501 U.S. 252, 276 (1991) (holding that "[i]f the power is executive, the Constitution does not permit an agent of Congress to exercise it"). Similarly, the President may not exercise the legislative power to authorize the seizure of private property for public use. *Youngstown.* And, the judicial power to decide cases and controversies does not include the provision of purely advisory opinions to the Executive, or permit the federal courts to resolve non justiciable questions.

Of course the lines between the powers of the three branches are not always neatly defined. But in this case there is no suggestion that the Federal Judiciary is being asked to perform any function that might in some way be described as "executive." Respondent is merely asking the courts to exercise their core Article III jurisdiction to decide cases and controversies. Whatever the outcome of this case, there is no possibility that the decision will curtail the scope of the official powers of the Executive Branch. The litigation of questions that relate entirely to the unofficial conduct of the individual who happens to be the President poses no perceptible risk of misallocation of either judicial power or executive power.

Rather than arguing that the decision of the case will produce either an aggrandizement of judicial power or a narrowing of executive power, petitioner contends that—as a by-product of an otherwise traditional exercise of judicial power—burdens will be placed on the President that will hamper the performance of his official duties. We have recognized that "[e]ven when a branch does not arrogate power to itself *** the separation-of-powers doctrine requires that a branch not impair another in the performance of its constitutional duties." As a factual matter, petitioner contends that this particular case—as well as the potential additional litigation that an affirmance of the Court of Appeals judgment might spawn—may impose an

---

[29] We noted in *Fitzgerald*: "Article II, § 1, of the Constitution provides that '[t]he executive Power shall be vested in a President of the United States. *** ' This grant of authority establishes the President as the chief constitutional officer of the Executive Branch, entrusted with supervisory and policy responsibilities of utmost discretion and sensitivity. *** "

unacceptable burden on the President's time and energy, and thereby impair the effective performance of his office.

Petitioner's predictive judgment finds little support in either history or the relatively narrow compass of the issues raised in this particular case. As we have already noted, in the more than 200–year history of the Republic, only three sitting Presidents have been subjected to suits for their private actions. If the past is any indicator, it seems unlikely that a deluge of such litigation will ever engulf the Presidency. As for the case at hand, if properly managed by the District Court, it appears to us highly unlikely to occupy any substantial amount of petitioner's time.

Of greater significance, petitioner errs by presuming that interactions between the Judicial Branch and the Executive, even quite burdensome interactions, necessarily rise to the level of constitutionally forbidden impairment of the Executive's ability to perform its constitutionally mandated functions. "[O]ur *** system imposes upon the Branches a degree of overlapping responsibility, a duty of interdependence as well as independence the absence of which 'would preclude the establishment of a Nation capable of governing itself effectively.'" As Madison explained, separation of powers does not mean that the branches "ought to have no partial agency in, or no control over the acts of each other." The fact that a federal court's exercise of its traditional Article III jurisdiction may significantly burden the time and attention of the Chief Executive is not sufficient to establish a violation of the Constitution. Two long-settled propositions, first announced by CHIEF JUSTICE MARSHALL, support that conclusion.

First, we have long held that when the President takes official action, the Court has the authority to determine whether he has acted within the law. *** Second, it is also settled that the President is subject to judicial process in appropriate circumstances. Although Thomas Jefferson apparently thought otherwise, CHIEF JUSTICE MARSHALL, when presiding in the treason trial of Aaron Burr, ruled that a subpoena duces tecum could be directed to the President. *United States v. Burr*, 25 F.Cas. 30 (C.C.Va. 1807). We unequivocally and emphatically endorsed Marshall's position when we held that President Nixon was obligated to comply with a subpoena commanding him to produce certain tape recordings of his conversations with his aides. *United States v. Nixon.* As we explained, "neither the doctrine of separation of powers, nor the need for confidentiality of high-level communications, without more, can sustain an absolute, unqualified Presidential privilege of immunity from judicial process under all circumstances."[39]

Sitting Presidents have responded to court orders to provide testimony and other information with sufficient frequency that such interactions between the Judicial and Executive Branches can scarcely be thought a novelty. President Monroe responded to written interrogatories, ***

---

[39] Of course, it does not follow that a court may "'proceed against the president as against an ordinary individual,'" *United States v. Nixon.* Special caution is appropriate if the materials or testimony sought by the court relate to a President's official activities ***.

President Nixon—as noted above—produced tapes in response to a subpoena duces tecum, *** President Ford complied with an order to give a deposition in a criminal trial, *** and President Clinton has twice given videotaped testimony in criminal proceedings ***. Moreover, sitting Presidents have also voluntarily complied with judicial requests for testimony. President Grant gave a lengthy deposition in a criminal case *** and President Carter similarly gave videotaped testimony for use at a criminal trial ***.

In sum, "[i]t is settled law that the separation-of-powers doctrine does not bar every exercise of jurisdiction over the President of the United States." *Fitzgerald.* If the Judiciary may severely burden the Executive Branch by reviewing the legality of the President's official conduct, and if it may direct appropriate process to the President himself, it must follow that the federal courts have power to determine the legality of his unofficial conduct. The burden on the President's time and energy that is a mere by-product of such review surely cannot be considered as onerous as the direct burden imposed by judicial review and the occasional invalidation of his official actions. We therefore hold that the doctrine of separation of powers does not require federal courts to stay all private actions against the President until he leaves office.

The reasons for rejecting such a categorical rule apply as well to a rule that would require a stay "in all but the most exceptional cases." Indeed, if the Framers of the Constitution had thought it necessary to protect the President from the burdens of private litigation, we think it far more likely that they would have adopted a categorical rule than a rule that required the President to litigate the question whether a specific case belonged in the "exceptional case" subcategory. In all events, the question whether a specific case should receive exceptional treatment is more appropriately the subject of the exercise of judicial discretion than an interpretation of the Constitution. Accordingly, we turn to the question whether the District Court's decision to stay the trial until after petitioner leaves office was an abuse of discretion.

VII

The Court of Appeals described the District Court's discretionary decision to stay the trial as the "functional equivalent" of a grant of temporary immunity. *** Strictly speaking the stay was not the functional equivalent of the constitutional immunity that petitioner claimed, because the District Court ordered discovery to proceed. Moreover, a stay of either the trial or discovery might be justified by considerations that do not require the recognition of any constitutional immunity. The District Court has broad discretion to stay proceedings as an incident to its power to control its own docket. *** Although we have rejected the argument that the potential burdens on the President violate separation of powers principles, those burdens are appropriate matters for the District Court to evaluate in its management of the case. The high respect that is owed to the office of the Chief Executive, though not justifying a rule of categorical immunity, is a matter that should inform the conduct of the entire proceeding, including the timing and scope of discovery.

Nevertheless, we are persuaded that it was an abuse of discretion for the District Court to defer the trial until after the President leaves office. Such a lengthy and categorical stay takes no account whatever of the respondent's interest in bringing the case to trial. The complaint was filed within the statutory limitations period—albeit near the end of that period—and delaying trial would increase the danger of prejudice resulting from the loss of evidence, including the inability of witnesses to recall specific facts, or the possible death of a party.

The decision to postpone the trial was, furthermore, premature. The proponent of a stay bears the burden of establishing its need. In this case, at the stage at which the District Court made its ruling, there was no way to assess whether a stay of trial after the completion of discovery would be warranted. Other than the fact that a trial may consume some of the President's time and attention, there is nothing in the record to enable a judge to assess the potential harm that may ensue from scheduling the trial promptly after discovery is concluded. We think the District Court may have given undue weight to the concern that a trial might generate unrelated civil actions that could conceivably hamper the President in conducting the duties of his office. If and when that should occur, the court's discretion would permit it to manage those actions in such fashion (including deferral of trial) that interference with the President's duties would not occur. But no such impingement upon the President's conduct of his office was shown here.

VIII

We add a final comment on two matters that are discussed at length in the briefs: the risk that our decision will generate a large volume of politically motivated harassing and frivolous litigation, and the danger that national security concerns might prevent the President from explaining a legitimate need for a continuance.

We are not persuaded that either of these risks is serious. Most frivolous and vexatious litigation is terminated at the pleading stage or on summary judgment, with little if any personal involvement by the defendant. Moreover, the availability of sanctions provides a significant deterrent to litigation directed at the President in his unofficial capacity for purposes of political gain or harassment. History indicates that the likelihood that a significant number of such cases will be filed is remote. Although scheduling problems may arise, there is no reason to assume that the District Courts will be either unable to accommodate the President's needs or unfaithful to the tradition— especially in matters involving national security—of giving "the utmost deference to Presidential responsibilities." Several Presidents, including petitioner, have given testimony without jeopardizing the Nation's security. In short, we have confidence in the ability of our federal judges to deal with both of these concerns.

If Congress deems it appropriate to afford the President stronger protection, it may respond with appropriate legislation. *** If the Constitution embodied the rule that the President advocates, Congress, of course, could not repeal it. But our holding today raises no barrier to a statutory response to these concerns. *** Accordingly, the judgment of the Court of Appeals is affirmed.

JUSTICE BREYER, concurring in the judgment.

I agree with the majority that the Constitution does not automatically grant the President an immunity from civil lawsuits based upon his private conduct. Nor does the "doctrine of separation of powers *** require federal courts to stay" virtually "all private actions against the President until he leaves office." *** In my view, however, once the President sets forth and explains a conflict between judicial proceeding and public duties, the matter changes. At that point, the Constitution permits a judge to schedule a trial in an ordinary civil damages action (where postponement normally is possible without overwhelming damage to a plaintiff) only within the constraints of a constitutional principle—a principle that forbids a federal judge in such a case to interfere with the President's discharge of his public duties. *** I think it important to explain how the Constitution's text, history, and precedent support this principle of judicial noninterference with Presidential functions in ordinary civil damages actions.

I

The Constitution states that the "executive Power shall be vested in a President." U.S. Const., Art. II, § 1. This constitutional delegation means that a sitting President is unusually busy, that his activities have an unusually important impact upon the lives of others, and that his conduct embodies an authority bestowed by the entire American electorate. *** This constitutional delegation means still more. Article II makes a single President responsible for the actions of the Executive Branch in much the same way that the entire Congress is responsible for the actions of the Legislative Branch, or the entire Judiciary for those of the Judicial Branch. It thereby creates a constitutional equivalence between a single President, on the one hand, and many legislators, or judges, on the other.

The Founders created this equivalence by consciously deciding to vest Executive authority in one person rather than several. They did so in order to focus, rather than to spread, Executive responsibility thereby facilitating accountability. They also sought to encourage energetic, vigorous, decisive, and speedy execution of the laws by placing in the hands of a single, constitutionally indispensable, individual the ultimate authority that, in respect to the other branches, the Constitution divides among many. *** It means that, unlike Congress, which is regularly out of session, U.S. Const., Art. I, §§ 4, 5, 7, the President never adjourns.

More importantly, these constitutional objectives explain why a President, though able to delegate duties to others, cannot delegate ultimate responsibility or the active obligation to supervise that goes with it. And the related constitutional equivalence between President, Congress, and the Judiciary, means that judicial scheduling orders in a private civil case must not only take reasonable account of, say, a particularly busy schedule, or a job on which others critically depend, or an underlying electoral mandate. They must also reflect the fact that interference with a President's ability to carry out his public responsibilities is constitutionally equivalent to interference with the ability of the entirety of Congress, or the Judicial Branch, to carry out their public obligations.

II

The leading case regarding Presidential immunity from suit is *Nixon v. Fitzgerald*. Before discussing *Fitzgerald*, it is helpful to understand the historical precedent on which it relies. ***

Three of the historical sources this Court cited in *Fitzgerald*—a commentary by Joseph Story, an argument attributed to John Adams and Oliver Ellsworth, and a letter written by Thomas Jefferson—each make clear that this is so.

First, Joseph Story wrote in his Commentaries:

"There are *** incidental powers, belonging to the executive department, which are necessarily implied from the nature of the functions, which are confided to it. Among those, must necessarily be included the power to perform them, without any obstruction or impediment whatsoever. The president cannot, therefore, be liable to arrest, imprisonment, or detention, while he is in the discharge of the duties of his office; and for this purpose his person must be deemed, in civil cases at least, to possess an official inviolability."

As interpreted by this Court in *Nixon v. Fitzgerald*, the words "for this purpose" would seem to refer to the President's need for "official inviolability" in order to "perform" the duties of his office without "obstruction or impediment." As so read, Story's commentary does not explicitly define the contours of "official inviolability." But it does suggest that the "inviolability" is time bound ("while *** in the discharge of the duties of his office"); that it applies in private lawsuits (for it attaches to the President's "person" in "civil cases"); and that it is functional ("necessarily implied from the nature of the [President's] functions").

Since *Nixon* did not involve a physical constraint, the Court's reliance upon JUSTICE STORY's commentary makes clear, in the Court's view, that the commentary does not limit the scope of "inviolability" to an immunity from a physical imprisonment, physical detention, or physical "arrest"—a now abandoned procedure that permitted the arrest of certain civil case defendants (e.g., those threatened by bankruptcy) during a civil proceeding. ***

Second, during the first Congress, then-Vice President John Adams and then-Senator Oliver Ellsworth expressed a view of an applicable immunity far broader than any currently asserted. Speaking of a sitting President, they said that the "'President, personally, was not the subject to any process whatever ***. For [that] would *** put it in the power of a common justice to exercise any authority over him and stop the whole machine of Government.'"

They included in their claim a kind of immunity from criminal, as well as civil, process. *** This court's rejection of Adams' and Ellsworth's views in the context of criminal proceedings does not deprive those views of authority here. ***

Third, *** Jefferson, like Adams and Ellsworth, argued strongly for an immunity from both criminal and civil judicial process—an immunity greater in scope than any immunity, or any special scheduling factor, now at issue in the civil case before us. The significance of his views for present purposes lies in his conviction that the Constitution protected a sitting President from litigation that would "withdraw" a President from his current "constitutional duties." That concern may not have applied to Mr. Fitzgerald's 1982 case against a former President, but it is at issue in the current litigation.

Precedent that suggests to the contrary—that the Constitution does not offer a sitting President significant protections from potentially distracting civil litigation—consists of the following: (1) In several instances sitting Presidents have given depositions or testified at criminal trials, and (2) this Court has twice authorized the enforcement of subpoenas seeking documents from a sitting President for use in a criminal case. ***

The first set of precedents tells us little about what the Constitution commands, for they amount to voluntary actions on the part of a sitting President. The second set of precedents amounts to a search for documents, rather than a direct call upon Presidential time. More important, both sets of precedents involve criminal proceedings in which the President participated as a witness. Criminal proceedings, unlike private civil proceedings, are public acts initiated and controlled by the Executive Branch; they are not normally subject to postponement; and ordinarily they put at risk, not a private citizen's hope for monetary compensation, but a private citizen's freedom from enforced confinement. Nor is it normally possible in a criminal case, unlike many civil cases, to provide the plaintiff with interest to compensate for scheduling delay.

The remaining precedent to which the majority refers does not seem relevant in this case. That precedent, *Youngstown Sheet & Tube Co. v. Sawyer*, concerns official action. And any Presidential time spent dealing with, or action taken in response to, that kind of case is part of a President's official duties. Hence court review in such circumstances could not interfere with, or distract from, official duties. Insofar as a court orders a President, in any such a proceeding, to act or to refrain from action, it defines, or determines, or clarifies, the legal scope of an official duty. ***

Case law, particularly, *Nixon v. Fitzgerald*, strongly supports the principle that judges hearing a private civil damages action against a sitting President may not issue orders that could significantly distract a President from his official duties. In *Fitzgerald*, the Court held that former President Nixon was absolutely immune from civil damage lawsuits based upon any conduct within the "outer perimeter" of his official responsibilities. The holding rested upon six determinations that are relevant here.

First, the Court found that the Constitution assigns the President singularly important duties (thus warranting an "absolute," rather than a "qualified," immunity). Second, the Court held that "recognition of immunity" does not require a "specific textual basis" in the Constitution. Third, although physical constraint of the President was not at issue, the Court nevertheless considered JUSTICE STORY's constitutional analysis "persuasive." Fourth, the Court distinguished contrary precedent on the ground that it involved criminal, not civil, proceedings. Fifth, the Court's concerns encompassed the fact that "the sheer prominence of the President's office" could make him "an easily identifiable target for suits for civil damages." Sixth, and most important, the Court rested its conclusion in important part upon the fact that civil lawsuits "could distract a President from his public duties, to the detriment of not only the President and his office but also the Nation that the Presidency was designed to serve."

The majority argues that this critical, last-mentioned, feature of the case is dicta. *** The majority, however, overlooks the fact that *Fitzgerald* set forth a single immunity (an absolute immunity) applicable both to sitting and former Presidents. Its reasoning focused upon both. Its key paragraph, explaining why the President enjoys an absolute immunity rather than a qualified immunity, contains seven sentences, four of which focus primarily upon time and energy distraction and three of which focus primarily upon official decision distortion. *** The cases ultimately turn on an assessment that the threat that a civil damage lawsuit poses to a public official's ability to perform his job properly. And, whether they provide an absolute immunity, a qualified immunity, or merely a special procedure, they ultimately balance consequent potential public harm against private need. ***

III

The majority points to the fact that private plaintiffs have brought civil damage lawsuits against a sitting President only three times in our Nation's history; and it relies upon the threat of sanctions to discourage, and "the court's discretion" to manage, such actions so that "interference with the President's duties would not occur." I am less sanguine. Since 1960, when the last such suit was filed, the number of civil lawsuits filed annually in Federal District Courts has increased from under 60,000 to about 240,000 ***. And this Court has now made clear that such lawsuits may proceed against a sitting President. ***

I concede the possibility that district courts, supervised by the Courts of Appeals and perhaps this Court, might prove able to manage private civil damage actions against sitting Presidents without significantly interfering with the discharge of Presidential duties—at least if they manage those actions with the constitutional problem in mind. Nonetheless, predicting the future is difficult, and I am skeptical. Should the majority's optimism turn out to be misplaced, then, in my view, courts will have to develop administrative rules applicable to such cases (including postponement rules of the sort at issue in this case) in order to implement the basic constitutional directive. *** I agree with the majority's determination that a constitutional defense must await a more specific showing of need; I do not agree with what I believe to be an understatement of the "danger." And I believe that ordinary case-management principles are unlikely to prove sufficient to deal with private civil lawsuits for damages unless supplemented with a constitutionally based requirement that district courts schedule proceedings so as to avoid significant interference with the President's ongoing discharge of his official responsibilities.

IV

*** Yet, I agree with the majority that there is no automatic temporary immunity and that the President should have to provide the District Court with a reasoned explanation of why the immunity is needed; and I also agree that, in the absence of that explanation, the court's postponement of the trial date was premature. For those reasons, I concur in the result.

Notes

1. **Fallout.** Did the Supreme Court fail to understand the ramifications of its decision in *Clinton v. Jones*? Do you recall the role this decision played in President Clinton's being impeached by the House and tried by the Senate?

2. **Other Privileges?** Are the President's conversations with the First Spouse privileged? Consider whether Secret Service agents who guard the President should be immune from a subpoena by Paula Jones' lawyers requiring them to appear for depositions concerning extramarital sexual activity by the President during his time in the White House. What arguments would you make on both sides of this issue? Would your answer change if the subpoena came from the Office of Independent Counsel? If it came from a House committee considering the possibility of impeaching the President? If the request concerned not alleged sexual activities but alleged diversion of government money for personal use?

3. **Independent Counsels.** Do you support the appointment of independent counsels? Can you think of any alternative to independent counsels to control wrongdoing in the Executive Branch? Should independent counsels be appointed to deal with alleged wrongdoing by Members of Congress? To prosecute allegations involving Supreme Court Justices and other federal judges? Revisit these questions after reading *Morrison v. Olson, infra* p. 192.

C. LEGISLATIVE AUTHORITY

Until the New Deal era, it was generally assumed that Congress could not delegate lawmaking functions other than by establishing an "intelligible principle" by which others administering the law would thereafter be guided. The two cases which most exemplify this approach are *Panama Refining Co. v. Ryan*, 293 U.S. 388 (1935) (statute authorizing the President to prohibit interstate transportation of "hot oil" unconstitutionally delegated legislative powers since it provided no standards for the President to follow) and *A.L.A. Schechter Poultry Corp. v. United States*, 295 U.S. 495 (1935) (statute prohibiting "unfair competition" under "rules of competition deemed fair for each industry by representative members of that industry" unconstitutionally delegated legislative power). *Schechter* marks the last time the Supreme

Court invalidated a legislative delegation of authority; it has approved statutes commanding agencies to act "in the public interest," to outlaw "unreasonable risks," and so forth. Occasionally, various members of the Court have said that the possibility of unconstitutional delegation was a reason for construing a statute more narrowly, but the nondelegation doctrine has not been revived. See *Loving v. United States*, 517 U.S. 748 (1996), upholding a delegation that courts-martial "may, under such limitations as the President [as Commander-in-Chief] may prescribe, adjudge any punishment *** including the penalty of death."

In *Whitman v. American Trucking Associations, Inc.*, 531 U.S. 457 (2001), the Supreme Court rejected the argument that § 109(b)(1) of the Clean Air Act [setting "ambient air quality standards" allowing "an adequate margin of safety" "requisite to protect the public health"] unconstitutionally delegated legislative power to the Environmental Protection Agency. JUSTICE SCALIA explained for the majority:

> *** [W]e repeatedly have said that when Congress confers decisionmaking authority upon agencies Congress must "lay down by legislative act an intelligible principle to which the person or body authorized to [act] is directed to conform." *J.W. Hampton, Jr., & Co. v. United States*, 276 U.S. 394, 409 (1928). We have never suggested that an agency can cure an unlawful delegation of legislative power by adopting in its discretion a limiting construction of the statute. *** [T]he text of § 109(b)(1) of the CAA at a minimum requires that "[f]or a discrete set of pollutants and based on published air quality criteria that reflect the latest scientific knowledge, [the] EPA must establish uniform national standards at a level that is requisite to protect public health from the adverse effects of the pollutant in the ambient air." Requisite, in turn, "mean[s] sufficient, but not more than necessary." *** It is true enough that the degree of agency discretion that is acceptable varies according to the scope of the power congressionally conferred. *** But even in sweeping regulatory schemes we have never demanded, as the Court of Appeals did here, that statutes provide a "determinate criterion" for saying "how much [of the regulated harm] is too much." *** "[A] certain degree of discretion, and thus of lawmaking, inheres in most executive or judicial action." Section 109(b)(1) of the CAA, which to repeat we interpret as requiring the EPA to set air quality standards at the level that is "requisite"—that is, not lower or higher than is necessary—to protect the public health with an adequate margin of safety, fits comfortably within the scope of discretion permitted by our precedent. ***

If the Court were to revive the nondelegation doctrine, Congress would either have to leave more private activity unregulated or work much harder to specify more precise standards to cover the same territory as one broad standard. Less obviously, a consequence of the demise of the nondelegation doctrine has been Congress' search for ways to control the President and agencies to whom broad authority is delegated.

The following opinions concerning whether Congress has overreached its boundaries vis-a-vis the President seem inconsistent: some are highly formalistic exercises in definitions of constitutional terms; others seem more functional, focusing on whether Congress is intruding into the Executive branch's functions. Dissatisfaction with the Court's body of work in these cases has led some to suggest that the Court ought to simply stay out of the business of serving as referee for the two political branches and focus on individual rights matters. As you read the following cases, consider whether you agree with this assessment.

1. DOMESTIC AFFAIRS

INS v. CHADHA
462 U.S. 919, 103 S.Ct. 2764, 77 L.Ed.2d 317 (1983).

CHIEF JUSTICE BURGER delivered the opinion of the Court.

*** Chadha is an East Indian who was born in Kenya and holds a British passport. He was lawfully admitted to the United States in 1966 on a nonimmigrant student visa. His visa expired on June 30, 1972. On October 11, 1973, the District Director of the Immigration and Naturalization Service [INS] ordered Chadha to show cause why he should not be deported for having "remained in the United States for a longer time than permitted." [At] a deportation hearing *** before an immigration judge, *** Chadha conceded that he was deportable for overstaying his visa and the hearing was adjourned to enable him to file an application for suspension of deportation under [the Immigration and Nationality Act].

*** On the basis of evidence adduced at the hearing, affidavits submitted with the application, and the results of a character investigation conducted by the INS, the immigration judge ordered that Chadha's deportation be suspended. The immigration judge found that Chadha met the requirements of [an exception provided for in the Act]: he had resided continuously in the United States for over seven years, was of good moral character, and would suffer "extreme hardship" if deported. Pursuant to § 244(c)(1) of the Act, the immigration judge suspended Chadha's deportation and a report of the suspension was transmitted to Congress. [The Attorney General recommended that Chadha's deportation be suspended as provided for under the Act.] Once the recommendation for suspension of Chadha's deportation was conveyed to Congress, Congress had the power under § 244(c)(2) of the Act to veto the Attorney General's determination that Chadha should not be deported.

On December 12, 1975, Representative Eilberg, Chairman of the Judiciary Subcommittee on Immigration, Citizenship, and International Law, introduced a resolution opposing "the granting of permanent residence in the United States to [six] aliens", including Chadha. The resolution was referred to the House Committee on the Judiciary. On December 16, 1975, the resolution was discharged from further consideration by the House

Committee on the Judiciary and submitted to the House of Representatives for a vote. *** The resolution was passed without debate or recorded vote. Since the House action was pursuant to § 244(c)(2), the resolution was not treated as an Article I legislative act; it was not submitted to the Senate or presented to the President for his action.

After the House veto of the Attorney General's decision to allow Chadha to remain in the United States, the immigration judge reopened the deportation proceedings to implement the House order deporting Chadha. Chadha moved to terminate the proceedings on the ground that § 244(c)(2) is unconstitutional. The immigration judge held that he had no authority to rule on the constitutional validity of § 244(c)(2). On November 8, 1976, Chadha was ordered deported pursuant to the House action.

Chadha appealed the deportation order to the Board of Immigration Appeals again contending that § 244(c)(2) is unconstitutional. The Board held that it had "no power to declare unconstitutional an act of Congress" and Chadha's appeal was dismissed.

Pursuant to § 106(a) of the Act Chadha filed a petition for review of the deportation order in the United States Court of Appeals for the Ninth Circuit. The Immigration and Naturalization Service agreed with Chadha's position before the Court of Appeals and joined him in arguing that § 244(c)(2) is unconstitutional. After full briefing and oral argument, the Court of Appeals held that the House was without constitutional authority to order Chadha's deportation; accordingly it directed the Attorney General "to cease and desist from taking any steps to deport this alien based upon the resolution enacted by the House of Representatives." The essence of its holding was that § 244(c)(2) violates the constitutional doctrine of separation of powers.

We granted certiorari and we now affirm.

Before we address the important question of the constitutionality of the one-House veto provision of § 244(c)(2), we first consider several challenges to the authority of this Court to resolve the issue raised. [The Court determined, inter alia, that it had jurisdiction, that Chadha had standing, that the veto provision was severable for judicial purposes from the remainder of the Act, and that the issue was not a non-justiciable political question.]

*** We turn now to the question whether action of one House of Congress under § 244(c)(2) violates strictures of the Constitution. We begin, of course, with the presumption that the challenged statute is valid. Its wisdom is not the concern of the courts; if a challenged action does not violate the Constitution, it must be sustained.

*** By the same token, the fact that a given law or procedure is efficient, convenient, and useful in facilitating functions of government, standing alone, will not save it if it is contrary to the Constitution. Convenience and efficiency are not the primary objectives—or the hallmarks—of democratic government and our inquiry is sharpened rather than blunted by the fact that Congressional veto provisions are appearing with increasing frequency in statutes which delegate authority to executive and independent agencies:

"Since 1932, when the first veto provision was enacted into law, 295 congressional veto-type procedures have been inserted in 196 different statutes as follows: from 1932 to 1939, five statutes were affected; from 1940–49, nineteen statutes; between 1950–59, thirty-four statutes; and from 1960–69, forty-nine. From the year 1970 through 1975, at least one hundred sixty-three such provisions were included in eighty-nine laws."

JUSTICE WHITE undertakes to make a case for the proposition that the one-House veto is a useful "political invention," and we need not challenge that assertion. *** But policy arguments supporting even useful "political inventions" are subject to the demands of the Constitution which defines powers and, with respect to this subject, sets out just how those powers are to be exercised.

Explicit and unambiguous provisions of the Constitution prescribe and define the respective functions of the Congress and of the Executive in the legislative process. Art. I provides: "All legislative Powers herein granted shall be vested in a Congress of the United States, which shall consist of a Senate and a House of Representatives." Art. I, § 1. "Every Bill which shall have passed the House of Representatives and the Senate, shall, before it becomes a Law, be presented to the President of the United States; *** " Art. I, § 7, cl. 2. "Every Order, Resolution, or Vote to which the Concurrence of the Senate and House of Representatives may be necessary (except on a question of Adjournment) shall be presented to the President of the United States; and before the Same shall take Effect, shall be approved by him, or being disapproved by him, shall be repassed by two thirds of the Senate and House of Representatives, according to the Rules and Limitations prescribed in the Case of a Bill." Art. I, § 7, cl. 3. (Emphasis added).

These provisions of Art. I are integral parts of the constitutional design for the separation of powers. *** The very structure of the articles delegating and separating powers under Arts. I, II, and III exemplify the concept of separation of powers and we now turn to Art I. The records of the Constitutional Convention reveal that the requirement that all legislation be presented to the President before becoming law was uniformly accepted by the Framers. Presentment to the President and the Presidential veto were considered so imperative that the draftsmen took special pains to assure that these requirements could not be circumvented.

The decision to provide the President with a limited and qualified power to nullify proposed legislation by veto was based on the profound conviction of the Framers that the powers conferred on Congress were the powers to be most carefully circumscribed. It is beyond doubt that lawmaking was a power to be shared by both Houses and the President. *** The bicameral requirement of Art. I, §§ 1, 7 was of scarcely less concern to the Framers than was the Presidential veto and indeed the two concepts are interdependent. By providing that no law could take effect without the concurrence of the prescribed majority of the Members of both Houses, the Framers reemphasized their belief *** that legislation should not be enacted unless it has been carefully and fully considered by the Nation's elected officials.

*** We see therefore that the Framers were acutely conscious that the bicameral requirement and the Presentment Clauses would serve essential constitutional functions. *** It emerges clearly that the prescription for legislative action in Art. I, §§ 1, 7 represents the Framers' decision that the legislative power of the Federal government be exercised in accord with a single, finely wrought and exhaustively considered, procedure.

*** The Constitution sought to divide the delegated powers of the new federal government into three defined categories, legislative, executive and judicial, to assure, as nearly as possible, that each Branch of government would confine itself to its assigned responsibility. *** When any Branch acts, it is presumptively exercising the power the Constitution has delegated to it. When the Executive acts, it presumptively acts in an executive or administrative capacity as defined in Art. II. And when, as here, one House of Congress purports to act, it is presumptively acting within its assigned sphere.

Beginning with this presumption, we must nevertheless establish that the challenged action under § 244(c)(2) is of the kind to which the procedural requirements of Art. I, § 7 apply. Not every action taken by either House is subject to the bicameralism and presentment requirements of Art. I. Whether actions taken by either House are, in law and fact, an exercise of legislative power depends not on their form but upon "whether they contain matter which is properly to be regarded as legislative in its character and effect."

Examination of the action taken here by one House pursuant to § 244(c)(2) reveals that it was essentially legislative in purpose and effect. In purporting to exercise power defined in Art. I, § 8, cl. 4 to "establish an uniform Rule of Naturalization," the House took action that had the purpose and effect of altering the legal rights, duties and relations of persons, including the Attorney General, Executive Branch officials and Chadha, all outside the legislative branch. The one-House veto operated in this case to overrule the Attorney General and mandate Chadha's deportation; absent the House action, Chadha would remain in the United States. Congress has acted and its action has altered Chadha's status.

The legislative character of the one-House veto in this case is confirmed by the character of the Congressional action it supplants. Neither the House of Representatives nor the Senate contends that, absent the veto provision in § 244(c)(2), either of them, or both of them acting together, could effectively require the Attorney General to deport an alien once the Attorney General, in the exercise of legislatively delegated authority, had determined the alien should remain in the United States. Without the challenged provision in § 244(c)(2), this could have been achieved, if at all, only by legislation requiring deportation.

*** The nature of the decision implemented by the one-House veto in this case further manifests its legislative character. After long experience with the clumsy, time consuming private bill procedure, Congress made a deliberate choice to delegate to the Executive Branch, and specifically to the Attorney General, the authority to allow deportable aliens to remain in this country in certain specified circumstances. It is not disputed that this choice to delegate authority is precisely the kind of decision that can be implemented only in accordance with the procedures set out in Art. I. Disagreement with the Attorney General's decision on Chadha's deportation—that is, Congress' decision to deport Chadha—no less than Congress' original choice to delegate to the Attorney General the authority to make that decision, involves determinations of policy that Congress can implement in only one way; bicameral passage followed by presentment to the President. Congress must abide by its delegation of authority until that delegation is legislatively altered or revoked.

Finally, we see that when the Framers intended to authorize either House of Congress to act alone and outside of its prescribed bicameral legislative role, they narrowly and precisely defined the procedure for such action. There are but four provisions in the Constitution, explicit and unambiguous, by which one House may act alone with the unreviewable force of law, not subject to the President's veto:

(a) The House of Representatives alone was given the power to initiate impeachments. Art. I, § 2, cl. 6;

(b) The Senate alone was given the power to conduct trials following impeachment on charges initiated by the House and to convict following trial. Art. I, § 3, cl. 5;

(c) The Senate alone was given final unreviewable power to approve or to disapprove presidential appointments. Art. II, § 2, cl. 2;

(d) The Senate alone was given unreviewable power to ratify treaties negotiated by the President. Art. II, § 2, cl. 2.

Clearly, when the Draftsmen sought to confer special powers on one House, independent of the other House, or of the President, they did so in explicit, unambiguous terms. ***[21] The bicameral requirement, the Presentment Clauses, the President's veto, and Congress' power to override a veto were intended to erect enduring checks on each Branch and to protect

---

[21] JUSTICE POWELL's position is that the one-House veto in this case is a judicial act and therefore unconstitutional as beyond the authority vested in Congress by the Constitution. We agree that there is a sense in which one-House action pursuant to s 244(c)(2) has a judicial cast, since it purports to "review" Executive action. *** To be sure, it is normally up to the courts to decide whether an agency has complied with its statutory mandate. But the attempted analogy between judicial action and the one-House veto is less than perfect. Federal courts do not enjoy a roving mandate to correct alleged excesses of administrative agencies; we are limited by Art. III to hearing cases and controversies and no justiciable case or controversy was presented by the Attorney General's decision to allow Chadha to remain in this country. We are aware of no decision, and JUSTICE POWELL has cited none, where a federal court has reviewed a decision of the Attorney General suspending deportation of an alien pursuant to the standards set out in § 244(a)(1). This is not surprising, given that no party to such action has either the motivation or the right to appeal from it. As JUSTICE WHITE correctly notes, "the courts have not been given the authority to review whether an alien should be given permanent status; review is limited to whether the Attorney General has properly applied the statutory standards for" denying a request for suspension of deportation. Thus, JUSTICE POWELL's statement that the one-House veto in this case is "clearly adjudicatory," simply is not supported by his accompanying assertion that the House has "assumed a function ordinarily entrusted to the federal courts."

the people from the improvident exercise of power by mandating certain prescribed steps. To preserve those checks, and maintain the separation of powers, the carefully defined limits on the power of each Branch must not be eroded. To accomplish what has been attempted by one House of Congress in this case requires action in conformity with the express procedures of the Constitution's prescription for legislative action: passage by a majority of both Houses and presentment to the President.[22]

*** The choices we discern as having been made in the Constitutional Convention impose burdens on governmental processes that often seem clumsy, inefficient, even unworkable, but those hard choices were consciously made by men who had lived under a form of government that permitted arbitrary governmental acts to go unchecked. There is no support in the Constitution or decisions of this Court for the proposition that the cumbersomeness and delays often encountered in complying with explicit Constitutional standards may be avoided, either by the Congress or by the President. *See Youngstown Sheet & Tube Co. v. Sawyer*, 343 U.S. 579 (1952). With all the obvious flaws of delay, untidiness, and potential for abuse, we have not yet found a better way to preserve freedom than by making the exercise of power subject to the carefully crafted restraints spelled out in the Constitution.

We hold that the Congressional veto provision in § 244(c)(2) is severable from the Act and that it is unconstitutional. ***

JUSTICE POWELL, concurring in the judgment.

*** The Constitution does not establish three branches with precisely defined boundaries. *See Buckley v. Valeo*, 424 U.S. 1, 121 (1976) (per curiam). Rather, as JUSTICE JACKSON wrote, "[w]hile the Constitution diffuses power the better to secure liberty, it also contemplates that practice will integrate the dispersed powers into a workable government. It enjoins upon its branches separateness but interdependence, autonomy but reciprocity." *Youngstown Sheet & Tube Co. v. Sawyer*, 343 U.S. 579, 635 (1952) (concurring opinion). The Court thus has been mindful that the boundaries between each branch should be fixed "according to common sense and the inherent necessities of the governmental co-ordination."

*** On its face, the House's action appears clearly adjudicatory. The House did not enact a general rule; rather it made its own determination that

---

[22] Neither can we accept the suggestion that the one-House veto provision in § 244(c)(2) either removes or modifies the bicameralism and presentation requirements for the enactment of future legislation affecting aliens. JUSTICE WHITE suggests that the Attorney General's action under § 244(c)(1) suspending deportation is equivalent to a proposal for legislation and that because Congressional approval is indicated "by failure to veto, the one-House veto satisfies the requirement of bicameral approval." However, as the Court of Appeals noted, that approach "would analogize the effect of the one house disapproval to the failure of one house to vote affirmatively on a private bill." Even if it were clear that Congress entertained such an arcane theory when it enacted § 244(c)(2), which JUSTICE WHITE does not suggest, this would amount to nothing less than an amending of Art. I. The legislative steps outlined in Art. I are not empty formalities; they were designed to assure that both Houses of Congress and the President participate in the exercise of lawmaking authority.

six specific persons did not comply with certain statutory criteria. It thus undertook the type of decision that traditionally has been left to other branches. Even if the House did not make a de novo determination, but simply reviewed the Immigration and Naturalization Service's findings, it still assumed a function ordinarily entrusted to the federal courts.

*** The impropriety of the House's assumption of this function is confirmed by the fact that its action raises the very danger the Framers sought to avoid—the exercise of unchecked power. In deciding whether Chadha deserves to be deported, Congress is not subject to any internal constraints that prevent it from arbitrarily depriving him of the right to remain in this country. Unlike the judiciary or an administrative agency, Congress is not bound by established substantive rules. Nor is it subject to the procedural safeguards, such as the right to counsel and a hearing before an impartial tribunal, that are present when a court or an agency adjudicates individual rights. The only effective constraint on Congress' power is political, but Congress is most accountable politically when it prescribes rules of general applicability. When it decides rights of specific persons, those rights are subject to "the tyranny of a shifting majority." *** In my view, when Congress undertook to apply its rules to Chadha, it exceeded the scope of its constitutionally prescribed authority. I would not reach the broader question whether legislative vetoes are invalid under the Presentment Clauses.

JUSTICE WHITE, dissenting.

Today the Court not only invalidates § 244(c)(2) of the Immigration and Nationality Act, but also sounds the death knell for nearly 200 other statutory provisions in which Congress has reserved a "legislative veto." For this reason, the Court's decision is of surpassing importance. And it is for this reason that the Court would have been well-advised to decide the case, if possible, on the narrower grounds of separation of powers, leaving for full consideration the constitutionality of other congressional review statutes operating on such varied matters as war powers and agency rulemaking, some of which concern the independent regulatory agencies.

The prominence of the legislative veto mechanism in our contemporary political system and its importance to Congress can hardly be overstated. It has become a central means by which Congress secures the accountability of executive and independent agencies. Without the legislative veto, Congress is faced with a Hobson's choice: either to refrain from delegating the necessary authority, leaving itself with a hopeless task of writing laws with the requisite specificity to cover endless special circumstances across the entire policy landscape, or in the alternative, to abdicate its law-making function to the executive branch and independent agencies. To choose the former leaves major national problems unresolved; to opt for the latter risks unaccountable policymaking by those not elected to fill that role. Accordingly, over the past five decades, the legislative veto has been placed in nearly 200 statutes. The device is known in every field of governmental concern: reorganization, budgets, foreign affairs, war powers, and regulation of trade, safety, energy, the environment and the economy.

*** [A] brief review [of its history] suffices to demonstrate that the legislative veto is more than "efficient, convenient, and useful." It is an important if not indispensable political invention that allows the President and Congress to resolve major constitutional and policy differences, assures the accountability of independent regulatory agencies, and preserves Congress' control over lawmaking. Perhaps there are other means of accommodation and accountability, but the increasing reliance of Congress upon the legislative veto suggests that the alternatives to which Congress must now turn are not entirely satisfactory.

The history of the legislative veto also makes clear that it has not been a sword with which Congress has struck out to aggrandize itself at the expense of the other branches—the concerns of Madison and Hamilton. Rather, the veto has been a means of defense, a reservation of ultimate authority necessary if Congress is to fulfill its designated role under Article I as the nation's lawmaker. While the President has often objected to particular legislative vetoes, generally those left in the hands of congressional committees, the Executive has more often agreed to legislative review as the price for a broad delegation of authority. To be sure, the President may have preferred unrestricted power, but that could be precisely why Congress thought it essential to retain a check on the exercise of delegated authority.

*** The Constitution does not directly authorize or prohibit the legislative veto. Thus, our task should be to determine whether the legislative veto is consistent with the purposes of Art. I and the principles of Separation of Powers which are reflected in that Article and throughout the Constitution. We should not find the lack of a specific constitutional authorization for the legislative veto surprising, and I would not infer disapproval of the mechanism from its absence. From the summer of 1787 to the present the government of the United States has become an endeavor far beyond the contemplation of the Framers. Only within the last half century has the complexity and size of the Federal Government's responsibilities grown so greatly that the Congress must rely on the legislative veto as the most effective if not the only means to insure their role as the nation's lawmakers. But the wisdom of the Framers was to anticipate that the nation would grow and new problems of governance would require different solutions. Accordingly, our Federal Government was intentionally chartered with the flexibility to respond to contemporary needs without losing sight of fundamental democratic principles. *** I do not dispute the Court's truismatic exposition of the[ ] clauses [of Article I]. There is no question that a bill does not become a law until it is approved by both the House and the Senate, and presented to the President. Similarly, I would not hesitate to strike an action of Congress in the form of a concurrent resolution which constituted an exercise of original lawmaking authority. I agree with the Court that the President's qualified veto power is a critical element in the distribution of powers under the Constitution, widely endorsed among the Framers, and intended to serve the President as a defense against legislative encroachment and to check the "passing of bad laws through haste, inadvertence, or design." The Federalist No. 73 (A. Hamilton). The records of the Convention reveal that it is the first purpose which figured most prominently but I acknowledge the vitality of the second. I also agree that the bicameral approval required by Art. I, §§ 1, 7 "was of scarcely less concern to the Framers than was the Presidential veto," and that the need to divide and disperse legislative power figures significantly in our scheme of Government. All of this, the Third Part of the Court's opinion, is entirely unexceptionable.

[Presentment and bicameralism do] not, however, answer the constitutional question before us. The power to exercise a legislative veto is not the power to write new law without bicameral approval or presidential consideration. The veto must be authorized by statute and may only negative what an Executive department or independent agency has proposed. On its face, the legislative veto no more allows one House of Congress to make law than does the presidential veto confer such power upon the President. Accordingly, the Court properly recognizes that it "must establish that the challenged action under § 244(c)(2) is of the kind to which the procedural requirements of Art. I, § 7 apply" and admits that "not every action taken by either House is subject to the bicameralism and presentation requirements of Art. I."

The terms of the Presentment Clauses suggest only that bills and their equivalent are subject to the requirements of bicameral passage and presentment to the President. *** Although the Clause does not specify the actions for which the concurrence of both Houses is "necessary," the proceedings at the Philadelphia Convention suggest its purpose was to prevent Congress from circumventing the presentation requirement in the making of new legislation. ***

When the Convention [turned] its attention to the scope of Congress' lawmaking power, the Framers were expansive. The Necessary and Proper Clause, Art. I, § 8, cl. 18, vests Congress with the power "to make all laws which shall be necessary and proper for carrying into Execution the foregoing Powers [the enumerated powers of § 8], and all other Powers vested by this Constitution in the government of the United States, or in any Department or Officer thereof." It is long-settled that Congress may "exercise its best judgment in the selection of measures, to carry into execution the constitutional powers of the government," and "avail itself of experience, to exercise its reason, and to accommodate its legislation to circumstances." *McCulloch v. Maryland*, 4 Wheat. 316 (1819).

The Court heeded this counsel in approving the modern administrative state. The Court's holding today that all legislative-type action must be enacted through the lawmaking process ignores that legislative authority is routinely delegated to the Executive branch, to the independent regulatory agencies, and to private individuals and groups. "The rise of administrative bodies probably has been the most significant legal trend of the last century. *** They have become a veritable fourth branch of the Government, which has deranged our three-branch legal theories ***." *Federal Trade Commission v. Ruberoid Co.*, 343 U.S. 470 (1952) (JACKSON, J. dissenting).

This Court's decisions sanctioning such delegations make clear that Article I does not require all action with the effect of legislation to be passed as a law.

Theoretically, agencies and officials were asked only to "fill up the details," and the rule was that "Congress cannot delegate any part of its legislative power except under a limitation of a prescribed standard." *** In practice, however, restrictions on the scope of the power that could be delegated diminished and all but disappeared.

*** The wisdom and the constitutionality of these broad delegations are matters that still have not been put to rest. But for present purposes, these cases establish that by virtue of congressional delegation, legislative power can be exercised by independent agencies and Executive departments without the passage of new legislation. For some time, the sheer amount of law—the substantive rules that regulate private conduct and direct the operation of government—made by the agencies has far outnumbered the lawmaking engaged in by Congress through the traditional process. There is no question but that agency rulemaking is lawmaking in any functional or realistic sense of the term.

*** If Congress may delegate lawmaking power to independent and executive agencies, it is most difficult to understand Article I as forbidding Congress from also reserving a check on legislative power for itself. Absent the veto, the agencies receiving delegations of legislative or quasi-legislative power may issue regulations having the force of law without bicameral approval and without the President's signature. It is thus not apparent why the reservation of a veto over the exercise of that legislative power must be subject to a more exacting test. In both cases, it is enough that the initial statutory authorizations comply with the Article I requirements.

Nor are there strict limits on the agents that may receive such delegations of legislative authority so that it might be said that the legislature can delegate authority to others but not to itself. While most authority to issue rules and regulations is given to the executive branch and the independent regulatory agencies, statutory delegations to private persons have also passed this Court's scrutiny.

*** More fundamentally, even if the Court correctly characterizes the Attorney General's authority under § 244 as an Article II Executive power, the Court concedes that certain administrative agency action, such as rulemaking, "may resemble lawmaking" and recognizes that "[t]his Court has referred to agency activity as being 'quasi-legislative' in character. *Humphrey's Executor v. United States*, 295 U.S. 602, 628 (1935)." Such rules and adjudications by the agencies meet the Court's own definition of legislative action for they "alter *** the legal rights, duties, and relations of persons *** outside the legislative branch," and involve "determinations of policy." Under the Court's analysis, the Executive Branch and the independent agencies may make rules with the effect of law while Congress, in whom the Framers confided the legislative power, Art. I, § 1, may not exercise a veto which precludes such rules from having operative force. If the effective functioning of a complex modern government requires the delegation of vast authority which, by virtue of its breadth, is legislative or "quasi-legislative" in character, I cannot accept that Article I—which is, after all, the source of the non-delegation doctrine—should forbid Congress from qualifying that grant with a legislative veto.

The Court also takes no account of perhaps the most relevant consideration: However resolutions of disapproval under § 244(c)(2) are formally characterized, in reality, a departure from the status quo occurs only upon the concurrence of opinion among the House, Senate, and President. Reservations of legislative authority to be exercised by Congress should be upheld if the exercise of such reserved authority is consistent with the distribution of and limits upon legislative power that Article I provides.

*** [T]he history of the separation of powers doctrine is *** a history of accommodation and practicality. Apprehensions of an overly powerful branch have not led to undue prophylactic measures that handicap the effective working of the national government as a whole. The Constitution does not contemplate total separation of the three branches of Government. ***

The legislative veto provision does not "prevent the Executive Branch from accomplishing its constitutionally assigned functions." First, it is clear that the Executive Branch has no "constitutionally assigned" function of suspending the deportation of aliens. "'Over no conceivable subject is the legislative power of Congress more complete than it is over' the admission of aliens." *** Moreover, the Court believes that the legislative veto we consider today is best characterized as an exercise of legislative or quasi-legislative authority. Under this characterization, the practice does not, even on the surface, constitute an infringement of executive or judicial prerogative. The Attorney General's suspension of deportation is equivalent to a proposal for legislation. The nature of the Attorney General's role as recommendatory is not altered because § 244 provides for congressional action through disapproval rather than by ratification. In comparison to private bills, which must be initiated in the Congress and which allow a Presidential veto to be overriden by a two-thirds majority in both Houses of Congress, § 244 augments rather than reduces the executive branch's authority. So understood, congressional review does not undermine, as the Court of Appeals thought, the "weight and dignity" that attends the decisions of the Executive Branch.

Nor does § 244 infringe on the judicial power, as JUSTICE POWELL would hold. Section 244 makes clear that Congress has reserved its own judgment as part of the statutory process. Congressional action does not substitute for judicial review of the Attorney General's decisions. The Act provides for judicial review of the refusal of the Attorney General to suspend a deportation and to transmit a recommendation to Congress.

*** I do not suggest that all legislative vetoes are necessarily consistent with separation of powers principles. A legislative check on an inherently executive function, for example that of initiating prosecutions, poses an entirely different question. But the legislative veto device here—and in many other settings—is far from an instance of legislative tyranny over the Executive. It is a necessary check on the unavoidably expanding power of the agencies, both executive and independent, as they engage in exercising authority delegated by Congress.

*** [The Court's holding] reflects a profoundly different conception of the Constitution than that held by the Courts which sanctioned the modern administrative state. Today's decision strikes down in one fell swoop provisions in more laws enacted by Congress than the Court has cumulatively invalidated in its history. I fear it will now be more difficult "to insure that the fundamental policy decisions in our society will be made not by an appointed official but by the body immediately responsible to the people," *Arizona v. California*, 373 U.S. 546, 626 (1963) (HARLAN, J., dissenting). I must dissent.

JUSTICE REHNQUIST, with whom JUSTICE WHITE joins, dissenting [on the ground that § 244(c) was not severable]. [omitted]

Notes

1. **Theory.** Consider the extent to which constitutional text provides guidance in *Chadha.* Do legislative vetoes involve legislative encroachment on the executive branch? Should the President be deemed to have waived objections to such encroachment when he (or a predecessor) signs into law a bill containing a legislative veto?

2. **Scope of *Chadha.*** Does the case invalidate all legislative vetoes? Only "one-house" vetoes? Only committee-driven legislative vetoes? Only "adjudicatory" exercises of the legislative veto?

3. **Questions.** What effect, if any, do you see of *Chadha* on (a) congressional oversight processes where legislation is not forthcoming, or even contemplated, but Congress wants to deter executive action by increasing the visibility of disfavored decisions, (b) requirements that rules be submitted to Congress before they become final to allow Congress to legislate, and (c) automatic "sunset" legislation whereby agencies disappear if not reauthorized by new legislation?

BOWSHER v. SYNAR
478 U.S. 714, 106 S.Ct. 3181, 92 L.Ed.2d 583 (1986).

CHIEF JUSTICE BURGER delivered the opinion of the Court.

The question presented by these appeals is whether the assignment by Congress to the Comptroller General of the United States of certain functions under the Balanced Budget and Emergency Deficit Control Act of 1985 violates the doctrine of separation of powers.

On December 12, 1985, the President signed into law the Balanced Budget and Emergency Deficit Control Act of 1985, popularly known as the "Gramm-Rudman–Hollings Act." The purpose of the Act is to eliminate the federal budget deficit. To that end, the Act sets a "maximum deficit amount" for federal spending for each of fiscal years 1986 through 1991. The size of that maximum deficit amount progressively reduces to zero in fiscal year

1991. If in any fiscal year the federal budget deficit exceeds the maximum deficit amount by more than a specified sum, the Act requires across-the-board cuts in federal spending to reach the targeted deficit level, with half of the cuts made to defense programs and the other half made to nondefense programs.

These "automatic" reductions are accomplished through a rather complicated procedure, spelled out in § 251, the so-called "reporting provisions" of the Act. Each year, the Directors of the Office of Management and Budget (OMB) and the Congressional Budget Office (CBO) independently estimate the amount of the federal budget deficit for the upcoming fiscal year. If that deficit exceeds the maximum targeted deficit amount for that fiscal year by more than a specified amount, the Directors of OMB and CBO independently calculate, on a program-by-program basis, the budget reductions necessary to ensure that the deficit does not exceed the maximum deficit amount. The Act then requires the Directors to report jointly their deficit estimates and budget reduction calculations to the Comptroller General.

The Comptroller General, after reviewing the Directors' reports, then reports his conclusions to the President. § 251(b). The President in turn must issue a "sequestration" order mandating the spending reductions specified by the Comptroller General. There follows a period during which Congress may by legislation reduce spending to obviate, in whole or in part, the need for the sequestration order. If such reductions are not enacted, the sequestration order becomes effective and the spending reductions included in that order are made.

Anticipating constitutional challenge to these procedures, the Act also contains a "fallback" deficit reduction process to take effect "[i]n the event that any of the reporting procedures described in section 251 are invalidated." Under these provisions, the report prepared by the Directors of OMB and the CBO is submitted directly to a specially created Temporary Joint Committee on Deficit Reduction, which must report in five days to both Houses a joint resolution setting forth the content of the Directors' report. Congress then must vote on the resolution under special rules, which render amendments out of order. If the resolution is passed and signed by the President, it then serves as the basis for a Presidential sequestration order.

Within hours of the President's signing of the Act, Congressman Synar, who had voted against the Act, filed a complaint seeking declaratory relief that the Act was unconstitutional. Eleven other Members later joined Congressman Synar's suit. A virtually identical lawsuit was also filed by the National Treasury Employees Union. The Union alleged that its members had been injured as a result of the Act's automatic spending reduction provisions, which have suspended certain cost-of-living benefit increases to the Union's members.

*** [T]he District Court *** held that the role of the Comptroller General in the deficit reduction process violated the constitutionally imposed separation of powers. The court explained that the Comptroller General exercises executive functions under the Act. However, the Comptroller General, while appointed by the President with the advice and consent of the Senate, is removable not by the President but only by a joint resolution of Congress or by impeachment. The District Court reasoned that this arrangement could not be sustained [because] Congress may not retain the power of removal over an officer performing executive functions. The congressional removal power created a "here-and-now subservience" of the Comptroller General to Congress.

[Appeal was taken directly to the Supreme Court as provided in the Act.]

*** The Constitution does not contemplate an active role for Congress in the supervision of officers charged with the execution of the laws it enacts. The President appoints "Officers of the United States" with the "Advice and Consent of the Senate. *** " Art. II, § 2. Once the appointment has been made and confirmed, however, the Constitution explicitly provides for removal of Officers of the United States by Congress only upon impeachment by the House of Representatives and conviction by the Senate. ***

This Court first directly addressed this issue in *Myers v. United States*, 272 U.S. 52 (1926). At issue in Myers was a statute providing that certain postmasters could be removed only "by and with the advice and consent of the Senate." The President removed one such Postmaster without Senate approval, and a lawsuit ensued. CHIEF JUSTICE TAFT, writing for the Court, declared the statute unconstitutional on the ground that for Congress to "draw to itself, or to either branch of it, the power to remove or the right to participate in the exercise of that power *** would be *** to infringe the constitutional principle of the separation of governmental powers."

A decade later, in *Humphrey's Executor v. United States*, 295 U.S. 602 (1935), relied upon heavily by appellants, a Federal Trade Commissioner who had been removed by the President sought backpay. *Humphrey's Executor* involved an issue not presented either in the *Myers* case or in this case—i.e., the power of Congress to limit the President's powers of removal of a Federal Trade Commissioner. The relevant statute permitted removal "by the President," but only "for inefficiency, neglect of duty, or malfeasance in office." JUSTICE SUTHERLAND, speaking for the Court, upheld the statute, holding that "illimitable power of removal is not possessed by the President [with respect to Federal Trade Commissioners]." The Court distinguished *Myers*, reaffirming its holding that congressional participation in the removal of executive officers is unconstitutional.

*** In light of these precedents, we conclude that Congress cannot reserve for itself the power of removal of an officer charged with the execution of the laws except by impeachment. To permit the execution of the laws to be vested in an officer answerable only to Congress would, in practical terms, reserve in Congress control over the execution of the laws. The structure of the Constitution does not permit Congress to execute the laws; it follows that Congress cannot grant to an officer under its control what it does not possess.

*** Appellants urge that the Comptroller General performs his duties independently and is not subservient to Congress. We agree with the District Court that this contention does not bear close scrutiny.

III–3. "Another Boundary Dispute" by Walter J. Enright. Appeared in the *Evening World*, ca. 1929–30.

*** The [Budget and Accounting Act of 1921] permits removal [of the Comptroller General] for "inefficiency," "neglect of duty," or "malfeasance." These terms are very broad and, as interpreted by Congress, could sustain removal of a Comptroller General for any number of actual or perceived transgressions of the legislative will. The Constitutional Convention chose to permit impeachment of executive officers only for "Treason, Bribery, or other high Crimes and Misdemeanors." It rejected language that would have permitted impeachment for "maladministration," with Madison arguing that "[s]o vague a term will be equivalent to a tenure during pleasure of the Senate."

*** [Further,] [i]t is clear that Congress has consistently viewed the Comptroller General as an officer of the Legislative Branch. The Reorganization Acts of 1945 and 1949, for example, both stated that the Comptroller General and the [General Accounting Office] are "a part of the legislative branch of the Government." Similarly, in the Accounting and Auditing Act of 1950, Congress required the Comptroller General to conduct audits "as an agent of the Congress."

Over the years, the Comptrollers General have also viewed themselves as part of the Legislative Branch. In one of the early Annual Reports of Comptroller General, the official seal of his office was described as reflecting "the independence of judgment to be exercised by the General Accounting Office, subject to the control of the legislative branch. *** The combination represents an agency of the Congress independent of other authority auditing and checking the expenditures of the Government as required by law and subjecting any questions arising in that connection to quasi-judicial determination."

*** Against this background, we see no escape from the conclusion that, because Congress has retained removal authority over the Comptroller General, he may not be entrusted with executive powers. The remaining question is whether the Comptroller General has been assigned such powers in the Balanced Budget and Emergency Deficit Control Act of 1985.

*** Appellants suggest that the duties assigned to the Comptroller General in the Act are essentially ministerial and mechanical so that their performance does not constitute "execution of the law" in a meaningful sense. On the contrary, we view these functions as plainly entailing execution of the law in constitutional terms. Interpreting a law enacted by Congress to implement the legislative mandate is the very essence of "execution" of the law. Under § 251, the Comptroller General must exercise judgment concerning facts that affect the application of the Act. He must also interpret the provisions of the Act to determine precisely what budgetary calculations are required. Decisions of that kind are typically made by officers charged with executing a statute.

The executive nature of the Comptroller General's functions under the Act is revealed in § 252(a)(3) which gives the Comptroller General the ultimate authority to determine the budget cuts to be made. Indeed, the Comptroller General commands the President himself to carry out, without the slightest variation (with exceptions not relevant to the constitutional issues presented), the directive of the Comptroller General as to the budget reductions.

*** Congress of course initially determined the content of the Balanced Budget and Emergency Deficit Control Act; and undoubtedly the content of the Act determines the nature of the executive duty. However, as *Chadha* makes clear, once Congress makes its choice in enacting legislation, its participation ends. Congress can thereafter control the execution of its enactment only indirectly—by passing new legislation. By placing the responsibility for execution of the Balanced Budget and Emergency Deficit Control Act in the hands of an officer who is subject to removal only by itself, Congress in effect has retained control over the execution of the Act and has intruded into the executive function. The Constitution does not permit such intrusion.

*** No one can doubt that Congress and the President are confronted with fiscal and economic problems of unprecedented magnitude, but "the fact that a given law or procedure is efficient, convenient, and useful in facilitating functions of government, standing alone, will not save it if it is contrary to the Constitution. Convenience and efficiency are not the primary objectives—or the hallmarks—of democratic government. *** " *Chadha*, supra, 462 U.S., at 944.

We conclude that the District Court correctly held that the powers vested in the Comptroller General under § 251 violate the command of the Constitution that the Congress play no direct role in the execution of the laws. ***

JUSTICE STEVENS, with whom JUSTICE MARSHALL joins, concurring in the judgment.

*** I agree with the Court that the "Gramm–Rudman–Hollings" Act contains a constitutional infirmity so severe that the flawed provision may not stand. I disagree with the Court, however, on the reasons why the Constitution prohibits the Comptroller General from exercising the powers assigned to him by § 251(b) and § 251(c)(2) of the Act. It is not the dormant, carefully circumscribed congressional removal power that represents the primary constitutional evil. Nor do I agree with the conclusion of both the majority and the dissent that the analysis depends on a labeling of the functions assigned to the Comptroller General as "executive powers." Rather, I am convinced that the Comptroller General must be characterized as an agent of Congress because of his longstanding statutory responsibilities; that the powers assigned to him under the Gramm–Rudman–Hollings Act require him to make policy that will bind the Nation; and that, when Congress, or a component or an agent of Congress, seeks to make policy that will bind the Nation, it must follow the procedures mandated by Article I of the Constitution—through passage by both Houses and presentment to the President. In short, Congress may not exercise its fundamental power to formulate national policy by delegating that power to one of its two Houses, to a legislative committee, or to an individual agent of the Congress such as the Speaker of the House of Representatives, the Sergeant at Arms of the Senate, or the Director of the Congressional Budget Office. That principle, I believe, is applicable to the Comptroller General.

*** The Court concludes that the Gramm–Rudman–Hollings Act impermissibly assigns the Comptroller General "executive powers." JUSTICE WHITE's dissent agrees that "the powers exercised by the Comptroller under the Act may be characterized as 'executive' in that they involve the interpretation and carrying out of the Act's mandate." This conclusion is not only far from obvious but also rests on the unstated and unsound premise that there is a definite line that distinguishes executive power from legislative power.

*** The powers delegated to the Comptroller General by § 251 of the Act before us today have a *** chameleon-like quality. The District Court persuasively explained why they may be appropriately characterized as executive powers. But, when that delegation is held invalid, the "fallback provision" provides that the report that would otherwise be issued by the Comptroller General shall be issued by Congress itself. In the event that the resolution is enacted, the congressional report will have the same legal consequences as if it had been issued by the Comptroller General. In that event, moreover, surely no one would suggest that Congress had acted in any capacity other than "legislative."

*** Under the *** analysis adopted by the majority today, it would therefore appear that the function at issue is "executive" if performed by the Comptroller General but "legislative" if performed by the Congress. In my view, however, the function may appropriately be labeled "legislative" even if performed by the Comptroller General or by an executive agency.

Despite the statement in Article I of the Constitution that "All legislative Powers herein granted shall be vested in a Congress of the United States," it is far from novel to acknowledge that independent agencies do indeed exercise legislative powers. As JUSTICE WHITE explained in his *Chadha* dissent, after reviewing our cases upholding broad delegations of legislative power: "[T]hese cases establish that by virtue of congressional delegation, legislative power can be exercised by independent agencies and Executive departments without the passage of new legislation."

*** Thus, I do not agree that the Comptroller General's responsibilities under the Gramm–Rudman–Hollings Act must be termed "executive powers," or even that our inquiry is much advanced by using that term. For, whatever the label given the functions to be performed by the Comptroller General under § 251—or by the Congress under [the fallback provisions]—the District Court had no difficulty in concluding that Congress could delegate the performance of those functions to another branch of the Government. If the delegation to a stranger is permissible, why may not Congress delegate the same responsibilities to one of its own agents? That is the central question before us today.

*** The Gramm–Rudman–Hollings Act assigns to the Comptroller General the duty to make policy decisions that have the force of law. *** Article I of the Constitution specifies the procedures that Congress must follow when it makes policy that binds the Nation: its legislation must be approved by both of its Houses and presented to the President. ***

In my opinion, Congress itself could not exercise the [Act's] functions through a concurrent resolution. The fact that the fallback provision *** requires a joint resolution indicates that Congress [agrees]. I think it equally clear that Congress may not simply delegate those functions to an agent ***. Since I am persuaded that the Comptroller General is *** an agent of Congress, he too cannot exercise such functions. In short, even though it is well settled that Congress may delegate legislative power to independent agencies or to the Executive, and thereby divest itself of a portion of its lawmaking power, when it elects to exercise such power itself, it may not authorize a lesser representative of the Legislative Branch to act on its behalf. It is for this reason that I believe § 251(b) and § 251(c)(2) of the Act are unconstitutional. ***

JUSTICE WHITE, dissenting.

The Court, acting in the name of separation of powers, takes upon itself to strike down the Gramm–Rudman–Hollings Act, one of the most novel and far-reaching legislative responses to a national crisis since the New Deal. The basis of the Court's action is a solitary provision of another statute that was passed over 60 years ago and has lain dormant since that time. I cannot concur in the Court's action. Like the Court, I will not purport to speak to the wisdom of the policies incorporated in the legislation the Court invalidates; that is a matter for the Congress and the Executive, both of which expressed their assent to the statute barely half a year ago. I will, however, address the wisdom of the Court's willingness to interpose its distressingly formalistic view of separation of powers as a bar to the attainment of governmental objectives through the means chosen by the Congress and the President in the legislative process established by the Constitution. *** The Court's decision rests on a feature of the legislative scheme that is of minimal practical significance and that presents no substantial threat to the basic scheme of separation of powers. In attaching dispositive significance to what should be regarded as a triviality, the Court neglects what has in the past been recognized as a fundamental principle governing consideration of disputes over separation of powers: "The actual art of governing under our Constitution does not and cannot conform to judicial definitions of the power of any of its branches based on isolated clauses or even single Articles torn from context. While the Constitution diffuses power the better to secure liberty, it also contemplates that practice will integrate the dispersed powers into a workable government." *Youngstown Sheet & Tube Co. v. Sawyer*, 343 U.S. 579, 635 (1952) (JACKSON, J., concurring).

Before examining the merits of the Court's argument, I wish to emphasize what it is that the Court quite pointedly and correctly does not hold: namely, that "executive" powers of the sort granted the Comptroller by the Act may only be exercised by officers removable at will by the President. *** In an earlier day, in which simpler notions of the role of government in society prevailed, it was perhaps plausible to insist that all "executive" officers be subject to an unqualified Presidential removal power, *see Myers v. United States*, 272 U.S. 52 (1926); but with the advent and triumph of the administrative state and the accompanying multiplication of the tasks undertaken by the Federal Government, the Court has been virtually compelled to recognize that Congress may reasonably deem it "necessary and proper" to vest some among the broad new array of governmental functions in officers who are free from the partisanship that may be expected of agents wholly dependent upon the President.

The Court's recognition of the legitimacy of legislation vesting "executive" authority in officers independent of the President does not imply derogation of the President's own constitutional authority—indeed, duty—to "take Care that the Laws be faithfully executed," Art. II, § 3, for any such duty is necessarily limited to a great extent by the content of the laws enacted by the Congress. *** [T]here are undoubtedly executive functions that, regardless of the enactments of Congress, must be performed by officers subject to removal at will by the President. Whether a particular function falls within this class or within the far larger class that may be relegated to independent officers "will depend upon the character of the office." *Humphrey's Executor*, supra, 295 U.S., at 631.

*** It is evident (and nothing in the Court's opinion is to the contrary) that the powers exercised by the Comptroller General under the Gramm–Rudman–Hollings Act are not such that vesting them in an officer not subject to removal at will by the President would in itself improperly interfere with Presidential powers. Determining the level of spending by the Federal Government is not by nature a function central either to the exercise of the President's enumerated powers or to his general duty to ensure execution of the laws; rather, appropriating funds is a peculiarly legislative function.

*** [T]he question remains whether, as the Court concludes, the fact that the officer to whom Congress has delegated the authority to implement the Act is removable by a joint resolution of Congress should require invalidation of the Act. *** I have no quarrel with the proposition that the powers exercised by the Comptroller under the Act may be characterized as "executive" in that they involve the interpretation and carrying out of the Act's mandate. I can also accept the general proposition that although Congress has considerable authority in designating the officers who are to execute legislation the constitutional scheme of separated powers does prevent Congress from reserving an executive role for itself or for its "agents." *Buckley v. Valeo*, 424 U.S., at 120–141 (WHITE, J., concurring in part and dissenting in part). I cannot accept, however, that the exercise of authority by an officer removable for cause by a joint resolution of Congress is analogous to the impermissible execution of the law by Congress itself, nor would I hold that the congressional role in the removal process renders the Comptroller an "agent" of the Congress, incapable of receiving "executive" power.

*** The deficiencies in the Court's reasoning are apparent. First, the Court baldly mischaracterizes the removal provision when it suggests that it allows Congress to remove the Comptroller for "executing the laws in any fashion found to be unsatisfactory"; in fact, Congress may remove the Comptroller only for one or more of five specified reasons, which "although not so narrow as to deny Congress any leeway, circumscribe Congress' power to some extent by providing a basis for judicial review of congressional removal." Second, and more to the point, the Court overlooks or deliberately ignores the decisive difference between the congressional removal provision and the legislative veto struck down in *Chadha*: under the Budget and Accounting Act, Congress may remove the Comptroller only through a joint resolution, which by definition must be passed by both Houses and signed by the President. *See United States v. California*, 332 U.S. 19, 28 (1947). In other words, a removal of the Comptroller under the statute satisfies the requirements of bicameralism and presentment laid down in *Chadha*. The majority's citation of *Chadha* for the proposition that Congress may only control the acts of officers of the United States "by passing new legislation" in no sense casts doubt on the legitimacy of the removal provision, for that provision allows Congress to effect removal only through action that constitutes legislation as defined in *Chadha*.

*** That such action may represent a more or less successful attempt by Congress to "control" the actions of an officer of the United States surely does not in itself indicate that it is unconstitutional, for no one would dispute that Congress has the power to "control" administration through legislation imposing duties or substantive restraints on executive officers, through legislation increasing or decreasing the funds made available to such officers, or through legislation actually abolishing a particular office. Indeed, *Chadha* expressly recognizes that while congressional meddling with administration of the laws outside of the legislative process is impermissible, congressional control over executive officers exercised through the legislative process is valid.

*** The practical result of the removal provision is not to render the Comptroller unduly dependent upon or subservient to Congress, but to render him one of the most independent officers in the entire federal establishment. Those who have studied the office agree that the procedural and substantive limits on the power of Congress and the President to remove the Comptroller make dislodging him against his will practically impossible.

*** The majority's contrary conclusion rests on the rigid dogma that, outside of the impeachment process, any "direct congressional role in the removal of officers charged with the execution of the laws *** is inconsistent with separation of powers." Reliance on such an unyielding principle to strike down a statute posing no real danger of aggrandizement of congressional power is extremely misguided and insensitive to our constitutional role. The wisdom of vesting "executive" powers in an officer removable by joint resolution may indeed be debatable—as may be the wisdom of the entire scheme of permitting an unelected official to revise the budget enacted by Congress—but such matters are for the most part to be worked out between the Congress and the President through the legislative process, which affords each branch ample opportunity to defend its interests. The Act vesting budget-cutting authority in the Comptroller General represents Congress' judgment that the delegation of such authority to counteract ever-mounting deficits is "necessary and proper" to the exercise of the powers granted the Federal Government by the Constitution; and the President's approval of the statute signifies his unwillingness to reject the choice made by Congress. Under such circumstances, the role of this Court should be limited to determining whether the Act so alters the balance of authority among the branches of government as to pose a genuine threat to the basic division between the lawmaking power and the power to execute the law. Because I see no such threat, I cannot join the Court in striking down the Act.

I dissent.

JUSTICE BLACKMUN, dissenting. [omitted]

Notes

1. **Background Cases.** *Bowsher* discusses two cases, *Myers* and *Humphrey's Executor*, which involve congressional limits on the President's removal of officials. In *Myers*, a majority of the Court found congressional limits on the

President's removal of a postmaster unconstitutional, stating variously that removal was an executive act, that the President (not his subordinates) has a duty to "take Care" to enforce the law, and that Article II vests all executive power in the President. The dissenters (including JUSTICE HOLMES) thought that because Congress had created the office, it could "prescribe a term of life to it free from any interference." In *Humphrey's Executor*, along with *Wiener v. United States*, 357 U.S. 349 (1958), the Court concluded that Congress could limit the President's removal of members of regulatory agencies. In *Humphrey's Executor*, the Court said the Federal Trade Commission, since it was created to effectuate Congressional policies, was not "in any proper sense" "an arm or an eye of the executive." *Wiener* held that the War Claims Commission's adjudicatory nature implied a limit on the President's removal power. Another pre-*Bowsher* case, *Buckley v. Valeo*, 424 U.S. 1 (1976), held that (a) Congress could appoint members of the Federal Election Commission to the extent that their duties were "essentially of an investigative and informative nature" because Congress could delegate such tasks to its own committees, but (b) Congress could not vest rulemaking and adjudicatory powers in a commission that has any members appointed by Congress. Consider the following questions about these cases:

(a) What does the Constitution say about appointment and removal of officers of the United States?

(b) Are these cases consistent or inconsistent?

(c) Do they authorize a "headless fourth branch" of government not subject to control by either the President or Congress?

(d) Are these cases simply reflective of necessity in the modern administrative state?

(e) Is there a difference between Congress controlling agencies and Congress limiting the President's control of agencies?

2. **Case Comparison.** Compare the Court's analytical approaches in *Chadha* and *Bowsher*. The former holds Congress to formal processes when it legislates, while the latter says the defect was that Congress was not legislating, but executing. Do you see these approaches as being consistent? Which do you think is preferable (and why)?

3. **Question.** If the Comptroller General's actions are executive, why isn't the "fall-back" provision, under which Congress would enact the budget cuts, also executive and therefore unconstitutional?

4. **Problems On "Framework" Statutes.** While many commentators call statutes like Gramm–Rudman–Hollings "quasi-constitutional" statutes, that term is confusing: such statutes can be repealed or amended by a majority vote in both houses of Congress and the President's signature, just like any other legislation.

(a) Is there any constitutional problem with Congress passing a statute tying its hands for the future, such as by requiring a 3/5ths or 2/3rds vote to engage in deficit spending, raise taxes, etc.?

(b) Is there a constitutional problem with the Senate's cloture rule, requiring a supermajority vote to cut off debate on a measure favored by the majority (3/5) of Senators?

(c) If a statute could demand a balanced budget, why would so many members of Congress favor a balanced budget Constitutional Amendment? Sunstein et. al. argue in their casebook (at page 455) that: "To the extent that the amendment forces this generation to restrict borrowing, it is unnecessary because Congress can accomplish this goal by ordinary legislative processes. To the extent that it attempts to bind future generations, it is illegitimate because these generations have no role in the ratification process." Do you agree?

5. **Problem.** Congress passes domestic legislation giving the Department of Labor authority to make "all appropriate rules and regulations to effectuate the policy of the Labor Act." Shortly thereafter, to meet budget reduction goals, the President issues an Executive Order requiring all agency rules to be prescreened by the President's Office of Management and Budget (OMB). OMB prescreens the Department of Labor's regulations, finds that they would create a "significant impact on federal spending," and refuses to release the regulations. Is OMB's action constitutional?

MORRISON v. OLSON
487 U.S. 654, 108 S.Ct. 2597, 101 L.Ed.2d 569 (1988).

CHIEF JUSTICE REHNQUIST delivered the opinion of the Court.

This case presents us with a challenge to the independent counsel provisions of the Ethics in Government Act of 1978, 28 U.S.C. §§ 49, 591 et seq. We hold today that these provisions of the Act do not violate the Appointments Clause of the Constitution, Art. II, § 2, cl. 2, or the limitations of Article III, nor do they impermissibly interfere with the President's authority under Article II in violation of the constitutional principle of separation of powers.

Briefly stated, Title VI of the Ethics in Government Act (Title VI or the Act), 28 U.S.C. §§ 591–599, allows for the appointment of an "independent counsel" to investigate and, if appropriate, prosecute certain high-ranking Government officials for violations of federal criminal laws. The Act requires the Attorney General, upon receipt of information that he determines is "sufficient to constitute grounds to investigate whether any person [covered by the Act] may have violated any Federal criminal law," to conduct a preliminary investigation of the matter. When the Attorney General has completed this investigation, or 90 days has elapsed, he is required to report to a special court (the Special Division) created by the Act "for the purpose of appointing independent counsels." If the Attorney General determines that "there are no reasonable grounds to believe that further investigation is warranted," then he must notify the Special Division of this result. In such a case, "the division of the court shall have no power to appoint an independent counsel." If, however, the Attorney General has determined that there are "reasonable grounds to believe that further investigation or prosecution is warranted," then he "shall apply to the division of the court for the appointment of an independent counsel." The Attorney General's application to the court "shall contain sufficient information to assist the [court] in selecting an independent counsel and in defining that independent counsel's prosecutorial jurisdiction." Upon receiving this application, the Special Division "shall appoint an appropriate independent counsel and shall define that independent counsel's prosecutorial jurisdiction."

*** Two statutory provisions govern the length of an independent counsel's tenure in office. The first defines the procedure for removing an independent counsel. Section 596(a)(1) provides: "An independent counsel appointed under this chapter may be removed from office, other than by impeachment and conviction, only by the personal action of the Attorney General and only for good cause, physical disability, mental incapacity, or any other condition that substantially impairs the performance of such independent counsel's duties." If an independent counsel is removed pursuant to this section, the Attorney General is required to submit a report to both the Special Division and the Judiciary Committees of the Senate and the House "specifying the facts found and the ultimate grounds for such removal." Under the current version of the Act, an independent counsel can obtain judicial review of the Attorney General's action by filing a civil action in the United States District Court for the District of Columbia. Members of the Special Division "may not hear or determine any such civil action or any appeal of a decision in any such civil action." The reviewing court is authorized to grant reinstatement or "other appropriate relief."

The other provision governing the tenure of the independent counsel defines the procedures for "terminating" the counsel's office. Under § 596(b)(1), the office of an independent counsel terminates when he or she notifies the Attorney General that he or she has completed or substantially completed any investigations or prosecutions undertaken pursuant to the Act. In addition, the Special Division, acting either on its own or on the suggestion of the Attorney General, may terminate the office of an independent counsel at any time if it finds that "the investigation of all matters within the prosecutorial jurisdiction of such independent counsel *** have been completed or so substantially completed that it would be appropriate for the Department of Justice to complete such investigations and prosecutions."

*** The Appointments Clause of Article II reads as follows:

"[The President] shall nominate, and by and with the Advice and Consent of the Senate, shall appoint Ambassadors, other public Ministers and Consuls, Judges of the Supreme Court, and all other Officers of the United States, whose Appointments are not herein otherwise provided for, and which shall be established by Law: but the Congress may by Law vest the Appointment of such inferior Officers, as they think proper, in the President alone, in the Courts of Law, or in the Heads of Departments."

U.S. Const., Art. II, § 2, cl. 2.

The parties do not dispute that "[t]he Constitution for purposes of appointment *** divides all its officers into two classes." As we stated in *Buckley v. Valeo*, 424 U.S. 1, 132 (1976): "[P]rincipal officers are selected by the President with the advice and consent of the Senate. Inferior officers

Congress may allow to be appointed by the President alone, by the heads of departments, or by the Judiciary." The initial question is, accordingly, whether appellant is an "inferior" or a "principal" officer. If she is the latter, as the Court of Appeals concluded, then the Act is in violation of the Appointments Clause.

The line between "inferior" and "principal" officers is one that is far from clear, and the Framers provided little guidance into where it should be drawn. *** We need not attempt here to decide exactly where the line falls between the two types of officers, because in our view appellant clearly falls on the "inferior officer" side of that line. Several factors lead to this conclusion.

First, appellant is subject to removal by a higher Executive Branch official. Although appellant may not be "subordinate" to the Attorney General (and the President) insofar as she possesses a degree of independent discretion to exercise the powers delegated to her under the Act, the fact that she can be removed by the Attorney General indicates that she is to some degree "inferior" in rank and authority. Second, appellant is empowered by the Act to perform only certain, limited duties. *** Third, appellant's office is limited in jurisdiction. *** Finally, appellant's office is limited in tenure. There is concededly no time limit on the appointment of a particular counsel. Nonetheless, the office of independent counsel is "temporary" in the sense that an independent counsel is appointed essentially to accomplish a single task, and when that task is over the office is terminated, either by the counsel herself or by action of the Special Division.

*** This does not, however, end our inquiry under the Appointments Clause. Appellees argue that even if appellant is an "inferior" officer, the Clause does not empower Congress to place the power to appoint such an officer outside the Executive Branch. They contend that the Clause does not contemplate congressional authorization of "interbranch appointments," in which an officer of one branch is appointed by officers of another branch. The relevant language of the Appointments Clause is worth repeating. It reads: " *** but the Congress may by Law vest the Appointment of such inferior Officers, as they think proper, in the President alone, in the courts of Law, or in the Heads of Departments." On its face, the language of this "excepting clause" admits of no limitation on interbranch appointments. Indeed, the inclusion of "as they think proper" seems clearly to give Congress significant discretion to determine whether it is "proper" to vest the appointment of, for example, executive officials in the "courts of Law."

*** We do not mean to say that Congress' power to provide for interbranch appointments of "inferior officers" is unlimited. In addition to separation-of-powers concerns, which would arise if such provisions for appointment had the potential to impair the constitutional functions assigned to one of the branches, Siebold itself suggested that Congress' decision to vest the appointment power in the courts would be improper if there was some "incongruity" between the functions normally performed by the courts and the performance of their duty to appoint. In this case, however, we do not think it impermissible for Congress to vest the power to appoint independent counsel in a specially created federal court. We thus disagree with the Court of Appeals' conclusion that there is an inherent incongruity about a court having the power to appoint prosecutorial officers.[13] We have recognized that courts may appoint private attorneys to act as prosecutor for judicial contempt judgments. *** Congress, of course, was concerned when it created the office of independent counsel with the conflicts of interest that could arise in situations when the Executive Branch is called upon to investigate its own high-ranking officers. If it were to remove the appointing authority from the Executive Branch, the most logical place to put it was in the Judicial Branch. In the light of the Act's provision making the judges of the Special Division ineligible to participate in any matters relating to an independent counsel they have appointed we do not think that appointment of the independent counsel by the court runs afoul of the constitutional limitation on "incongruous" interbranch appointments.

Appellees next contend that the powers vested in the Special Division by the Act conflict with Article III of the Constitution.

Leaving aside for the moment the Division's power to terminate an independent counsel, we do not think that Article III absolutely prevents Congress from vesting *** miscellaneous powers in the Special Division pursuant to the Act. As we observed above, one purpose of the broad prohibition upon the courts' exercise of "executive or administrative duties of a nonjudicial nature" is to maintain the separation between the Judiciary and the other branches of the Federal Government by ensuring that judges do not encroach upon executive or legislative authority or undertake tasks that are more properly accomplished by those branches. In this case, the miscellaneous powers described above do not impermissibly trespass upon the authority of the Executive Branch. Some of these allegedly "supervisory" powers conferred on the court are passive: the Division merely "receives" reports from the counsel or the Attorney General, it is not entitled to act on them or to specifically approve or disapprove of their contents. Other provisions of the Act do require the court to exercise some judgment and discretion, but the powers granted by these provisions are themselves essentially ministerial. The Act simply does not give the Division the power to "supervise" the independent counsel in the exercise of his or her investigative or prosecutorial authority.

We are more doubtful about the Special Division's power to terminate the office of the independent counsel pursuant to § 596(b)(2). *** Nonetheless, we do not, as did the Court of Appeals, view this provision as a significant judicial encroachment upon executive power or upon the prosecutorial discretion of the independent counsel.

---

[13] Indeed, in light of judicial experience with prosecutors in criminal cases, it could be said that courts are especially well qualified to appoint prosecutors. This is not a case in which judges are given power to appoint an officer in an area in which they have no special knowledge or expertise, as in, for example, a statute authorizing the courts to appoint officials in the Department of Agriculture or the Federal Energy Regulatory Commission.

Nor do we believe, as appellees contend, that the Special Division's exercise of the various powers specifically granted to it under the Act poses any threat to the "impartial and independent federal adjudication of claims within the judicial power of the United States." We reach this conclusion for two reasons. First, the Act as it currently stands gives the Special Division itself no power to review any of the actions of the independent counsel or any of the actions of the Attorney General with regard to the counsel. Accordingly, there is no risk of partisan or biased adjudication of claims regarding the independent counsel by that court. Second, the Act prevents members of the Special Division from participating in "any judicial proceeding concerning a matter which involves such independent counsel while such independent counsel is serving in that office or which involves the exercise of such independent counsel's official duties, regardless of whether such independent counsel is still serving in that office." We think both the special court and its judges are sufficiently isolated by these statutory provisions from the review of the activities of the independent counsel so as to avoid any taint of the independence of the Judiciary such as would render the Act invalid under Article III.

*** We now turn to consider whether the Act is invalid under the constitutional principle of separation of powers. Two related issues must be addressed: The first is whether the provision of the Act restricting the Attorney General's power to remove the independent counsel to only those instances in which he can show "good cause," taken by itself, impermissibly interferes with the President's exercise of his constitutionally appointed functions. The second is whether, taken as a whole, the Act violates the separation of powers by reducing the President's ability to control the prosecutorial powers wielded by the independent counsel.

*** We held in *Bowsher* that "Congress cannot reserve for itself the power of removal of an officer charged with the execution of the laws except by impeachment." A primary antecedent for this ruling was our 1926 decision in *Myers v. United States*, 272 U.S. 52 (1926). ***

Unlike both *Bowsher* and *Myers*, this case does not involve an attempt by Congress itself to gain a role in the removal of executive officials other than its established powers of impeachment and conviction. The Act instead puts the removal power squarely in the hands of the Executive Branch; an independent counsel may be removed from office, "only by the personal action of the Attorney General, and only for good cause." There is no requirement of congressional approval of the Attorney General's removal decision, though the decision is subject to judicial review. In our view, the removal provisions of the Act make this case more analogous to *Humphrey's Executor v. United States*, 295 U.S. 602 (1935), and *Wiener v. United States*, 357 U.S. 349 (1958), than to *Myers* or *Bowsher*.

Appellees contend that *Humphrey's Executor* and *Wiener* are distinguishable from this case because they did not involve officials who performed a "core executive function." They argue that our decision in *Humphrey's Executor* rests on a distinction between "purely executive" officials and officials who exercise "quasi-legislative" and "quasi-judicial" powers. ***

We undoubtedly did rely on the terms "quasi-legislative" and "quasi-judicial" to distinguish the officials involved in *Humphrey's Executor* and *Wiener* from those in *Myers*, but our present considered view is that the determination of whether the Constitution allows Congress to impose a "good cause"-type restriction on the President's power to remove an official cannot be made to turn on whether or not that official is classified as "purely executive." The analysis contained in our removal cases is designed not to define rigid categories of those officials who may or may not be removed at will by the President, but to ensure that Congress does not interfere with the President's exercise of the "executive power" and his constitutionally appointed duty to "take care that the laws be faithfully executed" under Article II.

Considering for the moment the "good cause" removal provision in isolation from the other parts of the Act at issue in this case, we cannot say that the imposition of a "good cause" standard for removal by itself unduly trammels on executive authority. *** Although the counsel exercises no small amount of discretion and judgment in deciding how to carry out his or her duties under the Act, we simply do not see how the President's need to control the exercise of that discretion is so central to the functioning of the Executive Branch as to require as a matter of constitutional law that the counsel be terminable at will by the President.

Nor do we think that the "good cause" removal provision at issue here impermissibly burdens the President's power to control or supervise the independent counsel, as an executive official, in the execution of his or her duties under the Act. This is not a case in which the power to remove an executive official has been completely stripped from the President, thus providing no means for the President to ensure the "faithful execution" of the laws. Rather, because the independent counsel may be terminated for "good cause," the Executive, through the Attorney General, retains ample authority to assure that the counsel is competently performing his or her statutory responsibilities in a manner that comports with the provisions of the Act. Although we need not decide in this case exactly what is encompassed within the term "good cause" under the Act, the legislative history of the removal provision also makes clear that the Attorney General may remove an independent counsel for "misconduct." *** We do not think that this limitation as it presently stands sufficiently deprives the President of control over the independent counsel to interfere impermissibly with his constitutional obligation to ensure the faithful execution of the laws.

The final question to be addressed is whether the Act, taken as a whole, violates the principle of separation of powers by unduly interfering with the role of the Executive Branch. [W]e have never held that the Constitution requires that the three branches of Government "operate with absolute independence." *United States v. Nixon*, 418 U.S., at 707.

We observe first that this case does not involve an attempt by Congress to increase its own powers at the expense of the Executive Branch. Cf. *Commodity Futures Trading Comm'n v. Schor*, 478 U.S., at 856. Unlike some of our previous cases, most recently *Bowsher v. Synar*, this case simply does not pose a "dange[r] of congressional usurpation of Executive Branch functions." ***

Similarly, we do not think that the Act works any judicial usurpation of properly executive functions. As should be apparent from our discussion of the Appointments Clause above, the power to appoint inferior officers such as independent counsel is not in itself an "executive" function in the constitutional sense, at least when Congress has exercised its power to vest the appointment of an inferior office in the "courts of Law." We note nonetheless that under the Act the Special Division has no power to appoint an independent counsel sua sponte; it may only do so upon the specific request of the Attorney General, and the courts are specifically prevented from reviewing the Attorney General's decision not to seek appointment.

Finally, we do not think that the Act "impermissibly undermine[s]" the powers of the Executive Branch, *Schor,* supra, 478 U.S., at 856, 106 S.Ct., at 3260, or "disrupts the proper balance between the coordinate branches [by] prevent[ing] the Executive Branch from accomplishing its constitutionally assigned functions," *Nixon v. Administrator of General Services*, supra, 433 U.S., at 443. It is undeniable that the Act reduces the amount of control or supervision that the Attorney General and, through him, the President exercises over the investigation and prosecution of a certain class of alleged criminal activity. The Attorney General is not allowed to appoint the individual of his choice; he does not determine the counsel's jurisdiction; and his power to remove a counsel is limited. Nonetheless, the Act does give the Attorney General several means of supervising or controlling the prosecutorial powers that may be wielded by an independent counsel. ***

In sum, we conclude today that it does not violate the Appointments Clause for Congress to vest the appointment of independent counsel in the Special Division; that the powers exercised by the Special Division under the Act do not violate Article III; and that the Act does not violate the separation-of-powers principle by impermissibly interfering with the functions of the Executive Branch. The decision of the Court of Appeals is therefore

Reversed.

JUSTICE KENNEDY took no part in the consideration or decision of this case.

JUSTICE SCALIA, dissenting.

*** If to describe this case is not to decide it, the concept of a government of separate and coordinate powers no longer has meaning. The Court devotes most of its attention to such relatively technical details as the Appointments Clause and the removal power, addressing briefly and only at the end of its opinion the separation of powers. *** I think that has it backwards. Our opinions are full of the recognition that it is the principle of separation of powers, and the inseparable corollary that each department's "defense must *** be made commensurate to the danger of attack," Federalist No. 51, p. 322 (J. Madison), which gives comprehensible content to the Appointments Clause, and determines the appropriate scope of the removal power.

*** Article II, § 1, cl. 1, of the Constitution provides: "The executive Power shall be vested in a President of the United States." *** [T]his does not mean some of the executive power, but all of the executive power. It seems to me, therefore, that the decision of the Court of Appeals invalidating the present statute must be upheld on fundamental separation-of-powers principles if the following two questions are answered affirmatively: (1) Is the conduct of a criminal prosecution (and of an investigation to decide whether to prosecute) the exercise of purely executive power? (2) Does the statute deprive the President of the United States of exclusive control over the exercise of that power? Surprising to say, the Court appears to concede an affirmative answer to both questions, but seeks to avoid the inevitable conclusion that since the statute vests some purely executive power in a person who is not the President of the United States it is void.

The Court concedes that "[t]here is no real dispute that the functions performed by the independent counsel are 'executive'," though it qualifies that concession by adding "in the sense that they are law enforcement functions that typically have been undertaken by officials within the Executive Branch." The qualifier adds nothing but atmosphere. In what other sense can one identify "the executive Power" that is supposed to be vested in the President (unless it includes everything the Executive Branch is given to do) except by reference to what has always and everywhere—if conducted by government at all—been conducted never by the legislature, never by the courts, and always by the executive. There is no possible doubt that the independent counsel's functions fit this description.

*** As for the second question, whether the statute before us deprives the President of exclusive control over that quintessentially executive activity: The Court does not, and could not possibly, assert that it does not. That is indeed the whole object of the statute. Instead, the Court points out that the President, through his Attorney General, has at least some control. That concession is alone enough to invalidate the statute, but I cannot refrain from pointing out that the Court greatly exaggerates the extent of that "some" Presidential control. ***

The utter incompatibility of the Court's approach with our constitutional traditions can be made more clear, perhaps, by applying it to the powers of the other two branches. Is it conceivable that if Congress passed a statute depriving itself of less than full and entire control over some insignificant area of legislation, we would inquire whether the matter was "so central to the functioning of the Legislative Branch" as really to require complete control, or whether the statute gives Congress "sufficient control over the surrogate legislator to ensure that Congress is able to perform its constitutionally assigned duties"? Of course we would have none of that. Once we determined that a purely legislative power was at issue we would require it to be exercised, wholly and entirely, by Congress. Or to bring the point closer to home, consider a statute giving to non-Article III judges just a tiny bit of purely judicial power in a relatively insignificant field, with substantial control, though not total control, in the courts—perhaps "clear error" review, which would be a fair judicial equivalent of the Attorney General's "for cause" removal power here. Is there any doubt that we would not pause to inquire whether the matter was "so central to the functioning of the Judicial Branch" as really to require complete control, or whether we retained "sufficient control over the matters to be decided that we are able to perform our constitutionally assigned duties"? We would say that our "constitutionally assigned duties" include complete control over all exercises of the judicial power—or, as the plurality opinion said in *Northern Pipeline Construction Co. v. Marathon Pipe Line Co.*, 458 U.S. 50, 58–59 (1982): "The inexorable command of [Article III] is clear and definite: The judicial power of the United States must be exercised by courts having the attributes prescribed in Art. III." We should say here that the President's constitutionally assigned duties include complete control over investigation and prosecution of violations of the law, and that the inexorable command of Article II is clear and definite: the executive power must be vested in the President of the United States.

Is it unthinkable that the President should have such exclusive power, even when alleged crimes by him or his close associates are at issue? No more so than that Congress should have the exclusive power of legislation, even when what is at issue is its own exemption from the burdens of certain laws. No more so than that this Court should have the exclusive power to pronounce the final decision on justiciable cases and controversies, even those pertaining to the constitutionality of a statute reducing the salaries of the Justices. A system of separate and coordinate powers necessarily involves an acceptance of exclusive power that can theoretically be abused.

The Court has, nonetheless, replaced the clear constitutional prescription that the executive power belongs to the President with a "balancing test." What are the standards to determine how the balance is to be struck, that is, how much removal of Presidential power is too much? Many countries of the world get along with an executive that is much weaker than ours—in fact, entirely dependent upon the continued support of the legislature. Once we depart from the text of the Constitution, just where short of that do we stop? The most amazing feature of the Court's opinion is that it does not even purport to give an answer. It simply announces, with no analysis, that the ability to control the decision whether to investigate and prosecute the President's closest advisers, and indeed the President himself, is not "so central to the functioning of the Executive Branch" as to be constitutionally required to be within the President's control. Apparently that is so because we say it is so. Having abandoned as the basis for our decision-making the text of Article II that "the executive Power" must be vested in the President, the Court does not even attempt to craft a substitute criterion—a "justiciable standard," *see, e.g., Baker v. Carr*, 369 U.S. 186, 210 (1962), however remote from the Constitution—that today governs, and in the future will govern, the decision of such questions.

*** Besides weakening the Presidency by reducing the zeal of his staff, it must also be obvious that the institution of the independent counsel enfeebles him more directly in his constant confrontations with Congress, by eroding his public support. Nothing is so politically effective as the ability to charge that one's opponent and his associates are not merely wrongheaded, naive, ineffective, but, in all probability, "crooks." And nothing so effectively gives an appearance of validity to such charges as a Justice Department investigation and, even better, prosecution. The present statute provides ample means for that sort of attack, assuring that massive and lengthy investigations will occur, not merely when the Justice Department in the application of its usual standards believes they are called for, but whenever it cannot be said that there are "no reasonable grounds to believe" they are called for.

III–4. "Independent Counsel Act." AUTH © 1998 The Philadelphia Inquirer. Reprinted with permission of UNIVERSAL PRESS SYNDICATE. All rights reserved.

*** [T]he Court does not attempt to "decide exactly" what establishes the line between principal and "inferior" officers, but is confident that, whatever the line may be, appellant "clearly falls on the 'inferior officer' side" of it. The Court gives three reasons: First, she "is subject to removal by a higher Executive Branch official," namely, the Attorney General. Second, she is "empowered by the Act to perform only certain, limited duties." Third, her office is "limited in jurisdiction" and "limited in tenure."

The first of these lends no support to the view that appellant is an inferior officer. Appellant is removable only for "good cause" or physical or mental incapacity. 28 U.S.C. § 596(a)(1). By contrast, most (if not all) principal officers in the Executive Branch may be removed by the President at will. I fail to see how the fact that appellant is more difficult to remove than most principal officers helps to establish that she is an inferior officer.

*** The second reason offered by the Court—that appellant performs only certain, limited duties—may be relevant to whether she is an inferior officer, but it mischaracterizes the extent of her powers. As the Court states: "Admittedly, the Act delegates to appellant [the] 'full power and independent authority to exercise all investigative and prosecutorial functions and powers of the Department of Justice.'" Moreover, in addition to this general grant of power she is given a broad range of specifically enumerated powers, including a power not even the Attorney General possesses: to "contes[t] in court *** any claim of privilege or attempt to withhold evidence on grounds of national security." Once all of this is "admitted," it seems to me impossible to maintain that appellant's authority is so "limited" as to render her an inferior officer.

*** The final set of reasons given by the Court for why the independent counsel clearly is an inferior officer emphasizes the limited nature of her jurisdiction and tenure. Taking the latter first, I find nothing unusually limited about the independent counsel's tenure. To the contrary, unlike most high-ranking Executive Branch officials, she continues to serve until she (or the Special Division) decides that her work is substantially completed. *** As to the scope of her jurisdiction, there can be no doubt that is small (though far from unimportant). But within it she exercises more than the full power of the Attorney General.

*** I think it preferable to look to the text of the Constitution and the division of power that it establishes. These demonstrate, I think, that the independent counsel is not an inferior officer because she is not subordinate to any officer in the Executive Branch (indeed, not even to the President). Dictionaries in use at the time of the Constitutional Convention gave the word "inferior" two meanings which it still bears today: (1) "[l]ower in place, *** station, *** rank of life, *** value or excellency," and (2) "[s]ubordinate." In a document dealing with the structure *** of a government, one would naturally expect the word to bear the latter meaning—indeed, in such a context it would be unpardonably careless to use the word unless a relation of subordination was intended ***.

*** There is, of course, no provision in the Constitution stating who may remove executive officers, except the provisions for removal by impeachment. Before the present decision it was established, however, (1) that the President's power to remove principal officers who exercise purely executive powers could not be restricted, *see Myers v. United States*, 272 U.S. 52, 127 (1926), and (2) that his power to remove inferior officers who exercise purely executive powers, and whose appointment Congress had removed from the usual procedure of Presidential appointment with Senate consent, could be restricted, at least where the appointment had been made by an officer of the Executive Branch, *United States v. Perkins*, 116 U.S. 483, 485 (1886).

*** Since our 1935 decision in *Humphrey's Executor v. United States*, which was considered by many at the time the product of an activist, anti-New Deal Court bent on reducing the power of President Franklin

Roosevelt—it has been established that the line of permissible restriction upon removal of principal officers lies at the point at which the powers exercised by those officers are no longer purely executive. *** What *Humphrey's Executor* (and presumably *Myers*) really means, we are now told, is not that there are any "rigid categories of those officials who may or may not be removed at will by the President," but simply that Congress cannot "interfere with the President's exercise of the 'executive power' and his constitutionally appointed duty to 'take care that the laws be faithfully executed.'"

*** *Humphrey's Executor* at least had the decency formally to observe the constitutional principle that the President had to be the repository of all executive power, which, as *Myers* carefully explained, necessarily means that he must be able to discharge those who do not perform executive functions according to his liking. By contrast, "our present considered view" is simply that any executive officer's removal can be restricted, so long as the President remains "able to accomplish his constitutional role." There are now no lines. If the removal of a prosecutor, the virtual embodiment of the power to "take care that the laws be faithfully executed," can be restricted, what officer's removal cannot? This is an open invitation for Congress to experiment. What about a special Assistant Secretary of State, with responsibility for one very narrow area of foreign policy, who would not only have to be confirmed by the Senate but could also be removed only pursuant to certain carefully designed restrictions? Could this possibly render the President "[un]able to accomplish his constitutional role"? Or a special Assistant Secretary of Defense for Procurement? The possibilities are endless, and the Court does not understand what the separation of powers, what "[a]mbition *** counteract[ing] ambition," Federalist No. 51 (Madison), is all about, if it does not expect Congress to try them. As far as I can discern from the Court's opinion, it is now open season upon the President's removal power for all executive officers, with not even the superficially principled restriction of *Humphrey's Executor* as cover. The Court essentially says to the President: "Trust us. We will make sure that you are able to accomplish your constitutional role." I think the Constitution gives the President—and the people—more protection than that.

Notes

1. **Comparisons and Policies.** Can you reconcile *Bowsher* and *Morrison*? Does *Morrison* permit Congress to create pockets of federal governmental authority (what JUSTICE SCALIA calls "mini-Executives") not subject to control by any official elected by the people? Is it true that special prosecutors have nothing to do with Congress reducing the power of the President?

2. **Role of the Courts.** Are you comfortable with the role played by the judiciary in the appointment of special prosecutors? Don't special prosecutors ultimately answer to the courts, who oversee any criminal actions which the prosecutor may initiate? It is interesting to compare the Supreme Court's early refusal to give an advisory opinion to President Washington with the Court's blessing of the collateral duty given to judges in *Morrison*. See also *Mistretta v. United States*, 488 U.S. 361 (1989), in which the Court upheld the constitutionality of the United

States Sentencing Commission, "an independent commission located in the judicial branch" whose role is to create mandatory sentencing guidelines specifying narrow ranges of permissible sentences for various crimes in order to reduce the variation in sentences given by different judges. The seven members of the Sentencing Commission are appointed by the President; three of them must be federal judges. The Court held that "the participation of federal judges on the Sentencing Commission does not threaten, either in fact or in appearance, the impartiality of the judicial branch" because "sentencing will continue to be performed exclusively by the judicial branch." The Court said, of presidential appointment and removal power, that federal judges would not likely be influenced to "comport their actions to the wishes of the President for the purpose of receiving an appointment" and that removal from the commission was a "negligible threat" since removal would still leave the judge with a lifetime appointment. In a scathing dissent, JUSTICE SCALIA argued that *Mistretta* "is not about commingling, but *** about the creation of a new branch altogether, a sort of junior-varsity Congress." With whom do you agree?

3. **Problem.** The United States owns Washington National Airport and Dulles International Airport. In 1987, Congress passed and the President signed the Airports Act, which provides for the lease of these airports to an Authority established by the State of Virginia and the District of Columbia. As a condition of the lease, the Airports Act establishes a Board of Review empowered to disapprove of Authority decisions, including budgets, adoption of regulations, and appointment of the Authority's President. The Airports Act states that the five members of this Board of Review serve "in their individual capacities as representatives of users of the airports." They are appointed by the Authority from lists of Congressmen and Senators "currently serving on" specified congressional committees responsible for formulating national aviation policies. The Airports Act says nothing about removal of members of the Board of Review. The Airports Act also provides that invalidation of the provisions concerning the Board of Review will make the lease to the Authority "null and void." Were the lease voided, major expansions of both airports contemplated by the Authority would be delayed. Citizens for the Abatement of Aircraft Noise ("Citizens") has filed suit on behalf of individuals who claim they would face increased noise and pollution from the expansion of the airports. The suit alleges that the Airports Act provisions outlined above are unconstitutional. Discuss whether the Airports Act is constitutional. After you have independently outlined your thoughts on this problem, you might look at *Metropolitan Washington Airports Authority v. Citizens for the Abatement of Aircraft Noise*, 501 U.S. 252 (1991). As a review exercise, you might also consider whether Citizens' suit is justiciable.

2. FOREIGN AFFAIRS

In the late 1960's and early 1970's, America's involvement in military operations in Vietnam became increasingly unpopular. Disenchantment over America's lack of resolution of that conflict led President Lyndon B. Johnson not to seek reelection in 1968. Johnson's successor, Richard M. Nixon, vetoed the following resolution that Congress had passed in an effort to control future military actions by presidents. President Nixon, whose veto of this resolution was overridden, thought that the following statute unconstitutionally intruded on the President's Article II powers.

What provisions of the War Powers Resolution, if any, do you think intrude on the President's powers? Are there any other arguments you can find concerning the constitutionality of specific provisions of the resolution?

Critics have thought this resolution particularly ineffective. What makes it unlikely to be effective? What other tools in the Constitution could Congress use to keep presidents from engaging in military action?

WAR POWERS RESOLUTION
50 U.S.C.A. §§ 1541–1544, § 1547.

§ 1541. PURPOSE AND POLICY

(a) CONGRESSIONAL DECLARATION

It is the purpose of this chapter to fulfill the intent of the framers of the Constitution of the United States and insure that the collective judgment of both the Congress and the President will apply to the introduction of United States Armed Forces into hostilities, or into situations where imminent involvement in hostilities is clearly indicated by the circumstances, and to the continued use of such forces in hostilities or in such situations.

(b) CONGRESSIONAL LEGISLATIVE POWER UNDER NECESSARY AND PROPER CLAUSE

Under article I, section 8, of the Constitution, it is specifically provided that the Congress shall have the power to make all laws necessary and proper for carrying into execution, not only its own powers but also all other powers vested by the Constitution in the Government of the United States, or in any department or officer thereof.

(c) PRESIDENTIAL EXECUTIVE POWER AS COMMANDER-IN-CHIEF; LIMITATION

The constitutional powers of the President as Commander-in-Chief to introduce United States Armed Forces into hostilities, or into situations where imminent involvement in hostilities is clearly indicated by the circumstances, are exercised only pursuant to (1) a declaration of war, (2) specific statutory authorization, or (3) a national emergency created by attack upon the United States, its territories or possessions, or its armed forces.

§ 1542. CONSULTATION; INITIAL AND REGULAR CONSULTATIONS

The President in every possible instance shall consult with Congress before introducing United States Armed Forces into hostilities or into situations where imminent involvement in hostilities is clearly indicated by the circumstances, and after every such introduction shall consult regularly with the Congress until United States Armed Forces are no longer engaged in hostilities or have been removed from such situations.

§ 1543. REPORTING REQUIREMENT

(a) WRITTEN REPORT; TIME OF SUBMISSION; CIRCUMSTANCES NECESSITATING SUBMISSION; INFORMATION REPORTED

In the absence of a declaration of war, in any case in which United States Armed Forces are introduced—

(1) into hostilities or into situations where imminent involvement in hostilities is clearly indicated by the circumstances;

(2) into the territory, airspace or waters of a foreign nation, while equipped for combat, except for deployments which relate solely to supply, replacement, repair, or training of such forces; or

(3) in numbers which substantially enlarge United States Armed Forces equipped for combat already located in a foreign nation;

the President shall submit within 48 hours to the Speaker of the House of Representatives and to the President pro tempore of the Senate a report, in writing, setting forth—

(A) the circumstances necessitating the introduction of United States Armed Forces;

(B) the constitutional and legislative authority under which such introduction took place; and

(C) the estimated scope and duration of the hostilities or involvement.

(b) OTHER INFORMATION REPORTED

The President shall provide such other information as the Congress may request in the fulfillment of its constitutional responsibilities with respect to committing the Nation to war and to the use of United States Armed Forces abroad.

(c) PERIODIC REPORTS; SEMIANNUAL REQUIREMENT

Whenever United States Armed Forces are introduced into hostilities or into any situation described in subsection (a) of this section, the President shall, so long as such armed forces continue to be engaged in such hostilities or situation, report to the Congress periodically on the status of such hostilities or situation as well as on the scope and duration of such hostilities or situation, but in no event shall he report to the Congress less often than once every six months.

§ 1544. CONGRESSIONAL ACTION

(a) TRANSMITTAL OF REPORT AND REFERRAL TO CONGRESSIONAL COMMITTEES; JOINT REQUEST FOR CONVENING CONGRESS

Each report submitted pursuant to section 1543(a)(1) of this title shall be transmitted to the Speaker of the House of Representatives and to the President pro tempore of the Senate on the same calendar day. Each report so transmitted shall be referred to the Committee on Foreign Affairs of the House of Representatives and to the Committee on Foreign Relations of the Senate for appropriate action. If, when the report is transmitted, the Congress has adjourned sine die or has adjourned for any period in excess of three calendar days, the Speaker of the House of Representatives and the President pro tempore of the Senate, if they deem it advisable (or if petitioned by at least 30 percent of the membership of their respective Houses) shall jointly request the President to convene Congress in order that it may consider the report and take appropriate action pursuant to this section.

(b) TERMINATION OF USE OF UNITED STATES ARMED FORCES; EXCEPTIONS; EXTENSION PERIOD

Within sixty calendar days after a report is submitted or is required to be submitted pursuant to section 1543(a)(1) of this title, whichever is earlier, the President shall terminate any use of United States Armed Forces with respect to which such report was submitted (or required to be submitted), unless the Congress (1) has declared war or has enacted a specific authorization for such use of United States Armed Forces, (2) has extended by law such sixty-day period, or (3) is physically unable to meet as a result of an armed attack upon the United States. Such sixty-day period shall be extended for not more than an additional thirty days if the President determines and certifies to the Congress in writing that unavoidable military necessity respecting the safety of United States Armed Forces requires the continued use of such armed forces in the course of bringing about a prompt removal of such forces.

(c) CONCURRENT RESOLUTION FOR REMOVAL BY PRESIDENT OF UNITED STATES ARMED FORCES

Notwithstanding subsection (b) of this section, at any time that United States Armed Forces are engaged in hostilities outside the territory of the United States, its possessions and territories without a declaration of war or specific statutory authorization, such forces shall be removed by the President if the Congress so directs by concurrent resolution.

§ 1547. INTERPRETATION OF JOINT RESOLUTION

(a) INFERENCES FROM ANY LAW OR TREATY

Authority to introduce United States Armed Forces into hostilities or into situations wherein involvement in hostilities is clearly indicated by the circumstances shall not be inferred—

(1) from any provision of law (whether or not in effect before November 7, 1973), including any provision contained in any appropriation Act, unless such provision specifically authorizes the introduction of United States Armed Forces into hostilities or into such situations and states that it is intended to constitute specific statutory authorization within the meaning of this chapter; or

(2) from any treaty heretofore or hereafter ratified unless such treaty is implemented by legislation specifically authorizing the introduction of United States Armed Forces into hostilities or into such situations and stating that it is intended to constitute specific statutory authorization within the meaning of this chapter.

(b) JOINT HEADQUARTERS OPERATIONS OF HIGH-LEVEL MILITARY COMMANDS

Nothing in this chapter shall be construed to require any further specific statutory authorization to permit members of United States Armed Forces to participate jointly with members of the armed forces of one or more foreign countries in the headquarters operations of high-level military commands which were established prior to November 7, 1973, and pursuant to the United Nations Charter or any treaty ratified by the United States prior to such date.

(c) INTRODUCTION OF UNITED STATES ARMED FORCES

For purposes of this chapter, the term "introduction of United States Armed Forces" includes the assignment of members of such armed forces to command, coordinate, participate in the movement of, or accompany the regular or irregular military forces of any foreign country or government when such military forces are engaged, or there exists an imminent threat that such forces will become engaged, in hostilities.

(d) CONSTITUTIONAL AUTHORITIES OR EXISTING TREATIES UNAFFECTED; CONSTRUCTION AGAINST GRANT OF PRESIDENTIAL AUTHORITY RESPECTING USE OF UNITED STATES ARMED FORCES

Nothing in this chapter—

(1) is intended to alter the constitutional authority of the Congress or of the President, or the provisions of existing treaties; or

(2) shall be construed as granting any authority to the President with respect to the introduction of United States Armed Forces into hostilities or into situations wherein involvement in hostilities is clearly indicated by the circumstances which authority he would not have had in the absence of this chapter.

REVIEW PROBLEMS

Review Problem #1.

Assume that in response to public health concerns about tobacco, Congress passes and the President signs legislation creating a special commission to investigate health problems caused by tobacco use. This Tobacco Health Policy Commission (THPC) is composed of six members, selected as follows: two are chosen by the President; two are chosen by the Speaker of the House; and two are chosen by the Majority Leader of the Senate. The authorizing statute states the THPC is to make policy recommendations to Congress and the President, and that Congress and the President must seriously consider and act with all deliberate speed in response to the THPC recommendations.

After a year of careful study, the THPC issues a report identifying smoking by those under 18 years of age as presenting the most pressing health problem. The THPC recommends various measures, including a ban on the sale of tobacco to teenagers and restrictions on advertising. Relying on the THPC report, Congress enacts legislation banning the sale of tobacco to anyone under 18 years of age. The President then issues an executive order banning the advertising of tobacco products on any television program whose primary target audience consists of those under 18 years of age.

(a) Does the THPC violate the separation of powers?

(b) Does the President have the authority to issue this executive order?

Review Problem #2.

Congress recently enacted a foreign aid bill that provides for grants to dozens of countries around the world. Because of concern with the problem of terrorism directed at the United States, Congress included a provision in the legislation that requires the President to determine whether countries that receive foreign aid from the United States are terrorist nations. The legislation defines a terrorist nation as "a nation that supports, harbors, or encourages persons or organizations that use or support the use of violence against citizens of the United States." The foreign aid legislation authorizes (but does not require) the President to cancel foreign aid that would otherwise go to a nation that the President determines is a terrorist nation.

The legislation further provides that before a cancellation takes effect, the President must inform the chairs of the foreign affairs committees of the Senate and the House of Representatives of his or her intent to cancel. Cancellation does not take effect until two months after this notification. During the two-month interval, Congress may enact legislation (through the usual legislative process) reauthorizing the foreign aid and exempting it from presidential cancellation. If no legislation is enacted within two months, the presidential cancellation takes effect.

President Powell believes international narcotics trafficking poses as great a threat to the United States as international terrorism and "fosters violent crime in the United States." Accordingly, he issues an Executive Order canceling foreign aid for nations that harbor or support individuals who smuggle narcotics into the United States. With regard to these cancellations, the Executive Order sets out the same procedures that the foreign aid legislation provides for terrorist nations: informing the foreign affairs committee chairs of intent to cancel the expenditure and waiting two months before actual cancellation.

(a) Does the terrorist nation cancellation provision violate the separation of powers?

(b) Does President Powell have the authority to cancel foreign aid to nations that harbor or support drug traffickers?

IV

CONGRESS' POWERS

―――――

"This government is acknowledged by all, to be one of enumerated powers. The principle, that it can exercise only the powers granted to it, *** is now universally admitted. But the question respecting the extent of the powers actually granted, is perpetually arising, and will probably continue to arise, so long as our system shall exist. In discussing these questions, the conflicting powers of the general and state governments must be brought into view, and the supremacy of their respective laws, when they are in opposition, must be settled. *** [T]he government of the Union, though limited in its powers, is supreme within its sphere of action."

—CHIEF JUSTICE MARSHALL in *McCulloch v. Maryland*

The starting point to understanding the powers of Congress is the Constitution's text: "All legislative Powers herein granted shall be vested in a Congress of the United States, which shall consist of a Senate and House of Representatives." Art. I, § 1. The legislative powers given Congress fit, for the most part, into seventeen separate categories listed before the "necessary and proper" clause in Article I, § 8. REREAD this section. Another important power given Congress in § 5 of the Fourteenth Amendment is to "enforce, by appropriate legislation, the provisions of this article."

Part A of this chapter examines the breadth to be accorded the powers of Congress; it contains the classic interpretation given the "necessary and proper" clause. Part B assesses Congress' power "To regulate Commerce with foreign Nations, and among the several States, and with the Indian Tribes." This focus on the commerce power is appropriate: the power to regulate interstate commerce, if read broadly enough, moots the need for any other power. In other words, the Commerce Clause could permit Congress to pass any legislation it desires. Part C presents the other Article I powers of Congress, with emphasis on the taxing and spending powers and the treaty and war powers. Finally, Part D considers Congress' power to enforce the Fourteenth Amendment. To the extent that the Commerce Power is limited, the powers considered in Parts C and D have increased practical and theoretical interest.

Whatever legislative powers Congress does not have reside with the states or the people. On a conceptual level, both courts and commentators have had difficulty sorting out whether, concerning a particular matter: (1)

Congress has exclusive power, (2) Congress and the states have concurrent power, or (3) the states have exclusive power.

Chapter V explores the "background understanding" of the relationships between state and federal sovereignty, including the Tenth Amendment, as limitations on Congress' legislative power. It also evaluates the flip side of that coin, federalism's limits on State power. Another important issue, whether state legislation affecting interstate commerce is prohibited in the *absence* of congressional legislation, is reserved for Chapter VI.

A. BASIC FRAMEWORK: THE NECESSARY AND PROPER CLAUSE

After enumerating seventeen specific powers of Congress, Article I, § 8 provides that Congress has the power "To make all Laws which shall be necessary and proper for carrying into Execution the foregoing Powers, and all other Powers vested by this Constitution in the Government of the United States, or in any Department or Officer thereof." The following early Supreme Court opinion gives a broad reading to this phrase, thus expanding federal power and limiting state power.

A bit of historical context is useful here. The charter of the First Bank of the United States, created in 1790, lapsed in 1811. Alexander Hamilton had been a strong supporter of that bank, Thomas Jefferson a strong opponent. Each grounded his position on the Constitution. The First Bank was not subjected to definitive constitutional scrutiny, but when the Second Bank of the United States was created in 1815, many states opposed the bank and some, including Maryland, sought to tax it. By this time, Jefferson supported the Bank as a tool for controlling financial turmoil after the War of 1812.

McCULLOCH v. MARYLAND
17 U.S. (4 Wheat.) 316, 4 L.Ed. 579 (1819).

*** It is admitted by the parties in this cause, by their counsel, that there was passed, on the 10th day of April 1816, by the congress of the United States, an act, entitled, "an act to incorporate the subscribers to the Bank of the United States;" and that there was passed on the 11th day of February 1818, by the general assembly of Maryland, an act, entitled, "an act to impose a tax on all banks, or branches thereof, in the state of Maryland, not chartered by the legislature,"

It is further admitted, that the Bank of the United States did establish a branch, or an office of discount and deposit, in the city of Baltimore, in the state of Maryland, which has, from that time, until the first day of May 1818, ever since transacted and carried on business as a bank, or office of discount and deposit, and as a branch of the said Bank of the United States.

It is further admitted, that James William McCulloch, the defendant below, [was] the cashier of the said branch, [and] that the said president, directors and company of the Bank of the United States, and the said branch, or office of discount and deposit, have not, nor has either of them, paid in advance, or otherwise, the sum of $15,000, to the treasurer of the Western Shore, for the use of the state of Maryland, [as required by state law].

MARSHALL, CH. J., delivered the opinion of the court.

In the case now to be determined, the defendant, a sovereign state, denies the obligation of a law enacted by the legislature of the Union, and the plaintiff, on his part, contests the validity of an act which has been passed by the legislature of that state. The constitution of our country, in its most interesting and vital parts, is to be considered; the conflicting powers of the government of the Union and of its members, as marked in that constitution, are to be discussed; and an opinion given, which may essentially influence the great operations of the government. No tribunal can approach such a question without a deep sense of its importance, and of the awful responsibility involved in its decision. But it must be decided peacefully, or remain a source of hostile legislation, perhaps, of hostility of a still more serious nature; and if it is to be so decided, by this tribunal alone can the decision be made. On the supreme court of the United States has the constitution of our country devolved this important duty.

The first question made in the cause is—has congress power to incorporate a bank? It has been truly said, that this can scarcely be considered as an open question, entirely unprejudiced by the former proceedings of the nation respecting it. The principle now contested was introduced at a very early period of our history, has been recognised by many successive legislatures, and has been acted upon by the judicial department, in cases of peculiar delicacy, as a law of undoubted obligation. ***

The power now contested was exercised by the first congress elected under the present constitution. The bill for incorporating the Bank of the United States did not steal upon an unsuspecting legislature, and pass unobserved. Its principle was completely understood, and was opposed with equal zeal and ability. After being resisted, first, in the fair and open field of debate, and afterwards, in the executive cabinet, with as much persevering talent as any measure has ever experienced, and being supported by arguments which convinced minds as pure and as intelligent as this country can boast, it became a law. The original act was permitted to expire; but a short experience of the embarrassments to which the refusal to revive it exposed the government, convinced those who were most prejudiced against the measure of its necessity, and induced the passage of the present law. It would require no ordinary share of intrepidity, to assert that a measure adopted under these circumstances, was a bold and plain usurpation, to which the constitution gave no countenance. These observations belong to the cause; but they are not made under the impression, that, were the question entirely new, the law would be found irreconcilable with the constitution.

In discussing this question, the counsel for the state of Maryland have deemed it of some importance, in the construction of the constitution, to consider that instrument, not as emanating from the people, but as the act of sovereign and independent states. The powers of the general government, it has been said, are delegated by the states, who alone are truly sovereign; and must be exercised in subordination to the states, who alone possess supreme dominion.

It would be difficult to sustain this proposition. The convention which framed the constitution was indeed elected by the state legislatures. But the instrument, when it came from their hands, was a mere proposal, without obligation, or pretensions to it. It was reported to the then existing congress of the United States, with a request that it might "be submitted to a convention of delegates, chosen in each state by the people thereof, under the recommendation of its legislature, for their assent and ratification." This mode of proceeding was adopted; and by the convention, by congress, and by the state legislatures, the instrument was submitted to the people. They acted upon it in the only manner in which they can act safely, effectively and wisely, on such a subject, by assembling in convention. It is true, they assembled in their several states—and where else should they have assembled? No political dreamer was ever wild enough to think of breaking down the lines which separate the states, and of compounding the American people into one common mass. Of consequence, when they act, they act in their states. But the measures they adopt do not, on that account, cease to be the measures of the people themselves, or become the measures of the state governments.

From these conventions, the constitution derives its whole authority. The government proceeds directly from the people; is "ordained and established," in the name of the people; and is declared to be ordained, "in order to form a more perfect union, establish justice, insure domestic tranquillity, and secure the blessings of liberty to themselves and to their posterity." The assent of the states, in their sovereign capacity, is implied, in calling a convention, and thus submitting that instrument to the people. But the people were at perfect liberty to accept or reject it; and their act was final. It required not the affirmance, and could not be negatived, by the state governments. The constitution, when thus adopted, was of complete obligation, and bound the state sovereignties ***.

[T]he government of the Union, then (whatever may be the influence of this fact on the case), is, emphatically and truly, a government of the people. In form, and in substance, it emanates from them. Its powers are granted by them, and are to be exercised directly on them, and for their benefit.

This government is acknowledged by all, to be one of enumerated powers. The principle, that it can exercise only the powers granted to it, would seem too apparent, to have required to be enforced by all those arguments, which its enlightened friends, while it was depending before the people, found it necessary to urge; that principle is now universally admitted. But the question respecting the extent of the powers actually granted, is perpetually arising, and will probably continue to arise, so long as our system shall exist. In discussing these questions, the conflicting powers of the general and state governments must be brought into view, and the supremacy of their respective laws, when they are in opposition, must be settled.

If any one proposition could command the universal assent of mankind, we might expect it would be this—that the government of the Union, though limited in its powers, is supreme within its sphere of action. This would seem to result, necessarily, from its nature. It is the government of all; its powers are delegated by all; it represents all, and acts for all. Though any one state may be willing to control its operations, no state is willing to allow others to control them. The nation, on those subjects on which it can act, must necessarily bind its component parts. But this question is not left to mere reason: the people have, in express terms, decided it, by saying, "this constitution, and the laws of the United States, which shall be made in pursuance thereof," "shall be the supreme law of the land," and by requiring that the members of the state legislatures, and the officers of the executive and judicial departments of the states, shall take the oath of fidelity to it. The government of the United States, then, though limited in its powers, is supreme; and its laws, when made in pursuance of the constitution, form the supreme law of the land, "anything in the constitution or laws of any state to the contrary notwithstanding."

Among the enumerated powers, we do not find that of establishing a bank or creating a corporation. But there is no phrase in the instrument which, like the articles of confederation, excludes incidental or implied powers; and which requires that everything granted shall be expressly and minutely described. Even the 10th amendment, which was framed for the purpose of quieting the excessive jealousies which had been excited, omits the word "expressly," and declares only, that the powers "not delegated to the United States, nor prohibited to the states, are reserved to the states or to the people;" thus leaving the question, whether the particular power which may become the subject of contest, has been delegated to the one government, or prohibited to the other, to depend on a fair construction of the whole instrument. The men who drew and adopted this amendment had experienced the embarrassments resulting from the insertion of this word in the articles of confederation, and probably omitted it, to avoid those embarrassments. A constitution, to contain an accurate detail of all the subdivisions of which its great powers will admit, and of all the means by which they may be carried into execution, would partake of the prolixity of a legal code, and could scarcely be embraced by the human mind. It would, probably, never be understood by the public. Its nature, therefore, requires, that only its great outlines should be marked, its important objects designated, and the minor ingredients which compose those objects, be deduced from the nature of the objects themselves. That this idea was entertained by the framers of the American constitution, is not only to be inferred from the nature of the instrument, but from the language. Why else were some of the limitations, found in the 9th section of the 1st article, introduced? It is also, in some degree, warranted, by their having omitted to use any restrictive term which might prevent its receiving a fair and just interpretation. In considering this question, then, we must never forget that it is a constitution we are expounding.

Although, among the enumerated powers of government, we do not find the word "bank" or "incorporation," we find the great powers, to lay and collect taxes; to borrow money; to regulate commerce; to declare and conduct a war; and to raise and support armies and navies. The sword and the purse, all the external relations, and no inconsiderable portion of the industry of the nation, are intrusted to its government. It can never be pretended, that these vast powers draw after them others of inferior importance, merely because they are inferior. Such an idea can never be advanced. But it may with great reason be contended, that a government, intrusted with such ample powers, on the due execution of which the happiness and prosperity of the nation so vitally depends, must also be intrusted with ample means for their execution. The power being given, it is the interest of the nation to facilitate its execution. It can never be their interest, and cannot be presumed to have been their intention, to clog and embarrass its execution, by withholding the most appropriate means. Throughout this vast republic, from the St. Croix to the Gulf of Mexico, from the Atlantic to the Pacific, revenue is to be collected and expended, armies are to be marched and supported. The exigencies of the nation may require, that the treasure raised in the north should be transported to the south, that raised in the east, conveyed to the west, or that this order should be reversed. Is that construction of the constitution to be preferred, which would render these operations difficult, hazardous and expensive? Can we adopt that construction (unless the words imperiously require it), which would impute to the framers of that instrument, when granting these powers for the public good, the intention of impeding their exercise, by withholding a choice of means?

It is not denied, that the powers given to the government imply the ordinary means of execution. That, for example, of raising revenue, and applying it to national purposes, is admitted to imply the power of conveying money from place to place, as the exigencies of the nation may require, and of employing the usual means of conveyance ***.

But the constitution of the United States has not left the right of congress to employ the necessary means, for the execution of the powers conferred on the government, to general reasoning. To its enumeration of powers is added, that of making "all laws which shall be necessary and proper, for carrying into execution the foregoing powers, and all other powers vested by this constitution, in the government of the United States, or in any department thereof." The counsel for the state of Maryland have urged various arguments, to prove that this clause, though, in terms, a grant of power, is not so, in effect; but is really restrictive of the general right, which might otherwise be implied, of selecting means for executing the enumerated powers.

[T]he argument on which most reliance is placed, is drawn from that peculiar language of this clause. Congress is not empowered by it to make all laws, which may have relation to the powers conferred on the government, but such only as may be "necessary and proper" for carrying them into execution. The word "necessary" is considered as controlling the whole sentence, and as limiting the right to pass laws for the execution of the granted powers, to such as are indispensable, and without which the power would be nugatory. That it excludes the choice of means, and leaves to congress, in each case, that only which is most direct and simple.

Is it true, that this is the sense in which the word "necessary" is always used? Does it always import an absolute physical necessity, so strong, that one thing to which another may be termed necessary, cannot exist without that other? We think it does not. If reference be had to its use, in the common affairs of the world, or in approved authors, we find that it frequently imports no more than that one thing is convenient, or useful, or essential to another. To employ the means necessary to an end, is generally understood as employing any means calculated to produce the end, and not as being confined to those single means, without which the end would be entirely unattainable. Such is the character of human language, that no word conveys to the mind, in all situations, one single definite idea; and nothing is more common than to use words in a figurative sense. Almost all compositions contain words, which, taken in their rigorous sense, would convey a meaning different from that which is obviously intended. It is essential to just construction, that many words which import something excessive, should be understood in a more mitigated sense—in that sense which common usage justifies. The word "necessary" is of this description. It has not a fixed character, peculiar to itself. It admits of all degrees of comparison; and is often connected with other words, which increase or diminish the impression the mind receives of the urgency it imports. A thing may be necessary, very necessary, absolutely or indispensably necessary. To no mind would the same idea be conveyed by these several phrases. The comment on the word is well illustrated by the passage cited at the bar, from the 10th section of the 1st article of the constitution. It is, we think, impossible to compare the sentence which prohibits a state from laying 'imposts, or duties on imports or exports, except what may be absolutely necessary for executing its inspection laws,' with that which authorizes congress "to make all laws which shall be necessary and proper for carrying into execution" the powers of the general government, without feeling a conviction, that the convention understood itself to change materially the meaning of the word "necessary," by prefixing the word "absolutely." This word, then, like others, is used in various senses; and, in its construction, the subject, the context, the intention of the person using them, are all to be taken into view.

Let this be done in the case under consideration. The subject is the execution of those great powers on which the welfare of a nation essentially depends. It must have been the intention of those who gave these powers, to insure, so far as human prudence could insure, their beneficial execution. This could not be done, by confiding the choice of means to such narrow limits as not to leave it in the power of congress to adopt any which might be appropriate, and which were conducive to the end. This provision is made in a constitution, intended to endure for ages to come, and consequently, to be adapted to the various crises of human affairs. To have prescribed the means by which government should, in all future time, execute its powers, would have been to change, entirely, the character of the instrument, and give it the properties of a legal code. It would have been an unwise attempt to provide, by immutable rules, for exigencies which, if foreseen at all, must have been seen dimly, and which can be best provided for as they occur. To have declared, that the best means shall not be used, but those alone, without which the power given would be nugatory, would have been to deprive the legislature of the capacity to avail itself of experience, to exercise its reason, and to accommodate its legislation to circumstances.

So, with respect to the whole penal code of the United States: whence arises the power to punish, in cases not prescribed by the constitution? All admit, that the government may, legitimately, punish any violation of its laws; and yet, this is not among the enumerated powers of congress. The right to enforce the observance of law, by punishing its infraction, might be denied, with the more plausibility, because it is expressly given in some cases.

Congress is empowered "to provide for the punishment of counterfeiting the securities and current coin of the United States," and "to define and punish piracies and felonies committed on the high seas, and offences against the law of nations." The several powers of congress may exist, in a very imperfect state, to be sure, but they may exist and be carried into execution, although no punishment should be inflicted, in cases where the right to punish is not expressly given.

Take, for example, the power "to establish post-offices and post-roads." This power is executed, by the single act of making the establishment. But, from this has been inferred the power and duty of carrying the mail along the post-road, from one post-office to another. And from this implied power, has again been inferred the right to punish those who steal letters from the post-office, or rob the mail. It may be said, with some plausibility, that the right to carry the mail, and to punish those who rob it, is not indispensably necessary to the establishment of a post-office and post-road. This right is indeed essential to the beneficial exercise of the power, but not indispensably necessary to its existence. So, of the punishment of the crimes of stealing or falsifying a record or process of a court of the United States, or of perjury in such court. To punish these offences, is certainly conducive to the due administration of justice. But courts may exist, and may decide the causes brought before them, though such crimes escape punishment.

In ascertaining the sense in which the word "necessary" is used in this clause of the constitution, we may derive some aid from that with which it is associated. Congress shall have power "to make all laws which shall be necessary and proper to carry into execution" the powers of the government. If the word "necessary" was used in that strict and rigorous sense for which the counsel for the state of Maryland contend, it would be an extraordinary departure from the usual course of the human mind, as exhibited in composition, to add a word, the only possible effect of which is, to qualify that strict and rigorous meaning; to present to the mind the idea of some choice of means of legislation, not strained and compressed within the narrow limits for which gentlemen contend.

But the argument which most conclusively demonstrates the error of the construction contended for by the counsel for the state of Maryland, is founded on the intention of the convention, as manifested in the whole clause. To waste time and argument in proving that, without it, congress might carry its powers into execution, would be not much less idle, than to hold a lighted taper to the sun. As little can it be required to prove, that in the absence of this clause, congress would have some choice of means. That it might employ those which, in its judgment, would most advantageously effect the object to be accomplished. That any means adapted to the end, any means which tended directly to the execution of the constitutional powers of the government, were in themselves constitutional. This clause, as construed by the state of Maryland, would abridge, and almost annihilate, this useful and necessary right of the legislature to select its means. That this could not be intended, is, we should think, had it not been already controverted, too apparent for controversy.

We think so for the following reasons: 1st. The clause is placed among the powers of congress, not among the limitations on those powers. 2d. Its terms purport to enlarge, not to diminish the powers vested in the government. It purports to be an additional power, not a restriction on those already granted. No reason has been, or can be assigned, for thus concealing an intention to narrow the discretion of the national legislature, under words which purport to enlarge it.

The result of the most careful and attentive consideration bestowed upon this clause is, that if it does not enlarge, it cannot be construed to restrain the powers of congress, or to impair the right of the legislature to exercise its best judgment in the selection of measures to carry into execution the constitutional powers of the government. If no other motive for its insertion can be suggested, a sufficient one is found in the desire to remove all doubts respecting the right to legislate on that vast mass of incidental powers which must be involved in the constitution, if that instrument be not a splendid bauble.

We admit, as all must admit, that the powers of the government are limited, and that its limits are not to be transcended. But we think the sound construction of the constitution must allow to the national legislature that discretion, with respect to the means by which the powers it confers are to be carried into execution, which will enable that body to perform the high duties assigned to it, in the manner most beneficial to the people. Let the end be legitimate, let it be within the scope of the constitution, and all means which are appropriate, which are plainly adapted to that end, which are not prohibited, but consist with the letter and spirit of the constitution, are constitutional ***.

If a corporation may be employed, indiscriminately with other means, to carry into execution the powers of the government, no particular reason can be assigned for excluding the use of a bank, if required for its fiscal operations. To use one, must be within the discretion of congress, if it be an appropriate mode of executing the powers of government. That it is a convenient, a useful, and essential instrument in the prosecution of its fiscal operations, is not now a subject of controversy. All those who have been concerned in the administration of our finances, have concurred in representing its importance and necessity; and so strongly have they been felt, that statesmen of the first class, whose previous opinions against it had been confirmed by every circumstance which can fix the human judgment, have yielded those opinions to the exigencies of the nation. Under the confederation, congress, justifying the measure by its necessity, transcended, perhaps, its powers, to obtain the advantage of a bank; and our own legislation attests the universal conviction of the utility of this measure. The time has passed away, when it can be necessary to enter into any discussion, in order to prove the importance of this instrument, as a means to effect the legitimate objects of the government.

But were its necessity less apparent, none can deny its being an appropriate measure; and if it is, the decree of its necessity, as has been very justly observed, is to be discussed in another place. Should congress, in the execution of its powers, adopt measures which are prohibited by the constitution; or should congress, under the pretext of executing its powers, pass laws for the accomplishment of objects not intrusted to the government; it would become the painful duty of this tribunal, should a case requiring such a decision come before it, to say, that such an act was not the law of the land. But where the law is not prohibited, and is really calculated to effect any of the objects intrusted to the government, to undertake here to inquire into the degree of its necessity, would be to pass the line which circumscribes the judicial department, and to tread on legislative ground. This court disclaims all pretensions to such a power.

After this declaration, it can scarcely be necessary to say, that the existence of state banks can have no possible influence on the question. No trace is to be found in the constitution, of an intention to create a dependence of the government of the Union on those of the states, for the execution of the great powers assigned to it. Its means are adequate to its ends; and on those means alone was it expected to rely for the accomplishment of its ends. To impose on it the necessity of resorting to means which it cannot control, which another government may furnish or withhold, would render its course precarious, the result of its measures uncertain, and create a dependence on other governments, which might disappoint its most important designs, and is incompatible with the language of the constitution. But were it otherwise, the choice of means implies a right to choose a national bank in preference to state banks, and congress alone can make the election.

After the most deliberate consideration, it is the unanimous and decided opinion of this court, that the act to incorporate the Bank of the United States is a law made in pursuance of the constitution, and is a part of the supreme law of the land.

It being the opinion of the court, that the act incorporating the bank is constitutional; and that the power of establishing a branch in the state of Maryland might be properly exercised by the bank itself, we proceed to inquire—

2. Whether the state of Maryland may, without violating the constitution, tax that branch? That the power of taxation is one of vital importance; that it

is retained by the states; that it is not abridged by the grant of a similar power to the government of the Union; that it is to be concurrently exercised by the two governments—are truths which have never been denied. But such is the paramount character of the constitution, that its capacity to withdraw any subject from the action of even this power, is admitted. The states are expressly forbidden to lay any duties on imports or exports, except what may be absolutely necessary for executing their inspection laws. If the obligation of this prohibition must be conceded—if it may restrain a state from the exercise of its taxing power on imports and exports—the same paramount character would seem to restrain, as it certainly may restrain, a state from such other exercise of this power, as is in its nature incompatible with, and repugnant to, the constitutional laws of the Union. A law, absolutely repugnant to another, as entirely repeals that other as if express terms of repeal were used.

On this ground, the counsel for the bank place its claim to be exempted from the power of a state to tax its operations. There is no express provision for the case, but the claim has been sustained on a principle which so entirely pervades the constitution, is so intermixed with the materials which compose it, so interwoven with its web, so blended with its texture, as to be incapable of being separated from it, without rending it into shreds. This great principle is, that the constitution and the laws made in pursuance thereof are supreme; that they control the constitution and laws of the respective states, and cannot be controlled by them. From this, which may be almost termed an axiom, other propositions are deduced as corollaries, on the truth or error of which, and on their application to this case, the cause has been supposed to depend. These are, 1st. That a power to create implies a power to preserve: 2d. That a power to destroy, if wielded by a different hand, is hostile to, and incompatible with these powers to create and to preserve: 3d. That where this repugnancy exists, that authority which is supreme must control, not yield to that over which it is supreme. ***

The power of congress to create, and of course, to continue, the bank, was the subject of the preceding part of this opinion; and is no longer to be considered as questionable. That the power of taxing it by the states may be exercised so as to destroy it, is too obvious to be denied. But taxation is said to be an absolute power, which acknowledges no other limits than those expressly prescribed in the constitution, and like sovereign power of every other description, is intrusted to the discretion of those who use it. But the very terms of this argument admit, that the sovereignty of the state, in the article of taxation itself, is subordinate to, and may be controlled by the constitution of the United States. How far it has been controlled by that instrument, must be a question of construction. In making this construction, no principle, not declared, can be admissible, which would defeat the legitimate operations of a supreme government. It is of the very essence of supremacy, to remove all obstacles to its action within its own sphere, and so to modify every power vested in subordinate governments, as to exempt its own operations from their own influence. This effect need not be stated in terms. It is so involved in the declaration of supremacy, so necessarily implied in it, that the expression of it could not make it more certain. We must, therefore, keep it in view, while construing the constitution.

The argument on the part of the state of Maryland, is, not that the states may directly resist a law of congress, but that they may exercise their acknowledged powers upon it, and that the constitution leaves them this right, in the confidence that they will not abuse it. Before we proceed to examine this argument, and to subject it to test of the constitution, we must be permitted to bestow a few considerations on the nature and extent of this original right of taxation, which is acknowledged to remain with the states. It is admitted, that the power of taxing the people and their property, is essential to the very existence of government, and may be legitimately exercised on the objects to which it is applicable, to the utmost extent to which the government may choose to carry it. The only security against the abuse of this power, is found in the structure of the government itself. In imposing a tax, the legislature acts upon its constituents. This is, in general, a sufficient security against erroneous and oppressive taxation.

The people of a state, therefore, give to their government a right of taxing themselves and their property, and as the exigencies of government cannot be limited, they prescribe no limits to the exercise of this right, resting confidently on the interest of the legislator, and on the influence of the constituent over their representative, to guard them against its abuse. But the means employed by the government of the Union have no such security, nor is the right of a state to tax them sustained by the same theory. Those means are not given by the people of a particular state, not given by the constituents of the legislature, which claim the right to tax them, but by the people of all the states. They are given by all, for the benefit of all—and upon theory, should be subjected to that government only which belongs to all.

It may be objected to this definition, that the power of taxation is not confined to the people and property of a state. It may be exercised upon every object brought within its jurisdiction. This is true. But to what source do we trace this right? It is obvious, that it is an incident of sovereignty, and is co-extensive with that to which it is an incident. All subjects over which the sovereign power of a state extends, are objects of taxation; but those over which it does not extend, are, upon the soundest principles, exempt from taxation. This proposition may almost be pronounced self-evident.

The sovereignty of a state extends to everything which exists by its own authority, or is introduced by its permission; but does it extend to those means which are employed by congress to carry into execution powers conferred on that body by the people of the United States? We think it demonstrable, that it does not. Those powers are not given by the people of a single state. They are given by the people of the United States, to a government whose laws, made in pursuance of the constitution, are declared to be supreme. Consequently, the people of a single state cannot confer a sovereignty which will extend over them.

We find, then, on just theory, a total failure of this original right to tax the means employed by the government of the Union, for the execution of its powers. The right never existed, and the question whether it has been surrendered, cannot arise.

But, waiving this theory for the present, let us resume the inquiry, whether this power can be exercised by the respective states, consistently with a fair construction of the constitution? That the power to tax involves the power to destroy; that the power to destroy may defeat and render useless the power to create; that there is a plain repugnance in conferring on one government a power to control the constitutional measures of another, which other, with respect to those very measures, is declared to be supreme over that which exerts the control, are propositions not to be denied. But all inconsistencies are to be reconciled by the magic of the word confidence. Taxation, it is said, does not necessarily and unavoidably destroy. To carry it to the excess of destruction, would be an abuse, to presume which, would banish that confidence which is essential to all government. But is this a case of confidence? Would the people of any one state trust those of another with a power to control the most insignificant operations of their state government? We know they would not. Why, then, should we suppose, that the people of any one state should be willing to trust those of another with a power to control the operations of a government to which they have confided their most important and most valuable interests? In the legislature of the Union alone, are all represented. The legislature of the Union alone, therefore, can be trusted by the people with the power of controlling measures which concern all, in the confidence that it will not be abused. This, then, is not a case of confidence, and we must consider it is as it really is.

If we apply the principle for which the state of Maryland contends, to the constitution, generally, we shall find it capable of changing totally the character of that instrument. We shall find it capable of arresting all the measures of the government, and of prostrating it at the foot of the states. The American people have declared their constitution and the laws made in pursuance thereof, to be supreme; but this principle would transfer the supremacy, in fact, to the states. If the states may tax one instrument, employed by the government in the execution of its powers, they may tax any and every other instrument. They may tax the mail; they may tax the mint; they may tax patent-rights; they may tax the papers of the custom-house; they may tax judicial process; they may tax all the means employed by the government, to an excess which would defeat all the ends of government. This was not intended by the American people. They did not design to make their government dependent on the states.

It has also been insisted, that, as the power of taxation in the general and state governments is acknowledged to be concurrent, every argument which would sustain the right of the general government to tax banks chartered by the states, will equally sustain the right of the states to tax banks chartered by the general government. But the two cases are not on the same reason. The people of all the states have created the general government, and have conferred upon it the general power of taxation. The people of all the states, and the states themselves, are represented in congress, and, by their representatives, exercise this power. When they tax the chartered institutions of the states, they tax their constituents; and these taxes must be uniform. But when a state taxes the operations of the government of the United States, it acts upon institutions created, not by their own constituents, but by people over whom they claim no control. It acts upon the measures of a government created by others as well as themselves, for the benefit of others in common with themselves. The difference is that which always exists, and always must exist, between the action of the whole on a part, and the action of a part on the whole—between the laws of a government declared to be supreme, and those of a government which, when in opposition to those laws, is not supreme.

But if the full application of this argument could be admitted, it might bring into question the right of congress to tax the state banks, and could not prove the rights of the states to tax the Bank of the United States.

The court has bestowed on this subject its most deliberate consideration. The result is a conviction that the states have no power, by taxation or otherwise, to retard, impede, burden, or in any manner control, the operations of the constitutional laws enacted by congress to carry into execution the powers vested in the general government. This is, we think, the unavoidable consequence of that supremacy which the constitution has declared. We are unanimously of opinion, that the law passed by the legislature of Maryland, imposing a tax on the Bank of the United States, is unconstitutional and void.

This opinion does not deprive the states of any resources which they originally possessed. It does not extend to a tax paid by the real property of the bank, in common with the other real property within the state, nor to a tax imposed on the interest which the citizens of Maryland may hold in this institution, in common with other property of the same description throughout the state. But this is a tax on the operations of the bank, and is, consequently, a tax on the operation of an instrument employed by the government of the Union to carry its powers into execution. Such a tax must be unconstitutional.

Notes

1. **Structure.** *McCulloch v. Maryland* is often referred to as an opinion based on a "structural" approach to constitutional interpretation. Identify components of the opinion that support this view of the case.

2. **Logic and Limits.**

   (a) Does CHIEF JUSTICE MARSHALL's opinion support the notion that Congress has implied powers?

   (b) President Thomas Jefferson said that "the constitution allows only the means which are *necessary*, not merely 'convenient,' for effectuating the enumerated powers *** [Otherwise, the 'necessary and proper clause'] would swallow up all the delegated powers, and reduce the whole to one power." Do you agree or disagree with Jefferson?

(c) Do you agree or disagree with Virginia CHIEF JUSTICE SPENCER ROANE's argument that "[t]here is no earthly difference between an *unlimited* grant of power, and a grant limited to its terms, but accompanied with *unlimited* means of carrying it into execution"?

(d) What do you think of Marshall's mention of means-ends relationships and the Court's power to invalidate laws enacted "under the pretext" of exercising granted powers?

3. **Aphorisms.**

· Marshall's phrase "it is a *constitution* we are expounding" has proven powerful. What does this phrase mean to you? What bearing should it have on judicial decision making?

· Is Marshall's phrase "the power to tax involves the power to destroy" grounded in the Constitution?

4. **Policy.** Are the policy issues different concerning the two parts of the opinion, or are they really two sides to the same coin? Subsequent commentators have placed great emphasis on what they call the "representation-reinforcement" role played by the Court. Reread what Marshall says concerning the fact that Maryland is harming people not represented in its legislature and whether this is sufficient reason for the Supreme Court, rather than Congress, to protect unrepresented out-of-staters. Was the second part of the Court's opinion needed to preserve federal power?

5. **Federalism and Decentralization.** What is the distinction between a federal system and a governmental system that is merely decentralized?

6. **Intergovernmental Tax Immunity.** Prior to 1938, the intergovernmental tax immunity doctrine was broadly interpreted to prohibit federal and state governments from taxing the salaries of persons employed by other sovereign entities. Since 1939, however, the Court has held that the doctrine should be construed more narrowly. *See Graves v. New York ex rel. O'Keefe,* 306 U.S. 466 (1939) and *United States v. New Mexico,* 455 U.S. 720 (1982). In *Jefferson County, Ala. v. Acker,* 527 U.S. 423 (1999), an Alabama county imposed an occupational tax (as opposed to an income tax) on a group of professions pursuant to the federal Public Salary Tax Act. Two federal judges claimed that the tax on their salaries interfered with the operation of the federal judiciary and violated the intergovernmental tax immunity doctrine. In upholding the constitutionality of the County's ordinance, the Court reaffirmed its previous holding that a State's taxation of federal employees' salaries would be permissible provided that the tax was not directly imposed on one sovereign entity by another and was not discriminatory in nature.

B. THE COMMERCE CLAUSE POWER

Commercial interests were a driving force behind adoption of the Constitution, for the barriers to trade which blossomed under the Articles of Confederation were hindering the economic aspirations of the American people. In addition to specific disabilities placed by the Constitution on the States concerning tariffs and trade, Congress was given the power to regulate commerce, presumably so national commercial interests might prevail over what the Federalists called local protectionist "factions." The classic exposition of the reach of this power is contained in CHIEF JUSTICE MARSHALL's opinion in *Gibbons v. Ogden*, set forth below in Section 1.

As the nation grew during the nineteenth century and the early part of the twentieth century, many Americans were enamored of a laissez faire notion of government on the ground that this was the best way to facilitate commercial growth. During this period, Congress, with few exceptions, did not seek to regulate this growth. When Congress did exercise of this power, the Court sometimes attempted, with a notable lack of success, to cabin Congress' power. Various judicial formulae sought to limit Congress' power to the "direct" regulation of commerce, rather than manufacturing and the like. With the advent of the Great Depression and Franklin Roosevelt's election as President, the laissez faire approach to commerce was challenged as insufficient to guarantee the well being of the American people. Roosevelt's appointees to the Court gave Congress wide latitude to regulate commerce.

Section 2 presents some highlights of the New Deal and Post–New Deal approach of the Supreme Court to the reach of Congress' powers under the Commerce Clause. After reading these cases, you might well conclude that there are no judicially enforceable limits to the Commerce Power, a corollary of which is that the other powers given Congress in Article I, § 8 are superfluous.

This conclusion would be erroneous. Section 3 explores the extent to which the Supreme Court has recently cast doubt on this conventional wisdom, establishing some internal limits to the Commerce Power. How minor or extensive these limits are remains a matter of much debate.

1. CLASSICAL VIEW OF THE COMMERCE CLAUSE

GIBBONS v. OGDEN
22 U.S. (9 Wheat.) 1, 6 L.Ed. 23 (1824).

APPEAL from the Court for the Trial of Impeachments and Correction of Errors of the State of New–York. Aaron Ogden filed his bill in the Court of Chancery of that State, against Thomas Gibbons, setting forth the several acts of the Legislature thereof, enacted for the purpose of securing to Robert R. Livingston and Robert Fulton, the exclusive navigation of all the waters within the jurisdiction of that State, with boats moved by fire or steam, for a term of years which has not yet expired; and authorizing the Chancellor to award an injunction, restraining any person whatever from navigating those waters with boats of that description. The bill stated an assignment from Livingston and Fulton to one John R. Livingston, and from him to the complainant, Ogden, of the right to navigate the waters between Elizabethtown, and other places in New–Jersey, and the city of New–York; and that Gibbons, the defendant below, was in possession of two steam boats, called the Stoudinger and the Bellona, which were actually employed in running between New–York and Elizabethtown, in violation of the exclusive privilege conferred on the complainant, and praying an injunction to restrain the said Gibbons from using the said boats, or any other propelled by fire or steam, in navigating the waters within the territory of New–York. The injunction having been awarded, the answer of Gibbons was filed; in which he stated, that the boats employed by him were duly enrolled and licensed, to be employed in carrying on the coasting trade, under the act of Congress, passed the 18th of February, 1793, c. 3. entitled, "An act for enrolling and licensing ships and vessels to be employed in the coasting trade and fisheries, and for regulating the same." And the defendant insisted on his right, in virtue of such licenses, to navigate the waters between Elizabethtown and the city of New–York, the said acts of the Legislature of the State of New–York to the contrary notwithstanding. At the hearing, the Chancellor perpetuated the injunction, being of the opinion, that the said acts were not repugnant to the constitution and laws of the United States, and were valid. This decree was affirmed in the Court for the Trial of Impeachments and Correction of Errors, which is the highest Court of law and equity in the State, before which the cause could be carried, and it was thereupon brought to this Court by appeal.

MR. CHIEF JUSTICE MARSHALL delivered the opinion of the Court, and, after stating the case, proceeded as follows:

The appellant contends that this decree is erroneous, because the laws which purport to give the exclusive privilege it sustains, are repugnant to the constitution and laws of the United States.

They are said to be repugnant *** [t]o that clause in the constitution which authorizes Congress to regulate commerce ***.

As preliminary to the very able discussions of the constitution, which we have heard from the bar, and as having some influence on its construction, reference has been made to the political situation of these States, anterior to its formation. It has been said, that they were sovereign, were completely independent, and were connected with each other only by a league. This is true. But, when these allied sovereigns converted their league into a government, when they converted their Congress of Ambassadors, deputed to deliberate on their common concerns, and to recommend measures of general utility, into a Legislature, empowered to enact laws on the most interesting subjects, the whole character in which the States appear, underwent a change, the extent of which must be determined by a fair consideration of the instrument by which that change was effected.

[The constitution] contains an enumeration of powers expressly granted by the people to their government. It has been said, that these powers ought to be construed strictly. But why ought they to be so construed? Is there one sentence in the constitution which gives countenance to this rule? In the last of the enumerated powers, that which grants, expressly, the means for carrying all others into execution, Congress is authorized "to make all laws which shall be necessary and proper" for the purpose. But this limitation on the means which may be used, is not extended to the powers which are conferred; nor is there one sentence in the constitution, which has been pointed out by the gentlemen of the bar, or which we have been able to discern, that prescribes this rule. We do not, therefore, think ourselves justified in adopting it. *** If, from the imperfection of human language, there should be serious doubts respecting the extent of any given power, it is a well settled rule, that the objects for which it was given, especially when those objects are expressed in the instrument itself, should have great influence in the construction. We know of no reason for excluding this rule from the present case.

The words [of the constitution] are, "Congress shall have power to regulate commerce with foreign nations, and among the several States, and with the Indian tribes."

The subject to be regulated is commerce; and our constitution being, as was aptly said at the bar, one of enumeration, and not of definition, to ascertain the extent of the power, it becomes necessary to settle the meaning of the word. The counsel for the appellee would limit it to traffic, to buying and selling, or the interchange of commodities, and do not admit that it comprehends navigation. This would restrict a general term, applicable to many objects, to one of its significations. Commerce, undoubtedly, is traffic, but it is something more: it is intercourse. It describes the commercial intercourse between nations, and parts of nations, in all its branches, and is regulated by prescribing rules for carrying on that intercourse. The mind can scarcely conceive a system for regulating commerce between nations, which shall exclude all laws concerning navigation, which shall be silent on the admission of the vessels of the one nation into the ports of the other, and be confined to prescribing rules for the conduct of individuals, in the actual employment of buying and selling, or of barter.

If commerce does not include navigation, the government of the Union has no direct power over that subject, and can make no law prescribing what shall constitute American vessels, or requiring that they shall be navigated by American seamen. Yet this power has been exercised from the commencement of the government, has been exercised with the consent of all, and has been understood by all to be a commercial regulation. All America understands, and has uniformly understood, the word "commerce," to comprehend navigation. It was so understood, and must have been so understood, when the constitution was framed. The power over commerce, including navigation, was one of the primary objects for which the people of America adopted their government, and must have been contemplated in forming it. The convention must have used the word in that sense, because all have understood it in that sense; and the attempt to restrict it comes too late ***.

The word used in the constitution, then, comprehends, and has been always understood to comprehend, navigation within its meaning; and a power to regulate navigation, is as expressly granted, as if that term had been added to the word "commerce."

To what commerce does this power extend? The constitution informs us, to commerce "with foreign nations, and among the several States, and with the Indian tribes."

It has, we believe, been universally admitted, that these words comprehend every species of commercial intercourse between the United States and foreign nations. No sort of trade can be carried on between this country and any other, to which this power does not extend ***. The subject to which the power is next applied, is to commerce "among the several States." The word "among" means intermingled with. A thing which is among others, is intermingled with them. Commerce among the States, cannot stop at the external boundary line of each State, but may be introduced into the interior.

It is not intended to say that these words comprehend that commerce, which is completely internal, which is carried on between man and man in a State, or between different parts of the same State, and which does not extend to or affect other States. Such a power would be inconvenient, and is certainly unnecessary.

Comprehensive as the word "among" is, it may very properly be restricted to that commerce which concerns more States than one. The phrase is not one which would probably have been selected to indicate the completely interior traffic of a State, because it is not an apt phrase for that purpose; and the enumeration of the particular classes of commerce, to which the power was to be extended, would not have been made, had the intention been to extend the power to every description. The enumeration presupposes something not enumerated; and that something, if we regard the language or the subject of the sentence, must be the exclusively internal commerce of a State. The genius and character of the whole government seem to be, that its action is to be applied to all the external concerns of the nation, and to those internal concerns which affect the States generally; but not to those which are completely within a particular State, which do not affect other States, and with which it is not necessary to interfere, for the purpose of executing some of the general powers of the government. The completely internal commerce of a State, then, may be considered as reserved for the State itself.

But, in regulating commerce with foreign nations, the power of Congress does not stop at the jurisdictional lines of the several States. It would be a very useless power, if it could not pass those lines. The commerce of the United States with foreign nations, is that of the whole United States. Every district has a right to participate in it. The deep streams which penetrate our country in every direction, pass through the interior of almost every State in the Union, and furnish the means of exercising this right. If Congress has the power to regulate it, that power must be exercised whenever the subject exists. If it exists within the States, if a foreign voyage may commence or terminate at a port within a State, then the power of Congress may be exercised within a State.

This principle is, if possible, still more clear, when applied to commerce "among the several States." They either join each other, in which case they are separated by a mathematical line, or they are remote from each other, in which case other States lie between them. What is commerce "among" them; and how is it to be conducted? Can a trading expedition between two adjoining States, commence and terminate outside of each? And if the trading intercourse be between two States remote from each other, must it not commence in one, terminate in the other, and probably pass through a third? Commerce among the States must, of necessity, be commerce with the States. In the regulation of trade with the Indian tribes, the action of the law, especially when the constitution was made, was chiefly within a State. The power of Congress, then, whatever it may be, must be exercised within the territorial jurisdiction of the several States. The sense of the nation on this subject, is unequivocally manifested by the provisions made in the laws for transporting goods, by land, between Baltimore and Providence, between New–York and Philadelphia, and between Philadelphia and Baltimore.

We are now arrived at the inquiry—What is this power?

It is the power to regulate; that is, to prescribe the rule by which commerce is to be governed. This power, like all others vested in Congress, is complete in itself, may be exercised to its utmost extent, and acknowledges no limitations, other than are prescribed in the constitution. These are expressed in plain terms, and do not affect the questions which arise in this case, or which have been discussed at the bar. If, as has always been understood, the sovereignty of Congress, though limited to specified objects, is plenary as to those objects, the power over commerce with foreign nations, and among the several States, is vested in Congress as absolutely as it would be in a single government, having in its constitution the same restrictions on the exercise of the power as are found in the constitution of the United States. The wisdom and the discretion of Congress, their identity with the people, and the influence which their constituents possess at elections, are, in this, as in many other instances, as that, for example, of declaring war, the sole restraints on which they have relied, to secure them from its abuse. They are the restraints on which the people must often they solely, in all representative governments.

The power of Congress, then, comprehends navigation, within the limits of every State in the Union; so far as that navigation may be, in any manner, connected with "commerce with foreign nations, or among the several States, or with the Indian tribes." It may, of consequence, pass the jurisdictional line of New York, and act upon the very waters to which the prohibition now under consideration applies.

But it has been urged with great earnestness, that, although the power of Congress to regulate commerce with foreign nations, and among the several States, be co-extensive with the subject itself, and have no other limits than are prescribed in the constitution, yet the States may severally exercise the same power, within their respective jurisdictions.

[For example, t]he grant of the power to lay and collect taxes is, like the power to regulate commerce, made in general terms, and has never been understood to interfere with the exercise of the same power by the State; and hence has been drawn an argument which has been applied to the question under consideration. But the two grants are not, it is conceived, similar in their terms or their nature. Although many of the powers formerly exercised by the States, are transferred to the government of the Union, yet the State governments remain, and constitute a most important part of our system. The power of taxation is indispensable to their existence, and is a power which, in its own nature, is capable of residing in, and being exercised by, different authorities at the same time. We are accustomed to see it placed, for different purposes, in different hands. Taxation is the simple operation of taking small portions from a perpetually accumulating mass, susceptible of almost infinite division; and a power in one to take what is necessary for certain purposes, is not, in its nature, incompatible with a power in another to take what is necessary for other purposes. Congress is authorized to lay and collect taxes, &c. to pay the debts, and provide for the common defence and general welfare of the United States. This does not interfere with the power of the States to tax for the support of their own governments; nor is the exercise of that power by the States, an exercise of any portion of the power that is granted to the United States. In imposing taxes for State purposes, they are not doing what Congress is empowered to do. Congress is not empowered to tax for those purposes which are within the exclusive province of the States. When, then, each government exercises the power of taxation, neither is exercising the power of the other. But, when a State proceeds to regulate commerce with foreign nations, or among the several States, it is exercising the very power that is granted to Congress, and is doing the very thing which Congress is authorized to do. There is no analogy, then, between the power of taxation and the power of regulating commerce ***.

The sole question is, can a State regulate commerce with foreign nations and among the States, while Congress is regulating it?

The counsel for the respondent answer this question in the affirmative, and rely very much on the restrictions in the 10th section, as supporting their opinion. They say, very truly, that limitations of a power, furnish a strong argument in favour of the existence of that power, and that the section which prohibits the States from laying duties on imports or exports, proves that this power might have been exercised, had it not been expressly forbidden; and, consequently, that any other commercial regulation, not expressly forbidden, to which the original power of the State was competent, may still be made.

That this restriction shows the opinion of the Convention, that a State might impose duties on exports and imports, if not expressly forbidden, will be conceded; but that it follows as a consequence, from this concession, that a State may regulate commerce with foreign nations and among the States, cannot be admitted ***.

[I]nspection laws are said to be regulations of commerce, and are certainly recognised in the constitution, as being passed in the exercise of a power remaining with the States.

That inspection laws may have a remote and considerable influence on commerce, will not be denied; but that a power to regulate commerce is the source from which the right to pass them is derived, cannot be admitted. The object of inspection laws, is to improve the quality of articles produced by the labour of a country; to fit them for exportation; or, it may be, for domestic use. They act upon the subject before it becomes an article of foreign commerce, or of commerce among the States, and prepare it for that purpose. They form a portion of that immense mass of legislation, which embraces every thing within the territory of a State, not surrendered to the general government: all which can be most advantageously exercised by the States themselves. Inspection laws, quarantine laws, health laws of every description, as well as laws for regulating the internal commerce of a State, and those which respect turnpike roads, ferries, &c., are component parts of this mass.

No direct general power over these objects is granted to Congress; and, consequently, they remain subject to State legislation. If the legislative power of the Union can reach them, it must be for national purposes; it must be where the power is expressly given for a special purpose, or is clearly incidental to some power which is expressly given. It is obvious, that the government of the Union, in the exercise of its express powers, that, for example, of regulating commerce with foreign nations and among the States, may use means that may also be employed by a State, in the exercise of its acknowledged powers; that, for example, of regulating commerce within the State. If Congress license vessels to sail from one port to another, in the same State, the act is supposed to be, necessarily, incidental to the power expressly granted to Congress, and implies no claim of a direct power to regulate the purely internal commerce of a State, or to act directly on its system of police. So, if a State, in passing laws on subjects acknowledged to be within its control, and with a view to those subjects, shall adopt a measure of the same character with one which Congress may adopt, it does not derive its authority from the particular power which has been granted, but from some other, which remains with the State, and may be executed by the same means. ***

In pursuing this inquiry at the bar, it has been said, that the constitution does not confer the right of intercourse between State and State. That right derives its source from those laws whose authority is acknowledged by civilized man throughout the world. This is true. The constitution found it an existing right, and gave to Congress the power to regulate it. In the exercise of this power, Congress has passed "an act for enrolling or licensing ships or vessels to be employed in the coasting trade and fisheries, and for regulating the same." ***

This act demonstrates the opinion of Congress, that steam boats may be enrolled and licensed, in common with vessels using sails. They are, of course, entitled to the same privileges, and can no more be restrained from navigating waters, and entering ports which are free to such vessels, than if they were wafted on their voyage by the winds, instead of being propelled by the agency of fire. The one element may be as legitimately used as the other, for every commercial purpose authorized by the laws of the Union; and the act of a State inhibiting the use of either to any vessel having a license under the act of Congress, comes, we think, in direct collision with that act.

The Court is aware that, in stating the train of reasoning by which we have been conducted to this result, much time has been consumed in the attempt to demonstrate propositions which may have been thought axioms. It is felt that the tediousness inseparable from the endeavour to prove that which is already clear, is imputable to a considerable part of this opinion. But it was unavoidable. The conclusion to which we have come, depends on a chain of principles which it was necessary to preserve unbroken; and, although some of them were thought nearly self-evident, the magnitude of the question, the weight of character belonging to those from whose judgment we dissent, and the argument at the bar, demanded that we should assume nothing.

Powerful and ingenious minds, taking, as postulates, that the powers expressly granted to the government of the Union, are to be contracted by construction, into the narrowest possible compass, and that the original powers of the States are retained, if any possible construction will retain them, may, by a course of well digested, but refined and metaphysical reasoning, founded on these premises, explain away the constitution of our country, and leave it, a magnificent structure, indeed, to look at, but totally unfit for use. They may so entangle and perplex the understanding, as to obscure principles, which were before thought quite plain, and induce doubts where, if the mind were to pursue its own course, none would be perceived. In such a case, it is peculiarly necessary to recur to safe and fundamental principles to sustain those principles, and when sustained, to make them the tests of the arguments to be examined. ***

MR. JUSTICE JOHNSON. [concurring]

For a century the States [as Colonies] submitted, with murmurs, to the commercial restrictions imposed by the parent State; and [under the Articles of Confederation] finding themselves in the unlimited possession of those powers over their own commerce, which they had so long been deprived of, and so earnestly coveted, that selfish principle which, well controlled, is so salutary, and which, unrestricted, is so unjust and tyrannical, guided by inexperience and jealousy, began to show itself in iniquitous laws and impolitic measures, from which grew up a conflict of commercial regulations, destructive to the harmony of the States, and fatal to their commercial interests abroad.

This was the immediate cause, that led to the [Constitutional] convention. ***

The history of the times will, therefore, sustain the opinion, that the grant of power over commerce, if intended to be commensurate with the evils existing, and the purpose of remedying those evils, could be only commensurate with the power of the States over the subject. And this opinion is supported by a very remarkable evidence of the general understanding of the whole American people, when the grant was made.

There was not a State in the Union, in which there did not, at that time, exist a variety of commercial regulations, concerning which it is too much to suppose, that the whole ground covered by those regulations was immediately assumed by actual legislation, under the authority of the Union. But where was the existing statute on this subject, that a State attempted to execute? or by what State was it ever thought necessary to repeal those statutes? By common consent, those laws dropped lifeless from their statute books, for want of the sustaining power, that had been relinquished to Congress. ***

The "power to regulate commerce," here meant to be granted, was that power to regulate unquestionably, supreme; and each possessed that power over commerce, which is acknowledged to reside in every sovereign State. *** The power of a sovereign state over commerce, therefore, amounts to nothing more than a power to limit and restrain it at pleasure. And since the power to prescribe the limits to its freedom, necessarily implies the power to determine what shall remain unrestrained, it follows, that the power must be exclusive; it can reside but in one potentate; and hence, the grant of this power carries with it the whole subject, leaving nothing for the State to act upon. ***

It is impossible, with the views which I entertain of the principle on which the commercial privileges of the people of the United States, among themselves, rests, to concur in the view which this Court takes of the effect of the coasting license in this cause. I do not regard it as the foundation of the right set up in behalf of the appellant. If there was any one object riding over every other in the adoption of the constitution, it was to keep the commercial intercourse among the States free from all invidious and partial restraints. And I cannot overcome the conviction, that if the licensing act was repealed to-morrow, the rights of the appellant to a reversal of the decision complained of, would be as strong as it is under this license. One half the doubts in life arise form the defects of language, and if this instrument had been called an exemption instead of a license, it would have given a better idea of its character. Licensing acts, in fact, in legislation, are universally restraining acts; as, for example, acts licensing gaming houses, retailers of spiritous liquors, &c. ***

Yet there is one view, in which the license may be allowed considerable influence in sustaining the decision of this Court.

It has been contended, that the grants of power to the United States over any subject, do not, necessarily, paralyze the arm of the States, or deprive them of the capacity to act on the same subject. This can be the effect only of prohibitory provisions in their own constitutions, or in that of the general government. The vis vitae of power is still existing in the States, if not extinguished by the constitution of the United States. That, although as to all those grants of power which may be called aboriginal, with relation to the government, brought into existence by the constitution, they, of course, are out of the reach of State power; yet, as to all concessions of powers which previously existed in the States, it was otherwise. The practice of our government certainly has been, on many subjects, to occupy so much only of the field opened to them, as they think the public interests require. Witness the jurisdiction of the Circuit Courts, limited both as to cases and as to amount; and various other instances that might to be cited. But the license furnishes a full answer to this objection; for, although one grant of power over commerce, should not be deemed a total relinquishment of power over the subject, but amounting only to a power to assume, still the power of the States must be at an end, so far as the United States have, by their legislative act, taken the subject under their immediate superintendence. So far as relates to the commerce coastwise, the act under which this license is granted, contains a full expression of Congress on this subject.

But the principal objections to these opinions arise, 1st. From the unavoidable action of some of the municipal powers of the States, upon commercial subjects [and] 2d. From passages in the constitution, which are supposed to imply a concurrent power in the States in regulating commerce.

It is no objection to the existence of distinct, substantive powers, that in their application, they bear upon the same subject. The same bale of goods, the same cask of provisions, or the same ship, that may be the subject of commercial regulation, may also be the vehicle of disease. And the health laws that require them to be stopped and ventilated, are no more intended as regulations on commerce, than the laws which permit their importation, are intended to innoculate the community with disease. Their different purposes mark the distinction between the powers brought into action, and while frankly exercised, they can produce no serious collision. As to laws affecting ferries, turnpike roads, and other subjects of the same class, so far from meriting the epithet of commercial regulations, they are, in fact, commercial facilities, for which, by the consent of mankind, a compensation is paid, upon the same principle that the whole commercial world submit to pay light money to the Danes. Inspection laws are of a more equivocal nature, and it is obvious, that the constitution has viewed that subject with much solicitude. But so far from sustaining an inference in favour of the power of the States over commerce, I cannot but think that the guarded provisions of the 10th section, on this subject, furnish a strong argument against that inference. It was obvious, that inspection laws must combine municipal with commercial regulations; and, while the power over the subject is yielded to the States, for obvious reasons, an absolute control is given over State legislation on the subject, as far as that legislation may be exercised, so as to affect the commerce of the country. The inferences, to be correctly drawn, from this whole article, appear to me to be altogether in favour of the exclusive grants to Congress of power over commerce, and the reverse of that which the appellee contends for.

This section contains the positive restrictions imposed by the constitution upon State power. The first clause of it, specifies those powers which the states are precluded from exercising, even though the Congress were to permit them. The second, those which the States may exercise with the consent of Congress. And here the sedulous attention to the subject of State exclusion from commercial power, is strongly marked. Not satisfied with the express grant to the United States of the power over commerce, this clause negatives the exercise of that power to the States, as to the only two objects which could ever tempt them to assume the exercise of that power, to wit, the collection of a revenue from imposts and duties on imports and exports; or from a tonnage duty. As to imposts on imports or exports, such a revenue might have been aimed at directly, by express legislation, or indirectly, in the form of inspection laws; and it became necessary to guard against both. Hence, first, the consent of Congress to such imposts or duties, is made necessary; and as to inspection laws, it is limited to the minimum of expenses. Then, the money so raised shall be paid into the treasury of the United States, or may be sued for, since it is declared to be for their use. And lastly, all such laws may be modified, or repealed, by an act of Congress. It is impossible for a right to be more guarded.

It would be in vain to deny the possibility of a clashing and collision between the measures of the two governments. The line cannot be drawn with sufficient distinctness between the municipal powers of the one, and the commercial powers of the other. In some points they meet and blend so as scarcely to admit of separation. Hitherto the only remedy has been applied which the case admits of, that of a frank and candid co-operation for the general good. Witness the laws of Congress requiring its officers to respect the inspection laws of the States, and to aid in enforcing their health laws; that which surrenders to the States the superintendence of pilotage, and the many laws passed to permit a tonnage duty to be levied for the use of their ports. Other instances could be cited, abundantly to prove that collision must be sought to be produced; and when it does arise, the question must be decided how far the powers of Congress are adequate to put it down. Wherever the powers of the respective governments are frankly exercised, with a distinct view to the ends of such powers, they may act upon the same object, or use the same means and yet the powers be kept perfectly distinct. A resort to the same means, therefore, is no argument to prove the identity of their respective powers. ***

Notes

1. **Linguistic Limits.** Consider the Court's attempt to parse the language of the Commerce Clause.

• *Commerce.* How does CHIEF JUSTICE MARSHALL define this term and relate it to navigation? To state inspection laws?

• *Among the Several States.* How does Marshall view commerce that is "completely internal" and does not affect other states?

• *Regulate.* Why are inspection laws a problem for Marshall in defining regulation?

2. **Concurrence.** Compare and contrast JUSTICE JOHNSON's concurrence with CHIEF JUSTICE MARSHALL's opinion for the Court.

3. **Judicial Competence.** Is the Court or Congress in the better position to determine whether a particular statutory provision regulates commerce among the several states?

2. THE COMMERCE CLAUSE DURING AND AFTER THE NEW DEAL

WICKARD v. FILBURN
317 U.S. 111, 63 S.Ct. 82, 87 L.Ed. 122 (1942).

MR. JUSTICE JACKSON delivered the opinion of the Court.

The appellee filed his complaint against the Secretary of Agriculture of the United States [and others]. *** He sought to enjoin enforcement against himself of the marketing penalty imposed by the amendment of May 26, 1941 to the Agricultural Adjustment Act of 1938 upon that part of his 1941 wheat crop which was available for marketing in excess of the marketing quota established for his farm. He also sought a declaratory judgment that the wheat marketing quota provisions of the Act as amended and applicable to him were unconstitutional because not sustainable under the Commerce Clause or consistent with the Due Process Clause of the Fifth Amendment. ***

The appellee for many years past has owned and operated a small farm in Montgomery County, Ohio, maintaining a herd of dairy cattle, selling milk, raising poultry, and selling poultry and eggs. It has been his practice to raise a small acreage of winter wheat, sown in the Fall and harvested in the following July; to sell a portion of the crop; to feed part to poultry and livestock on the farm, some of which is sold; to use some in making flour for home consumption; and to keep the rest for the following seeding. The intended disposition of the crop here involved has not been expressly stated.

In July of 1940, pursuant to the Agricultural Adjustment Act of 1938, as then amended, there were established for the appellee's 1941 crop a wheat acreage allotment of 11.1 acres and a normal yield of 20.1 bushels of wheat an acre. He was given notice of such allotment in July of 1940 before the Fall planting of his 1941 crop of wheat, and again in July of 1941, before it was harvested. He sowed, however, 23 acres, and harvested from his 11.9 acres of excess acreage 239 bushels, which under the terms of the Act as amended on May 26, 1941, constituted farm marketing excess, subject to a penalty of 49 cents a bushel, or $117.11 in all. The appellee has not paid the penalty and he has not postponed or avoided it by storing the excess under regulations of the Secretary of Agriculture, or by delivering it up to the Secretary. The Committee, therefore, refused him a marketing card, which was, under the terms of Regulations promulgated by the Secretary, necessary to protect a buyer from liability to the penalty and upon its protecting lien.

The general scheme of the Agricultural Adjustment Act of 1938 as related to wheat is to control the volume moving in interstate and foreign commerce in order to avoid surpluses and shortages and the consequent abnormally low or high wheat prices and obstructions to commerce. Within prescribed limits and by prescribed standards the Secretary of Agriculture is directed to ascertain and proclaim each year a national acreage allotment for the next crop of wheat, which is then apportioned to the states and their counties, and is eventually broken up into allotments for individual farms. Loans and payments to wheat farmers are authorized in stated circumstances.

The Act provides further that whenever it appears that the total supply of wheat as of the beginning of any marketing year, beginning July 1, will exceed a normal year's domestic consumption and export by more than 35 per cent, the Secretary shall so proclaim not later than May 15 prior to the beginning of such marketing year; and that during the marketing year a compulsory national marketing quota shall be in effect with respect to the marketing of wheat. Between the issuance of the proclamation and June 10, the Secretary must, however, conduct a referendum of farmers who will be subject to the quota to determine whether they favor or oppose it; and if more than one-third of the farmers voting in the referendum do oppose, the Secretary must prior to the effective date of the quota by proclamation suspend its operation.

On May 19, 1941 the Secretary of Agriculture made a radio address to the wheat farmers of the United States in which he advocated approval of the quotas. ***

Pursuant to the Act, the referendum of wheat growers was held on May 31, 1941. According to the required published statement of the Secretary of Agriculture, 81 per cent of those voting favored the marketing quota, with 19 per cent opposed.

*** It is urged that under the Commerce Clause of the Constitution, Article I, s 8, clause 3, Congress does not possess the power it has in this instance sought to exercise. The question would merit little consideration since our decision in *United States v. Darby*, 312 U.S. 100, sustaining the federal power to regulate production of goods for commerce except for the fact that this Act extends federal regulation to production not intended in any part for commerce but wholly for consumption on the farm. *** [M]arketing quotas not only embrace all that may be sold without penalty but also what may be consumed on the premises. Wheat produced on excess acreage is designated as "available for marketing" as so defined and the penalty is imposed thereon. Penalties do not depend upon whether any part of the wheat either within or without the quota is sold or intended to be sold. The sum of this is that the Federal Government fixes a quota including all that the farmer may harvest for sale or for his own farm needs, and declares that wheat produced on excess acreage may neither be disposed of nor used except upon payment of the penalty or except it is stored as required by the Act or delivered to the Secretary of Agriculture.

Appellee says that this is a regulation of production and consumption of wheat. Such activities are, he urges, beyond the reach of Congressional power under the Commerce Clause, since they are local in character, and their effects upon interstate commerce are at most "indirect." In answer the Government argues that the statute regulates neither production nor consumption, but only marketing; and, in the alternative, that if the Act does go beyond the regulation of marketing it is sustainable as a "necessary and proper" implementation of the power of Congress over interstate commerce.

*** [Q]uestions of the power of Congress are not to be decided by reference to any formula which would give controlling force to nomenclature such as "production" and "indirect" and foreclose consideration of the actual effects of the activity in question upon interstate commerce.

At the beginning CHIEF JUSTICE MARSHALL described the Federal commerce power with a breadth never yet exceeded. *Gibbons v. Ogden*. He made emphatic the embracing and penetrating nature of this power by warning that effective restraints on its exercise must proceed from political rather than from judicial processes.

*** Not long after the decision of *United States v. E. C. Knight Co.*, [156 U.S. 1,] MR. JUSTICE HOLMES, in sustaining the exercise of national power over intrastate activity, stated for the Court that "commerce among the states is not a technical legal conception, but a practical one, drawn from the course of business." *Swift & Co. v. United States*, 196 U.S. 375, 398. It was soon demonstrated that the effects of many kinds of intrastate activity upon interstate commerce were such as to make them a proper subject of federal regulation. In some cases sustaining the exercise of federal power over intrastate matters the term "direct" was used for the purpose of stating, rather than of reaching, a result; in others it was treated as synonymous with "substantial" or "material;" and in others it was not used at all. Of late its use has been abandoned in cases dealing with questions of federal power under the Commerce Clause.

In the Shreveport Rate Cases the Court held that railroad rates of an admittedly intrastate character and fixed by authority of the state might, nevertheless, be revised by the Federal Government because of the economic effects which they had upon interstate commerce. The opinion of MR. JUSTICE HUGHES found federal intervention constitutionally authorized because of "matters having such a close and substantial relation to interstate traffic that the control is essential or appropriate to the security of that traffic, to the efficiency of the interstate service, and to the maintenance of the conditions under which interstate commerce may be conducted upon fair terms and without molestation or hindrance."

The Court's recognition of the relevance of the economic effects in the application of the Commerce Clause exemplified by this statement has made the mechanical application of legal formulas no longer feasible. Once an economic measure of the reach of the power granted to Congress in the Commerce Clause is accepted, questions of federal power cannot be decided simply by finding the activity in question to be "production" nor can consideration of its economic effects be foreclosed by calling them "indirect." ***

Whether the subject of the regulation in question was "production," "consumption," or "marketing" is, therefore, not material for purposes of deciding the question of federal power before us. That an activity is of local character may help in a doubtful case to determine whether Congress intended to reach it. The same consideration might help in determining whether in the absence of Congressional action it would be permissible for the state to exert its power on the subject matter, even though in so doing it to some degree affected interstate commerce. But even if appellee's activity be local and though it may not be regarded as commerce, it may still, whatever its nature, be reached by Congress if it exerts a substantial economic effect on interstate commerce and this irrespective of whether such effect is what might at some earlier time have been defined as "direct" or "indirect."

The parties have stipulated a summary of the economics of the wheat industry. Commerce among the states in wheat is large and important. Although wheat is raised in every state but one, production in most states is not equal to consumption. Sixteen states on average have had a surplus of wheat above their own requirements for feed, seed, and food. Thirty-two states and the District of Columbia, where production has been below consumption, have looked to these surplus-producing states for their supply as well as for wheat for export and carryover.

The wheat industry has been a problem industry for some years. Largely as a result of increased foreign production and import restrictions, annual exports of wheat and flour from the United States during the ten-year period ending in 1940 averaged less than 10 per cent of total production, while during the 1920's they averaged more than 25 per cent. The decline in the export trade has left a large surplus in production which in connection with an abnormally large supply of wheat and other grains in recent years caused congestion in a number of markets; tied up railroad cars; and caused elevators in some instances to turn away grains, and railroads to institute embargoes to prevent further congestion. *** In the absence of regulation the price of wheat in the United States would be much affected by world conditions. During 1941 producers who cooperated with the Agricultural Adjustment program received an average price on the farm of about $1.16 a bushel as compared with the world market price of 40 cents a bushel.

*** The effect of consumption of homegrown wheat on interstate commerce is due to the fact that it constitutes the most variable factor in the disappearance of the wheat crop. Consumption on the farm where grown appears to vary in an amount greater than 20 per cent of average production. The total amount of wheat consumed as food varies but relatively little, and use as seed is relatively constant.

The maintenance by government regulation of a price for wheat undoubtedly can be accomplished as effectively by sustaining or increasing the demand as by limiting the supply. The effect of the statute before us is to restrict the amount which may be produced for market and the extent as well to which one may forestall resort to the market by producing to meet his own needs. That appellee's own contribution to the demand for wheat may be trivial by itself is not enough to remove him from the scope of federal regulation where, as here, his contribution, taken together with that of many others similarly situated, is far from trivial.

*** [A] factor of such volume and variability as home-consumed wheat [will] have a substantial influence on price and market conditions. This may arise because being in marketable condition such wheat overhangs the market and if induced by rising prices tends to flow into the market and check price increases. But if we assume that it is never marketed, it supplies a need of the man who grew it which would otherwise be reflected by purchases in the open market. Home-grown wheat in this sense competes with wheat in commerce. The stimulation of commerce is a use of the regulatory function quite as definitely as prohibitions or restrictions thereon. This record leaves us in no doubt that Congress may properly have considered that wheat consumed on the farm where grown if wholly outside the scheme of regulation would have a substantial effect in defeating and obstructing its purpose to stimulate trade therein at increased prices.

It is said, however, that this Act, forcing some farmers into the market to buy what they could provide for themselves, is an unfair promotion of the markets and prices of specializing wheat growers. It is of the essence of regulation that it lays a restraining hand on the self-interest of the regulated and that advantages from the regulation commonly fall to others. The conflicts of economic interest between the regulated and those who advantage by it are wisely left under our system to resolution by the Congress under its more flexible and responsible legislative process. Such conflicts rarely lend themselves to judicial determination. And with the wisdom, workability, or fairness, of the plan of regulation we have nothing to do. ***

Notes

1. **History.** *Wickard* was decided more than a hundred years after *Gibbons*. Between the two decisions, the Civil War led to a redefinition of the power of the states relative to the federal government; the Great Depression led to an expanded appreciation of economic interdependence; and technological progress greatly expanded both the modes and matters of commerce. Is the Court still looking at the same Commerce Clause in the more recent case?

2. **Limits?** Five years before *Wickard*, in *NLRB v. Jones & Laughlin Steel Corp.*, 301 U.S. 1 (1937), the Court considered whether the National Labor Relations Act unconstitutionally attempted to regulate all commerce. The Court found that the NLRA was an attempt to "reach only what might be deemed to burden or obstruct [interstate] commerce." The Court stated that, whether the statute exceeded Congress' power should be looked at with respect to particular applications; the Court then proceeded to document the huge steel company's many involvements with interstate commerce and found that the statute could properly be applied to the company under the authority of the Commerce Clause. The outcome of *Wickard* would surely have been different if this approach had been used. Does the Court's approach in *Wickard* signal that the Court has abandoned all efforts to distinguish interstate from local commerce? What activities can be aggregated?

3. **Statutory Construction.** What do you think JUSTICE JACKSON meant when he said: "That an activity is of local character may help in a doubtful case to determine whether Congress intended to reach it"? What is a "doubtful case"? What does Congress intend to regulate when it says that any person convicted of a felony who "receives, possesses or transports in commerce or affecting commerce [any] firearm" shall be fined or imprisoned? *See United States v. Bass*, 404 U.S. 336 (1971).

HEART OF ATLANTA MOTEL v. UNITED STATES
379 U.S. 241, 85 S.Ct. 348, 13 L.Ed.2d 258 (1964).

MR. JUSTICE CLARK delivered the opinion of the Court

This is a declaratory judgment action, 28 U.S.C. § 2201 and § 2202, attacking the constitutionality of Title II of the Civil Rights Act of 1964.

*** Appellant owns and operates the Heart of Atlanta Motel which has 216 rooms available to transient guests [and] is readily accessible to interstate highways 75 and 85 and state highways 23 and 41. Appellant solicits patronage from outside the State of Georgia through various national advertising media, including magazines of national circulation; it maintains over 50 billboards and highway signs within the State, soliciting patronage for the motel; it accepts convention trade from outside Georgia and approximately 75% of its registered guests are from out of State. Prior to passage of the Act the motel had followed a practice of refusing to rent rooms to Negroes, and it alleged that it intended to continue to do so. In an effort to perpetuate that policy this suit was filed.

IV–1. Heart of Atlanta. Atlanta Braves Program.

*** [O]n June 19, 1963, the late President Kennedy called for civil rights legislation in a message to Congress to which he attached a proposed bill. Its stated purpose was "to promote the general welfare by eliminating discrimination based on race, color, religion, or national origin in *** public accommodations through the exercise by Congress of the powers conferred upon it *** to enforce the provisions of the fourteenth and fifteenth amendments, to regulate commerce among the several States, and to make laws necessary and proper to execute the powers conferred upon it by the Constitution." Bills were introduced in each House of the Congress, embodying the President's suggestion. [O]n July 2, 1964, upon the recommendation of President Johnson, that the Civil Rights Act of 1964, here under attack, was finally passed.

*** The Act as finally adopted was most comprehensive, undertaking to prevent through peaceful and voluntary settlement discrimination in voting, as well as in places of accommodation and public facilities, federally secured programs and in employment. Since Title II is the only portion under attack here, we confine our consideration to those public accommodation provisions.

This Title is divided into seven sections beginning with § 201(a) which provides that: "All persons shall be entitled to the full and equal enjoyment of the goods, services, facilities, privileges, advantages, and accommodations of any place of public accommodation, as defined in this section, without discrimination or segregation on the ground of race, color, religion, or national origin." There are listed in § 201(b) four classes of business establishments, each of which "serves the public" and "is a place of public accommodation" within the meaning of § 201(a) "if its operations affect commerce, or if discrimination or segregation by it is supported by State action." The covered establishments are: "(1) any inn, hotel, motel, or other establishment which provides lodging to transient guests, other than an establishment located within a building which contains not more than five rooms for rent or hire and which is actually occupied by the proprietor of such establishment as his residence *** [and others not at issue]." Section 201(c) defines the phrase "affect commerce" as applied to the above establishments. It first declares that "any inn, hotel, motel, or other establishment which provides lodging to transient guests" affects commerce per se.

*** It is admitted that the operation of the motel brings it within the provisions of § 201(a) of the Act and that appellant refused to provide lodging for transient Negroes because of their race or color and that it intends to continue that policy unless restrained.

The sole question posed is, therefore, the constitutionality of the Civil Rights Act of 1964 as applied to these facts. The legislative history of the Act indicates that Congress based the Act on § 5 and the Equal Protection Clause of the Fourteenth Amendment as well as its power to regulate interstate commerce under Art. I, § 8, cl. 3, of the Constitution. ***

*** In light of our ground for decision, it might be well at the outset to discuss the *Civil Rights Cases*, which declared provisions of the Civil Rights Act of 1875 unconstitutional. We think that decision inapposite, and without precedential value in determining the constitutionality of the present Act. Unlike Title II of the present legislation, the 1875 Act broadly proscribed discrimination in "inns, public conveyances on land or water, theaters, and other places of public amusement," without limiting the categories of affected businesses to those impinging upon interstate commerce. In contrast, the applicability of Title II is carefully limited to enterprises having a direct and substantial relation to the interstate flow of goods and people, except where state action is involved. Further, the fact that certain kinds of businesses may not in 1875 have been sufficiently involved in interstate commerce to warrant bringing them within the ambit of the commerce power is not necessarily dispositive of the same question today. Our populace had not reached its present mobility, nor were facilities, goods and services circulating as readily in interstate commerce as they are today. Although the principles which we apply today are those first formulated by CHIEF JUSTICE MARSHALL in *Gibbons v. Ogden*, 9 Wheat. 1 (1824), the conditions of transportation and commerce have changed dramatically, and we must apply those principles to the present state of commerce. The sheer increase in volume of interstate traffic alone would give discriminatory practices which inhibit travel a far larger impact upon the Nation's commerce than such practices had on the economy of another day. *** We, therefore, conclude that the Civil Rights Cases have no relevance to the basis of decision here where the Act explicitly relies upon the commerce power, and where the record is filled with testimony of obstructions and restraints resulting from the discriminations found to be existing. We now pass to that phase of the case.

While the Act as adopted carried no congressional findings the record of its passage through each house is replete with evidence of the burdens that discrimination by race or color places upon interstate commerce. This testimony included the fact that our people have become increasingly mobile with millions of people of all races traveling from State to State; that Negroes in particular have been the subject of discrimination in transient accommodations, having to travel great distances to secure the same; that often they have been unable to obtain accommodations and have had to call upon friends to put them up overnight, and that these conditions had become so acute as to require the listing of available lodging for Negroes in a special guidebook which was itself "dramatic testimony to the difficulties" Negroes encounter in travel. These exclusionary practices were found to be nationwide, the Under Secretary of Commerce testifying that there is "no question that this discrimination in the North still exists to a large degree" and in the West and Midwest as well. This testimony indicated a qualitative as well as quantitative effect on interstate travel by Negroes. The former was the obvious impairment of the Negro traveler's pleasure and convenience that resulted when he continually was uncertain of finding lodging. As for the latter, there was evidence that this uncertainty stemming from racial discrimination had the effect of discouraging travel on the part of a substantial portion of the Negro community. This was the conclusion not only of the Under Secretary of Commerce but also of the Administrator of the Federal Aviation Agency who wrote the Chairman of the Senate Commerce Committee that it was his "belief that air commerce is adversely affected by the denial to a substantial segment of the traveling public of adequate and desegregated public accommodations." We shall not burden this opinion with further details since the voluminous testimony presents overwhelming evidence that discrimination by hotels and motels impedes interstate travel.

The power of Congress to deal with these obstructions depends on the meaning of the Commerce Clause. *** In short, the determinative test of the exercise of power by the Congress under the Commerce Clause is simply whether the activity sought to be regulated is "Commerce which concerns more States than one" and has a real and substantial relation to the national interest.

*** The same interest in protecting interstate commerce which led Congress to deal with segregation in interstate carriers and the white-slave traffic has prompted it to extend the exercise of its power to gambling, *Lottery Case (Champion v. Ames)*, 188 U.S. 321 (1903); to criminal enterprises, *Brooks v. United States*, 267 U.S. 432 (1925); to deceptive practices in the sale of products, *Federal Trade Comm. v. Mandel Bros., Inc.*, 359 U.S. 385 (1959); to fraudulent security transactions, *Securities & Exchange Comm. v. Ralston Purina Co.*, 346 U.S. 119 (1953); to misbranding of drugs, *Weeks v. United States*, 245 U.S. 618 (1918); to wages and hours, *United States v. Darby*, 312 U.S. 100 (1941); to members of labor unions, *National Labor Relations Board v. Jones & Laughlin Steel Corp.*, 301 U.S. 1, (1937); to crop control, *Wickard v. Filburn*; to discrimination against shippers, *United States v. Baltimore & Ohio R. Co.*, 333 U.S. 169 (1948); to the protection of small business from injurious price cutting, *Moore v. Mead's Fine Bread Co.*, 348 U.S. 115 (1954); to resale price maintenance, *Hudson Distributors, Inc. v. Eli Lilly & Co.*, 377 U.S. 386 (1964); to professional football, *Radovich v. National Football League*, 352 U.S. 445 (1957); and to racial discrimination by owners and managers of terminal restaurants, *Boynton v. Com. of Virginia*, 364 U.S. 454 (1960).

That Congress was legislating against moral wrongs in many of these areas rendered its enactments no less valid. In framing Title II of this Act Congress was also dealing with what it considered a moral problem. But that fact does not detract from the overwhelming evidence of the disruptive effect that racial discrimination has had on commercial intercourse. It was this burden which empowered Congress to enact appropriate legislation, and, given this basis for the exercise of its power, Congress was not restricted by the fact that the particular obstruction to interstate commerce with which it was dealing was also deemed a moral and social wrong.

It is said that the operation of the motel here is of a purely local character. But, assuming this to be true, "[i]f it is interstate commerce that feels the pinch, it does not matter how local the operation which applies the squeeze." *** [T]he power of Congress to promote interstate commerce also includes the power to regulate the local incidents thereof, including local activities in both the States of origin and destination, which might have a substantial and harmful effect upon that commerce. One need only examine the evidence which we have discussed above to see that Congress may—as it has—prohibit racial discrimination by motels serving travelers, however "local" their operations may appear.

Nor does the Act deprive appellant of liberty or property under the Fifth Amendment. The commerce power invoked here by the Congress is a specific and plenary one authorized by the Constitution itself. The only questions are: (1) whether Congress had a rational basis for finding that racial discrimination by motels affected commerce, and (2) if it had such a basis, whether the means it selected to eliminate that evil are reasonable and appropriate. If they are, appellant has no "right" to select its guests as it sees fit, free from governmental regulation. ***

It is doubtful if in the long run appellant will suffer economic loss as a result of the Act. Experience is to the contrary where discrimination is completely obliterated as to all public accommodations. But whether this be true or not is of no consequence since this Court has specifically held that the fact that a "Member of the class which is regulated may suffer economic losses not shared by others *** has never been a barrier" to such legislation. ***

We, therefore, conclude that the action of the Congress in the adoption of the Act as applied here to a motel which concededly serves interstate travelers is within the power granted it by the Commerce Clause of the Constitution, as interpreted by this Court for 140 years. It may be argued that Congress could have pursued other methods to eliminate the obstructions it found in interstate commerce caused by racial discrimination. But this is a matter of policy that rests entirely with the Congress, not with the courts. How obstructions in commerce may be removed—what means are to be employed—is within the sound and exclusive discretion of the Congress. It is subject only to one caveat—that the means chosen by it must be reasonably adapted to the end permitted by the Constitution. We cannot say that its choice here was not so adapted. The Constitution requires no more.

[Concurrences of BLACK, DOUGLAS, and GOLDBERG omitted.]

Notes

1. **Commerce in People?** Is the interstate movement of people commerce? Heart of Atlanta's counsel argued that the Fourteenth Amendment did not prohibit "racial discrimination by an individual," that "the framers *** intended to cover commerce as commerce is known in business fields," that the Court had previously held that "People engage in commerce ***. But people themselves are not commerce." Does the Court answer these arguments?

2. **Commerce or Other Power?** Congress premised the Civil Rights Act of 1964 on the Commerce Clause. Was the proximity of the motel to I–75/85 a necessary component of the Court's decision? If you had been a member of Congress in 1964, would *Wickard* reassure you that the Civil Rights Act was within the scope of your constitutional authority? What do you think of the argument that the activity affecting commerce is discrimination? Would § 5 of the Fourteenth Amendment be a better (or additional) basis for the Civil Rights Act of 1964? Could the Court turn to § 5 if it found the Commerce Clause insufficient, even though Congress did not rest its legislation on the Fourteenth Amendment?

3. *Wickard + Heart of Atlanta.* In *Katzenbach v. McClung*, 379 U.S. 294 (1964), a companion case to *Heart of Atlanta*, the Court considered the constitutionality of applying the same statute to Ollie's Barbecue, a family restaurant in Birmingham, Alabama. Ollie's seated 220 (whites only), was located 11-miles from an interstate highway, and its customers were almost exclusively local. The court upheld application of Title II of the Civil Rights Act, noting that the restaurant had purchased about $150,000 worth of food, 46% from a local supplier who had in turn received it from out of state. The Court said that "viewed in isolation, the volume of food purchased by Ollie's Barbecue from sources supplied from out of state was insignificant when compared with the total foodstuffs moving in commerce." Nonetheless, citing *Wickard* and extensive Congressional findings on depressed per capita spending by African Americans, the Court upheld Congress' "conclusive presumption that restaurants meeting the criteria set out in the Act 'affect commerce.'"

3. MODERN LIMITATION OF THE COMMERCE CLAUSE

UNITED STATES v. LOPEZ
514 U.S. 549, 115 S.Ct. 1624, 131 L.Ed.2d 626 (1995).

CHIEF JUSTICE REHNQUIST delivered the opinion of the Court.

In the Gun–Free School Zones Act of 1990, Congress made it a federal offense "for any individual knowingly to possess a firearm at a place that the individual knows, or has reasonable cause to believe, is a school zone." 18 U.S.C. § 922(q)(1)(A). The Act neither regulates a commercial activity nor contains a requirement that the possession be connected in any way to interstate commerce. We hold that the Act exceeds the authority of Congress "[t]o regulate Commerce *** among the several States. *** "

On March 10, 1992, respondent, who was then a 12th-grade student, arrived at Edison High School in San Antonio, Texas, carrying a concealed .38 caliber handgun and five bullets. Acting upon an anonymous tip, school authorities confronted respondent, who admitted that he was carrying the weapon. He was arrested and charged under Texas law with firearm possession on school premises. The next day, the state charges were dismissed after federal agents charged respondent by complaint with violating the Gun–Free School Zones Act of 1990.[7] ***

We start with first principles. The Constitution creates a Federal Government of enumerated powers. As James Madison wrote, "[t]he powers delegated by the proposed Constitution to the federal government are few and defined. Those which are to remain in the State governments are numerous and indefinite." The Federalist No. 45. "Just as the separation and independence of the coordinate branches of the Federal Government serves to prevent the accumulation of excessive power in any one branch, a healthy balance of power between the States and the Federal Government will reduce the risk of tyranny and abuse from either front."

The Constitution delegates to Congress the power "[t]o regulate Commerce with foreign Nations, and among the several States, and with the Indian Tribes." *** CHIEF JUSTICE MARSHALL, first defined the nature of Congress' commerce power in *Gibbons v. Ogden*, 9 Wheat. 1, 189–190 (1824). The commerce power "is the power to regulate; that is, to prescribe the rule by which commerce is to be governed. This power, like all others vested in Congress, is complete in itself, may be exercised to its utmost extent, and acknowledges no limitations, other than are prescribed in the constitution." The *Gibbons* Court, however, acknowledged that limitations on the commerce power are inherent in the very language of the Commerce Clause. "It is not intended to say that these words comprehend that commerce, which is completely internal, which is carried on between man and man in a State, or between different parts of the same State, and which does not extend to or affect other States. Such a power would be inconvenient, and is certainly

---

[7] The term "school zone" is defined as "in, or on the grounds of, a public, parochial or private school" or "within a distance of 1,000 feet from the grounds of a public, parochial or private school." § 921(a)(25).

unnecessary. "Comprehensive as the word 'among' is, it may very properly be restricted to that commerce which concerns more States than one. *** The enumeration presupposes something not enumerated; and that something, if we regard the language or the subject of the sentence, must be the exclusively internal commerce of a State."

For nearly a century thereafter, the Court's Commerce Clause decisions dealt but rarely with the extent of Congress' power, and almost entirely with the Commerce Clause as a limit on state legislation that discriminated against interstate commerce. ***

In 1887, Congress enacted the Interstate Commerce Act and in 1890, Congress enacted the Sherman Antitrust Act. These laws ushered in a new era of federal regulation under the commerce power. When cases involving these laws first reached this Court, we imported from our negative Commerce Clause cases the approach that Congress could not regulate activities such as "production," "manufacturing," and "mining." Simultaneously, however, the Court held that, where the interstate and intrastate aspects of commerce were so mingled together that full regulation of interstate commerce required incidental regulation of intrastate commerce, the Commerce Clause authorized such regulation.

In *A.L.A. Schechter Poultry Corp. v. United States*, 295 U.S. 495 (1935), the Court struck down regulations that fixed the hours and wages of individuals employed by an intrastate business because the activity being regulated related to interstate commerce only indirectly. In doing so, the Court characterized the distinction between direct and indirect effects of intrastate transactions upon interstate commerce as "a fundamental one, essential to the maintenance of our constitutional system." Activities that affected interstate commerce directly were within Congress' power; activities that affected interstate commerce indirectly were beyond Congress' reach. The justification for this formal distinction was rooted in the fear that otherwise "there would be virtually no limit to the federal power and for all practical purposes we should have a completely centralized government."

Two years later, in the watershed case of *NLRB v. Jones & Laughlin Steel Corp.*, 301 U.S. 1 (1937), the Court upheld the National Labor Relations Act against a Commerce Clause challenge, and in the process, departed from the distinction between "direct" and "indirect" effects on interstate commerce. The Court held that intrastate activities that "have such a close and substantial relation to interstate commerce that their control is essential or appropriate to protect that commerce from burdens and obstructions" are within Congress' power to regulate.

In *United States v. Darby*, 312 U.S. 100 (1941), the Court upheld the Fair Labor Standards Act, stating: "The power of Congress over interstate commerce is not confined to the regulation of commerce among the states. It extends to those activities intrastate which so affect interstate commerce or the exercise of the power of Congress over it as to make regulation of them appropriate means to the attainment of a legitimate end, the exercise of the granted power of Congress to regulate interstate commerce."

Jones & Laughlin Steel, Darby, and *Wickard* ushered in an era of Commerce Clause jurisprudence that greatly expanded the previously defined authority of Congress under that Clause. In part, this was a recognition of the great changes that had occurred in the way business was carried on in this country. Enterprises that had once been local or at most regional in nature had become national in scope. But the doctrinal change also reflected a view that earlier Commerce Clause cases artificially had constrained the authority of Congress to regulate interstate commerce.

But even these modern-era precedents which have expanded congressional power under the Commerce Clause confirm that this power is subject to outer limits. In *Jones & Laughlin Steel,* the Court warned that the scope of the interstate commerce power "must be considered in the light of our dual system of government and may not be extended so as to embrace effects upon interstate commerce so indirect and remote that to embrace them, in view of our complex society, would effectually obliterate the distinction between what is national and what is local and create a completely centralized government." *** Consistent with this structure, we have identified three broad categories of activity that Congress may regulate under its commerce power. First, Congress may regulate the use of the channels of interstate commerce. See, e.g., *Darby, Heart of Atlanta Motel.* Second, Congress is empowered to regulate and protect the instrumentalities of interstate commerce, or persons or things in interstate commerce, even though the threat may come only from intrastate activities. *** Finally, Congress' commerce authority includes the power to regulate those activities having a substantial relation to interstate commerce, i.e., those activities that substantially affect interstate commerce.

Within this final category, admittedly, our case law has not been clear whether an activity must "affect" or "substantially affect" interstate commerce in order to be within Congress' power to regulate it under the Commerce Clause. We conclude, consistent with the great weight of our case law, that the proper test requires an analysis of whether the regulated activity "substantially affects" interstate commerce.

We now turn to consider the power of Congress, in the light of this framework, to enact § 922(q). The first two categories of authority may be quickly disposed of: § 922(q) is not a regulation of the use of the channels of interstate commerce, nor is it an attempt to prohibit the interstate transportation of a commodity through the channels of commerce; nor can § 922(q) be justified as a regulation by which Congress has sought to protect an instrumentality of interstate commerce or a thing in interstate commerce. Thus, if § 922(q) is to be sustained, it must be under the third category as a regulation of an activity that substantially affects interstate commerce.

*** Section 922(q) is a criminal statute that by its terms has nothing to do with "commerce" or any sort of economic enterprise, however broadly one might define those terms. Section 922(q) is not an essential part of a larger regulation of economic activity, in which the regulatory scheme could be undercut unless the intrastate activity were regulated. It cannot, therefore, be sustained under our cases upholding regulations of activities that arise out of or are connected with a commercial transaction, which viewed in the aggregate, substantially affects interstate commerce. ***

Second, § 922(q) contains no jurisdictional element which would ensure, through case-by-case inquiry, that the firearm possession in question affects interstate commerce. For example, in *United States v. Bass*, 404 U.S. 336 (1971), the Court interpreted [a statute] which made it a crime for a felon to "receiv[e], posses[s], or transpor[t] in commerce or affecting commerce *** any firearm." The Court interpreted the possession component of s 1202(a) to require an additional nexus to interstate commerce both because the statute was ambiguous and because "unless Congress conveys its purpose clearly, it will not be deemed to have significantly changed the federal-state balance." The *Bass* Court set aside the conviction because although the Government had demonstrated that Bass had possessed a firearm, it had failed "to show the requisite nexus with interstate commerce." The Court thus interpreted the statute to reserve the constitutional question whether Congress could regulate, without more, the "mere possession" of firearms. ***

Although as part of our independent evaluation of constitutionality under the Commerce Clause we of course consider legislative findings, and indeed even congressional committee findings, regarding effect on interstate commerce, the Government concedes that "[n]either the statute nor its legislative history contain[s] express congressional findings regarding the effects upon interstate commerce of gun possession in a school zone." We agree with the Government that Congress normally is not required to make formal findings as to the substantial burdens that an activity has on interstate commerce. But to the extent that congressional findings would enable us to evaluate the legislative judgment that the activity in question substantially affected interstate commerce, even though no such substantial effect was visible to the naked eye, they are lacking here. ***

The Government's essential contention, *in fine*, is that we may determine here that § 922(q) is valid because possession of a firearm in a local school zone does indeed substantially affect interstate commerce. The Government argues that possession of a firearm in a school zone may result in violent crime and that violent crime can be expected to affect the functioning of the national economy in two ways. First, the costs of violent crime are substantial, and, through the mechanism of insurance, those costs are spread throughout the population. Second, violent crime reduces the willingness of individuals to travel to areas within the country that are perceived to be unsafe. The Government also argues that the presence of guns in schools poses a substantial threat to the educational process by threatening the learning environment. A handicapped educational process, in turn, will result in a less productive citizenry. That, in turn, would have an adverse effect on the Nation's economic well-being. As a result, the Government argues that Congress could rationally have concluded that § 922(q) substantially affects interstate commerce.

We pause to consider the implications of the Government's arguments. The Government admits, under its "costs of crime" reasoning, that Congress could regulate not only all violent crime, but all activities that might lead to violent crime, regardless of how tenuously they relate to interstate commerce. Similarly, under the Government's "national productivity" reasoning, Congress could regulate any activity that it found was related to the economic productivity of individual citizens: family law (including marriage, divorce, and child custody), for example. Under the theories that the Government presents in support of § 922(q), it is difficult to perceive any limitation on federal power, even in areas such as criminal law enforcement or education where States historically have been sovereign. Thus, if we were to accept the Government's arguments, we are hard-pressed to posit any activity by an individual that Congress is without power to regulate. ***

Admittedly, a determination whether an intrastate activity is commercial or noncommercial may in some cases result in legal uncertainty. But, so long as Congress' authority is limited to those powers enumerated in the Constitution, and so long as those enumerated powers are interpreted as having judicially enforceable outer limits, congressional legislation under the Commerce Clause always will engender "legal uncertainty." *** The Constitution mandates this uncertainty by withholding from Congress a plenary police power that would authorize enactment of every type of legislation. *** [However,] the question of congressional power under the Commerce Clause "is necessarily one of degree."

These are not precise formulations, and in the nature of things they cannot be. But we think they point the way to a correct decision of this case. The possession of a gun in a local school zone is in no sense an economic activity that might, through repetition elsewhere, substantially affect any sort of interstate commerce. Respondent was a local student at a local school; there is no indication that he had recently moved in interstate commerce, and there is no requirement that his possession of the firearm have any concrete tie to interstate commerce.

To uphold the Government's contentions here, we would have to pile inference upon inference in a manner that would bid fair to convert congressional authority under the Commerce Clause to a general police power of the sort retained by the States. Admittedly, some of our prior cases have taken long steps down that road, giving great deference to congressional action. The broad language in these opinions has suggested the possibility of additional expansion, but we decline here to proceed any further. To do so would require us to conclude that the Constitution's enumeration of powers does not presuppose something not enumerated, cf. *Gibbons v. Ogden*, supra, and that there never will be a distinction between what is truly national and what is truly local, cf. *Jones & Laughlin Steel*, supra. This we are unwilling to do. ***

JUSTICE KENNEDY, with whom JUSTICE O'CONNOR joins, concurring.

*** The theory that two governments accord more liberty than one requires for its realization two distinct and discernable lines of political accountability: one between the citizens and the Federal Government; the second between the citizens and the States. If, as Madison expected, the Federal and State Governments are to control each other, see The Federalist

No. 51, and hold each other in check by competing for the affections of the people, see The Federalist No. 46, those citizens must have some means of knowing which of the two governments to hold accountable for the failure to perform a particular function. "Federalism serves to assign political responsibility, not to obscure it." *FTC v. Ticor Title Ins. Co.*, 504 U.S. 621, 636 (1992). Were the Federal Government to take over the regulation of entire areas of traditional state concern, areas having nothing to do with the regulation of commercial activities, the boundaries between the spheres of federal and state authority would blur and political responsibility would become illusory. The resultant inability to hold either branch of the government answerable to the citizens is more dangerous even than devolving too much authority to the remote central power.

*** The statute before us upsets the federal balance to a degree that renders it an unconstitutional assertion of the commerce power, and our intervention is required. As THE CHIEF JUSTICE explains, unlike the earlier cases to come before the Court here neither the actors nor their conduct have a commercial character, and neither the purposes nor the design of the statute have an evident commercial nexus. The statute makes the simple possession of a gun within 1,000 feet of the grounds of the school a criminal offense. In a sense any conduct in this interdependent world of ours has an ultimate commercial origin or consequence, but we have not yet said the commerce power may reach so far. If Congress attempts that extension, then at the least we must inquire whether the exercise of national power seeks to intrude upon an area of traditional state concern. ***

The statute now before us forecloses the States from experimenting and exercising their own judgment in an area to which States lay claim by right of history and expertise, and it does so by regulating an activity beyond the realm of commerce in the ordinary and usual sense of that term. The tendency of this statute to displace state regulation in areas of traditional state concern is evident from its territorial operation. There are over 100,000 elementary and secondary schools in the United States. Each of these now has an invisible federal zone extending 1,000 feet beyond the (often irregular) boundaries of the school property. In some communities no doubt it would be difficult to navigate without infringing on those zones. Yet throughout these areas, school officials would find their own programs for the prohibition of guns in danger of displacement by the federal authority unless the State chooses to enact a parallel rule. ***

JUSTICE THOMAS, concurring.

The Court today properly concludes that the Commerce Clause does not grant Congress the authority to prohibit gun possession within 1,000 feet of a school, as it attempted to do in the Gun–Free School Zones Act of 1990. Although I join the majority, I write separately to observe that our case law has drifted far from the original understanding of the Commerce Clause. In a future case, we ought to temper our Commerce Clause jurisprudence in a manner that both makes sense of our more recent case law and is more faithful to the original understanding of that Clause.

We have said that Congress may regulate not only "Commerce *** among the several states," U.S. Const., Art. I, § 8, cl. 3, but also anything that has a "substantial effect" on such commerce. This test, if taken to its logical extreme, would give Congress a "police power" over all aspects of American life. Unfortunately, we have never come to grips with this implication of our substantial effects formula. Although we have supposedly applied the substantial effects test for the past 60 years, we *always* have rejected readings of the Commerce Clause and the scope of federal power that would permit Congress to exercise a police power; our cases are quite clear that there are real limits to federal power. *** Indeed, on this crucial point, the majority and JUSTICE BREYER agree in principle: the Federal Government has nothing approaching a police power. *** At an appropriate juncture, I think we must modify our Commerce Clause jurisprudence. Today, it is easy enough to say that the Clause certainly does not empower Congress to ban gun possession within 1,000 feet of a school.

JUSTICE STEVENS, dissenting.

*** Guns are both articles of commerce and articles that can be used to restrain commerce. Their possession is the consequence, either directly or indirectly, of commercial activity. In my judgment, Congress' power to regulate commerce in firearms includes the power to prohibit possession of guns at any location because of their potentially harmful use; it necessarily follows that Congress may also prohibit their possession in particular markets. The market for the possession of handguns by school-age children is, distressingly, substantial. Whether or not the national interest in eliminating that market would have justified federal legislation in 1789, it surely does today.

JUSTICE SOUTER, dissenting.

*** The question for the courts, as all agree, is not whether as a predicate to legislation Congress in fact found that a particular activity substantially affects interstate commerce. The legislation implies such a finding, and there is no reason to entertain claims that Congress acted ultra vires intentionally. Nor is the question whether Congress was correct in so finding. The only question is whether the legislative judgment is within the realm of reason. Congressional findings do not, however, directly address the question of reasonableness; they tell us what Congress actually has found, not what it could rationally find. If, indeed, the Court were to make the existence of explicit congressional findings dispositive in some close or difficult cases something other than rationality review would be afoot. The resulting congressional obligation to justify its policy choices on the merits would imply either a judicial authority to review the justification (and, hence, the wisdom) of those choices, or authority to require Congress to act with some high degree of deliberateness, of which express findings would be evidence. But review for congressional wisdom would just be the old judicial pretension discredited and abandoned in 1937, and review for deliberateness would be as patently unconstitutional as an Act of Congress mandating long opinions from this Court. Such a legislative process requirement would function merely as an excuse for covert review of the merits of legislation under standards never expressed and more or less arbitrarily applied. Under such a regime, in any case, the rationality standard of review would be a thing of the past. ***

JUSTICE BREYER, with whom JUSTICE STEVENS, JUSTICE SOUTER, and JUSTICE GINSBURG join, dissenting.

The issue in this case is whether the Commerce Clause authorizes Congress to enact a statute that makes it a crime to possess a gun in, or near, a school. In my view, the statute falls well within the scope of the commerce power as this Court has understood that power over the last half-century.

In reaching this conclusion, I apply three basic principles of Commerce Clause interpretation. First, the power to "regulate Commerce *** among the several States," U.S. Const., Art. I, § 8, cl. 3, encompasses the power to regulate local activities insofar as they significantly affect interstate commerce. I use the word "significant" because the word "substantial" implies a somewhat narrower power than recent precedent suggests. But, to speak of "substantial effect" rather than "significant effect" would make no difference in this case.

Second, in determining whether a local activity will likely have a significant effect upon interstate commerce, a court must consider, not the effect of an individual act (a single instance of gun possession), but rather the cumulative effect of all similar instances (i.e., the effect of all guns possessed in or near schools). See, e.g., *Wickard*.

Third, the Constitution requires us to judge the connection between a regulated activity and interstate commerce, not directly, but at one remove. Courts must give Congress a degree of leeway in determining the existence of a significant factual connection between the regulated activity and interstate commerce—both because the Constitution delegates the commerce power directly to Congress and because the determination requires an empirical judgment of a kind that a legislature is more likely than a court to make with accuracy. The traditional words "rational basis" capture this leeway. *** I recognize that we must judge this matter independently. "[S]imply because Congress may conclude that a particular activity substantially affects interstate commerce does not necessarily make it so."

*** Congress could also have found, given the effect of education upon interstate and foreign commerce, that gun-related violence in and around schools is a commercial, as well as a human, problem. [Further,] Congress could have found that gun-related violence near the classroom poses a serious economic threat (1) to consequently inadequately educated workers who must endure low paying jobs, and (2) to communities and businesses that might (in today's "information society") otherwise gain, from a well-educated work force, an important commercial advantage of a kind that location near a railhead or harbor provided in the past. ***

To hold this statute constitutional is not to "obliterate" the "distinction of what is national and what is local," nor is it to hold that the Commerce Clause permits the Federal Government to "regulate any activity that it found was related to the economic productivity of individual citizens," to regulate "marriage, divorce, and child custody," or to regulate any and all aspects of education. For one thing, this statute is aimed at curbing a particularly acute threat to the educational process—the possession (and use) of life-threatening firearms in, or near, the classroom. The empirical evidence that I have discussed above unmistakably documents the special way in which guns and education are incompatible. ***

The majority's holding—that § 922 falls outside the scope of the Commerce Clause—creates three serious legal problems. First, the majority's holding runs contrary to modern Supreme Court cases that have upheld congressional actions despite connections to interstate or foreign commerce that are less significant than the effect of school violence. ***

The second legal problem the Court creates comes from its apparent belief that it can reconcile its holding with earlier cases by making a critical distinction between "commercial" and noncommercial "transaction[s]." That is to say, the Court believes the Constitution would distinguish between two local activities, each of which has an identical effect upon interstate commerce, if one, but not the other, is "commercial" in nature. As a general matter, this approach fails to heed this Court's earlier warning not to turn "questions of the power of Congress" upon "formula[s]" that would give "controlling force to nomenclature such as 'production' and 'indirect' and foreclose consideration of the actual effects of the activity in question upon interstate commerce." *Wickard*, supra ***. The third legal problem created by the Court's holding is that it threatens legal uncertainty in an area of law that, until this case, seemed reasonably well settled. ***

In sum, to find this legislation within the scope of the Commerce Clause would permit "Congress *** to act in terms of economic *** realities." [Further,] it would interpret the Clause as this Court has traditionally interpreted it. *** Upholding this legislation would do no more than simply recognize that Congress had a "rational basis" for finding a significant connection between guns in or near schools and (through their effect on education) the interstate and foreign commerce they threaten. For these reasons, I would reverse the judgment of the Court of Appeals. Respectfully, I dissent.

Notes

1. **Significance.** Commentators are divided as to whether *Lopez* represents a "constitutional moment" like the Civil War or the New Deal in the relationship between the federal government and the states. Do you think the Court has overruled *Wickard* and/or *Heart of Atlanta*?

2. **Ambiguities In *Lopez*.**

    • Is the lack of congressional findings critical? If Congress had made more extensive interstate commerce findings, could the Court look behind them?

- How important is it that criminal law and education are "traditional areas" for exercise of state powers? How should courts decide what areas are traditionally state matters and which are not?

- Is it relevant that the statute involved regulated guns?

- How important is it that the statute at issue blurred "discernible lines of political accountability"?

- Is it important that the activity involved was noncommercial? How should the courts distinguish that which is commercial from that which is noncommercial?

3. **Policy.** Has the Court forgotten its historically developed understanding that it is not a particularly effective institution for considering whether or not commerce has been substantially affected? Is it fearful of leaving Congress' power unchecked?

UNITED STATES v. MORRISON
529 U.S. 598, 120 S.Ct. 1740, 146 L.Ed.2d 658 (2000).

CHIEF JUSTICE REHNQUIST delivered the opinion of the Court.

In these cases we consider the constitutionality of 42 U.S.C. § 13981, which provides a federal civil remedy for the victims of gender-motivated violence. ***

I

Petitioner Christy Brzonkala enrolled at Virginia Polytechnic Institute (Virginia Tech) in the fall of 1994. In September of that year, Brzonkala met respondents Antonio Morrison and James Crawford, who were both students at Virginia Tech and members of its varsity football team. Brzonkala alleges that, within 30 minutes of meeting Morrison and Crawford, they assaulted and repeatedly raped her. *** Brzonkala alleges that this attack caused her to become severely emotionally disturbed and depressed. She sought assistance from a university psychiatrist, who prescribed antidepressant medication. Shortly after the rape Brzonkala stopped attending classes and withdrew from the university. *** In December 1995, Brzonkala sued Morrison, Crawford, and Virginia Tech ***. [She] alleged that Morrison's and Crawford's attack violated § 13981 ***. Morrison and Crawford moved to dismiss this complaint on the grounds that *** § 13981's civil remedy is unconstitutional. The United States intervened to defend § 13981's constitutionality.

Section 13981 was part of the Violence Against Women Act of 1994. It states that "[a]ll persons within the United States shall have the right to be free from crimes of violence motivated by gender." To enforce that right, subsection (c) declares [that "a person *** who commits a crime of violence motivated by gender *** shall be liable to the party injured"]. Section 13981 defines a "crim[e] of violence motivated by gender" as "a crime of violence committed because of gender or on the basis of gender, and due, at least in part, to an animus based on the victim's gender." ***

Every law enacted by Congress must be based on one or more of its powers enumerated in the Constitution. *** Congress explicitly identified the sources of federal authority on which it relied in enacting § 13981. It said that a "federal civil rights cause of action" is established "[p]ursuant to the affirmative power of Congress *** under section 5 of the Fourteenth Amendment to the Constitution, as well as under section 8 of Article I of the Constitution." We address Congress' authority to enact this remedy under each of these constitutional provisions in turn.

II

Due respect for the decisions of a coordinate branch of Government demands that we invalidate a congressional enactment only upon a plain showing that Congress has exceeded its constitutional bounds. *See United States v. Lopez.* *** As we discussed at length in *Lopez,* our interpretation of the Commerce Clause has changed as our Nation has developed. ***

Lopez emphasized, however, that even under our modern, expansive interpretation of the Commerce Clause, Congress' regulatory authority is not without effective bounds. *** Since *Lopez* most recently canvassed and clarified our case law governing this third category of Commerce Clause regulation [the power to regulate those activities having a substantial relation to interstate commerce], it provides the proper framework for conducting the required analysis of § 13981. In *Lopez,* *** [s]everal significant considerations contributed to our decision.

First, we observed that [it] was "a criminal statute that by its terms has nothing to do with 'commerce' or any sort of economic enterprise, however broadly one might define those terms." *** The second consideration that we found important *** was that the statute contained "no express jurisdictional element which might limit its reach to a discrete set of firearm possessions that additionally have an explicit connection with or effect on interstate commerce." *** Third, we noted that neither [the statute] "nor its legislative history contain[s] express congressional findings regarding the effects upon interstate commerce of gun possession in a school zone." While "Congress normally is not required to make formal findings as to the substantial burdens that an activity has on interstate commerce," the existence of such findings may "enable us to evaluate the legislative judgment that the activity in question substantially affect[s] interstate commerce, even though no such substantial effect [is] visible to the naked eye." Finally, our decision in *Lopez* rested in part on the fact that the link between gun possession and a substantial effect on interstate commerce was attenuated. ***

With these principles underlying our Commerce Clause jurisprudence as reference points, the proper resolution of the present cases is clear. Gender-motivated crimes of violence are not, in any sense of the phrase, economic activity. While we need not adopt a categorical rule against aggregating the effects of any noneconomic activity in order to decide these cases, thus far in our Nation's history our cases have upheld Commerce Clause regulation of intrastate activity only where that activity is economic in nature. *** [Moreover,] § 13981 contains no jurisdictional element establishing that the federal cause of action is in pursuance of Congress' power to regulate interstate commerce. ***

In contrast with the lack of congressional findings that we faced in *Lopez*, § 13981 is supported by numerous findings regarding the serious impact that gender-motivated violence has on victims and their families. But the existence of congressional findings is not sufficient, by itself, to sustain the constitutionality of Commerce Clause legislation. As we stated in *Lopez*, "'[S]imply because Congress may conclude that a particular activity substantially affects interstate commerce does not necessarily make it so.'" Rather, "'[w]hether particular operations affect interstate commerce sufficiently to come under the constitutional power of Congress to regulate them is ultimately a judicial rather than a legislative question, and can be settled finally only by this Court.'"

In these cases, Congress' findings are substantially weakened by the fact that they rely so heavily on a method of reasoning that we have already rejected as unworkable if we are to maintain the Constitution's enumeration of powers. Congress found that gender-motivated violence affects interstate commerce

> "by deterring potential victims from traveling interstate, from engaging in employment in interstate business, and from transacting with business, and in places involved in interstate commerce; *** by diminishing national productivity, increasing medical and other costs, and decreasing the supply of and the demand for interstate products."

Given these findings and petitioners' arguments, the concern that we expressed in *Lopez* that Congress might use the Commerce Clause to completely obliterate the Constitution's distinction between national and local authority seems well founded. The reasoning that petitioners advance seeks to follow the but-for causal chain from the initial occurrence of violent crime (the suppression of which has always been the prime object of the States' police power) to every attenuated effect upon interstate commerce. If accepted, petitioners' reasoning would allow Congress to regulate any crime as long as the nationwide, aggregated impact of that crime has substantial effects on employment, production, transit, or consumption. Indeed, if Congress may regulate gender-motivated violence, it would be able to regulate murder or any other type of violence since gender-motivated violence, as a subset of all violent crime, is certain to have lesser economic impacts than the larger class of which it is a part.

Petitioners' reasoning, moreover, will not limit Congress to regulating violence but may, as we suggested in *Lopez*, be applied equally as well to family law and other areas of traditional state regulation since the aggregate effect of marriage, divorce, and childrearing on the national economy is undoubtedly significant. Congress may have recognized this specter when it expressly precluded § 13981 from being used in the family law context. Under our written Constitution, however, the limitation of congressional authority is not solely a matter of legislative grace.

We accordingly reject the argument that Congress may regulate noneconomic, violent criminal conduct based solely on that conduct's aggregate effect on interstate commerce. The Constitution requires a distinction between what is truly national and what is truly local. In recognizing this fact we preserve one of the few principles that has been consistent since the Clause was adopted. ***

JUSTICE THOMAS, concurring.

*** I write separately only to express my view that the very notion of a "substantial effects" test under the Commerce Clause is inconsistent with the original understanding of Congress' powers and with this Court's early Commerce Clause cases. By continuing to apply this rootless and malleable standard, however circumscribed, the Court has encouraged the Federal Government to persist in its view that the Commerce Clause has virtually no limits. Until this Court replaces its existing Commerce Clause jurisprudence with a standard more consistent with the original understanding, we will continue to see Congress appropriating state police powers under the guise of regulating commerce.

JUSTICE SOUTER, with whom JUSTICE STEVENS, JUSTICE GINSBURG, and JUSTICE BREYER join, dissenting.

The Court says both that it leaves Commerce Clause precedent undisturbed and that the Civil Rights Remedy of the Violence Against Women Act of 1994 exceeds Congress's power under that Clause. I find the claims irreconcilable and respectfully dissent.

Our cases, which remain at least nominally undisturbed, stand for the following propositions. Congress has the power to legislate with regard to activity that, in the aggregate, has a substantial effect on interstate commerce. The fact of such a substantial effect is not an issue for the courts in the first instance, but for the Congress, whose institutional capacity for gathering evidence and taking testimony far exceeds ours. *** One obvious difference from *United States v. Lopez*, 514 U.S. 549 (1995), is the mountain of data assembled by Congress, here showing the effects of violence against women on interstate commerce. *** Congress thereby explicitly stated the predicate for the exercise of its Commerce Clause power. ***

Indeed, the legislative record here is far more voluminous than the record compiled by Congress and found sufficient in two prior cases upholding Title II of the Civil Rights Act of 1964 against Commerce Clause challenges. In *Heart of Atlanta Motel, Inc. v. United States*, 379 U.S. 241 (1964), and *Katzenbach v. McClung*, 379 U.S. 294 (1964), the Court referred to evidence showing the consequences of racial discrimination by motels and restaurants on interstate commerce. *** [G]ender-based violence in the 1990's was shown to operate in a manner similar to racial discrimination in the 1960's in reducing the mobility of employees and their production and consumption of goods shipped in interstate commerce. Like racial discrimination, "[g]ender-based violence bars its most likely targets—women—from full partic[ipation] in the national economy."

*** Supply and demand for goods in interstate commerce will [ ] be affected by the deaths of 2,000 to 4,000 women annually at the hands of domestic abusers, and by the reduction in the work force by the 100,000 or more rape victims who lose their jobs each year or are forced to quit. Violence against women may be found to affect interstate commerce and affect it substantially.

The Act would have passed muster at any time between *Wickard* in 1942 and *Lopez* in 1995, a period in which the law enjoyed a stable understanding that congressional power under the Commerce Clause, complemented by the authority of the Necessary and Proper Clause, Art. I. § 8 cl. 18, extended to all activity that, when aggregated, has a substantial effect on interstate commerce. *** The fact that the Act does not pass muster before the Court today is therefore proof, to a degree that *Lopez* was not, that the Court's nominal adherence to the substantial effects test is merely that. ***

Thus the elusive heart of the majority's analysis in these cases is its statement that Congress's findings of fact are "weakened" by the presence of a disfavored "method of reasoning." This seems to suggest that the "substantial effects" analysis is not a factual inquiry, for Congress in the first instance with subsequent judicial review looking only to the rationality of the congressional conclusion, but one of a rather different sort, dependent upon a uniquely judicial competence. *** The premise that the enumeration of powers implies that other powers are withheld is sound; the conclusion that some particular categories of subject matter are therefore presumptively beyond the reach of the commerce power is, however, a non sequitur. From the fact that Art. I, § 8, cl. 3 grants an authority limited to regulating commerce, it follows only that Congress may claim no authority under that section to address any subject that does not affect commerce. It does not at all follow that an activity affecting commerce nonetheless falls outside the commerce power, depending on the specific character of the activity, or the authority of a State to regulate it along with Congress. My disagreement with the majority is not, however, confined to logic, for history has shown that categorical exclusions have proven as unworkable in practice as they are unsupportable in theory.

Obviously, it would not be inconsistent with the text of the Commerce Clause itself to declare "noncommercial" primary activity beyond or presumptively beyond the scope of the commerce power. *** Since adherence to these formalistically contrived confines of commerce power in large measure provoked the judicial crisis of 1937, one might reasonably have doubted that Members of this Court would ever again toy with a return to the days before *NLRB v. Jones & Laughlin Steel Corp.*, 301 U.S. 1 (1937), which brought the earlier and nearly disastrous experiment to an end. And yet today's decision can only be seen as a step toward recapturing the prior mistakes. *** If we now ask why the formalistic economic/noneconomic distinction might matter today, after its rejection in *Wickard*, the answer is not that the majority fails to see causal connections in an integrated economic world. The answer is that in the minds of the majority there is a new animating theory that makes categorical formalism seem useful again. Just as the old formalism had value in the service of an economic conception, the new one is useful in serving a conception of federalism. *** The legitimacy of the Court's current emphasis on the noncommercial nature of regulated activity, then, does not turn on any logic serving the text of the Commerce Clause or on the realism of the majority's view of the national economy. The essential issue is rather the strength of the majority's claim to have a constitutional warrant for its current conception of a federal relationship enforceable by this Court through limits on otherwise plenary commerce power. *** The Court finds it relevant that the statute addresses conduct traditionally subject to state prohibition under domestic criminal law, a fact said to have some heightened significance when the violent conduct in question is not itself aimed directly at interstate commerce or its instrumentalities. *** The effort to carve out inviolable state spheres within the spectrum of activities substantially affecting commerce was, of course, just as irreconcilable with *Gibbons*'s explanation of the national commerce power as being as "absolut[e] as it would be in a single government."[14]

The objection to reviving traditional state spheres of action as a consideration in commerce analysis, however, not only rests on the portent of incoherence, but is compounded by a further defect just as fundamental. The defect, in essence, is the majority's rejection of the Founders' considered judgment that politics, not judicial review, should mediate between state and national interests as the strength and legislative jurisdiction of the National Government inevitably increased through the expected growth of the national economy. ***

All of this convinces me that today's ebb of the commerce power rests on error, and at the same time leads me to doubt that the majority's view will prove to be enduring law. *** The facts that cannot be ignored today are the facts of integrated national commerce and a political relationship between States and Nation much affected by their respective treasuries and constitutional modifications adopted by the people. The federalism of some earlier time is no more adequate to account for those facts today than the theory of laissez-faire was able to govern the national economy 70 years ago.

---

[14] The Constitution of 1787 did, in fact, forbid some exercises of the commerce power. Article I, § 9, cl. 6, barred Congress from giving preference to the ports of one State over those of another. More strikingly, the Framers protected the slave trade from federal interference, see Art. I, § 9, cl. 1, and confirmed the power of a State to guarantee the chattel status of slaves who fled to another State, see Art. IV, § 2, cl. 3. These reservations demonstrate the plenary nature of the federal power; the exceptions prove the rule. Apart from them, proposals to carve islands of state authority out of the stream of commerce power were entirely unsuccessful. Roger Sherman's proposed definition of federal legislative power as excluding "matters of internal police" met Gouverneur Morris's response that "[t]he internal police *** ought to be infringed in many cases" and was voted down eight to two. The Convention similarly rejected Sherman's attempt to include in Article V a proviso that "no state shall *** be affected in its internal police." 5 Elliot's Debates 551–552. Finally, Rufus King suggested an explicit bill of rights for the States, a device that might indeed have set aside the areas the Court now declares off-limits. That proposal, too, came to naught. In short, to suppose that enumerated powers must have limits is sensible; to maintain that there exist judicially identifiable areas of state regulation immune to the plenary congressional commerce power even though falling within the limits defined by the substantial effects test is to deny our constitutional history.

JUSTICE BREYER, with whom JUSTICE STEVENS joins, and with whom JUSTICE SOUTER and JUSTICE GINSBURG join as to Part I–A, dissenting.

No one denies the importance of the Constitution's federalist principles. Its state/federal division of authority protects liberty—both by restricting the burdens that government can impose from a distance and by facilitating citizen participation in government that is closer to home. The question is how the judiciary can best implement that original federalist understanding where the Commerce Clause is at issue.

The majority holds that the federal commerce power does not extend to such "noneconomic" activities as "noneconomic, violent criminal conduct" that significantly affects interstate commerce only if we "aggregate" the interstate "effect[s]" of individual instances. ***

Consider the problems. The "economic/noneconomic" distinction is not easy to apply. Does the local street corner mugger engage in "economic" activity or "noneconomic" activity when he mugs for money? Would evidence that desire for economic domination underlies many brutal crimes against women save the present statute?

The line becomes yet harder to draw given the need for exceptions. The Court itself would permit Congress to aggregate, hence regulate, "noneconomic" activity taking place at economic establishments. See *Heart of Atlanta Motel, Inc. v. United States*; *Katzenbach v. McClung*; *Lopez*. And it would permit Congress to regulate where that regulation is "an essential part of a larger regulation of economic activity, in which the regulatory scheme could be undercut unless the intrastate activity were regulated." *Lopez*, supra, at 561. Given the former exception, can Congress simply rewrite the present law and limit its application to restaurants, hotels, perhaps universities, and other places of public accommodation? Given the latter exception, can Congress save the present law by including it, or much of it, in a broader "Safe Transport" or "Workplace Safety" act?

More important, why should we give critical constitutional importance to the economic, or noneconomic, nature of an interstate-commerce-affecting cause? If chemical emanations through indirect environmental change cause identical, severe commercial harm outside a State, why should it matter whether local factories or home fireplaces release them? The Constitution itself refers only to Congress' power to "regulate Commerce *** among the several States," and to make laws "necessary and proper" to implement that power. The language says nothing about either the local nature, or the economic nature, of an interstate-commerce-affecting cause.

This Court has long held that only the interstate commercial effects, not the local nature of the cause, are constitutionally relevant. Nothing in the Constitution's language, or that of earlier cases prior to *Lopez*, explains why the Court should ignore one highly relevant characteristic of an interstate-commerce-affecting cause (how "local" it is), while placing critical constitutional weight upon a different, less obviously relevant, feature (how "economic" it is).

Most important, the Court's complex rules seem unlikely to help secure the very object that they seek, namely, the protection of "areas of traditional state regulation" from federal intrusion. The Court's rules, even if broadly interpreted, are underinclusive. The local pickpocket is no less a traditional subject of state regulation than is the local gender-motivated assault. Regardless, the Court reaffirms, as it should, Congress' well-established and frequently exercised power to enact laws that satisfy a commerce-related jurisdictional prerequisite—for example, that some item relevant to the federally regulated activity has at some time crossed a state line. ***

And in a world where most everyday products or their component parts cross interstate boundaries, Congress will frequently find it possible to redraft a statute using language that ties the regulation to the interstate movement of some relevant object, thereby regulating local criminal activity or, for that matter, family affairs. Although this possibility does not give the Federal Government the power to regulate everything, it means that any substantive limitation will apply randomly in terms of the interests the majority seeks to protect. How much would be gained, for example, were Congress to reenact the present law in the form of "An Act Forbidding Violence Against Women Perpetrated at Public Accommodations or by Those Who Have Moved in, or through the Use of Items that Have Moved in, Interstate Commerce"? Complex Commerce Clause rules creating fine distinctions that achieve only random results do little to further the important federalist interests that called them into being. That is why modern (pre-*Lopez*) case law rejected them.

The majority, aware of these difficulties, is nonetheless concerned with what it sees as an important contrary consideration. To determine the lawfulness of statutes simply by asking whether Congress could reasonably have found that aggregated local instances significantly affect interstate commerce will allow Congress to regulate almost anything. Virtually all local activity, when instances are aggregated, can have "substantial effects on employment, production, transit, or consumption." Hence Congress could "regulate any crime," and perhaps "marriage, divorce, and childrearing" as well, obliterating the "Constitution's distinction between national and local authority."

This consideration, however, while serious, does not reflect a jurisprudential defect, so much as it reflects a practical reality. We live in a Nation knit together by two centuries of scientific, technological, commercial, and environmental change. *** Since judges cannot change the world, the "defect" means that, within the bounds of the rational, Congress, not the courts, must remain primarily responsible for striking the appropriate state/federal balance. Congress is institutionally motivated to do so. Its Members represent state and local district interests. They consider the views of state and local officials when they legislate, and they have even developed formal procedures to ensure that such consideration takes place. Not surprisingly, the bulk of American law is still state law, and overwhelmingly so.

I would also note that Congress, when it enacted the statute, followed procedures that help to protect the federalism values at stake. It provided adequate notice to the States of its intent to legislate in an "are[a] of traditional state regulation." And in response, attorneys general in the overwhelming majority of States (38) supported congressional legislation, telling Congress that "[o]ur experience as Attorneys General strengthens our belief that the problem of violence against women is a national one, requiring federal attention, federal leadership, and federal funds."

Moreover, as JUSTICE SOUTER has pointed out, Congress compiled a "mountain of data" explicitly documenting the interstate commercial effects of gender-motivated crimes of violence. After considering alternatives, it focused the federal law upon documented deficiencies in state legal systems. And it tailored the law to prevent its use in certain areas of traditional state concern, such as divorce, alimony, or child custody. Consequently, the law before us seems to represent an instance, not of state/federal conflict, but of state/federal efforts to cooperate in order to help solve a mutually acknowledged national problem. ***

Notes

1. **Reviewing *Lopez.*** Which of the rationales in *Lopez* have prevailed?

2. **Problems.** Consider whether the following would be within Congress' commerce clause power after *Lopez* and *Morrison*:

- A federal law forbidding construction that would eliminate small ponds used by migrating birds.

- A federal law punishing parents who fail to pay past due support obligations with respect to a child who resides in another state.

- A federal law prohibiting any person from possessing a firearm who has previously been convicted of any crime involving domestic violence.

- A federal law criminalizing destruction of "real or personal property used in interstate commerce *** or in any activity affecting commerce," including arson of a private residence. *See Jones v. United States*, 120 S.Ct. 1904 (2000).

- A federal law prohibiting the use or threat of force or physical obstruction against a person seeking to obtain or provide reproductive health services, including abortions.

- A national anti-prostitution statute.

- A federal requirement that high school graduates demonstrate proficiency in math or a forgeign language.

3. **Judicial Myopia?** "In focusing narrowly on one target of the legislation—for example, on the gun-toting student and the alleged rapist—rather than on the intended beneficiaries, the ills triggering legislative action, or the ripple effects of regulatory intervention, *Lopez* and *Morrison* *** suggest a preference for a vantage point that diminishes the commercial connection." Robert A. Schapiro & William W. Buzbee, *Unidimensional Federalism: Power and Perspective in*

Commerce Clause Adjudication, 88 CORNELL L. REV. 1199 (2003). Do you agree that the Court should broaden its perspective? If so, what role would be left for the courts in assessing whether Congress had acted within the Commerce Clause power?

C. OTHER ARTICLE I POWERS

1. TAXING AND SPENDING POWERS

Taxing. Remember CHIEF JUSTICE MARSHALL's aphorism that "the power to tax is the power to destroy"? Consider the dramatic growth in the federal government that has occurred since 1913 when the Sixteenth Amendment gave the federal government the ability to tax incomes directly. Today, federal income taxes exceed $1 trillion, slightly more than 20% of the nation's gross national product.

After the Sixteenth Amendment, what limits, if any, are there to federal taxation? In 1922, the Court held an excise tax imposed on profits of mines and factories that used child labor unconstitutional on the ground that this was a penalty, not a tax. *Bailey v. Drexel Furniture Co.*, 259 U.S. 20 (1922). Subsequently, however, the Court has repeatedly upheld "regulatory" taxes on firearms, narcotics, etc., refusing to inquire into Congress' motive in enacting a tax. Is there any importance to the fact that the power to tax precedes the words "and provide for the common Defence and general Welfare of the United States"? Should we speak of a broader General Welfare Clause rather than the power to tax?

Spending. The Spending Power gives Congress power because, like regulation, spending facilitates Congress' efforts to require that particular things be done in exchange for federal money. The next case considers what limits there are to the exercise of this power other than that Congress may not use it to constrain speech, violate equal protection rights, and the like.

SOUTH DAKOTA v. DOLE
483 U.S. 203, 107 S.Ct. 2793, 97 L.Ed.2d 171 (1987).

CHIEF JUSTICE REHNQUIST delivered the opinion of the Court.

Petitioner South Dakota permits persons 19 years of age or older to purchase beer containing up to 3.2% alcohol. In 1984 Congress enacted [legislation] which directs the Secretary of Transportation to withhold a percentage of federal highway funds otherwise allocable from States "in which the purchase or public possession *** of any alcoholic beverage by a person who is less than twenty-one years of age is lawful." The State sued in United States District Court seeking a declaratory judgment that § 158 [of the Act] violates the constitutional limitations on congressional exercise of the spending power and violates the Twenty-first Amendment to the United States Constitution. ***

In this Court, the parties direct most of their efforts to defining the proper scope of the Twenty-first Amendment. Relying on our statement in *California Retail Liquor Dealers Assn. v. Midcal Aluminum, Inc.*, 445 U.S. 97,

110 (1980), that the "Twenty-first Amendment grants the States virtually complete control over whether to permit importation or sale of liquor and how to structure the liquor distribution system," South Dakota asserts that the setting of minimum drinking ages is clearly within the "core powers" reserved to the States under § 2 of the Amendment.[1] [The Act], petitioner claims, usurps that core power. The Secretary in response asserts that the Twenty-first Amendment is simply not implicated by § 158; the plain language of § 2 confirms the States' broad power to impose restrictions on the sale and distribution of alcoholic beverages but does not confer on them any power to permit sales that Congress seeks to prohibit. That Amendment, under this reasoning, would not prevent Congress from affirmatively enacting a national minimum drinking age more restrictive than that provided by the various state laws; and it would follow *a fortiori* that the indirect inducement involved here is compatible with the Twenty-first Amendment.

[W]e need not decide in this case whether that Amendment would prohibit an attempt by Congress to legislate directly a national minimum drinking age. Here, Congress has acted indirectly under its spending power to encourage uniformity in the States' drinking ages. As we explain below, we find this legislative effort within constitutional bounds even if Congress may not regulate drinking ages directly.

The Constitution empowers Congress to "lay and collect Taxes, Duties, Imposts, and Excises, to pay the Debts and provide for the common Defence and general Welfare of the United States." Art. I, § 8, cl. 1. Incident to this power, Congress may attach conditions on the receipt of federal funds, and has repeatedly employed the power "to further broad policy objectives by conditioning receipt of federal moneys upon compliance by the recipient with federal statutory and administrative directives." The breadth of this power was made clear in *United States v. Butler*, 297 U.S. 1 (1936), where the Court, resolving a longstanding debate over the scope of the Spending Clause, determined that "the power of Congress to authorize expenditure of public moneys for public purposes is not limited by the direct grants of legislative power found in the Constitution." Thus, objectives not thought to be within Article I's "enumerated legislative fields," may nevertheless be attained through the use of the spending power and the conditional grant of federal funds.

The spending power is of course not unlimited but is instead subject to several general restrictions articulated in our cases. The first of these limitations is derived from the language of the Constitution itself: the exercise of the spending power must be in pursuit of "the general welfare." In considering whether a particular expenditure is intended to serve general public purposes, courts should defer substantially to the judgment of Congress. Second, we have required that if Congress desires to condition the States' receipt of federal funds, it "must do so unambiguously ***, enabl[ing] the States to exercise their choice knowingly, cognizant of the consequences

---

[1] Section 2 of the Twenty-first Amendment provides: "The transportation or importation into any State, Territory, or possession of the United States for delivery or use therein of intoxicating liquors, in violation of the laws thereof, is hereby prohibited."

of their participation." Third, our cases have suggested (without significant elaboration) that conditions on federal grants might be illegitimate if they are unrelated "to the federal interest in particular national projects or programs." Finally, we have noted that other constitutional provisions may provide an independent bar to the conditional grant of federal funds.

South Dakota does not seriously claim that [the Act] is inconsistent with any of the first three restrictions mentioned above. We can readily conclude that the provision is designed to serve the general welfare, especially in light of the fact that "the concept of welfare or the opposite is shaped by Congress ***." Congress found that the differing drinking ages in the States created particular incentives for young persons to combine their desire to drink with their ability to drive, and that this interstate problem required a national solution. The means it chose to address this dangerous situation were reasonably calculated to advance the general welfare. The conditions upon which States receive the funds, moreover, could not be more clearly stated by Congress. And the State itself, rather than challenging the germaneness of the condition to federal purposes, admits that it "has never contended that the congressional action was *** unrelated to a national concern in the absence of the Twenty-first Amendment." Indeed, the condition imposed by Congress is directly related to one of the main purposes for which highway funds are expended—safe interstate travel. ***

The remaining question about the validity of § 158—and the basic point of disagreement between the parties—is whether the Twenty-first Amendment constitutes an "independent constitutional bar" to the conditional grant of federal funds. Petitioner, relying on its view that the Twenty-first Amendment prohibits direct regulation of drinking ages by Congress, asserts that "Congress may not use the spending power to regulate that which it is prohibited from regulating directly under the Twenty-first Amendment." But our cases show that this "independent constitutional bar" limitation on the spending power is not of the kind petitioner suggests. ***

We have also held that a perceived Tenth Amendment limitation on congressional regulation of state affairs did not concomitantly limit the range of conditions legitimately placed on federal grants. ***

[T]he "independent constitutional bar" limitation on the spending power is not, as petitioner suggests, a prohibition on the indirect achievement of objectives which Congress is not empowered to achieve directly. Instead, we think that the language in our earlier opinions stands for the unexceptionable proposition that the power may not be used to induce the States to engage in activities that would themselves be unconstitutional. Thus, for example, a grant of federal funds conditioned on invidiously discriminatory state action or the infliction of cruel and unusual punishment would be an illegitimate exercise of the Congress' broad spending power. But no such claim can be or is made here. Were South Dakota to succumb to the blandishments offered by Congress and raise its drinking age to 21, the State's action in so doing would not violate the constitutional rights of anyone.

Our decisions have recognized that in some circumstances the financial inducement offered by Congress might be so coercive as to pass the point at which "pressure turns into compulsion." Here, however, Congress has directed only that a State desiring to establish a minimum drinking age lower than 21 lose a relatively small percentage of certain federal highway funds. Petitioner contends that the coercive nature of this program is evident from the degree of success it has achieved. We cannot conclude, however, that a conditional grant of federal money of this sort is unconstitutional simply by reason of its success in achieving the congressional objective.

When we consider, for a moment, that all South Dakota would lose if she adheres to her chosen course as to a suitable minimum drinking age is 5% of the funds otherwise obtainable under specified highway grant programs, the argument as to coercion is shown to be more rhetoric than fact. As we said a half century ago in *Steward Machine Co. v. Davis*: "[E]very rebate from a tax when conditioned upon conduct is in some measure a temptation. But to hold that motive or temptation is equivalent to coercion is to plunge the law in endless difficulties. The outcome of such a doctrine is the acceptance of a philosophical determinism by which choice becomes impossible. Till now the law has been guided by a robust common sense which assumes the freedom of the will as a working hypothesis in the solution of its problems." 301 U.S., at 589–590. Here Congress has offered relatively mild encouragement to the States to enact higher minimum drinking ages than they would otherwise choose. But the enactment of such laws remains the prerogative of the States not merely in theory but in fact. Even if Congress might lack the power to impose a national minimum drinking age directly, we conclude that encouragement to state action found in § 158 is a valid use of the spending power. ***

JUSTICE BRENNAN, dissenting. [omitted]

JUSTICE O'CONNOR, dissenting.

The Court today upholds the National Minimum Drinking Age [§ 158] as a valid exercise of the spending power conferred by Article I, § 8. But § 158 is not a condition on spending reasonably related to the expenditure of federal funds and cannot be justified on that ground. Rather, it is an attempt to regulate the sale of liquor, an attempt that lies outside Congress' power to regulate commerce because it falls within the ambit of § 2 of the Twenty-first Amendment.

My disagreement with the Court is relatively narrow on the spending power issue: it is a disagreement about the application of a principle rather than a disagreement on the principle itself. I agree with the Court that Congress may attach conditions on the receipt of federal funds to further "the federal interest in particular national projects or programs." I also subscribe to the established proposition that the reach of the spending power "is not limited by the direct grants of legislative power found in the Constitution." Finally, I agree that there are four separate types of limitations on the spending power: the expenditure must be for the general welfare, the conditions imposed must be unambiguous, they must be reasonably related to the purpose of the expenditure, and the legislation may not violate any independent constitutional prohibition. Insofar as two of those limitations are concerned, the Court is clearly correct that § 158 is wholly unobjectionable. Establishment of a national minimum drinking age certainly fits within the broad concept of the general welfare and the statute is entirely unambiguous. I am also willing to assume, arguendo, that the Twenty-first Amendment does not constitute an "independent constitutional bar" to a spending condition.

But the Court's application of the requirement that the condition imposed be reasonably related to the purpose for which the funds are expended is cursory and unconvincing. We have repeatedly said that Congress may condition grants under the spending power only in ways reasonably related to the purpose of the federal program. In my view, establishment of a minimum drinking age of 21 is not sufficiently related to interstate highway construction to justify so conditioning funds appropriated for that purpose.

In support of its contrary conclusion, the Court relies on a supposed concession by counsel for South Dakota that the State "has never contended that the congressional action was *** unrelated to a national concern in the absence of the Twenty-first Amendment." In the absence of the Twenty-first Amendment, however, there is a strong argument that the Congress might regulate the conditions under which liquor is sold under the commerce power, just as it regulates the sale of many other commodities that are in or affect interstate commerce. The fact that the Twenty-first Amendment is crucial to the State's argument does not, therefore, amount to a concession that the condition imposed by § 158 is reasonably related to highway construction.

*** [The] Court asserts the reasonableness of the relationship between the supposed purpose of the expenditure—"safe interstate travel"—and the drinking age condition. The Court reasons that Congress wishes that the roads it builds may be used safely, that drunken drivers threaten highway safety, and that young people are more likely to drive while under the influence of alcohol under existing law than would be the case if there were a uniform national drinking age of 21. It hardly needs saying, however, that if the purpose of § 158 is to deter drunken driving, it is far too over and under-inclusive. It is over-inclusive because it stops teenagers from drinking even when they are not about to drive on interstate highways. It is under-inclusive because teenagers pose only a small part of the drunken driving problem in this Nation.

When Congress appropriates money to build a highway, it is entitled to insist that the highway be a safe one. But it is not entitled to insist as a condition of the use of highway funds that the State impose or change regulations in other areas of the State's social and economic life because of an attenuated or tangential relationship to highway use or safety. Indeed, if the rule were otherwise, the Congress could effectively regulate almost any area of a State's social, political, or economic life on the theory that use of the interstate transportation system is somehow enhanced. If, for example, the United States were to condition highway moneys upon moving the state capital, I suppose it might argue that interstate transportation is facilitated by locating local governments in places easily accessible to interstate highways—or, conversely, that highways might become overburdened if they had to carry traffic to and from the state capital. In my mind, such a relationship is hardly more attenuated than the one which the Court finds supports § 158.

There is a clear place at which the Court can draw the line between permissible and impermissible conditions on federal grants. *** The appropriate inquiry is whether the spending requirement or prohibition is a condition on a grant or whether it is regulation. The difference turns on whether the requirement specifies in some way how the money should be spent, so that Congress' intent in making the grant will be effectuated. Congress has no power under the Spending Clause to impose requirements on a grant that go beyond specifying how the money should be spent. A requirement that is not such a specification is not a condition, but a regulation, which is valid only if it falls within one of Congress' delegated regulatory powers.

*** If the spending power is to be limited only by Congress' notion of the general welfare, the reality, given the vast financial resources of the Federal Government, is that the Spending Clause gives "power to the Congress to tear down the barriers, to invade the states' jurisdiction, and to become a parliament of the whole people, subject to no restrictions save such as are self-imposed." This, of course, was not the Framers' plan and it is not the meaning of the Spending Clause.

*** As discussed above, a condition that a State will raise its drinking age to 21 cannot fairly be said to be reasonably related to the expenditure of funds for highway construction. The only possible connection, highway safety, has nothing to do with how the funds Congress has appropriated are expended. Rather than a condition determining how federal highway money shall be expended, it is a regulation determining who shall be able to drink liquor. As such it is not justified by the spending power.

Of the other possible sources of congressional authority for regulating the sale of liquor only the commerce power comes to mind. But in my view, the regulation of the age of the purchasers of liquor, just as the regulation of the price at which liquor may be sold, falls squarely within the scope of those powers reserved to the States by the Twenty-first Amendment. ***

The immense size and power of the Government of the United States ought not obscure its fundamental character. It remains a Government of enumerated powers. Because [the Act] cannot be justified as an exercise of any power delegated to the Congress, it is not authorized by the Constitution. The Court errs in holding it to be the law of the land, and I respectfully dissent.

Notes

1. **Background.** Prior to *Dole*, the Court's decisions disapproved conditional spending that provided funds to "special groups" and that coerced the states

excessively. As you can imagine, it was hard to define a special group and to distinguish between coercion and willing acceptance by the states.

2. **Analysis.** How well do you think the *Dole* analysis deals with the scope of the Spending Power? How does JUSTICE REHNQUIST define the outer limits to this power? Do you agree or disagree with JUSTICE O'CONNOR's dissent?

3. **Question.** Consider whether Congress could condition the receipt of any federal funds by a school district on prohibition of guns (or drugs) within 1000 feet of any school within the district. What if Congress conditioned a state's receipt of all federal funds on the same "no guns (or drugs) near schools" rule?

4. **Problems.** Consider how you might use the spending power post-*Dole* to accomplish the goals of the regulations hypothesized in problem 2, p. 263.

5. **Conditional Spending and Social Policy.** Cultural liberals might see conditional spending as a tool for progressive nationwide changes, a way to circumvent the Rehnquist Court's restricted readings of Congress' powers. Two scholars suggest this is short-sighted and that the following conditional spending schemes would be permissible under *Dole*: "(1) Congress conditions grants for state law enforcement on a state's enactment of right-to-carry laws and on enactment, and enforcement, of the death penalty; (2) Congress conditions Head Start funds on a state's prohibiting affirmative action even by private educational institutions; and (3) Congress conditions a package of funds designed to promote child welfare (perhaps in health and education) on a state's prohibiting homosexual couples from adopting." Lynn A. Baker & Mitchell N. Berman, *Getting off the Dole: Why the Court Should Abandon its Spending Doctrine, and How a Too-Clever Congress Could Provoke It to Do So*, 78 INDIANA L. J. 459, 482-83 (2003).

6. **Will the *Dole* Test Last?** If Congress uses conditional spending when it could not legislate, will the Court abandon or alter the *Dole* test to reestablish a federalist balance? JUSTICE KENNEDY, joined by CHIEF JUSTICE REHNQUIST, JUSTICE SCALIA and JUSTICE THOMAS said that "[T]he Spending Clause power, if wielded without concern for the federal balance, has the potential to obliterate distinctions between national and local spheres of interest and power by permitting the Federal Government to set policy in the most sensitive areas of traditional state concerns, areas which would otherwise be out of reach." *Davis v. Monroe County Bd. of Educ.*, 526 U.S. 629, 654-55 (1999). Consider what the Court might do with a challenge to the Religious Land Use and Institutionalized Persons Act of 2000 (programs receiving federal financial assistance may not "impose a substantial burden on the religious exercise" of an institutionalized person "even if the burden results from a rule of general applicability;" government must use the least restrictive means to meet a compelling interest when imposing such a general rule).

2. THE TREATY AND WAR POWERS

Treaty Power. The leading case on the treaty power, *Missouri v. Holland*, 252 U.S. 416 (1920), was written by JUSTICE HOLMES near the end of his career, during a time when the Commerce Power was viewed as much narrower than during and after the New Deal. Holmes wrote, inter alia: "Acts of Congress are the supreme law of the land only when made in pursuance of the Constitution, while treaties are declared to be so when made under the authority of the United States." While JUSTICE HOLMES noted that the treaty involved "does not contravene any prohibitory words to be found in the Constitution," the opinion might be read to mean that treaties may violate constitutional rights of American citizens.

In the early 1950s, a proposed constitutional amendment (the Bricker Amendment) provided (1) "a provision of a treaty which conflicts with this Constitution shall be of no force or effect," and (2) a treaty shall become effective as internal law [only] through legislation which would be valid in the absence of a treaty. While this amendment did not become part of the Constitution, the Supreme Court, in *Reid v. Covert*, 354 U.S. 1 (1957), said there was nothing in the supremacy clause "which intimates that treaties and laws enacted pursuant to them do not have to comply with the provisions of the Constitution."

Congress and the President have several tools at their disposal to limit the domestic effects of treaties. One is simply to supercede a treaty by legislation. As CHIEF JUSTICE (formerly President) TAFT noted: "A treaty may repeal a statute and a statute may repeal a treaty." Another way in which the President and Congress control application of treaties domestically is through expressing reservations to particular treaties. Professor Johan D. van der Vyver, in "Religious Fundamentalism and Human Rights," J. INT. AFF. (1996) at pp. 34–35, says United States reservations to treaties mean: "The United States shall abide by the principles enunciated in the concerned conventions and covenants in so far as it would make no difference to the country's municipal law." Do you agree?

War Power. Congress was given the power to "declare war" but not to "make war." Many analysts believe this change in language by the framers has greatly affected the balance of power between Congress and the President, especially in connection with numerous small-scale military actions taken by Presidents from early in the history of the United States until the present. But Congress has a number of other powers it can use to control the exercise of military power by the President. Review Article I, § 8.

Language in *Woods v. Cloyd W. Miller Co.*, 333 U.S. 138 (1948), supports the notion of Congress having a broad war power: (1) "the war power does not necessarily end with the cessation of hostilities," and (2) the war power, broadly construed, might "swallow up" the other powers and burst free from Ninth and Tenth Amendment constraints on Congress. JUSTICE JACKSON's concurrence cautioned that the war power "is the most dangerous one to free government" and that the "haste and excitement" accompanying exercise of the war power should lead to especially careful judicial protection of liberties.

Notes

1. **Treaty Power.** The North American Free Trade Agreement (NAFTA) was negotiated by President Clinton, passed by majorities of both houses of Congress, and signed by President Clinton. Is NAFTA unconstitutional since it was not ratified by 2/3rds of the Senate? What additional information concerning NAFTA would help you answer this question? Of what relevance, if any, is the

"Commerce with foreign Nations" provision of Art. 1, § 8, cl. 3? Can the President alone terminate a treaty, or must the Senate ratify its termination?

2.   **Choice of Powers.** What Article I powers might Congress rely upon (if any) to accomplish the following, and how might it exercise such powers:

- Punishing hate crimes based on the victims race, gender, or sexual orientation.

- Barring execution of pregnant women.

- Encouraging state and local school voucher programs.

- Prohibiting homosexual marriages and "no-fault" divorces.

- Outlawing bungee-jumping.

D. THE POWER TO ENFORCE THE RECONSTRUCTION AMENDMENTS

The 13th, 14th, 15th, 19th, 24th, and 26th amendments provide Congress power to "enforce" their provisions "by appropriate legislation." The following cases examine the scope of these enforcement powers. The first, which deals with whether Congress can prohibit private discrimination, will deepen your understanding of *Heart of Atlanta*. The other cases examine the substantive reach of the enforcement power. How far may Congress go in defining, facilitating, and limiting Fourteenth Amendment rights? And what do these rights encompass, anyway? The practical significance of this power will become clearer when you have finished all the materials in this and the next chapter. Significant expansion of your understanding of the reach of the Fourteenth Amendment and more problematical aspects of "state action" will be developed in later chapters.

1. STATE ACTION AND THE ENFORCEMENT POWER

THE CIVIL RIGHTS CASES
109 U.S. 3, 3 S.Ct. 18, 27 L.Ed. 835 (1883).

BRADLEY, J.

*** [T]he primary and important question in all the cases is the constitutionality of th[is] law ***: "That all persons within the jurisdiction of the United States shall be entitled to the full and equal enjoyment of the accommodations, advantages, facilities, and privileges of inns, public conveyances on land or water, theaters, and other places of public amusement; subject only to the conditions and limitations established by law, and applicable alike to citizens of every race and color, regardless of any previous condition of servitude [and that violations shall be remedied by civil suits by the "person aggrieved" and criminal sanctions.]"

Has congress constitutional power to make such a law? Of course, no one will contend that the power to pass it was contained in the constitution before the adoption of the last three amendments. The power is sought, first, in the fourteenth amendment ***. [In t]he first section of the fourteenth amendment *** it is state action of a particular character that is prohibited. Individual invasion of individual rights is not the subject-matter of the amendment. It has a deeper and broader scope. It nullifies and makes void all state legislation, and state action of every kind, which impairs the privileges and immunities of citizens of the United States, or which injures them in life, liberty, or property without due process of law, or which denies to any of them the equal protection of the laws. *** [T]he last section of the amendment invests congress with power to enforce it by appropriate legislation. To enforce what? To enforce the prohibition. To adopt appropriate legislation for correcting the effects of such prohibited state law and state acts, and thus to render them effectually null, void, and innocuous. This is the legislative power conferred upon congress, and this is the whole of it. It does not invest congress with power to legislate upon subjects which are within the domain of state legislation; but to provide modes of relief against state legislation, or state action, of the kind referred to. It does not authorize congress to create a code of municipal law for the regulation of private rights; but to provide modes of redress against the operation of state laws, and the action of state officers, executive or judicial, when these are subversive of the fundamental rights specified in the amendment. ***

An apt illustration of this distinction may be found in some of the provisions of the original constitution. Take the subject of contracts, for example. The constitution prohibited the states from passing any law impairing the obligation of contracts. This did not give to congress power to provide laws for the general enforcement of contracts; nor power to invest the courts of the United States with jurisdiction over contracts, so as to enable parties to sue upon them in those courts. It did, however, give the power to provide remedies by which the impairment of contracts by state legislation might be counteracted and corrected; and this power was exercised. *** Some obnoxious state law passed, or that might be passed, is necessary to be assumed in order to lay the foundation of any federal remedy in the case, and for the very sufficient reason that the constitutional prohibition is against state laws impairing the obligation of contracts.

And so in the present case, until some state law has been passed, or some state action through its officers or agents has been taken, adverse to the rights of citizens sought to be protected by the fourteenth amendment, no legislation of the United States under said amendment, nor any proceeding under such legislation, can be called into activity, for the prohibitions of the amendment are against state laws and acts done under state authority. *** An inspection of the law shows that it makes no reference whatever to any supposed or apprehended violation of the fourteenth amendment on the part of the states. *** In other words, it steps into the domain of local jurisprudence, and lays down rules for the conduct of individuals is society towards each other, and imposes sanctions for the enforcement of those rules, without referring in any manner to any supposed action of the state or its authorities.

If this legislation is appropriate for enforcing the prohibitions of the amendment, it is difficult to see where it is to stop. Why may not congress, with equal show of authority, enact a code of laws for the enforcement and vindication of all rights of life, liberty, and property? *** [This law] is repugnant to the tenth amendment of the constitution ***.

[C]ivil rights, such as are guarantied by the constitution against state aggression, cannot be impaired by the wrongful acts of individuals, unsupported by state authority in the shape of laws, customs, or judicial or executive proceedings. The wrongful act of an individual, unsupported by any such authority, is simply a private wrong, or a crime of that individual; an invasion of the rights of the injured party, it is true, whether they affect his person, his property, or his reputation; but if not sanctioned in some way by the state, or not done under state authority, his rights remain in full force, and may presumably be vindicated by resort to the laws of the state for redress. An individual cannot deprive a man of his right to vote, to hold property, to buy and to sell, to sue in the courts, or to be a witness or a juror; he may, by force or fraud, interfere with the enjoyment of the right in a particular case; he may commit an assault against the person, or commit murder, or use ruffian violence at the polls, or slander the good name of a fellow-citizen; but unless protected in these wrongful acts by some shield of state law or state authority, he cannot destroy or injure the right; he will only render himself amenable to satisfaction or punishment; and amenable therefor to the laws of the state where the wrongful acts are committed. Hence, in all those cases where the constitution seeks to protect the rights of the citizen against discriminative and unjust laws of the state by prohibiting such laws, it is not individual offenses, but abrogation and denial of rights, which it denounces, and for which it clothes the congress with power to provide a remedy. This abrogation and denial of rights, for which the states alone were or could be responsible, was the great seminal and fundamental wrong which was intended to be remedied. And the remedy to be provided must necessarily be predicated upon that wrong. It must assume that in the cases provided for, the evil or wrong actually committed rests upon some state law or state authority for its excuse and perpetration.

Of course, these remarks do not apply to those cases in which congress is clothed with direct and plenary powers of legislation over the whole subject, accompanied with an express or implied denial of such power to the states, as in the regulation of commerce with foreign nations, among the several states, and with the Indian tribes, the coining of money, the establishment of post-offices and post-roads, the declaring of war, etc. In these cases congress has power to pass laws for regulating the subjects specified, in every detail, and the conduct and transactions of individuals respect thereof. But where a subject is not submitted to the general legislative power of congress, but is only submitted thereto for the purpose of rendering effective some prohibition against particular state legislation or state action in reference to that subject, the power given is limited by its object, and any legislation by congress in the matter must necessarily be corrective in its character, adapted to counteract and redress the operation of such prohibited state laws or proceedings of state officers.

*** [T]he law in question cannot be sustained by any grant of legislative power made to congress by the fourteenth amendment. That amendment prohibits the states from denying to any person the equal protection of the laws, and declares that congress shall have power to enforce, by appropriate legislation, the provisions of the amendment. The law in question, without any reference to adverse state legislation on the subject, declares that all persons shall be entitled to equal accommodation and privileges of inns, public conveyances, and places of public amusement, and imposes a penalty upon any individual who shall deny to any citizen such equal accommodations and privileges. This is not corrective legislation; it is primary and direct; it takes immediate and absolute possession of the subject of the right of admission to inns, public conveyances, and places of amusement. It supersedes and displaces state legislation on the same subject, or only allows it permissive force. It ignores such legislation, and assumes that the matter is one that belongs to the domain of national regulation. Whether it would not have been a more effective protection of the rights of citizens to have clothed congress with plenary power over the whole subject, is not now the question. What we have to decide is, whether such plenary power has been conferred upon congress by the fourteenth amendment, and, in our judgment, it has not. ***

But the power of congress to adopt direct and primary, as distinguished from corrective, legislation on the subject in hand, is sought, in the second place, from the thirteenth amendment, which abolishes slavery. *** It is true that slavery cannot exist without law any more than property in lands and goods can exist without law, and therefore the thirteenth amendment may be regarded as nullifying all state laws which establish or uphold slavery. *** [I]t is assumed that the power vested in congress to enforce the article by appropriate legislation, clothes congress with power to pass all laws necessary and proper for abolishing all badges and incidents of slavery in the United Stated; and upon this assumption it is claimed that this is sufficient authority for declaring by law that all persons shall have equal accommodations and privileges in all inns, public conveyances, and places of public amusement; the argument being that the denial of such equal accommodations and privileges is in itself a subjection to a species of servitude within the meaning of the amendment. ***

But is there any similarity between such servitudes and a denial by the owner of an inn, a public conveyance, or a theater, of its accommodations and privileges to an individual, even through the denial be founded on the race or color of that individual? Where does any slavery or servitude, or badge of either, arise from such an act of denial? Whether it might not be a denial of a right which, if sanctioned by the state law, would be obnoxious to the prohibitions of the fourteenth amendment, is another question. But what has it to do with the question of slavery? It may be that by the black code, (as it was called,) in the times when slavery prevailed, the proprietors of inns and public conveyances were forbidden to receive persons of the African race, because it might assist slaves to escape from the control of their masters. This was merely a means of preventing such escapes, and was no part of the servitude itself. ***

We must not forget that the province and scope of the thirteenth and fourteenth amendments are different: the former simply abolished slavery ***. The only question under the present head, therefore, is, whether the refusal to any persons of the accommodations of an inn, or a public conveyance, or a place of public amusement, by an individual, and without any sanction or support from any state law or regulation, does inflict upon such persons any manner of servitude, or form of slavery, as those terms are understood in this country? ***

Now, conceding, for the sake of the argument, that the admission to an inn, a public conveyance, or a place of public amusement, on equal terms with all other citizens, is the right of every man and all classes of men, is it any more than one of those rights which the states by the fourteenth amendment are forbidden to deny to any person? And is the constitution violated until the denial of the right has some state sanction or authority? Can the act of a mere individual, the owner of the inn, the public conveyance, or place of amusement, refusing the accommodation, be justly regarded as imposing any badge of slavery or servitude upon the applicant, or only as inflicting an ordinary civil injury, properly cognizable by the laws of the state, and presumably subject to redress by those laws until the contrary appears? *** [S]uch an act of refusal has nothing to do with slavery or involuntary servitude, and that if it is violative of any right of the party, his redress is to be sought under the laws of the state; or, if those laws are adverse to his rights and do not protect him, his remedy will be found in the corrective legislation which congress has adopted, or may adopt, for counteracting the effect of state laws, or state action, prohibited by the fourteenth amendment. It would be running the slavery argument into the ground to make it apply to every act of discrimination which a person may see fit to make as to the guests he will entertain, or as to the people he will take into his coach or cab or car, or admit to his concert or theater, or deal with in other matters of intercourse or business. Innkeepers and public carriers, by the laws of all the states, so far as we are aware, are bound, to the extent of their facilities, to furnish proper accommodation to all unobjectionable persons who in good faith apply for them. If the laws themselves make any unjust discrimination, amenable to the prohibitions of the fourteenth amendment, congress has full power to afford a remedy under that amendment and in accordance with it.

When a man has emerged from slavery, and by the aid of beneficent legislation has shaken off the inseparable concomitants of that state, there must be some stage in the progress of his elevation when he takes the rank of a mere citizen, and ceases to be the special favorite of the laws, and when his rights as a citizen, or a man, are to be protected in the ordinary modes by which other men's rights are protected. There were thousands of free colored people in this country before the abolition of slavery, enjoying all the essential rights of life, liberty, and property the same as white citizens; yet no one, at that time, thought that it was any invasion of their personal status as freemen because they were not admitted to all the privileges enjoyed by white citizens, or because they were subjected to discriminations in the enjoyment of accommodations in inns, public conveyances, and places of amusement.

Mere discriminations on account of race or color were not regarded as badges of slavery. ***

HARLAN, J., dissenting.

The opinion in these cases proceeds, as it seems to me, upon grounds entirely too narrow and artificial. The substance and spirit of the recent amendments of the constitution have been sacrificed by a subtle and ingenious verbal criticism. ***

The thirteenth amendment, my brethren concede, did something more than to prohibit slavery as an institution, resting upon distinctions of race, and upheld by positive law. *** That there are burdens and disabilities which constitute badges of slavery and servitude, and that the express power delegated to congress to enforce, by appropriate legislation, the thirteenth amendment, may be exerted by legislation of a direct and primary character, for the eradication, not simply of the institution, but of its badges and incidents, are propositions which ought to be deemed indisputable. *** I do not contend that the thirteenth amendment invests congress with authority, by legislation, to regulate the entire body of the civil rights which citizens enjoy, or may enjoy, in the several states. But I do hold that since slavery, as the court has repeatedly declared, was the moving or principal cause of the adoption of that amendment, and since that institution rested wholly upon the inferiority, as a race, of those held in bondage, their freedom necessarily involved immunity from, and protection against, all discrimination against them, because of their race, in respect of such civil rights as belong to freemen of other races. ***

It remains now to inquire what are the legal rights of colored persons in respect of the accommodations, privileges, and facilities of public conveyances, inns, and places of public amusement. *** I am of opinion that such discrimination is a badge of servitude, the imposition of which congress may prevent under its power, through appropriate legislation, to enforce the thirteenth amendment; and consequently, without reference to its enlarged power under the fourteenth amendment, the act of March 1, 1875, is not, in my judgment, repugnant to the constitution.

It remains now to consider these cases with reference to the power congress has possessed since the adoption of the fourteenth amendment. *** [T]he court refers to the clause of the constitution forbidding the passage by a state of any law impairing the obligation of contracts. The clause does not, I submit, furnish a proper illustration of the scope and effect of the fifth section of the fourteenth amendment. No express power is given congress to enforce, by primary direct legislation, the prohibition upon state laws impairing the obligation of contracts. ***

[The § 1] prohibition upon a state is not a *power* in *congress* or *in the national government*. It is simply a denial of power to the state [enforceable by suit in federal court to invalidate any such law]. *** The fourteenth amendment presents the first instance in our history of the investiture of congress with affirmative power, by legislation, to enforce an express prohibition upon the states. It is not said that the judicial power of the nation may be exerted for the enforcement of that amendment. *** The power given is, in terms, by congressional legislation, to enforce the provisions of the amendment.

The assumption that this amendment consists wholly of prohibitions upon state laws and state proceedings in hostility to its provisions, is unauthorized by its language. *** The citizenship thus acquired by that race, in virtue of an affirmative grant by the nation, may be protected, not alone by the judicial branch of the government, but by congressional legislation of a primary direct character; this, because the power of congress is not restricted to the enforcement of prohibitions upon state laws or state action. It is, in terms distinct and positive, to enforce 'the provisions of this article' of amendment ***.

What are the privileges and immunities to which, by that clause of the constitution, they became entitled? *** [W]hat was secured to colored citizens of the United States—as between them and their respective states—by the grant to them of state citizenship? With what rights, privileges, or immunities did this grant from the nation invest them? There is one, if there be no others—exemption from race discrimination in respect of any civil right belonging to citizens of the white race in the same state. That, surely, is their constitutional privilege when within the jurisdiction of other states. And such must be their constitutional right, in their own state, unless the recent amendments be "splendid baubles," thrown out to delude those who deserved fair and generous treatment at the hands of the nation. Citizenship in this country necessarily imports equality of civil rights among citizens of every race in the same state. It is fundamental in American citizenship that, in respect of such rights, there shall be no discrimination by the state, or its officers, or by individuals, or corporations exercising public functions or authority, against any citizen because of his race or previous condition of servitude. ***

If, then, exemption from discrimination in respect of civil rights is a new constitutional right, secured by the grant of state citizenship to colored citizens of the United States, why may not the nation, by means of its own legislation of a primary direct character, guard, protect, and enforce that right? *** This court has always given a broad and liberal construction to the constitution, so as to enable congress, by legislation, to enforce rights secured by that instrument. *** *McCulloch v. Maryland.* *** If fugitive slave laws, providing modes and prescribing penalties whereby the master could seize and recover his fugitive slave, were legitimate exertions of an implied power to protect and enforce a right recognized by the constitution, why shall the hands of congress be tied, so that—under an express power, by appropriate legislation, to enforce a constitutional provision, granting citizenship—it may not, by means of direct legislation, bring the whole power of this nation to bear upon states and their officers, and upon such individuals and corporations exercising public functions, as assume to abridge, impair, or deny rights confessedly secured by the supreme law of the land? *** It was perfectly well known that the great danger to the equal enjoyment by citizens of their rights, as citizens, was to be apprehended, not altogether from unfriendly state legislation, but from the hostile action of corporations and individuals in the states. And it is to be presumed that it was intended, by that section, to clothe congress with power and authority to meet that danger. *** As to the prohibition in the fourteenth amendment upon the making or enforcing of state laws abridging the privileges of citizens of the United States, it was impossible for any state to have enforced laws of that character. The judiciary could have annulled all such legislation ***. The states were already under an implied prohibition not to abridge any privilege or immunity belonging to citizens of the United States as such. ***

It is said that any interpretation of the fourteenth amendment different from that adopted by the court, would authorize congress to enact a municipal code for all the states, covering every matter affecting the life, liberty, and property of the citizens of the several states. Not so. *** The rights and immunities of persons recognized in the prohibitive clauses of the amendments were always under the protection, primarily, of the states, while rights created by or derived from the United States have always been, and, in the nature of things, should always be, primarily, under the protection of the general government. Exemption from race discrimination in respect of the civil rights which are fundamental in citizenship in a republican government, is, as we have seen, a new constitutional right, created by the nation, with express power in congress, by legislation, to enforce the constitutional provision from which it is derived. *** In every material sense applicable to the practical enforcement of the fourteenth amendment, railroad corporations, keepers of inns, and managers of places of public amusement are agents of the state, because amenable, in respect of their public duties and functions, to public regulation. It seems to me that *** a denial by these instrumentalities of the state to the citizen, because of his race, of that equality of civil rights secured to him by law, is a denial by the state within the meaning of the fourteenth amendment. If it be not, then that race is left, in respect of the civil rights under discussion, practically at the mercy of corporations and individuals wielding power under public authority.

*** What I affirm is that no state, nor the officers of any state, nor any corporation or individual wielding power under state authority for the public benefit or the public convenience, can, consistently either with the freedom established by the fundamental law, or with that equality of civil rights which now belongs to every citizen, discriminate against freemen or citizens, in their civil rights, because of their race, or because they once labored under disabilities imposed upon them as a race. The rights which congress, by the act of 1875, endeavored to secure and protect are legal, not social, rights. The right, for instance, of a colored citizen to use the accommodations of a public highway upon the same terms as are permitted to white citizens is no more a social right than his right, under the law, to use the public streets of a city, or a town, or a turnpike road, or a public market, or a post-office, or his right to sit in a public building with others, of whatever race, for the purpose of hearing the political questions of the day discussed. Scarcely a day passes without our seeing in this court-room citizens of the white and black races sitting side by side watching the progress of our business. It would never occur to any one that the presence of a colored citizen in a court-house or court-room was an invasion of the social rights of white persons who may frequent such places. And yet such a suggestion would be quite as sound in law—I say it with all respect—as is the suggestion that the claim of a colored citizen to use, upon the same terms as is permitted to white citizens, the accommodations of public highways, or public inns, or places of public amusement, established under the license of the law, is an invasion of the social rights of the white race.

The court, in its opinion, reserves the question whether congress, in the exercise of its power to regulate commerce among the several states, might or might not pass a law regulating rights in public conveyances passing from one state to another. *** Has it ever been held that the judiciary should overturn a statute because the legislative department did not accurately recite therein the particular provision of the constitution authorizing its enactment? *** [Moreover,] the state of Louisiana, in 1869, passed a statute giving to passengers, without regard to race or color, equality of right in the accommodations of railroad and street cars, steam-boats, or other water-crafts, stage-coaches, omnibuses, or other vehicles. But in *Hall v. De Cuir*, 95 U.S. 485, that act was pronounced unconstitutional so far as it related to commerce between the states, this court saying that "if the public good requires such legislation it must come from congress and not from the states." I suggest that it may become a pertinent inquiry whether congress may, in the exertion of its power to regulate commerce among the states, enforce among passengers on public conveyances equality of right without regard to race, color, or previous condition of servitude, if it be true—which I do not admit—that such legislation would be an interference by government with the social rights of the people.

My brethren say that when a man has emerged from slavery, and by the aid of beneficient legislation has shaken off the inseparable concomitants of that state, there must be some stage in the progress of his elevation when he takes the rank of a mere citizen, and ceases to be the special favorite of the laws, and when his rights as a citizen, or a man, are to be protected in the ordinary modes by which other men's rights are protected. It is, I submit, scarcely just to say that the colored race has been the special favorite of the laws. *** To-day it is the colored race which is denied, by corporations and individuals wielding public authority, rights fundamental in their freedom and citizenship. At some future time it may be some other race that will fall under the ban. ***

Notes

1. **Holdings.** List the holdings of the case. For each, consider whether you think the majority or the dissent has the better of the argument and why.

2. **Or iginal intent.** Suppose the framers of the 13th and 14th Amendments thought they were authorized to pass the law invalidated in *The Civil Rights Cases*, a fair assumption since the same legislators who passed the law also approved these amendments. Neither the majority nor the dissent lays significant emphasis on this argument. Would you?

3. **Ramifications.** Consider the immediate effects of this decision on the development of race relations in this country. Why didn't Congress simply reenact the invalidated statute using the Commerce Clause powers discussed by the dissent? Why didn't the decision at least have the effect of nullifying the Jim Crow laws which relegated blacks to the back of public buses, to separate railroad cars, and to segregated classrooms for so many decades? *See Plessy v. Ferguson* and *Brown v. Board of Education,* infra Chapter IX.

4. **The *Civil Rights Cases* Today.** The *Civil Rights Cases* have been distinguished but not overruled, despite widespread academic commentary arguing that overruling is overdue. Here are excerpts from the portions of the majority and dissent in *United States v. Morrison,* supra p. 255, assessing whether the Violence Against Women Act could be supported by Congress' § 5 power:

> Shortly after the Fourteenth Amendment was adopted, we decided two cases interpreting the Amendment's provisions, *United States v. Harris,* 106 U.S. 629 (1883), and the *Civil Rights Cases,* 109 U.S. 3 (1883). In *Harris,* the Court considered a challenge to § 2 of the Civil Rights Act of 1871. That section sought to punish "private persons" for "conspiring to deprive any one of the equal protection of the laws enacted by the State." We concluded that this law exceeded Congress' § 5 power because the law was "directed exclusively against the action of private persons, without reference to the laws of the State, or their administration by her officers." *** We reached a similar conclusion in the *Civil Rights Cases.* In those consolidated cases, we held that the public accommodation provisions of the Civil Rights Act of 1875, which applied to purely private conduct, were beyond the scope of the § 5 enforcement power. *** The force of the doctrine of stare decisis behind these decisions stems not only from the length of time they have been on the books, but also from the insight attributable to the Members of the Court at that time. Every Member had been appointed by President Lincoln, Grant, Hayes, Garfield, or Arthur—and each of their judicial appointees obviously had intimate knowledge and familiarity with the events surrounding the adoption of the Fourteenth Amendment.

> *** Section 13981 is not aimed at proscribing discrimination by officials which the Fourteenth Amendment might not itself proscribe; it is directed not at any State or state actor, but at individuals who have committed criminal acts motivated by gender bias. *** Congress' power under § 5 does not extend to the enactment of § 13981. ***

JUSTICE BREYER, dissenting:

> *** The Federal Government's argument *** is that Congress used § 5 to remedy the actions of state actors, namely, those States which, through discriminatory design or the discriminatory conduct of their officials, failed to provide adequate (or any) state remedies for women injured by gender-motivated violence—a failure that the States, and Congress, documented in depth.

Neither *Harris* nor the *Civil Rights Cases* considered this kind of claim. The Court in *Harris* specifically said that it treated the federal laws in question as "directed exclusively against the action of private persons, without reference to the laws of the State, or their administration by her officers"; see also *Civil Rights Cases* (observing that the statute did "not profess to be corrective of any constitutional wrong committed by the States" and that it established "rules for the conduct of individuals in society towards each other, *** without referring in any manner to any supposed action of the State or its authorities").

The Court responds directly to the relevant "state actor" claim by finding that the present law lacks "congruence and proportionality" to the state discrimination that it purports to remedy. That is because the law, unlike federal laws prohibiting literacy tests for voting, imposing voting rights requirements, or punishing state officials who intentionally discriminated in jury selection, is not "directed *** at any State or state actor."

But why can Congress not provide a remedy against private actors? Those private actors, of course, did not themselves violate the Constitution. But this Court has held that Congress at least sometimes can enact remedial "[l]egislation *** [that] prohibits conduct which is not itself unconstitutional." *Flores*; see also *Katzenbach v. Morgan*; *South Carolina v. Katzenbach*. The statutory remedy does not in any sense purport to "determine what constitutes a constitutional violation." It intrudes little upon either States or private parties. It may lead state actors to improve their own remedial systems, primarily through example. It restricts private actors only by imposing liability for private conduct that is, in the main, already forbidden by state law. Why is the remedy "disproportionate"? And given the relation between remedy and violation—the creation of a federal remedy to substitute for constitutionally inadequate state remedies—where is the lack of "congruence"?

The majority adds that Congress found that the problem of inadequacy of state remedies "does not exist in all States, or even most States." But Congress had before it the task force reports of at least 21 States documenting constitutional violations. And it made its own findings about pervasive gender-based stereotypes hampering many state legal systems, sometimes unconstitutionally so. The record nowhere reveals a congressional finding that the problem "does not exist" elsewhere. Why can Congress not take the evidence before it as evidence of a national problem? This Court has not previously held that Congress must document the existence of a problem in every State prior to proposing a national solution.

How might Congress restrict § 13981 to make it constitutional? Could § 13981 be premised on protecting the citizenship of women (see the first sentence of § 1)?

5. **Scope of the Thirteenth Amendment Enforcement Power.** The Thirteenth Amendment abolishes "slavery or involuntary servitude," whether engaged in by

the state or private individuals, and gives Congress "power to enforce this article by appropriate legislation." The Thirteenth Amendment has been read to permit Congress to eliminate "badges of slavery" through statutes barring private race discrimination, *Jones v. Alfred H. Mayer Co.*, 392 U.S. 409 (1968), but not sex discrimination. *Runyon v. McCrary*, 427 U.S. 160 (1976). Could Congress forbid State Bar Associations from requiring lawyers to do pro bono work?

2. POWER TO "ENFORCE" THE FOURTEENTH AMENDMENT

KATZENBACH v. MORGAN
384 U.S. 641, 86 S.Ct. 1717, 16 L.Ed.2d 828 (1966).

MR. JUSTICE BRENNAN delivered the opinion of the Court.

These cases concern the constitutionality of § 4(e) of the Voting Rights Act of 1965. That law, in the respects pertinent in these cases, provides that no person who has successfully completed the sixth primary grade in a public school in, or a private school accredited by, the Commonwealth of Puerto Rico in which the language of instruction was other than English shall be denied the right to vote in any election because of his inability to read or write English. Appellees, registered voters in New York City, brought this suit to challenge the constitutionality of § 4(e) insofar as it pro tanto prohibits the enforcement of the election laws of New York requiring an ability to read and write English as a condition of voting. Under these laws many of the several hundred thousand New York City residents who have migrated there from the Commonwealth of Puerto Rico had previously been denied the right to vote, and appellees attack § 4(e) insofar as it would enable many of these citizens to vote.[3] *** The [District] court held that in enacting § 4(e) Congress exceeded the powers granted to it by the Constitution and therefore usurped powers reserved to the States by the Tenth Amendment. Appeals were taken directly to this Court. We reverse. We hold that, in the application challenged in these cases, § 4(e) is a proper exercise of the powers granted to Congress by § 5 of the Fourteenth Amendment[5] and that by force of the Supremacy Clause, Article VI, the New York English literacy requirement cannot be enforced to the extent that it is inconsistent with § 4(e).

---

[3] This limitation on appellees' challenge to § 4(e), and thus on the scope of our inquiry, does not distort the primary intent of § 4(e). *** The Solicitor General informs us in his brief to this Court, that in all probability the practical effect of § 4(e) will be limited to enfranchising those educated in Puerto Rican schools. He advises us that, aside from the schools in the Commonwealth of Puerto Rico, there are no public or parochial schools in the territorial limits of the United States in which the predominant language of instruction is other than English and which would have generally been attended by persons who are otherwise qualified to vote save for their lack of literacy in English.

[5] "Section 5. The Congress shall have power to enforce, by appropriate legislation, the provisions of this article." It is therefore unnecessary for us to consider whether s 4(e) could be sustained as an exercise of power under the Territorial Clause, Art. IV, § 3; or as a measure to discharge certain treaty obligations of the United States. Nor need we consider whether § 4(e) could be sustained insofar as it relates to the election of federal officers as an exercise of congressional power under Art. I, § 4; nor whether § 4(e) could be sustained, insofar as it relates to the election of state officers, as an exercise of congressional power to enforce the clause guaranteeing to each State a republican form of government.

Under the distribution of powers effected by the Constitution, the States establish qualifications for voting for state officers. But, of course, the States have no power to grant or withhold the franchise on conditions that are forbidden by the Fourteenth Amendment, or any other provision of the Constitution. Such exercises of state power are no more immune to the limitations of the Fourteenth Amendment than any other state action. The Equal Protection Clause itself has been held to forbid some state laws that restrict the right to vote.

The Attorney General of the State of New York argues that an exercise of congressional power under § 5 of the Fourteenth Amendment that prohibits the enforcement of a state law can only be sustained if the judicial branch determines that the state law is prohibited by the provisions of the Amendment that Congress sought to enforce. More specifically, he urges that § 4(e) cannot be sustained as appropriate legislation to enforce the Equal Protection Clause unless the judiciary decides—even with the guidance of a congressional judgment—that the application of the English literacy requirement prohibited by § 4(e) is forbidden by the Equal Protection Clause itself.

We disagree. Neither the language nor history of § 5 supports such a construction. As was said with regard to § 5 in *Ex Parte Virginia*, 100 U.S. 339, 345, "It is the power of Congress which has been enlarged. Congress is authorized to enforce the prohibitions by appropriate legislation. Some legislation is contemplated to make the amendments fully effective." A construction of § 5 that would require a judicial determination that the enforcement of the state law precluded by Congress violated the Amendment, as a condition of sustaining the congressional enactment, would depreciate both congressional resourcefulness and congressional responsibility for implementing the Amendment. It would confine the legislative power in this context to the insignificant role of abrogating only those state laws that the judicial branch was prepared to adjudge unconstitutional, or of merely informing the judgment of the judiciary by particularizing the "majestic generalities" of § 1 of the Amendment.

Thus our task in this case is not to determine whether the New York English literacy requirement as applied to deny the right to vote to a person who successfully completed the sixth grade in a Puerto Rican school violates the Equal Protection Clause. *** [The] question before us here [is]: Without regard to whether the judiciary would find that the Equal Protection Clause itself nullifies New York's English literacy requirement as so applied, could Congress prohibit the enforcement of the state law by legislating under § 5 of the Fourteenth Amendment? In answering this question, our task is limited to determining whether such legislation is, as required by § 5, appropriate legislation to enforce the Equal Protection Clause.

By including § 5 the draftsmen sought to grant to Congress, by a specific provision applicable to the Fourteenth Amendment, the same broad powers expressed in the Necessary and Proper Clause, Art. I, § 8, cl. 18. The classic formulation of the reach of those powers was established by CHIEF JUSTICE MARSHALL in *McCulloch v. Maryland*, "[l]et the end be legitimate, let it be within the scope of the constitution, and all means which are appropriate, which are plainly adapted to that end, which are not prohibited, but consist with the letter and spirit of the constitution, are constitutional." *** Correctly viewed, § 5 is a positive grant of legislative power authorizing Congress to exercise its discretion in determining whether and what legislation is needed to secure the guarantees of the Fourteenth Amendment.

We therefore proceed to the consideration whether § 4(e) is "appropriate legislation" to enforce the Equal Protection Clause, that is, under the *McCulloch v. Maryland* standard, whether § 4(e) may be regarded as an enactment to enforce the Equal Protection Clause, whether it is "plainly adapted to that end" and whether it is not prohibited by but is consistent with "the letter and spirit of the constitution."[10]

There can be no doubt that § 4(e) may be regarded as an enactment to enforce the Equal Protection Clause. Congress explicitly declared that it enacted § 4(e) "to secure the rights under the fourteenth amendment of persons educated in American-flag schools in which the predominant classroom language was other than English." The persons referred to include those who have migrated from the Commonwealth of Puerto Rico to New York and who have been denied the right to vote because of their inability to read and write English, and the Fourteenth Amendment rights referred to include those emanating from the Equal Protection Clause. More specifically, § 4(e) may be viewed as a measure to secure for the Puerto Rican community residing in New York nondiscriminatory treatment by government—both in the imposition of voting qualifications and the provision or administration of governmental services, such as public schools, public housing and law enforcement.

Section 4(e) may be readily seen as "plainly adapted" to furthering these aims of the Equal Protection Clause. The practical effect of § 4(e) is to prohibit New York from denying the right to vote to large segments of its Puerto Rican community. Congress has thus prohibited the State from denying to that community the right that is "preservative of all rights." This enhanced political power will be helpful in gaining nondiscriminatory treatment in public services for the entire Puerto Rican community. Section 4(e) thereby enables the Puerto Rican minority better to obtain "perfect equality of civil rights and the equal protection of the laws." It was well within congressional authority to say that this need of the Puerto Rican minority for the vote warranted federal intrusion upon any state interests served by the English literacy requirement. It was for Congress, as the branch that made this judgment, to assess and weigh the various conflicting considerations—the risk or pervasiveness of the discrimination in governmental services, the effectiveness of eliminating the state restriction

---

[10] *** § 5 does not grant Congress power to exercise discretion in the other direction and to enact "statutes so as in effect to dilute equal protection and due process decisions of this Court." We emphasize that Congress' power under § 5 is limited to adopting measures to enforce the guarantees of the Amendment; § 5 grants Congress no power to restrict, abrogate, or dilute these guarantees. Thus, for example, an enactment authorizing the States to establish racially segregated systems of education would not be—as required by § 5—a measure "to enforce" the Equal Protection Clause since that clause of its own force prohibits such state laws.

on the right to vote as a means of dealing with the evil, the adequacy or availability of alternative remedies, and the nature and significance of the state interests that would be affected by the nullification of the English literacy requirement as applied to residents who have successfully completed the sixth grade in a Puerto Rican school. It is not for us to review the congressional resolution of these factors. It is enough that we be able to perceive a basis upon which the Congress might resolve the conflict as it did. There plainly was such a basis to support § 4(e) in the application in question in this case. Any contrary conclusion would require us to be blind to the realities familiar to the legislators.

*** [I]t is enough that we perceive a basis upon which Congress might predicate a judgment that the application of New York's English literacy requirement to deny the right to vote to a person with a sixth grade education in Puerto Rican schools in which the language of instruction was other than English constituted an invidious discrimination in violation of the Equal Protection Clause.

There remains the question whether the congressional remedies adopted in § 4(e) constitute means which are not prohibited by, but are consistent "with the letter and spirit of the constitution." The only respect in which appellees contend that § 4(e) fails in this regard is that the section itself works an invidious discrimination in violation of the Fifth Amendment by prohibiting the enforcement of the English literacy requirement only for those educated in American-flag schools (schools located within United States jurisdiction) in which the language of instruction was other than English, and not for those educated in schools beyond the territorial limits of the United States in which the language of instruction was also other than English. This is not a complaint that Congress, in enacting § 4(e), has unconstitutionally denied or diluted anyone's right to vote but rather that Congress violated the Constitution by not extending the relief effected in § 4(e) to those educated in non-American-flag schools. *** [This] argument fails ***. We therefore conclude that § 4(e), in the application challenged in this case, is appropriate legislation to enforce the Equal Protection Clause ***.

MR. JUSTICE DOUGLAS joins the Court's opinion [except for the discussion whether the congressional remedies adopted are constitutional, an issue on which he reserves judgment].

MR. JUSTICE HARLAN, whom MR. JUSTICE STEWART joins, dissenting.

*** The pivotal question in this instance is what effect the added factor of a congressional enactment has on the straight equal protection argument. The Court declares that since § 5 of the Fourteenth Amendment gives to the Congress power to "enforce" the prohibitions of the Amendment by "appropriate" legislation, the test for judicial review of any congressional determination in this area is simply one of rationality; that is, in effect, was Congress acting rationally in declaring that the New York statute is irrational? Although § 5 most certainly does give to the Congress wide powers in the field of devising remedial legislation to effectuate the Amendment's prohibition on arbitrary state action, I believe the Court has confused the issue of how much enforcement power Congress possesses under § 5 with the distinct issue of what questions are appropriate for congressional determination and what questions are essentially judicial in nature.

When recognized state violations of federal constitutional standards have occurred, Congress is of course empowered by § 5 to take appropriate remedial measures to redress and prevent the wrongs. But it is a judicial question whether the condition with which Congress has thus sought to deal is in truth an infringement of the Constitution, something that is the necessary prerequisite to bringing the § 5 power into play at all. ***

Section 4(e), however, presents a significantly different type of congressional enactment. The question here is not whether the statute is appropriate remedial legislation to cure an established violation of a constitutional command, but whether there has in fact been an infringement of that constitutional command, that is, whether a particular state practice or, as here, a statute is so arbitrary or irrational as to offend the command of the Equal Protection Clause of the Fourteenth Amendment. That question is one for the judicial branch ultimately to determine. Were the rule otherwise, Congress would be able to qualify this Court's constitutional decisions under the Fourteenth and Fifteenth Amendments let alone those under other provisions of the Constitution, by resorting to congressional power under the Necessary and Proper Clause. In view of this Court's holding in *Lassiter*, that an English literacy test is a permissible exercise of state supervision over its franchise, I do not think it is open to Congress to limit the effect of that decision as it has undertaken to do by § 4(e). In effect the Court reads § 5 of the Fourteenth Amendment as giving Congress the power to define the substantive scope of the Amendment. If that indeed be the true reach of § 5, then I do not see why Congress should not be able as well to exercise its § 5 "discretion" by enacting statutes so as in effect to dilute equal protection and due process decisions of this Court. In all such cases there is room for reasonable men to differ as to whether or not a denial of equal protection or due process has occurred, and the final decision is one of judgment. Until today this judgment has always been one for the judiciary to resolve.

I do not mean to suggest in what has been said that a legislative judgment of the type incorporated in § 4(e) is without any force whatsoever. Decisions on questions of equal protection and due process are based not on abstract logic, but on empirical foundations. To the extent "legislative facts" are relevant to a judicial determination, Congress is well equipped to investigate them, and such determinations are of course entitled to due respect. ***

But no such factual data provide a legislative record supporting § 4(e) by way of showing that Spanish-speaking citizens are fully as capable of making informed decisions in a New York election as are English-speaking citizens. Nor was there any showing whatever to support the Court's alternative argument that § 4(e) should be viewed as but a remedial measure designed to cure or assure against unconstitutional discrimination of other varieties, e.g., in "public schools, public housing and law enforcement" to which Puerto Rican minorities might be subject in such communities as New York. There is simply no legislative record supporting such hypothesized discrimination of the sort we have hitherto insisted upon when congressional power is brought to bear on constitutionally reserved state concerns.

Thus, we have here not a matter of giving deference to a congressional estimate, based on its determination of legislative facts, bearing upon the validity vel non of a statute, but rather what can at most be called a legislative announcement that Congress believes a state law to entail an unconstitutional deprivation of equal protection. Although this kind of declaration is of course entitled to the most respectful consideration, coming as it does from a concurrent branch and one that is knowledgeable in matters of popular political participation, I do not believe it lessens our responsibility to decide the fundamental issue of whether in fact the state enactment violates federal constitutional rights.

*** Whichever way this case is decided, one statute will be rendered inoperative in whole or in part, and although it has been suggested that this Court should give somewhat more deference to Congress than to a state legislature such a simple weighing of presumptions is hardly a satisfying way of resolving a matter that touches the distribution of state and federal power in an area so sensitive as that of the regulation of the franchise. Rather it should be recognized that while the Fourteenth Amendment is a 'brooding omnipresence' over all state legislation, the substantive matters which it touches are all within the primary legislative competence of the States. Federal authority, legislative no less than judicial, does not intrude unless there has been a denial by state action of Fourteenth Amendment limitations, in this instance a denial of equal protection. At least in the area of primary state concern a state statute that passes constitutional muster under the judicial standard of rationality should not be permitted to be set at naught by a mere contrary congressional pronouncement unsupported by a legislative record justifying that conclusion.

To deny the effectiveness of this congressional enactment is not of course to disparage Congress' exertion of authority in the field of civil rights; it is simply to recognize that the Legislative Branch like the other branches of federal authority is subject to the governmental boundaries set by the Constitution. To hold, on this record, that § 4(e) overrides the New York literacy requirement seems to me tantamount to allowing the Fourteenth Amendment to swallow the State's constitutionally ordained primary authority in this field. For if Congress by what, as here, amounts to mere ipse dixit can set that otherwise permissible requirement partially at naught I see no reason why it could not also substitute its judgment for that of the States in other fields of their exclusive primary competence as well. ***

Notes

1. **Logic of *Katzenbach v. Morgan*.** The Fourteenth Amendment's first sentence creates a new notion of national citizenship that enhances the abolition of slavery in the Thirteenth Amendment. The second sentence, however, begins with the phrase "No State shall." Is Congress' § 5 authority to enforce the Fourteenth Amendment's protections contained in this second sentence limited to preventing

states from violating "privileges or immunities," "equal protection," and "due process"? How can Congress enact § 4(e) to "eliminat[e] an invidious discrimination in establishing voter qualifications" when New York's literacy requirement had been held constitutional? Is the scope of § 5 limited to judicial notions of what is encompassed by the concepts set forth in § 1?

2. Scope of *Katzenbach v. Morgan.* In *Oregon v. Mitchell,* 400 U.S. 112 (1970), the Supreme Court considered the constitutionality of a federal statute that lowered the voting age in both state and federal elections from 21 to 18. The Court upheld the age reduction for federal elections but found the state age reduction unconstitutional. JUSTICE BLACK's opinion, which provided the swing vote on both issues, stressed three limitations on Congress' § 5 Power: (1) there can be no legislative repeal of the Constitution, (2) the power was not intended to "strip the States of their power to govern themselves or to convert our national government of enumerated powers into a central government of unrestrained authority," and (3) the "appropriate legislation" language forbids Congress from undercutting "personal equality and freedom from discrimination" [citing *Katzenbach*], or undermining the Bill of Rights (which the Court by then, for the most part, had made applicable to the States). Can you square this case with *Katzenbach v. Morgan*? Incidentally, the Twenty-sixth Amendment (ratified in 1971) overturned *Oregon v. Mitchell,* providing that the right to vote of citizens 18 or older "shall not be denied or abridged by the United States or by any State on account of age."

CITY OF BOERNE v. FLORES
521 U.S. 507, 117 S.Ct. 2157, 138 L.Ed.2d 624 (1997).

KENNEDY, J.

A decision by local zoning authorities to deny a church a building permit was challenged under the Religious Freedom Restoration Act of 1993 (RFRA). The case calls into question the authority of Congress to enact RFRA. We conclude the statute exceeds Congress' power.

I

Situated on a hill in the city of Boerne, Texas, some 28 miles northwest of San Antonio, is St. Peter Catholic Church. Built in 1923, the church's structure replicates the mission style of the region's earlier history. The church seats about 230 worshippers, a number too small for its growing parish. Some 40 to 60 parishioners cannot be accommodated at some Sunday masses. In order to meet the needs of the congregation the Archbishop of San Antonio gave permission to the parish to plan alterations to enlarge the building.

A few months later, the Boerne City Council passed an ordinance authorizing the city's Historic Landmark Commission to prepare a preservation plan with proposed historic landmarks and districts. Under the ordinance, the Commission must preapprove construction affecting historic landmarks or buildings in a historic district.

Soon afterwards, the Archbishop applied for a building permit so construction to enlarge the church could proceed. City authorities, relying on the ordinance and the designation of a historic district (which, they argued, included the church), denied the application. The Archbishop brought this suit challenging the permit denial ***. The Archbishop relied upon RFRA as one basis for relief from the refusal to issue the permit. ***

II

Congress enacted RFRA in direct response to the Court's decision in *Employment Div., Dept. of Human Resources of Oregon v. Smith*, 494 U.S. 872 (1990). There we considered a Free Exercise Clause claim brought by members of the Native American Church who were denied unemployment benefits when they lost their jobs because they had used peyote. Their practice was to ingest peyote for sacramental purposes, and they challenged an Oregon statute of general applicability which made use of the drug criminal. In evaluating the claim, we declined to apply the balancing test set forth in *Sherbert v. Verner*, 374 U.S. 398 (1963), under which we would have asked whether Oregon's prohibition substantially burdened a religious practice and, if it did, whether the burden was justified by a compelling government interest. We stated:

> [G]overnment's ability to enforce generally applicable prohibitions of socially harmful conduct *** cannot depend on measuring the effects of a governmental action on a religious objector's spiritual development. To make an individual's obligation to obey such a law contingent upon the law's coincidence with his religious beliefs, except where the State's interest is "compelling" *** contradicts both constitutional tradition and common sense.

The application of the *Sherbert* test, the *Smith* decision explained, would have produced an anomaly in the law, a constitutional right to ignore neutral laws of general applicability. The anomaly would have been accentuated, the Court reasoned, by the difficulty of determining whether a particular practice was central to an individual's religion. We explained, moreover, that it "is not within the judicial ken to question the centrality of particular beliefs or practices to a faith, or the validity of particular litigants' interpretations of those creeds."

The only instances where a neutral, generally applicable law had failed to pass constitutional muster, the *Smith* Court noted, were cases in which other constitutional protections were at stake. In *Wisconsin v. Yoder*, 406 U.S. 205 (1972), for example, we invalidated Wisconsin's mandatory school-attendance law as applied to Amish parents who refused on religious grounds to send their children to school. That case implicated not only the right to the free exercise of religion but also the right of parents to control their children's education. *** By contrast, where a general prohibition, such as Oregon's, is at issue, "the sounder approach, and the approach in accord with the vast majority of our precedents, is to hold the test inapplicable to [free exercise] challenges." *Smith* held that neutral, generally applicable laws may be applied to religious practices even when not supported by a compelling governmental interest.

Four Members of the Court disagreed. They argued the law placed a substantial burden on the Native American Church members so that it could be upheld only if the law served a compelling state interest and was narrowly tailored to achieve that end. ***

These points of constitutional interpretation were debated by Members of Congress in hearings and floor debates. Many criticized the Court's reasoning, and this disagreement resulted in the passage of RFRA. Congress announced:

"(1) [T]he framers of the Constitution, recognizing free exercise of religion as an unalienable right, secured its protection in the First Amendment to the Constitution;

"(2) laws 'neutral' toward religion may burden religious exercise as surely as laws intended to interfere with religious exercise;

"(3) governments should not substantially burden religious exercise without compelling justification;

"(4) in *Employment Division v. Smith*, 494 U.S. 872 (1990), the Supreme Court virtually eliminated the requirement that the government justify burdens on religious exercise imposed by laws neutral toward religion; and

"(5) the compelling interest test as set forth in prior Federal court rulings is a workable test for striking sensible balances between religious liberty and competing prior governmental interests."

The Act's stated purposes are:

"(1) to restore the compelling interest test as set forth in *Sherbert v. Verner* and *Wisconsin v. Yoder*, and to guarantee its application in all cases where free exercise of religion is substantially burdened; and

"(2) to provide a claim or defense to persons whose religious exercise is substantially burdened by government."

RFRA prohibits "[g]overnment" from "substantially burden[ing]" a person's exercise of religion even if the burden results from a rule of general applicability unless the government can demonstrate the burden "(1) is in furtherance of a compelling governmental interest; and (2) is the least restrictive means of furthering that compelling governmental interest." The Act's mandate applies to any "branch, department, agency, instrumentality, and official (or other person acting under color of law) of the United States," as well as to any "State, or *** subdivision of a State." The Act's universal coverage is confirmed in § 2000bb–3(a), under which RFRA "applies to all Federal and State law, and the implementation of that law, whether statutory or otherwise, and whether adopted before or after [RFRA's enactment]." In accordance with RFRA's usage of the term, we shall use "state law" to include local and municipal ordinances.

III

A

*** Congress relied on its Fourteenth Amendment enforcement power in enacting the most far reaching and substantial of RFRA's provisions, those which impose its requirements on the States.

The parties disagree over whether RFRA is a proper exercise of Congress' § 5 power "to enforce" by "appropriate legislation" the constitutional guarantee that no State shall deprive any person of "life, liberty, or property, without due process of law" nor deny any person "equal protection of the laws."

In defense of the Act respondent contends, with support from the United States as amicus, that RFRA is permissible enforcement legislation. Congress, it is said, is only protecting by legislation one of the liberties guaranteed by the Fourteenth Amendment's Due Process Clause, the free exercise of religion, beyond what is necessary under *Smith*. It is said the congressional decision to dispense with proof of deliberate or overt discrimination and instead concentrate on a law's effects accords with the settled understanding that § 5 includes the power to enact legislation designed to prevent as well as remedy constitutional violations. It is further contended that Congress' § 5 power is not limited to remedial or preventive legislation.

All must acknowledge that § 5 is "a positive grant of legislative power" to Congress, *Katzenbach v. Morgan*. In *Ex parte Virginia*, 100 U.S. 339 (1879), we explained the scope of Congress' § 5 power in the following broad terms:

> Whatever legislation is appropriate, that is, adapted to carry out the objects the amendments have in view, whatever tends to enforce submission to the prohibitions they contain, and to secure to all persons the enjoyment of perfect equality of civil rights and the equal protection of the laws against State denial or invasion, if not prohibited, is brought within the domain of congressional power.

Legislation which deters or remedies constitutional violations can fall within the sweep of Congress' enforcement power even if in the process it prohibits conduct which is not itself unconstitutional and intrudes into "legislative spheres of autonomy previously reserved to the States." *Fitzpatrick v. Bitzer*, 427 U.S. 445 (1976). For example, the Court upheld a suspension of literacy tests and similar voting requirements under Congress' parallel power to enforce the provisions of the Fifteenth Amendment as a measure to combat racial discrimination in voting, *South Carolina v. Katzenbach*, 383 U.S. 301 (1966), despite the facial constitutionality of the tests under *Lassiter v. Northampton County Bd. of Elections*, 360 U.S. 45 (1959). We have also concluded that other measures protecting voting rights are within Congress' power to enforce the Fourteenth and Fifteenth Amendments, despite the burdens those measures placed on the States. *South Carolina v. Katzenbach*, supra (upholding several provisions of the Voting Rights Act of 1965); *Katzenbach v. Morgan*, supra (upholding ban on literacy tests that prohibited certain people schooled in Puerto Rico from voting); *Oregon v. Mitchell*, 400 U.S. 112 (1970) (upholding 5–year nationwide ban on literacy tests and similar voting requirements for registering to vote); *City of Rome v. United States*, 446 U.S. 156 (1980) (upholding 7–year extension of the Voting Rights Act's requirement that certain jurisdictions preclear any change to a "'standard, practice, or procedure with respect to voting'") ***.

It is also true, however, that "[a]s broad as the congressional enforcement power is, it is not unlimited." *Oregon v. Mitchell* (opinion of BLACK, J.). In assessing the breadth of § 5's enforcement power, we begin with its text. Congress has been given the power "to enforce" the "provisions of this article." We agree with respondent, of course, that Congress can enact legislation under § 5 enforcing the constitutional right to the free exercise of religion. The "provisions of this article," to which § 5 refers, include the Due Process Clause of the Fourteenth Amendment. Congress' power to enforce the Free Exercise Clause follows from our holding in *Cantwell v. Connecticut*, 310 U.S. 296 (1940), that the "fundamental concept of liberty embodied in [the Fourteenth Amendment's Due Process Clause] embraces the liberties guaranteed by the First Amendment." *** Congress' power under § 5, however, extends only to "enforc[ing]" the provisions of the Fourteenth Amendment. The Court has described this power as "remedial," *South Carolina v. Katzenbach*. The design of the Amendment and the text of § 5 are inconsistent with the suggestion that Congress has the power to decree the substance of the Fourteenth Amendment's restrictions on the States. Legislation which alters the meaning of the Free Exercise Clause cannot be said to be enforcing the Clause. Congress does not enforce a constitutional right by changing what the right is. It has been given the power "to enforce," not the power to determine what constitutes a constitutional violation. Were it not so, what Congress would be enforcing would no longer be, in any meaningful sense, the "provisions of [the Fourteenth Amendment]."

While the line between measures that remedy or prevent unconstitutional actions and measures that make a substantive change in the governing law is not easy to discern, and Congress must have wide latitude in determining where it lies, the distinction exists and must be observed. There must be a congruence and proportionality between the injury to be prevented or remedied and the means adopted to that end. Lacking such a connection, legislation may become substantive in operation and effect. History and our case law support drawing the distinction, one apparent from the text of the Amendment.

1

The Fourteenth Amendment's history confirms the remedial, rather than substantive, nature of the Enforcement Clause. The Joint Committee on Reconstruction of the 39th Congress began drafting what would become the Fourteenth Amendment in January 1866. The objections to the Committee's first draft of the Amendment, and the rejection of the draft, have a direct bearing on the central issue of defining Congress' enforcement power. In

February, Republican Representative John Bingham of Ohio reported the following draft amendment to the House of Representatives on behalf of the Joint Committee:

> The Congress shall have power to make all laws which shall be necessary and proper to secure to the citizens of each State all privileges and immunities of citizens in the several States, and to all persons in the several States equal protection in the rights of life, liberty, and property. Cong. Globe, 39th Cong., 1st Sess., 1034 (1866).

The proposal encountered immediate opposition, which continued through three days of debate. Members of Congress from across the political spectrum criticized the Amendment, and the criticisms had a common theme: The proposed Amendment gave Congress too much legislative power at the expense of the existing constitutional structure. Democrats and conservative Republicans argued that the proposed Amendment would give Congress a power to intrude into traditional areas of state responsibility, a power inconsistent with the federal design central to the Constitution. ***.

As a result of these objections ***, the House voted to table the proposal until April. The congressional action was seen as marking the defeat of the proposal. ***

Section 1 of the new draft Amendment imposed self-executing limits on the States. Section 5 prescribed that "[t]he Congress shall have power to enforce, by appropriate legislation, the provisions of this article." Under the revised Amendment, Congress' power was no longer plenary but remedial. Congress was granted the power to make the substantive constitutional prohibitions against the States effective. *** The revised Amendment proposal did not raise the concerns expressed earlier regarding broad congressional power to prescribe uniform national laws with respect to life, liberty, and property. After revisions not relevant here, the new measure passed both Houses and was ratified in July 1868 as the Fourteenth Amendment.

The significance of the defeat of the Bingham proposal was apparent even then. During the debates over the Ku Klux Klan Act only a few years after the Amendment's ratification, Representative James Garfield argued there were limits on Congress' enforcement power, saying "unless we ignore both the history and the language of these clauses we cannot, by any reasonable interpretation, give to [§ 5] *** the force and effect of the rejected [Bingham] clause." Scholars of successive generations have agreed with this assessment.

The design of the Fourteenth Amendment has proved significant also in maintaining the traditional separation of powers between Congress and the Judiciary. The first eight Amendments to the Constitution set forth self-executing prohibitions on governmental action, and this Court has had primary authority to interpret those prohibitions. The Bingham draft, some thought, departed from that tradition by vesting in Congress primary power to interpret and elaborate on the meaning of the new Amendment through legislation. *** While this separation of powers aspect did not occasion the widespread resistance which was caused by the proposal's threat to the federal balance, it nonetheless attracted the attention of various Members. As enacted, the Fourteenth Amendment confers substantive rights against the States which, like the provisions of the Bill of Rights, are self-executing. The power to interpret the Constitution in a case or controversy remains in the Judiciary.

2

The remedial and preventive nature of Congress' enforcement power, and the limitation inherent in the power, were confirmed in our earliest cases on the Fourteenth Amendment. In the *Civil Rights Cases*, 109 U.S. 3 (1883), the Court invalidated sections of the Civil Rights Act of 1875 which prescribed criminal penalties for denying to any person "the full enjoyment of" public accommodations and conveyances, on the grounds that it exceeded Congress' power by seeking to regulate private conduct. The Enforcement Clause, the Court said, did not authorize Congress to pass "general legislation upon the rights of the citizen, but corrective legislation; that is, such as may be necessary and proper for counteracting such laws as the States may adopt or enforce, and which, by the amendment, they are prohibited from making or enforcing. *** " The power to "legislate generally upon" life, liberty, and property, as opposed to the "power to provide modes of redress" against offensive state action, was "repugnant" to the Constitution. Although the specific holdings of these early cases might have been superseded or modified, their treatment of Congress' § 5 power as corrective or preventive, not definitional, has not been questioned.

Recent cases have continued to revolve around the question of whether § 5 legislation can be considered remedial. In *South Carolina v. Katzenbach*, supra, we emphasized that "[t]he constitutional propriety of [legislation adopted under the Enforcement Clause] must be judged with reference to the historical experience *** it reflects the Act's new remedies, which used the administrative resources of the Federal Government, included the suspension of both literacy tests and, pending federal review, all new voting regulations in covered jurisdictions, as well as the assignment of federal examiners to list qualified applicants enabling those listed to vote. The new, unprecedented remedies were deemed necessary given the ineffectiveness of the existing voting rights laws, and the slow costly character of case-by-case litigation." ***

3

Any suggestion that Congress has a substantive, non-remedial power under the Fourteenth Amendment is not supported by our case law. In *Oregon v. Mitchell*, a majority of the Court concluded Congress had exceeded its enforcement powers by enacting legislation lowering the minimum age of voters from 21 to 18 in state and local elections. The five Members of the Court who reached this conclusion explained that the legislation intruded into an area reserved by the Constitution to the States. Four of these five were explicit in rejecting the position that § 5 endowed Congress with the power to establish the meaning of constitutional provisions. JUSTICE BLACK's rejection of this position might be inferred from his disagreement with Congress' interpretation of the Equal Protection Clause.

*** Both rationales for upholding § 4(e) rested on unconstitutional discrimination by New York and Congress' reasonable attempt to combat it. As JUSTICE STEWART explained in *Oregon v. Mitchell*, interpreting *Morgan* to give Congress the power to interpret the Constitution "would require an enormous extension of that decision's rationale."

If Congress could define its own powers by altering the Fourteenth Amendment's meaning, no longer would the Constitution be "superior paramount law, unchangeable by ordinary means." It would be "on a level with ordinary legislative acts, and, like other acts, *** alterable when the legislature shall please to alter it." *Marbury v. Madison.* Under this approach, it is difficult to conceive of a principle that would limit congressional power. Shifting legislative majorities could change the Constitution and effectively circumvent the difficult and detailed amendment process contained in Article V.

We now turn to consider whether RFRA can be considered enforcement legislation under § 5 of the Fourteenth Amendment.

B

Respondent contends that RFRA is a proper exercise of Congress' remedial or preventive power. The Act, it is said, is a reasonable means of protecting the free exercise of religion as defined by *Smith*. It prevents and remedies laws which are enacted with the unconstitutional object of targeting religious beliefs and practices. To avoid the difficulty of proving such violations, it is said, Congress can simply invalidate any law which imposes a substantial burden on a religious practice unless it is justified by a compelling interest and is the least restrictive means of accomplishing that interest. If Congress can prohibit laws with discriminatory effects in order to prevent racial discrimination in violation of the Equal Protection Clause, then it can do the same, respondent argues, to promote religious liberty.

While preventive rules are sometimes appropriate remedial measures, there must be a congruence between the means used and the ends to be achieved. The appropriateness of remedial measures must be considered in light of the evil presented. Strong measures appropriate to address one harm may be an unwarranted response to another, lesser one.

A comparison between RFRA and the Voting Rights Act is instructive. In contrast to the record which confronted Congress and the judiciary in the voting rights cases, RFRA's legislative record lacks examples of modern instances of generally applicable laws passed because of religious bigotry. The history of persecution in this country detailed in the hearings mentions no episodes occurring in the past 40 years. The absence of more recent episodes stems from the fact that, as one witness testified, "deliberate persecution is not the usual problem in this country." Rather, the emphasis of the hearings was on laws of general applicability which place incidental burdens on religion. Much of the discussion centered upon anecdotal evidence of autopsies performed on Jewish individuals and Hmong immigrants in violation of their religious beliefs, and on zoning regulations and historic preservation laws (like the one at issue here), which as an incident of their normal operation, have adverse effects on churches and synagogues. It is difficult to maintain that they are examples of legislation enacted or enforced due to animus or hostility to the burdened religious practices or that they indicate some widespread pattern of religious discrimination in this country. Congress' concern was with the incidental burdens imposed, not the object or purpose of the legislation. This lack of support in the legislative record, however, is not RFRA's most serious shortcoming. Judicial deference, in most cases, is based not on the state of the legislative record Congress compiles but "on due regard for the decision of the body constitutionally appointed to decide." *Oregon v. Mitchell.* As a general matter, it is for Congress to determine the method by which it will reach a decision.

Regardless of the state of the legislative record, RFRA cannot be considered remedial, preventive legislation, if those terms are to have any meaning. RFRA is so out of proportion to a supposed remedial or preventive object that it cannot be understood as responsive to, or designed to prevent, unconstitutional behavior. It appears, instead, to attempt a substantive change in constitutional protections. Preventive measures prohibiting certain types of laws may be appropriate when there is reason to believe that many of the laws affected by the congressional enactment have a significant likelihood of being unconstitutional. Remedial legislation under § 5 "should be adapted to the mischief and wrong which the [Fourteenth] [A]mendment was intended to provide against." *Civil Rights Cases.*

RFRA is not so confined. Sweeping coverage ensures its intrusion at every level of government, displacing laws and prohibiting official actions of almost every description and regardless of subject matter. RFRA's restrictions apply to every agency and official of the Federal, State, and local Governments. RFRA applies to all federal and state law, statutory or otherwise, whether adopted before or after its enactment. RFRA has no termination date or termination mechanism. Any law is subject to challenge at any time by any individual who alleges a substantial burden on his or her free exercise of religion.

*** The stringent test RFRA demands of state laws reflects a lack of proportionality or congruence between the means adopted and the legitimate end to be achieved. If an objector can show a substantial burden on his free exercise, the State must demonstrate a compelling governmental interest and show that the law is the least restrictive means of furthering its interest. Claims that a law substantially burdens someone's exercise of religion will often be difficult to contest. Requiring a State to demonstrate a compelling interest and show that it has adopted the least restrictive means of achieving that interest is the most demanding test known to constitutional law. If "'compelling interest' really means what it says *** many laws will not meet the test. *** [The test] would open the prospect of constitutionally required religious exemptions from civic obligations of almost every conceivable kind."

Laws valid under *Smith* would fall under RFRA without regard to whether they had the object of stifling or punishing free exercise. We make these observations not to reargue the position of the majority in *Smith* but to illustrate the substantive alteration of its holding attempted by RFRA. Even assuming RFRA would be interpreted in effect to mandate some lesser test, say one equivalent to intermediate scrutiny, the statute nevertheless would require searching judicial scrutiny of state law with the attendant likelihood of invalidation. This is a considerable congressional intrusion into the States' traditional prerogatives and general authority to regulate for the health and welfare of their citizens.

The substantial costs RFRA exacts, both in practical terms of imposing a heavy litigation burden on the States and in terms of curtailing their traditional general regulatory power, far exceed any pattern or practice of unconstitutional conduct under the Free Exercise Clause as interpreted in *Smith*. Simply put, RFRA is not designed to identify and counteract state laws likely to be unconstitutional because of their treatment of religion. In most cases, the state laws to which RFRA applies are not ones which will have been motivated by religious bigotry. If a state law disproportionately burdened a particular class of religious observers, this circumstance might be evidence of an impermissible legislative motive. *Cf. Washington v. Davis*, 426 U.S. 229 (1976). RFRA's substantial burden test, however, is not even a discriminatory effects or disparate impact test. It is a reality of the modern regulatory state that numerous state laws, such as the zoning regulations at issue here, impose a substantial burden on a large class of individuals. When the exercise of religion has been burdened in an incidental way by a law of general application, it does not follow that the persons affected have been burdened any more than other citizens, let alone burdened because of their religious beliefs. In addition, the Act imposes in every case a least restrictive means requirement—a requirement that was not used in the pre-*Smith* jurisprudence RFRA purported to codify—which also indicates that the legislation is broader than is appropriate if the goal is to prevent and remedy constitutional violations. ***

Our national experience teaches that the Constitution is preserved best when each part of the government respects both the Constitution and the proper actions and determinations of the other branches. When the Court has interpreted the Constitution, it has acted within the province of the Judicial Branch, which embraces the duty to say what the law is. *Marbury v. Madison.* When the political branches of the Government act against the background of a judicial interpretation of the Constitution already issued, it must be understood that in later cases and controversies the Court will treat its precedents with the respect due them under settled principles, including *stare decisis*, and contrary expectations must be disappointed. RFRA was designed to control cases and controversies, such as the one before us; but as the provisions of the federal statute here invoked are beyond congressional authority, it is this Court's precedent, not RFRA, which must control. ***

It is for Congress in the first instance to "determin[e] whether and what legislation is needed to secure the guarantees of the Fourteenth

Amendment," and its conclusions are entitled to much deference. *Katzenbach v. Morgan*. Congress' discretion is not unlimited, however, and the courts retain the power, as they have since *Marbury v. Madison*, to determine if Congress has exceeded its authority under the Constitution. Broad as the power of Congress is under the Enforcement Clause of the Fourteenth Amendment, RFRA contradicts vital principles necessary to maintain separation of powers and the federal balance. ***

JUSTICE STEVENS, concurring.

In my opinion, the Religious Freedom Restoration Act of 1993 (RFRA) is a "law respecting an establishment of religion" that violates the First Amendment to the Constitution. ***

JUSTICE SCALIA, whom JUSTICE STEVENS joins, concurring in part. [omitted]

JUSTICE O'CONNOR, whom JUSTICE BREYER joins, dissenting.

I dissent from the Court's disposition of this case. I agree with the Court that the issue before us is whether the Religious Freedom Restoration Act (RFRA) is a proper exercise of Congress' power to enforce § 5 of the Fourteenth Amendment. *** I remain of the view that *Smith* was wrongly decided, and I would use this case to reexamine the Court's holding there. ***

JUSTICE SOUTER and JUSTICE BREYER'S dissents are omitted.

Notes

1. **Other RFRA Issues.** Could RFRA be reenacted under Congress' Commerce Clause power? Consider this question in light of *Seminole Tribe,* supra p. 98 and reconsider it after you read *Alden,* infra p. 351. Could Congress reenact RFRA but make it applicable only to the federal government, not the states? Seven states have enacted state legislation modeled on RFRA. Do you see any constitutional problems with state mini-RFRAs?

2. **Other Statutes at Risk?** Does this decision have any bearing on the constitutionality of statutes in which Congress has defined discrimination to include practices having a "disparate impact" as unlawful, even though such practices are not unlawful under § 1 of the Fourteenth Amendment? *See Washington v. Davis, infra* p. XXX.

3. **Remedial and not Substantive.** Is the Court's distinction between remedial and substantive power coherent? The law professor who argued the case for the losing side writes: "The ordinary meaning of "remedial" would be legislation that provides a remedy for a judicially determined violation. *** The ordinary meaning of "substantive" would be legislation that defines a statutory violation in some way different from the Court's definition of a constitutional violation. But a vast range of possible legislation is substantive in this sense." Laycock, *Conceptual Gulfs in City of Boerne v. Flores*, 39 WM. & MARY L. REV. 743 (1998).

4. **Congruence and Proportionality.** Is the Court's test of "congruence and proportionality" consistent with usual notions of judicial deference to Congress

and with the necessary and proper clause? Is that clause relevant when Congress uses its § 5 power?

UNIVERSITY OF ALABAMA
v. GARRETT
531 U.S. 356, 121 S.Ct. 955, 148 L. Ed. 2d 866 (2001).

CHIEF JUSTICE REHNQUIST delivered the opinion of the Court.

We decide here whether employees of the State of Alabama may recover money damages by reason of the State's failure to comply with the provisions of Title I of the Americans with Disabilities Act of 1990 (ADA or Act). We hold that such suits are barred by the Eleventh Amendment.

The ADA prohibits certain employers, including the States, from "discriminat[ing] against a qualified individual with a disability ***." To this end, the Act requires employers to "mak[e] reasonable accommodations to the known physical or mental limitations of an otherwise qualified individual with a disability who is an applicant or employee, unless [the employer] can demonstrate that the accommodation would impose an undue hardship on the operation of the [employer's] business." ***

[T]he ADA can apply to the States only to the extent that the statute is appropriate § 5 legislation. *** § 5 legislation reaching beyond the scope of § 1's actual guarantees must exhibit "congruence and proportionality between the injury to be prevented or remedied and the means adopted to that end."

The first step in applying these now familiar principles is to identify with some precision the scope of the constitutional right at issue. Here, that inquiry requires us to examine the limitations § 1 of the Fourteenth Amendment places upon States' treatment of the disabled. *** In *Cleburne v. Cleburne Living Center*, 473 U. S. 432 (1985), we considered *** whether *** mental retardation qualified as a "quasi-suspect" classification under our equal protection jurisprudence. We [concluded] *** that such legislation incurs only the minimum "rational-basis" review applicable to general social and economic legislation. *** Thus, the result of *Cleburne* is that States are not required by the Fourteenth Amendment to make special accommodations for the disabled, so long as their actions towards such individuals are rational. ***

Once we have determined the metes and bounds of the constitutional right in question, we examine whether Congress identified a history and pattern of unconstitutional employment discrimination by the States against the disabled. *** The legislative record of the ADA, however, simply fails to show that Congress did in fact identify a pattern of irrational state discrimination in employment against the disabled.

Respondents contend that the inquiry as to unconstitutional discrimination should extend not only to States themselves, but to units of local governments, such as cities and counties. All of these, they say, are "state actors" for purposes of the Fourteenth Amendment. This is quite true, but the Eleventh Amendment does not extend its immunity to units of local government. These entities are subject to private claims for damages under the ADA without Congress' ever having to rely on § 5 of the Fourteenth Amendment to render them so. It would make no sense to consider constitutional violations on their part, as well as by the States themselves, when only the States are the beneficiaries of the Eleventh Amendment. ***

Respondents in their brief cite half a dozen examples from the record that did involve States. *** Several of these incidents undoubtedly evidence an unwillingness on the part of state officials to make the sort of accommodations for the disabled required by the ADA. Whether they were irrational under our decision in *Cleburne* is more debatable, particularly when the incident is described out of context. But even if it were to be determined that each incident upon fuller examination showed unconstitutional action on the part of the State, these incidents taken together fall far short of even suggesting the pattern of unconstitutional discrimination on which § 5 legislation must be based. See *Kimel*; *City of Boerne*. Congress, in enacting the ADA, found that "some 43,000,000 Americans have one or more physical or mental disabilities." In 1990, the States alone employed more than 4.5 million people. It is telling, we think, that given these large numbers, Congress assembled only such minimal evidence of unconstitutional state discrimination in employment against the disabled.

JUSTICE BREYER maintains that Congress applied Title I of the ADA to the States in response to a host of incidents representing unconstitutional state discrimination in employment against persons with disabilities. A close review of the relevant materials, however, undercuts that conclusion. *** [H]ad Congress truly understood this information as reflecting a pattern of unconstitutional behavior by the States, one would expect some mention of that conclusion in the Act's legislative findings. There is none. *** [T]here is also strong evidence that Congress' failure to mention States in its legislative findings addressing discrimination in employment reflects that body's judgment that no pattern of unconstitutional state action had been documented.

Even were it possible to squeeze out of these examples a pattern of unconstitutional discrimination by the States, the rights and remedies created by the ADA against the States would raise the same sort of concerns as to congruence and proportionality as were found in *City of Boerne*. For example, whereas it would be entirely rational (and therefore constitutional) for a state employer to conserve scarce financial resources by hiring employees who are able to use existing facilities, the ADA requires employers to "mak[o] oxisting facilities used by employees readily accessible to and usable by individuals with disabilities." The ADA does except employers from the "reasonable accommodatio[n]" requirement where the employer "can demonstrate that the accommodation would impose an undue hardship on the operation of the business of such covered entity." However, even with this exception, the accommodation duty far exceeds what is constitutionally required in that it makes unlawful a range of alternate responses that would be reasonable but would fall short of imposing an "undue burden" upon the employer. The Act also makes it the employer's duty to prove that it would suffer such a burden, instead of requiring (as the Constitution does) that the complaining party negate reasonable bases for the employer's decision.

The ADA also forbids "utilizing standards, criteria, or methods of administration" that disparately impact the disabled, without regard to whether such conduct has a rational basis. Although disparate impact may be relevant evidence of racial discrimination, such evidence alone is insufficient even where the Fourteenth Amendment subjects state action to strict scrutiny.

The ADA's constitutional shortcomings are apparent when the Act is compared to Congress' efforts in the Voting Rights Act of 1965 to respond to a serious pattern of constitutional violations. *** In that Act, Congress documented a marked pattern of unconstitutional action by the States. State officials, Congress found, routinely applied voting tests in order to exclude African-American citizens from registering to vote. Congress also determined that litigation had proved ineffective and that there persisted an otherwise inexplicable 50-percentage-point gap in the registration of white and African-American voters in some States. Congress' response was to promulgate in the Voting Rights Act a detailed but limited remedial scheme designed to guarantee meaningful enforcement of the Fifteenth Amendment in those areas of the Nation where abundant evidence of States' systematic denial of those rights was identified.

The contrast between this kind of evidence, and the evidence that Congress considered in the present case, is stark. Congressional enactment of the ADA represents its judgment that there should be a "comprehensive national mandate for the elimination of discrimination against individuals with disabilities." Congress is the final authority as to desirable public policy, but in order to authorize private individuals to recover money damages against the States, there must be a pattern of discrimination by the States which violates the Fourteenth Amendment, and the remedy imposed by Congress must be congruent and proportional to the targeted violation. Those requirements are not met here, and to uphold the Act's application to the States would allow Congress to rewrite the Fourteenth Amendment law laid down by this Court in *Cleburne*. Section 5 does not so broadly enlarge congressional authority. ***

JUSTICE KENNEDY, with whom JUSTICE O'CONNOR joins, concurring.

*** If the States had been transgressing the Fourteenth Amendment by their mistreatment or lack of concern for those with impairments, one would have expected to find in decisions of the courts of the States and also the courts of the United States extensive litigation and discussion of the constitutional violations. This confirming judicial documentation does not exist. *** It must be noted, moreover, that what is in question is not whether the Congress, acting pursuant to a power granted to it by the Constitution, can compel the States to act. What is involved is only the question whether the States can be subjected to liability in suits brought not by the Federal Government, but by private persons seeking to collect moneys from the state treasury without the consent of the State. ***

JUSTICE BREYER, with whom JUSTICE STEVENS, JUSTICE SOUTER and JUSTICE GINSBURG join, dissenting.

Reviewing the congressional record as if it were an administrative agency record, the Court holds the statutory provision before us unconstitutional. The Court concludes that Congress assembled insufficient evidence of unconstitutional discrimination, that Congress improperly attempted to "re-write" the law we established in *Cleburne v. Cleburne Living Center, Inc.*, and that the law is not sufficiently tailored to address unconstitutional discrimination. *** In my view, Congress reasonably could have concluded that the remedy before us constitutes an "appropriate" way to enforce this basic equal protection requirement. And that is all the Constitution requires.

The Court says that its primary problem with this statutory provision is one of legislative evidence. It says that "Congress assembled only *** minimal evidence of unconstitutional state discrimination in employment." In fact, Congress compiled a vast legislative record documenting "'massive, society-wide discrimination'" against persons with disabilities. *** The powerful evidence of discriminatory treatment throughout society in general, including discrimination by private persons and local governments, implicates state governments as well, for state agencies form part of that same larger society. There is no particular reason to believe that they are immune from the "stereotypic assumptions" and pattern of "purposeful unequal treatment" that Congress found prevalent. *** In any event, there is no need to rest solely upon evidence of discrimination by local governments or general societal discrimination. There are roughly 300 examples of discrimination by state governments themselves in the legislative record. *** [O]ne study that was before Congress revealed that "most *** governmental agencies in [one State] discriminated in hiring against job applicants for an average period of five years after treatment for cancer," based in part on coworkers' misguided belief that "cancer is contagious." *** Congress could have reasonably believed that these examples represented signs of a widespread problem of unconstitutional discrimination.

The Court's failure to find sufficient evidentiary support may well rest upon its decision to hold Congress to a strict, judicially created evidentiary standard, particularly in respect to lack of justification. *** The problem with the Court's approach is that neither the "burden of proof" that favors States nor any other rule of restraint applicable to *judges* applies to *Congress* when it exercises its § 5 power. "Limitations stemming from the nature of the judicial process *** have no application to Congress." Rational-basis review with its presumptions favoring constitutionality–is "a paradigm of judicial restraint." And the Congress of the United States is not a lower court. *** There is simply no reason to require Congress, seeking to determine facts relevant to the exercise of its § 5 authority, to adopt rules or presumptions that reflect a court's institutional limitations. Unlike courts, Congress can readily gather facts from across the Nation, assess the magnitude of a problem, and more easily find an appropriate remedy. Unlike courts, Congress directly reflects public attitudes and beliefs, enabling Congress better to understand where, and to what extent, refusals to accommodate a disability amount to behavior that is callous or unreasonable to the point of lacking constitutional justification. Unlike judges, Members of Congress can directly obtain information from constituents who have firsthand experience with discrimination and related issues.

The Court argues in the alternative that the statute's damage remedy is not "congruent" with and "proportional" to the equal protection problem that Congress found. The Court suggests that the Act's "reasonable accommodation" requirement, and disparate-impact standard, "far excee[d] what is constitutionally required." But we have upheld disparate-impact standards in contexts where they were not "constitutionally required."

And what is wrong with a remedy that, in response to unreasonable employer behavior, requires an employer to make accommodations that are reasonable? Of course, what is "reasonable" in the statutory sense and what is "unreasonable" in the constitutional sense might differ. In other words, the requirement may exceed what is necessary to avoid a constitutional violation. But it is just that power—the power to require more than the minimum—that § 5 grants to Congress, as this Court has repeatedly confirmed. *** § 5's "draftsmen sought to grant to Congress, by a specific provision applicable to the Fourteenth Amendment, the same broad powers expressed in the Necessary and Proper Clause." *** Nothing in the words "reasonable accommodation" suggests that the requirement has no "tend[ency] to enforce" the Equal Protection Clause that it is an irrational way to achieve the objective, that it would fall outside the scope of the Necessary and Proper Clause, or that it somehow otherwise exceeds the bounds of the "appropriate." ***

The Court's harsh review of Congress' use of its § 5 power is reminiscent of the similar (now-discredited) limitation that it once imposed upon Congress' Commerce Clause power. I could understand the legal basis for such a review were we judging a statute that discriminated against those of a particular race or gender, or a statute that threatened a basic constitutionally protected liberty such as free speech. The legislation before us, however, does not discriminate against anyone, nor does it pose any threat to basic liberty. And it is difficult to understand why the Court, which applies "minimum 'rational-basis' review" to statutes that *burden* persons with disabilities, subjects to far stricter scrutiny a statute that seeks to *help* those same individuals. *** The Court, through its evidentiary demands, its non-deferential review, and its failure to distinguish between judicial and legislative constitutional competencies, improperly invades a power that the Constitution assigns to Congress. Its decision saps § 5 of independent force, effectively "confin[ing] the legislative power *** to the insignificant role of abrogating only those state laws that the judicial branch [is] prepared to adjudge unconstitutional." Whether the Commerce Clause does or does not enable Congress to enact this provision, in my view, § 5 gives Congress the necessary authority. ***

Notes

1. **Adequate Legislative Record.** With respect to state actions that would be subjected to "rational basis" review, States are not required to articulate their reasons for enacting legislation or regulations prior to passage. This is a primary difference between rational basis review and the Court's intermediate scrutiny standard for gender distinctions, as well as its strict scrutiny standard for racial distinctions. *See* Chapter IX. The Court has also required discriminatory intent for governmental action to run afoul of the equal protection clause—disparate impact that results from the challenged state action is not sufficient. The majority in *Garrett* found the lack of a legislative record demonstrating a pattern of unconstitutional discrimination by the States fatal to the ADA's application to the States as an "appropriate" exercise of Congress's § 5 power. Since the State does not need to articulate its reasoning before enacting legislation that disadvantages disabled individuals, and that intent to discriminate must be proven for a violation of § 1 of the Fourteenth Amendment to lie, how could Congress ever assemble a legislative record that would allow the ADA to apply to the States?

2. **"State" in the Eleventh and Fourteenth Amendments.** Respondents claimed that local government discrimination against the disabled should be considered in assessing whether a pattern of discrimination supported passage of the ADA. In rejecting that argument, CHIEF JUSTICE REHNQUIST recognized that the term "State" in the Fourteenth Amendment encompasses local governments, but noted that "the Eleventh Amendment does not extend its immunity to units of local government. *** These entities are subject to private claims for damages under the ADA without Congress ever having to rely on § 5 of the Fourteenth Amendment to render them so. It would make no sense to consider constitutional violations on their part, as well as by the States themselves, when only the states are the beneficiaries of the Eleventh Amendment."

- How can the Eleventh Amendment's definition of the term "State" control what kinds of state action support an exercise of Congress' § 5 powers? Doesn't this have it backwards? The Fourteenth Amendment limited state sovereignty and trumped the Eleventh Amendment, just as the Eleventh Amendment trumped Congress' earlier Article I powers.

- Congress can use Article I powers against local governments without being limited by the Eleventh Amendment and Congress is not required to show that § 5 is the only grant of legislative authority supporting particular legislation. Even if application of the ADA to local government is supported by the commerce clause power, can't it also be supported by the § 5 power?

- Is the Court's point that aggregating state and local government discrimination in making a legislative record is not appropriate when Congress passes legislation limiting state as well as local sovereignty? If so, could that be because local government discrimination is (a) contrary to state law or (b) without the knowledge of the state government? If so, it will be very hard for Congress to amass a record that is adequate: state governments can avoid suits under federal laws by delegating broad authority to local government.

- Perhaps it would have been better to leave the aggregation point out of the analysis if the real concern was that individual acts of discrimination by local officials are simply not sufficiently numerous and notorious to support imposition of federal restrictions on state-level actors. Must Congress be more careful in articulating the local-state ties when it passes legislation applicable to state as well as local entities?

3. **Level of Scrutiny and Factual Predicate.** In *Katzenbach v. Morgan*, 384 U.S. 641 (1966) the Supreme Court noted that "[I]t is enough that we perceive a basis upon which Congress *might* predicate a judgment that the application of New York's English literacy requirement to deny the right to vote to a person with a sixth grade education in Puerto Rican schools in which the language of instruction was other than English constituted an invidious discrimination in violation of the Equal Protection Clause." (emphasis added). Though racial classifications by the States are subjected to the most stringent of constitutional tests, the Supreme Court clearly states with respect to the legislative record in *Morgan* that "it need only perceive a basis" for congressional action under § 5. Compare this with the heightened scrutiny the legislative records in *Garrett* when Congress sought to combat age or disability discrimination on the part of the states—classifications subjected to only rational basis review. Yet, in these cases, the Supreme Court insisted upon a showing of a pattern and history of pervasive discrimination committed by the States at the state level and found the ADA lacking in this regard. Does this suggest that there is an inverse relationship between the Court's level of constitutional scrutiny of State classifications and the Court's scrutiny of congressional findings supportive of § 5 legislation? Is it paradoxical that Congressional findings amassed in support of remedial legislation dealing with racial classifications would be subjected to more lenient level of scrutiny than similar findings compiled by Congress in support of statutes similar to the ADA? Or is this simply a tool the Court uses to keep Congress from expanding its power under § 5 excessively?

4. **Congruence and Proportionality in *Garrett*.** CHIEF JUSTICE REHNQUIST's majority opinion explains that the ADA is unconstitutional as applied to the States in two respects: (1) Congress failed to establish a history and pattern of unconstitutional discrimination by the states; and, (2) the ADA does not meet the "congruent and proportional" test for § 5 legislation enunciated in *City of Boerne*. The decision as to which forms of state action may be considered part of the legislative record used to establish the requisite pattern of discrimination is important to resolution of both issues. Assume for the moment that the Court included the actions of local governmental entities in its assessment of the Congressional record, and found the requisite pattern of discrimination. The ADA might nevertheless fail to meet the "congruence and proportionality" test because "[T]he accommodation duty far exceeds what is constitutionally required in that it makes unlawful a wide range of alternate responses that would be reasonable but would fall short of imposing an 'undue burden' on the employer. The Act also makes it the employer's duty to prove that it would suffer such a burden, instead of requiring (as the Constitution does) that the complaining party negate reasonable bases for the employer's decision." If the necessary pattern existed, could Congress cure the remaining constitutional defect by making the ADA less demanding on employers? Would it be "congruent and proportional" if costs of access exceeding a certain amount were subsidized by the government? If the undue burden standard required only "reasonable" alternative responses?

5. **Public Accommodations.** Title II of the ADA requires that public "services, programs or activities" be accessible to people with disabilities." Responding to Title II suits by a wheelchair-impaired plaintiff who had to crawl up two flights of stairs at a county courthouse to make a required court appearance and a disabled court reporter who could not gain access to several courthouses where she had been hired to record proceedings, states argue the suits are barred by sovereign immunity. Are these cases controlled by *Garrett*?

NEVADA DEPARTMENT OF HUMAN RESOURCES v. HIBBS
123 S.Ct. 1972, 155 L.Ed. 2d 953, 71 USLW 4375 (2003).

CHIEF JUSTICE REHNQUIST delivered the opinion of the Court.

The Family and Medical Leave Act of 1993 (FMLA or Act) entitles eligible employees to take up to 12 work weeks of unpaid leave annually for any of several reasons, including the onset of a "serious health condition" in an employee's spouse, child, or parent. The Act creates a private right of action to seek both equitable relief and money damages "against any employer (including a public agency) in any Federal or State court of competent jurisdiction," should that employer "interfere with, restrain, or deny the exercise of" FMLA rights. We hold that employees of the State of Nevada may recover money damages in the event of the State's failure to comply with the family-care provision of the Act. *** Respondent sued petitioners in the United States District Court seeking damages and injunctive and declaratory relief for [FMLA] violations. *** This case turns, then, on whether Congress acted within its constitutional authority when it sought to abrogate the States' immunity for purposes of the FMLA's family-leave provision. ***

The FMLA aims to protect the right to be free from gender-based discrimination in the workplace. We have held that statutory classifications that distinguish between males and females are subject to heightened scrutiny. For a gender-based classification to withstand such scrutiny, it must "serv[e] important governmental objectives," and "the discriminatory means employed [must be] substantially related to the achievement of those objectives." The State's justification for such a classification "must not rely on overbroad generalizations about the different talents, capacities, or preferences of males and females." We now inquire whether Congress had evidence of a pattern of constitutional violations on the part of the States in this area.

The history of the many state laws limiting women's employment opportunities is chronicled in—and, until relatively recently, was sanctioned by—this Court's own opinions. *** Congress responded to this history of discrimination by abrogating States' sovereign immunity in Title VII of the Civil Rights Act of 1964. *** But state gender discrimination did not cease. *** According to evidence that was before Congress when it enacted the FMLA, States continue to rely on invalid gender stereotypes in the employment context, specifically in the administration of leave benefits. Reliance on such stereotypes cannot justify the States' gender discrimination in this area. The long and extensive history of sex discrimination prompted us to hold that measures that differentiate on the basis of gender warrant heightened scrutiny; here, as in *Fitzpatrick*, the persistence of such unconstitutional discrimination by the States justifies Congress' passage of prophylactic § 5 legislation.

As the FMLA's legislative record reflects, a 1990 Bureau of Labor Statistics (BLS) survey stated that 37 percent of surveyed private-sector employees were covered by maternity leave policies, while only 18 percent were covered by paternity leave policies. *** Congress also heard testimony that "[p]arental leave for fathers *** is rare. Even *** [w]here child-care leave policies do exist, men, *both in the public and private sectors*, receive notoriously discriminatory treatment in their requests for such leave." Many States offered women extended "maternity" leave that far exceeded the typical 4- to 8-week period of physical disability due to pregnancy and childbirth, but very few States granted men a parallel benefit ***. This and other differential leave policies were not attributable to any differential physical needs of men and women, but rather to the pervasive sex-role stereotype that caring for family members is women's work.

Finally, Congress had evidence that, even where state laws and policies were not facially discriminatory, they were applied in discriminatory ways. It was aware of the "serious problems with the discretionary nature of family leave," because when "the authority to grant leave and to arrange the length of that leave rests with individual supervisors," it leaves "employees open to discretionary and possibly unequal treatment." Testimony supported that conclusion, explaining that "[t]he lack of uniform parental and medical leave policies in the work place has created an environment where [sex] discrimination is rampant."

In spite of all of the above evidence, JUSTICE KENNEDY argues in dissent that Congress' passage of the FMLA was unnecessary because "the States appear to have been ahead of Congress in providing gender-neutral family leave benefits," and points to Nevada's leave policies in particular. However, it was only "[s]ince Federal family leave legislation was first introduced" that the States had even "begun to consider similar family leave initiatives."

Furthermore, the dissent's statement that some States "had adopted some form of family-care leave" before the FMLA's enactment glosses over important shortcomings of some state policies. First, seven States had childcare leave provisions that applied to women only. Indeed, Massachusetts required that notice of its leave provisions be posted only in "establishment[s] in which females are employed." These laws reinforced the very stereotypes that Congress sought to remedy through the FMLA. Second, 12 States provided their employees no family leave, beyond an initial childbirth or adoption, to care for a seriously ill child or family member. Third, many States provided no statutorily guaranteed right to family leave, offering instead only voluntary or discretionary leave programs. *** Finally, four States provided leave only through administrative regulations or personnel policies, which Congress could reasonably conclude offered significantly less firm protection than a federal law. Against the above backdrop of limited state leave policies, *** Congress was justified in enacting the FMLA as remedial legislation.[10]

In sum, the States' record of unconstitutional participation in, and fostering of, gender-based discrimination in the administration of leave benefits is weighty enough to justify the enactment of prophylactic § 5 legislation. *** Because the standard for demonstrating the constitutionality of a gender-based classification is more difficult to meet than our rational-basis test—it must "serv[e] important governmental objectives" and be "substantially related to the achievement of those objectives,"—it was easier for Congress to show a pattern of state constitutional violations. *** Stereotypes about women's domestic roles are reinforced by parallel stereotypes presuming a lack of domestic responsibilities for men. Because employers continued to regard the family as the woman's domain, they often denied men similar accommodations or discouraged them from taking leave. ***

We believe that Congress' chosen remedy, the family-care leave provision of the FMLA, is "congruent and proportional to the targeted violation." Congress had already tried unsuccessfully to address this problem through Title VII and the amendment of Title VII by the Pregnancy Discrimination Act. Here, *** Congress again confronted a "difficult and intractable proble[m]," where previous legislative attempts had failed. Such problems may justify added prophylactic measures in response. *** By setting a minimum standard of family leave for *all* eligible employees, irrespective of gender, the FMLA attacks the formerly state-sanctioned stereotype that only women are responsible for family caregiving, thereby reducing employers' incentives to engage in discrimination by basing hiring and promotion decisions on stereotypes.

The dissent characterizes the FMLA as a "substantive entitlement program" rather than a remedial statute because it establishes a floor of 12 weeks' leave. In the dissent's view, in the face of evidence of gender-based discrimination by the States in the provision of leave benefits, Congress could do no more in exercising its § 5 power than simply proscribe such discrimination. But this position cannot be squared with our recognition that Congress "is not confined to the enactment of legislation that merely parrots the precise wording of the Fourteenth Amendment," but may prohibit "a somewhat broader swath of conduct, including that which is not itself forbidden by the Amendment's text." ***

Indeed, in light of the evidence before Congress, a statute mirroring Title

---

10 Contrary to the dissent's belief, we do not hold that Congress may "abrogat[e] state immunity from private suits whenever the State's social benefits program is not enshrined in the statutory code and provides employers with discretion,' or when a State does not confer social benefits 'as generous or extensive as Congress would later deem appropriate." The dissent misunderstands the purpose of the FMLA's family leave provision. The FMLA is not a "substantive entitlement program"; Congress did not create a particular leave policy for its own sake. Rather, Congress sought to adjust family leave policies in order to eliminate their reliance on and perpetuation of invalid stereotypes, and thereby dismantle persisting gender-based barriers to the hiring, retention, and promotion of women in the workplace. ***

VII, that simply mandated gender equality in the administration of leave benefits, would not have achieved Congress' remedial object. Such a law would allow States to provide for no family leave at all. Where "[t]wo-thirds of the nonprofessional caregivers for older, chronically ill, or disabled persons are working women," and state practices continue to reinforce the stereotype of women as caregivers, such a policy would exclude far more women than men from the workplace.

Unlike the statutes at issue in *City of Boerne, Kimel*, and *Garrett*, which applied broadly to every aspect of state employers' operations, the FMLA is narrowly targeted at the fault line between work and family–precisely where sex-based overgeneralization has been and remains strongest–and affects only one aspect of the employment relationship. *** We also find significant the many other limitations that Congress placed on the scope of this measure. The FMLA requires only unpaid leave, and applies only to employees who have worked for the employer for at least one year and provided 1,250 hours of service within the last 12 months. *** [O]f particular importance to the States, the FMLA expressly excludes from coverage state elected officials, their staffs, and appointed policymakers. *** In choosing 12 weeks as the appropriate leave floor, Congress chose "a middle ground, a period long enough to serve 'the needs of families' but not so long that it would upset 'the legitimate interests of employers.'" Moreover, the cause of action under the FMLA is a restricted one: The damages recoverable are strictly defined and measured by actual monetary losses, and the accrual period for backpay is limited by the Act's 2-year statute of limitations. ***

JUSTICE SOUTER, with whom JUSTICE GINSBURG and JUSTICE BREYER join, concurring. [omitted]

JUSTICE STEVENS, concurring in the judgment. [omitted]

JUSTICE SCALIA, dissenting.

*** The constitutional violation that is a prerequisite to "prophylactic" congressional action to "enforce" the Fourteenth Amendment is a violation *by the State against which the enforcement action is taken*. There is no guilt by association, enabling the sovereignty of one State to be abridged under § 5 of the Fourteenth Amendment because of violations by another State, or by most other States, or even by 49 other States. Congress has sometimes displayed awareness of this self-evident limitation. That is presumably why the most sweeping provisions of the Voting Rights Act of 1965–which we upheld *** –were restricted to States "with a demonstrable history of intentional racial discrimination in voting."

Today's opinion for the Court does not even attempt to demonstrate that each one of the 50 States covered *** was in violation of the Fourteenth Amendment. It treats "the States" as some sort of collective entity which is guilty or innocent as a body. "[T]he States' record of unconstitutional participation in, and fostering of, gender-based discrimination," it concludes, "is weighty enough to justify the enactment of prophylactic § 5 legislation." This will not do. Prophylaxis in the sense of extending the remedy beyond the violation is one thing; prophylaxis in the sense of extending the remedy beyond the violator is something else. ***

JUSTICE KENNEDY, with whom JUSTICE SCALIA and JUSTICE THOMAS join, dissenting.

*** In examining whether Congress was addressing a demonstrated "pattern of unconstitutional employment discrimination by the States," the Court gives superficial treatment to the requirement that we "identify with some precision the scope of the constitutional right at issue." The Court suggests the issue is "the right to be free from gender-based discrimination in the workplace," and then it embarks on a survey of our precedents speaking to "[t]he history of the many state laws limiting women's employment opportunities." All would agree that women historically have been subjected to conditions in which their employment opportunities are more limited than those available to men. As the Court acknowledges, however, Congress responded to this problem by abrogating States' sovereign immunity in Title VII of the Civil Rights Act of 1964. The provision now before us has a different aim than Title VII. It seeks to ensure that eligible employees, irrespective of gender, can take a minimum amount of leave time to care for an ill relative.

The relevant question, as the Court seems to acknowledge, is whether, notwithstanding the passage of Title VII and similar state legislation, the States continued to engage in widespread discrimination on the basis of gender in the provision of family leave benefits. If such a pattern were shown, the Eleventh Amendment would not bar Congress from devising a congruent and proportional remedy. *** As the Court seems to recognize, the evidence considered by Congress concerned discriminatory practices of the private sector, not those of state employers. The statistical information compiled by the Bureau of Labor Statistics (BLS), which are the only factual findings the Court cites, surveyed only private employers. While the evidence of discrimination by private entities may be relevant, it does not, by itself, justify the abrogation of States' sovereign immunity. ***

The Court maintains the evidence pertaining to the parenting leave is relevant because both parenting and family leave provisions respond to "the same gender stereotype: that women's family duties trump those of the workplace." Thi s sets the contours of the inquiry at too high a level of abstraction. The question is not whether the family leave provision is a congruent and proportional response to general gender-based stereotypes in employment which "ha[ve] historically produced discrimination in the hiring and promotion of women;" the question is whether it is a proper remedy to an alleged pattern of unconstitutional discrimination by States in the grant of family leave. The evidence of gender-based stereotypes is too remote to support the required showing.

The Court next argues that "even where state laws and policies were not facially discriminatory, they were applied in discriminatory ways." This charge is based on an allegation that many States did not guarantee the right to family leave by statute ***. The study from which the Court derives this conclusion examined "the parental leave policies of Federal executive branch agencies," not those of the States. The study explicitly stated that its conclusions concerned federal employees ***. A history of discrimination on the part of the Federal Government may, in some situations, support an inference of similar conduct by the States, but the Court does not explain why the inference is justified here. ***

The federal-state equivalence upon which the Court places such emphasis is a deficient rationale at an even more fundamental level, however; for the States appear to have been ahead of Congress in providing gender-neutral family leave benefits. Thirty States, the District of Columbia, and Puerto Rico had adopted some form of family-care leave in the years preceding the Act's adoption. *** Given that the States assumed a pioneering role in the creation of family leave schemes, it is not surprising these early efforts may have been imperfect. This is altogether different, however, from purposeful discrimination. ***

Stripped of the conduct which exhibits no constitutional infirmity, the Court's "exten[sive] and specifi[c] *** record of unconstitutional state conduct," boils down to the fact that three States, Massachusetts, Kansas, and Tennessee, provided parenting leave only to their female employees, and had no program for granting their employees (male or female) family leave. ***

Our concern with gender discrimination, which is subjected to heightened scrutiny, as opposed to age- or disability-based distinctions, which are reviewed under rational standard, does not alter this conclusion. The application of heightened scrutiny is designed to ensure gender-based classifications are not based on the entrenched and pervasive stereotypes which inhibit women's progress in the workplace. This consideration does not divest respondents of their burden to show that "Congress identified a history and pattern of unconstitutional employment discrimination by the States." *** The paucity of evidence to support the case the Court tries to make demonstrates that Congress was not responding with a congruent and proportional remedy to a perceived course of unconstitutional conduct. Instead, it enacted a substantive entitlement program of its own. If Congress had been concerned about different treatment of men and women with respect to family leave, a congruent remedy would have sought to ensure the benefits of any leave program enacted by a State are available to men and women on an equal basis. Instead, the Act imposes, across the board, a requirement that States grant a minimum of 12 weeks of leave per year. This requirement may represent Congress' considered judgment as to the optimal balance between the family obligations of workers and the interests of employers, and the States may decide to follow these guidelines in designing their own family leave benefits. It does not follow, however, that if the States choose to enact a different benefit scheme, they should be deemed to engage in unconstitutional conduct and forced to open their treasuries to private suits for damages.

*** [T]he abrogation of state sovereign immunity pursuant to Title VII was a legitimate congressional response to a pattern of gender-based discrimination in employment. The family leave benefit conferred by the Act discrimination in employment. The family leave benefit conferred by the Act is, by contrast, a substantive benefit Congress chose to confer upon state employees. *** What is at issue is only whether the States can be subjected, without consent, to suits brought by private persons seeking to collect moneys from the state treasury. Their immunity cannot be abrogated without documentation of a pattern of unconstitutional acts by the States, and only then by a congruent and proportional remedy. There has been a complete failure by respondents to carry their burden to establish each of these necessary propositions. ***

Notes

1. **Gender and Race v. Age and Disability?** Is the level of scrutiny given under § 1 the key to the intensity of scrutiny given to congressional evidence and findings when the Court assesses whether Congress legitimately engaged in its § 5 enforcement authority? Would JUSTICE REHNQUIST'S rationale in *Hibbs* allow Congress to mandate caretaker leave for women but not men? *Hibbs* does not explain how the FMLA differs from the VAWA (see *Morrison*) in terms of Congress' § 5 enforcement power. Are these two sex discrimination statutes distinguishable?

2. **Title VII Ramifications?** Do all members of the Court concede that Title VII was a proportional and congruent exercise of enforcement power? Are the parts of Title VII that concern religious and national origin discrimination more vulnerable than the race and sex discrimination prohibitions? May Congress use its § 5 enforcement power to prohibit otherwise permissible (but not required) race-based affirmative action in state university admissions processes?

3. **§ 5 Power and the Content of § 1.** Until you have studied the materials in Chapters VIII and IX you cannot fully appreciate the extent of the difficulties in deciding whether or not a particular statute was enacted under Congress' § 5 power. Nevertheless, the following questions provide a fair prelude to this issue.

   - Assume the Supreme Court has held equal that payment of male and female state employees who occupy *different* jobs of "comparable worth" is not required by the Equal Protection Clause. Could Congress nevertheless require "comparable worth" pay based on its § 5 Power?

   - Would a federal statute denying students the "in-state" tuition rate until the student had lived in the state for one year be a proper exercise of § 5 power?

   - Would a federal statute making false and misleading advertising unlawful be within the § 5 power?

4. **Contrasting Commerce Clause and § 5 Power.** Could § 5 serve as a basis for any of the legislation suggested in note 2, p. 263 and note 2, p. 272?

5. **Religious Accommodation.** May a state employee sue her state employer for failing to reasonably accommodate her "religious observances and practices," as § 701 (j) of Title VII of the Civil Rights Act of 1964 requires? Is § 701(j) appropriate legislation to "enforce" the equal protection clause? Does the provision pass the "congruence and proportionality" test? Is it important that (1) there was little Civil Rights Act legislative history about religious discrimination, (2) religion was

considered an aspect of race when the Fourteenth Amendment was ratified, and (3) anti-Jewish, anti-Catholic, anti-Mormon, and anti-Muslim sentiments have been widespread at various times in American history? See *Endres v. Indiana State Police*, 334 F. 3d 618 (7th Cir. 2003).

REVIEW PROBLEM

Sally Smart is a United States Senator from the State of New Hope. On her way to the office one morning, she heard the following story on the radio:

"State legislators in the State of Bessland just passed legislation establishing two single-sex state colleges. Currently Bessland has no public single-sex colleges. The sponsor of the legislation, state senator Brenda Bright, commented, 'Social science evidence proves that some students of both genders perform better in college in a single-sex environment. Those students should have the option of a public, single-sex college education.' It appears that other states may well follow the lead of Bessland. Legislation to establish single-sex colleges is currently pending in the legislatures of 30 other states."

Senator Smart arrived at her office enraged. She called in her chief legislative counsel and declared, "I have a Ph.D. in sociology. I know those studies claiming that students perform better in single-sex colleges, and those studies are a load of rubbish. Single-sex colleges are a return to the old days when women went to finishing schools to learn flower arranging and men went to all-male colleges to get their fancy education without the need to compete against well-qualified women. We have to stop that from happening again."

Senator Smart, who chairs the Senate Education Committee, held hearings about single-sex education. About 20 education scholars testified. Fifteen of the education scholars testified that no reliable, social scientific data proves that any students perform better in single-sex colleges. These fifteen scholars further testified that the most reliable studies showed that both men and women perform better in mixed-gender (that is, coeducational) colleges. By contrast, the five other scholars testified that they believed that reliable social scientific studies, such as those studies relied on by the Bessland legislature, did prove that some men and women perform better in single-sex colleges. In addition, about 10 historians appeared before the committee, and all testified that in the past, the great majority of public and private colleges were single-sex, the women's colleges had much less funding, and that the prior system of single-sex colleges interfered with the ability of women to receive an education equal to men.

Following the hearings, Senator Smart introduced the following legislation, which passed both houses of Congress and was signed by President Rumsfeld:

EQUAL ACCESS TO COLLEGE ACT

1. Findings:
    (a) Single-sex colleges in the past have interfered with the educational opportunities of women.
    (b) Social scientific evidence demonstrates that single-sex colleges do not enhance the educational opportunities of men or women.
    (c) Mixed-gender educational environments are essential for men and women to learn to function together in society.
    (d) Providing the best possible educational environment is essential for the economic welfare of the United States.
    (e) Single-gender education impairs interstate commerce and violates the guarantee of equal protection.

2. Therefore:
    (a) No state college may deny admission to any student on the basis of gender.
    (b) To ensure proper enforcement of this Act, every state college shall prepare a report on an annual basis containing the following information on each applicant: the applicant's gender, the applicant's test scores on the SAT, ACT or similar standardized test, and whether the applicant was admitted.
    (c) Violation of any provision of this Act shall constitute a misdemeanor, for which the state college may be fined up to $10,000.

1. Is the Equal Access to College Act a valid exercise of Congress's powers to regulate interstate commerce?

2. Is the Equal Access to College Act a valid exercise of Congress's powers to enforce the provisions of the Equal Protection clause of the Fourteenth Amendment?

***

At the signing ceremony for the Equal Access to College Act, President Rumsfeld held a news conference at which he said: "I am four-square behind the intent of this legislation. In Iraq, men and women fought together. It is essential that they learn to work together in civilian life as well." Shortly thereafter, President Rumsfeld issued an executive order specifying steps the Executive Branch would take to "further the goals of the Equal Access to College Act." This order provided that military recruiters would not visit any public or private single-sex college, that no graduate of such a college would be eligible to be an officer in the military, and that no government contracts would be awarded to any college having less than a 20% representation of either gender among its student body.

3. Is President Rumsfeld's order constitutional?

V

FEDERALISM'S LIMITS ON CONGRESS AND THE STATES

"Federalism was our Nation's own discovery. The Framers split the atom of sovereignty. It was the genius of their idea that our citizens would have two political capacities, one state and one federal, each protected from incursion by the other. The resulting Constitution created a legal system unprecedented in form and design, establishing two orders of government, each with its own direct relationship, its own privity, its own set of mutual rights and obligations to the people who sustain it and are governed by it."

—JUSTICE KENNEDY, concurring in
U.S. Term Limits v. Thornton

There is considerable controversy concerning where federalism locates the boundary lines between federal and state spheres of authority. Whether Congress possesses certain powers, an aspect of this controversy, was considered in the previous chapter. This chapter examines when other portions of the Constitution, such as the 10th and 11th Amendments, impose barriers on federal authority. It also looks at the Constitution's "vertical federalism" restrictions on state power imposed by federal functions and federal regulation. Constitutional restrictions on state relations with other states (sometimes called "horizontal federalism") are addressed elsewhere in this book, primarily in the next chapter.

A. LIMITS ON CONGRESS

Assuming Congress has a substantive power justifying regulation in a particular area, are there any federalism bars to its exercise of power vis-à-vis the states? Another way of phrasing the question considered in the next cases is: even if a law is within Congress' powers, is it unconstitutional if it intrudes too much on state authority? If so, when is intrusion on state authority excessive?

Section 1 below considers the extent to which Congress can regulate the States using its extensive, if not limitless, Commerce Clause powers. Section 2 examines the extent to which Congress may specifically command a state to engage in regulation and require that states assist in executing federal laws.

Finally, Section 3 assesses the role of state sovereign immunity in insulating the states from suits authorized by Congress.

1. SUBSTANTIVE REGULATION OF THE STATES

GARCIA v. SAN ANTONIO METROPOLITAN TRANSIT AUTHORITY
469 U.S. 528, 105 S.Ct. 1005, 83 L.Ed.2d 1016 (1985).

JUSTICE BLACKMUN delivered the opinion of the Court.

We revisit in these cases an issue raised in *National League of Cities v. Usery*, 426 U.S. 833 (1976). In that litigation, this Court, by a sharply divided vote, ruled that the Commerce Clause does not empower Congress to enforce the minimum-wage and overtime provisions of the Fair Labor Standards Act (FLSA) against the States "in areas of traditional governmental functions." Although *National League of Cities* supplied some examples of "traditional governmental functions," it did not offer a general explanation of how a "traditional" function is to be distinguished from a "nontraditional" one. Since then, federal and state courts have struggled with the task, thus imposed, of identifying a traditional function for purposes of state immunity under the Commerce Clause.

In the present cases, a Federal District Court concluded that municipal ownership and operation of a mass-transit system is a traditional governmental function and thus, under *National League of Cities*, is exempt from the obligations imposed by the FLSA. Faced with the identical question, three Federal Courts of Appeals and one state appellate court have reached the opposite conclusion.

Our examination of this "function" standard applied in these and other cases over the last eight years now persuades us that the attempt to draw the boundaries of state regulatory immunity in terms of "traditional governmental function" is not only unworkable but is also inconsistent with established principles of federalism and, indeed, with those very federalism principles on which *National League of Cities* purported to rest. That case, accordingly, is overruled. ***

Appellees have not argued that SAMTA is immune from regulation under the FLSA on the ground that it is a local transit system engaged in intrastate commercial activity. In a practical sense, SAMTA's operations might well be characterized as "local." Nonetheless, it long has been settled that Congress' authority under the Commerce Clause extends to intrastate economic activities that affect interstate commerce. Were SAMTA a privately owned and operated enterprise, it could not credibly argue that Congress exceeded the bounds of its Commerce Clause powers in prescribing minimum wages and overtime rates for SAMTA's employees. Any constitutional exemption from the requirements of the FLSA therefore must rest on SAMTA's status as a governmental entity rather than on the "local" nature of its operations.

*** [U]nder *National League of Cities*, four conditions must be satisfied before a state activity may be deemed immune from a particular federal regulation under the Commerce Clause. First, it is said that the federal statute at issue must regulate "the 'States as States.'" Second, the statute must "address matters that are indisputably 'attribute[s] of state sovereignty.'" Third, state compliance with the federal obligation must "directly impair [the States'] ability 'to structure integral operations in areas of traditional governmental functions.'" "Finally, the relation of state and federal interests must not be such that 'the nature of the federal interest *** justifies state submission.'"

The controversy in the present cases has focused on the third requirement—that the challenged federal statute trench on "traditional governmental functions." The District Court voiced a common concern: "Despite the abundance of adjectives, identifying which particular state functions are immune remains difficult." Just how troublesome the task has been is revealed by the results reached in other federal cases. *** We find it difficult, if not impossible, to identify an organizing principle that places each of the cases in the first group on one side of a line and each of the cases in the second group on the other side. The constitutional distinction between licensing drivers and regulating traffic, for example, or between operating a highway authority and operating a mental health facility, is elusive at best.

*** The most obvious defect of a historical approach to state immunity is that it prevents a court from accommodating changes in the historical functions of States, changes that have resulted in a number of once-private functions like education being assumed by the States and their subdivisions. At the same time, the only apparent virtue of a rigorous historical standard, namely, its promise of a reasonably objective measure for state immunity, is illusory. Reliance on history as an organizing principle results in line-drawing of the most arbitrary sort; the genesis of state governmental functions stretches over a historical continuum from before the Revolution to the present, and courts would have to decide by fiat precisely how longstanding a pattern of state involvement had to be for federal regulatory authority to be defeated.

A nonhistorical standard for selecting immune governmental functions is likely to be just as unworkable as is a historical standard. The goal of identifying "uniquely" governmental functions, for example, has been rejected by the Court [in] part because the notion of a "uniquely" governmental function is unmanageable. ***

We believe, however, that there is a more fundamental problem at work here, a problem that explains why the Court was never able to provide a basis for the governmental/proprietary distinction in the intergovernmental tax-immunity cases and why an attempt to draw similar distinctions with respect to federal regulatory authority under *National League of Cities* is unlikely to succeed regardless of how the distinctions are phrased. The problem is that neither the governmental/proprietary distinction nor any other that purports to separate out important governmental functions can be faithful to the role of federalism in a democratic society. The essence of our federal system is that within the realm of authority left open to them under the Constitution, the States must be equally free to engage in any activity that their citizens choose for the common weal, no matter how unorthodox or unnecessary anyone else—including the judiciary—deems state involvement to be. Any rule of state immunity that looks to the "traditional," "integral," or "necessary" nature of governmental functions inevitably invites an unelected federal judiciary to make decisions about which state policies it favors and which ones it dislikes. ***

We therefore now reject, as unsound in principle and unworkable in practice, a rule of state immunity from federal regulation that turns on a judicial appraisal of whether a particular governmental function is "integral" or "traditional." Any such rule leads to inconsistent results at the same time that it disserves principles of democratic self-governance, and it breeds inconsistency precisely because it is divorced from those principles. If there are to be limits on the Federal Government's power to interfere with state functions—as undoubtedly there are—we must look elsewhere to find them. We accordingly return to the underlying issue that confronted this Court in *National League of Cities*—the manner in which the Constitution insulates States from the reach of Congress' power under the Commerce Clause.

The central theme of *National League of Cities* was that the States occupy a special position in our constitutional system and that the scope of Congress' authority under the Commerce Clause must reflect that position. Of course, the Commerce Clause by its specific language does not provide any special limitation on Congress' actions with respect to the States. It is equally true, however, that the text of the Constitution provides the beginning rather than the final answer to every inquiry into questions of federalism, for "[b]ehind the words of the constitutional provisions are postulates which limit and control." *Monaco v. Mississippi*, 292 U.S. 313, 322 (1934). *National League of Cities* reflected the general conviction that the Constitution precludes "the National Government [from] devour[ing] the essentials of state sovereignty." In order to be faithful to the underlying federal premises of the Constitution, courts must look for the "postulates which limit and control."

What has proved problematic is not the perception that the Constitution's federal structure imposes limitations on the Commerce Clause, but rather the nature and content of those limitations. ***

The States unquestionably do "retai[n] a significant measure of sovereign authority." *EEOC v. Wyoming*, 460 U.S., at 269 (POWELL, J., dissenting). They do so, however, only to the extent that the Constitution has not divested them of their original powers and transferred those powers to the Federal Government. In the words of James Madison to the Members of the First Congress: "Interference with the power of the States was no constitutional criterion of the power of Congress. If the power was not given, Congress could not exercise it; if given, they might exercise it, although it should interfere with the laws, or even the Constitution of the States." 2 Annals of Cong. 1897 (1791).

As a result, to say that the Constitution assumes the continued role of the States is to say little about the nature of that role. Only recently, this Court recognized that the purpose of the constitutional immunity recognized in

National League of Cities is not to preserve "a sacred province of state autonomy." With rare exceptions, like the guarantee, in Article IV, § 3, of state territorial integrity, the Constitution does not carve out express elements of state sovereignty that Congress may not employ its delegated powers to displace. The power of the Federal Government is a "power to be respected" as well, and the fact that the States remain sovereign as to all powers not vested in Congress or denied them by the Constitution offers no guidance about where the frontier between state and federal power lies. In short, we have no license to employ freestanding conceptions of state sovereignty when measuring congressional authority under the Commerce Clause.

When we look for the States' "residuary and inviolable sovereignty," The Federalist No. 39, p. 285 (B. Wright ed. 1961) (J. Madison), in the shape of the constitutional scheme rather than in predetermined notions of sovereign power, a different measure of state sovereignty emerges. Apart from the limitation on federal authority inherent in the delegated nature of Congress' Article I powers, the principal means chosen by the Framers to ensure the role of the States in the federal system lies in the structure of the Federal Government itself. It is no novelty to observe that the composition of the Federal Government was designed in large part to protect the States from overreaching by Congress.

[The extent to which the structure of the Federal Government itself was relied on to insulate the interests of the States is evident in the views of the Framers. James Madison explained that the Federal Government "will partake sufficiently of the spirit [of the States], to be disinclined to invade the rights of the individual States, or the prerogatives of their governments." The Federalist No. 46, p. 332.] *** In short, the Framers chose to rely on a federal system in which special restraints on federal power over the States inhered principally in the workings of the National Government itself, rather than in discrete limitations on the objects of federal authority. State sovereign interests, then, are more properly protected by procedural safeguards inherent in the structure of the federal system than by judicially created limitations on federal power.

The effectiveness of the federal political process in preserving the States' interests is apparent even today in the course of federal legislation. On the one hand, the States have been able to direct a substantial proportion of federal revenues into their own treasuries in the form of general and program-specific grants in aid. The federal role in assisting state and local governments is a longstanding one. *** Moreover, at the same time that the States have exercised their influence to obtain federal support, they have been able to exempt themselves from a wide variety of obligations imposed by Congress under the Commerce Clause. For example, the Federal Power Act, the National Labor Relations Act, the Labor–Management Reporting and Disclosure Act, the Occupational Safety and Health Act, the Employee Retirement Income Security Act, and the Sherman Act all contain express or implied exemptions for States and their subdivisions. The fact that some federal statutes such as the FLSA extend general obligations to the States cannot obscure the extent to which the political position of the States in the federal system has served to minimize the burdens that the States bear under the Commerce Clause.

We realize that changes in the structure of the Federal Government have taken place since 1789, not the least of which has been the substitution of popular election of Senators by the adoption of the Seventeenth Amendment in 1913, and that these changes may work to alter the influence of the States in the federal political process. Nonetheless, against this background, we are convinced that the fundamental limitation that the constitutional scheme imposes on the Commerce Clause to protect the "States as States" is one of process rather than one of result. Any substantive restraint on the exercise of Commerce Clause powers must find its justification in the procedural nature of this basic limitation, and it must be tailored to compensate for possible failings in the national political process rather than to dictate a "sacred province of state autonomy."

Insofar as the present cases are concerned, then, we need go no further than to state that we perceive nothing in the overtime and minimum-wage requirements of the FLSA, as applied to SAMTA, that is destructive of state sovereignty or violative of any constitutional provision. SAMTA faces nothing more than the same minimum-wage and overtime obligations that hundreds of thousands of other employers, public as well as private, have to meet. ***

This analysis makes clear that Congress' action in affording SAMTA employees the protections of the wage and hour provisions of the FLSA contravened no affirmative limit on Congress' power under the Commerce Clause. The judgment of the District Court therefore must be reversed.

Of course, we continue to recognize that the States occupy a special and specific position in our constitutional system and that the scope of Congress' authority under the Commerce Clause must reflect that position. But the principal and basic limit on the federal commerce power is that inherent in all congressional action—the built-in restraints that our system provides through state participation in federal governmental action. The political process ensures that laws that unduly burden the States will not be promulgated. In the factual setting of these cases the internal safeguards of the political process have performed as intended.

These cases do not require us to identify or define what affirmative limits the constitutional structure might impose on federal action affecting the States under the Commerce Clause. ***

JUSTICE POWELL, with whom THE CHIEF JUSTICE, JUSTICE REHNQUIST, and JUSTICE O'CONNOR join, dissenting.

The Court today, in its 5–4 decision, overrules *National League of Cities v. Usery*, 426 U.S. 833 (1976), a case in which we held that Congress lacked authority to impose the requirements of the Fair Labor Standards Act on state and local governments. Because I believe this decision substantially alters the federal system embodied in the Constitution, I dissent. *** Whatever effect the Court's decision may have in weakening the application of *stare decisis*, it is likely to be less important than what the Court has done to the Constitution itself. A unique feature of the United States is the federal system of government guaranteed by the Constitution and implicit in the very name of our country. Despite some genuflecting in the Court's opinion to the concept of federalism, today's decision effectively reduces the Tenth Amendment to meaningless rhetoric when Congress acts pursuant to the Commerce Clause. ***

Today's opinion does not explain how the States' role in the electoral process guarantees that particular exercises of the Commerce Clause power will not infringe on residual state sovereignty.[7] Members of Congress are elected from the various States, but once in office they are Members of the Federal Government.[8] Although the States participate in the Electoral College, this is hardly a reason to view the President as a representative of the States' interest against federal encroachment. We noted recently "[t]he hydraulic pressure inherent within each of the separate Branches to exceed the outer limits of its power. *** " *INS v. Chadha*, 462 U.S. 919, 951 (1983). The Court offers no reason to think that this pressure will not operate when Congress seeks to invoke its powers under the Commerce Clause, notwithstanding the electoral role of the States.[9]

The Court apparently thinks that the State's success at obtaining federal funds for various projects and exemptions from the obligations of some federal statutes is indicative of the "effectiveness of the federal political process in preserving the States' interests. *** " But such political success is not relevant to the question whether the political processes are the proper means of enforcing constitutional limitations.[11] The fact that Congress

---

[7] Late in its opinion, the Court suggests that after all there may be some "affirmative limits the constitutional structure might impose on federal action affecting the States under the Commerce Clause." The Court asserts that "[i]n the factual setting of these cases the internal safeguards of the political process have performed as intended." The Court does not explain the basis for this judgment. Nor does it identify the circumstances in which the "political process" may fail and "affirmative limits" are to be imposed. Presumably, such limits are to be determined by the Judicial Branch even though it is "unelected." Today's opinion, however, has rejected the balancing standard and suggests no other standard that would enable a court to determine when there has been a malfunction of the "political process." The Court's failure to specify the "affirmative limits" on federal power, or when and how these limits are to be determined, may well be explained by the transparent fact that any such attempt would be subject to precisely the same objections on which it relies to overrule *National League of Cities*.

[8] One can hardly imagine this Court saying that because Congress is composed of individuals, individual rights guaranteed by the Bill of Rights are amply protected by the political process. Yet, the position adopted today is indistinguishable in principle. The Tenth Amendment also is an essential part of the Bill of Rights.

[9] *** The adoption of the Seventeenth Amendment (providing for direct election of Senators), the weakening of political parties on the local level, and the rise of national media, among other things, have made Congress increasingly less representative of state and local interests, and more likely to be responsive to the demands of various national constituencies. Thus, even if one were to ignore the numerous problems with the Court's position in terms of constitutional theory, there would remain serious questions as to its factual premises.

[11] Apparently in an effort to reassure the States, the Court identifies several major statutes that thus far have not been made applicable to state governments. The Court does not suggest that this restraint will continue after its decision here. Indeed, it is unlikely that special interest

generally does not transgress constitutional limits on its power to reach state activities does not make judicial review any less necessary to rectify the cases in which it does do so.[12] The States' role in our system of government is a matter of constitutional law, not of legislative grace. "The powers not delegated to the United States by the Constitution, nor prohibited by it to the States, are reserved to the States, respectively, or to the people." U.S. Const., Amdt. 10.

More troubling than the logical infirmities in the Court's reasoning is the result of its holding, i.e., that federal political officials, invoking the Commerce Clause, are the sole judges of the limits of their own power. This result is inconsistent with the fundamental principles of our constitutional system. See, e.g., The Federalist No. 78 (Hamilton). At least since *Marbury v. Madison*, it has been the settled province of the federal judiciary "to say what the law is" with respect to the constitutionality of Acts of Congress. In rejecting the role of the judiciary in protecting the States from federal overreaching, the Court's opinion offers no explanation for ignoring the teaching of the most famous case in our history.[13]

In our federal system, the States have a major role that cannot be pre-empted by the National Government. As contemporaneous writings and the debates at the ratifying conventions make clear, the States' ratification of the Constitution was predicated on this understanding of federalism. Indeed, the Tenth Amendment was adopted specifically to ensure that the important role promised the States by the proponents of the Constitution was realized.

Much of the initial opposition to the Constitution was rooted in the fear that the National Government would be too powerful and eventually would eliminate the States as viable political entities. This concern was voiced repeatedly until proponents of the Constitution made assurances that a Bill of Rights, including a provision explicitly reserving powers in the States, would be among the first business of the new Congress. *** This history,

---

groups will fail to accept the Court's open invitation to urge Congress to extend these and other statutes to apply to the States and their local subdivisions.

[12] This Court has never before abdicated responsibility for assessing the constitutionality of challenged action on the ground that affected parties theoretically are able to look out for their own interests through the electoral process. As the Court noted in *National League of Cities*, a much stronger argument as to inherent structural protections could have been made in either *Buckley v. Valeo*, 424 U.S. 1 (1976), or *Myers v. United States*, 272 U.S. 52 (1926), than can be made here. In these cases, the President signed legislation that limited his authority with respect to certain appointments and thus arguably "it was *** no concern of this Court that the law violated the Constitution." The Court nevertheless held the laws unconstitutional because they infringed on Presidential authority, the President's consent notwithstanding. The Court does not address this point; nor does it cite any authority for its contrary view.

[13] The Court states that the decision in *National League of Cities* "invites an unelected federal judiciary to make decisions about which state policies it favors and which ones its dislikes." Curiously, the Court then suggests that under the application of the "traditional" governmental function analysis, "the States cannot serve as laboratories for social and economic experiment." Apparently the Court believes that when "an unelected federal judiciary" makes decisions as to whether a particular function is one for the Federal or State Governments, the States no longer may engage in "social and economic experiment." The Court does not explain how leaving the States virtually at the mercy of the Federal Government, without recourse to judicial review, will enhance their opportunities to experiment and serve as "laboratories."

which the Court simply ignores, documents the integral role of the Tenth Amendment in our constitutional theory. It exposes as well, I believe, the fundamental character of the Court's error today. Far from being "unsound in principle," judicial enforcement of the Tenth Amendment is essential to maintaining the federal system so carefully designed by the Framers and adopted in the Constitution.

The Framers had definite ideas about the nature of the Constitution's division of authority between the Federal and State Governments. *** The Framers believed that the separate sphere of sovereignty reserved to the States would ensure that the States would serve as an effective "counterpoise" to the power of the Federal Government. The States would serve this essential role because they would attract and retain the loyalty of their citizens. The roots of such loyalty, the Founders thought, were found in the objects peculiar to state government. *** Thus, the harm to the States that results from federal overreaching under the Commerce Clause is not simply a matter of dollars and cents. Nor is it a matter of the wisdom or folly of certain policy choices. Rather, by usurping functions traditionally performed by the States, federal overreaching under the Commerce Clause undermines the constitutionally mandated balance of power between the States and the Federal Government, a balance designed to protect our fundamental liberties. *** [T]he Court today propounds a view of federalism that pays only lip service to the role of the States. Although it says that the States "unquestionably do 'retai[n] a significant measure of sovereign authority,'" it fails to recognize the broad, yet specific areas of sovereignty that the Framers intended the States to retain. *** [The] Court's view of federalism appears to relegate the States to precisely the trivial role that opponents of the Constitution feared they would occupy.

In *National League of Cities*, we spoke of fire prevention, police protection, sanitation, and public health as "typical of [the services] performed by state and local governments in discharging their dual functions of administering the public law and furnishing public services." Not only are these activities remote from any normal concept of interstate commerce, they are also activities that epitomize the concerns of local, democratic self-government. In emphasizing the need to protect traditional governmental functions, we identified the kinds of activities engaged in by state and local governments that affect the everyday lives of citizens. These are services that people are in a position to understand and evaluate, and in a democracy, have the right to oversee.[18] We recognized that "it is functions such as these which governments are created to provide *** " and that the States and local governments are better able than the National Government to perform them.

The Court maintains that the standard approved in *National League of Cities* "disserves principles of democratic self-goverance." In reaching this conclusion, the Court looks myopically only to persons elected to positions in

---

[18] The Framers recognized that the most effective democracy occurs at local levels of government, where people with firsthand knowledge of local problems have more ready access to public officials responsible for dealing with them. This is as true today as it was when the Constitution was adopted.

the Federal Government. It disregards entirely the far more effective role of democratic self-government at the state and local levels. One must compare realistically the operation of the state and local governments with that of the Federal Government. Federal legislation is drafted primarily by the staffs of the congressional committees. In view of the hundreds of bills introduced at each session of Congress and the complexity of many of them, it is virtually impossible for even the most conscientious legislators to be truly familiar with many of the statutes enacted. Federal departments and agencies customarily are authorized to write regulations. Often these are more important than the text of the statutes. As is true of the original legislation, these are drafted largely by staff personnel. The administration and enforcement of federal laws and regulations necessarily are largely in the hands of staff and civil service employees. These employees may have little or no knowledge of the States and localities that will be affected by the statutes and regulations for which they are responsible. In any case, they hardly are as accessible and responsive as those who occupy analogous positions in state and local governments.

In drawing this contrast, I imply no criticism of these federal employees or the officials who are ultimately in charge. The great majority are conscientious and faithful to their duties. My point is simply that members of the immense federal bureaucracy are not elected, know less about the services traditionally rendered by States and localities, and are inevitably less responsive to recipients of such services, than are state legislatures, city councils, boards of supervisors, and state and local commissions, boards, and agencies. It is at these state and local levels—not in Washington as the Court so mistakenly thinks—that "democratic self-government" is best exemplified.

The question presented in these cases is whether the extension of the FLSA to the wages and hours of employees of a city-owned transit system unconstitutionally impinges on fundamental state sovereignty. The Court's sweeping holding does far more than simply answer this question in the negative. In overruling *National League of Cities*, today's opinion apparently authorizes federal control, under the auspices of the Commerce Clause, over the terms and conditions of employment of all state and local employees. ***

I return now to the balancing test approved in *National League of Cities*. The Court does not find in this case that the "federal interest is demonstrably greater." No such finding could have been made, for the state interest is compelling. The financial impact on States and localities of displacing their control over wages, hours, overtime regulations, pensions, and labor relations with their employees could have serious, as well as unanticipated, effects on state and local planning, budgeting, and the levying of taxes. ***

The Court emphasizes that municipal operation of an intra-city mass transit system is relatively new in the life of our country. It nevertheless is a classic example of the type of service traditionally provided by local government. It is local by definition. It is indistinguishable in principle from the traditional services of providing and maintaining streets, public lighting, traffic control, water, and sewerage systems. Services of this kind are precisely those with which citizens are more "familiarly and minutely conversant." The Federalist No. 46. State and local officials of course must be intimately familiar with these services and sensitive to their quality as well as cost. Such officials also know that their constituents and the press respond to the adequacy, fair distribution, and cost of these services. It is this kind of state and local control and accountability that the Framers understood would insure the vitality and preservation of the federal system that the Constitution explicitly requires. *** As I view the Court's decision today as rejecting the basic precepts of our federal system and limiting the constitutional role of judicial review, I dissent.

JUSTICE REHNQUIST, dissenting. [omitted]

JUSTICE O'CONNOR, with whom JUSTICE POWELL and JUSTICE REHNQUIST join, dissenting.

*** In my view, federalism cannot be reduced to the weak "essence" distilled by the majority today. There is more to federalism than the nature of the constraints that can be imposed on the States in "the realm of authority left open to them by the Constitution." The central issue of federalism, of course, is whether any realm is left open to the States by the Constitution— whether any area remains in which a State may act free of federal interference. ***

Due to the emergence of an integrated and industrialized national economy, this Court has been required to examine and review a breathtaking expansion of the powers of Congress. In doing so the Court correctly perceived that the Framers of our Constitution intended Congress to have sufficient power to address national problems. But the Framers were not single-minded. The Constitution is animated by an array of intentions. Just as surely as the Framers envisioned a National Government capable of solving national problems, they also envisioned a republic whose vitality was assured by the diffusion of power not only among the branches of the Federal Government, but also between the Federal Government and the States. In the 18th century these intentions did not conflict because technology had not yet converted every local problem into a national one. A conflict has now emerged, and the Court today retreats rather than reconcile the Constitution's dual concerns for federalism and an effective commerce power.

*** Incidental to this expansion of the commerce power, Congress has been given an ability it lacked prior to the emergence of an integrated national economy. Because virtually every state activity, like virtually every activity of a private individual, arguably "affects" interstate commerce, Congress can now supplant the States from the significant sphere of activities envisioned for them by the Framers. It is in this context that recent changes in the workings of Congress, such as the direct election of Senators and the expanded influence of national interest groups become relevant. These changes may well have lessened the weight Congress gives to the legitimate interests of States as States. As a result, there is now a real risk that Congress will gradually erase the diffusion of power between State and Nation on which the Framers based their faith in the efficiency and vitality of our Republic.

*** With the abandonment of *National League of Cities*, all that stands between the remaining essentials of state sovereignty and Congress is the latter's underdeveloped capacity for self-restraint.

The problems of federalism in an integrated national economy are capable of more responsible resolution than holding that the States as States retain no status apart from that which Congress chooses to let them retain. The proper resolution, I suggest, lies in weighing state autonomy as a factor in the balance when interpreting the means by which Congress can exercise its authority on the States as States. It is insufficient, in assessing the validity of congressional regulation of a State pursuant to the commerce power, to ask only whether the same regulation would be valid if enforced against a private party. *** If state autonomy is ignored in assessing the means by which Congress regulates matters affecting commerce, then federalism becomes irrelevant simply because the set of activities remaining beyond the reach of such a commerce power "may well be negligible."

It has been difficult for this Court to craft bright lines defining the scope of the state autonomy protected by *National League of Cities*. Such difficulty is to be expected whenever constitutional concerns as important as federalism and the effectiveness of the commerce power come into conflict. Regardless of the difficulty, it is and will remain the duty of this Court to reconcile these concerns in the final instance. ***

2. "COMMANDEERING" THE STATES

NEW YORK v. UNITED STATES
505 U.S. 144, 112 S.Ct. 2408, 120 L.Ed.2d 120 (1992).

JUSTICE O'CONNOR delivered the opinion of the Court.

This case implicates one of our Nation's newest problems of public policy and perhaps our oldest question of constitutional law. The public policy issue involves the disposal of radioactive waste: In this case, we address the constitutionality of three provisions of the Low–Level Radioactive Waste Policy Amendments Act of 1985. The constitutional question is as old as the Constitution: It consists of discerning the proper division of authority between the Federal Government and the States. We conclude that while Congress has substantial power under the Constitution to encourage the States to provide for the disposal of the radioactive waste generated within their borders, the Constitution does not confer upon Congress the ability simply to compel the States to do so. ***

We live in a world full of low level radioactive waste. *** The waste must be isolated from humans for long periods of time, often for hundreds of years. Millions of cubic feet of low level radioactive waste must be disposed of each year. *** [By] 1979, [only] South Carolina [was left] to shoulder the responsibility of storing low level radioactive waste produced in every part of the country. The Governor of South Carolina, understandably perturbed, ordered a 50% reduction in the quantity of waste accepted at the site.

Faced with the possibility that the Nation would be left with no disposal sites for low level radioactive waste, Congress responded by enacting the Low-Level Radioactive Waste Policy Act. Relying largely on a report submitted by the National Governors' Association, Congress declared a federal policy of holding each State "responsible for providing for the availability of capacity either within or outside the State for the disposal of low-level radioactive waste generated within its borders." *** The 1980 Act authorized States to enter into regional compacts that, once ratified by Congress, would have the authority beginning in 1986 to restrict the use of their disposal facilities to waste generated within member States.

By 1985, only three approved regional compacts had operational disposal facilities ***. Congress once again took up the issue of waste disposal. The result was the legislation challenged here, the Low–Level Radioactive Waste Policy Amendments Act of 1985.

The 1985 Act was again based largely on a proposal submitted by the National Governors' Association. In broad outline, the Act embodies a compromise among the sited and unsited States. The sited States agreed to extend for seven years the period in which they would accept low level radioactive waste from other States. In exchange, the unsited States agreed to end their reliance on the sited States by 1992. *** The Act authorizes States to "enter into such [interstate] compacts as may be necessary to provide for the establishment and operation of regional disposal facilities for low-level radioactive waste." *** [T]hrough the end of 1992, the existing disposal sites "shall make disposal capacity available for low-level radioactive waste generated by any source." But the States in which the disposal sites are located are permitted to exact a graduated surcharge for waste arriving from outside the regional compact. After the 7–year transition period expires, approved regional compacts may exclude radioactive waste generated outside the region.

The Act provides three types of incentives to encourage the States to comply with their statutory obligation to provide for the disposal of waste generated within their borders.

1. Monetary incentives. One quarter of the surcharges collected by the sited States must be transferred to an escrow account held by the Secretary of Energy. The Secretary then makes payments from this account to each State that has *** ratified legislation either joining a regional compact or indicating an intent to develop a disposal facility within the State. ***

2. Access incentives. The second type of incentive involves the denial of access to disposal sites. States that fail to meet the July 1986 deadline may be charged twice the ordinary surcharge for the remainder of 1986 and may be denied access to disposal facilities thereafter. ***

3. The take title provision. The third type of incentive is the most severe. The Act provides: "If a State (or, where applicable, a compact region) in which low-level radioactive waste is generated is unable to provide for the disposal of all such waste generated within such State or compact region by January 1, 1996, each State in which such waste is generated *** shall take title to

the waste, be obligated to take possession of the waste, and shall be liable for all damages directly or indirectly incurred by such generator or owner as a consequence of the failure of the State to take possession of the waste." ***

New York, a State whose residents generate a relatively large share of the Nation's low level radioactive waste, did not join a regional compact. Instead, the State complied with the Act's requirements by enacting legislation providing for the siting and financing of a disposal facility in New York.

*** [A]s the case stands before us, petitioners claim only that the Act is inconsistent with the Tenth Amendment and the Guarantee Clause. *** While no one disputes the proposition that "[t]he Constitution created a Federal Government of limited powers," and while the Tenth Amendment makes explicit that "[t]he powers not delegated to the United States by the Constitution, nor prohibited by it to the States, are reserved to the States respectively, or to the people"; the task of ascertaining the constitutional line between federal and state power has given rise to many of the Court's most difficult and celebrated cases. At least as far back as *Martin v. Hunter's Lessee*, 1 Wheat. 304, 324 (1816), the Court has resolved questions "of great importance and delicacy" in determining whether particular sovereign powers have been granted by the Constitution to the Federal Government or have been retained by the States.

These questions can be viewed in either of two ways. In some cases the Court has inquired whether an Act of Congress is authorized by one of the powers delegated to Congress in Article I of the Constitution. In other cases the Court has sought to determine whether an Act of Congress invades the province of state sovereignty reserved by the Tenth Amendment. *See, e.g., Garcia v. San Antonio Metropolitan Transit Authority*, 469 U.S. 528 (1985). In a case like this one, involving the division of authority between federal and state governments, the two inquiries are mirror images of each other. If a power is delegated to Congress in the Constitution, the Tenth Amendment expressly disclaims any reservation of that power to the States; if a power is an attribute of state sovereignty reserved by the Tenth Amendment, it is necessarily a power the Constitution has not conferred on Congress.

*** Congress exercises its conferred powers subject to the limitations contained in the Constitution. Thus, for example, under the Commerce Clause Congress may regulate publishers engaged in interstate commerce, but Congress is constrained in the exercise of that power by the First Amendment. The Tenth Amendment likewise restrains the power of Congress, but this limit is not derived from the text of the Tenth Amendment itself, which is essentially a tautology. Instead, the Tenth Amendment confirms that the power of the Federal Government is subject to limits that may, in a given instance, reserve power to the States. The Tenth Amendment thus directs us to determine whether an incident of state sovereignty is protected by a limitation on an Article I power.

The benefits of this federal structure have been extensively catalogued elsewhere, but they need not concern us here. Our task would be the same even if one could prove that federalism secured no advantages to anyone. It consists not of devising our preferred system of government, but of understanding and applying the framework set forth in the Constitution. "The question is not what power the Federal Government ought to have but what powers in fact have been given by the people." *United States v. Butler*, 297 U.S. 1, 63 (1936).

This framework has been sufficiently flexible over the past two centuries to allow for enormous changes in the nature of government. The Federal Government undertakes activities today that would have been unimaginable to the Framers in two senses; first, because the Framers would not have conceived that any government would conduct such activities; and second, because the Framers would not have believed that the Federal Government, rather than the States, would assume such responsibilities. Yet the powers conferred upon the Federal Government by the Constitution were phrased in language broad enough to allow for the expansion of the Federal Government's role. Among the provisions of the Constitution that have been particularly important in this regard, three concern us here [the Commerce Clause, the General Welfare Clause, and the Supremacy Clause]. ***

The actual scope of the Federal Government's authority with respect to the States has changed over the years, therefore, but the constitutional structure underlying and limiting that authority has not. In the end, just as a cup may be half empty or half full, it makes no difference whether one views the question at issue in this case as one of ascertaining the limits of the power delegated to the Federal Government under the affirmative provisions of the Constitution or one of discerning the core of sovereignty retained by the States under the Tenth Amendment. Either way, we must determine whether any of the three challenged provisions of the Low–Level Radioactive Waste Policy Amendments Act of 1985 oversteps the boundary between federal and state authority.

Petitioners do not contend that Congress lacks the power to regulate the disposal of low level radioactive waste. *** *Cf. Philadelphia v. New Jersey*, 437 U.S. 617. Petitioners likewise do not dispute that under the Supremacy Clause Congress could, if it wished, pre-empt state radioactive waste regulation. Petitioners contend only that the Tenth Amendment limits the power of Congress to regulate in the way it has chosen.

Most of our recent cases interpreting the Tenth Amendment have concerned the authority of Congress to subject state governments to generally applicable laws. *** This case presents no occasion to apply or revisit the holdings of any of these cases, as this is not a case in which Congress has subjected a State to the same legislation applicable to private parties.

This case instead concerns the circumstances under which Congress may use the States as implements of regulation; that is, whether Congress may direct or otherwise motivate the States to regulate in a particular field or a particular way.

As an initial matter, Congress may not simply "commandee[r] the legislative processes of the States by directly compelling them to enact and enforce a federal regulatory program." *** While Congress has substantial powers to govern the Nation directly, including in areas of intimate concern to the States, the Constitution has never been understood to confer upon Congress the ability to require the States to govern according to Congress' instructions. ***

Indeed, the question whether the Constitution should permit Congress to employ state governments as regulatory agencies was a topic of lively debate among the Framers. Under the Articles of Confederation, Congress lacked the authority in most respects to govern the people directly. *** Alexander Hamilton observed: "The great and radical vice in the construction of the existing Confederation is in the principle of LEGISLATION for STATES or GOVERNMENTS, in their CORPORATE or COLLECTIVE CAPACITIES, and as contra-distinguished from the INDIVIDUALS of whom they consist." The Federalist No. 15.

In the end, the [Constitutional] Convention opted for a Constitution in which Congress would exercise its legislative authority directly over individuals rather than over States. This choice was made clear to the subsequent state ratifying conventions. Oliver Ellsworth, a member of the Connecticut delegation in Philadelphia, explained the distinction to his State's convention: "This Constitution does not attempt to coerce sovereign bodies, states, in their political capacity. *** But this legal coercion singles out the *** individual." 2 J. Elliot, Debates on the Federal Constitution 197 (2d ed. 1863). ***

In providing for a stronger central government, therefore, the Framers explicitly chose a Constitution that confers upon Congress the power to regulate individuals, not States. We have always understood that even where Congress has the authority under the Constitution to pass laws requiring or prohibiting certain acts, it lacks the power directly to compel the States to require or prohibit those acts. The allocation of power contained in the Commerce Clause, for example, authorizes Congress to regulate interstate commerce directly; it does not authorize Congress to regulate state governments' regulation of interstate commerce.

This is not to say that Congress lacks the ability to encourage a State to regulate in a particular way, or that Congress may not hold out incentives to the States as a method of influencing a State's policy choices. Our cases have identified a variety of methods, short of outright coercion, by which Congress may urge a State to adopt a legislative program consistent with federal interests. Two of these methods are of particular relevance here.

First, under Congress' spending power, "Congress may attach conditions on the receipt of federal funds." *South Dakota v. Dole*, 483 U.S., at 206. *** Second, where Congress has the authority to regulate private activity under the Commerce Clause, we have recognized Congress' power to offer States the choice of regulating that activity according to federal standards or having state law pre-empted by federal regulation. This arrangement, which has been termed "a program of cooperative federalism," is replicated in numerous federal statutory schemes.

*** Where Congress encourages state regulation rather than compelling it, state governments remain responsive to the local electorate's preferences; state officials remain accountable to the people.

By contrast, where the Federal Government compels States to regulate, the accountability of both state and federal officials is diminished. If the citizens of New York, for example, do not consider that making provision for the disposal of radioactive waste is in their best interest, they may elect state officials who share their view. That view can always be preempted under the Supremacy Clause if it is contrary to the national view, but in such a case it is the Federal Government that makes the decision in full view of the public, and it will be federal officials that suffer the consequences if the decision turns out to be detrimental or unpopular. But where the Federal Government directs the States to regulate, it may be state officials who will bear the brunt of public disapproval, while the federal officials who devised the regulatory program may remain insulated from the electoral ramifications of their decision. Accountability is thus diminished when, due to federal coercion, elected state officials cannot regulate in accordance with the views of the local electorate in matters not preempted by federal regulation. ***

[The Court then turned to the challenged incentives, upholding the first two.] *** The take title provision is of a different character. This third so-called "incentive" offers States, as an alternative to regulating pursuant to Congress' direction, the option of taking title to and possession of the low level radioactive waste generated within their borders and becoming liable for all damages waste generators suffer as a result of the States' failure to do so promptly. In this provision, Congress has crossed the line distinguishing encouragement from coercion.

The take title provision offers state governments a "choice" of either accepting ownership of waste or regulating according to the instructions of Congress. On one hand, the Constitution would not permit Congress simply to transfer radioactive waste from generators to state governments. Such a forced transfer, standing alone, would in principle be no different than a congressionally compelled subsidy from state governments to radioactive waste producers. The same is true of the provision requiring the States to become liable for the generators' damages. Standing alone, this provision would be indistinguishable from an Act of Congress directing the States to assume the liabilities of certain state residents. Either type of federal action would "commandeer" state governments into the service of federal regulatory purposes, and would for this reason be inconsistent with the Constitution's division of authority between federal and state governments. On the other hand, the second alternative held out to state governments—regulating pursuant to Congress' direction—would, standing alone, present a simple command to state governments to implement legislation enacted by Congress. As we have seen, the Constitution does not empower Congress to subject state governments to this type of instruction.

Because an instruction to state governments to take title to waste, standing alone, would be beyond the authority of Congress, and because a direct order to regulate, standing alone, would also be beyond the authority of

Congress, it follows that Congress lacks the power to offer the States a choice between the two. Unlike the first two sets of incentives, the take title incentive does not represent the conditional exercise of any congressional power enumerated in the Constitution. In this provision, Congress has not held out the threat of exercising its spending power or its commerce power; it has instead held out the threat, should the States not regulate according to one federal instruction, of simply forcing the States to submit to another federal instruction. A choice between two unconstitutionally coercive regulatory techniques is no choice at all. Either way, "the Act commandeers the legislative processes of the States by directly compelling them to enact and enforce a federal regulatory program," an outcome that has never been understood to lie within the authority conferred upon Congress by the Constitution.

Respondents emphasize the latitude given to the States to implement Congress' plan. The Act enables the States to regulate pursuant to Congress' instructions in any number of different ways. States may avoid taking title by contracting with sited regional compacts, by building a disposal site alone or as part of a compact, or by permitting private parties to build a disposal site. States that host sites may employ a wide range of designs and disposal methods, subject only to broad federal regulatory limits. This line of reasoning, however, only underscores the critical alternative a State lacks: A State may not decline to administer the federal program. No matter which path the State chooses, it must follow the direction of Congress.

The take title provision appears to be unique. No other federal statute has been cited which offers a state government no option other than that of implementing legislation enacted by Congress. Whether one views the take title provision as lying outside Congress' enumerated powers, or as infringing upon the core of state sovereignty reserved by the Tenth Amendment, the provision is inconsistent with the federal structure of our Government established by the Constitution. ***

The United States proposes three alternative views of the constitutional line separating state and federal authority. *** First, the United States argues that the Constitution's prohibition of congressional directives to state governments can be overcome where the federal interest is sufficiently important to justify state submission. This argument contains a kernel of truth: In determining whether the Tenth Amendment limits the ability of Congress to subject state governments to generally applicable laws, the Court has in some cases stated that it will evaluate the strength of federal interests in light of the degree to which such laws would prevent the State from functioning as a sovereign, that is, the extent to which such generally applicable laws would impede a state government's responsibility to represent and be accountable to the citizens of the State. *** But whether or not a particularly strong federal interest enables Congress to bring state governments within the orbit of generally applicable federal regulation, no Member of the Court has ever suggested that such a federal interest would enable Congress to command a state government to enact state regulation. No matter how powerful the federal interest involved, the Constitution simply does not give Congress the authority to require the States to regulate. The Constitution instead gives Congress the authority to regulate matters directly and to pre-empt contrary state regulation. Where a federal interest is sufficiently strong to cause Congress to legislate, it must do so directly; it may not conscript state governments as its agents.

Second, the United States argues that the Constitution does, in some circumstances, permit federal directives to state governments. Various cases are cited for this proposition, but none support it. Some of these cases discuss the well established power of Congress to pass laws enforceable in state courts. These cases involve no more than an application of the Supremacy Clause's provision that federal law "shall be the supreme Law of the Land," enforceable in every State. More to the point, all involve congressional regulation of individuals, not congressional requirements that States regulate. Federal statutes enforceable in state courts do, in a sense, direct state judges to enforce them, but this sort of federal "direction" of state judges is mandated by the text of the Supremacy Clause. No comparable constitutional provision authorizes Congress to command state legislatures to legislate. ***

Third, the United States argues that the Constitution envisions a role for Congress as an arbiter of interstate disputes. The United States observes that federal courts, and this Court in particular, have frequently resolved conflicts among States. Many of these disputes have involved the allocation of shared resources among the States, a category perhaps broad enough to encompass the allocation of scarce disposal space for radioactive waste. The United States suggests that if the Court may resolve such interstate disputes, Congress can surely do the same under the Commerce Clause. ***

While the Framers no doubt endowed Congress with the power to regulate interstate commerce in order to avoid further instances of the interstate trade disputes that were common under the Articles of Confederation, the Framers did not intend that Congress should exercise that power through the mechanism of mandating state regulation. The Constitution established Congress as "a superintending authority over the reciprocal trade" among the States, The Federalist No. 42, by empowering Congress to regulate that trade directly, not by authorizing Congress to issue trade-related orders to state governments. As Madison and Hamilton explained, "a sovereignty over sovereigns, a government over governments, a legislation for communities, as contradistinguished from individuals, as it is a solecism in theory, so in practice it is subversive of the order and ends of civil polity."

The sited state respondents focus their attention on the process by which the Act was formulated. *** How can a federal statute be found an unconstitutional infringement of state sovereignty when state officials consented to the statute's enactment?

The answer follows from an understanding of the fundamental purpose served by our Government's federal structure. The Constitution does not protect the sovereignty of States for the benefit of the States or state governments as abstract political entities, or even for the benefit of the public officials governing the States. To the contrary, the Constitution divides authority between federal and state governments for the protection of individuals. State sovereignty is not just an end in itself: "Rather, federalism secures to citizens the liberties that derive from the diffusion of sovereign power." *Coleman v. Thompson*, 501 U.S. 722, 759 (1991) (BLACKMUN, J., dissenting). "Just as the separation and independence of the coordinate branches of the Federal Government serves to prevent the accumulation of excessive power in any one branch, a healthy balance of power between the States and the Federal Government will reduce the risk of tyranny and abuse from either front." *Gregory v. Ashcroft*, 501 U.S., at 458.

Where Congress exceeds its authority relative to the States, therefore, the departure from the constitutional plan cannot be ratified by the "consent" of state officials. An analogy to the separation of powers among the branches of the Federal Government clarifies this point. The Constitution's division of power among the three branches is violated where one branch invades the territory of another, whether or not the encroached-upon branch approves the encroachment. The constitutional authority of Congress cannot be expanded by the "consent" of the governmental unit whose domain is thereby narrowed, whether that unit is the Executive Branch or the States.

State officials thus cannot consent to the enlargement of the powers of Congress beyond those enumerated in the Constitution. Indeed, the facts of this case raise the possibility that powerful incentives might lead both federal and state officials to view departures from the federal structure to be in their personal interests. Most citizens recognize the need for radioactive waste disposal sites, but few want sites near their homes. As a result, while it would be well within the authority of either federal or state officials to choose where the disposal sites will be, it is likely to be in the political interest of each individual official to avoid being held accountable to the voters for the choice of location. If a federal official is faced with the alternatives of choosing a location or directing the States to do it, the official may well prefer the latter, as a means of shifting responsibility for the eventual decision. If a state official is faced with the same set of alternatives—choosing a location or having Congress direct the choice of a location—the state official may also prefer the latter, as it may permit the avoidance of personal responsibility. The interests of public officials thus may not coincide with the Constitution's intergovernmental allocation of authority. Where state officials purport to submit to the direction of Congress in this manner, federalism is hardly being advanced. ***

Some truths are so basic that, like the air around us, they are easily overlooked. Much of the Constitution is concerned with setting forth the form of our government, and the courts have traditionally invalidated measures deviating from that form. The result may appear "formalistic" in a given case to partisans of the measure at issue, because such measures are typically the product of the era's perceived necessity. But the Constitution protects us from our own best intentions: It divides power among sovereigns and among branches of government precisely so that we may resist the temptation to concentrate power in one location as an expedient solution to the crisis of the day. The shortage of disposal sites for radioactive waste is a pressing national problem, but a judiciary that licensed extra-constitutional government with each issue of comparable gravity would, in the long run, be far worse.

States are not mere political subdivisions of the United States. State governments are neither regional offices nor administrative agencies of the Federal Government. The positions occupied by state officials appear nowhere on the Federal Government's most detailed organizational chart. The Constitution instead "leaves to the several States a residuary and inviolable sovereignty," The Federalist No. 39, reserved explicitly to the States by the Tenth Amendment.

Whatever the outer limits of that sovereignty may be, one thing is clear: The Federal Government may not compel the States to enact or administer a federal regulatory program. The Constitution permits both the Federal Government and the States to enact legislation regarding the disposal of low level radioactive waste. The Constitution enables the Federal Government to pre-empt state regulation contrary to federal interests, and it permits the Federal Government to hold out incentives to the States as a means of encouraging them to adopt suggested regulatory schemes. It does not, however, authorize Congress simply to direct the States to provide for the disposal of the radioactive waste generated within their borders. While there may be many constitutional methods of achieving regional self-sufficiency in radioactive waste disposal, the method Congress has chosen is not one of them. ***

JUSTICE WHITE, with whom JUSTICE BLACKMUN and JUSTICE STEVENS join, dissenting in part [as to the "take title" holding].

My disagreement with the Court's analysis begins at the basic descriptive level of how the legislation at issue in this case came to be enacted ***. The Low–Level Radioactive Waste Policy Act of 1980, and its amendatory 1985 Act, resulted from the efforts of state leaders to achieve a state-based set of remedies to the waste problem. They sought not federal pre-emption or intervention, but rather congressional sanction of interstate compromises they had reached. *** [T]he 1985 Act was very much the product of cooperative federalism, in which the States bargained among themselves to achieve compromises for Congress to sanction. *** New York's actions subsequent to enactment of the 1980 and 1985 Acts fairly indicate its approval of the interstate agreement process embodied in those laws within the meaning of Art. I, § 10, cl. 3, of the Constitution, which provides that "[n]o State shall, without the Consent of Congress, *** enter into any Agreement or Compact with another State." *** [T]hese statutes are best understood as the products of collective state action, rather than as impositions placed on States by the Federal Government. ***

[S]een as a term of an agreement entered into between the several States, this measure proves to be less constitutionally odious than the Court opines. First, the practical effect of New York's position is that because it is unwilling to honor its obligations to provide in-state storage facilities for its low-level radioactive waste, other States with such plants must accept New York's waste, whether they wish to or not. Otherwise, the many economically and socially beneficial producers of such waste in the State would have to cease their operations. The Court's refusal to force New York to accept responsibility for its own problem inevitably means that some other State's sovereignty will be impinged by it being forced, for public health reasons, to accept New York's low-level radioactive waste. I do not understand the principle of federalism to impede the National Government from acting as referee among the States to prohibit one from bullying another.

Moreover, it is utterly reasonable that, in crafting a delicate compromise between the three overburdened States that provided low-level radioactive waste disposal facilities and the rest of the States, Congress would have to ratify some punitive measure as the ultimate sanction for noncompliance. ***

The Court announces that it has no occasion to revisit such decisions as *Gregory v. Ashcroft*, and *Garcia v. San Antonio Metropolitan Transit Authority*, because "this is not a case in which Congress has subjected a State to the same legislation applicable to private parties." Although this statement sends the welcome signal that the Court does not intend to cut a wide swath through our recent Tenth Amendment precedents, it nevertheless is unpersuasive. ***

The Court's distinction between a federal statute's regulation of States and private parties for general purposes, as opposed to a regulation solely on the activities of States, is unsupported by our recent Tenth Amendment cases. *** Moreover, the Court makes no effort to explain why this purported distinction should affect the analysis of Congress' power under general principles of federalism and the Tenth Amendment. *** An incursion on state sovereignty hardly seems more constitutionally acceptable if the federal statute that "commands" specific action also applies to private parties. The alleged diminution in state authority over its own affairs is not any less because the federal mandate restricts the activities of private parties. ***

*** [T]he more appropriate analysis should flow from *Garcia*, even if this case does not involve a congressional law generally applicable to both States and private parties. In *Garcia*, we stated the proper inquiry: "[W]e are convinced that the fundamental limitation that the constitutional scheme imposes on the Commerce Clause to protect the 'States as States' is one of process rather than one of result. Any substantive restraint on the exercise of Commerce Clause powers must find its justification in the procedural nature of this basic limitation, and it must be tailored to compensate for possible failings in the national political process rather than to dictate a 'sacred province of state autonomy.'" *** We face a crisis of national proportions in the disposal of low-level radioactive waste, and Congress has acceded to the wishes of the States by permitting local decisionmaking rather than imposing a solution from Washington. New York itself participated and supported passage of this legislation at both the gubernatorial and federal representative levels, and then enacted state laws specifically to comply with the deadlines and timetables agreed upon by the States in the 1985 Act. For me, the Court's civics lecture has a decidedly hollow ring at a time when action, rather than rhetoric, is needed to solve a national problem.[3] ***

The ultimate irony of the decision today is that in its formalistically rigid obeisance to "federalism," the Court gives Congress fewer incentives to defer to the wishes of state officials in achieving local solutions to local problems. This legislation was a classic example of Congress acting as arbiter among the States in their attempts to accept responsibility for managing a problem of grave import. The States urged the National Legislature not to impose from Washington a solution to the country's low-level radioactive waste management problems. Instead, they sought a reasonable level of local and regional autonomy consistent with Art. I, § 10, cl. 3, of the Constitution. By invalidating the measure designed to ensure compliance for recalcitrant States, such as New York, the Court upsets the delicate compromise achieved among the States and forces Congress to erect several additional formalistic hurdles to clear before achieving exactly the same objective. ***

JUSTICE STEVENS, concurring in part and dissenting in part.

Under the Articles of Confederation, the Federal Government had the power to issue commands to the States. See Arts. VIII, IX. Because that indirect exercise of federal power proved ineffective, the Framers of the Constitution empowered the Federal Government to exercise legislative authority directly over individuals within the States, even though that direct authority constituted a greater intrusion on state sovereignty. Nothing in that history suggests that the Federal Government may not also impose its will upon the several States as it did under the Articles. The Constitution enhanced, rather than diminished, the power of the Federal Government.

The notion that Congress does not have the power to issue "a simple command to state governments to implement legislation enacted by Congress," is incorrect and unsound. There is no such limitation in the Constitution. *** To the contrary, the Federal Government directs state governments in many realms. The Government regulates state-operated railroads, state school systems, state prisons, state elections, and a host of

---

[3] [I] do not read the majority's many invocations of history to be anything other than elaborate window dressing. *** Moreover, *** the majority's historical analysis has a distinctly wooden quality. One would not know from reading the majority's account, for instance, that the nature of federal-state relations changed fundamentally after the Civil War. That conflict produced in its wake a tremendous expansion in the scope of the Federal Government's law-making authority, so much so that the persons who helped to found the Republic would scarcely have recognized the many added roles the National Government assumed for itself. Moreover, the majority fails to mention the New Deal era, in which the Court recognized the enormous growth in Congress' power under the Commerce Clause. While I believe we should not be blind to history, neither should we read it so selectively as to restrict the proper scope of Congress' powers under Article I, especially when the history not mentioned by the majority fully supports a more expansive understanding of the legislature's authority than may have existed in the late 18th century. Given the scanty textual support for the majority's position, it would be far more sensible to defer to a coordinate branch of government in its decision to devise a solution to a national problem of this kind. Certainly in other contexts, principles of federalism have not insulated States from mandates by the National Government. The Court has upheld statutes that impose clear directives on state officials *** pursuant to the extradition clause [and]the post-Civil War Amendments, as well as congressional statutes that require state courts to hear certain actions.

other state functions. Similarly, there can be no doubt that, in time of war, Congress could either draft soldiers itself or command the States to supply their quotas of troops. I see no reason why Congress may not also command the States to enforce federal water and air quality standards or federal standards for the disposition of low-level radioactive wastes. ***

PRINTZ v. UNITED STATES
521 U.S. 898, 117 S.Ct. 2365, 138 L.Ed.2d 914 (1997).

JUSTICE SCALIA delivered the opinion of the Court.

The question presented in these cases is whether certain interim provisions of the Brady Handgun Violence Prevention Act, commanding state and local law enforcement officers to conduct background checks on prospective handgun purchasers and to perform certain related tasks, violate the Constitution.

I

The Gun Control Act of 1968 (GCA) establishes a detailed federal scheme governing the distribution of firearms. It prohibits firearms dealers from transferring handguns to any person under 21, not resident in the dealer's State, or prohibited by state or local law from purchasing or possessing firearms. It also forbids possession of a firearm by, and transfer of a firearm to, convicted felons, fugitives from justice, unlawful users of controlled substances, persons adjudicated as mentally defective or committed to mental institutions, aliens unlawfully present in the United States, persons dishonorably discharged from the Armed Forces, persons who have renounced their citizenship, and persons who have been subjected to certain restraining orders or been convicted of a misdemeanor offense involving domestic violence.

In 1993, Congress amended the GCA by enacting the Brady Act. The Act requires the Attorney General to establish a national instant background check system by November 30, 1998 and immediately puts in place certain interim provisions until that system becomes operative. Under the interim provisions, a firearms dealer who proposes to transfer a handgun must first: (1) receive from the transferee a statement (the Brady Form), containing the name, address and date of birth of the proposed transferee along with a sworn statement that the transferee is not among any of the classes of prohibited purchasers; (2) verify the identity of the transferee by examining an identification document; and (3) provide the "chief law enforcement officer" (CLEO) of the transferee's residence with notice of the contents (and a copy) of the Brady Form. With some exceptions, the dealer must then wait five business days before consummating the sale, unless the CLEO earlier notifies the dealer that he has no reason to believe the transfer would be illegal.

The Brady Act creates two significant alternatives to the foregoing scheme. A dealer may sell a handgun immediately if the purchaser possesses a state handgun permit issued after a background check, or if state law provides for an instant background check. In States that have not rendered one of these alternatives applicable to all gun purchasers, CLEOs are required to perform certain duties. When a CLEO receives the required notice of a proposed transfer from the firearms dealer, the CLEO must "make a reasonable effort to ascertain within 5 business days whether receipt or possession would be in violation of the law, including research in whatever State and local recordkeeping systems are available and in a national system designated by the Attorney General." The Act does not require the CLEO to take any particular action if he determines that a pending transaction would be unlawful; he may notify the firearms dealer to that effect, but is not required to do so. If, however, the CLEO notifies a gun dealer that a prospective purchaser is ineligible to receive a handgun, he must, upon request, provide the would-be purchaser with a written statement of the reasons for that determination. Moreover, if the CLEO does not discover any basis for objecting to the sale, he must destroy any records in his possession relating to the transfer, including his copy of the Brady Form. Under a separate provision of the GCA, any person who "knowingly violates [the section of the GCA amended by the Brady Act] shall be fined under this title, imprisoned for no more than 1 year, or both."

Petitioners Jay Printz and Richard Mack, the CLEOs for Ravalli County, Montana, and Graham County, Arizona, respectively, filed separate actions challenging the constitutionality of the Brady Act's interim provisions. ***

II

From the description set forth above, it is apparent that the Brady Act purports to direct state law enforcement officers to participate, albeit only temporarily, in the administration of a federally enacted regulatory scheme. Regulated firearms dealers are required to forward Brady Forms not to a federal officer or employee, but to the CLEOs, whose obligation to accept those forms is implicit in the duty imposed upon them to make "reasonable efforts" within five days to determine whether the sales reflected in the forms are lawful. While the CLEOs are subjected to no federal requirement that they prevent the sales determined to be unlawful (it is perhaps assumed that their state-law duties will require prevention or apprehension), they are empowered to grant, in effect, waivers of the federally prescribed 5–day waiting period for handgun purchases by notifying the gun dealers that they have no reason to believe the transactions would be illegal.

The petitioners here object to being pressed into federal service, and contend that congressional action compelling state officers to execute federal laws is unconstitutional. Because there is no constitutional text speaking to this precise question, the answer to the CLEOs' challenge must be sought in historical understanding and practice, in the structure of the Constitution, and in the jurisprudence of this Court. We treat those three sources, in that order, in this and the next two sections of this opinion.

Petitioners contend that compelled enlistment of state executive officers for the administration of federal programs is, until very recent years at least, unprecedented. The Government contends, to the contrary, that "the earliest

Congresses enacted statutes that required the participation of state officials in the implementation of federal laws." The Government's contention demands our careful consideration, since early congressional enactments "provid[e] 'contemporaneous and weighty evidence' of the Constitution's meaning," ***.

These early laws establish, at most, that the Constitution was originally understood to permit imposition of an obligation on state judges to enforce federal prescriptions, insofar as those prescriptions related to matters appropriate for the judicial power. That assumption was perhaps implicit in one of the provisions of the Constitution, and was explicit in another. In accord with the so-called Madisonian Compromise, Article III, § 1, established only a Supreme Court, and made the creation of lower federal courts optional with the Congress—even though it was obvious that the Supreme Court alone could not hear all federal cases throughout the United States. And the Supremacy Clause, Art. VI, cl. 2, announced that "the Laws of the United States *** shall be the supreme Law of the Land; and the Judges in every State shall be bound thereby." It is understandable why courts should have been viewed distinctively in this regard; unlike legislatures and executives, they applied the law of other sovereigns all the time. The principle underlying so-called "transitory" causes of action was that laws which operated elsewhere created obligations in justice that courts of the forum state would enforce. The Constitution itself, in the Full Faith and Credit Clause, Art. IV, § 1, generally required such enforcement with respect to obligations arising in other States.

For these reasons, we do not think the early statutes imposing obligations on state courts imply a power of Congress to impress the state executive into its service. *** The only early federal law the Government has brought to our attention that imposed duties on state executive officers is the Extradition Act of 1793, which required the "executive authority" of a State to cause the arrest and delivery of a fugitive from justice upon the request of the executive authority of the State from which the fugitive had fled. That was in direct implementation, however, of the Extradition Clause of the Constitution itself, see Art. IV, § 2.

Not only do the enactments of the early Congresses, as far as we are aware, contain no evidence of an assumption that the Federal Government may command the States' executive power in the absence of a particularized constitutional authorization, they contain some indication of precisely the opposite assumption. On September 23, 1789—the day before its proposal of the Bill of Rights, see 1 Annals of Congress 912–913—the First Congress *** "recommended to the legislatures of the several States to pass laws, making it expressly the duty of the keepers of their goals, to receive and safe keep therein all prisoners committed under the authority of the United States," and offered to pay 50 cents per month for each prisoner. Moreover, when Georgia refused to comply with the request, Congress's only reaction was a law authorizing the marshal in any State that failed to comply with the Recommendation of September 23, 1789, to rent a temporary jail until provision for a permanent one could be made.

*** To complete the historical record, we must note that there is not only an absence of executive-commandeering statutes in the early Congresses, but there is an absence of them in our later history as well, at least until very recent years. [The Court distinguishes these statutes as authorizing rather than commanding local enforcement of federal law.] *** The Government points to a number of federal statutes enacted within the past few decades that require the participation of state or local officials in implementing federal regulatory schemes. *** Their persuasive force is far outweighed by almost two centuries of apparent congressional avoidance of the practice. Compare *INS v. Chadha*, 462 U.S. 919 (1983), in which the legislative veto, though enshrined in perhaps hundreds of federal statutes, most of which were enacted in the 1970's and the earliest of which was enacted in 1932, was nonetheless held unconstitutional.

III

The constitutional practice we have examined above tends to negate the existence of the congressional power asserted here, but is not conclusive. We turn next to consideration of the structure of the Constitution, to see if we can discern among its "essential postulate[s]" a principle that controls the present cases.

It is incontestible that the Constitution established a system of "dual sovereignty." *** The Framers' experience under the Articles of Confederation had persuaded them that using the States as the instruments of federal governance was both ineffectual and provocative of federal-state conflict. Preservation of the States as independent political entities being the price of union, and "[t]he practicality of making laws, with coercive sanctions, for the States as political bodies" having been, in Madison's words, "exploded on all hands," 2 Records of the Federal Convention of 1787, p. 9 (M. Farrand ed.1911), the Framers rejected the concept of a central government that would act upon and through the States, and instead designed a system in which the state and federal governments would exercise concurrent authority over the people—who were, in Hamilton's words, "the only proper objects of government," The Federalist No. 15, at 109. We have set forth the historical record in more detail elsewhere, see *New York v. United States*, and need not repeat it here. It suffices to repeat the conclusion: "The Framers explicitly chose a Constitution that confers upon Congress the power to regulate individuals, not States." The great innovation of this design was that "our citizens would have two political capacities, one state and one federal, each protected from incursion by the other"—"a legal system unprecedented in form and design, establishing two orders of government, each with its own direct relationship, its own privity, its own set of mutual rights and obligations to the people who sustain it and are governed by it." *U.S. Term Limits, Inc. v. Thornton*, 514 U.S. 779, 838 (1995) (KENNEDY, J., concurring). The Constitution thus contemplates that a State's government will represent and remain accountable to its own citizens. *** The power of the Federal Government would be augmented immeasurably if it were able to impress into its service—and at no cost to itself—the police officers of the 50 States.

We have thus far discussed the effect that federal control of state officers would have upon the first element of the "double security" alluded to by Madison: the division of power between State and Federal Governments. It would also have an effect upon the second element: the separation and equilibration of powers between the three branches of the Federal Government itself. The Constitution does not leave to speculation who is to administer the laws enacted by Congress; the President, it says, "shall take Care that the Laws be faithfully executed," Art. II, § 3, personally and through officers whom he appoints (save for such inferior officers as Congress may authorize to be appointed by the "Courts of Law" or by "the Heads of Departments" who are themselves presidential appointees), Art. II, § 2. The Brady Act effectively transfers this responsibility to thousands of CLEOs in the 50 States, who are left to implement the program without meaningful Presidential control (if indeed meaningful Presidential control is possible without the power to appoint and remove). The insistence of the Framers upon unity in the Federal Executive—to insure both vigor and accountability—is well known. That unity would be shattered, and the power of the President would be subject to reduction, if Congress could act as effectively without the President as with him, by simply requiring state officers to execute its laws.

The dissent of course resorts to the last, best hope of those who defend ultra vires congressional action, the Necessary and Proper Clause. *** What destroys the dissent's Necessary and Proper Clause argument, however, is not the Tenth Amendment but the Necessary and Proper Clause itself. When a "La[w] *** for carrying into Execution" the Commerce Clause violates the principle of state sovereignty reflected in the various constitutional provisions we mentioned earlier, it is not a "La[w] *** proper for carrying into Execution the Commerce Clause," and is thus, in the words of The Federalist, "merely [an] ac[t] of usurpation" which "deserve[s] to be treated as such." We in fact answered the dissent's Necessary and Proper Clause argument in *New York*: "[E]ven where Congress has the authority under the Constitution to pass laws requiring or prohibiting certain acts, it lacks the power directly to compel the States to require or prohibit those acts *** . [T]he Commerce Clause, for example, authorizes Congress to regulate interstate commerce directly; it does not authorize Congress to regulate state governments' regulation of interstate commerce."

The dissent perceives a simple answer in that portion of Article VI which requires that "all executive and judicial Officers, both of the United States and of the several States, shall be bound by Oath or Affirmation, to support this Constitution," arguing that by virtue of the Supremacy Clause this makes "not only the Constitution, but every law enacted by Congress as well," binding on state officers, including laws requiring state-officer enforcement. The Supremacy Clause, however, makes "Law of the Land" only "Laws of the United States which shall be made in Pursuance [of the Constitution]"; so the Supremacy Clause merely brings us back to the question discussed earlier, whether laws conscripting state officers violate state sovereignty and are thus not in accord with the Constitution.

IV

Finally, and most conclusively in the present litigation, we turn to the prior jurisprudence of this Court. *** The Government contends that *New York* is distinguishable on the following ground: unlike the "take title" provisions invalidated there, the background-check provision of the Brady Act does not require state legislative or executive officials to make policy, but instead issues a final directive to state CLEOs. *** The Government's distinction between "making" law and merely "enforcing" it, between "policymaking" and mere "implementation," is an interesting one. It is perhaps not meant to be the same as, but it is surely reminiscent of, the line that separates proper congressional conferral of Executive power from unconstitutional delegation of legislative authority for federal separation-of-powers purposes. See *A.L.A. Schechter Poultry Corp. v. United States*, 295 U.S. 495, 530 (1935); *Panama Refining Co. v. Ryan*, 293 U.S. 388, 428–429 (1935). This Court has not been notably successful in describing the latter line; indeed, some think we have abandoned the effort to do so. *** We are doubtful that the new line the Government proposes would be any more distinct. Executive action that has utterly no policymaking component is rare, particularly at an executive level as high as a jurisdiction's chief law-enforcement officer. Is it really true that there is no policymaking involved in deciding, for example, what "reasonable efforts" shall be expended to conduct a background check? It may well satisfy the Act for a CLEO to direct that (a) no background checks will be conducted that divert personnel time from pending felony investigations, and (b) no background check will be permitted to consume more than one-half hour of an officer's time. But nothing in the Act requires a CLEO to be so parsimonious; diverting at least some felony-investigation time, and permitting at least some background checks beyond one-half hour would certainly not be unreasonable. Is this decision whether to devote maximum "reasonable efforts" or minimum "reasonable efforts" not preeminently a matter of policy? It is quite impossible, in short, to draw the Government's proposed line at "no policymaking," and we would have to fall back upon a line of "not too much policymaking." How much is too much is not likely to be answered precisely; and an imprecise barrier against federal intrusion upon state authority is not likely to be an effective one.

Even assuming, moreover, that the Brady Act leaves no "policymaking" discretion with the States, we fail to see how that improves rather than worsens the intrusion upon state sovereignty. Preservation of the States as independent and autonomous political entities is arguably less undermined by requiring them to make policy in certain fields than (as Judge Sneed aptly described it over two decades ago) by "reduc[ing] [them] to puppets of a ventriloquist Congress," *Brown v. EPA*, 521 F.2d, at 839. It is an essential attribute of the States' retained sovereignty that they remain independent and autonomous within their proper sphere of authority. It is no more compatible with this independence and autonomy that their officers be "dragooned" into administering federal law, than it would be compatible with the independence and autonomy of the United States that its officers be impressed into service for the execution of state laws. ***

The Government also maintains that requiring state officers to perform discrete, ministerial tasks specified by Congress does not violate the principle of *New York* because it does not diminish the accountability of state or federal officials. This argument fails even on its own terms. By forcing state governments to absorb the financial burden of implementing a federal regulatory program, Members of Congress can take credit for "solving" problems without having to ask their constituents to pay for the solutions with higher federal taxes. And even when the States are not forced to absorb the costs of implementing a federal program, they are still put in the position of taking the blame for its burdensomeness and for its defects. Under the present law, for example, it will be the CLEO and not some federal official who stands between the gun purchaser and immediate possession of his gun. And it will likely be the CLEO, not some federal official, who will be blamed for any error (even one in the designated federal database) that causes a purchaser to be mistakenly rejected.

The dissent makes no attempt to defend the Government's basis for distinguishing *New York*, but instead advances what seems to us an even more implausible theory. The Brady Act, the dissent asserts, is different from the "take title" provisions invalidated in *New York* because the former is addressed to individuals—namely CLEOs—while the latter were directed to the State itself. That is certainly a difference, but it cannot be a constitutionally significant one. While the Brady Act is directed to "individuals," it is directed to them in their official capacities as state officers; it controls their actions, not as private citizens, but as the agents of the State. *** To say that the Federal Government cannot control the State, but can control all of its officers, is to say nothing of significance.[15] Indeed, it merits the description "empty formalistic reasoning of the highest order." By resorting to this, the dissent not so much distinguishes *New York* as disembowels it.

Finally, the Government puts forward a cluster of arguments that can be grouped under the heading: "The Brady Act serves very important purposes, is most efficiently administered by CLEOs during the interim period, and places a minimal and only temporary burden upon state officers." There is considerable disagreement over the extent of the burden, but we need not pause over that detail. Assuming all the mentioned factors were true, *** [i]t is the very principle of separate state sovereignty that such a law offends, and no comparative assessment of the various interests can overcome that fundamental defect. *** The mandatory obligation imposed on CLEOs to perform background checks on prospective handgun purchasers plainly runs afoul of that rule.

---

[15] Contrary to the dissent's suggestion, the distinction in our Eleventh Amendment jurisprudence between States and municipalities is of no relevance here. We long ago made clear that the distinction is peculiar to the question of whether a governmental entity is entitled to Eleventh Amendment sovereign immunity; we have refused to apply it to the question of whether a governmental entity is protected by the Constitution's guarantees of federalism, including the Tenth Amendment.

V

What we have said makes it clear enough that the central obligation imposed upon CLEOs by the interim provisions of the Brady Act—the obligation to "make a reasonable effort to ascertain within 5 business days whether receipt or possession [of a handgun] would be in violation of the law, including research in whatever State and local recordkeeping systems are available and in a national system designated by the Attorney General,"—is unconstitutional. Extinguished with it, of course, is the duty implicit in the background-check requirement that the CLEO accept notice of the contents of, and a copy of, the completed Brady Form, which the firearms dealer is required to provide to him.

Petitioners also challenge, however, two other provisions of the Act: (1) the requirement that any CLEO "to whom a [Brady Form] is transmitted" destroy the form and any record containing information derived from it, and (2) the requirement that any CLEO who "determines that an individual is ineligible to receive a handgun" provide the would-be purchaser, upon request, a written statement of the reasons for that determination. With the background-check and implicit receipt-of-forms requirements invalidated, however, these provisions require no action whatsoever on the part of the CLEO. *** [Other] provisions burden only firearms dealers and purchasers, and no plaintiff in either of those categories is before us here. We decline to speculate regarding the rights and obligations of parties not before the Court. ***

We held in *New York* that Congress cannot compel the States to enact or enforce a federal regulatory program. Today we hold that Congress cannot circumvent that prohibition by conscripting the State's officers directly. The Federal Government may neither issue directives requiring the States to address particular problems, nor command the States' officers, or those of their political subdivisions, to administer or enforce a federal regulatory program. It matters not whether policymaking is involved, and no case-by-case weighing of the burdens or benefits is necessary; such commands are fundamentally incompatible with our constitutional system of dual sovereignty. Accordingly, the judgment of the Court of Appeals for the Ninth Circuit is reversed.

JUSTICE O'CONNOR, concurring. [omitted]

JUSTICE THOMAS, concurring.

*** In my "revisionist" view, the Federal Government's authority under the Commerce Clause, which merely allocates to Congress the power "to regulate Commerce *** among the several states," does not extend to the regulation of wholly *intra* state, point-of-sale transactions. See *United States v. Lopez*. *** Even if we construe Congress' authority to regulate interstate commerce to encompass those intrastate transactions that "substantially affect" interstate commerce, I question whether Congress can regulate the particular transactions at issue here. The Constitution, in addition to delegating certain enumerated powers to Congress, places whole areas outside the reach of Congress' regulatory authority. *** If [ ] the Second

Amendment is read to confer a *personal* right to "keep and bear arms," a colorable argument exists that the Federal Government's regulatory scheme, at least as it pertains to the purely intrastate sale or possession of firearms, runs afoul of that Amendment's protections. ***

JUSTICE STEVENS, with whom JUSTICE SOUTER, JUSTICE GINSBURG, and JUSTICE BREYER join, dissenting.

When Congress exercises the powers delegated to it by the Constitution, it may impose affirmative obligations on executive and judicial officers of state and local governments as well as ordinary citizens. *** These cases do not implicate the more difficult questions associated with congressional coercion of state legislatures ***. The question is whether Congress, acting on behalf of the people of the entire Nation, may require local law enforcement officers to perform certain duties during the interim needed for the development of a federal gun control program. It is remarkably similar to the question, heavily debated by the Framers of the Constitution, whether the Congress could require state agents to collect federal taxes. ***

Indeed, since the ultimate issue is one of power, we must consider its implications in times of national emergency. Matters such as the enlistment of air raid wardens, the administration of a military draft, the mass inoculation of children to forestall an epidemic, or perhaps the threat of an international terrorist, may require a national response before federal personnel can be made available to respond. If the Constitution empowers Congress and the President to make an appropriate response, is there anything in the Tenth Amendment, "in historical understanding and practice, in the structure of the Constitution, [or] in the jurisprudence of this Court," that forbids the enlistment of state officers to make that response effective? More narrowly, what basis is there in any of those sources for concluding that it is the Members of this Court, rather than the elected representatives of the people, who should determine whether the Constitution contains the unwritten rule that the Court announces today? *** There is not a clause, sentence, or paragraph in the entire text of the Constitution of the United States that supports the proposition that a local police officer can ignore a command contained in a statute enacted by Congress pursuant to an express delegation of power enumerated in Article I.

Under the Articles of Confederation the National Government had the power to issue commands to the several sovereign states, but it had no authority to govern individuals directly. *** That method of governing proved to be unacceptable, not because it demeaned the sovereign character of the several States, but rather because it was cumbersome and inefficient. *** Hamilton made clear that the new Constitution, "by extending the authority of the federal head to the individual citizens of the several States, will enable the government to employ the ordinary magistracy of each, in the execution of its laws." The Federalist No. 27, at 180. Hamilton's meaning was unambiguous; the federal government was to have the power to demand that local officials implement national policy programs. As he went on to explain: "It is easy to perceive that this will tend to destroy, in the common apprehension, all distinction between the sources from which [the state and federal governments] might proceed; and will give the federal government the same advantage for securing a due obedience to its authority which is enjoyed by the government of each State."

More specifically, during the debates concerning the ratification of the Constitution, it was assumed that state agents would act as tax collectors for the federal government. *** Bereft of support in the history of the founding, the Court rests its conclusion on the claim that there is little evidence the National Government actually exercised such a power in the early years of the Republic. This reasoning is misguided in principle and in fact. *** [W]e have never suggested that the failure of the early Congresses to address the scope of federal power in a particular area or to exercise a particular authority was an argument against its existence. That position, if correct, would undermine most of our post-New Deal Commerce Clause jurisprudence. *** More importantly, the fact that Congress did elect to rely on state judges and the clerks of state courts to perform a variety of executive functions is surely evidence of a contemporary understanding that their status as state officials did not immunize them from federal service. The majority's description of these early statutes is both incomplete and at times misleading. ***

The Court's "structural" arguments are not sufficient to rebut that presumption. The fact that the Framers intended to preserve the sovereignty of the several States simply does not speak to the question whether individual state employees may be required to perform federal obligations, such as registering young adults for the draft, creating state emergency response commissions designed to manage the release of hazardous substances, collecting and reporting data on underground storage tanks that may pose an environmental hazard, and reporting traffic fatalities, and missing children to a federal agency.

As we explained in *Garcia*: "[T]he principal means chosen by the Framers to ensure the role of the States in the federal system lies in the structure of the Federal Government itself. It is no novelty to observe that the composition of the Federal Government was designed in large part to protect the States from overreaching by Congress." Given the fact that the Members of Congress are elected by the people of the several States, with each State receiving an equivalent number of Senators in order to ensure that even the smallest States have a powerful voice in the legislature, it is quite unrealistic to assume that they will ignore the sovereignty concerns of their constituents. ***

Perversely, the majority's rule seems more likely to damage than to preserve the safeguards against tyranny provided by the existence of vital state governments. By limiting the ability of the Federal Government to enlist state officials in the implementation of its programs, the Court creates incentives for the National Government to aggrandize itself. In the name of State's rights, the majority would have the Federal Government create vast national bureaucracies to implement its policies. ***

Finally, the Court advises us that the "prior jurisprudence of this Court" is the most conclusive support for its position. That "prior jurisprudence" is *New York v. United States*. *** The "take title" provision at issue in New York was beyond Congress' authority to enact because it was "in principle *** no different than a congressionally compelled subsidy from state governments to radioactive waste producers," almost certainly a legislative act. *** [I]t is hard to characterize the minimal requirement that CLEOs perform background checks as one involving the exercise of substantial policymaking discretion on that essentially legislative scale. *** [T]he majority asserts that the difference between a federal command addressed to individuals and one addressed to the State itself "cannot be a constitutionally significant one." But as I have already noted, there is abundant authority in our Eleventh Amendment jurisprudence recognizing a constitutional distinction between local government officials, such as the CLEO's who brought this action, and State entities that are entitled to sovereign immunity. To my knowledge, no one has previously thought that the distinction "disembowels," the Eleventh Amendment.[28] ***

The provision of the Brady Act that crosses the Court's newly defined constitutional threshold is more comparable to a statute requiring local police officers to report the identity of missing children to the Crime Control Center of the Department of Justice than to an offensive federal command to a sovereign state. If Congress believes that such a statute will benefit the people of the Nation, and serve the interests of cooperative federalism better than an enlarged federal bureaucracy, we should respect both its policy judgment and its appraisal of its constitutional power. ***

JUSTICE SOUTER, dissenting. [omitted]

JUSTICE BREYER, with whom JUSTICE STEVENS joins, dissenting.

I would add to the reasons JUSTICE STEVENS sets forth the fact that the United States is not the only nation that seeks to reconcile the practical need for a central authority with the democratic virtues of more local control. At least some other countries, facing the same basic problem, have found that local control is better maintained through application of a principle that is the direct opposite of the principle the majority derives from the silence of our Constitution. The federal systems of Switzerland, Germany, and the European Union, for example, all provide that constituent states, not federal bureaucracies, will themselves implement many of the laws, rules, regulations, or decrees enacted by the central "federal" body. They do so in part because they believe that such a system interferes less, not more, with the independent authority of the "state," member nation, or other subsidiary government, and helps to safeguard individual liberty as well.

---

[28] Ironically, the distinction that the Court now finds so preposterous can be traced to the majority opinion in *National League of Cities*. The fact that the distinction did not provide an adequate basis for curtailing the power of Congress to extend the coverage of the Fair Labor Standards Act to state employees does not speak to the question whether it may identify a legitimate difference between a directive to local officers to provide information or assistance to the Federal Government and a directive to a State to enact legislation.

Of course, we are interpreting our own Constitution, not those of other nations, and there may be relevant political and structural differences between their systems and our own. But their experience may nonetheless cast an empirical light on the consequences of different solutions to a common legal problem—in this case the problem of reconciling central authority with the need to preserve the liberty-enhancing autonomy of a smaller constituent governmental entity. And that experience here offers empirical confirmation of the implied answer to a question JUSTICE STEVENS asks: Why, or how, would what the majority sees as a constitutional alternative—the creation of a new federal gun-law bureaucracy, or the expansion of an existing federal bureaucracy—better promote either state sovereignty or individual liberty?

As comparative experience suggests, there is no need to interpret the Constitution as containing an absolute principle—forbidding the assignment of virtually any federal duty to any state official. Nor is there a need to read the Brady Act as permitting the Federal Government to overwhelm a state civil service. The statute uses the words "reasonable effort," 18 U.S.C. § 922(s)(2)—words that easily can encompass the considerations of, say, time or cost, necessary to avoid any such result. *** [T]here is neither need nor reason to find in the Constitution an absolute principle, the inflexibility of which poses a surprising and technical obstacle to the enactment of a law that Congress believed necessary to solve an important national problem. ***

Notes

1. **Overruling?** JUSTICE BLACKMUN's switch of sides between 1976 and 1985 explains *Garcia*'s overruling of *National League of Cities*. The addition of Reagan appointees Scalia (1986) and Kennedy (1988) as well as Bush appointees Souter (1990) and Thomas (1991) may be viewed as critical to the outcome of *New York* and *Printz*. But these cases do not explicitly overrule *Garcia*. Can you reconcile these cases?

2. **Judicial "Commandeering."** The Court attempts to distinguish "commandeering" the states in the context of "requirements that the States regulate" (unconstitutional under *New York*) or execute the laws (unconstitutional under *Printz*) from the "well established power of Congress to pass laws enforceable in state courts" (not unconstitutional under *Hunter v. Martin's Lessee*). Is this distinction justified by the text of the Constitution?

3. **Limits to "Commandeering."** The distinction between imposing a federal rule and commandeering the states is critical. In *Reno v. Condon*, 528 U.S. 141 (2000), the Court unanimously upheld the 1994 Driver's Privacy Protection Act, which restricts disclosure by state motor vehicle departments and private parties of "personal information about any individual" contained in motor vehicle records. The Court held that the states, as owners of databases, were properly regulated under Congress' Commerce Clause powers; the statute commandeered neither legislative nor executive components of state governments.

4. **Federalism and Social Policy.** "Mormons moved from Illinois to Utah, while African-Americans migrated from the Jim Crow South. Rail travel and, later, automobiles and airplanes enabled residents of conservative states to escape constraints on divorce and remarriage.*** [W]omen from states with restrictive

abortion laws sought reproductive autonomy in more sympathetic jurisdictions. Today, the lesbian who finds herself in Utah, like the gun lover who lives in Washington, D.C., and the gambler in Pennsylvania, need only cross a state border to be free of constraining rules. There are liberties that come only with the variations in local norms made possible by federalism." Seth F. Kreimer, *Federalism and Freedom*, 574 ANNALS AM. ACAD. POL. & SCI. 66, 72 (2001).

3. STATE SOVEREIGN IMMUNITY

ALDEN v. MAINE
527 U.S. 706, 119 S.Ct. 2240, 144 L.Ed.2d 636 (1999).

JUSTICE KENNEDY delivered the opinion of the Court.

In 1992, petitioners, a group of probation officers, *** alleged the State had violated the overtime provisions of the Fair Labor Standards Act of 1938 (FLSA), and sought compensation and liquidated damages. While the suit was pending, this Court decided *Seminole Tribe of Fla. v. Florida,* 517 U.S. 44 (1996), which made it clear that Congress lacks power under Article I to abrogate the States' sovereign immunity from suits commenced or prosecuted in the federal courts. *** We hold that the powers delegated to Congress under Article I of the United States Constitution do not include the power to subject nonconsenting States to private suits for damages in state courts. ***

I

The Eleventh Amendment makes explicit reference to the States' immunity from suits "commenced or prosecuted against one of the United States by Citizens of another State, or by Citizens or Subjects of any Foreign State." We have, as a result, sometimes referred to the States' immunity from suit as "Eleventh Amendment immunity." The phrase is convenient shorthand but something of a misnomer, for the sovereign immunity of the States neither derives from nor is limited by the terms of the Eleventh Amendment. Rather, as the Constitution's structure, and its history, and the authoritative interpretations by this Court make clear, the States' immunity from suit is a fundamental aspect of the sovereignty which the States enjoyed before the ratification of the Constitution, and which they retain today (either literally or by virtue of their admission into the Union upon an equal footing with the other States) except as altered by the plan of the Convention or certain constitutional Amendments.

*** The federal system established by our Constitution preserves the sovereign status of the States in two ways. First, it reserves to them a substantial portion of the Nation's primary sovereignty ***. Second, even as to matters within the competence of the National Government, the constitutional design secures the founding generation's rejection of "the concept of a central government that would act upon and through the States" in favor of "a system in which the State and Federal Governments would exercise concurrent authority over the people ***. The States thus retain "a residuary and inviolable sovereignty." They are not relegated to the role of mere provinces or political corporations, but retain the dignity, though not the full authority, of sovereignty.

*** Although the American people had rejected other aspects of English political theory, the doctrine that a sovereign could not be sued without its consent was universal in the States when the Constitution was drafted and ratified. *** [For example, Alexander Hamilton in The Federalist No. 81 wrote:]

> "It is inherent in the nature of sovereignty not to be amenable to the suit of an individual without its consent. This is the general sense, and the general practice of mankind; and the exemption, as one of the attributes of sovereignty, is now enjoyed by the government of every State in the Union. *** The contracts between a nation and individuals are only binding on the conscience of the sovereign, and have no pretensions to a compulsive force. They confer no right of action independent of the sovereign Will. To what purpose would it be to authorize suits against States for the debts they owe? How could recoveries be enforced? It is evident that it could not be done without waging war against the contracting State; and to ascribe to the federal courts, by mere implication, and in destruction of the preexisting right of the State governments, a power which would involve such a consequence, would be altogether forced and unwarrantable."

*** Although the state conventions which addressed the issue of sovereign immunity in their formal ratification documents sought to clarify the point by constitutional amendment, they made clear that they, like Hamilton *** understood the Constitution as drafted to preserve the States' immunity from private suits. The Rhode Island Convention thus proclaimed that "it is declared by the Convention, that the judicial power of the United States, in cases in which a state may be a party, does not extend to criminal prosecutions, or to authorize any suit by any person against a state." ***

Despite the persuasive assurances of the Constitution's leading advocates and the expressed understanding of the only state conventions to address the issue in explicit terms, this Court held, just five years after the Constitution was adopted, that Article III authorized a private citizen of another State to sue the State of Georgia without its consent. *Chisholm v. Georgia, 2 Dall. 419 (1793)*. Each of the four Justices who concurred in the judgment issued a separate opinion. The common theme of the opinions was that the case fell within the literal text of Article III ***. JUSTICE IREDELL dissented, relying on American history, English history, and the principles of enumerated powers and separate sovereignty ***.

The Court's decision "fell upon the country with a profound shock." *** The States, in particular, responded with outrage to the decision. The Massachusetts Legislature, for example, denounced the decision as "repugnant to the first principles of a federal government," and called upon the State's Senators and Representatives to take all necessary steps to "remove any clause or article of the Constitution, which can be construed to imply or justify a decision, that, a State is compellable to answer in any suit by an individual or individuals in any Court of the United States." Georgia's response was more intemperate: Its House of Representatives passed a bill providing that anyone attempting to enforce the Chisholm decision would be "'guilty of felony and shall suffer death, without benefit of clergy, by being hanged.'"

An initial proposal to amend the Constitution was introduced in the House of Representatives the day after *Chisholm* was announced; the proposal adopted as the Eleventh Amendment was introduced in the Senate promptly following an intervening recess. *** Each House spent but a single day discussing the Amendment, and the vote in each House was close to unanimous. All attempts to weaken the Amendment were defeated. ***

The text and history of the Eleventh Amendment also suggest that Congress acted not to change but to restore the original constitutional design. *** Although the dissent attempts to rewrite history to reflect a different original understanding, its evidence is unpersuasive. *** Simply put, "The Constitution never would have been ratified if the States and their courts were to be stripped of their sovereign authority except as expressly provided by the Constitution itself." *** [S]overeign immunity derives not from the Eleventh Amendment but from the structure of the original Constitution itself. ***

II

In this case we must determine whether Congress has the power, under Article I, to subject nonconsenting States to private suits in their own courts. As the foregoing discussion makes clear, the fact that the Eleventh Amendment by its terms limits only "the Judicial power of the United States" does not resolve the question. To rest on the words of the Amendment alone would be to engage in the type of historical literalism we have rejected in interpreting the scope of the States' sovereign immunity since the discredited decision in *Chisholm*. *Seminole Tribe*.

While the constitutional principle of sovereign immunity does pose a bar to federal jurisdiction over suits against nonconsenting States, this is not the only structural basis of sovereign immunity implicit in the constitutional design. Rather, "there is also the postulate that States of the Union, still possessing attributes of sovereignty, shall be immune from suits, without their consent, save where there has been 'a surrender of this immunity in the plan of the convention.'" *** This separate and distinct structural principle is not directly related to the scope of the judicial power established by Article III, but inheres in the system of federalism established by the Constitution. In exercising its Article I powers Congress may subject the States to private suits in their own courts only if there is "compelling evidence" that the States were required to surrender this power to Congress pursuant to the constitutional design. ***

Petitioners contend the text of the Constitution and our recent sovereign immunity decisions establish that the States were required to relinquish this portion of their sovereignty. *** The Supremacy Clause *** enshrines as "the supreme Law of the Land" only those federal Acts that accord with the constitutional design. Appeal to the Supremacy Clause alone merely raises the question whether a law is a valid exercise of the national power. *Printz* .

The Constitution, by delegating to Congress the power to establish the supreme law of the land when acting within its enumerated powers, does not foreclose a State from asserting immunity to claims arising under federal law merely because that law derives not from the State itself but from the national power. A contrary view could not be reconciled with *Hans v. Louisiana,* which sustained Louisiana's immunity in a private suit arising under the Constitution itself. *** We reject any contention that substantive federal law by its own force necessarily overrides the sovereign immunity of the States. When a State asserts its immunity to suit, the question is not the primacy of federal law but the implementation of the law in a manner consistent with the constitutional sovereignty of the States.

Nor can we conclude that the specific Article I powers delegated to Congress necessarily include, by virtue of the Necessary and Proper Clause or otherwise, the incidental authority to subject the States to private suits as a means of achieving objectives otherwise within the scope of the enumerated powers. *** "When a 'Law *** for carrying into Execution' the Commerce Clause violates the principle of state sovereignty reflected in the various constitutional provisions *** it is not a 'Law *** proper for carrying into Execution the Commerce Clause,' and is thus, in the words of The Federalist, 'merely [an] act of usurpation' which 'deserves to be treated as such.'" *Printz* ***.

The cases we have cited, of course, came at last to the conclusion that neither the Supremacy Clause nor the enumerated powers of Congress confer authority to abrogate the States' immunity from suit in federal court. The logic of the decisions, however, does not turn on the forum in which the suits were prosecuted but extends to state-court suits as well. *** Although the sovereign immunity of the States derives at least in part from the common-law tradition, the structure and history of the Constitution make clear that the immunity exists today by constitutional design. *** Despite the dissent's assertion to the contrary, the fact that a right is not defeasible by statute means only that it is protected by the Constitution, not that it derives from natural law. ***

There are isolated statements in some of our cases suggesting that the Eleventh Amendment is inapplicable in state courts. *** This, of course, is a truism as to the literal terms of the Eleventh Amendment. As we have explained, however, the bare text of the Amendment is not an exhaustive description of the States' constitutional immunity from suit. The cases, furthermore, do not decide the question presented here—whether the States retain immunity from private suits in their own courts notwithstanding an attempted abrogation by the Congress. *** Whether Congress has authority under Article I to abrogate a State's immunity from suit in its own courts is, then, a question of first impression. In determining whether there is "compelling evidence" that this derogation of the States' sovereignty is "inherent in the constitutional compact," *** we continue our discussion of history, practice, precedent, and the structure of the Constitution.

We look first to evidence of the original understanding of the Constitution. Petitioners contend that because the ratification debates and the events surrounding the adoption of the Eleventh Amendment focused on the States' immunity from suit in federal courts, the historical record gives no instruction as to the founding generation's intent to preserve the States' immunity from suit in their own courts.

We believe, however, that the founders' silence is best explained by the simple fact that no one, not even the Constitution's most ardent opponents, suggested the document might strip the States of the immunity. In light of the overriding concern regarding the States' war-time debts, together with the well known creativity, foresight, and vivid imagination of the Constitution's opponents, the silence is most instructive. It suggests the sovereign's right to assert immunity from suit in its own courts was a principle so well established that no one conceived it would be altered by the new Constitution.

The arguments raised against the Constitution confirm this strong inference. *** The point of the argument was that federal jurisdiction under Article III would circumvent the States' immunity from suit in their own courts. The argument would have made little sense if the States were understood to have relinquished the immunity in all events.

The response the Constitution's advocates gave to the argument is also telling. Relying on custom and practice—and, in particular, on the States' immunity from suit in their own courts—they contended that no individual could sue a sovereign without its consent. It is true the point was directed toward the power of the Federal Judiciary, for that was the only question at issue. The logic of the argument, however, applies with even greater force in the context of a suit prosecuted against a sovereign in its own courts, for in this setting, more than any other, sovereign immunity was long established and unquestioned. Similarly, while the Eleventh Amendment by its terms addresses only "the Judicial power of the United States," nothing in *Chisholm*, the catalyst for the Amendment, suggested the States were not immune from suits in their own courts. ***

In light of the language of the Constitution and the historical context, it is quite apparent why neither the ratification debates nor the language of the Eleventh Amendment addressed the States' immunity from suit in their own courts. The concerns voiced at the ratifying conventions, the furor raised by *Chisholm*, and the speed and unanimity with which the Amendment was adopted, moreover, underscore the jealous care with which the founding generation sought to preserve the sovereign immunity of the States. To read this history as permitting the inference that the Constitution stripped the States of immunity in their own courts and allowed Congress to subject them to suit there would turn on its head the concern of the founding generation— that Article III might be used to circumvent state-court immunity. In light of the historical record it is difficult to conceive that the Constitution would have been adopted if it had been understood to strip the States of immunity from suit in their own courts and cede to the Federal Government a power to subject nonconsenting States to private suits in these fora.

Our historical analysis is supported by early congressional practice, which provides "contemporaneous and weighty evidence of the Constitution's meaning." *Printz* *** Although early Congresses enacted various statutes authorizing federal suits in state court, *** we have discovered no instance in which they purported to authorize suits against nonconsenting States in these fora. The "numerousness of these statutes [authorizing suit in state court], contrasted with the utter lack of statutes" subjecting States to suit, "suggests an assumed absence of such power." It thus appears early Congresses did not believe they had the power to authorize private suits against the States in their own courts.

Not only were statutes purporting to authorize private suits against nonconsenting States in state courts not enacted by early Congresses, statutes purporting to authorize such suits in any forum are all but absent from our historical experience. *** The provisions of the FLSA at issue here, *** are among the first statutory enactments purporting in express terms to subject nonconsenting States to private suits. Although similar statutes have multiplied in the last generation, " *** [t]heir persuasive force is far outweighed by almost two centuries of apparent congressional avoidance of the practice."

Even the recent statutes, moreover, do not provide evidence of an understanding that Congress has a greater power to subject States to suit in their own courts than in federal courts. On the contrary, the statutes purport to create causes of actions against the States which are enforceable in federal, as well as state, court. ***

The theory and reasoning of our earlier cases suggest the States do retain a constitutional immunity from suit in their own courts. *** We have said on many occasions, furthermore, that the States retain their immunity from private suits prosecuted in their own courts. *** In particular, the exception to our sovereign immunity doctrine recognized in *Ex parte Young*, 209 U.S. 123 (1908), is based in part on the premise that sovereign immunity bars relief against States and their officers in both state and federal courts, and that certain suits for declaratory or injunctive relief against state officers must therefore be permitted if the Constitution is to remain the supreme law of the land. *** Had we not understood the States to retain a constitutional immunity from suit in their own courts, the need for the *Ex parte Young* rule would have been less pressing, and the rule would not have formed so essential a part of our sovereign immunity doctrine. ***

Our final consideration is whether a congressional power to subject nonconsenting States to private suits in their own courts is consistent with the structure of the Constitution. We look both to the essential principles of federalism and to the special role of the state courts in the constitutional design.

Although the Constitution grants broad powers to Congress, our federalism requires that Congress treat the States in a manner consistent with their status as residuary sovereigns and joint participants in the governance of the Nation. See, e.g., *United States v. Lopez, Printz, New York*. The founding generation thought it "neither becoming nor convenient that the several States of the Union, invested with that large residuum of sovereignty which had not been delegated to the United States, should be summoned as defendants to answer the complaints of private persons."

Petitioners contend that immunity from suit in federal court suffices to preserve the dignity of the States. Private suits against nonconsenting States, however, present "the indignity of subjecting a State to the coercive process of judicial tribunals at the instance of private parties," regardless of the forum. Not only must a State defend or default but also it must face the prospect of being thrust, by federal fiat and against its will, into the disfavored status of a debtor, subject to the power of private citizens to levy on its treasury or perhaps even government buildings or property which the State administers on the public's behalf.

In some ways, of course, a congressional power to authorize private suits against nonconsenting States in their own courts would be even more offensive to state sovereignty than a power to authorize the suits in a federal forum. *** A power to press a State's own courts into federal service to coerce the other branches of the State, furthermore, is the power first to turn the State against itself and ultimately to commandeer the entire political machinery of the State against its will and at the behest of individuals. *** Such plenary federal control of state governmental processes denigrates the separate sovereignty of the States.

It is unquestioned that the Federal Government retains its own immunity from suit not only in state tribunals but also in its own courts. In light of our constitutional system recognizing the essential sovereignty of the States, we are reluctant to conclude that the States are not entitled to a reciprocal privilege.

Underlying constitutional form are considerations of great substance. Private suits against nonconsenting States—especially suits for money damages—may threaten the financial integrity of the States. It is indisputable that, at the time of the founding, many of the States could have been forced into insolvency but for their immunity from private suits for money damages. Even today, an unlimited congressional power to authorize suits in state court to levy upon the treasuries of the States for compensatory damages, attorney's fees, and even punitive damages could create staggering burdens, giving Congress a power and a leverage over the States that is not contemplated by our constitutional design. The potential national power would pose a severe and notorious danger to the States and their resources.

A congressional power to strip the States of their immunity from private suits in their own courts would pose more subtle risks as well. *** While the States have relinquished their immunity from suit in some special contexts— at least as a practical matter—see Part III, infra, this surrender carries with it substantial costs to the autonomy, the decisionmaking ability, and the sovereign capacity of the States.

A general federal power to authorize private suits for money damages would place unwarranted strain on the States' ability to govern in accordance with the will of their citizens. Today, as at the time of the founding, the allocation of scarce resources among competing needs and interests lies at the heart of the political process. While the judgment creditor of the State may have a legitimate claim for compensation, other important needs and worthwhile ends compete for access to the public fisc. Since all cannot be satisfied in full, it is inevitable that difficult decisions involving the most sensitive and political of judgments must be made. If the principle of representative government is to be preserved to the States, the balance between competing interests must be reached after deliberation by the political process established by the citizens of the State, not by judicial decree mandated by the Federal Government and invoked by the private citizen. *** When the Federal Government asserts authority over a State's most fundamental political processes, it strikes at the heart of the political accountability so essential to our liberty and republican form of government.

The asserted authority would blur not only the distinct responsibilities of the State and National Governments but also the separate duties of the judicial and political branches of the state governments, displacing "state decisions that 'go to the heart of representative government.'" *** If Congress could displace a State's allocation of governmental power and responsibility, the judicial branch of the State, whose legitimacy derives from fidelity to the law, would be compelled to assume a role not only foreign to its experience but beyond its competence as defined by the very constitution from which its existence derives. ***

The resulting anomaly cannot be explained by reference to the special role of the state courts in the constitutional design. Although Congress may not require the legislative or executive branches of the States to enact or administer federal regulatory programs, see *Printz, New York,* it may require state courts of "adequate and appropriate" jurisdiction, "to enforce federal prescriptions, insofar as those prescriptions relate to matters appropriate for the judicial power," *Printz.* It would be an unprecedented step, however, to infer from the fact that Congress may declare federal law binding and enforceable in state courts the further principle that Congress' authority to pursue federal objectives through the state judiciaries exceeds not only its power to press other branches of the State into its service but even its control over the federal courts themselves. The conclusion would imply that Congress may in some cases act only through instrumentalities of the States. Yet, as CHIEF JUSTICE MARSHALL explained, "No trace is to be found in the constitution of an intention to create a dependence of the government of the Union on those of the States, for the execution of the great powers assigned to it. Its means are adequate to its ends; and on those means alone was it expected to rely for the accomplishment of its ends." *McCulloch v. Maryland* ***.

The provisions of the Constitution upon which we have relied in finding the state courts peculiarly amenable to federal command, moreover, do not distinguish those courts from the Federal Judiciary. The Supremacy Clause does impose specific obligations on state judges. There can be no serious contention, however, that the Supremacy Clause imposes greater obligations on state-court judges than on the Judiciary of the United States itself. The text of Article III, § 1, which extends federal judicial power to enumerated classes of suits but grants Congress discretion whether to establish inferior federal courts, does give strong support to the inference that state courts may be opened to suits falling within the federal judicial power. The Article in no way suggests, however, that state courts may be required to assume jurisdiction that could not be vested in the federal courts and forms no part of the judicial power of the United States.

*** We are aware of no constitutional precept that would admit of a congressional power to require state courts to entertain federal suits which are not within the judicial power of the United States and could not be heard in federal courts. *** In light of history, practice, precedent, and the structure of the Constitution, we hold that the States retain immunity from private suit in their own courts, an immunity beyond the congressional power to abrogate by Article I legislation.

III

The constitutional privilege of a State to assert its sovereign immunity in its own courts does not confer upon the State a concomitant right to disregard the Constitution or valid federal law. The States and their officers are bound by obligations imposed by the Constitution and by federal statutes that comport with the constitutional design. We are unwilling to assume the States will refuse to honor the Constitution or obey the binding laws of the United States. *** Sovereign immunity, moreover, does not bar all judicial review of state compliance with the Constitution and valid federal law. Rather, certain limits are implicit in the constitutional principle of state sovereign immunity.

The first of these limits is that sovereign immunity bars suits only in the absence of consent. *** Nor, subject to constitutional limitations, does the Federal Government lack the authority or means to seek the States' voluntary consent to private suits. Cf. *South Dakota v. Dole*. The States have consented, moreover, to some suits pursuant to the plan of the Convention or to subsequent constitutional amendments. In ratifying the Constitution, the States consented to suits brought by other States or by the Federal Government ***. A suit which is commenced and prosecuted against a State in the name of the United States by those who are entrusted with the constitutional duty to "take Care that the Laws be faithfully executed," U.S. Const., Art. II, § 3, differs in kind from the suit of an individual: While the Constitution contemplates suits among the members of the federal system as an alternative to extralegal measures, the fear of private suits against nonconsenting States was the central reason given by the founders who chose to preserve the States' sovereign immunity. Suits brought by the United

States itself require the exercise of political responsibility for each suit prosecuted against a State, a control which is absent from a broad delegation to private persons to sue nonconsenting States.

We have held also that in adopting the Fourteenth Amendment, the people required the States to surrender a portion of the sovereignty that had been preserved to them by the original Constitution, so that Congress may authorize private suits against nonconsenting States pursuant to its § 5 enforcement power. *Fitzpatrick v. Bitzer,* 427 U.S. 445 (1976). ***

The second important limit to the principle of sovereign immunity is that it bars suits against States but not lesser entities. *** Nor does sovereign immunity bar all suits against state officers. Some suits against state officers are barred by the rule that sovereign immunity is not limited to suits which name the State as a party if the suits are, in fact, against the State ***. The rule, however, does not bar certain actions against state officers for injunctive or declaratory relief. *** Even a suit for money damages may be prosecuted against a state officer in his individual capacity for unconstitutional or wrongful conduct fairly attributable to the officer himself, so long as the relief is sought not from the state treasury but from the officer personally. ***

The sole remaining question is whether Maine has waived its immunity. *** The State, we conclude, has not consented to suit.

*** The Framers of the Constitution did not share our dissenting colleagues' belief that the Congress may circumvent the federal design by regulating the States directly when it pleases to do so, including by a proxy in which individual citizens are authorized to levy upon the state treasuries absent the States' consent to jurisdiction.

The case before us depends upon these principles. The State of Maine has not questioned Congress' power to prescribe substantive rules of federal law to which it must comply. Despite an initial good-faith disagreement about the requirements of the FLSA, it is conceded by all that the State has altered its conduct so that its compliance with federal law cannot now be questioned. The Solicitor General of the United States has appeared before this Court, however, and asserted that the federal interest in compensating the States' employees for alleged past violations of federal law is so compelling that the sovereign State of Maine must be stripped of its immunity and subjected to suit in its own courts by its own employees. Yet, despite specific statutory authorization, see 29 U.S.C. § 216(c), the United States apparently found the same interests insufficient to justify sending even a single attorney to Maine to prosecute this litigation. The difference between a suit by the United States on behalf of the employees and a suit by the employees implicates a rule that the National Government must itself deem the case of sufficient importance to take action against the State; and history, precedent, and the structure of the Constitution make clear that, under the plan of the Convention, the States have consented to suits of the first kind but not of the second. ***

JUSTICE SOUTER, with whom JUSTICE STEVENS, JUSTICE GINSBURG, and JUSTICE BREYER join, dissenting.

In *Seminole Tribe* *** a majority of this Court invoked the Eleventh Amendment to declare that the federal judicial power under Article III of the Constitution does not reach a private action against a State, even on a federal question. *** The Court does not, however, offer today's holding as a mere corollary to its reasoning in *Seminole Tribe*, substituting the Tenth Amendment for the Eleventh as the occasion demands, and it is fair to read its references to a "fundamental aspect" of state sovereignty as referring not to a prerogative inherited from the Crown, but to a conception necessarily implied by statehood itself. The conception is thus not one of common law so much as of natural law, a universally applicable proposition discoverable by reason. This, I take it, is the sense in which the Court so emphatically relies on Alexander Hamilton's reference in The Federalist No. 81 to the States' sovereign immunity from suit as an "inherent" right, a characterization that does not require, but is at least open to, a natural law reading.   *** The apparent novelty and uniqueness of Hamilton's employment of natural law terminology to explain the sovereign immunity of the States is worth remarking, because it stands in contrast to formulations indicating no particular position on the natural-law-versus-common-law origin, to the more widespread view that sovereign immunity derived from common law, and to the more radical stance that the sovereignty of the people made sovereign immunity out of place in the United States. Hamilton's view is also worth noticing because, in marked contrast to its prominence in the Court's opinion today *** it found no favor in the early Supreme Court. *** At the farthest extreme from Hamilton, James Wilson made several comments in the Pennsylvania Convention that suggested his hostility to any idea of state sovereign immunity. *** For Wilson, "the answer [was] plain and easy: the government of each state ought to be subordinate to the government of the United States." *** [This] expressed the major premise of what would later become JUSTICE WILSON's position in *Chisholm*: that because the people, and not the States, are sovereign, sovereign immunity has no applicability to the States. ***

At the close of the ratification debates, the issue of the sovereign immunity of the States under Article III had not been definitively resolved, and in some instances the indeterminacy led the ratification conventions to respond in ways that point to the range of thinking about the doctrine. Several state ratifying conventions proposed amendments and issued declarations that would have exempted States from subjection to suit in federal court. ***

In sum, then, in *Chisholm* two JUSTICES (JAY and WILSON), both of whom had been present at the Constitutional Convention, took a position suggesting that States should not enjoy sovereign immunity (however conceived) even in their own courts; one (CUSHING) was essentially silent on the issue of sovereign immunity in state court; one (BLAIR) took a cautious position affirming the pragmatic view that sovereign immunity was a continuing common law doctrine and that States would permit suit against themselves as of right; and one (IREDELL) expressly thought that state sovereign immunity at common-law rightly belonged to the sovereign States. Not a single Justice suggested that sovereign immunity was an inherent and indefeasible right of statehood, and neither counsel for Georgia before the Circuit Court, nor JUSTICE IREDELL seems even to have conceived the possibility that the new Tenth Amendment produced the equivalent of such a doctrine. This dearth of support makes it very implausible for today's Court to argue that a substantial (let alone a dominant) body of thought at the time of the framing understood sovereign immunity to be an inherent right of statehood, adopted or confirmed by the Tenth Amendment.

The Court's discomfort is evident in its obvious recognition that its natural law or Tenth Amendment conception of state sovereign immunity is insupportable if *Chisholm* stands. Hence the Court's attempt to discount the *Chisholm* opinions, an enterprise in which I believe it fails. ***

Nor can the Court make good on its claim that the enactment of the Eleventh Amendment retrospectively reestablished the view that had already been established at the time of the framing (though eluding the perception of all but one Member of the Supreme Court), and hence "acted *** to restore the original constitutional design." There was nothing "established" about the position espoused by Georgia in the effort to repudiate its debts *** [and] no received view either of the role this sovereign immunity would play in the circumstances of the case or of a conceptual foundation for immunity doctrine at odds with *Chisholm's* reading of Article III. *** The federal citizen-state diversity jurisdiction was settled by the Eleventh Amendment; Article III was not "restored." *** Alden's suit should go forward.

The Court's rationale for today's holding based on a conception of sovereign immunity as somehow fundamental to sovereignty or inherent in statehood fails for the lack of any substantial support for such a conception in the thinking of the founding era. The Court cannot be counted out yet, however, for it has a second line of argument looking not to a clause-based reception of the natural law conception or even to its recognition as a "background principle," but to a structural basis in the Constitution's creation of a federal system. *** "In America, the powers of sovereignty are divided between the government of the Union, and those of the States. They are each sovereign, with respect to the objects committed to it, and neither sovereign with respect to the objects committed to the other." *McCulloch v. Maryland.*

Hence the flaw in the Court's appeal to federalism. The State of Maine is not sovereign with respect to the national objective of the FLSA. It is not the authority that promulgated the FLSA, on which the right of action in this case depends. That authority is the United States acting through the Congress, whose legislative power under Article I of the Constitution to extend FLSA coverage to state employees has already been decided, see *Garcia v. San Antonio Metropolitan Transit Authority,* 469 U.S. 528 (1985), and is not contested here. *** Maine has advanced no "'valid excuse,'" *** for its courts' refusal to hear federal-law claims in which Maine is a defendant, and sovereign immunity cannot be that excuse, simply because the State is not sovereign with respect to the subject of the claim against it. ***

It is symptomatic of the weakness of the structural notion proffered by the Court that it seeks to buttress the argument by relying on "the dignity and respect afforded a State, which the immunity is designed to protect," and by invoking the many demands on a State's fisc. *** The "judgment creditor" in question is not a dunning bill-collector, but a citizen whose federal rights have been violated, and a constitutional structure that stints on enforcing federal rights out of an abundance of delicacy toward the States has substituted politesse in place of respect for the rule of law.

If neither theory nor structure can supply the basis for the Court's conceptions of sovereign immunity and federalism, then perhaps history might. The Court apparently believes that because state courts have not historically entertained Commerce Clause-based federal-law claims against the States, such an innovation carries a presumption of unconstitutionality. *** But *** in light of *Garcia,* the law is settled that federal legislation enacted under the Commerce Clause may bind the States without having to satisfy a test of undue incursion into state sovereignty. "The fundamental limitation that the constitutional scheme imposes on the Commerce Clause to protect the 'States as States' is one of process rather than one of result." Because the commerce power is no longer thought to be circumscribed, the dearth of prior private federal claims entertained against the States in state courts does not tell us anything, and reflects nothing but an earlier and less expansive application of the commerce power.

Least of all is it to the point for the Court to suggest that because the Framers would be surprised to find States subjected to a federal-law suit in their own courts under the commerce power, the suit must be prohibited by the Constitution. *** If the Framers would be surprised to see States subjected to suit in their own courts under the commerce power, they would be astonished by the reach of Congress under the Commerce Clause generally. The proliferation of Government, State and Federal, would amaze the Framers, and the administrative state with its reams of regulations would leave them rubbing their eyes. *** *Garcia* remains good law, its reasoning has not been repudiated, and it has not been challenged here.

The FLSA has not, however, fared as well in practice as it has in theory. The Court in *Seminole Tribe* created a significant impediment to the statute's practical application by rendering its damages provisions unenforceable against the States by private suit in federal court. Today's decision blocking private actions in state courts makes the barrier to individual enforcement a total one.

The Court might respond to the charge that in practice it has vitiated *Garcia* by insisting, as counsel for Maine argued, that the United States may bring suit in federal court against a State for damages under the FLSA. *** [T]he allusion to enforcement of private rights by the National Government is probably not much more than whimsy. Facing reality, Congress specifically found, as long ago as 1974, "that the enforcement capability of the Secretary of Labor is not alone sufficient to provide redress in all or even a substantial portion of the situations where compliance is not forthcoming voluntarily." One hopes that such voluntary compliance will prove more popular than it has in Maine, for there is no reason today to suspect that enforcement by the Secretary of Labor alone would likely prove adequate to assure compliance with this federal law in the multifarious circumstances of some 4.7 million employees of the 50 States of the Union. *** Denying private enforcement of an FLSA claim is thus on par with closing the courthouse door to state tort victims unaccompanied by a lawyer from Washington.

So there is much irony in the Court's profession that it grounds its opinion on a deeply rooted historical tradition of sovereign immunity, when the Court abandons a principle nearly as inveterate, and much closer to the hearts of the Framers: that where there is a right, there must be a remedy. *** The generation of the Framers thought the principle so crucial that several States put it into their constitutions. And when CHIEF JUSTICE MARSHALL asked about Marbury, "If he has a right, and that right has been violated, do the laws of his country afford him a remedy?" *Marbury v. Madison,* the question was rhetorical, and the answer clear:

> "The very essence of civil liberty certainly consists in the right of every individual to claim the protection of the laws, whenever he receives an injury. One of the first duties of government is to afford that protection. In Great Britain the king himself is sued in the respectful form of a petition, and he never fails to comply with the judgment of his court."

Yet today the Court has no qualms about saying frankly that the federal right to damages afforded by Congress under the FLSA cannot create a concomitant private remedy. *** The resemblance of today's state sovereign immunity to the *Lochner* era's industrial due process is striking. *** I expect the Court's late essay into immunity doctrine will prove the equal of its earlier experiment in laissez-faire, the one being as unrealistic as the other, as indefensible, and probably as fleeting.

Notes

1. **Judicial Reasoning.** Do you find the majority's or the dissent's view of sovereign immunity more compelling? Why?

2. *Alden* **and** *Garcia.* If you had been in the dissent in *Garcia*, would you have found this case an appropriate vehicle for overruling *Garcia*? Why didn't the Court overrule *Garcia*?

3. *Alden, Seminole Tribe,* **and the § 5 Power.** *Alden* makes the § 5 power even more critical than *Seminole Tribe* and *Boerne* made it. It may now be difficult for Congress to prohibit the states from discriminating based on pregnancy, age, or disability, or to keep states from infringing on property rights, even those specifically mentioned in the Constitution. For example, *College Savings Bank v. Florida Prepaid Postsecondary Education Expense Board*, 527 U.S. 666 (1999), held that federal prohibitions on false and misleading advertising were not premised on the § 5 power to enforce the due process clause ("nor shall any State deprive any person of *** property without due process of law"). Therefore, suit in federal court was barred under the Eleventh Amendment. After *Alden*, it seems likely the same suit would also be barred in state courts.

4. *Alden* and the Powers to Tax and Spend. Can't Congress simply use its 16th Amendment power to enhance federal power while reducing the resources available to the states? Can Congress engage in spending conditioned upon the states waiving their sovereign immunity?

5. **Amendment.** Consider whether you would support either of the following proposed constitutional amendments:

(a) "The Eleventh Amendment is hereby repealed."

(b) "No State shall interpose sovereign immunity as a defense in any action brought in state or federal court when that action is premised upon a federal statute or a treaty of the United States."

FEDERAL MARITIME COMMISSION
v.
SOUTH CAROLINA STATE PORTS AUTHORITY
535 U.S. 743, 122 S.Ct. 1864, 152 L.Ed.2d 962 (2002).

JUSTICE THOMAS delivered the opinion of the Court.

This case presents the question whether state sovereign immunity precludes petitioner Federal Maritime Commission (FMC or Commission) from adjudicating a private party's complaint that a state-run port has violated the Shipping Act of 1984. We hold that state sovereign immunity bars such an adjudicative proceeding.

On five occasions, South Carolina Maritime Services, Inc. (Maritime Services), asked respondent South Carolina State Ports Authority (SCSPA) for permission to berth a cruise ship, the M/V *Tropic Sea,* at the SCSPA's port facilities in Charleston, South Carolina. *** The SCSPA repeatedly denied Maritime Services' requests, contending that it had an established policy of denying berths in the Port of Charleston to vessels whose primary purpose was gambling. As a result, Maritime Services filed a complaint with the FMC, contending that the SCSPA's refusal to provide berthing space to the M/V *Tropic Sea* violated the Shipping Act. *** Maritime Services' complaint was referred to an administrative law judge (ALJ). The SCSPA *** filed a motion to dismiss, asserting *** that the SCSPA, as an arm of the State of South Carolina, was "entitled to Eleventh Amendment immunity" from Maritime Services' suit. The SCSPA argued that "the Constitution prohibits Congress from passing a statute authorizing Maritime Services to file [this] Complaint before the Commission and, thereby, sue the State of South Carolina for damages and injunctive relief." ***

We now consider whether the sovereign immunity enjoyed by States as part of our constitutional framework applies to adjudications conducted by the FMC. *** For purposes of this case, we will assume, *arguendo,* that in adjudicating complaints filed by private parties under the Shipping Act, the FMC does not exercise the judicial power of the United States. Such an assumption, however, does not end our inquiry as this Court has repeatedly held that the sovereign immunity enjoyed by the States extends beyond the literal text of the Eleventh Amendment. ***

"[L]ook[ing] first to evidence of the original understanding of the Constitution," *Alden v. Maine*, 527 U.S., at 741, as well as early congressional practice, we find a relatively barren historical record, from which the parties draw radically different conclusions. *** The Framers, who envisioned a limited Federal Government, could not have anticipated the vast growth of the administrative state. Because formalized administrative adjudications were all but unheard of in the late 18th century and early 19th century, the dearth of specific evidence indicating whether the Framers believed that the States' sovereign immunity would apply in such proceedings is unsurprising.

This Court, however, has applied a presumption—first explicitly stated in *Hans* v. *Louisiana*—that the Constitution was not intended to "rais[e] up" any proceedings against the States that were "anomalous and unheard of when the Constitution was adopted." We therefore attribute great significance to the fact that States were not subject to private suits in administrative adjudications at the time of the founding or for many years thereafter. For instance, while the United States asserts that "state entities have long been subject to similar administrative enforcement proceedings," the earliest example it provides did not occur until 1918.

To decide whether the *Hans* presumption applies here, however, we must examine FMC adjudications to determine whether they are the type of proceedings from which the Framers would have thought the States possessed immunity when they agreed to enter the Union.

In another case asking whether an immunity present in the judicial context also applied to administrative adjudications, this Court considered whether ALJs share the same absolute immunity from suit as do Article III judges. See *Butz* v. *Economou*, 438 U.S. 478 (1978). Examining in that case the duties performed by an ALJ, this Court observed:

> "There can be little doubt that the role of the modern federal hearing examiner or administrative law judge *** is 'functionally comparable' to that of a judge. His powers are often, if not generally, comparable to those of a trial judge: He may issue subpoenas, rule on proffers of evidence, regulate the course of the hearing, and make or recommend decisions. More importantly, the process of agency adjudication is currently structured so as to assure that the hearing examiner exercises his independent judgment on the evidence before him, free from pressures by the parties or other officials within the agency."

*** Turning to FMC adjudications specifically, neither the Commission nor the United States disputes the Court of Appeals' characterization below that such a proceeding "walks, talks, and squawks very much like a lawsuit." Nor do they deny that the similarities identified in *Butz* between administrative adjudications and trial court proceedings are present here. ***

The preeminent purpose of state sovereign immunity is to accord States the dignity that is consistent with their status as sovereign entities. *** Simply put, if the Framers thought it an impermissible affront to a State's dignity to be required to answer the complaints of private parties in federal courts, we cannot imagine that they would have found it acceptable to compel a State to do exactly the same thing before the administrative tribunal of an agency, such as the FMC. Cf. *Alden*. The affront to a State's dignity does not lessen when an adjudication takes place in an administrative tribunal as opposed to an Article III court. In both instances, a State is required to defend itself in an adversarial proceeding against a private party before an impartial federal officer. Moreover, it would be quite strange to prohibit Congress from exercising its Article I powers to abrogate state sovereign immunity in Article III judicial proceedings, see *Seminole Tribe*, 517 U.S., at 72, but permit the use of those same Article I powers to create court-like administrative tribunals where sovereign immunity does not apply.

The United States suggests two reasons why we should distinguish FMC administrative adjudications from judicial proceedings for purposes of state sovereign immunity. *** The United States first contends that sovereign immunity should not apply to FMC adjudications because the Commission's orders are not self-executing. Whereas a court may enforce a judgment through the exercise of its contempt power, the FMC cannot enforce its own orders. Rather, the Commission's orders can only be enforced by a federal district court. *** The United States next suggests that sovereign immunity should not apply to FMC proceedings because they do not present the same threat to the financial integrity of States as do private judicial suits. *** This argument, however, reflects a fundamental misunderstanding of the purposes of sovereign immunity. *** Sovereign immunity does not merely constitute a defense to monetary liability or even to all types of liability. Rather, it provides an immunity from suit. The statutory scheme, as interpreted by the United States, is thus no more permissible than if Congress had allowed private parties to sue States in federal court for violations of the Shipping Act but precluded a court from awarding them any relief.

It is also worth noting that an FMC order that a State pay reparations to a private party may very well result in the withdrawal of funds from that State's treasury. *** The United States, moreover, does not even dispute that the FMC could impose a civil penalty on a State for failing to obey a nonreparation order, which, if enforced by the Attorney General, would also result in a levy upon that State's treasury.

Two final arguments raised by the FMC and the United States remain to be addressed. *** The FMC maintains that sovereign immunity should not bar the Commission from adjudicating Maritime Services' complaint because "[t]he constitutional necessity of uniformity in the regulation of maritime commerce limits the States' sovereignty with respect to the Federal Government's authority to regulate that commerce." *** *Seminole Tribe* precludes us from creating a new "maritime commerce" exception to state sovereign immunity. *** Finally, the United States maintains that even if sovereign immunity were to bar the FMC from adjudicating a private party's complaint against a state-run port for purposes of issuing a reparation order, the FMC should not be precluded from considering a private party's request for other forms of relief, such as a cease-and-desist order. *** [W]e explained in *Seminole Tribe* that "the relief sought by a plaintiff suing a State is irrelevant to the question whether the suit is barred by the Eleventh Amendment." *** Although the Framers likely did not envision the intrusion on state sovereignty at issue in today's case, we are nonetheless confident that it is contrary to their constitutional design ***.

JUSTICE STEVENS, dissenting. [omitted]

JUSTICE BREYER, with whom JUSTICE STEVENS, JUSTICE SOUTER, and JUSTICE GINSBURG join, dissenting.

The Court holds that a private person cannot bring a complaint against a State to a federal administrative agency where the agency (1) will use an internal adjudicative process to decide if the complaint is well founded, and (2) if so, proceed to court to enforce the law. *** The legal body conducting the proceeding, the Federal Maritime Commission, is an "independent" federal agency. Constitutionally speaking, an "independent" agency belongs neither to the Legislative Branch nor to the Judicial Branch of Government. *** The agencies derive their legal powers from congressionally enacted statutes. And the agencies enforce those statutes, *i.e.*, they "execute" them, in part by making rules or by adjudicating matters in dispute. *** Where then can the Court find its constitutional principle—the principle that the Constitution forbids an Executive Branch agency to determine through ordinary adjudicative processes whether such a private complaint is justified? *** The Court's principle lacks any firm anchor in the Constitution's text. *** Federal administrative agencies do not exercise the "[j]udicial power of the United States." *** [The Court] has never said that the words "[j]udicial power of the United States" mean "the executive power of the United States." Nor should it.

The Tenth Amendment cannot help. *** The Constitution has "delegated to the United States" the power here in question, the power "[t]o regulate Commerce with foreign Nations, and among the several States." *** [T]he Court refers for textual support only to an earlier case, namely *Alden* v. *Maine,* 527 U.S. 706 (1999), and, through *Alden*, to the texts that *Alden* mentioned. These textual references include: (1) what Alexander Hamilton described as a constitutional "postulate," namely that the States retain their immunity from "suits, without their consent," unless there has been a "surrender" of that immunity "in the plan of the convention"; (2) what the *Alden* majority called "the system of federalism established by the Constitution"; and (3) what the *Alden* majority called "the constitutional design." *** [U]nless supported by considerations of history, of constitutional purpose, or of related consequence, those abstract phrases cannot support today's result.

Conceding that its conception of sovereign immunity is ungrounded in the Constitution's text, the Court attempts to support its holding with history. But this effort is similarly destined to fail, because the very history to which the majority turned in *Alden* here argues against the Court's basic analogy—between a federal administrative proceeding triggered by a private citizen and a private citizen's lawsuit against a State.

In *Alden* the Court said that feudal law had created an 18th-century legal norm to the effect that "'no lord could be sued by a vassal in his own court, but each petty lord was subject to suit in the courts of a higher lord.'" *** Here that same norm argues against immunity, for the forum at issue is federal—belonging by analogy to the "higher lord." *** The Framers enunciated in the "plan of the convention" the principle that the Federal Government may sue a State without its consent. *** A private citizen, believing that a State has violated federal law, seeks a determination by an Executive Branch agency that he is right; the agency will make that determination through use of its own adjudicatory agency processes; and, if the State fails to comply, the Federal Government may bring an action against the State in federal court to enforce the federal law.

Twentieth-century legal history reinforces the appropriateness of this description. The growth of the administrative state has led this Court to determine that administrative agencies are not Article III courts, that they have broad discretion to proceed either through agency adjudication or through rulemaking, and that they may bring administrative enforcement proceedings against States. ***

The Court argues that the basic purpose of "sovereign immunity" doctrine —namely preservation of a State's "dignity"—requires application of that doctrine here. It rests this argument upon *** its claim that the agency proceedings constitute a form of "compulsion" exercised by a private individual against the State. *** Viewed from a purely legal perspective, the "compulsion" claim is far too weak. *** Only the Federal Government, acting through the Commission or the Attorney General, has the authority to compel the State to act. *** Without a court proceeding the private individual cannot legally force the State to act, to pay, or to desist; only the Federal Government may institute a court proceeding; and, in deciding whether to do so, the Federal Government will exercise appropriate political responsibility. *** The statutes clearly provide the State with full judicial review of the initial agency decision should the State choose to seek that review. That review cannot "affront" the State's "dignity, for it takes place in a court proceeding in which the Commission, not the private party, will oppose the State." ***

*** The Court's decision may undermine enforcement against state employers of many laws designed to protect worker health and safety. See, *e.g.,* 42 U.S.C. § 7622 (1994 ed.) (Clean Air Act); 33 U.S.C. § 1367 (1994 ed.) (Clean Water Act); 15 U.S.C. § 2622 (Toxic Substances Control Act); 42 U.S.C. § 6971 (1994 ed.) (Solid Waste Disposal Act). And it may inhibit the development of federal fair, rapid, and efficient, informal nonjudicial responses to complaints, for example, of improper medical care (involving state hospitals). ***

Notes

1. **Flip-flopping Formalists?** Have the traditionally conservative and formalist justices in the majority abandoned textualism, history, and strict constructionist principles in this case?

2. **Particular Procedures.** If an ALJ or other decision-maker for a federal agency operates under procedures that depart significantly from the procedures used by courts, is sovereign immunity available to a State defendant in such a proceeding? How closely would such procedures need to mirror court procedures?

3. **Trials and Deportation Proceedings.** The public and the press have a right to attend civil trials. Deportation proceedings resemble civil trials. Is there a comparable right to attend deportation proceedings, or may the Attorney General close proceedings that he believes relate to terrorism without having a case-by-case hearing on that issue? Compare *Detroit Free Press v. Ashcroft*, 303 F. 3d 681 (6th Cir. 2002) with *North Jersey Media Group v. Ashcroft*, 308 F. 3d 198 (3rd Cir. 2002).

4. **Review Problem.** In *Jinks v. Richland County*, 123 S.Ct. 1667 (2003), the Court unanimously upheld a federal statute providing that, when certain claims are dismissed from federal court, state statutes of limitations are tolled to allow the claims to be refiled in state court. Justice Scalia said the statute was "necessary and proper" to Congress' Art. I power "[t]o constitute Tribunals inferior to the supreme Court" and facilitated fair exercise of "[t]he judicial Power of the United States." The Court rejected the argument that *Printz* precluded federal regulation of state court procedures because statutes of limitation are substantive, not procedural; it also rejected the county's Eleventh Amendment argument because only states receive that immunity. Would a federal statute be constitutional that required jury trials in state court civil cases that, if tried in federal courts, would be tried before juries because of the Seventh Amendment?

B. LIMITS ON THE STATES

Just as "our federalism" imposes limits on the federal government, it imposes limits on the states. States have residual powers and benefit from limits on Congress' powers, but the states also suffer both from structural limits implicit in the Constitution and from the operation of the Supremacy Clause. Section 1 below presents the framework of the implicit limits federalism places on the states in relation to the federal government; Section 2 deals with the preemptive effect of federal law over state law under the Supremacy Clause.

1. IMPLICIT FEDERAL LIMITS

U.S. TERM LIMITS v. THORNTON
514 U.S. 779, 115 S.Ct. 1842, 131 L.Ed.2d 881 (1995).

JUSTICE STEVENS delivered the opinion of the Court.

The Constitution sets forth qualifications for membership in the Congress of the United States. Article I, § 2, cl. 2, which applies to the House of Representatives, provides: "No Person shall be a Representative who shall not have attained to the Age of twenty five Years, and been seven Years a Citizen of the United States, and who shall not, when elected, be an Inhabitant of that State in which he shall be chosen." Article I, § 3, cl. 3, which applies to the Senate, similarly provides: "No Person shall be a Senator who shall not have attained to the Age of thirty Years, and been nine Years a

Citizen of the United States, and who shall not, when elected, be an Inhabitant of that State for which he shall be chosen."

Today's cases present a challenge to an amendment to the Arkansas State Constitution that prohibits the name of an otherwise-eligible candidate for Congress from appearing on the general election ballot if that candidate has already served three terms in the House of Representatives or two terms in the Senate. The Arkansas Supreme Court held that the amendment violates the Federal Constitution. We agree with that holding. Such a state-imposed restriction is contrary to the "fundamental principle of our representative democracy," embodied in the Constitution, that "the people should choose whom they please to govern them." *Powell v. McCormack*, 395 U.S. 486, 547 (1969) (internal quotation marks omitted). Allowing individual States to adopt their own qualifications for congressional service would be inconsistent with the Framers' vision of a uniform National Legislature representing the people of the United States. If the qualifications set forth in the text of the Constitution are to be changed, that text must be amended.

At the general election on November 3, 1992, the voters of Arkansas adopted Amendment 73 to their State Constitution. Proposed as a "Term Limitation Amendment," its preamble stated: "The people of Arkansas find and declare that elected officials who remain in office too long become preoccupied with reelection and ignore their duties as representatives of the people. Entrenched incumbency has reduced voter participation and has led to an electoral system that is less free, less competitive, and less representative than the system established by the Founding Fathers. Therefore, the people of Arkansas, exercising their reserved powers, herein limit the terms of the elected officials." ***

II

As the opinions of the Arkansas Supreme Court suggest, the constitutionality of Amendment 73 depends critically on the resolution of two distinct issues. The first is whether the Constitution forbids States from adding to or altering the qualifications specifically enumerated in the Constitution. The second is, if the Constitution does so forbid, whether the fact that Amendment 73 is formulated as a ballot access restriction rather than as an outright disqualification is of constitutional significance. Our resolution of these issues draws upon our prior resolution of a related but distinct issue: whether Congress has the power to add to or alter the qualifications of its Members.

Twenty-six years ago, in *Powell v. McCormack*, 395 U.S. 486 (1969), we reviewed the history and text of the Qualifications Clauses in a case involving an attempted exclusion of a duly elected Member of Congress. The principal issue was whether the power granted to each House in Art. I, § 5, to judge the "Qualifications of its own Members" includes the power to impose qualifications other than those set forth in the text of the Constitution. In an opinion by CHIEF JUSTICE WARREN for eight Members of the Court, we held that it does not. *** We concluded that, during the first 100 years of its existence, "Congress strictly limited its power to judge the qualifications of its members to those enumerated in the Constitution." *** We thus conclude now, as we did in *Powell*, that history shows that, with respect to Congress, the Framers intended the Constitution to establish fixed qualifications.

In *Powell*, of course, we did not rely solely on an analysis of the historical evidence, but instead complemented that analysis with "an examination of the basic principles of our democratic system." We noted that allowing Congress to impose additional qualifications would violate that "fundamental principle of our representative democracy *** 'that the people should choose whom they please to govern them.'"

Our opinion made clear that this broad principle incorporated at least two fundamental ideas. First, we emphasized the egalitarian concept that the opportunity to be elected was open to all. *** Second, we recognized the critical postulate that sovereignty is vested in the people, and that sovereignty confers on the people the right to choose freely their representatives to the National Government. ***

III

Our reaffirmation of *Powell* does not necessarily resolve the specific questions presented in these cases. For petitioners argue that whatever the constitutionality of additional qualifications for membership imposed by Congress, the historical and textual materials discussed in *Powell* do not support the conclusion that the Constitution prohibits additional qualifications imposed by States. In the absence of such a constitutional prohibition, petitioners argue, the Tenth Amendment and the principle of reserved powers require that States be allowed to add such qualifications. ***

Petitioners argue that the Constitution contains no express prohibition against state-added qualifications, and that Amendment 73 is therefore an appropriate exercise of a State's reserved power to place additional restrictions on the choices that its own voters may make. We disagree for two independent reasons. First, we conclude that the power to add qualifications is not within the "original powers" of the States, and thus is not reserved to the States by the Tenth Amendment. Second, even if States possessed some original power in this area, we conclude that the Framers intended the Constitution to be the exclusive source of qualifications for members of Congress, and that the Framers thereby "divested" States of any power to add qualifications.***

In short, as the Framers recognized, electing representatives to the National Legislature was a new right, arising from the Constitution itself. The Tenth Amendment thus provides no basis for concluding that the States possess reserved power to add qualifications to those that are fixed in the Constitution. Instead, any state power to set the qualifications for membership in Congress must derive not from the reserved powers of state sovereignty, but rather from the delegated powers of national sovereignty. In the absence of any constitutional delegation to the States of power to add qualifications to those enumerated in the Constitution, such a power does not exist.

Even if we believed that States possessed as part of their original powers some control over congressional qualifications, the text and structure of the Constitution, the relevant historical materials, and, most importantly, the "basic principles of our democratic system" all demonstrate that the Qualifications Clauses were intended to preclude the States from exercising any such power and to fix as exclusive the qualifications in the Constitution.

The available affirmative evidence indicates the Framers' intent that States have no role in the setting of qualifications. *** The provisions in the Constitution governing federal elections confirm the Framers' intent that States lack power to add qualifications. The Framers feared that the diverse interests of the States would undermine the National Legislature, and thus they adopted provisions intended to minimize the possibility of state interference with federal elections. *** In light of the Framers' evident concern that States would try to undermine the National Government, they could not have intended States to have the power to set qualifications. Indeed, one of the more anomalous consequences of petitioners' argument is that it accepts federal supremacy over the procedural aspects of determining the times, places, and manner of elections while allowing the states carte blanche with respect to the substantive qualifications for membership in Congress.

The dissent nevertheless contends that the Framers' distrust of the States with respect to elections does not preclude the people of the States from adopting eligibility requirements to help narrow their own choices. As the dissent concedes, however, the Framers were unquestionably concerned that the States would simply not hold elections for federal officers, and therefore the Framers gave Congress the power to "make or alter" state election regulations. Yet under the dissent's approach, the States could achieve exactly the same result by simply setting qualifications for federal office sufficiently high that no one could meet those qualifications. In our view, it is inconceivable that the Framers would provide a specific constitutional provision to ensure that federal elections would be held while at the same time allowing States to render those elections meaningless by simply ensuring that no candidate could be qualified for office. Given the Framers' wariness over the potential for state abuse, we must conclude that the specification of fixed qualifications in the constitutional text was intended to prescribe uniform rules that would preclude modification by either Congress or the States. *** The Constitution's provision for each House to be the judge of its own qualifications thus provides further evidence that the Framers believed that the primary source of those qualifications would be federal law.

We also find compelling the complete absence in the ratification debates of any assertion that States had the power to add qualifications. In those debates, the question whether to require term limits, or "rotation," was a major source of controversy. The draft of the Constitution that was submitted for ratification contained no provision for rotation.[22] In arguments that echo in the preamble to Arkansas' Amendment 73, opponents of ratification condemned the absence of a rotation requirement, noting that "there is no doubt that senators will hold their office perpetually; and in this situation, they must of necessity lose their dependence, and their attachments to the people." Even proponents of ratification expressed concern about the "abandonment in every instance of the necessity of rotation in office." At several ratification conventions, participants proposed amendments that would have required rotation.

The Federalists' responses to those criticisms and proposals addressed the merits of the issue, arguing that rotation was incompatible with the people's right to choose. ***

In short, if it had been assumed that States could add additional qualifications, that assumption would have provided the basis for a powerful rebuttal to the arguments being advanced. The failure of intelligent and experienced advocates to utilize this argument must reflect a general agreement that its premise was unsound, and that the power to add qualifications was one that the Constitution denied the States. *** [Additionally,] Congress' subsequent experience with state-imposed qualifications provides further evidence of the general consensus on the lack of state power in this area. *** We recognize, as we did in *Powell*, that "congressional practice has been erratic" and that the precedential value of congressional exclusion cases is "quite limited." *Powell*, 395 U.S., at 545–546. Nevertheless, those incidents lend support to the result we reach today.

Our conclusion that States lack the power to impose qualifications vindicates the same "fundamental principle of our representative democracy" that we recognized in *Powell*, namely that "the people should choose whom they please to govern them."

As we noted earlier, the *Powell* Court recognized that an egalitarian ideal—that election to the National Legislature should be open to all people of merit—provided a critical foundation for the Constitutional structure. This egalitarian theme echoes throughout the constitutional debates. *** Additional qualifications pose the same obstacle to open elections whatever their source. The egalitarian ideal, so valued by the Framers, is thus compromised to the same degree by additional qualifications imposed by States as by those imposed by Congress.

Similarly, we believe that state-imposed qualifications, as much as congressionally imposed qualifications, would undermine the second critical idea recognized in *Powell*: that an aspect of sovereignty is the right of the people to vote for whom they wish. Again, the source of the qualification is of little moment in assessing the qualification's restrictive impact.

---

[22] A proposal requiring rotation for members of the House was proposed at the Convention, *see* 1 Farrand 20, but was defeated unanimously. There is no record of any debate on either occasion.

Finally, state-imposed restrictions, unlike the congressionally imposed restrictions at issue in *Powell*, violate a third idea central to this basic principle: that the right to choose representatives belongs not to the States, but to the people. ***

Consistent with these views, the constitutional structure provides for a uniform salary to be paid from the national treasury, allows the States but a limited role in federal elections, and maintains strict checks on state interference with the federal election process. The Constitution also provides that the qualifications of the representatives of each State will be judged by the representatives of the entire Nation. The Constitution thus creates a uniform national body representing the interests of a single people.

Permitting individual States to formulate diverse qualifications for their representatives would result in a patchwork of state qualifications, undermining the uniformity and the national character that the Framers envisioned and sought to ensure. Such a patchwork would also sever the direct link that the Framers found so critical between the National Government and the people of the United States.

Petitioners attempt to overcome this formidable array of evidence against the States' power to impose qualifications by arguing that the practice of the States immediately after the adoption of the Constitution demonstrates their understanding that they possessed such power. One may properly question the extent to which the States' own practice is a reliable indicator of the contours of restrictions that the Constitution imposed on States, especially when no court has ever upheld a state-imposed qualification of any sort. But petitioners' argument is unpersuasive even on its own terms. At the time of the Convention, "[a]lmost all the State Constitutions required members of their Legislatures to possess considerable property." *** The contemporaneous state practice with respect to term limits is similar. At the time of the Convention, States widely supported term limits in at least some circumstances. The Articles of Confederation contained a provision for term limits.[36] As we have noted, some members of the Convention had sought to impose term limits for Members of Congress. In addition, many States imposed term limits on state officers, four placed limits on delegates to the Continental Congress, and several States voiced support for term limits for Members of Congress.[40] Despite this widespread support, no State sought to impose any term limits on its own federal representatives. Thus, a proper assessment of contemporaneous state practice provides further persuasive evidence of a general understanding that the qualifications in the Constitution were unalterable by the States. *** In sum, the available historical and textual evidence, read in light of the basic principles of democracy underlying the Constitution and recognized by this Court in *Powell*, reveal the Framers' intent that neither Congress nor the States

---

[36] *** ("[N]o person shall be capable of being a delegate for more than three years in any term of six years").

[40] [During the ratification debates] at least three states proposed some form of constitutional amendment supporting term limits for Members of Congress.

should possess the power to supplement the exclusive qualifications set forth in the text of the Constitution.

IV

Petitioners argue that, even if States may not add qualifications, Amendment 73 is constitutional because it is not such a qualification, and because Amendment 73 is a permissible exercise of state power to regulate the "Times, Places and Manner of Holding Elections." We reject these contentions. *** In our view, an amendment with the avowed purpose and obvious effect of evading the requirements of the Qualifications Clauses by handicapping a class of candidates cannot stand. To argue otherwise is to suggest that the Framers spent significant time and energy in debating and crafting Clauses that could be easily evaded. More importantly, allowing States to evade the Qualifications Clauses by "dress[ing] eligibility to stand for Congress in ballot access clothing" trivializes the basic principles of our democracy that underlie those Clauses.

Petitioners make the related argument that Amendment 73 merely regulates the "Manner" of elections, and that the Amendment is therefore a permissible exercise of state power under Article I, § 4, cl. 1 (the Elections Clause) to regulate the "Times, Places and Manner" of elections. We cannot agree.

A necessary consequence of petitioners' argument is that Congress itself would have the power to "make or alter" a measure such as Amendment 73. That the Framers would have approved of such a result is unfathomable. As our decision in *Powell* and our discussion above make clear, the Framers were particularly concerned that a grant to Congress of the authority to set its own qualifications would lead inevitably to congressional self-aggrandizement and the upsetting of the delicate constitutional balance. *** Moreover, petitioners' broad construction of the Elections Clause is fundamentally inconsistent with the Framers' view of that Clause. The Framers intended the Elections Clause to grant States authority to create procedural regulations, not to provide States with license to exclude classes of candidates from federal office. ***

We do not understand the dissent to contest our primary thesis, namely that if the qualifications for Congress are fixed in the Constitution, then a State-passed measure with the avowed purpose of imposing indirectly such an additional qualification violates the Constitution. The dissent, instead, raises two objections, challenging the assertion that the Arkansas amendment has the likely effect of creating a qualification, and suggesting that the true intent of Amendment 73 was not to evade the Qualifications Clause but rather to simply "level the playing field. Neither of these objections has merit." ***

V

The merits of term limits, or "rotation," have been the subject of debate since the formation of our Constitution, when the Framers unanimously rejected a proposal to add such limits to the Constitution. The cogent arguments on both sides of the question that were articulated during the process of ratification largely retain their force today. Over half the States have adopted measures that impose such limits on some offices either directly or indirectly, and the Nation as a whole, notably by constitutional amendment, has imposed a limit on the number of terms that the President may serve.[49] ***

We are, however, firmly convinced that allowing the several States to adopt term limits for congressional service would effect a fundamental change in the constitutional framework. Any such change must come not by legislation adopted either by Congress or by an individual State, but rather— as have other important changes in the electoral process[50]—through the Amendment procedures set forth in Article V. The Framers decided that the qualifications for service in the Congress of the United States be fixed in the Constitution and be uniform throughout the Nation. That decision reflects the Framers' understanding that Members of Congress are chosen by separate constituencies, but that they become, when elected, servants of the people of the United States. They are not merely delegates appointed by separate, sovereign States; they occupy offices that are integral and essential components of a single National Government. In the absence of a properly passed constitutional amendment, allowing individual States to craft their own qualifications for Congress would thus erode the structure envisioned by the Framers, a structure that was designed, in the words of the Preamble to our Constitution, to form a "more perfect Union." ***

JUSTICE KENNEDY, concurring.

The majority and dissenting opinions demonstrate the intricacy of the question whether or not the Qualifications Clauses are exclusive. In my view, however, it is well settled that the whole people of the United States asserted their political identity and unity of purpose when they created the federal system. The dissent's course of reasoning suggesting otherwise might be construed to disparage the republican character of the National Government, and it seems appropriate to add these few remarks to explain why that course of argumentation runs counter to fundamental principles of federalism.

Federalism was our Nation's own discovery. The Framers split the atom of sovereignty. It was the genius of their idea that our citizens would have two political capacities, one state and one federal, each protected from incursion by the other. The resulting Constitution created a legal system unprecedented in form and design, establishing two orders of government, each with its own direct relationship, its own privity, its own set of mutual rights and obligations to the people who sustain it and are governed by it. It is appropriate to recall these origins, which instruct us as to the nature of the two different governments created and confirmed by the Constitution.

---

[49] See U.S. Const., Amdt. 22 (1951) (limiting Presidents to two 4–year terms).

[50] See, e.g., Amdt. 17 (1913) (direct elections of Senators); Amdt. 19 (1920) (extending suffrage to women); Amdt. 22 (1951) (Presidential term limits); Amdt. 24 (1964) (prohibition against poll taxes); Amdt. 26 (1971) (lowering age of voter eligibility to 18).

A distinctive character of the National Government, the mark of its legitimacy, is that it owes its existence to the act of the whole people who created it. ***

In one sense it is true that "the people of each State retained their separate political identities," for the Constitution takes care both to preserve the States and to make use of their identities and structures at various points in organizing the federal union. It does not at all follow from this that the sole political identity of an American is with the State of his or her residence. It denies the dual character of the Federal Government which is its very foundation to assert that the people of the United States do not have a political identity as well, one independent of, though consistent with, their identity as citizens of the State of their residence. ***

It might be objected that because the States ratified the Constitution, the people can delegate power only through the States or by acting in their capacities as citizens of particular States. But in *McCulloch v. Maryland*, the Court set forth its authoritative rejection of this idea:

> " *** [The Constitution] was submitted to the people. *** It is true, they assembled in their several States—and where else should they have assembled? No political dreamer was ever wild enough to think of breaking down the lines which separate the States, and of compounding the American people into one common mass. Of consequence, when they act, they act in their States. But the measures they adopt do not, on that account, cease to be the measures of the people themselves, or become the measures of the state governments."

The political identity of the entire people of the Union is reinforced by the proposition. Which I take to be beyond dispute, that, though limited as to its objects, the National Government is, and must be, controlled by the people without collateral interference by the States. *McCulloch* affirmed this proposition as well, when the Court rejected the suggestion that States could interfere with federal powers. *** The States have no power, reserved or otherwise, over the exercise of federal authority within its proper sphere. *** That the States may not invade the sphere of federal sovereignty is as incontestable, in my view, as the corollary proposition that the Federal Government must be held within the boundaries of its own power when it intrudes upon matters reserved to the States. See *United States v. Lopez*, 514 U.S. 549 (1995).

Of course, because the Framers recognized that state power and identity were essential parts of the federal balance, see The Federalist No. 39, the Constitution is solicitous of the prerogatives of the States, even in an otherwise sovereign federal province. *** Nothing in the Constitution or The Federalist Papers, however, supports the idea of state interference with the most basic relation between the National Government and its citizens, the selection of legislative representatives. *** There can be no doubt, if we are to respect the republican origins of the Nation and preserve its federal character, that there exists a federal right of citizenship, a relationship between the people of the Nation and their National Government, with which the States may not interfere. Because the Arkansas enactment intrudes upon this federal domain, it exceeds the boundaries of the Constitution.

JUSTICE THOMAS, with whom THE CHIEF JUSTICE, JUSTICE O'CONNOR, and JUSTICE SCALIA join, dissenting.

It is ironic that the Court bases today's decision on the right of the people to "choose whom they please to govern them." Under our Constitution, there is only one State whose people have the right to "choose whom they please" to represent Arkansas in Congress. The Court holds, however, that neither the elected legislature of that State nor the people themselves (acting by ballot initiative) may prescribe any qualifications for those representatives. The majority therefore defends the right of the people of Arkansas to "choose whom they please to govern them" by invalidating a provision that won nearly 60% of the votes cast in a direct election and that carried every congressional district in the State.

I dissent. Nothing in the Constitution deprives the people of each State of the power to prescribe eligibility requirements for the candidates who seek to represent them in Congress. The Constitution is simply silent on this question. And where the Constitution is silent, it raises no bar to action by the States or the people.

I

Because the majority fundamentally misunderstands the notion of "reserved" powers, I start with some first principles. Contrary to the majority's suggestion, the people of the States need not point to any affirmative grant of power in the Constitution in order to prescribe qualifications for their representatives in Congress, or to authorize their elected state legislators to do so.

Our system of government rests on one overriding principle: all power stems from the consent of the people. To phrase the principle in this way, however, is to be imprecise about something important to the notion of "reserved" powers. The ultimate source of the Constitution's authority is the consent of the people of each individual State, not the consent of the undifferentiated people of the Nation as a whole.

When they adopted the Federal Constitution, of course, the people of each State surrendered some of their authority to the United States (and hence to entities accountable to the people of other States as well as to themselves). They affirmatively deprived their States of certain powers, see, e.g., Art. I, § 10, and they affirmatively conferred certain powers upon the Federal Government, see, e.g., Art. I, § 8. Because the people of the several States are the only true source of power, however, the Federal Government enjoys no authority beyond what the Constitution confers: the Federal Government's powers are limited and enumerated. ***

In each State, the remainder of the people's powers—"[t]he powers not delegated to the United States by the Constitution, nor prohibited by it to the

States," Amdt. 10—are either delegated to the state government or retained by the people. The Federal Constitution does not specify which of these two possibilities obtains; it is up to the various state constitutions to declare which powers the people of each State have delegated to their state government. As far as the Federal Constitution is concerned, then, the States can exercise all powers that the Constitution does not withhold from them. The Federal Government and the States thus face different default rules: where the Constitution is silent about the exercise of a particular power— that is, where the Constitution does not speak either expressly or by necessary implication—the Federal Government lacks that power and the States enjoy it.

These basic principles are enshrined in the Tenth Amendment, which declares that all powers neither delegated to the Federal Government nor prohibited to the States "are reserved to the States respectively, or to the people." With this careful last phrase, the Amendment avoids taking any position on the division of power between the state governments and the people of the States: it is up to the people of each State to determine which "reserved" powers their state government may exercise. But the Amendment does make clear that powers reside at the state level except where the Constitution removes them from that level. All powers that the Constitution neither delegates to the Federal Government nor prohibits to the States are controlled by the people of each State.

To be sure, when the Tenth Amendment uses the phrase "the people," it does not specify whether it is referring to the people of each State or the people of the Nation as a whole. But the latter interpretation would make the Amendment pointless: there would have been no reason to provide that where the Constitution is silent about whether a particular power resides at the state level, it might or might not do so. In addition, it would make no sense to speak of powers as being reserved to the undifferentiated people of the Nation as a whole, because the Constitution does not contemplate that those people will either exercise power or delegate it. The Constitution simply does not recognize any mechanism for action by the undifferentiated people of the Nation. Thus, the amendment provision of Article V calls for amendments to be ratified not by a convention of the national people, but by conventions of the people in each State or by the state legislatures elected by those people. Likewise, the Constitution calls for Members of Congress to be chosen State by State, rather than in nationwide elections. Even the selection of the President—surely the most national of national figures—is accomplished by an electoral college made up of delegates chosen by the various States, and candidates can lose a Presidential election despite winning a majority of the votes cast in the Nation as a whole. ***

Any ambiguity in the Tenth Amendment's use of the phrase "the people" is cleared up by the body of the Constitution itself. Article I begins by providing that the Congress of the United States enjoys "[a]ll legislative Powers herein granted," § 1, and goes on to give a careful enumeration of Congress' powers, § 8. It then concludes by enumerating certain powers that are prohibited to the States. The import of this structure is the same as the import of the Tenth Amendment: if we are to invalidate Arkansas' Amendment 73, we must point to something in the Federal Constitution that deprives the people of Arkansas of the power to enact such measures.

*** The majority's essential logic is that the state governments could not "reserve" any powers that they did not control at the time the Constitution was drafted. But it was not the state governments that were doing the reserving. The Constitution derives its authority instead from the consent of the people of the States. Given the fundamental principle that all governmental powers stem from the people of the States, it would simply be incoherent to assert that the people of the States could not reserve any powers that they had not previously controlled.

The Tenth Amendment's use of the word "reserved" does not help the majority's position. If someone says that the power to use a particular facility is reserved to some group, he is not saying anything about whether that group has previously used the facility. He is merely saying that the people who control the facility have designated that group as the entity with authority to use it. The Tenth Amendment is similar: the people of the States, from whom all governmental powers stem, have specified that all powers not prohibited to the States by the Federal Constitution are reserved "to the States respectively, or to the people."

The majority is therefore quite wrong to conclude that the people of the States cannot authorize their state governments to exercise any powers that were unknown to the States when the Federal Constitution was drafted. Indeed, the majority's position frustrates the apparent purpose of the Amendment's final phrase. The Amendment does not pre-empt any limitations on state power found in the state constitutions, as it might have done if it simply had said that the powers not delegated to the Federal Government are reserved to the States. But the Amendment also does not prevent the people of the States from amending their state constitutions to remove limitations that were in effect when the Federal Constitution and the Bill of Rights were ratified.

*** As for the fact that a State has no reserved power to establish qualifications for the office of President, it surely need not follow that a State has no reserved power to establish qualifications for the Members of Congress who represent the people of that State. Because powers are reserved to the States "respectively," it is clear that no State may legislate for another State: even though the Arkansas legislature enjoys the reserved power to pass a minimum-wage law for Arkansas, it has no power to pass a minimum-wage law for Vermont. For the same reason, Arkansas may not decree that only Arkansas citizens are eligible to be President of the United States; the selection of the President is not up to Arkansas alone, and Arkansas can no more prescribe the qualifications for that office than it can set the qualifications for Members of Congress from Florida. But none of this suggests that Arkansas cannot set qualifications for Members of Congress from Arkansas. ***

In a final effort to deny that the people of the States enjoy "reserved" powers over the selection of their representatives in Congress, the majority suggests that the Constitution expressly delegates to the States certain powers over congressional elections. Such delegations of power, the majority argues, would be superfluous if the people of the States enjoyed reserved powers in this area.

Only one constitutional provision—the Times, Places and Manner Clause of Article I, § 4—even arguably supports the majority's suggestion. *** Contrary to the majority's assumption, however, this Clause does not delegate any authority to the States. Instead, it simply imposes a duty upon them. The majority gets it exactly right: by specifying that the state legislatures "shall" prescribe the details necessary to hold congressional elections, the Clause "expressly requires action by the States." This command meshes with one of the principal purposes of Congress' "make or alter" power: to ensure that the States hold congressional elections in the first place, so that Congress continues to exist. *** Constitutional provisions that impose affirmative duties on the States are hardly inconsistent with the notion of reserved powers.

Of course, the second part of the Times, Places and Manner Clause does grant a power rather than impose a duty. As its contrasting uses of the words "shall" and "may" confirm, however, the Clause grants power exclusively to Congress, not to the States. If the Clause did not exist at all, the States would still be able to prescribe the times, places, and manner of holding congressional elections; the deletion of the provision would simply deprive Congress of the power to override these state regulations. ***

II

I take it to be established, then, that the people of Arkansas do enjoy "reserved" powers over the selection of their representatives in Congress. *** Whatever one might think of the wisdom of this arrangement, we may not override the decision of the people of Arkansas unless something in the Federal Constitution deprives them of the power to enact such measures. ***

[JUSTICE THOMAS indicates the "Qualifications Clauses are merely straightforward recitations of the minimum eligibility requirements that the Framers thought it essential for every Member of Congress to meet. They restrict state power only in that they prevent the States from abolishing all eligibility," discusses "the democratic principles that contributed to the Framers' decision to withhold this power from Congress do not prove that the Framers also deprived the people of the States of their reserved authority to set eligibility requirements for their own representatives," and argues that "the historical evidence refutes any notion that the Qualifications Clauses were generally understood to be exclusive."]

*** This conclusion is buttressed by our reluctance to read constitutional provisions to preclude state power by negative implication. The very structure of the Constitution counsels such hesitation. After all, § 10 of Article I contains a brief list of express prohibitions on the States. *** The majority responds that "a patchwork of state qualifications" would "undermin[e] the uniformity and the national character that the Framers envisioned and sought to ensure." Yet the Framers thought it perfectly consistent with the "national character" of Congress for the Senators and Representatives from each State to be chosen by the legislature or the people of that State. The majority never explains why Congress' fundamental character permits this state-centered system, but nonetheless prohibits the people of the States and their state legislatures from setting any eligibility requirements for the candidates who seek to represent them.

*** Although the Qualifications Clauses neither state nor imply the prohibition that it finds in them, the majority infers from the Framers' "democratic principles" that the Clauses must have been generally understood to preclude the people of the States and their state legislatures from prescribing any additional qualifications for their representatives in Congress. But the majority's evidence on this point establishes only two more modest propositions: (1) the Framers did not want the Federal Constitution itself to impose a broad set of disqualifications for congressional office, and (2) the Framers did not want the Federal Congress to be able to supplement the few disqualifications that the Constitution does set forth. The logical conclusion is simply that the Framers did not want the people of the States and their state legislatures to be constrained by too many qualifications imposed at the national level. The evidence does not support the majority's more sweeping conclusion that the Framers intended to bar the people of the States and their state legislatures from adopting additional eligibility requirements to help narrow their own choices. ***

As the majority argues, democratic principles also contributed to the Framers' decision to withhold the qualification-setting power from Congress. But the majority is wrong to suggest that the same principles must also have led the Framers to deny this power to the people of the States and the state legislatures. In particular, it simply is not true that "the source of the qualification is of little moment in assessing the qualification's restrictive impact." There is a world of difference between a self-imposed constraint and a constraint imposed from above.

Congressional power over qualifications would have enabled the representatives from some States, acting collectively in the National Legislature, to prevent the people of another State from electing their preferred candidates. *** Yet this is simply to say that qualifications should not be set at the national level for offices whose occupants are selected at the state level. The majority never identifies the democratic principles that would have been violated if a state legislature, in the days before the Constitution was amended to provide for the direct election of Senators, had imposed some limits of its own on the field of candidates that it would consider for appointment. Likewise, the majority does not explain why democratic principles forbid the people of a State from adopting additional eligibility requirements to help narrow their choices among candidates seeking to represent them in the House of Representatives. Indeed, the invocation of democratic principles to invalidate Amendment 73 seems particularly difficult in the present case, because Amendment 73 remains fully within the control of the people of Arkansas. If they wanted to repeal it (despite the 20–point margin by which they enacted it less than three years ago), they could do so by a simple majority vote.

The majority appears to believe that restrictions on eligibility for office are inherently undemocratic. But the Qualifications Clauses themselves prove that the Framers did not share this view; eligibility requirements to which the people of the States consent are perfectly consistent with the Framers' scheme. In fact, we have described "the authority of the people of the States to determine the qualifications of their most important government officials" as "an authority that lies at the heart of representative government." *Gregory v. Ashcroft*, 501 U.S. 452, 463 (1991) (internal quotation marks omitted) (refusing to read federal law to preclude States from imposing a mandatory retirement age on state judges who are subject to periodic retention elections). When the people of a State themselves decide to restrict the field of candidates whom they are willing to send to Washington as their representatives, they simply have not violated the principle that "the people should choose whom they please to govern them."

At one point, the majority suggests that the principle identified by Hamilton encompasses not only the electorate's right to choose, but also "the egalitarian concept that the opportunity to be elected [is] open to all." To the extent that the second idea has any content independent of the first, the majority apparently would read the Qualifications Clauses to create a personal right to be a candidate for Congress, and then to set that right above the authority of the people of the States to prescribe eligibility requirements for public office. But we have never suggested that "the opportunity to be elected" is open even to those whom the voters have decided not to elect. On that rationale, a candidate might have a right to appear on the ballot in the general election even though he lost in the primary. *** In fact, the authority to narrow the field of candidates in this way may be part and parcel of the right to elect Members of Congress. That is, the right to choose may include the right to winnow. ***

But one need not agree with me that the people of each State may delegate their qualification-setting power in order to uphold Arkansas' Amendment 73. Amendment 73 is not the act of a state legislature; it is the act of the people of Arkansas, adopted at a direct election and inserted into the state constitution. The majority never explains why giving effect to the people's decision would violate the "democratic principles" that undergird the Constitution. Instead, the majority's discussion of democratic principles is directed entirely to attacking eligibility requirements imposed on the people of a State by an entity other than themselves.

The majority protests that any distinction between the people of the States and the state legislatures is "untenable" and "astonishing." In the limited area of congressional elections, however, the Framers themselves drew this distinction: they specifically provided for Senators to be chosen by the state legislatures and for Representatives to be chosen by the people. In the context of congressional elections, the Framers obviously saw a meaningful difference between direct action by the people of each State and action by their state legislatures ***.

In addition to its arguments about democratic principles, the majority asserts that more specific historical evidence supports its view that the Framers did not intend to permit supplementation of the Qualifications Clauses. But when one focuses on the distinction between congressional power to add qualifications for congressional office and the power of the people or their state legislatures to add such qualifications, one realizes that this assertion has little basis.

In particular, the detail with which the majority recites the historical evidence set forth in *Powell v. McCormack*, 395 U.S. 486, 489 (1969), should not obscure the fact that this evidence has no bearing on the question now before the Court. As the majority ultimately concedes, it does not establish "the Framers' intent that the qualifications in the Constitution be fixed and exclusive;" it shows only that the Framers did not intend Congress to be able to enact qualifications laws. If anything, the solidity of the evidence supporting *Powell*'s view that Congress lacks the power to supplement the constitutional disqualifications merely highlights the weakness of the majority's evidence that the States and the people of the States also lack this power. ***

III

It is radical enough for the majority to hold that the Constitution implicitly precludes the people of the States from prescribing any eligibility requirements for the congressional candidates who seek their votes. This holding, after all, does not stop with negating the term limits that many States have seen fit to impose on their Senators and Representatives. Today's decision also means that no State may disqualify congressional candidates whom a court has found to be mentally incompetent, who are currently in prison, or who have past vote-fraud convictions. Likewise, after today's decision, the people of each State must leave open the possibility that they will trust someone with their vote in Congress even though they do not trust him with a vote in the election for Congress. ***

I do not mean to suggest that States have unbridled power to handicap particular classes of candidates, even when those candidates enjoy federally conferred advantages that may threaten to skew the electoral process. But laws that allegedly have the purpose and effect of handicapping a particular class of candidates traditionally are reviewed under the First and Fourteenth Amendments rather than the Qualifications Clauses. Term-limit measures have tended to survive such review without difficulty.

To analyze such laws under the Qualifications Clauses may open up whole new vistas for courts. If it is true that "the current congressional campaign finance system *** has created an electoral system so stacked against challengers that in many elections voters have no real choices," are the Federal Election Campaign Act Amendments of 1974 unconstitutional under (of all things) the Qualifications Clauses? If it can be shown that nonminorities are at a significant disadvantage when they seek election in districts dominated by minority voters, would the intentional creation of "majority-minority districts" violate the Qualifications Clauses even if it were to survive scrutiny under the Fourteenth Amendment? More generally, if "[d]istrict lines are rarely neutral phenomena" and if "districting inevitably has and is intended to have substantial political consequences," *Gaffney v. Cummings*, 412 U.S. 735 (1973), will plausible Qualifications Clause challenges greet virtually every redistricting decision?

The majority's opinion may not go so far, although it does not itself suggest any principled stopping point. No matter how narrowly construed, however, today's decision reads the Qualifications Clauses to impose substantial implicit prohibitions on the States and the people of the States. I would not draw such an expansive negative inference from the fact that the Constitution requires Members of Congress to be a certain age, to be inhabitants of the States that they represent, and to have been United States citizens for a specified period. Rather, I would read the Qualifications Clauses to do no more than what they say. I respectfully dissent.

Notes

1. **Two Preliminary Exercises.**

   (a) If you had been an Arkansas voter presented with the opportunity to vote for or against this term limits initiative, how would you have voted and why? Make a list of the factors on both sides of the question that you would consider.

   (b) Outline the positions of the majority and dissenting opinions on (1) the meaning of the textual language, (2) historical evidence concerning the intent of the Framers, (3) use of precedent, and (4) first principles. After contemplation, consider whether you find the majority or the dissent to be more persuasive and be prepared to articulate why.

2. **History.** As you can tell, historians may have differing views on the issue before the Court. Should the Supreme Court provide definitive historical analysis, especially when few (if any) members of the Court are trained historians? Do you think the answer to the historical question would have come out differently if the issue had been exclusion of a convicted felon from congressional service?

3. **Alternatives.**

   • What alternatives do you see to historical analysis when the text is indeterminate? Would you find a Supreme Court decision more (or less) satisfying which argued that "current democratic principles within our federal system now demand" uniformity of qualifications for Senators and Representatives, even if that was not required two centuries ago?

   • Should the Supreme Court have considered that its decision is unlikely to be reversed since the virtually exclusive mode of amending the Constitution to date has been through the process of a 2/3 majority vote in the Senate and House, whose members are unlikely to support term limits?

What potential would there be for amendment if the decision had gone 5–4 the other way?

4. **Principles and Term Limits?** ASSOCIATE JUSTICE BREYER, *in Judicial Review: A Practicing Judge's Perspective*, 78 TEX. L. REV. 761, 769 (2000), wrote that in *Term Limits*:

> "The ordinary 'nonsubjective' factors [language, history, purpose, and structure] *** were close to equipoise. The more one sees the Constitution as providing a stable democratic government over time, the more one sees a state term limits requirement as making a major change (with unforeseeable but certainly important institutional consequences) ***. The more one sees in the Constitution's division of powers an insistence upon the continued influence, power, and authority of the individual states, the more one would likely believe that the Constitution, without amendment, permits a state to impose the additional requirements. *** I find it difficult to characterize the resulting conclusion as unusually 'political' or particularly 'ideological' or even highly 'subjective,' as those terms are normally used. Rather, differences in outcome reflect somewhat different views of the same constitutional framework ***."

Do you agree with JUSTICE BREYER that this fundamental choice is not political, ideological, or subjective?

5. **Elections Clause Analysis.** Petitioners in *U.S. Term Limits* raised two separate arguments: (1) that Arkansas' Amendment 73 was a proper exercise of the state's reserved powers under the Tenth Amendment; and (2) that the term limits amendment was a ballot access restriction supported by the State's power under the Elections Clause to regulate the "Times, Places, and Manner of holding Elections." In rejecting the argument that the amendment regulated the manner of elections, the Court said: "The Framers intended the Elections Clause to grant States the authority to create procedural regulations, not to provide States with license to exclude classes of candidates from federal office." Because the States could not reserve any power in setting the qualifications for federal office, those who sought to advance the cause of term limits next couched their arguments in terms of Elections Clause procedures.

An amendment to Article VIII of the Missouri State Constitution required those elected as U.S. Representatives and Senators from Missouri to use all their powers to bring about passage of an amendment to the federal constitution that would "limit service in the U.S. Congress to three terms in the House of Representatives and two terms in the Senate." *Cook v. Gralike*, 531 U.S. 510 (2001), held this amendment unconstitutional:

> *** Three provisions in Article VIII combine to advance its purpose. Section 17 prescribes that the statement "DISREGARDED VOTERS' INSTRUCTION ON TERM LIMITS" be printed on all primary and general ballots adjacent to the name of a Senator or Representative who fails to take any one of eight legislative acts in support of the proposed amendment. Section 18 provides that the statement "DECLINED TO PLEDGE TO SUPPORT TERM LIMITS" be printed on all primary and general election ballots next to the name of every nonincumbent congressional candidate who

refuses to take a "Term Limit" pledge that commits the candidate, if elected, to performing the legislative acts enumerated in § 17. And § 19 directs the Missouri Secretary of State to determine and declare, *** whether either statement should be printed alongside the name of each candidate for Congress. *** Article VIII furthers the State's interest in adding a term limits amendment to the Federal Constitution in two ways. It encourages Missouri's congressional delegation to support such an amendment in order to avoid an unfavorable ballot designation when running for reelection. And it encourages the election of representatives who favor such an amendment. *** Article VIII is not a procedural regulation. It does not regulate the time of elections; it does not regulate the place of elections; nor, we believe, does it regulate the manner of elections. *** Rather, Article VIII is plainly designed to favor candidates who are willing to support the particular form of a term limits amendment set forth in its text and to disfavor those who either oppose term limits entirely or would prefer a different proposal. *** In describing the two labels, the courts below have employed terms such as "pejorative," "negative," "derogatory," "intentionally intimidating," "particularly harmful," "politically damaging," "a serious sanction," "a penalty," and "official denunciation." *** Thus, far from regulating the procedural mechanisms of elections, Article VIII attempts to "dictate electoral outcomes." *U.S. Term Limits*.***

6. **Political Questions and the Elections Clause.** Consider the six *Baker v. Carr* political question factors. Doesn't the text of the Elections Clause commit resolution of disputes regarding the exercise of state power under the clause to Congress? If it is not clear whether an action by a state is procedural or substantive, does this indicate a lack of judicially discoverable and manageable standards? Is the Supreme Court in a better position than Congress to discern what works a substantive change in the congressional electoral process? What does this indicate about the respect Congress receives as a coequal, coordinate branch of the federal government? The Supreme Court in *U.S. Term Limits* could have allowed Congress to revise Arkansas' action by statute, so long as Congress did not substantively change the electoral process in contravention of the Qualifications Clauses. But instead, the Court held the states had no power to add to the qualifications; the Court rather than Congress defined federalism's limits on the states.

2. FEDERAL PREEMPTION OF STATE LAW

Federal and State powers overlap extensively. Such overlap guarantees that there will be conflicts between the laws of the two sovereigns. The doctrine for resolving such conflicts, preemption, stems from Article VI, cl. 2 of the Constitution:

> "This Constitution, and the Laws of the United States which shall be made in Pursuance thereof; and all Treaties made, or which shall be made, under the Authority of the United States, shall be the supreme Law of the Land; and the Judges in every State shall be bound thereby, any Thing in the Constitution or Laws of any State to the Contrary notwithstanding."

An analogous clause of the Articles of Confederation, Article XIII, reads:

> "Every State shall abide by the determinations of the United States in Congress assembled, on all questions which by this confederation are submitted to them."

The Constitution's Supremacy Clause is stronger than its counterpart in the Articles of Confederation. First, it clearly requires state courts to implement the priority of the laws passed by Congress "pursuant to" the powers surveyed in Chapter IV. Arguably, implementing legislation was required from the state legislatures under Article XIII. Second, it establishes the rule that federal law trumps state law, just as the rule "later in time, first in priority" governs the relationship between two statutes passed by the same sovereign's legislature. Third, as discussed in Chapter II, the ultimate arbiter of such conflicts is the United States Supreme Court. No such institution existed under the Articles.

The Supreme Court has decided hundreds of preemption cases, a fact that has led some commentators to deem preemption the most active field of constitutional law. Commentators also have observed that preemption is a "muddle," "chaos," an "awful mess," and "confused," largely because the *extent* to which federal law ought to prevail in our federal system remains ambiguous. Yet this casebook devotes only two cases to this topic, and some professors who use the book will not assign either of them.

Why such a cursory treatment of such an important subject? First, preemption is often covered as a substantive component of other law school courses. Second, preemption cases generally involve extensive construction of both federal and state law; the constitutional framework within which such decisions are made is secondary.

The following cases raise basic constitutional framework issues about the scope of preemption relatively directly. They also demonstrate deep disagreements, not predictably grounded in specific visions of federalism.

GEIER v. AMERICAN HONDA MOTOR COMPANY
529 U.S. 861, 120 S.Ct. 1913, 146 L.Ed.2d 914 (2000).

JUSTICE BREYER delivered the opinion of the Court.

This case focuses on the 1984 version of a Federal Motor Vehicle Safety Standard promulgated by the Department of Transportation under the authority of the National Traffic and Motor Vehicle Safety Act of 1966. The standard, FMVSS 208, required auto manufacturers to equip some but not all of their 1987 vehicles with passive restraints [airbags]. We ask whether the Act pre-empts a state common-law tort action in which the plaintiff claims that the defendant auto manufacturer, who was in compliance with the standard, should nonetheless have equipped a 1987 automobile with airbags. [Alexis Geier, while driving a 1987 Honda Accord equipped with manual shoulder and lap belts which Geier had buckled, collided with a tree and was seriously injured. Geier sued under D.C. tort law, claiming that American Honda had designed his car negligently and defectively by not providing a driver's side airbag.] *** The basic question, then, is whether a common-law "no airbag" action like the one before us actually conflicts with FMVSS 208. We hold that it does.

In petitioners' and the dissent's view, FMVSS 208 sets a minimum airbag standard. As far as FMVSS 208 is concerned, the more airbags, and the sooner, the better. But that was not the Secretary's view. DOT's comments, which accompanied the promulgation of FMVSS 208, make clear that the standard deliberately provided the manufacturer with a range of choices among different passive restraint devices. Those choices would bring about a mix of different devices introduced gradually over time; and FMVSS 208 would thereby lower costs, overcome technical safety problems, encourage technological development, and win widespread consumer acceptance—all of which would promote FMVSS 208's safety objectives. *** DOT's own contemporaneous explanation of FMVSS 208 makes clear that the 1984 version of FMVSS 208 reflected the following significant considerations. First, buckled up seatbelts are a vital ingredient of automobile safety. Second, despite the enormous and unnecessary risks that a passenger runs by not buckling up manual lap and shoulder belts, more than 80% of front seat passengers would leave their manual seatbelts unbuckled. Third, airbags could make up for the dangers caused by unbuckled manual belts, but they could not make up for them entirely. Fourth, passive restraint systems had their own disadvantages, for example, the dangers associated with, intrusiveness of, and corresponding public dislike for, nondetachable automatic belts. Fifth, airbags brought with them their own special risks to safety, such as the risk of danger to out-of-position occupants (usually children) in small cars. Sixth, airbags were expected to be significantly more expensive than other passive restraint devices, raising the average cost of a vehicle price $320 for full frontal airbags over the cost of a car with manual lap and shoulder seatbelts (and potentially much more if production volumes were low). And the agency worried that the high replacement cost—estimated to be $800—could lead car owners to refuse to replace them after deployment. Seventh, the public, for reasons of cost, fear, or physical intrusiveness, might resist installation or use of any of the then-available passive restraint devices—a particular concern with respect to airbags.

FMVSS 208 *** deliberately sought variety—a mix of several different passive restraint systems. It did so by setting a performance requirement for passive restraint devices and allowing manufacturers to choose among different passive restraint mechanisms, such as airbags, automatic belts, or other passive restraint technologies to satisfy that requirement. *** The 1984 FMVSS 208 standard also deliberately sought a gradual phase-in of passive restraints. *** Of course, as the dissent points out, FMVSS 208 did not guarantee the mix by setting a ceiling for each different passive restraint device. In fact, it provided a form of extra credit for airbag installation (and other nonbelt passive restraint devices) under which each airbag-installed vehicle counted as 1.5 vehicles for purposes of meeting FMVSS 208's passive restraint requirement. But why should DOT have bothered to impose an airbag ceiling when the practical threat to the mix it desired arose from the likelihood that manufacturers would install, not too many airbags too quickly, but too few or none at all? *** The credit provision reinforces the point that FMVSS 208 sought a gradually developing mix of passive restraint devices; it does not show the contrary. ***

In effect, petitioners' tort action depends upon its claim that manufacturers had a duty to install an airbag when they manufactured the 1987 Honda Accord. Such a state law—i.e., a rule of state tort law imposing such a duty—by its terms would have required manufacturers of all similar cars to install airbags rather than other passive restraint systems, such as automatic belts or passive interiors. It thereby would have presented an obstacle to the variety and mix of devices that the federal regulation sought. It would have required all manufacturers to have installed airbags in respect to the entire District-of-Columbia-related portion of their 1987 new car fleet, even though FMVSS 208 at that time required only that 10% of a manufacturer's nationwide fleet be equipped with any passive restraint device at all. It thereby also would have stood as an obstacle to the gradual passive restraint phase-in that the federal regulation deliberately imposed. In addition, it could have made less likely the adoption of a state mandatory buckle-up law. Because the rule of law for which petitioners contend would have stood "as an obstacle to the accomplishment and execution of" the important means-related federal objectives that we have just discussed, it is pre-empted.

Petitioners ask this Court to calculate the precise size of the "obstacle," with the aim of minimizing it, by considering the risk of tort liability and a successful tort action's incentive-related or timing-related compliance effects. But this Court's pre-emption cases do not ordinarily turn on such compliance-related considerations as whether a private party in practice would ignore state legal obligations—paying, say, a fine instead—or how likely it is that state law actually would be enforced. Rather, this Court's pre-emption cases ordinarily assume compliance with the state law duty in question. The Court has on occasion suggested that tort law may be somewhat different, and that related considerations—for example, the ability to pay damages instead of modifying one's behavior—may be relevant for pre-emption purposes. We need not try to resolve these differences here, however, for the incentive or compliance considerations upon which the dissent relies cannot, by themselves, change the legal result. Some of those considerations rest on speculation; some rest in critical part upon the dissenters' own view of FMVSS 208's basic purposes—a view which we reject; and others, if we understand them correctly, seem less than persuasive. And in so concluding, we do not "put the burden" of proving pre-emption on petitioners. We simply find unpersuasive their arguments attempting to undermine the Government's demonstration of actual conflict. ***

The dissent would require a formal agency statement of pre-emptive intent as a prerequisite to concluding that a conflict exists. It relies on cases, or portions thereof, that did not involve conflict pre-emption. And conflict pre-emption is different in that it turns on the identification of "actual conflict," and not on an express statement of pre-emptive intent. While "[p]re-emption fundamentally is a question of congressional intent," this Court traditionally distinguishes between "express" and "implied" pre-emptive intent, and treats "conflict" pre-emption as an instance of the latter. And though the Court has looked for a specific statement of pre-emptive intent where it is claimed that the mere "volume and complexity" of agency regulations demonstrate an implicit intent to displace all state law in a particular area—so-called "field pre-emption"—the Court has never before required a specific, formal agency statement identifying conflict in order to conclude that such a conflict in fact exists. Indeed, one can assume that Congress or an agency ordinarily would not intend to permit a significant conflict. While we certainly accept the dissent's basic position that a court should not find pre-emption too readily in the absence of clear evidence of a conflict, for the reasons set out above we find such evidence here. To insist on a specific expression of agency intent to pre-empt, made after notice-and-comment rulemaking, would be in certain cases to tolerate conflicts that an agency, and therefore Congress, is most unlikely to have intended. The dissent, as we have said, apparently welcomes that result, at least where "frustration-of-purpos[e]" pre-emption by agency regulation is at issue. We do not.

Nor do we agree with the dissent that the agency's views, as presented here, lack coherence. *** It is possible that some special design-related circumstance concerning a particular kind of car might require airbags, rather than automatic belts, and that a suit seeking to impose that requirement could escape pre-emption—say, because it would affect so few cars that its rule of law would not create a legal "obstacle" to 208's mixed-fleet, gradual objective. But that is not what petitioners claimed. They have argued generally that, to be safe, a car must have an airbag. *** FMVSS 208 sought a gradually developing mix of alternative passive restraint devices for safety-related reasons. The rule of state tort law for which petitioners argue would stand as an "obstacle" to the accomplishment of that objective. And the statute foresees the application of ordinary principles of pre-emption in cases of actual conflict. Hence, the tort action is pre-empted. ***

JUSTICE STEVENS, with whom JUSTICE SOUTER, JUSTICE THOMAS, and JUSTICE GINSBURG join, dissenting.

*** "This is a case about federalism," that is, about respect for "the constitutional role of the States as sovereign entities." *Alden v. Maine*, 527 U.S. 706 (1999). It raises important questions concerning the way in which the Federal Government may exercise its undoubted power to oust state courts of their traditional jurisdiction over common-law tort actions. The rule the Court enforces today was not enacted by Congress and is not to be found in the text of any Executive Order or regulation. It has a unique origin: it is the product of the Court's interpretation of the final commentary accompanying an interim administrative regulation and the history of airbag regulation generally. Like many other judge-made rules, its contours are not precisely defined. *** Perhaps such a rule would be a wise component of a legislative reform of our tort system. I express no opinion about that possibility. It is, however, quite clear to me that Congress neither enacted any such rule itself nor authorized the Secretary of Transportation to do so. It is equally clear to me that the objectives that the Secretary intended to achieve through the adoption of Federal Motor Vehicle Safety Standard 208 would not be frustrated one whit by allowing state courts to determine whether in 1987 the life-saving advantages of airbags had become sufficiently obvious that their omission might constitute a design defect in some new cars. Finally, I submit that the Court is quite wrong to characterize its rejection of the presumption against pre-emption, and its reliance on history and regulatory commentary rather than either statutory or regulatory text, as "ordinary experience-proved principles of conflict pre-emption."

The question presented is whether either the National Traffic and Motor Vehicle Safety Act of 1966 (Safety Act or Act), or the version of Standard 208 promulgated by the Secretary of Transportation in 1984, pre-empts common-law tort claims that an automobile manufactured in 1987 was negligently and defectively designed because it lacked "an effective and safe passive restraint system, including, but not limited to, airbags." *** The purpose of the Act, as stated by Congress, was "to reduce traffic accidents and deaths and injuries to persons resulting from traffic accidents." The Act directed the Secretary of Transportation or his delegate to issue motor vehicle safety standards that "shall be practicable, shall meet the need for motor vehicle safety, and shall be stated in objective terms." The Act defines the term "safety standard" as a "minimum standard for motor vehicle performance, or motor vehicle equipment performance."

Standard 208 covers "[o]ccupant crash protection." Its purpose "is to reduce the number of deaths of vehicle occupants, and the severity of injuries, by specifying vehicle crashworthiness requirements *** [and] equipment requirements for active and passive restraint systems." *** The 1984 standard provided for a phase-in of passive restraint requirements beginning with the 1987 model year. *** While the 1987 Honda Accord driven by Ms. Geier was not so equipped, it is undisputed that Honda complied with the 10% minimum by installing passive restraints in certain other 1987 models. *** Although the standard did not require airbags in all cars, it is clear that the Secretary did intend to encourage wider use of airbags. *** [T]here is no mention, either in the text of the final standard or in the accompanying comments, of the possibility that the risk of potential tort liability would provide an incentive for manufacturers to install airbags. Nor is there any other specific evidence of an intent to preclude common-law tort actions. ***

When a state statute, administrative rule, or common-law cause of action conflicts with a federal statute, it is axiomatic that the state law is without effect. U.S. Const., Art. VI, cl. 2; *Cipollone v. Liggett Group, Inc.*, 505 U.S. 504 (1992). On the other hand, it is equally clear that the Supremacy Clause does not give unelected federal judges carte blanche to use federal law as a means of imposing their own ideas of tort reform on the States. Because of the role of States as separate sovereigns in our federal system, we have long presumed that state laws—particularly those, such as the provision of tort remedies to compensate for personal injuries, that are within the scope of the States' historic police powers—are not to be pre-empted by a federal statute unless it is the clear and manifest purpose of Congress to do so. ***

*** Honda [argues] that the imposition of common-law liability for failure to install an airbag would frustrate the purposes and objectives of Standard 208. Both the text of the statute and the text of the standard provide persuasive reasons for rejecting this argument. *** [T]he text of Standard 208 says nothing about pre-emption, and I am not persuaded that Honda has overcome our traditional presumption that it lacks any implicit pre-emptive effect.

Honda argues, and the Court now agrees, that the risk of liability presented by common-law claims that vehicles without airbags are negligently and defectively designed would frustrate the policy decision that the Secretary made in promulgating Standard 208. This decision, in their view, was that safety—including a desire to encourage "public acceptance of the airbag technology and experimentation with better passive restraint systems"—would best be promoted through gradual implementation of a passive restraint requirement making airbags only one of a variety of systems that a manufacturer could install in order to comply, rather than through a requirement mandating the use of one particular system in every vehicle. ***

There are at least three flaws in this argument that provide sufficient grounds for rejecting it. First, the entire argument is based on an unrealistic factual predicate. Whatever the risk of liability on a no-airbag claim may have been prior to the promulgation of the 1984 version of Standard 208, that risk did not lead any manufacturer to install airbags in even a substantial portion of its cars. *** Second, even if the manufacturers' assessment of their risk of liability ultimately proved to be wrong, the purposes of Standard 208 would not be frustrated. In light of the inevitable time interval between the eventual filing of a tort action alleging that the failure to install an airbag is a design defect and the possible resolution of such a claim against a manufacturer, *** it is obvious that the phase-in period would have ended long before its purposes could have been frustrated by the specter of tort liability. Thus, even without pre-emption, the public would have been given the time that the Secretary deemed necessary to gradually adjust to the increasing use of airbag technology and allay their unfounded concerns about it. Moreover, even if any no-airbag suits were ultimately resolved against manufacturers, *** manufacturers held liable for failing to install passive restraints would have been free to respond by modifying their designs to include such a system instead of an airbag.[18] *** Third, despite its

_____

[18] The Court's failure to "understand [this point] correctly," is directly attributable to its fundamental misconception of the nature of duties imposed by tort law. A general verdict of liability in a case seeking damages for negligent and defective design of a vehicle that (like Ms. Geier's) lacked any passive restraints does not amount to an immutable, mandatory "rule of state tort law imposing *** a duty [to install an airbag]." Rather, that verdict merely reflects the jury's judgment that the manufacturer of a vehicle without any passive restraint system breached its duty of due care by designing a product that was not reasonably safe because a reasonable alternative design—"including, but not limited to, airbags"—could have reduced the foreseeable risks of harm posed by the product. Such a verdict obviously does not foreclose the possibility that more than one alternative design exists the use of which would render the vehicle reasonably safe and satisfy the manufacturer's duty of due care. Thus, the Court is quite wrong

acknowledgement that the saving clause "preserves those actions that seek to establish greater safety than the minimum safety achieved by a federal regulation intended to provide a floor," the Court completely ignores the important fact that by definition all of the standards established under the Safety Act—like the British regulations that governed the number and capacity of lifeboats aboard the Titanic—impose minimum, rather than fixed or maximum, requirements. The phase-in program authorized by Standard 208 thus set minimum percentage requirements for the installation of passive restraints ***. Those requirements were not ceilings, and it is obvious that the Secretary favored a more rapid increase. The possibility that exposure to potential tort liability might accelerate the rate of increase would actually further the only goal explicitly mentioned in the standard itself: reducing the number of deaths and severity of injuries of vehicle occupants. ***

My disagreement with Honda and the Government runs deeper than these flaws, however. In its brief, the Government concedes that "[a] claim that a manufacturer should have chosen to install airbags rather than another type of passive restraint in a certain model of car because of other design features particular to that car *** would not necessarily frustrate Standard 208's purposes." Petitioners' claims here are quite similar to the claim described by the Government: their complaint discusses other design features particular to the 1987 Accord (such as the driver's seat) that allegedly rendered it unreasonably dangerous to operate without an airbag. The only distinction is that in this case, the particular 1987 Accord driven by Ms. Geier included no passive restraint of any kind because Honda chose to comply with Standard 208's 10% minimum requirement by installing passive restraints in other 1987 models. I fail to see how this distinction makes a difference to the purposes of Standard 208, however. If anything, the type of claim favored by the Government—e.g., that a particular model of car should have contained an airbag instead of an automatic seatbelt—would seem to trench even more severely upon the purposes that the Government and Honda contend were behind the promulgation of Standard 208: that having a variety of passive restraints, rather than only airbags, was necessary to promote safety. Thus, I conclude that the Government, on the Secretary's behalf, has failed to articulate a coherent view of the policies behind Standard 208 that would be frustrated by the petitioners' claims.

For these reasons, it is evident that Honda has not crossed the high threshold established by our decisions regarding pre-emption of state laws that allegedly frustrate federal purposes: it has not demonstrated that allowing a common-law no-airbag claim to go forward would impose an obligation on manufacturers that directly and irreconcilably contradicts any primary objective that the Secretary set forth with clarity in Standard 208. Furthermore, it is important to note that the text of Standard 208 *** does not contain any expression of an intent to displace state law. Given our repeated emphasis on the importance of the presumption against pre-emption, this silence lends additional support to the conclusion that the

---

to suggest that, as a consequence of such a verdict, only the installation of airbags would enable manufacturers to avoid liability in the future.

continuation of whatever common-law liability may exist in a case like this poses no danger of frustrating any of the Secretary's primary purposes in promulgating Standard 208. ***

Our presumption against pre-emption is rooted in the concept of federalism. It recognizes that when Congress legislates "in a field which the States have traditionally occupied *** [,] we start with the assumption that the historic police powers of the States were not to be superseded by the Federal Act unless that was the clear and manifest purpose of Congress." The signal virtues of this presumption are its placement of the power of pre-emption squarely in the hands of Congress, which is far more suited than the Judiciary to strike the appropriate state/federal balance (particularly in areas of traditional state regulation), and its requirement that Congress speak clearly when exercising that power. In this way, the structural safeguards inherent in the normal operation of the legislative process operate to defend state interests from undue infringement. In addition, the presumption serves as a limiting principle that prevents federal judges from running amok with our potentially boundless (and perhaps inadequately considered) doctrine of implied conflict pre-emption based on frustration of purposes—i.e., that state law is pre-empted if it "stands as an obstacle to the accomplishment and execution of the full purposes and objectives of Congress."

While the presumption is important in assessing the pre-emptive reach of federal statutes, it becomes crucial when the pre-emptive effect of an administrative regulation is at issue. Unlike Congress, administrative agencies are clearly not designed to represent the interests of States, yet with relative ease they can promulgate comprehensive and detailed regulations that have broad pre-emption ramifications for state law. We have addressed the heightened federalism and nondelegation concerns that agency pre-emption raises by using the presumption to build a procedural bridge across the political accountability gap between States and administrative agencies. Thus, even in cases where implied regulatory pre-emption is at issue, we generally "expect an administrative regulation to declare any intention to pre-empt state law with some specificity." This expectation, which is shared by the Executive Branch, serves to ensure that States will be able to have a dialog with agencies regarding pre-emption decisions ex ante through the normal notice-and-comment procedures of the Administrative Procedure Act (APA).

When the presumption and its underpinnings are properly understood, it is plain that Honda has not overcome the presumption in this case. Neither Standard 208 nor its accompanying commentary includes the slightest specific indication of an intent to pre-empt common-law no-airbag suits. Indeed, the only mention of such suits in the commentary tends to suggest that they would not be pre-empted. In the Court's view, however, "[t]he failure of the Federal Register to address pre-emption explicitly is *** not determinative," because the Secretary's consistent litigating position since 1989, the history of airbag regulation, and the commentary accompanying the final version of Standard 208 reveal purposes and objectives of the Secretary that would be frustrated by no-airbag suits. Pre-empting on these three bases blatantly contradicts the presumption against pre-emption. When the 1984 version of Standard 208 was under consideration, the States obviously were not afforded any notice that purposes might someday be discerned in the history of airbag regulation that would support pre-emption. Nor does the Court claim that the notice of proposed rulemaking that led to Standard 208 provided the States with notice either that the final version of the standard might contain an express pre-emption provision or that the commentary accompanying it might contain a statement of purposes with arguable pre-emptive effect. Finally, the States plainly had no opportunity to comment upon either the commentary accompanying the final version of the standard or the Secretary's ex post litigating position that the standard had implicit pre-emptive effect.

Furthermore, the Court identifies no case in which we have upheld a regulatory claim of frustration-of-purposes implied conflict pre-emption based on nothing more than an ex post administrative litigating position and inferences from regulatory history and final commentary. The latter two sources are even more malleable than legislative history. Thus, when snippets from them are combined with the Court's broad conception of a doctrine of frustration-of-purposes pre-emption untempered by the presumption, a vast, undefined area of state law becomes vulnerable to pre-emption by any related federal law or regulation. In my view, however, "preemption analysis is, or at least should be, a matter of precise statutory [or regulatory] construction rather than an exercise in free-form judicial policymaking." 1 L. Tribe, American Constitutional Law § 6–28, p. 1177 (3d ed. 2000).

As to the Secretary's litigating position, it is clear that "an interpretation contained in a [legal brief], not one arrived at after, for example, a formal adjudication or notice-and-comment rulemaking[,] *** do[es] not warrant [extensive] deference." Moreover, our pre-emption precedents and the APA establish that even if the Secretary's litigating position were coherent, the lesser deference paid to it by the Court today would be inappropriate. Given the Secretary's contention that he has the authority to promulgate safety standards that pre-empt state law and the fact that he could promulgate a standard *** with relative ease, we should be quite reluctant to find pre-emption based only on the Secretary's informal effort to recast the 1984 version of Standard 208 into a pre-emptive mold. Requiring the Secretary to put his pre-emptive position through formal notice-and-comment rulemaking—whether contemporaneously with the promulgation of the allegedly pre-emptive regulation or at any later time that the need for pre-emption becomes apparent—respects both the federalism and nondelegation principles that underlie the presumption against pre-emption in the regulatory context and the APA's requirement of new rulemaking when an agency substantially modifies its interpretation of a regulation.

Because neither the text of the statute nor the text of the regulation contains any indication of an intent to pre-empt petitioners' cause of action, and because I cannot agree with the Court's unprecedented use of inferences from regulatory history and commentary as a basis for implied pre-emption, I am convinced that Honda has not overcome the presumption against preemption in this case. I therefore respectfully dissent.

Notes

1. **Judicial Inconsistency?** The Justices line up differently in preemption and federalism cases. Is this a sign of judicial inconsistency, judicial integrity or other factors?

2. **Federalism and Presumptions.** Do you agree that federalism requires a presumption against preemption? If so, what should it take to overcome that presumption? Should the presumption be different depending on the nature of the federal lawmaker and its mode of communication (Congress' text, congressional intent, agency regulations, or agency interpretations of regulations)? If Congress' intent should be clear, what evidence shows clear intent?

3. **Commandeering and Commands.** Is federal commandeering more threatening to state autonomy than preempting state acts? Is preemption more threatening than requiring states to adopt specific regulations or submit to a federal regulatory scheme? More threatening than cutting off federal funds if the state doesn't do what Congress wants?

4. **Foreign Affairs.** Should there be a presumption of preemption when foreign affairs are involved? *See Crosby v. National Foreign Trade Council,* 530 U.S. 363 (2000) (state law barring state agency purchases of goods and services from companies doing business in Burma preempted by a federal statute). The following case provides insight as to whether preemption operates differently in the foreign affairs arena than it does in domestic law contexts.

AMERICAN INSURANCE ASSOCIATION
v.
GARAMENDI
539 U.S. XXX, 123 S.Ct. 2374, 156 L.Ed. 2d 376 (2003).

JUSTICE SOUTER delivered the opinion of the Court.

California's Holocaust Victim Insurance Relief Act of 1999 (HVIRA or Act), requires any insurer doing business in that State to disclose information about all policies sold in Europe between 1920 and 1945 by the company itself or any one "related" to it. The issue here is whether HVIRA interferes with the National Government's conduct of foreign relations. We hold that it does, with the consequence that the state statute is preempted.

I

The Nazi Government of Germany engaged not only in genocide and enslavement but theft of Jewish assets, including the value of insurance policies, and in particular policies of life insurance, a form of savings held by many Jews in Europe before the Second World War. *** These confiscations and frustrations of claims fell within the subject of reparations, which became a principal object of Allied diplomacy soon after the war. *** Ensuing negotiations at the national level produced the German Foundation

Agreement, signed by President Clinton and German Chancellor Schroeder in July 2000, in which Germany agreed to enact legislation establishing a foundation funded with 10 billion deutsch marks contributed equally by the German Government and German companies, to be used to compensate all those "who suffered at the hands of German companies during the National Socialist era."

The willingness of the Germans to create a voluntary compensation fund was conditioned on some expectation of security from lawsuits in United States courts, and after extended dickering President Clinton put his weight behind two specific measures toward that end. First, the Government agreed that whenever a German company was sued on a Holocaust-era claim in an American court, the Government of the United States would submit a statement that "it would be in the foreign policy interests of the United States for the Foundation to be the exclusive forum and remedy for the resolution of all asserted claims against German companies arising from their involvement in the National Socialist era and World War II. *** On top of that undertaking, the Government promised to use its "best efforts, in a manner it considers appropriate," to get state and local governments to respect the foundation as the exclusive mechanism.

As for insurance claims specifically, both countries agreed that the German Foundation would work with the International Commission on Holocaust Era Insurance Claims (ICHEIC), a voluntary organization formed in 1998 ***. The job of the ICHEIC, chaired by former Secretary of State Eagleburger, includes negotiation with European insurers to provide information about unpaid insurance policies issued to Holocaust victims and settlement of claims brought under them. It has thus set up procedures for handling demands against participating insurers, including "a reasonable review *** of the participating companies' files" for production of unpaid policies, "an investigatory process to determine the current status" of insurance policies for which claims are filed, and a "claims and valuation process to settle and pay individual claims," employing "relaxed standards of proof." ***

While these international efforts were underway, California's Department of Insurance began its own enquiry into the issue of unpaid claims under Nazi-era insurance policies, prompting state legislation designed to force payment by defaulting insurers. *** The section of the [1998] bill codified as HVIRA, at issue here, requires "[a]ny insurer currently doing business in the state" to disclose the details of "life, property, liability, health, annuities, dowry, educational, or casualty insurance policies" issued "to persons in Europe, which were in effect between 1920 and 1945." The duty is to make disclosure not only about policies the particular insurer sold, but also about those sold by any "related company," including "any parent, subsidiary, reinsurer, successor in interest, managing general agent, or affiliate company of the insurer," whether or not the companies were related during the time when the policies subject to disclosure were sold. Nor is the obligation restricted to policies sold to "Holocaust victims" as defined in the Act; it covers policies sold to anyone during that time. The insurer must report the current status of each policy, the city of origin, domicile, or address of each policyholder, and the names of the beneficiaries, all of which is to be put in a central registry open to the public. The mandatory penalty for default is suspension of the company's license to do business in the State, and there are misdemeanor criminal sanctions for falsehood in certain required representations about whether and to whom the proceeds of each policy have been distributed. *** While the legislature acknowledged that "[t]he international Jewish community is in active negotiations with responsible insurance companies through the [ICHEIC] to resolve all outstanding insurance claims issues," it still thought the Act "necessary to protect the claims and interests of California residents, as well as to encourage the development of a resolution to these issues through the international process or through direct action by the State of California, as necessary."

After HVIRA was enacted, administrative subpoenas were issued against several subsidiaries of European insurance companies participating in the ICHEIC. Immediately, in November 1999, Deputy Secretary Eizenstat wrote to the insurance commissioner of California that although HVIRA "reflects a genuine commitment to justice for Holocaust victims and their families, it has the unfortunate effect of damaging the one effective means now at hand to process quickly and completely unpaid insurance claims from the Holocaust period, the [ICHEIC]." *** The same day, Deputy Secretary Eizenstat also wrote to California's Governor making the same points ***. These expressions of the National Government's concern proved to be of no consequence, for the state commissioner announced at an investigatory hearing in December 1999 that he would enforce HVIRA to its fullest, requiring the affected insurers to make the disclosures, leave the State voluntarily, or lose their licenses. ***

III

The principal argument for preemption made by petitioners and the United States as *amicus curiae* is that HVIRA interferes with foreign policy of the Executive Branch, as expressed principally in the executive agreements with Germany, Austria, and France. The major premises of the argument, at least, are beyond dispute. There is, of course, no question that at some point an exercise of state power that touches on foreign relations must yield to the National Government's policy, given the "concern for uniformity in this country's dealings with foreign nations" that animated the Constitution's allocation of the foreign relations power to the National Government in the first place.

Nor is there any question generally that there is executive authority to decide what that policy should be. *** At a more specific level, our cases have recognized that the President has authority to make "executive agreements" with other countries, requiring no ratification by the Senate or approval by Congress, this power having been exercised since the early years of the Republic. *** Given the fact that the practice goes back over 200 years to the first Presidential administration, and has received congressional acquiescence throughout its history, the conclusion "[t]hat the President's control of foreign relations includes the settlement of claims is indisputable."

The executive agreements at issue here do differ in one respect from those just mentioned insofar as they address claims associated with formerly belligerent states, but against corporations, not the foreign governments. But the distinction does not matter. Historically, wartime claims against even nominally private entities have become issues in international diplomacy, and three of the postwar settlements dealing with reparations implicating private parties were made by the Executive alone. *** While a sharp line between public and private acts works for many purposes in the domestic law, insisting on the same line in defining the legitimate scope of the Executive's international negotiations would hamstring the President in settling international controversies.

Generally, then, valid executive agreements are fit to preempt state law, just as treaties are, and if the agreements here had expressly preempted laws like HVIRA, the issue would be straightforward. But petitioners and the United States as *amicus curiae* both have to acknowledge that the agreements include no preemption clause, and so leave their claim of preemption to rest on asserted interference with the foreign policy those agreements embody. Reliance is placed on our decision in *Zschernig v. Miller,* 389 U.S. 429 (1968).

Zschernig dealt with an Oregon probate statute prohibiting inheritance by a nonresident alien, absent showings that the foreign heir would take the property "without confiscation" by his home country and that American citizens would enjoy reciprocal rights of inheritance there. *** [I]t was clear that the Oregon law in practice had invited "minute inquiries concerning the actual administration of foreign law," and so was providing occasions for state judges to disparage certain foreign regimes, employing the language of the anti-Communism prevalent here at the height of the Cold War. Although the Solicitor General, speaking for the State Department, denied that the state statute "unduly interfere[d] with the United States' conduct of foreign relations," the Court was not deterred from exercising its own judgment to invalidate the law as an "intrusion by the State into the field of foreign affairs which the Constitution entrusts to the President and the Congress."

The *Zschernig* majority relied on statements in a number of previous cases open to the reading that state action with more than incidental effect on foreign affairs is preempted, even absent any affirmative federal activity in the subject area of the state law, and hence without any showing of conflict. *** JUSTICE HARLAN, joined substantially by JUSTICE WHITE, disagreed with the *Zschernig* majority on this point, arguing that its implication of preemption of the entire field of foreign affairs was at odds with some other cases suggesting that in the absence of positive federal action "the States may legislate in areas of their traditional competence even though their statutes may have an incidental effect on foreign relations." ***

It is a fair question whether respect for the executive foreign relations power requires a categorical choice between the contrasting theories of field and conflict preemption evident in the *Zschernig* opinions,[11] but the question requires no answer here. For even on JUSTICE HARLAN's view, the likelihood that state legislation will produce something more than incidental effect in conflict with express foreign policy of the National Government would require preemption of the state law. And since on his view it is legislation within "areas of *** traditional competence" that gives a State any claim to prevail, it would be reasonable to consider the strength of the state interest, judged by standards of traditional practice, when deciding how serious a conflict must be shown before declaring the state law preempted. Judged by these standards, we think petitioners and the Government have demonstrated a sufficiently clear conflict to require finding preemption here.

IV

To begin with, resolving Holocaust-era insurance claims that may be held by residents of this country is a matter well within the Executive's responsibility for foreign affairs. Since claims remaining in the aftermath of hostilities may be "sources of friction" acting as an "impediment to resumption of friendly relations" between the countries involved, there is a "longstanding practice" of the national Executive to settle them in discharging its responsibility to maintain the Nation's relationships with other countries, *Dames & Moore,* 453 U.S., at 679. The issue of restitution for Nazi crimes has in fact been addressed in Executive Branch diplomacy and formalized in treaties and executive agreements over the last half century, and although resolution of private claims was postponed by the Cold War, securing private interests is an express object of diplomacy today, just as it was addressed in agreements soon after the Second World War. Vindicating victims injured by acts and omissions of enemy corporations in wartime is thus within the traditional subject matter of foreign policy in which national, not state, interests are overriding, and which the National Government has addressed.

The exercise of the federal executive authority means that state law must give way where, as here, there is evidence of clear conflict between the policies adopted by the two. The foregoing account of negotiations toward the three settlement agreements is enough to illustrate that the consistent Presidential foreign policy has been to encourage European governments and companies to volunteer settlement funds in preference to litigation or coercive sanctions. As for insurance claims in particular, the national position, expressed unmistakably in the executive agreements signed by the President

---

[11] The two positions can be seen as complementary. If a State were simply to take a position on a matter of foreign policy with no serious claim to be addressing a traditional state responsibility, field preemption might be the appropriate doctrine, whether the National Government had acted and, if it had, without reference to the degree of any conflict, the principle having been established that the Constitution entrusts foreign policy exclusively to the National Government. Where, however, a State has acted within what JUSTICE HARLAN called its "traditional competence," but in a way that affects foreign relations, it might make good sense to require a conflict, of a clarity or substantiality that would vary with the strength or the traditional importance of the state concern asserted. Whether the strength of the federal foreign policy interest should itself be weighed is, of course, a further question.

with Germany and Austria, has been to encourage European insurers to work with the ICHEIC to develop acceptable claim procedures, including procedures governing disclosure of policy information. This position, of which the agreements are exemplars, has also been consistently supported in the high levels of the Executive Branch ***. The approach taken serves to resolve the several competing matters of national concern apparent in the German Foundation Agreement: the national interest in maintaining amicable relationships with current European allies; survivors' interests in a "fair and prompt" but nonadversarial resolution of their claims so as to "bring some measure of justice *** in their lifetimes"; and the companies' interest in securing "legal peace" when they settle claims in this fashion. As a way for dealing with insurance claims, moreover, the voluntary scheme protects the companies' ability to abide by their own countries' domestic privacy laws limiting disclosure of policy information.

California has taken a different tack of providing regulatory sanctions to compel disclosure and payment, supplemented by a new cause of action for Holocaust survivors if the other sanctions should fail. HVIRA's economic compulsion to make public disclosure, of far more information about far more policies than ICHEIC rules require, employs "a different, state system of economic pressure," and in doing so undercuts the President's diplomatic discretion and the choice he has made exercising it. Whereas the President's authority to provide for settling claims in winding up international hostilities requires flexibility in wielding "the coercive power of the national economy" as a tool of diplomacy, HVIRA denies this, by making exclusion from a large sector of the American insurance market the automatic sanction for noncompliance with the State's own policies on disclosure. "Quite simply, if the [California] law is enforceable the President has less to offer and less economic and diplomatic leverage as a consequence." The law thus "compromise[s] the very capacity of the President to speak for the Nation with one voice in dealing with other governments" to resolve claims against European companies arising out of World War II.[14]

*** HVIRA threatens to frustrate the operation of the particular mechanism the President has chosen. The letters from Deputy Secretary Eizenstat to California officials show well enough how the portent of further litigation and sanctions has in fact placed the Government at a disadvantage in obtaining practical results from persuading "foreign governments and foreign companies to participate voluntarily in organizations such as ICHEIC." In addition to thwarting the Government's policy of repose for companies that pay through the ICHEIC, California's indiscriminate disclosure provisions place a handicap on the ICHEIC's effectiveness (and raise a further irritant to the European allies) by undercutting European privacy protections. It is true, of course, as it is probably true of all elements

---

[14] It is true that the President in this case is acting without express congressional authority, and thus does not have the "plenitude of Executive authority" that "controll[ed] the issue of preemption" in *Crosby*. But in *Crosby* we were careful to note that the President possesses considerable independent constitutional authority to act on behalf of the United States on international issues, and conflict with the exercise of that authority is a comparably good reason to find preemption of state law.

of HVIRA, that the disclosure requirement's object of obtaining compensation for Holocaust victims is a goal espoused by the National Government as well. But "[t]he fact of a common end hardly neutralizes conflicting means," and here HVIRA is an obstacle to the success of the National Government's chosen "calibration of force" in dealing with the Europeans using a voluntary approach.

The express federal policy and the clear conflict raised by the state statute are alone enough to require state law to yield. If any doubt about the clarity of the conflict remained, however, it would have to be resolved in the National Government's favor, given the weakness of the State's interest, against the backdrop of traditional state legislative subject matter, in regulating disclosure of European Holocaust-era insurance policies in the manner of HVIRA. *** Indeed, there is no serious doubt that the state interest actually underlying HVIRA is concern for the several thousand Holocaust survivors said to be living in the State. ***   [T]he very same objective dignifies the interest of the National Government in devising its chosen mechanism for voluntary settlements, there being about 100,000 survivors in the country, only a small fraction of them in California. As against the responsibility of the United States of America, the humanity underlying the state statute could not give the State the benefit of any doubt in resolving the conflict with national policy.

The basic fact is that California seeks to use an iron fist where the President has consistently chosen kid gloves. *** [D]issatisfaction should be addressed to the President or, perhaps, Congress. The question relevant to preemption in this case is conflict, and the evidence here is "more than sufficient to demonstrate that the state Act stands in the way of [the President's] diplomatic objectives." *Crosby*.

V

The State's remaining submission is that even if HVIRA does interfere with Executive Branch foreign policy, Congress authorized state law of this sort in the McCarran-Ferguson Act, and the more recent U.S. Holocaust Assets Commission Act of 1998 (Holocaust Commission Act). There is, however, no need to consider the possible significance for preemption doctrine of tension between an Act of Congress and Presidential foreign policy, for neither statute does the job the commissioner ascribes to it. *** Indeed, it is worth noting that Congress has done nothing to express disapproval of the President's policy. Legislation along the lines of HVIRA has been introduced in Congress repeatedly, but none of the bills has come close to making it into law. *** Given the President's independent authority "in the areas of foreign policy and national security, *** congressional silence is not to be equated with congressional disapproval." ***

JUSTICE GINSBURG, with whom JUSTICE STEVENS, JUSTICE SCALIA, and JUSTICE THOMAS join, dissenting.

*** Although the federal approach differs from California's, no executive agreement or other formal expression of foreign policy disapproves state disclosure laws like the HVIRA. Absent a clear statement aimed at disclosure requirements by the "one voice" to which courts properly defer in matters of foreign affairs, I would leave intact California's enactment.

*** In the late 1990s, litigation in American courts provided a spur to action. Holocaust survivors and their descendents initiated class-action suits against German and other European firms seeking compensation for *** the failure to pay Jewish insurance claims. *** [T]he litigation propelled a number of European companies to agree on a framework for resolving unpaid claims outside the courts. This concord prompted the 1998 creation of the International Commission on Holocaust Era Insurance Claims (ICHEIC). *** As the Court observes, ICHEIC has formulated procedures for the filing, investigation, valuation, and resolution of Holocaust-era insurance claims. At least until very recently, however, ICHEIC's progress has been slow and insecure. Initially, ICHEIC's insurance company members represented little more than one-third of the Holocaust-era insurance market. *** Moreover, ICHEIC has thus far settled only a tiny proportion of the claims it has received. Evidence submitted in a series of class actions filed against Italian insurer Generali indicated that by November 2001, ICHEIC had resolved only 797 of 77,000 claims. ***

Finally, although ICHEIC has directed its members to publish lists of unpaid Holocaust-era policies, that non-binding directive had not yielded significant compliance at the time this case reached the Court. *** But other insurers have been less forthcoming. For a prime example, Generali—which may have sold more life insurance and annuity policies in Eastern Europe during the Holocaust than any other company—reportedly maintains a 340,000-name list of persons to whom it sold insurance between 1918 and 1945, but has refused to disclose the bulk of the information on the list.

California's disclosure law, the HVIRA, was enacted a year after ICHEIC's formation. *** These measures, the HVIRA declares, are "necessary to protect the claims and interests of California residents, as well as to encourage the development of a resolution to these issues through the international process or through direct action by the State of California, as necessary." *** The HVIRA imposes no duty to pay any claim, nor does it authorize litigation on any claim. It mandates only information *disclosure,* and our assessment of the HVIRA is properly confined to that requirement alone. ***

The President's primacy in foreign affairs, I agree with the Court, empowers him to conclude executive agreements with other countries. Our cases do not catalog the subject matter meet for executive agreement, but we have repeatedly acknowledged the President's authority to make such agreements to settle international claims. And in settling such claims, we have recognized, an executive agreement may preempt otherwise permissible state laws or litigation. *** The Court states that if the executive "agreements here had expressly preempted laws like HVIRA, the issue would be straightforward." One can safely demur to that statement, for, as the Court acknowledges, no executive agreement before us expressly preempts the HVIRA. Indeed, no agreement so much as mentions the HVIRA's sole concern: public disclosure.

Despite the absence of express preemption, the Court holds that the HVIRA interferes with foreign policy objectives implicit in the executive agreements. I would not venture down that path.

The Court's analysis draws substantially on *Zschernig v. Miller,* 389 U.S. 429 (1968). *** We have not relied on *Zschernig* since it was decided, and I would not resurrect that decision here. The notion of "dormant foreign affairs preemption" with which *Zschernig* is associated resonates most audibly when a state action "reflect[s] a state policy critical of foreign governments and involve[s] 'sitting in judgment' on them." The HVIRA entails no such state action or policy. It takes no position on any contemporary foreign government and requires no assessment of any existing foreign regime. It is directed solely at private insurers doing business in California, and it requires them solely to disclose information in their or their affiliates' possession or control. I would not extend *Zschernig* into this dissimilar domain.[14]

*** Here, *** none of the executive agreements extinguish any underlying claim for relief. The United States has agreed to file precatory statements advising courts that dismissing Holocaust-era claims accords with American foreign policy, but the German Foundation Agreement confirms that such statements have no legally binding effect. It remains uncertain, therefore, whether even *litigation* on Holocaust-era insurance claims must be abated in deference to the German Foundation Agreement or the parallel agreements with Austria and France. Indeed, ambiguity on this point appears to have been the studied aim of the American negotiating team.

If it is uncertain whether insurance *litigation* may continue given the executive agreements on which the Court relies, it should be abundantly clear that those agreements leave *disclosure* laws like the HVIRA untouched. *** Here, the Court invalidates a state disclosure law on grounds of conflict with foreign policy "embod[ied]" in certain executive agreements, although those agreements do not refer to state disclosure laws specifically, or even to information disclosure generally. It therefore is surely an exaggeration to assert that the "HVIRA threatens to frustrate the operation of the particular mechanism the President has chosen" to resolve Holocaust-era claims. If that were so, one might expect to find some reference to laws like the HVIRA in the later-in-time executive agreements. There is none.

To fill the agreements' silences, the Court points to statements by individual members of the Executive Branch. But we have never premised foreign affairs preemption on statements of that order. We should not do so here lest we place the considerable power of foreign affairs preemption in the hands of individual sub-Cabinet members of the Executive Branch. *** The displacement of state law by preemption properly requires a considerably

---

[14] The Court also places considerable weight on *Crosby.* As the Court acknowledges, however, *Crosby* was a statutory preemption case. The state law there at issue posed "an obstacle to the accomplishment of Congress's full objectives under the [relevant] federal Act." That statutory decision provides little support for preempting a state law by inferring preclusive foreign policy objectives from precatory language in executive agreements.

more formal and binding federal instrument. *** As I see it, courts step out of their proper role when they rely on no legislative or even executive text, but only on inference and implication, to preempt state laws on foreign affairs grounds. ***

Notes

1. **Foreign and domestic preemption.** Is the Court's preemption analysis consistent with the analysis in *Geier v. American Honda*, or is preemption broader when foreign affairs interests are opposed to state interests instead of federal domestic interests?

2. **Dormant Foreign Commerce Clause.** Is this case about preemption at all? Or is this a judicial exercise of power rather than a Presidential exercise of power? Perhaps this is an exercise of dormant federal authority comparable to the dormant interstate commerce clause power dealt with in the next chapter.

REVIEW PROBLEMS

Review Problem #1.

Determine if the following hypothetical legislation is a valid exercise of Congress' powers under § 5 of the Fourteenth Amendment:

SEXUAL ORIENTATION ANTI–DISCRIMINATION ACT OF 2005

1. **Findings:**

   (a) Discrimination against gays and lesbians has historically been pervasive, profound, and irrational, and such discrimination continues today;

   (b) Because of this history of discrimination and the irrationality of discrimination against gays and lesbians, gays and lesbians constitute a suspect class that merits heightened constitutional protection;

   (c) Discrimination by state and local governments is particularly pervasive and sets an improper example for society as a whole; and

   (d) Whatever the supposed purposes, governmental actions that discriminate against gays and lesbians generally reflect irrational animus.

2. **Therefore:**

   No state or local government may discriminate in any manner, including employment and contracting, against any person on the basis of sexual orientation.

Review Problem #2.

In the wake of several highly publicized incidents in which gays and lesbians were the targets of violent acts, Congress held hearings on the problem of crime motivated by anti-gay and lesbian bias. At the hearings, several witnesses testified that state and local police forces did not provide adequate protection for gays and lesbians. The witnesses suggested that the police officers, themselves, often had anti-gay and lesbian feelings and that because of these feelings, the police officers did not adequately patrol areas prone to anti-gay and lesbian violence and did not adequately investigate violent acts against gays and lesbians. After the hearings, Congress enacted and the President signed the following legislation:

EQUAL POLICE PROTECTION ACT OF 2000

1. **Findings:**

   (a) Gays and lesbians are disproportionately the targets of violent crime;

   (b) Because of bias against gays and lesbians, state and local police forces often do not provide adequate protection for gays and lesbians; and

   (c) Violent crime against gays and lesbians interferes with their ability to work, shop, transact business and otherwise engage in commerce, including interstate commerce.

2. **Therefore:**

   (a) In performing their law enforcement functions, including crime-prevention activity and criminal investigation, state and local police forces shall not discriminate based on the sexual orientation of the victim or intended victim of the crime.

   (b) Any person who suffers injury because a state or local police force violates section 2(a) of this Act shall have a cause of action for damages not to exceed $250,000 against that state or locality.

   (c) In any action brought to enforce this Act, the state or locality may not assert a defense of sovereign immunity.

New Hope is a state in the United States. The National Gay and Lesbian Coalition ("NGLC") organized a weekend symposium at Woody Hollow, a state park in New Hope, for March 17, 2000. The New Hope State Police are the police with jurisdiction over Woody Hollow. A week before the symposium, the NGLC notified the New Hope State Police that it had received threats that anti-gay and lesbian violence might occur at the symposium. The NGLC also notified the New Hope State Police that some of NGLC's prior events have been disrupted by violent attacks.

The New Hope State Police generally provide police protection for events at state parks. However, no police protection was provided for the NGLC symposium. The symposium events were disrupted by violent anti-gay and lesbian protests, and several of the participants were severely injured. A seminar participant who was injured has threatened to sue NGLC and the symposium organizer.

Invoking the Equal Police Protection Act ("EPPA"), the symposium organizer files suit against New Hope in state court seeking compensatory damages of $250,000.

1. Is the EPPA a valid exercise of Congress's powers: (a) To regulate interstate commerce or (b) To enforce the Equal Protection Clause of the Fourteenth Amendment?

2. Do (a) standing or (b) sovereign immunity bar the suit?

Review Problem #3:

Under the laws of every state, privately owned and operated hazardous waste disposal facilities may only be built and operated if the state grants permits for their construction and operation. The standards for granting the permits have been determined solely by state law. Congress, however, has become concerned that areas with significant racial minority populations bear a disproportionate burden of these facilities. Congress has enacted, and the President has signed, the following legislation:

FEDERAL ENVIRONMENTAL JUSTICE ACT

1. **Findings:**

   (a) Hazardous waste disposal facilities ("HWDF's") pose great potential health risks for people living close to the facilities;

   (b) Statistical studies clearly demonstrate that HWDF's appear disproportionately in communities in which racial minorities are a significant proportion of the population; and

   (c) State decisions about where to grant HDWF permits contribute to placement of HDWF's in areas with large racial minority populations. States apparently undertake no efforts to promote a more equitable distribution of these facilities across a wide variety of communities.

2. **Therefore:**

   (a) No HWDF may be constructed or operated without a state permit.

   (b) Every state shall collect information on the racial composition of the communities in which HWDF's are located in that state. In particular, states shall calculate the proportion of the state's overall HWDF's that are located in "minority communities," defined as communities in which racial minorities constitute a majority of the population.

   (c) If the proportion of HWDF's in "minority communities" exceeds the proportion of racial minorities in the population of the state as a whole, then the state may not issue any a new permits for constructing a HWDF in a "minority community," unless no suitable location for the facility exists in a non-minority community in that state. In such circumstances, both the party applying for the permit and the state must certify that no alternative location in a non-minority community in that state is suitable.

   (d) Any citizen suffering harm by a violation of this Act may sue to enforce the provisions of this Act. Suit may be brought against the state, the applicant for the permit, or both. In addition to all other relief, prevailing plaintiffs shall be entitled to liquidated damages in the amount of $50,000.

(e) In any action brought against a state under this Act, the state may not assert a defense of sovereign immunity.

Gambrell is a state in the United States. Waste Management, Inc. ("WMI") has applied for and received a permit to operate a HWDF in Smythe, a city in southern Gambrell. It is undisputed that racial minority groups constitute 20% of the population of Gambrell, that 40% of Gambrell's HWDF's are in minority communities, and that Smythe is a minority community. However, WMI and the state of Gambrell certified that no suitable location for the HWDF existed in a non-minority community.

Pat, a citizen of Gambrell, lives in Tull, a city in northern Gambrell. Pat believes, contrary to this certification, that several suitable locations for HWDF's exist in Gambrell's non-minority communities. Invoking the Federal Environmental Justice Act, Pat sues Gambrell and WMI in state court to enjoin construction of the facility and collect liquidated damages. Pat's complaint asserts that Pat frequently travels to Smythe, enjoys its natural beauty, and that construction of the HWDF would destroy Smythe's natural beauty.

1. Does Pat have standing to bring the suit?

2. Assuming Pat has standing, is the statute a valid exercise of Congress's powers to (a) regulate interstate commerce or (b) enforce the 14th Amendment equal protection clause?

3. Does sovereign immunity bar all or part of Pat's suit?

Review Problem #4:

Assume that police officers may make investigative stops of vehicles that arouse their suspicion, even without any evidence of criminal activity, may search the vehicle if they have reasonable suspicion of criminal activity. Police officers may not actually arrest the driver or any other occupants of the car unless the police discover actual evidence of criminal activity.

***

News reports alleged that police target African Americans and other racial minorities for such investigative stops disproportionately. They, emphasized the large number of African American drivers stopped, but not arrested, as evidence of police bias. Congress held hearings to investigate these allegations of racial bias and debated various legislative proposals. One of the concerns expressed in these debates was that a future President might not fully enforce the provisions of the legislation. Ultimately, Congress enacted and the President signed the following legislation, effective in December 2002:

DRIVING WITHOUT DISCRIMINATION ACT OF 2002

1. Findings:

(a) The vast majority of law enforcement agents nationwide discharge their duties professionally, without bias, and protect the safety of their communities;

(b) Statistical evidence demonstrates that racial profiling (police officers' use of race or ethnicity in deciding which drivers should be subject to investigative stops) is a real and measurable phenomenon;

(c) A Department of Justice report found that, although African-American and Hispanic motorists were more likely to be stopped and searched, they were less likely to be in possession of contraband than white drivers; and

(d) Racial profiling violates the guarantee of equal protection and may discourage individuals from driving freely, impairing both interstate and intrastate commerce.

2. **Therefore:**

(a) No state or local law enforcement officer shall stop a driver based on the driver's race or ethnicity.

(b) Every state and local police department shall keep a record of all investigative traffic stops, including the race and ethnicity of the driver and whether an arrest was made. By February 1 of each year, every state and local police department shall transmit the investigative stop record for the preceding calendar year to the United States Department of Justice.

(c) In a given calendar year, no state or local police department shall stop but not arrest drivers of one race or ethnicity in a substantially greater percentage than their proportion of the drivers in that state or locality. Substantially greater percentage shall mean more than 10 percentage points.

(d) If a state or local police department violates section 2(c) of this Act, such police department shall be subject to suit for damages by any driver who (i) was stopped but not arrested by that police department during the calendar year and (ii) is a member of a racial or ethnic group subject to substantially greater percentage stops without arrests by that police department during that calendar year. If such a suit is successful, the plaintiff shall be entitled to liquidated damages in the amount of $10,000 and a reasonable attorney's fee.

(e) There shall be created, in the United States Department of Justice, an official known as the Racial Justice Coordinator ("RJC"). The United States Supreme Court shall appoint the RJC, and the appointment must be confirmed by a majority of the Senate. The RJC may not be removed except by impeachment and shall have the authority to seek an injunction against any state or local police force to enforce the provisions of this Act.

A New Jersey State Police officer stopped Janice Joiner, an African American from Princeton, New Jersey, in February 2003, while she was driving to visit her father in a nearby New Jersey town. The officer checked her driver's license, which was valid. He then told her that he thought he smelled marijuana. He searched her car. When the police officer found no contraband, he allowed Janice to continue on her way. The stop lasted approximately 30 minutes, and Janice had to wait on the side of the highway while the car was searched.

The February 1, 2004 investigative stop record required by section 2(b) of the Driving Without Discrimination Act ("DWDA") revealed that, during 2003, thirty percent (30%) of the drivers stopped but not arrested by the New Jersey State Police were African American. It is undisputed that African Americans constituted only ten percent (10%) of the drivers in New Jersey. It is thus undisputed that the New Jersey State Police violated section 2(c) of the DWDA.

Invoking the DWDA, Janice files suit against the New Jersey State Police in New Jersey state court seeking liquidated damages of $10,000 for the inconvenience and embarrassment of the stop plus attorney's fees.

1. Is the DWDA a valid exercise of Congress's powers (a) To regulate interstate commerce; or (b) To enforce the provisions of the 14th Amendment equal protection clause?

2. Does DWDA section 2(e) violate the separation of powers?

VI

JUDICIAL PROTECTION OF
INTERSTATE COMMERCE

"[To] the extent that we have gone beyond guarding against rank discrimination against citizens of other States—which is regulated not by the Commerce Clause but by the Privileges and Immunities Clause—the Court for over a century has engaged in an enterprise that it has been unable to justify by textual support or even coherent nontextual theory, that it was almost certainly not intended to undertake, and that it has not undertaken very well ***." There is no conceivable reason why congressional inaction under the Commerce Clause should be deemed to have the same preemptive effect elsewhere accorded only to congressional action. There, as elsewhere, "Congress' silence is just that—silence."

—JUSTICE SCALIA in *Tyler Pipe Industries v. Washington State Department of Revenue*, 483 U.S. 232 (1987).

The cases in this section generally involve situations in which Congress has **not** exercised legislative power pursuant to the Commerce Clause. Rather, the Supreme Court considers whether to invalidate state regulations on the theory that what the state has done is inconsistent with the policies behind the constitutional allocation of power to Congress to regulate interstate commerce.

Typically, these cases have both economic and political components. The economic component involves whether a state or local law discriminates against or has an adverse effect on interstate commercial transactions, reducing efficiency in the delivery of goods and services. The political component deals with whether the citizens of a state are seeking to impose burdens on those not part of the state's polity or to confer benefits on the state's citizens at the expense of outsiders. Often these components are intertwined, but it is sometimes useful to evaluate the economic and political factors separately.

Another common characteristic of these cases is their contingent nature as constitutional law: Congress can reverse Supreme Court decisions in this area by passing legislation validating a state burden on commerce invalidated by the Court. Conversely, Congress can statutorily override the Court's approval of a state regime that Congress believes should be regulated nationally.

Section A reviews the origins of the Court's active role in protecting interstate commerce. Se ction B examines the doctrinal frameworks that have developed for evaluating explicitly discriminatory state legislation. Section C considers neutral state laws having negative effects on interstate commerce. Section D looks at the market participant exception to the Court's dormant commerce clause jurisprudence. Finally, Section E explores a related constitutional provision, the privileges and immunities clause of Article IV.

As you read these materials, assess when the Court **should** step in to invalidate state law that interferes with interstate commerce.

A. ORIGINS OF THE DORMANT COMMERCE CLAUSE

WILLSON v. THE BLACK BIRD CREEK MARSH COMPANY
27 U.S. (2 Pet.) 245, 7 L.Ed. 412 (1829).

THIS was a writ of error to the high court of errors and appeals of the state of Delaware. The Black Bird Creek Marsh Company *** [was] empowered to make and construct a good and sufficient dam across said creek ***. [T]he company proceeded to erect and place in the creek a dam, by which the navigation of the creek was obstructed ***. The defendants being the owners of a sloop called the Sally, regularly licensed and enrolled according to the navigation laws of the United States, broke and injured the dam so erected by the company; and thereupon an action of trespass *** was instituted against them ***.

MR. CHIEF JUSTICE MARSHALL delivered the opinion of the Court.

*** [The appeal] denies the state's capacity to authorize the construction of a dam across a navigable stream, in which the tide ebbs and flows; and in which there was, and of right ought to have been, a certain common and public way in the nature of a highway. This plea draws nothing into question but the validity of the act; and the judgment of the [Delaware] court must have been in favor of its validity. Its consistency with, or repugnancy to the constitution of the United States, necessarily arises upon these pleadings, and must have been determined [in the action below]. This Court has repeatedly decided in favor of its jurisdiction in such a case. Martin *vs.* Hunter's lessee [and other cases] are expressly in point. They establish, as far as precedents can establish any thing, that it is not necessary to state in terms on the record, that the constitution or a law of the United States was drawn in question. It is sufficient to bring the case within the provisions of the 25th section of the judicial act, if the record shows, that the constitution or a law or a treaty of the United States must have been misconstrued, or the decision could not be made. Or, as in this case, that the constitutionality of a state law was questioned, and the decision has been in favor of the party claiming under such law.

The jurisdiction of the Court being established, the more doubtful question is to be considered, whether the act incorporating the Black Bird Creek Marsh Company is repugnant to the constitution, so far as it authorizes a dam across the creek. The plea states the creek to be navigable, in the nature of a highway, through which the tide ebbs and flows.

The act of assembly by which the plaintiffs were authorized to construct their dam, shows plainly that this is one of those many creeks, passing through a deep level marsh adjoining the Delaware, up which the tide flows for some distance. The value of the property on its banks must be enhanced by excluding the water from the marsh, and the health of the inhabitants probably improved. Measures calculated to produce these objects, provided they do not come into collision with the powers of the general government, are undoubtedly within those which are reserved to the states. But the measure authorized by this act stops a navigable creek, and must be supposed to abridge the rights of those who have been accustomed to use it. But this abridgment, unless it comes in conflict with the constitution or a law of the United States, is an affair between the government of Delaware and its citizens, of which this Court can take no cognizance.

The counsel for the plaintiffs in error insist that it comes in conflict with the power of the United States "to regulate commerce with foreign nations and among the several states."

If congress had passed any act which bore upon the case; any act in execution of the power to regulate commerce, the object of which was to control state legislation over those small navigable creeks into which the tide flows, and which abound throughout the lower country of the middle and southern states; we should feel not much difficulty in saying that a state law coming in conflict with such act would be void. But congress has passed no such act. The repugnancy of the law of Delaware to the constitution is placed entirely on its repugnancy to the power to regulate commerce with foreign nations and among the several states; a power which has not been so exercised as to affect the question.

We do not think that the act empowering the Black Bird Creek Marsh Company to place a dam across the creek, can, under all the circumstances of the case, be considered as repugnant to the power to regulate commerce in its dormant state, or as being in conflict with any law passed on the subject. ***

Notes

1. **Language.** The Commerce clause spoke only to Congress' power, not the Court's power. How do the federal courts even have jurisdiction if Congress has not enacted legislation arguably in conflict with Delaware's authorization of a dam?

2. **Precedent.** Isn't there such a federal law, the licensing act which controlled the outcome of *Gibbons v. Ogden*, supra p. 225? Shouldn't *Gibbons* control this case? If not, what is different?

3. **The *Willson* Reasoning and Dormant Commerce Clause Policy.**

- Why did the Court stress Delaware's police power to enhance property values and the health of its people? Isn't it true that, whatever Delaware's purpose, the effect of the dam was to block a navigable waterway? Do you think the Court would have decided the case differently if the Hudson River (rather than Black Bird Creek) had been dammed?

- Do you think the Court would have viewed this case differently if the owners of the sloop Sally had sued to enjoin construction rather than asserting a Commerce Clause defense to a trespass action for damaging the dam?

- Should it be relevant that the dam's benefits inured exclusively (so far as we know) to Delaware residents? That the disadvantages of the dam fell equally on Delaware and non-Delaware sloop owners?

B. DISCRIMINATION AGAINST OUT-OF-STATERS

PHILADELPHIA v. NEW JERSEY
437 U.S. 617, 98 S.Ct. 2531, 57 L.Ed.2d 475 (1978).

MR. JUSTICE STEWART delivered the opinion of the Court.

A New Jersey law prohibits the importation of most "solid or liquid waste which originated or was collected outside the territorial limits of the State ***." In this case we are required to decide whether this statutory prohibition violates the Commerce Clause of the United States Constitution.

The statutory provision in question *** provides: "No person shall bring into this State any solid or liquid waste which originated or was collected outside the territorial limits of the State, except garbage to be fed to swine in the State of New Jersey, until the commissioner [of the State Department of Environmental Protection] shall determine that such action can be permitted without endangering the public health, safety and welfare and has promulgated regulations permitting and regulating the treatment and disposal of such waste in this State."

As authorized by [the Act], the Commissioner promulgated regulations permitting four categories of waste to enter the State. Apart from these narrow exceptions, however, New Jersey closed its borders to all waste from other States.

Immediately affected by these developments were the operators of private landfills in New Jersey, and several cities in other States that had agreements with these operators for waste disposal. They brought suit against New Jersey and its Department of Environmental Protection in state court, attacking the statute and regulations on [preemption and other constitutional] grounds. *** The New Jersey Supreme Court *** found that [the Act] advanced vital health and environmental objectives with no economic discrimination against, and with little burden upon, interstate commerce, and that the law was therefore permissible under the Commerce Clause of the Constitution. The court also found no congressional intent to pre-empt.

*** We agree with the New Jersey court that the state law has not been pre-empted by federal legislation. The dispositive question, therefore, is whether the law is constitutionally permissible in light of the Commerce Clause of the Constitution.

Before it addressed the merits of the appellants' claim, the New Jersey Supreme Court questioned whether the interstate movement of those wastes banned by ch. 363 is "commerce" at all within the meaning of the Commerce Clause. Any doubts on that score should be laid to rest at the outset. *** The state court found that ch. 363 as narrowed by the state regulations banned only "those wastes which can[not] be put to effective use," and therefore those wastes were not commerce at all, unless "the mere transportation and disposal of valueless waste between states constitutes interstate commerce within the meaning of the constitutional provision."

We think the state court misread our cases, and thus erred in assuming that they require a two-tiered definition of commerce. *** All objects of interstate trade merit Commerce Clause protection; none is excluded by definition at the outset. *** Hence, we reject the state court's suggestion that the banning of "valueless" out-of-state wastes *** implicates no constitutional protection. Just as Congress has power to regulate the interstate movement of these wastes, States are not free from constitutional scrutiny when they restrict that movement.

Although the Constitution gives Congress the power to regulate commerce among the States, many subjects of potential federal regulation under that power inevitably escape congressional attention "because of their local character and their number and diversity." *South Carolina State Highway Dept. v. Barnwell Bros., Inc.*, 303 U.S. 177, 185. In the absence of federal legislation, these subjects are open to control by the States so long as they act within the restraints imposed by the Commerce Clause itself. The bounds of these restraints appear nowhere in the words of the Commerce Clause, but have emerged gradually in the decisions of this Court giving effect to its basic purpose. That broad purpose was well expressed by MR. JUSTICE JACKSON in his opinion for the Court in *H. P. Hood & Sons, Inc. v. Du Mond*, 336 U.S. 525, 537–538: "This principle that our economic unit is the Nation, which alone has the gamut of powers necessary to control of the economy, including the vital power of erecting customs barriers against foreign competition, has as its corollary that the states are not separable economic units. *** [W]hat is ultimate is the principle that one state in its dealings with another may not place itself in a position of economic isolation." [internal quotation marks omitted.]

The opinions of the Court through the years have reflected an alertness to the evils of "economic isolation" and protectionism, while at the same time recognizing that incidental burdens on interstate commerce may be unavoidable when a State legislates to safeguard the health and safety of its people. Thus, where simple economic protectionism is effected by state legislation, a virtually per se rule of invalidity has been erected. The clearest example of such legislation is a law that overtly blocks the flow of interstate commerce at a State's borders. But where other legislative objectives are credibly advanced and there is no patent discrimination against interstate trade, the Court has adopted a much more flexible approach, the general contours of which were outlined in *Pike v. Bruce Church, Inc.*, 397 U.S. 137, 142:

> "Where the statute regulates evenhandedly to effectuate a legitimate local public interest, and its effects on interstate commerce are only incidental, it will be upheld unless the burden imposed on such commerce is clearly excessive in relation to the putative local benefits. *** If a legitimate local purpose is found, then the question becomes one of degree. And the extent of the burden that will be tolerated will of course depend on the nature of the local interest involved, and on whether it could be promoted as well with a lesser impact on interstate activities."

The crucial inquiry, therefore, must be directed to determining whether ch. 363 is basically a protectionist measure, or whether it can fairly be viewed as a law directed to legitimate local concerns, with effects upon interstate commerce that are only incidental.

The purpose of ch. 363 is set out in the statute itself as follows:

> "The Legislature finds and determines that *** the volume of solid and liquid waste continues to rapidly increase, that the treatment and disposal of these wastes continues to pose an even greater threat to the quality of the environment of New Jersey, that the available and appropriate land fill sites within the State are being diminished, that the environment continues to be threatened by the treatment and disposal of waste which originated or was collected outside the State, and that the public health, safety and welfare require that the treatment and disposal within this State of all wastes generated outside of the State be prohibited."

The New Jersey Supreme Court accepted this statement of the state legislature's purpose. The state court additionally found that New Jersey's existing landfill sites will be exhausted within a few years; that to go on using these sites or to develop new ones will take a heavy environmental toll, both from pollution and from loss of scarce open lands; that new techniques to divert waste from landfills to other methods of disposal and resource recovery processes are under development, but that these changes will require time; and finally, that "the extension of the lifespan of existing landfills, resulting from the exclusion of out-of-state waste, may be of crucial importance in preventing further virgin wetlands or other undeveloped lands from being devoted to landfill purposes." Based on these findings, the court concluded that ch. 363 was designed to protect, not the State's economy, but its environment, and that its substantial benefits outweigh its "slight" burden on interstate commerce.

The appellants strenuously contend that ch. 363, "while outwardly cloaked 'in the currently fashionable garb of environmental protection,' *** is actually no more than a legislative effort to suppress competition and stabilize the cost of solid waste disposal for New Jersey residents ***." They cite passages of legislative history suggesting that the problem addressed by ch. 363 is primarily financial: Stemming the flow of out-of-state waste into certain landfill sites will extend their lives, thus delaying the day when New Jersey cities must transport their waste to more distant and expensive sites.

The appellees, on the other hand, deny that ch. 363 was motivated by financial concerns or economic protectionism. In the words of their brief, "[n]o New Jersey commercial interests stand to gain advantage over competitors from outside the state as a result of the ban on dumping out-of-state waste." Noting that New Jersey landfill operators are among the plaintiffs, the appellee's brief argues that "[t]he complaint is not that New Jersey has forged an economic preference for its own commercial interests, but rather that it has denied a small group of its entrepreneurs an economic opportunity to traffic in waste in order to protect the health, safety and welfare of the citizenry at large."

This dispute about ultimate legislative purpose need not be resolved, because its resolution would not be relevant to the constitutional issue to be decided in this case. Contrary to the evident assumption of the state court and the parties, the evil of protectionism can reside in legislative means as well as legislative ends. Thus, it does not matter whether the ultimate aim of ch. 363 is to reduce the waste disposal costs of New Jersey residents or to save remaining open lands from pollution, for we assume New Jersey has every right to protect its residents' pocketbooks as well as their environment. And it may be assumed as well that New Jersey may pursue those ends by slowing the flow of all waste into the State's remaining landfills, even though interstate commerce may incidentally be affected. But whatever New Jersey's ultimate purpose, it may not be accomplished by discriminating against articles of commerce coming from outside the State unless there is some reason, apart from their origin, to treat them differently. Both on its face and in its plain effect, ch. 363 violates this principle of nondiscrimination.

The Court has consistently found parochial legislation of this kind to be constitutionally invalid, whether the ultimate aim of the legislation was to assure a steady supply of milk by erecting barriers to allegedly ruinous outside competition, or to create jobs by keeping industry within the State, or to preserve the State's financial resources from depletion by fencing out indigent immigrants. In each of these cases, a presumably legitimate goal was sought to be achieved by the illegitimate means of isolating the State from the national economy.

Also relevant here are the Court's decisions holding that a State may not accord its own inhabitants a preferred right of access over consumers in other States to natural resources located within its borders. These cases stand for the basic principle that a "State is without power to prevent privately owned articles of trade from being shipped and sold in interstate commerce on the ground that they are required to satisfy local demands or because they are needed by the people of the State."

The New Jersey law at issue in this case falls squarely within the area that the Commerce Clause puts off limits to state regulation. On its face, it imposes on out-of-state commercial interests the full burden of conserving the State's remaining landfill space. It is true that in our previous cases the scarce natural resource was itself the article of commerce, whereas here the scarce resource and the article of commerce are distinct. But that difference is without consequence. In both instances, the State has overtly moved to slow or freeze the flow of commerce for protectionist reasons. It does not matter that the State has shut the article of commerce inside the State in one case and outside the State in the other. What is crucial is the attempt by one State to isolate itself from a problem common to many by erecting a barrier against the movement of interstate trade.

The appellees argue that not all laws which facially discriminate against out-of-state commerce are forbidden protectionist regulations. In particular, they point to quarantine laws, which this Court has repeatedly upheld even though they appear to single out interstate commerce for special treatment. In the appellees' view, ch. 363 is analogous to such health-protective measures, since it reduces the exposure of New Jersey residents to the allegedly harmful effects of landfill sites.

It is true that certain quarantine laws have not been considered forbidden protectionist measures, even though they were directed against out-of-state commerce. But those quarantine laws banned the importation of articles such as diseased livestock that required destruction as soon as possible because their very movement risked contagion and other evils. Those laws thus did not discriminate against interstate commerce as such, but simply prevented traffic in noxious articles, whatever their origin.

The New Jersey statute is not such a quarantine law. There has been no claim here that the very movement of waste into or through New Jersey endangers health, or that waste must be disposed of as soon and as close to its point of generation as possible. The harms caused by waste are said to arise after its disposal in landfill sites, and at that point, as New Jersey concedes, there is no basis to distinguish out-of-state waste from domestic waste. If one is inherently harmful, so is the other. Yet New Jersey has banned the former while leaving its landfill sites open to the latter. The New Jersey law blocks the importation of waste in an obvious effort to saddle those outside the State with the entire burden of slowing the flow of refuse into New Jersey's remaining landfill sites. That legislative effort is clearly impermissible under the Commerce Clause of the Constitution.

Today, cities in Pennsylvania and New York find it expedient or necessary to send their waste into New Jersey for disposal, and New Jersey claims the right to close its borders to such traffic. Tomorrow, cities in New Jersey may find it expedient or necessary to send their waste into Pennsylvania or New York for disposal, and those States might then claim the right to close their borders. The Commerce Clause will protect New Jersey in the future, just as it protects her neighbors now, from efforts by one State to isolate itself in the stream of interstate commerce from a problem shared by all. ***

MR. JUSTICE REHNQUIST, with whom THE CHIEF JUSTICE joins, dissenting.

A growing problem in our Nation is the sanitary treatment and disposal of solid waste. For many years, solid waste was incinerated. Because of the significant environmental problems attendant on incineration, however, this method of solid waste disposal has declined in use in many localities, including New Jersey. "Sanitary" landfills have replaced incineration as the principal method of disposing of solid waste. In ch. 363 of the 1973 N.J. Laws, the State of New Jersey legislatively recognized the unfortunate fact that landfills also present extremely serious health and safety problems. First, in New Jersey, "virtually all sanitary landfills can be expected to produce leachate, a noxious and highly polluted liquid which is seldom visible and frequently pollutes *** ground and surface waters." The natural decomposition process which occurs in landfills also produces large quantities of methane and thereby presents a significant explosion hazard. Landfills can also generate "health hazards caused by rodents, fires and scavenger birds" and, "needless to say, do not help New Jersey's aesthetic appearance nor New Jersey's noise or water or air pollution problems."

The health and safety hazards associated with landfills present appellees with a currently unsolvable dilemma. Other, hopefully safer, methods of disposing of solid wastes are still in the development stage and cannot presently be used. But appellees obviously cannot completely stop the tide of solid waste that its citizens will produce in the interim. For the moment, therefore, appellees must continue to use sanitary landfills to dispose of New Jersey's own solid waste despite the critical environmental problems thereby created.

The question presented in this case is whether New Jersey must also continue to receive and dispose of solid waste from neighboring States, even though these will inexorably increase the health problems discussed above. The Court answers this question in the affirmative. New Jersey must either prohibit all landfill operations, leaving itself to cast about for a presently nonexistent solution to the serious problem of disposing of the waste generated within its own borders, or it must accept waste from every portion of the United States, thereby multiplying the health and safety problems which would result if it dealt only with such wastes generated within the State. Because past precedents establish that the Commerce Clause does not present appellees with such a Hobson's choice, I dissent.

The Court recognizes that States can prohibit the importation of items "'which, on account of their existing condition, would bring in and spread disease, pestilence, and death, such as rags or other substances infected with the germs of yellow fever or the virus of small-pox, or cattle or meat or other provisions that are diseased or decayed or otherwise, from their condition and quality, unfit for human use or consumption.'" As the Court points out, such "quarantine laws have not been considered forbidden protectionist measures, even though they were directed against out-of-state commerce."

In my opinion, [quarantine] cases are dispositive of the present one. Under them, New Jersey may require germ-infected rags or diseased meat to be disposed of as best as possible within the State, but at the same time prohibit the importation of such items for disposal at the facilities that are set up within New Jersey for disposal of such material generated within the State. The physical fact of life that New Jersey must somehow dispose of its own noxious items does not mean that it must serve as a depository for those of every other State. Similarly, New Jersey should be free under our past precedents to prohibit the importation of solid waste because of the health and safety problems that such waste poses to its citizens. The fact that New Jersey continues to, and indeed must continue to, dispose of its own solid waste does not mean that New Jersey may not prohibit the importation of even more solid waste into the State. I simply see no way to distinguish solid waste, on the record of this case, from germ-infected rags, diseased meat, and other noxious items.

The Court's effort to distinguish these prior cases is unconvincing. It first asserts that the quarantine laws which have previously been upheld "banned the importation of articles such as diseased livestock that required destruction as soon as possible because their very movement risked contagion and other evils." According to the Court, the New Jersey law is distinguishable from these other laws, and invalid, because the concern of New Jersey is not with the movement of solid waste but with the present inability to safely dispose of it once it reaches its destination. But I think it far from clear that the State's law has as limited a focus as the Court imputes to it: Solid waste which is a health hazard when it reaches its destination may in all likelihood be an equally great health hazard in transit.

Even if the Court is correct in its characterization of New Jersey's concerns, I do not see why a State may ban the importation of items whose movement risks contagion, but cannot ban the importation of items which, although they may be transported into the State without undue hazard, will then simply pile up in an ever increasing danger to the public's health and safety. The Commerce Clause was not drawn with a view to having the validity of state laws turn on such pointless distinctions.

Second, the Court implies that the challenged laws must be invalidated because New Jersey has left its landfills open to domestic waste. But, as the Court notes, this Court has repeatedly upheld quarantine laws "even though they appear to single out interstate commerce for special treatment." The fact that New Jersey has left its landfill sites open for domestic waste does not, of course, mean that solid waste is not innately harmful. Nor does it mean that New Jersey prohibits importation of solid waste for reasons other than the health and safety of its population. New Jersey must out of sheer necessity treat and dispose of its solid waste in some fashion, just as it must treat New Jersey cattle suffering from hoof-and-mouth disease. It does not follow that New Jersey must, under the Commerce Clause, accept solid waste or diseased cattle from outside its borders and thereby exacerbate its problems.

The Supreme Court of New Jersey expressly found that ch. 363 was passed "to preserve the health of New Jersey residents by keeping their exposure to solid waste and landfill areas to a minimum." The Court points to absolutely no evidence that would contradict this finding by the New Jersey

Supreme Court. Because I find no basis for distinguishing the laws under challenge here from our past cases upholding state laws that prohibit the importation of items that could endanger the population of the State, I dissent.

Notes

1. **Benefits and Burdens Analysis.** What is the commerce in *Philadelphia*? Who gains the benefits and who bears the burdens of the New Jersey statute (consider out-of-state waste producers, out-of-state landfill operators, in-state waste producers, and in-state landfill operators)? Note that it may be difficult to determine whether the locality's overall economic benefits exceed its overall costs. When you read *Carbone* later in this chapter, repeat this analysis on its facts. There are substantial differences based on the fact that waste elimination is the good in this case and processing services the good in *Carbone*.

2. **Facial Discrimination.** Does the Court really care about the aggregate benefits and burdens when there is facial discrimination against outsiders? Maybe the Court has simply established a default rule: discriminatory legislation is normally (per se?) unconstitutional unless and until Congress acts to permit such discrimination. On the other hand, there are a few cases in which the Court has found compelling local justifications sufficient to validate even facially discriminatory local statutes. *See Maine v. Taylor*, 477 U.S. 131 (1986) (prohibition on import of live baitfish permissible to protect local species when there is no way to inspect imported baitfish for harmful parasites).

3. **Discriminatory Taxation.** State taxes that discriminate against foreign or out-of-state firms, like discriminatory regulations, frequently violate the Commerce Clause. What should the Court do with facially different but potentially offsetting taxes between local and out-of-state entities? *South Central Bell Telephone Co. v. Alabama*, 526 U.S. 160 (1999), concerned an Alabama statute that required all foreign and out-of-state companies to pay a franchise tax equal to 0.3% of the value of the actual amount of capital employed in the State. In-state firms, however, were required to pay a franchise tax equal to 1% of the par value of the firm's stock. Local firms thus were taxed at a nominally higher rate, but had considerable flexibility to set their own levels of tax liability by setting the par value much lower than the market value of their stock. The Court determined that the statute was facially discriminatory in light of the different tax standards set for out-of-state and in-state firms. It then noted that a "discriminatory tax cannot be upheld as 'compensatory' unless the State proves that the special burden that the franchise tax imposes upon foreign corporations is 'roughly *** approximate' to the special burden on domestic corporations, and that the taxes are similar enough 'in substance' to serve as 'mutually exclusive' proxies for one another." *See Oregon Waste Systems, Inc. v. Department of Environmental Quality of Oregon*, 511 U.S. 93 (1994). Alabama did not prove that its taxes met this standard.

4. **Problem.** Many states prohibit direct shipment of wine to their residents by out-of-state shippers. Do such laws run afoul of the dormant commerce clause? How, if at all, does the Twenty-First Amendment affect your assessment?

C. NEUTRAL STATUTES BURDENING
INTERSTATE COMMERCE

KASSEL v. CONSOLIDATED FREIGHTWAYS
450 U.S. 662, 101 S.Ct. 1309, 67 L.Ed.2d 580 (1981).

JUSTICE POWELL announced the judgment of the Court and delivered an opinion, in which JUSTICE WHITE, JUSTICE BLACKMUN, and JUSTICE STEVENS joined.

The question is whether an Iowa statute that prohibits the use of certain large trucks within the State unconstitutionally burdens interstate commerce.

I

Appellee Consolidated Freightways Corporation of Delaware (Consolidated) is one of the largest common carriers in the country. It offers service in 48 States under a certificate of public convenience and necessity issued by the Interstate Commerce Commission. Among other routes, Consolidated carries commodities through Iowa on Interstate 80, the principal east-west route linking New York, Chicago, and the west coast, and on Interstate 35, a major north-south route.

Consolidated mainly uses two kinds of trucks. One consists of a three-axle tractor pulling a 40–foot two-axle trailer. This unit, commonly called a single, or "semi," is 55 feet in length overall. Such trucks have long been used on the Nation's highways. Consolidated also uses a two-axle tractor pulling a single-axle trailer which, in turn, pulls a single-axle dolly and a second single-axle trailer. This combination, known as a double, or twin, is 65 feet long overall. Many trucking companies, including Consolidated, increasingly prefer to use doubles to ship certain kinds of commodities. Doubles have larger capacities, and the trailers can be detached and routed separately if necessary. Consolidated would like to use 65–foot doubles on many of its trips through Iowa.

The State of Iowa, however, by statute restricts the length of vehicles that may use its highways. Unlike all other States in the West and Midwest, Iowa generally prohibits the use of 65–foot doubles within its borders. Instead, most truck combinations are restricted to 55 feet in length. Doubles, mobile homes, trucks carrying vehicles such as tractors and other farm equipment, and singles hauling livestock are permitted to be as long as 60 feet. Notwithstanding these restrictions, Iowa's statute permits cities abutting the state line by local ordinance to adopt the length limitations of the adjoining State. Where a city has exercised this option, otherwise oversized trucks are permitted within the city limits and in nearby commercial zones.[6]

---

[6] The Iowa Legislature in 1974 passed House Bill 671, which would have permitted 65–foot doubles. But Iowa Governor Ray vetoed the bill, noting that it "would benefit only a few Iowa-based companies while providing a great advantage for out-of-state trucking firms and competitors at the expense of our Iowa citizens." Governor's Veto Message of March 2, 1974 ***.

Iowa also provides for two other relevant exemptions. An Iowa truck manufacturer may obtain a permit to ship trucks that are as large as 70 feet. Permits also are available to move oversized mobile homes, provided that the unit is to be moved from a point within Iowa or delivered for an Iowa resident.[7]

Because of Iowa's statutory scheme, Consolidated cannot use its 65–foot doubles to move commodities through the State. Instead, the company must do one of four things: (i) use 55–foot singles; (ii) use 60–foot doubles; (iii) detach the trailers of a 65–foot double and shuttle each through the State separately; or (iv) divert 65–foot doubles around Iowa.

Dissatisfied with these options, Consolidated filed this suit in the District Court averring that Iowa's statutory scheme unconstitutionally burdens interstate commerce. Iowa defended the law as a reasonable safety measure enacted pursuant to its police power. The State asserted that 65–foot doubles are more dangerous than 55–foot singles and, in any event, that the law promotes safety and reduces road wear within the State by diverting much truck traffic to other States.

In a 14–day trial, both sides adduced evidence on safety, and on the burden on interstate commerce imposed by Iowa's law. On the question of safety, the District Court found that the "evidence clearly establishes that the twin is as safe as the semi." For that reason,

"There is no valid safety reason for barring twins from Iowa's highways because of their configuration.

"The evidence convincingly, if not overwhelmingly, establishes that the 65 foot twin is as safe as, if not safer than, the 60 foot twin and the 55 foot semi ***.

"Twins and semis have different characteristics. Twins are more maneuverable, are less sensitive to wind, and create less splash and spray. However, they are more likely than semis to jackknife or upset. They can be backed only for a short distance. The negative characteristics are not such that they render the twin less safe than semis overall. Semis are more stable but are more likely to 'rear end' another vehicle."

In light of these findings, the District Court applied the standard we enunciated in *Raymond Motor Transportation, Inc. v. Rice*, 434 U.S. 429 (1978), and concluded that the state law impermissibly burdened interstate commerce:

The "border-cities exemption" was passed by the General Assembly and signed by the Governor shortly thereafter. ***

[7] The parochial restrictions in the mobile home provision were enacted after Governor Ray vetoed a bill that would have permitted the interstate shipment of all mobile homes through Iowa. Governor Ray commented, in his veto message: "This bill *** would make Iowa a bridge state as these oversized units are moved into Iowa after being manufactured in another state and sold in a third. None of this activity would be of particular economic benefit to Iowa."

"[T]he balance here must be struck in favor of the federal interests. The *total effect* of the law as a safety measure in reducing accidents and casualties is so slight and problematical that it does not outweigh the national interest in keeping interstate commerce free from interferences that seriously impede it."

*** The Court of Appeals for the Eighth Circuit affirmed.

II

*** The Commerce Clause does not, of course, invalidate all state restrictions on commerce. It has long been recognized that, "in the absence of conflicting legislation by Congress, there is a residuum of power in the state to make laws governing matters of local concern which nevertheless in some measure affect interstate commerce or even, to some extent, regulate it." *Southern Pacific Co. v. Arizona*, 325 U.S. 761 (1945). The extent of permissible state regulation is not always easy to measure. It may be said with confidence, however, that a State's power to regulate commerce is never greater than in matters traditionally of local concern. For example, regulations that touch upon safety—especially highway safety—are those that "the Court has been most reluctant to invalidate." *Raymond*, supra, 434 U.S., at 443. Indeed, "if safety justifications are not illusory, the Court will not second-guess legislative judgment about their importance in comparison with related burdens on interstate commerce." *Raymond*, at 449 (BLACKMUN, J., concurring). Those who would challenge such bona fide safety regulations must overcome a "strong presumption of validity." *Bibb v. Navajo Freight Lines, Inc.*, 359 U.S. 520, 524 (1959).

But the incantation of a purpose to promote the public health or safety does not insulate a state law from Commerce Clause attack. Regulations designed for that salutary purpose nevertheless may further the purpose so marginally, and interfere with commerce so substantially, as to be invalid under the Commerce Clause. In the Court's recent unanimous decision in *Raymond*, we declined to "accept the State's contention that the inquiry under the Commerce Clause is ended without a weighing of the asserted safety purpose against the degree of interference with interstate commerce." This "weighing" by a court requires—and indeed the constitutionality of the state regulation depends on—"a sensitive consideration of the weight and nature of the state regulatory concern in light of the extent of the burden imposed on the course of interstate commerce."

III

Applying these general principles, we conclude that the Iowa truck-length limitations unconstitutionally burden interstate commerce.

In *Raymond Motor Transportation, Inc. v. Rice*, the Court held that a Wisconsin statute that precluded the use of 65–foot doubles violated the Commerce Clause. This case is *Raymond* revisited. Here, as in *Raymond*, the State failed to present any persuasive evidence that 65–foot doubles are less safe than 55–foot singles. Moreover, Iowa's law is now out of step with the laws of all other Midwestern and Western States. Iowa thus substantially burdens the interstate flow of goods by truck. In the absence of congressional action to set uniform standards, some burdens associated with state safety regulations must be tolerated. But where, as here, the State's safety interest has been found to be illusory, and its regulations impair significantly the federal interest in efficient and safe interstate transportation, the state law cannot be harmonized with the Commerce Clause.[12]

Iowa made a more serious effort to support the safety rationale of its law than did Wisconsin in *Raymond*, but its effort was no more persuasive. As noted above, the District Court found that the "evidence clearly establishes that the twin is as safe as the semi." The record supports this finding.

The trial focused on a comparison of the performance of the two kinds of trucks in various safety categories. The evidence showed, and the District Court found, that the 65–foot double was at least the equal of the 55–foot single in the ability to brake, turn, and maneuver. The double, because of its axle placement, produces less splash and spray in wet weather. And, because of its articulation in the middle, the double is less susceptible to dangerous "off-tracking," to wind.

None of these findings is seriously disputed by Iowa. Indeed, the State points to only three ways in which the 55–foot single is even arguably superior: singles take less time to be passed and to clear intersections; they may back up for longer distances; and they are somewhat less likely to jackknife.

The first two of these characteristics are of limited relevance on modern interstate highways. As the District Court found, the negligible difference in the time required to pass, and to cross intersections, is insignificant on 4–lane divided highways because passing does not require crossing into oncoming traffic lanes, and interstates have few, if any, intersections. The concern over backing capability also is insignificant because it seldom is necessary to back up on an interstate. In any event, no evidence suggested any difference in backing capability between the 60–foot doubles that Iowa permits and the 65–foot doubles that it bans. Similarly, although doubles tend to jackknife somewhat more than singles, 65–foot doubles actually are less likely to jackknife than 60–foot doubles.

Statistical studies supported the view that 65–foot doubles are at least as safe overall as 55–foot singles and 60–foot doubles. ***[16]

Consolidated, meanwhile, demonstrated that Iowa's law substantially burdens interstate commerce. Trucking companies that wish to continue to

---

[12] It is highly relevant that here, as in *Raymond*, the state statute contains exemptions that weaken the deference traditionally accorded to a state safety regulation.

[16] In suggesting that Iowa's law actually promotes safety, the dissenting opinion ignores the findings of the courts below and relies on largely discredited statistical evidence. The dissent implies that a statistical study identified doubles as more dangerous than singles. At trial, however, the author of that study—Iowa's own statistician—conceded that his calculations were statistically biased, and therefore "not very meaningful." ***

use 65–foot doubles must route them around Iowa or detach the trailers of the doubles and ship them through separately. Alternatively, trucking companies must use the smaller 55–foot singles or 60–foot doubles permitted under Iowa law. Each of these options engenders inefficiency and added expense. The record shows that Iowa's law added about $12.6 million each year to the costs of trucking companies. Consolidated alone incurred about $2 million per year in increased costs.

In addition to increasing the costs of the trucking companies (and, indirectly, of the service to consumers), Iowa's law may aggravate, rather than ameliorate, the problem of highway accidents. Fifty-five foot singles carry less freight than 65–foot doubles. Either more small trucks must be used to carry the same quantity of goods through Iowa, or the same number of larger trucks must drive longer distances to bypass Iowa. In either case, as the District Court noted, the restriction requires more highway miles to be driven to transport the same quantity of goods. Other things being equal, accidents are proportional to distance traveled. Thus, if 65–foot doubles are as safe as 55–foot singles, Iowa's law tends to increase the number of accidents, and to shift the incidence of them from Iowa to other States.[18]

IV

Perhaps recognizing the weakness of the evidence supporting its safety argument, and the substantial burden on commerce that its regulations create, Iowa urges the Court simply to "defer" to the safety judgment of the State. It argues that the length of trucks is generally, although perhaps imprecisely, related to safety. The task of drawing a line is one that Iowa contends should be left to its legislature.

The Court normally does accord "special deference" to state highway safety regulations. *Raymond*. This traditional deference "derives in part from the assumption that where such regulations do not discriminate on their face against interstate commerce, their burden usually falls on local economic interests as well as other States' economic interests, thus insuring that a State's own political processes will serve as a check against unduly burdensome regulations." Less deference to the legislative judgment is due, however, where the local regulation bears disproportionately on out-of-state residents and businesses. Such a disproportionate burden is apparent here. Iowa's scheme, although generally banning large doubles from the State, nevertheless has several exemptions that secure to Iowans many of the benefits of large trucks while shunting to neighboring States many of the costs associated with their use.

At the time of trial there were two particularly significant exemptions. First, singles hauling livestock or farm vehicles were permitted to be as long

---

[18] The District Court *** noted that Iowa's law causes "more accidents, more injuries, more fatalities and more fuel consumption." Appellant Kassel conceded as much at trial. Kassel explained, however, that most of these additional accidents occur in States other than Iowa because truck traffic is deflected around the State. He noted: "Our primary concern is the citizens of Iowa and our own highway system we operate in this state."

as 60 feet. As the Court of Appeals noted, this provision undoubtedly was helpful to local interests. *Cf. Raymond* (exemption in Wisconsin for milk shippers). Second, cities abutting other States were permitted to enact local ordinances adopting the larger length limitation of the neighboring State. This exemption offered the benefits of longer trucks to individuals and businesses in important border cities without burdening Iowa's highways with interstate through traffic. *Cf. Raymond* (exemption in Wisconsin for shipments from local plants).

The origin of the "border cities exemption" also suggests that Iowa's statute may not have been designed to ban dangerous trucks, but rather to discourage interstate truck traffic. In 1974, the legislature passed a bill that would have permitted 65–foot doubles in the State. Governor Ray vetoed the bill. He said:

> "I find sympathy with those who are doing business in our state and whose enterprises could gain from increased cargo carrying ability by trucks. However, with this bill, the Legislature has pursued a course that would benefit only a few Iowa-based companies while providing a great advantage for out-of-state trucking firms and competitors at the expense of our Iowa citizens."

After the veto, the "border cities exemption" was immediately enacted and signed by the Governor.

It is thus far from clear that Iowa was motivated primarily by a judgment that 65–foot doubles are less safe than 55–foot singles. Rather, Iowa seems to have hoped to limit the use of its highways by deflecting some through traffic. In the District Court and Court of Appeals, the State explicitly attempted to justify the law by its claimed interest in keeping trucks out of Iowa. The Court of Appeals correctly concluded that a State cannot constitutionally promote its own parochial interests by requiring safe vehicles to detour around it. *** Because Iowa has imposed this burden without any significant countervailing safety interest, its statute violates the Commerce Clause. ***

JUSTICE BRENNAN, with whom JUSTICE MARSHALL joins, concurring in the judgment.

Iowa's truck-length regulation challenged in this case is nearly identical to the Wisconsin regulation struck down in *Raymond Motor Transportation, Inc. v. Rice* as in violation of the Commerce Clause. In my view the same Commerce Clause restrictions that dictated that holding also require invalidation of Iowa's regulation insofar as it prohibits 65–foot doubles.

The reasoning bringing me to that conclusion does not require, however, that I engage in the debate between my Brothers POWELL and REHNQUIST over what the District Court record shows on the question whether 65–foot doubles are more dangerous than shorter trucks. With all respect, my Brothers ask and answer the wrong question.

For me, analysis of Commerce Clause challenges to state regulations must take into account three principles: (1) The courts are not empowered to second-guess the empirical judgments of lawmakers concerning the utility of legislation. (2) The burdens imposed on commerce must be balanced against the local benefits actually sought to be achieved by the State's lawmakers, and not against those suggested after the fact by counsel. (3) Protectionist legislation is unconstitutional under the Commerce Clause, even if the burdens and benefits are related to safety rather than economics.

I

Both the opinion of my Brother POWELL and the opinion of my Brother REHNQUIST are predicated upon the supposition that the constitutionality of a state regulation is determined by the factual record created by the State's lawyers in trial court. But that supposition cannot be correct, for it would make the constitutionality of state laws and regulations depend on the vagaries of litigation rather than on the judgments made by the State's lawmakers.

In considering a Commerce Clause challenge to a state regulation, the judicial task is to balance the burden imposed on commerce against the local benefits sought to be achieved by the State's *lawmakers*. In determining those benefits, a court should focus ultimately on the regulatory purposes identified by the lawmakers and on the evidence before or available to them that might have supported their judgment. *See generally, Minnesota v. Clover Leaf Creamery Co.*, 449 U.S. 456, 464 (1981). Since the court must confine its analysis to the purposes the lawmakers had for maintaining the regulation, the only relevant evidence concerns whether the lawmakers could rationally have believed that the challenged regulation would foster those purposes. *** It is not the function of the court to decide whether in fact the regulation promotes its intended purpose, so long as an examination of the evidence before or available to the lawmaker indicates that the regulation is not wholly irrational in light of its purposes. *See Clover Leaf Creamery Co.*, at 469, 473.[10]

II

My Brothers POWELL and REHNQUIST make the mistake of disregarding the intention of Iowa's lawmakers and assuming that resolution of the case must hinge upon the argument offered by Iowa's attorneys: that 65–foot doubles are more dangerous than shorter trucks. They then canvass the factual record and findings of the courts below and reach opposite conclusions as to whether the evidence adequately supports that empirical judgment. I repeat: my Brothers POWELL and REHNQUIST have asked and

---

[10] Moreover, I would emphasize that in the field of safety—and perhaps in other fields where the decisions of state lawmakers are deserving of a heightened degree of deference—the role of the courts is not to balance asserted burdens against intended benefits as it is in other fields. In the field of safety, once the court has established that the intended safety benefit is not illusory, insubstantial, or nonexistent, it must defer to the State's lawmakers on the appropriate balance to be struck against other interests. I therefore disagree with my Brother POWELL when he asserts that the degree of interference with interstate commerce may in the first instance be "weighed" against the State's safety interests ***.

answered the wrong question. For although Iowa's lawyers in this litigation have defended the truck-length regulation on the basis of the safety advantages of 55–foot singles and 60–foot doubles over 65–foot doubles, Iowa's actual rationale for maintaining the regulation had nothing to do with these purported differences. Rather, Iowa sought to discourage interstate truck traffic on Iowa's highways. Thus, the safety advantages and disadvantages of the types and lengths of trucks involved in this case are irrelevant to the decision.[3] ***

Although the Court has stated that "[i]n no field has *** deference to state regulation been greater than that of highway safety," *Raymond*, at 443, it has declined to go so far as to presume that size restrictions are inherently tied to public safety. The Court has emphasized that the "strong presumption of validity" of size restrictions "cannot justify a court in closing its eyes to uncontroverted evidence of record,"—here the obvious fact that the safety characteristics of 65–foot doubles did not provide the motivation for either legislators or Governor in maintaining the regulation.

III

Though my Brother POWELL recognizes that the State's actual purpose in maintaining the truck-length regulation was "to limit the use of its highways by deflecting some through traffic," he fails to recognize that this purpose, being protectionist in nature, is impermissible under the Commerce Clause. The Governor admitted that he blocked legislative efforts to raise the length of trucks because the change "would benefit only a few Iowa-based companies while providing a great advantage for out-of-state trucking firms and competitors at the expense of our Iowa citizens." Appellant Raymond Kassel, Director of the Iowa Department of Transportation, while admitting that the greater 65–foot length standard would be safer overall, defended the more restrictive regulations because of their benefits within Iowa :

---

[3] *** The extent to which we may rely upon *post hoc* justifications of counsel depends on the circumstances surrounding passage of the legislation. Where there is no evidence bearing on the actual purpose for a legislative classification, our analysis necessarily focuses on the suggestions of counsel. Even then, "marginally more demanding scrutiny" is appropriate to "test the plausibility of the tendered purpose." But where the lawmakers' purposes in enacting a statute are explicitly set forth, or are clearly discernible from the legislative history, this Court should not take *** the extraordinary step of disregarding the *actual* purpose in favor of some "imaginary basis or purpose." The principle of separation of powers requires, after all, that we defer to the elected lawmakers' judgment as to the appropriate means to accomplish an end, not that we defer to the arguments of lawyers.

If, as here, the only purpose ever articulated by the State's lawmakers for maintaining a regulation is illegitimate, I consider it contrary to precedent as well as to sound principles of constitutional adjudication for the courts to base their analysis on purposes never conceived by the lawmakers. This is especially true where, as the dissent's strained analysis of the relative safety of 65–foot doubles to shorter trucks amply demonstrates, the *post hoc* justifications are implausible as well as imaginary. I would emphasize that, although my Brother Powell's plurality opinion does not give as much weight to the illegitimacy of Iowa's actual purpose as I do, both that opinion and this concurrence have found the actual motivation of the Iowa lawmakers in maintaining the truck-length regulation highly relevant to, if not dispositive of, the case.

"Q: Overall, there would be fewer miles of operation, fewer accidents and fewer fatalities?

"A: Yes, on the national scene.

"Q: Does it not concern the Iowa Department of Transportation that banning 65–foot twins causes more accidents, more injuries and more fatalities?

"A: Do you mean outside of our state border?

"Q: Overall.

"A: Our primary concern is the citizens of Iowa and our own highway system we operate in this state."

The regulation has had its predicted effect. As the District Court found:

> "Iowa's length restriction causes the trucks affected by the ban to travel more miles over more dangerous roads in other states which means a greater overall exposure to accidents and fatalities. More miles of highway are subjected to wear. More fuel is consumed and greater transportation costs are incurred."

Iowa may not shunt off its fair share of the burden of maintaining interstate truck routes, nor may it create increased hazards on the highways of neighboring States in order to decrease the hazards on Iowa highways. Such an attempt has all the hallmarks of the "simple *** protectionism" this Court has condemned in the economic area. Just as a State's attempt to avoid interstate competition in economic goods may damage the prosperity of the Nation as a whole, so Iowa's attempt to deflect interstate truck traffic has been found to make the Nation's highways as a whole more hazardous. That attempt should therefore be subject to "a virtually per se rule of invalidity."

This Court's heightened deference to the judgments of state lawmakers in the field of safety is largely attributable to a judicial disinclination to weigh the interests of safety against other societal interests, such as the economic interest in the free flow of commerce. Thus, "if safety justifications are not illusory, the Court will not second-guess legislative judgment about their importance in comparison with related burdens on interstate commerce." *Raymond* (BLACKMUN, J., concurring). Here, the decision of Iowa's lawmakers to promote Iowa's safety and other interests at the direct expense of the safety and other interests of neighboring States merits no such deference. No special judicial acuity is demanded to perceive that this sort of parochial legislation violates the Commerce Clause. As JUSTICE CARDOZO has written, the Commerce Clause "was framed upon the theory that the peoples of the several states must sink or swim together, and that in the long run prosperity and salvation are in union and not division."

I therefore concur in the judgment.

JUSTICE REHNQUIST, with whom THE CHIEF JUSTICE and JUSTICE STEWART join, dissenting.

The result in this case suggests, to paraphrase JUSTICE JACKSON, that the only state truck-length limit "that is valid is one which this Court has not been able to get its hands on." Although the plurality opinion and the opinion concurring in the judgment strike down Iowa's law by different routes, I believe the analysis in both opinions oversteps our "limited authority to review state legislation under the commerce clause" and seriously intrudes upon the fundamental right of the States to pass laws to secure the safety of their citizens. Accordingly, I dissent.

It is necessary to elaborate somewhat on the facts as presented in the plurality opinion to appreciate fully what the Court does today. Iowa's action in limiting the length of trucks which may travel on its highways is in no sense unusual. Every State in the Union regulates the length of vehicles permitted to use the public roads. Nor is Iowa a renegade in having length limits which operate to exclude the 65-foot doubles favored by Consolidated. These trucks are prohibited in other areas of the country as well, some 17 States and the District of Columbia, including all of New England and most of the Southeast. While pointing out that Consolidated carries commodities through Iowa on Interstate 80, "the principal east-west route linking New York, Chicago, and the west coast," the plurality neglects to note that both Pennsylvania and New Jersey, through which Interstate 80 runs before reaching New York, also ban 65–foot doubles. In short, the persistent effort in the plurality opinion to paint Iowa as an oddity standing alone to block commerce carried in 65–foot doubles is simply not supported by the facts.

Nor does the plurality adequately convey the extent to which the lower courts permitted the 65–foot doubles to operate in Iowa. Consolidated sought to have the 60–foot length limit declared an unconstitutional burden on commerce when applied to the seven Interstate Highways in Iowa and "access routes to and from Plaintiff's terminals, and reasonable access from said Interstate Highways to facilities for food, fuel, repairs, or rest." The lower courts granted this relief, permitting the 65–foot doubles to travel *off the Interstates* as far as five miles for access to terminal and other facilities, or less if closer facilities were available. To the extent the plurality relies on characteristics of the Interstate Highways in rejecting Iowa's asserted safety justifications, it fails to recognize the scope of the District Court order it upholds.

With these additions to the relevant facts, we can now examine the appropriate analysis to be applied. *** A determination that a state law is a rational safety measure does not end the Commerce Clause inquiry. A "sensitive consideration" of the safety purpose in relation to the burden on commerce is required. *Raymond*, at 441. When engaging in such a consideration the Court does not directly compare safety benefits to commerce costs and strike down the legislation if the latter can be said in some vague sense to "outweigh" the former. Such an approach would make an empty gesture of the strong presumption of validity accorded state safety measures, particularly those governing highways. It would also arrogate to this Court functions of forming public policy, functions which, in the absence of congressional action, were left by the Framers of the Constitution to state legislatures. "[I]n reviewing a state highway regulation where Congress has not acted, a court is not called upon, as are state legislatures, to determine what, in its judgment, is the most suitable restriction to be applied of those that are possible, or to choose that one which in its opinion is best adapted to all the diverse interests affected." *Barnwell Brothers*, at 190. [This admonition is] peculiarly apt when, as here, the question involves the difficult comparison of financial losses and "the loss of lives and limbs of workers and people using the highways." *** [4]

The purpose of the "sensitive consideration" referred to above is rather to determine if the asserted safety justification, although rational, is merely a pretext for discrimination against interstate commerce. We will conclude that it is if the safety benefits from the regulation are demonstrably trivial while the burden on commerce is great. *** The cases *** demonstrate that the safety benefits of a state law must be slight indeed before it will be struck down under the dormant Commerce Clause.

Iowa defends its statute as a highway safety regulation. There can be no doubt that the challenged statute is a valid highway safety regulation and thus entitled to the strongest presumption of validity against Commerce Clause challenges. As noted, all 50 States regulate the length of trucks which may use their highways. The Iowa Supreme Court has long viewed the provision in question as intended to promote highway safety, and "[t]his Court has also had occasion to point out that the sizes and weights of automobiles have an important relation to the safe and convenient use of the highways, which are matters of state control."*** There can also be no question that the particular limit chosen by Iowa—60 feet—is rationally related to Iowa's safety objective. Most truck limits are between 55 and 65 feet and Iowa's choice is thus well within the widely accepted range.

Iowa adduced evidence supporting the relation between vehicle length and highway safety. The evidence indicated that longer vehicles take greater time to be passed, thereby increasing the risks of accidents, particularly during the inclement weather not uncommon in Iowa. The 65–foot vehicle exposes a passing driver to visibility-impairing splash and spray during bad weather for a longer period than do the shorter trucks permitted in Iowa. Longer trucks are more likely to clog intersections, and although there are no intersections on the Interstate Highways, the order below went beyond the highways themselves and the concerns about greater length at intersections would arise "[a]t every trip origin, every trip destination, every intermediate stop for picking up trailers, reconfiguring loads, change of drivers, eating, refueling—every intermediate stop would generate this type of situation." The Chief of the Division of Patrol in the Iowa Department of Public Safety testified that longer vehicles pose greater problems at the scene of an

---

[4] It should not escape notice that a majority of the Court goes on record today as agreeing that courts in Commerce Clause cases do not sit to weigh safety benefits against burdens on commerce when the safety benefits are not illusory. Even the plurality gives lipservice to this principle. I do not agree with my Brother BRENNAN, however, that only those safety benefits somehow articulated by the legislature as the motivation for the challenged statute can be considered in supporting the state law.

accident. For example, trucks involved in accidents often must be unloaded at the scene, which would take longer the bigger the load.

In rebuttal of Consolidated's evidence on the relative safety of 65–foot doubles to trucks permitted on Iowa's highways, Iowa introduced evidence that doubles are more likely than singles to jackknife or upset. The District Court concluded that this was so and that singles are more stable than doubles. Iowa also introduced evidence from Consolidated's own records showing that Consolidated's overall accident rate for doubles exceeded that of semis for three of the last four years, and that some of Consolidated's own drivers expressed a preference for the handling characteristics of singles over doubles.

In addition Iowa elicited evidence undermining the probative value of Consolidated's evidence. For example, Iowa established that the more experienced drivers tended to drive doubles, because they have seniority and driving doubles is a higher paying job than driving singles. Since the leading cause of accidents was driver error, Consolidated's evidence of the relative safety record of doubles may have been based in large part not on the relative safety of the vehicles themselves but on the experience of the drivers. Although the District Court, the Court of Appeals, and the plurality all fail to recognize the fact, Iowa also negated much of Consolidated's evidence by establishing that it considered the relative safety of doubles to singles, and not the question of length alone. Consolidated introduced much evidence that its doubles were as safe as singles. Such evidence is beside the point. The trucks which Consolidated wants to run in Iowa are prohibited because of their length, not their configuration. Doubles are allowed in Iowa, up to a length of 60 feet, and Consolidated in fact operates 60–foot doubles in Iowa. Consolidated's experts were often forced to admit that they could draw no conclusions about the relative safety of 65–foot doubles and 60–foot doubles, as opposed to doubles and singles. Conclusions that the double configuration is as safe as the single do not at all mean the 65–foot double is as safe as the 60–foot double, or that length is not relevant to vehicle safety. For example, one of Consolidated's experts testified that doubles "off track" better than singles, because of their axle placement, but conceded on cross-examination that a 60–foot double would off-track better than a 65–foot double. In sum, there was sufficient evidence presented at trial to support the legislative determination that length is related to safety, and nothing in Consolidated's evidence undermines this conclusion.

The District Court approached the case as if the question were whether Consolidated's 65–foot trucks were as safe as others permitted on Iowa highways, and the Court of Appeals as if its task were to determine if the District Court's factual findings in this regard were "clearly erroneous." The question, however, is whether the Iowa Legislature has acted rationally in regulating vehicle lengths and whether the safety benefits from this regulation are more than slight or problematical. "The classification of the traffic for the purposes of regulation *** is a legislative, not a judicial, function. Its merits are not to be weighed in the judicial balance and the classification rejected merely because the weight of the evidence in court appears to favor a different standard." *Clark v. Paul Gray, Inc.*, 306 U.S. 583, 594 (1939). "Since the adoption of one weight or width regulation, rather than another, is a legislative and not a judicial choice, its constitutionality is not to be determined by weighing in the judicial scales the merits of the legislative choice and rejecting it if the weight of evidence presented in court appears to favor a different standard." *Barnwell Brothers*, 303 U.S., at 191.[8]

The answering of the relevant question is not appreciably advanced by comparing trucks slightly over the length limit with those at the length limit. It is emphatically not our task to balance any incremental safety benefits from prohibiting 65–foot doubles as opposed to 60–foot doubles against the burden on interstate commerce. Lines drawn for safety purposes will rarely pass muster if the question is whether a slight increment can be permitted without sacrificing safety. ***

The question is rather whether it can be said that the benefits flowing to Iowa from a rational truck-length limitation are "slight or problematical." See *Bibb*, at 524. The particular line chosen by Iowa—60 feet—is relevant only to the question whether the limit is a rational one. Once a court determines that it is, it considers the overall safety benefits from the regulation against burdens on interstate commerce, and not any marginal benefits from the scheme the State established as opposed to that the plaintiffs desire.

The difficulties with the contrary approach are patent. While it may be clear that there are substantial safety benefits from a 55–foot truck as compared to a 105–foot truck, these benefits may not be discernible in 5–foot jumps. Appellee's approach would permit what could not be accomplished in one lawsuit to be done in 10 separate suits, each challenging an additional five feet.

Any direct balancing of marginal safety benefits against burdens on commerce would make the burdens on commerce the sole significant factor, and make likely the odd result that similar state laws enacted for identical safety reasons might violate the Commerce Clause in one part of the country but not another. For example, Mississippi and Georgia prohibit trucks over 55 feet. Since doubles are not operated in the Southeast, the demonstrable burden on commerce may not be sufficient to strike down these laws, while

---

[8] The opinion of my Brother BRENNAN concurring in the judgment mischaracterizes this dissent when it states that I assume "resolution of the case must hinge upon the argument offered by Iowa's attorneys: that 65–foot doubles are more dangerous than shorter trucks." I assume nothing of the sort. As noted in the immediately preceding paragraph, the point of this dissent is that the District Court and the Court of Appeals erred when they undertook to determine if the prohibited trucks were as safe as the permitted ones on the basis of evidence presented at trial. As I read this Court's opinions, the State must simply prove, aided by a "strong presumption of validity," that the safety benefits of its law are not illusory. I review the evidence presented at trial simply to demonstrate that Iowa made such a showing in this case, not because the validity of Iowa's law depends on its proving by a preponderance of the evidence that the excluded trucks are unsafe. As I thought was made clear, it is my view that Iowa must simply show a relation between vehicle length limits and safety, and that the benefits from its length limit are not illusory. Iowa's arguments on passing time, intersection obstruction, and problems at the scene of accidents have validity beyond a comparison of the 65–and 60–foot trucks. In sum, I fully agree with JUSTICE BRENNAN that the validity of Iowa's length limit does not turn on whether 65–foot trucks are less safe than 60–foot trucks.

Consolidated maintains that it is in this case, even though the doubles here are given an additional five feet. On the other hand, if Consolidated were to win this case it could shift its 65–foot doubles to routes leading into Mississippi or Georgia (both States border States in which 65–foot trucks are permitted) and claim the same constitutional violation it claims in this case. Consolidated Freightways, and not this Court, would become the final arbiter of the Commerce Clause.

It must be emphasized that there is nothing in the laws of nature which make 65–foot doubles an obvious norm. *** Striking down Iowa's law because Consolidated has made a voluntary business decision to employ 65–foot doubles, a decision based on the actions of other state legislatures, would essentially be compelling Iowa to yield to the policy choices of neighboring States. Under our constitutional scheme, however, there is only one legislative body which can pre empt the rational policy determination of the Iowa Legislature and that is Congress. Forcing Iowa to yield to the policy choices of neighboring States perverts the primary purpose of the Commerce Clause, that of vesting power to regulate interstate commerce in Congress, where all the States are represented. In *Barnwell Brothers*, the Court upheld a South Carolina width limit of 90 inches even though "all other states permit a width of 96 inches which is the standard width of trucks engaged in interstate commerce." 303 U.S., at 184. Then JUSTICE STONE, writing for the Court, stressed: "The fact that many states have adopted a different standard is not persuasive. *** The legislature, being free to exercise its own judgment, is not bound by that of other legislatures. It would hardly be contended that if all the states had adopted a single standard none, in the light of its own experience and in the exercise of its judgment upon all the complex elements which enter into the problem, could change it."

*** [T]he exception to the Wisconsin prohibition which the Court specifically noted in *Raymond* finds no parallel in this case. The exception in *Raymond* permitted oversized vehicles to travel from plant to plant in Wisconsin or between a Wisconsin plant and the border. As the Court noted, this discriminated on its face between Wisconsin industries and the industries of other States. The border-cities exception to the Iowa length limit does not. Iowa shippers in cities with border-city ordinances may use longer vehicles in interstate commerce, but interstate shippers coming into such cities may do so as well. Cities without border-city ordinances may neither export nor import on oversized vehicles. Nor can the border-cities exception be "[v]iewed realistically," as was the Wisconsin exception, to "be the product of compromise between forces within the State that seek to retain the State's general truck-length limit, and industries within the State that complain that the general limit is unduly burdensome." The Wisconsin exception was available to all Wisconsin industries wanting to ship out of State from Wisconsin plants. The border-cities exception is of much narrower applicability: only 5 of Iowa's 16 largest cities and only 8 cities in all permit oversized trucks under the border-cities exception. The population of the eight cities with border-city ordinances is only 13 percent of the population of the State.

My Brother BRENNAN argues that the Court should consider only the purpose the Iowa legislators actually sought to achieve by the length limit, and not the purposes advanced by Iowa's lawyers in defense of the statute. This argument calls to mind what was said of the Roman Legions: that they may have lost battles, but they never lost a war, since they never let a war end until they had won it. The argument has been consistently rejected by the Court in other contexts, and JUSTICE BRENNAN can cite no authority for the proposition that possible legislative purposes suggested by a State's lawyers should not be considered in Commerce Clause cases. The problems with a view such as that advanced in the opinion concurring in the judgment are apparent. To name just a few, it assumes that individual legislators are motivated by one discernible "actual" purpose, and ignores the fact that different legislators may vote for a single piece of legislation for widely different reasons. How, for example, would a court adhering to the views expressed in the opinion concurring in the judgment approach a statute, the legislative history of which indicated that 10 votes were based on safety considerations, 10 votes were based on protectionism, and the statute passed by a vote of 40–20? What would the actual purpose of the legislature have been in that case? This Court has wisely "never insisted that a legislative body articulate its reasons for enacting a statute."

*** Both the plurality and the concurrence attach great significance to the Governor's veto of a bill passed by the Iowa Legislature permitting 65–foot doubles. Whatever views one may have about the significance of legislative motives, it must be emphasized that the law which the Court strikes down today was not passed to achieve the protectionist goals the plurality and the concurrence ascribe to the Governor. Iowa's 60–foot length limit was established in 1963, at a time when very few States permitted 65–foot doubles. Striking down legislation on the basis of asserted legislative motives is dubious enough, but the plurality and concurrence strike down the legislation involved in this case because of asserted impermissible motives for not enacting other legislation, motives which could not possibly have been present when the legislation under challenge here was considered and passed. Such action is, so far as I am aware, unprecedented in this Court's history.

Furthermore, the effort in both the plurality and the concurrence to portray the legislation involved here as protectionist is in error. Whenever a State enacts more stringent safety measures than its neighbors, in an area which affects commerce, the safety law will have the incidental effect of deflecting interstate commerce to the neighboring States. Indeed, the safety and protectionist motives cannot be separated: The whole purpose of safety regulation of vehicles is to protect the State from unsafe vehicles. If a neighboring State chooses not to protect its citizens from the danger discerned by the enacting State, that is its business, but the enacting State should not be penalized when the vehicles it considers unsafe travel through the neighboring State.

The other States with truck-length limits that exclude Consolidated's 65–foot doubles would not at all be paranoid in assuming that they might be next on Consolidated's "hit list." The true problem with today's decision is that it gives no guidance whatsoever to these States as to whether their laws are valid or how to defend them. For that matter, the decision gives no guidance to Consolidated or other trucking firms either. Perhaps, after all is said and done, the Court today neither says nor does very much at all. We know only that Iowa's law is invalid and that the jurisprudence of the "negative side" of the Commerce Clause remains hopelessly confused.

Notes

1. **Background.** Does the analysis proceed any differently because Iowa's statute was facially neutral? Consider for a moment a facially neutral state statute that has an adverse effect only on out-of-state companies, benefits some local businesses, and which may adversely affect in-state consumers. Should the Court use Dormant Commerce Clause power to invalidate the statute? *See, e.g., Exxon Corp. v. Governor of Maryland*, 437 U.S. 117 (1978) (upholding by an 8–1 margin a statute providing that a producer or refiner of petroleum products could not operate a retail service station in the state; the statute had been enacted following a gasoline shortage in which refiners provided gasoline products to stations they owned in preference to stations owned by independent operators).

2. *Kassel* **Analysis.**

   • What is the effect of the statutory exceptions to Iowa's 55–foot maximum length rule? Are there nondiscriminatory explanations for these exceptions?

   • What do you think of JUSTICE BRENNAN's point that Iowa must bear its "fair share" of safety problems in the region?

   • Do you think that courts are more or less institutionally capable than state legislatures and Congress in assessing burdens on interstate commerce?

   • Is the Court's balancing a purely economic calculus or does it have a political dimension also?

3. **Judicial Activism.** The most fundamental question about this case is why the Court should do anything about such state statutes. Is there cost-exporting or benefits-reserving activity similar to that involved in *Philadelphia* (involving a facially discriminatory statute)? Or is there merely a redistributive effect of the statutes, both among commercial players within the state and commercial players outside the state? Is the Court seeking to discourage the states from drafting facially neutral statutes that accomplish most of what the states could do with facially discriminatory statutes? Can the Court deal with such issues better or worse than Congress?

4. **Burdening Commerce.** Does the Constitution express a preference for free trade over nondiscriminatory but regulated interstate commerce?

5. **The Surface Transportation Act.** In 1982, Congress imposed an excise tax on fuel and eliminated state restrictions on double-long trucks on interstate highways. A 1984 amendment allowed the Secretary of Transportation, on safety grounds, to exclude "doubles" from portions of the interstate system; the Secretary may also, with the Governor's consent, open portions of the state's

noninterstate highways to "doubles." What, if any, bearing does this legislation have on your thinking about the Court's decision in *Kassel*?

6. **Internet Commerce.** Could a state ban internet "spam" to residents of the state? How would this legislation fare under benefits/burdens analysis?

CARBONE v. TOWN OF CLARKSTOWN
511 U.S. 383, 114 S.Ct. 1677, 128 L.Ed.2d 399 (1994).

JUSTICE KENNEDY delivered the opinion of the Court.

*** We consider a so-called flow control ordinance, which requires all solid waste to be processed at a designated transfer station before leaving the municipality. The avowed purpose of the ordinance is to retain the processing fees charged at the transfer station to amortize the cost of the facility. Because it attains this goal by depriving competitors, including out-of-state firms, of access to a local market, we hold that the flow control ordinance violates the Commerce Clause.

The town of Clarkstown, New York *** entered into a consent decree with the New York State Department of Environmental Conservation. The town agreed to close its landfill and build a new solid waste transfer station on the same site. The station would receive bulk solid waste and separate recyclable from nonrecyclable items. Recyclable waste would be baled for shipment to a recycling facility; nonrecyclable waste, to a suitable landfill or incinerator.

The cost of building the transfer station was estimated at $1.4 million. A local private contractor agreed to construct the facility and operate it for five years, after which the town would buy it for one dollar. During those five years, the town guaranteed a minimum waste flow of 120,000 tons per year, for which the contractor could charge the hauler a so-called tipping fee of $81 per ton. If the station received less than 120,000 tons in a year, the town promised to make up the tipping fee deficit. *** The town would finance its new facility with the income generated by the tipping fees.

The problem of [how] to meet the yearly guarantee *** was compounded by the fact that the tipping fee of $81 per ton exceeded the disposal cost of unsorted solid waste on the private market. The solution the town adopted was the flow control ordinance here in question. The ordinance requires all nonhazardous solid waste within the town to be deposited at the *** transfer station. Noncompliance is punishable by as much as a $1,000 fine and up to 15 days in jail.

The petitioner in this case [operates] a recycling center in Clarkstown, where it receives bulk solid waste, sorts and bales it, and then ships it to other processing facilities—much as occurs at the town's new transfer station. While the flow control ordinance permits recyclers like Carbone to continue receiving solid waste, it requires them to bring the nonrecyclable residue from that waste to the [transfer] station *** and it requires Carbone to pay a tipping fee on trash that Carbone has already sorted.

*** At the outset we confirm that the flow control ordinance does regulate interstate commerce, despite the town's position to the contrary. The town says that its ordinance reaches only waste within its jurisdiction and is in practical effect a quarantine: It prevents garbage from entering the stream of interstate commerce until it is made safe. This reasoning is premised, however, on an outdated and mistaken concept of what constitutes interstate commerce.

While the immediate effect of the ordinance is to direct local transport of solid waste to a designated site within the local jurisdiction, its economic effects are interstate in reach. The Carbone facility in Clarkstown receives and processes waste from places other than Clarkstown, including from out of State. By requiring Carbone to send the nonrecyclable portion of this waste to the transfer station at an additional cost, the flow control ordinance drives up the cost for out-of-state interests to dispose of their solid waste. Furthermore, even as to waste originant in Clarkstown, the ordinance prevents everyone except the favored local operator from performing the initial processing step. The ordinance thus deprives out-of-state businesses of access to a local market. These economic effects are more than enough to bring the Clarkstown ordinance within the purview of the Commerce Clause. ***

The real question is whether the flow control ordinance is valid despite its undoubted effect on interstate commerce. For this inquiry, our case law yields two lines of analysis: first, whether the ordinance discriminates against interstate commerce, and second, whether the ordinance imposes a burden on interstate commerce that is "clearly excessive in relation to the putative local benefits." As we find that the ordinance discriminates against interstate commerce, we need not resort to the [other] test.

The central rationale for the rule against discrimination is to prohibit state or municipal laws whose object is local economic protectionism, laws that would excite those jealousies and retaliatory measures the Constitution was designed to prevent. We have interpreted the Commerce Clause to invalidate local laws that impose commercial barriers or discriminate against an article of commerce by reason of its origin or destination out of State. *See, e.g., Philadelphia v. New Jersey.*

Clarkstown protests that its ordinance does not discriminate because it does not differentiate solid waste on the basis of its geographic origin. All solid waste, regardless of origin, must be processed at the designated transfer station before it leaves the town. Unlike the statute in Philadelphia, says the town, the ordinance erects no barrier to the import or export of any solid waste but requires only that the waste be channeled through the designated facility.

Our initial discussion of the effects of the ordinance on interstate commerce goes far toward refuting the town's contention that there is no discrimination in its regulatory scheme. The town's own arguments go the rest of the way. As the town itself points out, what makes garbage a profitable business is not its own worth but the fact that its possessor must pay to get rid of it. In other words, the article of commerce is not so much the solid waste itself, but rather the service of processing and disposing of it.

With respect to this stream of commerce, the flow control ordinance discriminates, for it allows only the favored operator to process waste that is within the limits of the town. The ordinance is no less discriminatory because in-state or in-town processors are also covered by the prohibition. In *Dean Milk Co. v. Madison*, 340 U.S. 349 (1951), we struck down a city ordinance that required all milk sold in the city to be pasteurized within five miles of the city lines. We found it "immaterial that Wisconsin milk from outside the Madison area is subjected to the same proscription as that moving in interstate commerce."

In this light, the flow control ordinance is just one more instance of local processing requirements that we long have held invalid. The essential vice in laws of this sort is that they bar the import of the processing service. Out-of-state meat inspectors, or shrimp hullers, or milk pasteurizers, are deprived of access to local demand for their services. Put another way, the offending local laws hoard a local resource—be it meat, shrimp, or milk—for the benefit of local businesses that treat it.

The flow control ordinance has the same design and effect. It hoards solid waste, and the demand to get rid of it, for the benefit of the preferred processing facility. The only conceivable distinction from the cases cited above is that the flow control ordinance favors a single local proprietor. But this difference just makes the protectionist effect of the ordinance more acute. In *Dean Milk*, the local processing requirement at least permitted pasteurizers within five miles of the city to compete. An out-of-state pasteurizer who wanted access to that market might have built a pasteurizing facility within the radius. The flow control ordinance at issue here squelches competition in the waste-processing service altogether, leaving no room for investment from outside.

Discrimination against interstate commerce in favor of local business or investment is per se invalid, save in a narrow class of cases in which the municipality can demonstrate, under rigorous scrutiny, that it has no other means to advance a legitimate local interest. A number of amici contend that the flow control ordinance fits into this narrow class. They suggest that as landfill space diminishes and environmental cleanup costs escalate, measures like flow control become necessary to ensure the safe handling and proper treatment of solid waste.

The teaching of our cases is that these arguments must be rejected absent the clearest showing that the unobstructed flow of interstate commerce itself is unable to solve the local problem. The Commerce Clause presumes a national market free from local legislation that discriminates in favor of local interests. Here Clarkstown has any number of nondiscriminatory alternatives for addressing the health and environmental problems alleged to justify the ordinance in question. The most obvious would be uniform safety regulations enacted without the object to discriminate. These regulations would ensure that competitors like Carbone do not underprice the market by cutting corners on environmental safety.

Nor may Clarkstown justify the flow control ordinance as a way to steer solid waste away from out-of-town disposal sites that it might deem harmful to the environment. To do so would extend the town's police power beyond its jurisdictional bounds. States and localities may not attach restrictions to exports or imports in order to control commerce in other states. ***

The flow control ordinance does serve a central purpose that a nonprotectionist regulation would not: It ensures that the town-sponsored facility will be profitable, so that the local contractor can build it and Clarkstown can buy it back at nominal cost in five years. In other words, as the most candid of amici and even Clarkstown admit, the flow control ordinance is a financing measure. By itself, of course, revenue generation is not a local interest that can justify discrimination against interstate commerce. Otherwise States could impose discriminatory taxes against solid waste originating outside the State.

Clarkstown maintains that special financing is necessary to ensure the long-term survival of the designated facility. If so, the town may subsidize the facility through general taxes or municipal bonds. *New Energy Co. of Indiana v. Limbach*, 486 U.S. 269 (1988). But having elected to use the open market to earn revenues for its project, the town may not employ discriminatory regulation to give that project an advantage over rival businesses from out of State.

Though the Clarkstown ordinance may not in explicit terms seek to regulate interstate commerce, it does so nonetheless by its practical effect and design. In this respect the ordinance is not far different from the state law this Court found invalid in *Buck v. Kuykendall*, 267 U.S. 307 (1925). That statute prohibited common carriers from using state highways over certain routes without a certificate of public convenience. Writing for the Court, JUSTICE BRANDEIS said of the law: "Its primary purpose is not regulation with a view to safety or to conservation of the highways, but the prohibition of competition. It determines not the manner of use, but the persons by whom the highways may be used. It prohibits such use to some persons while permitting it to others for the same purpose and in the same manner."

State and local governments may not use their regulatory power to favor local enterprise by prohibiting patronage of out-of-state competitors or their facilities. ***

JUSTICE O'CONNOR, concurring in the judgment.

*** The Court holds today that [the Clarkstown] ordinance violates the Commerce Clause because it discriminates against interstate commerce. I agree with the majority's ultimate conclusion that the ordinance violates the dormant Commerce Clause. In my view, however, the town's ordinance is unconstitutional not because of facial or effective discrimination against interstate commerce, but rather because it imposes an excessive burden on interstate commerce.

The scope of the dormant Commerce Clause is a judicial creation. *** This Court long ago concluded [that] the Clause not only empowers Congress to regulate interstate commerce, but also imposes limitations on the States in the absence of congressional action ***.

We have generally distinguished between two types of impermissible regulations. A facially nondiscriminatory regulation supported by a legitimate state interest which incidentally burdens interstate commerce is constitutional unless the burden on interstate trade is clearly excessive in relation to the local benefits. Where, however, a regulation "affirmatively" or "clearly" discriminates against interstate commerce on its face or in practical effect, it violates the Constitution unless the discrimination is demonstrably justified by a valid factor unrelated to protectionism. Of course, there is no clear line separating these categories. "In either situation the critical consideration is the overall effect of the statute on both local and interstate activity."

Local Law 9 prohibits anyone except the town-authorized transfer station operator from processing discarded waste and shipping it out of town. In effect, the town has given a waste processing monopoly to the transfer station. The majority concludes that this processing monopoly facially discriminates against interstate commerce. In support of this conclusion, the majority cites previous decisions of this Court striking down regulatory enactments requiring that a particular economic activity be performed within the jurisdiction.

Local Law 9, however, lacks an important feature common to the regulations at issue in [those previous] cases—namely, discrimination on the basis of geographic origin. *** [In] *Dean Milk*, on which the majority heavily relies, the city of Madison drew a line around its perimeter and required that all milk sold in the City be pasteurized only by dairies located inside the line. This type of geographic distinction, which confers an economic advantage on local interests in general, is common to all the local processing cases cited by the majority. And the Court has, I believe, correctly concluded that these arrangements are protectionist either in purpose or practical effect, and thus amount to virtually per se discrimination.

In my view, the majority fails to come to terms with a significant distinction between the laws in the local processing cases discussed above and Local Law 9. Unlike the regulations we have previously struck down, Local Law 9 does not give more favorable treatment to local interests as a group as compared to out-of-state or out-of-town economic interests. Rather, the garbage sorting monopoly is achieved at the expense of all competitors, be they local or nonlocal. That the ordinance does not discriminate on the basis of geographic origin is vividly illustrated by the identity of the plaintiff in this very action: petitioner is a local recycler, physically located in Clarkstown, that desires to process waste itself, and thus bypass the town's designated transfer facility. Because in-town processors—like petitioner—and out-of-town processors are treated equally, I cannot agree that Local Law 9 "discriminates" against interstate commerce. Rather, Local Law 9 "discriminates" evenhandedly against all potential participants in the waste processing business, while benefiting only the chosen operator of the transfer facility.

I believe this distinction has more doctrinal significance than the majority acknowledges. In considering state health and safety regulations such as Local Law 9, we have consistently recognized that the fact that interests within the regulating jurisdiction are equally affected by the challenged enactment counsels against a finding of discrimination. And for good reason. The existence of substantial in-state interests harmed by a regulation is "a powerful safeguard" against legislative discrimination. The Court generally defers to health and safety regulations because "their burden usually falls on local economic interests as well as other States' economic interests, thus insuring that a State's own political processes will serve as a check against unduly burdensome regulations." *Raymond Motor Transportation, Inc. v. Rice*, 434 U.S. 429, 444, n. 18 (1978). Thus, while there is no bright line separating those enactments which are virtually per se invalid and those which are not, the fact that in-town competitors of the transfer facility are equally burdened by Local Law 9 leads me to conclude that Local Law 9 does not discriminate against interstate commerce.

That the ordinance does not discriminate against interstate commerce does not, however, end the Commerce Clause inquiry. Even a nondiscriminatory regulation may nonetheless impose an excessive burden on interstate trade when considered in relation to the local benefits conferred. Indeed, we have long recognized that "a burden imposed by a State upon interstate commerce is not to be sustained simply because the statute imposing it applies alike to *** the people of the State enacting such statute." ***

The local interest in proper disposal of waste is obviously significant. But this interest could be achieved by simply requiring that all waste disposed of in the town be properly processed somewhere. For example, the town could ensure proper processing by setting specific standards with which all town processors must comply.

In fact, however, the town's purpose is narrower than merely ensuring proper disposal. Local Law 9 is intended to ensure the financial viability of the transfer facility. I agree with the majority that this purpose can be achieved by other means that would have a less dramatic impact on the flow of goods. For example, the town could finance the project by imposing taxes, by issuing municipal bonds, or even by lowering its price for processing to a level competitive with other waste processing facilities. But by requiring that all waste be processed at the town's facility, the ordinance "squelches competition in the waste-processing service altogether, leaving no room for investment from outside."

In addition, "[t]he practical effect of [Local Law 9] must be evaluated not only by considering the consequences of the statute itself, but also by considering how the challenged statute may interact with the legitimate regulatory regimes of the other States and what effect would arise if not one, but many or every, [jurisdiction] adopted similar legislation." This is not a hypothetical inquiry. Over 20 states have enacted statutes authorizing local governments to adopt flow control laws. If the localities in these States impose the type of restriction on the movement of waste that Clarkstown has adopted, the free movement of solid waste in the stream of commerce will be severely impaired. Indeed, pervasive flow control would result in the type of balkanization the Clause is primarily intended to prevent.

Given that many jurisdictions are contemplating or enacting flow control, the potential for conflicts is high. For example, in the State of New Jersey, just south of Clarkstown, local waste may be removed from the State for the sorting of recyclables "as long as the residual solid waste is returned to New Jersey." Under Local Law 9, however, if petitioners bring waste from New Jersey for recycling at their Clarkstown operation, the residual waste may not be returned to New Jersey, but must be transported to Clarkstown's transfer facility. As a consequence, operations like petitioners' cannot comply with the requirements of both jurisdictions. Nondiscriminatory state or local laws which actually conflict with the enactments of other States are constitutionally infirm if they burden interstate commerce. The increasing number of flow control regimes virtually ensures some inconsistency between jurisdictions, with the effect of eliminating the movement of waste between jurisdictions. I therefore conclude that the burden Local Law 9 imposes on interstate commerce is excessive in relation to Clarkstown's interest in ensuring a fixed supply of waste to supply its project. ***

JUSTICE SOUTER, with whom THE CHIEF JUSTICE and JUSTICE BLACKMUN join, dissenting.

*** Previous cases have held that the "negative" or "dormant" aspect of the Commerce Clause renders state or local legislation unconstitutional when it discriminates against out-of-state or out-of-town businesses such as those that pasteurize milk, hull shrimp, or mill lumber, and the majority relies on these cases because of what they have in common with this one: out-of-state processors are excluded from the local market (here, from the market for trash processing services). What the majority ignores, however, are the differences between our local processing cases and this one: the exclusion worked by Clarkstown's Local Law 9 bestows no benefit on a class of local private actors, but instead directly aids the government in satisfying a traditional governmental responsibility. The law does not differentiate between all local and all out-of-town providers of a service, but instead between the one entity responsible for ensuring that the job gets done and all other enterprises, regardless of their location. The ordinance thus falls outside that class of tariff or protectionist measures that the Commerce Clause has traditionally been thought to bar States from enacting against each other, and when the majority subsumes the ordinance within the class of laws this Court has struck down as facially discriminatory (and so avails itself of our "virtually per se rule" against such statutes, *see Philadelphia v. New Jersey*, 437 U.S. 617, 624 (1978)), the majority is in fact greatly extending the Clause's dormant reach.

There are, however, good and sufficient reasons against expanding the Commerce Clause's inherent capacity to trump exercises of state authority such as the ordinance at issue here. There is no indication in the record that any out-of-state trash processor has been harmed, or that the interstate movement or disposition of trash will be affected one whit. To the degree Local Law 9 affects the market for trash processing services, it does so only by subjecting Clarkstown residents and businesses to burdens far different from the burdens of local favoritism that dormant Commerce Clause jurisprudence seeks to root out. The town has found a way to finance a public improvement, not by transferring its cost to out-of-state economic interests, but by spreading it among the local generators of trash, an equitable result with tendencies that should not disturb the Commerce Clause and should not be disturbed by us ***.

We are not called upon to judge the ultimate wisdom of creating this local monopoly, but we are asked to say whether Clarkstown's monopoly violates the Commerce Clause, as long read by this Court to limit the power of state and local governments to discriminate against interstate commerce. *** This limitation on the state and local power has been seen implicit in the Commerce Clause because, as the majority recognizes, the Framers sought to dampen regional jealousies in general and, in particular, to eliminate retaliatory tariffs, which had poisoned commercial relations under the Articles of Confederation. Laws that hoard for local businesses the right to serve local markets or develop local resources work to isolate States from each other and to incite retaliation, since no State would stand by while another advanced the economic interests of its own business classes at the expense of its neighbors.

The majority argues that resolution of the issue before us is controlled by a line of cases in which we have struck down state or local laws that discriminate against out-of-state or out-of-town providers of processing services. [The] laws invalidated in those cases were patently discriminatory, differentiating by their very terms between in-state and out-of-state (or local and nonlocal) processors. One ordinance, for example, forbad selling pasteurized milk "'unless the same shall have been pasteurized and bottled *** within a radius of five miles from the central portion of the City of Madison. *** '" *Dean Milk Co. v. Madison*, 340 U.S. 349, 350, n. 1 (1951). The other laws expressly discriminated against commerce crossing state lines, placing these local processing cases squarely within the larger class of cases in which this Court has invalidated facially discriminatory legislation.

As the majority recognizes, Local Law 9 shares two features with these local processing cases. It regulates a processing service available in interstate commerce, i.e., the sorting and baling of solid waste for disposal. And it does so in a fashion that excludes out-of-town trash processors by its very terms. These parallels between Local Law 9 and the statutes previously invalidated confer initial plausibility on the majority's classification of this case with those earlier ones on processing, and they even bring this one within the most general language of some of the earlier cases, abhorring the tendency of such statutes "to impose an artificial rigidity on the economic pattern of the industry."

There are, however, both analytical and practical differences between this and the earlier processing cases, differences the majority underestimates or overlooks but which, if given their due, should prevent this case from being decided the same way. First, the terms of Clarkstown's ordinance favor a single processor, not the class of all such businesses located in Clarkstown. Second, the one proprietor so favored is essentially an agent of the municipal government, which (unlike Carbone or other private trash processors) must ensure the removal of waste according to acceptable standards of public health. Any discrimination worked by Local Law 9 thus fails to produce the sort of entrepreneurial favoritism we have previously defined and condemned as protectionist.

The outstanding feature of the statutes reviewed in the local processing cases is their distinction between two classes of private economic actors according to location, favoring *** milk pasteurizers within five miles of the center of Madison, and so on. Since nothing in these local processing laws prevented a proliferation of local businesses within the State or town, the out-of-town processors were not excluded as part and parcel of a general exclusion of private firms from the market, but as a result of discrimination among such firms according to geography alone. It was because of that discrimination in favor of local businesses, preferred at the expense of their out-of-town or out-of-state competitors, that the Court struck down those local processing laws as classic examples of the economic protectionism the dormant Commerce Clause jurisprudence aims to prevent. In the words of one commentator summarizing our case law, it is laws "adopted for the purpose of improving the competitive position of local economic actors, just because they are local, vis-a-vis their foreign competitors" that offend the Commerce Clause. The Commerce Clause does not otherwise protect access to local markets.

The majority recognizes, but discounts, this difference between laws favoring all local actors and this law favoring a single municipal one. According to the majority, "this difference just makes the protectionist effect of the ordinance more acute" because outside investors cannot even build competing facilities within Clarkstown. But of course Clarkstown investors face the same prohibition, which is to say that Local Law 9's exclusion of outside capital is part of a broader exclusion of private capital, not a discrimination against out-of-state investors as such. Thus, while these differences may underscore the ordinance's anticompetitive effect, they substantially mitigate any protectionist effect, for subjecting out-of-town investors and facilities to the same constraints as local ones is not economic protectionism.

Nor is the monopolist created by Local Law 9 just another private company successfully enlisting local government to protect the jobs and profits of local citizens. While our previous local processing cases have barred discrimination in markets served by private companies, Clarkstown's transfer station is essentially a municipal facility, built and operated under a contract with the municipality and soon to revert entirely to municipal ownership. ***

The majority ignores this distinction between public and private enterprise, equating Local Law 9's "hoarding" of solid waste for the municipal transfer station with the design and effect of ordinances that restrict access to local markets for the benefit of local private firms. But private businesses, whether local or out of State, first serve the private interests of their owners, and there is therefore only rarely a reason other than economic protectionism for favoring local businesses over their out-of-town competitors. The local government itself occupies a very different market position, however, being the one entity that enters the market to serve the public interest of local citizens quite apart from private interest in private gain. Reasons other than economic protectionism are accordingly more likely to explain the design and effect of an ordinance that favors a public facility. The facility as constructed might, for example, be one that private economic actors, left to their own devices, would not have built, but which the locality needs in order to abate (or guarantee against creating) a public nuisance. *** An ordinance that favors a municipal facility, in any event, is one that favors the public sector, and if "we continue to recognize that the States occupy a special and specific position in our constitutional system and that the scope of Congress' authority under the Commerce Clause must reflect that position," *Garcia v. San Antonio Metropolitan Transit Authority*, 469 U.S. 528, 556 (1985), then surely this Court's dormant Commerce Clause jurisprudence must itself see that favoring state-sponsored facilities differs from discriminating among private economic actors, and is much less likely to be protectionist.

*** The justification for subjecting the local processing laws and the broader class of clearly discriminatory commercial regulation to near-fatal scrutiny is the virtual certainty that such laws, at least in their discriminatory aspect, serve no legitimate, nonprotectionist purpose. Whether we find the "the evil of protectionism" in the clear import of specific statutory provisions or in the legislature's ultimate purpose, the discriminatory scheme is almost always designed either to favor local industry, as such, or to achieve some other goal while exporting a disproportionate share of the burden of attaining it, which is merely a subtler form of local favoritism.

On the other hand, in a market served by a municipal facility, a law that favors that single facility over all others is a law that favors the public sector over all private-sector processors, whether local or out of State. Because the favor does not go to local private competitors of out-of-state firms, out-of-state governments will at the least lack a motive to favor their own firms in order to equalize the positions of private competitors. While a preference in favor of the government may incidentally function as local favoritism as well, a more particularized enquiry is necessary before a court can say whether such a law does in fact smack too strongly of economic protectionism. ***

We have said that when legislation that does not facially discriminate "comes into conflict with the Commerce Clause's overriding requirement of a national 'common market,' we are confronted with the task of effecting an accommodation of the competing national and local interests." *Hunt v. Washington State Apple Advertising Comm'n*, 432 U.S. 333, 350 (1977).

Although this analysis of competing interests has sometimes been called a "balancing test," it is not so much an open-ended weighing of an ordinance's pros and cons, as an assessment of whether an ordinance discriminates in practice or otherwise unjustifiably operates to isolate a State's economy from the national common market.

*** The primary burden Carbone attributes to flow control ordinances such as Local Law 9 is that they "prevent trash from being sent to the most cost-effective disposal facilities, and insulate the designated facility from all price competition." In this case, customers must pay $11 per ton more for dumping trash at the Clarkstown transfer station than they would pay at Carbone's facility, although this dollar figure presumably overstates the burden by disguising some differences between the two: according to its state permit, 90 percent of Carbone's waste stream comprises recyclable cardboard, while the Clarkstown facility takes all manner of less valuable waste, which it treats with state-of-the-art environmental technology not employed at Carbone's more rudimentary plant.

Fortunately, the dollar cost of the burden need not be pinpointed, its nature being more significant than its economic extent. When we look to its nature, it should be clear that the monopolistic character of Local Law 9's effects is not itself suspicious for purposes of the Commerce Clause. Although the right to compete is a hallmark of the American economy and local monopolies are subject to challenge under the century-old Sherman Act, the bar to monopolies (or, rather, the authority to dismember and penalize them) arises from a statutory, not a constitutional, mandate. *** The dormant Commerce Clause does not "protec[t] the particular structure or methods of operation in a[ny] *** market." *Exxon Corp. v. Governor of Md.*, 437 U.S. 117, 127 (1978). The only right to compete that it protects is the right to compete on terms independent of one's location.

While the monopolistic nature of the burden may be disregarded, any geographically discriminatory elements must be assessed with care. We have already observed that there is no geographically based selection among private firms, and it is clear from the face of the ordinance that nothing hinges on the source of trash that enters Clarkstown or upon the destination of the processed waste that leaves the transfer station. There is, to be sure, an incidental local economic benefit, for the need to process Clarkstown's trash in Clarkstown will create local jobs. But this local boon is mitigated by another feature of the ordinance, in that it finances whatever benefits it confers on the town from the pockets of the very citizens who passed it into law. On the reasonable assumption that no one can avoid producing some trash, every resident of Clarkstown must bear a portion of the burden Local Law 9 imposes to support the municipal monopoly, an uncharacteristic feature of statutes claimed to violate the Commerce Clause.

By way of contrast, most of the local processing statutes we have previously invalidated imposed requirements that made local goods more expensive as they headed into the national market, so that out-of-state economies bore the bulk of any burden. *** Courts step in through the dormant Commerce Clause to prevent such exports because legislative action imposing a burden "'principally upon those without the state *** is not likely to be subjected to those political restraints which are normally exerted on legislation where it affects adversely some interests within the state.'" Here, in contrast, every voter in Clarkstown pays to fund the benefits of flow control, however high the tipping fee is set. Since, indeed, the mandate to use the town facility will only make a difference when the tipping fee raises the cost of using the facility above what the market would otherwise set, the Clarkstown voters are funding their benefit by assessing themselves and paying an economic penalty. Any whiff of economic protectionism is far from obvious.

An examination of the record confirms skepticism that enforcement of the ordinance portends a Commerce Clause violation, for it shows that the burden falls entirely on Clarkstown residents. If the record contained evidence that Clarkstown's ordinance burdened out-of-town providers of garbage sorting and baling services, rather than just the local business that is a party in this case, that fact might be significant. But petitioner has presented no evidence that there are transfer stations outside Clarkstown capable of handling the town's business, and the record is devoid of evidence that such enterprises have lost business as a result of this ordinance. Similarly, if the record supported an inference that above-market pricing at the Clarkstown transfer station caused less trash to flow to out-of-state landfills and incinerators, that, too, might have constitutional significance. There is, however, no evidence of any disruption in the flow of trash from curbsides in Clarkstown to landfills in Florida and Ohio. Here we can confidently say that the only business lost as a result of this ordinance is business lost in Clarkstown, as customers who had used Carbone's facility drift away in response to any higher fees Carbone may have to institute to afford its share of city services; but business lost in Clarkstown as a result of a Clarkstown ordinance is not a burden that offends the Constitution.

This skepticism that protectionism is afoot here is confirmed again when we examine the governmental interests apparently served by the local law. As mentioned already, the State and its municipalities need prompt, sanitary trash processing, which is imperative whether or not the private market sees fit to serve this need at an affordable price and to continue doing so dependably into the future. The state and local governments also have a substantial interest in the flow-control feature to minimize the risk of financing this service, for while there may be an element of exaggeration in the statement that "[r]esource recovery facilities cannot be built unless they are guaranteed a supply of discarded material," there is no question that a "put or pay" contract of the type Clarkstown signed will be a significant inducement to accept municipal responsibility to guarantee efficiency and sanitation in trash processing. Waste disposal with minimal environmental damage requires serious capital investment and there are limits on any municipality's ability to incur debt or to finance facilities out of tax revenues. Protection of the public fisc is a legitimate local benefit directly advanced by the ordinance and quite unlike the generalized advantage to local businesses that we have condemned as protectionist in the past.

Moreover, flow control offers an additional benefit that could not be gained by financing through a subsidy derived from general tax revenues, in spreading the cost of the facility among all Clarkstown residents who generate trash. *** In proportioning each resident's burden to the amount of trash generated, the ordinance has the added virtue of providing a direct and measurable deterrent to the generation of unnecessary waste in the first place. And in any event it is far from clear that the alternative to flow control (i.e., subsidies from general tax revenues or municipal bonds) would be less disruptive of interstate commerce than flow control, since a subsidized competitor can effectively squelch competition by underbidding it.

There is, in short, no evidence that Local Law 9 causes discrimination against out-of-town processors, because there is no evidence in the record that such processors have lost business as a result of it. Instead, we know only that the ordinance causes the local residents who adopted it to pay more for trash disposal services. But local burdens are not the focus of the dormant Commerce Clause, and this imposition is in any event readily justified by the ordinance's legitimate benefits in reliable and sanitary trash processing.

The Commerce Clause was not passed to save the citizens of Clarkstown from themselves. It should not be wielded to prevent them from attacking their local garbage problems with an ordinance that does not discriminate between local and out-of-town participants in the private market for trash disposal services and that is not protectionist in its purpose or effect. Local Law 9 conveys a privilege on the municipal government alone, the only market participant that bears responsibility for ensuring that adequate trash processing services continue to be available to Clarkstown residents. Because the Court's decision today is neither compelled by our local processing cases nor consistent with this Court's reason for inferring a dormant or negative aspect to the Commerce Clause in the first place, I respectfully dissent.

Notes

1. **State and Local Legislation.** Do you think the Court should treat local (municipal) facially discriminatory legislation as presumptively unconstitutional to the same extent that it treats statewide discriminatory legislation as presumptively unconstitutional? What about the fact that out-of-town in-staters are treated the same as out-of-town out-of-staters? Can you explain why local governments are treated like states in Eleventh Amendment cases?

2. **Independent or Dependent Discrimination and Balkanization.** Consider JUSTICE O'CONNOR's evaluation of the Balkanizing impact of local regulation: "how the challenged statute may interact with the legitimate regulatory regimes of the other States and what effect would arise if not one, but many and every [jurisdiction] adopted similar legislation." Did such concerns play a role in *Kassel*? Should the Court seek evidence concerning whether other jurisdictions have adopted or are likely to adopt similar legislation?

3. **Tax and Subsidize.** The Court in *West Lynn Creamery, Inc. v. Healy*, 512 U.S. 186 (1994), used Dormant Commerce Clause analysis to invalidate a Massachusetts program in which a nondiscriminatory tax levied on all milk dealers (both in-state and out-of-state) was coupled with a subsidy to local milk

producers. A concurrence by JUSTICES SCALIA and THOMAS said it would have been permissible for the State to "subsidize its domestic industry so long as it does so from nondiscriminatory taxes that go into the State's general revenue fund." CHIEF JUSTICE REHNQUIST and JUSTICE BLACKMUN dissented. One academic has distinguished regulation from spending programs because the latter are "less coercive," "less hostile to other states [and the notion of union]," "positively beneficial [and] would not exist [if not local]," "expensive [and therefore] less likely to proliferate than measures like tariffs," and "less likely to produce resentment and retaliation." Regan, "The Supreme Court and State Protectionism: Making Sense of the Dormant Commerce Clause," 84 MICH. L. REV. 1091 (1986). Are you convinced? *Pharmaceutical Research and Manufacturers of America v. Walsh*, 123 S.Ct. 1855 (2003), distinguished *West Lynn Creamery*. The petitioners argued that Maine's program of providing discounted prescription drugs to its uninsured citizens funded through state-negotiated rebates from drug manufacturers discriminated against interstate commerce to subsidize in-state retail sales. The Court said: "Unlike the situation in *West Lynn*, however, the Maine Rx Program will not impose a disparate burden on any competitors. A manufacturer could not avoid its rebate obligation by opening production facilities in Maine and would receive no benefit from the rebates even if it did so; the payments to the local pharmacists provide no special benefit to competitors of rebate-paying manufacturers."

D. THE MARKET PARTICIPANT EXCEPTION

SOUTH-CENTRAL TIMBER DEVELOPMENT
v. WUNNICKE
467 U.S. 82, 104 S.Ct. 2237, 81 L.Ed.2d 71 (1984).

JUSTICE WHITE announced the judgment of the Court and delivered the opinion of the Court with respect to Parts I and II, and an opinion with respect to Parts III and IV, in which JUSTICE BRENNAN, JUSTICE BLACKMUN, and JUSTICE STEVENS joined.

We granted certiorari in this case to review a decision of the Court of Appeals for the Ninth Circuit that held that Alaska's requirement that timber taken from state lands be processed within the State prior to export was "implicitly authorized" by Congress and therefore does not violate the Commerce Clause. We hold that it was not authorized and reverse the judgment of the Court of Appeals.

I

In September 1980, the Alaska Department of Natural Resources published a notice that it would sell approximately 49 million board-feet of timber in the area of Icy Cape, Alaska, on October 23, 1980. The notice of sale, the prospectus, and the proposed contract for the sale all provided, pursuant to [Alaska law], that "[p]rimary manufacture within the State of Alaska will be required as a special provision of the contract." Under the primary-manufacture requirement, the successful bidder must partially process the timber prior to shipping it outside of the State. *** The stated purpose of the requirement is to "protect existing industries, provide for the establishment of new industries, derive revenue from all timber resources, and manage the State's forests on a sustained yield basis." When it imposes the requirement, the State charges a significantly lower price for the timber than it otherwise would.

Petitioner, South–Central Timber Development, Inc., is an Alaska corporation engaged in the business of purchasing standing timber, logging the timber, and shipping the logs into foreign commerce, almost exclusively to Japan. It does not operate a mill in Alaska and customarily sells unprocessed logs. When it learned that the primary-manufacture requirement was to be imposed on the Icy Cape sale, it brought an action in Federal District Court seeking an injunction, arguing that the requirement violated the negative implications of the Commerce Clause. The District Court agreed and issued an injunction. The Court of Appeals for the Ninth Circuit reversed, finding it unnecessary to reach the question whether, standing alone, the requirement would violate the Commerce Clause, because it found implicit congressional authorization in the federal policy of imposing a primary-manufacture requirement on timber taken from federal land in Alaska.

We must first decide whether the court was correct in concluding that Congress has authorized the challenged requirement. If Congress has not, we must respond to respondents' submission that we should affirm the judgment on two grounds not reached by the Court of Appeals: (1) whether in the absence of congressional approval Alaska's requirement is permissible because Alaska is acting as a market participant, rather than as a market regulator; and (2), if not, whether the local-processing requirement is forbidden by the Commerce Clause.

[In Part II, JUSTICE WHITE found no approval, since Congressional consent was not "unmistakably clear."]

III

We now turn to the issues left unresolved by the Court of Appeals. The first of these issues is whether Alaska's restrictions on export of unprocessed timber from state-owned lands are exempt from Commerce Clause scrutiny under the "market-participant doctrine."

Our cases make clear that if a State is acting as a market participant, rather than as a market regulator, the dormant Commerce Clause places no limitation on its activities. *See White v. Massachusetts Council of Construction Employers, Inc.*, 460 U.S., at 206–208 (1983); *Reeves, Inc. v. Stake*, 447 U.S. 429, 436–437 (1980); *Hughes v. Alexandria Scrap Corp.*, 426 U.S. 794, 810 (1976). The precise contours of the market-participant doctrine have yet to be established, however, the doctrine having been applied in only three cases of this Court to date.

The first of the cases, *Hughes v. Alexandria Scrap Corp.*, supra, involved a Maryland program designed to reduce the number of junked automobiles in the State. A "bounty" was established on Maryland-licensed junk cars, and the State imposed more stringent documentation requirements on out-of-state scrap processors than on in-state ones. The Court rejected a Commerce Clause attack on the program, although it noted that under traditional Commerce Clause analysis the program might well be invalid because it had the effect of reducing the flow of goods in interstate commerce. The Court concluded that Maryland's action was not "the kind of action with which the Commerce Clause is concerned" because "[n]othing in the purposes animating the Commerce Clause prohibits a State, in the absence of congressional action, from participating in the market and exercising the right to favor its own citizens over others."

In *Reeves, Inc. v. Stake*, the Court upheld a South Dakota policy of restricting the sale of cement from a state-owned plant to state residents, declaring that "[t]he basic distinction drawn in *Alexandria Scrap* between States as market participants and States as market regulators makes good sense and sound law." The Court relied upon "'the long recognized right of trader or manufacturer, engaged in an entirely private business, freely to exercise his own independent discretion as to parties with whom he will deal.'" In essence, the Court recognized the principle that the Commerce Clause places no limitations on a State's refusal to deal with particular parties when it is participating in the interstate market in goods.

The most recent of this Court's cases developing the market-participant doctrine is *White v. Massachusetts Council of Construction Employers, Inc.*, in which the Court sustained against a Commerce Clause challenge an executive order of the Mayor of Boston that required all construction projects funded in whole or in part by city funds or city-administered funds to be performed by a work force of at least 50% city residents. The Court rejected the argument that the city was not entitled to the protection of the doctrine because the order had the effect of regulating employment contracts between public contractors and their employees. Recognizing that "there are some limits on a state or local government's ability to impose restrictions that reach beyond the immediate parties with which the government transacts business," the Court found it unnecessary to define those limits because "[e]veryone affected by the order [was], in a substantial if informal sense, 'working for the city.'" The fact that the employees were "working for the city" was "crucial" to the market-participant analysis in *White*. *See United Building and Construction Trades Council v. Mayor of Camden*, 465 U.S. 208, 219 (1984) [reprinted below].

The State of Alaska contends that its primary-manufacture requirement fits squarely within the market-participant doctrine, arguing that "Alaska's entry into the market may be viewed as precisely the same type of subsidy to local interests that the Court found unobjectionable in Alexandria Scrap." However, when Maryland became involved in the scrap market it was as a purchaser of scrap; Alaska, on the other hand, participates in the timber market, but imposes conditions downstream in the timber-processing market. Alaska is not merely subsidizing local timber processing in an amount "roughly equal to the difference between the price the timber would fetch in the absence of such a requirement and the amount the state actually receives." If the State directly subsidized the timber-processing industry by such an amount, the purchaser would retain the option of taking advantage of the subsidy by processing timber in the State or forgoing the benefits of the subsidy and exporting unprocessed timber. Under the Alaska requirement, however, the choice is made for him: if he buys timber from the State he is not free to take the timber out of state prior to processing.

The State also would have us find *Reeves* controlling. It states that "*Reeves* made it clear that the Commerce Clause imposes no limitation on Alaska's power to choose the terms on which it will sell its timber." Such an unrestrained reading of *Reeves* is unwarranted. Although the Court in *Reeves* did strongly endorse the right of a State to deal with whomever it chooses when it participates in the market, it did not—and did not purport to—sanction the imposition of any terms that the State might desire. For example, the Court expressly noted in *Reeves* that "Commerce Clause scrutiny may well be more rigorous when a restraint on foreign commerce is alleged" that a natural resource "like coal, timber, wild game, or minerals," was not involved, but instead the cement was "the end product of a complex process whereby a costly physical plant and human labor act on raw materials," and that South Dakota did not bar resale of South Dakota cement to out-of-state purchasers. In this case, all three of the elements that were not present in Reeves—foreign commerce, a natural resource, and restrictions on resale—are present.

Finally, Alaska argues that since the Court in *White* upheld a requirement that reached beyond "the boundary of formal privity of contract," then, a fortiori, the primary-manufacture requirement is permissible, because the State is not regulating contracts for resale of timber or regulating the buying and selling of timber, but is instead "a seller of timber, pure and simple." Yet it is clear that the State is more than merely a seller of timber. In the commercial context, the seller usually has no say over, and no interest in, how the product is to be used after sale; in this case, however, payment for the timber does not end the obligations of the purchaser, for, despite the fact that the purchaser has taken delivery of the timber and has paid for it, he cannot do with it as he pleases. Instead, he is obligated to deal with a stranger to the contract after completion of the sale.

That privity of contract is not always the outer boundary of permissible state activity does not necessarily mean that the Commerce Clause has no application within the boundary of formal privity. The market-participant doctrine permits a State to influence "a discrete, identifiable class of economic activity in which [it] is a major participant." *White* at 211. Contrary to the State's contention, the doctrine is not carte blanche to impose any conditions that the State has the economic power to dictate, and does not validate any requirement merely because the State imposes it upon someone with whom it is in contractual privity.

The limit of the market-participant doctrine must be that it allows a State to impose burdens on commerce within the market in which it is a participant, but allows it to go no further. The State may not impose conditions, whether by statute, regulation, or contract, that have a substantial regulatory effect outside of that particular market. Unless the "market" is relatively narrowly defined, the doctrine has the potential of swallowing up the rule that States may not impose substantial burdens on interstate commerce even if they act with the permissible state purpose of fostering local industry.

At the heart of the dispute in this case is disagreement over the definition of the market. Alaska contends that it is participating in the processed timber market, although it acknowledges that it participates in no way in the actual processing. South–Central argues, on the other hand, that although the State may be a participant in the timber market, it is using its leverage in that market to exert a regulatory effect in the processing market, in which it is not a participant. We agree with the latter position.

There are sound reasons for distinguishing between a State's preferring its own residents in the initial disposition of goods when it is a market participant and a State's attachment of restrictions on dispositions subsequent to the goods coming to rest in private hands. First, simply as a matter of intuition a state market participant has a greater interest as a "private trader" in the immediate transaction than it has in what its purchaser does with the goods after the State no longer has an interest in them. The common law recognized such a notion in the doctrine of restraints on alienation. Similarly, the antitrust laws place limits on vertical restraints. It is no defense in an action charging vertical trade restraints that the same end could be achieved through vertical integration; if it were, there would be virtually no antitrust scrutiny of vertical arrangements. We reject the contention that a State's action as a market regulator may be upheld against Commerce Clause challenge on the ground that the State could achieve the same end as a market participant. We therefore find it unimportant for present purposes that the State could support its processing industry by selling only to Alaska processors, by vertical integration, or by direct subsidy.

Second, downstream restrictions have a greater regulatory effect than do limitations on the immediate transaction. Instead of merely choosing its own trading partners, the State is attempting to govern the private, separate economic relationships of its trading partners; that is, it restricts the post-purchase activity of the purchaser, rather than merely the purchasing activity. In contrast to the situation in *White*, this restriction on private economic activity takes place after the completion of the parties' direct commercial obligations, rather than during the course of an ongoing commercial relationship in which the city retained a continuing proprietary interest in the subject of the contract. In sum, the State may not avail itself of the market-participant doctrine to immunize its downstream regulation of the timber-processing market in which it is not a participant.

IV

Finally, the State argues that even if we find that Congress did not authorize the processing restriction, and even if we conclude that its actions do not qualify for the market-participant exception, the restriction does not substantially burden interstate or foreign commerce under ordinary Commerce Clause principles. We need not labor long over that contention.

Viewed as a naked restraint on export of unprocessed logs, there is little question that the processing requirement cannot survive scrutiny under the precedents of the Court. *** Because of the protectionist nature of Alaska's local-processing requirement and the burden on commerce resulting therefrom, we conclude that it falls within the rule of virtual per se invalidity of laws that "bloc[k] the flow of interstate commerce at a State's borders." *City of Philadelphia v. New Jersey*, 437 U.S. 617, 624 (1978).

We are buttressed in our conclusion that the restriction is invalid by the fact that foreign commerce is burdened by the restriction. It is a well-accepted rule that state restrictions burdening foreign commerce are subjected to a more rigorous and searching scrutiny. It is crucial to the efficient execution of the Nation's foreign policy that "the Federal Government *** speak with one voice when regulating commercial relations with foreign governments." *Michelin Tire Corp. v. Wages*, 423 U.S. 276, 285 (1976). In light of the substantial attention given by Congress to the subject of export restrictions on unprocessed timber, it would be peculiarly inappropriate to permit state regulation of the subject. ***

JUSTICE MARSHALL took no part in the decision of this case.

JUSTICE BRENNAN, concurring. I join JUSTICE WHITE's opinion in full because I believe Alaska's in-state processing requirement constitutes market regulation that is not authorized by Congress. In my view, JUSTICE WHITE's treatment of the market-participant doctrine and the response of JUSTICE REHNQUIST point up the inherent weakness of the doctrine. *See Hughes v. Alexandria Scrap Corp.*, 426 U.S. 794, 817 (1976) (BRENNAN, J., dissenting).

JUSTICE POWELL, with whom THE CHIEF JUSTICE joins, concurring in part and concurring in the judgment.

I join Parts I and II of JUSTICE WHITE's opinion. I would remand the case to the Court of Appeals to allow that court to consider whether Alaska was acting as a "market participant" and whether Alaska's primary-manufacture requirement substantially burdened interstate commerce.

JUSTICE REHNQUIST, with whom JUSTICE O'CONNOR joins, dissenting.

In my view, the line of distinction drawn in the plurality opinion between the State as market participant and the State as market regulator is both artificial and unconvincing. The plurality draws this line "simply as a matter of intuition," but then seeks to bolster its intuition through a series of remarks more appropriate to antitrust law than to the Commerce Clause.[1]

---

[1] The plurality does offer one other reason for its demarcation of the boundary between these two concepts. "[D]ownstream restrictions have a greater regulatory effect than do limitations on the immediate transaction. Instead of merely choosing its own trading partners, the State is attempting to govern the private, separate economic relationships of its trading partners; that in it restricts the post-purchase activity of the purchaser, rather than merely the purchasing activity." But, of course, this is not a "reason" at all, but merely a restatement of the conclusion. The line between participation and regulation is what we are trying to determine. To invoke that very distinction in support of the line drawn is merely to fall back again on intuition.

Perhaps the State's actions do raise antitrust problems. But what the plurality overlooks is that the antitrust laws apply to a State only when it is acting as a market participant. When the State acts as a market regulator, it is immune from antitrust scrutiny. Of course, the line of distinction in cases under the Commerce Clause need not necessarily parallel the line drawn in antitrust law. But the plurality can hardly justify placing Alaska in the market-regulator category, in this Commerce Clause case, by relying on antitrust cases that are relevant only if the State is a market participant.

The contractual term at issue here no more transforms Alaska's sale of timber into "regulation" of the processing industry than the resident-hiring preference imposed by the city of Boston in *White v. Massachusetts Council of Construction Employers, Inc.*, 460 U.S. 204 (1983), constituted regulation of the construction industry. Alaska is merely paying the buyer of the timber indirectly, by means of a reduced price, to hire Alaska residents to process the timber. Under existing precedent, the State could accomplish that same result in any number of ways. For example, the State could choose to sell its timber only to those companies that maintain active primary-processing plants in Alaska. [*Reeves, Inc. v. Stake*]. Or the State could directly subsidize the primary-processing industry within the State. [*Hughes v. Alexandria Scrap Corp.*]. The State could even pay to have the logs processed and then enter the market only to sell processed logs. It seems to me unduly formalistic to conclude that the one path chosen by the State as best suited to promote its concerns is the path forbidden it by the Commerce Clause. ***

Notes

1. **Downstream Regulation.** Do you find the Court's exception to the market participant exception convincing?

2. **Natural Resources.** Why didn't the Court simply decide that Alaska could not hoard a natural resource like timber? Should a State be permitted more latitude to manufacture goods than to "hoard" natural resources for the benefit of its own citizens? In *Reeves*, the Court found that "Cement is not a natural resource, like coal, timber, wild game or minerals." Does it trouble you that the Court might have reached a different result if it had looked at the components of cement (such as limestone and sand)?

3. **Regulation versus Participation.** "The line between state market participation and state market regulation is a fuzzy one that has perplexed courts and commentators alike." *Big Country Foods, Inc. v. Board of Educ.*, 952 F.2d 1173 (9th Cir. 1992). In *Hughes*, the state did not go into the auto wrecking business or the scrap processing business. How then was it a market participant at all? What is the test for whether the State is regulating or is a market participant?

4. **Questions on Scope of Market Participation Exception.**

   - There is no indication that the framers of the Commerce Clause distinguished between the state as regulator and the state as market participant. Adam Smith, whose work preceded the American Revolution, discussed extensively the evils of mercantilism, including state bounties which distorted free markets. Should this matter?

- Some of the impetus for the market participant doctrine comes from analogizing the state to "just another private party." Given the State's power to tax as well as its other coercive powers, isn't this a flawed analogy?

- Is this a return to the governmental/proprietary distinction rejected by the Court in the "active" Commerce Clause context in *Garcia*? Why does this distinction only apply in Dormant Commerce Clause cases?

5. **Definition of Market.** If a state owns and operates a farmer's market and assigns inferior sales locations to nonresident sellers, is it acting as a regulator or market participant? Does the answer turn on whether the market is selling/leasing space or selling market produce? *Smith v. Department of Agric.*, 630 F.2d 1081 (5th Cir.1980), cert. denied, 452 U.S. 910 (1981).

E. STATE PRIVILEGES AND IMMUNITIES

UNITED BUILDING AND CONSTRUCTION TRADES COUNCIL v. CITY OF CAMDEN
465 U.S. 208, 104 S.Ct. 1020, 79 L.Ed.2d 249 (1984).

JUSTICE REHNQUIST delivered the opinion of the Court.

A municipal ordinance of the city of Camden, New Jersey requires that at least 40% of the employees of contractors and subcontractors working on city construction projects be Camden residents. Appellant, the United Building and Construction Trades Council of Camden and Vicinity (the Council), challenges that ordinance as a violation of the Privileges and Immunities Clause, Article IV, § 2, of the United States Constitution.[1] The Supreme Court of New Jersey rejected appellant's privileges and immunities attack on the ground that the ordinance discriminates on the basis of municipal, not state, residency. The court "decline[d] to apply the Privileges and Immunities Clause in the context of a municipal ordinance that has identical effects upon out-of-state citizens and New Jersey citizens not residing in the locality." ***

Because of changes [in the posture of the case since the appeal was filed], the only question left for our consideration is whether the Camden ordinance, as now written, violates the Privileges and Immunities Clause. We first address the argument, accepted by the Supreme Court of New Jersey, that the Clause does not even apply to a municipal ordinance such as this. Two separate contentions are advanced in support of this position: first, that the Clause only applies to laws passed by a State and, second, that the Clause only applies to laws that discriminate on the basis of state citizenship.

The first argument can be quickly rejected. The fact that the ordinance in question is a municipal, rather than a state, law does not somehow place it outside the scope of the Privileges and Immunities Clause. First of all, one cannot easily distinguish municipal from state action in this case: the municipal ordinance would not have gone into effect without express approval by the State Treasurer.

---

[1] "The citizens of each State shall be entitled to all the Privileges and Immunities of Citizens in the several States." United States Constitution, Art. IV, § 2, cl. 1.

More fundamentally, a municipality is merely a political subdivision of the State from which its authority derives. It is as true of the Privileges and Immunities Clause as of the Equal Protection Clause that what would be unconstitutional if done directly by the State can no more readily be accomplished by a city deriving its authority from the State. Thus, even if the ordinance had been adopted solely by Camden, and not pursuant to a state program or with state approval, the hiring preference would still have to comport with the Privileges and Immunities Clause.

The second argument merits more consideration. The New Jersey Supreme Court concluded that the Privileges and Immunities Clause does not apply to an ordinance that discriminates solely on the basis of municipal residency. The Clause is phrased in terms of state citizenship and was designed "to place the citizens of each State upon the same footing with citizens of other States, so far as the advantages resulting from citizenship in those States are concerned." *Paul v. Virginia*, 8 Wall. 168, 180 (1869).

> "The primary purpose of this clause, like the clauses between which it is located—those relating to full faith and credit and to interstate extradition of fugitives from justice—was to help fuse into one Nation a collection of independent, sovereign States. It was designed to insure to a citizen of State A who ventures into State B the same privileges which the citizens of State B enjoy. For protection of such equality the citizen of State A was not to be restricted to the uncertain remedies afforded by diplomatic processes and official retaliation."

Toomer v. Witsell, 334 U.S. 385, 395 (1948). Municipal residency classifications, it is argued, simply do not give rise to the same concerns.

We cannot accept this argument. We have never read the Clause so literally as to apply it only to distinctions based on state citizenship. *** A person who is not residing in a given State is ipso facto not residing in a city within that State. Thus, whether the exercise of a privilege is conditioned on state residency or on municipal residency he will just as surely be excluded.

Given the Camden ordinance, an out-of-state citizen who ventures into New Jersey will not enjoy the same privileges as the New Jersey citizen residing in Camden. It is true that New Jersey citizens not residing in Camden will be affected by the ordinance as well as out-of-state citizens. And it is true that the disadvantaged New Jersey residents have no claim under the Privileges and Immunities Clause. *The Slaughter–House Cases*, 16 Wall. 36, 77 (1872). But New Jersey residents at least have a chance to remedy at the polls any discrimination against them. Out-of-state citizens have no similar opportunity and they must "not be restricted to the uncertain remedies afforded by diplomatic processes and official retaliation."[9] We

---

[9] The dissent suggests that New Jersey citizens not residing in Camden will adequately protect the interests of out-of-state residents and that the scope of the Privileges and Immunities Clause should be measured in light of this political reality. What the dissent fails to appreciate is that the Camden ordinance at issue in this case was adopted pursuant to a comprehensive, state-wide program applicable in all New Jersey cities. The Camden resident-preference ordinance has

conclude that Camden's ordinance is not immune from constitutional review at the behest of out-of-state residents merely because some in-state residents are similarly disadvantaged.

Application of the Privileges and Immunities Clause to a particular instance of discrimination against out-of-state residents entails a two-step inquiry. As an initial matter, the court must decide whether the ordinance burdens one of those privileges and immunities protected by the Clause. Not all forms of discrimination against citizens of other States are constitutionally suspect. *** As a threshold matter, then, we must determine whether an out-of-state resident's interest in employment on public works contracts in another State is sufficiently "fundamental" to the promotion of interstate harmony so as to "fall within the purview of the Privileges and Immunities Clause."

Certainly, the pursuit of a common calling is one of the most fundamental of those privileges protected by the Clause. Many, if not most, of our cases expounding the Privileges and Immunities Clause have dealt with this basic and essential activity. Public employment, however, is qualitatively different from employment in the private sector; it is a subspecies of the broader opportunity to pursue a common calling. We have held that there is no fundamental right to government employment for purposes of the Equal Protection Clause. *Massachusetts v. Murgia*, 427 U.S. 307, 313 (1976) (per curiam). And in *White* [discussed in *Wunnicke*, above], we held that for purposes of the Commerce Clause everyone employed on a city public works project is, "in a substantial if informal sense, 'working for the city.'"

It can certainly be argued that for purposes of the Privileges and Immunities Clause everyone affected by the Camden ordinance is also "working for the city" and, therefore, has no grounds for complaint when the city favors its own residents. But we decline to transfer mechanically into this context an analysis fashioned to fit the Commerce Clause. Our decision in *White* turned on a distinction between the city acting as a market participant and the city acting as a market regulator. The question whether employees of contractors and subcontractors on public works projects were or were not, in some sense, working for the city was crucial to that analysis. The question had to be answered in order to chart the boundaries of the

---

already received state sanction and approval, and every New Jersey city is free to adopt a similar protectionist measure. Some h ave already done so. Thus, it is hard to see how New Jersey residents living outside Camden will protect the interests of out-of-state citizens.

More fundamentally, the dissent's proposed blanket exemption for all classifications that are less than state-wide would provide States with a simple means for evading the strictures of the Privileges and Immunities Clause. Suppose, for example, that California wanted to guarantee that all employees of contractors and subcontractors working on construction projects funded in whole or in part by state funds are state residents. Under the dissent's analysis, the California legislature need merely divide the State in half, providing one resident-hiring preference for Northern Californians on all such projects taking place in Northern California, and one for Southern Californians on all projects taking place in Southern California. State residents generally would benefit from the law at the expense of out-of-state residents; yet, the law would be immune from scrutiny under the Clause simply because it was not phrased in terms of state citizenship or residency. Such a formalistic construction would effectively write the Clause out of the Constitution.

distinction. But the distinction between market participant and market regulator relied upon in *White* to dispose of the Commerce Clause challenge is not dispositive in this context. The two Clauses have different aims and set different standards for state conduct.

The Commerce Clause acts as an implied restraint upon state regulatory powers. Such powers must give way before the superior authority of Congress to legislate on (or leave unregulated) matters involving interstate commerce. When the State acts solely as a market participant, no conflict between state regulation and federal regulatory authority can arise. The Privileges and Immunities Clause, on the other hand, imposes a direct restraint on state action in the interests of interstate harmony. This concern with comity cuts across the market regulator-market participant distinction that is crucial under the Commerce Clause. It is discrimination against out-of-state residents on matters of fundamental concern which triggers the Clause, not regulation affecting interstate commerce. Thus, the fact that Camden is merely setting conditions on its expenditures for goods and services in the marketplace does not preclude the possibility that those conditions violate the Privileges and Immunities Clause.

In *Hicklin v. Orbeck*, 437 U.S. 518 (1978), we struck down as a violation of the Privileges and Immunities Clause an "Alaska Hire" statute containing a resident hiring preference for all employment related to the development of the State's oil and gas resources. Alaska argued in that case "that because the oil and gas that are the subject of Alaska Hire are owned by the State, this ownership, of itself, is sufficient justification for the Act's discrimination against nonresidents, and takes the Act totally without the scope of the Privileges and Immunities Clause." We concluded, however, that the State's interest in controlling those things it claims to own is not absolute. "Rather than placing a statute completely beyond the Clause, a State's ownership of the property with which the statute is concerned is a factor—although often the crucial factor—to be considered in evaluating whether the statute's discrimination against non-citizens violates the Clause." Much the same analysis, we think, is appropriate to a city's efforts to bias private employment decisions in favor of its residents on construction projects funded with public monies. The fact that Camden is expending its own funds or funds it administers in accordance with the terms of a grant is certainly a factor—perhaps the crucial factor—to be considered in evaluating whether the statute's discrimination violates the Privileges and Immunities Clause. But it does not remove the Camden ordinance completely from the purview of the Clause.

In sum, Camden may, without fear of violating the Commerce Clause, pressure private employers engaged in public works projects funded in whole or in part by the city to hire city residents. But that same exercise of power to bias the employment decisions of private contractors and subcontractors against out-of-state residents may be called to account under the Privileges and Immunities Clause. A determination of whether a privilege is "fundamental" for purposes of that Clause does not depend on whether the employees of private contractors and subcontractors engaged in public works projects can or cannot be said to be "working for the city." The opportunity to seek employment with such private employers is "sufficiently basic to the livelihood of the Nation" as to fall within the purview of the Privileges and Immunities Clause even though the contractors and subcontractors are themselves engaged in projects funded in whole or part by the city.

The conclusion that Camden's ordinance discriminates against a protected privilege does not, of course, end the inquiry. We have stressed in prior cases that "[l]ike many other constitutional provisions, the privileges and immunities clause is not an absolute." *Toomer v. Witsell*, 334 U.S. 385, 396 (1948). It does not preclude discrimination against citizens of other States where there is a "substantial reason" for the difference in treatment. "[T]he inquiry in each case must be concerned with whether such reasons do exist and whether the degree of discrimination bears a close relation to them." As part of any justification offered for the discriminatory law, nonresidents must somehow be shown to "constitute a peculiar source of the evil at which the statute is aimed."

The city of Camden contends that its ordinance is necessary to counteract grave economic and social ills. Spiralling unemployment, a sharp decline in population, and a dramatic reduction in the number of businesses located in the city have eroded property values and depleted the city's tax base. The resident hiring preference is designed, the city contends, to increase the number of employed persons living in Camden and to arrest the "middle class flight" currently plaguing the city. The city also argues that all non-Camden residents employed on city public works projects, whether they reside in New Jersey or Pennsylvania, constitute a "source of the evil at which the statute is aimed." That is, they "live off" Camden without "living in" Camden. Camden contends that the scope of the discrimination practiced in the ordinance, with its municipal residency requirement, is carefully tailored to alleviate this evil without unreasonably harming nonresidents, who still have access to 60% of the available positions.

Every inquiry under the Privileges and Immunities Clause "must *** be conducted with due regard for the principle that the states should have considerable leeway in analyzing local evils and in prescribing appropriate cures." This caution is particularly appropriate when a government body is merely setting conditions on the expenditure of funds it controls. The Alaska Hire statute at issue in *Hicklin v. Orbeck* swept within its strictures not only contractors and subcontractors dealing directly with the State's oil and gas; it also covered suppliers who provided goods and services to those contractors and subcontractors. We invalidated the Act as "an attempt to force virtually all businesses that benefit in some way from the economic ripple effect of Alaska's decision to develop its oil and gas resources to bias their employment practices in favor of the State's residents." No similar "ripple effect" appears to infect the Camden ordinance. It is limited in scope to employees working directly on city public works projects.

Nonetheless, we find it impossible to evaluate Camden's justification on the record as it now stands. No trial has ever been held in the case. No findings of fact have been made. *** We, therefore, deem it wise to remand the case to the New Jersey Supreme Court. That court may decide, consistent with state procedures, on the best method for making the necessary findings. ***

JUSTICE BLACKMUN, dissenting.

For over a century the underlying meaning of the Privileges and Immunities Clause of the Constitution's Article IV has been regarded as settled: at least absent some substantial, non-invidious justification, a State may not discriminate between its own residents and residents of other States on the basis of state citizenship.

Today, however, the Court casually extends the scope of the Clause by holding that it applies to laws that discriminate among state residents on the basis of municipal residence, simply because discrimination on the basis of municipal residence disadvantages citizens of other States "ipso facto." This novel interpretation arrives accompanied by little practical justification and no historical or textual support whatsoever. Because I believe that the Privileges and Immunities Clause was not intended to apply to the kind of municipal discrimination presented by this case, I would affirm the judgment of the Supreme Court of New Jersey.

The historical underpinnings of the Privileges and Immunities Clause are not in serious dispute. The Clause was derived from the fourth Article of Confederation and was designed to carry forward that provision's prescription of interstate comity. Both the text of the Clause and the historical record confirm that the Framers meant to foreclose any one State from denying citizens of other States the same "privileges and immunities" accorded its own citizens. While the Framers thus conceived of the Privileges and Immunities Clause as an instrument for frustrating discrimination based on state citizenship, there is no evidence of any sort that they were concerned by intrastate discrimination based on municipal residence. The most obvious reason for this is also the most simple one: by the time the Constitution was enacted, such discrimination was rarely practiced and even more rarely successful. Even had attempts to practice the kind of economic localism at issue here been more widespread, moreover, there is little reason to believe that the Framers would have devoted their limited institutional resources to bringing such conduct within the ambit of the Privileges and Immunities Clause. Whatever the weaknesses of the new state governments in suppressing sectional conflicts that gave rise to outright physical violence, like Shays' Rebellion in 1786–1787, the States had more than adequate powers to prevent localities from disrupting the States' internal economic affairs through discriminatory ordinances and regulations. By the time the Constitution was adopted, most state legislatures had assumed the power to grant and alter municipal charters and the power to legislate with respect to municipal affairs. *** As a result, the Framers had every reason to believe that intrastate discrimination based on municipal residence could and would be dealt with by the States themselves in those instances where it persisted.

In light of the historical context in which the Privileges and Immunities Clause was adopted, it hardly is surprising that none of this Court's intervening decisions has suggested that the Clause applies to discrimination on the basis of municipal residence. To the contrary, while the Court never has addressed the question directly, it repeatedly has proceeded on the assumption that the "Privileges and Immunities of Citizens" to which the Clause refers are entitlements held equally by all citizens of a State. ***

Indeed, I had understood the Court to have reaffirmed this principle only two Terms ago in *Zobel v. Williams*, 457 U.S. 55 (1982). In *Zobel*, the Court held that an Alaska statute which allocated state treasury refunds to state residents on the basis of the length of their residence violated the Equal Protection Clause. The Court declined, however, to hold that the statute violated the Privileges and Immunities Clause. It observed that the statute "does not simply make distinctions between native-born Alaskans and those who migrate to Alaska from other States;" instead, it "also discriminates among long-time residents and even native-born residents." As a result: "The statute does not involve the kind of discrimination which the Privileges and Immunities Clause of Art. IV was designed to prevent. That Clause 'was designed to insure to a citizen of State A who ventures into State B the same privileges which the citizens of State B enjoy.'" *Toomer*, 334 U.S. at 395.

I am somewhat at a loss to understand how the Court's decision today can be reconciled with its reasoning in *Zobel*. The Alaska statute at issue in *Zobel* fell outside the scope of the Privileges and Immunities Clause for the elementary reason that it did not discriminate between state residents and nonresidents on the basis of state residence; rather, it discriminated among state residents in a way that disadvantaged nonresidents as well but did not thereby implicate the underlying concerns of the Privileges and Immunities Clause. The Camden ordinance presently before the Court occupies precisely the same position.

*** The Court recognizes, as it must, that the Privileges and Immunities Clause does not afford state residents any protection against their own State's laws. When this settled rule is combined with the Court's newly-fashioned rule concerning municipal discrimination, however, it has the perverse effect of vesting non-New Jersey residents with constitutional privileges that are not enjoyed by most New Jersey residents themselves. This result is directly contrary to the Court's longstanding position that the Privileges and Immunities Clause does not give nonresidents "higher and greater privileges than are enjoyed by the citizens of the state itself." When judicial alchemy transmutes gold into lead in this fashion, it is time for the Court to re-examine its reasoning.

Finally, the Court fails to attend to the functional considerations that underlie the Privileges and Immunities Clause. The Clause has been a necessary limitation on state autonomy not simply because of the self-interest of individual States, but because state parochialism is likely to go unchecked by state political processes when those who are disadvantaged are by definition disenfranchised as well. The Clause remedies this breakdown in the representative process by requiring state residents to bear the same burdens that they choose to place on nonresidents; "by constitutionally tying the fate of outsiders to the fate of those possessing political power, the framers insured that their interests would be well looked after." J. Ely, Democracy and Distrust 83 (1980). As a practical matter, therefore, the scope of the Clause may be measured by asking whether failure to link the interests of those who are disadvantaged with the interests of those who are preferred will consign the former group to "the uncertain remedies afforded by diplomatic processes and official retaliation." *Toomer*, at 395.

Contrary to the Court's tacit assumption, discrimination on the basis of municipal residence is substantially different in this regard from discrimination on the basis of state citizenship. The distinction is simple but fundamental: discrimination on the basis of municipal residence penalizes persons within the State's political community as well as those without. The Court itself points out that while New Jersey citizens who reside outside Camden are not protected by the Privileges and Immunities Clause, they may resort to the State's political processes to protect themselves. What the Court fails to appreciate is that this avenue of relief for New Jersey residents works to protect residents of other States as well; disadvantaged state residents who turn to the state legislature to displace ordinances like Camden's further the interests of nonresidents as well as their own. In short, discrimination on the basis of municipal residence simply does not consign residents of other States, in the words of *Toomer, supra*, to "the uncertain remedies afforded by diplomatic processes and official retaliation." The Court thus has applied the Privileges and Immunities Clause without regard for the political ills that it was designed to cure.

Needless to say, my view of the constitutional question in this case does not depend on my personal opinion about the desirability of the course on which Camden has embarked. I do not find "beggar thy neighbor" economic policies any more attractive when practiced by municipalities than when practiced by States or nations. The unedifying sight of localities fighting for parochial gain at one another's expense gives new urgency to Benjamin Franklin's reputed warning that "we must *** all hang together, or most assuredly we shall all hang separately." At the risk of restating the obvious, however, the issue before us is not the desirability of the ordinance but its constitutionality—more particularly, its constitutionality under the Privileges and Immunities Clause. Because I believe that the Clause does not apply to discrimination based on municipal residence, I dissent.

Notes

1.   **Different Provisions.** Are you troubled that different provisions of the Constitution yield different results in *White* and *Camden*? Why is that any different from saying that whipping of all prisoners constitutes cruel and unusual punishment but not a violation of the equal protection clause? Perhaps the problem overlap is so considerable: discrimination against out-of-staters is at the heart of both the Dormant Commerce Clause and the Privileges and Immunities Clause. However, aliens and corporations cannot invoke the more favorable Privileges and Immunities Clause. Indeed, there is some truth to the view that the Dormant Commerce Clause deals with goods and services while the Privileges and Immunities Clause deals with people.

2. **Origins and Meanings.** The Privileges and Immunities Clause of Article IV is based on the fourth Article of the Articles of Confederation. Consult Appendix A for this language and compare the two provisions. Consider also this statement of the clause's meaning in *Paul v. Virginia*, 75 U.S. (8 Wall.) 168 (1869):

> "It was undoubtedly the object of this clause *** to place the citizens of each State on the same footing with citizens of other States, so far as the advantages resulting from citizenship in those States are concerned. It relieves them from the disabilities of alienage in other States; it inhibits discriminating legislation against them by other States; it gives them the right of free ingress into other States, and egress from them; it insures to them in other States the same freedom possessed by the citizens of those States in the acquisition and enjoyment of property and in the pursuit of happiness; and it secures to them in other States the equal protection of their laws. *** [W]ithout some provision of the kind *** the Republic would have constituted little more than a league of States."

3. **Remand of *Camden*.** As an advocate, what would you seek to present to the court on remand?

4. ***Carbone, Wunnicke,* and *Camden*.** Review JUSTICE SOUTER's observation in *Carbone* that, once the plant is bought by the city, the flow control ordinance would not violate the commerce clause. Do you agree? How do you think the *Carbone* flow control ordinance would fare in the face of an Article IV Privileges and Immunities claim?

5. **Problem.** Many states charge higher state university tuition for nonresidents than for residents. Do such differential tuition charges violate the Commerce Clause? The Privileges and Immunities Clause?

REVIEW PROBLEMS

Review Problem #1.

Medical technology allows doctors to transplant human organs, such as lungs, kidneys, and livers. The organs are "harvested" from people after death and transplanted into recipients whose own organs are not functioning properly. The transplants must generally take place within a short period of time following death of the donor. The need for transplanted organs greatly exceeds the supply, and many people die while awaiting transplants. Consent for transplant must be obtained in advance from the potential donor or from that person's family after his or her death. Many organs suitable for transplant are not transplanted because the potential donor fails to consent in advance, family cannot be located in time, and family may be reluctant to consent. To address these problems, the State General Assembly recently enacted this legislation:

State Organ Donation Act

1. Findings:

    (a) The State should strongly encourage potential donors to consent in advance to transplant and encourage families to consent to transplant following the death of a potential donor;

(b) It is fair and appropriate for State citizens to benefit from the State's expenditures to encourage its citizens to become organ donors;

(c) Organ donations are more likely to be successful if there is the shortest time possible between harvesting and transplanting organs into recipients. When organs are removed in State, transplantation will likely be quicker if the recipient is a State citizen; and

(d) Organ donations are more likely to be successful if the donor and recipient have a similar genetic make up. It may be time consuming to perform a comprehensive genetic screening of potential organ donors and potential organ recipients. People of the same races or ethnic backgrounds are more likely to have a similar genetic make up.

2. **Therefore:**

(a) $10 million is appropriated for a public education campaign to encourage State citizens to become organ donors.

(b) To further encourage organ donations, the State shall pay $1000 to the family of any person who dies in the State, if the person consents in advance to become an organ donor.

(c) All organs harvested in the State must be transplanted in accordance with a "recipient priority" list drawn up by the State Health Department and it shall be unlawful to transplant organs harvested in the State except in accordance with this list.

(d) In determining the "recipient priority" list, the State Health Department shall give preference to citizens of the State.

Assume that the Federal Government does not regulate organ transplants. Does the State Organ Donation Act violate the Dormant Commerce Clause? The Article IV Privileges and Immunities Clause?

Review Problem #2:

Gambrel is a State in the United States. State health officials in Gambrel are very concerned about the spread of the worldwide epidemic of Severe Acute Deficiency Syndrome ("SADS"). So far, about 200 people in the United States have been diagnosed with SADS, and 20 people have died. So far, no cases of SADS have been diagnosed in the State of Gambrel. SADS has an incubation period of two to ten days when no symptoms are present, but a person is very contagious. When it first breaks out, SADS has mild symptoms, similar to those of a common cold, and the person remains contagious. In roughly half the cases, victims develop their own immunities to the disease, recover without treatment, are no longer contagious, and are no longer susceptible to further SADS infection. In roughly half the cases, however, SADS can become very debilitating and require several weeks in the hospital. SADS is sometimes fatal.

A new drug, Interaxin, has been developed to check the spread of SADS. Interaxin does not prevent a person from contracting SADS, nor does Interaxin affect the symptoms of a person suffering from SADS. But Interaxin does prevent infected people from transmitting the disease to others—though Interaxin is effective only about half the time. Interaxin is effective only if given in two injections approximately three hours apart.

The Governor of Gambrel, Sam Perdition, decides that a bold plan is necessary to ensure that Gambrel does not suffer an outbreak of SADS. The Governor decides that the best way to fight SADS is by Interaxin because a lengthy (20 day) quarantine would be impossible to enforce. Perdition proposes and the legislature passes a law providing that all Gambrel residents must receive treatment with Interaxin. No Gambrel resident who leaves the State may return unless he or she receives Interaxin treatment. All non-resident visitors to Gambrel must receive Interaxin treatment or leave the State immediately. Anyone who fails to comply will be charged with a felony punishable by up to five years in prison.

The legislation provides that the ten large State hospitals will serve as the exclusive Interaxin treatment centers, and as the only hospitals certified to house SADS patients. The hospitals will charge patients a fee for administering the Interaxin. These fees will be used to pay for the administration of the plan—including providing the Interaxin and the hospital beds, paying for the law enforcement necessary to ensure compliance, and subsidizing the cost of the treatment for those who cannot afford the fees. Because of these broad intended uses of the fee, the State hospitals will be charging a fee for the Interaxin greater than the cost of Interaxin in the open market.

Does Gambrel's SADS program violate Dormant Commerce Clause or Privileges and Immunities principles?

VII

CITIZENSHIP, PRIVILEGES,
AND IMMUNITIES

The remainder of this book, after this chapter, explores how the Supreme Court has interpreted § 1 of the Fourteenth Amendment. As a reminder, here is the text of § 1:

All persons born or naturalized in the United States, and subject to the jurisdiction thereof, are citizens of the United States and of the State wherein they reside. No State shall make or enforce any law which shall abridge the privileges or immunities of citizens of the United States; nor shall any State deprive any person of life, liberty, or property, without due process of law; nor deny to any person within its jurisdiction the equal protection of the laws.

At the risk of gross oversimplification, two themes dominate the remainder of this book:

- First, precisely how much did the Fourteenth Amendment restructure the relationship between the United States and the individual states? The Court's decisions in this portion of the materials obviously relate powerfully to materials covered earlier in this book, especially those in Chapters IV and V.

- Second—and more centrally—how has the Court interpreted the Fourteenth Amendment's grand but vague guarantees of privileges or immunities, due process, and equal protection? These phrases are a lynchpin for the Court's work as expositor of individual rights rather than as umpire over the structural boundaries between governmental units.

This short chapter begins with the most reviled opinion in the history of the United States Supreme Court, *Dred Scott v. Sandford*. *Dred Scott* highlights the legal regime the Thirteenth, Fourteenth, and Fifteenth Amendments changed. It also raises issues of judicial interpretation of the Constitution, the potential for evil as well as good from the work of the Court, and the relationship between the Court and the larger society. The second case, the *Slaughter-House Cases*, is an early interpretation by the Supreme Court of the Fourteenth Amendment. Along with *The Civil Rights Cases*, with which you became familiar in Chapter IV, and *Plessy v. Ferguson*, which you will read in Chapter VIII, this case has been pilloried by modern critics. Finally, the chapter concludes with a recent decision that may (or may not) foreshadow a revival of the Privileges or Immunities Clause.

A. ORIGINS OF THE THIRTEENTH, FOURTEENTH, AND FIFTEENTH AMENDMENTS

Antislavery forces before the Civil War argued that slavery was unconstitutional, despite clauses in the Constitution that prohibited Congress from abolishing the slave trade until 1808, apportioned representatives on the whole number of free persons plus "three fifths of all other persons," and required states to "[deliver] up" escaped slaves. For example, abolitionist William Lloyd Garrison in 1831 told the Philadelphia Convention of the Free People of Color that "The Constitution *** knows nothing of white or black men *** those State Laws which disenfranchise and degrade you are unconstitutional[.] *** [I]f they fall upon the Constitution, they will be dashed to pieces. I say it is your duty to carry this question up to the Supreme Court of the United States, and have it settled forever[.] *** [G]et yourself acknowledged, by that august tribunal, as citizens of the United States ***." Frederick Douglass in an 1852 speech argued that "the constitution is a glorious liberty document. Read its preamble, consider its purposes. Is slavery among them? *** [I]f the Constitution were intended to be, by its framers and adopters, a slave-holding instrument, why [can] neither *slavery, slaveholding,* nor *slave* *** anywhere be found in it[?]"

During the first half of the 19th century, the North and South (other than abolitionists) were reconciled to the former remaining "free" and the latter "slave." The problem lay in the territories: neither side wanted the other to obtain control over the slavery issue in Congress through admission of disproportionate numbers of free or slave states as the country rapidly expanded westward. Congress believed it had the power (Art. IV, § 3, cl. 2) to prohibit or protect slavery in the territories, and exercised that power several times, most famously in the Northwest Ordinance of 1789 and the Missouri Compromise of 1820.

The Supreme Court, however, threw cold water on further political compromise of the slavery issue when it decided, in the following case, that the Missouri Compromise was unconstitutional and that a slave taken to a free state by his master was not a citizen of the United States. As you read this case, pay particular attention to the components of citizenship, the relationship between citizenship and legal rights, and the extent to which control over these matters is entrusted to the states and to the federal government.

DRED SCOTT v. SANDFORD
60 U.S. (19 How.) 393, 15 L.Ed. 691 (1856).

MR. CHIEF JUSTICE TANEY delivered the opinion of the court.

*** The question is simply this: Can a negro, whose ancestors were imported into this country, and sold as slaves, become a member of the political community formed and brought into existence by the Constitution of the United States, and as such become entitled to all the rights, and privileges, and immunities, guaranteed by that instrument to the citizen?

One of which rights is the privilege of suing in a court of the United States in the cases specified in the Constitution. ***

The situation of this population was altogether unlike that of the Indian race. The latter, it is true, formed no part of the colonial communities, and never amalgamated with them in social connections or in government. But although they were uncivilized, they were yet a free and independent people, associated together in nations or tribes, and governed by their own laws. *** [T]hey may, without doubt, like the subjects of any other foreign Government, be naturalized by the authority of Congress, and become citizens of a State, and of the United States; and if an individual should leave his nation or tribe, and take up his abode among the white population, he would be entitled to all the rights and privileges which would belong to an emigrant from any other foreign people. ***

The words "people of the United States" and "citizens" are synonymous terms, and mean the same thing. They both describe the political body who, according to our republican institutions, form the sovereignty, and who hold the power and conduct the Government through their representatives. They are what we familiarly call the "sovereign people," and every citizen is one of this people, and a constituent member of this sovereignty. The question before us is, whether [descendants of slaves] compose a portion of this people, and are constituent members of this sovereignty? We think they are not, and that they are not included, and were not intended to be included, under the word "citizens" in the Constitution, and can therefore claim none of the rights and privileges which that instrument provides for and secures to citizens of the United States. On the contrary, they were at that time considered as a subordinate and inferior class of beings, who had been subjugated by the dominant race, and, whether emancipated or not, yet remained subject to their authority, and had no rights or privileges but such as those who held the power and the Government might choose to grant them.

It is not the province of the court to decide upon the justice or injustice, the policy or impolicy, of these laws. The decision of that question belonged to the political or law-making power; to those who formed the sovereignty and framed the Constitution. The duty of the court is, to interpret the instrument they have framed, with the best lights we can obtain on the subject, and to administer it as we find it, according to its true intent and meaning when it was adopted.

In discussing this question, we must not confound the rights of citizenship which a State may confer within its own limits, and the rights of citizenship as a member of the Union. It does not by any means follow, because he has all the rights and privileges of a citizen of a State, that he must be a citizen of the United States. He may have all of the rights and privileges of the citizen of a State, and yet not be entitled to the rights and privileges of a citizen in any other State. For, previous to the adoption of the Constitution of the United States, every State had the undoubted right to confer on whomsoever it pleased the character of citizen, and to endow him with all its rights. But this character of course was confined to the boundaries of the State, and gave him no rights or privileges in other States beyond those secured to him by the laws of nations and the comity of States. Nor have the several States surrendered the power of conferring these rights and privileges by adopting the Constitution of the United States. Each State may still confer them upon an alien, or any one it thinks proper, or upon any class or description of persons; yet he would not be a citizen in the sense in which that word is used in the Constitution of the United States, nor entitled to sue as such in one of its courts, nor to the privileges and immunities of a citizen in the other States. The rights which he would acquire would be restricted to the State which gave them. The Constitution has conferred on Congress the right to establish an uniform rule of naturalization, and this right is evidently exclusive, and has always been held by this court to be so. Consequently, no State, since the adoption of the Constitution, can by naturalizing an alien invest him with the rights and privileges secured to a citizen of a State under the Federal Government, although, so far as the State alone was concerned, he would undoubtedly be entitled to the rights of a citizen, and clothed with all the rights and immunities which the Constitution and laws of the State attached to that character.

It is very clear, therefore, that no State can, by any act or law of its own, passed since the adoption of the Constitution, introduce a new member into the political community created by the Constitution of the United States. It cannot make him a member of this community by making him a member of its own. And for the same reason it cannot introduce any person, or description of persons, who were not intended to be embraced in this new political family, which the Constitution brought into existence, but were intended to be excluded from it.

The question then arises, whether the provisions of the Constitution, in relation to the personal rights and privileges to which the citizen of a State should be entitled, embraced the negro African race, at that time in this country, or who might afterwards be imported, who had then or should afterwards be made free in any State; and to put it in the power of a single State to make him a citizen of the United States, and endue him with the full rights of citizenship in every other State without their consent? Does the Constitution of the United States act upon him whenever he shall be made free under the laws of a State, and raised there to the rank of a citizen, and immediately clothe him with all the privileges of a citizen in every other State, and in its own courts?

The court think the affirmative of these propositions cannot be maintained. And if it cannot, the plaintiff in error could not be a citizen of the State of Missouri, within the meaning of the Constitution of the United States, and, consequently, was not entitled to sue in its courts.

It is true, every person, and every class and description of persons, who were at the time of the adoption of the Constitution recognized as citizens in the several States, became also citizens of this new political body; but none other; it was formed by them, and for them and their posterity, but for no one else. And the personal rights and privileges guaranteed to citizens of this new sovereignty were intended to embrace those only who were then members of the several State communities, or who should afterwards by birthright or otherwise become members, according to the provisions of the Constitution and the principles on which it was founded. It was the union of those who were at that time members of distinct and separate political communities into one political family, whose power, for certain specified purposes, was to extend over the whole territory of the United States. And it gave to each citizen rights and privileges outside of his State which he did not before possess, and placed him in every other State upon a perfect equality with its own citizens as to rights of person and rights of property; it made him a citizen of the United States.

It becomes necessary, therefore, to determine who were citizens of the several States when the Constitution was adopted. And in order to do this, we must recur to the Governments and institutions of the thirteen colonies, when they separated from Great Britain and formed new sovereignties, and took their places in the family of independent nations. We must inquire who, at that time, were recognized as the people or citizens of a State, whose rights and liberties had been outraged by the English Government; and who declared their independence, and assumed the powers of Government to defend their rights by force of arms.

In the opinion of the court, the legislation and histories of the times, and the language used in the Declaration of Independence, show, that neither the class of persons who had been imported as slaves, nor their descendants, whether they had become free or not, were then acknowledged as a part of the people, nor intended to be included in the general words used in that memorable instrument. *** They had for more than a century before been regarded as beings of an inferior order, and altogether unfit to associate with the white race, either in social or political relations; and so far inferior, that they had no rights which the white man was bound to respect; and that the negro might justly and lawfully be reduced to slavery for his benefit. He was bought and sold, and treated as an ordinary article of merchandise and traffic, whenever a profit could be made by it. This opinion was at that time fixed and universal in the civilized portion of the white race. *** The opinion thus entertained and acted upon in England was naturally impressed upon the colonies they founded on this side of the Atlantic. And, accordingly, a negro of the African race was regarded by them as an article of property, and held, and bought and sold as such, in every one of the thirteen colonies which united in the Declaration of Independence, and afterwards formed the Constitution of the United States. The slaves were more or less numerous in the different colonies, as slave labor was found more or less profitable. But no one seems to have doubted the correctness of the prevailing opinion of the time.

The legislation of the different colonies furnishes positive and indisputable proof of this fact. [CHIEF JUSTICE TANEY discusses Maryland and Massachusetts laws criminalizing miscegenation.] *** And no distinction in this respect was made between the free negro or mulatto and the slave, but this stigma, of the deepest degradation, was fixed upon the whole race. ***

The language of the Declaration of Independence is equally conclusive: *** "We hold these truths to be self-evident: that all men are created equal;

that they are endowed by their Creator with certain unalienable rights; that among them is life, liberty, and the pursuit of happiness; that to secure these rights, Governments are instituted, deriving their just powers from the consent of the governed."

The general words above quoted would seem to embrace the whole human family, and if they were used in a similar instrument at this day would be so understood. But it is too clear for dispute, that the enslaved African race were not intended to be included, and formed no part of the people who framed and adopted this declaration; for if the language, as understood in that day, would embrace them, the conduct of the distinguished men who framed the Declaration of Independence would have been utterly and flagrantly inconsistent with the principles they asserted; and instead of the sympathy of mankind, to which they so confidently appealed, they would have deserved and received universal rebuke and reprobation.

Yet the men who framed this declaration were great men—high in literary acquirements—high in their sense of honor, and incapable of asserting principles inconsistent with those on which they were acting. They perfectly understood the meaning of the language they used, and how it would be understood by others; and they knew that it would not in any part of the civilized world be supposed to embrace the negro race, which, by common consent, had been excluded from civilized Governments and the family of nations, and doomed to slavery. They spoke and acted according to the then established doctrines and principles, and in the ordinary language of the day, and no one misunderstood them. The unhappy black race were separated from the white by indelible marks, and laws long before established, and were never thought of or spoken of except as property, and when the claims of the owner or the profit of the trader were supposed to need protection.

This state of public opinion had undergone no change when the Constitution was adopted, as is equally evident from its provisions and language. ***

[T]here are two clauses in the Constitution which point directly and specifically to the negro race as a separate class of persons, and show clearly that they were not regarded as a portion of the people or citizens of the Government then formed.

One of these clauses reserves to each of the thirteen States the right to import slaves until the year 1808, if it thinks proper. *** And by the other provision the States pledge themselves to each other to maintain the right of property of the master, by delivering up to him any slave who may have escaped from his service, and be found within their respective territories. *** And these two provisions show, conclusively, that neither the description of persons therein referred to, nor their descendants, were embraced in any of the other provisions of the Constitution; for certainly these two clauses were not intended to confer on them or their posterity the blessings of liberty, or any of the personal rights so carefully provided for the citizen.

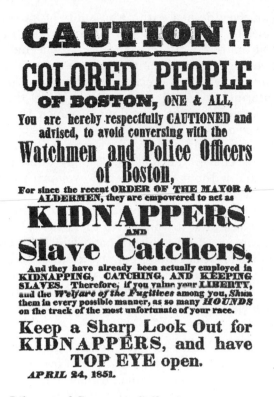

CAUTION!!

COLORED PEOPLE
OF BOSTON, ONE & ALL,

You are hereby respectfully CAUTIONED and
advised, to avoid conversing with the

Watchmen and Police Officers
of Boston,

For since the recent ORDER OF THE MAYOR &
ALDERMEN, they are empowered to act as

KIDNAPPERS
AND
Slave Catchers,

And they have already been actually employed in
KIDNAPPING, CATCHING, AND KEEPING
SLAVES. Therefore, if you value your LIBERTY,
and the *Welfare of the Fugitives* among you, *Shun*
them in every possible manner, as so many *HOUNDS*
on the track of the most unfortunate of your race.

Keep a Sharp Look Out for
KIDNAPPERS, and have
TOP EYE open.
APRIL 24, 1851.

VII–1. Poster from Library of Congress Collection.

*** And if we turn to the legislation of the States where slavery had worn out, or measures taken for its speedy abolition, we shall find the same opinion[ ] ***. Massachusetts, in 1786, passed [an antimiscegenation] law similar to the colonial one of which we have spoken. *** So, too, in Connecticut. *** Chancellor Kent, whose accuracy and research no one will question, states in the sixth edition of his Commentaries, that in no part of the country except Maine, did the African race, in point of fact, participate equally with the whites in the exercise of civil and political rights.

The legislation of the States therefore shows, in a manner not to be mistaken, the inferior and subject condition of that race at the time the Constitution was adopted, and long afterwards, throughout the thirteen States by which that instrument was framed; and it is hardly consistent with the respect due to these States, to suppose that they regarded at that time, as fellow-citizens and members of the sovereignty, a class of beings whom they had thus stigmatized; whom, as we are bound, out of respect to the State sovereignties, to assume they had deemed it just and necessary thus to stigmatize, and upon whom they had impressed such deep and enduring marks of inferiority and degradation; or, that when they met in convention to form the Constitution, they looked upon them as a portion of their constituents, or designed to include them in the provisions so carefully inserted for the security and protection of the liberties and rights of their citizens. It cannot be supposed that they intended to secure to them rights, and privileges, and rank, in the new political body throughout the Union, which every one of them denied within the limits of its own dominion. More especially, it cannot be believed that the large slaveholding States regarded them as included in the word citizens, or would have consented to a Constitution which might compel them to receive them in that character from another State. For if they were so received, and entitled to the privileges and immunities of citizens, it would exempt them from the operation of the special laws and from the police regulations which they considered to be necessary for their own safety. It would give to persons of the negro race, who were recognized as citizens in any one State of the Union, the right to enter every other State whenever they pleased, singly or in companies, without pass or passport, and without obstruction, to sojourn there as long as they pleased, to go where they pleased at every hour of the day or night without molestation, unless they committed some violation of law for which a white man would be punished; and it would give them the full liberty of speech in public and in private upon all subjects upon which its own citizens might speak; to hold public meetings upon political affairs, and to keep and carry arms wherever they went. And all of this would be done in the face of the subject race of the same color, both free and slaves, and inevitably producing discontent and insubordination among them, and endangering the peace and safety of the State.

It is impossible, it would seem, to believe that the great men of the slaveholding States, who took so large a share in framing the Constitution of the United States, and exercised so much influence in procuring its adoption, could have been so forgetful or regardless of their own safety and the safety of those who trusted and confided in them.

Besides, this want of foresight and care would have been utterly inconsistent with the caution displayed in providing for the admission of new members into this political family. For, when they gave to the citizens of each State the privileges and immunities of citizens in the several States, they at the same time took from the several States the power of naturalization, and confined that power exclusively to the Federal Government. *** [T]hey could never have left with the States a much more important power—that is, the power of transforming into citizens a numerous class of persons, who in that character would be much more dangerous to the peace and safety of a large portion of the Union, than the few foreigners one of the States might improperly naturalize. *** And no law of a State, therefore, passed since the Constitution was adopted, can give any right of citizenship outside of its own territory.

A clause similar to the one in the Constitution, in relation to the rights and immunities of citizens of one State in the other States, was contained in the Articles of Confederation. But there is a difference of language, which is worthy of note. The provision in the Articles of Confederation was, "that the *free inhabitants* of each of the States, paupers, vagabonds, and fugitives from justice, excepted, should be entitled to all the privileges and immunities of free citizens in the several States." ***

But although this clause of the Articles of Confederation is the same in principle with that inserted in the Constitution, yet the comprehensive word inhabitant, which might be construed to include an emancipated slave, is omitted; and the privilege is confined to citizens of the State. And this alteration in words would hardly have been made, unless a different meaning was intended to be conveyed, or a possible doubt removed. ***

To all this mass of proof we have still to add, that Congress has repeatedly legislated upon the same construction of the Constitution that we have given. Three laws, two of which were passed almost immediately after the Government went into operation, will be abundantly sufficient to show this. ***

The first of these acts is the naturalization law, which was passed at the second session of the first Congress, March 26, 1790, and confines the right of becoming citizens "*to aliens being free white persons.*" *** [The first militia law, passed in 1792] directs that every "free able-bodied white male citizen" shall be enrolled in the militia. *** The third act *** provides: "That from and after the termination of the war in which the United States are now engaged with Great Britain, it shall not be lawful to employ, on board of any public or private vessels of the United States, any person or persons except citizens of the United States, *or* persons of color, natives of the United States.

Here the line of distinction is drawn in express words. Persons of color, in the judgment of Congress, were not included in the word citizens ***. The conduct of the Executive Department of the Government has been in perfect harmony upon this subject with this course of legislation. ***

But it is said that a person may be a citizen, and entitled to that character, although he does not possess all the rights which may belong to other citizens; as, for example, the right to vote, or to hold particular offices; and that yet, when he goes into another State, he is entitled to be recognized there as a citizen, although the State may measure his rights by the rights which it allows to persons of a like character or class resident in the State, and refuse to him the full rights of citizenship. *** Undoubtedly, a person may be a citizen, that is, a member of the community who form the sovereignty, although he exercises no share of the political power, and is incapacitated from holding particular offices. Women and minors, who form a part of the political family, cannot vote; and when a property qualification is required to vote or hold a particular office, those who have not the necessary qualification cannot vote or hold the office, yet they are citizens.

So, too, a person may be entitled to vote by the law of the State, who is not a citizen even of the State itself. And in some of the States of the Union foreigners not naturalized are allowed to vote. And the State may give the right to free negroes and mulattoes, but that does not make them citizens of the State, and still less of the United States. And the provision in the Constitution giving privileges and immunities in other States, does not apply to them.

Neither does it apply to a person who, being the citizen of a State, migrates to another State. For then he becomes subject to the laws of the State in which he lives, and he is no longer a citizen of the State from which he removed. And the State in which he resides may then, unquestionably, determine his *status* or condition, and place him among the class of persons who are not recognized as citizens, but belong to an inferior and subject race; and may deny him the privileges and immunities enjoyed by its citizens.

But so far as mere rights of person are concerned, the provision in question is confined to citizens of a State who are temporarily in another State without taking up their residence there. It gives them no political rights in the State, as to voting or holding office, or in any other respect. For a citizen of one State has no right to participate in the government of another. But if he ranks as a citizen in the State to which he belongs, within the meaning of the Constitution of the United States, then, whenever he goes into another State, the Constitution clothes him, as to the rights of person, with all the privileges and immunities which belong to citizens of the State. And if persons of the African race are citizens of a State, and of the United States, they would be entitled to all of these privileges and immunities in every State, and the State could not restrict them; for they would hold these privileges and immunities under the paramount authority of the Federal Government, and its courts would be bound to maintain and enforce them, the Constitution and laws of the State to the contrary notwithstanding. And if the States could limit or restrict them, or place the party in an inferior grade, this clause of the Constitution would be unmeaning, and could have no operation; and would give no rights to the citizen when in another State. He would have none but what the State itself chose to allow him. This is evidently not the construction or meaning of the clause in question. It guaranties rights to the citizen, and the State cannot withhold them. And these rights are of a character and would lead to consequences which make it absolutely certain that the African race were not included under the name of citizens of a State, and were not in the contemplation of the framers of the Constitution when these privileges and immunities were provided for the protection of the citizen in other States. *** Dred Scott was not a citizen of Missouri within the meaning of the Constitution of the United States, and not entitled as such to sue in its courts. ***

[B]ut if that plea is regarded as waived, or out of the case upon any other ground, [we proceed to the merits of Dred Scott's claim to freedom under federal law]. ***

The act of Congress, upon which the plaintiff relies, declares that slavery and involuntary servitude, except as a punishment for crime, shall be forever prohibited in all that part of the territory ceded by France, under the name of Louisiana, which lies north of thirty-six degrees thirty minutes north latitude, and not included within the limits of Missouri. *** [Was] Congress authorized to pass this law under any of the powers granted to it by the Constitution [?] *** The counsel for the plaintiff has laid much stress upon that article in the Constitution which confers on Congress the power 'to dispose of and make all needful rules and regulations respecting the territory or other property belonging to the United States;' but, in the judgment of the court, that provision has no bearing on the present controversy. *** The power is given in relation only to the territory of the United States—that is, to a territory then in existence, and then known or claimed as the territory of the United States. ***

This brings us to examine by what provision of the Constitution the present Federal Government, under its delegated and restricted powers, is authorized to acquire territory outside of the original limits of the United States, and what powers it may exercise therein over the person or property of a citizen of the United States, while it remains a Territory, and until it shall be admitted as one of the States of the Union. *** [C]itizens of the United States who migrate to a Territory belonging to the people of the United States, cannot be ruled as mere colonists, dependent upon the will of the General Government, and to be governed by any laws it may think proper to impose. The principle upon which our Governments rest, and upon which alone they continue to exist, is the union of States, sovereign and independent within their own limits in their internal and domestic concerns, and bound together as one people by a General Government, possessing certain enumerated and restricted powers. *** A power, therefore, in the General Government to obtain and hold colonies and dependent territories, over which they might legislate without restriction, would be inconsistent with its own existence in its present form. *** [T]he act of Congress which prohibited a citizen from holding and owning property of this kind in the territory of the United States north of the line therein mentioned, is not warranted by the Constitution, and is therefore void; and that neither Dred Scott himself, nor any of his family, were made free by being carried into this territory; even if they had been carried there by the owner, with the intention of becoming a permanent resident.

*** And it is contended, on the part of the plaintiff, that he is made free by being taken to Rock Island, in the State of Illinois, independently of his residence in the territory of the United States; and being so made free, he was not again reduced to a state of slavery by being brought back to Missouri. *** As Scott was a slave when taken into the State of Illinois by his owner, and was there held as such, and brought back in that character, his status, as free or slave, depended on the laws of Missouri, and not of Illinois.

It has, however, been urged in the argument, that by the laws of Missouri he was free on his return ***. [W]e are satisfied, upon a careful examination of all the cases decided in the State courts of Missouri referred to, that it is now firmly settled by the decisions of the highest court in the State, that Scott and his family upon their return were not free, but were, by the laws of Missouri, the property of the defendant; and that the Circuit Court of the United States had no jurisdiction, when, by the laws of the State, the plaintiff was a slave, and not a citizen. ***

MR. JUSTICE WAYNE, concurring opinion. [omitted]

MR. JUSTICE NELSON, concurring opinion. [omitted]

MR. JUSTICE GRIER, concurring opinion. [omitted]

MR. JUSTICE DANIEL, concurring.

*** For who, it may be asked, is a citizen? *** It is difficult to conceive by what magic the mere *surcease* or renunciation of an interest in a subject of *property*, by an individual possessing that interest, can alter the essential character of that property with respect to persons or communities unconnected with such renunciation. *** The institution of slavery, as it exists and has existed from the period of its introduction into the United States, though more humane and mitigated in character than was the same institution, either under the republic or the empire of Rome, bears, both in its tenure and in the simplicity incident to the mode of its exercise, a closer resemblance to Roman slavery than it does to the condition of *villanage*, as it formerly existed in England. *** [W]ith regard to slavery amongst the Romans, it is by no means true that emancipation, either during the republic or the empire, conferred, by the act itself, or implied, the *status* or the rights of citizenship.

The proud title of Roman citizen, with the immunities and rights incident thereto, and as contradistinguished alike from the condition of conquered subjects or of the lower grades of native domestic residents, was maintained throughout the duration of the republic ***. Whatever these Constitutions and laws validly determine to be property, it is the duty of the Federal Government, through the domain of jurisdiction merely Federal, to recognize to be property. *** Wherever a master is entitled to go within the United States, his slave may accompany him, without any impediment from, or fear of, Congressional legislation or interference. ***

MR. JUSTICE CAMPBELL, concurring opinion. [omitted]

MR. JUSTICE CATRON, concurring opinion. [omitted]

MR. JUSTICE MCLEAN, dissenting.

*** Being born under our Constitution and laws, no naturalization is required, as one of foreign birth, to make him a citizen. The most general and appropriate definition of the term citizen is "a freeman." Being a freeman, and having his domicil in a State different from that of the defendant, he is a citizen within the act of Congress, and the courts of the Union are open to him. *** To constitute a good plea to the jurisdiction, it must negative those qualities and rights which enable an individual to sue in the Federal courts. This has not been done; and on this ground the plea was defective, and the demurrer was properly sustained. *** No injustice can result to the master, from an exercise of jurisdiction in this cause. Such a decision does not in any degree affect the merits of the case; it only enables the plaintiff to assert his claims to freedom before this tribunal. If the jurisdiction be ruled against him, on the ground that he is a slave, it is decisive of his fate.

It has been argued that, if a colored person be made a citizen of a State, he cannot sue in the Federal court. *** In the argument, it was said that a colored citizen would not be an agreeable member of society. This is more a matter of taste than of law. Several of the States have admitted persons of color to the right of suffrage, and in this view have recognized them as citizens; and this has been done in the slave as well as the free States. On the question of citizenship, it must be admitted that we have not been very fastidious. Under the late treaty with Mexico, we have made citizens of all grades, combinations, and colors. The same was done in the admission of Louisiana and Florida. No one ever doubted, and no court ever held, that the people of these Territories did not become citizens under the treaty. They have exercised all the rights of citizens, without being naturalized under the acts of Congress.

There are several important principles involved in this case, which have been argued, and which may be considered under the following heads:

1.   The locality of slavery, as settled by this court and the courts of the States.

2.   The relation which the Federal Government bears to slavery in the States.

3.   The power of Congress to establish Territorial Governments, and to prohibit the introduction of slavery therein.

4.   The effect of taking slaves into a new State or Territory, and so holding them, where slavery is prohibited.

5.   Whether the return of a slave under the control of his master, after being entitled to his freedom, reduces him to his former condition.

6.   Are the decisions of the Supreme Court of Missouri, on the questions before us, binding on this court, within the rule adopted. ***

[1.] As to the locality of slavery. The civil law throughout the Continent of Europe, it is believed, without an exception, is, that slavery can exist only within the territory where it is established; and that, if a slave escapes, or is carried beyond such territory, his master cannot reclaim him, unless by virtue of some express stipulation. ***

[2.] Slavery is emphatically a State institution. *** [U]nder the commercial power, Congress had a right to regulate the slave trade among the several States; but the court held that Congress had no power to interfere with slavery as it exists in the States, or to regulate what is called the slave trade among them. If this trade were subject to the commercial power, it would follow that Congress could abolish or establish slavery in every State of the Union. *** We need not refer to the mercenary spirit which introduced the infamous traffic in slaves, to show the degradation of negro slavery in our country. Our independence was a great epoch in the history of freedom; and while I admit the Government was not made especially for the colored race, yet many of them were citizens of the New England States, and exercised, the rights of suffrage when the Constitution was adopted, and it was not doubted by any intelligent person that its tendencies would greatly ameliorate their condition. *** But if we are to turn our attention to the dark ages of the world, why confine our view to colored slavery? On the same principles, white men were made slaves. All slavery has its origin in power, and is against right.

[3.] The power of Congress to establish Territorial Governments, and to prohibit the introduction of slavery therein, is the next point to be considered.

*** It would be singular, if in 1804 Congress had power to prohibit the introduction of slaves in Orleans Territory from any other part of the Union, under the penalty of freedom to the slave, if the same power, embodied in the Missouri compromise, could not be exercised in 1820.

But this law of Congress, which prohibits slavery north of Missouri and of thirty-six degrees thirty minutes, is declared to have been null and void by my brethren. And this opinion is founded mainly, as I understand, on the distinction drawn between the ordinance of 1787 and the Missouri compromise line. *** If Congress may establish a Territorial Government in the exercise of its discretion, it is a clear principle that a court cannot control that discretion. This being the case, I do not see on what ground the act is held to be void. It did not purport to forfeit property, or take it for public purposes. It only prohibited slavery; in doing which, it followed the ordinance of 1787. ***

[4.] [In *Prigg v. Commonwealth of Pennsylvania*, 41 U.S. 539 (1842),] the court says: "The state of slavery is deemed to be a mere municipal regulation, founded upon and limited to the range of the territorial laws." If this be so, slavery can exist nowhere except under the authority of law, founded on usage having the force of law, or by statutory recognition. And the court further says: "It is manifest, from this consideration, that if the Constitution had not contained the clause requiring the rendition of fugitives from labor, every non-slaveholding State in the Union would have been at liberty to have declared free all runaway slaves coming within its limits, and to have given them entire immunity and protection against the claims of their masters."

Now, if a slave absconds, he may be reclaimed; but if he accompany his master into a State or Territory where slavery is prohibited, such slave cannot be said to have left the service of his master where his services were legalized. And if slavery be limited to the range of the territorial laws, how can the slave be coerced to serve in a State or Territory, not only without the authority of law, but against its express provisions? What gives the master the right to control the will of his slave? ***

By virtue of what law is it, that a master may take his slave into free territory, and exact from him the duties of a slave? The law of the Territory does not sanction it. No authority can be claimed under the Constitution of the United States, or any law of Congress. Will it be said that the slave is taken as property, the same as other property which the master may own? To this I answer, that colored persons are made property by the law of the State, and no such power has been given to Congress. Does the master carry with him the law of the State from which he removes into the Territory? And does that enable him to coerce his slave in the Territory? Let us test this theory. If this may be done by a master from one slave State, it may be done by a master from every other slave State. This right is supposed to be connected with the person of the master, by virtue of the local law. Is it transferable? May it be negotiated, as a promissory note or bill of exchange? If it be assigned to a man from a free State, may he coerce the slave by virtue of it? What shall this thing be denominated? Is it personal or real property? Or is it an indefinable fragment of sovereignty, which every person carries with him from his late domicil? One thing is certain, that its origin has been very recent, and it is unknown to the laws of any civilized country.

*** It is said the Territories are common property of the States, and that every man has a right to go there with his property. This is not controverted. But the court say a slave is not property beyond the operation of the local law which makes him such. *** Now, unless the fugitive escape from a place where, by the municipal law, he is held to labor, this provision affords no remedy to the master. What can be more conclusive than this? Suppose a slave escape from a Territory where slavery is not authorized by law, can he be reclaimed?

In this case, a majority of the court have said that a slave may be taken by his master into a Territory of the United States, the same as a horse, or any other kind of property. *** The question of jurisdiction, being before the court, was decided by them authoritatively, but nothing beyond that question. A slave is not a mere chattel. He bears the impress of his Maker, and is amenable to the laws of God and man; and he is destined to an endless existence. ***

[5.] The slave States have generally adopted the rule, that where the master, by a residence with his slave in a State or Territory where slavery is prohibited, the slave was entitled to his freedom everywhere. *** Illinois has declared in the most solemn and impressive form that there shall be neither slavery nor involuntary servitude in that State, and that any slave brought into it, with a view of becoming a resident, shall be emancipated. With a full knowledge of these facts, a slave is brought from Missouri to Rock Island, in the State of Illinois, and is retained there as a slave for two years, and then taken to Fort Snelling, where slavery is prohibited by the Missouri compromise act, and there he is detained two years longer in a state of slavery. Harriet, his wife, was also kept at the same place four years as a slave, having been purchased in Missouri. They were then removed to the State of Missouri, and sold as slaves, and in the action before us they are not only claimed as slaves, but a majority of my brethren have held that on their being returned to Missouri the status of slavery attached to them.

I am not able to reconcile this result with the respect due to the State of Illinois. ***

[6.] "[W]hether the decisions of the Supreme Court of Missouri, on the question before us, are binding on this court." *** The Supreme Court of Missouri refused to notice the act of Congress or the Constitution of Illinois, under which Dred Scott, his wife and children, claimed that they are entitled to freedom. *** The Missouri court disregards the express provisions of an act of Congress and the Constitution of a sovereign State, both of which laws for twenty-eight years it had not only regarded, but carried into effect.

If a State court may do this, on a question involving the liberty of a human being, what protection do the laws afford? So far from this being a Missouri question, it is a question, as it would seem, within the twenty-fifth section of the judiciary act, where a right to freedom being set up under the act of Congress, and the decision being against such right, it may be brought for revision before this court, from the Supreme Court of Missouri. ***

MR. JUSTICE CURTIS, dissenting.

*** [T]he question is, whether any person of African descent, whose ancestors were sold as slaves in the United States, can be a citizen of the United States. *** The first section of the second article of the Constitution uses the language, "a citizen of the United States at the time of the adoption of the Constitution." *** Citizens of the United States at the time of the adoption of the Constitution can have been no other than citizens of the United States under the Confederation. *** To determine whether any free persons, descended from Africans held in slavery, were citizens of the United States under the Confederation, and consequently at the time of the adoption of the Constitution of the United States, it is only necessary to know whether any such persons were citizens of either of the States under the Confederation, at the time of the adoption of the Constitution.

Of this there can be no doubt. At the time of the ratification of the Articles of Confederation, all free native-born inhabitants of the States of New Hampshire, Massachusetts, New York, New Jersey, and North Carolina, though descended from African slaves, were not only citizens of those States, but such of them as had the other necessary qualifications possessed the franchise of electors, on equal terms with other citizens. *** [I]n some of the original thirteen States, free colored persons, before and at the time of the formation of the Constitution, were citizens of those States.

The fourth of the fundamental articles of the Confederation was as follows: "The free inhabitants of each of these States, paupers, vagabonds, and fugitives from justice, excepted, shall be entitled to all the privileges and immunities of free citizens in the several States."

*** [F]ree persons of color were citizens of some of the several States, [with] the consequence, that this fourth article of the Confederation would have the effect to confer on such persons the privileges and immunities of general citizenship. *** Did the Constitution of the United States deprive them or their descendants of citizenship? *** I can find nothing in the Constitution which, *proprio vigore*, deprives of their citizenship any class of persons who were citizens of the United States at the time of its adoption, or who should be native-born citizens of any State after its adoption; nor any power enabling Congress to disfranchise persons born on the soil of any State, and entitled to citizenship of such State by its Constitution and laws. And my opinion is, that, under the Constitution of the United States, every free person born on the soil of a State, who is a citizen of that State by force of its Constitution or laws, is also a citizen of the United States.

I will proceed to state the grounds of that opinion.

*** Among the powers expressly granted to Congress is "the power to establish a uniform rule of naturalization." *** [T]he only power expressly granted to Congress to legislate concerning citizenship, is confined to the removal of the disabilities of foreign birth. *** Among the powers unquestionably possessed by the several States, was that of determining what persons should and what persons should not be citizens. ***

"The citizens of each State shall be entitled to all the privileges and immunities of citizens of the several States." Nowhere else in the Constitution is there anything concerning a general citizenship; but here, privileges and immunities to be enjoyed throughout the United States, under and by force of the national compact, are granted and secured. In selecting those who are to enjoy these national rights of citizenship, how are they described? As citizens of each State. It is to them these national rights are secured. The qualification for them is not to be looked for in any provision of the Constitution or laws of the United States. They are to be citizens of the several States, and, as such, the privileges and immunities of general citizenship, derived from and guarantied by the Constitution, are to be enjoyed by them. *** [T]he citizens of the several States are to enjoy the privileges and immunities of citizens in every State, and their franchise as electors under the Constitution depends on their citizenship in the several States. ***

It has been often asserted that the Constitution was made exclusively by and for the white race. It has already been shown that in five of the thirteen original States, colored persons then possessed the elective franchise, and were among those by whom the Constitution was ordained and established. If so, it is not true, in point of fact, that the Constitution was made exclusively by the white race. *** What civil rights shall be enjoyed by its citizens, and whether all shall enjoy the same, or how they may be gained or lost, are to be determined in the same way.

One may confine the right of suffrage to white male citizens; another may extend it to colored persons and females; one may allow all persons above a prescribed age to convey property and transact business; another may exclude married women. But whether native-born women, or persons under age, or under guardianship because insane or spendthrifts, be excluded from voting or holding office, or allowed to do so, I apprehend no one will deny that they are citizens of the United States. ***

It has been suggested, that in adopting it into the Constitution, the words "free inhabitants" were changed for the word "citizens." An examination of the forms of expression commonly used in the State papers of that day, and an attention to the substance of this article of the Confederation, will show that the words "free inhabitants," as then used, were synonymous with citizens. ***

It may be further objected, that if free colored persons may be citizens of the United States, it depends only on the will of a master whether he will emancipate his slave, and thereby make him a citizen. Not so. The master is subject to the will of the State. Whether he shall be allowed to emancipate his slave at all; if so, on what conditions; and what is to be the political status of the freed man, depend, not on the will of the master, but on the will of the State, upon which the political status of all its native-born inhabitants depends. Under the Constitution of the United States, each State has retained this power of determining the political status of its native-born inhabitants, and no exception thereto can be found in the Constitution. And if a master in a slaveholding State should carry his slave into a free State, and there emancipate him, he would not thereby make him a native-born citizen of that State, and consequently no privileges could be claimed by such emancipated slave as a citizen of the United States. For, whatever powers the States may exercise to confer privileges of citizenship on persons not born on their soil, the Constitution of the United States does not recognize such citizens. As has already been said, it recognizes the great principle of public law, that allegiance and citizenship spring from the place of birth. It leaves to the States the application of that principle to individual cases. It secured to the citizens of each State the privileges and immunities of citizens in every other State. But it does not allow to the States the power to make aliens citizens, or permit one State to take persons born on the soil of another State, and, contrary to the laws and policy of the State where they were born, make them its citizens, and so citizens of the United States. No such deviation from the great rule of public law was contemplated by the Constitution; and when any such attempt shall be actually made, it is to be met by applying to it those rules of law and those principles of good faith which will be sufficient to decide it, and not, in my judgment, by denying that all the free native-born inhabitants of a State, who are its citizens under its Constitution and laws, are also citizens of the United States. ***

If, then, this clause does contain a power to legislate respecting the territory, what are the limits of that power? *** Looking at the power of Congress over the Territories as of the extent just described, what positive prohibition exists in the Constitution, which restrained Congress from enacting a law in 1820 to prohibit slavery north of thirty-six degrees thirty minutes north latitude?

The only one suggested is that clause in the fifth article of the amendments of the Constitution which declares that no person shall be deprived of his life, liberty, or property, without due process of law. *** Slavery, being contrary to natural right, is created only by municipal law. *** The Constitution refers to slaves as "persons held to service in one State, under the laws thereof." Nothing can more clearly describe a status created by municipal law. *** It was certainly understood by the Convention which framed the Constitution, and has been so understood ever since, that, under the power to regulate commerce, Congress could prohibit the importation of slaves; and the exercise of the power was restrained till 1808. A citizen of the United States owns slaves in Cuba, and brings them to the United States, where they are set free by the legislation of Congress. Does this legislation deprive him of his property without due process of law? If so, what becomes of the laws prohibiting the slave trade? If not, how can similar regulation respecting a Territory violate the fifth amendment of the Constitution? ***

Notes

1. **Critique of *Dred Scott*.** What was wrong about the decision as a matter of constitutional theory (as opposed to theories of fundamental human rights and

morality)? Could the Court have reached a different result with a textual, as opposed to an original intent, approach? Was the Court wrong to ignore the language of the Declaration of Independence ("All men are created equal *** ") in assessing original intent? Would structural interpretation have been of use to the Court in reaching a contrary decision? Should the Court have envisioned the Constitution as growing and changing to embody societal aspirations? Should the Court have held that slavery violated the natural law right of human freedom?

2. **The Limits of the Court's Power.** Quite erroneously, the Court thought its decision would take the slavery issue "out of politics." Instead, it inflamed preexisting passions. It encouraged the southern states to assert the power to leave the Union and it convinced the abolitionists that nothing short of superior force could undo the injustice of the Court's interpretation of the Constitution. For example, William Lloyd Garrison publicly burned a copy of the Constitution following the *Dred Scott* decision, calling the Constitution a "compact with the devil." What difference politically would a decision opposite that rendered by the Court have made? Would the Civil War have been averted? Would a contrary decision have freed the slaves? Consider the following proposed Thirteenth Amendment to the Constitution, which passed both houses of Congress less than a week before Lincoln's inauguration with the blessings of the Republican leadership in a Congress already missing representation from the Deep South:

> *No amendment shall be made to the Constitution which will authorize or give to Congress the power to abolish or interfere, within any State, with the domestic institutions thereof, including that of persons held to labor or service by the laws of said state.*

If northern Republicans were willing permanently to accept slavery in the South to avoid civil war, what hope did the Court have of resolving the issue? The rest—Lincoln's election, the Civil War, Reconstruction, and Jim Crow—is history.

3. **Reversing *Dred Scott*.** Three constitutional amendments were passed to overturn various aspects of this one decision. The Thirteenth Amendment (1865) abolished slavery. But this manumission did not give former slaves the benefits of being citizens. The first sentence of the Fourteenth Amendment (1868) established a national rule of citizenship for those born (like the former slaves) in the United States. This sentence gave the freed slaves, among other things, the right of citizens to sue in federal court. The second sentence of the Fourteenth Amendment guaranteed "privileges or immunities of citizens of the United States," and that states could not deprive "any person" of "due process of law" and "equal protection of the laws." This sentence did not mention race, slavery, or former condition of servitude. The Fifteenth Amendment (1870) prohibited the United States and the states from denying the right to vote "on account of race, color, or previous condition of servitude."

4 **Beyond Reversal.** Most of the remainder of this book examines judicial interpretation of the second sentence of the Fourteenth Amendment. Three further amendments addressed other situations alluded to in this case: the Nineteenth Amendment (1920) ended the era where females could be citizens but denied the right to vote; the Twenty–Fourth Amendment (1964) abolished poll taxes used covertly to deny African–Americans the right to vote on an equal basis with white citizens; and the Twenty–Sixth Amendment set a uniform age of 18 at which citizens were guaranteed the right to vote.

B. FEDERAL PRIVILEGES OR IMMUNITIES

Historian Edwin Corwin observed that "Unique among constitutional provisions, the privileges and immunities clause of the Fourteenth Amendment enjoys the distinction of having been rendered a 'practical nullity' by a single decision of the Supreme Court within five years after its ratification." The decision which accomplished this nullification, *The Slaughter–House Cases*, has not been overruled. The second case in this section, *Saenz v. Roe, may* signal that the Court is moving toward reopening the door it closed over a century ago.

SLAUGHTER-HOUSE CASES
83 U.S. (16 Wall.) 36, 21 L.Ed. 394 (1873).

MR. JUSTICE MILLER *** delivered the opinion of the court.

*** The statute *** [here] assailed as unconstitutional was passed March 8th, 1869, and is entitled "An act to protect the health of the city of New Orleans, to locate the stock-landings and slaughter-houses, and to incorporate the Crescent City Live–Stock Landing and Slaughter–House Company." *** It declares that the company *** shall have the sole and exclusive privilege of conducting and carrying on the live-stock landing and slaughter-house business within the limits and privilege granted by the act, and that all such animals shall be landed at the stock-landings and slaughtered at the slaughter-houses of the company, and nowhere else. Penalties are enacted for infractions of this provision, and prices fixed for the maximum charges of the company for each steamboat and for each animal landed. *** [The statute] makes it the duty of the company to permit any person to slaughter animals in their slaughter-houses under a heavy penalty for each refusal. Another section fixes a limit to the charges to be made by the company for each animal so slaughtered in their building, and another provides for an inspection of all animals intended to be so slaughtered, by an officer appointed by the governor of the State for that purpose.

These are the principal features of the statute, and are all that have any bearing upon the questions to be decided by us.

This statute is denounced not only as creating a monopoly and conferring odious and exclusive privileges upon a small number of persons at the expense of the great body of the community of New Orleans, but it is asserted that it deprives a large and meritorious class of citizens—the whole of the butchers of the city—of the right to exercise their trade, the business to which they have been trained and on which they depend for the support of themselves and their families, and that the unrestricted exercise of the business of butchering is necessary to the daily subsistence of the population of the city. ***

It is not, and cannot be successfully controverted, that it is both the right and the duty of the legislative body—the supreme power of the State or municipality—to prescribe and determine the localities where the business of slaughtering for a great city may be conducted. To do this effectively it is indispensable that all persons who slaughter animals for food shall do it in those places and nowhere else. ***

The [police] power here exercised by the legislature of Louisiana is, in its essential nature, one which has been, up to the present period in the constitutional history of this country, always conceded to belong to the States. *** The regulation of the place and manner of conducting the slaughtering of animals, and the business of butchering within a city, and the inspection of the animals to be killed for meat, and of the meat afterwards, are among the most necessary and frequent exercises of this power. It is not, therefore, needed that we should seek for a comprehensive definition, but rather look for the proper source of its exercise. ***

The proposition is, therefore, reduced to these terms: Can any exclusive privileges be granted to any of its citizens, or to a corporation, by the legislature of a State? ***

The plaintiffs in error accepting this issue, allege that the statute is a violation of the Constitution of the United States in these several particulars:

That it creates an involuntary servitude forbidden by the thirteenth article of amendment;

That it abridges the privileges and immunities of citizens of the United States;

That it denies to the plaintiffs the equal protection of the laws; and,

That it deprives them of their property without due process of law; contrary to the provisions of the first section of the fourteenth article of amendment.

This court is thus called upon for the first time to give construction to these articles. ***

[I]n the light of *** events, almost too recent to be called history, but which are familiar to us all; and on the most casual examination of the language of these amendments, no one can fail to be impressed with the one pervading purpose found in them all, lying at the foundation of each, and without which none of them would have been even suggested; we mean the freedom of the slave race, the security and firm establishment of that freedom, and the protection of the newly-made freeman and citizen from the oppressions of those who had formerly exercised unlimited dominion over him. It is true that only the fifteenth amendment, in terms, mentions the negro by speaking of his color and his slavery. But it is just as true that each of the other articles was addressed to the grievances of that race, and designed to remedy them as the fifteenth.

We do not say that no one else but the negro can share in this protection. *** But what we do say, and what we wish to be understood is, that in any fair and just construction of any section or phrase of these amendments, it is necessary to look to the purpose which we have said was the pervading spirit of them all, the evil which they were designed to remedy, and the process of continued addition to the Constitution, until that purpose was supposed to be accomplished, as far as constitutional law can accomplish it.

The first section of the fourteenth article, to which our attention is more specially invited, opens with a definition of citizenship—not only citizenship of the United States, but citizenship of the States. *** [T]o establish a clear and comprehensive definition of citizenship which should declare what should constitute citizenship of the United States, and also citizenship of a State, the first clause of the first section was framed.

"All persons born or naturalized in the United States, and subject to the jurisdiction thereof, are citizens of the United States and of the State wherein they reside."

*** [The clause] declares that persons may be citizens of the United States without regard to their citizenship of a particular State, and it overturns the *Dred Scott* decision by making all persons born within the United States and subject to its jurisdiction citizens of the United States.

*** [Here] the distinction between citizenship of the United States and citizenship of a State is clearly recognized and established. Not only may a man be a citizen of the United States without being a citizen of a State, but an important element is necessary to convert the former into the latter. He must reside within the State to make him a citizen of it, but it is only necessary that he should be born or naturalized in the United States to be a citizen of the Union. It is quite clear, then, that there is a citizenship of the United States, and a citizenship of a State, which are distinct from each other, and which depend upon different characteristics or circumstances in the individual.

We think this distinction and its explicit recognition in this amendment of great weight in this argument, because the next paragraph of this same section, which is the one mainly relied on by the plaintiffs in error, speaks only of privileges and immunities of citizens of the United States, and does not speak of those of citizens of the several States. The argument, however, in favor of the plaintiffs rests wholly on the assumption that the citizenship is the same, and the privileges and immunities guaranteed by the clause are the same.

The language is, "No State shall make or enforce any law which shall abridge the privileges or immunities of citizens of the United States." It is a little remarkable, if this clause was intended as a protection to the citizen of a State against the legislative power of his own State, that the word citizen of the State should be left out when it is so carefully used, and used in contradistinction to citizens of the United States, in the very sentence which precedes it. It is too clear for argument that the change in phraseology was adopted understandingly and with a purpose.

Of the privileges and immunities of the citizen of the United States, and of the privileges and immunities of the citizen of the State, and what they respectively are, we will presently consider; but we wish to state here that it is only the former which are placed by this clause under the protection of the

Federal Constitution, and that the latter, whatever they may be, are not intended to have any additional protection by this paragraph of the amendment.

If, then, there is a difference between the privileges and immunities belonging to a citizen of the United States as such, and those belonging to the citizen of the State as such the latter must rest for their security and protection where they have heretofore rested; for they are not embraced by this paragraph of the amendment.

*** [S]ection two of the fourth article [of the Constitution provides] *** : "The citizens of each State shall be entitled to all the privileges and immunities of citizens of the several States."

There can be but little question that the purpose of both these provisions is the same, and that the privileges and immunities intended are the same in each. In the article of the Confederation we have some of these specifically mentioned, and enough perhaps to give some general idea of the class of civil rights meant by the phrase. Fortunately we are not without judicial construction of this clause of the Constitution. The first and the leading case on the subject is that of *Corfield v. Coryell*, decided by MR. JUSTICE WASHINGTON in the Circuit Court for the District of Pennsylvania in 1823.

> "The inquiry *** is, what are the privileges and immunities of citizens of the several States? We feel no hesitation in confining these expressions to those privileges and immunities which are fundamental; which belong of right to the citizens of all free governments, and which have at all times been enjoyed by citizens of the several States which compose this Union, from the time of their becoming free, independent, and sovereign. What these fundamental principles are, it would be more tedious than difficult to enumerate. They may all, however, be comprehended under the following general heads: protection by the government, with the right to acquire and possess property of every kind, and to pursue and obtain happiness and safety, subject, nevertheless, to such restraints as the government may prescribe for the general good of the whole."

*** The constitutional provision there alluded to did not create those rights, which it called privileges and immunities of citizens of the States. It threw around them in that clause no security for the citizen of the State in which they were claimed or exercised. Nor did it profess to control the power of the State governments over the rights of its own citizens. Its sole purpose was to declare to the several States, that whatever those rights, as you grant or establish them to your own citizens, or as you limit or qualify, or impose restrictions on their exercise, the same, neither more nor less, shall be the measure of the rights of citizens of other States within your jurisdiction.

*** [U]p to the adoption of the recent amendments, no claim or pretence was set up that those rights depended on the Federal government for their existence or protection ***. Was it the purpose of the fourteenth amendment, by the simple declaration that no State should make or enforce any law which shall abridge the privileges and immunities of citizens of the United States, to transfer the security and protection of all the civil rights which we have mentioned, from the States to the Federal government? And where it is declared that Congress shall have the power to enforce that article, was it intended to bring within the power of Congress the entire domain of civil rights heretofore belonging exclusively to the States?

All this and more must follow, if the proposition of the plaintiffs in error be sound. For not only are these rights subject to the control of Congress whenever in its discretion any of them are supposed to be abridged by State legislation, but that body may also pass laws in advance, limiting and restricting the exercise of legislative power by the States, in their most ordinary and usual functions, as in its judgment it may think proper on all such subjects. And still further, such a construction *** would constitute this court a perpetual censor upon all legislation of the States, on the civil rights of their own citizens, with authority to nullify such as it did not approve as consistent with those rights, as they existed at the time of the adoption of this amendment. The argument we admit is not always the most conclusive which is drawn from the consequences urged against the adoption of a particular construction of an instrument. But when, as in the case before us, these consequences are so serious, so far-reaching and pervading, so great a departure from the structure and spirit of our institutions; when the effect is to fetter and degrade the State governments by subjecting them to the control of Congress, in the exercise of powers heretofore universally conceded to them of the most ordinary and fundamental character; when in fact it radically changes the whole theory of the relations of the State and Federal governments to each other and of both these governments to the people; the argument has a force that is irresistible, in the absence of language which expresses such a purpose too clearly to admit of doubt.

We are convinced that no such results were intended by the Congress which proposed these amendments, nor by the legislatures of the States which ratified them.

Having shown that the privileges and immunities relied on in the argument are those which belong to citizens of the States as such, and that they are left to the State governments for security and protection, and not by this article placed under the special care of the Federal government, we may hold ourselves excused from defining the privileges and immunities of citizens of the United States which no State can abridge, until some case involving those privileges may make it necessary to do so.

But lest it should be said that no such privileges and immunities are to be found if those we have been considering are excluded, we venture to suggest some which own their existence to the Federal government, its National character, its Constitution, or its laws.

One of these is well described in the case of *Crandall v. Nevada.* [73 U.S. 35 (1867).] It is said to be the right of the citizen of this great country, protected by implied guarantees of its Constitution, 'to come to the seat of government to assert any claim he may have upon that government, to transact any business he may have with it, to seek its protection, to share its offices, to engage in administering its functions. He has the right of free access to its seaports, through which all operations of foreign commerce are conducted, to the subtreasuries, land offices, and courts of justice in the several States.' ***

Another privilege of a citizen of the United States is to demand the care and protection of the Federal government over his life, liberty, and property when on the high seas or within the jurisdiction of a foreign government. Of this there can be no doubt, nor that the right depends upon his character as a citizen of the United States. The right to peaceably assemble and petition for redress of grievances, the privilege of the writ of habeas corpus, are rights of the citizen guaranteed by the Federal Constitution. The right to use the navigable waters of the United States, however they may penetrate the territory of the several States, all rights secured to our citizens by treaties with foreign nations, are dependent upon citizenship of the United States, and not citizenship of a State. One of these privileges is conferred by the very article under consideration. It is that a citizen of the United States can, of his own volition, become a citizen of any State of the Union by a bona fide residence therein, with the same rights as other citizens of that State. To these may be added the rights secured by the thirteenth and fifteenth articles of amendment, and by the other clause of the fourteenth, next to be considered.

But it is useless to pursue this branch of the inquiry, since we are of opinion that the rights claimed by these plaintiffs in error, if they have any existence, are not privileges and immunities of citizens of the United States within the meaning of the clause of the fourteenth amendment under consideration. ***

[The Court also rejected the Petitioners' claims against the statute under the Thirteenth and Fourteenth Amendments.]

MR. JUSTICE FIELD, dissenting:

*** The amendment does not attempt to confer any new privileges or immunities upon citizens, or to enumerate or define those already existing. It assumes that there are such privileges and immunities which belong of right to citizens as such, and ordains that they shall not be abridged by State legislation. If this inhibition has no reference to privileges and immunities of this character, but only refers, as held by the majority of the court in their opinion, to such privileges and immunities as were before its adoption specially designated in the Constitution or necessarily implied as belonging to citizens of the United States, it was a vain and idle enactment, which accomplished nothing, and most unnecessarily excited Congress and the people on its passage. With privileges and immunities thus designated or implied no State could ever have interfered by its laws, and no new constitutional provision was required to inhibit such interference. The supremacy of the Constitution and the laws of the United States always controlled any State legislation of that character. But if the amendment refers to the natural and inalienable rights which belong to all citizens, the inhibition has a profound significance and consequence.

What, then, are the privileges and immunities which are secured against abridgment by State legislation? *** In *Corfield v. Coryell*, MR. JUSTICE WASHINGTON said he had "no hesitation in confining these expressions to those privileges and immunities which were, in their nature, fundamental; which belong of right to citizens of all free governments, and which have at all times been enjoyed by the citizens of the several States which compose the Union, from the time of their becoming free, independent, and sovereign." *** This appears to me to be a sound construction of the clause in question. The privileges and immunities designated are *those which of right belong to the citizens of all free governments*. Clearly among these must be placed the right to pursue a lawful employment in a lawful manner, without other restraint than such as equally affects all persons. ***

What [Article IV, § 2] did for the protection of the citizens of one State against hostile and discriminating legislation of other States, the fourteenth amendment does for the protection of every citizen of the United States against hostile and discriminating legislation against him in favor of others, whether they reside in the same or in different States. If under the fourth article of the Constitution equality of privileges and immunities is secured between citizens of different States, under the fourteenth amendment the same equality is secured between citizens of the United States.

It will not be pretended that under the fourth article of the Constitution any State could create a monopoly in any known trade or manufacture in favor of her own citizens, or any portion of them, which would exclude an equal participation *** by citizens of other States. She could not confer, for example, upon any of her citizens the sole right to manufacture shoes, or boots, or silk, or the sole right to sell those articles in the State so as to exclude non-resident citizens from engaging in a similar manufacture or sale. *** Now, what [Article IV, § 2] does for the protection of citizens of one State against the creation of monopolies in favor of citizens of other States, the fourteenth amendment does for the protection of every citizen of the United States against the creation of any monopoly whatever. The privileges and immunities of citizens of the United States, of every one of them, is secured against abridgment in any form by any State. The fourteenth amendment places them under the guardianship of the National authority. All monopolies in any known trade or manufacture are an invasion of these privileges, for they encroach upon the liberty of citizens to acquire property and pursue happiness. ***

So fundamental has this privilege of every citizen to be free from disparaging and unequal enactments, in the pursuit of the ordinary avocations of life, been regarded, that few instances have arisen where the principle has been so far violated as to call for the interposition of the courts. But whenever this has occurred, with the exception of the present cases from Louisiana, which are the most barefaced and flagrant of all, the enactment interfering with the privilege of the citizen has been pronounced illegal and void. ***

This equality of right, with exemption from all disparaging and partial enactments, in the lawful pursuits of life, throughout the whole country, is the distinguishing privilege of citizens of the United States. To them, everywhere, all pursuits, all professions, all avocations are open without other restrictions than such as are imposed equally upon all others of the same age, sex, and condition. The State may prescribe such regulations for every pursuit and calling of life as will promote the public health, secure the good order and advance the general prosperity of society, but when once prescribed, the pursuit or calling must be free to be followed by every citizen who is within the conditions designated, and will conform to the regulations. This is the fundamental idea upon which our institutions rest, and unless adhered to in the legislation of the country our government will be a republic only in name. The fourteenth amendment, in my judgment, makes it essential to the validity of the legislation of every State that this equality of right should be respected. ***

I am authorized by the CHIEF JUSTICE, MR. JUSTICE SWAYNE, and MR. JUSTICE BRADLEY, to state that they concur with me in this dissenting opinion.

MR. JUSTICE BRADLEY, also dissenting:

*** The right of a State to regulate the conduct of its citizens is undoubtedly a very broad and extensive one, and not to be lightly restricted. But there are certain fundamental rights which this right of regulation cannot infringe. It may prescribe the manner of their exercise, but it cannot subvert the rights themselves. I speak now of the rights of citizens of any free government. Granting for the present that the citizens of one government cannot claim the privileges of citizens in another government; that prior to the union of our North American States the citizens of one State could not claim the privileges of citizens in another State; or, that after the union was formed the citizens of the United States, as such, could not claim the privileges of citizens in any particular State; yet the citizens of each of the States and the citizens of the United States would be entitled to certain privileges and immunities as citizens, at the hands of their own government—privileges and immunities which their own governments respectively would be bound to respect and maintain. In this free country, the people of which inherited certain traditionary rights and privileges from their ancestors, citizenship means something. It has certain privileges and immunities attached to it which the government, whether restricted by express or implied limitations, cannot take away or impair. It may do so temporarily by force, but it cannot do so by right. And these privileges and immunities attach as well to citizenship of the United States as to citizenship of the States.

The people of this country brought with them to its shores the rights of Englishmen; the rights which had been wrested from English sovereigns at various periods of the nation's history. *** Blackstone classifies these fundamental rights under three heads, as the absolute rights of individuals, to wit: the right of personal security, the right of personal liberty, and the right of private property. And of the last he says: 'The third absolute right, inherent in every Englishman, is that of property, which consists in the free use, enjoyment, and disposal of all his acquisitions, without any control or diminution save only by the laws of the land.' *** These are the fundamental rights which can only be taken away by due process of law, and which can only be interfered with, or the enjoyment of which can only be modified, by lawful regulations necessary or proper for the mutual good of all; and these rights, I contend, belong to the citizens of every free government.

*** [The] right to choose one's calling is an essential part of that liberty which it is the object of government to protect; and a calling, when chosen, is a man's property and right. Liberty and property are not protected where these rights are arbitrarily assailed. *** The keeping of a slaughter-house is part of, and incidental to, the trade of a butcher—one of the ordinary occupations of human life. To compel a butcher, or rather all the butchers of a large city and an extensive district, to slaughter their cattle in another person's slaughter-house and pay him a toll therefor, is such a restriction upon the trade as materially to interfere with its prosecution. It is onerous, unreasonable, arbitrary, and unjust. It has none of the qualities of a police regulation. If it were really a police regulation, it would undoubtedly be within the power of the legislature. That portion of the act which requires all slaughter-houses to be located below the city, and to be subject to inspection, &c., is clearly a police regulation. That portion which allows no one but the favored company to build, own, or have slaughter-houses is not a police regulation, and has not the faintest semblance of one. It is one of those arbitrary and unjust laws made in the interest of a few scheming individuals, by which some of the Southern States have, within the past few years, been so deplorably oppressed and impoverished. It seems to me strange that it can be viewed in any other light.

*** [G]reat fears are expressed that this construction of the amendment will lead to enactments by Congress interfering with the internal affairs of the States, and establishing therein civil and criminal codes of law for the government of the citizens, and thus abolishing the State governments in everything but name; or else, that it will lead the Federal courts to draw to their cognizance the supervision of State tribunals on every subject of judicial inquiry, on the plea of ascertaining whether the privileges and immunities of citizens have not been abridged.

In my judgment no such practical inconveniences would arise. Very little, if any, legislation on the part of Congress would be required to carry the amendment into effect. *** As the privileges and immunities protected are only those fundamental ones which belong to every citizen, they would soon become so far defined as to cause but a slight accumulation of business in the Federal courts. ***

MR. JUSTICE SWAYNE, dissenting. [omitted]

Notes

1. **Some "Irrelevant" History.** What did the drafters and ratifiers of the Fourteenth Amendment intend to accomplish through the Privileges or

Immunities Clause? Granting to the former slaves the same rights which white citizens had enjoyed was a paramount consideration. But what were these rights? Consider the following possibilities:

(a) Many historians have argued that the clause was intended to constitutionalize, and thus insulate from congressional reversal, the Civil Rights Act of 1866, which guaranteed "all persons born in the United States the same rights as white citizens to make and enforce contracts, to sue, be parties, and give evidence, to inherit, purchase, lease, sell, hold, and convey real and personal property, and to full and equal benefit of all laws and proceedings for the security of person and property *** and shall be subject to like punishment, pains, and penalties, and to none other." *The Slaughter-House Cases* read the Privileges or Immunities Clause much more narrowly than this statute even though, on its face, the Clause might easily have been read more broadly than the statute.

(b) The clause could have been read as elevating to national status all the rights which might previously have been given to any citizen under any state law. Do you see any problem with such an interpretation?

(c) Should the clause be read to accord with the views of its chief sponsor in Congress, Representative Bingham, who said: "the privileges and immunities of citizens of the United States [are] chiefly defined in the first eight amendments to the Constitution"? Cong. Globe, 42d Cong., 1st Sess., app. 85 (1871). Should we be concerned that Representative Bingham's view seems anomalous in light of the fact that the similarly-phrased Privileges and Immunities Clause of Article IV preceded the Bill of Rights? Does this concern fade if we view the Bill of Rights as merely expressive of generally understood natural law rights? But then there would have been no need for a written Bill of Rights, would there?

(d) Assuming a rough congruence between the Article IV Privileges and Immunities Clause and the Fourteenth Amendment Privileges or Immunities Clause would not help to clarify the clause much. Remember the vagueness of the former clause from the *City of Camden* case?

(e) The Privileges or Immunities Clause stated only vague aspirations. Perhaps Representative Bingham was a sloppy draftsman, perhaps he and other astute politicians thought vagueness made ratification more likely, or perhaps the clause was deliberately left to be filled out by the judiciary over time.

(f) One exploration of the clause's history concludes that it "ensures that all the citizens of every state shall be entitled to the privileges and immunities of state citizenship, thereby mandating equality of rights." John Harrison, "Reconstructing the Privileges or Immunities Clause," 101 YALE L.J. 1385 (1992). So read, would the clause support the existence of any nationwide privileges and immunities of all United States citizens (either trivial ones, as *The Slaughter-House Cases* held, or substantial ones, considered earlier in this note)?

2. Ironies of the *Slaughter-House Cases*.

   · The plaintiffs were white, not black.

- The plaintiffs were asserting business rights, not personal rights.

- The plaintiffs did not pursue a Dormant Commerce Clause theory.

- The Court undid (or at least delayed) the transformation of the Constitution by the post-Civil War amendments.

3.   **The "Dead Hand" of the** *Slaughter-House Cases*. The untimely death of the substantive rights which might have been articulated as "Privileges or Immunities" has been a driving force in the twentieth century for expansive interpretation of two other clauses of Section 1 of the Fourteenth Amendment: the Due Process Clause and the Equal Protection Clause. As you read the following case, and again after you read Chapters VIII and IX of these materials, consider whether the Privileges or Immunities Clause might provide a different (and perhaps more straightforward) source of some or all the substantive due process rights the Court has created over the past century.

SAENZ v. ROE
526 U.S. 489, 119 S.Ct. 1518, 143 L.Ed.2d 689 (1999).

JUSTICE STEVENS delivered the opinion of the Court.

In 1992, California enacted a statute limiting the maximum welfare benefits available to newly arrived residents. The scheme limits the amount payable to a family that has resided in the State for less than 12 months to the amount payable by the State of the family's prior residence. ***

On December 21, 1992, three California residents who were eligible for AFDC benefits filed an action in the Eastern District of California challenging the constitutionality of the durational residency requirement in § 11450.03. Each plaintiff alleged that she had recently moved to California to live with relatives in order to escape abusive family circumstances. *** Relying primarily on our decisions in *Shapiro v. Thompson*, 394 U.S. 618 (1969), and *Zobel v. Williams*, 457 U.S. 55 (1982), [the courts below] concluded that the statute placed "a penalty on the decision of new residents to migrate to the State and be treated on an equal basis with existing residents." ***

III

The word "travel" is not found in the text of the Constitution. Yet the "constitutional right to travel from one State to another" is firmly embedded in our jurisprudence. Indeed, as JUSTICE STEWART reminded us in *Shapiro v. Thompson*, 394 U.S. 618 (1969), the right is so important that it is "assertable against private interference as well as governmental action *** a virtually unconditional personal right, guaranteed by the Constitution to us all." (concurring opinion).

In *Shapiro*, we reviewed the constitutionality of three statutory provisions that denied welfare assistance to residents of Connecticut, the District of Columbia, and Pennsylvania, who had resided within those respective jurisdictions less than one year immediately preceding their applications for assistance. Without pausing to identify the specific source of the right, we began by noting that the Court had long "recognized that the nature of our Federal Union and our constitutional concepts of personal liberty unite to require that all citizens be free to travel throughout the length and breadth of our land uninhibited by statutes, rules, or regulations which unreasonably burden or restrict this movement." We squarely held that it was "constitutionally impermissible" for a State to enact durational residency requirements for the purpose of inhibiting the migration by needy persons into the State. We further held that a classification that had the effect of imposing a penalty on the exercise of the right to travel violated the Equal Protection Clause "unless shown to be necessary to promote a compelling governmental interest," and that no such showing had been made.

In this case California argues that § 11450.03 was not enacted for the impermissible purpose of inhibiting migration by needy persons and that, unlike the legislation reviewed in *Shapiro*, it does not penalize the right to travel because new arrivals are not ineligible for benefits during their first year of residence. California submits that, instead of being subjected to the strictest scrutiny, the statute should be upheld if it is supported by a rational basis and that the State's legitimate interest in saving over $10 million a year satisfies that test. Although the United States did not elect to participate in the proceedings in the District Court or the Court of Appeals, it has participated as amicus curiae in this Court. It has advanced the novel argument that the enactment of PRWORA allows the States to adopt a "specialized choice-of-law-type provision" that "should be subject to an intermediate level of constitutional review," merely requiring that durational residency requirements be "substantially related to an important governmental objective." The debate about the appropriate standard of review, together with the potential relevance of the federal statute, persuades us that it will be useful to focus on the source of the constitutional right on which respondents rely.

IV

The "right to travel" discussed in our cases embraces at least three different components. It protects the right of a citizen of one State to enter and to leave another State, the right to be treated as a welcome visitor rather than an unfriendly alien when temporarily present in the second State, and, for those travelers who elect to become permanent residents, the right to be treated like other citizens of that State.

It was the right to go from one place to another, including the right to cross state borders while en route, that was vindicated in *Edwards v. California*, 314 U.S. 160 (1941), which invalidated a state law that impeded the free interstate passage of the indigent. We reaffirmed that right in *United States v. Guest*, 383 U.S. 745 (1966), which afforded protection to the "'right to travel freely to and from the State of Georgia and to use highway facilities and other instrumentalities of interstate commerce within the State of Georgia.'" Given that § 11450.03 imposed no obstacle to respondents' entry into California, we think the State is correct when it argues that the statute does not directly impair the exercise of the right to free interstate movement.

For the purposes of this case, therefore, we need not identify the source of that particular right in the text of the Constitution. The right of "free ingress and regress to and from" neighboring States, which was expressly mentioned in the text of the Articles of Confederation, may simply have been "conceived from the beginning to be a necessary concomitant of the stronger Union the Constitution created."

The second component of the right to travel is, however, expressly protected by the text of the Constitution. The first sentence of Article IV, § 2, provides:

> "The Citizens of each State shall be entitled to all Privileges
> and Immunities of Citizens in the several States."

Thus, by virtue of a person's state citizenship, a citizen of one State who travels in other States, intending to return home at the end of his journey, is entitled to enjoy the "Privileges and Immunities of Citizens in the several States" that he visits.[14] *** It provides important protections for nonresidents who enter a State whether to obtain employment, *Hicklin v. Orbeck,* 437 U.S. 518 (1978), to procure medical services, *Doe v. Bolton,* 410 U.S. 179, 200 (1973), or even to engage in commercial shrimp fishing, *Toomer v. Witsell,* 334 U.S. 385 (1948). Those protections are not "absolute," but the Clause "does bar discrimination against citizens of other States where there is no substantial reason for the discrimination beyond the mere fact that they are citizens of other States." There may be a substantial reason for requiring the nonresident to pay more than the resident for a hunting license, see *Baldwin v. Fish and Game Comm'n of Mont.,* 436 U.S. 371, 390–391 (1978), or to enroll in the state university, see *Vlandis v. Kline,* 412 U.S. 441 (1973), but our cases have not identified any acceptable reason for qualifying the protection afforded by the Clause for "the 'citizen of State A who ventures into State B' to settle there and establish a home." *Zobel,* 457 U.S. at 74 (O'CONNOR, J., concurring in judgment). Permissible justifications for discrimination between residents and nonresidents are simply inapplicable to a nonresident's exercise of the right to move into another State and become a resident of that State.

What is at issue in this case, then, is this third aspect of the right to travel—the right of the newly arrived citizen to the same privileges and immunities enjoyed by other citizens of the same State. That right is protected not only by the new arrival's status as a state citizen, but also by her status as a citizen of the United States.[15] ***

---

[14] *Corfield v. Coryell,* 6 F. Cas. 546 (C.C.E.D.Pa.1823) (WASHINGTON, J., on circuit) ("fundamental" rights protected by the privileges and immunities clause include "the right of a citizen of one state to pass through, or to reside in any other state").

[15] The Framers of the Fourteenth Amendment modeled this Clause upon the "Privileges and Immunities" Clause found in Article IV. Cong. Globe, 39th Cong., 1st Sess., 1033–1034 (1866) (statement of Rep. Bingham). In *Dred Scott v. Sandford,* 60 U.S. 393 (1857), this Court had limited the protection of Article IV to rights under state law and concluded that free blacks could not claim citizenship. The Fourteenth Amendment overruled this decision. The Amendment's Privileges and Immunities Clause and Citizenship Clause guaranteed the rights of newly freed

Despite fundamentally differing views concerning the coverage of the Privileges or Immunities Clause of the Fourteenth Amendment, most notably expressed in the majority and dissenting opinions in the *Slaughter-House Cases*, 83 U.S. 36 (1873), it has always been common ground that this Clause protects the third component of the right to travel. Writing for the majority in the *Slaughter-House Cases*, JUSTICE MILLER explained that one of the privileges conferred by this Clause "is that a citizen of the United States can, of his own volition, become a citizen of any State of the Union by a bona fide residence therein, with the same rights as other citizens of that State." JUSTICE BRADLEY, in dissent, used even stronger language to make the same point:

> "The states have not now, if they ever had, any power to restrict their citizenship to any classes or persons. A citizen of the United States has a perfect constitutional right to go to and reside in any State he chooses, and to claim citizenship therein, and an equality of rights with every other citizen; and the whole power of the nation is pledged to sustain him in that right. He is not bound to cringe to any superior, or to pray for any act of grace, as a means of enjoying all the rights and privileges enjoyed by other citizens."

That newly arrived citizens "have two political capacities, one state and one federal," adds special force to their claim that they have the same rights as others who share their citizenship. Neither mere rationality nor some intermediate standard of review should be used to judge the constitutionality of a state rule that discriminates against some of its citizens because they have been domiciled in the State for less than a year. The appropriate standard may be more categorical than that articulated in *Shapiro*, but it is surely no less strict.

V

Because this case involves discrimination against citizens who have completed their interstate travel, the State's argument that its welfare scheme affects the right to travel only "incidentally" is beside the point. Were we concerned solely with actual deterrence to migration, we might be persuaded that a partial withholding of benefits constitutes a lesser incursion on the right to travel than an outright denial of all benefits. See *Dunn v. Blumstein*, 405 U.S. 330, 339 (1972). But since the right to travel embraces the citizen's right to be treated equally in her new State of residence, the discriminatory classification is itself a penalty.

It is undisputed that respondents and the members of the class that they represent are citizens of California and that their need for welfare benefits is unrelated to the length of time that they have resided in California. We thus have no occasion to consider what weight might be given to a citizen's length of residence if the bona fides of her claim to state citizenship were questioned.

---

black citizens by ensuring that they could claim the state citizenship of any State in which they resided and by precluding that State from abridging their rights of national citizenship.

Moreover, because whatever benefits they receive will be consumed while they remain in California, there is no danger that recognition of their claim will encourage citizens of other States to establish residency for just long enough to acquire some readily portable benefit, such as a divorce or a college education, that will be enjoyed after they return to their original domicile. See, *e.g., Sosna v. Iowa*, 419 U.S. 393 (1975); *Vlandis v. Kline*, 412 U.S. 441 (1973).

The classifications challenged in this case—and there are many—are defined entirely by (a) the period of residency in California and (b) the location of the prior residences of the disfavored class members. The favored class of beneficiaries includes all eligible California citizens who have resided there for at least one year, plus those new arrivals who last resided in another country or in a State that provides benefits at least as generous as California's. Thus, within the broad category of citizens who resided in California for less than a year, there are many who are treated like lifetime residents. And within the broad sub-category of new arrivals who are treated less favorably, there are many smaller classes whose benefit levels are determined by the law of the States from whence they came. To justify § 11450.03, California must therefore explain not only why it is sound fiscal policy to discriminate against those who have been citizens for less than a year, but also why it is permissible to apply such a variety of rules within that class.

These classifications may not be justified by a purpose to deter welfare applicants from migrating to California for three reasons. First, although it is reasonable to assume that some persons may be motivated to move for the purpose of obtaining higher benefits, the empirical evidence reviewed by the District Judge, which takes into account the high cost of living in California, indicates that the number of such persons is quite small—surely not large enough to justify a burden on those who had no such motive. Second, California has represented to the Court that the legislation was not enacted for any such reason. Third, even if it were, as we squarely held in *Shapiro v. Thompson*, 394 U.S. 618 (1969), such a purpose would be unequivocally impermissible.

Disavowing any desire to fence out the indigent, California has instead advanced an entirely fiscal justification ***. The question is not whether such saving is a legitimate purpose but whether the State may accomplish that end by the discriminatory means it has chosen. An evenhanded, across-the-board reduction of about 72 cents per month for every beneficiary would produce the same result. But our negative answer to the question does not rest on the weakness of the State's purported fiscal justification. It rests on the fact that the Citizenship Clause of the Fourteenth Amendment expressly equates citizenship with residence: "That Clause does not provide for, and does not allow for, degrees of citizenship based on length of residence." *Zobel.* It is equally clear that the Clause does not tolerate a hierarchy of 45 subclasses of similarly situated citizens based on the location of their prior residence. Thus § 11450.03 is doubly vulnerable: Neither the duration of respondents' California residence, nor the identity of their prior States of residence, has any relevance to their need for benefits. Nor do those factors bear any relationship to the State's interest in making an equitable allocation of the funds to be distributed among its needy citizens. As in *Shapiro*, we reject any contributory rationale for the denial of benefits to new residents:

"But we need not rest on the particular facts of these cases. Appellants' reasoning would logically permit the State to bar new residents from schools, parks, and libraries or deprive them of police and fire protection. Indeed it would permit the State to apportion all benefits and services according to the past tax contributions of its citizens."

In short, the State's legitimate interest in saving money provides no justification for its decision to discriminate among equally eligible citizens.

VI

The question that remains is whether congressional approval of durational residency requirements in the 1996 amendment to the Social Security Act somehow resuscitates the constitutionality of § 11450.03. That question is readily answered, for we have consistently held that Congress may not authorize the States to violate the Fourteenth Amendment. Moreover, the protection afforded to the citizen by the Citizenship Clause of that Amendment is a limitation on the powers of the National Government as well as the States. *** Citizens of the United States, whether rich or poor, have the right to choose to be citizens "of the State wherein they reside." U.S. Const., Amdt. 14, § 1. The States, however, do not have any right to select their citizens. The Fourteenth Amendment, like the Constitution itself, was, as JUSTICE CARDOZO put it, "framed upon the theory that the peoples of the several states must sink or swim together, and that in the long run prosperity and salvation are in union and not division." *Baldwin v. G. A. F. Seelig, Inc.*, 294 U.S. 511, 523 (1935). ***

CHIEF JUSTICE REHNQUIST, with whom JUSTICE THOMAS joins, dissenting.

The Court today breathes new life into the previously dormant Privileges or Immunities Clause of the Fourteenth Amendment—a Clause relied upon by this Court in only one other decision, *Colgate v. Harvey*, 296 U.S. 404 (1935), overruled five years later by *Madden v. Kentucky*, 309 U.S. 83 (1940). It uses this Clause to strike down what I believe is a reasonable measure falling under the head of a "good-faith residency requirement." Because I do not think any provision of the Constitution—and surely not a provision relied upon for only the second time since its enactment 130 years ago—requires this result, I dissent. ***

But I cannot see how the right to become a citizen of another State is a necessary "component" of the right to travel, or why the Court tries to marry these separate and distinct rights. A person is no longer "traveling" in any sense of the word when he finishes his journey to a State which he plans to make his home. Indeed, under the Court's logic, the protections of the Privileges or Immunities Clause recognized in this case come into play only when an individual stops traveling with the intent to remain and become a citizen of a new State. The right to travel and the right to become a citizen are distinct, their relationship is not reciprocal, and one is not a "component" of the other. Indeed, the same dicta from the *Slaughter-House Cases* quoted by the Court actually treats the right to become a citizen and the right to travel as separate and distinct rights under the Privileges or Immunities Clause of the Fourteenth Amendment. At most, restrictions on an individual's right to become a citizen indirectly affect his calculus in deciding whether to exercise his right to travel in the first place, but such an attenuated and uncertain relationship is no ground for folding one right into the other.

No doubt the Court has, in the past 30 years, essentially conflated the right to travel with the right to equal state citizenship in striking down durational residence requirements similar to the one challenged here. These cases marked a sharp departure from the Court's prior right-to-travel cases because in none of them was travel itself prohibited. Instead, the Court in these cases held that restricting the provision of welfare benefits, votes, or certain medical benefits to new citizens for a limited time impermissibly "penalized" them under the Equal Protection Clause of the Fourteenth Amendment for having exercised their right to travel. The Court thus settled for deciding what restrictions amounted to "deprivations of very important benefits and rights" that operated to indirectly "penalize" the right to travel. In other cases, the Court recognized that laws dividing new and old residents had little to do with the right to travel and merely triggered an inquiry into whether the resulting classification rationally furthered a legitimate government purpose. While *Zobel* and *Hooper* reached the wrong result in my view, they at least put the Court on the proper track in identifying exactly what interests it was protecting; namely, the right of individuals not to be subject to unjustifiable classifications as opposed to infringements on the right to travel.

The Court today tries to clear much of the underbrush created by these prior right-to-travel cases, abandoning its effort to define what residence requirements deprive individuals of "important rights and benefits" or "penalize" the right to travel. Under its new analytical framework, a State, outside certain ill-defined circumstances, cannot classify its citizens by the length of their residence in the State without offending the Privileges or Immunities Clause of the Fourteenth Amendment. The Court thus departs from *Shapiro* and its progeny, and, while paying lipservice to the right to travel, the Court does little to explain how the right to travel is involved at all. Instead, as the Court's analysis clearly demonstrates, this case is only about respondents' right to immediately enjoy all the privileges of being a California citizen in relation to that State's ability to test the good-faith assertion of this right. The Court has thus come full circle by effectively disavowing the analysis of *Shapiro*, segregating the right to travel and the rights secured by Article IV from the right to become a citizen under the Privileges or Immunities Clause, and then testing the residence requirement here against this latter right. For all its misplaced efforts to fold the right to become a citizen into the right to travel, the Court has essentially returned to its original understanding of the right to travel.

In unearthing from its tomb the right to become a state citizen and to be treated equally in the new State of residence, however, the Court ignores a State's need to assure that only persons who establish a bona fide residence receive the benefits provided to current residents of the State. The *Slaughter-House* dicta at the core of the Court's analysis specifically conditions a United States citizen's right to "become a citizen of any state of the Union" and to enjoy the "same rights as other citizens of that State" on the establishment of a "bona fide residence therein." Even when redefining the right to travel in *Shapiro* and its progeny, the Court has "always carefully distinguished between bona fide residence requirements, which seek to differentiate between residents and nonresidents, and residence requirements, such as durational, fixed date, and fixed point residence requirements, which treat established residents differently based on the time they migrated into the State." ***

If States can require individuals to reside in-state for a year before exercising the right to educational benefits, the right to terminate a marriage, or the right to vote in primary elections that all other state citizens enjoy, then States may surely do the same for welfare benefits. Indeed, there is no material difference between a 1–year residence requirement applied to the level of welfare benefits given out by a State, and the same requirement applied to the level of tuition subsidies at a state university. The welfare payment here and in-state tuition rates are cash subsidies provided to a limited class of people, and California's standard of living and higher education system make both subsidies quite attractive. Durational residence requirements were upheld when used to regulate the provision of higher education subsidies, and the same deference should be given in the case of welfare payments. See *Dandridge v. Williams,* 397 U.S. 471 (1970) ("The Constitution does not empower this Court to second-guess state officials charged with the difficult responsibility of allocating limited public welfare funds among the myriad of potential recipients").

The Court today recognizes that States retain the ability to determine the bona fides of an individual's claim to residence, but then tries to avoid the issue. It asserts that because respondents' need for welfare benefits is unrelated to the length of time they have resided in California, it has "no occasion to consider what weight might be given to a citizen's length of residence if the bona fides of her claim to state citizenship were questioned." But I do not understand how the absence of a link between need and length of residency bears on the State's ability to objectively test respondents' resolve to stay in California. There is no link between the need for an education or for a divorce and the length of residence, and yet States may use length of residence as an objective yardstick to channel their benefits to those whose intent to stay is legitimate.

In one respect, the State has a greater need to require a durational residence for welfare benefits than for college eligibility. The impact of a large number of new residents who immediately seek welfare payments will have a far greater impact on a State's operating budget than the impact of new residents seeking to attend a state university. In the case of the welfare recipients, a modest durational residence requirement to allow for the completion of an annual legislative budget cycle gives the State time to decide how to finance the increased obligations.

The Court tries to distinguish education and divorce benefits by contending that the welfare payment here will be consumed in California, while a college education or a divorce produces benefits that are "portable" and can be enjoyed after individuals return to their original domicile. But this "you can't take it with you" distinction is more apparent than real, and offers little guidance to lower courts who must apply this rationale in the future. Welfare payments are a form of insurance, giving impoverished individuals and their families the means to meet the demands of daily life while they receive the necessary training, education, and time to look for a job. The cash itself will no doubt be spent in California, but the benefits from receiving this income and having the opportunity to become employed or employable will stick with the welfare recipients if they stay in California or go back to their true domiciles. Similarly, tuition subsidies are "consumed" in-state but the recipient takes the benefits of a college education with him wherever he goes. A welfare subsidy is thus as much an investment in human capital as is a tuition subsidy, and their attendant benefits are just as "portable." More importantly, this foray into social economics demonstrates that the line drawn by the Court borders on the metaphysical, and requires lower courts to plumb the policies animating certain benefits like welfare to define their "essence" and hence their "portability." As this Court wisely recognized almost 30 years ago, "the intractable economic, social, and even philosophical problems presented by public welfare assistance programs are not the business of this Court." *Dandridge*, 397 U.S. at 487.

I therefore believe that the durational residence requirement challenged here is a permissible exercise of the State's power to "assur[e] that services provided for its residents are enjoyed only by residents." *** Finally, Congress' express approval in 42 U.S.C. § 604(c) of durational residence requirements for welfare recipients like the one established by California only goes to show the reasonableness of a law like § 11450.03. *** California has reasonably exercised it through an objective, narrowly tailored residence requirement. I see nothing in the Constitution that should prevent the enforcement of that requirement.

JUSTICE THOMAS, with whom the CHIEF JUSTICE joins, dissenting.

*** [T]he Court all but read the Privileges or Immunities Clause out of the Constitution in the *Slaughter-House Cases*, 83 U.S. 36 (1873). *** Unlike the majority, I would look to history to ascertain the original meaning of the Clause.[11] At least in American law, the phrase (or its close approximation) appears to stem from the 1606 Charter of Virginia, which provided that "all and every the Persons being our Subjects, which shall dwell and inhabit within every or any of the said several Colonies *** shall HAVE and enjoy all Liberties, Franchises, and Immunities *** as if they had been abiding and

---

[11] Legal scholars agree on little beyond the conclusion that the Clause does not mean what the Court said it meant in 1873.

born, within this our Realme of England." Other colonial charters contained similar guarantees. Years later, as tensions between England and the American Colonies increased, the colonists adopted resolutions reasserting their entitlement to the privileges or immunities of English citizenship.

The colonists' repeated assertions that they maintained the rights, privileges and immunities of persons "born within the realm of England" and "natural born" persons suggests that, at the time of the founding, the terms "privileges" and "immunities" (and their counterparts) were understood to refer to those fundamental rights and liberties specifically enjoyed by English citizens, and more broadly, by all persons. Presumably members of the Second Continental Congress so understood these terms when they employed them in the Articles of Confederation, which guaranteed that "the free inhabitants of each of these States, paupers, vagabonds and fugitives from justice excepted, shall be entitled to all privileges and immunities of free citizens in the several States." Art. IV. The Constitution, which superceded the Articles of Confederation, similarly guarantees that "[t]he Citizens of each State shall be entitled to all Privileges and Immunities of Citizens in the several States." Art. IV, § 2, cl. 1.

JUSTICE BUSHROD WASHINGTON's landmark opinion in *Corfield v. Coryell* reflects this historical understanding. In *Corfield*, a citizen of Pennsylvania challenged a New Jersey law that prohibited any person who was not an "actual inhabitant and resident" of New Jersey from harvesting oysters from New Jersey waters. JUSTICE WASHINGTON, sitting as Circuit Justice, rejected the argument that the New Jersey law violated Article IV's Privileges and Immunities Clause. He reasoned, "we cannot accede to the proposition *** that, under this provision of the constitution, the citizens of the several states are permitted to participate in all the rights which belong exclusively to the citizens of any other particular state, merely upon the ground that they are enjoyed by those citizens." Instead, Washington concluded:

> "We feel no hesitation in confining these expressions to those privileges and immunities which are, in their nature, fundamental; which belong, of right, to the citizens of all free governments; and which have, at all times, been enjoyed by the citizens of the several states which compose this Union, from the time of their becoming free, independent, and sovereign. What these fundamental principles are, it would perhaps be more tedious than difficult to enumerate. They may, however, be all comprehended under the following general heads: Protection by the government; the enjoyment of life and liberty, with the right to acquire and possess property of every kind, and to pursue and obtain happiness and safety; subject nevertheless to such restraints as the government may justly prescribe for the general good of the whole. The right of a citizen of one state to pass through, or to reside in any other state, for purposes of trade, agriculture, professional pursuits, or otherwise; to claim the benefit of the writ of habeas corpus; to institute and maintain actions of any kind in the courts of the state; *** and an exemption

from higher taxes or impositions than are paid by the other citizens of the state; *** the elective franchise, as regulated and established by the laws or constitution of the state in which it is to be exercised. These, and many others which might be mentioned, are, strictly speaking, privileges and immunities."

Washington rejected the proposition that the Privileges and Immunities Clause guaranteed equal access to all public benefits (such as the right to harvest oysters in public waters) that a State chooses to make available. Instead, he endorsed the colonial-era conception of the terms "privileges" and "immunities," concluding that Article IV encompassed only *fundamental* rights that belong to all citizens of the United States.

JUSTICE WASHINGTON's opinion in *Corfield* indisputably influenced the Members of Congress who enacted the Fourteenth Amendment. When Congress gathered to debate the Fourteenth Amendment, members frequently, if not as a matter of course, appealed to *Corfield*, arguing that the Amendment was necessary to guarantee the fundamental rights that JUSTICE WASHINGTON identified in his opinion. *** That Members of the 39th Congress appear to have endorsed the wisdom of JUSTICE WASHINGTON's opinion does not, standing alone, provide dispositive insight into their understanding of the Fourteenth Amendment's Privileges or Immunities Clause. Nevertheless, their repeated references to the *Corfield* decision, combined with what appears to be the historical understanding of the Clause's operative terms, supports the inference that, at the time the Fourteenth Amendment was adopted, people understood that "privileges or immunities of citizens" were fundamental rights, rather than every public benefit established by positive law. Accordingly, the majority's conclusion—that a State violates the Privileges or Immunities Clause when it "discriminates" against citizens who have been domiciled in the State for less than a year in the distribution of welfare benefit appears contrary to the original understanding and is dubious at best.

As THE CHIEF JUSTICE points out, it comes as quite a surprise that the majority relies on the Privileges or Immunities Clause at all in this case. *** Although the majority appears to breathe new life into the Clause today, it fails to address its historical underpinnings or its place in our constitutional jurisprudence. Because I believe that the demise of the Privileges or Immunities Clause has contributed in no small part to the current disarray of our Fourteenth Amendment jurisprudence, I would be open to reevaluating its meaning in an appropriate case. Before invoking the Clause, however, we should endeavor to understand what the framers of the Fourteenth Amendment thought that it meant. We should also consider whether the Clause should displace, rather than augment, portions of our equal protection and substantive due process jurisprudence. The majority's failure to consider these important questions raises the specter that the Privileges or Immunities Clause will become yet another convenient tool for inventing new rights, limited solely by the "predilections of those who happen at the time to be Members of this Court." *Moore v. East Cleveland*, 431 U.S. 494 (1977). ***

Notes

1. **Significance.** Try writing a one paragraph opinion affirming or reversing based on *Shapiro v. Thompson.* Why didn't the Court do this? The fact that it revisited a clause that had been "dead" for over 100 years may signify that the Court is moving toward reviving the Privileges or Immunities clause of the Fourteenth Amendment. Make sure you understand the points made in JUSTICE THOMAS' dissent, which are not addressed by the majority.

2. **Portability.** If you study the law of your State (rather than the federal and generic state law covered in this course) in your law school, how portable is your education? If a State premises health care benefits on durational residency, would that be constitutional after *Saenz?* Isn't your restored health portable? Many states once required durational residency for candidates sitting for the state bar exam. Suc h requirements were struck down based on *Shapiro.* I f reinstituted now, could a state argue that its bar membership is not portable under *Saenz?*

3. **Other Privileges and Immunities.** What privileges and immunities can you think of which this case might foreshadow? Reconsider this question after you have read the Substantive Due Process materials in the next chapter.

VIII

DUE PROCESS, PROCEDUREAL
AND SUBSTANTIVE

———

"Due process has not been reduced to any formula; its content cannot be determined by reference to any code. The best that can be said is that through the course of this Court's decisions it has represented the balance which our Nation, built upon postulates of respect for the liberty of the individual, has struck between that liberty and the demands of organized society. *** A decision of this Court which radically departs from it could not long survive, while a decision which builds on what has survived is likely to be sound. No formula could serve as a substitute, in this area, for judgment and restraint."

—JUSTICE HARLAN, dissenting in *Poe v. Ullmann* (1961)

A. PROCEDURAL DUE PROCESS

Most of the materials in this chapter concern "substantive," rather than "procedural," due process. If you think about it, the notion of substantive due process is an oxymoron, what Professor John Hart Ely called "red pastel greenness." More of substantive due process in Section B.

The more straightforward meaning of "due process" is procedural. In the criminal law field, there are elaborate procedures, many required by the Constitution, that the federal, state, and local authorities must observe before they can convict and imprison a person. These are components of due process in a broad sense, but criminal procedures are left to other courses and will not be examined here.

The following cases involve governmental procedures challenged as inadequate when someone is deprived of "life, liberty or property." As the cases show, it is essential to understand (1) when there is a constitutionally protected deprivation of "life, liberty or property" and (2) what process is due when there is such a deprivation. The cases presented here concern three matters that affect millions of people: government employment, government benefits, and immigration processes.

1. PROPERTY AND LIBERTY DEPRIVATIONS

With approximately 20% of the civilian workforce employed by federal, state, and local governments, dismissal of an employee is likely to be met with arguments that the employee's statutory or constitutional rights were violated. We have already looked at the constitutionality of federal substantive law protecting state and local employees (*Garcia* and *Garrett*), and restrictions on suits against state governments (*Seminole Tribe* and *Alden*). Does the Constitution, unaided by federal legislation, protect a "property" right of such employees in continued employment? The next case involves the due process clause of the Fourteenth Amendment, but the issues would be the same under the due process clause of the Fifth Amendment.

Two background cases mentioned in the opinion may be worth preliminary mention. The Court in *Board of Regents v. Roth*, 408 U.S. 564 (1972), said that "property interests protected by procedural due process extend well beyond actual ownership of real estate, chattels, or money" and that more than a "unilateral expectation" of continued employment was needed to constitute a property interest. The Court held that nonrenewal of a one-year contract to teach at a state university did not require any explanation because there was no reasonable expectation of continued employment. *Perry v. Sindermann*, 408 U.S. 593 (1972), decided the same day, involved a tenth-year employee who had worked under a succession of one-year contracts and was told that his contract would not be renewed. The Court said that this employee was entitled to attempt to prove that he had "de facto tenure," and that such an implied contract would be a property interest under the Fourteenth Amendment.

CLEVELAND BOARD OF EDUCATION
v. LOUDERMILL
470 U.S. 532, 105 S.Ct. 1487 , 84 L.Ed.2d 494 (1985).

JUSTICE WHITE delivered the opinion of the Court.

In these cases we consider what pretermination process must be accorded a public employee who can be discharged only for cause.

In 1979 the Cleveland Board of Education hired respondent James Loudermill as a security guard. On his job application, Loudermill stated that he had never been convicted of a felony. Eleven months later, as part of a routine examination of his employment records, the Board discovered that in fact Loudermill had been convicted of grand larceny in 1968. By letter dated November 3, 1980, the Board's Business Manager informed Loudermill that he had been dismissed because of his dishonesty in filling out the employment application. Loudermill was not afforded an opportunity to respond to the charge of dishonesty or to challenge his dismissal. On November 13, the Board adopted a resolution officially approving the discharge.

Under Ohio law, Loudermill was a "classified civil servant." Such employees can be terminated only for cause, and may obtain administrative review if discharged. Pursuant to this provision, Loudermill filed an appeal with the Cleveland Civil Service Commission on November 12. On July 20, 1981, the full Commission heard argument and orally announced that it would uphold the dismissal.

Respondents' federal constitutional claim depends on [his] having had a property right in continued employment. If [he] did, the State could not deprive [him] of this property without due process. *Board of Regents v. Roth*, 408 U.S. 564 (1972).

Property interests are not created by the Constitution, "they are created and their dimensions are defined by existing rules or understandings that stem from an independent source such as state law ***." *Roth*, at 577. The Ohio statute plainly creates such an interest. Respondents were "classified civil service employees," entitled to retain their positions "during good behavior and efficient service," who could not be dismissed "except *** for *** misfeasance, malfeasance, or nonfeasance in office." The statute plainly supports the conclusion, reached by both lower courts, that respondents possessed property rights in continued employment. Indeed, this question does not seem to have been disputed below.

The *** Board argues, however, that the property right is defined by, and conditioned on, the legislature's choice of procedures for its deprivation. The Board stresses that in addition to specifying the grounds for termination, the statute sets out procedures by which termination may take place. The procedures were adhered to in these cases. According to petitioner, "[t]o require additional procedures would in effect expand the scope of the property interest itself."

This argument, which was accepted by the District Court, has its genesis in the plurality opinion in *Arnett v. Kennedy*, 416 U.S. 134 (1974). *Arnett* involved a challenge by a former federal employee to the procedures by which he was dismissed. The plurality reasoned that where the legislation conferring the substantive right also sets out the procedural mechanism for enforcing that right, the two cannot be separated:

> "The employee's statutorily defined right is not a guarantee against removal without cause in the abstract, but such a guarantee as enforced by the procedures which Congress has designated for the determination of cause. *** " [W]here the grant of a substantive right is inextricably intertwined with the limitations on the procedures which are to be employed in determining that right, a litigant in the position of appellee must take the bitter with the sweet."

This view garnered three votes in *Arnett*, but was specifically rejected by the other six Justices. Since then, this theory has at times seemed to gather some additional support. More recently, however, the Court has clearly rejected it. In *Vitek v. Jones*, 445 U.S. 480, 491 (1980), we pointed out that "minimum [procedural] requirements [are] a matter of federal law, they are not diminished by the fact that the State may have specified its own procedures that it may deem adequate for determining the preconditions to adverse official action." ***

In light of [recent cases], it is settled that the "bitter with the sweet" approach misconceives the constitutional guarantee. If a clearer holding is needed, we provide it today. The point is straightforward: the Due Process

Clause provides that certain substantive rights—life, liberty, and property— cannot be deprived except pursuant to constitutionally adequate procedures. The categories of substance and procedure are distinct. Were the rule otherwise, the Clause would be reduced to a mere tautology. "Property" cannot be defined by the procedures provided for its deprivation any more than can life or liberty. The right to due process "is conferred, not by legislative grace, but by constitutional guarantee. While the legislature may elect not to confer a property interest in [public] employment, it may not constitutionally authorize the deprivation of such an interest, once conferred, without appropriate procedural safeguards." *Arnett v. Kennedy* ***.

Opinions by JUSTICE MARSHALL, JUSTICE BRENNAN, and JUSTICE POWELL are omitted.

JUSTICE REHNQUIST, dissenting.

In *Arnett v. Kennedy*, six Members of this Court agreed that a public employee could be dismissed for misconduct without a full hearing prior to termination. A plurality of Justices agreed that the employee was entitled to exactly what Congress gave him, and no more. THE CHIEF JUSTICE, JUSTICE STEWART, and I said:

> "Here appellee did have a statutory expectancy that he not be removed other than for 'such cause as will promote the efficiency of [the] service.' But the very section of the statute which granted him that right, a right which had previously existed only by virtue of administrative regulation, expressly provided also for the procedure by which 'cause' was to be determined, and expressly omitted the procedural guarantees which appellee insists are mandated by the Constitution. Only by bifurcating the very sentence of the Act of Congress which conferred upon appellee the right not to be removed save for cause could it be said that he had an expectancy of that substantive right without the procedural limitations which Congress attached to it. In the area of federal regulation of government employees, where in the absence of statutory limitation the governmental employer has had virtually uncontrolled latitude in decisions as to hiring and firing, we do not believe that a statutory enactment such as the Lloyd–La Follette Act may be parsed as discretely as appellee urges. Congress was obviously intent on according a measure of statutory job security to governmental employees which they had not previously enjoyed, but was likewise intent on excluding more elaborate procedural requirements which it felt would make the operation of the new scheme unnecessarily burdensome in practice. Where the focus of legislation was thus strongly on the procedural mechanism for enforcing the substantive right which was simultaneously conferred, we decline to conclude that the substantive right may be viewed wholly apart from the procedure provided for its enforcement. The employee's statutorily defined right is not a guarantee against removal without cause in the

abstract, but such a guarantee as enforced by the procedures which Congress has designated for the determination of cause."

In [this case], the relevant Ohio statute provides in its first paragraph that "[t]he tenure of every officer or employee in the classified service of the state *** shall be during good behavior and efficient service ***." The very next paragraph of this section of the Ohio Revised Code provides that in the event of suspension of more than three days or removal the appointing authority shall furnish the employee with the stated reasons for his removal. The next paragraph provides that within 10 days following the receipt of such a statement, the employee may appeal in writing to the State Personnel Board of Review or the Commission, such appeal shall be heard within 30 days from the time of its filing, and the Board may affirm, disaffirm, or modify the judgment of the appointing authority.

Thus in one legislative breath Ohio has conferred upon civil service employees such as respondents in these cases a limited form of tenure during good behavior, and prescribed the procedures by which that tenure may be terminated. Here, as in Arnett, "[t]he employee's statutorily defined right is not a guarantee against removal without cause in the abstract, but such a guarantee as enforced by the procedures which [the Ohio Legislature] has designated for the determination of cause." *** We ought to recognize the totality of the State's definition of the property right in question, and not merely seize upon one of several paragraphs in a unitary statute to proclaim that in that paragraph the State has inexorably conferred upon a civil service employee something which it is powerless under the United States Constitution to qualify in the next paragraph of the statute. *** Because I believe that the Fourteenth Amendment of the United States Constitution does not support the conclusion that Ohio's effort to confer a limited form of tenure upon respondents resulted in the creation of a "property right" in their employment, I dissent.

Notes

1. **Context of Notice and Hearing.** The Constitution says nothing specific about notice and hearing requirements to congressional lawmaking or presidential actions. *See Bi–Metallic Investment Co. v. State Board of Equalization*, 239 U.S. 441 (1915) (legislative bodies need not provide notice and opportunity to be heard, both because representative processes legitimize decisions and because such due process is impracticable in legislative contexts). Administrative proceedings, not contemplated under the original constitutional framework, provide the context for virtually all the Supreme Court's procedural due process cases. In essence, the Court has established more relaxed and flexible procedural requirements for agency adjudications than for civil trials. Why should agencies be able to decide cases adversely affecting individuals without the full panoply of protections given in court proceedings? Consider that there may be two very different benefits to procedural requirements in adjudications: (1) more accurate factual determinations and (2) enhanced dignity for the affected individuals. Are jury trials, counsel, and the like not mandated by the Court because the traditional trial procedures may not be the only or even the best way to afford these benefits? Trial processes are costly and the Court's hybrid processes may be much cheaper

than full trials. Why are there relatively few procedural due process cases concerning property interests adjudicated in civil litigation or liberty restrictions following criminal conviction?

2. **"Property" and "Liberty" Definitions.** You have a right to a hearing if and only if you have an entitlement, a Court-approved "property" or "liberty" interest. Property seems to encompass benefits you are receiving, but not benefits for which you would like to qualify (see discussion in *Loudermill*). In short, the government has total discretion as to whether to create a benefit which will become property to the recipient, but is constrained concerning the procedures available to protect the entitlement it has created. Liberty interests, not the focus of the procedural due process cases in these materials, include certain "grievous losses" to the individual but not other losses which seem almost equally serious. *See Ingraham v. Wright*, 430 U.S. 651 (1977) (paddling of student implicates a liberty interest). Compare *Owen v. City of Independence*, 445 U.S. 622 (1980) (right to reputation when combined from at-will employment is liberty interest) with *Paul v. Davis*, 424 U.S. 693 (1976) (reputation alone of one accused of being a shoplifter is not a liberty interest) and with *Board of Regents of State Colleges v. Roth*, 408 U.S. 564 (1972) (untenured assistant professor who is at-will employee has no liberty or property interest in continued employment).

3. **A Conundrum.** Why should a "for cause" provision in a statute, ordinance, or rule create a property interest, while the procedural restrictions in the same statute, ordinance, or rule are ignored? Don't the procedures in fact define the worth of the substantive entitlement? Is it possible that people don't read the procedures (like fine print in a boilerplate contract)? Does the Constitution distinguish "life, liberty, and property" from "due process"? Would failure to let the courts decide how much process is due "end judicial enforcement of the due process clause [because any legislature] that wishes to limit procedural rights need only make the limitation part of the definition of the underlying substantive right"? Douglas Laycock, *Due Process and Separation of Powers: The Effort to Make the Due Process Clauses Nonjusticiable*, 60 TEX. L. REV. 875 (1982).

2. PROCESS DUE

MATHEWS v. ELDRIDGE
424 U.S. 319, 96 S.Ct. 893, 47 L.Ed.2d 18 (1976).

MR. JUSTICE POWELL delivered the opinion of the Court.

The issue in this case is whether the Due Process Clause of the Fifth Amendment requires that prior to the termination of Social Security disability benefit payments the recipient be afforded an opportunity for an evidentiary hearing.

Cash benefits are provided to workers during periods in which they are completely disabled under the disability insurance benefits program created by the 1956 amendments to Title II of the Social Security Act. Respondent Eldridge was first awarded benefits in June 1968. In March 1972, he received a questionnaire from the state agency charged with monitoring his medical condition. Eldridge completed the questionnaire, indicating that his condition had not improved and identifying the medical sources, including physicians, from whom he had received treatment recently. The state agency then obtained reports from his physician and a psychiatric consultant. After considering these reports and other information in his file the agency informed Eldridge by letter that it had made a tentative determination that his disability had ceased in May 1972. The letter included a statement of reasons for the proposed termination of benefits, and advised Eldridge that he might request reasonable time in which to obtain and submit additional information pertaining to his condition.

In his written response, Eldridge disputed one characterization of his medical condition and indicated that the agency already had enough evidence to establish his disability. The state agency then made its final determination that he had ceased to be disabled in May 1972. This determination was accepted by the Social Security Administration (SSA), which notified Eldridge in July that his benefits would terminate after that month. The notification also advised him of his right to seek reconsideration by the state agency of this initial determination within six months.

Instead of requesting reconsideration Eldridge commenced this action challenging the constitutional validity of the administrative procedures established by the Secretary of Health, Education, and Welfare for assessing whether there exists a continuing disability. ***

Procedural due process imposes constraints on governmental decisions which deprive individuals of "liberty" or "property" interests within the meaning of the Due Process Clause of the Fifth or Fourteenth Amendment. The Secretary does not contend that procedural due process is inapplicable to terminations of Social Security disability benefits. He recognizes, as has been implicit in our prior decisions, that the interest of an individual in continued receipt of these benefits is a statutorily created "property" interest protected by the Fifth Amendment. Rather, the Secretary contends that the existing administrative procedures *** provide all the process that is constitutionally due before a recipient can be deprived of that interest.

This Court consistently has held that some form of hearing is required before an individual is finally deprived of a property interest. The "right to be heard before being condemned to suffer grievous loss of any kind, even though it may not involve the stigma and hardships of a criminal conviction, is a principle basic to our society." *Joint Anti–Fascist Comm. v. McGrath*, 341 U.S. 123, 168 (1951) (FRANKFURTER, J., concurring). The fundamental requirement of due process is the opportunity to be heard "at a meaningful time and in a meaningful manner." Eldridge agrees that the review procedures available to a claimant before the initial determination of ineligibility becomes final would be adequate if disability benefits were not terminated until after the evidentiary hearing stage of the administrative process. The dispute centers upon what process is due prior to the initial termination of benefits, pending review.

In recent years this Court increasingly has had occasion to consider the extent to which due process requires an evidentiary hearing prior to the deprivation of some type of property interest even if such a hearing is provided thereafter. In only one case, *Goldberg v. Kelly*, 397 U.S. 254 (1970), has the Court held that a hearing closely approximating a judicial trial is necessary. In other cases requiring some type of pretermination hearing as a matter of constitutional right the Court has spoken sparingly about the requisite procedures. ***

[The Court's] decisions underscore the truism that "'(d)ue process,' unlike some legal rules, is not a technical conception with a fixed content unrelated to time, place and circumstances." "(D)ue process is flexible and calls for such procedural protections as the particular situation demands." Accordingly, resolution of the issue whether the administrative procedures provided here are constitutionally sufficient requires analysis of the governmental and private interests that are affected. More precisely, our prior decisions indicate that identification of the specific dictates of due process generally requires consideration of three distinct factors: First, the private interest that will be affected by the official action; second, the risk of an erroneous deprivation of such interest through the procedures used, and the probable value, if any, of additional or substitute procedural safeguards; and finally, the Government's interest, including the function involved and the fiscal and administrative burdens that the additional or substitute procedural requirement would entail. ***

In order to establish initial and continued entitlement to disability benefits a worker must demonstrate that he is unable "to engage in any substantial gainful activity by reason of any medically determinable physical or mental impairment ***." To satisfy this test the worker bears a continuing burden of showing, by means of "medically acceptable clinical and laboratory diagnostic techniques," that he has a physical or mental impairment of such severity that "he is not only unable to do his previous work but cannot *** engage in any other kind of substantial gainful work which exists in the national economy." ***

The continuing-eligibility investigation is made by a state agency acting through a "team" consisting of a physician and a nonmedical person trained in disability evaluation. The agency periodically communicates with the disabled worker, usually by mail in which case he is sent a detailed questionnaire or by telephone, and requests information concerning his present condition, including current medical restrictions and sources of treatment, and any additional information that he considers relevant to his continued entitlement to benefits.

Information regarding the recipient's current condition is also obtained from his sources of medical treatment. If there is a conflict between the information provided by the beneficiary and that obtained from medical sources such as his physician, or between two sources of treatment, the agency may arrange for an examination by an independent consulting physician. Whenever the agency's tentative assessment of the beneficiary's condition differs from his own assessment, the beneficiary is informed that benefits may be terminated, provided a summary of the evidence upon which the proposed determination to terminate is based, and afforded an opportunity to review the medical reports and other evidence in his case file. He also may respond in writing and submit additional evidence.

The state agency then makes its final determination, which is reviewed by an examiner in the SSA Bureau of Disability Insurance. If, as is usually the case, the SSA accepts the agency determination it notifies the recipient in writing, informing him of the reasons for the decision, and of his right to seek *** reconsideration by the state agency. Upon acceptance by the SSA, benefits are terminated effective two months after the month in which medical recovery is found to have occurred.

If the recipient seeks reconsideration by the state agency and the determination is adverse, the SSA reviews the reconsideration determination and notifies the recipient of the decision. He then has a right to an evidentiary hearing before an SSA administrative law judge. The hearing is nonadversary and the SSA is not represented by counsel. As at all prior and subsequent stages of the administrative process, however, the claimant may be represented by counsel or other spokesmen. If this hearing results in an adverse decision, the claimant is entitled to request discretionary review by the SSA Appeals Council and finally may obtain judicial review.

Should it be determined at any point after termination of benefits, that the claimant's disability extended beyond the date of cessation initially established, the worker is entitled to retroactive payments. If, on the other hand, a beneficiary receives any payments to which he is later determined not to be entitled, the statute authorizes the Secretary to attempt to recoup these funds in specified circumstances.

Despite the elaborate character of the administrative procedures provided by the Secretary, the courts below held them to be constitutionally inadequate, concluding that due process requires an evidentiary hearing prior to termination. In light of the private and governmental interests at stake here and the nature of the existing procedures, we think this was error.

Since a recipient whose benefits are terminated is awarded full retroactive relief if he ultimately prevails, his sole interest is in the uninterrupted receipt of this source of income pending final administrative decision on his claim. His potential injury is thus similar in nature to that of the welfare recipient in *Goldberg* v. *Kelly*, 397 U.S. 254 (1970).

Only in *Goldberg* has the Court held that due process requires an evidentiary hearing prior to a temporary deprivation. It was emphasized there that welfare assistance is given to persons on the very margin of subsistence. *** Eligibility for disability benefits, in contrast, is not based upon financial need. Indeed, it is wholly unrelated to the worker's income or support from many other sources, such as earnings of other family members, workmen's compensation awards, tort claims awards, savings, private insurance, public or private pensions, veterans' benefits, food stamps, public assistance, or the "many other important programs, both public and private, which contain provisions for disability payments affecting a substantial portion of the work force ***."

As *Goldberg* illustrates, the degree of potential deprivation that may be created by a particular decision is a factor to be considered in assessing the validity of any administrative decisionmaking process. The potential deprivation here is generally likely to be less than in *Goldberg*, although the degree of difference can be overstated. As the District Court emphasized, to remain eligible for benefits a recipient must be "unable to engage in substantial gainful activity." Thus, in contrast to the discharged federal employee in *Arnett*, there is little possibility that the terminated recipient will be able to find even temporary employment to ameliorate the interim loss. [Moreover,] "the possible length of wrongful deprivation of *** benefits (also) is an important factor in assessing the impact of official action on the private interests." The Secretary concedes that the delay between a request for a hearing before an administrative law judge and a decision on the claim is currently between 10 and 11 months. Since a terminated recipient must first obtain a reconsideration decision as a prerequisite to invoking his right to an evidentiary hearing, the delay between the actual cutoff of benefits and final decision after a hearing exceeds one year.

In view of the torpidity of this administrative review process, and the typically modest resources of the family unit of the physically disabled worker, the hardship imposed upon the erroneously terminated disability recipient may be significant. Still, the disabled worker's need is likely to be less than that of a welfare recipient. In addition to the possibility of access to private resources, other forms of government assistance will become available where the termination of disability benefits places a worker or his family below the subsistence level. In view of these potential sources of temporary income, there is less reason here than in *Goldberg* to depart from the ordinary principle, established by our decisions, that something less than an evidentiary hearing is sufficient prior to adverse administrative action.

An additional factor to be considered here is the fairness and reliability of the existing pretermination procedures, and the probable value, if any, of additional procedural safeguards. Central to the evaluation of any administrative process is the nature of the relevant inquiry. In order to remain eligible for benefits the disabled worker must demonstrate by means of "medically acceptable clinical and laboratory diagnostic techniques," that he is unable "to engage in any substantial gainful activity by reason of any medically determinable physical or mental impairment ***." In short, a medical assessment of the worker's physical or mental condition is required. This is a more sharply focused and easily documented decision than the typical determination of welfare entitlement. In the latter case, a wide variety of information may be deemed relevant, and issues of witness credibility and veracity often are critical to the decisionmaking process. Goldberg noted that in such circumstances "written submissions are a wholly unsatisfactory basis for decision."

By contrast, the decision whether to discontinue disability benefits will turn, in most cases, upon "routine, standard, and unbiased medical reports by physician specialists," concerning a subject whom they have personally examined. *** To be sure, credibility and veracity may be a factor in the ultimate disability assessment in some cases. But procedural due process rules are shaped by the risk of error inherent in the truthfinding process as applied to the generality of cases, not the rare exceptions. The potential value of an evidentiary hearing, or even oral presentation to the decisionmaker, is substantially less in this context than in *Goldberg*.

The decision in *Goldberg* also was based on the Court's conclusion that written submissions were an inadequate substitute for oral presentation because they did not provide an effective means for the recipient to communicate his case to the decisionmaker. Written submissions were viewed as an unrealistic option, for most recipients lacked the "educational attainment necessary to write effectively" and could not afford professional assistance. In addition, such submissions would not provide the "flexibility of oral presentations" or "permit the recipient to mold his argument to the issues the decision maker appears to regard as important." In the context of the disability-benefits-entitlement assessment the administrative procedures under review here fully answer these objections. ***

A further safeguard against mistake is the policy of allowing the disability recipient's representative full access to all information relied upon by the state agency. In addition, prior to the cutoff of benefits the agency informs the recipient of its tentative assessment, the reasons therefor, and provides a summary of the evidence that it considers most relevant. Opportunity is then afforded the recipient to submit additional evidence or arguments, enabling him to challenge directly the accuracy of information in his file as well as the correctness of the agency's tentative conclusions. These procedures, again as contrasted with those before the Court in *Goldberg*, enable the recipient to "mold" his argument to respond to the precise issues which the decisionmaker regards as crucial.

Despite these carefully structured procedures, amici point to the significant reversal rate for appealed cases as clear evidence that the current process is inadequate. Depending upon the base selected and the line of analysis followed, the relevant reversal rates urged by the contending parties vary from a high of 58.6% For appealed reconsideration decisions to an overall reversal rate of only 3.3%. Bare statistics rarely provide a satisfactory measure of the fairness of a decisionmaking process. Their adequacy is especially suspect here since the administrative review system is operated on an open-file basis. A recipient may always submit new evidence, and such submissions may result in additional medical examinations. Such fresh examinations were held in approximately 30% To 40% Of the appealed cases, in fiscal 1973, either at the reconsideration or evidentiary hearing stage of the administrative process. In this context, the value of reversal rate statistics as one means of evaluating the adequacy of the pretermination process is diminished. Thus, although we view such information as relevant, it is certainly not controlling in this case.

In striking the appropriate due process balance the final factor to be assessed is the public interest. This includes the administrative burden and other societal costs that would be associated with requiring, as a matter of constitutional right, an evidentiary hearing upon demand in all cases prior to the termination of disability benefits. The most visible burden would be the incremental cost resulting from the increased number of hearings and the expense of providing benefits to ineligible recipients pending decision. No one can predict the extent of the increase, but the fact that full benefits would continue until after such hearings would assure the exhaustion in most cases of this attractive option. Nor would the theoretical right of the Secretary to recover undeserved benefits result, as a practical matter, in any substantial offset to the added outlay of public funds. The parties submit widely varying estimates of the probable additional financial cost. We only need say that experience with the constitutionalizing of government procedures suggests that the ultimate additional cost in terms of money and administrative burden would not be insubstantial.

Financial cost alone is not a controlling weight in determining whether due process requires a particular procedural safeguard prior to some administrative decision. But the Government's interest, and hence that of the public, in conserving scarce fiscal and administrative resources is a factor that must be weighed. At some point the benefit of an additional safeguard to the individual affected by the administrative action and to society in terms of increased assurance that the action is just, may be outweighed by the cost. Significantly, the cost of protecting those whom the preliminary administrative process has identified as likely to be found undeserving may in the end come out of the pockets of the deserving since resources available for any particular program of social welfare are not unlimited.

But more is implicated in cases of this type than ad hoc weighing of fiscal and administrative burdens against the interests of a particular category of claimants. The ultimate balance involves a determination as to when, under our constitutional system, judicial-type procedures must be imposed upon administrative action to assure fairness. We reiterate the wise admonishment of MR. JUSTICE FRANKFURTER that differences in the origin and function of administrative agencies "preclude wholesale transplantation of the rules of procedure, trial and review which have evolved from the history and experience of courts." The judicial model of an evidentiary hearing is neither a required, nor even the most effective, method of decisionmaking in all circumstances. The essence of due process is the requirement that "a person in jeopardy of serious loss (be given) notice of the case against him and opportunity to meet it." All that is necessary is that the procedures be tailored, in light of the decision to be made, to "the capacities and circumstances of those who are to be heard," *Goldberg* at 268–269, to insure that they are given a meaningful opportunity to present their case. In assessing what process is due in this case, substantial weight must be given to the good-faith judgments of the individuals charged by Congress with the administration of social welfare programs that the procedures they have provided assure fair consideration of the entitlement claims of individuals. ***

We conclude that an evidentiary hearing is not required prior to the termination of disability benefits and that the present administrative procedures fully comport with due process. ***

MR. JUSTICE STEVENS took no part in the consideration or decision of this case.

MR. JUSTICE BRENNAN, with whom MR. JUSTICE MARSHALL concurs, dissenting.

*** I agree with the District Court and the Court of Appeals that, prior to termination of benefits, Eldridge must be afforded an evidentiary hearing of the type required for welfare beneficiaries under Title IV of the Social Security Act. *See Goldberg v. Kelly.* I would add that the Court's consideration that a discontinuance of disability benefits may cause the recipient to suffer only a limited deprivation is no argument. It is speculative. Moreover, the very legislative determination to provide disability benefits, without any prerequisite determination of need in fact, presumes a need by the recipient which is not this Court's function to denigrate. Indeed, in the present case, it is indicated that because disability benefits were terminated there was a foreclosure upon the Eldridge home and the family's furniture was repossessed, forcing Eldridge, his wife, and their children to sleep in one bed. Finally, it is also no argument that a worker, who has been placed in the untenable position of having been denied disability benefits, may still seek other forms of public assistance.

Notes

1. **Utilitarian Balancing or "How Much Process is Due?"**

    • *Mathews* is the classic statement of the Court's three-part balancing test and therefore you should commit its components—degree of potential deprivation, fairness of procedure and value of additional safeguards, and the public interest—to memory.

    • Does the Court ignore the "dignitary value" of full procedures before adverse things are done to individuals by government?

    • Aren't the three things balanced by the Court incommensurable? That is, how does one weigh individual hardship versus social costs?

    • Is the Court evenhanded in balancing the factors, or does it put its finger on the scales by calling individual hardships "speculative" and accepting at face value what JUSTICE STEVENS calls "obscure suggestions of necessity" by the government?

    • How does one know what extra processes will be productive in arriving at "the truth"? For example, is it really true that a technical medical determination rather than subjective impressions and credibility are at the heart of termination of disability benefits?

    • Note that the *Mathews* balancing is NOT a balancing of the costs and benefits of the substantive regulations themselves, but only of the procedures connected with terminating the benefit conferred by the regulations.

2. **Balancing in the Employment Termination Context.** In a portion of *Loudermill* not reproduced above, the Court held that Loudermill was not entitled to a full adversary hearing prior to termination of his employment, but that some "opportunity to respond prior to termination" was necessary. The Court balanced the competing interests of "the private interests in retaining employment, the

governmental interest in the expeditious removal of unsatisfactory employees and the avoidance of administrative burdens, and the risk of erroneous termination." It found that all required was "notice and an opportunity to respond [to the reasons given for termination]" where Loudermill was accorded a "full post-termination hearing." JUSTICES MARSHALL and BRENNAN dissented, the former on the ground that a nine-month delay after wage termination until the full hearing might be "devastating" to the employee, the latter on the ground that there should be a remand to examine the issue of "overlong delay."

3. **Policy.** There is substantial debate concerning the wisdom of the procedural due process revolution inaugurated by *Goldberg v. Kelly*. JUSTICE BRENNAN once said that this case was the decision of which he was most proud. Critics argue that *Goldberg*'s due process revolution has in fact hurt the poor, in effect transferring money from programs for the poor to middle-class government officials who administer the procedural aspects of programs for the poor. If you were a welfare recipient, how much would you be willing to pay for notice and a full due process hearing prior to termination of benefits? If you were running a school, would you rather have more freedom to implement what you believed were educationally-desirable programs or more money with your discretion limited by due process considerations? Is any of this policy debate relevant to the decisions you have read in this unit?

4. **Problems.**

(a) State law makes discharge for age, disability and other reasons unlawful and provides that where a claim is filed, the state agency must begin a proceeding within 120 days to consider the claim. The agency inadvertently scheduled the proceeding on the 125th day, and state courts held that the agency was without jurisdiction to hear the matter at this time. Consider the claimant's procedural due process claim. *See Logan v. Zimmerman Brush Co.*, 455 U.S. 422 (1982).

(b) Suppose a state university decides to dismiss a student for cheating on an examination. How would you apply procedural due process to this situation? Would your analysis differ if the university proposed to dismiss the student for not maintaining the required grade-point average? What if the proposed dismissal was for drunken and disorderly conduct and sexually harassing advances at a fraternity party?

(c) Assume that the President and Congress agree to a package of welfare reforms that limit a recipient to two years of benefits in a lifetime. No process is provided prior to termination; once a person receives a 24th monthly check, a letter is issued saying "That's it for you. Get a job." Does the new welfare package violate procedural due process requirements?

3. PROCEDURE AND SUBSTANCE

The next two cases consider the liberty of aliens in deportation contexts. Has the Court altered the framework established in *Mathews*?

ZADVYDAS v. DAVIS
533 U.S. 678, 121 S.Ct. 2492, 150 L.Ed.2d 653 (2001).

JUSTICE BREYER delivered the opinion of the Court.

When an alien has been found to be unlawfully present in the United States and a final order of removal has been entered, the Government ordinarily secures the alien's removal during a subsequent 90-day statutory "removal period," during which time the alien normally is held in custody.

A special statute authorizes further detention if the Government fails to remove the alien during those 90 days. *** The post-removal-period detention statute applies to *** inadmissible aliens, criminal aliens, aliens who have violated their nonimmigrant status conditions, and aliens removable for certain national security or foreign relations reasons, as well as any alien "who has been determined by the Attorney General to be a risk to the community or unlikely to comply with the order of removal." *** The Government argues that *** "whether to continue to detain such an alien and, if so, in what circumstances and for how long" is up to the Attorney General, not up to the courts. *** In our view, the statute, read in light of the Constitution's demands, limits an alien's post-removal-period detention to a period reasonably necessary to bring about that alien's removal from the United States. It does not permit indefinite detention.

*** Freedom from imprisonment–from government custody, detention, or other forms of physical restraint–lies at the heart of the liberty that Clause protects. *** The proceedings at issue here are civil, not criminal, and we assume that they are nonpunitive in purpose and effect. *** The statute, says the Government, has two regulatory goals: "ensuring the appearance of aliens at future immigration proceedings" and "[p]reventing danger to the community." But by definition the first justification–preventing flight–is weak or nonexistent where removal seems a remote possibility at best. *** The second justification–protecting the community–does not necessarily diminish in force over time. But we have upheld preventive detention based on dangerousness only when limited to specially dangerous individuals and subject to strong procedural protections. In cases in which preventive detention is of potentially *indefinite* duration, we have also demanded that the dangerousness rationale be accompanied by some other special circumstance, such as mental illness, that helps to create the danger.

*** Moreover, the sole procedural protections available to the alien are found in administrative proceedings, where the alien bears the burden of proving he is not dangerous, without (in the Government's view) significant later judicial review. This Court has suggested, however, that the Constitution may well preclude granting 'an administrative body the unreviewable authority to make determinations implicating fundamental rights.' *Superintendent, Mass. Correctional Institution at Walpole v. Hill*, 472 U. S. 445, 450 (1985) (O'CONNOR, J.). The Constitution demands greater procedural protection even for property. The serious constitutional problem arising out of a statute that, in these circumstances, permits an indefinite, perhaps permanent, deprivation of human liberty without any such protection is obvious.

The Government argues that, from a constitutional perspective, alien status itself can justify indefinite detention, and points to *Shaughnessy v. United States ex rel. Mezei*, 345 U. S. 206 (1953), as support. *** The Court held that Mezei's detention did not violate the Constitution. Although *Mezei*, like the present cases, involves indefinite detention, it differs from the present cases in a critical respect. As the Court emphasized, the alien's extended departure from the United States required him to seek entry into this country once again. His presence on Ellis Island did not count as entry into the United States. Hence, he was "treated," for constitutional purposes, "as if stopped at the border." And that made all the difference. *** [O]nce an alien enters the country, the legal circumstance changes, for the Due Process Clause applies to all "persons" within the United States, including aliens, whether their presence here is lawful, unlawful, temporary, or permanent. Indeed, this Court has held that the Due Process Clause protects an alien subject to a final order of deportation, see *Wong Wing v. United States*, 163 U. S. 228, 238 (1896), though the nature of that protection may vary depending upon status and circumstance. ***

Finally, the Government argues that, whatever liberty interest the aliens possess, it is "greatly diminished" by their lack of a legal right to "liv[e] at large in this country." The choice, however, is not between imprisonment and the alien "living at large." It is between imprisonment and supervision under release conditions that may not be violated. And, for the reasons we have set forth, we believe that an alien's liberty interest is, at the least, strong enough to raise a serious question as to whether, irrespective of the procedures used, the Constitution permits detention that is indefinite and potentially permanent. *** [I]nterpreting the statute to avoid a serious constitutional threat, we conclude that, once removal is no longer reasonably foreseeable, continued detention is no longer authorized by statute. ***

JUSTICE SCALIA, with whom JUSTICE THOMAS joins, dissenting.

*** A criminal alien under final order of removal who allegedly will not be accepted by any other country in the reasonably foreseeable future claims a constitutional right of supervised release into the United States. This claim can be repackaged as freedom from "physical restraint" or freedom from "indefinite detention," but it is at bottom a claimed right of release into this country by an individual who *concededly* has no legal right to be here. *** Like a criminal alien under final order of removal, an inadmissible alien at the border has no right to be in the United States. *The Chinese Exclusion Case*, 130 U. S. 581, 603 (1889). *** Insofar as a claimed legal right to release into this country is concerned, an alien under final order of removal stands on an equal footing with an inadmissible alien at the threshold of entry: He has no such right. ***

JUSTICE KENNEDY, with whom The CHIEF JUSTICE joins, and with whom JUSTICE SCALIA and JUSTICE THOMAS join ***, dissenting.

*** The Court's amendment of the statute reads out of the provision the congressional decision that dangerousness alone is a sufficient basis for detention, and reads out as well any meaningful structure for supervised release. ***

As the Government represents to us, judicial orders requiring release of removable aliens, even on a temporary basis, have the potential to undermine the obvious necessity that the Nation speak with one voice on immigration and foreign affairs matters. *** The interference with sensitive foreign relations becomes even more acute where hostility or tension characterizes the relationship, for other countries can use the fact of judicially mandated release to their strategic advantage, refusing the return of their nationals to force dangerous aliens upon us. One of the more alarming aspects of the Court's new venture into foreign affairs management is the suggestion that the district court can expand or contract the reasonable period of detention based on its own assessment of the course of negotiations with foreign powers. ***

The majority does say that the release of terrorists or other "special circumstances" might justify "heightened deference to the judgments of the political branches with respect to matters of national security." *** Because other nations may refuse to admit aliens who have committed certain crimes[,] *** often the aliens who have committed the most serious crimes will be those who may be released immediately under the majority's rule. *** Today's result may well mandate the release of those aliens who first gained entry illegally or by fraud, and, indeed, is broad enough to require even that inadmissible and excludable aliens detained at the border be set free in our community. ***

*** The reason detention is permitted at all is that a removable alien does not have the same liberty interest as a citizen does. The Court cannot bring itself to acknowledge this established proposition. *** As persons within our jurisdiction, the aliens are entitled to the protection of the Due Process Clause. Liberty under the Due Process Clause includes protection against unlawful or arbitrary personal restraint or detention. The liberty rights of the aliens before us here are subject to limitations and conditions not applicable to citizens, however. *** They are removable, and their rights must be defined in accordance with that status. The due process analysis must begin with a "careful description of the asserted right." *Reno v. Flores*, 507 U. S. 292, 302 (1993). We have "long held that an alien seeking initial admission to the United States requests a privilege and has no constitutional rights regarding his application, for the power to admit or exclude aliens is a sovereign prerogative." *Landon v. Plasencia*, 459 U. S. 21, 32 (1982). The same is true for those aliens like Zadvydas and Ma, who face a final order of removal. When an alien is removable, he or she has no right under the basic immigration laws to remain in this country. The removal orders reflect the determination that the aliens' ties to this community are insufficient to justify their continued presence in the United States. *** It is neither arbitrary nor capricious to detain the aliens when necessary to avoid the risk of flight or danger to the community.

Whether a due process right is denied when removable aliens who are flight risks or dangers to the community are detained turns, then, not on the substantive right to be free, but on whether there are adequate procedures to review their cases, allowing persons once subject to detention to show that through rehabilitation, new appreciation of their responsibilities, or under other standards, they no longer present special risks or danger if put at large.

*** Neither Zadvydas nor Ma argues that the Attorney General has applied the procedures in an improper manner; they challenge only the Attorney General's authority to detain at all where removal is no longer foreseeable. ***

DEMORE v. KIM
123 S. Ct. 1708, 125 L.Ed.2d 724 (2003).

CHIEF JUSTICE REHNQUIST delivered the opinion of the Court.

Section 236(c) of the Immigration and Nationality Act, provides that "[t]he Attorney General shall take into custody any alien who" is removable from this country because he has been convicted of one of a specified set of crimes. Respondent is a citizen of the Republic of South Korea. He entered the United States in 1984, at the age of six, and became a lawful permanent resident of the United States two years later. In July 1996, he was convicted of first- degree burglary in state court in California and, in April 1997, he was convicted of a second crime, "petty theft with priors." The Immigration and Naturalization Service (INS) charged respondent with being deportable from the United States in light of these convictions, and detained him pending his removal hearing. We hold that Congress, justifiably concerned that deportable criminal aliens who are not detained continue to engage in crime and fail to appear for their removal hearings in large numbers, may require that persons such as respondent be detained for the brief period necessary for their removal proceedings. *** In conceding that he was deportable, respondent forwent a hearing at which he would have been entitled to raise any nonfrivolous argument available to demonstrate that he was not properly included in a mandatory detention category. Respondent instead filed a habeas corpus action ***. He argued that his detention under § 1226(c) violated due process because the INS had made no determination that he posed either a danger to society or a flight risk. ***

*** Section 1226(c) mandates detention during removal proceedings for a limited class of deportable aliens–including those convicted of an aggravated felony. Congress adopted this provision against a backdrop of wholesale failure by the INS to deal with increasing rates of criminal activity by aliens. Criminal aliens were the fastest growing segment of the federal prison population, already constituting roughly 25% of all federal prisoners, and they formed a rapidly rising share of state prison populations as well. Congress' investigations showed, however, that the INS could not even *identify* most deportable aliens, much less locate them and remove them from the country. One study showed that, at the then-current rate of deportation, it would take 23 years to remove every criminal alien already subject to deportation. Making matters worse, criminal aliens who were deported swiftly reentered the country illegally in great numbers.

The agency's near-total inability to remove deportable criminal aliens imposed more than a monetary cost on the Nation. First, as Congress explained, "[a]liens who enter or remain in the United States in violation of our law are effectively taking immigration opportunities that might otherwise be extended to others." Second, deportable criminal aliens who remained in the United States often committed more crimes before being removed. One 1986 study showed that, after criminal aliens were identified as deportable, 77% were arrested at least once more and 45%—nearly half— were arrested multiple times before their deportation proceedings even began.

Congress also had before it evidence that one of the major causes of the INS' failure to remove deportable criminal aliens was the agency's failure to detain those aliens during their deportation proceedings. *** Once released, more than 20% of deportable criminal aliens failed to appear for their removal hearings. *** Congress amended the immigration laws several times toward the end of the 1980's. *** Congress enacted 8 U.S.C. § 1226, requiring the Attorney General to detain a subset of deportable criminal aliens pending a determination of their removability.

"In the exercise of its broad power over naturalization and immigration, Congress regularly makes rules that would be unacceptable if applied to citizens." *Mathews v. Diaz,* 426 U.S. 67 (1976). The dissent seeks to avoid this fundamental premise of immigration law by repeatedly referring to it as "dictum." The Court in *Mathews,* however, made the statement the dissent now seeks to avoid in reliance on clear precedent establishing that "'any policy toward aliens is vitally and intricately interwoven with contemporaneous policies in regard to the conduct of foreign relations, the war power, and the maintenance of a republican form of government.'" And, since *Mathews,* this Court has firmly and repeatedly endorsed the proposition that Congress may make rules as to aliens that would be unacceptable if applied to citizens.

In his habeas corpus challenge, respondent did not contest Congress' general authority to remove criminal aliens from the United States. Nor did he argue that he himself was not "deportable" ***. Rather, respondent argued that the Government may not, consistent with the Due Process Clause of the Fifth Amendment, detain him for the brief period necessary for his removal proceedings. *** Respondent, like the four Courts of Appeals that have held § 1226(c) to be unconstitutional, relies heavily upon our recent opinion in *Zadvydas v. Davis,* 533 U.S. 678 (2001). *** But *Zadvydas* is materially different from the present case in two respects.

First, in *Zadvydas,* the aliens challenging their detention following final orders of deportation were ones for whom removal was "no longer practically attainable." The Court thus held that the detention there did not serve its purported immigration purpose. In so holding, the Court rejected the Government's claim that, by detaining the aliens involved, it could prevent them from fleeing prior to their removal. The Court observed that where, as there, "detention's goal is no longer practically attainable, detention no longer bears a reasonable relation to the purpose for which the individual was committed."

In the present case, the statutory provision at issue governs detention of deportable criminal aliens *pending their removal proceedings.* Such detention necessarily serves the purpose of preventing deportable criminal aliens from fleeing prior to or during their removal proceedings, thus increasing the chance that, if ordered removed, the aliens will be successfully removed. *** The evidence Congress had before it certainly supports the approach it selected even if other, hypothetical studies might have suggested different courses of action.

Zadvydas is materially different from the present case in a second respect as well. While the period of detention at issue in *Zadvydas* was "indefinite" and "potentially permanent," the detention here is of a much shorter duration.

Zadvydas distinguished the statutory provision it was there considering from § 1226 on these very grounds, noting that "post-removal-period detention, *unlike detention pending a determination of removability*, has no obvious termination point." Under 1226(c), not only does detention have a definite termination point, in the majority of cases it lasts for less than the 90 days we considered presumptively valid in *Zadvydas*. The Executive Office for Immigration Review has calculated that, in 85% of the cases in which aliens are detained pursuant to § 1226(c), removal proceedings are completed in an average time of 47 days and a median of 30 days. In the remaining 15% of cases, in which the alien appeals the decision of the Immigration Judge to the Board of Immigration Appeals, appeal takes an average of four months, with a median time that is slightly shorter.

These statistics do not include the many cases in which removal proceedings are completed while the alien is still serving time for the underlying conviction. In those cases, the aliens involved are never subjected to mandatory detention at all. *** Respondent was detained for somewhat longer than the average–spending six months in INS custody prior to the District Court's order granting habeas relief, but respondent himself had requested a continuance of his removal hearing. ***

JUSTICE KENNEDY, concurring.

*** Respondent was entitled to a hearing in which he could have "raise[d] any nonfrivolous argument available to demonstrate that he was not properly included in a mandatory detention category." *** Respondent, however, did not seek relief under these procedures, and the Court had no occasion here to determine their adequacy. ***

JUSTICE O'CONNOR, with whom JUSTICE SCALIA and JUSTICE THOMAS join, concurring in part and concurring in the judgment. [omitted]

JUSTICE SOUTER, with whom JUSTICE STEVENS and JUSTICE GINSBURG join, concurring in part and dissenting in part.

*** The constitutional protection of an alien's person and property is particularly strong in the case of aliens lawfully admitted to permanent residence (LPRs). The immigration laws give LPRs the opportunity to establish a life permanently in this country by developing economic, familial, and social ties indistinguishable from those of a citizen. *** Once they are admitted to permanent residence, LPRs share in the economic freedom enjoyed by citizens: they may compete for most jobs in the private and public sectors without obtaining job-specific authorization, and apart from the franchise, jury duty, and certain forms of public assistance, their lives are generally indistinguishable from those of United States citizens. That goes for obligations as well as opportunities. *** "Resident aliens, like citizens, pay taxes, support the economy, serve in the Armed Forces, and contribute in myriad other ways to our society." And if they choose, they may apply for full membership in the national polity through naturalization. *** The law therefore considers an LPR to be at home in the United States, and even when the Government seeks removal, we have accorded LPRs greater protections than other aliens under the Due Process Clause. *** In evaluating Kim's challenge to his mandatory detention *** the only reasonable starting point is the traditional doctrine concerning the Government's physical confinement of individuals.

Kim's claim is a limited one: not that the Government may not detain LPRs to ensure their appearance at removal hearings, but that due process under the Fifth Amendment conditions a potentially lengthy detention on a hearing and an impartial decisionmaker's finding that detention is necessary to a governmental purpose. *** The substantive demands of due process necessarily go hand in hand with the procedural, and the cases insist at the least on an opportunity for a detainee to challenge the reason claimed for committing him. *** In none of the cases cited did we ever suggest that the government could avoid the Due Process Clause *** by selecting a class of people for confinement on a categorical basis and denying members of that class any chance to dispute the necessity of putting them away. *** And if procedure could be dispensed with so expediently, so presumably could the substantive requirements that the class of detainees be narrow and the detention period strictly limited. *** Kim's detention without particular justification in these respects, or the opportunity to enquire into it, violates both components of due process ***. This is surely little enough, given the fact that 8 U.S.C. § 1536 gives an LPR charged with being a foreign terrorist the right to a release hearing pending a determination that he be removed.

*** The Court spends much effort trying to distinguish *Zadvydas*, ***. First, the Court says that § 1226(c) "serves the purpose of preventing deportable criminal aliens from fleeing prior to or during their removal proceedings." Yes it does, and the statute in *Zadvydas*, viewed outside the context of any individual alien's detention, served the purpose of preventing aliens ordered to be deported from fleeing prior to actual deportation. In each case, the fact that a statute serves its purpose in general fails to justify the detention of an individual in particular. *** The Court's second effort is its claim that mandatory detention under § 1226(c) is generally of a "much shorter duration" than the incarceration at issue in *Zadvydas*. While it is true that removal proceedings are unlikely to prove "indefinite and potentially permanent," they are not formally limited to any period, and often extend beyond the time suggested by the Court ***. Even taking these averages on their face, however, they are no legitimate answer to the due process claim to individualized treatment and hearing.

In the first place, the average time from receipt of charging documents to decision obscures the fact that the alien may receive charging documents only after being detained for a substantial period. Kim, for example, was not charged until five weeks after the INS detained him. *** [Moreover,] the length of the average detention period in great part reflects the fact that the vast majority of cases involve aliens who raise no challenge to removability at all. *** Unlike many illegal entrants and temporary nonimmigrants, LPRs are the aliens most likely to press substantial challenges to removability requiring lengthy proceedings. *** The potential for several months of confinement requires an individualized finding of necessity under *Zadvydas*.[24] *** [N]o impartial decisionmaker has determined that detaining Kim is required for any purpose at all, and neither the Government nor the Court even claims such a need. ***

JUSTICE BREYER, concurring in part and dissenting in part.

*** If I believed (as the majority apparently believes) that Kim had conceded that he is deportable, then I would conclude that the Government could detain him without bail for the few weeks ordinarily necessary for formal entry of a removal order. ***

Notes

1. **The effect of setting different levels of generality.** The *Zadvydas* majority defines the liberty interest at a relatively high level of generality: The right to be free from indefinite civil detention, absent a governmental showing that either removal to another country is reasonably foreseeable, the detained individual presents a flight risk, or that the individual presents a danger to the community. The majority would allow supervision, but not detention, of individuals released due to the Government's inability to deport them. What distinguishes indefinite supervision from detention of indefinite duration? JUSTICE SCALIA's dissenting opinion frames the right in rather specific terms: "[I]t is at bottom a claimed right of release into this country by an individual who concededly has no right to be here." Is JUSTICE SCALIA focusing upon the right being asserted, or the remedy required to vindicate that right?

2. **A continuum of due process rights.** Does the 5th Amendment Due Process draw a citizen/alien distinction? JUSTICE KENNEDY's dissent in *Zadvydas* views due process rights in the immigration law context as resting on a continuum; persons stopped at the border are located at one extreme, and citizens are located at the other. The process due to each individual depends upon where a person happens to fall on this continuum. For a convicted criminal subject to a final removal order, perhaps indefinite detention is warranted, so long as it is not arbitrary or capricious. In what other areas can this analytical framework be applied?

---

[24] The Court calls several months of unnecessary imprisonment a "very limited time." *** The 90-day removal period in § 1231(a)(1) not only has a fixed endpoint, but also applies only after the alien has been adjudged removable. The discussion of that provision in *Zadvydas* cannot be read to indicate any standard of permissible treatment of an LPR who has not yet been found removable.

3. **Procedures: Half Full or Half Empty?** In *Demore*, is an individual determination likely to improve the odds of the alien showing up at the hearing? Is there an absconder rate that would convince the dissenters? Is the detention here very limited or potentially lengthy? Who determines the length of detention, the government or the alien?

4. **Jurisdiction.** A preliminary hurdle in *Demore* was whether the courts had jurisdiction in light of 8 U.S.C. § 1226(e): "The Attorney General's discretionary judgment regarding the application of this section shall not be subject to review." The Court said that the LPR did not challenge a "discretionary judgment" by the Attorney General or a "decision" the Attorney General made regarding detention or release. Rather, respondent challenges the statutory framework that permits his detention without bail. *** Sec tion 1226(e) contains no explicit provision barring habeas review ***." Are you convinced? JUSTICES O'CONNOR, SCALIA, and THOMAS weren't.

5. **Procedural or Substantive Due Process?** In *Zadvydas*, is the majority reading a substantive due process limitation into the challenged statutory provisions? In *Demore*, is the majority ignoring substantive due process limits? How do substance and procedure relate to each other?

6. **Deportation and the War on Terrorism.** The Chief Immigration Judge, under the Attorney General's authorization, has closed "special interest" deportation cases in which there may be some relation to terrorism. Indeed, such cases are not even registered on a public docket. Do these closures pose due process problems? Would monitoring attorney-client conversations in "special interest" cases violate due process?

B. SUBSTANTIVE DUE PROCESS

The Supreme Court first recognized a non-procedural component to the Due Process Clause of the Fourteenth Amendment in the late 19th century. That era of the Court's work is often called the *Lochner* era of substantive due process.

Even after the Court abandoned *Lochner*, it continued to find certain actions of governmental bodies unconstitutional under the Due Process Clause. Preventing the government from taking certain actions even if it follows majoritarian and constitutional processes is a powerful application of judicial review. Blocking democratic processes is the most controversial aspect of the Court's work, especially when the Constitution lacks or provides very weak textual support for the Court's decisions.

1. ECONOMIC RIGHTS

LOCHNER v. NEW YORK
198 U.S. 45, 25 S.Ct. 539, 49 L.Ed. 937 (1905).

MR. JUSTICE PECKHAM *** delivered the opinion of the Court:

[The Court reviewed the following section of a New York statute, violations of which carried criminal penalties:

§ 110, Hours of labor in bakeries and confectionery establishments.—No employee shall be required or permitted to work in a biscuit, bread, or cake bakery or confectionery establishment more than sixty hours in any one week, or more than ten hours in any one day, unless for the purpose of making a shorter work day on the last day of the week; nor more hours in any one week than will make an average of ten hours per day for the number of days during such week in which such employee shall work.

The petitioner had been indicted under the statute, and claimed it violated the Due Process clause.]

*** The statute necessarily interferes with the right of contract between the employer and employees, concerning the number of hours in which the latter may labor in the bakery of the employer. The general right to make a contract in relation to his business is part of the liberty of the individual protected by the 14th Amendment of the Federal Constitution. *Allgeyer v. Louisiana*, 165 U. S. 578. Under that provision no state can deprive any person of life, liberty, or property without due process of law. The right to purchase or to sell labor is part of the liberty protected by this amendment, unless there are circumstances which exclude the right. There are, however, certain powers, existing in the sovereignty of each state in the Union, somewhat vaguely termed police powers, the exact description and limitation of which have not been attempted by the courts. Those powers, broadly stated, and without, at present, any attempt at a more specific limitation, relate to the safety, health, morals, and general welfare of the public. Both property and liberty are held on such reasonable conditions as may be imposed by the governing power of the state in the exercise of those powers, and with such conditions the 14th Amendment was not designed to interfere. *Mugler v. Kansas*, 123 U. S. 623.

The state, therefore, has power to prevent the individual from making certain kinds of contracts, and in regard to them the Federal Constitution offers no protection. If the contract be one which the state, in the legitimate exercise of its police power, has the right to prohibit, it is not prevented from prohibiting it by the 14th Amendment. Contracts in violation of a statute, either of the Federal or state government, or a contract to let one's property for immoral purposes, or to do any other unlawful act, could obtain no protection from the Federal Constitution, as coming under the liberty of person or of free contract. Therefore, when the state, by its legislature, in the assumed exercise of its police powers, has passed an act which seriously limits the right to labor or the right of contract in regard to their means of livelihood between persons who are sui juris (both employer and employee), it becomes of great importance to determine which shall prevail,—the right of the individual to labor for such time as he may choose, or the right of the state to prevent the individual from laboring, or from entering into any contract to labor, beyond a certain time prescribed by the state.

This court has recognized the existence and upheld the exercise of the police powers of the states in many cases which might fairly be considered as border ones, and it has, in the course of its determination of questions regarding the asserted invalidity of such statutes, on the ground of their violation of the rights secured by the Federal Constitution, been guided by rules of a very liberal nature, the application of which has resulted, in numerous instances, in upholding the validity of state statutes thus assailed. Among the later cases where the state law has been upheld by this court is that of *Holden v. Hardy*. A provision in the act of the legislature of Utah was there under consideration, the act limiting the employment of workmen in all underground mines or workings, to eight hours per day, 'except in cases of emergency, where life or property is in imminent danger.' *** The act was held to be a valid exercise of the police powers of the state. *** It was held that the kind of employment, mining, smelting, etc., and the character of the employees in such kinds of labor, were such as to make it reasonable and proper for the state to interfere to prevent the employees from being constrained by the rules laid down by the proprietors in regard to labor. [However, there] is nothing in *Holden v. Hardy* which covers the case now before us. ***

It must, of course, be conceded that there is a limit to the valid exercise of the police power by the state. There is no dispute concerning this general proposition. Otherwise the 14th Amendment would have no efficacy and the legislatures of the states would have unbounded power, and it would be enough to say that any piece of legislation was enacted to conserve the morals, the health, or the safety of the people; such legislation would be valid, no matter how absolutely without foundation the claim might be. *** In every case that comes before this court, therefore, where legislation of this character is concerned, and where the protection of the Federal Constitution is sought, the question necessarily arises: Is this a fair, reasonable, and appropriate exercise of the police power of the state, or is it an unreasonable, unnecessary, and arbitrary interference with the right of the individual to his personal liberty, or to enter into those contracts in relation to labor which may seem to him appropriate or necessary for the support of himself and his family? Of course the liberty of contract relating to labor includes both parties to it. The one has as much right to purchase as the other to sell labor.

This is not a question of substituting the judgment of the court for that of the legislature. If the act be within the power of the state it is valid, although the judgment of the court might be totally opposed to the enactment of such a law. But the question would still remain: Is it within the police power of the state? ***

The question whether this act is valid as a labor law, pure and simple, may be dismissed in a few words. There is no reasonable ground for interfering with the liberty of person or the right of free contract, by determining the hours of labor, in the occupation of a baker. There is no contention that bakers as a class are not equal in intelligence and capacity to men in other trades or manual occupations, or that they are not able to assert their rights and care for themselves without the protecting arm of the state, interfering with their independence of judgment and of action. They are in no sense wards of the state. Viewed in the light of a purely labor law, with no reference whatever to the question of health, we think that a law like the one before us involves neither the safety, the morals, nor the welfare, of the public, and that the interest of the public is not in the slightest degree affected by such an act. The law must be upheld, if at all, as a law pertaining to the health of the individual engaged in the occupation of a baker. It does not affect any other portion of the public than those who are engaged in that occupation. Clean and wholesome bread does not depend upon whether the baker works but ten hours per day or only sixty hours a week. The limitation of the hours of labor does not come within the police power on that ground.

It is a question of which of two powers or rights shall prevail,—the power of the state to legislate or the right of the individual to liberty of person and freedom of contract. The mere assertion that the subject relates, though but in a remote degree, to the public health, does not necessarily render the enactment valid. The act must have a more direct relation, as a means to an end, and the end itself must be appropriate and legitimate, before an act can be held to be valid which interferes with the general right of an individual to be free in his person and in his power to contract in relation to his own labor. ***

VIII–1. Joseph Lochner's Bakery. Photograph by Dante Tranquille for the Utica Observer–Dispatch, ca. 1930.

We think the limit of the police power has been reached and passed in this case. There is, in our judgment, no reasonable foundation for holding this to be necessary or appropriate as a health law to safeguard the public health, or the health of the individuals who are following the trade of a baker. If this statute be valid, and if, therefore, a proper case is made out in which to deny the right of an individual, sui juris, as employer or employee, to make contracts for the labor of the latter under the protection of the provisions of the Federal Constitution, there would seem to be no length to which legislation of this nature might not go. ***

We think that there can be no fair doubt that the trade of a baker, in and of itself, is not an unhealthy one to that degree which would authorize the legislature to interfere with the right to labor, and with the right of free contract on the part of the individual, either as employer or employee. In looking through statistics regarding all trades and occupations, it may be true that the trade of a baker does not appear to be as healthy as some other trades, and is also vastly more healthy than still others. To the common understanding the trade of a baker has never been regarded as an unhealthy one. Very likely physicians would not recommend the exercise of that or of any other trade as a remedy for ill health. Some occupations are more healthy than others, but we think there are none which might not come under the power of the legislature to supervise and control the hours of working therein, if the mere fact that the occupation is not absolutely and perfectly healthy is to confer that right upon the legislative department of the government. It might be safely affirmed that almost all occupations more or less affect the health. There must be more than the mere fact of the possible existence of some small amount of unhealthiness to warrant legislative interference with liberty. It is unfortunately true that labor, even in any department, may possibly carry with it the seeds of unhealthiness. But are we all, on that account, at the mercy of legislative majorities? *** No trade, no occupation, no mode of earning one's living, could escape this all-pervading power, and the acts of the legislature in limiting the hours of labor in all employments would be valid, although such limitation might seriously cripple the ability of the laborer to support himself and his family. ***

It is also urged, pursuing the same line of argument, that it is to the interest of the state that its population should be strong and robust, and therefore any legislation which may be said to tend to make people healthy must be valid as health laws, enacted under the police power. If this be a valid argument and a justification for this kind of legislation, it follows that the protection of the Federal Constitution from undue interference with liberty of person and freedom of contract is visionary, wherever the law is sought to be justified as a valid exercise of the police power. Scarcely any law but might find shelter under such assumptions, and conduct, properly so called, as well as contract, would come under the restrictive sway of the legislature. Not only the hours of employees, but the hours of employers, could be regulated, and doctors, lawyers, scientists, all professional men, as well as athletes and artisans, could be forbidden to fatigue their brains and bodies by prolonged hours of exercise, lest the fighting strength of the state be impaired. We mention these extreme cases because the contention is extreme. We do not believe in the soundness of the views which uphold this law. On the contrary, we think that such a law as this, although passed in the assumed exercise of the police power, and as relating to the public health, or the health of the employees named, is not within that power, and is invalid. The act is not, within any fair meaning of the term, a health law, but is an illegal interference with the rights of individuals, both employers and employees, to make contracts regarding labor upon such terms as they may think best, or which they may agree upon with the other parties to such contracts. Statutes of the nature of that under review, limiting the hours in which grown and intelligent men may labor to earn their living, are mere meddlesome interferences with the rights of the individual, and they are not saved from condemnation by the claim that they are passed in the exercise of the police power and upon the subject of the health of the individual whose rights are interfered with, unless there be some fair ground, reasonable in and of itself, to say that there is material danger to the public health, or to the health of the employees, if the hours of labor are not curtailed. If this be not clearly the case, the individuals whose rights are thus made the subject of legislative interference are under the protection of the Federal Constitution regarding their liberty of contract as well as of person; and the legislature of the state has no power to limit their right as proposed in this statute. All that it could properly do has been done by it with regard to the conduct of bakeries, as provided for in the other sections of the act, [which] provide for the inspection of the premises where the bakery is carried on, with regard to furnishing proper wash rooms and waterclosets, *** with regard to providing proper drainage, plumbing, and painting, *** and for other things of that nature. ***

It was further urged *** that restricting the hours of labor in the case of bakers was valid because it tended to cleanliness on the part of the workers, as a man was more apt to be cleanly when not overworked, and if cleanly then his "output" was also more likely to be so ***. We do not admit the reasoning to be sufficient to justify the claimed right of such interference. The state in that case would assume the position of a supervisor, or pater familias, over every act of the individual ***. In our judgment it is not possible in fact to discover the connection between the number of hours a baker may work in the bakery and the healthful quality of the bread made by the workman. The connection, if any exist, is too shadowy and thin to build any argument for the interference of the legislature. *** When assertions such as we have adverted to become necessary in order to give, if possible, a plausible foundation for the contention that the law is a 'health law,' it gives rise to at least a suspicion that there was some other motive dominating the legislature than the purpose to subserve the public health or welfare.

This interference on the part of the legislatures of the several states with the ordinary trades and occupations of the people seems to be on the increase. *** It is impossible for us to shut our eyes to the fact that many of the laws of this character, while passed under what is claimed to be the police power for the purpose of protecting the public health or welfare, are, in reality, passed from other motives. We are justified in saying so when, from the character of the law and the subject upon which it legislates, it is apparent that the public health or welfare bears but the most remote relation to the law. The purpose of a statute must be determined from the natural and legal effect of the language employed; and whether it is or is not repugnant to the Constitution of the United States must be determined from the natural effect of such statutes when put into operation, and not from their proclaimed purpose. The court looks beyond the mere letter of the law in such cases. *Yick Wo v. Hopkins*, 118 U. S. 356.

It is manifest to us that *** the statute under which the indictment was found, and the plaintiff in error convicted, has no such direct relation to, and no such substantial effect upon, the health of the employee, as to justify us in regarding the section as really a health law. It seems to us that the real object and purpose were simply to regulate the hours of labor between the master and his employees (all being men, sui juris), in a private business, not dangerous in any degree to morals, or in any real and substantial degree to the health of the employees. Under such circumstances the freedom of master and employee to contract with each other in relation to their employment, and in defining the same, cannot be prohibited or interfered with, without violating the Federal Constitution. ***

MR. JUSTICE HOLMES dissenting:

*** This case is decided upon an economic theory which a large part of the country does not entertain. If it were a question whether I agreed with that theory, I should desire to study it further and long before making up my mind. But I do not conceive that to be my duty, because I strongly believe that my agreement or disagreement has nothing to do with the right of a majority to embody their opinions in law. It is settled by various decisions of this court that state constitutions and state laws may regulate life in many ways which we as legislators might think as injudicious, or if you like as tyrannical, as this, and which, equally with this, interfere with the liberty to contract. Sunday laws and usury laws are ancient examples. A more modern one is the prohibition of lotteries. The liberty of the citizen to do as he likes so long as he does not interfere with the liberty of others to do the same, which has been a shibboleth for some well-known writers, is interfered with by school laws, by the Post Office, by every state or municipal institution which takes his money for purposes thought desirable, whether he likes it or not. The 14th Amendment does not enact Mr. Herbert Spencer's Social Statics. The other day we sustained the Massachusetts vaccination law. *Jacobson v. Massachusetts*, 197 U. S. 11. United States and State statutes and decisions cutting down the liberty to contract by way of combination are familiar to this court. *** The decision sustaining an eight-hour law for miners is still recent. *Holden v. Hardy*. Some of these laws embody convictions or prejudices which judges are likely to share. Some may not. But a Constitution is not intended to embody a particular economic theory, whether of paternalism and the organic relation of the citizen to the state or of laissez faire. It is made for people of fundamentally differing views, and the accident of our finding certain opinions natural and familiar, or novel, and even shocking, ought not to conclude our judgment upon the question whether statutes embodying them conflict with the Constitution of the United States.

General propositions do not decide concrete cases. The decision will depend on a judgment or intuition more subtle than any articulate major premise. But I think that the proposition just stated, if it is accepted, will carry us far toward the end. Every opinion tends to become a law. I think that the word "liberty," in the 14th Amendment, is perverted when it is held to prevent the natural outcome of a dominant opinion, unless it can be said that a rational and fair man necessarily would admit that the statute proposed would infringe fundamental principles as they have been understood by the traditions of our people and our law. It does not need research to show that no such sweeping condemnation can be passed upon the statute before us. A reasonable man might think it a proper measure on the score of health. Men whom I certainly could not pronounce unreasonable would uphold it as a first instalment of a general regulation of the hours of work. ***

MR. JUSTICE HARLAN (with whom MR. JUSTICE WHITE and MR. JUSTICE DAY concurred) dissenting:

*** It is plain that this statute was enacted in order to protect the physical well-being of those who work in bakery and confectionery establishments. It may be that the statute had its origin, in part, in the belief that employers and employees in such establishments were not upon an equal footing, and that the necessities of the latter often compelled them to submit to such exactions as unduly taxed their strength. Be this as it may, the statute must be taken as expressing the belief of the people of New York that, as a general rule, and in the case of the average man, labor in excess of sixty hours during a week in such establishments may endanger the health of those who thus labor. Whether or not this be wise legislation it is not the province of the court to inquire. Under our systems of government the courts are not concerned with the wisdom or policy of legislation. So that, in determining the question of power to interfere with liberty of contract, the court may inquire whether the means devised by the state are germane to an end which may be lawfully accomplished and have a real or substantial relation to the protection of health, as involved in the daily work of the persons, male and female, engaged in bakery and confectionery establishments. But when this inquiry is entered upon I find it impossible, in view of common experience, to say that there is here no real or substantial relation between the means employed by the state and the end sought to be accomplished by its legislation. Nor can I say that the statute has no appropriate or direct connection with that protection to health which each state owes to her citizens or that it is not promotive of the health of the employees in question, or that the regulation prescribed by the state is utterly unreasonable and extravagant or wholly arbitrary. Still less can I say that the statute is, beyond question, a plain, palpable invasion of rights secured by the fundamental law. ***

Professor Hirt in his treatise on the "Diseases of the Workers" has said:

"The labor of the bakers is among the hardest and most laborious imaginable, because it has to be performed under conditions injurious to the health of those engaged in it. It is hard, very hard, work, not only because it requires a great deal of physical exertion in an overheated workshop and during unreasonably long hours, but more so because of the erratic demands of the public, compelling the baker to perform the greater part of his work at night, thus depriving him of an opportunity to enjoy the necessary rest and sleep,—a fact which is highly injurious to his health."

Another writer says:

"The constant inhaling of flour dust causes inflammation of the lungs and of the bronchial tubes. The eyes also suffer through this dust, which is responsible for the many cases of running eyes among the bakers. The long hours of toil to which all bakers are subjected produce rheumatism, cramps, and swollen legs. The intense heat in the workshops induces the workers to resort to cooling drinks, which, together with their habit of exposing the greater part of their bodies to the change in the atmosphere, is another source of a number of diseases of various organs."

*** We judicially know that the question of the number of hours during which a workman should continuously labor has been, for a long period, and is yet, a subject of serious consideration among civilized peoples, and by those having special knowledge of the laws of health. *** But the statute before us *** may be said to occupy a middle ground in respect of the hours of labor. What is the true ground for the state to take between legitimate protection, by legislation, of the public health and liberty of contract is not a question easily solved, nor one in respect of which there is or can be absolute certainty. ***

I do not stop to consider whether any particular view of this economic question presents the sounder theory. What the precise facts are it may be difficult to say. It is enough for the determination of this case, and it is enough for this court to know, that the question is one about which there is room for debate and for an honest difference of opinion. There are many reasons of a weighty, substantial character, based upon the experience of mankind, in support of the theory that, all things considered, more than ten hours' steady work each day, from week to week, in a bakery or confectionery establishment, may endanger the health and shorten the lives of the workmen, thereby diminishing their physical and mental capacity to serve the state and to provide for those dependent upon them.

If such reasons exist that ought to be the end of this case, for the state is not amenable to the judiciary, in respect of its legislative enactments, unless such enactments are plainly, palpably, beyond all question, inconsistent with the Constitution of the United States. We are not to presume that the state of New York has acted in bad faith. Nor can we assume that its legislature acted without due deliberation, or that it did not determine this question upon the fullest attainable information and for the common good. We cannot say that the state has acted without reason, nor ought we to proceed upon the theory that its action is a mere sham. Our duty, I submit, is to sustain the statute as not being in conflict with the Federal Constitution, for the reason—and such is an all-sufficient reason—it is not shown to be plainly and palpably inconsistent with that instrument. Let the state alone in the management of its purely domestic affairs, so long as it does not appear beyond all question that it has violated the Federal Constitution. This view necessarily results from the principle that the health and safety of the people of a state are primarily for the state to guard and protect. ***

WEST COAST HOTEL CO. v. PARRISH
300 U.S. 379, 57 S.Ct. 578, 81 L.Ed. 703 (1937).

MR. CHIEF JUSTICE HUGHES delivered the opinion of the Court.

This case presents the question of the constitutional validity of the minimum wage law of the state of Washington. The act, entitled "Minimum Wages for Women," authorizes the fixing of minimum wages for women and minors. It provides:

"Sec. 1. The welfare of the State of Washington demands that women and minors be protected from conditions of labor which have a pernicious effect on their health and morals. The State of Washington, therefore, exercising herein its police and sovereign power declares that inadequate wages and unsanitary conditions of labor exert such pernicious effect.

"Sec. 2. It shall be unlawful to employ women or minors in any industry or occupation within the State of Washington under conditions of labor detrimental to their health or morals; and it shall be unlawful to employ women workers in any industry within the State of Washington at wages which are not adequate for their maintenance.

"Sec. 3. There is hereby created a commission to be known as the 'Industrial Welfare Commission' for the State of Washington, to establish such standards of wages and conditions of labor for women and minors employed within the State of Washington, as shall be held hereunder to be reasonable and not detrimental to health and morals, and which shall be sufficient for the decent maintenance of women.'

The appellant conducts a hotel. The appellee Elsie Parrish was employed as a chambermaid and (with her husband) brought this suit to recover the difference between the wages paid her and the minimum wage fixed pursuant to the state law.

The appellant relies upon the decision of this Court in *Adkins v. Children's Hospital*, 261 U.S. 525, which held invalid the District of Columbia Minimum Wage Act which was attacked under the due process clause of the Fifth Amendment. On the argument at bar, counsel for the appellees attempted to distinguish the *Adkins* Case upon the ground that the appellee was employed in a hotel and that the business of an innkeeper was affected with a public interest. That effort at distinction is obviously futile, as it appears that in one of the cases ruled by the *Adkins* opinion the employee was a woman employed as an elevator operator in a hotel.

*** The Supreme Court of Washington has upheld the minimum wage statute of that state. It has decided that the statute is a reasonable exercise of the police power of the state. In reaching that conclusion, the state court has invoked principles long established by this Court in the application of the

Fourteenth Amendment. The state court has refused to regard the decision in the *Adkins* Case as determinative and has pointed to our decisions both before and since that case as justifying its position. We are of the opinion that this ruling of the state court demands on our part a re-examination of the *Adkins* Case. The importance of the question, in which many states having similar laws are concerned, the close division by which the decision in the *Adkins* Case was reached, and the economic conditions which have supervened, and in the light of which the reasonableness of the exercise of the protective power of the state must be considered, make it not only appropriate, but we think imperative, that in deciding the present case the subject should receive fresh consideration. ***

The principle which must control our decision is not in doubt. The constitutional provision invoked is the due process clause of the Fourteenth Amendment governing the states, as the due process clause invoked in the *Adkins* Case governed Congress. In each case the violation alleged by those attacking minimum wage regulation for women is deprivation of freedom of contract. What is this freedom? The Constitution does not speak of freedom of contract. It speaks of liberty and prohibits the deprivation of liberty without due process of law. In prohibiting that deprivation, the Constitution does not recognize an absolute and uncontrollable liberty. Liberty in each of its phases has its history and connotation. But the liberty safeguarded is liberty in a social organization which requires the protection of law against the evils which menace the health, safety, morals, and welfare of the people. Liberty under the Constitution is thus necessarily subject to the restraints of due process, and regulation which is reasonable in relation to its subject and is adopted in the interests of the community is due process. ***

This power under the Constitution to restrict freedom of contract has had many illustrations. That it may be exercised in the public interest with respect to contracts between employer and employee is undeniable. *** In dealing with the relation of employer and employed, the Legislature has necessarily a wide field of discretion in order that there may be suitable protection of health and safety, and that peace and good order may be promoted through regulations designed to insure wholesome conditions of work and freedom from oppression. ***

The minimum wage to be paid under the Washington statute is fixed after full consideration by representatives of employers, employees, and the public. It may be assumed that the minimum wage is fixed in consideration of the services that are performed in the particular occupations under normal conditions. Provision is made for special licenses at less wages in the case of women who are incapable of full service. The statement of MR. JUSTICE HOLMES in the *Adkins* Case is pertinent: "This statute does not compel anybody to pay anything. It simply forbids employment at rates below those fixed as the minimum requirement of health and right living. It is safe to assume that women will not be employed at even the lowest wages allowed unless they earn them, or unless the employer's business can sustain the burden. In short the law in its character and operation is like hundreds of so-called police laws that have been up-held." 261 U.S. 525, at 570. ***

VIII–2. "New Deal Plan for Enlarged Supreme Court" by Clifford K. Berryman. © 1937, The Washington Post. Reprinted with permission.

We think that the view thus expressed [is] sound and that the decision in the *Adkins* Case was a departure from the true application of the principles governing the regulation by the state of the relation of employer and employed. Those principles have been reinforced by our subsequent decisions. ***

With full recognition of the earnestness and vigor which characterize the prevailing opinion in the *Adkins* Case, we find it impossible to reconcile that ruling with these well-considered declarations. What can be closer to the public interest than the health of women and their protection from unscrupulous and overreaching employers? And if the protection of women is a legitimate end of the exercise of state power, how can it be said that the requirement of the payment of a minimum wage fairly fixed in order to meet the very necessities of existence is not an admissible means to that end? The Legislature of the state was clearly entitled to consider the situation of women in employment, the fact that they are in the class receiving the least pay, that their bargaining power is relatively weak, and that they are the ready victims of those who would take advantage of their necessitous circumstances. The Legislature was entitled to adopt measures to reduce the evils of the "sweating system," the exploiting of workers at wages so low as to be insufficient to meet the bare cost of living, thus making their very helplessness the occasion of a most injurious competition. The Legislature had the right to consider that its minimum wage requirements would be an important aid in carrying out its policy of protection. The adoption of similar requirements by many states evidences a deep-seated conviction both as to the presence of the evil and as to the means adapted to check it. Legislative response to that conviction cannot be regarded as arbitrary or capricious and that is all we have to decide. Even if the wisdom of the policy be regarded as debatable and its effects uncertain, still the Legislature is entitled to its judgment.

There is an additional and compelling consideration which recent economic experience has brought into a strong light. The exploitation of a class of workers who are in an unequal position with respect to bargaining power and are thus relatively defenseless against the denial of a living wage is not only detrimental to their health and well being, but casts a direct burden for their support upon the community. What these workers lose in wages the taxpayers are called upon to pay. The bare cost of living must be met. We may take judicial notice of the unparalleled demands for relief which arose during the recent period of depression and still continue to an alarming extent despite the degree of economic recovery which has been achieved. *** The community is not bound to provide what is in effect a subsidy for unconscionable employers. The community may direct its law-making power to correct the abuse which springs from their selfish disregard of the public interest. The argument that the legislation in question constitutes an arbitrary discrimination, because it does not extend to men, is unavailing. This Court has frequently held that the legislative authority, acting within its proper field, is not bound to extend its regulation to all cases which it might possibly reach. The Legislature "is free to recognize degrees of harm and it may confine its restrictions to those classes of cases where the need is deemed to be clearest." If "the law presumably hits the evil where it is most felt, it is not to be overthrown because there are other instances to which it might have been applied." There is no 'doctrinaire requirement' that the legislation should be couched in all embracing terms. *** *Adkins v. Children's Hospital*, should be, and it is, overruled. ***

MR. JUSTICE SUTHERLAND, MR. JUSTICE VAN DEVANTER, MR. JUSTICE MCREYNOLDS, and MR. JUSTICE BUTLER, [dissenting].

*** Under our form of government, where the written Constitution, by its own terms, is the supreme law, some agency, of necessity, must have the power to say the final word as to the validity of a statute assailed as unconstitutional. The Constitution makes it clear that the power has been entrusted to this court when the question arises in a controversy within its jurisdiction; and so long as the power remains there, its exercise cannot be avoided without betrayal of the trust. *** [T]his judicial duty is one of gravity and delicacy; and that rational doubts must be resolved in favor of the constitutionality of the statute. *** Undoubtedly it is the duty of a member of the court, in the process of reaching a right conclusion, to give due weight to the opposing views of his associates; but in the end, the question which he must answer is not whether such views seem sound to those who entertain them, but whether they convince him that the statute is constitutional or engender in his mind a rational doubt upon that issue. *** He cannot subordinate his convictions to that extent and keep faith with his oath or retain his judicial and moral independence.

The suggestion that the only check upon the exercise of the judicial power, when properly invoked, to declare a constitutional right superior to an unconstitutional statute is the judge's own faculty of self-restraint, is both ill considered and mischievous. Self-restraint belongs in the domain of will and not of judgment. The check upon the judge is that imposed by his oath of office, by the Constitution, and by his own conscientious and informed convictions; and since he has the duty to make up his own mind and adjudge accordingly, it is hard to see how there could be any other restraint. ***

It is urged that the question involved should now receive fresh consideration, among other reasons, because of "the economic conditions which have supervened"; but the meaning of the Constitution does not change with the ebb and flow of economic events. *** The judicial function is that of interpretation; it does not include the power of amendment under the guise of interpretation. To miss the point of difference between the two is to miss all that the phrase "supreme law of the land" stands for and to convert what was intended as inescapable and enduring mandates into mere moral reflections.

If the Constitution, intelligently and reasonably construed in the light of these principles, stands in the way of desirable legislation, the blame must rest upon that instrument, and not upon the court for enforcing it according to its terms. The remedy in that situation—and the only true remedy—is to amend the Constitution. ***

In support of minimum-wage legislation, it has been urged, on the one hand, that great benefits will result in favor of underpaid labor, and, on the other hand, that the danger of such legislation is that the minimum will tend to become the maximum and thus bring down the earnings of the more efficient toward the level of the less-efficient employees. But with these speculations we have nothing to do. We are concerned only with the question of constitutionality. ***

The Washington statute, like the one for the District of Columbia, fixes minimum wages for adult women. Adult men and their employers are left free to bargain as they please; and it is a significant and an important fact that all state statutes to which our attention has been called are of like character. The common-law rules restricting the power of women to make contracts have, under our system, long since practically disappeared. Women today stand upon a legal and political equality with men. There is no longer any reason why they should be put in different classes in respect of their legal right to make contracts; nor should they be denied, in effect, the right to compete with men for work paying lower wages which men may be willing to accept. And it is an arbitrary exercise of the legislative power to do so. ***

An appeal to the principle that the Legislature is free to recognize degrees of harm and confine its restrictions accordingly, is but to beg the question, which is—Since the contractual rights of men and women are the same, does the legislation here involved, by restricting only the rights of women to make contracts as to wages, create an arbitrary discrimination? We think it does. Difference of sex affords no reasonable ground for making a restriction applicable to the wage contracts of all working women from which like contracts of all working men are left free. Certainly a suggestion that the bargaining ability of the average woman is not equal to that of the average man would lack substance. The ability to make a fair bargain, as every one knows, does not depend upon sex.

If, in the light of the facts, the state legislation, without reason or for reasons of mere expediency, excluded men from the provisions of the legislation, the power was exercised arbitrarily. On the other hand, if such legislation in respect of men was properly omitted on the ground that it would be unconstitutional, the same conclusion of unconstitutionality is inescapable in respect of similar legislative restraint in the case of women. ***

Notes

1. **Critique of *Lochner*.**

   · The Constitution says nothing about theories of economics.

   · The state had legitimate justifications for regulation.

   · There is no "private" sphere of worker-management "liberty."

   · The Court took as a given an inappropriate common law "baseline."

2. **Defense of *Lochner*.**

   · The decision was good policy, at least for consumers of baked goods.

   · The statute was not a health measure at all, nor the result of bargaining inequality; it was rent-seeking by big unions and large employers.

   · There was more Constitutional text (if you include the Contracts and Takings Clauses) than with other substantive due process interpretations.

3. **Modern Economic Substantive Due Process.** Does the following case indicate a revival of economic substantive due process? Are there other parts of the constitutional scheme that underlie the application of due process here?

STATE FARM v. CAMPBELL
123 S. Ct. 1513, 155 L.Ed.2d 585 (2003).

JUSTICE KENNEDY delivered the opinion of the Court.

We address once again the measure of punishment, by means of punitive damages, a State may impose upon a defendant in a civil case. The question is whether, in the circumstances we shall recount, an award of $145 million in punitive damages, where full compensatory damages are $1 million, is excessive and in violation of the Due Process Clause of the Fourteenth Amendment to the Constitution of the United States.

In 1981, Curtis Campbell (Campbell) was driving with his wife, Inez Preece Campbell, in Cache County, Utah. He decided to pass six vans traveling ahead of them on a two-lane highway. *** In the ensuing wrongful death and tort action, *** "a consensus was reached early on by the investigators and witnesses that Mr. Campbell's unsafe pass had indeed caused the crash." Campbell's insurance company, petitioner State Farm Mutual Automobile Insurance Company (State Farm), nonetheless decided to contest liability and declined offers *** to settle the claims for the policy limit of $50,000 ($25,000 per claimant). State Farm also ignored the advice of one of its own investigators and took the case to trial, assuring the Campbells that "their assets were safe, that they had no liability for the accident, that [State Farm] would represent their interests, and that they did not need to procure separate counsel." To the contrary, a jury determined that Campbell was 100 percent at fault, and a judgment was returned for $185,849, far more than the amount offered in settlement.

At first State Farm refused to cover the $135,849 in excess liability. *** In 1989, the Utah Supreme Court denied Campbell's appeal in the wrongful death and tort actions. State Farm then paid the entire judgment, including the amounts in excess of the policy limits. The Campbells nonetheless filed a complaint against State Farm alleging bad faith, fraud, and intentional infliction of emotional distress. *** [At trial] the jury determined that State Farm's decision not to settle was unreasonable because there was a substantial likelihood of an excess verdict.

Before the second phase of the action against State Farm we decided *BMW of North America, Inc. v. Gore,* 517 U.S. 559 (1996), and refused to sustain a $2 million punitive damages award which accompanied a verdict of only $4,000 in compensatory damages. *** The jury awarded the Campbells $2.6 million in compensatory damages [later reduced to $1 million] and $145 million in punitive damages. *** [I]n our judicial system compensatory and punitive damages, although usually awarded at the same time by the same decisionmaker, serve different purposes. Compensatory damages "are intended to redress the concrete loss that the plaintiff has suffered by reason of the defendant's wrongful conduct." By contrast, punitive damages serve a broader function; they are aimed at deterrence and retribution.

While States possess discretion over the imposition of punitive damages, it is well established that there are procedural and substantive constitutional limitations on these awards. The Due Process Clause of the Fourteenth Amendment prohibits the imposition of grossly excessive or arbitrary punishments on a tortfeasor. *** To the extent an award is grossly excessive, it furthers no legitimate purpose and constitutes an arbitrary deprivation of property. *** "[T]he most important indicium of the reasonableness of a punitive damages award is the degree of reprehensibility of the defendant's conduct. *** [W]e must acknowledge that State Farm's handling of the claims against the Campbells merits no praise. *** While we do not suggest there was error in awarding punitive damages based upon State Farm's conduct toward the Campbells, a more modest punishment for this reprehensible conduct could have satisfied the State's legitimate objectives, and the Utah courts should have gone no further.

This case, instead, was used as a platform to expose, and punish, the perceived deficiencies of State Farm's operations throughout the country. The Utah Supreme Court's opinion makes explicit that State Farm was being condemned for its nationwide policies rather than for the conduct direct toward the Campbells. This was, as well, an explicit rationale of the trial court's decision in approving the award ***. The Campbells contend that State Farm has only itself to blame for the reliance upon dissimilar and out-of-state conduct evidence. The record does not support this contention. From their opening statements onward the Campbells framed this case as a chance to rebuke State Farm for its nationwide activities. *** A State cannot punish a defendant for conduct that may have been lawful where it occurred. Nor, as a general rule, does a State have a legitimate concern in imposing punitive damages to punish a defendant for unlawful acts committed outside of the State's jurisdiction. Any proper adjudication of conduct that occurred outside Utah to other persons would require their inclusion, and, to those parties, the Utah courts, in the usual case, would need to apply the laws of their relevant jurisdiction.

Here, the Campbells do not dispute that much of the out- of-state conduct was lawful where it occurred. They argue, however, that such evidence was not the primary basis for the punitive damages award and was relevant to the extent it demonstrated, in a general sense, State Farm's motive against its insured. This argument misses the mark. Lawful out-of-state conduct may be probative when it demonstrates the deliberateness and culpability of the defendant's action in the State where it is tortious, but that conduct must have a nexus to the specific harm suffered by the plaintiff. A jury must be instructed, furthermore, that it may not use evidence of out-of-state conduct to punish a defendant for action that was lawful in the jurisdiction where it occurred. A basic principle of federalism is that each State may make its own reasoned judgment about what conduct is permitted or proscribed within its borders, and each State alone can determine what measure of punishment, if any, to impose on a defendant who acts within its jurisdiction.

For a more fundamental reason, however, the Utah courts erred in relying upon this and other evidence: The courts awarded punitive damages to punish and deter conduct that bore no relation to the Campbells' harm. A defendant's dissimilar acts, independent from the acts upon which liability was premised, may not serve as the basis for punitive damages. A defendant should be punished for the conduct that harmed the plaintiff, not for being an unsavory individual or business. Due process does not permit courts, in the calculation of punitive damages, to adjudicate the merits of other parties' hypothetical claims against a defendant under the guise of the reprehensibility analysis, but we have no doubt the Utah Supreme Court did that here. Punishment on these bases creates the possibility of multiple punitive damages awards for the same conduct; for in the usual case nonparties are not bound by the judgment some other plaintiff obtains. ***

[W]e have been reluctant to identify concrete constitutional limits on the ratio between harm, or potential harm, to the plaintiff and the punitive damages award. We decline again to impose a bright-line ratio which a punitive damages award cannot exceed. Our jurisprudence and the principles it has now established demonstrate, however, that, in practice, few awards exceeding a single-digit ratio between punitive and compensatory damages, to a significant degree, will satisfy due process. In [earlier cases,] in upholding a punitive damages award, we concluded that an award of more than four times the amount of compensatory damages might be close to the line of constitutional impropriety. *** The Court further referenced a long legislative history, dating back over 700 years and going forward to today, providing for sanctions of double, treble, or quadruple damages to deter and punish. While these ratios are not binding, they are instructive. They demonstrate what should be obvious: Single-digit multipliers are more likely to comport with due process, while still achieving the State's goals of deterrence and retribution, than awards with ratios in range of 500 to 1, or, in this case, of 145 to 1.

Nonetheless, because there are no rigid benchmarks that a punitive damages award may not surpass, ratios greater than those we have previously upheld may comport with due process where "a particularly egregious act has resulted in only a small amount of economic damages." The converse is also true, however. When compensatory damages are substantial, then a lesser ratio, perhaps only equal to compensatory damages, can reach the outermost limit of the due process guarantee. The precise award in any case, of course, must be based upon the facts and circumstances of the defendant's conduct and the harm to the plaintiff.

In sum, courts must ensure that the measure of punishment is both reasonable and proportionate to the amount of harm to the plaintiff and to the general damages recovered. In the context of this case, we have no doubt that there is a presumption against an award that has a 145-to-1 ratio. The compensatory award in this case was substantial; the Campbells were awarded $1 million for a year and a half of emotional distress. This was complete compensation. The harm arose from a transaction in the economic realm, not from some physical assault or trauma; there were no physical injuries; and State Farm paid the excess verdict before the complaint was filed, so the Campbells suffered only minor economic injuries for the 18-month period in which State Farm refused to resolve the claim against them. The compensatory damages for the injury suffered here, moreover, likely were based on a component which was duplicated in the punitive award. Much of the distress was caused by the outrage and humiliation the Campbells suffered at the actions of their insurer; and it is a major role of punitive damages to condemn such conduct. Compensatory damages, however, already contain this punitive element.

The Utah Supreme Court sought to justify the massive award by pointing to State Farm's purported failure to report a prior $100 million punitive damages award in Texas to its corporate headquarters; the fact that State Farm's policies have affected numerous Utah consumers; the fact that State Farm will only be punished in one out of every 50,000 cases as a matter of statistical probability; and State Farm's enormous wealth. Since the Supreme Court of Utah discussed the Texas award when applying the ratio guidepost, we discuss it here. The Texas award, however, should have been analyzed in the context of the reprehensibility guidepost only. The failure of the company to report the Texas award is out-of-state conduct that, if the conduct were similar, might have had some bearing on the degree of reprehensibility, subject to the limitations we have described. Here, it was dissimilar, and of such marginal relevance that it should have been accorded little or no weight. The award was rendered in a first-party lawsuit; no judgment was entered in the case; and it was later settled for a fraction of the verdict. With respect to the Utah Supreme Court's second justification, the Campbells' inability to direct us to testimony demonstrating harm to the people of Utah (other than those directly involved in this case) indicates that the adverse effect on the State's general population was in fact minor.

The remaining premises for the Utah Supreme Court's decision bear no relation to the award's reasonableness or proportionality to the harm. They are, rather, arguments that seek to defend a departure from well-established constraints on punitive damages. While States enjoy considerable discretion in deducing when punitive damages are warranted, each award must comport with the principles set forth in *Gore.* Here the argument that State Farm will be punished in only the rare case, coupled with reference to its assets (which, of course, are what other insured parties in Utah and other States must rely upon for payment of claims) had little to do with the actual harm sustained by the Campbells. The wealth of a defendant cannot justify an otherwise unconstitutional punitive damages award. The principles set forth in *Gore* must be implemented with care, to ensure both reasonableness and proportionality.

The third guidepost in *Gore* is the disparity between the punitive damages award and the "civil penalties authorized or imposed in comparable cases." *** Great care must be taken to avoid use of the civil process to assess criminal penalties that can be imposed only after the heightened protections of a criminal trial have been observed, including, of course, its higher standards of proof. Punitive damages are not a substitute for the criminal process ***. The most relevant civil sanction under Utah state law for the wrong done to the Campbells appears to be a $10,000 fine for an act of fraud, an amount dwarfed by the $145 million punitive damages award. The Supreme Court of Utah speculated about the loss of State Farm's business license, the disgorgement of profits, and possible imprisonment, but here again its references were to the broad fraudulent scheme drawn from evidence of out-of-state and dissimilar conduct. This analysis was insufficient to justify the award. *** The punitive award of $145 million, therefore, was neither reasonable nor proportionate to the wrong committed, and it was an irrational and arbitrary deprivation of the property of the defendant. The proper calculation of punitive damages under the principles we have discussed should be resolved, in the first instance, by the Utah courts. ***

JUSTICE SCALIA, dissenting.

*** [T]he Due Process Clause provides no substantive protections against "excessive" or "'unreasonable'" awards of punitive damages. ***

JUSTICE THOMAS, dissenting.

*** "I continue to believe that the Constitution does not constrain the size of punitive damages awards." ***

JUSTICE GINSBURG, dissenting.

Not long ago, this Court was hesitant to impose a federal check on state-court judgments awarding punitive damages. *** It was not until 1996, in *Gore*, that the Court, for the first time, invalidated a state-court punitive damages assessment as unreasonably large. If our activity in this domain is now "well-established," it takes place on ground not long held. *** The large size of the award upheld by the Utah Supreme Court in this case indicates why damage-capping legislation may be altogether fitting and proper. Neither the amount of the award nor the trial record, however, justifies this Court's substitution of its judgment for that of Utah's competent decisionmakers. In this regard, I count it significant that, on the key criterion "reprehensibility," there is a good deal more to the story than the Court's abbreviated account tells. *** State Farm's "policies and practices," the trial evidence thus bore out, were "responsible for the injuries suffered by the Campbells," and the means used to implement those policies could be found "callous, clandestine, fraudulent, and dishonest." The Utah Supreme Court, relying on the trial court's record-based recitations, understandably characterized State Farm's behavior as "egregious and malicious." ***

What is infirm about the Campbells' theory that their experience with State Farm exemplifies and reflects an overarching underpayment scheme, one that caused "repeated misconduct of the sort that injured them"? The Court's silence on that score is revealing: Once one recognizes that the Campbells did show "conduct by State Farm similar to that which harmed them," it becomes impossible to shrink the reprehensibility analysis to this sole case, or to maintain, at odds with the determination of the trial court, that "the adverse effect on the State's general population was in fact minor."

Evidence of out-of-state conduct, the Court acknowledges, may be "probative [even if the conduct is lawful in the state where it occurred] when it demonstrates the deliberateness and culpability of the defendant's action in the State where it is tortuous ***." "Other acts" evidence concerning practices both in and out of State was introduced in this case to show just such "deliberateness" and "culpability." The evidence was admissible, the trial court ruled: (1) to document State Farm's "reprehensible" PP & R program; and (2) to "rebut [State Farm's] assertion that [its] actions toward the Campbells were inadvertent errors or mistakes in judgment." Viewed in this light, there surely was "a nexus" between much of the "other acts" evidence and "the specific harm suffered by [the Campbells]."

When the Court first ventured to override state-court punitive damages awards, it did so moderately. The Court recalled that "[i]n our federal system, States necessarily have considerable flexibility in determining the level of punitive damages that they will allow in different classes of cases and in any particular case." Today's decision exhibits no such respect and restraint. No longer content to accord state-court judgments "a strong presumption of validity," the Court announces that "few awards exceeding a single-digit ratio between punitive and compensatory damages, to a significant degree, will satisfy due process." Moreover, the Court adds, when compensatory damages are substantial, doubling those damages "can reach the outermost limit of the due process guarantee." In a legislative scheme or a state high court's design to cap punitive damages, the handiwork in setting single-digit and 1-to-1 benchmarks could hardly be questioned; in a judicial decree imposed on the States by this Court under the banner of substantive due process, the numerical controls today's decision installs seem to me boldly out of order. ***

Notes

1. **Horizontal Federalism.** Is the protection of states from overreaching by their neighbors work that should be done by the Due Process Clause? Isn't this as much a federalism concern as those covered in earlier chapters of this book? Why couldn't this case have been handled through the Full Faith and Credit Clause or the Article IV Privileges and Immunities Clause? Would pre-constitutional practices be relevant in deciding this case?

2. **Dormant Commerce Clause.** Is the Court using Due Process Clause analysis like Dormant Commerce Clause analysis in Chapter VI to restrict states from exporting economic consequences outside their borders? Consider this language: "[A] State [does not] have a legitimate concern in imposing punitive damages to punish a defendant for unlawful acts committed outside of the State's jurisdiction. Any proper adjudication of conduct that occurred outside Utah to other persons would require their inclusion, and, to those parties, the Utah courts, in the usual case, would need to apply the laws of their relevant jurisdiction." Should discrimination or burdens on commerce analysis have been argued here?

3. **Federal Legislation.** Does the Court's decision point to the need for a Congressional solution to tort liability issues?

4. **The Contracts Clause.** Review the Constitution in search of provisions which explicitly protect economic liberty or property interests. One clause that jumps out is the bold assertion of Article I, § 10, cl. 1 that "No State shall [pass any Law] impairing the Obligation of Contracts." In *Fletcher v. Peck*, 10 U.S. (6 Cranch) 87 (1810), and the *Dartmouth College Case*, 17 U.S. (4 Wheat.) 518 (1819), the Marshall Court used this clause to invalidate Georgia's rescission of land grants and a New Hampshire law changing the provisions of Dartmouth's state charter. The Marshall Court also used this clause to limit state regulation of business corporations. The Taney Court (1836–64) retreated from these cases, however, most notably in *Charles River Bridge v. Warren Bridge*, 36 U.S. (11 Pet.) 420 (1837), in which it permitted Massachusetts to adopt new policies which abrogated a public charter to a ferry company. In *Home Building & Loan Association v. Blaisdell*, 290 U.S. 398 (1934), the Court held, in the midst of the Great Depression, that a Minnesota statute reducing lenders' contractual rights of foreclosure did not violate the Contracts Clause. Thereafter, the Contracts Clause was believed dead until the late 1970s, when two cases, *United States Trust Co. v. New Jersey*, 431 U.S. 1 (1977) and *Allied Structural Steel Co. v. Spannaus*, 438 U.S. 234 (1978), struck down state statutes abrogating contractual commitments in circumstances where the public justifications were

far weaker than in *Blaisdell*. More recent cases, however, seem to give more deference to state laws which abrogate contractual expectations. *See, e.g., Energy Reserves Group, Inc. v. Kansas Power & Light Co.*, 459 U.S. 400 (1983) (upholding abrogation of natural gas contracts where the state was not a beneficiary of a law concerning a "highly regulated industry" to avoid "unforeseen windfall profits"). The bottom line is that the Court's decisions can be viewed as involving either great deference to state law contract abrogations or as involving more careful scrutiny when the Court thinks that is justified.

5. **The Takings Clause.** Another clause protecting property interests is the final clause of the Fifth Amendment: "nor shall private property be taken for public use, without just compensation." Generally, American law schools cover the Takings Clause in Property rather than Constitutional Law. Despite this, a few words about this clause are appropriate. The most obvious application of the clause is to situations where governments condemn real estate for roads and other public projects. Th e clause has also been applied to situations where governmental activity, from flooding connected with damming rivers to noise associated with a public airport, renders private real estate unusable or virtually unusable. In such cases, only the "just" amount of compensation is at issue. More complex issues are raised when governmental regulation reduces the value of individual or business properties. Compare *Pennsylvania Coal v. Mahon*, 260 U.S. 393 (1922) (regulation making coal mining completely uneconomical violates Takings Clause) with *Keystone Bituminous Coal Association v. DeBenedictis*, 480 U.S. 470 (1987) (regulation does not violate clause absent findings that coal holdings were worthless). The Court has recognized that "Government hardly could go on if to some extent values incident to property could not be diminished without paying for every such change *** [therefore] government may execute laws or programs that adversely affect recognized economic values." *Penn Central Transportation Co. v. City of New York*, 438 U.S. 104 (1978). However, even in a regulatory context, it has sometimes required the state to compensate property owners for loss of "all beneficial uses" unless the state can "identify background principles of nuisance and property law that prohibit the uses he now intends in the circumstances in which the property is presently found." *Lucas v. South Carolina Coastal Council*, 505 U.S. 1003 (1992). To date, the Supreme Court has not addressed what compensation, if any, would be required if a regulation partially takes a person's property nor have they considered how damages should be measured in regulatory takings cases.

6. **Other Early Substantive Due Process Cases.** Even during the "heyday" of economic substantive due process, the Court upheld more state regulations than it invalidated. Moreover, the Court decided some substantive due process cases that did not involve economics. See *Meyer v. Nebraska*, 262 U.S. 390 (1923) (invalidating Nebraska law that prohibited teaching young children in any public or private school in a language other than English), and *Pierce v. Society of Sisters*, 268 U.S. 510 (1925) (invalidating state requirement that all children attend public schools).

2. PERSONAL RIGHTS

PREFATORY NOTE: INCORPORATION OF THE BILL OF RIGHTS

While strongly repudiating economic substantive due process, the Court has taken a very different course in interpreting what "personal rights" are protected by the Due Process Clause of the Fourteenth Amendment. This introductory note will examine how this clause has come to protect virtually all the personal rights enumerated in the first eight amendments to the Constitution. It will also touch on how the Due Process Clause of the Fifth Amendment, applicable to the federal government, has come to encompass an equal protection component. The remainder of the chapter will focus on personal rights other than those explicitly applicable against either the state or federal government that have come to be protected through judicial interpretation.

Both the Fifth and Fourteenth Amendments require "due process of law." The former provision was adopted to ensure that the federal government did not dispense with basic protections of rights with origins going back to the English Magna Carta of 1215. The latter added a similarly worded limitation applicable to the states. The textual parallelism appears to end here, however. The Fifth Amendment does not contain any reference to the "equal protection of the laws" and the Fourteenth Amendment does not say anything about matters contained in the Bill of Rights (freedom of speech, freedom of religion, the right to bear arms, cruel and unusual punishment, jury trials, double jeopardy, self-incrimination, etc.). During the end of the 19th century and the first half of the 20th century, the Supreme Court struggled over the meaning of these textual differences between constitutional rights asserted against the United States and its agents and those asserted against the states and their agents.

James Madison, who introduced the Bill of Rights in Congress, initially proposed that some of the protections adopted in the Bill of Rights be applied also to the states. *See* Appendix B. In making these proposals, Madison was of course aware that most states had their own bills of rights, and that the wording and content of these protections varied somewhat from state to state. Thus, Madison would have established certain minimum standards or a "floor" below which a state could not go in denying certain citizen rights. But Madison's views did not prevail, and the Bill of Rights as adopted made no mention of application to the states.   The Ninth Amendment reserved "certain rights" not enumerated to "the people" without specifying whether these rights would apply against the federal government, the states, or both. Further, the Tenth Amendment reserved the "powers not delegated to the United States" to "the States respectively, or to the people."

Thus, it should come as no shock to you that, prior to adoption of the Fourteenth Amendment, the Supreme Court held the Bill of Rights inapplicable to the states. *Barron v. Mayor and City Council of Baltimore*, 32 U.S. (7 Pet.) 243 (1833). Less forthright is the course by which the Bill of Rights has been held by the Court to apply, for the most part, to the states. The easiest route for this to happen would have been for the Court to hold that the "privileges or immunities" of the Fourteenth Amendment established the Bill of Rights guarantees as a minimum floor of United States citizens' rights. But, as we have seen, that route was foreclosed by the *Slaughter-House Cases*.

The *Slaughter-House Cases* were far less definitive in restricting the reach of the Due Process Clause of the Fourteenth Amendment. JUSTICE MILLER's famous opinion had concluded that the Due Process Clause of the Fourteenth Amendment was limited to procedural due process. In the late 1800s, however, several justices were appointed to the Supreme Court who saw the Due Process Clause in economic terms. *See Lochner*, supra. Within a few years, the Court would state that if a law "purporting to have been enacted to protect the public health, the public morals, or the public safety, has no real or substantial relations to those objects, or is a palpable invasion of rights secured by the fundamental law, it is the duty of the courts to so adjudge, and thereby give effect to the Constitution." *Mugler v. Kansas*, 123 U.S. 623 (1887). Beginning with *Chicago, Burlington & Quincy Railroad v. Chicago*, 166 U.S. 226 (1897), the Court began incorporating the various Bill of Rights provisions into the Due Process Clause of the Fourteenth Amendment. This case held that the Takings Clause of the Fifth Amendment applied to state takings of property.

The full expansion of the Due Process Clause of the Fourteenth Amendment to accommodate the Bill of Rights protections came during the middle third of the twentieth century. In *Palko v. Connecticut*, 302 U.S. 319 (1937), JUSTICE CARDOZO wrote what has become the leading case concerning whether the Bill of Rights applies to the States through the Due Process Clause of the Fourteenth Amendment. Cardozo rejected the notion that all the Bill of Rights provisions were incorporated, whether substantive (like free speech) or procedural (like grand jury indictment). He first summarized a significant number of the Court's apparently inconsistent decisions, including cases which had guaranteed against free speech infringement by the states but had rejected the need for states to commence criminal prosecutions by grand jury indictment. Then Cardozo wrote that only those portions of the Bill of Rights "implicit in the concept of ordered liberty," those matters "so rooted in the traditions and conscience of our people as to be ranked as fundamental" were part of the "due process" limiting state power. The problem, of course, is in deciding what specific matters fit these general descriptions without resorting to concepts of natural law (see the discussion of *Calder v. Bull*, supra p. 40). In *Palko*, the state retried a defendant because the first trial court had erroneously excluded evidence and misinstructed the jury on the difference between first and second-degree murder; the defendant claimed this was double jeopardy. How would you decide the issue in *Palko*? Although opaque, Cardozo's definition of fundamental rights (i.e. those "*implicit in the concept of ordered liberty*," and "*so rooted in the traditions and conscience of our people as to be ranked as fundamental*") has lasted since it was written in 1937 and is used by today's Court in determining what constitutes a fundamental right. *See Washington v. Glucksberg*, 521 U.S. 702 (1997), infra p. 651.

Another leading case, *Adamson v. California*, 332 U.S. 46 (1947), concerned whether the Fifth Amendment's privilege against self-incrimination, applicable in federal court, applied in state court. *Adamson* contains a spirited exchange between JUSTICE FELIX FRANKFURTER (an erudite former Harvard Law School teacher appointed by FDR) and JUSTICE

HUGO BLACK (a populist former Alabama Senator also appointed by FDR). JUSTICE FRANKFURTER reaffirmed the *Palko* approach, saying that 42 of the 43 Supreme Court Justices who had looked at the scope of the Fourteenth Amendment's Due Process Clause agreed with that approach. Only one "eccentric exception," wrote Frankfurter, "indicated a belief that the Fourteenth Amendment was a shorthand summary of the first eight Amendments." JUSTICE BLACK, in response, derided "the 'natural law' theory of the Constitution" which "degrade[s] the constitutional safeguards of the Bill of Rights" and "simultaneously appropriate[s] for this Court a broad power which we are not authorized by the Constitution to exercise." In the long run, JUSTICE BLACK prevailed. The only provisions of the first eight amendments not "selectively incorporated" are the Second and Third Amendments, the Fifth Amendment requirement of grand jury indictment, and the Seventh Amendment right to jury trial in civil cases. Many of these developments are reviewed in *Duncan v. Louisiana*, 391 U.S. 145 (1968), in which the Court rephrased the inquiry as whether "given this kind of system a particular procedure is fundamental—whether, that is, a procedure is necessary to an Anglo–American regime of ordered liberty."

JUSTICE THOMAS' concurrence in *Zelman v. Simmons-Harris*, 536 U.S. 639 (2002), which upheld Cleveland's school voucher program, suggests a new approach to at least some selective incorporations of the Bill of Rights.

*** The Establishment Clause originally protected States, and by extension their citizens, from the imposition of an established religion by the Federal Government. Whether and how this Clause should constrain state action under the Fourteenth Amendment is a more difficult question. *** When rights are incorporated against the States through the Fourteenth Amendment they should advance, not constrain, individual liberty.

Consequently, in the context of the Establishment Clause, it may well be that state action should be evaluated on different terms than similar action by the Federal Government. *** Thus, while the Federal Government may "make no law respecting an establishment of religion," the States may pass laws that include or touch on religious matters so long as these laws do not impede free exercise rights or any other individual religious liberty interest. By considering the particular religious liberty right alleged to be invaded by a State, federal courts can strike a proper balance between the demands of the Fourteenth Amendment on the one hand and the federalism prerogatives of States on the other. ***

Faced with a severe educational crisis, the State of Ohio enacted wide-ranging educational reform that allows voluntary participation of private and religious schools in educating poor urban children otherwise condemned to failing public schools. The program does not force any individual to submit to religious indoctrination or education. It simply gives parents a greater choice as to where and in what manner to educate their children. This is a choice that those with greater means have routinely exercised. *** [S]chool choice programs that involve religious schools appear unconstitutional only to those who would twist the Fourteenth Amendment against itself by expansively incorporating the Establishment Clause. Converting the Fourteenth Amendment from a guarantee of opportunity to an obstacle against education reform distorts our constitutional values and disserves those in the greatest need.

There is perhaps even less textual support for applying the Fourteenth Amendment to constrain the federal government than there is textual or historical support for incorporating the Bill of Rights into the Fourteenth Amendment as a constraint on state governments. Yet that is precisely what has happened. The equal protection component of the Fourteenth Amendment has been "reverse incorporated" into the Due Process Clause of the Fifth Amendment. The seminal case, *Bolling v. Sharpe*, 347 U.S. 497 (1954), held that segregation of schools in the District of Columbia violated the "equal protection component" of the Due Process Clause of the Fifth Amendment.

The cases below go one step beyond those discussed above: they involve application of rights mentioned neither in the Bill of Rights nor in the Fourteenth Amendment.

a. *Origins of Unenumerated Personal Rights*

GRISWOLD v. CONNECTICUT
381 U.S. 479, 85 S.Ct. 1678, 14 L.Ed.2d 510 (1965).

MR. JUSTICE DOUGLAS delivered the opinion of the Court.

Appellant Griswold is Executive Director of the Planned Parenthood League of Connecticut. Appellant Buxton is a licensed physician and a professor at the Yale Medical School who served as Medical Director for the League at its Center in New Haven—a center open and operating from November 1 to November 10, 1961, when appellants were arrested.

They gave information, instruction, and medical advice to married persons as to the means of preventing conception. They examined the wife and prescribed the best contraceptive device or material for her use. Fees were usually charged, although some couples were serviced free.

The statutes whose constitutionality is involved in this appeal *** provide: "Any person who uses any drug, medicinal article or instrument for the purpose of preventing conception shall be fined not less than fifty dollars or imprisoned not less than sixty days nor more than one year or be both fined and imprisoned." [and] "Any person who assists, abets, counsels, causes, hires or commands another to commit any offense may be prosecuted and punished as if he were the principal offender."

The appellants were found guilty as accessories and fined $100 each, against the claim that the accessory statute as so applied violated the Fourteenth Amendment.

We think that appellants have standing to raise the constitutional rights of the married people with whom they had a professional relationship. *** Certainly the accessory should have standing to assert that the offense which he is charged with assisting is not, or cannot constitutionally be a crime. ***

Coming to the merits, we are met with a wide range of questions that implicate the Due Process Clause of the Fourteenth Amendment. Overtones of some arguments suggest that *Lochner* should be our guide. But we decline that invitation as we did in *West Coast Hotel Co. v. Parrish*, 300 U.S. 379 [and others]. We do not sit as a super-legislature to determine the wisdom, need, and propriety of laws that touch economic problems, business affairs, or social conditions. This law, however, operates directly on an intimate relation of husband and wife and their physician's role in one aspect of that relation.

The association of people is not mentioned in the Constitution nor in the Bill of Rights. The right to educate a child in a school of the parents' choice—whether public or private or parochial—is also not mentioned. Nor is the right to study any particular subject or any foreign language. Yet the First Amendment has been construed to include certain of those rights.

*** [The] State may not, consistently with the spirit of the First Amendment, contract the spectrum of available knowledge. The right of freedom of speech and press includes not only the right to utter or to print, but the right to distribute, the right to receive, the right to read, and freedom of inquiry, freedom of thought, and freedom to teach. Without those peripheral rights the specific rights would be less secure. ***

In *NAACP v. State of Alabama*, 357 U.S. 449, 462, we protected the "freedom to associate and privacy in one's associations," noting that freedom of association was a peripheral First Amendment right. Disclosure of membership lists of a constitutionally valid association, we held, was invalid "as entailing the likelihood of a substantial restraint upon the exercise by petitioner's members of their right to freedom of association." In other words, the First Amendment has a penumbra where privacy is protected from governmental intrusion. In like context, we have protected forms of "association" that are not political in the customary sense but pertain to the social, legal, and economic benefit of the members. ***

[Specific] guarantees in the Bill of Rights have penumbras, formed by emanations from those guarantees that help give them life and substance. Various guarantees create zones of privacy. The right of association contained in the penumbra of the First Amendment is one, as we have seen. The Third Amendment in its prohibition against the quartering of soldiers "in any house" in time of peace without the consent of the owner is another facet of that privacy. The Fourth Amendment explicitly affirms the "right of the people to be secure in their persons, houses, papers, and effects, against unreasonable searches and seizures." The Fifth Amendment in its Self–Incrimination Clause enables the citizen to create a zone of privacy which government may not force him to surrender to his detriment. The Ninth Amendment provides: "The enumeration in the Constitution, of certain rights, shall not be construed to deny or disparage others retained by the people."

The Fourth and Fifth Amendments were described in *Boyd v. United States*, 116 U.S. 616, 630, as protection against all governmental invasions "of the sanctity of a man's home and the privacies of life." We recently referred in *Mapp v. Ohio*, 367 U.S. 643, 656, to the Fourth Amendment as creating a "right to privacy, no less important than any other right carefully and particularly reserved to the people."

We have had many controversies over these penumbral rights of "privacy and repose." *See, e.g.,* *** *Skinner v. State of Oklahoma*, 316 U.S. 535, 541. [*Skinner* and other] cases bear witness that the right of privacy which presses for recognition here is a legitimate one.

The present case, then, concerns a relationship lying within the zone of privacy created by several fundamental constitutional guarantees. And it concerns a law which, in forbidding the use of contraceptives rather than regulating their manufacture or sale, seeks to achieve its goals by means having a maximum destructive impact upon that relationship. Such a law cannot stand in light of the familiar principle, so often applied by this Court, that a "governmental purpose to control or prevent activities constitutionally subject to state regulation may not be achieved by means which sweep unnecessarily broadly and thereby invade the area of protected freedoms." *NAACP v. Alabama.* Would we allow the police to search the sacred precincts of marital bedrooms for telltale signs of the use of contraceptives? The very idea is repulsive to the notions of privacy surrounding the marriage relationship.

We deal with a right of privacy older than the Bill of Rights—older than our political parties, older than our school system. Marriage is a coming together for better or for worse, hopefully enduring, and intimate to the degree of being sacred. It is an association that promotes a way of life, not causes; a harmony in living, not political faiths; a bilateral loyalty, not commercial or social projects. Yet it is an association for as noble a purpose as any involved in our prior decisions.

MR. JUSTICE GOLDBERG, whom THE CHIEF JUSTICE and MR. JUSTICE BRENNAN join, concurring.

*** This Court, in a series of decisions, has held that the Fourteenth Amendment absorbs and applies to the States those specifics of the first eight amendments which express fundamental personal rights. The language and history of the Ninth Amendment reveal that the Framers of the Constitution believed that there are additional fundamental rights, protected from governmental infringement, which exist alongside those fundamental rights specifically mentioned in the first eight constitutional amendments. ***

The Ninth Amendment reads, "The enumeration in the Constitution, of certain rights, shall not be construed to deny or disparage others retained by the people." The Amendment is almost entirely the work of James Madison. It was introduced in Congress by him and passed the House and Senate with little or no debate and virtually no change in language. It was proffered to quiet expressed fears that a bill of specifically enumerated rights could not be sufficiently broad to cover all essential rights and that the specific mention of certain rights would be interpreted as a denial that others were protected. ***

While this Court has had little occasion to interpret the Ninth Amendment, "(i)t cannot be presumed that any clause in the constitution is intended to be without effect." *Marbury v. Madison*, 1 Cranch 137, 174. In interpreting the Constitution, "real effect should be given to all the words it uses." *** To hold that a right so basic and fundamental and so deep-rooted in our society as the right of privacy in marriage may be infringed because that right is not guaranteed in so many words by the first eight amendments to the Constitution is to ignore the Ninth Amendment and to give it no effect whatsoever. ***

The entire fabric of the Constitution and the purposes that clearly underlie its specific guarantees demonstrate that the rights to marital privacy and to marry and raise a family are of similar order and magnitude as the fundamental rights specifically protected.

Although the Constitution does not speak in so many words of the right of privacy in marriage, I cannot believe that it offers these fundamental rights no protection. The fact that no particular provision of the Constitution explicitly forbids the State from disrupting the traditional relation of the family *** surely does not show that the Government was meant to have the power to do so. Rather, as the Ninth Amendment expressly recognizes, there are fundamental personal rights such as this one, which are protected from abridgment by the Government though not specifically mentioned in the Constitution. ***

The logic of the dissents would sanction federal or state legislation that seems to me even more plainly unconstitutional than the statute before us. Surely the Government, absent a showing of a compelling subordinating state interest, could not decree that all husbands and wives must be sterilized after two children have been born to them. Yet by their reasoning such an invasion of marital privacy would not be subject to constitutional challenge because, while it might be "silly," no provision of the Constitution specifically prevents the Government from curtailing the marital right to bear children and raise a family. ***

In sum, I believe that the right of privacy in the marital relation is fundamental and basic—a personal right "retained by the people" within the meaning of the Ninth Amendment. Connecticut cannot constitutionally abridge this fundamental right, which is protected by the Fourteenth Amendment from infringement by the States. ***

MR. JUSTICE HARLAN, concurring in the judgment.

I fully agree with the judgment of reversal, but find myself unable to join the Court's opinion. *** In my view, the proper constitutional inquiry in this case is whether this Connecticut statute infringes the Due Process Clause of the Fourteenth Amendment because the enactment violates basic values "implicit in the concept of ordered liberty," *Palko v. State of Connecticut*, 302 U.S. 319, 325. For reasons stated at length in my dissenting opinion in *Poe v. Ullman*, [367 U.S. 497 (1961)], I believe that it does. While the relevant inquiry may be aided by resort to one or more of the provisions of the Bill of Rights, it is not dependent on them or any of their radiations. The Due Process Clause of the Fourteenth Amendment stands, in my opinion, on its own bottom. ***

[What follows is an edited version of JUSTICE HARLAN's dissent in *Poe v. Ullman*, in which the Court declined to reach the merits of the constitutionality of the same Connecticut statute.

*** Due process has not been reduced to any formula; its content cannot be determined by reference to any code. The best that can be said is that through the course of this Court's decisions it has represented the balance which our Nation, built upon postulates of respect for the liberty of the individual, has struck between that liberty and the demands of organized society. *** A decision of this Court which radically departs from it could not long survive, while a decision which builds on what has survived is likely to be sound. No formula could serve as a substitute, in this area, for judgment and restraint. *** Appellants contend that the Connecticut statute deprives them, as it unquestionably does, of a substantial measure of liberty in carrying on the most intimate of all personal relationships, and that it does so arbitrarily and without any rational, justifying purpose. The State, on the other hand, asserts that it is acting to protect the moral welfare of its citizenry, both directly, in that it considers the practice of contraception immoral in itself, and instrumentally, in that the availability of contraceptive materials tends to minimize "the disastrous consequence of dissolute action," that is fornication and adultery.

It is argued by appellants that the judgment, implicit in this statute—that the use of contraceptives by married couples is immoral—is an irrational one, that in effect it subjects them in a very important matter to the arbitrary whim of the legislature, and that it does so for no good purpose. *** Yet the very inclusion of the category of morality among state concerns indicates that society is not limited in its objects only to the physical well-being of the community, but has traditionally concerned itself with the moral soundness of its people as well. Indeed to attempt a line between public behavior and that which is purely consensual or solitary would be to withdraw from community concern a range of subjects with which every society in civilized times has found it necessary to deal. The laws regarding marriage which provide both when the sexual powers may be used and the legal and societal context in which children are born and brought up, as well as laws forbidding adultery, fornication and homosexual practices which express the negative of the proposition, confining sexuality to lawful marriage, form a pattern so deeply pressed into the substance of our social life that any Constitutional doctrine in this area must build upon that basis.

It is in this area of sexual morality, which contains many proscriptions of consensual behavior having little or no direct impact on others, that the State of Connecticut has expressed its moral judgment that all use of contraceptives is improper. Appellants cite an impressive list of authorities who, from a great variety of points of view, commend the considered use of contraceptives by married couples. What they do not emphasize is that not too long ago the current of opinion was very probably quite the opposite, and that even today the issue is not free of controversy. Certainly, Connecticut's judgment is no more demonstrably correct or incorrect than are the varieties of judgment, expressed in law, on marriage and divorce, on adult consensual homosexuality, abortion, and sterilization, or euthanasia and suicide. If we had a case before us which required us to decide simply, and in abstraction, whether the moral judgment implicit in the application of the present statute to married couples was a sound one, the very controversial nature of these questions would, I think, require us to hesitate long before concluding that the Constitution precluded Connecticut from choosing as it has among these various views.

But, as might be expected, we are not presented simply with this moral judgment to be passed on as an abstract proposition. The secular state is not an examiner of consciences: it must operate in the realm of behavior, of overt actions, and where it does so operate, not only the underlying, moral purpose of its operations, but also the choice of means becomes relevant to any Constitutional judgment on what is done. The moral presupposition on which appellants ask us to pass judgment could form the basis of a variety of legal rules and administrative choices, each presenting a different issue for adjudication. For example, one practical expression of the moral view propounded here might be the rule that a marriage in which only contraceptive relations had taken place had never been consummated and could be annulled. Again, the use of contraceptives might be made a ground for divorce, or perhaps tax benefits and subsidies could be provided for large families. ***

Precisely what is involved here is this: the State is asserting the right to enforce its moral judgment by intruding upon the most intimate details of the marital relation with the full power of the criminal law. *** This, then, is the precise character of the enactment whose Constitutional measure we must take. The statute must pass a more rigorous Constitutional test than that going merely to the plausibility of its underlying rationale. This enactment involves what, by common understanding throughout the English-speaking world, must be granted to be a most fundamental aspect of "liberty," the privacy of the home in its most basic sense, and it is this which requires that the statute be subjected to "strict scrutiny." ***

Of this whole "private realm of family life" it is difficult to imagine what is more private or more intimate than a husband and wife's marital relations. We would indeed be straining at a gnat and swallowing a camel were we to show concern for the niceties of property law involved in our recent decision, under the Fourth Amendment, in *Chapman v. United States*, 365 U.S. 610, and yet fail at least to see any substantial claim here.

Of course, just as the requirement of a warrant is not inflexible in carrying out searches and seizures, so there are countervailing considerations at this more fundamental aspect of the right involved. "(T)he family *** is not beyond regulation," and it would be an absurdity to suggest either that offenses may not be committed in the bosom of the family or that the home can be made a sanctuary for crime. The right of privacy most manifestly is not an absolute. Thus, I would not suggest that adultery, homosexuality, fornication and incest are immune from criminal enquiry, however privately practiced. So much has been explicitly recognized in acknowledging the State's rightful concern for its people's moral welfare. But not to discriminate between what is involved in this case and either the traditional offenses against good morals or crimes which, though they may be committed anywhere, happen to have been committed or concealed in the home, would entirely misconceive the argument that is being made.

Adultery, homosexuality and the like are sexual intimacies which the State forbids altogether, but the intimacy of husband and wife is necessarily an essential and accepted feature of the institution of marriage, an institution which the State not only must allow, but which always and in every age it has fostered and protected. It is one thing when the State exerts its power either to forbid extra-marital sexuality altogether, or to say who may marry, but it is quite another when, having acknowledged a marriage and the intimacies inherent in it, it undertakes to regulate by means of the criminal law the details of that intimacy.

In sum, even though the State has determined that the use of contraceptives is as iniquitous as any act of extra-marital sexual immorality, the intrusion of the whole machinery of the criminal law into the very heart of marital privacy, requiring husband and wife to render account before a criminal tribunal of their uses of that intimacy, is surely a very different thing indeed from punishing those who establish intimacies which the law has always forbidden and which can have no claim to social protection.

In my view the appellants have presented a very pressing claim for Constitutional protection. *** Since, as it appears to me, the statute marks an abridgment of important fundamental liberties protected by the Fourteenth Amendment, it will not do to urge in justification of that abridgment simply that the statute is rationally related to the effectuation of a proper state purpose. A closer scrutiny and stronger justification than that are required. ***

[C]onclusive, in my view, is the utter novelty of this enactment. Although the Federal Government and many States have at one time or other had on their books statutes forbidding or regulating the distribution of contraceptives, none, so far as I can find, has made the use of contraceptives a crime. Indeed, a diligent search has revealed that no nation, including several which quite evidently share Connecticut's moral policy, has seen fit to effectuate that policy by the means presented here. ***]

MR. JUSTICE WHITE, concurring in the judgment.

In my view this Connecticut law as applied to married couples deprives them of "liberty" without due process of law, as that concept is used in the Fourteenth Amendment. I therefore concur in the judgment of the Court reversing these convictions under Connecticut's aiding and abetting statute.

It would be unduly repetitious, and belaboring the obvious, to expound on the impact of this statute on the liberty guaranteed by the Fourteenth Amendment against arbitrary or capricious denials or on the nature of this liberty. Suffice it to say that this is not the first time this Court has had occasion to articulate that the liberty entitled to protection under the Fourteenth Amendment includes the right "to marry, establish a home and bring up children," [*Meyer v. Nebraska*] and "the liberty ***to direct the upbringing and education of children," [*Pierce v. Society of Sisters*] and that these are among the "basic civil rights of man." [*Skinner v. Oklahoma*]. These decisions affirm that there is a "realm of family life which the state cannot enter" without substantial justification. Surely the right invoked in this case, to be free of regulation of the intimacies of the marriage relationship, "come(s) to this Court with a momentum for respect lacking when appeal is made to liberties which derive merely from shifting economic arrangements." ***

As I read the opinions of the Connecticut courts and the argument of Connecticut in this Court, the State claims but one justification for its anti-use statute. There is no serious contention that Connecticut thinks the use of artificial or external methods of contraception immoral or unwise in itself, or that the anti-use statute is founded upon any policy of promoting population expansion. Rather, the statute is said to serve the State's policy against all forms of promiscuous or illicit sexual relationships, be they premarital or extramarital, concededly a permissible and legitimate legislative goal. ***

In these circumstances one is rather hard pressed to explain how the ban on use by married persons in any way prevents use of such devices by persons engaging in illicit sexual relations and thereby contributes to the State's policy against such relationships. Neither the state courts nor the State before the bar of this Court has tendered such an explanation. It is purely fanciful to believe that the broad proscription on use facilitates discovery of use by persons engaging in a prohibited relationship or for some other reason makes such use more unlikely and thus can be supported by any sort of administrative consideration. Perhaps the theory is that the flat ban on use prevents married people from possessing contraceptives and without the ready availability of such devices for use in the marital relationship, there will be no or less temptation to use them in extramarital ones. *** At most the broad ban is of marginal utility to the declared objective. A statute limiting its prohibition on use to persons engaging in the prohibited relationship would serve the end posited by Connecticut in the same way, and with the same effectiveness, or ineffectiveness, as the broad anti-use statute under attack in this case. I find nothing in this record justifying the sweeping scope of this statute, with its telling effect on the freedoms of married persons, and therefore conclude that it deprives such persons of liberty without due process of law.

MR. JUSTICE BLACK, with whom MR. JUSTICE STEWART joins, dissenting.

*** The Court talks about a constitutional "right of privacy" as though there is some constitutional provision or provisions forbidding any law ever to be passed which might abridge the "privacy" of individuals. But there is not. *** One of the most effective ways of diluting or expanding a constitutionally guaranteed right is to substitute for the crucial word or words of a constitutional guarantee another word or words, more or less flexible and more or less restricted in meaning. This fact is well illustrated by the use of the term "right of privacy" as a comprehensive substitute for the Fourth Amendment's guarantee against "unreasonable searches and seizures." "Privacy" is a broad, abstract and ambiguous concept which can easily be shrunken in meaning but which can also, on the other hand, easily be interpreted as a constitutional ban against many things other than searches and seizures. I have expressed the view many times that First Amendment freedoms, for example, have suffered from a failure of the courts to stick to the simple language of the First Amendment in construing it, instead of invoking multitudes of words substituted for those the Framers used. For these reasons I get nowhere in this case by talk about a constitutional "right or privacy" as an emanation from one or more constitutional provisions. I like my privacy as well as the next one, but I am nevertheless compelled to admit that government has a right to invade it unless prohibited by some specific constitutional provision.

*** I think that if properly construed neither the Due Process Clause nor the Ninth Amendment, nor both together, could under any circumstances be a proper basis for invalidating the Connecticut law. I discuss the due process and Ninth Amendment arguments together because on analysis they turn out to be the same thing—merely using different words to claim for this Court and the federal judiciary power to invalidate any legislative act which the judges find irrational, unreasonable or offensive. ***

I realize that many good and able men have eloquently spoken and written, sometimes in rhapsodical strains, about the duty of this Court to keep the Constitution in tune with the times. The idea is that the Constitution must be changed from time to time and that this Court is charged with a duty to make those changes. For myself, I must with all deference reject that philosophy. The Constitution makers knew the need for change and provided for it. Amendments suggested by the people's elected representatives can be submitted to the people or their selected agents for ratification. *** And so, I cannot rely on the Due Process Clause or the Ninth Amendment or any mysterious and uncertain natural law concept as a reason for striking down this state law. The Due Process Clause with an "arbitrary and capricious" or "shocking to the conscience" formula was liberally used by this Court to strike down economic legislation in the early decades of this century, threatening, many people thought, the tranquility and stability of the Nation. That formula, based on subjective considerations of "natural justice," is no less dangerous when used to enforce this Court's views about personal rights than those about economic rights. *** So far as I am concerned, Connecticut's law as applied here is not forbidden by any provision of the Federal Constitution as that Constitution was written, and I would therefore affirm.

MR. JUSTICE STEWART, whom MR. JUSTICE BLACK joins, dissenting.

Since 1879 Connecticut has had on its books a law which forbids the use of contraceptives by anyone. I think this is an uncommonly silly law. But we are not asked in this case to say whether we think this law is unwise, or even asinine. We are asked to hold that it violates the United States Constitution. And that I cannot do.

In the course of its opinion the Court refers to no less than six Amendments to the Constitution: the First, the Third, the Fourth, the Fifth, the Ninth, and the Fourteenth. But the Court does not say which of these Amendments, if any, it thinks is infringed by this Connecticut law.

We are told that the Due Process Clause of the Fourteenth Amendment is not, as such, the "guide" in this case. With that much I agree. There is no claim that this law, duly enacted by the Connecticut Legislature, is unconstitutionally vague. There is no claim that the appellants were denied any of the elements of procedural due process at their trial, so as to make their convictions constitutionally invalid. And, as the Court says, the day has long passed since the Due Process Clause was regarded as a proper instrument for determining "the wisdom, need, and propriety" of state laws. *** What provision of the Constitution, then, does make this state law invalid? The Court says it is the right of privacy "created by several fundamental constitutional guarantees." With all deference, I can find no such general right of privacy in the Bill of Rights, in any other part of the Constitution, or in any case ever before decided by this Court.

At the oral argument in this case we were told that the Connecticut law does not "conform to current community standards." But it is not the function of this Court to decide cases on the basis of community standards. We are here to decide cases "agreeably to the Constitution and laws of the United States." It is the essence of judicial duty to subordinate our own personal views, our own ideas of what legislation is wise and what is not. If, as I should surely hope, the law before us does not reflect the standards of the people of Connecticut, the people of Connecticut can freely exercise their true Ninth and Tenth Amendment rights to persuade their elected representatives to repeal it. That is the constitutional way to take this law off the books.

Notes

1. **Methodology.** Summarize the approaches of each opinion, then consider the strengths and weaknesses of each. Which opinion do you like best? Why?

2. **Unmarried People.**

(a) If the plaintiffs in *Griswold* had been single (or doctors asserting the right to provide contraceptive advice and devices to unmarried people), would the case come out differently? See *Eisenstadt v. Baird*, 405 U.S. 438 (1972), which decided on equal protection grounds that a law prohibiting the sale of contraceptives to unmarried individuals was unconstitutional.

(b) In *Eisenstadt*, the Court said: "It is true that in *Griswold* the right of privacy in question inhered in the marital relationship. Yet the marital couple is not an independent entity with a mind and a heart of its own, but an association of two individuals each with a separate intellectual and emotional makeup. If the right of privacy means anything, it is the right of the individual, married or single, to be free from unwarranted government intrusion into matters so fundamentally affecting a person as the decision whether to bear or beget a child."

(c) Do you agree with Judge Posner of the Seventh Circuit that *Eisenstadt* means that "unmarried persons have a right to engage in sexual intercourse"?

3. **Access to Contraceptives.** What should the Court do with a state law that says nothing about use of contraceptives but prohibits any person other than a licensed physician from distributing contraceptives? *See Carey v. Population Services*, 431 U.S. 678 (1977).

4. **Privacy Theory.** There are two main branches of privacy theory. The first is a negative theory, originally formulated as "the right to be let alone" (Brandeis and Warren, *The Right to Privacy*, 4 HARV. L. REV. 193 (1890)). The second is a more positive theory, concerned not so much with legal intrusion but with the law's role in forming "the totality of a person's life." Rubenfeld, *The Right to Privacy*, 102 HARV. L. REV. 737 (1989).

5. **Alternatives.** Since lack of birth control consequences fall more heavily on those who get pregnant than those who do not, should Connecticut's statute be viewed as gender discriminatory? If only poor people have trouble receiving birth control information and supplies, should this be considered an equal protection issue? Since the Roman Catholic Church was the primary source of continued support for the Connecticut statute, should the statute (whose secular purposes were minimal) be found unconstitutional under the First Amendment? The first two questions can be analyzed with the tools you will obtain in Chapter IX; the last one, alas, is for First Amendment courses.

b. Abortion

ROE v. WADE
410 U.S. 113, 93 S.Ct. 705, 35 L.Ed.2d 147 (1973).

MR. JUSTICE BLACKMUN delivered the opinion of the Court.

*** [These cases] present constitutional challenges to state criminal abortion legislation. *** The Texas statutes *** make it a crime to "procure an abortion," as therein defined, or to attempt one, except with respect to "an abortion procured or attempted by medical advice for the purpose of saving the life of the mother." Similar statutes are in existence in a majority of the States.

Jane Roe, a single woman who was residing in Dallas County, Texas, instituted this federal action in March 1970 against the District Attorney of the county. She sought a declaratory judgment that the Texas criminal abortion statutes were unconstitutional on their face, and an injunction restraining the defendant from enforcing the statutes.

Roe alleged that she was unmarried and pregnant; that she wished to terminate her pregnancy by an abortion "performed by a competent, licensed physician, under safe, clinical conditions"; that she was unable to get a "legal" abortion in Texas because her life did not appear to be threatened by the continuation of her pregnancy; and that she could not afford to travel to another jurisdiction in order to secure a legal abortion under safe conditions. She claimed that the Texas statutes were unconstitutionally vague and that they abridged her right of personal privacy, protected by the First, Fourth, Fifth, Ninth, and Fourteenth Amendments. *** Roe purported to sue "on behalf of herself and all other women" similarly situated. ***

The principal thrust of appellant's attack on the Texas statutes is that they improperly invade a right, said to be possessed by the pregnant woman, to choose to terminate her pregnancy. Appellant would discover this right in the concept of personal "liberty" embodied in the Fourteenth Amendment's Due Process Clause; or in personal marital, familial, and sexual privacy said to be protected by the Bill of Rights or its penumbras, *see Griswold v. Connecticut*, 381 U.S. 479 (1965); or among those rights reserved to the people by the Ninth Amendment, *Griswold v. Connecticut*, 381 U.S., at 486 (GOLDBERG, J., concurring). Before addressing this claim, we feel it desirable briefly to survey, in several aspects, the history of abortion, for such insight as that history may afford us, and then to examine the state purposes and interests behind the criminal abortion laws.

It perhaps is not generally appreciated that the restrictive criminal abortion laws in effect in a majority of States today are of relatively recent vintage. Those laws, generally proscribing abortion or its attempt at any time during pregnancy except when necessary to preserve the pregnant woman's life, are not of ancient or even of common-law origin. Instead, they derive from statutory changes effected, for the most part, in the latter half of the 19th century. *** We are [told] that abortion was practiced in Greek times as well as in the Roman Era, and that "it was resorted to without scruple." *** Greek and Roman law afforded little protection to the unborn. If abortion was prosecuted in some places, it seems to have been based on a concept of a violation of the father's right to his offspring. Ancient religion did not bar abortion. [In fact, most] Greek thinkers *** commended abortion, at least prior to viability. *** It is undisputed that at common law, abortion performed before "quickening"-the first recognizable movement of the fetus in utero, appearing usually from the 16th to the 18th week of pregnancy-was not an indictable offense. *** England's first criminal abortion statute came in 1803. It made abortion of a quick fetus a capital crime, but *** it provided lesser penalties for the felony of abortion before quickening, and thus preserved the "quickening" distinction. *** In this country, [however,] the law in effect in all but a few States until mid–19th century was the pre-existing English common law. *** Gradually, in the middle and late 19th century the quickening distinction disappeared from the statutory law of most States and the degree of the offense and the penalties were increased. By the end of the

1950's a large majority of the jurisdictions banned abortion, however and whenever performed, unless done to save or preserve the life of the mother.

It is thus apparent that at common law, at the time of the adoption of our Constitution, and throughout the major portion of the 19th century, abortion was viewed with less disfavor than under most American statutes currently in effect. Phrasing it another way, a woman enjoyed a substantially broader right to terminate a pregnancy than she does in most States today. At least with respect to the early stage of pregnancy, and very possibly without such a limitation, the opportunity to make this choice was present in this country well into the 19th century. ***

Three reasons have been advanced to explain historically the enactment of criminal abortion laws in the 19th century and to justify their continued existence.

It has been argued occasionally that these laws were the product of a Victorian social concern to discourage illicit sexual conduct. Texas, however, does not advance this justification in the present case, and it appears that no court or commentator has taken the argument seriously. *** A second reason is concerned with abortion as a medical procedure. When most criminal abortion laws were first enacted, the procedure was a hazardous one. *** Modern medical techniques have altered this situation. *** Mortality rates for women undergoing early abortions, where the procedure is legal, appear to be as low as or lower than the rates for normal childbirth. Consequently, any interest of the State in protecting the woman from an inherently hazardous procedure, except when it would be equally dangerous for her to forgo it, has largely disappeared. Of course, important state interests in the areas of health and medical standards do remain. The State has a legitimate interest in seeing to it that abortion, like any other medical procedure, is performed under circumstances that insure maximum safety for the patient *** [and] the State retains a definite interest in protecting the woman's own health and safety when an abortion is proposed at a late stage of pregnancy. *** The third reason is the State's interest *** in protecting prenatal life. Some of the argument for this justification rests on the theory that a new human life is present from the moment of conception. *** [However, in] assessing the State's interest, recognition may be given to the less rigid claim that as long as at least potential life is involved, the State may assert interests beyond the protection of the pregnant woman alone.

It is with these interests, and the weight to be attached to them, that this case is concerned.

The Constitution does not explicitly mention any right of privacy. *** [However,] the Court has recognized that a right of personal privacy, or a guarantee of certain areas or zones of privacy, does exist under the Constitution. In varying contexts, the Court or individual Justices have, indeed, found at least the roots of that right in the First Amendment, in the Fourth and Fifth Amendments, in the penumbras of the Bill of Rights, [*Griswold*], in the Ninth Amendment, or in the concept of liberty guaranteed by the first section of the Fourteenth Amendment, *see Meyer v. Nebraska.*

These decisions make it clear that only personal rights that can be deemed "fundamental" or "implicit in the concept of ordered liberty," are included in this guarantee of personal privacy. They also make it clear that the right has some extension to activities relating to marriage, *Loving v. Virginia*, 388 U.S. 1, 12; procreation, *Skinner v. Oklahoma*, 316 U.S. 535, 541–542 (1942); contraception, *Eisenstadt v. Baird*, 405 U.S., at 453–454; family relationships, *Prince v. Massachusetts*, 321 U.S. 158, 166 (1944); and child rearing and education, *Pierce v. Society of Sisters*, 268 U.S. 510, *Meyer v. Nebraska*.

This right of privacy, whether it be founded in the Fourteenth Amendment's concept of personal liberty and restrictions upon state action, as we feel it is, or [in] the Ninth Amendment's reservation of rights to the people, is broad enough to encompass a woman's decision whether or not to terminate her pregnancy. The detriment that the State would impose upon the pregnant woman by denying this choice altogether is apparent. Specific and direct harm medically diagnosable even in early pregnancy may be involved. Maternity, or additional offspring, may force upon the woman a distressful life and future. Psychological harm may be imminent. Mental and physical health may be taxed by child care. There is also the distress, for all concerned, associated with the unwanted child, and there is the problem of bringing a child into a family already unable, psychologically and otherwise, to care for it. In other cases, as in this one, the additional difficulties and continuing stigma of unwed motherhood may be involved. All these are factors the woman and her responsible physician necessarily will consider in consultation.

On the basis of elements such as these, appellant [argues] that the woman's right is absolute and that she is entitled to terminate her pregnancy at whatever time, in whatever way, and for whatever reason she alone chooses. With this we do not agree. *** The Court's decisions recognizing a right of privacy also acknowledge that some state regulation in areas protected by that right is appropriate. As noted above, a State may properly assert important interests in safeguarding health, in maintaining medical standards, and in protecting potential life. *** The privacy right involved, therefore, cannot be said to be absolute. *** We, therefore, conclude that the right of personal privacy includes the abortion decision, but that this right is not unqualified and must be considered against important state interests in regulation. *** Where certain "fundamental rights" are involved, the Court has held that regulation limiting these rights may be justified only by a "compelling state interest," and that legislative enactments must be narrowly drawn to express only the legitimate state interests at stake.

*** Appellant, as has been indicated, claims an absolute right that bars any state imposition of criminal penalties in the area. Appellee argues that the State's determination to recognize and protect prenatal life from and after conception constitutes a compelling state interest. As noted above, we do not agree fully with either formulation.

The appellee [argues] that the fetus is a "person" within the language and meaning of the Fourteenth Amendment. *** If this suggestion of personhood is established, the appellant's case, of course, collapses, for the fetus' right to life would then be guaranteed specifically by the Amendment. The appellant conceded as much on reargument. On the other hand, the appellee conceded on reargument that no case could be cited that holds that a fetus is a person within the meaning of the Fourteenth Amendment.

The Constitution does not define "person" in so many words. Section 1 of the Fourteenth Amendment contains three references to "person." The first, in defining "citizens," speaks of "persons born or naturalized in the United States." The word also appears both in the Due Process Clause and in the Equal Protection Clause. "Person" is used in other places in the Constitution: in the listing of qualifications for Representatives and Senators, Art. I, § 2, cl. 2, and § 3, cl. 3; in the Apportionment Clause, Art. I, § 2, cl. 3; in the Migration and Importation provision, Art. I, § 9, cl. 1; in the Emolument Clause, Art. I, § 9, cl. 8; in the Electors provisions, Art. II, § 1, cl. 2, and the superseded cl. 3; in the provision outlining qualifications for the office of President, Art. II, § 1, cl. 5; in the Extradition provisions, Art. IV, § 2, cl. 2, and the superseded Fugitive Slave Clause 3; and in the Fifth, Twelfth, and Twenty-second Amendments, as well as in §§ 2 and 3 of the Fourteenth Amendment. But in nearly all these instances, the use of the word is such that it has application only postnatally. None indicates, with any assurance, that it has any possible prenatal application.[54]

All this, together with our observation, supra, that throughout the major portion of the 19th century prevailing legal abortion practices were far freer than they are today, persuades us that the word "person," as used in the Fourteenth Amendment, does not include the unborn. *** This conclusion, however, does not of itself fully answer the contentions raised by Texas, and we pass on to other considerations.

The pregnant woman cannot be isolated in her privacy. She carries an embryo and, later, a fetus, if one accepts the medical definitions of the developing young in the human uterus. The situation therefore is inherently different from marital intimacy, or bedroom possession of obscene material, or marriage, or procreation, or education, with which *Eisenstadt* and *Griswold, Stanley, Loving, Skinner* and *Pierce* and *Meyer* were respectively concerned. As we have intimated above, it is reasonable and appropriate for a State to decide that at some point in time another interest, that of health of the mother or that of potential human life, becomes significantly involved. The woman's privacy is no longer sole and any right of privacy she possesses must be measured accordingly.

Texas urges that, apart from the Fourteenth Amendment, life begins at conception and is present throughout pregnancy, and that, therefore, the

---

[54] When Texas urges that a fetus is entitled to Fourteenth Amendment protection as a person, it faces a dilemma. Neither in Texas nor in any other State are all abortions prohibited. Despite broad proscription, an exception always exists. The exception [in Texas] for an abortion procured or attempted by medical advice for the purpose of saving the life of the mother, is typical. But if the fetus is a person who is not to be deprived of life without due process of law, and if the mother's condition is the sole determinant, does not the Texas exception appear to be out of line with the Amendment's command?

State has a compelling interest in protecting that life from and after conception. We need not resolve the difficult question of when life begins. When those trained in the respective disciplines of medicine, philosophy, and theology are unable to arrive at any consensus, the judiciary, at this point in the development of man's knowledge, is not in a position to speculate as to the answer.

It should be sufficient to note briefly the wide divergence of thinking on this most sensitive and difficult question. There has always been strong support for the view that life does not begin until live birth. This was the belief of the Stoics. It appears to be the predominant, though not the unanimous, attitude of the Jewish faith. It may be taken to represent also the position of a large segment of the Protestant community, insofar as that can be ascertained; organized groups that have taken a formal position on the abortion issue have generally regarded abortion as a matter for the conscience of the individual and her family. As we have noted, the common law found greater significance in quickening. Physicians and their scientific colleagues have regarded that event with less interest and have tended to focus either upon conception, upon live birth, or upon the interim point at which the fetus becomes "viable," that is, potentially able to live outside the mother's womb, albeit with artificial aid. Viability is usually placed at about seven months (28 weeks) but may occur earlier, even at 24 weeks. *** [Official] Roman Catholic dogma [is now] the existence of life from the moment of conception. *** [This] is a view strongly held by many non-Catholics as well, and by many physicians. ***

In areas other than criminal abortion, the law has been reluctant to endorse any theory that life, as we recognize it, begins before life birth or to accord legal rights to the unborn except in narrowly defined situations and except when the rights are contingent upon life birth. ***

In view of all this, we do not agree that, by adopting one theory of life, Texas may override the rights of the pregnant woman that are at stake. We repeat, however, that the State does have an important and legitimate interest in preserving and protecting the health of the pregnant woman, *** and that it has still another important and legitimate interest in protecting the potentiality of human life. These interests are separate and distinct. Each grows in substantiality as the woman approaches term and, at a point during pregnancy, each becomes "compelling."

With respect to the State's important and legitimate interest in the health of the mother, the "compelling" point, in the light of present medical knowledge, is at approximately the end of the first trimester. This is so because of the now-established medical fact that until the end of the first trimester mortality in abortion may be less than mortality in normal childbirth. It follows that, from and after this point, a State may regulate the abortion procedure to the extent that the regulation reasonably relates to the preservation and protection of maternal health. Examples of permissible state regulation in this area are requirements as to the qualifications of the person who is to perform the abortion; as to the licensure of that person; as to the facility in which the procedure is to be performed, that is, whether it must be a hospital or may be a clinic or some other place of less-than-hospital status; as to the licensing of the facility; and the like.

This means, on the other hand, that, for the period of pregnancy prior to this "compelling" point, the attending physician, in consultation with his patient, is free to determine, without regulation by the State, that, in his medical judgment, the patient's pregnancy should be terminated. If that decision is reached, the judgment may be effectuated by an abortion free of interference by the State.

With respect to the State's important and legitimate interest in potential life, the "compelling" point is at viability. This is so because the fetus then presumably has the capability of meaningful life outside the mother's womb. State regulation protective of fetal life after viability thus has both logical and biological justifications. If the State is interested in protecting fetal life after viability, it may go so far as to proscribe abortion during that period, except when it is necessary to preserve the life or health of the mother.

Measured against these standards, [the Texas statute], in restricting legal abortions to those "procured or attempted by medical advice for the purpose of saving the life of the mother," sweeps too broadly. The statute makes no distinction between abortions performed early in pregnancy and those performed later, and it limits to a single reason, "saving" the mother's life, the legal justification for the procedure. The statute, therefore, cannot survive the constitutional attack made upon it here.

To summarize and to repeat:

1. A state criminal abortion statute of the current Texas type, that excepts from criminality only a life-saving procedure on behalf of the mother, without regard to pregnancy stage and without recognition of the other interests involved, is violative of the Due Process Clause of the Fourteenth Amendment.

(a) For the stage prior to approximately the end of the first trimester, the abortion decision and its effectuation must be left to the medical judgment of the pregnant woman's attending physician.

(b) For the stage subsequent to approximately the end of the first trimester, the State, in promoting its interest in the health of the mother, may, if it chooses, regulate the abortion procedure in ways that are reasonably related to maternal health.

(c) For the stage subsequent to viability, the State in promoting its interest in the potentiality of human life may, if it chooses, regulate, and even proscribe, abortion except where it is necessary, in appropriate medical judgment, for the preservation of the life or health of the mother. ***

This holding, we feel, is consistent with the relative weights of the respective interests involved, with the lessons and examples of medical and legal history, with the lenity of the common law, and with the demands of the profound problems of the present day. ***

Mr. Justice Stewart, concurring.

*** The Constitution nowhere mentions a specific right of personal choice in matters of marriage and family life, but the "liberty" protected by the Due Process Clause of the Fourteenth Amendment covers more than those freedoms explicitly named in the Bill of Rights. *** As recently as last Term, in *Eisenstadt v. Baird*, 405 U.S. 438, 453, we recognized "the right of the individual, married or single, to be free from unwarranted governmental intrusion into matters so fundamentally affecting a person as the decision whether to bear or beget a child." That right necessarily includes the right of a woman to decide whether or not to terminate her pregnancy.

The asserted state interests are protection of the health and safety of the pregnant woman, and protection of the potential future human life within her. These are legitimate objectives, amply sufficient to permit a State to regulate abortions as it does other surgical procedures, and perhaps sufficient to permit a State to regulate abortions more stringently or even to prohibit them in the late stages of pregnancy. But such legislation is not before us, and I think the Court today has thoroughly demonstrated that these state interests cannot constitutionally support the broad abridgment of personal liberty worked by the existing Texas law. Accordingly, I join the Court's opinion holding that that law is invalid under the Due Process Clause of the Fourteenth Amendment.

MR. JUSTICE BURGER, concurring. [omitted]

MR. JUSTICE DOUGLAS, concurring. [omitted]

MR. JUSTICE REHNQUIST, dissenting.

*** I have difficulty in concluding, as the Court does, that the right of "privacy" is involved in this case. Texas, by the statute here challenged, bars the performance of a medical abortion by a licensed physician on a plaintiff such as Roe. A transaction resulting in an operation such as this is not "private" in the ordinary usage of that word. Nor is the "privacy" that the Court finds here even a distant relative of the freedom from searches and seizures protected by the Fourth Amendment to the Constitution, which the Court has referred to as embodying a right to privacy.

If the Court means by the term "privacy" no more than that the claim of a person to be free from unwanted state regulation of consensual transactions may be a form of "liberty" protected by the Fourteenth Amendment, there is no doubt that similar claims have been upheld in our earlier decisions on the basis of that liberty. I agree with the statement of MR. JUSTICE STEWART in his concurring opinion that the "liberty," against deprivation of which without due process the Fourteenth Amendment protects, embraces more than the rights found in the Bill of Rights. But that liberty is not guaranteed absolutely against deprivation, only against deprivation without due process of law. The test traditionally applied in the area of social and economic legislation is whether or not a law such as that challenged has a rational relation to a valid state objective. *Williamson v. Lee Optical Co.*, 348 U.S. 483, 491 (1955). The Due Process Clause of the Fourteenth Amendment undoubtedly does place a limit, albeit a broad one, on legislative power to enact laws such as this. If the Texas statute were to prohibit an abortion even where the mother's life is in jeopardy, I have little doubt that such a statute would lack a rational relation to a valid state objective under the test stated in *Williamson*. But the Court's sweeping invalidation of any restrictions on abortion during the first trimester is impossible to justify under that standard, and the conscious weighing of competing factors that the Court's opinion apparently substitutes for the established test is far more appropriate to a legislative judgment than to a judicial one.

The Court eschews the history of the Fourteenth Amendment in its reliance on the "compelling state interest" test. *** But the Court adds a new wrinkle to this test by transposing it from the legal considerations associated with the Equal Protection Clause of the Fourteenth Amendment to this case arising under the Due Process Clause of the Fourteenth Amendment. Unless I misapprehend the consequences of this transplanting of the "compelling state interest test," the Court's opinion will accomplish the seemingly impossible feat of leaving this area of the law more confused than it found it.

While the Court's opinion quotes from the dissent of MR. JUSTICE HOLMES in *Lochner*, the result it reaches is more closely attuned to the majority opinion of MR. JUSTICE PECKHAM in that case. As in *Lochner* and similar cases applying substantive due process standards to economic and social welfare legislation, the adoption of the compelling state interest standard will inevitably require this Court to examine the legislative policies and pass on the wisdom of these policies in the very process of deciding whether a particular state interest put forward may or may not be 'compelling.' The decision here to break pregnancy into three distinct terms and to outline the permissible restrictions the State may impose in each one, for example, partakes more of judicial legislation than it does of a determination of the intent of the drafters of the Fourteenth Amendment.

The fact that a majority of the States reflecting, after all the majority sentiment in those States, have had restrictions on abortions for at least a century is a strong indication, it seems to me, that the asserted right to an abortion is not "so rooted in the traditions and conscience of our people as to be ranked as fundamental." Even today, when society's views on abortion are changing, the very existence of the debate is evidence that the "right" to an abortion is not so universally accepted as the appellant would have us believe.

To reach its result, the Court necessarily has had to find within the Scope of the Fourteenth Amendment a right that was apparently completely unknown to the drafters of the Amendment. *** By the time of the adoption of the Fourteenth Amendment in 1868, there were at least 36 laws enacted by state or territorial legislatures limiting abortion.

There apparently was no question concerning the validity of this provision or of any of the other state statutes when the Fourteenth Amendment was adopted. The only conclusion possible from this history is that the drafters did not intend to have the Fourteenth Amendment withdraw from the States the power to legislate with respect to this matter.

Even if one were to agree that the case that the Court decides were here, and that the enunciation of the substantive constitutional law in the Court's opinion were proper, the actual disposition of the case by the Court is still difficult to justify. The Texas statute is struck down in toto, even though the Court apparently concedes that at later periods of pregnancy Texas might impose these selfsame statutory limitations on abortion. My understanding of past practice is that a statute found to be invalid as applied to a particular plaintiff, but not unconstitutional as a whole, is not simply 'struck down' but is, instead, declared unconstitutional as applied to the fact situation before the Court. ***

PLANNED PARENTHOOD v. CASEY
505 U.S. 833, 112 S.Ct. 2791, 120 L.Ed.2d 674 (1992).

JUSTICE O'CONNOR, JUSTICE KENNEDY, and JUSTICE SOUTER announced the judgment of the Court and delivered the opinion of the Court with respect to Parts I, II, III, V–A, V–C, and VI, an opinion with respect to Part V-E, in which JUSTICE STEVENS joins, and an opinion with respect to Parts IV, V-B, and V–D.

I

Liberty finds no refuge in a jurisprudence of doubt. Yet 19 years after our holding that the Constitution protects a woman's right to terminate her pregnancy in its early stages, *Roe v. Wade*, 410 U.S. 113 (1973), that definition of liberty is still questioned. Joining the respondents as amicus curiae, the United States, as it has done in five other cases in the last decade, again asks us to overrule *Roe*.

At issue in these cases are five provisions of the Pennsylvania Abortion Control Act of 1982, as amended in 1988 and 1989. *** The Act requires that a woman seeking an abortion give her informed consent prior to the abortion procedure, and specifies that she be provided with certain information at least 24 hours before the abortion is performed. For a minor to obtain an abortion, the Act requires the informed consent of one of her parents, but provides for a judicial bypass option if the minor does not wish to or cannot obtain a parent's consent. Another provision of the Act requires that, unless certain exceptions apply, a married woman seeking an abortion must sign a statement indicating that she has notified her husband of her intended abortion. The Act exempts compliance with these three requirements in the event of a "medical emergency." In addition to the above provisions regulating the performance of abortions, the Act imposes certain reporting requirements on facilities that provide abortion services. *** After considering the fundamental constitutional questions resolved by *Roe*, principles of institutional integrity, and the rule of stare decisis, we are led to conclude this: the essential holding of *Roe v. Wade* should be retained and once again reaffirmed.

It must be stated at the outset and with clarity that *Roe*'s essential holding, the holding we reaffirm, has three parts. First is a recognition of the right of the woman to choose to have an abortion before viability and to obtain it without undue interference from the State. Before viability, the State's interests are not strong enough to support a prohibition of abortion or the imposition of a substantial obstacle to the woman's effective right to elect the procedure. Second is a confirmation of the State's power to restrict abortions after fetal viability, if the law contains exceptions for pregnancies which endanger the woman's life or health. And third is the principle that the State has legitimate interests from the outset of the pregnancy in protecting the health of the woman and the life of the fetus that may become a child. These principles do not contradict one another; and we adhere to each.

II

Constitutional protection of the woman's decision to terminate her pregnancy derives from the Due Process Clause of the Fourteenth Amendment. Although a literal reading of the Clause might suggest that it governs only the procedures by which a State may deprive persons of liberty, for at least 105 years, the Clause has been understood to contain a substantive component as well, one "barring certain government actions regardless of the fairness of the procedures used to implement them." ***

It is also tempting *** to suppose that the Due Process Clause protects only those practices, defined at the most specific level, that were protected against government interference by other rules of law when the Fourteenth Amendment was ratified. But such a view would be inconsistent with our law. It is a promise of the Constitution that there is a realm of personal liberty which the government may not enter. We have vindicated this principle before. Marriage is mentioned nowhere in the Bill of Rights and interracial marriage was illegal in most States in the 19th century, but the Court was no doubt correct in finding it to be an aspect of liberty protected against state interference by the substantive component of the Due Process Clause in *Loving v. Virginia*, 388 U.S. 1, 12 (1967). *** Neither the Bill of Rights nor the specific practices of States at the time of the adoption of the Fourteenth Amendment marks the outer limits of the substantive sphere of liberty which the Fourteenth Amendment protects. *See* U.S. Const., Amdt. 9.

*** Abortion is a unique act. It is an act fraught with consequences for others: for the woman who must live with the implications of her decision; for the persons who perform and assist in the procedure; for the spouse, family, and society which must confront the knowledge that these procedures exist, procedures some deem nothing short of an act of violence against innocent human life; and, depending on one's beliefs, for the life or potential life that is aborted. Though abortion is conduct, it does not follow that the State is entitled to proscribe it in all instances. That is because the liberty of the woman is at stake in a sense unique to the human condition and so unique to the law. The mother who carries a child to full term is subject to anxieties, to physical constraints, to pain that only she must bear. That these sacrifices have from the beginning of the human race been endured by woman with a pride that ennobles her in the eyes of others and gives to the infant a bond of love cannot alone be grounds for the State to insist she make the sacrifice. Her suffering is too intimate and personal for the State to insist, without more, upon its own vision of the woman's role, however dominant that vision has been in the course of our history and our culture. The destiny of the woman must be shaped to a large extent on her own conception of her spiritual imperatives and her place in society.

It should be recognized, moreover, that in some critical respects the abortion decision is of the same character as the decision to use contraception, to which *Griswold v. Connecticut*, *Eisenstadt v. Baird*, and *Carey v. Population Services International* afford constitutional protection. We have no doubt as to the correctness of those decisions. They support the reasoning in *Roe* *** because they involve personal decisions concerning not only the meaning of procreation but also human responsibility and respect for it. ***

IV

*** [We] conclude that the basic decision in *Roe* was based on a constitutional analysis which we cannot now repudiate. The woman's liberty is not so unlimited, however, that from the outset the State cannot show its concern for the life of the unborn, and at a later point in fetal development the State's interest in life has sufficient force so that the right of the woman to terminate the pregnancy can be restricted. ***

We conclude the line should be drawn at viability, so that before that time the woman has a right to choose to terminate her pregnancy. We adhere to this principle for two reasons. First, as we have said, is the doctrine of stare decisis. *** The second reason is that the concept of viability, as we noted in *Roe*, is the time at which there is a realistic possibility of maintaining and nourishing a life outside the womb, so that the independent existence of the second life can in reason and all fairness be the object of state protection that now overrides the rights of the woman. *** *Roe v. Wade* speaks with clarity in establishing not only the woman's liberty but also the State's "important and legitimate interest in potential life." That portion of the decision in *Roe* has been given too little acknowledgment and implementation by the Court in its subsequent cases. Those cases decided that any regulation touching upon the abortion decision must survive strict scrutiny, to be sustained only if drawn in narrow terms to further a compelling state interest. Not all of the cases decided under that formulation can be reconciled with the holding in *Roe* itself that the State has legitimate interests in the health of the woman and in protecting the potential life within her. In resolving this tension, we choose to rely upon *Roe*, as against the later cases.

Roe established a trimester framework to govern abortion regulations. *** We reject the trimester framework, which we do not consider to be part of the essential holding of *Roe*. *** The trimester framework suffers from these basic flaws: in its formulation it misconceives the nature of the pregnant woman's interest; and in practice it undervalues the State's interest in potential life, as recognized in *Roe*. ***

Numerous forms of state regulation might have the incidental effect of increasing the cost or decreasing the availability of medical care, whether for abortion or any other medical procedure. The fact that a law which serves a valid purpose, one not designed to strike at the right itself, has the incidental effect of making it more difficult or more expensive to procure an abortion cannot be enough to invalidate it. Only where state regulation imposes an undue burden on a woman's ability to make this decision does the power of the State reach into the heart of the liberty protected by the Due Process Clause. *** These considerations of the nature of the abortion right illustrate that it is an overstatement to describe it as a right to decide whether to have an abortion "without interference from the State." *** Not all governmental intrusion is of necessity unwarranted; and that brings us to the other basic flaw in the trimester framework: even in *Roe*'s terms, in practice it undervalues the State's interest in the potential life within the woman. *** Not all burdens on the right to decide whether to terminate a pregnancy will be undue. In our view, the undue burden standard is the appropriate means of reconciling the State's interest with the woman's constitutionally protected liberty.

A finding of an undue burden is a shorthand for the conclusion that a state regulation has the purpose or effect of placing a substantial obstacle in the path of a woman seeking an abortion of a nonviable fetus. A statute with this purpose is invalid because the means chosen by the State to further the interest in potential life must be calculated to inform the woman's free choice, not hinder it. And a statute which, while furthering the interest in potential life or some other valid state interest, has the effect of placing a substantial obstacle in the path of a woman's choice cannot be considered a permissible means of serving its legitimate ends. *** Understood another way, we answer the question, left open in previous opinions discussing the undue burden formulation, whether a law designed to further the State's interest in fetal life which imposes an undue burden on the woman's decision before fetal viability could be constitutional. The answer is no.

Some guiding principles should emerge. What is at stake is the woman's right to make the ultimate decision, not a right to be insulated from all others in doing so. Regulations which do no more than create a structural mechanism by which the State, or the parent or guardian of a minor, may express profound respect for the life of the unborn are permitted, if they are not a substantial obstacle to the woman's exercise of the right to choose. Unless it has that effect on her right of choice, a state measure designed to persuade her to choose childbirth over abortion will be upheld if reasonably related to that goal. Regulations designed to foster the health of a woman seeking an abortion are valid if they do not constitute an undue burden.

*** We give this summary:

(a) To protect the central right recognized by *Roe v. Wade* while at the same time accommodating the State's profound interest in potential life, we will employ the undue burden analysis as explained in this opinion. An undue burden exists, and therefore a provision of law is invalid, if its purpose or effect is to place a substantial obstacle in the path of a woman seeking an abortion before the fetus attains viability.

(b) We reject the rigid trimester framework of *Roe v. Wade*. To promote the State's profound interest in potential life, throughout pregnancy the State may take measures to ensure that the woman's choice is informed, and measures designed to advance this interest will not be invalidated as long as their purpose is to persuade the woman to choose childbirth over abortion. These measures must not be an undue burden on the right.

(c) As with any medical procedure, the State may enact regulations to further the health or safety of a woman seeking an abortion. Unnecessary health regulations that have the purpose or effect of presenting a substantial obstacle to a woman seeking an abortion impose an undue burden on the right.

(d) Our adoption of the undue burden analysis does not disturb the central holding of *Roe v. Wade*, and we reaffirm that holding. Regardless of whether exceptions are made for particular circumstances, a State may not prohibit any woman from making the ultimate decision to terminate her pregnancy before viability.

(e) We also reaffirm *Roe*'s holding that "subsequent to viability, the State in promoting its interest in the potentiality of human life may, if it chooses, regulate, and even proscribe, abortion except where it is necessary, in appropriate medical judgment, for the preservation of the life or health of the mother."

These principles control our assessment of the Pennsylvania statute, and we now turn to the issue of the validity of its challenged provisions.

V

*** We now consider the separate statutory sections at issue.

A

Because it is central to the operation of various other requirements, we begin with the statute's definition of medical emergency. Under the statute, a medical emergency is "[t]hat condition which, on the basis of the physician's good faith clinical judgment, so complicates the medical condition of a pregnant woman as to necessitate the immediate abortion of her pregnancy to avert her death or for which a delay will create serious risk of substantial and irreversible impairment of a major bodily function." ***

The District Court found that there were three serious conditions which would not be covered by the statute: preeclampsia, inevitable abortion, and premature ruptured membrane. Yet, as the Court of Appeals observed, it is undisputed that under some circumstances each of these conditions could lead to an illness with substantial and irreversible consequences. While the definition could be interpreted in an unconstitutional manner, the Court of Appeals construed the phrase "serious risk" to include those circumstances.

*** We *** conclude that, as construed by the Court of Appeals, the medical emergency definition imposes no undue burden on a woman's abortion right.

B

We next consider the informed consent requirement. Except in a medical emergency, the statute requires that at least 24 hours before performing an abortion a physician inform the woman of the nature of the procedure, the health risks of the abortion and of childbirth, and the "probable gestational age of the unborn child." The physician or a qualified nonphysician must inform the woman of the availability of printed materials published by the State describing the fetus and providing information about medical assistance for childbirth, information about child support from the father, and a list of agencies which provide adoption and other services as alternatives to abortion. An abortion may not be performed unless the woman certifies in writing that she has been informed of the availability of these printed materials and has been provided them if she chooses to view them.

To the extent *Akron I* [462 U.S. 416 (1983)] and *Thornburgh* [476 U.S. 747 (1986)] find a constitutional violation when the government requires, as it does here, the giving of truthful, nonmisleading information about the nature of the procedure, the attendant health risks and those of childbirth, and the "probable gestational age" of the fetus, those cases go too far, are inconsistent with *Roe*'s acknowledgment of an important interest in potential life, and are overruled. *** In attempting to ensure that a woman apprehend the full consequences of her decision, the State furthers the legitimate purpose of reducing the risk that a woman may elect an abortion, only to discover later, with devastating psychological consequences, that her decision was not fully informed. If the information the State requires to be made available to the woman is truthful and not misleading, the requirement may be permissible.

We also see no reason why the State may not require doctors to inform a woman seeking an abortion of the availability of materials relating to the consequences to the fetus, even when those consequences have no direct relation to her health. *** The Pennsylvania statute also requires us to reconsider the holding in *Akron I* that the State may not require that a physician, as opposed to a qualified assistant, provide information relevant to a woman's informed consent. Since there is no evidence on this record that requiring a doctor to give the information as provided by the statute would amount in practical terms to a substantial obstacle to a woman seeking an abortion, we conclude that it is not an undue burden. ***

Our analysis of Pennsylvania's 24–hour waiting period between the provision of the information deemed necessary to informed consent and the performance of an abortion under the undue burden standard requires us to reconsider the premise behind the decision in *Akron I* invalidating a parallel requirement. In *Akron* I we said: "Nor are we convinced that the State's legitimate concern that the woman's decision be informed is reasonably served by requiring a 24–hour delay as a matter of course." We consider that conclusion to be wrong. The idea that important decisions will be more informed and deliberate if they follow some period of reflection does not strike us as unreasonable, particularly where the statute directs that important information become part of the background of the decision. ***

Whether the mandatory 24–hour waiting period is nonetheless invalid because in practice it is a substantial obstacle to a woman's choice to terminate her pregnancy is a closer question. The *** District Court found that for those women who have the fewest financial resources, those who must travel long distances, and those who have difficulty explaining their whereabouts to husbands, employers, or others, the 24–hour waiting period will be "particularly burdensome."

These findings are troubling in some respects, but they do not demonstrate that the waiting period constitutes an undue burden. *** [As] we have stated, under the undue burden standard a State is permitted to enact persuasive measures which favor childbirth over abortion, even if those measures do not further a health interest. And while the waiting period does limit a physician's discretion, that is not, standing alone, a reason to invalidate it. *** We also disagree with the District Court's conclusion that the "particularly burdensome" effects of the waiting period on some women require its invalidation. A particular burden is not of necessity a substantial obstacle. *** We are left with the argument that the various aspects of the informed consent requirement are unconstitutional because they place barriers in the way of abortion on demand. Even the broadest reading of *Roe*, however, has not suggested that there is a constitutional right to abortion on demand. Rather, the right protected by *Roe* is a right to decide to terminate a pregnancy free of undue interference by the State. Because the informed consent requirement facilitates the wise exercise of that right, it cannot be classified as an interference with the right *Roe* protects. The informed consent requirement is not an undue burden on that right.

C

Section 3209 of Pennsylvania's abortion law provides, except in cases of medical emergency, that no physician shall perform an abortion on a married woman without receiving a signed statement from the woman that she has notified her spouse that she is about to undergo an abortion. The woman has the option of providing an alternative signed statement certifying that her husband is not the man who impregnated her; that her husband could not be located; that the pregnancy is the result of spousal sexual assault which she has reported; or that the woman believes that notifying her husband will cause him or someone else to inflict bodily injury upon her. A physician who performs an abortion on a married woman without receiving the appropriate signed statement will have his or her license revoked, and is liable to the husband for damages.

The District Court heard the testimony of numerous expert witnesses, and made detailed findings of fact regarding the effect of this statute[, which suggested that women in a physically abusive relationship are unlikely to take the exceptions to the notification requirement provided in section 3209]. ***

These findings are supported by studies of domestic violence. *** Other studies fill in the rest of this troubling picture. Physical violence is only the most visible form of abuse. Psychological abuse, particularly forced social and economic isolation of women, is also common. Many victims of domestic violence remain with their abusers, perhaps because they perceive no superior alternative. Returning to one's abuser can be dangerous. Recent Federal Bureau of Investigation statistics disclose that 8.8 percent of all homicide victims in the United States are killed by their spouses. Thirty percent of female homicide victims are killed by their male partners.

The limited research that has been conducted with respect to notifying one's husband about an abortion, although involving samples too small to be representative, also supports the District Court's findings of fact. *** If anything in this field is certain, it is that [millions of] victims of spousal sexual assault are extremely reluctant to report the abuse to the government; hence, a great many spousal rape victims will not be exempt from the notification requirement imposed by § 3209.

Respondents attempt to avoid the conclusion that § 3209 is invalid by pointing out that it imposes almost no burden at all for the vast majority of women seeking abortions. *** We disagree with respondents' basic method of analysis.

The analysis does not end with the one percent of women upon whom the statute operates; it begins there. Legislation is measured for consistency with the Constitution by its impact on those whose conduct it affects. *** The proper focus of constitutional inquiry is the group for whom the law is a restriction, not the group for whom the law is irrelevant. *** The unfortunate yet persisting conditions we document above will mean that in a large fraction of the cases in which § 3209 is relevant, it will operate as a substantial obstacle to a woman's choice to undergo an abortion. It is an undue burden, and therefore invalid.

This conclusion is in no way inconsistent with our decisions upholding parental notification or consent requirements. Those enactments, and our judgment that they are constitutional, are based on the quite reasonable assumption that minors will benefit from consultation with their parents and that children will often not realize that their parents have their best interests at heart. We cannot adopt a parallel assumption about adult women. ***

Before birth, however, the issue takes on a very different cast. It is an inescapable biological fact that state regulation with respect to the child a woman is carrying will have a far greater impact on the mother's liberty than on the father's. The effect of state regulation on a woman's protected liberty is doubly deserving of scrutiny in such a case, as the State has touched not only upon the private sphere of the family but upon the very bodily integrity of the pregnant woman. The Court has held that "when the wife and the husband disagree on this decision, the view of only one of the two marriage partners can prevail. Inasmuch as it is the woman who physically bears the child and who is the more directly and immediately affected by the pregnancy, as between the two, the balance weighs in her favor." This conclusion rests upon the basic nature of marriage and the nature of our Constitution: "[T]he marital couple is not an independent entity with a mind and heart of its own, but an association of two individuals each with a separate intellectual and emotional makeup. If the right of privacy means anything, it is the right of the individual, married or single, to be free from unwarranted governmental intrusion into matters so fundamentally affecting a person as the decision whether to bear or beget a child." *Eisenstadt v. Baird*, 405 U.S., at 453 (1972). The Constitution protects individuals, men and women alike, from unjustified state interference, even when that interference is enacted into law for the benefit of their spouses.

There was a time, not so long ago, when a different understanding of the family and of the Constitution prevailed. In *Bradwell v. State*, 16 Wall. 130 (1873), three Members of this Court reaffirmed the common-law principle that "a woman had no legal existence separate from her husband, who was regarded as her head and representative in the social state. These views, of course, are no longer consistent with our understanding of the family, the individual, or the Constitution." ***

The husband's interest in the life of the child his wife is carrying does not permit the State to empower him with this troubling degree of authority over his wife. The contrary view leads to consequences reminiscent of the common law. A husband has no enforceable right to require a wife to advise him before she exercises her personal choices. If a husband's interest in the potential life of the child outweighs a wife's liberty, the State could require a married woman to notify her husband before she uses a postfertilization contraceptive. Perhaps next in line would be a statute requiring pregnant married women to notify their husbands before engaging in conduct causing risks to the fetus. After all, if the husband's interest in the fetus' safety is a sufficient predicate for state regulation, the State could reasonably conclude that pregnant wives should notify their husbands before drinking alcohol or smoking. *** A State may not give to a man the kind of dominion over his wife that parents exercise over their children. ***

D

We next consider the parental consent provision. Except in a medical emergency, an unemancipated young woman under 18 may not obtain an abortion unless she and one of her parents (or guardian) provides informed consent as defined above. If neither a parent nor a guardian provides consent, a court may authorize the performance of an abortion upon a determination that the young woman is mature and capable of giving informed consent and has in fact given her informed consent, or that an abortion would be in her best interests. ***

The only argument made by petitioners respecting this provision and to which our prior decisions do not speak is the contention that the parental consent requirement is invalid because it requires informed parental consent. For the most part, petitioners' argument is a reprise of their argument with respect to the informed consent requirement in general, and we reject it for the reasons given above. Indeed, some of the provisions regarding informed consent have particular force with respect to minors: the waiting period, for example, may provide the parent or parents of a pregnant young woman the opportunity to consult with her in private, and to discuss the consequences of her decision in the context of the values and moral or religious principles of their family.

E

Under the recordkeeping and reporting requirements of the statute, every facility which performs abortions is required to file a report stating its name and address as well as the name and address of any related entity, such as a controlling or subsidiary organization. In the case of state-funded institutions, the information becomes public. *** In *Danforth*, 428 U.S., at 80, we held that recordkeeping and reporting provisions "that are reasonably directed to the preservation of maternal health and that properly respect a patient's confidentiality and privacy are permissible." We think that under this standard, all the provisions at issue here, except that relating to spousal notice, are constitutional. Although they do not relate to the State's interest in informing the woman's choice, they do relate to health. *** Nor do we find that the requirements impose a substantial obstacle to a woman's choice. At most they might increase the cost of some abortions by a slight amount. While at some point increased cost could become a substantial obstacle, there is no such showing on the record before us. ***

JUSTICE STEVENS, concurring in part and dissenting in part.

*** In my opinion, a correct application of the "undue burden" standard leads to the [following] conclusion concerning the constitutionality of these requirements. A state-imposed burden on the exercise of a constitutional right is measured both by its effects and by its character: A burden may be "undue" either because the burden is too severe or because it lacks a legitimate, rational justification. *** The 24–hour delay requirement fails both parts of this test. *** The counseling provisions are similarly infirm. Whenever government commands private citizens to speak or to listen, careful review of the justification for that command is particularly appropriate. In these cases, the Pennsylvania statute directs that counselors provide women seeking abortions with information concerning alternatives to abortion, the availability of medical assistance benefits, and the possibility of child-support payments. The statute requires that this information be given to all women seeking abortions, including those for whom such information is clearly useless, such as those who are married, those who have undergone the procedure in the past and are fully aware of the options, and those who are fully convinced that abortion is their only reasonable option. Moreover, the statute requires physicians to inform all of their patients of "[t]he probable gestational age of the unborn child." This information is of little decisional value in most cases, because 90% of all abortions are performed during the first trimester when fetal age has less relevance than when the fetus nears viability. ***

JUSTICE BLACKMUN, concurring in part, concurring in the judgment in part, and dissenting in part. [JUSTICE BLACKMUN reiterated his belief in the correctness of the entire holding of *Roe v. Wade*. He dissented from the parts of the plurality's opinion which overruled portions of *Roe*, substituting the undue burden test for strict scrutiny.]

CHIEF JUSTICE REHNQUIST, with whom JUSTICE WHITE, JUSTICE SCALIA, and JUSTICE THOMAS join, concurring in the judgment in part and dissenting in part.

The joint opinion, following its newly minted variation on stare decisis, retains the outer shell of *Roe v. Wade*, but beats a wholesale retreat from the substance of that case. We believe that *Roe* was wrongly decided, and that it can and should be overruled consistently with our traditional approach to stare decisis in constitutional cases. We would adopt the approach of the plurality in *Webster v. Reproductive Health Services*, 492 U.S. 490 (1989), and uphold the challenged provisions of the Pennsylvania statute in their entirety.

*** In *Roe v. Wade*, the Court recognized a "guarantee of personal privacy" which "is broad enough to encompass a woman's decision whether or not to terminate her pregnancy." We are now of the view that, in terming this right fundamental, the Court in *Roe* read the earlier opinions upon which it based its decision much too broadly. Unlike marriage, procreation, and contraception, abortion "involves the purposeful termination of a potential life." *Harris v. McRae*, 448 U.S. 297, 325 (1980). *** One cannot ignore the fact that a woman is not isolated in her pregnancy, and that the decision to abort necessarily involves the destruction of a fetus. *** Nor do the historical traditions of the American people support the view that the right to terminate one's pregnancy is "fundamental." The common law which we inherited from England made abortion after "quickening" an offense. At the time of the adoption of the Fourteenth Amendment, statutory prohibitions or restrictions on abortion were commonplace. *** We think, therefore, both in view of this history and of our decided cases dealing with substantive liberty under the Due Process Clause, that the Court was mistaken in *Roe* when it classified a woman's decision to terminate her pregnancy as a "fundamental right" that could be abridged only in a manner which withstood "strict scrutiny." ***

[Does] the spousal notification requirement rationally further any legitimate state interests[?] We conclude that it does. First, a husband's interests in procreation within marriage and in the potential life of his unborn child are certainly substantial ones. *** By providing that a husband will usually know of his spouse's intent to have an abortion, the provision makes it more likely that the husband will participate in deciding the fate of his unborn child, a possibility that might otherwise have been denied him. This participation might in some cases result in a decision to proceed with the pregnancy. *** The State also has a legitimate interest in promoting "the integrity of the marital relationship." *** In our view, the spousal notice requirement is a rational attempt by the State to improve truthful communication between spouses and encourage collaborative decisionmaking, and thereby fosters marital integrity. ***

JUSTICE SCALIA, with whom CHIEF JUSTICE REHNQUIST, JUSTICE WHITE, and JUSTICE THOMAS join, concurring in the judgment in part and dissenting in part.

*** A State's choice between two positions on which reasonable people can disagree is constitutional even when (as is often the case) it intrudes upon a "liberty" in the absolute sense. Laws against bigamy, for example— with which entire societies of reasonable people disagree—intrude upon men and women's liberty to marry and live with one another. But bigamy happens not to be a liberty specially "protected" by the Constitution.

That is, quite simply, the issue in these cases: not whether the power of a woman to abort her unborn child is a "liberty" in the absolute sense; or even whether it is a liberty of great importance to many women. Of course it is both. The issue is whether it is a liberty protected by the Constitution of the United States. I am sure it is not. I reach that conclusion *** for the same reason I reach the conclusion that bigamy is not constitutionally protected— because of two simple facts: (1) the Constitution says absolutely nothing about it, and (2) the longstanding traditions of American society have permitted it to be legally proscribed.

The Court destroys the proposition, evidently meant to represent my position, that "liberty" includes "only those practices, defined at the most specific level, that were protected against government interference by other rules of law when the Fourteenth Amendment was ratified," That is not, however, what *Michael H.* says; it merely observes that, in defining "liberty," we may not disregard a specific, "relevant tradition protecting, or denying protection to, the asserted right."

*** The emptiness of the "reasoned judgment" that produced *Roe* is displayed in plain view by the fact that, after more than 19 years of effort by some of the brightest (and most determined) legal minds in the country, after more than 10 cases upholding abortion rights in this Court, and after dozens upon dozens of amicus briefs submitted in these and other cases, the best the Court can do to explain how it is that the word "liberty" must be thought to include the right to destroy human fetuses is to rattle off a collection of adjectives that simply decorate a value judgment and conceal a political choice. ***

The Court's description of the place of *Roe* in the social history of the United States is unrecognizable. Not only did *Roe* not, as the Court suggests, resolve the deeply divisive issue of abortion; it did more than anything else to nourish it, by elevating it to the national level where it is infinitely more difficult to resolve. National politics were not plagued by abortion protests, national abortion lobbying, or abortion marches on Congress before *Roe v. Wade* was decided. Profound disagreement existed among our citizens over the issue—as it does over other issues, such as the death penalty—but that disagreement was being worked out at the state level. *** *Roe*'s mandate for abortion on demand destroyed the compromises of the past, rendered compromise impossible for the future, and required the entire issue to be resolved uniformly, at the national level. ***

There is a poignant aspect to today's opinion. Its length, and what might be called its epic tone, suggest that its authors believe they are bringing to an end a troublesome era in the history of our Nation and of our Court. "It is the dimension" of authority, they say, to "cal[l] the contending sides of national controversy to end their national division by accepting a common mandate rooted in the Constitution."

There comes vividly to mind a portrait by Emanuel Leutze that hangs in the Harvard Law School: Roger Brooke Taney, painted in 1859, the 82d year of his life, the 24th of his Chief Justiceship, the second after his opinion in *Dred Scott*. He is all in black, sitting in a shadowed red armchair, left hand resting upon a pad of paper in his lap, right hand hanging limply, almost lifelessly, beside the inner arm of the chair. He sits facing the viewer and staring straight out. There seems to be on his face, and in his deep-set eyes, an expression of profound sadness and disillusionment. Perhaps he always looked that way, even when dwelling upon the happiest of thoughts. But those of us who know how the lustre of his great Chief Justiceship came to be eclipsed by *Dred Scott* cannot help believing that he had that case—its already apparent consequences for the Court and its soon-to-be-played-out consequences for the Nation—burning on his mind. I expect that two years earlier he, too, had thought himself "call[ing] the contending sides of national controversy to end their national division by accepting a common mandate rooted in the Constitution."

It is no more realistic for us in this litigation, than it was for him in that, to think that an issue of the sort they both involved—an issue involving life and death, freedom and subjugation—can be "speedily and finally settled" by the Supreme Court, as President James Buchanan in his inaugural address said the issue of slavery in the territories would be. Quite to the contrary, by foreclosing all democratic outlet for the deep passions this issue arouses, by banishing the issue from the political forum that gives all participants, even the losers, the satisfaction of a fair hearing and an honest fight, by continuing the imposition of a rigid national rule instead of allowing for regional differences, the Court merely prolongs and intensifies the anguish.

We should get out of this area, where we have no right to be, and where we do neither ourselves nor the country any good by remaining.

Notes

1. **Criticisms of *Roe*.** Scholars were very critical of *Griswold's* methodology but the case led to no popular protests or legislative reactions in Connecticut or elsewhere. *Roe*, conversely, has fueled a political firestorm for over twenty-five years. Consider the following commonly-articulated views of why *Roe* has been so controversial, and decide whether or not you agree:

  • In *Roe*, the Court acted like a legislature rather than a court.

  • *Roe* is the *Dred Scott* of the Court's work in the 20th Century.

  • *Roe* ended the possibility of political compromise on abortion rather than initiating a dialogue on the topic.

- *Roe* shifted the debate over abortion from the States, where it might be resolved, to the nation, where it is far harder to resolve.

- *Roe* is merely *Lochner* in liberal garb.

- The Court's decision "reads like a set of hospital rules" which will be "destroyed with new statistics" concerning medical advances.

2. **Defenses of *Roe*.** Do you agree or disagree with the following?

- *Roe* involves a stronger case for privacy than *Griswold:* the woman's interest in controlling her own body and her bodily integrity.

- *Roe* is essential to the lives and well-being of millions of women. It needs no further justification.

- The result in *Roe* was correct, but it should have been decided on gender-discrimination grounds.

- The outcome in *Roe* is strongly supported by First Amendment freedom of religion considerations.

3. **Other Perspectives on *Roe*.**

- Does it matter whether we phrase the right in *Roe* as one of "abortion" or "control over reproduction"?

- "Is the pregnant woman being required to confer a benefit on the fetus, or is she being prevented from harming it? This depends on whether the baseline is a world in which women control their pregnancies, or one in which pregnancies proceed to term." Farber, Eskridge, and Frickey, CONSTITUTIONAL LAW: THEMES FOR THE CONSTITUTION'S THIRD CENTURY, pp. 512–13 (West 1993).

- The right to obtain an abortion "does not free women, it frees male sexual aggression. The availability of abortion [removes] the one remaining legitimized reason that women have had for refusing sex besides the headache." MacKinnon, *Roe v. Wade: A Study in Male Ideology*, in ABORTION: MORAL AND LEGAL PERSPECTIVES 45, 49–51 (J. Garfield ed. 1985).

- Consider a hypothetical situation in which your circulatory system is involuntarily hooked up to a concert violinist who will die if detached from you in less than nine months. Are you morally justified in detaching the violinist? Can government compel you not to do so, under penalty of imprisonment? How, if at all, does this hypothetical differ from the situation of a woman carrying a fetus? *See* Thomson, *A Defense of Abortion*, 1 PHIL. & PUB. AFF. 47 (1971).

4. ***Roe* and *Casey*.** How much of *Roe* survives and how much is discarded in *Casey*? What problems, if any, does the "undue burden" framework resolve? What new problems, if any, does it create? Do you find the Joint Opinion's selective use of stare decisis troubling or appropriate? Should the Court be more reluctant to correct big errors than small ones? Is it right to say that *Lochner* and *Plessy* primarily involved factual errors?

5. *Casey.*

• Many people's views on abortion are determined by whether they consider the fetus a "person." Consider whether the state can regulate abortion even if the fetus is not a person within the meaning of the Constitution. If you are pro-choice, are you barred from recognizing the fetus as potential life? If you are pro-life, are there any circumstances where you might find abortion justifiable? Why isn't the State's interest in protection of fetal life compelling enough at every stage of pregnancy to permit regulation, even to the point of prohibition?

• The Joint Opinion approaches the meaning of "liberty" as an exercise in common law analogical thinking. JUSTICE SCALIA's dissent argues that "liberty" should only be protected when it is an outgrowth of deductive logic. Which is the correct approach? Does this component of *Casey* remind you of Frankfurter and Black's argument in *Adamson*?

• Consider the Court's analysis of Pennsylvania's spousal notification, parental consent, and waiting period provisions. Construct variations on each that would at least arguably lead to different results than those of the Court. What does this exercise tell you about the definitiveness of the Court's decision?

STENBERG v. CARHART
530 U.S. 914, 120 S.Ct. 2597, 147 L.Ed.2d 743 (2000).

JUSTICE BREYER delivered the opinion of the Court.

We again consider the right to an abortion. *** Three established principles determine the issue before us. We shall set them forth in the language of the joint opinion in *Casey*. First, before "viability *** the woman has a right to choose to terminate her pregnancy." Second, "a law designed to further the State's interest in fetal life which imposes an undue burden on the woman's decision before fetal viability" is unconstitutional. An "undue burden is *** shorthand for the conclusion that a state regulation has the purpose or effect of placing a substantial obstacle in the path of a woman seeking an abortion of a nonviable fetus." Third, "subsequent to viability, the State in promoting its interest in the potentiality of human life may, if it chooses, regulate, and even proscribe, abortion except where it is necessary, in appropriate medical judgment, for the preservation of the life or health of the mother."

We apply these principles to a Nebraska law banning "partial birth abortion." The statute reads as follows:

"No partial birth abortion shall be performed in this state, unless such procedure is necessary to save the life of the mother whose life is endangered by a physical disorder, physical illness, or physical injury, including a life-endangering physical condition caused by or arising from the pregnancy itself."

The statute defines "partial birth abortion" as:

"an abortion procedure in which the person performing the abortion partially delivers vaginally a living unborn child before killing the unborn child and completing the delivery."

It further defines "partially delivers vaginally a living unborn child before killing the unborn child" to mean

"deliberately and intentionally delivering into the vagina a living unborn child, or a substantial portion thereof, for the purpose of performing a procedure that the person performing such procedure knows will kill the unborn child and does kill the unborn child."

The law classifies violation of the statute as a "Class III felony" carrying a prison term of up to 20 years, and a fine of up to $25,000. It also provides for the automatic revocation of a doctor's license to practice medicine in Nebraska.

We hold that this statute violates the Constitution.

I

Dr. Leroy Carhart is a Nebraska physician who performs abortions in a clinical setting. He brought this lawsuit in Federal District Court seeking a declaration that the Nebraska statute violates the Federal Constitution, and asking for an injunction forbidding its enforcement. *** Because Nebraska law seeks to ban one method of aborting a pregnancy, we must describe and then discuss several different abortion procedures. Considering the fact that those procedures seek to terminate a potential human life, our discussion may seem clinically cold or callous to some, perhaps horrifying to others. There is no alternative way, however, to acquaint the reader with the technical distinctions among different abortion methods ***.

1. About 90% of all abortions performed in the United States take place during the first trimester of pregnancy, before 12 weeks of gestational age. During the first trimester, the predominant abortion method is "vacuum aspiration," which involves insertion of a vacuum tube (cannula) into the uterus to evacuate the contents. Such an abortion is typically performed on an outpatient basis under local anesthesia. *** As the fetus grows in size, however, the vacuum aspiration method becomes increasingly difficult to use.

2. Approximately 10% of all abortions are performed during the second trimester of pregnancy (12 to 24 weeks). In the early 1970's, inducing labor through the injection of saline into the uterus was the predominant method of second trimester abortion. Today, however, the medical profession has switched from medical induction of labor to surgical procedures for most second trimester abortions. The most commonly used procedure is called "dilation and evacuation" (D & E). That procedure (together with a modified form of vacuum aspiration used in the early second trimester) accounts for about 95% of all abortions performed from 12 to 20 weeks of gestational age.

3. D & E "refers generically to transcervical procedures performed at 13 weeks gestation or later." *** [T]he common points are that D & E involves

(1) dilation of the cervix; (2) removal of at least some fetal tissue using nonvacuum instruments; and (3) (after the 15th week) the potential need for instrumental disarticulation or dismemberment of the fetus or the collapse of fetal parts to facilitate evacuation from the uterus.

4. When instrumental disarticulation incident to D & E is necessary, it typically occurs as the doctor pulls a portion of the fetus through the cervix into the birth canal. ***

8. The American College of Obstetricians and Gynecologists describes the D & X procedure in a manner corresponding to a breech-conversion intact D & E, including the following steps:

"1. deliberate dilatation of the cervix, usually over a sequence of days;

"2. instrumental conversion of the fetus to a footling breech;

"3. breech extraction of the body excepting the head; and

"4. partial evacuation of the intracranial contents of a living fetus to effect vaginal delivery of a dead but otherwise intact fetus."

Despite the technical differences we have just described, intact D & E and D & X are sufficiently similar for us to use the terms interchangeably. ***

11. There are no reliable data on the number of D & X abortions performed annually. Estimates have ranged between 640 and 5,000 per year. ***

<hr>

II

The question before us is whether Nebraska's statute, making criminal the performance of a "partial birth abortion," violates the Federal Constitution ***. We conclude that it does for at least two independent reasons. First, the law lacks any exception "for the preservation of the *** health of the mother." "Second, it 'imposes an undue burden on a woman's ability' to choose a D & E abortion, thereby unduly burdening the right to choose abortion itself." ***

The *Casey* joint opinion reiterated what the Court held in *Roe*; that "subsequent to viability, the State in promoting its interest in the potentiality of human life may, if it chooses, regulate, and even proscribe, abortion except where it is necessary, in appropriate medical judgment, for the preservation of the life or health of the mother." *** The fact that Nebraska's law applies both pre-and postviability aggravates the constitutional problem presented. The State's interest in regulating abortion previability is considerably weaker than postviability. Since the law requires a health exception in order to validate even a postviability abortion regulation, it at a minimum requires the same in respect to previability regulation.

The quoted standard also depends on the state regulations "promoting [the State's] interest in the potentiality of human life." The Nebraska law, of course, does not directly further an interest "in the potentiality of human life" by saving the fetus in question from destruction, as it regulates only a method of performing abortion. Nebraska describes its interests differently. It says the law "show[s] concern for the life of the unborn," "prevent[s] cruelty to partially born children," and "preserve[s] the integrity of the medical profession." But we cannot see how the interest-related differences could make any difference to the question at hand, namely, the application of the "health" requirement.

Consequently, the governing standard requires an exception "where it is necessary, in appropriate medical judgment for the preservation of the life or health of the mother," for this Court has made clear that a State may promote but not endanger a woman's health when it regulates the methods of abortion.

JUSTICE THOMAS says that the cases just cited limit this principle to situations where the pregnancy itself creates a threat to health. He is wrong. The cited cases, reaffirmed in *Casey*, recognize that a State cannot subject women's health to significant risks both in that context, and also where state regulations force women to use riskier methods of abortion. Our cases have repeatedly invalidated statutes that in the process of regulating the methods of abortion, imposed significant health risks. They make clear that a risk to a women's health is the same whether it happens to arise from regulating a particular method of abortion, or from barring abortion entirely. Our holding does not go beyond those cases, as ratified in *Casey*.

Nebraska responds that the law does not require a health exception unless there is a need for such an exception. And here there is no such need, it says. It argues that "safe alternatives remain available" and "a ban on partial-birth abortion/D & X would create no risk to the health of women." The problem for Nebraska is that the parties strongly contested this factual question in the trial court below; and the findings and evidence support Dr. Carhart. The State fails to demonstrate that banning D & X without a health exception may not create significant health risks for women, because the record shows that significant medical authority supports the proposition that in some circumstances, D & X would be the safest procedure. *** The D & X is an infrequently used abortion procedure; but the health exception question is whether protecting women's health requires an exception for those infrequent occasions. A rarely used treatment might be necessary to treat a rarely occurring disease that could strike anyone—the State cannot prohibit a person from obtaining treatment simply by pointing out that most people do not need it. ***

The upshot is a District Court finding that D & X significantly obviates health risks in certain circumstances, a highly plausible record-based explanation of why that might be so, a division of opinion among some medical experts over whether D & X is generally safer, and an absence of controlled medical studies that would help answer these medical questions. Given these medically related evidentiary circumstances, we believe the law requires a health exception. *** For another thing, the division of medical opinion about the matter at most means uncertainty, a factor that signals the presence of risk, not its absence. That division here involves highly qualified knowledgeable experts on both sides of the issue. Where a significant body of medical opinion believes a procedure may bring with it greater safety for some patients and explains the medical reasons supporting that view, we cannot say that the presence of a different view by itself proves the contrary. Rather, the uncertainty means a significant likelihood that those who believe that D & X is a safer abortion method in certain circumstances may turn out to be right. If so, then the absence of a health exception will place women at an unnecessary risk of tragic health consequences. If they are wrong, the exception will simply turn out to have been unnecessary.

In sum, Nebraska has not convinced us that a health exception is "never necessary to preserve the health of women." ***

The Eighth Circuit found the Nebraska statute unconstitutional because, in *Casey's* words, it has the "effect of placing a substantial obstacle in the path of a woman seeking an abortion of a nonviable fetus." It thereby places an "undue burden" upon a woman's right to terminate her pregnancy before viability. Nebraska does not deny that the statute imposes an "undue burden" if it applies to the more commonly used D & E procedure as well as to D & X. And we agree with the Eighth Circuit that it does so apply.

Our earlier discussion of the D & E procedure shows that it falls within the statutory prohibition. The statute forbids "deliberately and intentionally delivering into the vagina a living unborn child, or a substantial portion thereof, for the purpose of performing a procedure that the person performing such procedure knows will kill the unborn child." We do not understand how one could distinguish, using this language, between D & E (where a foot or arm is drawn through the cervix) and D & X (where the body up to the head is drawn through the cervix). Evidence before the trial court makes clear that D & E will often involve a physician pulling a "substantial portion" of a still living fetus, say, an arm or leg, into the vagina prior to the death of the fetus. Indeed D & E involves dismemberment that commonly occurs only when the fetus meets resistance that restricts the motion of the fetus: "The dismemberment occurs between the traction of *** [the] instrument and the counter-traction of the internal os of the cervix." And these events often do not occur until after a portion of a living fetus has been pulled into the vagina.

Even if the statute's basic aim is to ban D & X, its language makes clear that it also covers a much broader category of procedures. The language does not track the medical differences between D & E and D & X—though it would have been a simple matter, for example, to provide an exception for the performance of D & E and other abortion procedures. *** The plain language covers both procedures. *** Both procedures can involve the introduction of a "substantial portion" of a still living fetus, through the cervix, into the vagina—the very feature of an abortion that leads JUSTICE THOMAS to characterize such a procedure as involving "partial birth."

The Nebraska State Attorney General [Stenberg] argues that the statute does differentiate between the two procedures. *** We cannot accept the Attorney General's narrowing interpretation of the Nebraska statute *** for it conflicts with the statutory language ***. That definition does not include the Attorney General's restriction—"the child up to the head." Its words, "substantial portion," indicate the contrary. *** In any event, the statute itself specifies that it applies both to delivering "an intact unborn child" or "a substantial portion thereof." The dissents cannot explain how introduction of a substantial portion of a fetus into the vagina pursuant to D & X is a "delivery," while introduction pursuant to D & E is not. *** In sum, using this law some present prosecutors and future Attorneys General may choose to pursue physicians who use D & E procedures, the most commonly used method for performing previability second trimester abortions. All those who perform abortion procedures using that method must fear prosecution, conviction, and imprisonment. The result is an undue burden upon a woman's right to make an abortion decision. We must consequently find the statute unconstitutional. ***

JUSTICE STEVENS, with whom JUSTICE GINSBURG joins, concurring.

*** [It is] impossible for me to understand how a State has any legitimate interest in requiring a doctor to follow any procedure other than the one that he or she reasonably believes will best protect the woman in her exercise of this constitutional liberty. But one need not even approach this view today to conclude that Nebraska's law must fall. For the notion that either of these two equally gruesome procedures performed at this late stage of gestation is more akin to infanticide than the other, or that the State furthers any legitimate interest by banning one but not the other, is simply irrational.

JUSTICE O'CONNOR, concurring.

*** First, the Nebraska statute is inconsistent with *Casey* because it lacks an exception for those instances when the banned procedure is necessary to preserve the health of the mother. *** [A]s the majority explains, where, as here, "a significant body of medical opinion believes a procedure may bring with it greater safety for some patients and explains the medical reasons supporting that view," then Nebraska cannot say that the procedure will not, in some circumstances, be "necessary to preserve the life or health of the mother." *** Second, Nebraska's statute is unconstitutional on the alternative and independent ground that it imposes an undue burden on a woman's right to choose to terminate her pregnancy before viability. ***

It is important to note that, unlike Nebraska, some other States have enacted statutes more narrowly tailored to proscribing the D & X procedure alone. *** By restricting their prohibitions to the D & X procedure exclusively, the Kansas, Utah, and Montana statutes avoid a principal defect of the Nebraska law. If Nebraska's statute limited its application to the D & X procedure and included an exception for the life and health of the mother, the question presented would be quite different than the one we face today. As we held in *Casey*, an abortion regulation constitutes an undue burden if it "has the purpose or effect of placing a substantial obstacle in the path of a woman seeking an abortion of a nonviable fetus." If there were adequate alternative methods for a woman safely to obtain an abortion before viability, it is unlikely that prohibiting the D & X procedure alone would "amount in

practical terms to a substantial obstacle to a woman seeking an abortion."
Thus, a ban on partial-birth abortion that only proscribed the D & X method
of abortion and that included an exception to preserve the life and health of
the mother would be constitutional in my view. ***

JUSTICE GINSBURG, with whom JUSTICE STEVENS joins, concurring.

*** Nebraska's "partial birth abortion" law *** does not save any fetus
from destruction, for it targets only "a method of performing abortion." Nor
does the statute seek to protect the lives or health of pregnant women.
Moreover, the most common method of performing previability second
trimester abortions is no less distressing or susceptible to gruesome
description. *** [T]he law prohibits the procedure because the State
legislators seek to chip away at the private choice shielded by *Roe v. Wade*,
even as modified by *Casey*. ***

CHIEF JUSTICE REHNQUIST, dissenting.

*** I believe JUSTICE KENNEDY and JUSTICE THOMAS have correctly
applied *Casey's* principles and join their dissenting opinions.

JUSTICE SCALIA, dissenting.

I am optimistic enough to believe that, one day, *Stenberg v. Carhart* will
be assigned its rightful place in the history of this Court's jurisprudence
beside *Korematsu* and *Dred Scott*. *** The notion that the Constitution ***
prohibits the States from simply banning this visibly brutal means of
eliminating our half-born posterity is quite simply absurd. *** It would be
unfortunate, however, if those who disagree with the result were induced to
regard it as merely a regrettable misapplication of *Casey*. It is not that, but is
Casey's logical and entirely predictable consequence. *** [W]hat I consider to
be an "undue burden" is different from what the majority considers to be an
"undue burden"—a conclusion that can not be demonstrated true or false by
factual inquiry or legal reasoning. It is a value judgment, dependent upon
how much one respects (or believes society ought to respect) the life of a
partially delivered fetus, and how much one respects (or believes society
ought to respect) the freedom of the woman who gave it life to kill it.
Evidently, the five Justices in today's majority value the former less, or the
latter more, (or both), than the four of us in dissent. Case closed. There is no
cause for anyone who believes in *Casey* to feel betrayed by this outcome. It
has been arrived at by precisely the process *Casey* promised—a democratic
vote by nine lawyers, not on the question whether the text of the Constitution
has anything to say about this subject (it obviously does not); nor even on the
question (also appropriate for lawyers) whether the legal traditions of the
American people would have sustained such a limitation upon abortion (they
obviously would); but upon the pure policy question whether this limitation
upon abortion is "undue"—i.e., goes too far.

In my dissent in *Casey*, I wrote that the "undue burden" test made law by
the joint opinion created a standard that was "as doubtful in application as it
is unprincipled in origin"; "hopelessly unworkable in practice"; "ultimately
standardless". Today's decision is the proof. *** The most that we can
honestly say is that we disagree with the majority on their policy-judgment-

couched-as-law. And those who believe that a 5–to–4 vote on a policy matter by unelected lawyers should not overcome the judgment of 30 state legislatures have a problem, not with the application of *Casey*, but with its existence. *** If only for the sake of its own preservation, the Court should return this matter to the people—where the Constitution, by its silence on the subject, left it—and let them decide, State by State, whether this practice should be allowed. *Casey* must be overruled.

JUSTICE KENNEDY, with whom THE CHIEF JUSTICE joins, dissenting.

*** Having concluded Nebraska's law survives the scrutiny dictated by a proper understanding of *Casey*, I dissent from the judgment invalidating it.

The Court's failure to accord any weight to Nebraska's interest in prohibiting partial-birth abortion is erroneous and undermines its discussion and holding. The Court's approach in this regard is revealed by its description of the abortion methods at issue, which the Court is correct to describe as "clinically cold or callous." The majority views the procedures from the perspective of the abortionist, rather than from the perspective of a society shocked when confronted with a new method of ending human life. *** Thus it seems necessary at the outset to set forth what may happen during an abortion. ***

Of the two described procedures, Nebraska seeks only to ban the D & X. In light of the description of the D & X procedure, it should go without saying that Nebraska's ban on partial-birth abortion furthers purposes States are entitled to pursue. *** The State's brief describes its interests as including concern for the life of the unborn and "for the partially-born," in preserving the integrity of the medical profession, and in "erecting a barrier to infanticide." A review of *Casey* demonstrates the legitimacy of these policies. The Court should say so. ***

Nebraska was entitled to find the existence of a consequential moral difference between the procedures. We are referred to substantial medical authority that D & X perverts the natural birth process to a greater degree than D & E, commandeering the live birth process until the skull is pierced. *** Witnesses to the procedure relate that the fingers and feet of the fetus are moving prior to the piercing of the skull; when the scissors are inserted in the back of the head, the fetus' body, wholly outside the woman's body and alive, reacts as though startled and goes limp. D & X's stronger resemblance to infanticide means Nebraska could conclude the procedure presents a greater risk of disrespect for life and a consequent greater risk to the profession and society, which depend for their sustenance upon reciprocal recognition of dignity and respect. The Court is without authority to second-guess this conclusion.

Those who oppose abortion would agree, indeed would insist, that both procedures are subject to the most severe moral condemnation, condemnation reserved for the most repulsive human conduct. This is not inconsistent, however, with the further proposition that as an ethical and moral matter D & X is distinct from D & E and is a more serious concern for medical ethics and the morality of the larger society the medical profession must serve. ***

The differentiation between the procedures is itself a moral statement, serving to promote respect for human life; and if the woman and her physician in contemplating the moral consequences of the prohibited procedure conclude that grave moral consequences pertain to the permitted abortion process as well, the choice to elect or not to elect abortion is more informed; and the policy of promoting respect for life is advanced. ***

Demonstrating a further and basic misunderstanding of *Casey*, the Court holds the ban on the D & X procedure fails because it does not include an exception permitting an abortionist to perform a D & X whenever he believes it will best preserve the health of the woman. *** Nebraska, however, was entitled to conclude that its ban, while advancing important interests regarding the sanctity of life, deprived no woman of a safe abortion and therefore did not impose a substantial obstacle on the rights of any woman. *** Substantial evidence supports Nebraska's conclusion that its law denies no woman a safe abortion. *** It is also important to recognize that the D & X is effective only when the fetus is close to viable or, in fact, viable; thus the State is regulating the process at the point where its interest in life is nearing its peak.

Courts are ill-equipped to evaluate the relative worth of particular surgical procedures. The legislatures of the several States have superior factfinding capabilities in this regard. ***

The Court's next holding is that Nebraska's ban forbids both the D & X procedure and the more common D & E procedure. *** The text demonstrates the law applies only to the D & X procedure. Nebraska's intention is demonstrated at three points in the statutory language: references to "partial-birth abortion" and to the "delivery" of a fetus; and the requirement that the delivery occur "before" the performance of the death-causing procedure. *** The majority and, even more so, the concurring opinion by JUSTICE O'CONNOR, ignore the settled rule against deciding unnecessary constitutional questions. The State of Nebraska conceded, under its understanding of *Casey*, that if this law must be interpreted to bar D & E as well as D & X it is unconstitutional. Since the majority concludes this is indeed the case, that should have been the end of the matter. Yet the Court and JUSTICE O'CONNOR go much farther. They conclude that the statute requires a health exception which, for all practical purposes and certainly in the circumstances of this case, allows the physician to make the determination in his own professional judgment. This is an immense constitutional holding. It is unnecessary; and, for the reasons I have sought to explain, it is incorrect. While it is not clear which of the two halves of the majority opinion is dictum, both are wrong. *** The State chose to forbid a procedure many decent and civilized people find so abhorrent as to be among the most serious of crimes against human life, while the State still protected the woman's autonomous right of choice as reaffirmed in Casey. The Court closes its eyes to these profound concerns. ***

JUSTICE THOMAS, with whom THE CHIEF JUSTICE and JUSTICE SCALIA join, dissenting.

*** Although a State may permit abortion, nothing in the Constitution dictates that a State must do so. *** Even assuming, however, as I will for the remainder of this dissent, that *Casey's* fabricated undue-burden standard merits adherence (which it does not), today's decision is extraordinary. Today, the Court inexplicably holds that the States cannot constitutionally prohibit a method of abortion that millions find hard to distinguish from infanticide and that the Court hesitates even to describe. This holding cannot be reconciled with *Casey's* undue-burden standard, as that standard was explained to us by the authors of the joint opinion, and the majority hardly pretends otherwise. In striking down this statute—which expresses a profound and legitimate respect for fetal life and which leaves unimpeded several other safe forms of abortion—the majority opinion gives the lie to the promise of *Casey* that regulations that do no more than "express profound respect for the life of the unborn are permitted, if they are not a substantial obstacle to the woman's exercise of the right to choose" whether or not to have an abortion. Today's decision is so obviously irreconcilable with *Casey's* explication of what its undue-burden standard requires, let alone the Constitution, that it should be seen for what it is, a reinstitution of the pre-*Webster* abortion-on-demand era in which the mere invocation of "abortion rights" trumps any contrary societal interest. If this statute is unconstitutional under *Casey*, then *Casey* meant nothing at all, and the Court should candidly admit it. ***

In the almost 30 years since *Roe*, this Court has never described the various methods of aborting a second-or third-trimester fetus. From reading the majority's sanitized description, one would think that this case involves state regulation of a widely accepted routine medical procedure. Nothing could be further from the truth. The most widely used method of abortion during this stage of pregnancy is so gruesome that its use can be traumatic even for the physicians and medical staff who perform it. And the particular procedure at issue in this case, "partial birth abortion," so closely borders on infanticide that 30 States have attempted to ban it. *** Although the Nebraska statute purports to prohibit only "partial birth abortion," a phrase which is commonly used *** to refer to the breech extraction version of intact D & E, the majority concludes that this statute could also be read in some future case to prohibit ordinary D & E, the first procedure described above. According to the majority, such an application would pose a substantial obstacle to some women seeking abortions and, therefore, the statute is unconstitutional. The majority errs with its very first step. I think it is clear that the Nebraska statute does not prohibit the D & E procedure. ***

Having resolved that Nebraska's partial birth abortion statute permits doctors to perform D & E abortions, the question remains whether a State can constitutionally prohibit the partial birth abortion procedure without a health exception. Although the majority and JUSTICE O'CONNOR purport to rely on the standard articulated in the *Casey* joint opinion in concluding that a State may not, they in fact disregard it entirely. *** The *Casey* joint opinion expressly noted that prior case law had undervalued the State's interest in potential life, and had invalidated regulations of abortion that "in no real sense deprived women of the ultimate decision." *** A regulation imposes an "undue burden" only if it "has the effect of placing a substantial obstacle in the path of a woman's choice."

There is no question that the State of Nebraska has a valid interest—one not designed to strike at the right itself—in prohibiting partial birth abortion. Casey itself noted that States may "express profound respect for the life of the unborn." *** The AMA has recognized that this procedure is "ethically different from other destructive abortion techniques because the fetus, normally twenty weeks or longer in gestation, is killed *outside* the womb." *** Thirty States have concurred with this view. ***

The next question, therefore, is whether the Nebraska statute is unconstitutional because it does not contain an exception that would allow use of the procedure whenever "necessary in appropriate medical judgment, for the preservation of the *** health of the mother." "According to the majority, *** unless a State can conclusively establish that an abortion procedure is no safer than other procedures, the State cannot regulate that procedure without including a health exception. *** The rule set forth by the majority and JUSTICE O'CONNOR dramatically expands on our prior abortion cases and threatens to undo any state regulation of abortion procedures. *** *Roe* and *Casey* say nothing at all about cases in which a physician considers one prohibited method of abortion to be preferable to permissible methods. Today's majority and JUSTICE O'CONNOR twist *Roe* and *Casey* to apply to the situation in which a woman desires—for whatever reason—an abortion and wishes to obtain the abortion by some particular method." ***

As if this state of affairs were not bad enough, the majority expands the health exception rule articulated in Casey in one additional and equally pernicious way. Although *Roe* and *Casey* mandated a health exception for cases in which abortion is "necessary" for a woman's health, the majority concludes that a procedure is "necessary" if it has any comparative health benefits. In other words, according to the majority, so long as a doctor can point to support in the profession for his (or the woman's) preferred procedure, it is "necessary" and the physician is entitled to perform it. But such a health exception requirement eviscerates *Casey's* undue burden standard and imposes unfettered abortion-on-demand. The exception entirely swallows the rule. In effect, no regulation of abortion procedures is permitted because there will always be some support for a procedure and there will always be some doctors who conclude that the procedure is preferable. If Nebraska reenacts its partial birth abortion ban with a health exception, the State will not be able to prevent physicians like Dr. Carhart from using partial birth abortion as a routine abortion procedure. This Court has now expressed its own conclusion that there is "highly plausible" support for the view that partial birth abortion is safer, which, in the majority's view, means that the procedure is therefore "necessary." Any doctor who wishes to perform such a procedure under the new statute will be able to do so with impunity. ***

The majority assiduously avoids addressing the actual standard articulated in *Casey*—whether prohibiting partial birth abortion without a health exception poses a substantial obstacle to obtaining an abortion. And for good reason: Such an obstacle does not exist. There are two essential reasons why the Court cannot identify a substantial obstacle. First, the Court cannot identify any real, much less substantial, barrier to any woman's ability to obtain an abortion. And second, the Court cannot demonstrate that any such obstacle would affect a sufficient number of women to justify invalidating the statute on its face. ***

Even if I were willing to assume that the partial birth method of abortion is safer for some small set of women, such a conclusion would not require invalidating the Act, because this case comes to us on a facial challenge. The only question before us is whether respondent has shown that "'no set of circumstances exists under which the Act would be valid.'" *Ohio v. Akron Center for Reproductive Health*, 497 U.S. 502, 514 (1990). *** In *Casey*, the Court was presented with a facial challenge to, among other provisions, a spousal notice requirement. The question, according to the majority was whether the spousal notice provision operated as a "substantial obstacle" to the women "whose conduct it affects," namely, "married women seeking abortions who do not wish to notify their husbands of their intentions and who do not qualify for one of the statutory exceptions to the notice requirement." The Court determined that a "large fraction" of the women in this category were victims of psychological or physical abuse. For this subset of women, according to the Court, the provision would pose a substantial obstacle to the ability to obtain an abortion because their husbands could exercise an effective veto over their decision. None of the opinions supporting the majority so much as mentions the large fraction standard, undoubtedly because the Nebraska statute easily survives it. *** In fact, it is not clear that any woman would be deprived of a safe abortion by her inability to obtain a partial birth abortion. ***

Notes

1. **Circumventing *Stenberg*?** Assume you work as a special assistant in the Attorney General's office. Can you draft a constitutional statute which will accomplish what the legislature desired?

2. **Question.** Does it violate substantive due process for the State to impose criminal punishment for harm to the fetus on a woman who uses illegal drugs during her pregnancy?

3. **Facial unconstitutionality and substantive due process.** In *United States v. Salerno*, 481 U.S. 739 (1987), the Court upheld provisions of The Bail Reform Act of 1984 (Act) allowing federal courts to detain arrestees pending trial if the Government shows that no release conditions "will reasonably assure *** the safety of any other person and the community." The challengers of the statute did not argue that the statute had been applied in a way that violated their Due Process rights, but that the procedures established in the act were facially unconstitutional. Rejecting this challenge, the Court said:

> "A facial challenge to a legislative Act is, of course, the most difficult challenge to mount successfully, since the challenger must establish that no set of circumstances exists under which the Act would be valid. The fact that the Bail Reform Act might operate

unconstitutionally under some conceivable set of circumstances is insufficient to render it wholly invalid, since we have not recognized an 'overbreadth' doctrine outside the limited context of the First Amendment. *** To sustain [the procedures of the Bail Reform Act] against such a challenge, we need only find them 'adequate to authorize the pretrial detention of at least some [persons] charged with crimes,' whether or not they might be insufficient in some particular circumstances. We think they pass that test. *** '[T]here is nothing inherently unattainable about a prediction of future criminal conduct.'

Under the Bail Reform Act, *** [d]etainees have a right to counsel at the detention hearing. They may testify in their own behalf, present information by proffer or otherwise, and cross-examine witnesses who appear at the hearing. The judicial officer charged with the responsibility of determining the appropriateness of detention is guided by statutorily enumerated factors, which include the nature and the circumstances of the charges, the weight of the evidence, the history and characteristics of the putative offender, and the danger to the community. *** The Government must prove its case by clear and convincing evidence. *** Finally, the judicial officer must include written findings of fact and a written statement of reasons for a decision to detain. *** The Act's review provisions provide for immediate appellate review of the detention decision.

We think these extensive safeguards suffice to repel a facial challenge. *** The protections are more exacting than those we found sufficient in the juvenile context, and they far exceed what we found necessary to effect limited postarrest detention. *** Given the legitimate and compelling regulatory purpose of the Act and the procedural protections it offers, we conclude that the Act is not facially invalid under the Due Process Clause of the Fifth Amendment." ***

After *Stenberg*, is the *Salerno* approach to facial unconstitutionality still valid?

4. **Problem.** Consider whether the following hypothetical federal legislation would violate due process:

FAMILY PRESERVATION ACT

1. FINDINGS.—The Congress finds that:

(a) Medical technology has now made it possible for people to give birth long after their natural biological processes would normally allow;

(b) Such artificially induced births in older people will have the effect of increasing the number of children whose parents die before the children reach maturity;

(c) The resulting increased number of parentless children will undermine the family structure central to American values and will increase the number of children who require public financial support;

(d) Both the undermining of family structure and the increased need for public funds will impair the nation's economy.

2. THEREFORE-

(a) *Age Limitation of Artificial Conception.* No one may implant a fertilized egg in a human being over age 65.

(b) *Punishment.* Violation of this statute shall be a misdemeanor punishable by a fine not to exceed $10,000 and imprisonment of not more than 6 months.

c. Family and Marriage

MOORE v. CITY OF EAST CLEVELAND, OHIO
431 U.S. 494, 97 S.Ct. 1932, 52 L.Ed.2d 531 (1977).

MR. JUSTICE POWELL announced the judgment of the Court, and delivered an opinion in which MR. JUSTICE BRENNAN, MR. JUSTICE MARSHALL, and MR. JUSTICE BLACKMUN joined.

East Cleveland's housing ordinance, like many throughout the country, limits occupancy of a dwelling unit to members of a single family. But the ordinance contains an unusual and complicated definitional section that recognizes as a "family" only a few categories of related individuals. Because her family, living together in her home, fits none of those categories, appellant stands convicted of a criminal offense. The question in this case is whether the ordinance violates the Due Process Clause of the Fourteenth Amendment.

Appellant, Mrs. Inez Moore, lives in her East Cleveland home together with her son, Dale Moore Sr., and her two grandsons, Dale, Jr., and John Moore, Jr. The two boys are first cousins rather than brothers; we are told that John came to live with his grandmother and with the elder and younger Dale Moores after his mother's death.

In early 1973, Mrs. Moore received a notice of violation from the city, stating that John was an "illegal occupant" and directing her to comply with the ordinance. When she failed to remove him from her home, the city filed a criminal charge. Mrs. Moore moved to dismiss, claiming that the ordinance was constitutionally invalid on its face. Her motion was overruled, and upon conviction she was sentenced to five days in jail and a $25 fine.

The city argues that our decision in *Village of Belle Terre v. Boraas*, 416 U.S. 1 (1974), requires us to sustain the ordinance attacked here. Belle Terre, like East Cleveland, imposed limits on the types of groups that could occupy a single dwelling unit. Applying the constitutional standard announced in this Court's leading land-use case, *Euclid v. Ambler Realty Co.*, 272 U.S. 365 (1926), we sustained the Belle Terre ordinance on the ground that it bore a rational relationship to permissible state objectives. *Euclid* held that land-use regulations violate the Due Process Clause if they are "clearly arbitrary and unreasonable, having no substantial relation to the public health, safety, morals, or general welfare." Later cases have emphasized that the general welfare is not to be narrowly understood; it embraces a broad range of governmental purposes. But our cases have not departed from the requirement that the government's chosen means must rationally further some legitimate state purpose.

But one overriding factor sets this case apart from *Belle Terre*. The ordinance there affected only unrelated individuals. It expressly allowed all who were related by "blood, adoption, or marriage" to live together, and in sustaining the ordinance we were careful to note that it promoted "family needs" and "family values." East Cleveland, in contrast, has chosen to regulate the occupancy of its housing by slicing deeply into the family itself. This is no mere incidental result of the ordinance. On its face it selects certain categories of relatives who may live together and declares that others may not. In particular, it makes a crime of a grandmother's choice to live with her grandson in circumstances like those presented here.

When a city undertakes such intrusive regulation of the family, *** the usual judicial deference to the legislature is inappropriate. "This Court has long recognized that freedom of personal choice in matters of marriage and family life is one of the liberties protected by the Due Process Clause of the Fourteenth Amendment." A host of cases *** have consistently acknowledged a "private realm of family life which the state cannot enter." *** Of course, the family is not beyond regulation. But when the government intrudes on choices concerning family living arrangements, this Court must examine carefully the importance of the governmental interests advanced and the extent to which they are served by the challenged regulation.

When thus examined, this ordinance cannot survive. The city seeks to justify it as a means of preventing overcrowding, minimizing traffic and parking congestion, and avoiding an undue financial burden on East Cleveland's school system. Although these are legitimate goals, the ordinance before us serves them marginally, at best. For example, the ordinance permits any family consisting only of husband, wife, and unmarried children to live together, even if the family contains a half dozen licensed drivers, each with his or her own car. At the same time it forbids an adult brother and sister to share a household, even if both faithfully use public transportation. The ordinance would permit a grandmother to live with a single dependent son and children, even if his school-age children number a dozen, yet it forces Mrs. Moore to find another dwelling for her grandson John, simply because of the presence of his uncle and cousin in the same household. ***

*** Substantive due process has at times been a treacherous field for this Court. There are risks when the judicial branch gives enhanced protection to certain substantive liberties without the guidance of the more specific provisions of the Bill of Rights. As the history of the *Lochner* era demonstrates, there is reason for concern lest the only limits to such judicial intervention become the predilections of those who happen at the time to be Members of this Court. That history counsels caution and restraint. But it does not counsel abandonment, nor does it require what the city urges here: cutting off any protection of family rights at the first convenient, if arbitrary boundary the boundary of the nuclear family.

Appropriate limits on substantive due process come not from drawing arbitrary lines but rather from careful "respect for the teachings of history (and), solid recognition of the basic values that underlie our society". *Griswold*, at 501 (HARLAN, J., concurring). Our decisions establish that the Constitution protects the sanctity of the family precisely because the institution of the family is deeply rooted in this Nation's history and tradition. It is through the family that we inculcate and pass down many of our most cherished values, moral and cultural.

Ours is by no means a tradition limited to respect for the bonds uniting the members of the nuclear family. The tradition of uncles, aunts, cousins, and especially grandparents sharing a household along with parents and children has roots equally venerable and equally deserving of constitutional recognition. *** Even if conditions of modern society have brought about a decline in extended family households, they have not erased the accumulated wisdom of civilization, gained over the centuries and honored throughout our history, that supports a larger conception of the family. Out of choice, necessity, or a sense of family responsibility, it has been common for close relatives to draw together and participate in the duties and the satisfactions of a common home. *** Whether or not such a household is established because of personal tragedy, the choice of relatives in this degree of kinship to live together may not lightly be denied by the State. ***

MR. JUSTICE BRENNAN, with whom MR. JUSTICE MARSHALL joins, concurring.

I join the plurality's opinion. *** [Z]oning power is not a license for local communities to enact senseless and arbitrary restrictions which cut deeply into private areas of protected family life. East Cleveland may not constitutionally define "family" as essentially confined to parents and the parents' own children. *** I write only to underscore the cultural myopia of the arbitrary boundary drawn by the East Cleveland ordinance in the light of the tradition of the American home that has been a feature of our society since our beginning as a Nation the "tradition" in the plurality's words, "of uncles, aunts, cousins, and especially grandparents sharing a household along with parents and children ***." The line drawn by this ordinance displays a depressing insensitivity toward the economic and emotional needs of a very large part of our society. ***

MR. JUSTICE STEVENS, concurring in the judgment.

In my judgment the critical question presented by this case is whether East Cleveland's housing ordinance is a permissible restriction on appellant's right to use her own property as she sees fit.

Long before the original States adopted the Constitution, the common law protected an owner's right to decide how best to use his own property. This basic right has always been limited by the law of nuisance which proscribes uses that impair the enjoyment of other property in the vicinity. But the question whether an individual owner's use could be further limited by a municipality's comprehensive zoning plan was not finally decided until this century.

The holding in *Euclid v. Ambler Realty Co.*, 272 U.S. 365, that a city could use its police power *** to create and implement a comprehensive plan for the use of land in the community, vastly diminished the rights of individual property owners. It did not, however, totally extinguish those rights. The intrusion on that basic property right has not previously gone beyond the point where the ordinance defines a family to include only persons related by blood, marriage, or adoption. *** The city has failed totally to explain the need for a rule which would allow a homeowner to have two grandchildren live with her if they are brothers, but not if they are cousins. Since this ordinance has not been shown to have any "substantial relation to the public health, safety, morals, or general welfare" of the city of East Cleveland, and since it cuts so deeply into a fundamental right normally associated with the ownership of residential property that of an owner to decide who may reside on his or her property it must fall under the limited standard of review of zoning decisions which this Court preserved in *Euclid* ***. Under that standard, East Cleveland's unprecedented ordinance constitutes a taking of property without due process and without just compensation.

For these reasons, I concur in the Court's judgment.

MR. CHIEF JUSTICE BURGER, dissenting. [omitted]

MR. JUSTICE STEWART, with whom MR. JUSTICE REHNQUIST joins, dissenting.

*** In my view, the appellant's claim that the ordinance in question invades constitutionally protected rights of association and privacy is in large part answered by the *Belle Terre* decision. *** To be sure, the ordinance involved in *Belle Terre* did not prevent blood relatives from occupying the same dwelling, and the Court's decision in that case does not, therefore, foreclose the appellant's arguments based specifically on the ties of kinship present in this case. Nonetheless, I would hold *** that the existence of those ties does not elevate either the appellant's claim of associational freedom or her claim of privacy to a level invoking constitutional protection.

To suggest that the biological fact of common ancestry necessarily gives related persons constitutional rights of association superior to those of unrelated persons is to misunderstand the nature of the associational freedoms that the Constitution has been understood to protect. The "association" in this case is not for any purpose relating to the promotion of speech, assembly, the press, or religion. And wherever the outer boundaries of constitutional protection of freedom of association may eventually turn out to be, they surely do not extend to those who assert no interest other than the gratification, convenience, and economy of sharing the same residence.

The appellant is considerably closer to the constitutional mark in asserting that the East Cleveland ordinance intrudes upon "the private realm of family life which the state cannot enter." *** Although the appellant's desire to share a single-dwelling unit also involves "private family life" in a sense, that desire can hardly be equated with any of the interests protected in the cases just cited. The ordinance about which the appellant complains did not impede her choice to have or not to have children, and it did not dictate to her how her own children were to be nurtured and reared. The ordinance clearly does not prevent parents from living together or living with their unemancipated offspring. *** Viewed in the light of these principles, I do not think East Cleveland's definition of "family" offends the Constitution. The city has undisputed power to ordain single-family residential occupancy. [*Belle Terre*; *Euclid*] And that power plainly carries with it the power to say what a "family" is. ***

MR. JUSTICE WHITE, dissenting.

*** [The] Court should be extremely reluctant to breathe still further substantive content into the Due Process Clause so as to strike down legislation adopted by a State or city to promote its welfare. Whenever the Judiciary does so, it unavoidably pre-empts for itself another part of the governance of the country without express constitutional authority.

*** I think it evident that the threshold question in any due process attack on legislation, whether the challenge is procedural or substantive, is whether there is a deprivation of life, liberty, or property. *** It would not be consistent with prior cases to restrict the liberties protected by the Due Process Clause to those fundamental interests "implicit in the concept of ordered liberty." *** [Previous] cases at most assert that only fundamental liberties will be given substantive protection; and they may be understood as merely identifying certain fundamental interests that the Court has deemed deserving of a heightened degree of protection under the Due Process Clause. ***

There are various "liberties," *** which require that infringing legislation be given closer judicial scrutiny, not only with respect to existence of a purpose and the means employed, but also with respect to the importance of the purpose itself relative to the invaded interest. Some interest would appear almost impregnable to invasion, such as the freedoms of speech, press, and religion, and the freedom from cruel and unusual punishments. Other interests, for example, the right of association, the right to vote, and various claims sometimes referred to under the general rubric of the right to privacy, also weigh very heavily against state claims of authority to regulate. *** Under our cases, the Due Process Clause extends substantial protection to various phases of family life, but none requires that the claim made here be sustained. I cannot believe that the interest in residing with more than one set of grandchildren is one that calls for any kind of heightened protection under the Due Process Clause. To say that one has a personal right to live with all, rather than some, of one's grandchildren and that this right is implicit in ordered liberty is, as my Brother STEWART says, "to extend the limited substantive contours of the Due Process Clause beyond recognition." ***

MR. JUSTICE POWELL would apparently construe the Due Process Clause to protect from all but quite important state regulatory interests any right or privilege that in his estimate is deeply rooted in the country's traditions. For me, this suggests a far too expansive charter for this Court and a far less meaningful and less confining guiding principle than MR. JUSTICE STEWART would use for serious substantive due process review. What the deeply rooted traditions of the country are is arguable; which of them deserve the protection of the Due Process Clause is even more debatable. The suggested view would broaden enormously the horizons of the Clause; and, if the interest involved here is any measure of what the States would be forbidden to regulate, the courts would be substantively weighing and very likely invalidating a wide range of measures that Congress and state legislatures think appropriate to respond to a changing economic and social order. ***

ZABLOCKI v. REDHAIL
434 U.S. 374, 98 S.Ct. 673, 54 L.Ed.2d 618 (1978).

MR. JUSTICE MARSHALL delivered the opinion of the Court.

At issue in this case is the constitutionality of a Wisconsin statute which provides that [any Wisconsin resident having minor issue not in his custody and which he is under obligation to support by any court order or judgment] may not marry, within the State or elsewhere, without first obtaining a court order granting permission to marry. *** The statute specifies that court permission cannot be granted unless the marriage applicant submits proof of compliance with the support obligation and, in addition, demonstrates that the children covered by the support order "are not then and are not likely thereafter to become public charges." ***

After being denied a marriage license because of his failure to comply with [the Act], appellee brought this class action challenging the statute as violative of the Equal Protection and Due Process Clauses of the Fourteenth Amendment ***.

Appellee Redhail is a Wisconsin resident who is unable to enter into a lawful marriage in Wisconsin or elsewhere so long as he maintains his Wisconsin residency. In January 1972, when appellee was a minor and a high school student, a paternity action was instituted against him in Milwaukee County Court, alleging that he was the father of a baby girl born out of wedlock on July 5, 1971. After he appeared and admitted that he was the child's father, the court entered an order on May 12, 1972, adjudging appellee the father and ordering him to pay $109 per month as support for the child until she reached 18 years of age. From May 1972 until August 1974, appellee was unemployed and indigent, and consequently was unable to make any support payments. On September 27, 1974, appellee filed an application for a marriage license with appellant Zablocki, the County Clerk of Milwaukee County, and a few days later the application was denied on the sole ground that appellee had not obtained a court order granting him permission to marry, as required by [the Act]. Although appellee did not petition a state court thereafter, it is stipulated that he would not have been able to satisfy either of the statutory prerequisites for an order granting permission to marry. ***

On December 24, 1974, appellee filed his complaint in the District Court, on behalf of himself and the class of all Wisconsin residents who had been rcfused a marriage license pursuant to [the Act] by one of the county clerks in Wisconsin. *** The statute was attacked on the grounds that it deprived appellee, and the class he sought to represent of equal protection and due process rights secured by the First, Fifth, Ninth, and Fourteenth Amendments to the United States Constitution. ***

[In *Loving v. Virginia*] the Court [held] that [Virginia's antimiscegenation] laws arbitrarily deprived [citizens] of a fundamental liberty protected by the Due Process Clause, the freedom to marry. The Court's language on the latter point bears repeating: "The freedom to marry has long been recognized as one of the vital personal rights essential to the orderly pursuit of happiness by free men." "Marriage is one of the 'basic civil rights of man,' fundamental to our very existence and survival." *** More recent decisions have established that the right to marry is part of the fundamental "right of privacy" implicit in the Fourteenth Amendment's Due Process Clause. *** It is not surprising that the decision to marry has been placed on the same level of importance as decisions relating to procreation, childbirth, child rearing, and family relationships. As the facts of this case illustrate, it would make little sense to recognize a right of privacy with respect to other matters of family life and not with respect to the decision to enter the relationship that is the foundation of the family in our society. *** [If] appellee's right to procreate means anything at all, it must imply some right to enter the only relationship in which the State of Wisconsin allows sexual relations legally to take place.

By reaffirming the fundamental character of the right to marry, we do not mean to suggest that every state regulation which relates in any way to the incidents of or prerequisites for marriage must be subjected to rigorous scrutiny. To the contrary, reasonable regulations that do not significantly interfere with decisions to enter into the marital relationship may legitimately be imposed. The statutory classification at issue here, however, clearly does interfere directly and substantially with the right to marry.

Under the challenged statute, no Wisconsin resident in the affected class may marry in Wisconsin or elsewhere without a court order, and marriages contracted in violation of the statute are both void and punishable as criminal offenses. Some of those in the affected class, like appellee, will never be able to obtain the necessary court order, because they either lack the financial means to meet their support obligations or cannot prove that their children will not become public charges. These persons are absolutely prevented from getting married. Many others, able in theory to satisfy the statute's requirements, will be sufficiently burdened by having to do so that thoy will in effect be coerced into forgoing their right to marry. And even those who can be persuaded to meet the statute's requirements suffer a serious intrusion into their freedom of choice in an area in which we have held such freedom to be fundamental. ***

When a statutory classification significantly interferes with the exercise of a fundamental right, it cannot be upheld unless it is supported by sufficiently important state interests and is closely tailored to effectuate only those interests. Appellant asserts that two interests are served by the challenged statute: the permission-to-marry proceeding furnishes an opportunity to counsel the applicant as to the necessity of fulfilling his prior support obligations; and the welfare of the out-of-custody children is protected. We may accept for present purposes that these are legitimate and substantial interests, but, since the means selected by the State for achieving these interests unnecessarily impinge on the right to marry, the statute cannot be sustained.

*** With regard to safeguarding the welfare of the out-of-custody children, appellant's brief does not make clear the connection between the State's interest and the statute's requirements. At argument, appellant's counsel suggested that, since permission to marry cannot be granted unless the applicant shows that he has satisfied his court-determined support obligations to the prior children and that those children will not become public charges, the statute provides incentive for the applicant to make support payments to his children. This "collection device" rationale cannot justify the statute's broad infringement on the right to marry. First, with respect to individuals who are unable to meet the statutory requirements, the statute merely prevents the applicant from getting married, without delivering any money at all into the hands of the applicant's prior children. More importantly, regardless of the applicant's ability or willingness to meet the statutory requirements, the State already has numerous other means for exacting compliance with support obligations, means that are at least as effective as the instant statute's and yet do not impinge upon the right to marry. ***

The statutory classification created by [the Act] thus cannot be justified by the interests advanced in support of it.

MR. CHIEF JUSTICE BURGER, concurring. [omitted]

MR. JUSTICE STEWART, concurring in the judgment.

I cannot join the opinion of the Court. To hold, as the Court does, that the Wisconsin statute violates the Equal Protection Clause seems to me to misconceive the meaning of that constitutional guarantee. *** The problem in this case is not one of discriminatory classifications, but of unwarranted encroachment upon a constitutionally protected freedom. I think that the Wisconsin statute is unconstitutional because it exceeds the bounds of permissible state regulation of marriage, and invades the sphere of liberty protected by the Due Process Clause of the Fourteenth Amendment.

I do not agree with the Court that there is a "right to marry" in the constitutional sense. That right, or more accurately that privilege, is under our federal system peculiarly one to be defined and limited by state law. A State may not only "significantly interfere with decisions to enter into marital relationship," but may in many circumstances absolutely prohibit it. Surely, for example, a State may legitimately say that no one can marry his or her sibling, that no one can marry who is not at least 14 years old, that no one can marry without first passing an examination for venereal disease, or that no one can marry who has a living husband or wife. But, just as surely, in regulating the intimate human relationship of marriage, there is a limit beyond which a State may not constitutionally go.

The Constitution does not specifically mention freedom to marry, but it is settled that the "liberty" protected by the Due Process Clause of the Fourteenth Amendment embraces more than those freedoms expressly enumerated in the Bill of Rights. And the decisions of this Court have made clear that freedom of personal choice in matters of marriage and family life is one of the liberties so protected. *** It is evident that the Wisconsin law now before us directly abridges that freedom. The question is whether the state interests that support the abridgment can overcome the substantive protections of the Constitution.

The Wisconsin law makes permission to marry turn on the payment of money in support of one's children by a previous marriage or liaison. Those who cannot show both that they have kept up with their support obligations and that their children are not and will not become wards of the State are altogether prohibited from marrying. ***

On several occasions this Court has held that a person's inability to pay money demanded by the State does not justify the total deprivation of a constitutionally protected liberty. *** The Wisconsin law makes no allowance for the truly indigent. The State flatly denies a marriage license to anyone who cannot afford to fulfill his support obligations and keep his children from becoming wards of the State. We may assume that the State has legitimate interests in collecting delinquent support payments and in reducing its welfare load. We may also assume that, as applied to those who can afford to meet the statute's financial requirements but choose not to do so, the law advances the State's objectives in ways superior to other means available to the State. The fact remains that some people simply cannot afford to meet the statute's financial requirements. To deny these people permission to marry penalizes them for failing to do that which they cannot do. Insofar as it applies to indigents, the state law is an irrational means of achieving these objectives of the State. ***

MR. JUSTICE POWELL, concurring in the judgment.

*** The Court apparently would subject all state regulation which "directly and substantially" interferes with the decision to marry in a traditional family setting to "critical examination" or "compelling state interest" analysis. Presumably, "reasonable regulations that do not significantly interfere with decisions to enter into the marital relationship may legitimately be imposed." The Court does not present, however, any principled means for distinguishing between the two types of regulations. Since state regulation in this area typically takes the form of a prerequisite or barrier to marriage or divorce, the degree of "direct" interference with the decision to marry or to divorce is unlikely to provide either guidance for state legislatures or a basis for judicial oversight. ***

In my view, analysis must start from the recognition of domestic relations as "an area that has long been regarded as a virtually exclusive province of the States." *** The State, representing the collective expression of moral aspirations, has an undeniable interest in ensuring that its rules of domestic relations reflect the widely held values of its people. *** State regulation has included bans on incest, bigamy, and homosexuality, as well as various preconditions to marriage, such as blood tests. Likewise, a showing of fault on the part of one of the partners traditionally has been a prerequisite to the dissolution of an unsuccessful union. A "compelling state purpose" inquiry would cast doubt on the network of restrictions that the States have fashioned to govern marriage and divorce.

State power over domestic relations is not without constitutional limits. The Due Process Clause requires a showing of justification "when the government intrudes on choices concerning family living arrangements" in a manner which is contrary to deeply rooted traditions. *** Furthermore, under the Equal Protection Clause the means chosen by the State in this case must bear "'a fair and substantial relation'" to the object of the legislation.

The Wisconsin measure in this case does not pass muster under either due process or equal protection standards. Appellant identifies three objectives which are supposedly furthered by the statute in question: (i) a counseling function; (ii) an incentive to satisfy outstanding support obligations; and (iii) a deterrent against incurring further obligations. The opinion of the Court amply demonstrates that the asserted counseling objective bears no relation to this statute. *** The so-called "collection device" rationale presents a somewhat more difficult question. I do not agree with the suggestion in the Court's opinion that a State may never condition the right to marry on satisfaction of existing support obligations simply because the State has alternative methods of compelling such payments. To the extent this restriction applies to persons who are able to make the required support payments but simply wish to shirk their moral and legal obligation, the Constitution interposes no bar to this additional collection mechanism. The vice inheres, not in the collection concept, but in the failure to make provision for those without the means to comply with child-support obligations. *** Because the State has not established a justification for this unprecedented foreclosure of marriage to many of its citizens solely because of their indigency, I concur in the judgment of the Court.

MR. JUSTICE STEVENS, concurring in the judgment.

*** A classification based on marital status is fundamentally different from a classification which determines who may lawfully enter into the marriage relationship. The individual's interest in making the marriage decision independently is sufficiently important to merit special constitutional protection. It is not, however, an interest which is constitutionally immune from evenhanded regulation. Thus, laws prohibiting marriage to a child, a close relative, or a person afflicted with venereal disease, are unchallenged even though they "interfere directly and substantially with the right to marry." This Wisconsin statute has a different character.

Under this statute, a person's economic status may determine his eligibility to enter into a lawful marriage. A noncustodial parent whose children are "public charges" may not marry even if he has met his court-ordered obligations. Thus, within the class of parents who have fulfilled their court-ordered obligations, the rich may marry and the poor may not. This type of statutory discrimination is, I believe, totally unprecedented, as well as inconsistent with our tradition of administering justice equally to the rich and to the poor.

*** The statute prevents impoverished parents from marrying even though their intended spouses are economically independent. Presumably, the Wisconsin Legislature assumed (a) that only fathers would be affected by the legislation, and (b) that they would never marry employed women. The first assumption ignores the fact that fathers are sometimes awarded custody, and the second ignores the composition of today's work force. To the extent that the statute denies a hard-pressed parent any opportunity to prove that an intended marriage will ease rather than aggravate his financial straits, it not only rests on unreliable premises, but also defeats its own objectives.

In sum, the public-charge provision is either futile or perverse insofar as it applies to childless couples, couples who will have illegitimate children if they are forbidden to marry, couples whose economic status will be improved by marriage, and couples who are so poor that the marriage will have no impact on the welfare status of their children in any event. Even assuming that the right to marry may sometimes be denied on economic grounds, this clumsy and deliberate legislative discrimination between the rich and the poor is irrational in so many ways that it cannot withstand scrutiny under the Equal Protection Clause of the Fourteenth Amendment.

MR. JUSTICE REHNQUIST, dissenting.

*** I think that under the Equal Protection Clause the statute need pass only the "rational basis test." The statute so viewed is a permissible exercise of the State's power to regulate family life and to assure the support of minor children, despite its possible imprecision in the extreme cases envisioned in the concurring opinions. ***

Notes

1. **Limits to *Moore*.**

   (a) Is this case distinguishable from *Belle Terre*? Compare the definitions of family in the two statutes.

   (b) If this distinction holds, it is because there is some tradition defining the reach of constitutional rights to some particular conception of family. Isn't the Court likely to be torn between the precise tradition (e.g. nuclear family) and the broader tradition (biologically related individuals) in many cases?

   (c) Can a city, after these two cases, prohibit biologically unrelated individuals who "feel like a family" or "significant others" from living together?

(d) What, if any, ramifications do you see in these cases for "adult communities" which exclude children (defined as anyone under 21) from living there for more than two weeks in any 52–week period?

2. *Moore* **and Class.** Would your views of this case change if you were told that the case involved an effort by a mainly black middle-class neighborhood to define itself as different from mainly black lower-class surrounding neighborhoods? Consider whether you agree with the comment that "The Court in *Moore* myopically saw the case as a dispute between 'a family' and 'the state' rather than as a dispute among citizens about the meaning of 'family.'" Burt, *The Constitution of the Family*, 1979 SUP. CT. REV. 329, 391.

3.   **Comparisons of** *Moore* **and** *Zablocki.*

(a) *Moore* was a pure substantive due process decision; *Zablocki* was actually decided on equal protection grounds though the various opinions sound like substantive due process. Which approach do you think preferable? Would you agree that "[Judicial] discovery of fundamental [values] outside the constitutional text [should] be grounded in the due process clause. [The] equality strand [should] not bear a substantive content"? Lupu, *Untangling the Strands of the Fourteenth Amendment*, 77 MICH. L. REV. 981, 985(1979).

(b) *Moore* is often considered for the proposition that there is a fundamental right to family; *Zablocki* that there is a fundamental right to marry. Yet both may be contextually limited, the former to prohibited living arrangements, the latter to debt-based bars to marriage. Should the Court invalidate an AFDC requirement that recipient families include within the family unit all children living within the household, including those receiving child support payments from noncustodial parents, with a consequent reduction of the family's benefit levels? *See Bowen v. Gilliard*, 483 U.S. 587 (1987) ("That some families may decide to modify their living arrangements" because of the regulation is not an impermissible intrusion on family). What should the Court do about a Social Security Act provision providing that benefits received by a disabled dependent child of a covered wage earner shall terminate when the child marries an individual who is not independently entitled to benefits, even if the spouse is also disabled? *See Califano v. Jobst*, 434 U.S. 47 (1977)(rule valid despite fact that "some persons who might otherwise have married were deterred by the rule or because some who did marry were burdened thereby"). What distinguishes these cases from *Moore* and *Zablocki*?

4.   **Family and Marriage Traditions.** Does the substantive due process protection of the family reach to a family which includes adopted children? Illegitimate children? Remote cousins, aunts and uncles? Likewise, does the protection of marriage extend to homosexual marriage?   Multiple marriages (polygamy)? Incestuous marriages?   Marriages which, for physical reasons, cannot be consummated? Perhaps the most fascinating case dealing with such issues is *Reynolds v. United States*, 98 U.S. 145 (1878), in which a Mormon convicted of violating an antibigamy statute countered that his conviction violated his free exercise of religion. The Court unanimously rejected his claim. While the First Amendment issue is not within the scope of this book, what the Court said about marriage may have ramifications today on some of the above questions:

"[T]here never has been a time in any State of the Union when polygamy has not been an offense against society, cognizable by the civil courts and punishable with more or less severity. In the face of all this evidence, it is impossible to believe that the constitutional guarantee of religious freedom was intended to prohibit legislation in respect to this most important feature of social life. Marriage, while from its very nature a sacred obligation, is nevertheless, in most civilized nations, a civil contract, and usually regulated by law. Upon it society may be said to be built, and out of its fruits spring social relations and social obligations and duties, with which government is frequently required to deal. *** [It] is within the legitimate scope of the power of every civil government to determine whether polygamy or monogamy shall be the law of social life under its dominion."

5. **Specificity of Traditions.** In *Michael H. v. Gerald D.*, 491 U.S. 110 (1989), the Court considered whether preclusion of visitation rights by the genetic father of a child under a California statute providing that a child born to a married woman living with her husband is conclusively presumed to be a child of the marriage was constitutional. JUSTICE SCALIA's plurality opinion upheld the statute on the ground that the interest asserted by the father was not "an interest traditionally protected by our society." In a footnote responding to JUSTICE BRENNAN's suggestion that "parenthood is an interest that historically has received our attention and protection," Scalia argued that Brennan's formulation of the tradition was too broad, and that the Court should look to "the most specific level at which a relevant tradition protecting, or denying protection to, the asserted right can be identified." He found that the "more specific tradition" "unqualifiedly denies protection to [the natural father of a child adulterously conceived]." Brennan responded that, had the Court followed Scalia's methodology, "many a decision would have reached a different result." Brennan noted, "We are not an assimilative, homogeneous society, but a facilitative, pluralistic one *** it is absurd to assume that we can agree on the content of those terms [like 'family' and 'parenthood'] and destructive to pretend that we do." With whom do you agree and why?

6. **Problems.**

(a) Does an unwed father have a constitutional right to custody of his illegitimate children when the mother dies? Does that right survive a state statute that denies him the right to veto the adoption of his illegitimate children by the mother's husband? Compare *Stanley v. Illinois*, 405 U.S. 645 (1972), with *Quilloin v. Walcott*, 434 U.S. 246 (1978).

(b) Is a prison rule that inmates may not marry anyone unless the warden concludes that there are compelling reasons for marriage constitutional? Pregnancy and birth of a child outside marriage are the only such reasons accepted to date. *See Turner v. Safley*, 482 U.S. 78 (1987).

(c) Are state bans on homosexual marriages constitutional? Senate candidate, Hilary Rodham Clinton in January 2000, opposing such marriages, said "Marriage has got historic, religious, and moral content that goes back to the beginning of time, and I think a marriage is as a marriage always has been: between a man and a woman." In *State of the Union*, THE NEW REPUBLIC, May 8, 2000, Andrew Sullivan responds: "The institution of human marriage, like most human institutions, has undergone vast changes over the last two millennia. If marriage were the same today as it has been for 2,000 years, it would be possible to marry a twelve-year-old you had never met, to own a wife as property and dispose of her at will, or to imprison a person who married someone of a different race. And it would be impossible to get a divorce." If this were a due process argument in court, who would have the better of it? See Lawrence v. Texas, infra.

TROXEL v. GRANVILLE
530 U.S. 57, 120 S.Ct. 2054, 147 L.Ed.2d 49 (2000).

JUSTICE O'CONNOR announced the judgment of the court and delivered an opinion, in which THE CHIEF JUSTICE, JUSTICE GINSBURG, and JUSTICE BREYER join.

Section 26.10.160(3) of the Revised Code of Washington permits "[a]ny person" to petition a superior court for visitation rights "at any time," and authorizes that court to grant such visitation rights whenever "visitation may serve the best interest of the child." ***

Tommie Granville and Brad Troxel shared a relationship that ended in June 1991. The two never married, but they had two daughters, Isabelle and Natalie. Jenifer and Gary Troxel are Brad's parents, and thus the paternal grandparents of Isabelle and Natalie. After Tommie and Brad separated in 1991, Brad lived with his parents and regularly brought his daughters to his parents' home for weekend visitation. Brad committed suicide in May 1993. Although the Troxels at first continued to see Isabelle and Natalie on a regular basis after their son's death, Tommie Granville informed the Troxels in October 1993 that she wished to limit their visitation with her daughters to one short visit per month.

In December 1993, the Troxels commenced the present action by filing, in the Washington Superior Court for Skagit County, a petition to obtain visitation rights with Isabelle and Natalie. *** At trial, the Troxels requested two weekends of overnight visitation per month and two weeks of visitation each summer. Granville did not oppose visitation altogether, but instead asked the court to order one day of visitation per month with no overnight stay. In 1995, the Superior Court issued an oral ruling and entered a visitation decree ordering visitation one weekend per month, one week during the summer, and four hours on both of the petitioning grandparents' birthdays.

Granville appealed, during which time she married Kelly Wynn. *** Granville's husband formally adopted Isabelle and Natalie.

The demographic changes of the past century make it difficult to speak of an average American family. *** In 1996, children living with only one parent accounted for 28 percent of all children under age 18 in the United States. Understandably, in these single-parent households, persons outside the nuclear family are called upon with increasing frequency to assist in the everyday tasks of child rearing. In many cases, grandparents play an important role. For example, in 1998, approximately 4 million children—or

5.6 percent of all children under age 18—lived in the household of their grandparents.

The nationwide enactment of nonparental visitation statutes is assuredly due, in some part, to the States' recognition of these changing realities of the American family. Because grandparents and other relatives undertake duties of a parental nature in many households, States have sought to ensure the welfare of the children therein by protecting the relationships those children form with such third parties. The States' nonparental visitation statutes are further supported by a recognition, which varies from State to State, that children should have the opportunity to benefit from relationships with statutorily specified persons—for example, their grandparents. The extension of statutory rights in this area to persons other than a child's parents, however, comes with an obvious cost. For example, the State's recognition of an independent third-party interest in a child can place a substantial burden on the traditional parent-child relationship. *** In this case, we are presented with just such a question. Specifically, we are asked to decide whether § 26.10.160(3), as applied to Tommie Granville and her family, violates the Federal Constitution. ***

The liberty interest at issue in this case—the interest of parents in the care, custody, and control of their children—is perhaps the oldest of the fundamental liberty interests recognized by this Court. More than 75 years ago, in *Meyer v. Nebraska*, 262 U.S. 390 (1923), we held that the "liberty" protected by the Due Process Clause includes the right of parents to "establish a home and bring up children" and "to control the education of their own." Two years later, in *Pierce v. Society of Sisters*, 268 U.S. 510 (1925), we again held that the "liberty of parents and guardians" includes the right "to direct the upbringing and education of children under their control." *** We returned to the subject in *Prince v. Massachusetts*, 321 U.S. 158 (1944), and again confirmed that there is a constitutional dimension to the right of parents to direct the upbringing of their children. "It is cardinal with us that the custody, care and nurture of the child reside first in the parents, whose primary function and freedom include preparation for obligations the state can neither supply nor hinder."

In subsequent cases also, we have recognized the fundamental right of parents to make decisions concerning the care, custody, and control of their children. See, e.g., *Stanley v. Illinois*, 405 U.S. 645 (1972) ("It is plain that the interest of a parent in the companionship, care, custody, and management of his or her children 'come[s] to this Court with a momentum for respect lacking when appeal is made to liberties which derive merely from shifting economic arrangements'"); *Wisconsin v. Yoder*, 406 U.S. 205 (1972) ("The history and culture of Western civilization reflect a strong tradition of parental concern for the nurture and upbringing of their children. This primary role of the parents in the upbringing of their children is now established beyond debate as an enduring American tradition"). *** In light of this extensive precedent, it cannot now be doubted that the Due Process Clause of the Fourteenth Amendment protects the fundamental right of parents to make decisions concerning the care, custody, and control of their children.

Section 26.10.160(3), as applied to Granville and her family in this case, unconstitutionally infringes on that fundamental parental right. The Washington nonparental visitation statute is breathtakingly broad. According to the statute's text, "[a]ny person may petition the court for visitation rights at any time," and the court may grant such visitation rights whenever "visitation may serve the best interest of the child." That language effectively permits any third party seeking visitation to subject any decision by a parent concerning visitation of the parent's children to state-court review. Once the visitation petition has been filed in court and the matter is placed before a judge, a parent's decision that visitation would not be in the child's best interest is accorded no deference. Section 26.10.160(3) contains no requirement that a court accord the parent's decision any presumption of validity or any weight whatsoever. Instead, the Washington statute places the best-interest determination solely in the hands of the judge. Should the judge disagree with the parent's estimation of the child's best interests, the judge's view necessarily prevails. Thus, in practical effect, in the State of Washington a court can disregard and overturn any decision by a fit custodial parent concerning visitation whenever a third party affected by the decision files a visitation petition, based solely on the judge's determination of the child's best interests. The Washington Supreme Court had the opportunity to give § 26.10.160(3) a narrower reading, but it declined to do so.

Turning to the facts of this case, the record reveals that the Superior Court's order was based on precisely the type of mere disagreement we have just described and nothing more. The Superior Court's order was not founded on any special factors that might justify the State's interference with Granville's fundamental right to make decisions concerning the rearing of her two daughters. To be sure, this case involves a visitation petition filed by grandparents soon after the death of their son—the father of Isabelle and Natalie—but the combination of several factors here compels our conclusion that § 26.10.160(3), as applied, exceeded the bounds of the Due Process Clause.

First, the Troxels did not allege, and no court has found, that Granville was an unfit parent. That aspect of the case is important, for there is a presumption that fit parents act in the best interests of their children. *** Accordingly, so long as a parent adequately cares for his or her children (i.e., is fit), there will normally be no reason for the State to inject itself into the private realm of the family to further question the ability of that parent to make the best decisions concerning the rearing of that parent's children. *** The judge's comments suggest that he presumed the grandparents' request should be granted unless the children would be "impact[ed] adversely." In effect, the judge placed on Granville, the fit custodial parent, the burden of disproving that visitation would be in the best interest of her daughters. The judge reiterated moments later: "I think [visitation with the Troxels] would be in the best interest of the children and I haven't been shown it is not in [the] best interest of the children."

The decisional framework employed by the Superior Court directly contravened the traditional presumption that a fit parent will act in the best interest of his or her child. In that respect, the court's presumption failed to provide any protection for Granville's fundamental constitutional right to make decisions concerning the rearing of her own daughters. *** In an ideal world, parents might always seek to cultivate the bonds between grandparents and their grandchildren. Needless to say, however, our world is far from perfect, and in it the decision whether such an intergenerational relationship would be beneficial in any specific case is for the parent to make in the first instance. And, if a fit parent's decision of the kind at issue here becomes subject to judicial review, the court must accord at least some special weight to the parent's own determination.

Finally, we note that there is no allegation that Granville ever sought to cut off visitation entirely. Rather, the present dispute originated when Granville informed the Troxels that she would prefer to restrict their visitation with Isabelle and Natalie to one short visit per month and special holidays. In the Superior Court proceedings Granville did not oppose visitation but instead asked that the duration of any visitation order be shorter than that requested by the Troxels. *** Significantly, many other States expressly provide by statute that courts may not award visitation unless a parent has denied (or unreasonably denied) visitation to the concerned third party. ***

Considered together with the Superior Court's reasons for awarding visitation to the Troxels, the combination of these factors demonstrates that the visitation order in this case was an unconstitutional infringement on Granville's fundamental right to make decisions concerning the care, custody, and control of her two daughters. The Washington Superior Court failed to accord the determination of Granville, a fit custodial parent, any material weight. In fact, the Superior Court made only two formal findings in support of its visitation order. First, the Troxels "are part of a large, central, loving family, all located in this area, and the [Troxels] can provide opportunities for the children in the areas of cousins and music." Second, "[t]he children would be benefitted from spending quality time with the [Troxels], provided that that time is balanced with time with the childrens' [sic] nuclear family." These slender findings, in combination with the court's announced presumption in favor of grandparent visitation and its failure to accord significant weight to Granville's already having offered meaningful visitation to the Troxels, show that this case involves nothing more than a simple disagreement between the Washington Superior Court and Granville concerning her children's best interests. The Superior Court's announced reason for ordering one week of visitation in the summer demonstrates our conclusion well: "I look back on some personal experiences ***. We always spen[t] as kids a week with one set of grandparents and another set of grandparents, [and] it happened to work out in our family that [it] turned out to be an enjoyable experience. Maybe that can, in this family, if that is how it works out." As we have explained, the Due Process Clause does not permit a State to infringe on the fundamental right of parents to make childrearing decisions simply because a state judge believes a "better" decision could be made. Neither the Washington nonparental visitation statute generally—which places no limits on either the persons who may petition for visitation or the circumstances in which such a petition may be granted—nor the Superior Court in this specific case required anything more. Accordingly, we hold that § 26.10.160(3), as applied in this case, is unconstitutional.

Because we rest our decision on the sweeping breadth of § 26.10.160(3) and the application of that broad, unlimited power in this case, we do not consider the primary constitutional question passed on by the Washington Supreme Court—whether the Due Process Clause requires all nonparental visitation statutes to include a showing of harm or potential harm to the child as a condition precedent to granting visitation. We do not, and need not, define today the precise scope of the parental due process right in the visitation context. In this respect, we agree with JUSTICE KENNEDY that the constitutionality of any standard for awarding visitation turns on the specific manner in which that standard is applied and that the constitutional protections in this area are best "elaborated with care." Because much state-court adjudication in this context occurs on a case-by-case basis, we would be hesitant to hold that specific nonparental visitation statutes violate the Due Process Clause as a per se matter. ***

JUSTICE SOUTER, concurring in the judgment. [omitted]

JUSTICE THOMAS, concurring in the judgment.

I write separately to note that neither party has argued that our substantive due process cases were wrongly decided and that the original understanding of the Due Process Clause precludes judicial enforcement of unenumerated rights under that constitutional provision. As a result, I express no view on the merits of this matter, and I understand the plurality as well to leave the resolution of that issue [and any challenge based on the Privileges and Immunities Clause] for another day. *** I would apply strict scrutiny to infringements of fundamental rights. Here, the State of Washington lacks even a legitimate governmental interest—to say nothing of a compelling one—in second-guessing a fit parent's decision regarding visitation with third parties. On this basis, I would affirm the judgment below.

JUSTICE STEVENS, dissenting.

*** In response to Tommie Granville's federal constitutional challenge, the State Supreme Court broadly held that Wash. Rev.Code § 26.10.160(3) (Supp.1996) was invalid on its face under the Federal Constitution. Despite the nature of this judgment, JUSTICE O'CONNOR would hold that the Washington visitation statute violated the Due Process Clause of the Fourteenth Amendment only as applied. I agree with JUSTICE SOUTER that this approach is untenable. *** We are thus presented with the unconstrued terms of a state statute and a State Supreme Court opinion that, in my view, significantly misstates the effect of the Federal Constitution upon any construction of that statute. Given that posture, I believe the Court should identify and correct the two flaws in the reasoning of the state court's majority opinion, and remand for further review of the trial court's disposition of this specific case.

In my view, the State Supreme Court erred in its federal constitutional analysis because neither the provision granting "any person" the right to petition the court for visitation, nor the absence of a provision requiring a "threshold *** finding of harm to the child," provides a sufficient basis for holding that the statute is invalid in all its applications. *** Under the Washington statute, there are plainly any number of cases—indeed, one suspects, the most common to arise—in which the "person" among "any" seeking visitation is a once-custodial caregiver, an intimate relation, or even a genetic parent. Even the Court would seem to agree that in many circumstances, it would be constitutionally permissible for a court to award some visitation of a child to a parent or previous caregiver in cases of parental separation or divorce, cases of disputed custody, cases involving temporary foster care or guardianship, and so forth. As the statute plainly sweeps in a great deal of the permissible, the State Supreme Court majority incorrectly concluded that a statute authorizing "any person" to file a petition seeking visitation privileges would invariably run afoul of the Fourteenth Amendment.

The second key aspect of the Washington Supreme Court's holding—that the Federal Constitution requires a showing of actual or potential "harm" to the child before a court may order visitation continued over a parent's objections—finds no support in this Court's case law. While, as the Court recognizes, the Federal Constitution certainly protects the parent-child relationship from arbitrary impairment by the State, we have never held that the parent's liberty interest in this relationship is so inflexible as to establish a rigid constitutional shield, protecting every arbitrary parental decision from any challenge absent a threshold finding of harm. The presumption that parental decisions generally serve the best interests of their children is sound, and clearly in the normal case the parent's interest is paramount. But even a fit parent is capable of treating a child like a mere possession.

Cases like this do not present a bipolar struggle between the parents and the State over who has final authority to determine what is in a child's best interests. There is at a minimum a third individual, whose interests are implicated in every case to which the statute applies—the child.

It has become standard practice in our substantive due process jurisprudence to begin our analysis with an identification of the "fundamental" liberty interests implicated by the challenged state action. My colleagues are of course correct to recognize that the right of a parent to maintain a relationship with his or her child is among the interests included most often in the constellation of liberties protected through the Fourteenth Amendment. Our cases leave no doubt that parents have a fundamental liberty interest in caring for and guiding their children, and a corresponding privacy interest—absent exceptional circumstances—in doing so without the undue interference of strangers to them and to their child. Moreover, and critical in this case, our cases applying this principle have explained that with this constitutional liberty comes a presumption (albeit a rebuttable one) that "natural bonds of affection lead parents to act in the best interests of their children."

Despite this Court's repeated recognition of these significant parental liberty interests, these interests have never been seen to be without limits. In *Lehr v. Robertson*, 463 U.S. 248 (1983), for example, this Court held that a putative biological father who had never established an actual relationship with his child did not have a constitutional right to notice of his child's adoption by the man who had married the child's mother. *** Conversely, in *Michael H. v. Gerald D.*, 491 U.S. 110 (1989), this Court concluded that despite both biological parenthood and an established relationship with a young child, a father's due process liberty interest in maintaining some connection with that child was not sufficiently powerful to overcome a state statutory presumption that the husband of the child's mother was the child's parent. As a result of the presumption, the biological father could be denied even visitation with the child because, as a matter of state law, he was not a "parent." A plurality of this Court there recognized that the parental liberty interest was a function, not simply of "isolated factors" such as biology and intimate connection, but of the broader and apparently independent interest in family.

A parent's rights with respect to her child have thus never been regarded as absolute, but rather are limited by the existence of an actual, developed relationship with a child, and are tied to the presence or absence of some embodiment of family. ***

While this Court has not yet had occasion to elucidate the nature of a child's liberty interests in preserving established familial or family-like bonds, it seems to me extremely likely that, to the extent parents and families have fundamental liberty interests in preserving such intimate relationships, so, too, do children have these interests, and so, too, must their interests be balanced in the equation. At a minimum, our prior cases recognizing that children are, generally speaking, constitutionally protected actors require that this Court reject any suggestion that when it comes to parental rights, children are so much chattel. The constitutional protection against arbitrary state interference with parental rights should not be extended to prevent the States from protecting children against the arbitrary exercise of parental authority that is not in fact motivated by an interest in the welfare of the child.

This is not, of course, to suggest that a child's liberty interest in maintaining contact with a particular individual is to be treated invariably as on a par with that child's parents' contrary interests. Because our substantive due process case law includes a strong presumption that a parent will act in the best interest of her child, it would be necessary, were the state appellate courts actually to confront a challenge to the statute as applied, to consider whether the trial court's assessment of the "best interest of the child" incorporated that presumption. *** But presumptions notwithstanding, we should recognize that there may be circumstances in which a child has a stronger interest at stake than mere protection from serious harm caused by the termination of visitation by a "person" other than a parent. The almost infinite variety of family relationships that pervade our ever-changing society strongly counsel against the creation by this Court of a constitutional rule that treats a biological parent's liberty interest in the care and supervision of her child as an isolated right that may be exercised arbitrarily. It is indisputably the business of the States, rather than a federal court employing a national standard, to assess in the first instance the relative importance of the conflicting interests that give rise to disputes such as this. Far from guaranteeing that parents' interests will be trammeled in the sweep of cases arising under the statute, the Washington law merely gives an individual—with whom a child may have an established relationship—the procedural right to ask the State to act as arbiter, through the entirely well-known best-interests standard, between the parent's protected interests and the child's. It seems clear to me that the Due Process Clause of the Fourteenth Amendment leaves room for States to consider the impact on a child of possibly arbitrary parental decisions that neither serve nor are motivated by the best interests of the child. ***

JUSTICE SCALIA, dissenting.

In my view, a right of parents to direct the upbringing of their children is among the "unalienable Rights" with which the Declaration of Independence proclaims "all Men *** are endowed by their Creator." And in my view that right is also among the "othe[r] [rights] retained by the people" which the Ninth Amendment says the Constitution's enumeration of rights "shall not be construed to deny or disparage." The Declaration of Independence, however, is not a legal prescription conferring powers upon the courts; and the Constitution's refusal to "deny or disparage" other rights is far removed from affirming any one of them, and even farther removed from authorizing judges to identify what they might be, and to enforce the judges' list against laws duly enacted by the people. Consequently, while I would think it entirely compatible with the commitment to representative democracy set forth in the founding documents to argue, in legislative chambers or in electoral campaigns, that the state has no power to interfere with parents' authority over the rearing of their children, I do not believe that the power which the Constitution confers upon me as a judge entitles me to deny legal effect to laws that (in my view) infringe upon what is (in my view) that unenumerated right.

Only three holdings of this Court rest in whole or in part upon a substantive constitutional right of parents to direct the upbringing of their children—two of them from an era rich in substantive due process holdings that have since been repudiated. See *Meyer v. Nebraska,* 262 U.S. 390 (1923); *Pierce v. Society of Sisters,* 268 U.S. 510 (1925); *Wisconsin v. Yoder,* 406 U.S. 205 (1972). The sheer diversity of today's opinions persuades me that the theory of unenumerated parental rights underlying these three cases has small claim to stare decisis protection. A legal principle that can be thought to produce such diverse outcomes in the relatively simple case before us here is not a legal principle that has induced substantial reliance. While I would not now overrule those earlier cases (that has not been urged), neither would I extend the theory upon which they rested to this new context.

*** If we embrace this unenumerated right, I think it obvious—whether we affirm or reverse the judgment here, or remand as JUSTICE STEVENS or JUSTICE KENNEDY would do—that we will be ushering in a new regime of judicially prescribed, and federally prescribed, family law. I have no reason to believe that federal judges will be better at this than state legislatures; and state legislatures have the great advantages of doing harm in a more circumscribed area, of being able to correct their mistakes in a flash, and of being removable by the people. ***

JUSTICE KENNEDY, dissenting.

*** Turning to the question whether harm to the child must be the controlling standard in every visitation proceeding, there is a beginning point that commands general, perhaps unanimous, agreement in our separate opinions: As our case law has developed, the custodial parent has a constitutional right to determine, without undue interference by the state, how best to raise, nurture, and educate the child. The parental right stems from the liberty protected by the Due Process Clause of the Fourteenth Amendment. *** The principle exists, then, in broad formulation; yet courts must use considerable restraint, including careful adherence to the incremental instruction given by the precise facts of particular cases, as they seek to give further and more precise definition to the right. ***

While it might be argued as an abstract matter that in some sense the child is always harmed if his or her best interests are not considered, the law of domestic relations, as it has evolved to this point, treats as distinct the two standards, one harm to the child and the other the best interests of the child. The judgment of the Supreme Court of Washington rests on that assumption, and I, too, shall assume that there are real and consequential differences between the two standards.

On the question whether one standard must always take precedence over the other in order to protect the right of the parent or parents, "[o]ur Nation's history, legal traditions, and practices" do not give us clear or definitive answers. *** As a general matter, however, contemporary state-court decisions acknowledge that "[h]istorically, grandparents had no legal right of visitation," *Campbell v. Campbell*, 896 P.2d 635, 642, n. 15 (Utah App.1995), and it is safe to assume other third parties would have fared no better in court. ***

My principal concern is that the holding seems to proceed from the assumption that the parent or parents who resist visitation have always been the child's primary caregivers and that the third parties who seek visitation have no legitimate and established relationship with the child. That idea, in turn, appears influenced by the concept that the conventional nuclear family ought to establish the visitation standard for every domestic relations case. As we all know, this is simply not the structure or prevailing condition in many households. See, *e.g., Moore v. East Cleveland*, 431 U.S. 494 (1977). For many boys and girls a traditional family with two or even one permanent and caring parent is simply not the reality of their childhood. This may be so whether their childhood has been marked by tragedy or filled with considerable happiness and fulfillment.

Cases are sure to arise—perhaps a substantial number of cases—in which a third party, by acting in a caregiving role over a significant period of time, has developed a relationship with a child which is not necessarily subject to absolute parental veto. See *Michael H. v. Gerald D.*, 491 U.S. 110 (1989) (putative natural father not entitled to rebut state law presumption that child born in a marriage is a child of the marriage); *Quilloin v. Walcott*, 434 U.S. 246 (1978) (best interests standard sufficient in adoption proceeding to protect interests of natural father who had not legitimated the child) ***. In the design and elaboration of their visitation laws, States may be entitled to consider that certain relationships are such that to avoid the risk of harm, a best interests standard can be employed by their domestic relations courts in some circumstances.

Indeed, contemporary practice should give us some pause before rejecting the best interests of the child standard in all third-party visitation cases, as the Washington court has done. The standard has been recognized for many years as a basic tool of domestic relations law in visitation proceedings. Since 1965 all 50 States have enacted a third-party visitation statute of some sort. Each of these statutes, save one, permits a court order to issue in certain cases if visitation is found to be in the best interests of the child. While it is unnecessary for us to consider the constitutionality of any particular provision in the case now before us, it can be noted that the statutes also include a variety of methods for limiting parents' exposure to third-party visitation petitions and for ensuring parental decisions are given respect. Many States limit the identity of permissible petitioners by restricting visitation petitions to grandparents, or by requiring petitioners to show a substantial relationship with a child, or both. The statutes vary in other respects—for instance, some permit visitation petitions when there has been a change in circumstances such as divorce or death of a parent, and some apply a presumption that parental decisions should control. Georgia's is the sole State Legislature to have adopted a general harm to the child standard, and it did so only after the Georgia Supreme Court held the State's prior visitation statute invalid under the Federal and Georgia Constitutions.

In light of the inconclusive historical record and case law, as well as the almost universal adoption of the best interests standard for visitation disputes, I would be hard pressed to conclude the right to be free of such review in all cases is itself "implicit in the concept of ordered liberty." *** We must keep in mind that family courts in the 50 States confront these factual variations each day, and are best situated to consider the unpredictable, yet inevitable, issues that arise.

It must be recognized, of course, that a domestic relations proceeding in and of itself can constitute state intervention that is so disruptive of the parent-child relationship that the constitutional right of a custodial parent to make certain basic determinations for the child's welfare becomes implicated. The best interests of the child standard has at times been criticized as indeterminate, leading to unpredictable results. If a single parent who is struggling to raise a child is faced with visitation demands from a third party, the attorney's fees alone might destroy her hopes and plans for the child's future. Our system must confront more often the reality that litigation can itself be so disruptive that constitutional protection may be required; and I do not discount the possibility that in some instances the best interests of the child standard may provide insufficient protection to the parent-child relationship. We owe it to the Nation's domestic relations legal structure, however, to proceed with caution.

It should suffice in this case to reverse the holding of the State Supreme Court that the application of the best interests of the child standard is always unconstitutional in third-party visitation cases. ***

Notes

1. **Circumventing *Troxel*?** Was the Court criticizing only the Washington law, or all laws that provide for grandparent visitations? Can you suggest any way for the State to rewrite its statute so it will pass muster under the due process clause?

2. **Mothers and Fathers.** If the children's father (rather than mother) had been raising the children, would that make a difference to the Court's analysis or holding?

3. **Biology Versus Caregiving.** Would the decision be different if the children were being raised by a stepmother and her second husband? What if she had adopted the children, either before or after the death of the biological father? Would it matter if the stepmother's new relationship was not with a second husband but with a gay partner? On this last question, see the following cases and *Romer v. Evans*, infra p. 817.

d. Homosexuality

LAWRENCE v. TEXAS
123 S.Ct. 2472, 156 L.Ed.2d 508 (2003)

JUSTICE KENNEDY delivered the opinion of the Court.

Liberty protects the person from unwarranted government intrusions into a dwelling or other private places. *** Freedom extends beyond spatial bounds. Liberty presumes an autonomy of self that includes freedom of thought, belief, expression, and certain intimate conduct. The instant case involves liberty of the person both in its spatial and more transcendent dimensions.

The question before the Court is the validity of a Texas statute making it a crime for two persons of the same sex to engage in certain intimate sexual conduct. *** [O]fficers of the Harris County Police Department *** entered an apartment where one of the petitioners, John Geddes Lawrence, resided. *** The officers observed Lawrence and another man, Tyron Garner, engaging in a sexual act. The two petitioners were arrested, held in custody over night, and charged and convicted before a Justice of the Peace.

The complaints described their crime as "deviate sexual intercourse, namely anal sex, with a member of the same sex (man)." *** Tex. Penal Code Ann. § 21.06(a) (2003) *** provides: "A person commits an offense if he engages in deviate sexual intercourse with another individual of the same sex." The statute defines "[d]eviate sexual intercourse" as follows:

"(A) any contact between any part of the genitals of one person and the mouth or anus of another person; or
"(B) the penetration of the genitals or the anus of another person with an object." § 21.01(1).

The petitioners *** challenged the statute as a violation of the Equal Protection Clause of the Fourteenth Amendment and of a like provision of the Texas Constitution. *** The petitioners were adults at the time of the alleged offense. Their conduct was in private and consensual.

We conclude the case should be resolved by determining whether the petitioners were free as adults to engage in the private conduct in the exercise of their liberty under the Due Process Clause of the Fourteenth Amendment to the Constitution. For this inquiry we deem it necessary to reconsider the Court's holding in *Bowers*. *** The facts in *Bowers* had some similarities to the instant case. A police officer *** observed Hardwick, in his own bedroom, engaging in intimate sexual conduct with another adult male. The conduct was in violation of a Georgia statute making it a criminal offense to engage in sodomy. One difference between the two cases is that the Georgia statute prohibited the conduct whether or not the participants were of the same sex, while the Texas statute, as we have seen, applies only to participants of the same sex. Hardwick was not prosecuted, but he brought an action in federal court to declare the state statute invalid. He alleged he was a practicing homosexual and that the criminal prohibition violated rights guaranteed to him by the Constitution. The Court, in an opinion by JUSTICE WHITE, sustained the Georgia law. *** Four Justices dissented.

The Court began its substantive discussion in *Bowers* as follows: "The issue presented is whether the Federal Constitution confers a fundamental right upon homosexuals to engage in sodomy and hence invalidates the laws of the many States that still make such conduct illegal and have done so for a very long time." That statement, we now conclude, discloses the Court's own failure to appreciate the extent of the liberty at stake. To say that the issue in *Bowers* was simply the right to engage in certain sexual conduct demeans the claim the individual put forward, just as it would demean a married couple were it to be said marriage is simply about the right to have sexual intercourse. The laws involved in *Bowers* and here are, to be sure, statutes that purport to do no more than prohibit a particular sexual act. Their penalties and purposes, though, have more far-reaching consequences, touching upon the most private human conduct, sexual behavior, and in the most private of places, the home. The statutes do seek to control a personal relationship that, whether or not entitled to formal recognition in the law, is within the liberty of persons to choose without being punished as criminals. *** When sexuality finds overt expression in intimate conduct with another person, the conduct can be but one element in a personal bond that is more enduring. The liberty protected by the Constitution allows homosexual persons the right to make this choice.

Having misapprehended the claim of liberty there presented to it, and thus stating the claim to be whether there is a fundamental right to engage in consensual sodomy, the *Bowers* Court said: "Proscriptions against that conduct have ancient roots.' *** [T]he following considerations counsel against adopting the definitive conclusions upon which *Bowers* placed such reliance.

*** [T]here is no longstanding history in this country of laws directed at homosexual conduct as a distinct matter. Beginning in colonial times there were prohibitions of sodomy derived from the English criminal laws passed in the first instance by the Reformation Parliament of 1533. The English prohibition was understood to include relations between men and women as well as relations between men and men. *** The absence of legal prohibitions focusing on homosexual conduct may be explained in part by noting that according to some scholars the concept of the homosexual as a distinct category of person did not emerge until the late 19th century. Thus early American sodomy laws were not directed at homosexuals as such but instead sought to prohibit nonprocreative sexual activity more generally. *** Instead of targeting relations between consenting adults in private, 19th-century sodomy prosecutions typically involved relations between men and minor girls or minor boys, relations between adults involving force, relations between adults implicating disparity in status, or relations between men and animals. *** But far from possessing "ancient roots," *Bowers*, American laws targeting same-sex couples did not develop until the last third of the 20th century. The reported decisions concerning the prosecution of consensual, homosexual sodomy between adults for the years 1880-1995 are not always clear in the details, but a significant number involved conduct in a public place.

It was not until the 1970's that any State singled out same-sex relations for criminal prosecution, and only nine States have done so. Post-*Bowers* even some of these States did not adhere to the policy of suppressing homosexual conduct. Over the course of the last decades, States with same-sex prohibitions have moved toward abolishing them.

In summary, the historical grounds relied upon in *Bowers* *** are not without doubt and, at the very least, are overstated.

It must be acknowledged, of course, that the Court in *Bowers* was making the broader point that for centuries there have been powerful voices to condemn homosexual conduct as immoral. *** CHIEF JUSTICE BURGER joined the opinion for the Court in *Bowers* and further explained his views as follows: "Decisions of individuals relating to homosexual conduct have been subject to state intervention throughout the history of Western civilization. Condemnation of those practices is firmly rooted in Judeao-Christian moral and ethical standards." As with JUSTICE WHITE's assumptions about history, scholarship casts some doubt on the sweeping nature of the statement by CHIEF JUSTICE BURGER as it pertains to private homosexual conduct between consenting adults. In all events we think that our laws and traditions in the past half century are of most relevance here. These references show an emerging awareness that liberty gives substantial protection to adult persons in deciding how to conduct their private lives in matters pertaining to sex. "[H]istory and tradition are the starting point but not in all cases the ending point of the substantive due process inquiry." *County of Sacramento v. Lewis*, 523 U. S. 833, 857 (1998) (KENNEDY, J., concurring).

This emerging recognition should have been apparent when *Bowers* was decided. In 1955 the American Law Institute promulgated the Model Penal Code and made clear that it did not recommend or provide for "criminal penalties for consensual sexual relations conducted in private." *** In 1961 Illinois changed its laws to conform to the Model Penal Code. Other States soon followed.

In *Bowers* the Court referred to the fact that before 1961 all 50 States had outlawed sodomy, and that at the time of the Court's decision 24 States and the District of Columbia had sodomy laws. JUSTICE POWELL pointed out that these prohibitions often were being ignored, however. *** The sweeping references by CHIEF JUSTICE BURGER to the history of Western civilization and to Judeo-Christian moral and ethical standards did not take account of other authorities pointing in an opposite direction. A committee advising the British Parliament recommended in 1957 repeal of laws punishing homosexual conduct. Parliament enacted the substance of those recommendations 10 years later. *** [A]lmost five years before *Bowers* was decided the European Court of Human Rights *** held that the laws proscribing the conduct were invalid under the European Convention on Human Rights. *Dudgeon v. United Kingdom*, 45 Eur. Ct. H. R. (1981). Authoritative in all countries that are members of the Council of Europe (21 nations then, 45 nations now), the decision is at odds with the premise in *Bowers* that the claim put forward was insubstantial in our Western civilization.

In our own constitutional system the deficiencies in *Bowers* became even more apparent in the years following its announcement. The 25 States with laws prohibiting the relevant conduct referenced in the *Bowers* decision are reduced now to 13, of which 4 enforce their laws only against homosexual conduct. In those States where sodomy is still proscribed, whether for same-sex or heterosexual conduct, there is a pattern of nonenforcement with respect to consenting adults acting in private. *** Two principal cases decided after *Bowers* cast its holding into even more doubt. In *Planned Parenthood of Southeastern Pa. v. Casey*, 505 U. S. 833 (1002), the Court reaffirmed the substantive force of the liberty protected by the Due Process Clause. *** The decision in *Bowers* would deny them this right.

The second post-*Bowers* case of principal relevance is *Romer v. Evans*, 517 U. S. 620 (1996). There the Court struck down class-based legislation directed at homosexuals as a violation of the Equal Protection Clause. *Romer* invalidated an amendment to Colorado's constitution which named as a solitary class persons who were homosexuals, lesbians, or bisexual either by "orientation, conduct, practices or relationships," and deprived them of protection under state antidiscrimination laws. *** Were we to hold the statute invalid under the Equal Protection Clause some might question whether a prohibition would be valid if drawn differently, say, to prohibit the conduct both between same-sex and different-sex participants.

Equality of treatment and the due process right to demand respect for conduct protected by the substantive guarantee of liberty are linked in important respects, and a decision on the latter point advances both interests. If protected conduct is made criminal and the law which does so remains unexamined for its substantive validity, its stigma might remain even if it were not enforceable as drawn for equal protection reasons. When homosexual conduct is made criminal by the law of the State, that declaration in and of itself is an invitation to subject homosexual persons to discrimination both in the public and in the private spheres. The central holding of *Bowers* has been brought in question by this case, and it should be addressed. Its continuance as precedent demeans the lives of homosexual persons.

The stigma this criminal statute imposes, moreover, is not trivial. *** The petitioners will bear on their record the history of their criminal convictions. *** We are advised that if Texas convicted an adult for private, consensual homosexual conduct under the statute here in question the convicted person would come within the [sex offender] registration laws of a least four States were he or she to be subject to their jurisdiction. *** Furthermore, the Texas criminal conviction carries with it the other collateral consequences always following a conviction, such as notations on job application forms, to mention but one example.

The foundations of *Bowers* have sustained serious erosion from our recent decisions in *Casey* and *Romer*. When our precedent has been thus weakened, criticism from other sources is of greater significance. In the United States criticism of *Bowers* has been substantial and continuing, disapproving of its reasoning in all respects, not just as to its historical assumptions. The courts of five different States have declined to follow it in interpreting provisions in their own state constitutions parallel to the Due Process Clause of the Fourteenth Amendment, see *Jegley v. Picado*, 349 Ark. 600, 80 S. W. 3d 332 (2002); *Powell v. State*, 270 Ga. 327, 510 S. E. 2d 18, 24 (1998); *Gryczan v. State*, 283 Mont. 433, 942 P. 2d 112 (1997); *Campbell v. Sundquist*, 926 S. W. 2d 250 (Tenn. App. 1996); *Commonwealth v. Wasson*, 842 S. W. 2d 487 (Ky. 1992).

To the extent *Bowers* relied on values we share with a wider civilization, it should be noted that the reasoning and holding in *Bowers* have been rejected elsewhere. The European Court of Human Rights has followed not *Bowers* but its own decision in *Dudgeon v. United Kingdom*. Other nations, too, have taken action consistent with an affirmation of the protected right of homosexual adults to engage in intimate, consensual conduct. ***

The doctrine of *stare decisis* is essential to the respect accorded to the judgments of the Court and to the stability of the law. It is not, however, an inexorable command. In *Casey* we noted that when a Court is asked to overrule a precedent recognizing a constitutional liberty interest, individual or societal reliance on the existence of that liberty cautions with particular strength against reversing course. The holding in *Bowers*, however, has not induced detrimental reliance comparable to some instances where recognized individual rights are involved. Indeed, there has been no individual or societal reliance on *Bowers* of the sort that could counsel against overturning its holding once there are compelling reasons to do so. *Bowers* itself causes uncertainty, for the precedents before and after its issuance contradict its central holding.

The rationale of *Bowers* does not withstand careful analysis. In his dissenting opinion in *Bowers* JUSTICE STEVENS came to these conclusions:

> "Our prior cases make two propositions abundantly clear. First, the fact that the governing majority in a State has traditionally viewed a particular practice as immoral is not a sufficient reason for upholding a law prohibiting the practice; neither history nor tradition could save a law prohibiting miscegenation from constitutional attack. Second, individual decisions by married persons, concerning the intimacies of their physical relationship, even when not intended to produce offspring, are a form of 'liberty' protected by the Due Process Clause of the Fourteenth Amendment. Moreover, this protection extends to intimate choices by unmarried as well as married persons."

JUSTICE STEVENS' analysis, in our view, should have been controlling in *Bowers* and should control here.

Bowers was not correct when it was decided, and it is not correct today. It ought not to remain binding precedent. *Bowers v. Hardwick* should be and now is overruled.

The present case does not involve minors. It does not involve persons who might be injured or coerced or who are situated in relationships where consent might not easily be refused. It does not involve public conduct or prostitution. It does not involve whether the government must give formal recognition to any relationship that homosexual persons seek to enter. The case does involve two adults who, with full and mutual consent from each other, engaged in sexual practices common to a homosexual lifestyle. The petitioners are entitled to respect for their private lives. The State cannot demean their existence or control their destiny by making their private sexual conduct a crime. Their right to liberty under the Due Process Clause gives them the full right to engage in their conduct without intervention of the government. "It is a promise of the Constitution that there is a realm of personal liberty which the government may not enter." The Texas statute furthers no legitimate state interest which can justify its intrusion into the personal and private life of the individual. ***

JUSTICE O'CONNOR, concurring in the judgment.

The Court today overrules *Bowers v. Hardwick*, 478 U. S. 186 (1986). ***

Rather than relying on the substantive component of the Fourteenth Amendment's Due Process Clause, as the Court does, I base my conclusion on the Fourteenth Amendment's Equal Protection Clause. *** When a law exhibits *** a desire to harm a politically unpopular group, we have applied a more searching form of rational basis review to strike down such laws under the Equal Protection Clause.

We have been most likely to apply rational basis review to hold a law unconstitutional under the Equal Protection Clause where, as here, the challenged legislation inhibits personal relationships. In *Department of Agriculture v. Moreno*, for example, we held that a law preventing those households containing an individual unrelated to any other member of the household from receiving food stamps violated equal protection because the purpose of the law was to "'discriminate against hippies.'" The asserted governmental interest in preventing food stamp fraud was not deemed sufficient to satisfy rational basis review. In *Eisenstadt v. Baird*, 405 U. S. 438, 447-455 (1972), we refused to sanction a law that discriminated between married and unmarried persons by prohibiting the distribution of contraceptives to single persons. Likewise, in *Cleburne v. Cleburne Living Center, supra,* we held that it was irrational for a State to require a home for the mentally disabled to obtain a special use permit when other residences– like fraternity houses and apartment buildings–did not have to obtain such a permit. And in *Romer v. Evans,* we disallowed a state statute that "impos[ed] a broad and undifferentiated disability on a single named group"– specifically, homosexuals. The dissent apparently agrees that if these cases have *stare decisis* effect, Texas' sodomy law would not pass scrutiny under the Equal Protection Clause, regardless of the type of rational basis review that we apply.

The statute at issue here makes sodomy a crime only if a person "engages in deviate sexual intercourse with another individual of the same sex." Tex. Penal Code Ann. § 21.06(a) (2003). Sodomy between opposite-sex partners, however, is not a crime in Texas. That is, Texas treats the same conduct differently based solely on the participants. Those harmed by this law are people who have a same-sex sexual orientation and thus are more likely to engage in behavior prohibited by § 21.06.

The Texas statute makes homosexuals unequal in the eyes of the law by making particular conduct–and only that conduct–subject to criminal sanction. It appears that prosecutions under Texas' sodomy law are rare. *** Texas' sodomy law brands all homosexuals as criminals, thereby making it more difficult for homosexuals to be treated in the same manner as everyone else. Indeed, Texas itself has previously acknowledged the collateral effects of the law, stipulating in a prior challenge to this action that the law "legally sanctions discrimination against [homosexuals] in a variety of ways unrelated to the criminal law," including in the areas of "employment, family issues, and housing."

Texas attempts to justify its law, and the effects of the law, by arguing that the statute satisfies rational basis review because it furthers the legitimate governmental interest of the promotion of morality. *** *Bowers* did not hold that moral disapproval of a group is a rational basis under the Equal Protection Clause to criminalize homosexual sodomy when heterosexual sodomy is not punished.

This case raises a different issue than *Bowers:* whether, under the Equal Protection Clause, moral disapproval is a legitimate state interest to justify by itself a statute that bans homosexual sodomy, but not heterosexual sodomy. It is not. Moral disapproval of this group, like a bare desire to harm the group, is an interest that is insufficient to satisfy rational basis review under the Equal Protection Clause. *** Texas argues, however, that the sodomy law does not discriminate against homosexual persons. Instead, the State maintains that the law discriminates only against homosexual conduct. While it is true that the law applies only to conduct, the conduct targeted by this law is conduct that is closely correlated with being homosexual. Under such circumstances, Texas' sodomy law is targeted at more than conduct. It is instead directed toward gay persons as a class. "After all, there can hardly be more palpable discrimination against a class than making the conduct that defines the class criminal." When a State makes homosexual conduct criminal, and not "deviate sexual intercourse" committed by persons of different sexes, "that declaration in and of itself is an invitation to subject homosexual persons to discrimination both in the public and in the private spheres."

Indeed, Texas law confirms that the sodomy statute is directed toward homosexuals as a class. In Texas, calling a person a homosexual is slander *per se* because the word "homosexual" "impute[s] the commission of a crime." The State has admitted that because of the sodomy law, *being* homosexual carries the presumption of being a criminal. *** A State can of course assign certain consequences to a violation of its criminal law. But the State cannot single out one identifiable class of citizens for punishment that does not apply to everyone else, with moral disapproval as the only asserted state interest for the law. The Texas sodomy statute subjects homosexuals to "a lifelong penalty and stigma. ***

Whether a sodomy law that is neutral both in effect and application, would violate the substantive component of the Due Process Clause is an issue that need not be decided today. *** That this law as applied to private, consensual conduct is unconstitutional under the Equal Protection Clause does not mean that other laws distinguishing between heterosexuals and homosexuals would similarly fail under rational basis review. Texas cannot assert any legitimate state interest here, such as national security or preserving the traditional institution of marriage. Unlike the moral disapproval of same-sex relations—the asserted state interest in this case—other reasons exist to promote the institution of marriage beyond mere moral disapproval of an excluded group. *** I therefore concur in the Court's judgment that Texas' sodomy law banning "deviate sexual intercourse" between consenting adults of the same sex, but not between consenting adults of different sexes, is unconstitutional.

JUSTICE SCALIA, with whom THE CHIEF JUSTICE and JUSTICE THOMAS join, dissenting.

*** Though there is discussion of "fundamental proposition[s]," and "fundamental decisions," nowhere does the Court's opinion declare that homosexual sodomy is a "fundamental right" under the Due Process Clause; nor does it subject the Texas law to the standard of review that would be appropriate (strict scrutiny) if homosexual sodomy *were* a "fundamental right." Thus, while overruling the *outcome* of *Bowers*, the Court leaves strangely untouched its central legal conclusion: "[R]espondent would have us announce *** a fundamental right to engage in homosexual sodomy. This we are quite unwilling to do." Instead the Court simply describes petitioners' conduct as "an exercise of their liberty"–which it undoubtedly is–and proceeds to apply an unheard-of form of rational-basis review that will have far-reaching implications beyond this case.

I begin with the Court's surprising readiness to reconsider a decision rendered a mere 17 years ago in *Bowers v. Hardwick*. I do not myself believe in rigid adherence to *stare decisis* in constitutional cases; but I do believe that we should be consistent rather than manipulative in invoking the doctrine. *** Today's approach to *stare decisis* invites us to overrule an erroneously decided precedent (including an "intensely divisive" decision) *if:* (1) its foundations have been "eroded" by subsequent decisions; (2) it has been subject to "substantial and continuing" criticism; and (3) it has not induced "individual or societal reliance" that counsels against overturning. The problem is that *Roe* itself–which today's majority surely has no disposition to overrule–satisfies these conditions to at least the same degree as *Bowers*.

*** I do not quarrel with the Court's claim that *Romer v. Evans*, 517 U. S. 620 (1996), "eroded" the "foundations" of *Bowers*' rational-basis holding. But *Roe* and *Casey* have been equally "eroded" by *Washington v. Glucksberg*, 521 U. S. 702, 721 (1997), which held that *only* fundamental rights which are "'deeply rooted in this Nation's history and tradition'" qualify for anything other than rational basis scrutiny under the doctrine of "substantive due process." *Roe* and *Casey*, of course, subjected the restriction of abortion to heightened scrutiny without even attempting to establish that the freedom to abort *was* rooted in this Nation's tradition.

*** "[T]here has been," the Court says, "no individual or societal reliance on *Bowers* of the sort that could counsel against overturning its holding ***." It seems to me that the "societal reliance" on the principles confirmed in *Bowers* and discarded today has been overwhelming. Countless judicial decisions and legislative enactments have relied on the ancient proposition that a governing majority's belief that certain sexual behavior is "immoral and unacceptable" constitutes a rational basis for regulation. We ourselves relied extensively on *Bowers* when we concluded, in *Barnes v. Glen Theatre, Inc.*, 501 U. S. 560, 569 (1991), that Indiana's public indecency statute furthered "a substantial government interest in protecting order and morality." State laws against bigamy, same-sex marriage, adult incest, prostitution, masturbation, adultery, fornication, bestiality, and obscenity are likewise sustainable only in light of *Bowers*' validation of laws based on moral choices. Every single one of these laws is called into question by today's decision; the Court makes no effort to cabin the scope of its decision to exclude them from its holding. The impossibility of distinguishing homosexuality from other traditional "morals" offenses is precisely why *Bowers* rejected the rational-basis challenge. "The law," it said, "is constantly based on notions of morality, and if all laws representing essentially moral choices are to be invalidated under the Due Process Clause, the courts will be very busy indeed." [2]

What a massive disruption of the current social order, therefore, the overruling of *Bowers* entails. Not so the overruling of *Roe*, which would simply have restored the regime that existed for centuries before 1973, in which the permissibility of and restrictions upon abortion were determined legislatively State-by-State. *** [T]he Court has chosen today to revise the standards of *stare decisis* set forth in *Casey*. It has thereby exposed *Casey*'s extraordinary deference to precedent for the result-oriented expedient that it is.

Having decided that it need not adhere to *stare decisis*, the Court still must establish that *Bowers* was wrongly decided and that the Texas statute, as applied to petitioners, is unconstitutional.

Texas Penal Code Ann. § 21.06(a) (2003) undoubtedly imposes constraints on liberty. So do laws prohibiting prostitution, recreational use of heroin, and, for that matter, working more than 60 hours per week in a bakery. But there is no right to "liberty" under the Due Process Clause, though today's opinion repeatedly makes that claim *** Our opinions applying the doctrine known as "substantive due process" hold that the Due Process Clause prohibits States from infringing *fundamental* liberty interests, unless the infringement is narrowly tailored to serve a compelling state interest. *Washington v. Glucksberg*, 521 U. S., at 721. We have held repeatedly, in cases the Court today does not overrule, that *only* fundamental rights qualify for this so-called "heightened scrutiny" protection—that is, rights which are

---

[2] While the Court does not overrule *Bowers'* holding that homosexual sodomy is not a "fundamental right," it is worth noting that the "societal reliance" upon that aspect of the decision has been substantial as well. See 10 U. S. C. § 654(b)(1) ("A member of the armed forces shall be separated from the armed forces *** if *** the member has engaged in *** a homosexual act or acts"); *Marcum v. McWhorter*, 308 F. 3d 635, 640-642 (C.A.6 2002) (relying on *Bowers* in rejecting a claimed fundamental right to commit adultery); *Mullins v. Oregon*, 57 F. 3d 789, 793-794 (C.A.9 1995) (relying on *Bowers* in rejecting a grandparent's claimed "fundamental liberty interes[t]" in the adoption of her grandchildren); *Doe v. Wigginton*, 21 F. 3d 733, 739-740 (C.A.6 1994) (relying on *Bowers* in rejecting a prisoner's claimed "fundamental right" to on-demand HIV testing); *Schowengerdt v. United States*, 944 F. 2d 483, 490 (C.A.9 1991) (relying on *Bowers* in upholding a bisexual's discharge from the armed services); *Charles v. Baesler*, 910 F. 2d 1349, 1353 (C.A.6 1990) (relying on *Bowers* in rejecting fire department captain's claimed "fundamental" interest in a promotion); *Henne v. Wright*, 904 F. 2d 1208, 1214-1215 (C.A.8 1990) (relying on *Bowers* in rejecting a claim that state law restricting surnames that could be given to children at birth implicates a "fundamental right"); *Walls v. Petersburg*, 895 F. 2d 188, 193 (C.A.4 1990) (relying on *Bowers* in rejecting substantive-due-process challenge to a police department questionnaire that asked prospective employees about homosexual activity); *High Tech Gays v. Defense Industrial Security Clearance Office*, 895 F. 2d 563, 570-571 (C.A.9 1988) (relying on *Bowers'* holding that homosexual activity is not a fundamental right in rejecting—on the basis of the rational-basis standard—an equal-protection challenge to the Defense Department's policy of conducting expanded investigations into backgrounds of gay and lesbian applicants for secret and top-secret security clearance).

"'deeply rooted in this Nation's history and tradition.'" *** All other liberty interests may be abridged or abrogated pursuant to a validly enacted state law if that law is rationally related to a legitimate state interest.

Bowers held, first, that criminal prohibitions of homosexual sodomy are not subject to heightened scrutiny because they do not implicate a "fundamental right" under the Due Process Clause. Noting that "[p]roscriptions against that conduct have ancient roots," that "[s]odomy was a criminal offense at common law and was forbidden by the laws of the original 13 States when they ratified the Bill of Rights," *ibid.*, and that many States had retained their bans on sodomy, *Bowers* concluded that a right to engage in homosexual sodomy was not "'deeply rooted in this Nation's history and tradition.'"

The Court today does not overrule this holding. Not once does it describe homosexual sodomy as a "fundamental right" or a "fundamental liberty interest," nor does it subject the Texas statute to strict scrutiny. Instead, having failed to establish that the right to homosexual sodomy is "'deeply rooted in this Nation's history and tradition,'" the Court concludes that the application of Texas's statute to petitioners' conduct fails the rational-basis test, and overrules *Bowers'* holding to the contrary. "The Texas statute furthers no legitimate state interest which can justify its intrusion into the personal and private life of the individual." ***

The Court's description of "the state of the law" at the time of *Bowers* only confirms that *Bowers* was right. The Court points to *Griswold v. Connecticut*, 381 U. S. 479, 481-482 (1965). But that case *expressly disclaimed* any reliance on the doctrine of "substantive due process," and grounded the so-called "right to privacy" in penumbras of constitutional provisions *other than* the Due Process Clause. *Eisenstadt v. Baird*, 405 U. S. 438 (1972), likewise had nothing to do with "substantive due process"; it invalidated a Massachusetts law prohibiting the distribution of contraceptives to unmarried persons solely on the basis of the Equal Protection Clause. Of course *Eisenstadt* contains well known dictum relating to the "right to privacy," but this referred to the right recognized in *Griswold*– a right penumbral to the *specific* guarantees in the Bill of Rights, and not a "substantive due process" right.

Roe v. Wade recognized that the right to abort an unborn child was a "fundamental right" protected by the Due Process Clause. The *Roe* Court, however, made no attempt to establish that this right was "'deeply rooted in this Nation's history and tradition'" ***. We have since rejected *Roe's* holding that regulations of abortion must be narrowly tailored to serve a compelling state interest–and thus, by logical implication, *Roe's* holding that the right to abort an unborn child is a "fundamental right."

*** [O]ur Nation has a longstanding history of laws prohibiting *sodomy in general*–regardless of whether it was performed by same-sex or opposite-sex couples ***. It is (as *Bowers* recognized) entirely irrelevant whether the laws in our long national tradition criminalizing homosexual sodomy were "directed at homosexual conduct as a distinct matter." *** The Court today agrees that homosexual sodomy was criminalized and thus does not dispute the facts on which *Bowers actually* relied.

Next the Court makes the claim, again unsupported by any citations, that "[l]aws prohibiting sodomy do not seem to have been enforced against consenting adults acting in private." *** If all the Court means by "acting in private" is "on private premises, with the doors closed and windows covered," it is entirely unsurprising that evidence of enforcement would be hard to come by. Surely that lack of evidence would not sustain the proposition that consensual sodomy on private premises with the doors closed and windows covered was regarded as a "fundamental right," even though all other consensual sodomy was criminalized. There are 203 prosecutions for consensual, adult homosexual sodomy reported in the West Reporting system and official state reporters from the years 1880-1995. There are also records of 20 sodomy prosecutions and 4 executions during the colonial period. *Bowers'* conclusion that homosexual sodomy is not a fundamental right "deeply rooted in this Nation's history and tradition" is utterly unassailable.

Realizing that fact, the Court instead says: "[W]e think that our laws and traditions in the past half century are of most relevance here. These references show *an emerging awareness* that liberty gives substantial protection to adult persons in deciding how to conduct their private lives *in matters pertaining to sex.*" Apart from the fact that such an "emerging awareness" does not establish a "fundamental right," the statement is factually false. States continue to prosecute all sorts of crimes by adults "in matters pertaining to sex": prostitution, adult incest, adultery, obscenity, and child pornography. Sodomy laws, too, have been enforced "in the past half century," in which there have been 134 reported cases involving prosecutions for consensual, adult, homosexual sodomy. In relying, for evidence of an "emerging recognition," upon the American Law Institute's 1955 recommendation not to criminalize "'consensual sexual relations conducted in private,'" the Court ignores the fact that this recommendation was "a point of resistance in most of the states that considered adopting the Model Penal Code."

In any event, an "emerging awareness" is by definition not "deeply rooted in this Nation's history and tradition[s]," as we have said "fundamental right" status requires. Constitutional entitlements do not spring into existence because some States choose to lessen or eliminate criminal sanctions on certain behavior. Much less do they spring into existence, as the Court seems to believe, because *foreign nations* decriminalize conduct. *** The Court's discussion of these foreign views (ignoring, of course, the many countries that have retained criminal prohibitions on sodomy) is therefore meaningless dicta. Dangerous dicta, however, since "this Court *** should not impose foreign moods, fads, or fashions on Americans."

I turn now to the ground on which the Court squarely rests its holding: the contention that there is no rational basis for the law here under attack *** The Texas statute undeniably seeks to further the belief of its citizens that certain forms of sexual behavior are "immoral and unacceptable"–the same interest furthered by criminal laws against fornication, bigamy, adultery, adult incest, bestiality, and obscenity. *Bowers* held that this *was* a legitimate state interest. The Court today reaches the opposite conclusion. The Texas statute, it says, "furthers *no legitimate state interest* which can justify its intrusion into the personal and private life of the individual." The Court embraces instead JUSTICE STEVENS' declaration in his *Bowers* dissent, that "the fact that the governing majority in a State has traditionally viewed a particular practice as immoral is not a sufficient reason for upholding a law prohibiting the practice." This effectively decrees the end of all morals legislation. If, as the Court asserts, the promotion of majoritarian sexual morality is not even a *legitimate* state interest, none of the above-mentioned laws can survive rational-basis review.

Finally, I turn to petitioners' equal-protection challenge, which no Member of the Court save JUSTICE O'CONNOR, embraces: On its face § 21.06(a) applies equally to all persons. Men and women, heterosexuals and homosexuals, are all subject to its prohibition of deviate sexual intercourse with someone of the same sex. To be sure, § 21.06 does distinguish between the sexes insofar as concerns the partner with whom the sexual acts are performed: men can violate the law only with other men, and women only with other women. But this cannot itself be a denial of equal protection, since it is precisely the same distinction regarding partner that is drawn in state laws prohibiting marriage with someone of the same sex while permitting marriage with someone of the opposite sex.

The objection is made, however, that the antimiscegenation laws invalidated in *Loving v. Virginia*, 388 U. S. 1, 8 (1967), similarly were applicable to whites and blacks alike, and only distinguished between the races insofar as the *partner* was concerned. In *Loving*, however, we correctly applied heightened scrutiny, rather than the usual rational-basis review, because the Virginia statute was "designed to maintain White Supremacy." A racially discriminatory purpose is always sufficient to subject a law to strict scrutiny, even a facially neutral law that makes no mention of race. See *Washington v. Davis*, 426 U. S. 229, 241-242 (1976). No purpose to discriminate against men or women as a class can be gleaned from the Texas law, so rational- basis review applies. That review is readily satisfied here by the same rational basis that satisfied it in *Bowers*–society's belief that certain forms of sexual behavior are "immoral and unacceptable." This is the same justification that supports many other laws regulating sexual behavior that make a distinction based upon the identity of the partner–for example, laws against adultery, fornication, and adult incest, and laws refusing to recognize homosexual marriage.

JUSTICE O'CONNOR argues that the discrimination in this law which must be justified is not its discrimination with regard to the sex of the partner but its discrimination with regard to the sexual proclivity of the principal actor.

*** Of course the same could be said of any law. A law against public nudity targets "the conduct that is closely correlated with being a nudist," and hence "is targeted at more than conduct"; it is "directed toward nudists as a class." But be that as it may. Even if the Texas law *does* deny equal protection to "homosexuals as a class," that denial *still* does not need to be justified by anything more than a rational basis, which our cases show is satisfied by the enforcement of traditional notions of sexual morality.

JUSTICE O'CONNOR simply decrees application of "a more searching form of rational basis review" to the Texas statute. The cases she cites do not recognize such a standard, and reach their conclusions only after finding, as required by conventional rational-basis analysis, that no conceivable legitimate state interest supports the classification at issue. *** Nor does JUSTICE O'CONNOR explain precisely what her "more searching form" of rational-basis review consists of. It must at least mean, however, that laws exhibiting "'a *** desire to harm a politically unpopular group,'" are invalid *even though* there may be a conceivable rational basis to support them.

This reasoning leaves on pretty shaky grounds state laws limiting marriage to opposite-sex couples. JUSTICE O'CONNOR seeks to preserve them by the conclusory statement that "preserving the traditional institution of marriage" is a legitimate state interest. But "preserving the traditional institution of marriage" is just a kinder way of describing the State's *moral disapproval* of same-sex couples. Texas's interest in § 21.06 could be recast in similarly euphemistic terms: "preserving the traditional sexual mores of our society." In the jurisprudence JUSTICE O'CONNOR has seemingly created, judges can validate laws by characterizing them as "preserving the traditions of society" (good); or invalidate them by characterizing them as "expressing moral disapproval" (bad).

***

Today's opinion is the product of a Court, which is the product of a law-profession culture, that has largely signed on to the so-called homosexual agenda, by which I mean the agenda promoted by some homosexual activists directed at eliminating the moral opprobrium that has traditionally attached to homosexual conduct. *** One of the most revealing statements in today's opinion is the Court's grim warning that the criminalization of homosexual conduct is "an invitation to subject homosexual persons to discrimination both in the public and in the private spheres." It is clear from this that the Court has taken sides in the culture war, departing from its role of assuring, as neutral observer, that the democratic rules of engagement are observed. Many Americans do not want persons who openly engage in homosexual conduct as partners in their business, as scoutmasters for their children, as teachers in their children's schools, or as boarders in their home. They view this as protecting themselves and their families from a lifestyle that they believe to be immoral and destructive. The Court views it as "discrimination" which it is the function of our judgments to deter. So imbued is the Court with the law profession's anti-anti-homosexual culture, that it is seemingly unaware that the attitudes of that culture are not obviously "mainstream"; that in most States what the Court calls "discrimination" against those who engage in homosexual acts is perfectly legal; that proposals to ban such "discrimination" under Title VII have repeatedly been rejected by Congress; that in some cases such "discrimination" is *mandated* by federal statute, see 10 U. S. C. § 654(b)(1) (mandating discharge from the armed forces of any service member who engages in or intends to engage in homosexual acts); and that in some cases such "discrimination" is a constitutional right, see *Boy Scouts of America v. Dale*, 530 U. S. 640 (2000).

Let me be clear that I have nothing against homosexuals, or any other group, promoting their agenda through normal democratic means. Social perceptions of sexual and other morality change over time, and every group has the right to persuade its fellow citizens that its view of such matters is the best. That homosexuals have achieved some success in that enterprise is attested to by the fact that Texas is one of the few remaining States that criminalize private, consensual homosexual acts. But persuading one's fellow citizens is one thing, and imposing one's views in absence of democratic majority will is something else. I would no more *require* a State to criminalize homosexual acts–or, for that matter, display *any* moral disapprobation of them–than I would *forbid* it to do so. *** But it is the premise of our system that those judgments are to be made by the people, and not imposed by a governing caste that knows best.

One of the benefits of leaving regulation of this matter to the people rather than to the courts is that the people, unlike judges, need not carry things to their logical conclusion. The people may feel that their disapprobation of homosexual conduct is strong enough to disallow homosexual marriage, but not strong enough to criminalize private homosexual acts–and may legislate accordingly. The Court today pretends that it possesses a similar freedom of action, so that that we need not fear judicial imposition of homosexual marriage, as has recently occurred in Canada (in a decision that the Canadian Government has chosen not to appeal). *** Today's opinion dismantles the structure of constitutional law that has permitted a distinction to be made between heterosexual and homosexual unions, insofar as formal recognition in marriage is concerned. If moral disapprobation of homosexual conduct is "no legitimate state interest" for purposes of proscribing that conduct; and if, as the Court coos (casting aside all pretense of neutrality), "[w]hen sexuality finds overt expression in intimate conduct with another person, the conduct can be but one element in a personal bond that is more enduring," what justification could there possibly be for denying the benefits of marriage to homosexual couples exercising "[t]he liberty protected by the Constitution"? Surely not the encouragement of procreation, since the sterile and the elderly are allowed to marry. This case "does not involve" the issue of homosexual marriage only if one entertains the belief that principle and logic have nothing to do with the decisions of this Court. Many will hope that, as the Court comfortingly assures us, this is so.

The matters appropriate for this Court's resolution are only three: Texas's prohibition of sodomy neither infringes a "fundamental right" (which the Court does not dispute), nor is unsupported by a rational relation to what the Constitution considers a legitimate state interest, nor denies the equal protection of the laws. I dissent.

JUSTICE THOMAS, dissenting.

*** I write separately to note that the law before the Court today "is ***

uncommonly silly." *Griswold v. Connecticut*, 381 U. S. 479, 527 (1965)
(STEWART, J., dissenting). If I were a member of the Texas Legislature, I
would vote to repeal it. *** Notwithstanding this, *** just like JUSTICE
STEWART, I "can find [neither in the Bill of Rights nor any other part of the
Constitution a] general right of privacy," or as the Court terms it today, the
"liberty of the person both in its spatial and more transcendent dimensions."

Notes

1.   **Overruling *Bowers*.** Do the Court's reasons justify overruling *Bowers*?

2.   **Neutral or Anti-homosexual?** Does the Texas statute discriminate against
homosexuals? Compare the Georgia statute in *Bowers*: "A person commits the
offense of sodomy when he performs or submits to any sexual act involving the
sex organs of one person and the mouth or anus of another." Was Georgia's
statute limited to homosexual sodomy? If not, how could the Court limit its
inquiry to homosexual sodomy? Would a statute making sodomy between
unmarried heterosexuals unlawful be unconstitutional?

3.   **Ramifications.** The majority and dissents have very different views of the
meaning of this case in other areas. Consider these:

   a. **Marriage.** How does this decision affect the political and legal status of
      efforts to legalize marriage by homosexual couples?

   b. **Military.** A federal statute, 10 U.S.C.A. § 654, bars homosexual   activity
      by service-members, requires separation from the service of those who
      admit being homosexual or bisexual, or who marry or   attempt   to
      marry someone "known to be of the same biological sex." Is this statute
      unconstitutional?

   c. **Adoption.** Only 11 states allow same-sex couples to adopt children. Are
      these prohibitions unconstitutional?

   d. **Employment.** Would a statute prohibiting employment of homosexuals in
      specific state jobs violate due process?

   e. **P olitics.** Does the Democratic or Republican Party benefit most from
      this decision? Why?

4.   **Practices of other Nations.** To what extent did the Court rely upon European
experience? Should it have also considered South American experience? Mid-
East experience? Asian experience? What weight should each be given?

5.   **State and Federal Constitutions.** State constitutions differ from the federal
constitution in several ways. First, each applies in one state, not fifty. Second,
they are easier to amend. For example, Alabama has amended its 1901
constitution almost 600 times. Third, state constitutions sometimes contain
slightly different words from the United States Constitution. Should these
factors affect judicial interpretations of such constitutions? Should the possibility
of broader interpretations of state constitutions affect the Supreme Court's
willingness to protect implied fundamental rights under the Fourteenth
Amendment? How can there be a fundamental right to engage in sodomy in
Georgia, but not in Florida?

e. The Right to Die

CRUZAN v. DIRECTOR, MISSOURI
DEPARTMENT OF HEALTH
497 U.S. 261, 110 S.Ct. 2841, 111 L.Ed.2d 224 (1990).

CHIEF JUSTICE REHNQUIST delivered the opinion of the Court.

*** On the night of January 11, 1983, Nancy Cruzan lost control of her car as she traveled down Elm Road in Jasper County, Missouri. The vehicle overturned, and Cruzan was discovered lying face down in a ditch without detectable respiratory or cardiac function. Paramedics were able to restore her breathing and heartbeat at the accident site, and she was transported to a hospital in an unconscious state. An attending neurosurgeon diagnosed her as having sustained probable cerebral contusions compounded by significant anoxia (lack of oxygen). The Missouri trial court in this case found that permanent brain damage generally results after 6 minutes in an anoxic state; it was estimated that Cruzan was deprived of oxygen from 12 to 14 minutes. She remained in a coma for approximately three weeks and then progressed to an unconscious state in which she was able to orally ingest some nutrition. In order to ease feeding and further the recovery, surgeons implanted a gastrostomy feeding and hydration tube in Cruzan with the consent of her then husband. Subsequent rehabilitative efforts proved unavailing. She now lies in a Missouri state hospital in what is commonly referred to as a persistent vegetative state: generally, a condition in which a person exhibits motor reflexes but evinces no indications of significant cognitive function. The State of Missouri is bearing the cost of her care.

After it had become apparent that Nancy Cruzan had virtually no chance of regaining her mental faculties, her parents asked hospital employees to terminate the artificial nutrition and hydration procedures. All agree that such a removal would cause her death. The employees refused to honor the request without court approval. ***

We granted certiorari to consider the question whether Cruzan has a right under the United States Constitution which would require the hospital to withdraw life-sustaining treatment from her under these circumstances.

At common law, even the touching of one person by another without consent and without legal justification was a battery. *** This notion of bodily integrity has been embodied in the requirement that informed consent is generally required for medical treatment. *** The logical corollary of the doctrine of informed consent is that the patient generally possesses the right not to consent, that is, to refuse treatment. Until about 15 years ago and the seminal decision in *In re Quinlan*, 355 A.2d 647, cert. denied *sub nom. Garger v. New Jersey*, 429 U.S. 922 (1976), the number of right-to-refuse-treatment decisions was relatively few. Most of the earlier cases involved patients who refused medical treatment forbidden by their religious beliefs, thus implicating First Amendment rights as well as common-law rights of self-determination. More recently, however, with the advance of medical technology capable of sustaining life well past the point where natural forces would have brought certain death in earlier times, cases involving the right to refuse life-sustaining treatment have burgeoned.

As [other] cases demonstrate, the common-law doctrine of informed consent is viewed as generally encompassing the right of a competent individual to refuse medical treatment. *** In this Court, the question is simply and starkly whether the United States Constitution prohibits Missouri from choosing the rule of decision which it did. This is the first case in which we have been squarely presented with the issue whether the United States Constitution grants what is in common parlance referred to as a "right to die." ***

The Fourteenth Amendment provides that no State shall "deprive any person of life, liberty, or property, without due process of law." The principle that a competent person has a constitutionally protected liberty interest in refusing unwanted medical treatment may be inferred from our prior decisions. In *Jacobson v. Massachusetts*, 197 U.S. 11, 24–30 (1905), for instance, the Court balanced an individual's liberty interest in declining an unwanted smallpox vaccine against the State's interest in preventing disease. *** Just this Term, in the course of holding that a State's procedures for administering antipsychotic medication to prisoners were sufficient to satisfy due process concerns, we recognized that prisoners possess "a significant liberty interest in avoiding the unwanted administration of antipsychotic drugs under the Due Process Clause of the Fourteenth Amendment." *Washington v. Harper*, 494 U.S. 210, 221–222 (1990). ***

But determining that a person has a "liberty interest" under the Due Process Clause does not end the inquiry; "whether respondent's constitutional rights have been violated must be determined by balancing his liberty interests against the relevant state interests." Petitioners insist that under the general holdings of our cases, the forced administration of life-sustaining medical treatment, and even of artificially delivered food and water essential to life, would implicate a competent person's liberty interest. Although we think the logic of the cases discussed above would embrace such a liberty interest, the dramatic consequences involved in refusal of such treatment would inform the inquiry as to whether the deprivation of that interest is constitutionally permissible. But for purposes of this case, we assume that the United States Constitution would grant a competent person a constitutionally protected right to refuse lifesaving hydration and nutrition.

Petitioners go on to assert that an incompetent person should possess the same right in this respect as is possessed by a competent person. *** The difficulty with petitioners' claim is that in a sense it begs the question: An incompetent person is not able to make an informed and voluntary choice to exercise a hypothetical right to refuse treatment or any other right. Such a "right" must be exercised for her, if at all, by some sort of surrogate. Here, Missouri has in effect recognized that under certain circumstances a surrogate may act for the patient in electing to have hydration and nutrition withdrawn in such a way as to cause death, but it has established a procedural safeguard to assure that the action of the surrogate conforms as best it may to the wishes expressed by the patient while competent. Missouri requires that evidence of the incompetent's wishes as to the withdrawal of treatment be proved by clear and convincing evidence. The question, then, is whether the United States Constitution forbids the establishment of this procedural requirement by the State. We hold that it does not.

*** Missouri relies on its interest in the protection and preservation of human life, and there can be no gainsaying this interest. *** [The] majority of States in this country have laws imposing criminal penalties on one who assists another to commit suicide. We do not think a State is required to remain neutral in the face of an informed and voluntary decision by a physically able adult to starve to death.

But in the context presented here, a State has more particular interests at stake. The choice between life and death is a deeply personal decision of obvious and overwhelming finality. We believe Missouri may legitimately seek to safeguard the personal element of this choice through the imposition of heightened evidentiary requirements. It cannot be disputed that the Due Process Clause protects an interest in life as well as an interest in refusing life-sustaining medical treatment. Not all incompetent patients will have loved ones available to serve as surrogate decisionmakers. And even where family members are present, "[t]here will, of course, be some unfortunate situations in which family members will not act to protect a patient." *In re Jobes*, 108 N.J. 394, 419 (1987). A State is entitled to guard against potential abuses in such situations. Similarly, a State is entitled to consider that a judicial proceeding to make a determination regarding an incompetent's wishes may very well not be an adversarial one, with the added guarantee of accurate factfinding that the adversary process brings with it. Finally, we think a State may properly decline to make judgments about the "quality" of life that a particular individual may enjoy, and simply assert an unqualified interest in the preservation of human life to be weighed against the constitutionally protected interests of the individual.

In our view, Missouri has permissibly sought to advance these interests through the adoption of a "clear and convincing" standard of proof to govern such proceedings. *** We think it self-evident that the interests at stake in the instant proceedings are more substantial, both on an individual and societal level, than those involved in a run-of-the-mine civil dispute. *** [However, we] believe that Missouri may permissibly place an increased risk of an erroneous decision on those seeking to terminate an incompetent individual's life-sustaining treatment. ***

The Supreme Court of Missouri held that in this case the testimony adduced at trial did not amount to clear and convincing proof of the patient's desire to have hydration and nutrition withdrawn. *** The testimony adduced at trial consisted primarily of Nancy Cruzan's statements made to a housemate about a year before her accident that she would not want to live should she face life as a "vegetable," and other observations to the same effect. The observations did not deal in terms with withdrawal of medical treatment or of hydration and nutrition. We cannot say that the Supreme Court of Missouri committed constitutional error in reaching the conclusion that it did.

Petitioners alternatively contend that Missouri must accept the "substituted judgment" of close family members even in the absence of substantial proof that their views reflect the views of the patient. They rely primarily upon our decisions in *Michael H. v. Gerald D.*, 491 U.S. 110 (1989), and *Parham v. J.R.*, 442 U.S. 584 (1979). But we do not think these cases support their claim. In *Michael H.*, we upheld the constitutionality of California's favored treatment of traditional family relationships; such a holding may not be turned around into a constitutional requirement that a State must recognize the primacy of those relationships in a situation like this. And in *Parham*, where the patient was a minor, we also upheld the constitutionality of a state scheme in which parents made certain decisions for mentally ill minors. Here again petitioners would seek to turn a decision which allowed a State to rely on family decisionmaking into a constitutional requirement that the State recognize such decisionmaking. But constitutional law does not work that way.

No doubt is engendered by anything in this record but that Nancy Cruzan's mother and father are loving and caring parents. If the State were required by the United States Constitution to repose a right of "substituted judgment" with anyone, the Cruzans would surely qualify. But we do not think the Due Process Clause requires the State to repose judgment on these matters with anyone but the patient herself. Close family members may have a strong feeling—a feeling not at all ignoble or unworthy, but not entirely disinterested, either—that they do not wish to witness the continuation of the life of a loved one which they regard as hopeless, meaningless, and even degrading. But there is no automatic assurance that the view of close family members will necessarily be the same as the patient's would have been had she been confronted with the prospect of her situation while competent. All of the reasons previously discussed for allowing Missouri to require clear and convincing evidence of the patient's wishes lead us to conclude that the State may choose to defer only to those wishes, rather than confide the decision to close family members. ***

JUSTICE O'CONNOR, concurring.

I agree that a protected liberty interest in refusing unwanted medical treatment may be inferred from our prior decisions, and that the refusal of artificially delivered food and water is encompassed within that liberty interest. *** [T]he Court does not today decide the issue whether a State must also give effect to the decisions of a surrogate decisionmaker. In my view, such a duty may well be constitutionally required to protect the patient's liberty interest in refusing medical treatment. Few individuals provide explicit oral or written instructions regarding their intent to refuse medical treatment should they become incompetent.

JUSTICE SCALIA, concurring.

The various opinions in this case portray quite clearly the difficult, indeed agonizing, questions that are presented by the constantly increasing power of science to keep the human body alive for longer than any reasonable person would want to inhabit it. The States have begun to grapple with these problems through legislation. I am concerned, from the tenor of today's opinions, that we are poised to confuse that enterprise as successfully as we have confused the enterprise of legislating concerning abortion—requiring it to be conducted against a background of federal constitutional imperatives that are unknown because they are being newly crafted from Term to Term. That would be a great misfortune.

While I agree with the Court's analysis today, and therefore join in its opinion, I would have preferred that we announce, clearly and promptly, that the federal courts have no business in this field; that American law has always accorded the State the power to prevent, by force if necessary, suicide—including suicide by refusing to take appropriate measures necessary to preserve one's life; that the point at which life becomes "worthless," and the point at which the means necessary to preserve it become "extraordinary" or "inappropriate," are neither set forth in the Constitution nor known to the nine Justices of this Court any better than they are known to nine people picked at random from the Kansas City telephone directory; and hence, that even when it is demonstrated by clear and convincing evidence that a patient no longer wishes certain measures to be taken to preserve his or her life, it is up to the citizens of Missouri to decide, through their elected representatives, whether that wish will be honored. *** Petitioners rely on three distinctions to separate Nancy Cruzan's case from ordinary suicide: (1) that she is permanently incapacitated and in pain; (2) that she would bring on her death not by any affirmative act but by merely declining treatment that provides nourishment; and (3) that preventing her from effectuating her presumed wish to die requires violation of her bodily integrity. None of these suffices. ***

What I have said above is not meant to suggest that I would think it desirable, if we were sure that Nancy Cruzan wanted to die, to keep her alive by the means at issue here. I assert only that the Constitution has nothing to say about the subject. To raise up a constitutional right here we would have to create out of nothing (for it exists neither in text nor tradition) some constitutional principle whereby, although the State may insist that an individual come in out of the cold and eat food, it may not insist that he take medicine; and although it may pump his stomach empty of poison he has ingested, it may not fill his stomach with food he has failed to ingest. Are there, then, no reasonable and humane limits that ought not to be exceeded in requiring an individual to preserve his own life? There obviously are, but they are not set forth in the Due Process Clause. What assures us that those limits will not be exceeded is the same constitutional guarantee that is the source of most of our protection—what protects us, for example, from being assessed a tax of 100% of our income above the subsistence level, from being forbidden to drive cars, or from being required to send our children to school for 10 hours a day, none of which horribles are categorically prohibited by the Constitution. Our salvation is the Equal Protection Clause, which requires the democratic majority to accept for themselves and their loved ones what they impose on you and me. This Court need not, and has no authority to, inject itself into every field of human activity where irrationality and oppression may theoretically occur, and if it tries to do so it will destroy itself.

JUSTICE BRENNAN, with whom JUSTICE MARSHALL and JUSTICE BLACKMUN join, dissenting.

*** The right to be free from medical attention without consent, to determine what shall be done with one's own body, is deeply rooted in this Nation's traditions, as the majority acknowledges. This right has long been "firmly entrenched in American tort law" and is securely grounded in the earliest common law. *** Thus, freedom from unwanted medical attention is unquestionably among those principles "so rooted in the traditions and conscience of our people as to be ranked as fundamental." *** No material distinction can be drawn between the treatment to which Nancy Cruzan continues to be subject—artificial nutrition and hydration—and any other medical treatment. ***

The only state interest asserted here is a general interest in the preservation of life. But the State has no legitimate general interest in someone's life, completely abstracted from the interest of the person living that life, that could outweigh the person's choice to avoid medical treatment. *** This is not to say that the State has no legitimate interests to assert here. As the majority recognizes, Missouri has a parens patriae interest in providing Nancy Cruzan, now incompetent, with as accurate as possible a determination of how she would exercise her rights under these circumstances. Second, if and when it is determined that Nancy Cruzan would want to continue treatment, the State may legitimately assert an interest in providing that treatment. But until Nancy's wishes have been determined, the only state interest that may be asserted is an interest in safe-guarding the accuracy of that determination.

Accuracy, therefore, must be our touchstone. Missouri may constitutionally impose only those procedural requirements that serve to enhance the accuracy of a determination of Nancy Cruzan's wishes or are at least consistent with an accurate determination. The Missouri "safeguard" that the Court upholds today does not meet that standard. *** Missouri's rule of decision imposes a markedly asymmetrical evidentiary burden. Only evidence of specific statements of treatment choice made by the patient when competent is admissible to support a finding that the patient, now in a persistent vegetative state, would wish to avoid further medical treatment. Moreover, this evidence must be clear and convincing. No proof is required to support a finding that the incompetent person would wish to continue treatment. ***

Even more than its heightened evidentiary standard, the Missouri court's categorical exclusion of relevant evidence dispenses with any semblance of accurate factfinding. The court *** failed to consider statements Nancy had made to family members and a close friend. The court also failed to consider testimony from Nancy's mother and sister that they were certain that Nancy would want to discontinue artificial nutrition and hydration, even after the court found that Nancy's family was loving and without malignant motive. The court also failed to consider the conclusions of the guardian ad litem, appointed by the trial court, that there was clear and convincing evidence that Nancy would want to discontinue medical treatment and that this was in her best interests. ***

Too few people execute living wills or equivalently formal directives for such an evidentiary rule to ensure adequately that the wishes of incompetent persons will be honored. While it might be a wise social policy to encourage people to furnish such instructions, no general conclusion about a patient's choice can be drawn from the absence of formalities. ***

As many as 10,000 patients are being maintained in persistent vegetative states in the United States, and the number is expected to increase significantly in the near future. Medical technology, developed over the past 20 or so years, is often capable of resuscitating people after they have stopped breathing or their hearts have stopped beating. *** The new medical technology can reclaim those who would have been irretrievably lost a few decades ago and restore them to active lives. For Nancy Cruzan, it failed, and for others with wasting incurable disease, it may be doomed to failure. In these unfortunate situations, the bodies and preferences and memories of the victims do not escheat to the State; nor does our Constitution permit the State or any other government to commandeer them. ***

JUSTICE STEVENS, dissenting.

*** To be constitutionally permissible, Missouri's intrusion upon *** fundamental liberties must, at a minimum, bear a reasonable relationship to a legitimate state end. Missouri asserts that its policy is related to a state interest in the protection of life. In my view, however, it is an effort to define life, rather than to protect it, that is the heart of Missouri's policy. Missouri insists, without regard to Nancy Cruzan's own interests, upon equating her life with the biological persistence of her bodily functions. Nancy Cruzan, it must be remembered, is not now simply incompetent. She is in a persistent vegetative state and has been so for seven years. The trial court found, and no party contested, that Nancy has no possibility of recovery and no consciousness. ***

In short, there is no reasonable ground for believing that Nancy Beth Cruzan has any personal interest in the perpetuation of what the State has decided is her life. *** Only because Missouri has arrogated to itself the power to define life, and only because the Court permits this usurpation, are Nancy Cruzan's life and liberty put into disquieting conflict. If Nancy Cruzan's life were defined by reference to her own interests, so that her life expired when her biological existence ceased serving any of her own interests, then her constitutionally protected interest in freedom from unwanted treatment would not come into conflict with her constitutionally protected interest in life. Conversely, if there were any evidence that Nancy Cruzan herself defined life to encompass every form of biological persistence by a human being, so that the continuation of treatment would serve Nancy's own liberty, then once again there would be no conflict between life and liberty. The opposition of life and liberty in this case are thus not the result of Nancy Cruzan's tragic accident, but are instead the artificial consequence of

Missouri's effort, and this Court's willingness, to abstract Nancy Cruzan's life from Nancy Cruzan's person. *** The Cruzan family's continuing concern provides a concrete reminder that Nancy Cruzan's interests did not disappear with her vitality or her consciousness. However commendable may be the State's interest in human life, it cannot pursue that interest by appropriating Nancy Cruzan's life as a symbol for its own purposes. Lives do not exist in abstraction from persons, and to pretend otherwise is not to honor but to desecrate the State's responsibility for protecting life. A State that seeks to demonstrate its commitment to life may do so by aiding those who are actively struggling for life and health. In this endeavor, unfortunately, no State can lack for opportunities: There can be no need to make an example of tragic cases like that of Nancy Cruzan. ***

VIII-8. By permission of Chip Bok and Creators Syndicate.

WASHINGTON v. GLUCKSBERG
521 U.S. 702, 117 S.Ct. 2258, 138 L.Ed.2d 772 (1997).

CHIEF JUSTICE REHNQUIST delivered the opinion of the Court.

The question presented in this case is whether Washington's prohibition against "caus[ing]" or "aid[ing]" a suicide offends the Fourteenth Amendment to the United States Constitution. We hold that it does not.

It has always been a crime to assist a suicide in the State of Washington. In 1854, Washington's first Territorial Legislature outlawed "assisting another in the commission of self-murder." Today, Washington law provides:

"A person is guilty of promoting a suicide attempt when he knowingly causes or aids another person to attempt suicide." "Promoting a suicide attempt" is a felony, punishable by up to five years' imprisonment and up to a $10,000 fine. At the same time, Washington's Natural Death Act, enacted in 1979, states that the "withholding or withdrawal of life-sustaining treatment" at a patient's direction "shall not, for any purpose, constitute a suicide."[2]

Petitioners in this case are the State of Washington and its Attorney General. Respondents Harold Glucksberg, M. D., Abigail Halperin, M. D., Thomas A. Preston, M. D., and Peter Shalit, M. D., are physicians who practice in Washington. These doctors occasionally treat terminally ill, suffering patients, and declare that they would assist these patients in ending their lives if not for Washington's assisted-suicide ban. In January 1994, respondents, along with three gravely ill, pseudonymous plaintiffs who have since died and Compassion in Dying, a nonprofit organization that counsels people considering physician-assisted suicide, sued in the United States District Court, seeking a declaration that Wash Rev.Code 9A.36.060(1) (1994) is, on its face, unconstitutional.

The plaintiffs asserted "the existence of a liberty interest protected by the Fourteenth Amendment which extends to a personal choice by a mentally competent, terminally ill adult to commit physician-assisted suicide." Relying primarily on *Planned Parenthood v. Casey* and *Cruzan v. Director, Missouri Dept. of Health* the District Court agreed and concluded that Washington's assisted-suicide ban is unconstitutional because it "places an undue burden on the exercise of [that] constitutionally protected liberty interest." *** A panel of the Court of Appeals for the Ninth Circuit reversed. The Ninth Circuit reheard the case en banc, reversed the panel's decision, and affirmed the District Court.

We begin, as we do in all due-process cases, by examining our Nation's history, legal traditions, and practices. In almost every State—indeed, in almost every western democracy—it is a crime to assist a suicide. The States' assisted-suicide bans are not innovations. Rather, they are longstanding expressions of the States' commitment to the protection and preservation of all human life. *** For the most part, the early American colonies adopted the common-law approach. For example, the legislators of the Providence Plantations, which would later become Rhode Island, declared, in 1647, that "[s]elf-murder is by all agreed to be the most unnatural, and it is by this present Assembly declared, to be that, wherein he that doth it, kills himself out of a premeditated hatred against his own life or other humor ***." Virginia also required ignominious burial for suicides, and their estates were forfeit to the crown. Over time, however, the American colonies abolished

---

[2] Under Washington's Natural Death Act, "adult persons have the fundamental right to control the decisions relating to the rendering of their own health care, including the decision to have life-sustaining treatment withheld or withdrawn in instances of a terminal condition or permanent unconscious condition." In Washington, "[a]ny adult person may execute a directive directing the withholding or withdrawal of life-sustaining treatment in a terminal condition or permanent unconscious condition," and a physician who, in accordance with such a directive, participates in the withholding or withdrawal of life-sustaining treatment is immune from civil, criminal, or professional liability.

these harsh common-law penalties. That suicide remained a grievous, though nonfelonious, wrong is confirmed by the fact that colonial and early state legislatures and courts did not retreat from prohibiting assisting suicide. *** And the prohibitions against assisting suicide never contained exceptions for those who were near death. ***

The earliest American statute explicitly to outlaw assisting suicide was enacted in New York in 1828 and many of the new States and Territories followed New York's example. In this century, the Model Penal Code also prohibited "aiding" suicide, prompting many States to enact or revise their assisted-suicide bans.

Though deeply rooted, the States' assisted-suicide bans have in recent years been reexamined and, generally, reaffirmed. Because of advances in medicine and technology, Americans today are increasingly likely to die in institutions, from chronic illnesses. Public concern and democratic action are therefore sharply focused on how best to protect dignity and independence at the end of life, with the result that there have been many significant changes in state laws and in the attitudes these laws reflect. Many States, for example, now permit "living wills," surrogate health-care decisionmaking, and the withdrawal or refusal of life-sustaining medical treatment. At the same time, however, voters and legislators continue for the most part to reaffirm their States' prohibitions on assisting suicide.

The Washington statute at issue in this case was enacted in 1975 as part of a revision of that State's criminal code. Four years later, Washington passed its Natural Death Act, which specifically stated that the "withholding or withdrawal of life-sustaining treatment *** shall not, for any purpose, constitute a suicide" and that "[n]othing in this chapter shall be construed to condone, authorize, or approve mercy killing." In 1991, Washington voters rejected a ballot initiative which, had it passed, would have permitted a form of physician-assisted suicide. Washington then added a provision to the Natural Death Act expressly excluding physician-assisted suicide.

California voters rejected an assisted-suicide initiative similar to Washington's in 1993. On the other hand, in 1994, voters in Oregon enacted, also through ballot initiative, that State's "Death With Dignity Act," which legalized physician-assisted suicide for competent, terminally ill adults. Since the Oregon vote, many proposals to legalize assisted-suicide have been and continue to be introduced in the States' legislatures, but none has been enacted. And just last year, Iowa and Rhode Island joined the overwhelming majority of States explicitly prohibiting assisted suicide. Also, on April 30, 1997, President Clinton signed the Federal Assisted Suicide Funding Restriction Act of 1997, which prohibits the use of federal funds in support of physician-assisted suicide.[16]

---

[16] Other countries are embroiled in similar debates: The Supreme Court of Canada recently rejected a claim that the Canadian Charter of Rights and Freedoms establishes a fundamental right to assisted suicide; the British House of Lords Select Committee on Medical Ethics refused to recommend any change in Great Britain's assisted-suicide prohibition; New Zealand's Parliament rejected a proposed "Death With Dignity Bill" that would have legalized physician-assisted suicide in August 1995; and the Northern Territory of Australia legalized assisted

Thus, the States are currently engaged in serious, thoughtful examinations of physician-assisted suicide and other similar issues. *** Against this backdrop of history, tradition, and practice, we now turn to respondents' constitutional claim.

*** Our established method of substantive-due-process analysis has two primary features: First, we have regularly observed that the Due Process Clause specially protects those fundamental rights and liberties which are, objectively, "deeply rooted in this Nation's history and tradition and 'implicit in the concept of ordered liberty,' such that 'neither liberty nor justice would exist if they were sacrificed,' *Palko v. Connecticut*, (1937). Second, we have required in substantive-due-process cases a 'careful description' of the asserted fundamental liberty interest." *Flores; Collins; Cruzan.* Our Nation's history, legal traditions, and practices thus provide the crucial "guideposts for responsible decisionmaking," that direct and restrain our exposition of the Due Process Clause. As we stated recently in *Flores*, the Fourteenth Amendment "forbids the government to infringe *** 'fundamental' liberty interests at all, no matter what process is provided, unless the infringement is narrowly tailored to serve a compelling state interest."

JUSTICE SOUTER, relying on JUSTICE HARLAN's dissenting opinion in *Poe v. Ullman*, would largely abandon this restrained methodology, and instead ask "whether [Washington's] statute sets up one of those 'arbitrary impositions' or 'purposeless restraints' at odds with the Due Process Clause of the Fourteenth Amendment." In our view, however, the development of this Court's substantive-due-process jurisprudence, described briefly above, has been a process whereby the outlines of the "liberty" specially protected by the Fourteenth Amendment—never fully clarified, to be sure, and perhaps not capable of being fully clarified—have at least been carefully refined by concrete examples involving fundamental rights found to be deeply rooted in our legal tradition. This approach tends to rein in the subjective elements that are necessarily present in due-process judicial review. In addition, by establishing a threshold requirement—that a challenged state action implicate a fundamental right—before requiring more than a reasonable relation to a legitimate state interest to justify the action, it avoids the need for complex balancing of competing interests in every case.

Turning to the claim at issue here, the Court of Appeals stated that "[p]roperly analyzed, the first issue to be resolved is whether there is a liberty interest in determining the time and manner of one's death," in other words, "[i]s there a right to die." Similarly, respondents assert a "liberty to choose how to die" and a right to "control of one's final days," and describe the asserted liberty as "the right to choose a humane, dignified death," and "the liberty to shape death." *** As noted above, we have a tradition of carefully formulating the interest at stake in substantive-due-process cases. For example, although *Cruzan* is often described as a "right to die" case, we were, in fact, more precise: We assumed that the Constitution granted competent persons a "constitutionally protected right to refuse lifesaving hydration and

---

suicide and voluntary euthanasia in. On the other hand, on May 20, 1997, Colombia's Constitutional Court legalized voluntary euthanasia for terminally ill people.

nutrition. The Washington statute at issue in this case prohibits 'aid[ing] another person to attempt suicide,' and, thus, the question before us is whether the 'liberty' specially protected by the Due Process Clause includes a right to commit suicide which itself includes a right to assistance in doing so." ***

Respondents contend, however, that the liberty interest they assert is consistent with this Court's substantive-due-process line of cases, if not with this Nation's history and practice. Pointing to *Casey* and *Cruzan*, respondents read our jurisprudence in this area as reflecting a general tradition of "self-sovereignty," and as teaching that the "liberty" protected by the Due Process Clause includes "basic and intimate exercises of personal autonomy." According to respondents, our liberty jurisprudence, and the broad, individualistic principles it reflects, protects the "liberty of competent, terminally ill adults to make end-of-life decisions free of undue government interference." The question presented in this case, however, is whether the protections of the Due Process Clause include a right to commit suicide with another's assistance. With this "careful description" of respondents' claim in mind, we turn to *Casey* and *Cruzan*.

Respondents contend that in *Cruzan* we "acknowledged that competent, dying persons have the right to direct the removal of life-sustaining medical treatment and thus hasten death," and that "the constitutional principle behind recognizing the patient's liberty to direct the withdrawal of artificial life support applies at least as strongly to the choice to hasten impending death by consuming lethal medication." Similarly, the Court of Appeals concluded that "*Cruzan*, by recognizing a liberty interest that includes the refusal of artificial provision of life-sustaining food and water, necessarily recognize[d] a liberty interest in hastening one's own death."

The right assumed in *Cruzan*, however, was not simply deduced from abstract concepts of personal autonomy. Given the common-law rule that forced medication was a battery, and the long legal tradition protecting the decision to refuse unwanted medical treatment, our assumption was entirely consistent with this Nation's history and constitutional traditions. The decision to commit suicide with the assistance of another may be just as personal and profound as the decision to refuse unwanted medical treatment, but it has never enjoyed similar legal protection. Indeed, the two acts are widely and reasonably regarded as quite distinct. ***

Respondents also rely on *Casey*. There, the Court's opinion concluded that "the essential holding of *Roe v. Wade* should be retained and once again reaffirmed." In reaching this conclusion, the opinion discussed in some detail this Court's substantive-due-process tradition of interpreting the Due Process Clause to protect certain fundamental rights and "personal decisions relating to marriage, procreation, contraception, family relationships, child rearing, and education," and noted that many of those rights and liberties "involv[e] the most intimate and personal choices a person may make in a lifetime." *** That many of the rights and liberties protected by the Due Process Clause sound in personal autonomy does not warrant the sweeping conclusion that any and all important, intimate, and personal decisions are so protected. *** *Casey* did not suggest otherwise.

The history of the law's treatment of assisted suicide in this country has been and continues to be one of the rejection of nearly all efforts to permit it. That being the case, our decisions lead us to conclude that the asserted "right" to assistance in committing suicide is not a fundamental liberty interest protected by the Due Process Clause. The Constitution also requires, however, that Washington's assisted-suicide ban be rationally related to legitimate government interests. This requirement is unquestionably met here.

First, Washington has an "unqualified interest in the preservation of human life." *Cruzan.* The State's prohibition on assisted suicide, like all homicide laws, both reflects and advances its commitment to this interest. Relatedly, all admit that suicide is a serious public-health problem, especially among persons in otherwise vulnerable groups. Those who attempt suicide— terminally ill or not—often suffer from depression or other mental disorders. Research indicates, however, that many people who request physician-assisted suicide withdraw that request if their depression and pain are treated. Thus, legal physician-assisted suicide could make it more difficult for the State to protect depressed or mentally ill persons, or those who are suffering from untreated pain, from suicidal impulses.

The State also has an interest in protecting the integrity and ethics of the medical profession. *** And physician-assisted suicide could, it is argued, undermine the trust that is essential to the doctor-patient relationship by blurring the time-honored line between healing and harming.

Next, the State has an interest in protecting vulnerable groups— including the poor, the elderly, and disabled persons—from abuse, neglect, and mistakes. The Court of Appeals dismissed the State's concern that disadvantaged persons might be pressured into physician-assisted suicide as "ludicrous on its face." We have recognized, however, the real risk of subtle coercion and undue influence in end-of-life situations. *Cruzan.* If physician-assisted suicide were permitted, many might resort to it to spare their families the substantial financial burden of end-of-life health-care costs.

The State's interest here goes beyond protecting the vulnerable from coercion; it extends to protecting disabled and terminally ill people from prejudice, negative and inaccurate stereotypes, and "societal indifference." ***

Finally, the State may fear that permitting assisted suicide will start it down the path to voluntary and perhaps even involuntary euthanasia. The Court of Appeals' decision, and its expansive reasoning, provide ample support for the State's concerns. Thus, it turns out that what is couched as a limited right to "physician-assisted suicide" is likely, in effect, a much broader license, which could prove extremely difficult to police and contain. Washington's ban on assisting suicide prevents such erosion.

This concern is further supported by evidence about the practice of euthanasia in the Netherlands. The Dutch government's own study revealed that in 1990, there were 2,300 cases of voluntary euthanasia (defined as "the deliberate termination of another's life at his request"), 400 cases of assisted suicide, and more than 1,000 cases of euthanasia without an explicit request. In addition to these latter 1,000 cases, the study found an additional 4,941 cases where physicians administered lethal morphine overdoses without the patients' explicit consent. This study suggests that, despite the existence of various reporting procedures, euthanasia in the Netherlands has not been limited to competent, terminally ill adults who are enduring physical suffering, and that regulation of the practice may not have prevented abuses in cases involving vulnerable persons, including severely disabled neonates and elderly persons suffering from dementia. Washington, like most other States, reasonably ensures against this risk by banning, rather than regulating, assisting suicide.

We need not weigh exactly the relative strengths of these various interests. They are unquestionably important and legitimate, and Washington's ban on assisted suicide is at least reasonably related to their promotion and protection. *** Throughout the Nation, Americans are engaged in an earnest and profound debate about the morality, legality, and practicality of physician-assisted suicide. Our holding permits this debate to continue, as it should in a democratic society. ***

[JUSTICE O'CONNOR, joined by JUSTICE GINSBERG and JUSTICE BREYER, concurred that "there is no generalized right to commit suicide" and noted that there was no reason to move beyond the facial challenges to the Washington statute mounted by Petitioners. She reserved the question whether "a mentally competent person who is experiencing great suffering has a constitutionally cognizable interest in controlling the circumstances of his or her imminent death." JUSTICE STEVENS concurred but argued that a decision "upholding a general statutory prohibition of assisted suicide does not mean that every possible application of the statute would be valid."]

JUSTICE SOUTER, concurring in the judgment.

*** My understanding of unenumerated rights in the wake of the *Poe* dissent and subsequent cases avoids the absolutist failing of many older cases without embracing the opposite pole of equating reasonableness with past practice described at a very specific level. *** The claims of arbitrariness that mark almost all instances of unenumerated substantive rights are those resting on "certain interests requir[ing] particularly careful scrutiny of the state needs asserted to justify their abridgment." In the face of an interest this powerful a State may not rest on threshold rationality or a presumption of constitutionality, but may prevail only on the ground of an interest sufficiently compelling to place within the realm of the reasonable a refusal to recognize the individual right asserted.

This approach calls for a court to assess the relative "weights" or dignities of the contending interests, and to this extent the judicial method is familiar to the common law. Common law method is subject, however, to two important constraints in the hands of a court engaged in substantive due process review. First, such a court is bound to confine the values that it recognizes to those truly deserving constitutional stature, either to those expressed in constitutional text, or those exemplified by "the traditions from which [the Nation] developed," or revealed by contrast with "the traditions from which it broke." *Poe.* ***

The argument supporting respondents' position thus progresses through three steps of increasing forcefulness. First, it emphasizes the decriminalization of suicide. Reliance on this fact is sanctioned under the standard that looks not only to the tradition retained, but to society's occasional choices to reject traditions of the legal past. The second step in the argument is to emphasize that the State's own act of decriminalization gives a freedom of choice much like the individual's option in recognized instances of bodily autonomy. One of these, abortion, is a legal right to choose in spite of the interest a State may legitimately invoke in discouraging the practice, just as suicide is now subject to choice, despite a state interest in discouraging it. The third step is to emphasize that respondents claim a right to assistance not on the basis of some broad principle that would be subject to exceptions if that continuing interest of the State's in discouraging suicide were to be recognized at all. There can be no stronger claim to a physician's assistance than at the time when death is imminent, a moral judgment implied by the State's own recognition of the legitimacy of medical procedures necessarily hastening the moment of impending death.

In my judgment, the importance of the individual interest here, as within that class of "certain interests" demanding careful scrutiny of the State's contrary claim cannot be gainsaid. Whether that interest might in some circumstances, or at some time, be seen as "fundamental" to the degree entitled to prevail is not, however, a conclusion that I need draw here, for I am satisfied that the State's interests *** are sufficiently serious to defeat the present claim that its law is arbitrary or purposeless.

The State has put forward several interests to justify the Washington law as applied to physicians treating terminally ill patients, even those competent to make responsible choices: protecting life generally, discouraging suicide even if knowing and voluntary, and protecting terminally ill patients from involuntary suicide and euthanasia, both voluntary and nonvoluntary.

It is not necessary to discuss the exact strengths of the first two claims of justification in the present circumstances, for the third is dispositive for me. That third justification is different from the first two, for it addresses specific features of respondents' claim, and it opposes that claim not with a moral judgment contrary to respondents', but with a recognized state interest in the protection of nonresponsible individuals and those who do not stand in relation either to death or to their physicians as do the patients whom respondents describe. The State claims interests in protecting patients from mistakenly and involuntarily deciding to end their lives, and in guarding against both voluntary and involuntary euthanasia. Leaving aside any difficulties in coming to a clear concept of imminent death, mistaken decisions may result from inadequate palliative care or a terminal prognosis that turns out to be error; coercion and abuse may stem from the large medical bills that family members cannot bear or unreimbursed hospitals decline to shoulder. ***

The mere assertion that the terminally sick might be pressured into suicide decisions by close friends and family members would not alone be very telling. Of course that is possible, not only because the costs of care might be more than family members could bear but simply because they might naturally wish to see an end of suffering for someone they love. But one of the points of restricting any right of assistance to physicians, would be to condition the right on an exercise of judgment by someone qualified to assess the patient's responsible capacity and detect the influence of those outside the medical relationship.

The State, however, goes further, to argue that dependence on the vigilance of physicians will not be enough. First, the lines proposed here (particularly the requirement of a knowing and voluntary decision by the patient) would be more difficult to draw than the lines that have limited other recently recognized due process rights. Limiting a state from prosecuting use of artificial contraceptives by married couples posed no practical threat to the State's capacity to regulate contraceptives in other ways that were assumed at the time of Poe to be legitimate; the trimester measurements of *Roe* and the viability determination of Casey were easy to make with a real degree of certainty. But the knowing and responsible mind is harder to assess. Second, this difficulty could become the greater by combining with another fact within the realm of plausibility, that physicians simply would not be assiduous to preserve the line. They have compassion, and those who would be willing to assist in suicide at all might be the most susceptible to the wishes of a patient, whether the patient were technically quite responsible or not. Physicians, and their hospitals, have their own financial incentives, too, in this new age of managed care. Whether acting from compassion or under some other influence, a physician who would provide a drug for a patient to administer might well go the further step of administering the drug himself; so, the barrier between assisted suicide and euthanasia could become porous, and the line between voluntary and involuntary euthanasia as well. The case for the slippery slope is fairly made out here, not because recognizing one due process right would leave a court with no principled basis to avoid recognizing another, but because there is a plausible case that the right claimed would not be readily containable by reference to facts about the mind that are matters of difficult judgment, or by gatekeepers who are subject to temptation, noble or not.

Respondents propose an answer to all this, the answer of state regulation with teeth. Legislation proposed in several States, for example, would authorize physician-assisted suicide but require two qualified physicians to confirm the patient's diagnosis, prognosis, and competence; and would mandate that the patient make repeated requests witnessed by at least two others over a specified time span; and would impose reporting requirements and criminal penalties for various acts of coercion.

But at least at this moment there are reasons for caution in predicting the effectiveness of the teeth proposed. Respondents' proposals, as it turns out, sound much like the guidelines now in place in the Netherlands, the only place where experience with physician-assisted suicide and euthanasia has yielded empirical evidence about how such regulations might affect actual practice. *** The Court should accordingly stay its hand to allow reasonable legislative consideration. While I do not decide for all time that respondents' claim should not be recognized, I acknowledge the legislative institutional competence as the better one to deal with that claim at this time.

Notes

1. **Concurrences.** What do you make of the concurrences? What if a state, unlike Washington, did not permit physicians to administer potentially lethal does of painkilling medications?

2. *Glucksburg, Bowers, and Lawrence.* Does the *Glucksburg* Court return to the analytical framework of *Bowers*? Is this return suspect after *Lawrence*?

3. **Executive Acts and Substantive Due Process.** Although the Court appears to have a set framework for the scrutiny to be applied to each type of case, this may not necessarily be so when dealing with actions of individual executive officers and the scenarios in which they performed their duties. *See County of Sacramento v. Lewis*, 523 U.S. 833 (1998) (the level of scrutiny applied to police officers' actions varies depending on whether the actions occurred during pursuit or while in a jail setting).

REVIEW PROBLEMS

Review Problem #1. Is the following hypothetical federal Constitutional?

THE ANTI–CLONING ACT

1. FINDINGS:

(a) Human reproduction historically has occurred only through processes in which each individual is created by a unique combination of genetic material from a male and a female;

(b) Biomedical advances have, for the first time in human history, enabled scientists to clone a genetic duplicate of a human being from the cells of a donor by introducing the donor's genetic material into an egg or ovum whose own genetic material has been destroyed;

(c) Reproduction of human beings through cloning poses profound religious and ethical questions for human beings and limits the genetic diversity of the human species;

(d) Cloning creates difficult legal problems (e.g. "Who is the clonee's family?"; "Is the clonor-clonee relationship a sibling or parent/child relationship?"; "Is a clonee a 'person' or 'human being' under United States law?"); and

(e) The states cannot prohibit cloning on a nationwide basis and have not exercised their powers to prohibit cloning within their jurisdictions.

2. THEREFORE:

(a) No state that permits its funds or facilities to be used to facilitate the cloning of human beings shall receive any federal financial assistance related to medical research or health care delivery.

(b) Any person who knowingly contributes genetic material intending that this genetic material be cloned, any person who contributes an ovum intending it to be used in cloning, and any person who knowingly permits her uterus to receive such genetic material in such an ovum shall be punished by imprisonment not to exceed one year.

Review Problem #2.

Ames is a state in the United States. Because of its wide sandy beaches and its good weather, Dale Beach, a city in Ames, has become a popular destination for college students on spring break. Many of the residents of Dale Beach have become concerned that during spring break, their community becomes a haven for students from out of town who wish to engage in conduct, including sexual conduct, that residents of Dale Beach consider immoral. Many residents have concluded that Dale Beach would be better off if the students went elsewhere for spring break.

After substantial debate, the Dale Beach City Council, "in order to discourage disease, extramarital birth, and immoral conduct, as well as to encourage marriage," passes an ordinance making it a misdemeanor, punishable by fine of up to $5,000 and imprisonment not to exceed two weeks, for people who are not married to each other to engage in sexual intercourse within the city limits. The ordinance has been enforced, following plea bargain or trial, several times when individuals came forward to report violations.

Does the ordinance violate the Due Process Clause of the Fourteenth Amendment?

IX

EQUAL PROTECTION OF THE LAWS

A. INTRODUCTION TO THE EQUAL PROTECTION CLAUSE

"No State shall make any distinction in civil rights and privileges among the naturalized citizens of the United States residing within its limits, or among persons born on its soil of parents permanently resident there, on account of race, color, or descent."

> —*National Anti–Slavery Standard*
> *editorial page banner,* July 22, 1865—
> March 31, 1866

As you study the materials in this chapter, consider how the Constitution would differ if the above language had been adopted. *Rice v. Cayetano*, 528 U.S. 495 (2000), a case in which voting had been limited to native Hawaiians, stated that race is a "prohibited classification." But that was a Fifteenth Amendment case based on this text: "The right of citizens of the United States to vote shall not be denied or abridged by the United States or any State on account of race, color, or previous condition of servitude." The Equal Protection Clause language ("No State shall *** deny to any person within its jurisdiction the equal protection of the laws") is both more general and more equivocal than that of the Fifteenth Amendment.

Hornbook Law. There is only one Equal Protection Clause. Nevertheless, the Supreme Court during the past half-century has adopted three "tiers" of equal protection analysis. The following is a useful oversimplification of the case law you will study:

(a) When dealing with a "suspect classification," such as race, or a "fundamental right," such as the right to vote, the Court has applied "strict scrutiny" to the governmental classification. Strict scrutiny means that, to sustain the classification, the government must prove it has a "compelling governmental interest" in the subject matter about which it has made the classification and that it has "narrowly tailored" its classification to fulfill that interest.

(b) When the Court is dealing with gender classifications made by government, it has applied "middle tier" scrutiny, which requires at least an "important governmental interest" which is "closely related" to the government's classification.

(c) "Rational basis" scrutiny, applied to all other governmental classifications, requires only that the classification be "rationally related" to some "legitimate governmental interest."

With three tiers of scrutiny, an obvious first problem is how to classify the classification at issue. If a legislative classification is deemed suspect, strict scrutiny is likely to be "fatal in fact" to the legislation. Conversely, if a legislative classification is not suspect, rational basis scrutiny will validate all but the most irrational legislation. Thus, a great deal turns on this first analytical step.

Theory of Heightened Scrutiny. The theory behind heightened scrutiny is often said to come from footnote four of *United States v. Carolene Products*, 304 U.S. 144 (1938). In *Carolene Products*, the Court upheld the constitutionality of a federal statute prohibiting interstate shipment of "filled milk" (milk having vegetable oil substituted for butter fat), despite Congress' finding that such milk was "injurious to the public health," that any danger could have been handled by a labeling requirement, and that the statute was undoubtedly the product of lobbying efforts by powerful dairy constituents. The footnote reads:

> "There may be narrower scope for operation of the presumption of constitutionality when legislation appears on its face to be within a specific prohibition of the Constitution, such as those of the first ten amendments ***. It is unnecessary to consider now whether legislation which restricts those political processes which can ordinarily be expected to bring about repeal of undesirable legislation, is to be subjected to more exacting judicial scrutiny. *** Nor need we enquire whether similar considerations enter into the review of statutes directed at particular religious *** or national *** or racial minorities[;] whether prejudice against discrete and insular minorities may be a special condition, which tends seriously to curtail the operation of those political processes ordinarily to be relied upon to protect minorities, and which may call for a correspondingly more searching judicial inquiry. ***"

As you read these materials, consider (as the Court did not in *Carolene Products*) when legislation (1) restricts ordinary political processes, (2) targets particular minorities, or (3) curtails processes that protect minorities. Do not, however, rely too heavily on this theory, for the courts often have not followed it. Moreover, modern political theory is quite skeptical of many components of this footnote; majoritarian political processes have regularly produced legislation benefiting "discrete and insular" minorities.

B. RACE AND EQUAL PROTECTION

The next two cases, which discuss the meaning of "equal" when state law requires "separate but equal" treatment of racial groups, provide an excellent opportunity to reconsider the interpretive issues discussed earlier in this course. What role do text, original understanding, precedent, and public policy play in these decisions? What should the role of the courts be in interpreting the Equal Protection Clause?

1. SEPARATE AND UNEQUAL

PLESSY v. FERGUSON
163 U.S. 537, 16 S.Ct. 1138, 41 L.Ed. 256 (1896).

[An 1890 Louisiana statute required railroad companies to provide "separate but equal" accommodations for whites and "colored races." Plessy, a United States citizen who resided in Louisiana, had seven-eighths Caucasian and one-eighth African blood. On June 7, 1892, he bought a first-class ticket on the East Louisiana Railway and took a vacant seat in a coach designated for white passengers. Plessy was required by the conductor to move to a coach for non-white passengers. When he refused to move, Plessy was (with the aid of a police officer) ejected from the coach, imprisoned, and charged with violating state law.]

MR. JUSTICE BROWN *** delivered the opinion of the court.

*** By the fourteenth amendment, all persons born or naturalized in the United States, and subject to the jurisdiction thereof, are made citizens of the United States and of the state wherein they reside; and the states are forbidden from making or enforcing any law which shall abridge the privileges or immunities of citizens of the United States, or shall deprive any person of life, liberty, or property without due process of law, or deny to any person within their jurisdiction the equal protection of the laws. ***

The object of the amendment was undoubtedly to enforce the absolute equality of the two races before the law, but, in the nature of things, it could not have been intended to abolish distinctions based upon color, or to enforce social, as distinguished from political, equality, or a commingling of the two races upon terms unsatisfactory to either. Laws permitting, and even requiring, their separation, in places where they are liable to be brought into contact, do not necessarily imply the inferiority of either race to the other, and have been generally, if not universally, recognized as within the competency of the state legislatures in the exercise of their police power. The most common instance of this is connected with the establishment of separate schools for white and colored children, which have been held to be a valid exercise of the legislative power even by courts of states where the political rights of the colored race have been longest and most earnestly enforced.

*** [I]t is *** suggested by the learned counsel for the plaintiff in error that the same argument that will justify the state legislature in requiring railways to provide separate accommodations for the two races will also authorize them to require separate cars to be provided for people whose hair is of a certain color, or who are aliens, or who belong to certain nationalities, or to enact laws requiring colored people to walk upon one side of the street, and white people upon the other, or requiring white men's houses to be painted white, and colored men's black, or their vehicles or business signs to be of different colors, upon the theory that one side of the street is as good as the other, or that a house or vehicle of one color is as good as one of another color. The reply to all this is that every exercise of the police power must be reasonable, and extend only to such laws as are enacted in good faith for the promotion of the public good, and not for the annoyance or oppression of a particular class. ***

So far, then, as a conflict with the fourteenth amendment is concerned, the case reduces itself to the question whether the statute of Louisiana is a reasonable regulation, and with respect to this there must necessarily be a large discretion on the part of the legislature. In determining the question of reasonableness, it is at liberty to act with reference to the established usages, customs, and traditions of the people, and with a view to the promotion of their comfort, and the preservation of the public peace and good order. Gauged by this standard, we cannot say that a law which authorizes or even requires the separation of the two races in public conveyances is unreasonable, or more obnoxious to the fourteenth amendment than the acts of congress requiring separate schools for colored children in the District of Columbia, the constitutionality of which does not seem to have been questioned, or the corresponding acts of state legislatures.

We consider the underlying fallacy of the plaintiff's argument to consist in the assumption that the enforced separation of the two races stamps the colored race with a badge of inferiority. If this be so, it is not by reason of anything found in the act, but solely because the colored race chooses to put that construction upon it. The argument necessarily assumes that if, as has been more than once the case, and is not unlikely to be so again, the colored race should become the dominant power in the state legislature, and should enact a law in precisely similar terms, it would thereby relegate the white race to an inferior position. We imagine that the white race, at least, would not acquiesce in this assumption. The argument also assumes that social prejudices may be overcome by legislation, and that equal rights cannot be secured to the negro except by an enforced commingling of the two races. We cannot accept this proposition. If the two races are to meet upon terms of social equality, it must be the result of natural affinities, a mutual appreciation of each other's merits, and a voluntary consent of individuals. *** Legislation is powerless to eradicate racial instincts, or to abolish distinctions based upon physical differences, and the attempt to do so can only result in accentuating the difficulties of the present situation. If the civil and political rights of both races be equal, one cannot be inferior to the other civilly or politically. If one race be inferior to the other socially, the constitution of the United States cannot put them upon the same plane. ***

MR. JUSTICE BREWER did not hear the argument or participate in the decision of this case.

MR. JUSTICE HARLAN dissenting.

*** In respect of civil rights, common to all citizens, the constitution of the United States does not, I think, permit any public authority to know the race of those entitled to be protected in the enjoyment of such rights. Every true man has pride of race, and under appropriate circumstances, when the rights of others, his equals before the law, are not to be affected, it is his privilege to express such pride and to take such action based upon it as to him seems proper. But I deny that any legislative body or judicial tribunal may have regard to the race of citizens when the civil rights of those citizens are involved. Indeed, such legislation as that here in question is inconsistent not only with that equality of rights which pertains to citizenship, national and state, but with the personal liberty enjoyed by every one within the United States. ***

It was said in argument that the statute of Louisiana does not discriminate against either race, but prescribes a rule applicable alike to white and colored citizens. But this argument does not meet the difficulty. Every one knows that the statute in question had its origin in the purpose, not so much to exclude white persons from railroad cars occupied by blacks, as to exclude colored people from coaches occupied by or assigned to white persons. Railroad corporations of Louisiana did not make discrimination among whites in the matter of accommodation for travelers. The thing to accomplish was, under the guise of giving equal accommodation for whites and blacks, to compel the latter to keep to themselves while traveling in railroad passenger coaches. No one would be so wanting in candor as to assert the contrary. The fundamental objection, therefore, to the statute, is that it interferes with the personal freedom of citizens. 'Personal liberty,' it has been well said, 'consists in the power of locomotion, of changing situation, or removing one's person to whatsoever places one's own inclination may direct, without imprisonment or restraint, unless by due course of law.' If a white man and a black man choose to occupy the same public conveyance on a public highway, it is their right to do so; and no government, proceeding alone on grounds of race, can prevent it without infringing the personal liberty of each.

It is one thing for railroad carriers to furnish, or to be required by law to furnish, equal accommodations for all whom they are under a legal duty to carry. It is quite another thing for government to forbid citizens of the white and black races from traveling in the same public conveyance, and to punish officers of railroad companies for permitting persons of the two races to occupy the same passenger coach. If a state can prescribe, as a rule of civil conduct, that whites and blacks shall not travel as passengers in the same railroad coach, why may it not so regulate the use of the streets of its cities and towns as to compel white citizens to keep on one side of a street, and black citizens to keep on the other? Why may it not, upon like grounds, punish whites and blacks who ride together in street cars or in open vehicles on a public road or street? Why may it not require sheriffs to assign whites to one side of a court room, and blacks to the other? And why may it not also prohibit the commingling of the two races in the galleries of legislative halls or in public assemblages convened for the consideration of the political questions of the day? Further, if this statute of Louisiana is consistent with the personal liberty of citizens, why may not the state require the separation in railroad coaches of native and naturalized citizens of the United States, or of Protestants and Roman Catholics?

The answer given at the argument to these questions was that regulations of the kind they suggest would be unreasonable, and could not, therefore, stand before the law. Is it meant that the determination of questions of legislative power depends upon the inquiry whether the statute whose validity is questioned is, in the judgment of the courts, a reasonable one, taking all the circumstances into consideration? A statute may be unreasonable merely because a sound public policy forbade its enactment. But I do not understand that the courts have anything to do with the policy or expediency of legislation. A statute may be valid, and yet, upon grounds of public policy, may well be characterized as unreasonable. ***

The white race deems itself to be the dominant race in this country. And so it is, in prestige, in achievements, in education, in wealth, and in power. So, I doubt not, it will continue to be for all time, if it remains true to its great heritage, and holds fast to the principles of constitutional liberty. But in view of the constitution, in the eye of the law, there is in this country no superior, dominant, ruling class of citizens. There is no caste here. Our constitution is color-blind, and neither knows nor tolerates classes among citizens. In respect of civil rights, all citizens are equal before the law. The humblest is the peer of the most powerful. The law regards man as man, and takes no account of his surroundings or of his color when his civil rights as guaranteed by the supreme law of the land are involved. It is therefore to be regretted that this high tribunal, the final expositor of the fundamental law of the land, has reached the conclusion that it is competent for a state to regulate the enjoyment by citizens of their civil rights solely upon the basis of race.

In my opinion, the judgment this day rendered will, in time, prove to be quite as pernicious as the decision made by this tribunal in the *Dred Scott* Case. *** [It] seems that we have yet, in some of the states, a dominant race—a superior class of citizens—which assumes to regulate the enjoyment of civil rights, common to all citizens, upon the basis of race. The present decision, it may well be apprehended, will not only stimulate aggressions, more or less brutal and irritating, upon the admitted rights of colored citizens, but will encourage the belief that it is possible, by means of state enactments, to defeat the beneficent purposes which the people of the United States had in view when they adopted the recent amendments of the constitution, by one of which the blacks of this country were made citizens of the United States and of the states in which they respectively reside, and whose privileges and immunities, as citizens, the states are forbidden to abridge. Sixty millions of whites are in no danger from the presence here of eight millions of blacks. The destinies of the two races, in this country, are indissolubly linked together, and the interests of both require that the common government of all shall not permit the seeds of race hate to be planted under the sanction of law. What can more certainly arouse race hate, what more certainly create and perpetuate a feeling of distrust between these races, than state enactments which, in fact, proceed on the ground that colored citizens are so inferior and degraded that they cannot be allowed to sit in public coaches occupied by white citizens? That, as all will admit, is the real meaning of such legislation as was enacted in Louisiana. ***

I am of opinion that the [Louisiana statute] is inconsistent with the personal liberty of citizens, white and black, in that state, and hostile to both the spirit and letter of the constitution of the United States. ***

Notes

1. **Judicial Discretion.** The *Plessy* Court had a social vision of appropriate race relations. The Court retained discretion to permit governmental practices matching that vision, while discarding those that did not match that vision. JUSTICE HARLAN's famous dissent is not only a call for racial equality, but for a Constitution not subject to change with judicial and societal whims. Do you think the Court should retain discretion on racial matters?

2. **Trains to Education.** *Plessy* involved trains, not education, but in *Cumming v. Board of Education of Richmond County*, 175 U.S. 528 (1899), the Court both upheld segregation in public education and leniently applied its requirement of equal facilities (the only black high school in Richmond County, Georgia was closed). JUSTICE HARLAN, seemingly inconsistently, wrote an opinion that said education was "a matter belonging to the respective states."

3. **Road to *Brown*.** The NAACP, formed in 1909 in conjunction with the hundredth anniversary of Lincoln's birth, submitted its first Supreme Court brief amicus curiae in 1915. This brief successfully urged the Supreme Court to use the Fifteenth Amendment to overturn an Oklahoma law which required a literacy test for all voters other than those entitled to vote prior to 1866 or descendants of those entitled to vote before 1866. Under the leadership of Howard Law Center Dean Charles Hamilton Houston, the NAACP repeatedly attacked Jim Crow (separate but equal) laws using the theory that separate facilities were in fact not equal. Despite some notable wins, the strategy seemed endless; it had to be carried out fact by fact and facility by facility. Yet the NAACP adhered to the strategy because it thought there was no hope of obtaining a reversal of the basic "separate but equal" holding of *Plessy.**

In 1938, Houston returned to private practice and leadership of the NAACP passed to 30 year-old Thurgood Marshall. During the 1940's, Marshall began working toward a frontal assault on *Plessy*. At first, the Court took a narrower course, holding in cases like *Sweatt v. Painter*, 339 U.S. 629 (1950), that separate was not in fact equal (separate Texas law schools would not provide the same

---

* *Plessy* was enforced by the courts for over half a century. Typical is *Carr v. Corning*, 182 F.2d 14 (D.C.Cir. 1950):

> We do not believe that the makers of the *** Fourteenth Amendment in 1866 meant to foreclose legislative treatment of the problem [of segregation] in this country. *** [T]he social and economic interrelationship of two races living together is a legislative problem, as yet not solved ***. We must remember that on this particular point we are interpreting a constitution *** ['Our question is merely whether the Federal Constitution prohibited segregation.'] *** [T]he actions of Congress [concerning the Fourteenth Amendment and Civil Rights Acts of 1866 and 1875], the discussion in the Civil Rights Cases, and the fact that in 1862, 1864, 1866, and 1874 Congress *** enacted legislation which specifically provided for separation of the races in the schools of the District of Columbia, conclusively support our view of the Amendment and its effect. [The court cites 12 Supreme Court and 16 lower court cases for the proposition that 'the races may be separated.'] [C]onstitutional invalidity does not arise from the mere fact of separation but may arise from an inequality of treatment.

professional opportunities even if facilities were equal). In 1952, the Court granted certiorari in four cases in which it was argued that segregated schools were unconstitutional. The Court was divided, however, and reargument was requested at the end of the 1952–53 term on the issue of the "original intent" of the Equal Protection Clause. During the course of the summer, CHIEF JUSTICE VINSON died and was replaced by Eisenhower appointee Earl Warren, who provided the leadership to pull the Court together for a unanimous opinion overruling *Plessy*. JUSTICE FELIX FRANKFURTER, who had favored overruling the "separate but equal" doctrine, thought such a dramatic move should be unanimous to put the full weight of the Court's authority behind the change. Frankfurter told a former law clerk that the change of Chief Justices was "the first indication I have ever had that there is a God."

BROWN v. BOARD OF EDUCATION
347 U.S. 483, 74 S.Ct. 686, 98 L.Ed. 873 (1954).

MR. CHIEF JUSTICE WARREN delivered the opinion of the Court.

*** [M]inors of the Negro race, through their legal representatives, seek the aid of the courts in obtaining admission to the public schools of their community on a nonsegregated basis. In each instance, they have been denied admission to schools attended by white children under laws requiring or permitting segregation according to race. This segregation was alleged to deprive the plaintiffs of the equal protection of the laws under the Fourteenth Amendment. ***

The plaintiffs contend that segregated public schools are not "equal" and cannot be made "equal," and that hence they are deprived of the equal protection of the laws. Because of the obvious importance of the question presented, the Court took jurisdiction. Argument was heard in the 1952 Term, and reargument was heard this Term on certain questions propounded by the Court.

Reargument was largely devoted to the circumstances surrounding the adoption of the Fourteenth Amendment in 1868. It covered exhaustively consideration of the Amendment in Congress, ratification by the states, then existing practices in racial segregation, and the views of proponents and opponents of the Amendment. This discussion and our own investigation convince us that, although these sources cast some light, it is not enough to resolve the problem with which we are faced. At best, they are inconclusive. The most avid proponents of the post-War Amendments undoubtedly intended them to remove all legal distinctions among "all persons born or naturalized in the United States." Their opponents, just as certainly, were antagonistic to both the letter and the spirit of the Amendments and wished them to have the most limited effect. What others in Congress and the state legislatures had in mind cannot be determined with any degree of certainty.

An additional reason for the inconclusive nature of the Amendment's history, with respect to segregated schools, is the status of public education at that time. In the South, the movement toward free common schools, supported by general taxation, had not yet taken hold. Education of white children was largely in the hands of private groups. Education of Negroes was almost nonexistent, and practically all of the race were illiterate. In fact, any education of Negroes was forbidden by law in some states. Today, in contrast, many Negroes have achieved outstanding success in the arts and sciences as well as in the business and professional world. It is true that public school education at the time of the Amendment had advanced further in the North, but the effect of the Amendment on Northern States was generally ignored in the congressional debates. Even in the North, the conditions of public education did not approximate those existing today. The curriculum was usually rudimentary; ungraded schools were common in rural areas; the school term was but three months a year in many states; and compulsory school attendance was virtually unknown. As a consequence, it is not surprising that there should be so little in the history of the Fourteenth Amendment relating to its intended effect on public education. ***

In approaching this problem, we cannot turn the clock back to 1868 when the Amendment was adopted, or even to 1896 when *Plessy v. Ferguson* was written. We must consider public education in the light of its full development and its present place in American life throughout the Nation. Only in this way can it be determined if segregation in public schools deprives these plaintiffs of the equal protection of the laws.

"I'VE DECIDED I WANT MY SEAT BACK."

IX–1. "I've Decided I Want My Seat Back" by Bill Mauldin. Reprinted with special permission from the Chicago Sun–Times, Inc. © 2000.

Today, education is perhaps the most important function of state and local governments. Compulsory school attendance laws and the great expenditures for education both demonstrate our recognition of the importance of education to our democratic society. It is required in the performance of our most basic public responsibilities, even service in the armed forces. It is the very foundation of good citizenship. Today it is a principal instrument in awakening the child to cultural values, in preparing him for later professional training, and in helping him to adjust normally to his environment. In these days, it is doubtful that any child may reasonably be expected to succeed in life if he is denied the opportunity of an education. Such an opportunity, where the state has undertaken to provide it, is a right which must be made available to all on equal terms.

We come then to the question presented: Does segregation of children in public schools solely on the basis of race, even though the physical facilities and other "tangible" factors may be equal, deprive the children of the minority group of equal educational opportunities? We believe that it does.

In *Sweatt v. Painter*, 339 U.S. 629, in finding that a segregated law school for Negroes could not provide them equal educational opportunities, this Court relied in large part on "those qualities which are incapable of objective measurement but which make for greatness in a law school." In *McLaurin v. Oklahoma State Regents*, 339 U.S. 637, the Court, in requiring that a Negro admitted to a white graduate school be treated like all other students, again resorted to intangible considerations: " *** his ability to study, to engage in discussions and exchange views with other students, and, in general, to learn his profession." Such considerations apply with added force to children in grade and high schools. To separate them from others of similar age and qualifications solely because of their race generates a feeling of inferiority as to their status in the community that may affect their hearts and minds in a way unlikely ever to be undone. The effect of this separation on their educational opportunities was well stated by a finding in the Kansas case by a court which nevertheless felt compelled to rule against the Negro plaintiffs:

> "Segregation of white and colored children in public schools has a detrimental effect upon the colored children. The impact is greater when it has the sanction of the law; for the policy of separating the races is usually interpreted as denoting the inferiority of the negro group. A sense of inferiority affects the motivation of a child to learn. Segregation with the sanction of law, therefore, has a tendency to (retard) the educational and mental development of Negro children and to deprive them of some of the benefits they would receive in a racial(ly) integrated school system."

Whatever may have been the extent of psychological knowledge at the time of *Plessy v. Ferguson*, this finding is amply supported by modern authority. Any language in *Plessy v. Ferguson* contrary to this finding is rejected.

We conclude that in the field of public education the doctrine of "separate but equal" has no place. Separate educational facilities are inherently unequal. Therefore, we hold that the plaintiffs and others similarly situated for whom the actions have been brought are, by reason of the segregation complained of, deprived of the equal protection of the laws guaranteed by the Fourteenth Amendment. ***

Notes

1.   **Rationale of *Brown*.** While there is virtually no dissent to the correctness of *Brown* as a matter of constitutional interpretation, there is substantial criticism of the Court's approach. Rather than returning to the language and original intent of the Fourteenth Amendment, the Court relied heavily on social science research and testimony presented to the lower courts, much of which was methodologically weak. Moreover, the Court's focus on how segregation "generates a feeling of inferiority" among blacks did not address the broader issue: how segregation disserved blacks and whites alike by dividing the citizenry into two racial groups with minimal opportunities for interchange and understanding between them.

2.   **Education to Trains.** Technically, the Court's decision dealt only with state-sponsored educational segregation; soon thereafter, however, the Court proceeded to grant certiorari on numerous cases involving other components of Jim Crow laws in the South and to summarily reverse or affirm decisions of the lower courts, citing *Brown*. Should the Court have articulated why it was extending *Brown*?

3.   **Remedies.** The Court held over for the following term the issue of the appropriate remedy for segregation. When it issued its decision in *Brown II*, it ambiguously required desegregation with "all deliberate speed." This was not very speedy in a South committed to a strategy of "massive resistance" to desegregation. Despite heroic efforts by the Fifth Circuit Court of Appeals (spanning the South from Texas to Georgia and Florida) to enforce *Brown*, it was not until the political branches of the government put their resources behind desegregation following the Civil Rights Act of 1964 that substantial changes in levels of segregation began to occur in southern public schools. Should one conclude that the Court was the catalyst for desegregation or that it was really powerless to act without the assistance of the rest of the Federal Government?

4.   **Other Issues Related to *Brown*.**

(a) <u>Desegregation or Integration?</u> In *Swann v. Charlotte–Mecklenburg Board of Education*, 402 U.S. 1 (1971), the Court said the "nature of the [constitutional] violation determines the scope of the remedy." It noted that, in light of the history of state-enforced segregation, it would apply "a presumption against schools that are substantially disproportionate in their racial composition." The Court upheld "sometimes drastic" remedies including pairing and clustering of schools, creation of noncontiguous school zones, and bussing of students to nonneighborhood schools. The Court did note that, at some point, when the school officials had achieved "full compliance" in creating a "unitary" school district, "further intervention by a district court should not be necessary."

(b) <u>De Facto Segregation</u>. In *Keyes v. School District No. 1, Denver, Colo.*, 413 U.S. 189 (1973), the State had never mandated segregation but the Denver School Board had gerrymandered the Park Hill section of the city to avoid racial integration. The Court permitted a Denver-wide remedy for this violation. Conversely, in *Milliken v. Bradley*, 418 U.S. 717 (1974), the Court held that federal courts lacked the power to impose interdistrict remedies for school segregation absent an interdistrict violation or interdistrict effects. The remedy was limited to the Detroit School System despite the involvement of the State of Michigan and state agencies in segregation of Detroit schools. Recently, in *Missouri v. Jenkins*, 515 U.S. 70 (1995), the Court stressed that *intra*district violations should not lead to *inter*district remedies (here attempts to attract white students into a core school system which was predominantly black). JUSTICE THOMAS' concurrence blasted the willingness of the courts "to assume that anything that is predominantly black must be inferior." He then pointed out "two threads" of dysfunctional Supreme Court jurisprudence: (1) its theory of "unspecified psychological harm" to blacks from segregation based on "questionable social science research" and "an assumption of black inferiority" and (2) its willingness to give "virtually unlimited equitable powers" to the courts, "trampl[ing] on principles of federalism and the separation of powers," letting courts "pursue other agendas unrelated to the narrow purpose of precisely remedying a constitutional harm." Four Justices dissented, complaining that the Court had retreated from the "redress the harms" component of earlier decisions.

(c) <u>Ending Judicial Oversight.</u> *Freeman v. Pitts*, 503 U.S. 467 (1992), held that courts can "relinquish supervision and control of school districts in incremental stages, before full compliance has been achieved in every area of school operations." In the Court's opinion, racial imbalance in the DeKalb County, Georgia school system was the result not of segregation but of "demographic factors not traceable to the initial violation." The dissent argued for continuing judicial oversight due to lack of a "proper unitary status record" including examination of test scores to see if the school system had "cured a deficiency in student achievement to the extent practicable."

2. INVIDIOUS RACE DISCRIMINATION

Outside the "separate but equal" context, how does the Equal Protection Clause deal with race discrimination? Are racial distinctions made by government always unconstitutional? Or are some racial distinctions permissible when the government's reasons for the distinction are strong or remedial? Does the prohibition apply even when the race discrimination does not fit the "black-white paradigm" stemming from slavery of African–Americans? When the discriminating entity is the federal government rather than state or local government? When all races are identically affected by a statute which draws a racial line? When a statute is facially neutral regarding race but has a disproportionate effect on one race? These are some of the questions addressed by the cases in the following sections.

STRAUDER v. WEST VIRGINIA
100 U.S. (10 Otto) 303, 25 L.Ed. 664 (1879).

MR. JUSTICE STRONG delivered the opinion of the court.

The plaintiff in error, a colored man, was indicted for murder in the Circuit Court of Ohio County, in West Virginia, on the 20th of October, 1874, and upon trial was convicted and sentenced. *** [I]t is now, in substance, averred that at the trial in the State court the defendant (now plaintiff in error) was denied rights to which he was entitled under the Constitution and laws of the United States. *** [Plaintiff argued that, by] virtue of the laws of the State of West Virginia no colored man was eligible to be a member of the grand jury or to serve on a petit jury in the State; that white men are so eligible, and that by reason of his being a colored man and having been a slave, he had reason to believe, and did believe, he could not have the full and equal benefit of all laws and proceedings in the State of West Virginia for the security of his person as is enjoyed by white citizens, and that he had less chance of enforcing in the courts of the State his rights on the prosecution, as a citizen of the United States, and that the probabilities of a denial of them to him as such citizen on every trial which might take place on the indictment in the courts of the State were much more enhanced than if he was a white man. *** [The question] is not whether a colored man, when an indictment has been preferred against him, has a right to a grand or a petit jury composed in whole or in part of persons of his own race or color, but it is whether, in the composition or selection of jurors by whom he is to be indicted or tried, all persons of his race or color may be excluded by law, solely because of their race or color, so that by no possibility can any colored man sit upon the jury. ***

[The Fourteenth Amendment] is one of a series of constitutional provisions having a common purpose; namely, securing to a race recently emancipated, a race that through many generations had been held in slavery, all the civil rights that the superior race enjoy. The true spirit and meaning of the amendments, as we said in the *Slaughter-House Cases*, cannot be understood without keeping in view the history of the times when they were adopted, and the general objects they plainly sought to accomplish. At the time when they were incorporated into the Constitution, it required little knowledge of human nature to anticipate that those who had long been regarded as an inferior and subject race would, when suddenly raised to the rank of citizenship, be looked upon with jealousy and positive dislike, and that State laws might be enacted or enforced to perpetuate the distinctions that had before existed. Discriminations against them had been habitual. It was well known that in some States laws making such discriminations then existed, and others might well be expected. The colored race, as a race, was abject and ignorant, and in that condition was unfitted to command the respect of those who had superior intelligence. Their training had left them mere children, and as such they needed the protection which a wise government extends to those who are unable to protect themselves. They especially needed protection against unfriendly action in the States where they were resident. It was in view of these considerations the Fourteenth Amendment was framed and adopted. It was designed to assure to the colored race the enjoyment of all the civil rights that under the law are enjoyed by white persons, and to give to that race the protection of the general government, in that enjoyment, whenever it should be denied by the

States. It not only gave citizenship and the privileges of citizenship to persons of color, but it denied to any State the power to withhold from them the equal protection of the laws, and authorized Congress to enforce its provisions by appropriate legislation. ***

What is this but declaring that the law in the States shall be the same for the black as for the white; that all persons, whether colored or white, shall stand equal before the laws of the States, and, in regard to the colored race, for whose protection the amendment was primarily designed, that no discrimination shall be made against them by law because of their color? The words of the amendment, it is true, are prohibitory, but they contain a necessary implication of a positive immunity, or right, most valuable to the colored race—the right to exemption from unfriendly legislation against them distinctively as colored—exemption from legal discriminations, implying inferiority in civil society, lessening the security of their enjoyment of the rights which others enjoy, and discriminations which are steps towards reducing them to the condition of a subject race.

That the West Virginia statute respecting juries—the statute that controlled the selection of the grand and petit jury in the case of the plaintiff in error—is such a discrimination ought not to be doubted. *** The very fact that colored people are singled out and expressly denied by a statute all right to participate in the administration of the law, as jurors, because of their color, though they are citizens, and may be in other respects fully qualified, is practically a brand upon them, affixed by the law, an assertion of their inferiority, and a stimulant to that race prejudice which is an impediment to securing to individuals of the race that equal justice which the law aims to secure to all others. *** It is well known that prejudices often exist against particular classes in the community, which sway the judgment of jurors, and which, therefore, operate in some cases to deny to persons of those classes the full enjoyment of that protection which others enjoy. ***

In view of these considerations, it is hard to see why the statute of West Virginia should not be regarded as discriminating against a colored man when he is put upon trial for an alleged criminal offense against the State. It is not easy to comprehend how it can be said that while every white man is entitled to a trial by a jury selected from persons of his own race or color, or, rather, selected without discrimination against his color, and a negro is not, the latter is equally protected by the law with the former. *** We do not say that within the limits from which it is not excluded by the amendment a State may not prescribe the qualifications of its jurors, and in so doing make discriminations. It may confine the selection to males, to freeholders, to citizens, to persons within certain ages, or to persons having educational qualifications. We do not believe the Fourteenth Amendment was ever intended to prohibit this. Looking at its history, it is clear it had no such purpose. Its aim was against discrimination because of race or color. ***

MR. JUSTICE FIELD and MR. JUSTICE CLIFFORD dissenting. [omitted]

YICK WO v. HOPKINS
118 U.S. 356, 6 S.Ct. 1064, 30 L.Ed. 220 (1886).

MATTHEWS, J.

*** [T]he supreme court of California *** considered these ordinances ["It shall be unlawful, from and after the passage of this order, for any person or persons to establish, maintain, or carry on a laundry, within the corporate limits of the city and county of San Francisco, without having first obtained the consent of the board of supervisors, except the same be located in a building constructed either of brick or stone,"] as vesting in the board of supervisors a not unusual discretion in granting or withholding their assent to the use of wooden buildings as laundries, to be exercised in reference to the circumstances of each case, with a view to the protection of the public against the dangers of fire. We are not able to concur in that interpretation of the power conferred upon the supervisors. There is nothing in the ordinances which points to such a regulation of the business of keeping and conducting laundries. They seem intended to confer, and actually to confer, not a discretion to be exercised upon a consideration of the circumstances of each case, but a naked and arbitrary power to give or withhold consent, not only as to places, but as to persons; so that, if an applicant for such consent, being in every way a competent and qualified person, and having complied with every reasonable condition demanded by any public interest, should, failing to obtain the requisite consent of the supervisors to the prosecution of his business, apply for redress by the judicial process of mandamus to require the supervisors to consider and act upon his case, it would be a sufficient answer for them to say that the law had conferred upon them authority to withhold their assent, without reason and without responsibility. The power given to them is not confided to their discretion in the legal sense of that term, but is granted to their mere will. It is purely arbitrary, and acknowledges neither guidance nor restraint. ***

The rights of the petitioners, as affected by the proceedings of which they complain, are not less because they are aliens and subjects of the emperor of China. *** The fourteenth amendment to the constitution is not confined to the protection of citizens. It says: "Nor shall any state deprive any person of life, liberty, or property without due process of law; nor deny to any person within its jurisdiction the equal protection of the laws." These provisions are universal in their application, to all persons within the territorial jurisdiction, without regard to any differences of race, of color, or of nationality; and the equal protection of the laws is a pledge of the protection of equal laws. ***

In the present cases, we are not obliged to reason from the probable to the actual, and pass upon the validity of the ordinances complained of, as tried merely by the opportunities which their terms afford, of unequal and unjust discrimination in their administration; for the cases present the ordinances in actual operation, and the facts shown establish an administration directed so exclusively against a particular class of persons as to warrant and require the conclusion that, whatever may have been the intent of the ordinances as adopted, they are applied by the public authorities charged with their administration, and thus representing the state itself, with a mind so unequal and oppressive as to amount to a practical denial by the state of that equal protection of the laws which is secured to the petitioners, as to all other persons, by the broad and benign provisions of the fourteenth amendment to the constitution of the United States. Though the law itself be fair on its face, and impartial in appearance, yet, if it is applied and administered by public authority with an evil eye and an unequal hand, so as practically to make unjust and illegal discriminations between persons in similar circumstances, material to their rights, the denial of equal justice is still within the prohibition of the constitution. ***

The present cases, as shown by the facts disclosed in the record, are within this class. It appears that both petitioners have complied with every requisite deemed by the law, or by the public officers charged with its administration, necessary for the protection of neighboring property from fire, or as a precaution against injury to the public health. No reason whatever, except the will of the supervisors, is assigned why they should not be permitted to carry on, in the accustomed manner, their harmless and useful occupation, on which they depend for a livelihood; and while this consent of the supervisors is withheld from them, and from 200 others who have also petitioned, all of whom happen to be Chinese subjects, 80 others, not Chinese subjects, are permitted to carry on the same business under similar conditions. The fact of this discrimination is admitted. No reason for it is shown, and the conclusion cannot be resisted that no reason for it exists except hostility to the race and nationality to which the petitioners belong, and which, in the eye of the law, is not justified. The discrimination is therefore illegal, and the public administration which enforces it is a denial of the equal protection of the laws, and a violation of the fourteenth amendment of the constitution. The imprisonment of the petitioners is therefore illegal, and they must be discharged. ***

KOREMATSU v. UNITED STATES
323 U.S. 214, 65 S.Ct. 193, 89 L.Ed. 194 (1944).

MR. JUSTICE BLACK delivered the opinion of the Court.

*** [An] Act of Congress of March 21, 1942 *** provides that " *** whoever shall enter, remain in, leave, or commit any act in any military area or military zone prescribed, under the authority of an Executive order of the President, *** by any military commander designated by the Secretary of War, contrary to *** the order of *** any such military commander, shall *** be guilty of a misdemeanor and upon conviction shall be liable to a fine of not to exceed $5,000 or to imprisonment for not more than one year, or both, for each offense."

Exclusion Order No. 34 *** was one of a number of military orders and proclamations, all of which were substantially based upon Executive Order No. 9066 ***. That order, issued after we were at war with Japan, declared that "the successful prosecution of the war requires every possible protection against espionage and against sabotage to national-defense material, national-defense premises, and national-defense utilities ***." [Persons of

Japanese descent, whether they were United States citizens, were forced to leave their homes and move to Relocation Centers. Petitioner "knowingly and willfully violated" the order.]

One of the series of orders and proclamations, a curfew order, which like the exclusion order here was promulgated pursuant to Executive Order 9066, subjected all persons of Japanese ancestry in prescribed West Coast military areas to remain in their residences from 8 p.m. to 6 a.m. [That order's constitutionality was upheld by the Court in a companion case, *Hirabayashi v. United States*, 320 U.S. 81 (1943).]

It should be noted, to begin with, that all legal restrictions which curtail the civil rights of a single racial group are immediately suspect. That is not to say that all such restrictions are unconstitutional. It is to say that courts must subject them to the most rigid scrutiny. Pressing public necessity may sometimes justify the existence of such restrictions; racial antagonism never can. ***

In the light of the principles we announced in the *Hirabayashi* case, we are unable to conclude that it was beyond the war power of Congress and the Executive to exclude those of Japanese ancestry from the West Coast war area at the time they did. True, exclusion from the area in which one's home is located is a far greater deprivation than constant confinement to the home from 8 p.m. to 6 a.m. Nothing short of apprehension by the proper military authorities of the gravest imminent danger to the public safety can constitutionally justify either. But exclusion from a threatened area, no less than curfew, has a definite and close relationship to the prevention of espionage and sabotage. The military authorities, charged with the primary responsibility of defending our shores, concluded that curfew provided inadequate protection and ordered exclusion. *** Here, as in the *Hirabayashi* case,

> " *** [W]e cannot reject as unfounded the judgment of the military authorities and of Congress that there were disloyal members of that population, whose number and strength could not be precisely and quickly ascertained. We cannot say that the war-making branches of the Government did not have ground for believing that in a critical hour such persons could not readily be isolated and separately dealt with, and constituted a menace to the national defense and safety, which demanded that prompt and adequate measures be taken to guard against it."

Like curfew, exclusion of those of Japanese origin was deemed necessary because of the presence of an unascertained number of disloyal members of the group, most of whom we have no doubt were loyal to this country. It was because we could not reject the finding of the military authorities that it was impossible to bring about an immediate segregation of the disloyal from the loyal that we sustained the validity of the curfew order as applying to the whole group. In the instant case, temporary exclusion of the entire group was rested by the military on the same ground. The judgment that exclusion of the whole group was for the same reason a military imperative answers the contention that the exclusion was in the nature of group punishment based on antagonism to those of Japanese origin. That there were members of the group who retained loyalties to Japan has been confirmed by investigations made subsequent to the exclusion. Approximately five thousand American citizens of Japanese ancestry refused to swear unqualified allegiance to the United States and to renounce allegiance to the Japanese Emperor, and several thousand evacuees requested repatriation to Japan.

We uphold the exclusion order as of the time it was made and when the petitioner violated it. In doing so, we are not unmindful of the hardships imposed by it upon a large group of American citizens. But hardships are part of war, and war is an aggregation of hardships. All citizens alike, both in and out of uniform, feel the impact of war in greater or lesser measure. Citizenship has its responsibilities as well as its privileges, and in time of war the burden is always heavier. Compulsory exclusion of large groups of citizens from their homes, except under circumstances of direst emergency and peril, is inconsistent with our basic governmental institutions. But when under conditions of modern warfare our shores are threatened by hostile forces, the power to protect must be commensurate with the threatened danger. ***

IX–2. Barrack homes at Manzanar relocation camp. Photograph by Dorothea Lange, volume 78 Section C WRA no. 838, *War Relocation Authority Photographs of Japanese–American Evacuation and Resettlement,* BANC PIC 1967.014—PIC, The Bancroft Library, University of California, Berkeley.

It is said that we are dealing here with the case of imprisonment of a citizen in a concentration camp solely because of his ancestry, without evidence or inquiry concerning his loyalty and good disposition towards the United States. Our task would be simple, our duty clear, were this a case involving the imprisonment of a loyal citizen in a concentration camp because of racial prejudice. Regardless of the true nature of the assembly and relocation centers—and we deem it unjustifiable to call them concentration camps with all the ugly connotations that term implies—we are dealing specifically with nothing but an exclusion order. To cast this case into outlines of racial prejudice, without reference to the real military dangers which were presented, merely confuses the issue. Korematsu was not excluded from the Military Area because of hostility to him or his race. He was excluded because we are at war with the Japanese Empire, because the properly constituted military authorities feared an invasion of our West Coast and felt constrained to take proper security measures, because they decided that the military urgency of the situation demanded that all citizens of Japanese ancestry be segregated from the West Coast temporarily, and finally, because Congress, reposing its confidence in this time of war in our military leaders—as inevitably it must—determined that they should have the power to do just this. There was evidence of disloyalty on the part of some, the military authorities considered that the need for action was great, and time was short. We cannot—by availing ourselves of the calm perspective of hindsight—now say that at that time these actions were unjustified.

MR. JUSTICE FRANKFURTER, concurring. [omitted]

MR. JUSTICE ROBERTS, dissenting. [omitted]

MR. JUSTICE MURPHY, dissenting.

This exclusion of "all persons of Japanese ancestry, both alien and non-alien," from the Pacific Coast area on a plea of military necessity in the absence of martial law ought not to be approved. Such exclusion goes over "the very brink of constitutional power" and falls into the ugly abyss of racism.

In dealing with matters relating to the prosecution and progress of a war, we must accord great respect and consideration to the judgments of the military authorities who are on the scene and who have full knowledge of the military facts. The scope of their discretion must, as a matter of necessity and common sense, be wide. And their judgments ought not to be overruled lightly by those whose training and duties ill-equip them to deal intelligently with matters so vital to the physical security of the nation.

At the same time, however, it is essential that there be definite limits to military discretion, especially where martial law has not been declared. Individuals must not be left impoverished of their constitutional rights on a plea of military necessity that has neither substance nor support. Thus, like other claims conflicting with the asserted constitutional rights of the individual, the military claim must subject itself to the judicial process of having its reasonableness determined and its conflicts with other interests reconciled. ***

It must be conceded that the military and naval situation in the spring of 1942 was such as to generate a very real fear of invasion of the Pacific Coast, accompanied by fears of sabotage and espionage in that area. The military command was therefore justified in adopting all reasonable means necessary to combat these dangers. In adjudging the military action taken in light of the then apparent dangers, we must not erect too high or too meticulous standards; it is necessary only that the action have some reasonable relation to the removal of the dangers of invasion, sabotage and espionage. But the exclusion, either temporarily or permanently, of all persons with Japanese blood in their veins has no such reasonable relation. And that relation is lacking because the exclusion order necessarily must rely for its reasonableness upon the assumption that all persons of Japanese ancestry may have a dangerous tendency to commit sabotage and espionage and to aid our Japanese enemy in other ways. It is difficult to believe that reason, logic or experience could be marshalled in support of such an assumption. ***

The main reasons relied upon by those responsible for the forced evacuation, therefore, do not prove a reasonable relation between the group characteristics of Japanese Americans and the dangers of invasion, sabotage and espionage. The reasons appear, instead, to be largely an accumulation of much of the misinformation, half-truths and insinuations that for years have been directed against Japanese Americans by people with racial and economic prejudices—the same people who have been among the foremost advocates of the evacuation. A military judgment based upon such racial and sociological considerations is not entitled to the great weight ordinarily given the judgments based upon strictly military considerations. Especially is this so when every charge relative to race, religion, culture, geographical location, and legal and economic status has been substantially discredited by independent studies made by experts in these matters. ***

No one denies, of course, that there were some disloyal persons of Japanese descent on the Pacific Coast who did all in their power to aid their ancestral land. Similar disloyal activities have been engaged in by many persons of German, Italian and even more pioneer stock in our country. But to infer that examples of individual disloyalty prove group disloyalty and justify discriminatory action against the entire group is to deny that under our system of law individual guilt is the sole basis for deprivation of rights. ***

MR. JUSTICE JACKSON, dissenting.

*** It would be impracticable and dangerous idealism to expect or insist that each specific military command in an area of probable operations will conform to conventional tests of constitutionality. When an area is so beset that it must be put under military control at all, the paramount consideration is that its measures be successful, rather than legal. *** But if we cannot confine military expedients by the Constitution, neither would I distort the Constitution to approve all that the military may deem expedient. This is what the Court appears to be doing, whether consciously or not. *** The limitation under which courts always will labor in examining the necessity for a military order are illustrated by this case. How does the Court know that these orders have a reasonable basis in necessity? No evidence whatever on that subject has been taken by this or any other court. ***

Much is said of the danger to liberty from the Army program for deporting and detaining these citizens of Japanese extraction. But a judicial construction of the due process clause that will sustain this order is a far more subtle blow to liberty than the promulgation of the order itself. A military order, however unconstitutional, is not apt to last longer than the military emergency. Even during that period a succeeding commander may revoke it all. But once a judicial opinion rationalizes such an order to show that it conforms to the Constitution, or rather rationalizes the Constitution to show that the Constitution sanctions such an order, the Court for all time has validated the principle of racial discrimination in criminal procedure and of transplanting American citizens. The principle then lies about like a loaded weapon ready for the hand of any authority that can bring forward a plausible claim of an urgent need. Every repetition imbeds that principle more deeply in our law and thinking and expands it to new purposes. ***

I should hold that a civil court cannot be made to enforce an order which violates constitutional limitations even if it is a reasonable exercise of military authority. The courts can exercise only the judicial power, can apply only law, and must abide by the Constitution, or they cease to be civil courts and become instruments of military policy.

Of course the existence of a military power resting on force, so vagrant, so centralized, so necessarily heedless of the individual, is an inherent threat to liberty. But I would not lead people to rely on this Court for a review that seems to me wholly delusive. The military reasonableness of these orders can only be determined by military superiors. If the people ever let command of the war power fall into irresponsible and unscrupulous hands, the courts wield no power equal to its restraint. The chief restraint upon those who command the physical forces of the country, in the future as in the past, must be their responsibility to the political judgments of their contemporaries and to the moral judgments of history.

My duties as a justice as I see them do not require me to make a military judgment as to whether General DeWitt's evacuation and detention program was a reasonable military necessity. I do not suggest that the courts should have attempted to interfere with the Army in carrying out its task. But I do not think they may be asked to execute a military expedient that has no place in law under the Constitution. I would reverse the judgment and discharge the prisoner.

Notes

1. **What is "Race"?** The Fourteenth Amendment's origins in the enslavement of African Americans makes it pretty clear why *Strauder* is a race case. Why are *Yick Wo* and *Korematsu*, which involved Asian immigrant groups, treated as race cases rather than "national origin" cases? CHIEF JUSTICE WARREN's opinion in *Hernandez v. Texas*, 347 U.S. 475 (1954), holds that the state can't exclude persons of Mexican descent from juries, but avoids calling the discrimination

"racial" or using the strict scrutiny model. The Court said that "the Fourteenth Amendment is not directed solely against discrimination due to a 'two-class theory'—that is, based upon differences between 'white' and Negro. *** The petitioner's initial burden in substantiating his charge of group discrimination was to prove that persons of Mexican descent constitute a separate class in Jackson County, distinct from 'whites.'" What do you make of this last comment? Consider further whether a statute discriminating against Native American Indians would be subject to strict scrutiny under the Equal Protection Clause. *See Morton v. Mancari*, 417 U.S. 535 (1974) (hiring preferences for Indians "does not constitute 'racial discrimination' ***. Here, where the preference is reasonable and rationally designed to further Indian self-government, we cannot say that Congress' classification violates due process."). Is there special constitutional treatment of Native American Indians that makes them different (for constitutional purposes) from other racial groups? Are religious groups (e.g. Jews or Muslims) racial for equal protection purposes? *See Shaare Tefila Congregation v. Cobb*, 481 U.S. 615 (1987), and *Saint Francis College v. Al-Khazraji*, 481 U.S. 604 (1987) (yes; authors of 1866 and 1870 civil rights acts believed them to be distinct races; "Congress intended to protect from discrimination identifiable classes of persons who are subjected to intentional discrimination solely because of their ancestry or ethnic characteristics *** whether or not it would be characterized as racial in terms of modern scientific theory.").

2. **Questions about *Strauder, Yick Wo*, and *Korematsu*.**

(a) *Strauder*. Is it fair to say that the Court finds a per se violation of the Fourteenth Amendment? What is the violation and how does Strauder get standing to litigate that violation? Would the historical approach of this case have provided an alternative rationale for *Brown*?

(b) *Yick Wo*. Is there an argument that the ordinance is unconstitutional on its face from a clause in the Constitution other than the Equal Protection Clause? Would the remedy differ if the case had been decided under the other clause? Is there any problem with the Court inferring invidious motives to laws like this one? How do you prove such a motive if you are Yick Wo's lawyer?

(c) *Korematsu*. Do you agree with the *Korematsu* majority or dissenters? Do the dissenters disagree as a matter of principle or application? Would this case have been a good precedent for the Court (or advocates) to cite in *Brown*?

3. **Theory.** Do these cases stand for the principle that race should not be taken into account by government? Do they speak to the question whether and to what extent the state may seek to rectify past discrimination (or "racial subordination")?

4. **Federal Equal Protection.** Despite "reverse incorporation," applying the Equal Protection component of the Fourteenth Amendment to the federal government through the Fifth Amendment's due process guarantee, *Korematsu* may be an application of the Court's observation that, "Not only does the language of the two amendments differ, but more importantly, there may be overriding national interests which justify federal legislation that would be unacceptable for an individual state [unless the federal law is only applicable to DC or another

limited territory]." *Hampton v. Mow Sun Wong*, 426 U.S. 88 (1976). For a more recent extended treatment of this topic, see *Adarand v. Pena*, infra p. 720.

5. **Immigration.** Despite *Yick Wo's* invocation of equal protection for persons, not just citizens, immigration may be an exception to normal equal protection principles on the basis that "the power of Congress over the admission of aliens to this country is absolute." *See The Chinese Exclusion Case*, 130 U.S. 581 (1889) (resident aliens returning from overseas visits could be excluded based on race) and *Fong Yue Ting v. United States*, 149 U.S. 698 (1893) (resident aliens may be deported if Congress concluded their race was undesirable). These decisions have been followed by the lower courts in recent years. *See Achacoso–Sanchez v. INS*, 779 F.2d 1260 (7th Cir. 1985) ("Congress has the power to make distinctions on account of race" in immigration context). Recent academic commentary argues that these cases should be overruled.

6. **Legislative Apportionment.** Is race discrimination more permissible when legislative districts are drawn which take account of race as well as other demographic and geographic factors? *See Miller v. Johnson*, 515 U.S. 900 (1995) (plaintiff in redistricting case must show "race was the predominant factor" by proving "the legislature subordinated traditional race-neutral districting principles"); *Bush v. Vera*, 517 U.S. 952 (1996) ("redistricting legislation that is so extremely irregular on its face that it rationally can be viewed only as an effort to segregate the races for purposes of voting" states an Equal Protection claim); and *Hunt v. Cromartie*, 526 U.S. 541 (1999) (political gerrymandering is permissible; "high correlation between race and party preference" does not suffice, without more, to demonstrate impermissible racial districting).

7. **Role of the Courts.** *Korematsu*, like *Dred Scott*, *Plessy*, and *Lochner*, is generally viewed as a low point of the Supreme Court's interpretation of the Constitution. Like *Ex parte McCardle* and *Ex parte Quirin*, supra, it may demonstrate the Court's reluctance to overrule the unified efforts of both the President and Congress on *constitutional* grounds during wartime. But the Court has been less reluctant to rule against military actions during war on *nonconstitutional* grounds. *Ex parte Endo*, 323 U.S. 283 (1944), announced the same day as *Korematsu*, illustrates the point. *Endo* unanimously invalidated the internment of Japanese-Americans as unsupported by the statute and order (held constitutional in *Korematsu*) that excluded them from the West Coast. Why would *Korematsu* be remembered so vividly and *Endo* forgotten almost entirely? *See* Patrick O. Gudridge, *Remember Endo?*, 116 HARV. L. REV. 1933 (2003).

LOVING v. VIRGINIA
388 U.S. 1, 87 S.Ct. 1817, 18 L.Ed.2d 1010 (1967).

MR. CHIEF JUSTICE WARREN delivered the opinion of the Court.

This case presents a constitutional question never addressed by this Court: whether a statutory scheme adopted by the State of Virginia to prevent marriages between persons solely on the basis of racial classifications violates the Equal Protection and Due Process Clauses of the Fourteenth Amendment. For reasons which seem to us to reflect the central meaning of those constitutional commands, we conclude that these statutes cannot stand consistently with the Fourteenth Amendment.

In June 1958, two residents of Virginia, Mildred Jeter, a Negro woman, and Richard Loving, a white man, were married in the District of Columbia pursuant to its laws. Shortly after their marriage, the Lovings returned to Virginia and *** a grand jury issued an indictment charging the Lovings with violating Virginia's ban on interracial marriages. On January 6, 1959, the Lovings pleaded guilty to the charge and were sentenced to one year in jail; however, the trial judge suspended the sentence for a period of 25 years on the condition that the Lovings leave the State and not return to Virginia together for 25 years. He stated in an opinion that: "Almighty God created the races white, black, yellow, malay and red, and he placed them on separate continents. And but for the interference with his arrangement there would be no cause for such marriages. The fact that he separated the races shows that he did not intend for the races to mix."

After their convictions, the Lovings took up residence in the District of Columbia. On *** October 28, 1964, the Lovings instituted a class action in the United States District Court for the Eastern District of Virginia requesting that a three-judge court be convened to declare the Virginia antimiscegenation statutes unconstitutional and to enjoin state officials from enforcing their convictions. *** [The] three-judge District Court continued the case to allow the Lovings to present their constitutional claims to the highest state court.

The Supreme Court of Appeals [of Virginia] upheld the constitutionality of the antimiscegenation statutes and *** affirmed the convictions. *** [The section of the Virginia Code,] which defines the penalty for miscegenation, provides:

"Punishment for marriage.—If any white person intermarry with a colored person, or any colored person intermarry with a white person, he shall be guilty of a felony and shall be punished by confinement in the penitentiary for not less than one nor more than five years. *** "

Virginia is now one of 16 States which prohibit and punish marriages on the basis of racial classifications. Penalties for miscegenation arose as an incident to slavery and have been common in Virginia since the colonial period. The present statutory scheme dates from the adoption of the Racial Integrity Act of 1924, passed during the period of extreme nativism which followed the end of the First World War. The central features of this Act, and current Virginia law, are the absolute prohibition of a "white person" marrying other than another "white person," a prohibition against issuing marriage licenses until the issuing official is satisfied that the applicants' statements as to their race are correct, certificates of "racial composition" to be kept by both local and state registrars, and the carrying forward of earlier prohibitions against racial intermarriage.

*** While the state court is no doubt correct in asserting that marriage is a social relation subject to the State's police power, *Maynard v. Hill*, 125 U.S. 190 (1888), the State does not contend in its argument before this Court that its powers to regulate marriage are unlimited notwithstanding the commands of the Fourteenth Amendment. *** Instead, the State argues that the meaning of the Equal Protection Clause, as illuminated by the statements of the Framers, is only that state penal laws containing an interracial element as part of the definition of the offense must apply equally to whites and Negroes in the sense that members of each race are punished to the same degree. Thus, the State contends that, because its miscegenation statutes punish equally both the white and the Negro participants in an interracial marriage, these statutes, despite their reliance on racial classifications do not constitute an invidious discrimination based upon race. ***

Because we reject the notion that the mere "equal application" of a statute containing racial classifications is enough to remove the classifications from the Fourteenth Amendment's proscription of all invidious racial discriminations, we do not accept the State's contention that these statutes should be upheld if there is any possible basis for concluding that they serve a rational purpose. The mere fact of equal application does not mean that our analysis of these statutes should follow the approach we have taken in cases involving no racial discrimination where the Equal Protection Clause has been arrayed against a statute discriminating between the kinds of advertising which may be displayed on trucks in New York City, *Railway Express Agency, Inc. v. People of State of New York*, 336 U.S. 106 (1949), or an exemption in Ohio's ad valorem tax for merchandise owned by a non-resident in a storage warehouse, *Allied Stores of Ohio, Inc. v. Bowers*, 358 U.S. 522 (1959). In these cases, involving distinctions not drawn according to race, the Court has merely asked whether there is any rational foundation for the discriminations, and has deferred to the wisdom of the state legislatures. In the case at bar, however, we deal with statutes containing racial classifications, and the fact of equal application does not immunize the statute from the very heavy burden of justification which the Fourteenth Amendment has traditionally required of state statutes drawn according to race ***.

There can be no question but that Virginia's miscegenation statutes rest solely upon distinctions drawn according to race. The statutes proscribe generally accepted conduct if engaged in by members of different races. Over the years, this Court has consistently repudiated "(d)istinctions between citizens solely because of their ancestry" as being "odious to a free people whose institutions are founded upon the doctrine of equality." *Hirabayashi v. United States*, 320 U.S. 81 (1943). At the very least, the Equal Protection Clause demands that racial classifications, especially suspect in criminal statutes, be subjected to the "most rigid scrutiny," *Korematsu v. United States*, 323 U.S. 214, 216 (1944), and, if they are ever to be upheld, they must be shown to be necessary to the accomplishment of some permissible state objective, independent of the racial discrimination which it was the object of the Fourteenth Amendment to eliminate. ***

There is patently no legitimate overriding purpose independent of invidious racial discrimination which justifies this classification. The fact that Virginia prohibits only interracial marriages involving white persons demonstrates that the racial classifications must stand on their own justification, as measures designed to maintain White Supremacy.[11] We have consistently denied the constitutionality of measures which restrict the rights of citizens on account of race. There can be no doubt that restricting the freedom to marry solely because of racial classifications violates the central meaning of the Equal Protection Clause. ***

MR. JUSTICE STEWART, concurring.

I have previously expressed the belief that "it is simply not possible for a state law to be valid under our Constitution which makes the criminality of an act depend upon the race of the actor." *McLaughlin v. State of Florida*, 379 U.S. 184, 198 (concurring opinion). Because I adhere to that belief, I concur in the judgment of the Court.

WASHINGTON v. DAVIS
426 U.S. 229, 96 S.Ct. 2040, 48 L.Ed.2d 597 (1976).

MR. JUSTICE WHITE delivered the opinion of the Court.

*** [Respondents argue] that the [District of Columbia Metropolitan Police] Department's recruiting procedures discriminated on the basis of race against black applicants by a series of practices including, but not limited to, a written personnel test which excluded a disproportionately high number of Negro applicants. *** [To] be accepted by the Department and to enter an intensive 17–week training program, the police recruit was required to satisfy certain physical and character standards, to be a high school graduate or its equivalent, and to receive a grade of at least 40 out of 80 on "Test 21," which is "an examination that is used generally throughout the federal service," which "was developed by the Civil Service Commission, not the Police Department," and which was "designed to test verbal ability, vocabulary, reading and comprehension." *** Respondents' evidence, the District Court said, warranted three conclusions: "(a) The number of black police officers, while substantial, is not proportionate to the population mix of the city. (b) A higher percentage of blacks fail the Test than whites. (c) The Test has not been validated to establish its reliability for measuring subsequent job performance." *** It was undisputed that the Department had systematically and affirmatively sought to enroll black officers many of whom passed the test but failed to report for duty. ***

The central purpose of the Equal Protection Clause of the Fourteenth Amendment is the prevention of official conduct discriminating on the basis of race. But our cases have not embraced the proposition that a law or other official act, without regard to whether it reflects a racially discriminatory

---

[11] Appellants point out that the State's concern in these statutes *** extends only to the integrity of the white race. While Virginia prohibits whites from marrying any nonwhite ([with] the exception for the descendants of Pocahontas), Negroes, Orientals, and any other racial class may intermarry without statutory interference. Appellants contend that this distinction renders [the] statutes arbitrary and unreasonable even assuming the constitutional validity of *** [a] purpose to preserve "racial integrity." We need not reach this contention because we find the racial classifications in these statutes repugnant to the Fourteenth Amendment, even assuming an even-handed state purpose to protect the "integrity" of all races.

purpose, is unconstitutional solely because it has a racially disproportionate impact.

Almost 100 years ago, *Strauder v. West Virginia* established that the exclusion of Negroes from grand and petit juries in criminal proceedings violated the Equal Protection Clause, but the fact that a particular jury or a series of juries does not statistically reflect the racial composition of the community does not in itself make out an invidious discrimination forbidden by the Clause. *** The rule is the same in other contexts. *Wright v. Rockefeller*, 376 U.S. 52 (1964), upheld a New York congressional apportionment statute against claims that district lines had been racially gerrymandered. The challenged districts were made up predominantly of whites or of minority races, and their boundaries were irregularly drawn. The challengers did not prevail because they failed to prove that [the] statute "was the product of a state contrivance to segregate on the basis of race or place of origin." ***

The school desegregation cases have also adhered to the basic equal protection principle that the invidious quality of a law claimed to be racially discriminatory must ultimately be traced to a racially discriminatory purpose. That there are both predominantly black and predominantly white schools in a community is not alone violative of the Equal Protection Clause. The essential element of De jure segregation is "a current condition of segregation resulting from intentional state action." The Court has also recently rejected allegations of racial discrimination based solely on the statistically disproportionate racial impact of various provisions of the Social Security Act because "(t)he acceptance of appellants' constitutional theory would render suspect each difference in treatment among the grant classes, however lacking in racial motivation and however otherwise rational the treatment might be." *Jefferson v. Hackney*, 406 U.S. 535, 548 (1972).

This is not to say that the necessary discriminatory racial purpose must be express or appear on the face of the statute, or that a law's disproportionate impact is irrelevant in cases involving Constitution-based claims of racial discrimination. A statute, otherwise neutral on its face, must not be applied so as invidiously to discriminate on the basis of race. ***

Necessarily, an invidious discriminatory purpose may often be inferred from the totality of the relevant facts, including the fact, if it is true, that the law bears more heavily on one race than another. It is also not infrequently true that the discriminatory impact in the jury cases for example, the total or seriously disproportionate exclusion of Negroes from jury venires may for all practical purposes demonstrate unconstitutionality because in various circumstances the discrimination is very difficult to explain on nonracial grounds. Nevertheless, we have not held that a law, neutral on its face and serving ends otherwise within the power of government to pursue, is invalid under the Equal Protection Clause simply because it may affect a greater proportion of one race than of another. Disproportionate impact is not irrelevant, but it is not the sole touchstone of an invidious racial discrimination forbidden by the Constitution. Standing alone, it does not trigger the rule that racial classifications are to be subjected to the strictest scrutiny and are justifiable only by the weightiest of considerations.

*** [W]e have difficulty understanding how a law establishing a racially neutral qualification for employment is nevertheless racially discriminatory and denies "any person *** equal protection of the laws" simply because a greater proportion of Negroes fail to qualify than members of other racial or ethnic groups. Had respondents, along with all others who had failed [the test], whether white or black, brought an action claiming that [it] denied each of them equal protection of the laws as compared with those who had passed with high enough scores to qualify them as police recruits, it is most unlikely that their challenge would have been sustained. [The test], which is administered generally to prospective Government employees, concededly seeks to ascertain whether those who take it have acquired a particular level of verbal skill; and it is untenable that the Constitution prevents the Government from seeking modestly to upgrade the communicative abilities of its employees rather than to be satisfied with some lower level of competence, particularly where the job requires special ability to communicate orally and in writing. Respondents, as Negroes, could no more successfully claim that the test denied them equal protection than could white applicants who also failed. The conclusion would not be different in the face of proof that more Negroes than whites had been disqualified by [the test]. That other Negroes also failed to score well would, alone, not demonstrate that respondents individually were being denied equal protection of the laws by the application of an otherwise valid qualifying test being administered to prospective police recruits.

Nor on the facts of the case before us would the disproportionate impact of [the test] warrant the conclusion that it is a purposeful device to discriminate against Negroes and hence an infringement of the constitutional rights of respondents as well as other black applicants. As we have said, the test is neutral on its face and rationally may be said to serve a purpose the Government is constitutionally empowered to pursue. Even agreeing with the District Court that the differential racial effect of [the test] called for further inquiry, we think the District Court correctly held that the affirmative efforts of the Metropolitan Police Department to recruit black officers, the changing racial composition of the recruit classes and of the force in general, and the relationship of the test to the training program negated any inference that the Department discriminated on the basis of race or that "a police officer qualifies on the color of his skin rather than ability." ***

A rule that a statute designed to serve neutral ends is nevertheless invalid, absent compelling justification, if in practice it benefits or burdens one race more than another would be far-reaching and would raise serious questions about, and perhaps invalidate, a whole range of tax, welfare, public service, regulatory, and licensing statutes that may be more burdensome to the poor and to the average black than to the more affluent white. ***

MR. JUSTICE STEVENS, concurring.

*** The requirement of purposeful discrimination is a common thread running through the cases summarized in [the majority's opinion]. These cases include criminal convictions which were set aside because blacks were excluded from the grand jury, a reapportionment case in which political boundaries were obviously influenced to some extent by racial considerations, a school desegregation case, and a case involving the unequal administration of an ordinance purporting to prohibit the operation of laundries in frame buildings. Although it may be proper to use the same language to describe the constitutional claim in each of these contexts, the burden of proving a prima facie case may well involve differing evidentiary considerations. The extent of deference that one pays to the trial court's determination of the factual issue, and indeed, the extent to which one characterizes the intent issue as a question of fact or a question of law, will vary in different contexts.

Frequently the most probative evidence of intent will be objective evidence of what actually happened rather than evidence describing the subjective state of mind of the actor. For normally the actor is presumed to have intended the natural consequences of his deeds. This is particularly true in the case of governmental action which is frequently the product of compromise, of collective decisionmaking, and of mixed motivation. It is unrealistic, on the one hand, to require the victim of alleged discrimination to uncover the actual subjective intent of the decisionmaker or, conversely, to invalidate otherwise legitimate action simply because an improper motive affected the deliberation of a participant in the decisional process. A law conscripting clerics should not be invalidated because an atheist voted for it.

My point in making this observation is to suggest that the line between discriminatory purpose and discriminatory impact is not nearly as bright, and perhaps not quite as critical, as the reader of the Court's opinion might assume. I agree, of course, that a constitutional issue does not arise every time some disproportionate impact is shown. On the other hand, when the disproportion is dramatic, *** it really does not matter whether the standard is phrased in terms of purpose or effect. Therefore, although I accept the statement of the general rule in the Court's opinion, I am not yet prepared to indicate how that standard should be applied in the many cases which have formulated the governing standard in different language. ***

MR. JUSTICE BRENNAN, dissenting. [omitted]

Notes

1. **Alternative Theories in** *Loving*.

(a) Does *Loving* involve a racial classification? While race is used to classify permissible and impermissible marriages, the statute affects individuals of various races; it is not directed at one race the way the legislation was in *Strauder* and *Korematsu*. How, if at all, should this affect the Court's equal protection analysis?

(b) If "strict scrutiny" applies, does the State have a "compelling interest" in preventing interracial marriage? If *Loving* does not involve a racial classification, does the state have a "rational basis" for its ban on interracial marriage?

(c) Does the Court's decision in *Loving* necessarily follow from the *Brown* decision? Consider the fact that segregation imposes a rule on both white and black school children. Consider also whether there is a difference between the education and the marriage contexts of the cases.

(d) Should the Court have treated *Loving* as a due process case? There is some discussion of this issue by CHIEF JUSTICE WARREN in a part of the opinion not reproduced here: "These statutes also deprive the Lovings of liberty without due process of law ***. The freedom to marry has long been recognized as one of the vital personal rights essential to the orderly pursuit of happiness ***. To deny this fundamental freedom on so unsupportable a basis as the racial classification embodied in these statutes [violates due process] ***."

(e) Should Mr. Loving (white) be able to raise all the arguments available to Mrs. Loving (black)?

2. *Washington v. Davis*: **Intent and Effects.**

(a) Why doesn't the Court use *Brown* and *Loving* or even *Yick Wo* to support the proposition that racially neutral classifications adversely affecting blacks are subject to strict scrutiny?

(b) How does a plaintiff prove discriminatory intent when the harm to her stems from a facially race-neutral statute?

(c) Consider the extent to which you agree or disagree with the following reasons for not applying strict scrutiny to statutes having a disparate impact:

(1) Disparate impact may be both unintended and unavoidable. Statutes may be passed not because of the impact, but despite the impact. *See Personnel Administrator v. Feeney*, 442 U.S. 256 (1979) (upholding Massachusetts veterans' preference for civil service jobs despite adverse effect on females).

(2) Judicial voiding of statutes having a disparate impact would mire the Court in a flood of litigation. How much impact would trigger unconstitutionality?

(3) Voiding statutes that have a disparate impact would show too little deference to legislatures and majoritarian processes.

(d) Is *Washington v. Davis* simply an instance of legislatures having to make hard decisions concerning allocation of scarce resources? See JUSTICE MARSHALL's dissent in *Rogers v. Lodge*, 458 U.S. 613 (1982), in which he distinguishes Fifteenth Amendment voting rights cases as not involving allocation of scarce resources and argues that an effect standard should be applied.

(e) Is *Washington v. Davis* merely an application of *Carolene Products* footnote four? Do these cases fail to deal adequately with perpetuation of past discrimination?

3. **More on Intent and Effects.** What is required to show discriminatory intent and is the intent requirement applied the same way in different contexts (sex

rather than race, group participation in politics rather than individual employment)? *Arlington Heights v. Metropolitan Housing Dev. Corp.*, 429 U.S. 252 (1977), rejected a challenge to a refusal to rezone from single to multi-family that might have had racial effects. The Court opined: "Rarely can it be said that a legislature or administrative body operating under a broad mandate made a decision motivated solely by a single concern, or even that a particular purpose was the 'dominant' or 'primary' one. *** Absent a pattern as stark as in *** *Yick Wo*, impact alone is not determinative." *Personnel Administrator of Mass. v. Feeney*, 442 U.S. 256 (1979), upheld an absolute veterans' preference for public employment even though 98.2% of all veterans were male. The Court held that "Equal laws, not equal results" was all equal protection required, the "distinction made [was] quite simply between veterans and nonveterans, not between men and women." To render the statute unconstitutional, the legislature must have acted "at least in part 'because of,' not merely 'in spite of,' its adverse effects" on females.

4. **Legislating Effects Tests.** Title VII of the Civil Rights Act of 1964 makes it unlawful for employers to engage in practices having a "disparate impact" by race or sex where the practices are not justified by "business necessity." Is this portion of Title VII within Congress' powers? Remember Chapter IV?

5. **Problem.** Assume, in connection with the question concerning the Organ Donation Act on page 457, that African Americans are 28% of the population of the State and 14% of the population of the United States. Assume further that, in the State, 28% of those in need of organ transplants are African Americans, but only 20% of the organs harvested in the State come from African American donors. Does the Organ Donation Act violate the Equal Protection Clause of the Fourteenth Amendment?

THE COALITION FOR ECONOMIC EQUITY v. WILSON
122 F.3d 692 (9th Cir.), cert. denied 522 U.S. 963 (1997).

O'SCANNLAIN, CIRCUIT JUDGE:

*** On November 5, 1996, the people of the State of California adopted the California Civil Rights Initiative as an amendment to their Constitution. The initiative, which appeared on the ballot as Proposition 209, provides in relevant part that: [t]he state shall not discriminate against, or grant preferential treatment to, any individual or group on the basis of race, sex, color, ethnicity, or national origin in the operation of public employment, public education, or public contracting. *** Proposition 209 passed by a margin of 54 to 46 percent; of nearly 9 million Californians casting ballots, 4,736,180 voted in favor of the initiative and 3,986,196 voted against it.

On the day after the election, *** plaintiffs [sought] a declaration that Proposition 209 is unconstitutional and a permanent injunction enjoining the State from implementing and enforcing it ***.

*** As a matter of "conventional" equal protection analysis, there is simply no doubt that Proposition 209 is constitutional. *** Proposition 209 provides that the State of California shall not discriminate against, or grant preferential treatment to, any individual or group on the basis of race or gender. Rather than classifying individuals by race or gender, Proposition

209 prohibits the State from classifying individuals by race or gender. A law that prohibits the State from classifying individuals by race or gender a fortiori does not classify individuals by race or gender. Proposition 209's ban on race and gender preferences, as a matter of law and logic, does not violate the Equal Protection Clause in any conventional sense.

V

As a matter of "political structure" analysis, however, plaintiffs challenge the level of government at which the State of California has prohibited race and gender preferences. Plaintiffs contend, along with the United States as amicus curiae, that Proposition 209 imposes an unequal "political structure" that denies women and minorities a right to seek preferential treatment from the lowest level of government. The district court agreed, relying on the so-called "*Hunter*" doctrine.

A

In *Hunter v. Erickson*, [393 U.S. 385 (1969),] the Supreme Court addressed the constitutionality of an amendment to the Charter of the City of Akron, Ohio. Before the charter amendment was enacted, the Akron City Council had authority to pass ordinances regulating the real estate market. Most ordinances became effective thirty days after the Council passed them. The charter amendment operated to prevent the city council from enacting ordinances addressing racial discrimination in housing without majority approval of the Akron voters. The plaintiff, Nellie Hunter, who wanted a fair housing ordinance enforced, claimed that the amendment violated her right to equal protection of the laws.

The Supreme Court found in the charter amendment "an explicitly racial classification treating racial housing matters differently from other racial and housing matters." The law disadvantaged those who would benefit from laws barring racial discrimination in the real estate market as against those who would benefit from other regulations of the real estate market. Absent a compelling state interest, the state "may no more disadvantage any particular group by making it more difficult to enact legislation in its behalf than it may dilute any person's vote or give any group a smaller representation than another of comparable size."

The Court later applied these principles to Washington State's educational decisionmaking structure in *Washington v. Seattle School District No. 1*[, 458 U.S. 457 (1982)]. A statewide initiative in *Washington* barred school boards from assigning students beyond their neighborhood schools. The initiative contained several broad exceptions, which effectively operated to preclude only desegregative busing. Certain school districts challenged the initiative under the Equal Protection Clause.

As in *Hunter*, the Court determined that the initiative effected a racial classification by removing "the authority to address a racial problem—and only a racial problem—from the existing decisionmaking body, in such a way as to burden minority interests." The initiative had restructured the State's educational decisionmaking process to differentiate "between the treatment of problems involving racial matters and that afforded other problems in the same area." That differentiation burdened minority interests "by lodging decisionmaking authority over the question at a new and remote level of government." Absent a compelling state interest, the initiative's unequal reordering of authority of school boards violated the Equal Protection Clause.

The district court applied *Hunter* and *Seattle* to invalidate Proposition 209. Proposition 209, the court found, effected a race and gender classification by singling out race and gender preferences for unique political burdens. The court concluded that race and gender preferences, like antidiscrimination laws and integrative busing, are of special interest to minorities and women. Before Proposition 209 was enacted, the court reasoned, women and minorities could petition local government for preferential treatment. To obtain preferential treatment now, the court concluded, women and minorities must appeal to the statewide electorate, a "new and remote level of government."

The district court next analyzed whether the classifications it gleaned from Proposition 209 withstood "heightened scrutiny." The court concluded that the classifications served no important government interest, let alone a compelling one, thus denying women and minorities equal protection of the laws.

B

The State contends that the district court's conclusion rests on an erroneous legal premise because Proposition 209, unlike the *Hunter* and *Seattle* initiatives, does not reallocate political authority in a discriminatory manner. [Intervenor Californians Against Discrimination and Preferences (CADP)] contends, additionally, that a majority of the electorate cannot restructure the political process to discriminate against itself. We address the second contention first.

1

Can a statewide ballot initiative deny equal protection to members of a group that constitutes a majority of the electorate that enacted it? Plaintiffs allege that Proposition 209 places procedural burdens in the path of women and minorities, who together constitute a majority of the California electorate. Is it possible for a majority of voters impermissibly to stack the political deck against itself? The Supreme Court leaves us, quite frankly, a little perplexed as to the answer.

The "political structure" equal protection cases, namely *Hunter* and *Seattle*, addressed the constitutionality of political obstructions that majorities had placed in the way of minorities to achieving protection against unequal treatment. *Hunter*, holding that the Akron amendment denied minorities equal protection of the laws, observed that "[t]he majority needs no protection against discrimination and if it did, a referendum might be bothersome but no more than that." *Hunter*. *Seattle* addressed a political structure held "to place special burdens on the ability of minority groups to achieve beneficial legislation." *Seattle*. In *Romer v. Evans*, 517 U.S. 620

(1996), the most recent "political structure" case, Colorado's Amendment 2 left homosexuals to "obtain specific protection against discrimination only by enlisting the citizenry of Colorado." It would seem to make little sense to apply "political structure" equal protection principles where the group alleged to face special political burdens itself constitutes a majority of the electorate.

The difficulty, however, lies in reconciling what seems to be that eminently sensible conclusion with the principle that the Fourteenth Amendment guarantees equal protection to individuals and not to groups. That the Fourteenth Amendment affords individuals, not groups, the right to demand equal protection is a fundamental first principle of "conventional" equal protection jurisprudence. *Adarand.* The Equal Protection Clause, after all, prohibits a state from denying "to any person within its jurisdiction the equal protection of the laws."

Where a state denies someone a job, an education, or a seat on the bus because of her race or gender, the injury to that individual is clear. The person who wants to work, study, or ride but cannot because she is black or a woman is denied equal protection. Where, as here, a state prohibits race or gender preferences at any level of government, the injury to any specific individual is utterly inscrutable. No one contends that individuals have a constitutional right to preferential treatment solely on the basis of their race or gender. Quite the contrary. What, then, is the personal injury that members of a group suffer when they cannot seek preferential treatment on the basis of their race or gender from local government? This question admits of no easy answer.

Hunter and *Seattle* suggest that the political structures they held unconstitutional imposed individual injuries analogous to "denying [members of a racial minority] the vote, on an equal basis with others. When the electorate votes up or down on a referendum alleged to burden a majority of the voters, it is hard to conceive how members of the majority have been denied the vote. If members of a majority somehow can deny their own right to ask local government for racial preferences, conceivably a statewide referendum affording preferential treatment to racial minorities would deny members of the racial majority the right to ask local governments to abolish racial preferences." "Consistency does recognize that any individual suffers an injury when he or she is disadvantaged by the government because of his or her race, whatever that race may be." *Adarand.*

Thankfully, the absence of any specific findings by the district court in this regard relieves us from having to reconcile "the long line of cases understanding equal protection as a personal right," with [the] admonition that "the majority needs no protection against discrimination," *Hunter.* Our task in this case is merely to determine whether the district court relied on an erroneous legal premise. We accept without questioning the district court's findings that Proposition 209 burdens members of insular minorities within the majority that enacted it who otherwise would seek to obtain race-based and gender-based preferential treatment from local entities.[13] The legal question for us to decide is whether a burden on achieving race-based or gender-based preferential treatment can deny individuals equal protection of the laws.

2

The Supreme Court has recognized an explicit distinction "between state action that discriminates on the basis of race and state action that addresses, in neutral fashion, race-related matters." *Crawford*. The former denies persons against whom the law discriminates equal protection of the laws; the latter does not. Into which category Proposition 209 falls we must now determine.

In *Crawford*, the Supreme Court considered an amendment to the California Constitution that prohibited state courts from mandating pupil assignment or transportation except to remedy a specific equal protection violation. Minority students had alleged that the amendment employed a racial classification that burdened minorities who sought to vindicate state-created rights. The Supreme Court disagreed, holding that the amendment did not employ a racial classification. Unlike the charter amendment in *Hunter*, "the simple repeal or modification of desegregation or antidiscrimination laws, without more, never has been viewed as embodying a presumptively invalid racial classification."

Crawford, thus, on the one hand, dictates that "the Equal Protection Clause is not violated by the mere repeal of race-related legislation or policies that were not required by the Federal Constitution in the first place ***." *Hunter* and *Seattle*, on the other hand, prohibited states from placing decisionmaking authority over certain racial issues at higher levels of government.

Plaintiffs attempt to align Proposition 209 with *Hunter* and *Seattle* and distinguish it from *Crawford*. *Crawford*, they argue, addressed an amendment that merely repealed a benefit that the state itself had afforded, not the authority of local subdivisions to afford the same benefit. *Hunter* and

---

[13] CADP's argument that *Hunter* and *Seattle* do not extend to gender-based laws because women themselves constitute a majority of the electorate is, nonetheless, compelling. Had the parties presented evidence, and had the district court found, that women constitute a majority of the California electorate, we likely would conclude as a matter of law, for that reason alone, that Proposition 209's ban on gender-based preferences does not deny women equal protection. By so concluding, to be sure, we would bring to a head the tension between the protection that the "political structure" cases afford to the "ability of minority groups to achieve beneficial legislation," *Seattle*, and the "fundamental principle of equal protection as a personal right." *Adarand*. On the one hand, "[t]he majority needs no protection against discrimination," *Hunter*, but, on the other, the Equal Protection Clause protects the individual members of the majority, not the majority as a group. Caught in the cross-fire of seemingly irreconcilable Supreme Court precedent, we would deem it better to err on the side of common sense. To hold that women as a majority could impose a political structure that denied themselves equal protection of the laws would subject to "political structure" scrutiny any state law that imposed benefits on those that shared a minority trait (e.g. veterans), with corresponding burdens on those that shared a majority trait (e.g. the non-veterans). Such a revolutionary concept is inimical to a constitutional scheme founded on democratic self-government.

Seattle, in their view, foreclose the authority of states to withdraw local jurisdiction to enact race and gender preferences unless the state also withdraws local jurisdiction to enact preferences based on any other criteria. Such an extraordinary proposition hardly follows from *Hunter* and *Seattle*. *** Rather, for the doctrine to apply at all, the state somehow must reallocate political authority in a discriminatory manner.

States have "extraordinarily wide latitude *** in creating various types of political subdivisions and conferring authority upon them. That a law resolves an issue at a higher level of state government says nothing in and of itself." Every statewide policy has the "procedural" effect of denying someone an inconsistent outcome at the local level. "[A] lawmaking procedure that 'disadvantages' a particular group does not always deny equal protection. Under any such holding, presumably a State would not be able to require referendums on any subject unless referendums were required on all, because they would always disadvantage some group."

Hunter and *Seattle* relied expressly on the states' existing educational and housing decisionmaking processes to find that they had reallocated authority in a racially discriminatory manner. In *Hunter*, the state obstructed equal housing by removing only racially fair housing prerogatives from the lawmaking procedure for all other housing matters. In *Seattle*, the state obstructed equal education by removing only racially desegregative prerogatives from the lawmaking procedure for all other educational matters.

As the *Seattle* Court explained:

> Before adoption of the initiative, the power to determine what programs would most appropriately fill a school district's educational needs—including programs involving student assignment and desegregation—was firmly committed to the local board's discretion. *** By placing power over desegregative busing at the state level, then, Initiative 350 plainly differentiates between the treatment of problems involving racial matters and that afforded other problems in the same area.

Plaintiffs would have us extrapolate from *Seattle* that a state may never treat race qua race differently from any other legal classification. *Seattle* itself, however, declined that invitation. *** The *Seattle* majority did not question "that the State might have vested all decisionmaking authority in itself." The State's prerogative in that regard was "irrelevant" in *Seattle*, though, because "the political structure it in fact erected impose[d] comparative burdens on minority interests. ^^^ " The State, of course, "could have reserved to state officials the right to make all decisions in the areas of education and student assignment." Conversely, the State had "not attempted to reserve to itself exclusive power to deal with racial issues generally." By removing desegregative prerogatives from these general grants of power, the State, as in *Hunter*, differentiated the treatment of racial problems in education from that afforded educational and racial issues generally.

When, in contrast, a state prohibits all its instruments from discriminating against or granting preferential treatment to anyone on the basis of race or gender, it has promulgated a law that addresses in neutral-fashion race-related and gender-related matters. It does not isolate race or gender antidiscrimination laws from any specific area over which the state has delegated authority to a local entity. Nor does it treat race and gender antidiscrimination laws in one area differently from race and gender antidiscrimination laws in another. Rather, it prohibits all race and gender preferences by state entities. ***

A denial of equal protection entails, at a minimum, a classification that treats individuals unequally. The "political structure" cases do not create some paradoxical exception to this sine qua non of any equal protection violation. In *Hunter*, the lawmaking procedure made it more difficult for Nellie Hunter to obtain protection against unequal treatment in the housing market. In *Seattle*, the lawmaking procedure made it more difficult for minority students to obtain protection against unequal treatment in education.[16] In *Romer*, Colorado's Amendment 2 denied homosexuals the ability to obtain "protection against discrimination," thus classifying homosexuals "not to further a proper legislative end but to make them unequal to everyone else."

Plaintiffs challenge Proposition 209 not as an impediment to protection against unequal treatment but as an impediment to receiving preferential treatment. The controlling words, we must remember, are "equal" and "protection." Impediments to preferential treatment do not deny equal protection.[17] It is one thing to say that individuals have equal protection rights against political obstructions to equal treatment; it is quite another to say that individuals have equal protection rights against political obstructions to preferential treatment. While the Constitution protects against obstructions to equal treatment, it erects obstructions to preferential treatment by its own terms.

---

[16] The district court perceived no relevant difference between the busing programs at issue in *Seattle* and the racial preference programs at issue here. We have recognized, however, that "'stacked deck' programs [such as race-based 'affirmative action'] trench on Fourteenth Amendment values in ways that 'reshuffle' programs [such as school desegregation] do not." Unlike racial preference programs, school desegregation programs are not inherently invidious, do not work wholly to the benefit of certain members of one group and correspondingly to the harm of certain members of another group, and do not deprive citizens of rights.

[17] We must be sure not to misread the district court's finding that those seeking race or gender preferences now must mount a statewide campaign while "those seeking preferences based on any ground other than race or gender, such as age, disability, or veteran status, continue to enjoy access to the political process at all levels of government." Proposition 209 only prohibits preferential treatment based on race or gender. "Those seeking preferences based on any ground other than race or gender, such as age, disability, or veteran status," who "continue to enjoy access to the political process at all levels of government," include, we must remember, everyone—members of all races and both genders. If the state ever prohibited women and minorities from seeking preferences on a basis available to everyone else, such as age, disability, or veteran status, the state would violate Proposition 209's prohibition against race or gender discrimination.

The alleged "equal protection" burden that Proposition 209 imposes on those who would seek race and gender preferences is a burden that the Constitution itself imposes. *** That the Constitution permits the rare race-based or gender-based preference hardly implies that the state cannot ban them altogether. States are free to make or not make any constitutionally permissible legislative classification. Nothing in the Constitution suggests the anomalous and bizarre result that preferences based on the most suspect and presumptively unconstitutional classifications—race and gender—must be readily available at the lowest level of government while preferences based on any other presumptively legitimate classification—such as wealth, age or disability—are at the mercy of statewide referenda.

After all, the "goal" of the Fourteenth Amendment, "to which the Nation continues to aspire," is "a political system in which race no longer matters." *Shaw.* *** The Constitution permits the people to grant a narrowly tailored racial preference only if they come forward with a compelling interest to back it up. *See, e.g., Adarand.* "[I]n the context of a Fourteenth Amendment challenge, courts must bear in mind the difference between what the law permits, and what it requires." *Shaw.* To hold that a democratically enacted affirmative action program is constitutionally permissible because the people have demonstrated a compelling state interest is hardly to hold that the program is constitutionally required. The Fourteenth Amendment, lest we lose sight of the forest for the trees, does not require what it barely permits.

A state law that prohibits classifications based on race or gender is a law that addresses in neutral-fashion race-related and gender-related matters. As in *Crawford*, "[i]t would be paradoxical to conclude that by adopting the Equal Protection Clause of the Fourteenth Amendment, the voters of the State thereby had violated it."[18] *Crawford.* For these reasons, we are persuaded that the district court relied on an erroneous legal premise when it concluded that plaintiffs have demonstrated a likelihood of success on their equal protection claim.

SCHROEDER, CIRCUIT JUDGE, with whom PREGERSON, NORRIS and TASHIMA, CIRCUIT JUDGES, join, dissenting from denial of rehearing en banc.

*** The panel opinion *** treats the case as if the state were merely repealing past remedies that it had determined were not constitutionally required. Proposition 209, however, is not merely a repeal of past remedies; it is a bar to future remedies to curb injustice ***. The panel is also incorrect when it characterizes the ordinance as "adopting the Equal Protection Clause." Unlike the amendment in *Crawford*, Prop. 209 does not merely conform California law to the federal constitution. Rather, it is specifically designed to bar remedies that are permissible under the Equal Protection Clause. Otherwise, the Proposition would be a nullity.

---

[18] To the extent that Proposition 209 prohibits race and gender preferences to a greater degree than the Equal Protection Clause, it provides greater protection to members of the gender and races otherwise burdened by the preference. *See PruneYard Shopping Ctr. v. Robins*, 447 U.S. 74 (1980) (noting a state's "sovereign right to adopt in its own Constitution individual liberties more expansive than those conferred by the Federal Constitution").

NORRIS, CIRCUIT JUDGE, with whom SCHROEDER, PREGERSON and TASHIMA, CIRCUIT JUDGES, join, respecting the denial of rehearing en banc.

*** Unless and until the Supreme Court overrules *Hunter* and *Seattle*, California simply does not have the constitutional authority to place minority groups at a disadvantage in the political process.

Proposition 209 strips the state legislature and all political subdivisions such as city councils, county boards of supervisors, local school boards, and the Board of Regents of the University of California, of all authority to adopt racial preferences in the future. It "lodg[es] decisionmaking authority over [affirmative action] at a new and remote level of government"—the entire electorate of California. The measure thereby deprives the proponents of affirmative action—and only the proponents of affirmative action—of the ordinary benefits of representative government ***. They must take their case directly to the voters of California.

It is hard to imagine a more onerous burden in the political process than mounting a statewide initiative campaign. *** Proposition 209 *** effectively shuts off all debate over racial preferences in the halls of representative government, depriving minorities even of the opportunity to persuade their elected and appointed officials that affirmative action programs make sense as a matter of social policy when they are narrowly tailored to achieve compelling remedial objectives. ***

In resting its decision on the view that affirmative action programs do not secure "equality," the panel injects into *Hunter-Seattle* analysis a test that looks to the personal views of individual judges about the relative merits of affirmative action programs and antidiscrimination laws. There is absolutely no reason to believe that the Supreme Court intended any such result. The relevant inquiry under *Hunter* and *Seattle* is simply to ask whether legislation is beneficial to minorities. The Court used language that is broad and unqualified. Nowhere has the Court suggested that the *Hunter-Seattle* doctrine permits judges to rely upon their own subjective impressions as to whether a particular measure aimed at benefiting minorities is also an effective means of securing equality, or whether the social costs associated with that measure are worth the potential benefits. ***

The question of the constitutionality of Proposition 209 has nothing to do with the wisdom of affirmative action programs. The *Hunter-Seattle* doctrine does not call for judges to determine whether constitutionally permissible, beneficial programs are also wise and just means of securing equality. Rather, the "equality" that the *Hunter-Seattle* doctrine secures is the equality of opportunity that the Constitution guarantees to minority groups to use the channels of representative government to "achieve legislation that is in their interest." *Hunter*. ***

The *Hunter-Seattle* doctrine does not ask whether any particular legislation is ever constitutionally required. The Supreme Court did not hold that either the antidiscrimination laws in *Hunter* or the remedial busing program in *Seattle* was constitutionally required. What the Court did hold is that states may not place political obstacles in the way of laws that favor minorities, nor may they remove such laws wholesale from the political process. All that is constitutionally required is that minorities have the opportunity, on equal terms, to seek "legislation in [their] behalf" within existing channels of government. *Hunter.*

The panel next suggests that Proposition 209 does not implicate the *Hunter-Seattle* doctrine because, in fact, it does not selectively restructure the political process. The panel argues that by forbidding race-related programs in employment, education, and contracting at every level of representative government—rather than doing so at only one level, as in *Seattle*—the State has "addresse[d] in neutral fashion race-related and gender-related matters" and so has not offended *Hunter* or *Seattle*. *** Neither *Hunter* nor *Seattle*—nor common sense, for that matter—supports the proposition that expanding the levels at which the State disadvantages minorities will render that action any less constitutionally suspect.

Next the panel would have us believe that *Hunter* and *Seattle* are inapposite because Proposition 209 burdens majority, not minority, interests. In putting forward this remarkable argument, the panel seizes upon a statement in *Hunter* that "[t]he majority needs no protection against discrimination." *Hunter.* It then puts its own spin on the word "majority" by turning women and racial minorities into one undifferentiated "group." *Hunter.* In other words, the panel transforms racial minorities into a numerical majority by lumping them together with women. Presto! Proposition 209 burdens the interests of the majority, not the minority. ***

Finally, the panel turns to *Crawford v. Board of Education of the City of Los Angeles*, in its attempt to distinguish *Hunter* and *Seattle*. For the same reason that the *Hunter-Seattle* doctrine controls this case, however, *Crawford* has no bearing upon the constitutionality of Proposition 209.

Crawford's focus is on the difference between the "mere repeal" of existing, minority-oriented legislation and the systematic obstruction of such legislation in the future. It holds that a "mere repeal," unlike systematic obstruction, does not violate equal protection ***. Proposition 209, of course, is not a mere repeal of existing affirmative action programs. *** A measure that places permanent political obstacles in the way of minority-oriented legislation violates the *Hunter-Seattle* doctrine and cannot fit itself within the "mere repeal" doctrine of *Crawford*. ***

HAWKINS, CIRCUIT JUDGE, commenting on the denial of rehearing en banc.

The panel was faced with the task of filtering a citizen initiative through its understanding and interpretation of the Constitution. Apparently because the panel believed there was no recent authority directly on point, it chose to do what courts often must do: interpret and apply existing authority to the legal challenge presented. At the end of the day, that is the same task in which the district court was engaged. I have no doubt that both the district court and my colleagues on the panel acted in the utmost good faith in doing so. But therein lies an interesting and important question of jurisprudence. It has nothing to do with the merits of affirmative action; it has everything to do with the way in which courts subject to review by higher authority carry out their duties. It is about the proper role of an inferior court faced with contrary, but apparently controlling, precedent that it honestly and earnestly believes will not be followed (or will be distinguished) by higher authority. Is it the role (the duty, if you will) of a court in that circumstance to attempt to accurately predict what the higher authority will do? Or is its duty to faithfully follow existing precedent? If an inferior court in such a circumstance is free to predict what the higher court will do, then this panel probably got the issue right. If, however, the duty of a lower court is to faithfully apply existing authority, then I have seen no persuasive argument that contradicts Judge Norris' *Carolene Products-Hunter-Seattle* analysis. The Supreme Court may well tell us that this case is not governed by that line of authority or that an exception to the application of those cases should be made for this particular measure. Until that happens, it is not our role to predict—however accurate our predictions might turn out to be.

Notes

1. **Repeals, Inaction, and Restructuring Political Processes.** Why shouldn't "mere repeals" of legislation benefiting blacks be subject to strict scrutiny? Why not apply strict scrutiny to a legislature's refusal to enact legislation benefiting blacks? In what sense did Seattle's Initiative 350 restructure the political process? Before *and* after the initiative, opponents of local school board policies could reverse such policies via statewide referendum. What, if anything, can the people of a state do after *Seattle* to stop local busing of school children?

2. **Distinguishing *Seattle* and *Crawford*.**

    (a) Consider that (1) in *Seattle*, a local program was repealed by statewide action, (2) in *Crawford*, both the program and the repeal were statewide, and (3) in *Hunter*, both the fair housing legislation and the referendum repealing it were local. Consider also that (1) after the Washington referendum, school boards could not bus to remedy de facto segregation and (2) after the California constitutional amendment, state courts could not bus to remedy de facto segregation.

    (b) One casebook suggests that *Washington v. Davis* and *Crawford* are "ultimately inconsistent" with *Brown*, *Loving*, and *Seattle*, and that the two lines of authority can only be reconciled if the Justices "articulate and justify a substantive theory about the distribution of resources among groups in our society. *** [While the Court hasn't done this,] trying to think about *Seattle* and *Crawford* without a theory of distribution is like trying to think about the race problem without a theory of justice." Stone, Seidman, Sunstein, and Tushnett CONSTITUTIONAL LAW (Little, Brown & Co., 3d Ed. 1996) at p. 648.

3. **Commentary on *Coalition for Economic Equality*.** A student note at 111 HARV. L.REV. 2081 (1998), argues that, notwithstanding the Ninth Circuit's decision, Prop 209 might well be held unconstitutional as applied. Do you agree?

4. **Racial Data and Descriptions.** California's Racial Privacy Initiative (RPI), which did not pass, would have prohibited any public entity (including schools, employers, and law enforcement agencies) from collecting any data on the basis of race or ethnicity. Would the RPI, if successful, violate the

Equal Protection Clause? Is collection of data by race permissible? On a more individualized level, may a police bulletin describe a suspect as "Black male, 6' tall, wearing jeans and an Eminem t-shirt?"

3. AFFIRMATIVE ACTION

CITY OF RICHMOND v. J.A. CROSON COMPANY
488 U.S. 469, 109 S.Ct. 706, 102 L.Ed.2d 854 (1989).

JUSTICE O'CONNOR announced the judgment of the Court and delivered the opinion of the Court with respect to Parts I, III–B, and IV, an opinion with respect to Part II, in which THE CHIEF JUSTICE and JUSTICE WHITE join, and an opinion with respect to Parts III–A and V, in which THE CHIEF JUSTICE, JUSTICE WHITE, and JUSTICE KENNEDY join.

In this case, we confront once again the tension between the Fourteenth Amendment's guarantee of equal treatment to all citizens, and the use of race-based measures to ameliorate the effects of past discrimination on the opportunities enjoyed by members of minority groups in our society. In *Fullilove v. Klutznick*, 448 U.S. 448 (1980), we held that a congressional program requiring that 10% of certain federal construction grants be awarded to minority contractors did not violate the equal protection principles embodied in the Due Process Clause of the Fifth Amendment. ***

I

On April 11, 1983, the Richmond City Council adopted the Minority Business Utilization Plan (the Plan). The Plan required prime contractors to whom the city awarded construction contracts to subcontract at least 30% of the dollar amount of the contract to one or more Minority Business Enterprises (MBE's). *** The Plan defined an MBE as "[a] business at least fifty-one (51) percent of which is owned and controlled *** by minority group members." "Minority group members" were defined as "[c]itizens of the United States who are Blacks, Spanish-speaking, Orientals, Indians, Eskimos, or Aleuts." *** [City set-aside rules provided that] "[no] partial or complete waiver of the [30% set-aside] requirement shall be granted by the city other than in exceptional circumstances. To justify a waiver, it must be shown that every feasible attempt has been made to comply, and it must be demonstrated that sufficient, relevant, qualified Minority Business Enterprises *** are unavailable or unwilling to participate in the contract to enable meeting the 30% MBE goal." ***

The Plan was adopted by the Richmond City Council after a public hearing. Seven members of the public spoke to the merits of the ordinance: five were in opposition, two in favor. Proponents of the set-aside provision relied on a study which indicated that, while the general population of Richmond was 50% black, only 0.67% of the city's prime construction contracts had been awarded to minority businesses in the 5–year period from 1978 to 1983. It was also established that a variety of contractors' associations, whose representatives appeared in opposition to the ordinance, had virtually no minority businesses within their membership. The city's legal counsel indicated his view that the ordinance was constitutional under this Court's decision in *Fullilove v. Klutznick*. Councilperson Marsh, a proponent of the ordinance, made the following statement: "There is some information, however, that I want to make sure that we put in the record. I have been practicing law in this community since 1961, and I am familiar with the practices in the construction industry in this area, in the State, and around the nation. And I can say without equivocation, that the general conduct of the construction industry in this area, and the State, and around the nation, is one in which race discrimination and exclusion on the basis of race is widespread."

There was no direct evidence of race discrimination on the part of the city in letting contracts or any evidence that the city's prime contractors had discriminated against minority-owned subcontractors. ***

II

*** In *Fullilove*, we upheld [a] minority set-aside [by Congress] *** against a challenge based on the equal protection component of the Due Process Clause. *** Appellant and its supporting *amici* rely heavily on *Fullilove* for the proposition that a city council, like Congress, need not make specific findings of discrimination to engage in race-conscious relief. Thus, appellant argues "[i]t would be a perversion of federalism to hold that the federal government has a compelling interest in remedying the effects of racial discrimination in its own public works program, but a city government does not."

What appellant ignores is that Congress, unlike any State or political subdivision, has a specific constitutional mandate to enforce the dictates of the Fourteenth Amendment. The power to "enforce" may at times also include the power to define situations which Congress determines threaten principles of equality and to adopt prophylactic rules to deal with those situations. *See Katzenbach v. Morgan*, 384 U.S., at 651. The Civil War Amendments themselves worked a dramatic change in the balance between congressional and state power over matters of race. Speaking of the Thirteenth and Fourteenth Amendments in *Ex parte Virginia*, 100 U.S. 339 (1880), the Court stated: "They were intended to be, what they really are, limitations of the powers of the States and enlargements of the power of Congress."

That Congress may identify and redress the effects of society-wide discrimination does not mean that, a fortiori, the States and their political subdivisions are free to decide that such remedies are appropriate. Section 1 of the Fourteenth Amendment is an explicit constraint on state power, and the States must undertake any remedial efforts in accordance with that provision. To hold otherwise would be to cede control over the content of the Equal Protection Clause to the 50 state legislatures and their myriad political subdivisions. The mere recitation of a benign or compensatory purpose for the use of a racial classification would essentially entitle the States to exercise the full power of Congress under § 5 of the Fourteenth Amendment and insulate any racial classification from judicial scrutiny under § 1. We believe that such a result would be contrary to the intentions of the Framers of the Fourteenth Amendment, who desired to place clear limits on the States' use of race as a criterion for legislative action, and to have the federal courts enforce those limitations. ***

It would seem equally clear, however, that a state or local subdivision (if delegated the authority from the State) has the authority to eradicate the effects of private discrimination within its own legislative jurisdiction. This authority must, of course, be exercised within the constraints of § 1 of the Fourteenth Amendment. Our decision in *Wygant* is not to the contrary. *Wygant* addressed the constitutionality of the use of racial quotas by local school authorities pursuant to an agreement reached with the local teachers' union. It was in the context of addressing the school board's power to adopt a race-based layoff program affecting its own work force that the *Wygant* plurality indicated that the Equal Protection Clause required "some showing of prior discrimination by the governmental unit involved." *Wygant*, 476 U.S., at 274. As a matter of state law, the city of Richmond has legislative authority over its procurement policies, and can use its spending powers to remedy private discrimination, if it identifies that discrimination with the particularity required by the Fourteenth Amendment. ***

Thus, if the city could show that it had essentially become a "passive participant" in a system of racial exclusion practiced by elements of the local construction industry, we think it clear that the city could take affirmative steps to dismantle such a system. It is beyond dispute that any public entity, state or federal, has a compelling interest in assuring that public dollars, drawn from the tax contributions of all citizens, do not serve to finance the evil of private prejudice.

III
A

The Equal Protection Clause of the Fourteenth Amendment provides that "[n]o State shall *** deny *to any person* within its jurisdiction the equal protection of the laws." *** The Richmond Plan denies certain citizens the opportunity to compete for a fixed percentage of public contracts based solely upon their race. To whatever racial group these citizens belong, their "personal rights" to be treated with equal dignity and respect are implicated by a rigid rule erecting race as the sole criterion in an aspect of public decisionmaking.

Absent searching judicial inquiry into the justification for such race-based measures, there is simply no way of determining what classifications are "benign" or "remedial" and what classifications are in fact motivated by illegitimate notions of racial inferiority or simple racial politics. Indeed, the purpose of strict scrutiny is to "smoke out" illegitimate uses of race by assuring that the legislative body is pursuing a goal important enough to warrant use of a highly suspect tool. The test also ensures that the means chosen "fit" this compelling goal so closely that there is little or no possibility that the motive for the classification was illegitimate racial prejudice or stereotype.

Classifications based on race carry a danger of stigmatic harm. Unless they are strictly reserved for remedial settings, they may in fact promote notions of racial inferiority and lead to a politics of racial hostility. *** [The] standard of review under the Equal Protection Clause is not dependent on the race of those burdened or benefited by a particular classification.

Our continued adherence to the standard of review employed in *Wygant* does not, as JUSTICE MARSHALL's dissent suggests, indicate that we view "racial discrimination as largely a phenomenon of the past" or that "government bodies need no longer preoccupy themselves with rectifying racial injustice." As we indicate [below], States and their local subdivisions have many legislative weapons at their disposal both to punish and prevent present discrimination and to remove arbitrary barriers to minority advancement. Rather, our interpretation of § 1 stems from our agreement with the view expressed by JUSTICE POWELL in *Bakke* that "[t]he guarantee of equal protection cannot mean one thing when applied to one individual and something else when applied to a person of another color."

Under the standard proposed by JUSTICE MARSHALL's dissent, "race-conscious classifications designed to further remedial goals" are forthwith subject to a relaxed standard of review. How the dissent arrives at the legal conclusion that a racial classification is "designed to further remedial goals," without first engaging in an examination of the factual basis for its enactment and the nexus between its scope and that factual basis, we are not told. However, once the "remedial" conclusion is reached, the dissent's standard is singularly deferential, and bears little resemblance to the close examination of legislative purpose we have engaged in when reviewing classifications based either on race or gender. The dissent's watered-down version of equal protection review effectively assures that race will always be relevant in American life ***.

Even were we to accept a reading of the guarantee of equal protection under which the level of scrutiny varies according to the ability of different groups to defend their interests in the representative process, heightened scrutiny would still be appropriate in the circumstances of this case. One of the central arguments for applying a less exacting standard to "benign" racial classifications is that such measures essentially involve a choice made by dominant racial groups to disadvantage themselves. *** In this case, blacks constitute approximately 50% of the population of the city of Richmond. Five of the nine seats on the city council are held by blacks. The concern that a political majority will more easily act to the disadvantage of a minority based on unwarranted assumptions or incomplete facts would seem to militate for, not against, the application of heightened judicial scrutiny in this case. ***

B

We think it clear that the factual predicate offered in support of the Richmond Plan suffers from the same two defects identified as fatal in *Wygant*. The District Court found the city council's "findings sufficient to ensure that, in adopting the Plan, it was remedying the present effects of past discrimination in the construction industry." *** [A] generalized assertion that there has been past discrimination in an entire industry provides no guidance for a legislative body to determine the precise scope of the injury it seeks to remedy. It "has no logical stopping point." *Wygant*, at 275 (plurality opinion). "Relief" for such an ill-defined wrong could extend until the percentage of public contracts awarded to MBE's in Richmond mirrored the percentage of minorities in the population as a whole.

Appellant argues that it is attempting to remedy various forms of past discrimination that are alleged to be responsible for the small number of minority businesses in the local contracting industry. Among these the city cites the exclusion of blacks from skilled construction trade unions and training programs. This past discrimination has prevented them "from following the traditional path from laborer to entrepreneur." The city also lists a host of nonracial factors which would seem to face a member of any racial group attempting to establish a new business enterprise, such as deficiencies in working capital, inability to meet bonding requirements, unfamiliarity with bidding procedures, and disability caused by an inadequate track record.

While there is no doubt that the sorry history of both private and public discrimination in this country has contributed to a lack of opportunities for black entrepreneurs, this observation, standing alone, cannot justify a rigid racial quota in the awarding of public contracts in Richmond, Virginia. *** It is sheer speculation how many minority firms there would be in Richmond absent past societal discrimination, just as it was sheer speculation how many minority medical students would have been admitted to the medical school at Davis absent past discrimination in educational opportunities. Defining these sorts of injuries as "identified discrimination" would give local governments license to create a patchwork of racial preferences based on statistical generalizations about any particular field of endeavor.

These defects are readily apparent in this case. The 30% quota cannot in any realistic sense be tied to any injury suffered by anyone. The District Court relied upon five predicate "facts" in reaching its conclusion that there was an adequate basis for the 30% quota: (1) the ordinance declares itself to be remedial; (2) several proponents of the measure stated their views that there had been past discrimination in the construction industry; (3) minority businesses received 0.67% of prime contracts from the city while minorities constituted 50% of the city's population; (4) there were very few minority contractors in local and state contractors' associations; and (5) in 1977, Congress made a determination that the effects of past discrimination had stifled minority participation in the construction industry nationally.

None of these "findings," singly or together, provide the city of Richmond with a "strong basis in evidence for its conclusion that remedial action was necessary." *Wygant*. There is nothing approaching a prima facie case of a constitutional or statutory violation by anyone in the Richmond construction industry.

The District Court accorded great weight to the fact that the city council designated the Plan as "remedial." But the mere recitation of a "benign" or legitimate purpose for a racial classification is entitled to little or no weight. *** The District Court also relied on the highly conclusionary statement of a proponent of the Plan that there was racial discrimination in the construction industry "in this area, and the State, and around the nation." It also noted that the city manager had related his view that racial discrimination still plagued the construction industry in his home city of Pittsburgh. These statements are of little probative value in establishing identified discrimination in the Richmond construction industry. The factfinding process of legislative bodies is generally entitled to a presumption of regularity and deferential review by the judiciary. *See Williamson v. Lee Optical.* But when a legislative body chooses to employ a suspect classification, it cannot rest upon a generalized assertion as to the classification's relevance to its goals. A governmental actor cannot render race a legitimate proxy for a particular condition merely by declaring that the condition exists. The history of racial classifications in this country suggests that blind judicial deference to legislative or executive pronouncements of necessity has no place in equal protection analysis.

Reliance on the disparity between the number of prime contracts awarded to minority firms and the minority population of the city of Richmond is similarly misplaced. *** In this case, the city does not even know how many MBE's in the relevant market are qualified to undertake prime or subcontracting work in public construction projects. Nor does the city know what percentage of total city construction dollars minority firms now receive as subcontractors on prime contracts let by the city.

To a large extent, the set-aside of subcontracting dollars seems to rest on the unsupported assumption that white prime contractors simply will not hire minority firms. *** Without any information on minority participation in subcontracting, it is quite simply impossible to evaluate overall minority representation in the city's construction expenditures.

The city and the District Court also relied on evidence that MBE membership in local contractors' associations was extremely low. Again, standing alone this evidence is not probative of any discrimination in the local construction industry. There are numerous explanations for this dearth of minority participation, including past societal discrimination in education and economic opportunities as well as both black and white career and entrepreneurial choices. Blacks may be disproportionately attracted to industries other than construction. ***

For low minority membership in these associations to be relevant, the city would have to link it to the number of local MBE's eligible for membership. If the statistical disparity between eligible MBE's and MBE membership were great enough, an inference of discriminatory exclusion could arise. In such a case, the city would have a compelling interest in preventing its tax dollars from assisting these organizations in maintaining a racially segregated construction market.

Finally, the city and the District Court relied on Congress' finding in connection with the set-aside approved in *Fullilove* that there had been nationwide discrimination in the construction industry. The probative value of these findings for demonstrating the existence of discrimination in Richmond is extremely limited. By its inclusion of a waiver procedure in the national program addressed in *Fullilove*, Congress explicitly recognized that the scope of the problem would vary from market area to market area. *** We have never approved the extrapolation of discrimination in one jurisdiction from the experience of another.

*** To accept Richmond's claim that past societal discrimination alone can serve as the basis for rigid racial preferences would be to open the door to competing claims for "remedial relief" for every disadvantaged group. The dream of a Nation of equal citizens in a society where race is irrelevant to personal opportunity and achievement would be lost in a mosaic of shifting preferences based on inherently unmeasurable claims of past wrongs. *** We think such a result would be contrary to both the letter and spirit of a constitutional provision whose central command is equality.

The foregoing analysis applies only to the inclusion of blacks within the Richmond set-aside program. There is *absolutely no evidence* of past discrimination against Spanish-speaking, Oriental, Indian, Eskimo, or Aleut persons in any aspect of the Richmond construction industry. The District Court took judicial notice of the fact that the vast majority of "minority" persons in Richmond were black. It may well be that Richmond has never had an Aleut or Eskimo citizen. The random inclusion of racial groups that, as a practical matter, may never have suffered from discrimination in the construction industry in Richmond suggests that perhaps the city's purpose was not in fact to remedy past discrimination.

If a 30% set-aside was "narrowly tailored" to compensate black contractors for past discrimination, one may legitimately ask why they are forced to share this "remedial relief" with an Aleut citizen who moves to Richmond tomorrow? The gross overinclusiveness of Richmond's racial preference strongly impugns the city's claim of remedial motivation.

IV

As noted by the court below, it is almost impossible to assess whether the Richmond Plan is narrowly tailored to remedy prior discrimination since it is not linked to identified discrimination in any way. We limit ourselves to two observations in this regard.

First, there does not appear to have been any consideration of the use of race-neutral means to increase minority business participation in city contracting. Many of the barriers to minority participation in the construction industry relied upon by the city to justify a racial classification appear to be race neutral. If MBE's disproportionately lack capital or cannot meet bonding requirements, a race-neutral program of city financing for small firms would, *a fortiori*, lead to greater minority participation. *** Second, the 30% quota cannot be said to be narrowly tailored to any goal, except perhaps outright racial balancing. It rests upon the "completely unrealistic" assumption that minorities will choose a particular trade in lockstep proportion to their representation in the local population.

Since the city must already consider bids and waivers on a case-by-case basis, it is difficult to see the need for a rigid numerical quota. As noted above, the congressional scheme upheld in *Fullilove* allowed for a waiver of the set-aside provision where an MBE's higher price was not attributable to the effects of past discrimination. Based upon proper findings, such programs are less problematic from an equal protection standpoint because they treat all candidates individually, rather than making the color of an applicant's skin the sole relevant consideration. Unlike the program upheld in *Fullilove*, the Richmond Plan's waiver system focuses solely on the availability of MBE's; there is no inquiry into whether or not the particular MBE seeking a racial preference has suffered from the effects of past discrimination by the city or prime contractors.

Given the existence of an individualized procedure, the city's only interest in maintaining a quota system rather than investigating the need for remedial action in particular cases would seem to be simple administrative convenience. *** Under Richmond's scheme, a successful black, Hispanic, or Oriental entrepreneur from anywhere in the country enjoys an absolute preference over other citizens based solely on their race. We think it obvious that such a program is not narrowly tailored to remedy the effects of prior discrimination.

V

Nothing we say today precludes a state or local entity from taking action to rectify the effects of identified discrimination within its jurisdiction. If the city of Richmond had evidence before it that nonminority contractors were systematically excluding minority businesses from subcontracting opportunities it could take action to end the discriminatory exclusion. Where there is a significant statistical disparity between the number of qualified minority contractors willing and able to perform a particular service and the number of such contractors actually engaged by the locality or the locality's prime contractors, an inference of discriminatory exclusion could arise. Under such circumstances, the city could act to dismantle the closed business system by taking appropriate measures against those who discriminate on the basis of race or other illegitimate criteria. In the extreme case, some form of narrowly tailored racial preference might be necessary to break down patterns of deliberate exclusion.

Nor is local government powerless to deal with individual instances of racially motivated refusals to employ minority contractors. Where such discrimination occurs, a city would be justified in penalizing the discriminator and providing appropriate relief to the victim of such discrimination. Moreover, evidence of a pattern of individual discriminatory acts can, if supported by appropriate statistical proof, lend support to a local government's determination that broader remedial relief is justified.

Even in the absence of evidence of discrimination, the city has at its disposal a whole array of race-neutral devices to increase the accessibility of city contracting opportunities to small entrepreneurs of all races. *** Business as usual should not mean business pursuant to the unthinking exclusion of certain members of our society from its rewards.

In the case at hand, the city has not ascertained how many minority enterprises are present in the local construction market nor the level of their participation in city construction projects. The city points to no evidence that qualified minority contractors have been passed over for city contracts or subcontracts, either as a group or in any individual case. ***

Proper findings in this regard are necessary to define both the scope of the injury and the extent of the remedy necessary to cure its effects. Such findings also serve to assure all citizens that the deviation from the norm of equal treatment of all racial and ethnic groups is a temporary matter, a measure taken in the service of the goal of equality itself. Absent such findings, there is a danger that a racial classification is merely the product of unthinking stereotypes or a form of racial politics. *** Because the city of Richmond has failed to identify the need for remedial action in the awarding of its public construction contracts, its treatment of its citizens on a racial basis violates the dictates of the Equal Protection Clause. ***

JUSTICE STEVENS, concurring in part and concurring in the judgment.

First, the city makes no claim that the public interest in the efficient performance of its construction contracts will be served by granting a preference to minority-business enterprises. *** Second, this litigation involves an attempt by a legislative body, rather than a court, to fashion a remedy for a past wrong. *** It is the judicial system, rather than the legislative process, that is best equipped to identify past wrongdoers and to fashion remedies that will create the conditions that presumably would have existed had no wrong been committed. *** Third, instead of engaging in a debate over the proper standard of review to apply in affirmative-action litigation, I believe it is more constructive to try to identify the characteristics of the advantaged and disadvantaged classes that may justify their disparate treatment. In this case that approach convinces me that, instead of carefully identifying the characteristics of the two classes of contractors that are respectively favored and disfavored by its ordinance, the Richmond City Council has merely engaged in the type of stereotypical analysis that is a hallmark of violations of the Equal Protection Clause. ***

JUSTICE KENNEDY, concurring in part and concurring in the judgment. [omitted]

JUSTICE SCALIA, concurring in the judgment.

I agree *** that strict scrutiny must be applied to all governmental classification by race, whether or not its asserted purpose is "remedial" or "benign." I do not agree, however, with JUSTICE O'CONNOR's dictum suggesting that, despite the Fourteenth Amendment, state and local governments may in some circumstances discriminate on the basis of race in

order (in a broad sense) "to ameliorate the effects of past discrimination." ***
At least where state or local action is at issue, only a social emergency rising
to the level of imminent danger to life and limb—for example, a prison race
riot, requiring temporary segregation of inmates—can justify an exception to
the principle embodied in the Fourteenth Amendment that "[o]ur
Constitution is color-blind, and neither knows nor tolerates classes among
citizens," *Plessy v. Ferguson*, (HARLAN, J., dissenting). ***

A sound distinction between federal and state (or local) action based on
race rests not only upon the substance of the Civil War Amendments, but
upon social reality and governmental theory. *** The struggle for racial
justice has historically been a struggle by the national society against
oppression in the individual States. And the struggle retains that character
in modern times. *Not all of that struggle has involved discrimination against
blacks, and not all of it has been in the Old South. What the record shows, in
other words, is that racial discrimination against any group finds a more
ready expression at the state and local than at the federal level. To the
children of the Founding Fathers, this should come as no surprise. An acute
awareness of the heightened danger of oppression from political factions in
small, rather than large, political units dates to the very beginning of our
national history.* ***

In my view there is only one circumstance in which the States may act by
race to "undo the effects of past discrimination": where that is necessary to
eliminate their own maintenance of a system of unlawful racial classification.
If, for example, a state agency has a discriminatory pay scale compensating
black employees in all positions at 20% less than their nonblack counterparts,
it may assuredly promulgate an order raising the salaries of "all black
employees" to eliminate the differential. This distinction explains our school
desegregation cases, in which we have made plain that States and localities
sometimes have an obligation to adopt race-conscious remedies. ***

I agree with the Court's dictum that a fundamental distinction must be
drawn between the effects of "societal" discrimination and the effects of
"identified" discrimination, and that the situation would be different if
Richmond's plan were "tailored" to identify those particular bidders who
"suffered from the effects of past discrimination by the city or prime
contractors." In my view, however, the reason that would make a difference is
not, as the Court states, that it would justify race-conscious action but rather
that it would enable race-neutral remediation. Nothing prevents Richmond
from according a contracting preference to identified victims of
discrimination. While most of the beneficiaries might be black, neither the
beneficiaries nor those disadvantaged by the preference would be identified
on the basis of their race. In other words, far from justifying racial
classification, identification of actual victims of discrimination makes it less
supportable than ever, because more obviously unneeded. ***

It is plainly true that in our society blacks have suffered discrimination
immeasurably greater than any directed at other racial groups. But those
who believe that racial preferences can help to "even the score" display, and
reinforce, a manner of thinking by race that was the source of the injustice

and that will, if it endures within our society, be the source of more injustice still. The relevant proposition is not that it was blacks, or Jews, or Irish who were discriminated against, but that it was individual men and women, "created equal," who were discriminated against. And the relevant resolve is that that should never happen again. Racial preferences appear to "even the score" (in some small degree) only if one embraces the proposition that our society is appropriately viewed as divided into races, making it right that an injustice rendered in the past to a black man should be compensated for by discriminating against a white. Nothing is worth that embrace. Since blacks have been disproportionately disadvantaged by racial discrimination, any race-neutral remedial program aimed at the disadvantaged as such will have a disproportionately beneficial impact on blacks. Only such a program, and not one that operates on the basis of race, is in accord with the letter and the spirit of our Constitution. ***

JUSTICE MARSHALL, with whom JUSTICE BRENNAN and JUSTICE BLACKMUN join, dissenting.

It is a welcome symbol of racial progress when the former capital of the Confederacy acts forthrightly to confront the effects of racial discrimination in its midst. In my view, nothing in the Constitution can be construed to prevent Richmond, Virginia, from allocating a portion of its contracting dollars for businesses owned or controlled by members of minority groups. Indeed, Richmond's set-aside program is indistinguishable in all meaningful respects from—and in fact was patterned upon—the federal set-aside plan which this Court upheld in *Fullilove v. Klutznick.*

A majority of this Court holds today, however, that the Equal Protection Clause of the Fourteenth Amendment blocks Richmond's initiative. The essence of the majority's position is that Richmond has failed to catalog adequate findings to prove that past discrimination has impeded minorities from joining or participating fully in Richmond's construction contracting industry. I find deep irony in second-guessing Richmond's judgment on this point. As much as any municipality in the United States, Richmond knows what racial discrimination is; a century of decisions by this and other federal courts has richly documented the city's disgraceful history of public and private racial discrimination. In any event, the Richmond City Council *has* supported its determination that minorities have been wrongly excluded from local construction contracting. Its proof includes statistics showing that minority-owned businesses have received virtually no city contracting dollars and rarely if ever belonged to area trade associations; testimony by municipal officials that discrimination has been widespread in the local construction industry; and the same exhaustive and widely publicized federal studies relied on in *Fullilove,* studies which showed that pervasive discrimination in the Nation's tight-knit construction industry had operated to exclude minorities from public contracting. These are precisely the types of statistical and testimonial evidence which, until today, this Court had credited in cases approving of race-conscious measures designed to remedy past discrimination.

More fundamentally, today's decision marks a deliberate and giant step backward in this Court's affirmative-action jurisprudence. Cynical of one municipality's attempt to redress the effects of past racial discrimination in a particular industry, the majority launches a grapeshot attack on race-conscious remedies in general. The majority's unnecessary pronouncements will inevitably discourage or prevent governmental entities, particularly States and localities, from acting to rectify the scourge of past discrimination. This is the harsh reality of the majority's decision, but it is not the Constitution's command. ***

Richmond has two powerful interests in setting aside a portion of public contracting funds for minority-owned enterprises. The first is the city's interest in eradicating the effects of past racial discrimination. *** Richmond has a second compelling interest in setting aside, where possible, a portion of its contracting dollars. That interest is the prospective one of preventing the city's own spending decisions from reinforcing and perpetuating the exclusionary effects of past discrimination. ***

The majority is wrong to trivialize the continuing impact of government acceptance or use of private institutions or structures once wrought by discrimination. When government channels all its contracting funds to a white-dominated community of established contractors whose racial homogeneity is the product of private discrimination, it does more than place its imprimatur on the practices which forged and which continue to define that community. It also provides a measurable boost to those economic entities that have thrived within it, while denying important economic benefits to those entities which, but for prior discrimination, might well be better qualified to receive valuable government contracts. ***

The remaining question with respect to the "governmental interest" prong of equal protection analysis is whether Richmond has proffered satisfactory proof of past racial discrimination to support its twin interests in remediation and in governmental nonperpetuation. *** The varied body of evidence on which Richmond relied provides a "strong," "firm," and "unquestionably legitimate" basis upon which the city council could determine that the effects of past racial discrimination warranted a remedial and prophylactic governmental response. *** Richmond acted against a backdrop of congressional and Executive Branch studies which demonstrated with such force the nationwide pervasiveness of prior discrimination that Congress presumed that "present economic inequities" in construction contracting resulted from "past discriminatory systems." The city's local evidence confirmed that Richmond's construction industry did not deviate from this pernicious national pattern. The fact that just 0.67% of public construction expenditures over the previous five years had gone to minority-owned prime contractors, despite the city's racially mixed population, strongly suggests that construction contracting in the area was rife with "present economic inequities." To the extent this enormous disparity did not itself demonstrate that discrimination had occurred, the descriptive testimony of Richmond's elected and appointed leaders drew the necessary link between the pitifully small presence of minorities in construction contracting and past exclusionary practices. That no one who testified challenged this depiction of widespread racial discrimination in area construction contracting lent significant weight to these accounts. The fact that area trade associations had virtually no minority members dramatized the extent of present inequities and suggested the lasting power of past discriminatory systems. In sum, to suggest that the facts on which Richmond has relied do not provide a sound basis for its finding of past racial discrimination simply blinks credibility.

*** The majority states *** that reliance on the disparity between the share of city contracts awarded to minority firms (0.67%) and the minority population of Richmond (approximately 50%) is "misplaced." It is true that, when the factual predicate needed to be proved is one of present discrimination, we have generally credited statistical contrasts between the racial composition of a work force and the general population as proving discrimination only where this contrast revealed "gross statistical disparities." But this principle does not impugn Richmond's statistical contrast, for two reasons. First, considering how minuscule the share of Richmond public construction contracting dollars received by minority-owned businesses is, it is hardly unreasonable to conclude that this case involves a "gross statistical disparit[y]." There are roughly equal numbers of minorities and nonminorities in Richmond—yet minority-owned businesses receive one-seventy-fifth of the public contracting funds that other businesses receive.

Second, and more fundamentally, where the issue is not present discrimination but rather whether past discrimination has resulted in the continuing exclusion of minorities from a historically tight-knit industry, a contrast between population and work force is entirely appropriate to help gauge the degree of the exclusion. ***

The majority's perfunctory dismissal of the testimony of Richmond's appointed and elected leaders is also deeply disturbing ***. When the legislatures and leaders of cities with histories of pervasive discrimination testify that past discrimination has infected one of their industries, armchair cynicism like that exercised by the majority has no place. *** Disbelief is particularly inappropriate here in light of the fact that appellee Croson, which had the burden of proving unconstitutionality at trial has at no point come forward with any direct evidence that the city council's motives were anything other than sincere. Finally, I vehemently disagree with the majority's dismissal of the congressional and Executive Branch findings noted in *Fullilove* as having "extremely limited" probative value in this case. ***

In my judgment, Richmond's set-aside plan also comports with the second prong of the equal protection inquiry, for it is substantially related to the interests it seeks to serve in remedying past discrimination and in ensuring that municipal contract procurement does not perpetuate that discrimination. The most striking aspect of the city's ordinance is the similarity it bears to the "appropriately limited" federal set-aside provision upheld in *Fullilove*. Like the federal provision, Richmond's is limited to five years in duration, and was not renewed when it came up for reconsideration in 1988. Like the federal provision, Richmond's contains a waiver provision freeing from its subcontracting requirements those nonminority firms that demonstrate that they cannot comply with its provisions. Like the federal provision, Richmond's has a minimal impact on innocent third parties. While the measure affects 30% of public contracting dollars, that translates to only 3% of overall Richmond area contracting.

Finally, like the federal provision, Richmond's does not interfere with any vested right of a contractor to a particular contract; instead it operates entirely prospectively. Richmond's initiative affects only future economic arrangements and imposes only a diffuse burden on nonminority competitors—here, businesses owned or controlled by nonminorities which seek subcontracting work on public construction projects.

*** The majority takes issue *** with two aspects of Richmond's tailoring: the city's refusal to explore the use of race-neutral measures to increase minority business participation in contracting and the selection of a 30% set-aside figure. The majority's first criticism is flawed in two respects. First, the majority overlooks the fact that since 1975, Richmond has barred both discrimination by the city in awarding public contracts and discrimination by public contractors. The virtual absence of minority businesses from the city's contracting rolls, indicated by the fact that such businesses have received less than 1% of public contracting dollars, strongly suggests that this ban has not succeeded in redressing the impact of past discrimination or in preventing city contract procurement from reinforcing racial homogeneity. Second, the majority's suggestion that Richmond should have first undertaken such race-neutral measures as a program of city financing for small firms ignores the fact that such measures, while theoretically appealing, have been discredited by Congress as ineffectual in eradicating the effects of past discrimination in this very industry. ***

As for Richmond's 30% target, the majority states that this figure "cannot be said to be narrowly tailored to any goal, except perhaps outright racial balancing." The majority ignores two important facts. First, the set-aside measure affects only 3% of overall city contracting; thus, any imprecision in tailoring has far less impact than the majority suggests. But more important, the majority ignores the fact that Richmond's 30% figure was patterned directly on the *Fullilove* precedent. Congress' 10% figure fell "roughly halfway between the present percentage of minority contractors and the percentage of minority group members in the Nation." *Fullilove*, at 513–514 (POWELL, J., concurring). The Richmond City Council's 30% figure similarly falls roughly halfway between the present percentage of Richmond-based minority contractors (almost zero) and the percentage of minorities in Richmond (50%). ***

Today, for the first time, a majority of this Court has adopted strict scrutiny as its standard of Equal Protection Clause review of race-conscious remedial measures. This is an unwelcome development. A profound difference separates governmental actions that themselves are racist, and governmental actions that seek to remedy the effects of prior racism or to prevent neutral governmental activity from perpetuating the effects of such racism. *** [T]he majority today does a grave disservice not only to those victims of past and present racial discrimination in this Nation whom government has sought to assist, but also to this Court's long tradition of approaching issues of race with the utmost sensitivity.

I am also troubled by the majority's assertion that, even if it did not believe generally in strict scrutiny of race-based remedial measures, "the circumstances of this case" require this Court to look upon the Richmond City Council's measure with the strictest scrutiny. The sole such circumstance which the majority cites, however, is the fact that blacks in Richmond are a "dominant racial grou[p]" in the city. In support of this characterization of dominance, the majority observes that "blacks constitute approximately 50% of the population of the city of Richmond" and that "[f]ive of the nine seats on the City Council are held by blacks."

While I agree that the numerical and political supremacy of a given racial group is a factor bearing upon the level of scrutiny to be applied, this Court has never held that numerical inferiority, standing alone, makes a racial group "suspect" and thus entitled to strict scrutiny review. Rather, we have identified other "traditional indicia of suspectness": whether a group has been "saddled with such disabilities, or subjected to such a history of purposeful unequal treatment, or relegated to such a position of political powerlessness as to command extraordinary protection from the majoritarian political process." *San Antonio Independent School Dist. v. Rodriguez*, 411 U.S. 1, 28 (1973).

It cannot seriously be suggested that nonminorities in Richmond have any "history of purposeful unequal treatment." Nor is there any indication that they have any of the disabilities that have characteristically afflicted those groups this Court has deemed suspect. ***

Richmond's own recent political history underscores the facile nature of the majority's assumption that elected officials' voting decisions are based on the color of their skins. In recent years, white and black councilmembers in Richmond have increasingly joined hands on controversial matters. When the Richmond City Council elected a black man mayor in 1982, for example, his victory was won with the support of the city council's four white members. The vote on the set-aside plan a year later also was not purely along racial lines. Of the four white councilmembers, one voted for the measure and another abstained. The majority's view that remedial measures undertaken by municipalities with black leadership must face a stiffer test of Equal Protection Clause scrutiny than remedial measures undertaken by municipalities with white leadership implies a lack of political maturity on the part of this Nation's elected minority officials that is totally unwarranted. Such insulting judgments have no place in constitutional jurisprudence.

Today's decision, finally, is particularly noteworthy for the daunting standard it imposes upon States and localities contemplating the use of race-conscious measures to eradicate the present effects of prior discrimination and prevent its perpetuation. The majority restricts the use of such measures to situations in which a State or locality can put forth "a prima facie case of a constitutional or statutory violation." *** To the degree that this parsimonious standard is grounded on a view that either § 1 or § 5 of the Fourteenth Amendment substantially disempowered States and localities from remedying past racial discrimination the majority is seriously mistaken. With respect, first, to § 5, our precedents have never suggested that this provision—or, for that matter, its companion federal-empowerment provisions in the Thirteenth and Fifteenth Amendments—was meant to pre-empt or limit state police power to undertake race-conscious remedial measures. ***

The majority today sounds a full-scale retreat from the Court's longstanding solicitude to race-conscious remedial efforts "directed toward deliverance of the century-old promise of equality of economic opportunity." *Fullilove*, 448 U.S., at 463. The new and restrictive tests it applies scuttle one city's effort to surmount its discriminatory past, and imperil those of dozens more localities. I, however, profoundly disagree with the cramped vision of the Equal Protection Clause which the majority offers today and with its application of that vision to Richmond, Virginia's, laudable set-aside plan. The battle against pernicious racial discrimination or its effects is nowhere near won. I must dissent.

JUSTICE BLACKMUN, with whom JUSTICE BRENNAN joins, dissenting.

I never thought that I would live to see the day when the city of Richmond, Virginia, the cradle of the Old Confederacy, sought on its own, within a narrow confine, to lessen the stark impact of persistent discrimination. But Richmond, to its great credit, acted. Yet this Court, the supposed bastion of equality, strikes down Richmond's efforts as though discrimination had never existed or was not demonstrated in this particular litigation. *** So the Court today regresses. I am confident, however, that, given time, it one day again will do its best to fulfill the great promises of the Constitution's Preamble and of the guarantees embodied in the Bill of Rights—a fulfillment that would make this Nation very special.

Notes

1. **Pros and Cons of Race–Conscious Affirmative Action.** Make two lists, one of reasons for and one of reasons against race-conscious affirmative action by governmental entities. Which list do you find more compelling? Why? Do any of these reasons have anything to do with legal reasoning as opposed to policy choices? Is your choice based on empirical evidence, or is it intuitive?

2. **Strict Scrutiny of Affirmative Action.** Think about how each of the following relates to whether strict scrutiny of racial affirmative action is appropriate:

    (a) Distrust of political processes where racial issues are involved.

    (b) Language of the Equal Protection Clause.

    (c) History and intent of the Equal Protection Clause.

    (d) Slavery, Jim Crow laws, and other racial subordination.

    (e) Concerns about "innocent victims."

(f) Difficulties in distinguishing between invidious and benign racial classifications.

3. **Meaning of Strict Scrutiny.** It is clear now that strict scrutiny applies to race-conscious affirmative action programs, but it is unclear what proportion of such programs that standard will invalidate. Will judicial strict scrutiny here be "fatal in fact" or not? Consider both the ends and means issues posed by strict scrutiny in this context:

(a) *Ends.* The Court seems willing to accept that some "compelling governmental purposes" may exist for "benign" race discrimination. Past discrimination is an acceptable reason, if the discrimination is by the governmental unit or within that unit's jurisdiction, at least if the discrimination continues into the present. Why is the Court uncomfortable with the notion that "societal discrimination" can justify affirmative action responses by governments? Other candidates for compelling purposes are "diversity" and "role modeling." Is diversity more acceptable in some contexts, like education, than in others, like employment or contracting? And what is meant by "diversity?" "Role modeling" was rejected by the Court in the context of layoff of a white teacher to retain a black teacher. *Wygant v. Jackson Bd. of Ed.*, 476 U.S. 267 (1986). Would it be legal for a city to demand that a person hired to counsel delinquent teen-agers in a predominantly-black neighborhood be black?

(b) *Means.* How specifically must the means and ends coincide? Why would Richmond define minorities to include Aleuts and other minorities, and what is it about such overinclusion that the Court finds objectionable? After *Croson*, must a city considering a set-aside for city contracting look separately at construction contracting and non-construction contracting? Must it look at plumbing versus roofing contracting?

4. **Exploring Race–Neutral Alternatives.** *Croson* requires exploration of race-neutral alternatives prior to adoption of race-conscious government programs. Would such alternatives be unconstitutional if adopted for the purpose of benefiting racial minorities? Would it be unlawful for a college to recognize all other forms of affirmative action (economics, geography, etc.) but not affirmative action based on societal race discrimination? In "gerrymandering" cases, where the lines drawn are not racial on their face, but purely geographic, the Court has held that "bizarre" lines "unexplainable on grounds other than race" are unconstitutional. The Court explained in *Miller v. Johnson*, 515 U.S. 900 (1995), that "The distinction between being aware of racial motivations and being motivated by them may be difficult to make *** a plaintiff must prove that the legislature subordinated traditional race-neutral districting principles, including but not limited to compactness, contiguity, respect for political subdivisions of communities defined by actual shared interests, to racial considerations."

5. *Brown* **and Affirmative Action.** Did the Court act in a race-neutral or race-conscious fashion in *Brown*? One commentator says, "The prohibition against discrimination established by *Brown* is not rooted in colorblindness at all. Instead, it is, like affirmative action, deeply race-conscious." Strauss, *The Myth of Colorblindness*, 1986 SUP. CT. REV. 99.

6. **Problem.** Advise a local governmental unit how to establish a constitutionally permissible race-conscious set-aside program.

7. **Federal Race–Consciousness.** *Croson* concerned state and local set-aside programs. Consider, as a matter of constitutional language, intent, and policy whether Congress should have more power than state and local governments to establish race-conscious affirmative action programs. Should this special competency, if you think it ought to exist, apply equally to federal agency affirmative action? Read the next case.

ADARAND CONSTRUCTORS v. PENA
515 U.S. 200, 115 S.Ct. 2097, 132 L.Ed.2d 158 (1995).

JUSTICE O'CONNOR announced the judgment of the Court and delivered an opinion with respect to Parts I, II, III–A, III–B, III–D, and IV, which is for the Court except insofar as it might be inconsistent with the views expressed in JUSTICE SCALIA's concurrence, and an opinion with respect to Part III–C in which JUSTICE KENNEDY joins. [III-C is not included in the excerpts below.]

Petitioner Adarand Constructors, Inc., claims that the Federal Government's practice of giving general contractors on Government projects a financial incentive to hire subcontractors controlled by "socially and economically disadvantaged individuals," and in particular, the Government's use of race-based presumptions in identifying such individuals, violates the equal protection component of the Fifth Amendment's Due Process Clause. ***

In 1989, the Central Federal Lands Highway Division (CFLHD), which is part of the United States Department of Transportation (DOT), awarded the prime contract for a highway construction project in Colorado to Mountain Gravel & Construction Company. *** The prime contract's terms provide that Mountain Gravel would receive additional compensation if it hired subcontractors certified as small businesses controlled by "socially and economically disadvantaged individuals." Gonzales is certified as such a business; Adarand is not. Mountain Gravel awarded the subcontract to Gonzales, despite Adarand's low bid, and Mountain Gravel's Chief Estimator has submitted an affidavit stating that Mountain Gravel would have accepted Adarand's bid, had it not been for the additional payment it received by hiring Gonzales instead. Federal law requires that a subcontracting clause similar to the one used here must appear in most federal agency contracts, and it also requires the clause to state that "[t]he contractor shall presume that socially and economically disadvantaged individuals include Black Americans, Hispanic Americans, Native Americans, Asian Pacific Americans, and other minorities, or any other individual found to be disadvantaged by the [Small Business] Administration pursuant to section 8(a) of the Small Business Act." Adarand claims that the presumption set forth in that statute discriminates on the basis of race in violation of the Federal Government's Fifth Amendment obligation not to deny anyone equal protection of the laws. ***

Respondents urge that "[t]he Subcontracting Compensation Clause program is *** a program based on disadvantage, not on race," and thus that it is subject only to "the most relaxed judicial scrutiny." To the extent that the statutes and regulations involved in this case are race neutral, we agree.

Respondents concede, however, that "the race-based rebuttable presumption used in some certification determinations under the Subcontracting Compensation Clause" is subject to some heightened level of scrutiny. The parties disagree as to what that level should be. *** Adarand's claim arises under the Fifth Amendment to the Constitution ***. Although this Court has always understood that Clause to provide some measure of protection against *arbitrary* treatment by the Federal Government, it is not as explicit a guarantee of equal treatment as the Fourteenth Amendment ***.

Through the 1940's, this Court had routinely taken the view in non-race-related cases that, "[u]nlike the Fourteenth Amendment, the Fifth contains no equal protection clause and it provides no guaranty against discriminatory legislation by Congress." *** *Korematsu v. United States*, 323 U.S. 214[, said in dictum,] "all legal restrictions which curtail the civil rights of a single racial group are immediately suspect *** [and] courts must subject them to the most rigid scrutiny." *** In *Bolling v. Sharpe*, 347 U.S. 497 (1954), the Court for the first time explicitly questioned the existence of any difference between the obligations of the Federal Government and the States to avoid racial classifications. *** Later cases *** did not distinguish between the duties of the States and the Federal Government to avoid racial classifications. *** Thus, in 1975, the Court stated explicitly that "[t]his Court's approach to Fifth Amendment equal protection claims has always been precisely the same as to equal protection claims under the Fourteenth Amendment." *Weinberger v. Wiesenfeld*, 420 U.S. 636, 638, n. 2. ***

The Court resolved the issue, at least in part, in 1989. *** But *Croson* of course had no occasion to declare what standard of review the Fifth Amendment requires for such action taken by the Federal Government. ***

Despite lingering uncertainty in the details, however, the Court's cases through *Croson* had established three general propositions with respect to governmental racial classifications. First, skepticism: "Any preference based on racial or ethnic criteria must necessarily receive a most searching examination." *** Second, consistency: "[T]he standard of review under the Equal Protection Clause is not dependent on the race of those burdened or benefited by a particular classification." *** And third, congruence: "Equal protection analysis in the Fifth Amendment area is the same as that under the Fourteenth Amendment." *** Taken together, these three propositions lead to the conclusion that any person, of whatever race, has the right to demand that any governmental actor subject to the Constitution justify any racial classification subjecting that person to unequal treatment under the strictest judicial scrutiny. ***

A year later, however, the Court took a surprising turn. *Metro Broadcasting, Inc. v. FCC*, 497 U.S. 547 (1990), involved a Fifth Amendment challenge to two race-based policies of the Federal Communications Commission (FCC). In *Metro Broadcasting*, the Court repudiated the long-held notion that "it would be unthinkable that the same Constitution would impose a lesser duty on the Federal Government" than it does on a State to afford equal protection of the laws. It did so by holding that "benign" federal racial classifications need only satisfy intermediate scrutiny, even though

Croson had recently concluded that such classifications enacted by a State must satisfy strict scrutiny. "[B]enign" federal racial classifications, the Court said, "—even if those measures are not 'remedial' in the sense of being designed to compensate victims of past governmental or societal discrimination—are constitutionally permissible to the extent that they serve important governmental objectives within the power of Congress and are *substantially related* to achievement of those objectives.'" The Court did not explain how to tell whether a racial classification should be deemed "benign," other than to express "confiden[ce] that an 'examination of the legislative scheme and its history' will separate benign measures from other types of racial classifications." ***

By adopting intermediate scrutiny as the standard of review for congressionally mandated "benign" racial classifications, *Metro Broadcasting* departed from prior cases in two significant respects. First, it turned its back on *Croson*'s explanation of why strict scrutiny of all governmental racial classifications is essential. *** Second, *Metro Broadcasting* squarely rejected one of the three propositions established by the Court's earlier equal protection cases, namely, congruence between the standards applicable to federal and state racial classifications, and in so doing also undermined the other two—skepticism of all racial classifications and consistency of treatment irrespective of the race of the burdened or benefited group. ***

The three propositions undermined by *Metro Broadcasting* all derive from the basic principle that the Fifth and Fourteenth Amendments to the Constitution protect *persons*, not *groups*. It follows from that principle that all governmental action based on race—a *group* classification long recognized as "in most circumstances irrelevant and therefore prohibited," should be subjected to detailed judicial inquiry to ensure that the personal right to equal protection of the laws has not been infringed. These ideas have long been central to this Court's understanding of equal protection, and holding "benign" state and federal racial classifications to different standards does not square with them. *** Accordingly, we hold today that all racial classifications, imposed by whatever federal, state, or local governmental actor, must be analyzed by a reviewing court under strict scrutiny. In other words, such classifications are constitutional only if they are narrowly tailored measures that further compelling governmental interests. To the extent that *Metro Broadcasting* is inconsistent with that holding, it is overruled. ***

But we need not decide today whether the program upheld in *Fullilove* would survive strict scrutiny as our more recent cases have defined it. *** We think that requiring strict scrutiny is the best way to ensure that courts will consistently give racial classifications that kind of detailed examination, both as to ends and as to means. *Korematsu* demonstrates vividly that even "the most rigid scrutiny" can sometimes fail to detect an illegitimate racial classification. *** Finally, we wish to dispel the notion that strict scrutiny is "strict in theory, but fatal in fact." The unhappy persistence of both the practice and the lingering effects of racial discrimination against minority groups in this country is an unfortunate reality, and government is not disqualified from acting in response to it. *** When race-based action is necessary to further a compelling interest, such action is within constitutional constraints if it satisfies the "narrow tailoring" test this Court has set out in previous cases.

Because our decision today alters the playing field in some important respects, we think it best to remand the case to the lower courts for further consideration in light of the principles we have announced. ***

JUSTICE SCALIA, concurring in part and concurring in the judgment.

*** In my view, government can never have a "compelling interest" in discriminating on the basis of race in order to "make up" for past racial discrimination in the opposite direction. Individuals who have been wronged by unlawful racial discrimination should be made whole; but under our Constitution there can be no such thing as either a creditor or a debtor race. That concept is alien to the Constitution's focus upon the individual *** and its rejection of dispositions based on race, see Amdt. 15, § 1 (prohibiting abridgment of the right to vote "on account of race"), or based on blood, see Art. III, § 3 ("[N]o Attainder of Treason shall work Corruption of Blood"); Art. I, § 9, cl. 8 ("No Title of Nobility shall be granted by the United States"). To pursue the concept of racial entitlement—even for the most admirable and benign of purposes—is to reinforce and preserve for future mischief the way of thinking that produced race slavery, race privilege and race hatred. In the eyes of government, we are just one race here. It is American. ***

JUSTICE THOMAS, concurring in part and concurring in the judgment.

*** I believe that there is a "moral [and] constitutional equivalence," between laws designed to subjugate a race and those that distribute benefits on the basis of race in order to foster some current notion of equality. *** That these programs may have been motivated, in part, by good intentions cannot provide refuge from the principle that under our Constitution, the government may not make distinctions on the basis of race. As far as the Constitution is concerned, it is irrelevant whether a government's racial classifications are drawn by those who wish to oppress a race or by those who have a sincere desire to help those thought to be disadvantaged. *** These programs not only raise grave constitutional questions, they also undermine the moral basis of the equal protection principle. Purchased at the price of immeasurable human suffering, the equal protection principle reflects our nation's understanding that such classifications ultimately have a destructive impact on the individual and our society. Unquestionably, "[i]nvidious [racial] discrimination is an engine of oppression." It is also true that "[r]emedial" racial preferences may reflect "a desire to foster equality in society." But there can be no doubt that racial paternalism and its unintended consequences can be as poisonous and pernicious as any other form of discrimination. So-called "benign" discrimination teaches many that because of chronic and apparently immutable handicaps, minorities cannot compete with them without their patronizing indulgence. Inevitably, such programs engender attitudes of superiority or, alternatively, provoke resentment among those who believe that they have been wronged by the government's use of race. These programs stamp minorities with a badge of inferiority and may cause them to develop dependencies or to adopt an attitude that they are "entitled" to preferences. *** In my mind, government-sponsored racial discrimination based on benign prejudice is just as noxious as discrimination inspired by malicious prejudice. In each instance, it is racial discrimination, plain and simple.

JUSTICE STEVENS, with whom JUSTICE GINSBURG joins, dissenting.

Instead of deciding this case in accordance with controlling precedent, the Court today delivers a disconcerting lecture about the evils of governmental racial classifications. *** The Court's concept of skepticism is, at least in principle, a good statement of law and of common sense. Undoubtedly, a court should be wary of a governmental decision that relies upon a racial classification. *** The Court's concept of "consistency" assumes that there is no significant difference between a decision by the majority to impose a special burden on the members of a minority race and a decision by the majority to provide a benefit to certain members of that minority notwithstanding its incidental burden on some members of the majority. In my opinion that assumption is untenable. There is no moral or constitutional equivalence between a policy that is designed to perpetuate a caste system and one that seeks to eradicate racial subordination. Invidious discrimination is an engine of oppression, subjugating a disfavored group to enhance or maintain the power of the majority. Remedial race-based preferences reflect the opposite impulse: a desire to foster equality in society. No sensible conception of the Government's constitutional obligation to "govern impartially," should ignore this distinction. *** We should reject a concept of "consistency" that would view the special preferences that the National Government has provided to Native Americans since 1834 as comparable to the official discrimination against African–Americans that was prevalent for much of our history.

The consistency that the Court espouses would disregard the difference between a "No Trespassing" sign and a welcome mat. *** An attempt by the majority to exclude members of a minority race from a regulated market is fundamentally different from a subsidy that enables a relatively small group of newcomers to enter that market. An interest in "consistency" does not justify treating differences as though they were similarities.

The Court's explanation for treating dissimilar race-based decisions as though they were equally objectionable is a supposed inability to differentiate between "invidious" and "benign" discrimination. But the term "affirmative action" is common and well understood. Its presence in everyday parlance shows that people understand the difference between good intentions and bad. *** Nothing is inherently wrong with applying a single standard to fundamentally different situations, as long as that standard takes relevant differences into account. *** Under such a standard, subsidies for disadvantaged businesses may be constitutional though special taxes on such businesses would be invalid. But a single standard that purports to equate remedial preferences with invidious discrimination cannot be defended in the name of "equal protection."

Moreover, the Court may find that its new "consistency" approach to race-based classifications is difficult to square with its insistence upon rigidly separate categories for discrimination against different classes of individuals. For example, as the law currently stands, the Court will apply "intermediate scrutiny" to cases of invidious gender discrimination and "strict scrutiny" to cases of invidious race discrimination, while applying the same standard for benign classifications as for invidious ones. If this remains the law, then today's lecture about "consistency" will produce the anomalous result that the Government can more easily enact affirmative-action programs to remedy discrimination against women than it can enact affirmative-action programs to remedy discrimination against African-Americans—even though the primary purpose of the Equal Protection Clause was to end discrimination against the former slaves. When a court becomes preoccupied with abstract standards, it risks sacrificing common sense at the altar of formal consistency. ***

The Court's concept of "congruence" assumes that there is no significant difference between a decision by the Congress of the United States to adopt an affirmative-action program and such a decision by a State or a municipality. In my opinion that assumption is untenable. It ignores important practical and legal differences between federal and state or local decisionmakers. *** An additional reason for giving greater deference to the National Legislature than to a local lawmaking body is that federal affirmative-action programs represent the will of our entire Nation's elected representatives, whereas a state or local program may have an impact on nonresident entities who played no part in the decision to enact it. Thus, in the state or local context, individuals who were unable to vote for the local representatives who enacted a race-conscious program may nonetheless feel the effects of that program. ***

The Fourteenth Amendment directly empowers Congress at the same time it expressly limits the States. This is no accident. It represents our Nation's consensus, achieved after hard experience throughout our sorry history of race relations, that the Federal Government must be the primary defender of racial minorities against the States, some of which may be inclined to oppress such minorities. A rule of "congruence" that ignores a purposeful "incongruity" so fundamental to our system of government is unacceptable. ***

JUSTICE SOUTER, with whom JUSTICE GINSBURG and JUSTICE BREYER join, dissenting. [omitted]

JUSTICE GINSBURG, with whom JUSTICE BREYER joins, dissenting. [omitted]

Notes

1. **Overruling.** Why didn't the Court overrule *Metro Broadcasting*? Are there any factors which distinguish it from *Adarand*? From *Adarand's* rationale?

2. **Flip-flopping Formalists?** Many of the formalist arguments are aligned against extension of *Croson* to the federal sphere. Consider the differences in text

between the Fifth and Fourteenth Amendments ("due process" versus "equal protection"), the history of affirmative action following the Civil War (Freedman's Bureau Acts, in which land, education, and other benefits were provided the former slaves), and Madisonian notions that the federal government would be more beyond factional politics than state and local governments. The Court's history in the race area (including *Dred Scott, Plessy*, and *Korematsu*) and the unseemliness of the federal government taking racial actions the states cannot take make the Court's decision more understandable. But these are functional arguments, and the majority in *Croson* and *Adarand* seem inclined to textualism. How do you account for this alignment?

GRUTTER v. BOLLINGER
123 S.Ct. 2325, 156 L.Ed.2d 304 (2003).

JUSTICE O'CONNOR delivered the opinion of the Court.

This case requires us to decide whether the use of race as a factor in student admissions by the University of Michigan Law School (Law School) is unlawful.

I

The Law School ranks among the Nation's top law schools. *** Seeking to "admit a group of students who individually and collectively are among the most capable," the Law School looks for individuals with "substantial promise for success in law school" and "a strong likelihood of succeeding in the practice of law and contributing in diverse ways to the well-being of others." More broadly, the Law School seeks "a mix of students with varying backgrounds and experiences who will respect and learn from each other." *** The [Law School's admissions] policy requires admissions officials to evaluate each applicant based on all the information available in the file, including a personal statement, letters of recommendation, and an essay describing the ways in which the applicant will contribute to the life and diversity of the Law School. In reviewing an applicant's file, admissions officials must consider the applicant's undergraduate grade point average (GPA) and Law School Admissions Test (LSAT) score because they are important (if imperfect) predictors of academic success in law school. *** The policy makes clear, however, that even the highest possible score does not guarantee admission to the Law School. Nor does a low score automatically disqualify an applicant. *** So-called "'soft' variables" such as "the enthusiasm of recommenders, the quality of the undergraduate institution, the quality of the applicant's essay, and the areas and difficulty of undergraduate course selection" are all brought to bear in assessing an "applicant's likely contributions to the intellectual and social life of the institution."

The policy aspires to "achieve that diversity which has the potential to enrich everyone's education and thus make a law school class stronger than the sum of its parts." The policy does not restrict the types of diversity contributions eligible for "substantial weight" in the admissions process, but instead recognizes "many possible bases for diversity admissions." The policy does, however, reaffirm the Law School's longstanding commitment to "one particular type of diversity," that is, "racial and ethnic diversity with special reference to the inclusion of students from groups which have been historically discriminated against, like African-Americans, Hispanics and Native Americans, who without this commitment might not be represented in our student body in meaningful numbers." By enrolling a "'critical mass' of [underrepresented] minority students," the Law School seeks to "ensur[e] their ability to make unique contributions to the character of the Law School." ***

Petitioner Barbara Grutter is a white Michigan resident who applied to the Law School in 1996 with a 3.8 grade point average and 161 LSAT score. The Law School initially placed petitioner on a waiting list, but subsequently rejected her application. *** Petitioner alleged that respondents discriminated against her on the basis of race in violation of the Fourteenth Amendment *** [and] that her application was rejected because the Law School uses race as a "predominant" factor, giving applicants who belong to certain minority groups "a significantly greater chance of admission than students with similar credentials from disfavored racial groups." Petitioner also alleged that respondents "had no compelling interest to justify their use of race in the admissions process." ***

II

We last addressed the use of race in public higher education over 25 years ago. In the landmark *Bakke* case, [438 U.S. 265 (1978),] we reviewed a racial set-aside program that reserved 16 out of 100 seats in a medical school class for members of certain minority groups. The decision produced six separate opinions, none of which commanded a majority of the Court. Four Justices would have upheld the program against all attack on the ground that the government can use race to "remedy disadvantages cast on minorities by past racial prejudice." Four other Justices avoided the constitutional question altogether and struck down the program on statutory grounds. JUSTICE POWELL provided a fifth vote not only for invalidating the set-aside program, but also for reversing the state court's injunction against any use of race whatsoever. The only holding for the Court in *Bakke* was that a "State has a substantial interest that legitimately may be served by a properly devised admissions program involving the competitive consideration of race and ethnic origin." Thus, we reversed that part of the lower court's judgment that enjoined the university "from any consideration of the race of any applicant." *** In the wake of our fractured decision in *Bakke*, courts have struggled to discern whether JUSTICE POWELL's diversity rationale, set forth in part of the opinion joined by no other Justice, is nonetheless binding precedent. *** [T]oday we endorse JUSTICE POWELL's view that student body diversity is a compelling state interest that can justify the use of race in university admissions. ***

III
A

*** The Law School's educational judgment that such diversity is essential to its educational mission is one to which we defer. *** We have long recognized that, given the important purpose of public education and the expansive freedoms of speech and thought associated with the university environment, universities occupy a special niche in our constitutional tradition. *** Our conclusion that the Law School has a compelling interest in a diverse student body is informed by our view that attaining a diverse student body is at the heart of the Law School's proper institutional mission, and that "good faith" on the part of a university is "presumed" absent "a showing to the contrary."

As part of its goal of "assembling a class that is both exceptionally academically qualified and broadly diverse," the Law School seeks to "enroll a 'critical mass' of minority students." The Law School's interest is not simply "to assure within its student body some specified percentage of a particular group merely because of its race or ethnic origin." That would amount to outright racial balancing, which is patently unconstitutional. Rather, the Law School's concept of critical mass is defined by reference to the educational benefits that diversity is designed to produce.

These benefits are substantial. *** [N]umerous studies show that student body diversity promotes learning outcomes, and "better prepares students for an increasingly diverse workforce and society, and better prepares them as professionals." *** [M]ajor American businesses have made clear that the skills needed in today's increasingly global marketplace can only be developed through exposure to widely diverse people, cultures, ideas, and viewpoints. What is more, high-ranking retired officers and civilian leaders of the United States military assert that, "[b]ased on [their] decades of experience," a "highly qualified, racially diverse officer corps *** is essential to the military's ability to fulfill its principle mission to provide national security." *** At present, "the military cannot achieve an officer corps that is *both* highly qualified *and* racially diverse unless the service academies and the ROTC used limited race-conscious recruiting and admissions policies." ***

We have repeatedly acknowledged the overriding importance of preparing students for work and citizenship, describing education as pivotal to "sustaining our political and cultural heritage" with a fundamental role in maintaining the fabric of society. *Plyler v. Doe*, 457 U. S. 202, 221 (1982). *** The United States, as *amicus curiae*, affirms that "[e]nsuring that public institutions are open and available to all segments of American society, including people of all races and ethnicities, represents a paramount government objective." And, "[n]owhere is the importance of such openness more acute than in the context of higher education." Effective participation by members of all racial and ethnic groups in the civic life of our Nation is essential if the dream of one Nation, indivisible, is to be realized.

Moreover, universities, and in particular, law schools, represent the training ground for a large number of our Nation's leaders. Individuals with law degrees occupy roughly half the state governorships, more than half the seats in the United States Senate, and more than a third of the seats in the United States House of Representatives. The pattern is even more striking when it comes to highly selective law schools. A handful of these schools accounts for 25 of the 100 United States Senators, 74 United States Courts of Appeals judges, and nearly 200 of the more than 600 United States District Court judges.

In order to cultivate a set of leaders with legitimacy in the eyes of the citizenry, it is necessary that the path to leadership be visibly open to talented and qualified individuals of every race and ethnicity. *** The Law School does not premise its need for critical mass on "any belief that minority students always (or even consistently) express some characteristic minority viewpoint on any issue." *** The Law School has determined, based on its experience and expertise, that a "critical mass" of underrepresented minorities is necessary to further its compelling interest in securing the educational benefits of a diverse student body.

B

*** To be narrowly tailored, a race-conscious admissions program cannot use a quota system—it cannot "insulat[e] each category of applicants with certain desired qualifications from competition with all other applicants." Instead, a university may consider race or ethnicity only as a "'plus' in a particular applicant's file," without "insulat[ing] the individual from comparison with all other candidates for the available seats." *** We are satisfied that the Law School's admissions program, like the Harvard plan described by JUSTICE POWELL, does not operate as a quota. Properly understood, a "quota" is a program in which a certain fixed number or proportion of opportunities are "reserved exclusively for certain minority groups." *Richmond v. J. A. Croson Co.* *** The Law School's goal of attaining a critical mass of underrepresented minority students does not transform its program into a quota. *** [B]etween 1993 and 2000, the number of African-American, Latino, and Native-American students in each class at the Law School varied from 13.5 to 20.1 percent, a range inconsistent with a quota.

*** [T]he number of underrepresented minority students who ultimately enroll in the Law School differs substantially from their representation in the applicant pool and varies considerably for each group from year to year.

That a race-conscious admissions program does not operate as a quota does not, by itself, satisfy the requirement of individualized consideration. *** Here, the Law School engages in a highly individualized, holistic review of each applicant's file, giving serious consideration to all the ways an applicant might contribute to a diverse educational environment. The Law School affords this individualized consideration to applicants of all races. *** Unlike the program at issue in *Gratz v. Bollinger*, the Law School awards no mechanical, predetermined diversity "bonuses" based on race or ethnicity. See *Gratz* (distinguishing a race-conscious admissions program that automatically awards 20 points based on race from the Harvard plan, which considered race but "did not contemplate that any single characteristic automatically ensured a specific and identifiable contribution to a university's diversity"). Like the Harvard plan, the Law School's admissions policy "is flexible enough to consider all pertinent elements of diversity in light of the particular qualifications of each applicant, and to place them on the same footing for consideration, although not necessarily according them the same weight."

We also find that, like the Harvard plan JUSTICE POWELL referenced in *Bakke*, the Law School's race-conscious admissions program adequately ensures that all factors that may contribute to student body diversity are meaningfully considered alongside race in admissions decisions. *** What is more, the Law School actually gives substantial weight to diversity factors besides race. The Law School frequently accepts nonminority applicants with grades and test scores lower than underrepresented minority applicants (and other nonminority applicants) who are rejected. *** JUSTICE KENNEDY speculates that "race is likely outcome determinative for many members of minority groups" who do not fall within the upper range of LSAT scores and grades. But the same could be said of the Harvard plan discussed approvingly by JUSTICE POWELL in *Bakke*, and indeed of any plan that uses race as one of many factors.

Petitioner and the United States argue that the Law School's plan is not narrowly tailored because race-neutral means exist to obtain the educational benefits of student body diversity that the Law School seeks. We disagree. Narrow tailoring does not require exhaustion of every conceivable race-neutral alternative. Nor does it require a university to choose between maintaining a reputation for excellence or fulfilling a commitment to provide educational opportunities to members of all racial groups. Narrow tailoring does, however, require serious, good faith consideration of workable race-neutral alternatives that will achieve the diversity the university seeks. *** The United States advocates "percentage plans," recently adopted by public undergraduate institutions in Texas, Florida, and California to guarantee admission to all students above a certain class-rank threshold in every high school in the State. The United States does not, however, explain how such plans could work for graduate and professional schools. More-over, even assuming such plans are race-neutral, they may preclude the university from conducting the individualized assessments necessary to assemble a student body that is not just racially diverse, but diverse along all the qualities valued by the university. *** [I]n the context of its individualized inquiry into the possible diversity contributions of all applicants, the Law School's race-conscious admissions program does not unduly harm nonminority applicants. *** [R]ace-conscious admissions policies must be limited in time. *** We see no reason to exempt race- conscious admissions programs from the requirement that all governmental use of race must have a logical end point. The Law School, too, concedes that all "race-conscious programs must have reasonable durational limits."

In the context of higher education, the durational requirement can be met by sunset provisions in race-conscious admissions policies and periodic reviews to determine whether racial preferences are still necessary to achieve student body diversity. Universities in California, Florida, and Washington State, where racial preferences in admissions are prohibited by state law, are currently engaged in experimenting with a wide variety of alternative approaches. Universities in other States can and should draw on the most promising aspects of these race-neutral alternatives as they develop. *** We take the Law School at its word that it would "like nothing better than to find a race-neutral admissions formula" and will terminate its race-conscious admissions program as soon as practicable. It has been 25 years since JUSTICE POWELL first approved the use of race to further an interest in student body diversity in the context of public higher education. Since that time, the number of minority applicants with high grades and test scores has indeed increased. We expect that 25 years from now, the use of racial preferences will no longer be necessary to further the interest approved today. ***

JUSTICE GINSBURG, with whom JUSTICE BREYER joins, concurring.

The Court's observation that race-conscious programs "must have a logical end point," accords with the international understanding of the office of affirmative action. *** It is well documented that conscious and unconscious race bias, even rank discrimination based on race, remain alive in our land, impeding realization of our highest values and ideals. As to public education, data for the years 2000-2001 show that 71.6% of African-American children and 76.3% of Hispanic children attended a school in which minorities made up a majority of the student body. And schools in predominantly minority communities lag far behind others measured by the educational resources available to them. *** From today's vantage point, one may hope, but not firmly forecast, that over the next generation's span, progress toward nondiscrimination and genuinely equal opportunity will make it safe to sunset affirmative action.

JUSTICE SCALIA, with whom JUSTICE THOMAS joins, concurring in part and dissenting in part.

*** The "educational benefit" that the University of Michigan seeks to achieve by racial discrimination consists, according to the Court, of "'cross-racial understanding,'" and "'better prepar[ation of] students for an increasingly diverse workforce and society,'" all of which is necessary not only for work, but also for good "citizenship". This is not, of course, an "educational benefit" on which students will be graded on their Law School transcript (Works and Plays Well with Others: B+) or tested by the bar examiners (Q: Describe in 500 words or less your cross-racial understanding). For it is a lesson of life rather than law—essentially the same lesson taught to (or rather learned by, for it cannot be "taught" in the usual sense) people three feet shorter and twenty years younger than the full-grown adults at the University of Michigan Law School, in institutions ranging from Boy Scout troops to public-school kindergartens. If properly considered an "educational benefit" at all, it is surely not one that is either uniquely relevant to law school or uniquely "teachable" in a formal educational setting. *And therefore:* If it is appropriate for the University of Michigan Law School to use racial discrimination for the purpose of putting together a "critical mass" that will convey generic lessons in socialization and good citizenship, surely it is no less appropriate—indeed, *particularly* appropriate—for the civil service system of the State of Michigan to do so. There, also, those exposed to "critical masses" of certain races will presumably become better Americans, better Michiganders, better civil servants. And surely private employers cannot be criticized–indeed, should be praised–if they also "teach" good citizenship to their adult employees through a patriotic, all-American system of racial discrimination in hiring. The nonminority individuals who are deprived of a legal education, a civil service job, or any job at all by reason of their skin color will surely understand.

*** [T]oday's *Grutter-Gratz* split double header seems perversely designed to prolong the controversy and the litigation. Some future lawsuits will presumably focus on whether the discriminatory scheme in question contains enough evaluation of the applicant "as an individual," and sufficiently avoids "separate admissions tracks" to fall under *Grutter* rather than *Gratz.* Some will focus on whether a university has gone beyond the bounds of a "'good faith effort'" and has so zealously pursued its "critical mass" as to make it an unconstitutional *de facto* quota system, rather than merely "'a permissible goal.'" Other lawsuits may focus on whether, in the particular setting at issue, any educational benefits flow from racial diversity. (That issue was not contested in *Grutter;* and while the opinion accords "a degree of deference to a university's academic decisions deference does not imply abandonment or abdication of judicial review.") Still other suits may challenge the bona fides of the institution's expressed commitment to the educational benefits of diversity that immunize the discriminatory scheme in *Grutter.* (Tempting targets, one would suppose, will be those universities that talk the talk of multiculturalism and racial diversity in the courts but walk the walk of tribalism and racial segregation on their campuses–through minority-only student organizations, separate minority housing opportunities, separate minority student centers, even separate minority-only graduation ceremonies.) And still other suits may claim that the institution's racial preferences have gone below or above the mystical *Grutter*-approved "critical mass." Finally, litigation can be expected on behalf of minority groups intentionally short changed in the institution's composition of its generic minority "critical mass." ***

JUSTICE THOMAS, with whom JUSTICE SCALIA joins ***, concurring in part and dissenting in part.

*** I believe blacks can achieve in every avenue of American life without the meddling of university administrators. Because I wish to see all students succeed whatever their color, I share, in some respect, the sympathies of those who sponsor the type of discrimination advanced by the University of Michigan Law School (Law School). The Constitution does not, however, tolerate institutional devotion to the status quo in admissions policies when such devotion ripens into racial discrimination. Nor does the Constitution countenance the unprecedented deference the Court gives to the Law School, an approach inconsistent with the very concept of "strict scrutiny." *** Nevertheless, I concur in part in the Court's opinion. First, I agree with the Court insofar as its decision, which approves of only one racial classification, confirms that further use of race in admissions remains unlawful. Second, I agree with the Court's holding that racial discrimination in higher education admissions will be illegal in 25 years. ***

The Law School's argument, as facile as it is, can only be understood in one way: Classroom aesthetics yield educational benefits, racially discriminatory admissions policies are required to achieve the right racial mix, and therefore the policies are required to achieve the educational benefits. It is the *educational benefits* that are the end, or allegedly compelling state interest, not "diversity." *** Under the proper standard, there is no pressing public necessity in maintaining a public law school at all and, it follows, certainly not an elite law school. Likewise, marginal improvements in legal education do not qualify as a compelling state interest. *** [T]he absence of a public, American Bar Association (ABA) accredited, law school in Alaska, Delaware, Massachusetts, New Hampshire, and Rhode Island, provides further evidence that Michigan's maintenance of the Law School does not constitute a compelling state interest.

As the foregoing makes clear, Michigan has no compelling interest in having a law school at all, much less an *elite* one. *** The only cognizable state interests vindicated by operating a public law school are, therefore, the education of that State's citizens and the training of that State's lawyers. *** The Law School today, however, does precious little training of those attorneys who will serve the citizens of Michigan. *** [W]hile a mere 27% of the Law School's 2002 entering class are from Michigan, only half of these, it appears, will stay in Michigan. *** Finally, even if the Law School's racial tinkering produces tangible educational benefits, a marginal improvement in legal education cannot justify racial discrimination where the Law School has no compelling interest in either its existence or in its current educational and admissions policies.

*** [T]he Court holds, implicitly and under the guise of narrow tailoring, that the Law School has a compelling state interest in doing what it wants to do. I cannot agree. First, under strict scrutiny, the Law School's assessment of the benefits of racial discrimination and devotion to the admissions status quo are not entitled to any sort of deference, grounded in the First Amendment or anywhere else. Second, even if its "academic selectivity" must be maintained at all costs along with racial discrimination, the Court ignores the fact that other top law schools have succeeded in meeting their aesthetic demands without racial discrimination. *** The Court's deference to the Law School's conclusion that its racial experimentation leads to educational benefits will, if adhered to, have serious collateral consequences. The Court relies heavily on social science evidence to justify its deference. The Court never acknowledges, however, the growing evidence that racial (and other sorts) of heterogeneity actually impairs learning among black students.

At oral argument in *Gratz v. Bollinger*, counsel for respondents stated that "most every single one of [the HBCs] do have diverse student bodies." What precisely counsel meant by "diverse" is indeterminate, but it is reported that in 2000 at Morehouse College, one of the most distinguished HBC's in the Nation, only 0.1% of the student body was white, and only 0.2% was Hispanic. And at Mississippi Valley State University, a public HBC, only 1.1% of the freshman class in 2001 was white. If there is a "critical mass" of whites at these institutions, then "critical mass" is indeed a very small proportion. *** It follows, therefore, that an HBC's assessment that racial homogeneity will yield educational benefits would similarly be given deference. *** Contained within today's majority opinion is the seed of a new constitutional justification for a concept I thought long and rightly rejected–racial segregation.

Moreover one would think, in light of the Court's decision in *United States v. Virginia,* 518 U. S. 515 (1996), that before being given license to use racial discrimination, the Law School would be required to radically reshape its admissions process, even to the point of sacrificing some elements of its character. *** [I]n the national debate on racial discrimination in higher education admissions, much has been made of the fact that elite institutions utilize a so-called "legacy" preference to give the children of alumni an advantage in admissions. This, and other, exceptions to a "true" meritocracy give the lie to protestations that merit admissions are in fact the order of the day at the Nation's universities. The Equal Protection Clause does not, however, prohibit the use of unseemly legacy preferences or many other kinds of arbitrary admissions procedures. What the Equal Protection Clause does prohibit are classifications made on the basis of race. So while legacy preferences can stand under the Constitution, racial discrimination cannot.[10] I will not twist the Constitution to invalidate legacy preferences or otherwise impose my vision of higher education admissions on the Nation. The majority should similarly stay its impulse to validate faddish racial discrimination the Constitution clearly forbids.

In any event, there is nothing ancient, honorable, or constitutionally protected about "selective" admissions. *** Columbia employed intelligence tests precisely because Jewish applicants, who were predominantly immigrants, scored worse on such tests. *** Similarly no modern law school can claim ignorance of the poor performance of blacks, relatively speaking, on the Law School Admissions Test (LSAT). Nevertheless, law schools continue to use the test and then attempt to "correct" for black underperformance by using racial discrimination in admissions so as to obtain their aesthetic student body. *** Having decided to use the LSAT, the Law School must accept the constitutional burdens that come with this decision. The Law School may freely continue to employ the LSAT and other allegedly merit-based standards in whatever fashion it likes. What the Equal Protection Clause forbids, but the Court today allows, is the use of these standards hand-in-hand with racial discrimination. *** [N]owhere in any of the filings in this Court is any evidence that the purported "beneficiaries" of this racial discrimination prove themselves by performing at (or even near) the same level as those students who receive no preferences.

The silence in this case is deafening to those of us who view higher education's purpose as imparting knowledge and skills to students, rather

---

[10] Were this Court to have the courage to forbid the use of racial discrimination in admissions, legacy preferences (and similar practices) might quickly become less popular–a possibility not lost, I am certain, on the elites (both individual and institutional) supporting the Law School in this case.

than a communal, rubber-stamp, credentialing process. The Law School is not looking for those students who, despite a lower LSAT score or undergraduate grade point average, will succeed in the study of law. The Law School seeks only a facade—it is sufficient that the class looks right, even if it does not perform right.

The Law School tantalizes unprepared students with the promise of a University of Michigan degree and all of the opportunities that it offers. These overmatched students take the bait, only to find that they cannot succeed in the cauldron of competition. *** Beyond the harm the Law School's racial discrimination visits upon its test subjects, no social science has disproved the notion that this discrimination "engender[s] attitudes of superiority or, alternatively, provoke[s] resentment among those who believe that they have been wronged by the government's use of race." "These programs stamp minorities with a badge of inferiority and may cause them to develop dependencies or to adopt an attitude that they are 'entitled' to preferences." ***

Finally, the Court's disturbing reference to the importance of the country's law schools as training grounds meant to cultivate "a set of leaders with legitimacy in the eyes of the citizenry," through the use of racial discrimination deserves discussion. As noted earlier, the Court has soundly rejected the remedying of societal discrimination as a justification for governmental use of race.

*** Under today's decision, it is still the case that racial discrimination that does not help a university to enroll an unspecified number, or "critical mass," of underrepresented minority students is unconstitutional. Thus, the Law School may not discriminate in admissions between similarly situated blacks and Hispanics, or between whites and Asians. *** The majority does not and cannot rest its time limitation on any evidence that the gap in credentials between black and white students is shrinking or will be gone in that timeframe. In recent years there has been virtually no change, for example, in the proportion of law school applicants with LSAT scores of 165 and higher who are black. *** Indeed, the very existence of racial discrimination of the type practiced by the Law School may impede the narrowing of the LSAT testing gap. *** Whites scoring between 163 and 167 on the LSAT are routinely rejected by the Law School, and thus whites aspiring to admission at the Law School have every incentive to improve their score to levels above that range. Blacks, on the other hand, are nearly guaranteed admission if they score above 155. As admission prospects approach certainty, there is no incentive for the black applicant to continue to prepare for the LSAT once he is reasonably assured of achieving the requisite score. ***

CHIEF JUSTICE REHNQUIST, with whom JUSTICE SCALIA, JUSTICE KENNEDY, and JUSTICE THOMAS join, dissenting.

*** Stripped of its "critical mass" veil, the Law School's program is revealed as a naked effort to achieve racial balancing. *** In practice, the Law School's program bears little or no relation to its asserted goal of achieving "critical mass." Respondents explain that the Law School seeks to accumulate a "critical mass" of *each* underrepresented minority group. But the record demonstrates that the Law School's admissions practices with respect to these groups differ dramatically and cannot be defended under any consistent use of the term "critical mass."

From 1995 through 2000, the Law School admitted between 1,130 and 1,310 students. Of those, between 13 and 19 were Native American, between 91 and 108 were African-Americans, and between 47 and 56 were Hispanic. If the Law School is admitting between 91 and 108 African-Americans in order to achieve "critical mass," thereby preventing African-American students from feeling "isolated or like spokespersons for their race," one would think that a number of the same order of magnitude would be necessary to accomplish the same purpose for Hispanics and Native Americans. ***

Respondents have *never* offered any race-specific arguments explaining why significantly more individuals from one underrepresented minority group are needed in order to achieve "critical mass" or further student body diversity. They certainly have not explained why Hispanics, who they have said are among "the groups most isolated by racial barriers in our country," should have their admission capped out in this manner. *** Only when the "critical mass" label is discarded does a likely explanation for these numbers emerge. The Court states that the Law School's goal of attaining a "critical mass" of underrepresented minority students is not an interest in merely "'assur[ing] within its student body some specified percentage of a particular group merely because of its race or ethnic origin.'" ***

But the correlation between the percentage of the Law School's pool of applicants who are members of the three minority groups and the percentage of the admitted applicants who are members of these same groups is far too precise to be dismissed as merely the result of the school paying "some attention to [the] numbers." *** [F]rom 1995 through 2000 the percentage of admitted applicants who were members of these minority groups closely tracked the percentage of individuals in the school's applicant pool who were from the same groups. *** For example, in 1995, when 9.7% of the applicant pool was African-American, 9.4% of the admitted class was African-American. By 2000, only 7.5% of the applicant pool was African-American, and 7.3% of the admitted class was African-American. *** The Law School cannot precisely control which of its admitted applicants decide to attend the university. But it can and, as the numbers demonstrate, clearly does employ racial preferences in extending offers of admission. ***

Finally, I believe that the Law School's program fails strict scrutiny because it is devoid of any reasonably precise time limit on the Law School's use of race in admissions. *** The Court suggests a possible 25-year limitation on the Law School's current program. Respondents, on the other hand, remain more ambiguous. *** These discussions of a time limit are the vaguest of assurances. In truth, they permit the Law School's use of racial preferences on a seemingly permanent basis. Thus, an important component of strict scrutiny—that a program be limited in time—is casually subverted.

***

JUSTICE KENNEDY, dissenting.

*** The opinion by JUSTICE POWELL, in my view, states the correct rule for resolving this case. The Court, however, does not apply strict scrutiny. *** Having approved the use of race as a factor in the admissions process, the majority proceeds to nullify the essential safeguard JUSTICE POWELL insisted upon as the precondition of the approval. The safeguard was rigorous judicial review, with strict scrutiny as the controlling standard. *** The Court confuses deference to a university's definition of its educational objective with deference to the implementation of this goal. *** It remains to point out how critical mass becomes inconsistent with individual consideration in some more specific aspects of the admissions process. *** There was little deviation among admitted minority students during the years from 1995 to 1998. The percentage of enrolled minorities fluctuated only by 0.3%, from 13.5% to 13.8%. *** The narrow fluctuation band raises an inference that the Law School subverted individual determination, and strict scrutiny requires the Law School to overcome the inference. *** If universities are given the latitude to administer programs that are tantamount to quotas, they will have few incentives to make the existing minority admissions schemes transparent and protective of individual review. The unhappy consequence will be to perpetuate the hostilities that proper consideration of race is designed to avoid. The perpetuation, of course, would be the worst of all outcomes. ***

Notes

1. *Grutter's* Sibling. The companion case to *Grutter*, *Gratz v. Bollinger*, 123 S.Ct. 2411 (2003), held that the UM undergraduate admissions point-bonus system was unconstitutional. Here are a few central points made in the *Gratz* opinions:

> CHIEF JUSTICE REHNQUIST for the Court: " *** OUA considers a number of factors in making admissions decisions, including high school grades, standardized test scores, high school quality, curriculum strength, geography, alumni relationships, and leadership. OUA also considers race. During all periods relevant to this litigation, the University has considered African-Americans, Hispanics, and Native Americans to be 'underrepresented minorities,' and it is undisputed that the University admits 'virtually every qualified *** applicant' from these groups. *** During 1999 and 2000, the OUA used the selection index, under which every applicant from an underrepresented racial or ethnic minority group was awarded 20 points. *** [T]he LSA's automatic distribution of 20 points has the effect of making 'the factor of race *** decisive' for virtually every minimally qualified underrepresented minority applicant. ***
>
> Respondents contend that '[t]he volume of applications and the presentation of applicant information make it impractical for [LSA] to use the *** admissions system' upheld by the Court today in *Grutter*. But the fact that the implementation of a program capable of providing individualized consideration might present

administrative challenges does not render constitutional an otherwise problematic system. *** [B]ecause the University's use of race in its current freshman admissions policy is not narrowly tailored to achieve respondents' asserted compelling interest in diversity, the admissions policy violates the Equal Protection Clause of the Fourteenth Amendment. *** "

JUSTICE O'CONNOR, concurring: " *** Even the most outstanding national high school leader could never receive more than five points for his or her accomplishments—a mere quarter of the points automatically assigned to an underrepresented minority solely based on the fact of his or her race. *** [T]he selection index, by setting up automatic, predetermined point allocations for the soft variables, ensures that the diversity contributions of applicants cannot be individually assessed. This policy stands in sharp contrast to the law school's admissions plan, which enables admissions officers to make nuanced judgments with respect to the contributions each applicant is likely to make to the diversity of the incoming class. *** "

JUSTICE THOMAS, concurring: " *** Under today's decisions, a university may not racially discriminate between the groups constituting the critical mass. *** "

JUSTICE SOUTER, with whom JUSTICE GINSBURG joins, dissenting: " *** The record does not describe a system with a quota like the one struck down in *Bakke*, which 'insulate[d]' all nonminority candidates from competition from certain seats. *** JUSTICE POWELL's plus factors necessarily are assigned some values. The college simply does by a numbered scale what the law school accomplishes in its 'holistic review,' *Grutter*; the distinction does not imply that applicants to the undergraduate college are denied individualized consideration or a fair chance to compete on the basis of all the various merits their applications may disclose. *** Any argument that the 'tailoring' amounts to a set-aside, then, boils down to the claim that a plus factor of 20 points makes some observers suspicious, where a factor of 10 points might not. *** Equal protection cannot become an exercise in which the winners are the ones who hide the ball. *** "

JUSTICE GINSBURG, with whom JUSTICE SOUTER joins, dissenting: " *** In the wake 'of a system of racial caste only recently ended,' large disparities endure. *** [A]s I see it, government decisionmakers may properly distinguish between policies of exclusion and inclusion. *** Our jurisprudence ranks race a 'suspect' category, 'not because [race] is inevitably an impermissible classification, but because it is one which usually, to our national shame, has been drawn for the purpose of maintaining racial inequality.' *** To avoid conflict with the equal protection clause, a classification that denies a benefit, causes harm, or imposes a burden must not be based on race. In that sense, the Constitution is color blind. But the Constitution is color conscious to prevent discrimination being perpetuated and to undo the effects of past discrimination.' *** The mere assertion of a laudable governmental purpose, of course, should not immunize a race-conscious measure from careful judicial inspection. Close review is needed 'to ferret out classifications in reality malign, but masquerading as benign,' and to 'ensure that preferences are not so large as to trammel unduly upon the opportunities of others or interfere too harshly with legitimate expectations of persons in once-preferred groups.' *** "

2.   **Litigation: Boom or Bust?** JUSTICE SCALIA predicts more litigation and describes what he believes are the fault lines. Do you agree? Consider what college and university admissions policies will read like after *Grutter*. Consider how these policies will be administered. How vulnerable are the institutions? How likely are you to prevail in a suit if you are a rejected white applicant and believe you would have been admitted were you a minority?

3.   **Other Academic Contexts.** How will *Grutter* affect scholarship programs that target minorities? Need-based scholarships mainly given to minority students? Will minority summer programs before college and law school remain viable? Will the deference to educators be as strong in these areas as in the admissions context?

4.   **Non-academic Contexts.** How, if at all, will affirmative action programs in government employment and set-asides be affected? Will *Grutter* have any effect on private employers' affirmative action programs?

5.   **Discrimination Among Minorities.** Will schools eliminate admissions processes that provide (either explicitly or implicitly) a larger plus for African-American candidates than Hispanic candidates? Can schools refuse to consider Asian-Americans as minorities entitled to any affirmative action plus?

C. GENDER AND EQUAL PROTECTION

The question addressed in this section is simple: To what extent does the Constitution mandate governmental gender equality?

The Declaration of Independence says "all men are created equal." Whether that phrase was intended as to be gender-specific or a generic reference to human kind is of little constitutional relevance.

The language of the original Constitution said nothing about women, but there are gender-specific references in several amendments. Section 2 of the Fourteenth Amendment repeals the 3/5 bargain concerning counting slaves for apportionment of the House of Representatives, but it explicitly notes that state representation will be tied to voting eligibility of the state's "male inhabitants." The right of women to vote in federal and state elections was not guaranteed until ratification of the Nineteenth Amendment in 1920.

Section 1 of the Fourteenth Amendment speaks of "equal protection of the laws" for all "persons," not just "male inhabitants," and the Supreme Court, in *Minor v. Happersett*, 88 U.S. (21 Wall.) 162 (1875), acknowledged that women are "persons" and "citizens," even though the right to vote was not then seen as a privilege of U.S. citizenship. In another case of about that vintage, *Bradwell v. Illinois*, 83 U.S. (16 Wall.) 130 (1873), the Court held that Illinois could refuse to license women to practice law. JUSTICE BRADLEY's concurring opinion contains this classic statement of the Court's attitude then toward gender discrimination:

"The natural and proper timidity and delicacy which belongs to the female sex evidently unfits it for many of the occupations of civil life. The constitution of the family organization, which is founded in the divine ordinance, as well as in the nature of things, indicates the domestic sphere as that which properly belongs to the domain and functions of womanhood. The harmony, not to say identity, of interests and views which belong or should belong to the family institution, is repugnant to the idea of a woman adopting a distinct and independent career from that of her husband. *** The paramount destiny and mission of woman are to fulfill the noble and benign offices of wife and mother. This is the law of the Creator. And the rules of civil society must be adapted to the general constitution of things, and cannot be based on exceptional cases."

Most of you will be glad that *Bradwell* does not represent the current state of the law.

For many decades, rational basis scrutiny was used in evaluating the constitutionality of laws that used gender categories. See, for example, *Muller v. Oregon*, 208 U.S. 412 (1908), upholding a statute prohibiting employment of women in factories more than ten hours a day. Then, in the 1960's and early 1970's, the Supreme Court began applying a more demanding explanation for gender differences in equal protection cases and came within one vote of applying strict scrutiny to invidious governmental discrimination against women. Soon thereafter, in 1972, Congress submitted to the states a proposed Equal Rights Amendment (ERA) for ratification. The ERA's operative language was: "Equality of rights under the law shall not be denied or abridged by the United States or by any State on account of sex."

The Court subsequently drew back from applying strict scrutiny to governmental gender distinctions and the ERA was not ratified by ¾ of the states. The following cases reveal the current state of equal protection gender jurisprudence.

CRAIG v. BOREN
429 U.S. 190, 97 S.Ct. 451, 50 L.Ed.2d 397 (1976).

MR. JUSTICE BRENNAN delivered the opinion of the Court.

The interaction of two sections of an Oklahoma statute prohibits the sale of "nonintoxicating" 3.2% beer to males under the age of 21 and to females under the age of 18. The question to be decided is whether such a gender-based differential constitutes a denial to males 18–20 years of age of the equal protection of the laws in violation of the Fourteenth Amendment. *** [S]tatutory classifications that distinguish between males and females are "subject to scrutiny under the Equal Protection Clause." To withstand constitutional challenge, previous cases establish that classifications by gender must serve important governmental objectives and must be substantially related to achievement of those objectives. Thus, in [*Reed v. Reed*, 404 U.S. 71 (1971)], the objectives of "reducing the workload on probate courts" and "avoiding intrafamily controversy" were deemed of insufficient importance to sustain use of an overt gender criterion in the appointment of administrators of intestate decedents' estates. Decisions following *Reed* similarly have rejected administrative ease and convenience as sufficiently important objectives to justify gender-based classifications. ***

Reed v. Reed has also provided the underpinning for decisions that have invalidated statutes employing gender as an inaccurate proxy for other, more germane bases of classification. Hence, "archaic and overbroad" generalizations could not justify use of a gender line in determining eligibility for certain governmental entitlements. Similarly, increasingly outdated misconceptions concerning the role of females in the home rather than in the "marketplace and world of ideas" were rejected as loose-fitting characterizations incapable of supporting state statutory schemes that were premised upon their accuracy. *** We turn then to the question whether, under *Reed*, the difference between males and females with respect to the purchase of 3.2% beer warrants the differential in age drawn by the Oklahoma statute. We conclude that it does not.

The District Court recognized that *Reed v. Reed* was controlling. In applying the teachings of that case, the court found the requisite important governmental objective in the traffic-safety goal proffered by the Oklahoma Attorney General. It then concluded that the statistics introduced by the appellees established that the gender-based distinction was substantially related to achievement of that goal.

We accept for purposes of discussion the District Court's identification of the objective underlying [the statute] as the enhancement of traffic safety. Clearly, the protection of public health and safety represents an important function of state and local governments. However, appellees' statistics in our view cannot support the conclusion that the gender-based distinction closely serves to achieve that objective and therefore the distinction cannot under Reed withstand equal protection challenge.

The appellees introduced a variety of statistical surveys. *** Conceding that "the case is not free from doubt," the District Court nonetheless concluded that this statistical showing substantiated "a rational basis for the legislative judgment underlying the challenged classification." *** Even were this statistical evidence accepted as accurate, it nevertheless offers only a weak answer to the equal protection question presented here. The most focused and relevant of the statistical surveys, arrests of 18–20–year-olds for alcohol-related driving offenses, exemplifies the ultimate unpersuasiveness of this evidentiary record. Viewed in terms of the correlation between sex and the actual activity that Oklahoma seeks to regulate driving while under the influence of alcohol the statistics broadly establish that .18% of females and 2% of males in that age group were arrested for that offense. While such a disparity is not trivial in a statistical sense, it hardly can form the basis for employment of a gender line as a classifying device. Certainly if maleness is to serve as a proxy for drinking and driving, a correlation of 2% must be considered an unduly tenuous "fit."[12] Indeed, prior cases have consistently rejected the use of sex as a decisionmaking factor even though the statutes in question certainly rested on far more predictive empirical relationships than this.[13]

Moreover, the statistics exhibit a variety of other shortcomings that seriously impugn their value to equal protection analysis. Setting aside the obvious methodological problems,[14] the surveys do not adequately justify the salient features of Oklahoma's gender-based traffic-safety law. None purports to measure the use and dangerousness of 3.2% beer as opposed to alcohol generally, a detail that is of particular importance since, in light of its low alcohol level, Oklahoma apparently considers the 3.2% beverage to be "nonintoxicating." Moreover, many of the studies, while graphically documenting the unfortunate increase in driving while under the influence of alcohol, make no effort to relate their findings to age-sex differentials as involved here. Indeed, the only survey that explicitly centered its attention upon young drivers and their use of beer albeit apparently not of the diluted 3.2% variety reached results that hardly can be viewed as impressive in justifying either a gender or age classification.

There is no reason to belabor this line of analysis. It is unrealistic to expect either members of the judiciary or state officials to be well versed in the rigors of experimental or statistical technique. But this merely illustrates that proving broad sociological propositions by statistics is a dubious business, and one that inevitably is in tension with the normative philosophy that underlies the Equal Protection Clause. Suffice to say that the showing offered by the appellees does not satisfy us that sex represents a legitimate, accurate proxy for the regulation of drinking and driving. In fact, when it is further recognized that Oklahoma's statute prohibits only the selling of 3.2% beer to young males and not their drinking the beverage once acquired (even after purchase by their 18–20–year-old female companions), the relationship between gender and traffic safety becomes far too tenuous to satisfy *Reed*'s requirement that the gender-based difference be substantially related to achievement of the statutory objective.

---

[12] Obviously, arrest statistics do not embrace all individuals who drink and drive. But for purposes of analysis, this "underinclusiveness" must be discounted somewhat by the shortcomings inherent in this statistical sample, see n. 14 In any event, we decide this case in light of the evidence offered by Oklahoma and know of no way of extrapolating these arrest statistics to take into account the driving and drinking population at large, including those who avoided arrest.

[13] For example, we can conjecture that in *Reed*, Idaho's apparent premise that women lacked experience in formal business matters (particularly compared to men) would have proved to be accurate in substantially more than 2% of all cases. And in both *Frontiero* and *Wiesenfeld*, we expressly found appellees' empirical defense of mandatory dependency tests for men but not women to be unsatisfactory, even though we recognized that husbands are still far less likely to be dependent on their wives than vice versa.

[14] The very social stereotypes that find reflection in age-differential laws are likely substantially to distort the accuracy of these comparative statistics. Hence "reckless" young men who drink and drive are transformed into arrest statistics, whereas their female counterparts are chivalrously escorted home. ***

We hold, therefore, that under *Reed*, Oklahoma's 3.2% beer statute invidiously discriminates against males 18–20 years of age. *** We conclude that the gender-based differential contained in [the statute] constitutes a denial of the equal protection of the laws to males aged 18–20 and reverse the judgment of the District Court.

MR. JUSTICE POWELL, concurring.

*** I view this as a relatively easy case. No one questions the legitimacy or importance of the asserted governmental objective: the promotion of highway safety. The decision of the case turns on whether the state legislature, by the classification it has chosen, had adopted a means that bears a "'fair and substantial relation'" to this objective.

It seems to me that the statistics offered by appellees and relied upon by the District Court do tend generally to support the view that young men drive more, possibly are inclined to drink more, and for various reasons are involved in more accidents than young women. Even so, I am not persuaded that these facts and the inferences fairly drawn from them justify this classification based on a three-year age differential between the sexes, and especially one that it so easily circumvented as to be virtually meaningless. Putting it differently, this gender-based classification does not bear a fair and substantial relation to the object of the legislation.

MR. JUSTICE STEVENS, concurring.

*** The classification is not totally irrational. For the evidence does indicate that there are more males than females in this age bracket who drive and also more who drink. Nevertheless, there are several reasons why I regard the justification as unacceptable. It is difficult to believe that the statute was actually intended to cope with the problem of traffic safety, since it has only a minimal effect on access to a not very intoxicating beverage and does not prohibit its consumption. Moreover, the empirical data submitted by the State accentuate the unfairness of treating all 18–21–year-old males as inferior to their female counterparts. The legislation imposes a restraint on 100% of the males in the class allegedly because about 2% of them have probably violated one or more laws relating to the consumption of alcoholic beverages. It is unlikely that this law will have a significant deterrent effect either on that 2% or on the law-abiding 98%. But even assuming some such slight benefit, it does not seem to me that an insult to all of the young men of the State can be justified by visiting the sins of the 2% on the 98%.

MR. JUSTICE BLACKMUN, concurring in part. [omitted]

MR. JUSTICE STEWART, concurring in the judgment. [omitted]

MR. CHIEF JUSTICE BURGER, dissenting. [omitted]

MR. JUSTICE REHNQUIST, dissenting.

The Court's disposition of this case is objectionable on two grounds. First is its conclusion that men challenging a gender-based statute which treats them less favorably than women may invoke a more stringent standard of judicial review than pertains to most other types of classifications. Second is the Court's enunciation of this standard, without citation to any source, as being that "classifications by gender must serve important governmental objectives and must be substantially related to achievement of those objectives." The only redeeming feature of the Court's opinion, to my mind, is that it apparently signals a retreat by those who joined the plurality opinion in *Frontiero v. Richardson*, 411 U.S. 677 (1973), from their view that sex is a "suspect" classification for purposes of equal protection analysis. I think the Oklahoma statute challenged here need pass only the "rational basis" equal protection analysis ***, and I believe that it is constitutional under that analysis. ***

The Court does not discuss the nature of the right involved, and there is no reason to believe that it sees the purchase of 3.2% beer as implicating any important interest, let alone one that is "fundamental" in the constitutional sense of invoking strict scrutiny. Indeed, the Court's accurate observation that the statute affects the selling but not the drinking of 3.2% beer, further emphasizes the limited effect that it has on even those persons in the age group involved. There is, in sum, nothing about the statutory classification involved here to suggest that it affects an interest, or works against a group, which can claim under the Equal Protection Clause that it is entitled to special judicial protection. ***

The Court's conclusion that a law which treats males less favorably than females "must serve important governmental objectives and must be substantially related to achievement of those objectives" apparently comes out of thin air. The Equal Protection Clause contains no such language, and none of our previous cases adopt that standard. I would think we have had enough difficulty with the two standards of review which our cases have recognized—the norm of "rational basis," and the "compelling state interest" required where a "suspect classification" is involved—so as to counsel weightily against the insertion of still another "standard" between those two. How is this Court to divine what objectives are important? How is it to determine whether a particular law is "substantially" related to the achievement of such objective, rather than related in some other way to its achievement? Both of the phrases used are so diaphanous and elastic as to invite subjective judicial preferences or prejudices relating to particular types of legislation, masquerading as judgments whether such legislation is directed at "important" objectives or, whether the relationship to those objectives is "substantial" enough.

*** The Court "accept(s) for purposes of discussion" the District Court's finding that the purpose of the provisions in question was traffic safety, and proceeds to examine the statistical evidence in the record in order to decide if "the gender-based distinction closely serves to achieve that objective." *** One need not immerse oneself in the fine points of statistical analysis, however, in order to see the weaknesses in the Court's attempted denigration of the evidence at hand.

One survey of arrest statistics assembled in 1973 indicated that males in the 18–20 age group were arrested for "driving under the influence" almost 18 times as often as their female counterparts, and for "drunkenness" in a ratio of almost 10 to 1. Accepting, as the Court does, appellants' comparison of the total figures with 1973 Oklahoma census data, this survey indicates a 2% arrest rate among males in the age group, as compared to a .18% rate among females. *** The Court's criticism of the statistics relied on by the District Court conveys the impression that a legislature in enacting a new law is to be subjected to the judicial equivalent of a doctoral examination in statistics. Legislatures are not held to any rules of evidence such as those which may govern courts or other administrative bodies, and are entitled to draw factual conclusions on the basis of the determination of probable cause which an arrest by a police officer normally represents. In this situation, they could reasonably infer that the incidence of drunk driving is a good deal higher than the incidence of arrest.

And while *** such statistics may be distorted as a result of stereotyping, the legislature is not required to prove before a court that its statistics are perfect. In any event, if stereotypes are as pervasive as the Court suggests, they may in turn influence the conduct of the men and women in question, and cause the young men to conform to the wild and reckless image which is their stereotype. *** Quite apart from these alleged methodological deficiencies in the statistical evidence, the Court appears to hold that that evidence, on its face, fails to support the distinction drawn in the statute. The Court notes that only 2% of males (as against .18% of females) in the age group were arrested for drunk driving, and that this very low figure establishes "an unduly tenuous 'fit'" between maleness and drunk driving in the 18 to 20-year-old group. *** Notwithstanding the Court's critique of the statistical evidence, that evidence suggests clear differences between the drinking and driving habits of young men and women. Those differences are grounds enough for the State reasonably to conclude that young males pose by far the greater drunk-driving hazard, both in terms of sheer numbers and in terms of hazard on a per-driver basis. The gender-based difference in treatment in this case is therefore not irrational.

The Court's argument that a 2% correlation between maleness and drunk driving is constitutionally insufficient therefore does not pose an equal protection issue concerning discrimination between males and females. The clearest demonstration of this is the fact that the precise argument made by the Court would be equally applicable to a flat bar on such purchases by anyone, male or female, in the 18–20 age group; in fact it would apply a fortiori in that case given the even more "tenuous 'fit'" between drunk-driving arrests and femaleness. The statistics indicate that about 1% of the age group population as a whole is arrested. What the Court's argument is relevant to is not equal protection, but due process whether there are enough persons in the category who drive while drunk to justify a bar against purchases by all members of the group.

This is not a case where the classification can only be justified on grounds of administrative convenience. There being no apparent way to single out persons likely to drink and drive, it seems plain that the legislature was faced here with the not atypical legislative problem of legislating in terms of broad categories with regard to the purchase and consumption of alcohol. I trust, especially in light of the Twenty-first Amendment, that there would be no due process violation if no one in this age group were allowed to purchase 3.2% beer. Since males drink and drive at a higher rate than the age group as a whole, I fail to see how a statutory bar with regard only to them can create any due process problem. ***

MICHAEL M. v. SUPERIOR COURT OF SONOMA COUNTY
450 U.S. 464, 101 S.Ct. 1200, 67 L.Ed.2d 437 (1981).

JUSTICE REHNQUIST announced the judgment of the Court and delivered an opinion, in which THE CHIEF JUSTICE, JUSTICE STEWART, and JUSTICE POWELL joined.

The question presented in this case is whether California's "statutory rape" law violates the Equal Protection Clause of the Fourteenth Amendment. [The law] defines unlawful sexual intercourse as "an act of sexual intercourse accomplished with a female not the wife of the perpetrator, where the female is under the age of 18 years." The statute thus makes men alone criminally liable for the act of sexual intercourse.

In July 1978, a complaint was filed in the Municipal Court of Sonoma County, Cal., alleging that petitioner, then a 17 1/2-year-old male, had had unlawful sexual intercourse with a female under the age of 18, in violation of [the law]. *** Prior to trial, petitioner sought to set aside the information on both state and federal constitutional grounds, asserting that [the law] unlawfully discriminated on the basis of gender. ***

*** [A] legislature may not "make overbroad generalizations based on sex which are entirely unrelated to any differences between men and women or which demean the ability or social status of the affected class." *Parham v. Hughes*, 441 U.S. 347, 354 (1979) (plurality opinion of STEWART, J.). But because the Equal Protection Clause does not "demand that a statute necessarily apply equally to all persons" or require "'things which are different in fact *** to be treated in law as though they were the same,'" this Court has consistently upheld statutes where the gender classification is not invidious, but rather realistically reflects the fact that the sexes are not similarly situated in certain circumstances.

Applying those principles to this case, the fact that the California Legislature criminalized the act of illicit sexual intercourse with a minor female is a sure indication of its intent or purpose to discourage that conduct. Precisely why the legislature desired that result is of course somewhat less clear. *** [For] example, the individual legislators may have voted for the statute for a variety of reasons. Some legislators may have been concerned about preventing teenage pregnancies, others about protecting young females from physical injury or from the loss of "chastity," and still others about promoting various religious and moral attitudes towards premarital sex.

The justification for the statute offered by the State, and accepted by the Supreme Court of California, is that the legislature sought to prevent illegitimate teenage pregnancies. That finding, of course, is entitled to great deference. *** We are satisfied not only that the prevention of illegitimate pregnancy is at least one of the "purposes" of the statute, but also that the State has a strong interest in preventing such pregnancy. ***

We need not be medical doctors to discern that young men and young women are not similarly situated with respect to the problems and the risks of sexual intercourse. Only women may become pregnant, and they suffer disproportionately the profound physical, emotional and psychological consequences of sexual activity. The statute at issue here protects women from sexual intercourse at an age when those consequences are particularly severe.[7]

The question thus boils down to whether a State may attack the problem of sexual intercourse and teenage pregnancy directly by prohibiting a male from having sexual intercourse with a minor female. We hold that such a statute is sufficiently related to the State's objectives to pass constitutional muster.

Because virtually all of the significant harmful and inescapably identifiable consequences of teenage pregnancy fall on the young female, a legislature acts well within its authority when it elects to punish only the participant who, by nature, suffers few of the consequences of his conduct. It is hardly unreasonable for a legislature acting to protect minor females to exclude them from punishment. Moreover, the risk of pregnancy itself constitutes a substantial deterrence to young females. No similar natural sanctions deter males. A criminal sanction imposed solely on males thus serves to roughly "equalize" the deterrents on the sexes.

*** [We] cannot say that a gender-neutral statute would be as effective as the statute California has chosen to enact. The State persuasively contends that a gender-neutral statute would frustrate its interest in effective enforcement. Its view is that a female is surely less likely to report violations of the statute if she herself would be subject to criminal prosecution. In an area already fraught with prosecutorial difficulties, we decline to hold that the Equal Protection Clause requires a legislature to enact a statute so broad that it may well be incapable of enforcement.

We similarly reject petitioner's argument that [the law] is impermissibly overbroad because it makes unlawful sexual intercourse with prepubescent females, who are, by definition, incapable of becoming pregnant. Quite apart from the fact that the statute could well be justified on the grounds that very young females are particularly susceptible to physical injury from sexual intercourse, it is ludicrous to suggest that the Constitution requires the California Legislature to limit the scope of its rape statute to older teenagers and exclude young girls.

---

[7] Although petitioner concedes that the State has a "compelling" interest in preventing teenage pregnancy, he contends that the "true" purpose of § 261.5 is to protect the virtue and chastity of young women. As such, the statute is unjustifiable because it rests on archaic stereotypes. What we have said above is enough to dispose of that contention. The question for us—and the only question under the Federal Constitution—is whether the legislation violates the Equal Protection Clause of the Fourteenth Amendment, not whether its supporters may have endorsed it for reasons no longer generally accepted. ***

There remains only petitioner's contention that the statute is unconstitutional as it is applied to him because he, like [his partner], was under 18 at the time of sexual intercourse. Petitioner argues that the statute is flawed because it presumes that as between two persons under 18, the male is the culpable aggressor. We find petitioner's contentions unpersuasive. Contrary to his assertions, the statute does not rest on the assumption that males are generally the aggressors. It is instead an attempt by a legislature to prevent illegitimate teenage pregnancy by providing an additional deterrent for men. The age of the man is irrelevant since young men are as capable as older men of inflicting the harm sought to be prevented. ***

JUSTICE STEWART, concurring. [omitted]

JUSTICE BLACKMUN, concurring in the judgment.

It is gratifying that the plurality recognizes that "[a]t the risk of stating the obvious, teenage pregnancies *** have increased dramatically over the last two decades" and "have significant social, medical, and economic consequences for both the mother and her child, and the State." There have been times when I have wondered whether the Court was capable of this perception, particularly when it has struggled with the different but not unrelated problems that attend abortion issues. ***

I, however, cannot vote to strike down the California statutory rape law, for I think it is a sufficiently reasoned and constitutional effort to control the problem at its inception. For me, there is an important difference between this state action and a State's adamant and rigid refusal to face, or even to recognize, the "significant *** consequences"—to the woman—of a forced or unwanted conception. I have found it difficult to rule constitutional, for example, state efforts to block, at that later point, a woman's attempt to deal with the enormity of the problem confronting her, just as I have rejected state efforts to prevent women from rationally taking steps to prevent that problem from arising. ***

I think, too, that it is only fair, with respect to this particular petitioner, to point out that his partner, Sharon, appears not to have been an unwilling participant in at least the initial stages of the intimacies that took place the night of June 3, 1978. Petitioner's and Sharon's nonacquaintance with each other before the incident; their drinking; their withdrawal from the others of the group; their foreplay, in which she willingly participated and seems to have encouraged; and the closeness of their ages (a difference of only one year and 18 days) are factors that should make this case an unattractive one to prosecute at all, and especially to prosecute as a felony, rather than as a misdemeanor. But the State has chosen to prosecute in that manner, and the facts, I reluctantly conclude, may fit the crime.

JUSTICE BRENNAN, with whom JUSTICES WHITE and MARSHALL join, dissenting.

It is disturbing to find the Court so splintered on a case that presents such a straightforward issue: Whether the admittedly gender-based classification in [the statute] bears a sufficient relationship to the State's asserted goal of preventing teenage pregnancies to survive the "mid-level" constitutional scrutiny mandated by *Craig v. Boren*, 429 U.S. 190 (1976). Applying the analytical framework provided by our precedents, I am convinced that there is only one proper resolution of this issue: the classification must be declared unconstitutional. I fear that the plurality opinion and JUSTICES STEWART and BLACKMUN reach the opposite result by placing too much emphasis on the desirability of achieving the State's asserted statutory goal—prevention of teenage pregnancy—and not enough emphasis on the fundamental question of whether the sex-based discrimination in the California statute is substantially related to the achievement of that goal. ***

The State of California vigorously asserts that the "important governmental objective" to be served by [the statute] is the prevention of teenage pregnancy. It claims that its statute furthers this goal by deterring sexual activity by males—the class of persons it considers more responsible for causing those pregnancies.[4] But even assuming that prevention of teenage pregnancy is an important governmental objective and that it is in fact an objective of [the statute], California still has the burden of proving that there are fewer teenage pregnancies under its gender-based statutory rape law than there would be if the law were gender neutral. To meet this burden, the State must show that because its statutory rape law punishes only males, and not females, it more effectively deters minor females from having sexual intercourse.

The plurality assumes that a gender-neutral statute would be less effective than [the statute] in deterring sexual activity because a gender-neutral statute would create significant enforcement problems. *** However, a State's bare assertion that its gender-based statutory classification substantially furthers an important governmental interest is not enough to meet its burden of proof under *Craig v. Boren*. Rather, the State must produce evidence that will persuade the court that its assertion is true. *** [Even] assuming that a gender-neutral statute would be more difficult to enforce, the State has still not shown that those enforcement problems would make such a statute less effective than a gender-based statute in deterring minor females from engaging in sexual intercourse. Common sense, however, suggests that a gender-neutral statutory rape law is potentially a greater deterrent of sexual activity than a gender-based law, for the simple reason that a gender-neutral law subjects both men and women to criminal sanctions and thus arguably has a deterrent effect on twice as many potential violators. Even if fewer persons were prosecuted under the gender-neutral law, as the State suggests, it would still be true that twice as many persons would be subject to arrest. The State's failure to prove that a gender-neutral law would be a less effective deterrent than a gender-based law, like the

---

[4] In a remarkable display of sexual stereotyping, the California Supreme Court stated: "The Legislature is well within its power in imposing criminal sanctions against males, alone, because they are the only persons who may physiologically cause the result which the law properly seeks to avoid."

State's failure to prove that a gender-neutral law would be difficult to enforce, should have led this Court to invalidate [the statute].

Until very recently, no California court or commentator had suggested that the purpose of California's statutory rape law was to protect young women from the risk of pregnancy. Indeed, the historical development of [the statute] demonstrates that the law was initially enacted on the premise that young women, in contrast to young men, were to be deemed legally incapable of consenting to an act of sexual intercourse. Because their chastity was considered particularly precious, those young women were felt to be uniquely in need of the State's protection. In contrast, young men were assumed to be capable of making such decisions for themselves; the law therefore did not offer them any special protection. ***

JUSTICE STEVENS, dissenting.

Local custom and belief—rather than statutory laws of venerable but doubtful ancestry—will determine the volume of sexual activity among unmarried teenagers. The empirical evidence cited by the plurality demonstrates the futility of the notion that a statutory prohibition will significantly affect the volume of that activity or provide a meaningful solution to the problems created by it. Nevertheless, as a matter of constitutional power *** I would have no doubt about the validity of a state law prohibiting all unmarried teenagers from engaging in sexual intercourse. The societal interests in reducing the incidence of venereal disease and teenage pregnancy are sufficient, in my judgment, to justify a prohibition of conduct that increases the risk of those harms. ***

The fact that the Court did not immediately acknowledge that the capacity to become pregnant is what primarily differentiates the female from the male does not impeach the validity of the plurality's newly found wisdom. I think the plurality is quite correct in making the assumption that the joint act that this law seeks to prohibit creates a greater risk of harm for the female than for the male. But the plurality surely cannot believe that the risk of pregnancy confronted by the female—any more than the risk of venereal disease confronted by males as well as females—has provided an effective deterrent to voluntary female participation in the risk-creating conduct. Yet the plurality's decision seems to rest on the assumption that the California Legislature acted on the basis of that rather fanciful notion.

In my judgment, the fact that a class of persons is especially vulnerable to a risk that a statute is designed to avoid is a reason for making the statute applicable to that class. The argument that a special need for protection provides a rational explanation for an exemption is one I simply do not comprehend.[14]

---

[14] A hypothetical racial classification will illustrate my point. Assume that skin pigmentation provides some measure of protection against cancer caused by exposure to certain chemicals in the atmosphere and, therefore, that white employees confront a greater risk than black employees in certain industrial settings. Would it be rational to require black employees to wear protective clothing but to exempt whites from that requirement? It seems to me that the greater

In this case, the fact that a female confronts a greater risk of harm than a male is a reason for applying the prohibition to her—not a reason for granting her a license to use her own judgment on whether or not to assume the risk. Surely, if we examine the problem from the point of view of society's interest in preventing the risk-creating conduct from occurring at all, it is irrational to exempt 50% of the potential violators. And, if we view the government's interest as that of a parens patriae seeking to protect its subjects from harming themselves, the discrimination is actually perverse. Would a rational parent making rules for the conduct of twin children of opposite sex simultaneously forbid the son and authorize the daughter to engage in conduct that is especially harmful to the daughter? That is the effect of this statutory classification. ***

In my opinion, the only acceptable justification for a general rule requiring disparate treatment of the two participants in a joint act must be a legislative judgment that one is more guilty than the other. The risk-creating conduct that this statute is designed to prevent requires the participation of two persons—one male and one female. In many situations it is probably true that one is the aggressor and the other is either an unwilling, or at least a less willing, participant in the joint act. If a statute authorized punishment of only one participant and required the prosecutor to prove that that participant had been the aggressor, I assume that the discrimination would be valid.

*** The fact that the California Legislature has decided to apply its prohibition only to the male may reflect a legislative judgment that in the typical case the male is actually the more guilty party. Any such judgment must, in turn, assume that the decision to engage in the risk-creating conduct is always—or at least typically—a male decision. If that assumption is valid, the statutory classification should also be valid. But what is the support for the assumption? *** [T]he possibility that such a habitual attitude may reflect nothing more than an irrational prejudice makes it an insufficient justification for discriminatory treatment that is otherwise blatantly unfair. ***

Nor do I find at all persuasive the suggestion that this discrimination is adequately justified by the desire to encourage females to inform against their male partners. Even if the concept of a wholesale informant's exemption were an acceptable enforcement device, what is the justification for defining the exempt class entirely by reference to sex rather than by reference to a more neutral criterion such as relative innocence? Indeed, if the exempt class is to be composed entirely of members of one sex, what is there to support the view that the statutory purpose will be better served by granting the informing license to females rather than to males? If a discarded male partner informs on a promiscuous female, a timely threat of prosecution might well prevent the precise harm the statute is intended to minimize.

---

risk of harm to white workers would be a reason for including them in the requirement—not for granting them an exemption.

Finally, even if my logic is faulty and there actually is some speculative basis for treating equally guilty males and females differently, I still believe that any such speculative justification would be outweighed by the paramount interest in evenhanded enforcement of the law. A rule that authorizes punishment of only one of two equally guilty wrongdoers violates the essence of the constitutional requirement that the sovereign must govern impartially.

UNITED STATES v. VIRGINIA
518 U.S. 515, 116 S.Ct. 2264, 135 L.Ed.2d 735 (1996).

JUSTICE GINSBURG delivered the opinion of the Court.

Virginia's public institutions of higher learning include an incomparable military college, Virginia Military Institute (VMI). The United States maintains that the Constitution's equal protection guarantee precludes Virginia from reserving exclusively to men the unique educational opportunities VMI affords. We agree.

Founded in 1839, VMI is today the sole single-sex school among Virginia's 15 public institutions of higher learning. VMI's distinctive mission is to produce "citizen-soldiers," men prepared for leadership in civilian life and in military service. *** Assigning prime place to character development, VMI uses an "adversative method" modeled on English public schools and once characteristic of military instruction. VMI constantly endeavors to instill physical and mental discipline in its cadets and impart to them a strong moral code. The school's graduates leave VMI with heightened comprehension of their capacity to deal with duress and stress, and a large sense of accomplishment for completing the hazardous course.

VMI has notably succeeded in its mission to produce leaders; among its alumni are military generals, Members of Congress, and business executives. The school's alumni overwhelmingly perceive that their VMI training helped them to realize their personal goals. VMI's endowment reflects the loyalty of its graduates; VMI has the largest per-student endowment of all public undergraduate institutions in the Nation.

Neither the goal of producing citizen-soldiers nor VMI's implementing methodology is inherently unsuitable to women. And the school's impressive record in producing leaders has made admission desirable to some women. Nevertheless, Virginia has elected to preserve exclusively for men the advantages and opportunities a VMI education affords.

From its establishment in 1839 as one of the Nation's first state military colleges, VMI has remained financially supported by Virginia and "subject to the control of the [Virginia] General Assembly" *** [and] VMI today enrolls about 1,300 men as cadets.[2] Its academic offerings in the liberal arts, sciences, and engineering are also available at other public colleges and universities in Virginia. But VMI's mission is special. *** VMI produces its

---

[2] Historically, most of Virginia's public colleges and universities were single-sex; by the mid–1970's, however, all except VMI had become coeducational. ***

"citizen-soldiers" through "an adversative, or doubting, model of education" which features "[p]hysical rigor, mental stress, absolute equality of treatment, absence of privacy, minute regulation of behavior, and indoctrination in desirable values." *** VMI cadets live in spartan barracks where surveillance is constant and privacy nonexistent; they wear uniforms, eat together in the mess hall, and regularly participate in drills. *** VMI attracts some applicants because of its reputation as an extraordinarily challenging military school, and "because its alumni are exceptionally close to the school." *** "[W]omen have no opportunity anywhere to gain the benefits of [the system of education at VMI]."

In 1990, prompted by a complaint filed with the Attorney General by a female high-school student seeking admission to VMI, the United States sued the Commonwealth of Virginia and VMI, alleging that VMI's exclusively male admission policy violated the Equal Protection Clause of the Fourteenth Amendment. ***

In the two years preceding the lawsuit, the District Court noted, VMI had received inquiries from 347 women, but had responded to none of them. *** [It] was also established that "some women are capable of all of the individual activities required of VMI cadets." *** The cross-petitions in this case present two ultimate issues. First, does Virginia's exclusion of women from the educational opportunities provided by VMI—extraordinary opportunities for military training and civilian leadership development—deny to women "capable of all of the individual activities required of VMI cadets," the equal protection of the laws guaranteed by the Fourteenth Amendment? Second, if VMI's "unique" situation—as Virginia's sole single-sex public institution of higher education—offends the Constitution's equal protection principle, what is the remedial requirement?

IV

We note, once again, the core instruction of this Court's pathmarking decisions in *J.E.B. v. Alabama ex rel. T. B.*, 511 U.S. 127, and *Mississippi Univ. for Women*, 458 U.S., at 724: Parties who seek to defend gender-based government action must demonstrate an "exceedingly persuasive justification" for that action. *** Without equating gender classifications, for all purposes, to classifications based on race or national origin,[6] the Court, in post-*Reed* decisions, has carefully inspected official action that closes a door or denies opportunity to women (or to men). To summarize the Court's current directions for cases of official classification based on gender· Focusing on the differential treatment or denial of opportunity for which relief is sought, the reviewing court must determine whether the proffered justification is "exceedingly persuasive." The burden of justification is demanding and it rests entirely on the State. The State must show "at least that the [challenged] classification serves 'important governmental objectives

---

[6] The Court has thus far reserved most stringent judicial scrutiny for classifications based on race or national origin, but last Term observed that strict scrutiny of such classifications is not inevitably "fatal in fact." *Adarand Constructors, Inc. v. Pena.* ***

and that the discriminatory means employed' are 'substantially related to the achievement of those objectives.'" The justification must be genuine, not hypothesized or invented post hoc in response to litigation. And it must not rely on overbroad generalizations about the different talents, capacities, or preferences of males and females.

The heightened review standard our precedent establishes does not make sex a proscribed classification. Supposed "inherent differences" are no longer accepted as a ground for race or national origin classifications. *See Loving v. Virginia*, 388 U.S. 1 (1967). Physical differences between men and women, however, are enduring: "[T]he two sexes are not fungible; a community made up exclusively of one [sex] is different from a community composed of both." *Ballard v. United States*, 329 U.S. 187 (1946).

"Inherent differences" between men and women, we have come to appreciate, remain cause for celebration, but not for denigration of the members of either sex or for artificial constraints on an individual's opportunity. Sex classifications may be used to compensate women "for particular economic disabilities [they have] suffered," to "promot[e] equal employment opportunity," to advance full development of the talent and capacities of our Nation's people.[7] But such classifications may not be used, as they once were, to create or perpetuate the legal, social, and economic inferiority of women. ***

V

*** Virginia *** asserts two justifications in defense of VMI's exclusion of women. First, the Commonwealth contends, "single-sex education provides important educational benefits," and the option of single-sex education contributes to "diversity in educational approaches". Second, the Commonwealth argues, "the unique VMI method of character development and leadership training," the school's adversative approach, would have to be modified were VMI to admit women. ***

Single-sex education affords pedagogical benefits to at least some students, Virginia emphasizes, and that reality is uncontested in this litigation. Similarly, it is not disputed that diversity among public educational institutions can serve the public good. But Virginia has not shown that VMI was established, or has been maintained, with a view to diversifying, by its categorical exclusion of women, educational opportunities within the State. In cases of this genre, our precedent instructs that "benign" justifications proffered in defense of categorical exclusions will not be

---

[7] Several amici have urged that diversity in educational opportunities is an altogether appropriate governmental pursuit and that single-sex schools can contribute importantly to such diversity. ** * We do not question the State's prerogative evenhandedly to support diverse educational opportunities. We address specifically and only an educational opportunity *** uniquely available only at Virginia's premier military institute, the State's sole single-sex public university or college. Cf. *Mississippi Univ. for Women v. Hogan*, 458 U.S. 718 (1982) ("Mississippi maintains no other single-sex public university or college. Thus, we are not faced with the question of whether States can provide 'separate but equal' undergraduate institutions for males and females.").

accepted automatically; a tenable justification must describe actual state purposes, not rationalizations for actions in fact differently grounded. ***

Neither recent nor distant history bears out Virginia's alleged pursuit of diversity through single-sex educational options. In 1839, when the State established VMI, a range of educational opportunities for men and women was scarcely contemplated. Higher education at the time was considered dangerous for women; reflecting widely held views about women's proper place, the Nation's first universities and colleges—for example, Harvard in Massachusetts, William and Mary in Virginia—admitted only men. *** Virginia eventually provided for several women's seminaries and colleges. *** By the mid–1970's, all four schools had become coeducational. *** Virginia describes the current absence of public single-sex higher education for women as "an historical anomaly." But the historical record indicates action more deliberate than anomalous: First, protection of women against higher education; next, schools for women far from equal in resources and stature to schools for men; finally, conversion of the separate schools to coeducation. The state legislature, prior to the advent of this controversy, had repealed "[a]ll Virginia statutes requiring individual institutions to admit only men or women." *** In sum, we find no persuasive evidence in this record that VMI's male-only admission policy "is in furtherance of a state policy of 'diversity.'" *** A purpose genuinely to advance an array of educational options *** is not served by VMI's historic and constant plan—a plan to "affor[d] a unique educational benefit only to males." However "liberally" this plan serves the State's sons, it makes no provision whatever for her daughters. That is not *equal* protection.

Virginia next argues that VMI's adversative method of training provides educational benefits that cannot be made available, unmodified, to women. *** Neither sex would be favored by the transformation, Virginia maintains: Men would be deprived of the unique opportunity currently available to them; women would not gain that opportunity because their participation would "eliminat[e] the very aspects of [the] program that distinguish [VMI] from *** other institutions of higher education in Virginia." *** It may be assumed, for purposes of this decision, that most women would not choose VMI's adversative method. *** The issue, however, is not whether "women—or men—should be forced to attend VMI"; rather, the question is whether the State can constitutionally deny to women who have the will and capacity, the training and attendant opportunities that VMI uniquely affords. The notion that admission of women would downgrade VMI's stature, destroy the adversative system and, with it, even the school, is a judgment hardly proved. *** Women's successful entry into the federal military academies, and their participation in the Nation's military forces, indicate that Virginia's fears for the future of VMI may not be solidly grounded. ***

The [State's] misunderstanding *** is apparent from VMI's mission: to produce "citizen-soldiers," individuals "'imbued with love of learning, confident in the functions and attitudes of leadership, possessing a high sense of public service, advocates of the American democracy and free enterprise system, and ready *** to defend their country in time of national peril.'"

Surely that goal is great enough to accommodate women, who today count as citizens in our American democracy equal in stature to men. Just as surely, the State's great goal is not substantially advanced by women's categorical exclusion, in total disregard of their individual merit, from the State's premier "citizen-soldier" corps.[16] Virginia, in sum, "has fallen far short of establishing the 'exceedingly persuasive justification,'" that must be the solid base for any gender-defined classification.

VI

In the second phase of the litigation, Virginia presented its remedial plan—maintain VMI as a male-only college and create VWIL [Virginia Women's Institute for Leadership at Mary Baldwin College] as a separate program for women. *** The Fourth Circuit *** decided that the two single-sex programs directly served Virginia's reasserted purposes: single-gender education, and "achieving the results of an adversative method in a military environment." *** The constitutional violation in this case is the categorical exclusion of women from an extraordinary educational opportunity afforded men. A proper remedy for an unconstitutional exclusion, we have explained, aims to "eliminate [so far as possible] the discriminatory effects of the past" and to "bar like discrimination in the future."

Virginia chose not to eliminate, but to leave untouched, VMI's exclusionary policy. For women only, however, Virginia proposed a separate program, different in kind from VMI and unequal in tangible and intangible facilities. *** Virginia described VWIL as a "parallel program," and asserted that VWIL shares VMI's mission of producing "citizen-soldiers" and VMI's goals of providing "education, military training, mental and physical discipline, character *** and leadership development." If the VWIL program could not "eliminate the discriminatory effects of the past," could it at least "bar like discrimination in the future"? A comparison of the programs said to be "parallel" informs our answer. *** VWIL affords women no opportunity to experience the rigorous military training for which VMI is famed. *** [It] "deemphasize[s]" military education, and uses a "cooperative method" of education "which reinforces self-esteem[.]" *** It is on behalf of these women that the United States has instituted this suit, and it is for them that a remedy must be crafted, a remedy that will end their exclusion from a state-supplied educational opportunity for which they are fit, a decree that will "bar like discrimination in the future."

In myriad respects other than military training, VWIL does not qualify as VMI's equal. VWIL's student body, faculty, course offerings, and facilities hardly match VMI's. Nor can the VWIL graduate anticipate the benefits associated with VMI's 157–year history, the school's prestige, and its influential alumni network. *** The VWIL student does not graduate with the advantage of a VMI degree. Her diploma does not unite her with the legions of VMI "graduates [who] have distinguished themselves" in military

---

[16] VMI has successfully managed another notable change. The school admitted its first African–American cadets in 1968. ***

and civilian life. "[VMI] alumni are exceptionally close to the school," and that closeness accounts, in part, for VMI's success in attracting applicants. A VWIL graduate cannot assume that the "network of business owners, corporations, VMI graduates and non-graduate employers *** interested in hiring VMI graduates," will be equally responsive to her search for employment. *** Virginia, in sum, while maintaining VMI for men only, has failed to provide any "comparable single-gender women's institution." *** Virginia's VWIL solution is reminiscent of the remedy Texas proposed 50 years ago, in response to a state trial court's 1946 ruling that, given the equal protection guarantee, African Americans could not be denied a legal education at a state facility. *See Sweatt v. Painter*, 339 U.S. 629 (1950). ***

VII

A generation ago, "the authorities controlling Virginia higher education," despite long established tradition, agreed "to innovate and favorably entertain[ed] the [then] relatively new idea that there must be no discrimination by sex in offering educational opportunity." Commencing in 1970, Virginia opened to women "educational opportunities at the Charlottesville campus that [were] not afforded in other [state-operated] institutions." *** VMI, too, offers an educational opportunity no other Virginia institution provides, and the school's "prestige"—associated with its success in developing "citizen-soldiers"—is unequaled. *** Women seeking and fit for a VMI-quality education cannot be offered anything less, under the State's obligation to afford them genuinely equal protection.

A prime part of the history of our Constitution, historian Richard Morris recounted, is the story of the extension of constitutional rights and protections to people once ignored or excluded. VMI's story continued as our comprehension of "We the People" expanded. There is no reason to believe that the admission of women capable of all the activities required of VMI cadets would destroy the Institute rather than enhance its capacity to serve the "more perfect Union."

THOMAS, J., took no part in the consideration or decision of the case.

CHIEF JUSTICE REHNQUIST, concurring in judgment.

*** Two decades ago in *Craig v. Boren*, 429 U.S. 190 (1976), we announced that "[t]o withstand constitutional challenge, *** classifications by gender must serve important governmental objectives and must be substantially related to achievement of those objectives." We have adhered to that standard of scrutiny ever since. While the majority adheres to this test today, it also says that the State must demonstrate an "'exceedingly persuasive justification'" to support a gender-based classification. It is unfortunate that the Court thereby introduces an element of uncertainty respecting the appropriate test. ***

Our cases dealing with gender discrimination also require that the proffered purpose for the challenged law be the actual purpose. It is on this ground that the Court rejects the first of two justifications Virginia offers for

VMI's single-sex admissions policy, namely, the goal of diversity among its public educational institutions.

*** [I]t is not the "exclusion of women" that violates the Equal Protection Clause, but the maintenance of an all-men school without providing any—much less a comparable—institution for women. Accordingly, the remedy should not necessarily require either the admission of women to VMI, or the creation of a VMI clone for women. An adequate remedy in my opinion might be a demonstration by Virginia that its interest in educating men in a single-sex environment is matched by its interest in educating women in a single-sex institution. *** It would be a sufficient remedy, I think, if the two institutions offered the same quality of education and were of the same overall calibre. *** In the end, the women's institution Virginia proposes, VWIL, fails as a remedy, because it is distinctly inferior to the existing men's institution and will continue to be for the foreseeable future. VWIL simply is not, in any sense, the institution that VMI is. In particular, VWIL is a program appended to a private college, not a self-standing institution; and VWIL is substantially underfunded as compared to VMI. I therefore ultimately agree with the Court that Virginia has not provided an adequate remedy.

JUSTICE SCALIA, dissenting.

Today the Court shuts down an institution that has served the people of the Commonwealth of Virginia with pride and distinction for over a century and a half. To achieve that desired result, it rejects (contrary to our established practice) the factual findings of two courts below, sweeps aside the precedents of this Court, and ignores the history of our people. As to facts: it explicitly rejects the finding that there exist "gender-based developmental differences" supporting Virginia's restriction of the "adversative" method to only a men's institution, and the finding that the all-male composition of the Virginia Military Institute (VMI) is essential to that institution's character. As to precedent: it drastically revises our established standards for reviewing sex-based classifications. And as to history: it counts for nothing the long tradition, enduring down to the present, of men's military colleges supported by both States and the Federal Government. *** The virtue of a democratic system with a First Amendment is that it readily enables the people, over time, to be persuaded that what they took for granted is not so, and to change their laws accordingly. *** The same cannot be said of this most illiberal Court, which has embarked on a course of inscribing one after another of the current preferences of the society (and in some cases only the counter-majoritarian preferences of the society's law-trained elite) into our Basic Law. Today it enshrines the notion that no substantial educational value is to be served by an all-men's military academy—so that the decision by the people of Virginia to maintain such an institution denies equal protection to women who cannot attend that institution but can attend others. Since it is entirely clear that the Constitution of the United States—the old one—takes no sides in this educational debate, I dissent.

I shall devote most of my analysis to evaluating the Court's opinion on the basis of our current equal protection jurisprudence, which regards this

Court as free to evaluate everything under the sun by applying one of three tests: "rational basis" scrutiny, intermediate scrutiny, or strict scrutiny. These tests are no more scientific than their names suggest, and a further element of randomness is added by the fact that it is largely up to us which test will be applied in each case. Strict scrutiny, we have said, is reserved for state "classifications based on race or national origin and classifications affecting fundamental rights." It is my position that the term "fundamental rights" should be limited to "interest[s] traditionally protected by our society," *Michael H. v. Gerald D*; but the Court has not accepted that view, so that strict scrutiny will be applied to the deprivation of whatever sort of right we consider "fundamental." We have no established criterion for "intermediate scrutiny" either, but essentially apply it when it seems like a good idea to load the dice. So far it has been applied to content-neutral restrictions that place an incidental burden on speech, to disabilities attendant to illegitimacy, and to discrimination on the basis of sex.

I have no problem with a system of abstract tests such as rational-basis, intermediate, and strict scrutiny (though I think we can do better than applying strict scrutiny and intermediate scrutiny whenever we feel like it). *** But in my view the function of this Court is to *preserve* our society's values regarding (among other things) equal protection, not to revise them; to prevent backsliding from the degree of restriction the Constitution imposed upon democratic government, not to prescribe, on our own authority, progressively higher degrees. *** And all the federal military colleges—West Point, the Naval Academy at Annapolis, and even the Air Force Academy, which was not established until 1954—admitted only males for most of their history. Their admission of women in 1976, came not by court decree, but because the people, through their elected representatives, decreed a change. ***

[T]he United States urged us to hold in this case "that strict scrutiny is the correct constitutional standard for evaluating classifications that deny opportunities to individuals based on their sex." The Court, while making no reference to the Government's argument, effectively accepts it. ***

Only the amorphous "exceedingly persuasive justification" phrase, and not the standard elaboration of intermediate scrutiny, can be made to yield this conclusion that VMI's single-sex composition is unconstitutional because there exist several women (or, one would have to conclude under the Court's reasoning, a single woman) willing and able to undertake VMI's program. Intermediate scrutiny has never required a least-restrictive-means analysis, but only a "substantial relation" between the classification and the state interests that it serves. Thus, in *Califano v. Webster*, 430 U.S. 313 (1977) (per curiam), we upheld a congressional statute that provided higher Social Security benefits for women than for men. We reasoned that "women *** as such have been unfairly hindered from earning as much as men," but we did not require proof that each woman so benefited had suffered discrimination or that each disadvantaged man had not; it was sufficient that even under the former congressional scheme "women on the average received lower retirement benefits than men." The reasoning in our other intermediate-scrutiny cases has similarly required only a substantial relation between end and means, not a perfect fit. In *Rostker v. Goldberg*, 453 U.S. 57 (1981), we held that selective-service registration could constitutionally exclude women, because even "assuming that a small number of women could be drafted for noncombat roles, Congress simply did not consider it worth the added burdens of including women in draft and registration plans." *** There is simply no support in our cases for the notion that a sex-based classification is invalid unless it relates to characteristics that hold true in every instance.

Not content to execute *a de facto* abandonment of the intermediate scrutiny that has been our standard for sex-based classifications for some two decades, the Court purports to reserve the question whether, even in principle, a higher standard (i.e., strict scrutiny) should apply. *** Our task is to clarify the law—not to muddy the waters, and not to exact over-compliance by intimidation. The States and the Federal Government are entitled to know before they act the standard to which they will be held, rather than be compelled to guess about the outcome of Supreme Court peek-a-boo. *** The question to be answered, I repeat, is whether the exclusion of women from VMI is "substantially related to an important governmental objective."

It is beyond question that Virginia has an important state interest in providing effective college education for its citizens. That single-sex instruction is an approach substantially related to that interest should be evident enough from the long and continuing history in this country of men's and women's colleges. *** But besides its single-sex constitution, VMI is different from other colleges in another way. It employs a "distinctive educational method," sometimes referred to as the "adversative, or doubting, model of education." *** No one contends that this method is appropriate for all individuals; education is not a "one size fits all" business. Just as a State may wish to support junior colleges, vocational institutes, or a law school that emphasizes case practice instead of classroom study, so too a State's decision to maintain within its system one school that provides the adversative method is "substantially related" to its goal of good education. ***

There can be no serious dispute that, as the District Court found, single-sex education and a distinctive educational method "represent legitimate contributions to diversity in the Virginia higher education system." *** In these circumstances, Virginia's election to fund one public all-male institution and one on the adversative model—and to concentrate its resources in a single entity that serves both these interests in diversity—is substantially related to the State's important educational interests. ***

Under the constitutional principles announced and applied today, single-sex public education is unconstitutional. *** And the rationale of today's decision is sweeping: for sex-based classifications, a redefinition of intermediate scrutiny that makes it indistinguishable from strict scrutiny. Indeed, the Court indicates that if any program restricted to one sex is "uniqu[e]," it must be opened to members of the opposite sex "who have the will and capacity" to participate in it. I suggest that the single-sex program that will not be capable of being characterized as "unique" is not only unique but nonexistent.[8]

In any event, regardless of whether the Court's rationale leaves some small amount of room for lawyers to argue, it ensures that single-sex public education is functionally dead. The costs of litigating the constitutionality of a single-sex education program, and the risks of ultimately losing that litigation, are simply too high to be embraced by public officials. *** There are few extant single-sex public educational programs. The potential of today's decision for widespread disruption of existing institutions lies in its application to *private* single-sex education. *** The issue will be not whether government assistance turns private colleges into state actors, but whether the government itself would be violating the Constitution by providing state support to single-sex colleges. *** The only hope for state-assisted single-sex private schools is that the Court will not apply in the future the principles of law it has applied today. That is a substantial hope, I am happy and ashamed to say. ***

Notes

1.   **General.** Is gender like race with respect to (1) history of the Fourteenth Amendment, (2) history of group repression or subordination, (3) the relative ability of women and minorities to win through majoritarian processes, and (4) other factors? Does your assessment of the similarities and differences explain the Court's use of "intermediate scrutiny"?

2.   *Craig v. Boren.*

(a) In *Craig*, the Court announced the intermediate scrutiny standard which had been building for some time. Do you see this as ironic in light of the fact that women were, at least superficially, the beneficiaries of Oklahoma's law? Ironic in light of the fact that the law was so trivial?

(b) Do you think the Oklahoma law meets either rational basis or intermediate scrutiny standards? Why?

(c) How do stereotypes or social assumptions relate to the Oklahoma law and to an appropriate response by the Supreme Court to that law?

3.   *Michael M.* Does the Court, in your opinion, adequately distinguish between real gender differences and sexist overgeneralizations?

4.   *United States v. Virginia.* Has the standard of scrutiny changed from *Craig*? How important are facts versus theory in this case? Do you agree with JUSTICE SCALIA that virtually all single-gender schools and components of schools that are single gender are now illegal?

5.   **From Schools to Bathrooms.** Are single-sex restrooms in a government office building constitutionally permissible? For those who have observed or endured

---

[8] In this regard, I note that the Court—which I concede is under no obligation to do so—provides no example of a program that would pass muster under its reasoning today: not even, for example, a football or wrestling program. On the Court's theory, any woman ready, willing, and physically able to participate in such a program would, as a constitutional matter, be entitled to do so.

the different-length bathroom waiting is "separate and unequal" alive and well despite the cases you have read? If so, when and why? Would pure strict scrutiny make a difference here? Would the ERA ("Equality of rights under the law shall not be denied or abridged by the United States or by any State on account of sex") affect the potty problem?

NGUYEN v. INS
533 U.S. 53, 121 S.Ct. 2053, 150 L.Ed.2d 115 (2001).

JUSTICE KENNEDY delivered the opinion of the Court.

*** 8 U.S.C. § 1409 governs the acquisition of United States citizenship by persons born to one United States citizen parent and one noncitizen parent when the parents are unmarried and the child is born outside of the United States or its possessions. The statute imposes different requirements for the child's acquisition of citizenship depending upon whether the citizen parent is the mother or the father. The question before us is whether the statutory distinction is consistent with the equal protection guarantee embedded in the Due Process Clause of the Fifth Amendment. *** [Section] 1409(a)(4) requires one of three affirmative steps to be taken if the citizen parent is the father, but not if the citizen parent is the mother: legitimation; a declaration of paternity under oath by the father; or a court order of paternity. Congress' decision to impose requirements on unmarried fathers that differ from those on unmarried mothers is based on the significant difference between their respective relationships to the potential citizen at the time of birth. Specifically, the imposition of the requirement for a paternal relationship, but not a maternal one, is justified by two important governmental objectives. *** The first governmental interest to be served is the importance of assuring that a biological parent-child relationship exists. In the case of the mother, the relation is verifiable from the birth itself. The mother's status is documented in most instances by the birth certificate or hospital records and the witnesses who attest to her having given birth. *** Section 1409(a)(4)'s provision of three options for a father seeking to establish paternity—legitimation, paternity oath, and court order of paternity—is designed to ensure an acceptable documentation of paternity.

Petitioners argue that the requirement *** that a father provide clear and convincing evidence of parentage, is sufficient to achieve the end of establishing paternity, given the sophistication of modern DNA tests. Section 1409(a)(1) does not actually mandate a DNA test, however. *** The requirement of § 1409(a)(4) represents a reasonable conclusion by the legislature that the satisfaction of one of several alternatives will suffice to establish the blood link between father and child required as a predicate to the child's acquisition of citizenship. Given the proof of motherhood that is inherent in birth itself, it is unremarkable that Congress did not require the same affirmative steps of mothers. ***

The second important governmental interest furthered in a substantial manner by § 1409(a)(4) is the determination to ensure that the child and the citizen parent have some demonstrated opportunity or potential to develop not just a relationship that is recognized, as a formal matter, by the law, but one that consists of the real, everyday ties that provide a connection between child and citizen parent and, in turn, the United States. In the case of a citizen mother and a child born overseas, the opportunity for a meaningful relationship between citizen parent and child inheres in the very event of birth, an event so often critical to our constitutional and statutory understandings of citizenship. The mother knows that the child is in being and is hers and has an initial point of contact with him. There is at least an opportunity for mother and child to develop a real, meaningful relationship.

The same opportunity does not result from the event of birth, as a matter of biological inevitability, in the case of the unwed father. *** This fact takes on particular significance in the case of a child born overseas and out of wedlock. One concern in this context has always been with young people, men for the most part, who are on duty with the Armed Forces in foreign countries. *** Even if a father knows of the fact of conception, moreover, it does not follow that he will be present at the birth of the child. Thus, unlike the case of the mother, there is no assurance that the father and his biological child will ever meet. ***

Congress is well within its authority in refusing, absent proof of at least the opportunity for the development of a relationship between citizen parent and child, to commit this country to embracing a child as a citizen entitled as of birth to the full protection of the United States, to the absolute right to enter its borders, and to full participation in the political process. *** There is nothing irrational or improper in the recognition that at the moment of birth—a critical event in the statutory scheme and in the whole tradition of citizenship law—the mother's knowledge of the child and the fact of parenthood have been established in a way not guaranteed in the case of the unwed father. This is not a stereotype.

*** [T]he question remains whether the means Congress chose to further its objective—the imposition of certain additional requirements upon an unwed father—substantially relate to that end. Under this test, the means Congress adopted must be sustained.

First, it should be unsurprising that Congress decided to require that an opportunity for a parent-child relationship occur during the formative years of the child's minority. *** Second, petitioners argue that § 1409(a)(4) is not effective. In particular, petitioners assert that, although a mother will know of her child's birth, "knowledge that one is a parent, no matter how it is acquired, does not guarantee a relationship with one's child." *** This line of argument misconceives the nature of both the governmental interest at issue and the manner in which we examine statutes alleged to violate equal protection. As to the former, Congress would of course be entitled to advance the interest of ensuring an actual, meaningful relationship in every case before citizenship is conferred. Or Congress could excuse compliance with the formal requirements when an actual father-child relationship is proved. It did neither here, perhaps because of the subjectivity, intrusiveness, and difficulties of proof that might attend an inquiry into any particular bond or tie. Instead, Congress enacted an easily administered scheme to promote the different but still substantial interest of ensuring at least an opportunity for a parent-child relationship to develop. ***

In this difficult context of conferring citizenship on vast numbers of persons, the means adopted by Congress are in substantial furtherance of important governmental objectives. The fit between the means and the important end is "exceedingly persuasive." *** In analyzing § 1409(a)(4), we are mindful that the obligation it imposes with respect to the acquisition of citizenship by the child of a citizen father is minimal. This circumstance shows that Congress has not erected inordinate and unnecessary hurdles to the conferral of citizenship on the children of citizen fathers in furthering its important objectives. Only the least onerous of the three options provided for in § 1409(a)(4) must be satisfied. *** The statute can be satisfied on the day of birth, or the next day, or for the next 18 years. In this case, the unfortunate, even tragic, circumstance is that Boulais did not pursue, or perhaps did not know of, these simple steps and alternatives. Any omission, however, does not nullify the statutory scheme.

Section 1409(a), moreover, is not the sole means by which the child of a citizen father can attain citizenship. An individual who fails to comply with § 1409(a), but who has substantial ties to the United States, can seek citizenship in his or her own right, rather than via reliance on ties to a citizen parent. ***

JUSTICE SCALIA, with whom JUSTICE THOMAS joins, concurring. [omitted]

JUSTICE O'CONNOR, with whom JUSTICE SOUTER, JUSTICE GINSBURG, and JUSTICE BREYER join, dissenting.

*** The Court *** departs from the guidance of our precedents concerning such classifications in several ways. *** [T]he majority glosses over the crucial matter of the burden of justification. *** For example, the majority hypothesizes about the interests served by the statute and fails adequately to inquire into the actual purposes of § 1409(a)(4). The Court also does not always explain adequately the importance of the interests that it claims to be served by the provision. The majority also fails carefully to consider whether the sex-based classification is being used impermissibly "as a 'proxy for other, more germane bases of classification,'" and instead casually dismisses the relevance of available sex-neutral alternatives. And, contrary to the majority's conclusion, the fit between the means and ends of § 1409(a)(4) is far too attenuated for the provision to survive heightened scrutiny. In all, the majority opinion represents far less than the rigorous application of heightened scrutiny that our precedents require.

According to the Court, "[t]he first governmental interest to be served is the importance of assuring that a biological parent-child relationship exists." *** [Section] 1409(a)(4) requires legitimation, an acknowledgment of paternity in writing under oath, or an adjudication of paternity before the child reaches the age of 18. *** The majority concedes that Congress could achieve the goal of assuring a biological parent-child relationship in a sex-neutral fashion [DNA testing], but then, in a surprising turn, dismisses the availability of sex-neutral alternatives as irrelevant. *** In our prior cases, the existence of comparable or superior sex-neutral alternatives has been a powerful reason to reject a sex-based classification. *** The majority's acknowledgment of the availability of sex-neutral alternatives scarcely confirms the point that "[t]he differential treatment is inherent in a sensible statutory scheme." The discussion instead demonstrates that, at most, differential impact will result from the fact that "[f]athers and mothers are not similarly situated with regard to the proof of biological parenthood." In other words, it will likely be easier for mothers to satisfy a sex-neutral proof of parentage requirement. But facially neutral laws that have a disparate impact are a different animal for purposes of constitutional analysis than laws that specifically provide for disparate treatment. ***

The Court states that "[t]he second important governmental interest furthered in a substantial manner by § 1409(a)(4) is the determination to ensure that the child and the citizen parent have some demonstrated opportunity or potential to develop not just a relationship that is recognized, as a formal matter, by the law, but one that consists of the real, everyday ties that provide a connection between child and citizen parent and, in turn, the United States." The Court again fails to demonstrate that this was Congress' actual purpose in enacting § 1409(a)(4). The majority's focus on "some demonstrated opportunity or potential to develop *** real, everyday ties," in fact appears to be the type of hypothesized rationale that is insufficient under heightened scrutiny. *** It is difficult to see how, in this citizenship-conferral context, anyone profits from a "demonstrated opportunity" for a relationship in the absence of the fruition of an actual tie. *** Even if it is important "to require that an opportunity for a parent-child relationship occur during the formative years of the child's minority," it is difficult to see how the requirement that *proof* of such opportunity be obtained before the child turns 18 substantially furthers the asserted interest. ***

Moreover, available sex-neutral alternatives would at least replicate, and could easily exceed, whatever fit there is between § 1409(a)(4)'s discriminatory means and the majority's asserted end. *** Congress could simply substitute for § 1409(a)(4) a requirement that the parent be present at birth or have knowledge of birth. Congress could at least allow proof of such presence or knowledge to be one way of demonstrating an opportunity for a relationship. *** Indeed, the idea that a mother's presence at birth supplies adequate assurance of an opportunity to develop a relationship while a father's presence at birth would appear to rest only on an overbroad sex-based generalization. *** There is no reason, other than stereotype, to say that fathers who are present at birth lack an opportunity for a relationship on similar terms. *** If Congress wishes to advance this end, it could easily do so by employing a sex-neutral classification that is a far "more germane bas[i]s of classification" than sex. For example, Congress could require some degree of regular contact between the child and the citizen parent over a period of time.

*** We have repeatedly rejected efforts to justify sex-based classifications on the ground of administrative convenience. There is no reason to think that this is a case where administrative convenience concerns are so powerful that they would justify the sex-based discrimination, especially where the use of sex as a proxy is so ill fit to the purported ends as it is here. ***

The claim that § 1409(a)(4) substantially relates to the achievement of the goal of a "real, practical relationship" thus finds support not in biological differences but instead in a stereotype–*i.e.*, "the generalization that mothers are significantly more likely than fathers *** to develop caring relationships with their children. Such a claim relies on "the very stereotype the law condemns," "lends credibility" to the generalization, and helps to convert that "assumption" into "a self-fulfilling prophecy." Indeed, contrary to this stereotype, Boulais has reared Nguyen, while Nguyen apparently has lacked a relationship with his mother. ***

The Court has also failed even to acknowledge the "volumes of history" to which "[t]oday's skeptical scrutiny of official action denying rights or opportunities based on sex responds." *** Section 1409 was first enacted as § 205 of the Nationality Act of 1940. The 1940 Act had been proposed by the President, forwarding a report by a specially convened Committee of Advisors, including the Attorney General. The Committee explained to Congress the rationale for § 205, whose sex-based classification remains in effect today:

> "[T]he Department of State has, at least since 1912, uniformly held that an illegitimate child born abroad of an American mother acquires at birth the nationality of the mother ***. This ruling is based *** on the ground that the mother in such case stands in the place of the father ***. [U]nder American law the mother has a right to custody and control of such child as against the putative father, and *is bound* to maintain it as its *natural guardian*. This rule seems to be in accord with the old Roman law and with the laws of Spain and France."

Section 1409(a)(4) is thus paradigmatic of a historic regime that left women with responsibility, and freed men from responsibility, for nonmarital children. ***

The Court also states that the obligation imposed by § 1409(a)(4) is "minimal" and does not present "inordinate and unnecessary hurdles" to the acquisition of citizenship by the nonmarital child of a citizen father. Even assuming that the burden is minimal (and the question whether the hurdle is "unnecessary" is quite different in kind from the question whether it is burdensome), it is well settled that "the 'absence of an insurmountable barrier' will not redeem an otherwise unconstitutionally discriminatory law." ***

Notes

1.   **Real, Not Hypothetical.** JUSTICE O' CONNOR calls attention to the reasons attributed to Congress for having enacted the gender-based classification and that this rationale was neither put forward by the INS nor contained in the statute's legislative history. If *United States v. Virginia*, requires the legislative rationale for passage of a gender-based classification to be articulated at or before

enactment, how can the majority of the court speculate regarding Congress' reasons for passing the statute?

2.   **Flexibility.** Does this case indicate that particular standards for assessing equal protection classifications (here, the middle-tier standard) are very flexible, depending upon the factual circumstances in which the standard is being employed?

3.   **Fact specificity.** Perhaps facts, more than doctrinal differences, explain (and limit) this decision. Here are some facts that may have influenced the outcome:

a. Context: Congress' power to make immigration law. If distinctions based upon race, why should gender-based classifications receive heightened scrutiny?

b. Conduct. The facts of this case are not very helpful to Nguyen, who was convicted of sexual assault. During his state criminal proceedings, he pleaded that he was a citizen of Vietnam, not the United States.

c. Burden. The burden on the defendant in this case to establish citizenship was not particularly onerous. Any one of three avenues could have been traveled to obtain citizenship. The petitioner did not seek to avail himself of any of these methods before his conviction for sexual assault.

d. Remedy. The majority clearly doubts the Court could fashion a suitable remedy, even though it attempts to put this issue off to the side.

e. Real Physical Differences. If the process of giving birth, perhaps the most telling physical distinction between men and women, does not pass intermediate scrutiny, what gender-based classification based upon physical characteristics would pass?

4.   **Other Suspect Classes.** There are a number of cases deciding whether aliens can be treated unequally to citizens (answer: sometimes yes, sometimes no, depending mainly on whether the federal government or a state government is making the distinction and the context of the distinction). Other cases hold that the law cannot treat illegitimate children differently from legitimate children.

5.   **Fundamental Interests.** The cases discussed in the preceding sections concern racial and gender classifications. Some of the cases in this chapter have involved fundamental interests as well as suspect classes. *See Strauder* (jury trial), *Korematsu* (liberty), *Loving* (marriage), and *Michael M.* (liberty). Another branch of equal protection law focuses on whether heightened scrutiny should be applied when discrimination occurs in relation to a person's "fundamental interests." We have examined comparable constitutional reasoning in Chapters VI and VIII.

D. FUNDAMENTAL INTERESTS AND EQUAL PROTECTION

SAN ANTONIO INDEPENDENT SCHOOL DISTRICT v. RODRIGUEZ
411 U.S. 1, 93 S.Ct. 1278, 36 L.Ed.2d 16 (1973).

MR. JUSTICE POWELL delivered the opinion of the Court.

This suit attacking the Texas system of financing public education was initiated by Mexican–American parents whose children attend the elementary and secondary schools in the Edgewood Independent School District, an urban school district in San Antonio, Texas. ***

I

*** Until recent times, Texas was a predominantly rural State and its population and property wealth were spread relatively evenly across the State. Sizable differences in the value of assessable property between local school districts became increasingly evident as the State became more industrialized and as rural-to-urban population shifts became more pronounced. The location of commercial and industrial property began to play a significant role in determining the amount of tax resources available to each school district. These growing disparities in population and taxable property between districts were responsible in part for increasingly notable differences in levels of local expenditure for education.

*** [A Foundation Program was begun in 1949 to ameliorate the problem.] The Program calls for state and local contributions to a fund earmarked specifically for teacher salaries, operating expenses, and transportation costs. The State, supplying funds from its general revenues, finances approximately 80% of the Program, and the school districts are responsible—as a unit—for providing the remaining 20%. ***

The school district in which appellees reside, the Edgewood Independent School District, has been compared throughout this litigation with the Alamo Heights Independent School District. This comparison between the least and most affluent districts in the San Antonio area serves to illustrate the manner in which the dual system of finance operates and to indicate the extent to which substantial disparities exist despite the State's impressive progress in recent years. Edgewood is one of seven public school districts in the metropolitan area. The district is situated in the core-city sector of San Antonio in a residential neighborhood that has little commercial or industrial property. The residents are predominantly of Mexican–American descent *** [and] [t]he average assessed property value per pupil is $5,960—the lowest in the metropolitan area. *** At an equalized tax rate of $1.05 per $100 of assessed property—the highest in the metropolitan area—the district contributed $26 to the education of each child for the 1967—1968 school year. *** The Foundation Program contributed $222 per pupil for a state-local total of $248. ***

Alamo Heights is the most affluent school district in San Antonio. Its six schools, housing approximately 5,000 students, are situated in a residential community quite unlike the Edgewood District. The school population is predominantly "Anglo," having only 18% Mexican–Americans and less than 1% Negroes. The assessed property value per pupil exceeds $49,000, and *** [i]n 1967—1968 the local tax rate of $.85 per $100 of valuation yielded $333 per pupil over and above its contribution to the Foundation Program. Coupled with the $225 provided from that Program, the district was able to supply $558 per student. *** For the 1970—1971 school year, the Foundation

School Program allotment for Edgewood was $356 per pupil. Alamo Heights *** net[ted] $491 per pupil in 1970—1971. *** Alamo Heights, because of its relative wealth, was required to contribute out of its local property tax collections approximately $100 per pupil, or about 20% of its Foundation grant. Edgewood, on the other hand, paid only $8.46 per pupil, which is about 2.4% of its grant. It appears then that, at least as to these two districts, the Local Fund Assignment does reflect a rough approximation of the relative taxpaying potential of each.

*** The District Court held that the Texas system discriminates on the basis of wealth in the manner in which education is provided for its people. Finding that wealth is a "suspect" classification and that education is a "fundamental" interest, the District Court held that the Texas system could be sustained only if the State could show that it was premised upon some compelling state interest. On this issue the court concluded that "(n)ot only are defendants unable to demonstrate compelling state interests *** they fail even to establish a reasonable basis for these classifications." *** We must decide, first, whether the Texas system of financing public education operates to the disadvantage of some suspect class or impinges upon a fundamental right explicitly or implicitly protected by the Constitution, thereby requiring strict judicial scrutiny. If so, the judgment of the District Court should be affirmed. If not, the Texas scheme must still be examined to determine whether it rationally furthers some legitimate, articulated state purpose and therefore does not constitute an invidious discrimination in violation of the Equal Protection Clause of the Fourteenth Amendment.

II

*** We are unable to agree that this case, which in significant aspects is sui generis, may be so neatly fitted into the conventional mosaic of constitutional analysis under the Equal Protection Clause. Indeed, *** we find neither the suspect-classification not the fundamental-interest analysis persuasive.

*** The individuals, or groups of individuals, who constituted the class discriminated against in our prior cases shared two distinguishing characteristics: because of their impecunity they were completely unable to pay for some desired benefit, and as a consequence, they sustained an absolute deprivation of a meaningful opportunity to enjoy that benefit. In *Griffin v. Illinois*, 351 U.S. 12 (1956), and its progeny, the Court invalidated state laws that prevented an indigent criminal defendant from acquiring a transcript, or an adequate substitute for a transcript, for use at several stages of the trial and appeal process. The payment requirements in each case were found to occasion de facto discrimination against those who, because of their indigency, were totally unable to pay for transcripts. And the Court in each case emphasized that no constitutional violation would have been shown if the State had provided some "adequate substitute" for a full stenographic transcript.

Likewise, in *Douglas v. California*, 372 U.S. 353 (1963), a decision establishing an indigent defendant's right to court-appointed counsel on direct appeal, the Court dealt only with defendants who could not pay for counsel from their own resources and who had no other way of gaining representation. *Douglas* provides no relief for those on whom the burdens of paying for a criminal defense are relatively speaking, great but not insurmountable. Nor does it deal with relative differences in the quality of counsel acquired by the less wealthy. *** Finally, in *Bullock v. Carter*, 405 U.S. 134 (1972), the Court invalidated the Texas filing-fee requirement for primary elections. Both of the relevant classifying facts found in the previous cases were present there. The size of the fee, often running into the thousands of dollars and, in at least one case, as high as $8,900, effectively barred all potential candidates who were unable to pay the required fee. As the system provided "no reasonable alternative means of access to the ballot", inability to pay occasioned an absolute denial of a position on the primary ballot.

Only appellees' first possible basis for describing the class disadvantaged by the Texas school-financing system—discrimination against a class of definably "poor" persons—might arguably meet the criteria established in these prior cases. Even a cursory examination, however, demonstrates that neither of the two distinguishing characteristics of wealth classifications can be found here. First, in support of their charge that the system discriminates against the "poor," appellees have made no effort to demonstrate that it operates to the peculiar disadvantage of any class fairly definable as indigent, or as composed of persons whose incomes are beneath any designated poverty level. Indeed, there is reason to believe that the poorest families are not necessarily clustered in the poorest property districts. *** [There] is no basis on the record in this case for assuming that the poorest people—defined by reference to any level of absolute impecunity—are concentrated in the poorest districts.

Second, neither appellees nor the District Court addressed the fact that, unlike each of the foregoing cases, lack of personal resources has not occasioned an absolute deprivation of the desired benefit. The argument here is not that the children in districts having relatively low assessable property values are receiving no public education; rather, it is that they are receiving a poorer quality education than that available to children in districts having more assessable wealth. Apart from the unsettled and disputed question whether the quality of education may be determined by the amount of money expended for it, a sufficient answer to appellees' argument is that, at least where wealth is involved, the Equal Protection Clause does not require absolute equality or precisely equal advantages. ***

For these two reasons—the absence of any evidence that the financing system discriminates against any definable category of "poor" people or that it results in the absolute deprivation of education—the disadvantaged class is not susceptible of identification in traditional terms. ***

In *Brown v. Board of Education*, a unanimous Court recognized that "education is perhaps the most important function of state and local governments." *** Nothing this Court holds today in any way detracts from our historic dedication to public education. We are in complete agreement with the conclusion of the three-judge panel below that "the grave significance of education both to the individual and to our society" cannot be doubted. But the importance of a service performed by the State does not determine whether it must be regarded as fundamental for purposes of examination under the Equal Protection Clause. ***

Lindsey v. Normet, 405 U.S. 56 (1972), decided only last Term, firmly reiterates that social importance is not the critical determinant for subjecting state legislation to strict scrutiny. MR. JUSTICE WHITE's analysis, in his opinion for the Court is instructive:

> "We do not denigrate the importance of decent, safe and sanitary housing. But the Constitution does not provide judicial remedies for every social and economic ill. We are unable to perceive in that document any constitutional guarantee of access to dwellings of a particular quality or any recognition of the right of a tenant to occupy the real property of his landlord beyond the term of his lease, without the payment of rent ***. Absent constitutional mandate, the assurance of adequate housing and the definition of landlord-tenant relationships are legislative, not judicial, functions."

Similarly, in *Dandridge v. Williams*, 397 U.S. 471 (1970), the Court's explicit recognition of the fact that the "administration of public welfare assistance *** involves the most basic economic needs of impoverished human beings," provided no basis for departing from the settled mode of constitutional analysis of legislative classifications involving questions of economic and social policy. ***

The lesson of these cases in addressing the question now before the Court is plain. It is not the province of this Court to create substantive constitutional rights in the name of guaranteeing equal protection of the laws. Thus, the key to discovering whether education is "fundamental" is not to be found in comparisons of the relative societal significance of education as opposed to subsistence or housing. Nor is it to be found by weighing whether education is as important as the right to travel. Rather, the answer lies in assessing whether there is a right to education explicitly or implicitly guaranteed by the Constitution. *Dunn v. Blumstein*, 405 U.S. 330 (1972);[74]

Police Dept. of City of Chicago v. Mosley, 408 U.S. 92, (1972);[75] *Skinner v. Oklahoma ex rel. Williamson*, 316 U.S. 535 (1942).[76]

---

[74] *Dunn* fully canvasses this Court's voting rights cases and explains that "this Court has made clear that a citizen has a constitutionally protected right to participate in elections on an equal basis with other citizens in the jurisdiction." The constitutional underpinnings of the right to equal treatment in the voting process can no longer be doubted even though, as the Court noted in *Harper v. Virginia Bd. of Elections*, 383 U.S., at 665, "the right to vote in state elections is nowhere expressly mentioned."

[75] In *Mosley*, the Court struck down a Chicago antipicketing ordinance that exempted labor picketing from its prohibitions. The ordinance was held invalid under the Equal Protection Clause after subjecting it to careful scrutiny and finding that the ordinance was not narrowly drawn. The stricter standard of review was appropriately applied since the ordinance was one "affecting First Amendment interests."

Education, of course, is not among the rights afforded explicit protection under our Federal Constitution. Nor do we find any basis for saying it is implicitly so protected. As we have said, the undisputed importance of education will not alone cause this Court to depart from the usual standard for reviewing a State's social and economic legislation. It is appellees' contention, however, that education is distinguishable from other services and benefits provided by the State because it bears a peculiarly close relationship to other rights and liberties accorded protection under the Constitution. Specifically, they insist that education is itself a fundamental personal right because it is essential to the effective exercise of First Amendment freedoms and to intelligent utilization of the right to vote. In asserting a nexus between speech and education, appellees urge that the right to speak is meaningless unless the speaker is capable of articulating his thoughts intelligently and persuasively. ***

A similar line of reasoning is pursued with respect to the right to vote.[78] Exercise of the franchise, it is contended, cannot be divorced from the educational foundation of the voter. The electoral process, if reality is to conform to the democratic ideal, depends on an informed electorate: a voter cannot cast his ballot intelligently unless his reading skills and thought processes have been adequately developed.

We need not dispute any of these propositions. The Court has long afforded zealous protection against unjustifiable governmental interference with the individual's rights to speak and to vote. Yet we have never presumed to possess either the ability or the authority to guarantee to the citizenry the most effective speech or the most informed electoral choice. That these may be desirable goals of a system of freedom of expression and of a representative form of government is not to be doubted. These are indeed goals to be pursued by a people whose thoughts and beliefs are freed from governmental interference. But they are not values to be implemented by judicial intrusion into otherwise legitimate state activities.

*** Whatever merit appellees' argument might have if a State's financing system occasioned an absolute denial of educational opportunities to any of its children, that argument provides no basis for finding an interference with fundamental rights where only relative differences in spending levels are involved and where—as is true in the present case—no charge fairly could be made that the system fails to provide each child with an opportunity to acquire the basic minimal skills necessary for the enjoyment of the rights of speech and of full participation in the political process.

---

[76] *Skinner* applied the standard of close scrutiny to a state law permitting forced sterilization of "habitual criminals." Implicit in the Court's opinion is the recognition that the right of procreation is among the rights of personal privacy protected under the Constitution. *See Roe v. Wade.*

[78] Since the right to vote, per se, is not a constitutionally protected right, we assume that appellees' references to that right are simply shorthand references to the protected right, implicit in our constitutional system, to participate in state elections on an equal basis with other qualified voters whenever the State has adopted an elective process for determining who will represent any segment of the State's population.

Furthermore, the logical limitations on appellees' nexus theory are difficult to perceive. How, for instance, is education to be distinguished from the significant personal interests in the basics of decent food and shelter? Empirical examination might well buttress an assumption that the ill-fed, ill-clothed, and ill-housed are among the most ineffective participants in the political process, and that they derive the least enjoyment from the benefits of the First Amendment. If so, appellees' thesis would cast serious doubt on the authority of *Dandridge v. Williams* and *Lindsey v. Normet.* ***

We need not rest our decision, however, solely on the inappropriateness of the strict-scrutiny test. A century of Supreme Court adjudication under the Equal Protection Clause affirmatively supports the application of the traditional standard of review, which requires only that the State's system be shown to bear some rational relationship to legitimate state purposes. This case represents far more than a challenge to the manner in which Texas provides for the education of its children. We have here nothing less than a direct attack on the way in which Texas has chosen to raise and disburse state and local tax revenues. We are asked to condemn the State's judgment in conferring on political subdivisions the power to tax local property to supply revenues for local interests. In so doing, appellees would have the Court intrude in an area in which it has traditionally deferred to state legislatures. This Court has often admonished against such interferences with the State's fiscal policies under the Equal Protection Clause. *** No scheme of taxation, whether the tax is imposed on property, income, or purchases of goods and services, has yet been devised which is free of all discriminatory impact. In such a complex arena in which no perfect alternatives exist, the Court does well not to impose too rigorous a standard of scrutiny lest all local fiscal schemes become subjects of criticism under the Equal Protection Clause.

In addition to matters of fiscal policy, this case also involves the most persistent and difficult questions of educational policy, another area in which this Court's lack of specialized knowledge and experience counsels against premature interference with the informed judgments made at the state and local levels. Education, perhaps even more than welfare assistance, presents a myriad of "intractable economic, social, and even philosophical problems." *Dandridge v. Williams.* *** In such circumstances, the judiciary is well advised to refrain from imposing on the States inflexible constitutional restraints that could circumscribe or handicap the continued research and experimentation so vital to finding even partial solutions to educational problems and to keeping abreast of ever-changing conditions. ***

III

*** The Texas system of school finance, *** [w]hile assuring a basic education for every child in the State, [also] permits and encourages a large measure of participation in and control of each district's schools at the local level. In an era that has witnessed a consistent trend toward centralization of the functions of government, local sharing of responsibility for public education has survived. *** [L]ocal control means *** the freedom to devote more money to the education of one's children. Equally important, however, is the opportunity it offers for participation in the decisionmaking process that determines how those local tax dollars will be spent. Each locality is free to tailor local programs to local needs. Pluralism also affords some opportunity for experimentation, innovation, and a healthy competition for educational excellence. ***

IX–3. "***One Nation***Indivisible***" by Herbert Block. © 1977 Herblock— from *Herblock On All Fronts* (New American Library, 1980).

Appellees do not question the propriety of Texas' dedication to local control of education. To the contrary, they attack the school-financing system precisely because, in their view, it does not provide the same level of local control and fiscal flexibility in all districts. Appellees suggest that local control could be preserved and promoted under other financing systems that resulted in more equality in education expenditures. While it is no doubt true that reliance on local property taxation for school revenues provides less freedom of choice with respect to expenditures for some districts than for others, the existence of "some inequality" in the manner in which the State's rationale is achieved is not alone a sufficient basis for striking down the entire system. *** Nor must the financing system fail because, as appellees suggest, other methods of satisfying the State's interest, which occasion "less drastic" disparities in expenditures, might be conceived. Only where state action impinges on the exercise of fundamental constitutional rights or liberties must it be found to have chosen the least restrictive alternative. It is also well to remember that even those districts that have reduced ability to make free decisions with respect to how much they spend on education still retain under the present system a large measure of authority as to how available funds will be allocated. They further enjoy the power to make numerous other decisions with respect to the operation of the schools. The people of Texas may be justified in believing that other systems of school financing, which place more of the financial responsibility in the hands of the State, will result in a comparable lessening of desired local autonomy. ***

In sum, to the extent that the Texas system of school financing results in unequal expenditures between children who happen to reside in different districts, we cannot say that such disparities are the product of a system that is so irrational as to be invidiously discriminatory. *** The constitutional standard under the Equal Protection Clause is whether the challenged state action rationally furthers a legitimate state purpose or interest. We hold that the Texas plan abundantly satisfies this standard. ***

MR. JUSTICE STEWERT, concurring. [omitted]

MR. JUSTICE BRENNAN, dissenting. [omitted]

MR. JUSTICE WHITE, with whom MR. JUSTICE DOUGLAS and MR. JUSTICE BRENNAN join, dissenting.

*** I cannot disagree with the proposition that local control and local decisionmaking play an important part in our democratic system of government. *** The difficulty with the Texas system, however, is that it provides a meaningful option to Alamo Heights and like school districts but almost none to Edgewood and those other districts with a low per-pupil real estate tax base. In these latter districts, *** the Texas system utterly fails to extend a realistic choice to parents because the property tax, which is the only revenue-raising mechanism extended to school districts, is practically and legally unavailable. *** In order to equal the highest yield in any other Bexar County district, Alamo Heights would be required to tax at the rate of 68 cents per $100 of assessed valuation. Edgewood would be required to tax at the prohibitive rate of $5.76 per $100. But state law places a $1.50 per $100 ceiling on the maintenance tax rate, a limit that would surely be reached long before Edgewood attained an equal yield. Edgewood is thus precluded in law, as well as in fact, from achieving a yield even close to that of some other districts. *** If the State aims at maximizing local initiative and local choice, by permitting school districts to resort to the real property tax if they choose to do so, it utterly fails in achieving its purpose in districts with property tax bases so low that there is little if any opportunity for interested parents, rich or poor, to augment school district revenues. Requiring the State to establish only that unequal treatment is in furtherance of a permissible goal, without also requiring the State to show that the means chosen to effectuate that goal are rationally related to its achievement, makes equal protection analysis no more than an empty gesture. In my view, the parents and children in Edgewood, and in like districts, suffer from an invidious discrimination violative of the Equal Protection Clause. ***

MR. JUSTICE MARSHALL, with whom MR. JUSTICE DOUGLAS concurs, dissenting.

*** To begin, I must once more voice my disagreement with the Court's rigidified approach to equal protection analysis. The Court apparently seeks to establish today that equal protection cases fall into one of two neat categories which dictate the appropriate standard of review—strict scrutiny or mere rationality. But this Court's decisions in the field of equal protection defy such easy categorization. A principled reading of what this Court has done reveals that it has applied a spectrum of standards in reviewing discrimination allegedly violative of the Equal Protection Clause. This spectrum clearly comprehends variations in the degree of care with which the Court will scrutinize particular classifications, depending, I believe, on the constitutional and societal importance of the interest adversely affected and the recognized invidiousness of the basis upon which the particular classification is drawn. ***

I therefore cannot accept the majority's labored efforts to demonstrate that fundamental interests, which call for strict scrutiny of the challenged classification, encompass only established rights which we are somehow bound to recognize from the text of the Constitution itself. To be sure, some interests which the Court has deemed to be fundamental for purposes of equal protection analysis are themselves constitutionally protected rights. Thus, discrimination against the guaranteed right of freedom of speech has called for strict judicial scrutiny. *See Police Dept. of City of Chicago v. Mosley*, 408 U.S. 92 (1972). Further, every citizen's right to travel interstate, although nowhere expressly mentioned in the Constitution, has long been recognized as implicit in the premises underlying that document ***. *Shapiro v. Thompson*[, 394 U.S. at 634]. But it will not do to suggest that the "answer" to whether an interest is fundamental for purposes of equal protection analysis is always determined by whether that interest "is a right *** explicitly or implicitly guaranteed by the Constitution."[59]

I would like to know where the Constitution guarantees the right to procreate, *Skinner v. Oklahoma ex rel. Williamson*, or the right to vote in state elections, e.g., *Reynolds v. Sims*, or the right to an appeal from a criminal conviction, e.g., *Griffin v. Illinois*. These are instances in which, due to the importance of the interests at stake, the Court has displayed a strong concern with the existence of discriminatory state treatment. But the Court has never said or indicated that these are interests which independently enjoy fullblown constitutional protection. ***

The majority is, of course, correct when it suggests that the process of determining which interests are fundamental is a difficult one. But I do not

---

[59] Indeed, the Court's theory would render the established concept of fundamental interests in the context of equal protection analysis superfluous, for the substantive constitutional right itself requires that this Court strictly scrutinize any asserted state interest for restricting or denying access to any particular guaranteed right.

think the problem is insurmountable. *** The task in every case should be to determine the extent to which constitutionally guaranteed rights are dependent on interests not mentioned in the Constitution. As the nexus between the specific constitutional guarantee and the nonconstitutional interest draws closer, the nonconstitutional interest becomes more fundamental and the degree of judicial scrutiny applied when the interest is infringed on a discriminatory basis must be adjusted accordingly. Thus, it cannot be denied that interests such as procreation, the exercise of the state franchise, and access to criminal appellate processes are not fully guaranteed to the citizen by our Constitution. But these interests have nonetheless been afforded special judicial consideration in the face of discrimination because they are, to some extent, interrelated with constitutional guarantees. Procreation is now understood to be important because of its interaction with the established constitutional right of privacy. The exercise of the state franchise is closely tied to basic civil and political rights inherent in the First Amendment. And access to criminal appellate processes enhances the integrity of the range of rights implicit in the Fourteenth Amendment guarantee of due process of law. Only if we closely protect the related interests from state discrimination do we ultimately ensure the integrity of the constitutional guarantee itself. This is the real lesson that must be taken from our previous decisions involving interests deemed to be fundamental. ***

Since the Court now suggests that only interests guaranteed by the Constitution are fundamental for purposes of equal protection analysis, and since it rejects the contention that public education is fundamental, it follows that the Court concludes that public education is not constitutionally guaranteed. It is true that this Court has never deemed the provision of free public education to be required by the Constitution. *** Nevertheless, the fundamental importance of education is amply indicated by the prior decisions of this Court, by the unique status accorded public education by our society, and by the close relationship between education and some of our most basic constitutional values. ***

Education directly affects the ability of a child to exercise his First Amendment rights, both as a source and as a receiver of information and ideas, whatever interests he may pursue in life. *** Education serves the essential function of instilling in our young an understanding of and appreciation for the principles and operation of our governmental processes. Education may instill the interest and provide the tools necessary for political discourse and debate. *** But of most immediate and direct concern must be the demonstrated effect of education on the exercise of the franchise by the electorate. *** It is this very sort of intimate relationship between a particular personal interest and specific constitutional guarantees that has heretofore caused the Court to attach special significance, for purposes of equal protection analysis, to individual interests such as procreation and the exercise of the state franchise.[74]

---

[74] I believe that the close nexus between education and our established constitutional values with respect to freedom of speech and participation in the political process makes this a different

*** The nature of our inquiry into the justifications for state discrimination is essentially the same in all equal protection cases: We must consider the substantiality of the state interests sought to be served, and we must scrutinize the reasonableness of the means by which the State has sought to advance its interests. Differences in the application of this test are, in my view, a function of the constitutional importance of the interests at stake and the invidiousness of the particular classification. *** The only justification offered by appellants to sustain the discrimination in educational opportunity caused by the Texas financing scheme is local educational control. Presented with this justification, the District Court concluded that "(n)ot only are defendants unable to demonstrate compelling state interests for their classifications based upon wealth, they fail even to establish a reasonable basis for these classifications." I must agree with this conclusion.

At the outset, I do not question that local control of public education, as an abstract matter, constitutes a very substantial state interest. *** The State's interest in local educational control—which certainly includes questions of educational funding—has deep roots in the inherent benefits of community support for public education. *** [However,] on this record, it is apparent that the State's purported concern with local control is offered primarily as an excuse rather than as a justification for interdistrict inequality. *** If Texas had a system truly dedicated to local fiscal control, one would expect the quality of the educational opportunity provided in each district to vary with the decision of the voters in that district as to the level of sacrifice they wish to make for public education. In fact, the Texas scheme produces precisely the opposite result. Local school districts cannot choose to have the best education in the State by imposing the highest tax rate. Instead, the quality of the educational opportunity offered by any particular district is largely determined by the amount of taxable property located in the district—a factor over which local voters can exercise no control. ***

In my judgment, any substantial degree of scrutiny of the operation of the Texas financing scheme reveals that the State has selected means wholly inappropriate to secure its purported interest in assuring its school districts local fiscal control.[96] At the same time, appellees have pointed out a variety of

---

case from our prior decisions concerning discrimination affecting public welfare, *see, e.g., Dandridge v. Williams*, or housing, *see, e.g., Lindsey v. Normet.* There can be no question that, as the majority suggests, constitutional rights may be less meaningful for someone without enough to eat or without decent housing. But the crucial difference lies in the closeness of the relationship. Whatever the severity of the impact of insufficient food or inadequate housing on a person's life, they have never been considered to bear the same direct and immediate relationship to constitutional concerns for free speech and for our political processes as education has long been recognized to bear. Perhaps, the best evidence of this fact is the unique status which has been accorded public education as the single public service nearly unanimously guaranteed in the constitutions of our States. Education, in terms of constitutional values, is much more analogous in my judgment, to the right to vote in state elections than to public welfare or public housing. Indeed, it is not without significance that we have long recognized education as an essential step in providing the disadvantaged with the tools necessary to achieve economic self-sufficiency.

[96] My Brother WHITE, in concluding that the Texas financing scheme runs afoul of the Equal Protection Clause, likewise finds on analysis that the means chosen by Texas—local property

alternative financing schemes which may serve the State's purported interest in local control as well as, if not better than, the present scheme without the current impairment of the educational opportunity of vast numbers of Texas schoolchildren. I see no need, however, to explore the practical or constitutional merits of those suggested alternatives at this time for, whatever their positive or negative features, experience with the present financing scheme impugns any suggestion that it constitutes a serious effort to provide local fiscal control. If for the sake of local education control, this Court is to sustain interdistrict discrimination in the educational opportunity afforded Texas school children, it should require that the State present something more than the mere sham now before us. *** I believe that the wide disparities in taxable district property wealth inherent in the local property tax element of the Texas financing scheme render that scheme violative of the Equal Protection Clause. ***

PLYLER v. DOE
457 U.S. 202, 102 S.Ct. 2382, 72 L.Ed.2d 786 (1982).

JUSTICE BRENNAN delivered the opinion of the Court.

The question presented by these cases is whether, consistent with the Equal Protection Clause of the Fourteenth Amendment, Texas may deny to undocumented school-age children the free public education that it provides to children who are citizens of the United States or legally admitted aliens.

*** Appellants argue at the outset that undocumented aliens, because of their immigration status, are not "persons within the jurisdiction" of the State of Texas, and that they therefore have no right to the equal protection of Texas law. We reject this argument. Whatever his status under the immigration laws, an alien is surely a "person" in any ordinary sense of that term. Aliens, even aliens whose presence in this country is unlawful, have long been recognized as "persons" guaranteed due process of law by the Fifth and Fourteenth Amendments. [*Yick Wo v. Hopkins*, 118 U.S. 356 (1886)]. *** The more difficult question is whether the Equal Protection Clause has been violated by the refusal of the State of Texas to reimburse local school boards for the education of children who cannot demonstrate that their presence within the United States is lawful, or by the imposition by those school boards of the burden of tuition on those children. It is to this question that we now turn.

III

taxation dependent upon local taxable wealth—is completely unsuited in its present form to the achievement of the asserted goal of providing local fiscal control. Although my Brother WHITE purports to reach this result by application of that lenient standard of mere rationality traditionally applied in the context of commercial interest, it seems to me that the care with which he scrutinizes the practical effectiveness of the present local property tax as a device for affording local fiscal control reflects the application of a more stringent standard of review, a standard which at the least is influenced by the constitutional significance of the process of public education.

*** A legislature must have substantial latitude to establish classifications that roughly approximate the nature of the problem perceived, that accommodate competing concerns both public and private, and that account for limitations on the practical ability of the State to remedy every ill. In applying the Equal Protection Clause to most forms of state action, we thus seek only the assurance that the classification at issue bears some fair relationship to a legitimate public purpose.

But we would not be faithful to our obligations under the Fourteenth Amendment if we applied so deferential a standard to every classification. The Equal Protection Clause was intended as a restriction on state legislative action inconsistent with elemental constitutional premises. Thus we have treated as presumptively invidious those classifications that disadvantage a "suspect class," or that impinge upon the exercise of a "fundamental right." With respect to such classifications, it is appropriate to enforce the mandate of equal protection by requiring the State to demonstrate that its classification has been precisely tailored to serve a compelling governmental interest. In addition, we have recognized that certain forms of legislative classification, while not facially invidious, nonetheless give rise to recurring constitutional difficulties; in these limited circumstances we have sought the assurance that the classification reflects a reasoned judgment consistent with the ideal of equal protection by inquiring whether it may fairly be viewed as furthering a substantial interest of the State. We turn to a consideration of the standard appropriate for the evaluation of [the Act].

Sheer incapability or lax enforcement of the laws barring entry into this country *** has resulted in the creation of a substantial "shadow population" of illegal migrants—numbering in the millions—within our borders. This situation raises the specter of a permanent caste of undocumented resident aliens, encouraged by some to remain here as a source of cheap labor, but nevertheless denied the benefits that our society makes available to citizens and lawful residents. The existence of such an underclass presents most difficult problems for a Nation that prides itself on adherence to principles of equality under law.[19]

The children who are plaintiffs in these cases are special members of this underclass. Persuasive arguments support the view that a State may withhold its beneficence from those whose very presence within the United States is the product of their own unlawful conduct. These arguments do not apply with the same force to classifications imposing disabilities on the minor

---

[19] We reject the claim that "illegal aliens" are a "suspect class." No case in which we have attempted to define a suspect class, has addressed the status of persons unlawfully in our country. Unlike most of the classifications that we have recognized as suspect, entry into this class, by virtue of entry into this country, is the product of voluntary action. Indeed, entry into the class is itself a crime. In addition, it could hardly be suggested that undocumented status is a "constitutional irrelevancy." With respect to the actions of the Federal Government, alienage classifications may be intimately related to the conduct of foreign policy, to the federal prerogative to control access to the United States, and to the plenary federal power to determine who has sufficiently manifested his allegiance to become a citizen of the Nation. No State may independently exercise a like power. But if the Federal Government has by uniform rule prescribed what it believes to be appropriate standards for the treatment of an alien subclass, the States may, of course, follow the federal direction.

children of such illegal entrants. At the least, those who elect to enter our territory by stealth and in violation of our law should be prepared to bear the consequences, including, but not limited to, deportation. But the children of those illegal entrants are not comparably situated. Their "parents have the ability to conform their conduct to societal norms," and presumably the ability to remove themselves from the State's jurisdiction; but the children who are plaintiffs in these cases "can affect neither their parents' conduct nor their own status." ***

Of course, undocumented status is not irrelevant to any proper legislative goal. Nor is undocumented status an absolutely immutable characteristic since it is the product of conscious, indeed unlawful, action. But [the Act] is directed against children, and imposes its discriminatory burden on the basis of a legal characteristic over which children can have little control. It is thus difficult to conceive of a rational justification for penalizing these children for their presence within the United States. Yet that appears to be precisely the effect of [the Act].

Public education is not a "right" granted to individuals by the Constitution. *San Antonio Independent School Dist. v. Rodriguez.* But neither is it merely some governmental "benefit" indistinguishable from other forms of social welfare legislation. Both the importance of education in maintaining our basic institutions, and the lasting impact of its deprivation on the life of the child, mark the distinction. *** In sum, education has a fundamental role in maintaining the fabric of our society. We cannot ignore the significant social costs borne by our Nation when select groups are denied the means to absorb the values and skills upon which our social order rests.

In addition to the pivotal role of education in sustaining our political and cultural heritage, denial of education to some isolated group of children poses an affront to one of the goals of the Equal Protection Clause: the abolition of governmental barriers presenting unreasonable obstacles to advancement on the basis of individual merit. *** Illiteracy is an enduring disability. The inability to read and write will handicap the individual deprived of a basic education each and every day of his life. The inestimable toll of that deprivation on the social economic, intellectual, and psychological well-being of the individual, and the obstacle it poses to individual achievement, make it most difficult to reconcile the cost or the principle of a status-based denial of basic education with the framework of equality embodied in the Equal Protection Clause. ***

These well settled principles allow us to determine the proper level of deference to be afforded [the Act]. Undocumented aliens cannot be treated as a suspect class because their presence in this country in violation of federal law is not a "constitutional irrelevancy." Nor is education a fundamental right; a State need not justify by compelling necessity every variation in the manner in which education is provided to its population. But more is involved in these cases than the abstract question whether [the Act] discriminates against a suspect class, or whether education is a fundamental right. [The Act] imposes a lifetime hardship on a discrete class of children not accountable for their disabling status. *** In light of these countervailing costs, the discrimination contained in [the Act] can hardly be considered rational unless it furthers some substantial goal of the State.

IV

It is the State's principal argument, and apparently the view of the dissenting Justices, that the undocumented status of these children *vel non* establishes a sufficient rational basis for denying them benefits that a State might choose to afford other residents. *** But we are unable to find in the congressional immigration scheme any statement of policy that might weigh significantly in arriving at an equal protection balance concerning the State's authority to deprive these children of an education.

The Constitution grants Congress the power to "establish an uniform Rule of Naturalization." Art. I., § 8, cl. 4. Drawing upon this power, upon its plenary authority with respect to foreign relations and international commerce, and upon the inherent power of a sovereign to close its borders, Congress has developed a complex scheme governing admission to our Nation and status within our borders. *** [T]he States do have some authority to act with respect to illegal aliens, at least where such action mirrors federal objectives and furthers a legitimate state goal. *** [Yet] there is no indication that the disability imposed by [the Act] corresponds to any identifiable congressional policy. The State does not claim that the conservation of state educational resources was ever a congressional concern in restricting immigration. More importantly, the classification *** does not operate harmoniously within the federal program.

To be sure, like all persons who have entered the United States unlawfully, these children are subject to deportation. But there is no assurance that a child subject to deportation will ever be deported. An illegal entrant might be granted federal permission to continue to reside in this country, or even to become a citizen. *** [W]e perceive no national policy that supports the State in denying these children an elementary education. ***

V

*** Apart from the asserted state prerogative to act against undocumented children solely on the basis of their undocumented status—an asserted prerogative that carries only minimal force in the circumstances of these cases—we discern three colorable state interests that might support [the Act].

First, appellants appear to suggest that the State may seek to protect itself from an influx of illegal immigrants. While a State might have an interest in mitigating the potentially harsh economic effects of sudden shifts in population, [the Act] hardly offers an effective method of dealing with an urgent demographic or economic problem. There is no evidence in the record suggesting that illegal entrants impose any significant burden on the State's economy. To the contrary, the available evidence suggests that illegal aliens underutilize public services, while contributing their labor to the local economy and tax money to the state fisc. ***

Second, while it is apparent that a State may "not *** reduce expenditures for education by barring [some arbitrarily chosen class of] children from its schools," appellants suggest that undocumented children are appropriately singled out for exclusion because of the special burdens they impose on the State's ability to provide high-quality public education. But the record in no way supports the claim that exclusion of undocumented children is likely to improve the overall quality of education in the State. *** [Further,] even if improvement in the quality of education were a likely result of barring some *number* of children from the schools of the State, the State must support its selection of *this* group as the appropriate target for exclusion. In terms of educational cost and need, however, undocumented children are "basically indistinguishable" from legally resident alien children.

Finally, appellants suggest that undocumented children are appropriately singled out because their unlawful presence within the United States renders them less likely than other children to remain within the boundaries of the State, and to put their education to productive social or political use within the State. Even assuming that such an interest is legitimate, it is an interest that is most difficult to quantify. The State has no assurance that any child, citizen or not, will employ the education provided by the State within the confines of the State's borders. In any event, the record is clear that many of the undocumented children disabled by this classification will remain in this country indefinitely, and that some will become lawful residents or citizens of the United States. It is difficult to understand precisely what the State hopes to achieve by promoting the creation and perpetuation of a subclass of illiterates within our boundaries, surely adding to the problems and costs of unemployment, welfare, and crime. It is thus clear that whatever savings might be achieved by denying these children an education, they are wholly insubstantial in light of the costs involved to these children, the State, and the Nation. ***

JUSTICE MARSHALL, concurring.

While I join the Court's opinion, I do so without in any way retreating from my opinion in *San Antonio Independent School District v. Rodriguez*. I continue to believe that an individual's interest in education is fundamental ***. Furthermore, I believe that the facts of these cases demonstrate the wisdom of rejecting a rigidified approach to equal protection analysis, and of employing an approach that allows for varying levels of scrutiny depending upon "the constitutional and societal importance of the interest adversely affected and the recognized invidiousness of the basis upon which the particular classification is drawn." It continues to be my view that a class-based denial of public education is utterly incompatible with the Equal Protection Clause of the Fourteenth Amendment.

JUSTICE BLACKMUN, concurring.

*** I joined JUSTICE POWELL's opinion for the Court in *Rodriguez*, and I continue to believe that it provides the appropriate model for resolving most equal protection disputes. *** [However,] I believe the Court's experience has demonstrated that the *Rodriguez* formulation does not settle every issue of "fundamental rights" arising under the Equal Protection Clause. Only a pedant would insist that there are *no* meaningful distinctions among the multitude of social and political interests regulated by the States, and *Rodriguez* does not stand for quite so absolute a proposition. To the contrary, *Rodriguez* implicitly acknowledged that certain interests, though not constitutionally guaranteed, must be accorded a special place in equal protection analysis. [JUSTICE BLACKMUN used the right to vote as an example]. ***

In my view, when the State provides an education to some and denies it to others, it immediately and inevitably creates class distinctions of a type fundamentally inconsistent with those purposes, mentioned above, of the Equal Protection Clause. Children denied an education are placed at a permanent and insurmountable competitive disadvantage, for an uneducated child is denied even the opportunity to achieve. And when those children are members of an identifiable group, that group—through the State's action—will have been converted into a discrete underclass. Other benefits provided by the State, such as housing and public assistance, are of course important; to an individual in immediate need, they may be more desirable than the right to be educated. But classifications involving the complete denial of education are in a sense unique, for they strike at the heart of equal protection values by involving the State in the creation of permanent class distinctions. In a sense, then, denial of an education is the analogue of denial of the right to vote: the former relegates the individual to second-class social status; the latter places him at a permanent political disadvantage.

This conclusion is fully consistent with *Rodriguez*. The Court there reserved judgment on the constitutionality of a state system that "occasioned an absolute denial of educational opportunities to any of its children." *** Here, *** the State has undertaken to provide an education to most of the children residing within its borders. And, in contrast to the situation in *Rodriguez*, it does not take an advanced degree to predict the effects of a complete denial of education upon those children targeted by the State's classification. In such circumstances, the voting decisions suggest that the State must offer something more than a rational basis for its classification. ***

JUSTICE POWELL, concurring.

I join the opinion of the Court, and write separately to emphasize the unique character of the case[ ] before us. *** Although the analogy is not perfect, our holding today does find support in decisions of this Court with respect to the status of illegitimates. *** "[V]isiting *** condemnation on the head of an infant" for the misdeeds of the parents is illogical, unjust, and "contrary to the basic concept of our system that legal burdens should bear some relationship to individual responsibility or wrongdoing." [Here], the State of Texas effectively denies to the school-age children of illegal aliens the opportunity to attend the free public schools that the State makes available to all residents. They are excluded only because of a status resulting from the violation by parents or guardians of our immigration laws and the fact that they remain in our country unlawfully. The appellee children are innocent in this respect. *** A legislative classification that threatens the creation of an underclass of future citizens and residents cannot be reconciled with one of the fundamental purposes of the Fourteenth Amendment. In these unique circumstances, the Court properly may require that the State's interests be substantial and that the means bear a "fair and substantial relation" to these interests.[14] In my view, the State's denial of education to these children bears no substantial relation to any substantial state interest. ***

CHIEF JUSTICE BURGER, with whom JUSTICE WHITE, JUSTICE REHNQUIST, and JUSTICE O'CONNOR join, dissenting.

Were it our business to set the Nation's social policy, I would agree without hesitation that it is senseless for an enlightened society to deprive any children—including illegal aliens—of an elementary education. I fully agree that it would be folly *** to tolerate creation of a segment of society made up of illiterate persons, many having a limited or no command of our language. However, the Constitution does not constitute us as "Platonic Guardians" nor does it vest in this Court the authority to strike down laws because they do not meet our standards of desirable social policy, "wisdom," or "common sense." We trespass on the assigned function of the political branches under our structure of limited and separated powers when we assume a policymaking role as the Court does today.

*** I have no quarrel with the conclusion that the Equal Protection Clause of the Fourteenth Amendment *applies* to aliens who, after their illegal entry into this country, are indeed physically "within the jurisdiction" of a state. However, as the Court concedes, this "only begins the inquiry." The Equal Protection Clause does not mandate identical treatment of different categories of persons. *** The dispositive issue in these cases, simply put, is whether, for purposes of allocating its finite resources, a state has a legitimate reason to differentiate between persons who are lawfully within the state and those who are unlawfully there. The distinction the State of Texas has drawn—based not only upon its own legitimate interests but on classifications established by the Federal Government in its immigration laws and policies—is not unconstitutional.

The Court acknowledges that, except in those cases when state classifications disadvantage a "suspect class" or impinge upon a "fundamental right," the Equal Protection Clause permits a state "substantial latitude" in distinguishing between different groups of persons. Moreover, the Court expressly—and correctly—rejects any suggestion that illegal aliens are a suspect class, or that education is a fundamental right. Yet by patching together bits and pieces of what might be termed quasi-

---

[14] The CHIEF JUSTICE argues in his dissenting opinion that this heightened standard of review is inconsistent with the Court's decision in [*Rodriguez*]. But in *Rodriguez* no group of children was singled out by the State and then penalized because of their parents' status. Rather, funding for education varied across the State because of the tradition of local control. Nor, in that case, was any group of children totally deprived of all education as in these cases. If the resident children of illegal aliens were denied welfare assistance, made available by government to all other children who qualify, this also—in my opinion—would be an impermissible penalizing of children because of their parents' status.

suspect-class and quasi-fundamental-rights analysis, the Court spins out a theory custom-tailored to the facts of these cases. In the end, we are told little more than that the level of scrutiny employed to strike down the Texas law applies only when illegal alien children are deprived of a public education. If ever a court was guilty of an unabashedly result-oriented approach, this case is a prime example.

The Court first suggests that these illegal alien children, although not a suspect class, are entitled to special solicitude under the Equal Protection Clause because they lack "control" over or "responsibility" for their unlawful entry into this country. Similarly, the Court appears to take the position that [the Act] is presumptively "irrational" because it has the effect of imposing "penalties" on "innocent" children. However, the Equal Protection Clause does not preclude legislators from classifying among persons on the basis of factors and characteristics over which individuals may be said to lack "control." *** [A] state legislature is not barred from considering, for example, relevant differences between the mentally healthy and the mentally ill, or between the residents of different counties, simply because these may be factors unrelated to individual choice or to any "wrongdoing." The Equal Protection Clause protects against arbitrary and irrational classifications, and against invidious discrimination stemming from prejudice and hostility; it is not an all-encompassing "equalizer" designed to eradicate every distinction for which persons are not "responsible." ***

The Court's analogy to cases involving discrimination against illegitimate children is grossly misleading. The State has not thrust any disabilities upon appellees due to their "status of birth." Rather, appellees' status is predicated upon the circumstances of their concededly illegal presence in this country. *** The second strand of the Court's analysis rests on the premise that, although public education is not a constitutionally guaranteed right, "neither is it merely some governmental 'benefit' indistinguishable from other forms of social welfare legislation." Whatever meaning or relevance this opaque observation might have in some other context, it simply has no bearing on the issues at hand. Indeed, it is never made clear what the Court's opinion means on this score.

The importance of education is beyond dispute. Yet we have held repeatedly that the importance of a governmental service does not elevate it to the status of a "fundamental right" for purposes of equal protection analysis. *** Moreover, the Court points to no meaningful way to distinguish between education and other governmental benefits in this context. Is the Court suggesting that education is more "fundamental" than food, shelter, or medical care?

The Equal Protection Clause guarantees similar treatment of similarly situated persons, but it does not mandate a constitutional hierarchy of governmental services. *** Yet that is precisely what the Court does today. ***

Once it is conceded—as the Court does—that illegal aliens are not a suspect class, and that education is not a fundamental right, our inquiry should focus on and be limited to whether the legislative classification at issue bears a rational relationship to a legitimate state purpose. ***

Without laboring what will undoubtedly seem obvious to many, it simply is not "irrational" for a state to conclude that it does not have the same responsibility to provide benefits for persons whose very presence in the state and this country is illegal as it does to provide for persons lawfully present. By definition, illegal aliens have no right whatever to be here, and the state may reasonably, and constitutionally, elect not to provide them with governmental services at the expense of those who are lawfully in the state. *** The Court has failed to offer even a plausible explanation why illegality of residence in this country is not a factor that may legitimately bear upon the bona fides of state residence and entitlement to the benefits of lawful residence.

It is significant that the Federal Government has seen fit to exclude illegal aliens from numerous social welfare programs, such as the food stamp program, the old-age assistance, aid to families with dependent children, aid to the blind, aid to the permanently and totally disabled, and supplemental security income programs, the Medicare hospital insurance benefits program, and the Medicaid hospital insurance benefits for the aged and disabled program. Although these exclusions do not conclusively demonstrate the constitutionality of the State's use of the same classification for comparable purposes, at the very least they tend to support the rationality of excluding illegal alien residents of a state from such programs so as to preserve the state's finite revenues for the benefit of lawful residents. *** [T]he fact that there are sound policy arguments against the Texas Legislature's choice does not render that choice an unconstitutional one.

The Constitution does not provide a cure for every social ill, nor does it vest judges with a mandate to try to remedy every social problem. Moreover, when this Court rushes in to remedy what it perceives to be the failings of the political processes, it deprives those processes of an opportunity to function. When the political institutions are not forced to exercise constitutionally allocated powers and responsibilities, those powers, like muscles not used, tend to atrophy. Today's case[ ], I regret to say, present yet another example of unwarranted judicial action which in the long run tends to contribute to the weakening of our political processes. ***

Notes

1.   **Two Approaches in** *Rodriguez.* Note the difference between the majority's recognition of "fundamental interests" under the Equal Protection Clause as encompassing only rights "explicitly or implicitly guaranteed by the Constitution" versus JUSTICE MARSHALL's focus on the "extent to which constitutionally protected rights are dependent on interests not mentioned in the Constitution." The Court also reaffirmed the "tiers" approach to equal protection claims (once two tiers, now three) versus JUSTICE MARSHALL's "sliding scale" approach. After *Rodriguez*, does the importance of the right affect Equal Protection Clause analysis? Compare these approaches to developments under the Due Process Clause, which you studied earlier.

2.   **Pragmatic Considerations.** Had the Court decided that education was a fundamental right under the Equal Protection Clause, how would it assess what kind of education and how much education a person was constitutionally entitled to receive? Can it avoid such difficulties by simply saying "this one won't work" and "remanding" the problem to the state legislature?

3.   **State Law.** The Supreme Court of Texas, more than 15 years later, decided that Rodriguez was correct in his claim that the Texas school financing system violated the *state* constitution's "free and equal" education clause.

4.   **Comparing *Rodriguez* and *Plyler*.** Which case is the norm, and which the special circumstance? Is *Plyler's* combination of a semi-suspect class with a semi-fundamental right analogous to "middle tier" scrutiny in the gender cases?

5.   **Judging.** We tend to think that justices are relatively consistent, at least in cases that look a lot like each other. JUSTICES POWELL and BLACKMUN, both of whom were with the majority in both cases, seem consistent in that *Plyler* involves total educational deprivation and a more narrowly defined class, children of illegal immigrants. What accounts for JUSTICE WHITE's dissents in both cases?

6.   **A Problem Concerning Wealth.** Suppose a city has a golf course for which it charges a green fee of $2000 per year. A golfer who recently declared bankruptcy can't afford the fee. Does she have an equal protection right to use the course? *See Kadrmas v. Dickinson Public Schools*, 487 U.S. 450 (1988) (upholding school bus fees covering 11% of actual costs). What if the city prohibited anyone not having an annual income of $50,000 per year from using the golf course? What if the city said that only those with a net worth of over $1,000,000 could use the course?

7.   **Other Equal Protection Fundamental Rights.**

   (a) Reproduction. *Skinner v. Oklahoma*, 316 U.S. 535 (1942), said the "right to have offspring" was fundamental. The Court found it was a denial of equal protection for the state to treat theft (of chickens, incidentally) differently from embezzlement (a more upscale crime?), with the consequence that a repeat offender of the former kind was sterilized while a repeat offender of the second variety was not.

   (b) Voting. Voting is sometimes viewed as a fundamental right, despite the fact that it has its own constitutional amendments (the 15th and the 19th). Representation-reinforcement notions play a role in these cases (see *McCulloch v. Maryland* from the early part of the course). While some of these cases are race cases, several of which are discussed in earlier notes, others involve denial or dilution of voting on other bases (e.g. party affiliation). *See Bush v. Gore*, infra.

   (c) Courts. There are also cases involving what the Court describes as "access to the judicial process." Access to judicial processes is a right explicitly treated in the Constitution. Federal court jurisdiction is limited under Article III (see Chapter I), but state court access, in both criminal and civil cases, is broader.

   (d) Interstate Travel. The issue of "travel" was reconceptualized in *Saenz v. Roe*, supra.

8. **Implied Rights Theory.** Do you agree with JUSTICE MARSHALL that "the Court's theory would render the established concept of fundamental interests in the context of equal protection analysis superfluous, for the substantive constitutional right itself requires that this Court strictly scrutinize any asserted state interest for restricting or denying access to any particular guaranteed right"?

BUSH v. GORE

531 U.S. 98, 121 S.Ct. 525, 148 L.Ed. 2d 388 (2000).

PER CURIAM.

I

On December 8, 2000, the Supreme Court of Florida ordered that the Circuit Court of Leon County tabulate by hand 9,000 ballots in Miami-Dade County. It also ordered the inclusion in the certified vote totals of 215 votes identified in Palm Beach County and 168 votes identified in Miami-Dade County for Vice President Albert Gore, Jr., and Senator Joseph Lieberman, Democratic Candidates for President and Vice President. The Supreme Court noted that petitioner, Governor George W. Bush asserted that the net gain for Vice President Gore in Palm Beach County was 176 votes, and directed the Circuit Court to resolve that dispute on remand. The court further held that relief would require manual recounts in all Florida counties where so-called "undervotes" had not been subject to manual tabulation. The court ordered all manual recounts to begin at once. Governor Bush and Richard Cheney, Republican Candidates for the Presidency and Vice Presidency, filed an emergency application for a stay of this mandate. On December 9, we granted the application, treated the application as a petition for a writ of certiorari, and granted certiorari. *** The petition presents the following questions: whether the Florida Supreme Court established new standards for resolving Presidential election contests, thereby violating Art. II, § 1, cl. 2, of the United States Constitution and failing to comply with 3 U.S.C. § 5, and whether the use of standardless manual recounts violates the Equal Protection and Due Process Clauses. With respect to the equal protection question, we find a violation of the Equal Protection Clause.

II

The closeness of this election, and the multitude of legal challenges which have followed in its wake, have brought into sharp focus a common, if heretofore unnoticed, phenomenon. Nationwide statistics reveal that an estimated 2% of ballots cast do not register a vote for President for whatever reason, including deliberately choosing no candidate at all or some voter error, such as voting for two candidates or insufficiently marking a ballot. In certifying election results, the votes eligible for inclusion in the certification are the votes meeting the properly established legal requirements.

This case has shown that punch card balloting machines can produce an unfortunate number of ballots, which are not punched in a clean, complete way by the voter. After the current counting, it is likely legislative bodies nationwide will examine ways to improve the mechanisms and machinery for voting.

The individual citizen has no federal constitutional right to vote for electors for the President of the United States unless and until the state legislature chooses a statewide election as the means to implement its power to appoint members of the Electoral College. U.S. Const., Art. II, § 1. This is the source for the statement in *McPherson v. Blacker*, 146 U.S. 1, 35 (1892), that the State legislature's power to select the manner for appointing electors is plenary; it may, if it so chooses, select the electors itself, which indeed was the manner used by State legislatures in several States for many years after the Framing of our Constitution. History has now favored the voter, and in each of the several States the citizens themselves vote for Presidential electors. When the state legislature vests the right to vote for President in its people, the right to vote as the legislature has prescribed is fundamental; and one source of its fundamental nature lies in the equal weight accorded to each vote and the equal dignity owed to each voter. The State, of course, after granting the franchise in the special context of Article II, can take back the power to appoint electors.

The right to vote is protected in more than the initial allocation of the franchise. Equal protection applies as well to the manner of its exercise. Having once granted the right to vote on equal terms, the State may not, by later arbitrary and disparate treatment, value one person's vote over that of anoter. See *e.g., Harper v. Virginia Bd. Of Elections*, 383 U.S. 663, 665 (1966) ("[O]nce the franchise is granted to the electorate, lines may not be drawn which are inconsistent with the Equal Protection Clause of the Fourteenth Amendment"). It must be remembered that "the right of suffrage can be denied by a debasement or dilution of the weight of the citizen's vote just as effectively as by wholly prohibiting the free exercise of the franchise." *Reynolds v. Sims*, 377 U.S. 533, 555 (1964).

There is no difference between the two sides of the present controversy on these basic propositions. Respondents say that the very purpose of vindicating the right to vote justifies the recount procedures now at issue. The question before us, however, is whether the recount procedures the Florida Supreme Court has adopted are consistent with its obligation to avoid arbitrary and disparate treatment of the members of its electorate.

Much of the controversy seems to revolve around ballot cards designed to be perforated by a stylus but which, either through error or deliberate omission, have not been perforated with sufficient precision for a machine to count them. In some cases a piece of the card–a chad–is hanging, say by two corners. In other cases there is no separation at all, just an indentation.

The Florida Supreme Court has ordered that the intent of the voter be discerned from such ballots. For purposes of resolving the equal protection challenge, it is not necessary to decide whether the Florida Supreme Court had the authority under the legislative scheme for resolving election disputes to define what a legal vote is and to mandate a manual recount implementing that definition. The recount mechanisms implemented in response to the decisions of the Florida Supreme Court do not satisfy the minimum requirement for nonarbitrary treatment of voters necessary to secure the fundamental right. Florida's basic command for the count of legally cast votes is to consider the "intent of the voter." This is unobjectionable as an abstract proposition and a starting principle. The problem inheres in the absence of specific standards to ensure its equal application. The formulation of uniform rules to determine intent based on these recurring circumstances is practicable and, we conclude, necessary.

The law does not refrain from searching for the intent of the actor in a multitude of circumstances; and in some cases the general command to ascertain intent is not susceptible to much further refinement. In this instance, however, the question is not whether to believe a witness but how to interpret the marks or holes or scratches on an inanimate object, a piece of cardboard or paper which, it is said, might not have registered as a vote during the machine count. The factfinder confronts a thing, not a person. The search for intent can be confined by specific rules designed to ensure uniform treatment.

The want of those rules here has led to unequal evaluation of ballots in various respects. See *Gore v. Harris*, 772 So.2d. 1243, at 1267 (2000) (WELLS, C.J., dissenting) ("Should a county canvassing board count or not count a 'dimpled chad' where the voter is able to successfully dislodge the chad in every other contest on that ballot? Here, the county canvassing boards disagree"). As seems to have been acknowledged at oral argument, the standards for accepting or rejecting contested ballots might vary not only from county to county but indeed within a single county from one recount team to another. ***

An early case in our one person, one vote jurisprudence arose when a State accorded arbitrary and disparate treatment to voters in its different counties. *Gray v. Sanders*, 372 U.S. 368 (1963). The Court found a constitutional violation. We relied on these principles in the context of the Presidential selection process in *Moore v. Ogilvie*, 394 U.S. 814 (1969), where we invalidated a county-based procedure that diluted the influence of citizens in larger counties in the nominating process. There we observed that "[t]he idea that one group can be granted greater voting strength than another is hostile to the one man, one vote basis of our representative government."

The State Supreme Court ratified this uneven treatment. It mandated that the recount totals from two counties, Miami-Dade and Palm Beach, be included in the certified total. The court also appeared to hold *sub silentio* that the recount totals from Broward County, which were not completed until after the original November 14 certification by the Secretary of State, were to be considered part of the new certified vote totals even though the county certification was not contested by Vice President Gore. Yet each of the counties used varying standards to determine what was a legal vote. Broward County used a more forgiving standard than Palm Beach County, and uncovered almost three times as many new votes, a result markedly disproportionate to the difference in population between the counties.

In addition, the recounts in these three counties were not limited to so-called undervotes but extended to all of the ballots. The distinction has real consequences. A manual recount of all ballots identifies not only those ballots which show no vote but also those which contain more than one, the so-called overvotes. Neither category will be counted by the machine. This is not a trivial concern. At oral argument, respondents estimated there are as many as 110,000 overvotes statewide. As a result, the citizen whose ballot was not read by a machine because he failed to vote for a candidate in a way readable by a machine may still have his vote counted in a manual recount; on the other hand, the citizen who marks two candidates in a way discernable by the machine will not have the same opportunity to have his vote count, even if a manual examination of the ballot would reveal the requisite indicia of intent. Furthermore, the citizen who marks two candidates, only one of which is discernable by the machine, will have his vote counted even though it should have been read as an invalid ballot. The State Supreme Court's inclusion of vote counts based on these variant standards exemplifies concerns with the remedial processes that were under way.

That brings the analysis to yet a further equal protection problem. The votes certified by the court included a partial total from one county, Miami-Dade. The Florida Supreme Court's decision thus gives no assurance that the recounts included in a final certification must be complete. Indeed, it is respondent's submission that it would be consistent with the rules of the recount procedures to include whatever partial counts are done by the time of final certification, and we interpret the Florida Supreme Court's decision to permit this. This accommodation no doubt results from the truncated contest period established by the Florida Supreme Court in *Palm Beach Canvassing Bd. v. Harris*, at respondents' own urging. The press of time does not diminish the constitutional concern. A desire for speed is not a general excuse for ignoring equal protection guarantees.

In addition to these difficulties the actual process by which the votes were to be counted under the Florida Supreme Court's decision raises further concerns. That order did not specify who would recount the ballots. The county canvassing boards were forced to pull together ad hoc teams comprised of judges from various Circuits who had no previous training in handling and interpreting ballots. Furthermore, while others were permitted to observe, they were prohibited from objecting during the recount.

The recount process, in its features here described, is inconsistent with the minimum procedures necessary to protect the fundamental right of each voter in the special instance of a statewide recount under the authority of a single state judicial officer. Our consideration is limited to the present circumstances, for the problem of equal protection in election processes generally presents many complexities.

The question before the Court is not whether local entities, in the exercise of their expertise, may develop different systems for implementing elections. Instead, we are presented with a situation where a state court with the power to assure uniformity has ordered a statewide recount with minimal procedural safeguards. When a court orders a statewide remedy, there must be at least some assurance that the rudimentary requirements of equal treatment and fundamental fairness are satisfied.

Given the Court's assessment that the recount process underway was probably being conducted in an unconstitutional manner, the Court stayed the order directing the recount so it could hear this case and render an expedited decision. The contest provision, as it was mandated by the State Supreme Court, is not well calculated to sustain the confidence that all citizens must have in the outcome of elections. The State has not shown that its procedures include the necessary safeguards. ***

Upon due consideration of the difficulties identified to this point, it is obvious that the recount cannot be conducted in compliance with the requirements of equal protection and due process without substantial additional work. It would require not only the adoption (after opportunity for argument) of adequate statewide standards for determining what is a legal vote, and practicable procedures to implement them, but also orderly judicial review of any disputed matters that might arise. In addition, the Secretary of State has advised that the recount of only a portion of the ballots requires that the vote tabulation equipment be used to screen out undervotes, a function for which the machines were not designed. If a recount of overvotes were also required, perhaps even a second screening would be necessary. Use of the equipment for this purpose, and any new software developed for it, would have to be evaluated for accuracy by the Secretary [of State] ***.

The Supreme Court of Florida has said that the legislature intended the State's electors to "participat[e] fully in the federal electoral process," as provided in 3 U.S.C. § 5. That statute, in turn, requires that any controversy or contest that is designed to lead to a conclusive selection of electors be completed by December 12. That date is upon us, and there is no recount procedure in place under the State Supreme Court's order that comports with minimal constitutional standards. Because it is evident that any recount seeking to meet the December 12 date will be unconstitutional for the reasons we have discussed, we reverse the judgment of the Supreme Court of Florida ordering a recount to proceed.

Seven Justices of the Court agree that there are constitutional problems with the recount ordered by the Florida Supreme Court that demand a remedy. The only disagreement is as to the remedy. Because the Florida Supreme Court has said that the Florida Legislature intended to obtain the safe-harbor benefits of 3 U.S.C. § 5, JUSTICE BREYER's proposed remedy—remanding to the Florida Supreme Court for its ordering of a constitutionally proper contest until December 18-contemplates action in violation of the Florida election code, and hence could not be part of an "appropriate" order ***.

None are more conscious of the vital limits on judicial authority than are the members of this Court, and none stand more in admiration of the Constitution's design to leave the selection of the President to the people, through their legislatures, and to the political sphere. When contending parties invoke the process of the courts, however, it becomes our unsought responsibility to resolve the federal and constitutional issues the judicial system has been forced to confront.

The judgment of the Supreme Court of Florida is reversed, and the case is remanded for further proceedings not inconsistent with this opinion. ***

CHIEF JUSTICE REHNQUIST, with whom JUSTICE SCALIA and JUSTICE THOMAS join, concurring.

We join the *per curiam* opinion. We write separately because we believe there are additional grounds that require us to reverse the Florida Supreme Court's decision.

We deal here not with an ordinary election, but with an election for the President of the United States. *** In most cases, comity and respect for federalism compel us to defer to the decisions of state courts on issues of state law. That practice reflects our understanding that the decisions of state courts are definitive pronouncements of the will of the States as sovereigns. *** But there are a few exceptional cases in which the Constitution imposes a duty or confers a power on a particular branch of a State's government. This is one of them. Article II, § 1, cl. 2, provides that "[e]ach State shall appoint, in such Manner as the *Legislature* thereof may direct," electors for President and Vice President. Thus, the text of the election law itself, and not just its interpretation by the courts of the States, takes on independent significance. ***

In Florida, the legislature has chosen to hold statewide elections to appoint the State's 25 electors. Importantly, the legislature has delegated the authority to run the elections and to oversee election disputes to the Secretary of State (Secretary), and to state circuit courts. Isolated sections of the code may well admit of more than one interpretation, but the general coherence of the legislative scheme may not be altered by judicial interpretation so as to wholly change the statutorily provided apportionment of responsibility among these various bodies. *** [W]ith respect to a Presidential election, the court must be both mindful of the legislature's role under Article II in choosing the manner of appointing electors and deferential to those bodies expressly empowered by the legislature to carry out its constitutional mandate.

In order to determine whether a state court has infringed upon the legislature's authority, we necessarily must examine the law of the State as it existed prior to the action of the court. Though we generally defer to state courts on the interpretation of state law, there are of course areas in which the Constitution requires this Court to undertake an independent, if still deferential, analysis of state law. *** What we would do in the present case is precisely parallel: Hold that the Florida Supreme Court's interpretation of the Florida election laws impermissibly distorted them beyond what a fair reading required, in violation of Article II.[1]

---

[1] Similarly, our jurisprudence requires us to analyze the "background principles" of state property law to determine whether there has been a taking of property in violation of the Takings Clause. That constitutional guarantee would, of course, afford no protection against state power if our inquiry could be concluded by a state supreme court holding that state property law accorded the plaintiff no rights. See *Lucas v. South Carolina Coastal Council,* 505

This inquiry does not imply a disrespect for state *courts* but rather a respect for the constitutionally prescribed role of state *legislatures.* To attach definitive weight to the pronouncement of a state court, when the very question at issue is whether the court has actually departed from the statutory meaning, would be to abdicate our responsibility to enforce the explicit requirements of Article II.

Acting pursuant to its constitutional grant of authority, the Florida Legislature has created a detailed, if not perfectly crafted, statutory scheme that provides for appointment of Presidential electors by direct election. *** After the election has taken place, the canvassing boards receive returns from precincts, count the votes, and in the event that a candidate was defeated by. 5% or less, conduct a mandatory recount. The county canvassing boards must file certified election returns with the Department of State by 5 p.m. on the seventh day following the election. The Elections Canvassing Commission must then certify the results of the election.

The state legislature has also provided mechanisms both for protesting election returns and for contesting certified election results. *** Any protest must be filed prior to the certification of election results by the county canvassing board. Once a protest has been filed, "the county canvassing board may authorize a manual recount." If a sample recount *** "indicates an error in the vote tabulation which could affect the outcome of the election," the county canvassing board is instructed to: "(a) Correct the error and recount the remaining precincts with the vote tabulation system; (b) Request the Department of State to verify the tabulation software; or (c) Manually recount all ballots." In the event a canvassing board chooses to conduct a manual recount of all ballots, [the statute] prescribes procedures for such a recount.

Contests to the certification of an election, on the other hand, are controlled by [another statute]. The grounds for contesting an election include "[r]eceipt of a number of illegal votes or rejection of a number of legal votes sufficient to change or place in doubt the result of the election." *** In Presidential elections, the contest period necessarily terminates on the date set by 3 U.S.C. § 5 for concluding the State's "final determination" of "election controversies."

In its first decision, *Palm Beach Canvassing Bd. v. Harris,* 772 So.2d 1220 (2000) (*Harris I*), the Florida Supreme Court extended the 7-day statutory certification deadline established by the legislature.[2] This modification of the code. by lengthening the protest period, necessarily

---

U.S. 1003 (1992). In one of our oldest cases, we similarly made an independent evaluation of state law in order to protect federal treaty guarantees. In *Fairfax's Devisee v. Hunter's Lessee,* 7 Cranch 603 (1813), we disagreed with the Supreme Court of Appeals of Virginia that a 1782 state law had extinguished the property interests of one Denny Fairfax, so that a 1789 ejectment order against Fairfax supported by a 1785 state law did not constitute a future confiscation under the 1783 peace treaty with Great Britain.

[2] We vacated that decision and remanded that case; the Florida Supreme Court reissued the same judgment with a new opinion on December 11, 2000, 772 So.2d, 1273.

shortened the contest period for Presidential elections. Underlying the extension of the certification deadline and the shortchanging of the contest period was, presumably, the clear implication that certification was a matter of significance: The certified winner would enjoy presumptive validity, making a contest proceeding by the losing candidate an uphill battle. In its latest opinion, however, the court empties certification of virtually all legal consequence during the contest, and in doing so departs from the provisions enacted by the Florida Legislature.

The court determined that canvassing boards' decisions regarding whether to recount ballots past the certification deadline (even the certification deadline established by *Harris I*) are to be reviewed *de novo*, although the election code clearly vests discretion whether to recount in the boards, and sets strict deadlines subject to the Secretary's rejection of late tallies and monetary fines for tardiness. Moreover, the Florida court held that all late vote tallies [specifically those from Palm Beach and Miami-Dade counties] arriving during the contest period should be automatically included in the certification regardless of the certification deadline (even the certification deadline established by *Harris I*), thus virtually eliminating both the deadline and the Secretary's discretion to disregard recounts that violate it.

Moreover, the court's interpretation of "legal vote," and hence its decision to order a contest-period recount, plainly departed from the legislative scheme. Florida statutory law cannot reasonably be thought to *require* the counting of improperly marked ballots. Each Florida precinct before election day provides instructions on how properly to cast a vote; each polling place on election day contains a working model of the voting machine it uses; and each voting booth contains a sample ballot. In precincts using punch-card ballots, voters are instructed to punch out the ballot cleanly:

"AFTER VOTING, CHECK YOUR BALLOT CARD TO BE SURE YOUR VOTING SELECTIONS ARE CLEARLY AND CLEANLY PUNCHED AND THERE ARE NO CHIPS LEFT HANGING ON THE BACK OF THE CARD.

No reasonable person would call it "an error in the vote tabulation," or a "rejection *** of legal votes,"[4] when electronic or electromechanical equipment performs precisely in the manner designed, and fails to count those ballots that are not marked in the manner that these voting instructions explicitly and prominently specify. The scheme that the Florida Supreme Court's opinion attributes to the legislature is one in which machines are *required* to be "capable of correctly counting votes," but which nonetheless regularly produces elections in which legal votes are predictably *not* tabulated, so that in close elections manual recounts are regularly required. This is of course absurd. The Secretary of State, who is authorized

---

[4] It is inconceivable that what constitutes a vote that must be counted under the "error in the vote tabulation" language of the protest phase is different from what constitutes a vote that must be counted under the "legal votes" language of the contest phase.

by law to issue binding interpretations of the election code, rejected this peculiar reading of the statutes. The Florida Supreme Court, although it must defer to the Secretary's interpretations, rejected her reasonable interpretation and embraced the peculiar one.

But as we indicated in our remand of the earlier case, in a Presidential election the clearly expressed intent of the legislature must prevail. And there is no basis for reading the Florida statutes as requiring the counting of improperly marked ballots, as an examination of the Florida Supreme Court's textual analysis shows. ***

The scope and nature of the remedy ordered by the Florida Supreme Court jeopardizes the "legislative wish" to take advantage of the safe harbor provided by 3 U.S.C. § 5. December 12, 2000, is the last date for a final determination of the Florida electors that will satisfy § 5. Yet in the late afternoon of December 8th–four days before this deadline–the Supreme Court of Florida ordered recounts of tens of thousands of so-called "undervotes" spread through 64 of the State's 67 counties. This was done in a search for elusive–perhaps delusive–certainty as to the exact count of 6 million votes. But no one claims that these ballots have not previously been tabulated; they were initially read by voting machines at the time of the election, and thereafter reread by virtue of Florida's automatic recount provision. No one claims there was any fraud in the election. The Supreme Court of Florida ordered this additional recount under the provision of the election code giving the circuit judge the authority to provide relief that is "appropriate under such circumstances."

Surely when the Florida Legislature empowered the courts of the State to grant "appropriate" relief, it must have meant relief that would have become final by the cut-off date of 3 U.S.C. § 5. In light of the inevitable legal challenges and ensuing appeals to the Supreme Court of Florida and petitions for certiorari to this Court, the entire recounting process could not possibly be completed by that date. ***

Given all these factors, and in light of the legislative intent identified by the Florida Supreme Court to bring Florida within the "safe harbor" provision of 3 U.S.C. § 5, the remedy prescribed by the Supreme Court of Florida cannot be deemed an "appropriate" one as of December 8. It significantly departed from the statutory framework in place on November 7, and authorized open-ended further proceedings, which could not be completed by December 12, thereby preventing a final determination by that date. ***

JUSTICE STEVENS, with whom JUSTICE GINSBURG and JUSTICE BREYER join, dissenting.

The Constitution assigns to the States the primary responsibility for determining the manner of selecting the Presidential electors. See Art. II, § 1 cl. 2. When questions arise about the meaning of state laws, including election laws, it is our settled practice to accept the opinions of the highest courts of the States as providing the final answers. On rare occasions, however, either federal statutes or the Federal Constitution may require federal judicial intervention in state elections. This is not such an occasion.

The federal questions that ultimately emerged in this case are not substantial. Article II provides that "[e]ach *State* shall appoint, in such Manner as the Legislature *thereof* may direct, a Number of Electors." It does not create state legislatures out of whole cloth, but rather takes them as they come—as creatures born of, and constrained by, their state constitutions. Lest there be any doubt, we stated over 100 years ago in *McPherson v. Blacker,* 146 U.S. 1, 25 (1892), that "[w]hat is forbidden or required to be done by a State" in the Article II context "is forbidden or required of the legislative power under state constitutions as they exist." In the same vein, we also observed that "[t]he [State's] legislative power is the supreme authority except as limited by the constitution of the State."[1] The legislative power in Florida is subject to judicial review pursuant to Article V of the Florida Constitution, and nothing in Article II of the Federal Constitution frees the state legislature from the constraints in the state constitution that created it. Moreover, the Florida Legislature's own decision to employ a unitary code for all elections indicates that it intended the Florida Supreme Court to play the same role in Presidential elections that it has historically played in resolving electoral disputes. The Florida Supreme Court's exercise of appellate jurisdiction therefore was wholly consistent with, and indeed contemplated by, the grant of authority in Article II.

It hardly needs stating that Congress, pursuant to 3 U.S.C. § 5, did not impose any affirmative duties upon the States that their governmental branches could "violate." Rather, § 5 provides a safe harbor for States to select electors in contested elections "by judicial or other methods" established by laws prior to the election day. Section 5, like Article II, assumes the involvement of the state judiciary in interpreting state election laws and resolving election disputes under those laws. Neither § 5 nor Article II grants federal judges any special authority to substitute their views for those of the state judiciary on matters of state law.

Nor are petitioners correct in asserting that the failure of the Florida Supreme Court to specify in detail the precise manner in which the "intent of the voter," is to be determined rises to the level of a constitutional violation.[2] We found such a violation when individual votes within the same State were weighted unequally, see, *e.g., Reynolds v. Sims,* 377 U.S. 533, 568 (1964), but we have never before called into question the substantive standard by which a State determines that a vote has been legally cast. And there is no reason to think that the guidance provided to the factfinders, specifically the various

---

[1] "Wherever the term 'legislature' is used in the Constitution it is necessary to consider the nature of the particular action in view." It is perfectly clear that the meaning of the words "Manner" and "Legislature" as used in Article II, § 1, parallels the usage in Article I, § 4, rather than the language in Article V. *U.S. Term Limits, Inc. v. Thornton,* 514 U.S. 779, 805 (1995). Article I, § 4, and Article II, § 1, both call upon legislatures to act in a lawmaking capacity whereas Article V simply calls on the legislative body to deliberate upon a binary decision. As a result, petitioners' reliance on *Leser v. Garnett,* 258 U.S. 130 (1922), and *Hawke v. Smith (No. 1),* 253 U.S. 221 (1920), is misplaced.

[2] The Florida statutory standard is consistent with the practice of the majority of States, which apply either an "intent of the voter" standard or an "impossible to determine the elector's choice" standard in ballot recounts. ***

canvassing boards, by the "intent of the voter" standard is any less sufficient—or will lead to results any less uniform—than, for example, the "beyond a reasonable doubt" standard employed everyday by ordinary citizens in courtrooms across this country.

Admittedly, the use of differing substandards for determining voter intent in different counties employing similar voting systems may raise serious concerns. Those concerns are alleviated—if not eliminated—by the fact that a single impartial magistrate will ultimately adjudicate all objections arising from the recount process. Of course, as a general matter, "[t]he interpretation of constitutional principles must not be too literal. We must remember that the machinery of government would not work if it were not allowed a little play in its joints." If it were otherwise, Florida's decision to leave to each county the determination of what balloting system to employ—despite enormous differences in accuracy[4]—might run afoul of equal protection. So, too, might the similar decisions of the vast majority of state legislatures to delegate to local authorities certain decisions with respect to voting systems and ballot design.

Even assuming that aspects of the remedial scheme might ultimately be found to violate the Equal Protection Clause, I could not subscribe to the majority's disposition of the case. As the majority explicitly holds, once a state legislature determines to select electors through a popular vote, the right to have one's vote counted is of constitutional stature. As the majority further acknowledges, Florida law holds that all ballots that reveal the intent of the voter constitute valid votes. Recognizing these principles, the majority nonetheless orders the termination of the contest proceeding before all such votes have been tabulated. Under their own reasoning, the appropriate course of action would be to remand to allow more specific procedures for implementing the legislature's uniform general standard to be established.

In the interest of finality, however, the majority effectively orders the disenfranchisement of an unknown number of voters whose ballots reveal their intent—and are therefore legal votes under state law—but were for some reason rejected by ballot-counting machines. It does so on the basis of the deadlines set forth in Title 3 of the United States Code. But, as I have already noted, those provisions merely provide rules of decision for Congress to follow when selecting among conflicting slates of electors. They do not prohibit a State from counting what the majority concedes to be legal votes until a bona fide winner is determined. ***

Finally, neither in this case, nor in its earlier opinion in *Palm Beach County Canvassing Bd. v. Harris*, 772 So.2d 1220 (2000), did the Florida Supreme Court make any substantive change in Florida electoral law. Its

---

[4] The percentage of nonvotes in this election in counties using a punch-card system was 3.92%; in contrast, the rate of error under the more modern optical-scan systems was only 1.43%. Put in other terms, for every 10,000 votes cast, punch-card systems result in 250 more nonvotes than optical-scan systems. A total of 3,718,305 votes were cast under punch-card systems, and 2,353,811 votes were cast under optical-scan systems.

decisions were rooted in long-established precedent and were consistent with the relevant statutory provisions, taken as a whole. It did what courts do—it decided the case before it in light of the legislature's intent to leave no legally cast vote uncounted. In so doing, it relied on the sufficiency of the general "intent of the voter" standard articulated by the state legislature, coupled with a procedure for ultimate review by an impartial judge, to resolve the concern about disparate evaluations of contested ballots. If we assume—as I do—that the members of that court and the judges who would have carried out its mandate are impartial, its decision does not even raise a colorable federal question.

What must underlie petitioners' entire federal assault on the Florida election procedures is an unstated lack of confidence in the impartiality and capacity of the state judges who would make the critical decisions if the vote count were to proceed. Otherwise, their position is wholly without merit. The endorsement of that position by the majority of this Court can only lend credence to the most cynical appraisal of the work of judges throughout the land. It is confidence in the men and women who administer the judicial system that is the true backbone of the rule of law. Time will one day heal the wound to that confidence that will be inflicted by today's decision. One thing, however, is certain. Although we may never know with complete certainty the identity of the winner of this year's Presidential election, the identity of the loser is perfectly clear. It is the Nation's confidence in the judge as an impartial guardian of the rule of law.

I respectfully dissent.

JUSTICE SOUTER, with whom JUSTICE BREYER joins and with whom JUSTICE STEVENS and JUSTICE GINSBURG join with regard to all but Part C, dissenting.

*** There are three issues: whether the State Supreme Court's interpretation of the statute providing for a contest of the state election results somehow violates 3 U.S.C. § 5; whether that court's construction of the state statutory provisions governing contests impermissibly changes a state law from what the State's legislature has provided, in violation of Article II, § 1, cl. 2, of the National Constitution; and whether the manner of interpreting markings on disputed ballots failing to cause machines to register votes for President (the undervote ballots) violates the equal protection or due process guaranteed by the Fourteenth Amendment. None of these issues is difficult to describe or to resolve.

The 3 U.S.C. § 5 issue is not serious. *** The second matter here goes to the State Supreme Court's interpretation of certain terms in the state statute governing election "contests," ***. What Bush does argue, as I understand the contention, is that the interpretation *** was so unreasonable as to transcend the accepted bounds of statutory interpretation, to the point of being a nonjudicial act and producing new law untethered to the legislative act in question. *** None of the state court's interpretations is unreasonable to the point of displacing the legislative enactment quoted. ***

It is only on the third issue before us that there is a meritorious argument for relief ***. It is an issue that might well have been dealt with adequately by the Florida courts if the state proceedings had not been interrupted, and if not disposed of at the state level it could have been considered by the Congress in any electoral vote dispute. But because the course of state proceedings has been interrupted, time is short, and the issue is before us, I think it sensible for the Court to address it.

Petitioners have raised an equal protection claim (or, alternatively, a due process claim), in the charge that unjustifiably disparate standards are applied in different electoral jurisdictions to otherwise identical facts. It is true that the Equal Protection Clause does not forbid the use of a variety of voting mechanisms within a jurisdiction, even though different mechanisms will have different levels of effectiveness in recording voters' intentions; local variety can be justified by concerns about cost, the potential value of innovation, and so on. But evidence in the record here suggests that a different order of disparity obtains under rules for determining a voter's intent that have been applied (and could continue to be applied) to identical types of ballots used in identical brands of machines and exhibiting identical physical characteristics (such as "hanging" or "dimpled" chads). *** I can conceive of no legitimate state interest served by these differing treatments of the expressions of voters' fundamental rights. The differences appear wholly arbitrary.

In deciding what to do about this, *** I would *** remand the case to the courts of Florida with instructions to establish uniform standards ***. I see no warrant for this Court to assume that Florida could not possibly comply with this requirement before the date set for the meeting of electors, December 18. *** There is no justification for denying the State the opportunity to try to count all disputed ballots now. ***

IX-4. By permission of Mike Luckovich and Creators Syndicate, Inc.

JUSTICE GINSBERG, with whom JUSTICE STEVENS joins and with whom JUSTICE SOUTER and JUSTICE BREYER join as to Part I, dissenting. [omitted]

JUSTICE BREYER, with whom JUSTICE STEVENS and JUSTICE GINSBERG join *** and with whom JUSTICE SOUTER joins as to Part I, dissenting. [omitted]

Notes

1.   **Rational Basis or Strict Scrutiny?** What is the Court's level of scrutiny for equal treatment of the votes to be recounted in *Bush v. Gore*? If it is "strict" or "middle-tier" scrutiny, is the theory that there was discriminatory treatment of a protected class? Or elevated scrutiny based on a fundamental interest? The per curiam opinion avoids these matter-or-fact equal protection fundamentals. Here are some issues such considerations might have raised:

- If rational basis is the standard, isn't it rational for the Florida Supreme Court to respond to Gore's strategy of seeking to recount votes only in heavily Democratic counties by ordering a statewide recount? Wasn't it rational for the court to rely on a broad general standard ("intent of the voter") supplemented by a statewide process supervised by a single ultimate decision-maker (Judge Lewis)? Isn't it rational to recount "undervotes" but not "overvotes," when "undervote" ballots are more readily identifiable?

- The strongest case for heightened scrutiny of the statewide recount would be if racial minorities (or majorities) or gender minorities (or majorities) were adversely treated. But nobody argued that was the case. Claims of racial exclusion (disparate treatment at the polls) or disparate impact (minorities disproportionately lived in counties using less accurate voting machinery) were considered and rejected. No case applies heightened scrutiny based on party affiliation (Democrat or Republican).

- It has been many years since the Court has used heightened scrutiny based on a "fundamental interest," such as voting rights. On an "original intent" basis, it is arguable that the Fourteenth Amendment was not intended to apply to voting at all. Since the Supreme Court has rejected that argument, however, it is appropriate to look how far the cases go in providing elevated scrutiny in voting cases. Though prior caselaw did not concern application of strict scrutiny to vote counting (or recounting), such an application is not much of a stretch: if one can win elections either at the polls or through vote counting after the polls, equal protection voting standards might well apply to vote counts and recounts. But the cases relied upon by the Court have facts very different from those of *Bush v. Gore*. Equal protection invalidation of voting restrictions adversely affecting poor citizens (at a time prior to *Rodriguez*) is weak precedent for invalidation of recounts that have no economic bias. Similarly, cases denying political majorities their fair say, when the courts were the only institution that could open up the political process, seem inapposite when other institutions (the Florida Legislature and Congress) could have resolved this election contest.

2.   **The Holding of *Bush v. Gore*.** On September 15, 2003, a Ninth Circuit panel postponed California's recall of Governor Gray Davis because the claim "presents almost precisely the same issue as the Court considered in *Bush*, that is, whether unequal methods of counting votes among counties constitutes a violation of the Equal Protection Clause. *** [U]sing error-prone voting equipment in some counties, but not in others will result in votes being counted differently among the counties." Reversing, and thus allowing the recall to proceed on October 7, as scheduled, an en banc panel held that "the plaintiffs have not established a clear probability of success on the merits of their equal protection claim." *Southwest Voter Registration Education Project v. Shelley*, 344 F.3d 882 (Sept. 15, 2003), rev'd 344 F.3d 914 (Sept. 23, 2003) (en banc). Which court read *Bush* correctly? Why?

3.   **Rationale versus remedy?** What is significant, for equal protection purposes, about the December 12, 2000 cutoff date? For equal protection purposes, is it important that the state legislature wished to avail itself of the "safe harbor" provision of Title 3? Did the per curiam opinion essentially adopt the analysis of the concurring opinion in refusing to remand for another effort by the Florida Supreme Court?

4.   **State Court, State Law, Federal Court, Federal Law.** Are the "Warren Court" era (1954-68) cases cited by the per curiam opinion regarding civil rights infractions in the Jim Crow South relevant in rejecting the Florida Supreme Court's method for counting votes cast for the presidency? What awakened the U.S. Supreme Court's latent "fundamental rights equal protection" jurisprudence to strike down the Florida Supreme Court's statewide standard?

5.   **Standing.** Did Bush have standing to raise an equal protection challenge to the recount process in the several Florida counties? Was it significant that the recount had not yet been completed? What injury-in-fact did Governor Bush experience that would satisfy the standing doctrine set forth in *Friends of the Earth v. Laidlaw*?

6.   **Review Questions and Comments:**

   a. Judicial function. Two hypothetical comments criticizing and supporting the U.S. Supreme Court and the Florida Supreme Court for the manner in which they conducted themselves in the post-election period follow. Consider the extent to which you agree or disagree with each.

   1. "The justices of the US Supreme Court allowed political considerations to dictate how they approached and resolved this case. The Court had already made up its mind to craft an opinion that would halt the recount proceedings in Florida and deliver the Presidency to Governor Bush. The best way to describe the per curiam's equal protection analysis is that it was contrived to justify the outcome. In language at the outset of the opinion, the Court desperately tries to limit the application of the broadest equal protection decision in decades. The refusal to remand the case and accept the final date for purposes of Title 3's 'safe harbor' provision cannot be justified on any grounds. Moreover, the Court resolved the election when that function was left to Congress, not the Court."

   2. "The justices of the U.S. Supreme Court were confronted with a scenario in which the Florida Supreme Court was willing to go to any

lengths necessary to deliver the election to Vice-President Gore. Faced with an openly defiant state supreme court, remanding the case for further consideration would have been futile. Why let the Florida Supreme Court bend the State's pre-existing election law again, with further recounts and additional political chaos? The per curiam opinion is sound and is appropriately limited to the unique set of facts that were before the Court. In any event, the concurring opinion's analysis of Article II requirements forcefully supports the need to end the recount process. The justices did the best they could with unclear constitutional provisions and precedents to prevent the will of the state legislature from being thwarted."

b. Separation of powers. Some constitutional scholars are concerned with the propensity of the Rehnquist Court to resolve what might have been considered political questions under *Baker v. Carr*, 369 U.S. 186. The text of Article II, § 1, cl. 2 specifically delegates to state legislatures the power to select the manner in which a state's slate of electors will be chosen to participate in the Electoral College. If no candidate is successful in garnering a majority of electoral votes, the outcome of the Presidential election is decided by the U.S. House of Representatives. Title 3, on which both the per curiam and concurring opinions place a great deal of emphasis, calls for Congress, not the courts, to be the final arbiter in settling disputes regarding competing slates of electors from a given state. Given the statutory and constitutional provisions delegating authority over various aspects of the presidential election process to Congress and the state legislatures (not the federal courts), did *Bush v. Gore* raise a political question calling for abstention rather than intervention?

c. Federalism. What is the appropriate scope of state judicial review of determinations made by the state legislature as to the manner in which electors will be appointed? CHIEF JUSTICE REHNQUIST's concurring opinion indicates that a large deviation from the electoral scheme enacted by the state legislature raises a federal question, which then allows the federal judiciary to take on an independent review of State law. In other words, the federal judiciary can intervene in a presidential election to preserve the appropriate balance of Article II power enjoyed by the state legislature and the state judiciary, ensuring that proper deference is paid to determinations made by the state legislature. The thrust of JUSTICE STEVENS' dissenting opinion is that Article II of the U.S. Constitution does not create state legislatures, "it takes them as they come," subject to state constitutional constraints even in the exercise of powers conferred by Article II. Gore's attorneys argued that the Florida State Constitution was the product of the state legislature. Does Title 3 impose any affirmative duties upon the States to appoint electors and take part in the Electoral College? If not, why do both the per curiam and concurring opinions place so much emphasis on this statute? Indeed, why do these opinions focus only on section five of the statute, when section fifteen (3 U.S.C. §15) specifically calls for Congress to resolve disputes that stem from competing slates of electors or other disputes relating to the process of appointing presidential electors?

E. RATIONAL BASIS AND HYBRID REVIEW

Legislative and administrative bodies classify people and things all the time. The Internal Revenue Code, for example, draws innumerable distinctions that govern how much tax a person or a corporation owes. Moreover, these often seemingly arbitrary distinctions change from year to year. If the Supreme Court applied strict scrutiny or even middle-tier scrutiny to such distinctions, it would be very busy indeed. In fact, most distinctions drawn by governmental bodies and officials are examined not at all or only cursorily. The cases in this section purport to examine a variety of governmental distinctions under this less searching "rational basis" standard. What makes the cases interesting is that the Court seems to bend this permissive standard sometimes. When and how it does so merit careful study.

First, however, a brief overview of traditional rational basis equal protection analysis is appropriate. The verbal formulations the Court has used for rational basis or low-level equal protection review have varied from case to case. Some examples are: (1) "the classification must be reasonable, not arbitrary, and must rest upon some ground of difference having a fair and substantial relation to the object of the legislation"; (2) "rationally related to a legitimate state interest"; and (3) "the classification [must not rest] on grounds wholly irrelevant to the achievement of the State's objective". While these standards sound progressively more tolerant of state conduct bordering on the irrational, if not totally irrational, "general propositions do not decide concrete cases," as JUSTICE HOLMES observed aphoristically in his *Lochner* dissent. Philosophical theories of equality, while fascinating intellectually, do not do so either.

So we turn to concrete cases. In addition to *Carolene Products*, discussed supra at p. 663, one frequently cited example of traditional rational basis review is *Railway Express Agency, Inc. v. New York*, 336 U.S. 106 (1949), which upheld an ordinance prohibiting advertising on sides of rented vehicles while permitting advertising of owner's products on side of vehicles. The Court said: "[T]he hireling may be put in a class by himself and may be dealt with differently than those who act on their own. *** [I]t is one thing to tolerate action from those who act on their own and it is another thing to permit the same action to be promoted for a price."

Another well-known example of cursory review is *Williamson v. Lee Optical of Okla., Inc.*, 348 U.S. 483 (1955), which upheld a statute making it unlawful for anyone not a licensed optometrist or opthalmologist to fit lenses or duplicate or replace lenses without a prescription from an opthalmologist or optometrist. Opticians, as a practical matter, were precluded by the state from engaging in such tasks. To add insult to injury, the statute exempted sellers of ready-to-wear glasses. The Court assumed that health factors justified the law favoring optometrists over opticians, even though the law was blatant interest-group legislation. JUSTICE DOUGLAS, zealous champion of individual rights in other areas, opined:

"The problem of legislative classification is a perennial one, admitting of no doctrinaire definition. Evils in the same field may be of different dimensions and proportions, requiring different remedies. Or so the legislature may think. Or the reform may take one step at a time ***. We cannot say that the point has been reached here. For all this record shows, the ready-to-wear branch of this business may not loom large in Oklahoma or may present problems or regulation distinct from the other branch."

Recently, in *Fitzgerald v. Racing Ass'n of Central Iowa*, 123 S.Ct. 2156 (2003), the Court unanimously upheld imposition of a 36% tax on slot machines at racetracks and a 20% tax on slot machines on riverboats on the ground that it might be supported by a "plausible policy reason."

Now that you have a flavor of traditional rational basis review, in which total discretion to certain legislative classifications is given, you are ready to move on to the more interesting cases.

NEW YORK CITY TRANSIT AUTHORITY v. BEAZER
440 U.S. 568, 99 S.Ct. 1355, 59 L.Ed.2d 587 (1979).

MR. JUSTICE STEVENS delivered the opinion of the Court.

The New York City Transit Authority refuses to employ persons who use methadone. The District Court found that this policy violates the Equal Protection Clause of the Fourteenth Amendment. *** The Court of Appeals affirmed ***. The departure by those courts from the procedure normally followed in addressing statutory and constitutional questions in the same case, as well as concern that the merits of these important questions had been decided erroneously, led us to grant certiorari. We now reverse.

The Transit Authority (TA) operates the subway system and certain bus lines in New York City. It employs about 47,000 persons, of whom many—perhaps most—are employed in positions that involve danger to themselves or to the public. *** TA enforces a general policy against employing persons who use narcotic drugs. The policy is reflected in *** TA's Rules and Regulations. *** [Methadone is considered by TA to be a narcotic, and though the Rules allow for an exception by the medical director of TA, no] written permission has ever been given by TA's medical director for the employment of a person using methadone. *** Methadone has been used legitimately in at least three ways—as a pain killer, in "detoxification units" of hospitals as an immediate means of taking addicts off of heroin, and in long-range "methadone maintenance programs" as part of an intended cure for heroin addiction. In such programs the methadone is taken orally in regular doses for a prolonged period. As so administered, it does not produce euphoria or any pleasurable effects associated with heroin; on the contrary, it prevents users from experiencing those effects when they inject heroin, and also alleviates the severe and prolonged discomfort otherwise associated with an addict's discontinuance of the use of heroin.

About 40,000 persons receive methadone maintenance treatment in New York City, of whom about 26,000 participate in the five major public or semipublic programs, and 14,000 are involved in about 25 private programs. The sole purpose of all these programs is to treat the addiction of persons who have been using heroin for at least two years.

The evidence indicates that methadone is an effective cure for the physical aspects of heroin addiction. But the District Court also found "that many persons attempting to overcome heroin addiction have psychological or life-style problems which reach beyond what can be cured by the physical taking of doses of methadone." *** [Further,] evidence relied upon by the District Court reveals that even among participants with more than 12 months' tenure in methadone maintenance programs, the incidence of drug and alcohol abuse may often approach and even exceed 25%. ***

This litigation was brought by the four respondents as a class action on behalf of all persons who have been, or would in the future be, subject to discharge or rejection as employees of TA by reason of participation in a methadone maintenance program. ***

The trial record contains extensive evidence concerning the success of methadone maintenance programs, the employability of persons taking methadone, and the ability of prospective employers to detect drug abuse or other undesirable characteristics of methadone users. In general, the District Court concluded that there are substantial numbers of methadone users who are just as employable as other members of the general population and that normal personnel-screening procedures—at least if augmented by some method of obtaining information from the staffs of methadone programs— would enable TA to identify the unqualified applicants on an individual basis. On the other hand, the District Court recognized that at least one-third of the persons receiving methadone treatment—and probably a good many more— would unquestionably be classified as unemployable.

After extensively reviewing the evidence, the District Court briefly stated its conclusion that TA's methadone policy is unconstitutional. The conclusion rested on the legal proposition that a public entity "cannot bar persons from employment on the basis of criteria which have no rational relation to the demands of the jobs to be performed." Because it is clear that substantial numbers of methadone users are capable of performing many of the jobs at TA, the court held that the Constitution will not tolerate a blanket exclusion of all users from all jobs.

The District Court enjoined TA from denying employment to any person solely because of participation in a methadone maintenance program. Recognizing, however, the special responsibility for public safety borne by certain TA employees and the correlation between longevity in a methadone maintenance program and performance capability, the injunction authorized TA to exclude methadone users from specific categories of safety-sensitive positions and also to condition eligibility on satisfactory performance in a methadone program for at least a year. In other words, the court held that TA could lawfully adopt general rules excluding all methadone users from some jobs and a large number of methadone users from all jobs. ***

At its simplest, the District Court's conclusion was that TA's rule is broader than necessary to exclude those methadone users who are not actually qualified to work for TA. We may assume not only that this conclusion is correct but also that it is probably unwise for a large employer like TA to rely on a general rule instead of individualized consideration of every job applicant. But these assumptions concern matters of personnel policy that do not implicate the principle safeguarded by the Equal Protection Clause. As the District Court recognized, the special classification created by TA's rule serves the general objectives of safety and efficiency. Moreover, the exclusionary line challenged by respondents "is not one which is directed 'against' any individual or category of persons, but rather it represents a policy choice *** made by that branch of Government vested with the power to make such choices." *Marshall v. United States*, 414 U.S. 417, 428. Because it does not circumscribe a class of persons characterized by some unpopular trait or affiliation, it does not create or reflect any special likelihood of bias on the part of the ruling majority. Under these circumstances, it is of no constitutional significance that the degree of rationality is not as great with respect to certain ill-defined subparts of the classification as it is with respect to the classification as a whole. ***

MR. JUSTICE POWELL, concurring in part and dissenting in part. [omitted]

MR. JUSTICE BRENNAN, dissenting.

I would affirm for the reasons stated in Part I of MR. JUSTICE WHITE's dissenting opinion.

MR. JUSTICE WHITE, with whom MR. JUSTICE MARSHALL joins, dissenting.

*** The question before us is the rationality of placing successfully maintained or recently cured persons in the same category as those just attempting to escape heroin addiction or who have failed to escape it, rather than in with the general population. The asserted justification for the challenged classification is the objective of a capable and reliable work force, and thus the characteristic in question is employability. "Employability," in this regard, does not mean that any particular applicant, much less every member of a given group of applicants, will turn out to be a model worker. Nor does it mean that no such applicant will ever become or be discovered to be a malingerer, thief, alcoholic, or even heroin addict. All employers take such risks. Employability, as the District Court used it in reference to successfully maintained methadone users, means only that the employer is no more likely to find a member of that group to be an unsatisfactory employee than he would an employee chosen from the general population.

Petitioners had every opportunity, but presented nothing to negative the employability of successfully maintained methadone users as distinguished from those who were unsuccessful. *** That 20% to 30% are unsuccessful after one year in a methadone program tells us nothing about the employability of the successful group, and it is the latter category of applicants that the District Court and the Court of Appeals held to be unconstitutionally burdened by the blanket rule disqualifying them from employment. *** Of course, the District Court's order permitting total exclusion of all methadone users maintained for less than one year, whether successfully or not, would still exclude some employables and would to this extent be overinclusive. "Overinclusiveness" as to the primary objective of employability is accepted for less successful methadone users because it fulfills a secondary purpose and thus is not "overinclusive" at all. Although many of those who have not been successfully maintained for a year are employable, as a class they, unlike the protected group, are not as employable as the general population. Thus, even assuming the bad risks could be identified, serving the end of employability would require unusual efforts to determine those more likely to revert. But that legitimate secondary goal is not fulfilled by excluding the protected class: The District Court found that the fact of successful participation for one year could be discovered through petitioners' normal screening process without additional effort and, I repeat, that those who meet that criterion are no more likely than the average applicant to turn out to be poor employees. Accordingly, the rule's classification of successfully maintained persons as dispositively different from the general population is left without any justification and, with its irrationality and invidiousness thus uncovered, must fall before the Equal Protection Clause. ***

Finally, even were the District Court wrong, and even were successfully maintained persons marginally less employable than the average applicant, the blanket exclusion of only these people, when but a few are actually unemployable and when many other groups have varying numbers of unemployable members, is arbitrary and unconstitutional. Many persons now suffer from or may again suffer from some handicap related to employability. But petitioners have singled out respondents—unlike ex-offenders, former alcoholics and mental patients, diabetics, epileptics, and those currently using tranquilizers, for example—for sacrifice to this at best ethereal and likely nonexistent risk of increased unemployability. Such an arbitrary assignment of burdens among classes that are similarly situated with respect to the proffered objectives is the type of invidious choice forbidden by the Equal Protection Clause.

Notes

1. **Rational Basis and Employment.** *Beazer* is pretty much a traditional rational basis equal protection case. But aren't drug users a "discrete and insular minority," to use the *Carolene Products* language? The Court assumes that the City's rule that it will not hire people who use methadone is "broader than necessary" and perhaps even "unwise" compared with "individualized consideration of every job applicant." Still, the Court says this is a permissible "policy choice" by the city which "does not circumscribe a class of persons characterized by some unpopular trait or affiliation." The Court dismisses the dissenters' concerns that methadone-maintained cured drug addicts are inappropriately lumped with those who are recovering or who have failed treatment as "of no constitutional significance." Do you agree?

2. **Prima Facie Case and Defenses.** Is *Beazer* explicable on the ground that the plaintiffs' evidence simply was too weak to make out a prima facie case? That the City's responses to this evidence were so straightforward as to be intuitively obvious?

3. **Contextual Factors.** What if the City were strongly supportive of methadone treatment programs for drug addiction and very conscious of the cost of welfare payments to drug addicts? What if New York required those in publicly funded methodone maintenance programs to seek jobs? Would New York be viewed as irrational for sending contradictory messages to recovering addicts in different programs? Does the nature of the jobs at issue make a difference?

CITY OF CLEBURNE, TEXAS v. CLEBURNE LIVING CENTER
473 U.S. 432, 105 S.Ct. 3249, 87 L.Ed.2d 313 (1985).

JUSTICE WHITE delivered the opinion of the Court.

A Texas city denied a special use permit for the operation of a group home for the mentally retarded, acting pursuant to a municipal zoning ordinance requiring permits for such homes. The Court of Appeals for the Fifth Circuit held that mental retardation is a "quasi-suspect" classification and that the ordinance violated the Equal Protection Clause because it did not substantially further an important governmental purpose. We hold that a lesser standard of scrutiny is appropriate, but conclude that under that standard the ordinance is invalid as applied in this case.

I

In July 1980, respondent Jan Hannah purchased a building *** in the city of Cleburne, Texas, with the intention of leasing it to Cleburne Living Center, Inc. (CLC), for the operation of a group home for the mentally retarded. It was anticipated that the home would house 13 retarded men and women *** under the constant supervision of CLC staff members. ***

The city informed CLC that a special use permit would be required for the operation of a group home at the site, and CLC accordingly submitted a permit application. In response to a subsequent inquiry from CLC, the city explained that under the zoning regulations applicable to the site, a special use permit, renewable annually, was required for the construction of "[h]ospitals for the insane or feeble-minded, or alcoholic [*sic*] or drug addicts, or penal or correctional institutions." The city had determined that the proposed group home should be classified as a "hospital for the feebleminded." After holding a public hearing on CLC's application, the City Council voted 3 to 1 to deny a special use permit.

CLC then filed suit in Federal District Court against the city and a number of its officials, alleging, *inter alia*, that the zoning ordinance was invalid on its face and as applied because it discriminated against the mentally retarded in violation of the equal protection rights of CLC and its potential residents. The District Court found that *** the City Counsel's decision "was motivated primarily by the fact that the residents of the home would be persons who are mentally retarded." Even so, the District Court held the ordinance and its application constitutional. Concluding that no fundamental right was implicated and that mental retardation was neither a suspect nor a quasi-suspect classification, the court employed the minimum level of judicial scrutiny applicable to equal protection claims. ***

The Court of Appeals for the Fifth Circuit reversed, determining that mental retardation was a quasi-suspect classification and that it should assess the validity of the ordinance under intermediate-level scrutiny. ***

II

The Equal Protection Clause of the Fourteenth Amendment commands that no State shall "deny to any person within its jurisdiction the equal protection of the laws," which is essentially a direction that all persons similarly situated should be treated alike. *Plyler v. Doe*, 457 U.S. 202, 216 (1982). *** The general rule is that legislation is presumed to be valid and will be sustained if the classification drawn by the statute is rationally related to a legitimate state interest. *** When social or economic legislation is at issue, the Equal Protection Clause allows the States wide latitude, *United States Railroad Retirement Board v. Fritz*, 449 U.S., at 174, and the Constitution presumes that even improvident decisions will eventually be rectified by the democratic processes.

The general rule gives way, however, when a statute classifies by race, alienage, or national origin. These factors are so seldom relevant to the achievement of any legitimate state interest that laws grounded in such considerations are deemed to reflect prejudice and antipathy—a view that those in the burdened class are not as worthy or deserving as others. For these reasons and because such discrimination is unlikely to be soon rectified by legislative means, these laws are subjected to strict scrutiny and will be sustained only if they are suitably tailored to serve a compelling state interest. *McLaughlin v. Florida*, 379 U.S. 184, 192 (1964). Similar oversight by the courts is due when state laws impinge on personal rights protected by the Constitution. ***

We have declined, however, to extend heightened review to differential treatment based on age: "While the treatment of the aged in this Nation has not been wholly free of discrimination, such persons, unlike, say, those who have been discriminated against on the basis of race or national origin, have not experienced a 'history of purposeful unequal treatment' or been subjected to unique disabilities on the basis of stereotyped characteristics not truly indicative of their abilities." *Massachusetts Board of Retirement v. Murgia*, 427 U.S. 307, 313 (1976).

The lesson of *Murgia* is that where individuals in the group affected by a law have distinguishing characteristics relevant to interests the State has the authority to implement, the courts have been very reluctant, as they should be in our federal system and with our respect for the separation of powers, to closely scrutinize legislative choices as to whether, how, and to what extent those interests should be pursued. In such cases, the Equal Protection Clause requires only a rational means to serve a legitimate end.

III

Against this background, we conclude for several reasons that the Court of Appeals erred in holding mental retardation a quasi-suspect classification calling for a more exacting standard of judicial review than is normally accorded economic and social legislation. First, it is undeniable, and it is not argued otherwise here, that those who are mentally retarded have a reduced ability to cope with and function in the everyday world. Nor are they all cut from the same pattern: as the testimony in this record indicates, they range from those whose disability is not immediately evident to those who must be constantly cared for. They are thus different, immutably so, in relevant respects, and the States' interest in dealing with and providing for them is plainly a legitimate one. How this large and diversified group is to be treated under the law is a difficult and often a technical matter, very much a task for legislators guided by qualified professionals and not by the perhaps ill-informed opinions of the judiciary. ***

Second, the distinctive legislative response, both national and state, to the plight of those who are mentally retarded demonstrates not only that they have unique problems, but also that the lawmakers have been addressing their difficulties in a manner that belies a continuing antipathy or prejudice and a corresponding need for more intrusive oversight by the judiciary. *** Such legislation thus singling out the retarded for special treatment reflects the real and undeniable differences between the retarded and others. That a civilized and decent society expects and approves such legislation indicates that governmental consideration of those differences in the vast majority of situations is not only legitimate but also desirable. It may be, as CLC contends, that legislation designed to benefit, rather than disadvantage, the retarded would generally withstand examination under a test of heightened scrutiny. The relevant inquiry, however, is whether heightened scrutiny is constitutionally mandated in the first instance. ***

Third, the legislative response, which could hardly have occurred and survived without public support, negates any claim that the mentally retarded are politically powerless in the sense that they have no ability to attract the attention of the lawmakers. Any minority can be said to be powerless to assert direct control over the legislature, but if that were a criterion for higher level scrutiny by the courts, much economic and social legislation would now be suspect.

Fourth, if the large and amorphous class of the mentally retarded were deemed quasi-suspect for the reasons given by the Court of Appeals, it would be difficult to find a principled way to distinguish a variety of other groups who have perhaps immutable disabilities setting them off from others, who cannot themselves mandate the desired legislative responses, and who can claim some degree of prejudice from at least part of the public at large. One need mention in this respect only the aging, the disabled, the mentally ill, and the infirm. *** Our refusal to recognize the retarded as a quasi-suspect class does not leave them entirely unprotected from invidious discrimination. To withstand equal protection review, legislation that distinguishes between the mentally retarded and others must be rationally related to a legitimate governmental purpose. This standard, we believe, affords government the latitude necessary both to pursue policies designed to assist the retarded in realizing their full potential, and to freely and efficiently engage in activities that burden the retarded in what is essentially an incidental manner. ***

IV

*** It is true, as already pointed out, that the mentally retarded as a group are indeed different from others not sharing their misfortune, and in this respect they may be different from those who would occupy other facilities that would be permitted. *** But this difference is largely irrelevant unless the *** home and those who would occupy it would threaten legitimate interests of the city in a way that other permitted uses such as boarding houses and hospitals would not. ***

The District Court found that the City Council's insistence on the permit rested on several factors. *** [T]he Council was concerned with the negative attitude of the majority of property owners located within 200 feet of the *** facility, as well as with the fears of elderly residents of the neighborhood. But mere negative attitudes, or fear, unsubstantiated by factors which are properly cognizable in a zoning proceeding, are not permissible bases for treating a home for the mentally retarded differently from apartment houses, multiple dwellings, and the like. It is plain that the electorate as a whole *** could not order city action violative of the Equal Protection Clause, and the City may not avoid the strictures of that Clause by deferring to the wishes or objections of some fraction of the body politic. "Private biases may be outside the reach of the law, but the law cannot, directly or indirectly, give them effect." *Palmore v. Sidoti*, 466 U.S. 429, 433 (1984).

*** [T]he Council had two objections to the location of the facility. It was concerned that the facility was across the street from a junior high school, and it feared that the students might harass the occupants of the *** home. But the school itself is attended by about 30 mentally retarded students, and denying a permit based on such vague, undifferentiated fears is again permitting some portion of the community to validate what would otherwise be an equal protection violation. The other objection to the home's location was that it was located on "a five hundred year flood plain." This concern with the possibility of a flood, however, can hardly be based on a distinction between the *** home and, for example, nursing homes, homes for convalescents or the aged, or sanitariums or hospitals, any of which could be located on the *** site without obtaining a special use permit. The same may be said of another concern of the Council—doubts about the legal responsibility for actions which the mentally retarded might take. If there is no concern about legal responsibility with respect to other uses that would be permitted in the area, such as boarding and fraternity houses, it is difficult to believe that the groups of mildly or moderately mentally retarded individuals who would live at [the home] would present any different or special hazard. *** [The] Council was concerned with the size of the home and the number of people that would occupy it. *** [However,] there would be no restrictions on the number of people who could occupy this home as a boarding house, nursing home, family dwelling, fraternity house, or dormitory. *** The short of it is that requiring the permit in this case appears to us to rest on an irrational prejudice against the mentally retarded, including those who would occupy the *** facility and who would live under the closely supervised and highly regulated conditions expressly provided for by state and federal law. ***

JUSTICE STEVENS, with whom *** CHIEF JUSTICE [BURGER] joins, concurring.

*** [Our] cases reflect a continuum of judgmental responses to differing classifications which have been explained in opinions by terms ranging from "strict scrutiny" at one extreme to "rational basis" at the other. I have never been persuaded that these so-called "standards" adequately explain the decisional process. Cases involving classifications based on alienage, illegal residency, illegitimacy, gender, age, or—as in this case—mental retardation, do not fit well into sharply defined classifications. *** In my own approach to these cases, I have always asked myself whether I could find a "rational basis" for the classification at issue. The term "rational," of course, includes a requirement that an impartial lawmaker could logically believe that the classification would serve a legitimate public purpose that transcends the harm to the members of the disadvantaged class. Thus, the word "rational"—for me at least—includes elements of legitimacy and neutrality that must always characterize the performance of the sovereign's duty to govern impartially.

The rational-basis test, properly understood, adequately explains why a law that deprives a person of the right to vote because his skin has a different pigmentation than that of other voters violates the Equal Protection Clause. It would be utterly irrational to limit the franchise on the basis of height or weight; it is equally invalid to limit it on the basis of skin color. None of these attributes has any bearing at all on the citizen's willingness or ability to exercise that civil right. We do not need to apply a special standard, or to apply "strict scrutiny," or even "heightened scrutiny," to decide such cases.

In every equal protection case, we have to ask certain basic questions. What class is harmed by the legislation, and has it been subjected to a "tradition of disfavor" by our laws? What is the public purpose that is being served by the law? What is the characteristic of the disadvantaged class that justifies the disparate treatment? In most cases the answer to these questions will tell us whether the statute has a "rational basis." *** [The] Court of Appeals correctly observed that through ignorance and prejudice the mentally retarded "have been subjected to a history of unfair and often grotesque mistreatment." The discrimination against the mentally retarded that is at issue in this case is the city's decision to require an annual special use permit before property in an apartment house district may be used as a group home for persons who are mildly retarded. The record convinces me that this permit was required because of the irrational fears of neighboring property owners, rather than for the protection of the mentally retarded persons who would reside in respondent's home. ***

JUSTICE MARSHALL, with whom JUSTICE BRENNAN and JUSTICE BLACKMUN join, concurring in the judgment in part and dissenting in part.

The Court holds that all retarded individuals cannot be grouped together as the "feebleminded" and deemed presumptively unfit to live in a community. Underlying this holding is the principle that mental retardation *per se* cannot be a proxy for depriving retarded people of their rights and interests without regard to variations in individual ability. With this holding and principle I agree. The Equal Protection Clause requires attention to the capacities and needs of retarded people as individuals.

I cannot agree, however, with the way in which the Court reaches its result or with the narrow, as-applied remedy it provides for the city of Cleburne's equal protection violation. The Court holds the ordinance invalid on rational-basis grounds and disclaims that anything special, in the form of heightened scrutiny, is taking place. Yet Cleburne's ordinance surely would be valid under the traditional rational-basis test applicable to economic and commercial regulation. *** [T]he Court's heightened-scrutiny discussion is even more puzzling given that Cleburne's ordinance is invalidated only after being subjected to precisely the sort of probing inquiry associated with heightened scrutiny. To be sure, the Court does not label its handiwork heightened scrutiny, and perhaps the method employed must hereafter be called "second order" rational-basis review rather than "heightened scrutiny." But however labeled, the rational basis test invoked today is most assuredly not the rational-basis test of *Williamson v. Lee Optical of Oklahoma, Inc.*, 348 U.S. 483 (1955), and [its] progeny.

The Court, for example, concludes that legitimate concerns for fire hazards or the serenity of the neighborhood do not justify singling out respondents to bear the burdens of these concerns, for analogous permitted uses appear to pose similar threats. Yet under the traditional and most minimal version of the rational-basis test, "reform may take one step at a time, addressing itself to the phase of the problem which seems most acute to the legislative mind." *Williamson v. Lee Optical of Oklahoma, Inc.*, supra, 348 U.S., at 489. The "record" is said not to support the ordinance's classifications, but under the traditional standard we do not sift through the record to determine whether policy decisions are squarely supported by a firm factual foundation. Finally, the Court further finds it "difficult to believe" that the retarded present different or special hazards inapplicable to other groups. In normal circumstances, the burden is not on the legislature to convince the Court that the lines it has drawn are sensible; legislation is presumptively constitutional, and a State "is not required to resort to close distinctions or to maintain a precise, scientific uniformity with reference" to its goals.

I share the Court's criticisms of the overly broad lines that Cleburne's zoning ordinance has drawn. But if the ordinance is to be invalidated for its imprecise classifications, it must be pursuant to more powerful scrutiny than the minimal rational-basis test used to review classifications affecting only economic and commercial matters. The same imprecision in a similar ordinance that required opticians but not optometrists to be licensed to practice, or that excluded new but not old businesses from parts of a community, would hardly be fatal to the statutory scheme.

*** [T]he mentally retarded have been subject to a "lengthy and tragic history" of segregation and discrimination that can only be called grotesque. *** By the latter part of the [19th] century and during the first decades of the new one, however, social views of the retarded underwent a radical transformation. Fueled by the rising tide of Social Darwinism *** and the extreme xenophobia of those years, leading medical authorities and others began to portray the "feeble-minded" as a "menace to society and civilization *** responsible in a large degree for many, if not all, of our social problems." A regime of state-mandated segregation and degradation soon emerged that in its virulence and bigotry rivaled, and indeed paralleled, the worst excesses of Jim Crow. *** Prejudice, once let loose, is not easily cabined. *** As of 1979, most States still categorically disqualified "idiots" from voting, without regard to individual capacity and with discretion to exclude left in the hands of low-level election officials. Not until Congress enacted the Education of the Handicapped Act were "the door[s] of public education" opened wide to handicapped children. But most important, lengthy and continuing isolation of the retarded has perpetuated the ignorance, irrational fears, and stereotyping that long have plagued them.

In light of the importance of the interest at stake and the history of discrimination the retarded have suffered, the Equal Protection Clause requires us to do more than review the distinctions drawn by Cleburne's zoning ordinance as if they appeared in a taxing statute or in economic or commercial legislation. The searching scrutiny I would give to restrictions on the ability of the retarded to establish community group homes leads me to conclude that Cleburne's vague generalizations for classifying the "feeble-minded" with drug addicts, alcoholics, and the insane, and excluding them where the elderly, the ill, the boarder, and the transient are allowed, are not substantial or important enough to overcome the suspicion that the ordinance rests on impermissible assumptions or outmoded and perhaps invidious stereotypes.

*** With respect to a liberty so valued as the right to establish a home in the community, and so likely to be denied on the basis of irrational fears and outright hostility, heightened scrutiny is surely appropriate.

In light of the scrutiny that should be applied here, Cleburne's ordinance sweeps too broadly to dispel the suspicion that it rests on a bare desire to treat the retarded as outsiders, pariahs who do not belong in the community. *** I must dissent from the novel proposition that "the preferred course of adjudication" is to leave standing a legislative Act resting on "irrational prejudice", thereby forcing individuals in the group discriminated against to continue to run the Act's gauntlet. *** In my view, the Court's remedial approach is both unprecedented in the equal protection area and unwise. *** [I]n focusing obsessively on the appropriate label to give its standard of review, the Court fails to identify the interests at stake or to articulate the principle that classifications based on mental retardation must be carefully examined to assure they do not rest on impermissible assumptions or false stereotypes regarding individual ability and need. *** I would *** strike down on its face the provision at issue. I therefore concur in the judgment in part and dissent in part.

Notes

1. *Cleburne* **and Equal Protection Theory.** Why does the Court find it necessary or appropriate to discuss "the plight of the mentally retarded"? Remember that in *Rodriguez*, the Court had refused to premise its analysis on "the plight of the poor," and that *Murgia* (discussed in *Rodriguez*) refused to elevate the level of scrutiny because of "the plight of the aged." Should the Court have cited *Plyler* more forcefully, saying the retarded were a blameless disadvantaged group (like children of immigrants) and that the city's zoning totally deprived them of a housing (like exclusion from schools)?

2. **Irrationality, Prejudice, and Close Scutiny.** Equal protection inquiry focuses on the "who," not the "what," of the city's special use permit denial. Pehaps the city's reasons were based on "vague, undifferentiated fears" masking "irrational prejudice." But ferreting out prejudice requires careful evidentiary assessments more common in strict than rational basis scrutiny. *See Yick Wo v. Hopkins*, supra p. 676. The Court in *Village of Willowbrook v. Olech*, 528 U.S. 1073 (2000), held, per curiam, that one person (a "class of one") may show an equal protection violation from "irrational and wholly arbitrary" official behavior "quite apart from *** subjective motivation." JUSTICE BREYER concurred, but opined that "vindictive action," "illegitimate animus," or "ill will" is needed to avoid "transforming run-of-the-mill zoning cases into cases of constitutional right." Should courts defer equally to elected officals' rule applications and their rule-making?

ROMER v. EVANS
517 U.S. 620, 116 S.Ct. 1620, 134 L.Ed.2d 855 (1996).

JUSTICE KENNEDY delivered the opinion of the Court.

*** The Equal Protection Clause enforces this principle and today requires us to hold invalid a provision of Colorado's Constitution.

I

The enactment challenged in this case is an amendment to the Constitution of the State of Colorado, adopted in a 1992 statewide referendum ["Amendment 2"]. *** The impetus for the amendment and the contentious campaign that preceded its adoption came in large part from ordinances that had been passed in various Colorado municipalities [prohibiting discrimination]. *** Amendment 2 repeals these ordinances to the extent they prohibit discrimination on the basis of "homosexual, lesbian or bisexual orientation, conduct, practices or relationships." Yet Amendment 2, in explicit terms, does more than repeal or rescind these provisions. It prohibits all legislative, executive or judicial action at any level of state or local government designed to protect the named class, a class we shall refer to as homosexual persons or gays and lesbians. ***

Soon after Amendment 2 was adopted, this litigation to declare its invalidity and enjoin its enforcement was commenced in the District Court for the City and County of Denver. Among the plaintiffs (respondents here) were homosexual persons, some of them government employees. They alleged that enforcement of Amendment 2 would subject them to immediate and substantial risk of discrimination on the basis of their sexual orientation. Other plaintiffs (also respondents here) included the three municipalities whose ordinances we have cited and certain other governmental entities which had acted earlier to protect homosexuals from discrimination but would be prevented by Amendment 2 from continuing to do so. Although Governor Romer had been on record opposing the adoption of Amendment 2, he was named in his official capacity as a defendant, together with the Colorado Attorney General and the State of Colorado. ***

II

The State's principal argument in defense of Amendment 2 is that it puts gays and lesbians in the same position as all other persons. So, the State says, the measure does no more than deny homosexuals special rights. This reading of the amendment's language is implausible. We rely not upon our own interpretation of the amendment but upon the authoritative construction of Colorado's Supreme Court. The state court, deeming it unnecessary to determine the full extent of the amendment's reach, found it invalid even on a modest reading of its implications. The critical discussion of the amendment, *** is as follows: "The immediate objective of Amendment 2 is, at a minimum, to repeal existing statutes, regulations, ordinances, and policies of state and local entities that barred discrimination based on sexual orientation. *** The 'ultimate effect' of Amendment 2 is to prohibit any governmental entity from adopting similar, or more protective statutes, regulations, ordinances, or policies in the future unless the state constitution is first amended to permit such measures."

Sweeping and comprehensive is the change in legal status effected by this law. *** Homosexuals, by state decree, are put in a solitary class with respect to transactions and relations in both the private and governmental spheres. The amendment withdraws from homosexuals, but no others, specific legal protection from the injuries caused by discrimination, and it forbids reinstatement of these laws and policies.

The change that Amendment 2 works in the legal status of gays and lesbians in the private sphere is far-reaching, both on its own terms and when considered in light of the structure and operation of modern anti-discrimination laws. That structure is well illustrated by contemporary statutes and ordinances prohibiting discrimination by providers of public accommodations. *** [It] was settled early that the Fourteenth Amendment did not give Congress a general power to prohibit discrimination in public accommodations, *Civil Rights Cases*, 109 U.S. 3, 25 (1883). In consequence, most States have chosen to counter discrimination by enacting detailed statutory schemes.

Colorado's state and municipal laws typify this emerging tradition of statutory protection and follow a consistent pattern. The laws first enumerate the persons or entities subject to a duty not to discriminate. The list goes well beyond the entities covered by the common law. The Boulder ordinance, for example, has a comprehensive definition of entities deemed places of "public accommodation." They include "any place of business engaged in any sales to the general public and any place that offers services, facilities, privileges, or advantages to the general public or that receives financial support through solicitation of the general public or through governmental subsidy of any kind." The Denver ordinance is of similar breadth, applying, for example, to hotels, restaurants, hospitals, dental clinics, theaters, banks, common carriers, travel and insurance agencies, and "shops and stores dealing with goods or services of any kind."

These statutes and ordinances also depart from the common law by enumerating the groups or persons within their ambit of protection. Enumeration is the essential device used to make the duty not to discriminate concrete and to provide guidance for those who must comply. In following this approach, Colorado's state and local governments have not limited anti-discrimination laws to groups that have so far been given the protection of heightened equal protection scrutiny under our cases. Rather, they set forth an extensive catalogue of traits which cannot be the basis for discrimination, including age, military status, marital status, pregnancy, parenthood, custody of a minor child, political affiliation, physical or mental disability of an individual or of his or her associates——and, in recent times, sexual orientation.

Amendment 2 bars homosexuals from securing protection against the injuries that these public-accommodations laws address. That in itself is a severe consequence, but there is more. Amendment 2, in addition, nullifies specific legal protections for this targeted class in all transactions in housing, sale of real estate, insurance, health and welfare services, private education, and employment.

Not confined to the private sphere, Amendment 2 also operates to repeal and forbid all laws or policies providing specific protection for gays or lesbians from discrimination by every level of Colorado government. The State Supreme Court cited two examples of protections in the governmental sphere that are now rescinded and may not be reintroduced. The first is Colorado Executive Order D0035 (1990), which forbids employment discrimination against "'all state employees, classified and exempt' on the basis of sexual orientation." Also repealed, and now forbidden, are "various provisions prohibiting discrimination based on sexual orientation at state colleges." The repeal of these measures and the prohibition against their future reenactment demonstrates that Amendment 2 has the same force and effect in Colorado's governmental sector as it does elsewhere and that it applies to policies as well as ordinary legislation.

Amendment 2's reach may not be limited to specific laws passed for the benefit of gays and lesbians. It is a fair, if not necessary, inference from the broad language of the amendment that it deprives gays and lesbians even of the protection of general laws and policies that prohibit arbitrary discrimination in governmental and private settings. At some point in the systematic administration of these laws, an official must determine whether homosexuality is an arbitrary and thus forbidden basis for decision. Yet a decision to that effect would itself amount to a policy prohibiting discrimination on the basis of homosexuality, and so would appear to be no more valid under Amendment 2 than the specific prohibitions against discrimination the state court held invalid.

If this consequence follows from Amendment 2, as its broad language suggests, it would compound the constitutional difficulties the law creates. The state court did not decide whether the amendment has this effect, however, and neither need we. In the course of rejecting the argument that Amendment 2 is intended to conserve resources to fight discrimination against suspect classes, the Colorado Supreme Court made the limited observation that the amendment is not intended to affect many anti-discrimination laws protecting non-suspect classes. In our view that does not resolve the issue. In any event, even if, as we doubt, homosexuals could find some safe harbor in laws of general application, we cannot accept the view that Amendment 2's prohibition on specific legal protections does no more than deprive homosexuals of special rights. To the contrary, the amendment imposes a special disability upon those persons alone. Homosexuals are forbidden the safeguards that others enjoy or may seek without constraint. They can obtain specific protection against discrimination only by enlisting the citizenry of Colorado to amend the State Constitution or perhaps, on the State's view, by trying to pass helpful laws of general applicability. This is so no matter how local or discrete the harm, no matter how public and widespread the injury. We find nothing special in the protections Amendment 2 withholds. These are protections taken for granted by most people either because they already have them or do not need them; these are protections against exclusion from an almost limitless number of transactions and endeavors that constitute ordinary civic life in a free society.

III

The Fourteenth Amendment's promise that no person shall be denied the equal protection of the laws must co-exist with the practical necessity that most legislation classifies for one purpose or another, with resulting disadvantage to various groups or persons. We have attempted to reconcile the principle with the reality by stating that, if a law neither burdens a fundamental right nor targets a suspect class, we will uphold the legislative classification so long as it bears a rational relation to some legitimate end.

Amendment 2 fails, indeed defies, even this conventional inquiry. First, the amendment has the peculiar property of imposing a broad and undifferentiated disability on a single named group, an exceptional and, as we shall explain, invalid form of legislation. Second, its sheer breadth is so discontinuous with the reasons offered for it that the amendment seems inexplicable by anything but animus toward the class that it affects; it lacks a rational relationship to legitimate state interests.

Taking the first point, even in the ordinary equal protection case calling for the most deferential of standards, we insist on knowing the relation between the classification adopted and the object to be attained. The search for the link between classification and objective gives substance to the Equal Protection Clause; it provides guidance and discipline for the legislature, which is entitled to know what sorts of laws it can pass; and it marks the limits of our own authority. In the ordinary case, a law will be sustained if it can be said to advance a legitimate government interest, even if the law seems unwise or works to the disadvantage of a particular group, or if the rationale for it seems tenuous. See *New Orleans v. Dukes*, 427 U.S. 297 (1976) (tourism benefits justified classification favoring pushcart vendors of certain longevity); *Williamson v. Lee Optical of Okla., Inc.*, 348 U.S. 483 (1955) (assumed health concerns justified law favoring optometrists over opticians); *Railway Express Agency, Inc. v. New York*, 336 U.S. 106 (1949) (potential traffic hazards justified exemption of vehicles advertising the owner's products from general advertising ban); *Kotch v. Board of River Port Pilot Comm'rs for Port of New Orleans*, 330 U.S. 552 (1947) (licensing scheme that disfavored persons unrelated to current river boat pilots justified by possible efficiency and safety benefits of a closely knit pilotage system). The laws challenged in the cases just cited were narrow enough in scope and grounded in a sufficient factual context for us to ascertain that there existed some relation between the classification and the purpose it served. By requiring that the classification bear a rational relationship to an independent and legitimate legislative end, we ensure that classifications are not drawn for the purpose of disadvantaging the group burdened by the law.

Amendment 2 confounds this normal process of judicial review. It is at once too narrow and too broad. It identifies persons by a single trait and then denies them protection across the board. The resulting disqualification of a class of persons from the right to seek specific protection from the law is unprecedented in our jurisprudence. The absence of precedent for Amendment 2 is itself instructive; "[d]iscriminations of an unusual character especially suggest careful consideration to determine whether they are obnoxious to the constitutional provision." *Louisville Gas & Elec. Co. v. Coleman*, 277 U.S. 32 (1928).

It is not within our constitutional tradition to enact laws of this sort. *** "'Equal protection of the laws is not achieved through indiscriminate imposition of inequalities.'" Respect for this principle explains why laws singling out a certain class of citizens for disfavored legal status or general hardships are rare. A law declaring that in general it shall be more difficult for one group of citizens than for all others to seek aid from the government is itself a denial of equal protection of the laws in the most literal sense. "The guaranty of 'equal protection of the laws is a pledge of the protection of equal laws.'" *Skinner v. Oklahoma*, 316 U.S. 535 (1942) (quoting *Yick Wo v. Hopkins*, 118 U.S. 356 (1886)).

Davis v. Beason, 133 U.S. 333 (1890), not cited by the parties but relied upon by the dissent, is not evidence that Amendment 2 is within our constitutional tradition, and any reliance upon it as authority for sustaining the amendment is misplaced. In *Davis*, the Court approved an Idaho territorial statute denying Mormons, polygamists, and advocates of polygamy the right to vote and to hold office because, as the Court construed the statute, it "simply excludes from the privilege of voting, or of holding any office of honor, trust or profit, those who have been convicted of certain offences, and those who advocate a practical resistance to the laws of the

Territory and justify and approve the commission of crimes forbidden by it." To the extent *Davis* held that persons advocating a certain practice may be denied the right to vote, it is no longer good law. *Brandenburg v. Ohio*, 395 U.S. 444 (1969) (per curiam). To the extent it held that the groups designated in the statute may be deprived of the right to vote because of their status, its ruling could not stand without surviving strict scrutiny, a most doubtful outcome. *Dunn v. Blumstein*, 405 U.S. 330 (1972). To the extent *Davis* held that a convicted felon may be denied the right to vote, its holding is not implicated by our decision and is unexceptionable.

A second and related point is that laws of the kind now before us raise the inevitable inference that the disadvantage imposed is born of animosity toward the class of persons affected. "[I]f the constitutional conception of 'equal protection of the laws' means anything, it must at the very least mean that a bare *** desire to harm a politically unpopular group cannot constitute a *legitimate* governmental interest." Even laws enacted for broad and ambitious purposes often can be explained by reference to legitimate public policies which justify the incidental disadvantages they impose on certain persons. Amendment 2, however, in making a general announcement that gays and lesbians shall not have any particular protections from the law, inflicts on them immediate, continuing, and real injuries that outrun and belie any legitimate justifications that may be claimed for it. We conclude that, in addition to the far-reaching deficiencies of Amendment 2 that we have noted, the principles it offends, in another sense, are conventional and venerable; a law must bear a rational relationship to a legitimate governmental purpose, and Amendment 2 does not.

The primary rationale the State offers for Amendment 2 is respect for other citizens' freedom of association, and in particular the liberties of landlords or employers who have personal or religious objections to homosexuality. Colorado also cites its interest in conserving resources to fight discrimination against other groups. The breadth of the amendment is so far removed from these particular justifications that we find it impossible to credit them. We cannot say that Amendment 2 is directed to any identifiable legitimate purpose or discrete objective. It is a status-based enactment divorced from any factual context from which we could discern a relationship to legitimate state interests; it is a classification of persons undertaken for its own sake, something the Equal Protection Clause does not permit. "[C]lass legislation *** [is] obnoxious to the prohibitions of the Fourteenth Amendment. *** "

We must conclude that Amendment 2 classifies homosexuals not to further a proper legislative end but to make them unequal to everyone else. This Colorado cannot do. A State cannot so deem a class of persons a stranger to its laws. Amendment 2 violates the Equal Protection Clause. ***

JUSTICE SCALIA, with whom THE CHIEF JUSTICE and JUSTICE THOMAS join, dissenting.

The Court has mistaken a Kulturkampf for a fit of spite. The constitutional amendment before us here is not the manifestation of a "'bare

*** desire to harm'" homosexuals, but is rather a modest attempt by seemingly tolerant Coloradans to preserve traditional sexual mores against the efforts of a politically powerful minority to revise those mores through use of the laws. That objective, and the means chosen to achieve it, are not only unimpeachable under any constitutional doctrine hitherto pronounced (hence the opinion's heavy reliance upon principles of righteousness rather than judicial holdings); they have been specifically approved by the Congress of the United States and by this Court.

In holding that homosexuality cannot be singled out for disfavorable treatment, the Court contradicts a decision, unchallenged here, pronounced only 10 years ago, see *Bowers v. Hardwick*, 478 U.S. 186 (1986), and places the prestige of this institution behind the proposition that opposition to homosexuality is as reprehensible as racial or religious bias. *** Since the Constitution of the United States says nothing about this subject, it is left to be resolved by normal democratic means, including the democratic adoption of provisions in state constitutions. ***

I

*** Part II of the Court's opinion *** is devoted to rejecting the State's arguments that Amendment 2 "puts gays and lesbians in the same position as all other persons," and "does no more than deny homosexuals special rights". The Court concludes that this reading of Amendment 2's language is "implausible" under the "authoritative construction" given Amendment 2 by the Supreme Court of Colorado. In reaching this conclusion, the Court considers it unnecessary to decide the validity of the State's argument that Amendment 2 does not deprive homosexuals of the "protection [afforded by] general laws and policies that prohibit arbitrary discrimination in governmental and private settings." I agree that we need not resolve that dispute, because the Supreme Court of Colorado has resolved it for us. *** [T]he Colorado court stated: "[I]t is significant to note that Colorado law currently proscribes discrimination against persons who are not suspect classes, including discrimination based on age, marital or family status, veterans' status, and for any legal, off-duty conduct such as smoking tobacco. *Of course Amendment 2 is not intended to have any effect on this legislation, but seeks only to prevent the adoption of antidiscrimination laws intended to protect gays, lesbians, and bisexuals.*" The Court utterly fails to distinguish this portion of the Colorado court's opinion. [The statute], which this passage authoritatively declares *not* to be affected by Amendment 2, was respondents' primary example of a generally applicable law whose protections would be unavailable to homosexuals under Amendment 2. The clear import of the Colorado court's conclusion that it is not affected is that "general laws and policies that prohibit arbitrary discrimination" would continue to prohibit discrimination on the basis of homosexual conduct as well. This analysis *** lays to rest such horribles, raised in the course of oral argument, as the prospect that assaults upon homosexuals could not be prosecuted. The amendment prohibits *special treatment* of homosexuals, and nothing more. ***

*** The only denial of equal treatment [the Court] contends homosexuals have suffered is this: They may not obtain *preferential* treatment without amending the State Constitution. That is to say, the principle underlying the Court's opinion is that one who is accorded equal treatment under the laws, but cannot as readily as others obtain *preferential* treatment under the laws, has been denied equal protection of the laws. If merely stating this alleged "equal protection" violation does not suffice to refute it, our constitutional jurisprudence has achieved terminal silliness.

The central thesis of the Court's reasoning is that any group is denied equal protection when, to obtain advantage (or, presumably, to avoid disadvantage), it must have recourse to a more general and hence more difficult level of political decisionmaking than others. The world has never heard of such a principle, which is why the Court's opinion is so long on emotive utterance and so short on relevant legal citation. And it seems to me most unlikely that any multilevel democracy can function under such a principle. For *whenever* a disadvantage is imposed, or conferral of a benefit is prohibited, at one of the higher levels of democratic decisionmaking (i.e., by the state legislature rather than local government, or by the people at large in the state constitution rather than the legislature), the affected group has (under this theory) been denied equal protection. To take the simplest of examples, consider a state law prohibiting the award of municipal contracts to relatives of mayors or city councilmen. Once such a law is passed, the group composed of such relatives must, in order to get the benefit of city contracts, persuade the state legislature—unlike all other citizens, who need only persuade the municipality. It is ridiculous to consider this a denial of equal protection, which is why the Court's theory is unheard of.

The Court might reply that the example I have given is *not* a denial of equal protection only because the same "rational basis" (avoidance of corruption) which renders constitutional the *substantive discrimination* against relatives (*i.e.,* the fact that they alone cannot obtain city contracts) also automatically suffices to sustain what might be called the *electoral-procedural discrimination* against them (*i.e.,* the fact that they must go to the state level to get this changed). This is of course a perfectly reasonable response, and would explain why "electoral-procedural discrimination" has not hitherto been heard of: a law that is valid in its substance is automatically valid in its level of enactment. But the Court cannot afford to make this argument, for *** there is no doubt of a rational basis for the substance of the prohibition at issue here. ***

II

I turn next to whether there was a legitimate rational basis for the substance of the constitutional amendment—for the prohibition of special protection for homosexuals.[1] It is unsurprising that the Court avoids

---

[1] The Court evidently agrees that "rational basis"—the normal test for compliance with the Equal Protection Clause—is the governing standard. The trial court rejected respondents' argument that homosexuals constitute a "suspect" or "quasi-suspect" class, and respondents elected not to appeal that ruling to the Supreme Court of Colorado. And the Court implicitly

discussion of this question, since the answer is so obviously yes. The case most relevant to the issue before us today is not even mentioned in the Court's opinion: In *Bowers v. Hardwick* we held that the Constitution does not prohibit what virtually all States had done from the founding of the Republic until very recent years—making homosexual conduct a crime. That holding is unassailable, except by those who think that the Constitution changes to suit current fashions. *** If it is constitutionally permissible for a State to make homosexual conduct criminal, surely it is constitutionally permissible for a State to enact other laws merely *disfavoring* homosexual conduct. *** And *a fortiori* it is constitutionally permissible for a State to adopt a provision *not even* disfavoring homosexual conduct, but merely prohibiting all levels of state government from bestowing *special protections* upon homosexual conduct. ***

But assuming that, in Amendment 2, a person of homosexual "orientation" is someone who does not engage in homosexual conduct but merely has a tendency or desire to do so, *Bowers* still suffices to establish a rational basis for the provision. If it is rational to criminalize the conduct, surely it is rational to deny special favor and protection to those with a self-avowed tendency or desire to engage in the conduct. Indeed, where criminal sanctions are not involved, homosexual "orientation" is an acceptable stand-in for homosexual conduct. A State "does not violate the Equal Protection Clause merely because the classifications made by its laws are imperfect," *Dandridge v. Williams*, 397 U.S. 471, 485 (1970) [*see New York City Transit Authority v. Beazer*, 440 U.S. 568 (1979)]. ***

Moreover, even if the provision regarding homosexual "orientation" were invalid, respondents' challenge to Amendment 2—which is a facial challenge—must fail. "A facial challenge to a legislative Act is, of course, the most difficult challenge to mount successfully, since the challenger must establish that no set of circumstances exists under which the Act would be valid." *United States v. Salerno*, 481 U.S. 739, 745 (1987). It would not be enough for respondents to establish (if they could) that Amendment 2 is unconstitutional as applied to those of homosexual "orientation"; since, under *Bowers*, Amendment 2 is unquestionably constitutional as applied to those who engage in homosexual conduct, the facial challenge cannot succeed. Some individuals of homosexual "orientation" who do not engage in homosexual acts might successfully bring an as-applied challenge to Amendment 2, but so far as the record indicates, none of the respondents is such a person.

III

The foregoing suffices to establish what the Court's failure to cite any case remotely in point would lead one to suspect: No principle set forth in the Constitution, nor even any imagined by this Court in the past 200 years, prohibits what Colorado has done here. But the case for Colorado is much

---

rejects the Supreme Court of Colorado's holding that Amendment 2 infringes upon a "fundamental right" of "independently identifiable class[es]" to "participate equally in the political process."

stronger than that. What it has done is not only unprohibited, but eminently reasonable, with close, congressionally approved precedent in earlier constitutional practice.

First, as to its eminent reasonableness. The Court's opinion contains grim, disapproving hints that Coloradans have been guilty of "animus" or "animosity" toward homosexuality, as though that has been established as un–American. Of course it is our moral heritage that one should not hate any human being or class of human beings. But I had thought that one could consider certain conduct reprehensible—murder, for example, or polygamy, or cruelty to animals—and could exhibit even "animus" toward such conduct. Surely that is the only sort of "animus" at issue here: moral disapproval of homosexual conduct, the same sort of moral disapproval that produced the centuries-old criminal laws that we held constitutional in *Bowers*. The Colorado amendment does not, to speak entirely precisely, prohibit giving favored status to people who are *homosexuals*; they can be favored for many reasons—for example, because they are senior citizens or members of racial minorities. But it prohibits giving them favored status *because of their homosexual conduct*—that is, it prohibits favored status for *homosexuality*. ***

Amendment 2 *** sought to counter both the geographic concentration and the disproportionate political power of homosexuals by (1) resolving the controversy at the statewide level, and (2) making the election a single-issue contest for both sides. It put directly, to all the citizens of the State, the question: Should homosexuality be given special protection? They answered no. The Court today asserts that this most democratic of procedures is unconstitutional. *** What the Court says is even demonstrably false at the constitutional level. The Eighteenth Amendment to the Federal Constitution, for example, deprived those who drank alcohol not only of the power to alter the policy of prohibition *locally* or through *state legislation*, but even of the power to alter it through *state constitutional amendment* or *federal legislation*. The Establishment Clause of the First Amendment prevents theocrats from having their way by converting their fellow citizens at the local, state, or federal statutory level; as does the Republican Form of Government Clause prevent monarchists.

But there is a much closer analogy, one that involves precisely the effort by the majority of citizens to preserve its view of sexual morality statewide, against the efforts of a geographically concentrated and politically powerful minority to undermine it. The constitutions of the States of Arizona, Idaho, New Mexico, Oklahoma, and Utah to this day contain provisions stating that polygamy is "forever prohibited." Polygamists, and those who have a polygamous "orientation," have been "singled out" by these provisions for much more severe treatment than merely denial of favored status; and that treatment can only be changed by achieving amendment of the state constitutions. The Court's disposition today suggests that these provisions are unconstitutional. *** The United States Congress *** *required* the inclusion of these antipolygamy provisions in the constitutions of Arizona, New Mexico, Oklahoma, and Utah, as a condition of their admission to statehood. *** Idaho adopted the constitutional provision on its own, but the 51st Congress, which admitted Idaho into the Union, found its constitution to be "republican in form *and *** in conformity with the Constitution of the United States*." Thus, this "singling out" of the sexual practices of a single group for statewide, democratic vote—so utterly alien to our constitutional system, the Court would have us believe—has not only happened, but has received the explicit approval of the United States Congress. *** [T]his Court *** approved a territorial statutory provision that went even further, depriving polygamists of the ability even to achieve a constitutional amendment, by depriving them of the power to vote. In *Davis v. Beason*, 133 U.S. 333 (1890), JUSTICE FIELD wrote for a unanimous Court: "In our judgment, § 501 of the Revised Statutes of Idaho Territory, which provides that 'no person *** who is a bigamist or polygamist *** is permitted to vote at any election, or to hold any position or office of honor, trust, or profit within this Territory,' is *not open to any constitutional or legal objection*." To the extent, if any, that this opinion permits the imposition of adverse consequences upon mere abstract advocacy of polygamy, it has of course been overruled by later cases. But the proposition that polygamy can be criminalized, and those engaging in that crime deprived of the vote, remains good law. *Beason* rejected the argument that "such discrimination is a denial of the equal protection of the laws."

This Court cited *Beason* with approval as recently as 1993, in an opinion authored by the same Justice who writes for the Court today. *** It remains to be explained how § 501 of the Idaho Revised Statutes was not an "impermissible targeting" of polygamists, but (the much more mild) Amendment 2 is an "impermissible targeting" of homosexuals. Has the Court concluded that the perceived social harm of polygamy is a "legitimate concern of government," and the perceived social harm of homosexuality is not?

IV

I strongly suspect that the answer to the last question is yes, which leads me to the last point I wish to make: The Court today *** employs a constitutional theory heretofore unknown to frustrate Colorado's reasonable effort to preserve traditional American moral values. *** I think it no business of the courts (as opposed to the political branches) to take sides in this culture war. *** When the Court takes sides in the culture wars, it tends to be with the knights rather than the villeins—and more specifically with the Templars, reflecting the views and values of the lawyer class from which the Court's Members are drawn. How that class feels about homosexuality will be evident to anyone who wishes to interview job applicants at virtually any of the Nation's law schools. The interviewer may refuse to offer a job because the applicant is a Republican; because he is an adulterer; because he went to the wrong prep school or belongs to the wrong country club; because he eats snails; because he is a womanizer; because she wears real-animal fur; or even because he hates the Chicago Cubs. But if the interviewer should wish not to be an associate or partner of an applicant because he disapproves of the applicant's homosexuality, *then* he will have violated the pledge which the Association of American Law Schools requires all its member-schools to exact from job interviewers: "assurance of the employer's willingness" to hire homosexuals. This law-school view of what "prejudices" must be stamped out may be contrasted with the more plebeian attitudes that apparently still prevail in the United States Congress, which has been unresponsive to repeated attempts to extend to homosexuals the protections of federal civil rights laws. ***

Today's opinion has no foundation in American constitutional law, and barely pretends to. The people of Colorado have adopted an entirely reasonable provision which does not even disfavor homosexuals in any substantive sense, but merely denies them preferential treatment. Amendment 2 is designed to prevent piecemeal deterioration of the sexual morality favored by a majority of Coloradans, and is not only an appropriate means to that legitimate end, but a means that Americans have employed before. Striking it down is an act, not of judicial judgment, but of political will. I dissent.

Notes

1. **Hearts and Heads.** "Since *Romer* came down, I have had many conversations about it with law professors and law students across the country. The initial consensus seems to be that while JUSTICE KENNEDY's language soared, JUSTICE SCALIA's logic held. JUSTICE KENNEDY won their hearts; JUSTICE SCALIA, their heads." Amar, *Attainder and Amendment 2: Romer's Rightness,* 95 MICH. L. REV. 203, 204 (1996). Do you agree with the "consensus"? Amar argues that Colorado's Amendment 2 is unconstitutional in light of the Attainder Clause of Article I, Section 9, which he calls "an early forebear of the Equal Protection Clause." It is unconstitutional as "legal and social outlawry in cowboy country—a targeting of outsiders, a badge of second-class citizenship, a tainting of queers, a scarlet Q." For a skeptical response by one of Amar's students, *see Hills, Is Amendment 2 Really a Bill of Attainder? Some Questions About Professor Amar's Analysis of Romer,* 95 MICH. L. REV. 236 (1996).

2. **Rational Basis Review.** If the standard is *really* whether there is a "legitimate state interest" "rationally related" to the categorization, should the Court have found Amendment 2 unconstitutional? This may be merely one of several cases in which the Court says one thing (rational basis standard) and does something different (heightened scrutiny). Do you think *Romer* is explicable as (1) an early step towards elevating sexual orientation to protected class status or (2) an anomaly caused by the breadth of Amendment 2 to deny homosexuals protection against discrimination regardless of the context?

3. *Romer* and *Coalition for Economic Equity.* Why wasn't more made of *Romer* in the challenge to Proposition 209 in *Coalition for Economic Equity v. Wilson*?

4. **Problems.**

    (a) Is the Clinton Administration's "don't ask, don't tell" policy in the military constitutional? The policy, codified at 10 U.S.C. § 654(b), provides for separation from the service when "the member has engaged in, attempted to engage in, or solicited another to engage in a homosexual act." The policy rests in part on testimony by military commanders that heterosexual personnel in the military do not want to serve alongside openly homosexual soldiers and that this would cause serious morale problems. Is this policy constitutional in the context of a case brought by a discharged service member who tells another service member that he is gay?

(b) Do state bans on homosexual marriages, city and state domestic partnership laws, and Vermont's "civil unions" for homosexuals in lieu of marriage violate the Equal Protection Clause? Consider the following argument in light of *Romer*:

> "'Separate but equal' was a failed and pernicious policy with regard to race; it will be a failed and pernicious policy with regard to sexual orientation. *** [T]here are no arguments for civil union that do not apply equally to marriage. To endorse one but not the other, to concede the substance of the matter while withholding the name and form of the relationship, is to engage in an act of pure stigmatization. *** Gay men and women are citizens of this country. After two centuries of invisibility and persecution, they deserve to be recognized as such." Sullivan, *State of the Union*, THE NEW REPUBLIC, May 8, 2000.

5.   **Question.** Assume a major U.S. city amends its charter to include the following language: "no special class status may be granted based upon sexual orientation, conduct or relationships." As a result of this amendment, the city may not enact, adopt, enforce, or administer any ordinance, regulation, rule, or policy which provides that homosexual, lesbian, or bisexual orientation, status, conduct, or relationship constitutes, entitles, or otherwise provides a person with the basis to have any claim of minority or protected status, quota preference, or other preferential treatment. The amendment also includes language that makes all previous city programs designed to give preferential treatment to homosexuals "null and void." Does this amendment violate the Equal Protection Clause of the Fourteenth Amendment? *See Equality Foundation of Greater Cincinnati, Inc. v. City of Cincinnati*, 128 F.3d 289 (6th Cir. 1997), *cert. denied*, 525 U.S. 943 (1998). **Review Problem # 1**

Justin Travis had felt uncomfortable "inhabiting a male body" ever since he was in junior high school. After attending college and beginning a career in California, Justin decided he would convert his body to match his psyche.

In 1999, Travis changed his name to Julienne Travis, began taking female hormones, and commenced to dress and groom as a female. In 2001, Travis had breast implants and began using women's restrooms. Finally, in early 2003, after saving diligently for the procedure over many months, Travis was prepared to take the final step to femininity: surgical conversion of his genitals from those of a male to those of a female. The very day that Travis made a down payment on the $10,000 operation, he was driving home listening to California Public Radio when he heard a news story that almost caused him to crash. A transcript of the story follows:

> "Today, the culture wars reached a new level of combat. Governor Ashcrafty signed legislation making it a felony for any physician, clinic or hospital in the State of California to perform 'any surgical procedure converting the genitals of a male to those of a female.' The Governor noted that over 100 California males

had such operations in the past year, that no comparable surgical procedure has been developed for converting females to males, and that the legislation would also prevent such tragedies as the one that befell a famous singer who died last year from complications arising out of such an operation. The Governor's statement also mentioned the widespread belief among most Californians that such legislation would keep mentally unstable individuals from being mutilated by predatory clinics and would reaffirm God's plan 'to divide the human species into two sexes, inalterably distinguishable, from birth to death.' Challenges to the legislation are expected, says Northern California law professor Larry Tribal."

Deciding (s)he would rather fight than run, Travis has teamed up with the "Be What You Wanna Be" Clinic, the site of the scheduled operation. **Travis and the Clinic have asked your advice concerning their chances of overturning the new legislation on either substantive due process or equal protection grounds.** They have asked for advice of another specialist as to whether the legislation is vulnerable on other grounds (such as the First Amendment), so you need not worry about those issues. You may also assume that the Governor Ashcrafty's statement that there is no comparable surgical procedure for female to male operations is accurate.

Review Problem # 2

Julienne (formerly Justin) Travis, who was in the process this time last year of converting his male body to match his female psyche, persuaded the California Supreme Court that the state had violated his rights when it prohibited "any surgical procedure converting the genitals of a male to those of a female." After the United States Supreme Court denied certiorari to the State of California, Travis completed his surgical procedure.

This year, Travis has a new problem. Julienne has fallen in love with a man and they are engaged to be married in July, when Travis' betrothed completes the California Bar Exam. Last week, however, Travis was driving on the freeway and heard the following story on California Public Radio:

"Today, Governor Ashcrafty signed legislation designed to restrict the ability of those he deemed 'freaks and perverts' from engaging in 'the sacred ceremony of marriage.' The legislation defines marriage as 'the union of one man and one woman' and specifies that gender at birth controls the determination of whether an individual is deemed a man or a woman for purposes of the statute. 'Transsexuals may have employment rights in this state under the state's laws against discrimination,' said the Governor, but they 'cannot enjoy the sanctity of marriage.' Our regular commentator on such matters, Northern California law professor Larry Tribal, says challenges to the legislation are expected. 'This law may meet the same fate as last year's surgical procedure law,' Tribal said, 'but the two laws raise somewhat different constitutional issues.'"

Not one to give up on marrying "the man of my dreams," Travis and the California Coalition for Transexual Rights (CTRAN) have asked you to prepare a memo assessing their chances of overturning the new legislation on substantive due process grounds. Other issues, including the status of the legislation under the Equal Protection Clause, the First Amendment, and the Full Faith and Credit clause, have been farmed out to attorneys at other firms specializing in such issues.

Discuss Travis' Due Process and Equal Protection rights.

X

STATE ACTION

"[In t]he first section of the fourteenth amendment, *** it is state action of a particular character that is prohibited. Individual invasion of individual rights is not the subject-matter of the amendment. It has a deeper and broader scope. It nullifies and makes void all state legislation, and state action of every kind, which impairs the privileges and immunities of citizens of the United States, or which injures them in life, liberty, or property without due process of law, or which denies to any of them the equal protection of the laws."

"It was perfectly well known that the great danger to the equal enjoyment by citizens of their rights, as citizens, was to be apprehended, not altogether from unfriendly state legislation, but from the hostile action of corporations and individuals in the states. And it is to be presumed that it was intended, by that section, to clothe congress with power and authority to meet that danger."

—Excerpts from the majority and dissenting opinions in *The Civil Rights Cases* (1883)

You may recall from Chapter IV the *Civil Rights Cases'* holdings (1) that the Equal Protection Clause regulates actions of state actors only, not private individuals, (2) that state action does not include entities regulated or chartered by the state or open to the public, such as common carriers or places of amusement, and (3) that state action only involves conduct by the government, not acquiescence in discrimination by private individuals. This chapter examines in more detail the minimum amount of state action required to trigger operation of the Fourteenth Amendment and when, if ever, state action can be found from the failure of the state to act.

A. MINIMUM AMOUNT OF STATE ACTION

SHELLEY v. KRAEMER
334 U.S. 1, 68 S.Ct. 836, 92 L.Ed. 1161 (1948).

MR. CHIEF JUSTICE VINSON delivered the opinion of the Court.

These cases present for our consideration questions relating to the validity of court enforcement of private agreements, generally described as restrictive covenants, which have as their purpose the exclusion of persons of designated race or color from the ownership or occupancy of real property. ***

On August 11, 1945, pursuant to a contract of sale, petitioners Shelley, who are Negroes, for valuable consideration received from one Fitzgerald a warranty deed to the parcel in question. The trial court found that petitioners had no actual knowledge of the restrictive agreement at the time of the purchase.

On October 9, 1945, respondents, as owners of other property subject to the terms of the restrictive covenant, brought suit in Circuit Court of the city of St. Louis praying that petitioners Shelley be restrained from taking possession of the property and that judgment be entered divesting title out of petitioners Shelley and revesting title in the immediate grantor or in such other person as the court should direct. ***

Whether the equal protection clause of the Fourteenth Amendment inhibits judicial enforcement by state courts of restrictive covenants based on race or color is a question which this Court has not heretofore been called upon to consider. *** [The Missouri] covenant declares that no part of the affected property shall be "occupied by any person not of the Caucasian race, it being intended hereby to restrict the use of said property *** against the occupancy as owners or tenants of any portion of said property for resident or other purpose by people of the Negro or Mongolian Race." Not only does the restriction seek to proscribe use and occupancy of the affected properties by members of the excluded class, but as construed by the Missouri courts, the agreement requires that title of any person who uses his property in violation of the restriction shall be divested. ***

It cannot be doubted that among the civil rights intended to be protected from discriminatory state action by the Fourteenth Amendment are the rights to acquire, enjoy, own and dispose of property. Equality in the enjoyment of property rights was regarded by the framers of that Amendment as an essential pre-condition to the realization of other basic civil rights and liberties which the Amendment was intended to guarantee. Thus, [42 U.S.C. § 1982], derived from § 1 of the Civil Rights Act of 1866 which was enacted by Congress while the Fourteenth Amendment was also under consideration, provides:

> "All citizens of the United States shall have the same right, in every State and Territory, as is enjoyed by white citizens thereof to inherit, purchase, lease, sell, hold, and convey real and personal property."

It is likewise clear that restrictions on the right of occupancy of the sort sought to be created by the private agreements in these cases could not be squared with the requirements of the Fourteenth Amendment if imposed by state statute or local ordinance. We do not understand respondents to urge the contrary. *** But the present cases do not involve action by state legislatures or city councils. Here the particular patterns of discrimination and the areas in which the restrictions are to operate, are determined, in the first instance, by the terms of agreements among private individuals. Participation of the State consists in the enforcement of the restrictions so defined. The crucial issue with which we are here confronted is whether this distinction removes these cases from the operation of the prohibitory provisions of the Fourteenth Amendment.

Since the decision of this Court in the *Civil Rights Cases,* the principle has become firmly embedded in our constitutional law that the action inhibited by the first section of the Fourteenth Amendment is only such action as may fairly be said to be that of the States. That Amendment erects no shield against merely private conduct, however discriminatory or wrongful.

We conclude, therefore, that the restrictive agreements standing alone cannot be regarded as a violation of any rights guaranteed to petitioners by the Fourteenth Amendment. So long as the purposes of those agreements are effectuated by voluntary adherence to their terms, it would appear clear that there has been no action by the State and the provisions of the Amendment have not been violated.

But here there was more. These are cases in which the purposes of the agreements were secured only by judicial enforcement by state courts of the restrictive terms of the agreements. The respondents urge that judicial enforcement of private agreements does not amount to state action; or, in any event, the participation of the State is so attenuated in character as not to amount to state action within the meaning of the Fourteenth Amendment. Finally, it is suggested, even if the States in these cases may be deemed to have acted in the constitutional sense, their action did not deprive petitioners of rights guaranteed by the Fourteenth Amendment. ***

That the action of state courts and of judicial officers in their official capacities is to be regarded as action of the State within the meaning of the Fourteenth Amendment, is a proposition which has long been established by decisions of this Court. *** One of the earliest applications of the prohibitions contained in the Fourteenth Amendment to action of state judicial officials occurred in cases in which Negroes had been excluded from jury service in criminal prosecutions by reason of their race or color. These cases demonstrate, also, the early recognition by this Court that state action in violation of the Amendment's provisions is equally repugnant to the constitutional commands whether directed by state statute or taken by a judicial official in the absence of statute. Thus, in *Strauder v. West Virginia*, 100 U.S. 303 (1880), this Court declared invalid a state statute restricting jury service to white persons as amounting to a denial of the equal protection of the laws to the colored defendant in that case. *** *Ex parte Virginia*, [100 U.S. 339 (1880)], held that a similar discrimination imposed by the action of a state judge denied rights protected by the Amendment, despite the fact that the language of the state statute relating to jury service contained no such restrictions.

The action of state courts in imposing penalties or depriving parties of other substantive rights without providing adequate notice and opportunity to defend, has, of course, long been regarded as a denial of the due process of law guaranteed by the Fourteenth Amendment.

In numerous cases, this Court has reversed criminal convictions in state courts for failure of those courts to provide the essential ingredients of a fair hearing. *** But the examples of state judicial action which have been held by this Court to violate the Amendment's commands are not restricted to situations in which the judicial proceedings were found in some manner to be procedurally unfair. It has been recognized that the action of state courts in enforcing a substantive common-law rule formulated by those courts, may result in the denial of rights guaranteed by the Fourteenth Amendment, even though the judicial proceedings in such cases may have been in complete accord with the most rigorous conceptions of procedural due process.

The short of the matter is that from the time of the adoption of the Fourteenth Amendment until the present, it has been the consistent ruling of this Court that the action of the States to which the Amendment has reference, includes action of state courts and state judicial officials. Although, in construing the terms of the Fourteenth Amendment, differences have from time to time been expressed as to whether particular types of state action may be said to offend the Amendment's prohibitory provisions, it has never been suggested that state court action is immunized from the operation of those provisions simply because the act is that of the judicial branch of the state government.

Against this background of judicial construction, extending over a period of some three-quarters of a century, we are called upon to consider whether enforcement by state courts of the restrictive agreements in these cases may be deemed to be the acts of those States; and, if so, whether that action has denied these petitioners the equal protection of the laws which the Amendment was intended to insure.

We have no doubt that there has been state action in these cases in the full and complete sense of the phrase. The undisputed facts disclose that petitioners were willing purchasers of properties upon which they desired to establish homes. The owners of the properties were willing sellers; and contracts of sale were accordingly consummated. It is clear that but for the active intervention of the state courts, supported by the full panoply of state power, petitioners would have been free to occupy the properties in question without restraint.

These are not cases, as has been suggested, in which the States have merely abstained from action, leaving private individuals free to impose such discriminations as they see fit. Rather, these are cases in which the States have made available to such individuals the full coercive power of government to deny to petitioners, on the grounds of race or color, the enjoyment of property rights in premises which petitioners are willing and financially able to acquire and which the grantors are willing to sell. The difference between judicial enforcement and nonenforcement of the restrictive covenants is the difference to petitioners between being denied rights of property available to other members of the community and being accorded full enjoyment of those rights on an equal footing. ***

Respondents urge, however, that since the state courts stand ready to enforce restrictive covenants excluding white persons from the ownership or occupancy of property covered by such agreements, enforcement of covenants excluding colored persons may not be deemed a denial of equal protection of the laws to the colored persons who are thereby affected. This contention does not bear scrutiny. The parties have directed our attention to no case in which a court, state or federal, has been called upon to enforce a covenant excluding members of the white majority from ownership or occupancy of real property on grounds of race or color. But there are more fundamental considerations. The rights created by the first section of the Fourteenth Amendment are, by its terms, guaranteed to the individual. The rights established are personal rights. It is, therefore, no answer to these petitioners to say that the courts may also be induced to deny white persons rights of ownership and occupancy on grounds of race or color. Equal protection of the laws is not achieved through indiscriminate imposition of inequalities.

Nor do we find merit in the suggestion that property owners who are parties to these agreements are denied equal protection of the laws if denied access to the courts to enforce the terms of restrictive covenants and to assert property rights which the state courts have held to be created by such agreements. The Constitution confers upon no individual the right to demand action by the State which results in the denial of equal protection of the laws to other individuals. And it would appear beyond question that the power of the State to create and enforce property interests must be exercised within the boundaries defined by the Fourteenth Amendment. Cf. *Marsh v. Alabama*, 326 U.S. 501 (1946).

The problem of defining the scope of the restrictions which the Federal Constitution imposes upon exertions of power by the States has given rise to many of the most persistent and fundamental issues which this Court has been called upon to consider. That problem was foremost in the minds of the framers of the Constitution, and since that early day, has arisen in a multitude of forms. The task of determining whether the action of a State offends constitutional provisions is one which may not be undertaken lightly. Where, however, it is clear that the action of the State violates the terms of the fundamental charter, it is the obligation of this Court so to declare.

The historical context in which the Fourteenth Amendment became a part of the Constitution should not be forgotten. Whatever else the framers sought to achieve, it is clear that the matter of primary concern was the establishment of equality in the enjoyment of basic civil and political rights and the preservation of those rights from discriminatory action on the part of the States based on considerations of race or color. *** [W]e find it unnecessary to consider whether petitioners have also been deprived of property without due process of law or denied privileges and immunities of citizens of the United States. ***

MR. JUSTICE REED, MR. JUSTICE JACKSON, and MR. JUSTICE RUTLEDGE took no part in the consideration or decision of these cases.

Notes

1. *Shelley* **Baseline for Judicial Action.** The covenant the beneficiaries sought to enforce in *Shelley* was private. What is not "neutral" about the Court's role if it simply enforces bargains, whatever they might be? Do the courts serve as enforcers of all private bargains? Is the problem that the bargain violates public policy? But isn't the public policy embodied in the Equal Protection Clause limited to race discrimination by the state?

2. **Narrowing** *Shelley.* Consider whether a private homeowner can exclude someone from her home on the basis of race without violating the Constitution. Before you answer "yes, because there is no state action," consider the homeowner's options: personal physical removal, which would not involve the state, and calling the police to evict the person. But if the police are called in to help with the removal, doesn't that involve state action under *Shelley*? Several possibilities for narrowing *Shelley* which might solve this hypothetical have been suggested: (1) since the common law disfavored restraints on alienation, the case merely applies that doctrine to a racial restraint on alienation; and (2) the land mass involved in *Shelley* was large (*see Marsh v. Alabama,* discussed infra), and the covenants therefore operated like zoning. Neither of these is very satisfactory, in part because neither is mentioned in the case. Another solution suggested by some is to say that the state is not doing anything *extraordinary* to encourage or ratify racial discrimination in the hypothetical, while it is "using its coercive power to allow persons tangential to the transaction (the complaining neighbors in *Shelley*) for racially discriminatory reasons to prevent a transaction between a willing, nondiscriminatory buyer and seller." Farber, Eskridge and Frickey, CONSTITUTIONAL LAW: THEMES FOR THE CONSTITUTION'S THIRD CENTURY (2d Ed. West 1998), at p. 195. Is this a satisfactory explanation?

EDMONSON v. LEESVILLE CONCRETE COMPANY
500 U.S. 614, 111 S.Ct. 2077, 114 L.Ed.2d 660 (1991).

JUSTICE KENNEDY delivered the opinion of the Court.

We must decide in the case before us whether a private litigant in a civil case may use peremptory challenges to exclude jurors on account of their race. ***

Thaddeus Donald Edmonson, a construction worker, was injured in a jobsite accident at Fort Polk, Louisiana, a federal enclave. Edmonson sued Leesville Concrete Company for negligence in the United States District Court for the Western District of Louisiana, claiming that a Leesville employee permitted one of the company's trucks to roll backward and pin him against some construction equipment. *** During *voir dire,* Leesville used two of its three peremptory challenges authorized by statute to remove black persons from the prospective jury. Citing our decision in *Batson v. Kentucky,* 476 U.S. 79 (1986), Edmonson, who is himself black, requested that the District Court require Leesville to articulate a race-neutral explanation for striking the two jurors. The District Court denied the request on the ground that *Batson* does not apply in civil proceedings. As empaneled, the jury included 11 white persons and 1 black person. ***

In *Powers v. Ohio*, 499 U.S. 400 (1991), we held that a criminal defendant, regardless of his or her race, may object to a prosecutor's race-based exclusion of persons from the petit jury. *** *Powers* relied upon over a century of jurisprudence dedicated to the elimination of race prejudice within the jury selection process. See, e.g., *Batson*, supra; *Strauder v. West Virginia*, 100 U.S. 303 (1880). While these decisions were for the most part directed at discrimination by a prosecutor or other government officials in the context of criminal proceedings, we have not intimated that race discrimination is permissible in civil proceedings. Indeed, discrimination on the basis of race in selecting a jury in a civil proceeding harms the excluded juror no less than discrimination in a criminal trial. In either case, race is the sole reason for denying the excluded venire person the honor and privilege of participating in our system of justice.

That an act violates the Constitution when committed by a government official, however, does not answer the question whether the same act offends constitutional guarantees if committed by a private litigant or his attorney. The Constitution's protections of individual liberty and equal protection apply in general only to action by the government. *National Collegiate Athletic Assn. v. Tarkanian*, 488 U.S. 179 (1988). Racial discrimination, though invidious in all contexts, violates the Constitution only when it may be attributed to state action. *Moose Lodge No. 107 v. Irvis*, 407 U.S. 163 (1972). Thus, the legality of the exclusion at issue here turns on the extent to which a litigant in a civil case may be subject to the Constitution's restrictions.

The Constitution structures the National Government, confines its actions, and, in regard to certain individual liberties and other specified matters, confines the actions of the States. With a few exceptions, such as the provisions of the Thirteenth Amendment, constitutional guarantees of individual liberty and equal protection do not apply to the actions of private entities. This fundamental limitation on the scope of constitutional guarantees "preserves an area of individual freedom by limiting the reach of federal law" and "avoids imposing on the State, its agencies or officials, responsibility for conduct for which they cannot fairly be blamed." *Lugar v. Edmondson Oil Co.*, 457 U.S. 922 (1982). One great object of the Constitution is to permit citizens to structure their private relations as they choose subject only to the constraints of statutory or decisional law.

To implement these principles, courts must consider from time to time where the governmental sphere ends and the private sphere begins. Although the conduct of private parties lies beyond the Constitution's scope in most instances, governmental authority may dominate an activity to such an extent that its participants must be deemed to act with the authority of the government and, as a result, be subject to constitutional constraints. This is the jurisprudence of state action, which explores the "essential dichotomy" between the private sphere and the public sphere, with all its attendant constitutional obligations. *Moose Lodge*, supra.

We begin our discussion within the framework for state-action analysis set forth in *Lugar*. There we considered the state-action question in the context of a due process challenge to a State's procedure allowing private parties to obtain prejudgment attachments. We asked first whether the claimed constitutional deprivation resulted from the exercise of a right or privilege having its source in state authority; and second, whether the private party charged with the deprivation could be described in all fairness as a state actor.

There can be no question that the first part of the *Lugar* inquiry is satisfied here. By their very nature, peremptory challenges have no significance outside a court of law. Their sole purpose is to permit litigants to assist the government in the selection of an impartial trier of fact. While we have recognized the value of peremptory challenges in this regard, particularly in the criminal context, there is no constitutional obligation to allow them. Peremptory challenges are permitted only when the government, by statute or decisional law, deems it appropriate to allow parties to exclude a given number of persons who otherwise would satisfy the requirements for service on the petit jury.

Legislative authorizations, as well as limitations, for the use of peremptory challenges date as far back as the founding of the Republic; and the common-law origins of peremptories predate that. *** In the case before us, the challenges were exercised under a federal statute that provides, inter alia: "In civil cases, each party shall be entitled to three peremptory challenges. *** " Without this authorization, granted by an Act of Congress itself, Leesville would not have been able to engage in the alleged discriminatory acts.

Given that the statutory authorization for the challenges exercised in this case is clear, the remainder of our state-action analysis centers around the second part of the *Lugar* test, whether a private litigant in all fairness must be deemed a government actor in the use of peremptory challenges. *** Our precedents establish that, in determining whether a particular action or course of conduct is governmental in character, it is relevant to examine the following: the extent to which the actor relies on governmental assistance and benefits, see *Burton v. Wilmington Parking Authority*, 365 U.S. 715 (1961); whether the actor is performing a traditional governmental function, see *Marsh v. Alabama*, 326 U.S. 501 (1946); and whether the injury caused is aggravated in a unique way by the incidents of governmental authority, see *Shelley v. Kraemer*, 334 U.S. 1 (1948). Based on our application of these three principles to the circumstances here, we hold that the exercise of peremptory challenges by the defendant in the District Court was pursuant to a course of state action.

Although private use of state-sanctioned private remedies or procedures does not rise, by itself, to the level of state action, our cases have found state action when private parties make extensive use of state procedures with "the overt, significant assistance of state officials"; see *Lugar v. Edmondson Oil Co.* (1982); *Sniadach v. Family Finance Corp. of Bay View*, 395 U.S. 337 (1969). It cannot be disputed that, without the overt, significant participation of the government, the peremptory challenge system, as well as the jury trial system of which it is a part, simply could not exist. *** In the federal system,

Congress has established the qualifications for jury service, and has outlined the procedures by which jurors are selected. To this end, each district court in the federal system must adopt a plan for locating and summoning to the court eligible prospective jurors. This plan, as with all other trial court procedures, must implement statutory policies of random juror selection from a fair cross section of the community, and non-exclusion on account of race, color, religion, sex, national origin, or economic status. Statutes prescribe many of the details of the jury plan defining the jury wheel, voter lists, and jury commissions. A statute also authorizes the establishment of procedures for assignment to grand and petit juries and for lawful excuse from jury service.

At the outset of the selection process, prospective jurors must complete jury qualification forms as prescribed by the Administrative Office of the United States Courts. *** The trial judge exercises substantial control over voir dire in the federal system. *** The judge oversees the exclusion of jurors for cause, in this way determining which jurors remain eligible for the exercise of peremptory strikes. In cases involving multiple parties, the trial judge decides how peremptory challenges shall be allocated among them. When a lawyer exercises a peremptory challenge, the judge advises the juror he or she has been excused.

As we have outlined here, a private party could not exercise its peremptory challenges absent the overt, significant assistance of the court. The government summons jurors, constrains their freedom of movement, and subjects them to public scrutiny and examination. The party who exercises a challenge invokes the formal authority of the court, which must discharge the prospective juror, thus effecting the "final and practical denial" of the excluded individual's opportunity to serve on the petit jury. Without the direct and indispensable participation of the judge, who beyond all question is a state actor, the peremptory challenge system would serve no purpose. By enforcing a discriminatory peremptory challenge, the court "has not only made itself a party to the [biased act], but has elected to place its power, property and prestige behind the [alleged] discrimination." *Burton v. Wilmington Parking Authority*, 365 U.S., at 725. In so doing, the government has "create[d] the legal framework governing the [challenged] conduct," *National Collegiate Athletic Assn.*, 488 U.S., at 192, and in a significant way has involved itself with invidious discrimination.

In determining Leesville's state-actor status, we next consider whether the action in question involves the performance of a traditional function of the government. A traditional function of government is evident here. The peremptory challenge is used in selecting an entity that is a quintessential governmental body, having no attributes of a private actor. The jury exercises the power of the court and of the government that confers the court's jurisdiction. ***

If a government confers on a private body the power to choose the government's employees or officials, the private body will be bound by the constitutional mandate of race neutrality. At least a plurality of the Court recognized this principle in *Terry v. Adams*, 345 U.S. 461 (1953). There we found state action in a scheme in which a private organization known as the Jaybird Democratic Association conducted whites-only elections to select candidates to run in the Democratic primary elections in Ford Bend County, Texas. The Jaybird candidate was certain to win the Democratic primary and the Democratic candidate was certain to win the general election. JUSTICE CLARK's concurring opinion drew from *Smith v. Allwright*, 321 U.S. 649, 664 (1944), the principle that "any 'part of the machinery for choosing officials' becomes subject to the Constitution's constraints." ***

The principle that the selection of state officials, other than through election by all qualified voters, may constitute state action applies with even greater force in the context of jury selection through the use of peremptory challenges. Though the motive of a peremptory challenge may be to protect a private interest, the objective of jury selection proceedings is to determine representation on a governmental body. Were it not for peremptory challenges, there would be no question that the entire process of determining who will serve on the jury constitutes state action. The fact that the government delegates some portion of this power to private litigants does not change the governmental character of the power exercised. The delegation of authority that in *Terry* occurred without the aid of legislation occurs here through explicit statutory authorization.

We find respondent's reliance on *Polk County v. Dodson*, 454 U.S. 312 (1981), unavailing. In that case, we held that a public defender is not a state actor in his general representation of a criminal defendant, even though he may be in his performance of other official duties. *** "[A] defense lawyer is not, and by the nature of his function cannot be, the servant of an administrative superior. Held to the same standards of competence and integrity as a private lawyer, a public defender works under canons of professional responsibility that mandate his exercise of independent judgment on behalf of the client."

In the ordinary context of civil litigation in which the government is not a party, an adversarial relation does not exist between the government and a private litigant. In the jury-selection process, the government and private litigants work for the same end. Just as a government employee was deemed a private actor because of his purpose and functions in *Dodson*, so here a private entity becomes a government actor for the limited purpose of using peremptories during jury selection. The selection of jurors represents a unique governmental function delegated to private litigants by the government and attributable to the government for purposes of invoking constitutional protections against discrimination by reason of race.

Our decision in *West v. Atkins*, 487 U.S. 42 (1988), provides a further illustration. We held there that a private physician who contracted with a state prison to attend to the inmates' medical needs was a state actor. He was not on a regular state payroll, but we held his "function[s] within the state system, not the precise terms of his employment, [determined] whether his actions can fairly be attributed to the State." ***

In the case before us, the parties do not act pursuant to any contractual relation with the government. Here, as in most civil cases, the initial decision whether to sue at all, the selection of counsel, and any number of ensuing tactical choices in the course of discovery and trial may be without the requisite governmental character to be deemed state action. That cannot be said of the exercise of peremptory challenges, however; when private litigants participate in the selection of jurors, they serve an important function within the government and act with its substantial assistance. If peremptory challenges based on race were permitted, persons could be required by summons to be put at risk of open and public discrimination as a condition of their participation in the justice system. The injury to excluded jurors would be the direct result of governmental delegation and participation.

Finally, we note that the injury caused by the discrimination is made more severe because the government permits it to occur within the courthouse itself. Few places are a more real expression of the constitutional authority of the government than a courtroom, where the law itself unfolds. Within the courtroom, the government invokes its laws to determine the rights of those who stand before it. In full view of the public, litigants press their cases, witnesses give testimony, juries render verdicts, and judges act with the utmost care to ensure that justice is done.

Race discrimination within the courtroom raises serious questions as to the fairness of the proceedings conducted there. Racial bias mars the integrity of the judicial system and prevents the idea of democratic government from becoming a reality. In the many times we have addressed the problem of racial bias in our system of justice, we have not "questioned the premise that racial discrimination in the qualification or selection of jurors offends the dignity of persons and the integrity of the courts." *Powers.* To permit racial exclusion in this official forum compounds the racial insult inherent in judging a citizen by the color of his or her skin. ***

JUSTICE O'CONNOR, with whom THE CHIEF JUSTICE and JUSTICE SCALIA join, dissenting.

The Court concludes that the action of a private attorney exercising a peremptory challenge is attributable to the government and therefore may compose a constitutional violation. This conclusion is based on little more than that the challenge occurs in the course of a trial. Not everything that happens in a courtroom is state action. A trial, particularly a civil trial is by design largely a stage on which private parties may act; it is a forum through which they can resolve their disputes in a peaceful and ordered manner. The government erects the platform; it does not thereby become responsible for all that occurs upon it. As much as we would like to eliminate completely from the courtroom the specter of racial discrimination, the Constitution does not sweep that broadly. Because I believe that a peremptory strike by a private litigant is fundamentally a matter of private choice and not state action, I dissent.

In order to establish a constitutional violation, Edmonson must first demonstrate that Leesville's use of a peremptory challenge can fairly be attributed to the government. Unfortunately, our cases deciding when private action might be deemed that of the state have not been a model of consistency. Perhaps this is because the state action determination is so closely tied to the "framework of the peculiar facts or circumstances present." *See Burton v. Wilmington Parking Authority*. Whatever the reason, and despite the confusion, a coherent principle has emerged. We have stated the rule in various ways, but at base, "constitutional standards are invoked only when it can be said that the [government] is responsible for the specific conduct of which the plaintiff complains." Constitutional "liability attaches only to those wrongdoers 'who carry a badge of authority of [the government] and represent it in some capacity.'"

The Court concludes that this standard is met in the present case. It rests this conclusion primarily on two empirical assertions. First, that private parties use peremptory challenges with the "overt, significant participation of the government." Second, that the use of a peremptory challenge by a private party "involves the performance of a traditional function of the government." Neither of these assertions is correct.

*** The peremptory challenge "allow[s] parties," in this case private parties, to exclude potential jurors. It is the nature of a peremptory that its exercise is left wholly within the discretion of the litigant. The purpose of this longstanding practice is to establish for each party an "'arbitrary and capricious species of challenge'" whereby the "'sudden impressions and unaccountable prejudices we are apt to conceive upon the bare looks and gestures of another'" may be acted upon. By allowing the litigant to strike jurors for even the most subtle of discerned biases, the peremptory challenge fosters both the perception and reality of an impartial jury. In both criminal and civil trials, the peremptory challenge is a mechanism for the exercise of private choice in the pursuit of fairness. The peremptory is, by design, an enclave of private action in a government-managed proceeding.

The Court amasses much ostensible evidence of the Federal Government's "overt, significant assistance" in the peremptory process. Most of this evidence is irrelevant to the issue at hand. The bulk of the practices the Court describes—the establishment of qualifications for jury service, the location and summoning of prospective jurors, the jury wheel, the voter lists, the jury qualification forms, the per diem for jury service—are independent of the statutory entitlement to peremptory strikes, or of their use. All of this Government action is in furtherance of the Government's distinct obligation to provide a qualified jury; the Government would do these things even if there were no peremptory challenges. All of this activity, as well as the trial judge's control over voir dire, is merely prerequisite to the use of a peremptory challenge; it does not constitute participation in the challenge. That these actions may be necessary to a peremptory challenge—in the sense that there could be no such challenge without a venire from which to select—no more makes the challenge state action than the building of roads and provision of public transportation makes state action of riding on a bus.

The entirety of the government's actual participation in the peremptory process boils down to a single fact: "When a lawyer exercises a peremptory challenge, the judge advises the juror he or she has been excused." This is not significant participation. *** As an initial matter, the judge does not "encourage" the use of a peremptory challenge at all. The decision to strike a juror is entirely up to the litigant, and the reasons for doing so are of no consequence to the judge. It is the attorney who strikes. ***

The alleged state action here is a far cry from that which the Court found, for example, in *Shelley v. Kraemer*, 334 U.S. 1 (1948). In that case, state courts were called upon to enforce racially restrictive covenants against sellers of real property who did not wish to discriminate. *** There is another important distinction between *Shelley* and this case. The state courts in *Shelley* used coercive force to impose conformance on parties who did not wish to discriminate. "Enforcement" of peremptory challenges, on the other hand, does not compel anyone to discriminate; the discrimination is wholly a matter of private choice. Judicial acquiescence does not convert private choice into that of the State.

Nor is this the kind of significant involvement found in *Tulsa Professional Collection Services, Inc. v. Pope*, 485 U.S. 478 (1988). There, we concluded that the actions of the executrix of an estate in providing notice to creditors that they might file claims could fairly be attributed to the State. The State's involvement in the notice process, we said, was "pervasive and substantial." In particular, a state statute directed the executrix to publish notice. *** There is no comparable state involvement here. No one is compelled by government action to use a peremptory challenge, let alone to use it in a racially discriminatory way.

The Court relies also on *Burton v. Wilmington Parking Authority*, 365 U.S. 715 (1961). But the decision in that case depended on the perceived symbiotic relationship between a restaurant and the state parking authority from whom it leased space in a public building. The State had "so far insinuated itself into a position of interdependence with" the restaurant that it had to be "recognized as a joint participant in the challenged activity." Among the "peculiar facts [and] circumstances" leading to that conclusion was that the State stood to profit from the restaurant's discrimination. As I have shown, the government's involvement in the use of peremptory challenges falls far short of "interdependence" or "joint participation." Whatever the continuing vitality of *Burton* beyond its facts, see *Jackson v. Metropolitan Edison Co.*, 419 U.S. 345 (1974), it does not support the Court's conclusion here.

Jackson is a more appropriate analogy to this case. Metropolitan Edison terminated Jackson's electrical service under authority granted it by the State, pursuant to a procedure approved by the state utility commission. Nonetheless, we held that Jackson could not challenge the termination procedure on due process grounds. The termination was not state action because the State had done nothing to encourage the particular termination practice: "Approval by a state utility commission of such a request from a regulated utility, where the commission has not put its own weight on the side of the proposed practice by ordering it, does not transmute a practice initiated by the utility and approved by the commission into 'state action.'

Respondent's exercise of the choice allowed by state law where the initiative comes from it and not from the State, does not make its action in doing so 'state action' for purposes of the Fourteenth Amendment."

The similarity to this case is obvious. The Court's "overt, significant" government participation amounts to the fact that the government provides the mechanism whereby a litigant can choose to exercise a peremptory challenge. That the government allows this choice and that the judge approves it, does not turn this private decision into state action.

To the same effect is *Flagg Bros., Inc. v. Brooks*, 436 U.S. 149 (1978). In that case, a warehouse company's proposed sale of goods entrusted to it for storage pursuant to the New York Uniform Commercial Code was not fairly attributable to the State. We held that "the State of New York is in no way responsible for Flagg Brothers' decision, a decision which the State in § 7–210 permits but does not compel, to threaten to sell these respondents' belongings." Similarly, in the absence of compulsion, or at least encouragement, from the government in the use of peremptory challenges, the government is not responsible.

"The essential nature of the peremptory challenge is that it is one exercised without a reason stated, without inquiry and without being subject to the court's control." *Swain.* The government neither encourages nor approves such challenges. Accordingly, there is no "overt, significant participation" by the government.

The Court errs also when it concludes that the exercise of a peremptory challenge is a traditional government function. In its definition of the peremptory challenge, the Court asserts, correctly, that jurors struck via peremptories "otherwise satisfy the requirements for service on the petit jury." Whatever reason a private litigant may have for using a peremptory challenge, it is not the government's reason. *** Peremptory challenges are not a traditional government function; the "tradition" is one of unguided private choice. *** The peremptory challenge forms no part of the government's responsibility in selecting a jury. *** In [various cases], the Court held that the performance of [traditional government functions], even if state regulated or state funded, was not state action unless the function had been one exclusively the prerogative of the State, or the State had provided such significant encouragement to the challenged action that the State could be held responsible for it. The use of a peremptory challenge by a private litigant meets neither criterion.

None of this should be news, as this case is fairly well controlled by *Polk County v. Dodson*, 454 U.S. 312 (1981). We there held that a public defender, employed by the State, does not act under color of state law when representing a defendant in a criminal trial.* In such a circumstance,

---

* *Dodson* was a case brought under 42 U.S.C. § 1983, the statutory mechanism for many constitutional claims. The issue in that case, therefore, was whether the public defender had acted "under color of state law." In *Lugar v. Edmondson Oil Co.*, 457 U.S. 922, 929 (1982), the Court held that the statutory requirement of action "under color of state law" is identical to the "state action" requirement for other constitutional claims.

government employment is not sufficient to create state action. More important for present purposes, neither is the performance of a lawyer's duties in a courtroom. This is because a lawyer, when representing a private client, cannot at the same time represent the government. *** The Court does not challenge the rule of *Dodson*, yet concludes that private attorneys performing this adversarial function are state actors. Where is the distinction?

The Court wishes to limit the scope of *Dodson* to the actions of public defenders in an adversarial relationship with the government. At a minimum then, the Court must concede that *Dodson* stands for the proposition that a criminal defense attorney is not a state actor when using peremptory strikes on behalf of a client, nor is an attorney representing a private litigant in a civil suit against the government. Both of these propositions are true, but the Court's distinction between this case and *Dodson* turns state action doctrine on its head. Attorneys in an adversarial relation to the state are not state actors, but that does not mean that attorneys who are not in such a relation are state actors.

The Court is plainly wrong when it asserts that "[i]n the jury selection process, the government and private litigants work for the same end." In a civil trial, the attorneys for each side are in "an adversarial relation"; they use their peremptory strikes in direct opposition to one another, and for precisely contrary ends. *** The government is simply not "responsible" for the use of peremptory strikes by private litigants.

Constitutional "liability attaches only to those wrongdoers 'who carry a badge of authority of [the government] and represent it in some capacity.'" A government attorney who uses a peremptory challenge on behalf of the client is, by definition, representing the government. The challenge thereby becomes state action. It is antithetical to the nature of our adversarial process, however, to say that a private attorney acting on behalf of a private client represents the government for constitutional purposes.

Beyond "significant participation" and "traditional function," the Court's final argument is that the exercise of a peremptory challenge by a private litigant is state action because it takes place in a courtroom. In the end, this is all the Court is left with; peremptories do not involve the "overt, significant participation of the government," nor do they constitute a "traditional function of the government." The Court is also wrong in its ultimate claim. If *Dodson* stands for anything, it is that the actions of a lawyer in a courtroom do not become those of the government by virtue of their location. This is true even if those actions are based on race.

Racism is a terrible thing. It is irrational, destructive, and mean. Arbitrary discrimination based on race is particularly abhorrent when manifest in a courtroom, a forum established by the government for the resolution of disputes through "quiet rationality." But not every opprobrious and inequitable act is a constitutional violation. The Fifth Amendment's Due Process Clause prohibits only actions for which the Government can be held responsible. The Government is not responsible for everything that occurs in a courtroom. The Government is not responsible for a peremptory challenge by a private litigant. I respectfully dissent.

JUSTICE SCALIA, dissenting.

*** The concrete benefits of the Court's newly discovered constitutional rule are problematic. It will not necessarily be a net help rather than hindrance to minority litigants in obtaining racially diverse juries. In criminal cases, *Batson v. Kentucky* already prevents the prosecution from using race-based strikes. The effect of today's decision (which logically must apply to criminal prosecutions) will be to prevent the defendant from doing so—so that the minority defendant can no longer seek to prevent an all-white jury, or to seat as many jurors of his own race as possible. To be sure, it is ordinarily more difficult to prove race-based strikes of white jurors, but defense counsel can generally be relied upon to do what we say the Constitution requires. So in criminal cases, today's decision represents a net loss to the minority litigant. In civil cases that is probably not true—but it does not represent an unqualified gain either. Both sides have peremptory challenges, and they are sometimes used to assure rather than to prevent a racially diverse jury.

The concrete costs of today's decision, on the other hand, are not at all doubtful; and they are enormous. We have now added to the duties of already-submerged state and federal trial courts the obligation to assure that race is not included among the other factors (sex, age, religion, political views, economic status) used by private parties in exercising their peremptory challenges. That responsibility would be burden enough if it were not to be discharged through the adversary process; but of course it is. When combined with our decision this Term in *Powers v. Ohio*, 499 U.S. 400 (1991), which held that the party objecting to an allegedly race-based peremptory challenge need not be of the same race as the challenged juror, today's decision means that both sides, in all civil jury cases, no matter what their race (and indeed, even if they are artificial entities such as corporations), may lodge racial-challenge objections and, after those objections have been considered and denied, appeal the denials—with the consequence, if they are successful, of having the judgments against them overturned. Thus, yet another complexity is added to an increasingly Byzantine system of justice that devotes more and more of its energy to sideshows and less and less to the merits of the case. Judging by the number of *Batson* claims that have made their way even as far as this Court under the pre-Powers regime, it is a certainty that the amount of judges' and lawyers' time devoted to implementing today's newly discovered Law of the Land will be enormous. That time will be diverted from other matters, and the overall system of justice will certainly suffer. Alternatively, of course, the States and Congress may simply abolish peremptory challenges, which would cause justice to suffer in a different fashion.

Although today's decision neither follows the law nor produces desirable concrete results, it certainly has great symbolic value. To overhaul the doctrine of state action in this fashion—what a magnificent demonstration of this institution's uncompromising hostility to race-based judgments, even by private actors! The price of the demonstration is, alas, high, and much of it will be paid by the minority litigants who use our courts. I dissent.

Notes

1. **State Involvement in Private Conduct.** As JUSTICE O'CONNOR's dissent discusses, *Burton* involved a private coffee shop's refusal to serve black customers prior to the Civil Rights Act of 1964. The coffee shop was located in a parking complex owned by a state agency which had the power to require the restaurant to adopt rules governing admission to the shop. The Court found sufficient state action. Is this because (as in *Shelley* and *Edmonson*) the case involves race discrimination? More recent cases have generally been reluctant to find state action from even significant state economic support of private entities. *See Jackson v. Metropolitan Edison,* described by JUSTICE O'CONNOR. *See Rendell–Baker v. Kohn,* 457 U.S. 830 (1982) (although 90–99% of school's budget comes from the state and its operations were closely regulated, no First Amendment protection for employees fired for voicing opinions concerning school policies).

2. **Public Functions.** In *Marsh v. Alabama,* 326 U.S. 501 (1946), Gulf Shipbuilding Corporation, a private company, owned the town of Chickasaw, Alabama. When a Jehovah's Witness sought to distribute religious literature on a sidewalk of the town, she was arrested for trespass. Her defense was that the First Amendment protected her distribution of literature on the sidewalk. In rejecting the state's response that she had no first Amendment rights on private property, the Court said "Ownership does not always mean absolute dominion," that the corporation had opened up its property "for use by the public in general," and that "there is no more reason for depriving [residents of company-owned towns] of the liberties guaranteed by the First and fourteenth Amendments than there is for curtailing these freedoms with respect to any other citizen." The Court pointed out that the State had "permitt[ed] a corporation to govern a community of citizens" and that such governance could not be free of constitutional rights. Should the holding of *Marsh* be extended to a remote sugar plantation which has no stores or other town amenities but which is so remote from any town that workers have to be driven there on weekends? To a large shopping center in a city? What exactly are public functions? In another context, remember the Court's reluctance to answer this question (*Garcia v. SAMTA*)?

BRENTWOOD ACADEMY
v.
TENNESSEE SECONDARY SCHOOL ATHLETIC ASSOCIATION
531 U.S. 288, 121 S.Ct. 924, 148 L. Ed. 2d 807 (2001).

JUSTICE SOUTER delivered the opinion of the Court.

The issue is whether a statewide association incorporated to regulate interscholastic athletic competition among public and private secondary schools may be regarded as engaging in state action when it enforces a rule against a member school. The association in question here includes most public schools located within the State, acts through their representatives, draws its officers from them, is largely funded by their dues and income received in their stead, and has historically been seen to regulate in lieu of the State Board of Education's exercise of its own authority. We hold that the association's regulatory activity may and should be treated as state action owing to the pervasive entwinement of state school officials in the structure of the association, there being no offsetting reason to see the association's acts in any other way. ***

Our cases try to plot a line between state action subject to Fourteenth Amendment scrutiny and private conduct (however exceptionable) that is not. The judicial obligation is not only to "preserv[e] an area of individual freedom by limiting the reach of federal law' and avoi[d] the imposition of responsibility on a State for conduct it could not control," but also to assure that constitutional standards are invoked "when it can be said that the State is *responsible* for the specific conduct of which the plaintiff complains". If the Fourteenth Amendment is not to be displaced, therefore, its ambit cannot be a simple line between States and people operating outside formally governmental organizations, and the deed of an ostensibly private organization or individual is to be treated sometimes as if a State had caused it to be performed. Thus, we say that state action may be found if, though only if, there is such a "close nexus between the State and the challenged action" that seemingly private behavior "may be fairly treated as that of the State itself."

What is fairly attributable is a matter of normative judgment, and the criteria lack rigid simplicity. From the range of circumstances that could point toward the State behind an individual face, no one fact can function as a necessary condition across the board for finding state action; nor is any set of circumstances absolutely sufficient, for there may be some countervailing reason against attributing activity to the government.

Our cases have identified a host of facts that can bear on the fairness of such an attribution. We have, for example, held that a challenged activity may be state action when it results from the State's exercise of "coercive power," when the State provides "significant encouragement, either overt or covert," or when a private actor operates as a "willful participant in joint activity with the State or its agents". We have treated a nominally private entity as a state actor when it is controlled by an "agency of the State," when it has been delegated a public function by the State, when it is "entwined with governmental policies" or when government is "entwined in [its] management or control," *Evans v. Newton,* 382 U.S. 296, 299, 301 (1966).

Amidst such variety, examples may be the best teachers, and examples from our cases are unequivocal in showing that the character of a legal entity is determined neither by its expressly private characterization in statutory law, nor by the failure of the law to acknowledge the entity's inseparability from recognized government officials or agencies. *** The nominally private character of the Association is overborne by the pervasive entwinement of public institutions and public officials in its composition and workings, and there is no substantial reason to claim unfairness in applying constitutional standards to it. ***

In sum, to the extent of 84% of its membership, the Association is an organization of public schools represented by their officials acting in their official capacity to provide an integral element of secondary public schooling. There would be no recognizable Association, legal or tangible, without the public school officials, who do not merely control but overwhelmingly perform all but the purely ministerial acts by which the Association exists and functions in practical terms. Only the 16% minority of private school memberships prevents this entwinement of the Association and the public school system from being total and their identities totally indistinguishable.

To complement the entwinement of public school officials with the Association from the bottom up, the State of Tennessee has provided for entwinement from top down. State Board members are assigned ex officio to serve as members of the board of control and legislative council, and the Association's ministerial employees are treated as state employees to the extent of being eligible for membership in the state retirement system.

It is, of course, true that the time is long past when the close relationship between the surrogate association and its public members and public officials acting as such was attested frankly. *** Today the State Board's member-designees continue to sit on the Association's committees as nonvoting members, and the State continues to welcome Association employees in its retirement scheme. The close relationship is confirmed by the Association's enforcement of the same preamendment rules and regulations reviewed and approved by the State Board (including the recruiting Rule challenged by Brentwood), and by the State Board's continued willingness to allow students to satisfy its physical education requirement by taking part in interscholastic athletics sponsored by the Association. The most one can say on the evidence is that the State Board once freely acknowledged the Association's official character but now does it by winks and nods. The amendment to the Rule in 1996 affected candor but not the "momentum" of the Association's prior involvement with the State Board. ***

The entwinement down from the State Board is therefore unmistakable, just as the entwinement up from the member public schools is overwhelming. Entwinement will support a conclusion that an ostensibly private organization ought to be charged with a public character and judged by constitutional standards; entwinement to the degree shown here requires it.

Entwinement is also the answer to the Association's several arguments offered to persuade us that the facts would not support a finding of state action under various criteria applied in other cases. These arguments are beside the point, simply because the facts justify a conclusion of state action under the criterion of entwinement, a conclusion in no sense unsettled merely because other criteria of state action may not be satisfied by the same facts.

The Association places great stress, for example, on the application of a public function test, as exemplified in *Rendell-Baker v. Kohn,* 457 U.S. 830 (1982). There, an apparently private school provided education for students whose special needs made it difficult for them to finish high school. The record, however, failed to show any tradition of providing public special education to students unable to cope with a regular school, who had historically been cared for (or ignored) according to private choice. It was true that various public school districts had adopted the practice of referring students to the school and paying their tuition, and no one disputed that providing the instruction aimed at a proper public objective and conferred a public benefit. But we held that the performance of such a public function did not permit a finding of state action on the part of the school unless the function performed was exclusively and traditionally public, as it was not in that case. The Association argues that application of the public function criterion would produce the same result here, and we will assume, *arguendo,* that it would. But this case does not turn on a public function test, any more than *Rendell-Baker* had anything to do with entwinement of public officials in the special school.

For the same reason, it avails the Association nothing to stress that the State neither coerced nor encouraged the actions complained of. "Coercion" and "encouragement" are like "entwinement" in referring to kinds of facts that can justify characterizing an ostensibly private action as public instead. Facts that address any of these criteria are significant, but no one criterion must necessarily be applied. When, therefore, the relevant facts show pervasive entwinement to the point of largely overlapping identity, the implication of state action is not affected by pointing out that the facts might not loom large under a different test. ***

JUSTICE THOMAS, with whom THE CHIEF JUSTICE, JUSTICE SCALIA, and JUSTICE KENNEDY join, dissenting.

We have never found state action based upon mere "entwinement." Until today, we have found a private organization's acts to constitute state action only when the organization performed a public function; was created, coerced, or encouraged by the government; or acted in a symbiotic relationship with the government. The majority's holding—that the Tennessee Secondary School Athletic Association's (TSSAA) enforcement of its recruiting rule is state action—not only extends state-action doctrine beyond its permissible limits but also encroaches upon the realm of individual freedom that the doctrine was meant to protect. I respectfully dissent.

*** The TSSAA was formed in 1925 as a private corporation to organize interscholastic athletics and to sponsor tournaments among its member schools. Any private or public secondary school may join the TSSAA by signing a contract agreeing to comply with its rules and decisions. Although public schools currently compose 84% of the TSSAA's membership, the TSSAA does not require that public schools constitute a set percentage of its membership, and, indeed, no public school need join the TSSAA. The TSSAA's rules are enforced not by a state agency but by its own board of control, which comprises high school principals, assistant principals, and superintendents, none of whom must work at a public school. Of course, at the time the recruiting rule was enforced in this case, all of the board members happened to be public school officials. However, each board member acts in a representative capacity on behalf of all the private and public schools in his region of Tennessee, and not simply his individual school.

The State of Tennessee did not create the TSSAA. The State does not fund the TSSAA and does not pay its employees. In fact, only 4% of the TSSAA's revenue comes from the dues paid by member schools; the bulk of its operating budget is derived from gate receipts at tournaments it sponsors. The State does not permit the TSSAA to use state-owned facilities for a discounted fee, and it does not exempt the TSSAA from state taxation. No Tennessee law authorizes the State to coordinate interscholastic athletics or empowers another entity to organize interscholastic athletics on behalf of the State. The only state pronouncement acknowledging the TSSAA's existence is a rule providing that the State Board of Education permits public schools to maintain membership in the TSSAA if they so choose.

Moreover, the State of Tennessee has never had any involvement in the particular action taken by the TSSAA in this case: the enforcement of the TSSAA's recruiting rule prohibiting members from using "undue influence" on students or their parents or guardians "to secure or to retain a student for athletic purposes." ***

The TSSAA has not performed a function that has been "traditionally exclusively reserved to the State." The organization of interscholastic sports is neither a traditional nor an exclusive public function of the States. Widespread organization and administration of interscholastic contests by schools did not begin until the 20th century. Certainly, in Tennessee, the State did not even show an interest in interscholastic athletics until 47 years after the TSSAA had been in existence and had been orchestrating athletic contests throughout the State. Even then, the State Board of Education merely acquiesced in the TSSAA's actions and did not assume the role of regulating interscholastic athletics. The TSSAA no doubt serves the public, particularly the public schools, but the mere provision of a service to the public does not render such provision a traditional and exclusive public function.

It is also obvious that the TSSAA is not an entity created and controlled by the government for the purpose of fulfilling a government objective, as was Amtrak in *Lebron v. National Railroad Passenger Corporation,* 513 U.S. 374, 394 (1995). Indeed, no one claims that the State of Tennessee played any role in the creation of the TSSAA as a private corporation in 1925. The TSSAA was designed to fulfill an objective—the organization of interscholastic athletic tournaments—that the government had not contemplated, much less pursued. And although the board of control currently is composed of public school officials, and although public schools currently account for the majority of the TSSAA's membership, this is not required by the TSSAA's constitution.

In addition, the State of Tennessee has not "exercised coercive power or *** provided such significant encouragement [to the TSSAA], either overt or covert," that the TSSAA's regulatory activities must in law be deemed to be those of the State. The State has not promulgated any regulations of interscholastic sports, and nothing in the record suggests that the State has encouraged or coerced the TSSAA in enforcing its recruiting rule. *** Furthermore, there is no evidence of "joint participation," between the State and the TSSAA in the TSSAA's enforcement of its recruiting rule. The

TSSAA's board of control enforces its recruiting rule solely in accordance with the authority granted to it under the contract that each member signs.

Finally, there is no "symbiotic relationship" between the State and the TSSAA. Contrary to the majority's assertion, the TSSAA's "fiscal relationship with the State is not different from that of many contractors performing services for the government." The TSSAA provides a service–the organization of athletic tournaments–in exchange for membership dues and gate fees, just as a vendor could contract with public schools to sell refreshments at school events. Certainly the public school could sell its own refreshments, yet the existence of that option does not transform the service performed by the contractor into a state action. Also, there is no suggestion in this case that, as was the case in *Burton,* th e State profits from the TSSAA's decision to enforce its recruiting rule. ***

Although the TSSAA's enforcement activities cannot be considered state action as a matter of common sense or under any of this Court's existing theories of state action, the majority presents a new theory. Under this theory, the majority holds that the combination of factors it identifies evidences "entwinement" of the State with the TSSAA, and that such entwinement converts private action into state action. The majority does not define "entwinement," and the meaning of the term is not altogether clear. But whatever this new "entwinement" theory may entail, it lacks any support in our state-action jurisprudence. *** [T]here is no case in which we have rested a finding of state action on entwinement alone.

Two of the cases on which the majority relies do not even use the word "entwinement." *** The majority's third example, *Evans v. Newton,* 382 U.S. 296 (1966), lends no more support to an "entwinement" theory ***. Although *Evans* at least uses the word "entwined," ("Conduct that is formally 'private' may become so entwined with governmental policies or so impregnated with a governmental character as to become subject to the constitutional limitations placed upon state action"), we did not discuss entwinement as a distinct concept, let alone one sufficient to transform a private entity into a state actor when traditional theories of state action do not. On the contrary, our analysis rested on the recognition that the subject of the dispute, a park, served a "public function," much like a fire department or a police department. A park, we noted, is a "public facility" that "serves the community." Even if the city severed all ties to the park and placed its operation in private hands, the park still would be "municipal in nature," analogous to other public facilities that have given rise to a finding of state action: the streets of a company town, the elective process, and the transit system. Because the park served public functions, the private trustees operating the park were considered to be state actors. ***

Because the majority never defines "entwinement," the scope of its holding is unclear. If we are fortunate, the majority's fact-specific analysis will have little bearing beyond this case. But if the majority's new entwinement test develops in future years, it could affect many organizations that foster activities, enforce rules, and sponsor extracurricular competition among high schools–not just in athletics, but in such diverse areas as agriculture, mathematics, music, marching bands, forensics, and cheerleading. Indeed, this entwinement test may extend to other organizations that are composed of, or controlled by, public officials or public entities, such as firefighters, policemen, teachers, cities, or counties. I am not prepared to say that any private organization that permits public entities and public officials to participate acts as the State in anything or everything it does, and our state-action jurisprudence has never reached that far. The state- action doctrine was developed to reach only those actions that are truly attributable to the State, not to subject private citizens to the control of federal courts hearing § 1983 actions. ***

Notes

1. **Leadership Organizations.** If a private entity produced many leaders in government, politics, and civic affairs, could its actions be deemed state action? In the First Amendment case of *Roberts v. United States Jaycees*, 468 U.S. 609 (1984), the Court was faced with the Jaycees' refusal to admit women to the organization as full-fledged members. Those challenging the practice couched their complaint in terms of statutory rights provided under the state law of Minnesota. The Jaycees countered that the application of the statute violated their First Amendment rights to Freedom of Association. Could the petitioner have claimed that the denial of membership constituted a violation of the Equal Protection Clause? Two of the *Roberts* justices (CHIEF JUSTICE BURGER and JUSTICE BLACKMUN) recused themselves from consideration of the case because of affiliation with the Jaycees.

2. **Unions.** Given the factors mentioned by the majority, would the actions of a union of governmental employees constitute state action? If such a union wanted to exclude or expel a member, would that individual be entitled to due process rights?

B. STATE INACTION

DESHANEY v. WINNEBAGO COUNTY DEPARTMENT OF SOCIAL SERVICES
489 U.S. 189, 109 S.Ct. 998, 103 L.Ed.2d 249 (1989).

CHIEF JUSTICE REHNQUIST delivered the opinion of the Court.

Petitioner is a boy who was beaten and permanently injured by his father, with whom he lived. Respondents are social workers and other local officials who received complaints that petitioner was being abused by his father and had reason to believe that this was the case, but nonetheless did not act to remove petitioner from his father's custody. Petitioner sued respondents claiming that their failure to act deprived him of his liberty in violation of the Due Process Clause of the Fourteenth Amendment to the United States Constitution. We hold that it did not.

The facts of this case are undeniably tragic. Petitioner Joshua DeShaney was born in 1979. In 1980, a Wyoming court granted his parents a divorce and awarded custody of Joshua to his father, Randy DeShaney. The father shortly thereafter moved to Neenah, a city located in Winnebago County,

Wisconsin, taking the infant Joshua with him. There he entered into a second marriage, which also ended in divorce.

The Winnebago County authorities first learned that Joshua DeShaney might be a victim of child abuse in January 1982, when his father's second wife complained to the police, at the time of their divorce, that he had previously "hit the boy causing marks and [was] a prime case for child abuse." The Winnebago County Department of Social Services (DSS) interviewed the father, but he denied the accusations, and DSS did not pursue them further. In January 1983, Joshua was admitted to a local hospital with multiple bruises and abrasions. The examining physician suspected child abuse and notified DSS, which immediately obtained an order from a Wisconsin juvenile court placing Joshua in the temporary custody of the hospital. Three days later, the county convened an ad hoc "Child Protection Team"—consisting of a pediatrician, a psychologist, a police detective, the county's lawyer, several DSS caseworkers, and various hospital personnel—to consider Joshua's situation. At this meeting, the Team decided that there was insufficient evidence of child abuse to retain Joshua in the custody of the court. The Team did, however, decide to recommend several measures to protect Joshua, including enrolling him in a preschool program, providing his father with certain counselling services, and encouraging his father's girlfriend to move out of the home. Randy DeShaney entered into a voluntary agreement with DSS in which he promised to cooperate with them in accomplishing these goals.

Based on the recommendation of the Child Protection Team, the juvenile court dismissed the child protection case and returned Joshua to the custody of his father. A month later, emergency room personnel called the DSS caseworker handling Joshua's case to report that he had once again been treated for suspicious injuries. The caseworker concluded that there was no basis for action. For the next six months, the caseworker made monthly visits to the DeShaney home, during which she observed a number of suspicious injuries on Joshua's head; she also noticed that he had not been enrolled in school, and that the girlfriend had not moved out. The caseworker dutifully recorded these incidents in her files, along with her continuing suspicions that someone in the DeShaney household was physically abusing Joshua, but she did nothing more. In November 1983, the emergency room notified DSS that Joshua had been treated once again for injuries that they believed to be caused by child abuse. On the caseworker's next two visits to the DeShaney home, she was told that Joshua was too ill to see her. Still DSS took no action.

In March 1984, Randy DeShaney beat 4–year-old Joshua so severely that he fell into a life-threatening coma. Emergency brain surgery revealed a series of hemorrhages caused by traumatic injuries to the head inflicted over a long period of time. Joshua did not die, but he suffered brain damage so severe that he is expected to spend the rest of his life confined to an institution for the profoundly retarded. Randy DeShaney was subsequently tried and convicted of child abuse.

Joshua and his mother brought this action under 42 U.S.C. § 1983 in the United States District Court for the Eastern District of Wisconsin against respondents Winnebago County, DSS, and various individual employees of DSS. The complaint alleged that respondents had deprived Joshua of his liberty without due process of law, in violation of his rights under the Fourteenth Amendment, by failing to intervene to protect him against a risk of violence at his father's hands of which they knew or should have known. The District Court granted summary judgment for respondents.

*** Petitioners contend that the State deprived Joshua of his liberty interest in "free[dom] from *** unjustified intrusions on personal security," by failing to provide him with adequate protection against his father's violence. The claim is one invoking the substantive rather than the procedural component of the Due Process Clause; petitioners do not claim that the State denied Joshua protection without according him appropriate procedural safeguards, but that it was categorically obligated to protect him in these circumstances.

But nothing in the language of the Due Process Clause itself requires the State to protect the life, liberty, and property of its citizens against invasion by private actors. The Clause is phrased as a limitation on the State's power to act, not as a guarantee of certain minimal levels of safety and security. It forbids the State itself to deprive individuals of life, liberty, or property without "due process of law," but its language cannot fairly be extended to impose an affirmative obligation on the State to ensure that those interests do not come to harm through other means. Nor does history support such an expansive reading of the constitutional text. ***

Consistent with these principles, our cases have recognized that the Due Process Clauses generally confer no affirmative right to governmental aid, even where such aid may be necessary to secure life, liberty, or property interests of which the government itself may not deprive the individual. *** As we said in *Harris v. McRae*[, 448 U.S. 297 (1980)]: "Although the liberty protected by the Due Process Clause affords protection against unwarranted *government* interference ***, it does not confer an entitlement to such [governmental aid] as may be necessary to realize all the advantages of that freedom." If the Due Process Clause does not require the State to provide its citizens with particular protective services, it follows that the State cannot be held liable under the Clause for injuries that could have been averted had it chosen to provide them. As a general matter, then, wc conclude that a State's failure to protect an individual against private violence simply does not constitute a violation of the Due Process Clause.

Petitioners contend, however, that even if the Due Process Clause imposes no affirmative obligation on the State to provide the general public with adequate protective services, such a duty may arise out of certain "special relationships" created or assumed by the State with respect to particular individuals. Petitioners argue that such a "special relationship" existed here because the State knew that Joshua faced a special danger of abuse at his father's hands, and specifically proclaimed, by word and by deed, its intention to protect him against that danger. Having actually undertaken to protect Joshua from this danger—which petitioners concede the State played no part in creating—the State acquired an affirmative "duty," enforceable through the Due Process Clause, to do so in a reasonably competent fashion. Its failure to discharge that duty, so the argument goes, was an abuse of governmental power that so "shocks the conscience" as to constitute a substantive due process violation.

We reject this argument. It is true that in certain limited circumstances the Constitution imposes upon the State affirmative duties of care and protection with respect to particular individuals. *** But these cases afford petitioners no help. Taken together, they stand only for the proposition that when the State takes a person into its custody and holds him there against his will, the Constitution imposes upon it a corresponding duty to assume some responsibility for his safety and general well-being. The rationale for this principle is simple enough: when the State by the affirmative exercise of its power so restrains an individual's liberty that it renders him unable to care for himself, and at the same time fails to provide for his basic human needs—e.g., food, clothing, shelter, medical care, and reasonable safety—it transgresses the substantive limits on state action set by the Eighth Amendment and the Due Process Clause. The affirmative duty to protect arises not from the State's knowledge of the individual's predicament or from its expressions of intent to help him, but from the limitation which it has imposed on his freedom to act on his own behalf. In the substantive due process analysis, it is the State's affirmative act of restraining the individual's freedom to act on his own behalf—through incarceration, institutionalization, or other similar restraint of personal liberty—which is the "deprivation of liberty" triggering the protections of the Due Process Clause, not its failure to act to protect his liberty interests against harms inflicted by other means. ***

It may well be that, by voluntarily undertaking to protect Joshua against a danger it concededly played no part in creating, the State acquired a duty under state tort law to provide him with adequate protection against that danger. *** But the claim here is based on the Due Process Clause of the Fourteenth Amendment, which, as we have said many times, does not transform every tort committed by a state actor into a constitutional violation. ***

Judges and lawyers, like other humans, are moved by natural sympathy in a case like this to find a way for Joshua and his mother to receive adequate compensation for the grievous harm inflicted upon them. But before yielding to that impulse, it is well to remember once again that the harm was inflicted not by the State of Wisconsin, but by Joshua's father. The most that can be said of the state functionaries in this case is that they stood by and did nothing when suspicious circumstances dictated a more active role for them. In defense of them it must also be said that had they moved too soon to take custody of the son away from the father, they would likely have been met with charges of improperly intruding into the parent-child relationship, charges based on the same Due Process Clause that forms the basis for the present charge of failure to provide adequate protection.

JUSTICE BRENNAN, with whom JUSTICE MARSHALL and JUSTICE BLACKMUN join, dissenting.

"The most that can be said of the state functionaries in this case," the Court today concludes, "is that they stood by and did nothing when suspicious circumstances dictated a more active role for them." Because I believe that this description of respondents' conduct tells only part of the story and that, accordingly, the Constitution itself "dictated a more active role" for respondents in the circumstances presented here, I cannot agree that respondents had no constitutional duty to help Joshua DeShaney.

It may well be, as the Court decides, that the Due Process Clause as construed by our prior cases creates no general right to basic governmental services. That, however, is not the question presented here ***. No one, in short, has asked the Court to proclaim that, as a general matter, the Constitution safeguards positive as well as negative liberties. *** In a constitutional setting that distinguishes sharply between action and inaction, one's characterization of the misconduct alleged *** may effectively decide the case. Thus, by leading off with a discussion (and rejection) of the idea that the Constitution imposes on the States an affirmative duty to take basic care of their citizens, the Court foreshadows—perhaps even preordains—its conclusion that no duty existed even on the specific facts before us. ***

The Court's baseline is the absence of positive rights in the Constitution and a concomitant suspicion of any claim that seems to depend on such rights. From this perspective, the DeShaneys' claim is first and foremost about inaction (the failure, here, of respondents to take steps to protect Joshua), and only tangentially about action (the establishment of a state program specifically designed to help children like Joshua). And from this perspective, holding these Wisconsin officials liable—where the only difference between this case and one involving a general claim to protective services is Wisconsin's establishment and operation of a program to protect children—would seem to punish an effort that we should seek to promote.

I would begin from the opposite direction. I would focus first on the action that Wisconsin *has* taken with respect to Joshua and children like him, rather than on the actions that the State failed to take. *** [T]o the Court, the only fact that seems to count as an "affirmative act of restraining the individual's freedom to act on his own behalf" is direct physical control. *** [However,] *I would recognize, as the Court apparently cannot, that "the State's knowledge of [an] individual's predicament [and] its expressions of intent to help him" can amount to a "limitation *** on his freedom to act on his own behalf" or to obtain help from others.* ***

Wisconsin has established a child-welfare system specifically designed to help children like Joshua. Wisconsin law places upon the local departments of social services such as respondent (DSS or Department) a duty to investigate reported instances of child abuse. *** Even when it is the sheriff's office or police department that receives a report of suspected child abuse, that report is referred to local social services departments for action; the only exception to this occurs when the reporter fears for the child's *immediate* safety. In this way, Wisconsin law invites—indeed, directs—citizens and other governmental entities to depend on local departments of social services such as respondent to protect children from abuse. ***

In these circumstances, a private citizen, or even a person working in a government agency other than DSS, would doubtless feel that her job was done as soon as she had reported her suspicions of child abuse to DSS. Through its child-welfare program, in other words, the State of Wisconsin has relieved ordinary citizens and governmental bodies other than the Department of any sense of obligation to do anything more than report their suspicions of child abuse to DSS. If DSS ignores or dismisses these suspicions, no one will step in to fill the gap. Wisconsin's child-protection program thus effectively confined Joshua DeShaney within the walls of Randy DeShaney's violent home until such time as DSS took action to remove him. Conceivably, then, children like Joshua are made worse off by the existence of this program when the persons and entities charged with carrying it out fail to do their jobs.

It simply belies reality, therefore, to contend that the State "stood by and did nothing" with respect to Joshua. Through its child-protection program, the State actively intervened in Joshua's life and, by virtue of this intervention, acquired ever more certain knowledge that Joshua was in grave danger. *** It will be meager comfort to Joshua and his mother to know that, if the State had "selectively den[ied] its protective services" to them because they were "disfavored minorities," their § 1983 suit might have stood on sturdier ground. Because of the posture of this case, we do not know why respondents did not take steps to protect Joshua; the Court, however, tells us that their reason is irrelevant so long as their inaction was not the product of invidious discrimination. Presumably, then, if respondents decided not to help Joshua because his name began with a "J," or because he was born in the spring, or because they did not care enough about him even to formulate an intent to discriminate against him based on an arbitrary reason, respondents would not be liable to the DeShaneys because they were not the ones who dealt the blows that destroyed Joshua's life. *** Today's opinion construes the Due Process Clause to permit a State to displace private sources of protection and then, at the critical moment, to shrug its shoulders and turn away from the harm that it has promised to try to prevent. Because I cannot agree that our Constitution is indifferent to such indifference, I respectfully dissent.

JUSTICE BLACKMUN, dissenting.

Today, the Court purports to be the dispassionate oracle of the law, unmoved by "natural sympathy." But, in this pretense, the Court itself retreats into a sterile formalism which prevents it from recognizing either the facts of the case before it or the legal norms that should apply to those facts. As JUSTICE BRENNAN demonstrates, the facts here involve not mere passivity, but active state intervention in the life of Joshua DeShaney—intervention that triggered a fundamental duty to aid the boy once the State learned of the severe danger to which he was exposed.

The Court fails to recognize this duty because it attempts to draw a sharp and rigid line between action and inaction. But such formalistic reasoning has no place in the interpretation of the broad and stirring Clauses of the Fourteenth Amendment. *** Like the antebellum judges who denied relief to fugitive slaves, the Court today claims that its decision, however harsh, is compelled by existing legal doctrine. On the contrary, the question presented by this case is an open one, and our Fourteenth Amendment precedents may be read more broadly or narrowly depending upon how one chooses to read them. Faced with the choice, I would adopt a "sympathetic" reading, one which comports with dictates of fundamental justice and recognizes that compassion need not be exiled from the province of judging.

Poor Joshua! Victim of repeated attacks by an irresponsible, bullying, cowardly, and intemperate father, and abandoned by respondents who placed him in a dangerous predicament and who knew or learned what was going on, and yet did essentially nothing except, as the Court revealingly observes, "dutifully recorded these incidents in [their] files." It is a sad commentary upon American life, and constitutional principles—so full of late of patriotic fervor and proud proclamations about "liberty and justice for all"—that this child, Joshua DeShaney, now is assigned to live out the remainder of his life profoundly retarded. Joshua and his mother, as petitioners here, deserve—but now are denied by this Court—the opportunity to have the facts of their case considered in the light of the constitutional protection that 42 U.S.C. § 1983 is meant to provide.

Notes

1. *DeShaney* Baseline for State Inaction. Is the difference between the majority and the dissent that the dissent assumes the State has a basic obligation to ensure citizen safety? Or is it more narrowly that, when the State establishes systems for dealing with violence on which the citizenry relies, it should be required to do its job with a minimum level of competence? Did the Department of Social Services act minimally competently? What would have been the likely upshot of *DeShaney* had the plaintiff prevailed?

2. A Thirteenth Amendment Approach to *DeShaney*? In *A Thirteenth Amendment Response to DeShaney*, 105 HARV. L. REV. 1359 (1992), Professors Amar and Widawsky suggest that the case should have been argued on the theory that Joshua had been subjected to "involuntary servitude," which they define as the "unconstrained power" of one person over another, so there is no meaningful consent to the exercise of that power. They argue that the Thirteenth Amendment prohibition applies to children, that it applies even in situations where the "master" is not seeking financial profit, and that "[u]nder the Thirteenth Amendment, a State has an obligation only in cases of slavery and involuntary servitude rather than in every case of interpersonal violence" to provide adequate assistance. Do you find this argument convincing? Would the Court likely find it so?

REVIEW PROBLEM

Plaintiff wants to sue a company and the state for copyright infringement under a federal law protecting copyright holders. The core of her factual allegation is that the company, with the knowledge and cooperation of state officials, under contract to and for the benefit of the state, used her copyrighted computer program without permission and without paying royalties. What problems you see with her suit? Consider, at a minimum (1) whether sovereign immunity would bar suing the state in federal or state court, and (2) whether the company can piggyback on that defense by arguing it should be considered a state actor.

Appendix A

THE ARTICLES OF CONFEDERATION

Agreed to by Congress November 15, 1777; ratified and in force, March 1, 1781.

Preamble

*** Whereas the Delegates of the United States of America in Congress assembled did *** agree to certain articles of Confederation and perpetual Union between the States of New Hampshire, Massachusetts bay, Rhode Island and Providence Plantations, Connecticut, New York, New Jersey, Pennsylvania, Delaware, Maryland, Virginia, North Carolina, South Carolina and Georgia ***.

Article I. The Style of this confederacy shall be "The United States of America."

Article II. Each state retains its sovereignty, freedom and independence, and every power, jurisdiction and right, which is not by this Confederation expressly delegated to the United States, in Congress assembled.

Article III. The said States hereby severally enter into a firm league of friendship with each other, for their common defence, the security of their liberties, and their mutual and general welfare, binding themselves to assist each other, against all force offered to, or attacks made upon them, or any of them, on account of religion, sovereignty, trade, or any other pretence whatever.

Article IV. The better to secure and perpetuate mutual friendship and intercourse among the people of the different States in this Union, the free inhabitants of each of these States, paupers, vagabonds and fugitives from justice excepted, shall be entitled to all privileges and immunities of free citizens in the several States; and the people of each state shall have free ingress and regress to and from any other State, and shall enjoy therein all the privileges of trade and commerce, subject to the same duties, impositions and restrictions as the inhabitants thereof respectively, provided that such restriction shall not extend so far as to prevent the removal of property imported into any state, to any other state of which the Owner is an inhabitant; provided also that no imposition, duties or restriction shall be laid by any state, on the property of the United States, or either of them.

If any person guilty of or charged with treason, felony, or other high misdemeanor in any state, shall flee from Justice, and be found in any of the United States, he shall upon demand of the governor or executive power of the state from which he fled, be delivered up and removed to the State having jurisdiction of his offence.

Full faith and credit shall be given in each of these States to the records, acts and judicial proceedings of the courts and magistrates of every other state.

Article V. For the more convenient management of the general interests of the United States, delegates shall be annually appointed in such manner as the legislature of each state shall direct, *** in every year, with a power reserved to each state, to recall its delegates, or any of them, at any time within the year ***. No state shall be represented in Congress by less than two, nor by more than seven Members; and no person shall be capable of being a delegate for more than three years in any term of six years; nor shall any person, being a delegate, be capable of holding any office under the United States, for which he, or another for his benefit receives any salary, fees or emolument of any kind. *** In determining questions in the United States, in Congress assembled, each State shall have one vote.

Freedom of speech and debate in Congress shall not be impeached or questioned in any Court, or place out of Congress, and the members of Congress shall be protected in their persons from arrests and imprisonments, during the time of their going to and from, and attendance on Congress, except for treason, felony, or breach of the peace.

Article VI. No state without the Consent of the United States in Congress assembled, shall send any embassy to, or receive any embassy from, or enter into any conference, agreement, or alliance or treaty with any king, prince or state; nor shall any person holding any office of profit or trust under the United States, or any of them, accept of any present, emolument, office or title of any kind whatever from any king, prince or foreign state; nor shall the United States in Congress assembled, or any of them, grant any title of nobility.

No two or more States shall enter into any treaty, confederation or alliance whatever between them, without the consent of the United States in Congress assembled, specifying accurately the purposes for which the same is to be entered into, and how long it shall continue.

No state shall lay any imposts or duties, which may interfere with any stipulations in treaties, entered into by the United States in Congress assembled, with any king, prince or state, in pursuance of any treaties already proposed by Congress, to the courts of France and Spain.

No vessels of war shall be kept up in time of peace by any State, except such number only, as shall be deemed necessary by the United States in Congress assembled, for the defence of such State or its trade; nor shall any body of forces be kept up by any State, in time of peace, except such number only, as in the judgment of the United States in Congress assembled, shall be deemed requisite to garrison the forts necessary for the defence of such State; but every State shall always keep up a well regulated and disciplined militia, sufficiently armed and accoutered, and shall provide and constantly have ready for use, in public stores, a due number of field pieces and tents, and a proper quantity of arms, ammunition and camp equipage.

No state shall engage in any war without the consent of the United States in Congress assembled, unless such state be actually invaded by enemies, or shall have received certain advice of a resolution being formed by some nation of Indians to invade such State, and the danger is so imminent as not to admit of a delay, till the United States in Congress assembled can be consulted: nor shall any state grant commissions to any ships or vessels of war, nor letters of marque or reprisal, except it be after a declaration of war by the United States in Congress assembled, and then only against the kingdom or State and the subjects thereof, against which war has been so declared, and under such regulations as shall be established by the United States in Congress assembled, unless such state be infested by pirates, in which case vessels of war may be fitted out for that occasion, and kept so long as the danger shall continue, or until the United States in Congress assembled shall determine otherwise.

Article VII. When land forces are raised by any state for the common defence, all officers of or under the rank of colonel, shall be appointed by the legislature of each state respectively by whom such forces shall be raised, or in such manner as such state shall direct, and all vacancies shall be filled up by the state which first made the appointment.

Article VIII. All charges of war, and all other expenses that shall be incurred for the common defence or general welfare, and allowed by the United States in Congress assembled, shall be defrayed out of a common treasury, which shall be supplied by the several States, in proportion to the value of all land within each state, granted to or surveyed for any person, as such land and the buildings and improvements thereon shall be estimated according to such mode as the United States in Congress assembled, shall from time to time direct and appoint. The taxes for paying that proportion shall be laid and levied by the authority and direction of the legislatures of the several States within the time agreed upon by the United States in Congress assembled.

Article IX. The United States in Congress assembled, shall have the sole and exclusive right and power of determining on peace and war, except in the cases mentioned in the sixth article-of sending and receiving ambassadors-entering into treaties and alliances, provided that no treaty of commerce shall be made whereby the legislative power of the respective States shall be restrained from imposing such imposts and duties on foreigners, as their own people are subjected to, or from prohibiting the exportation or importation of any species of goods or commodities whatsoever-of establishing rules for deciding in all cases, what captures on land or water shall be legal, and in what manner prizes taken by land or naval forces in the service of the United States shall be divided or appropriated-of granting letters of marque and reprisal in times of peace-appointing courts for the trial of piracies and felonies committed on the high seas and establishing courts for receiving and determining finally appeals in all cases of captures, provided that no member of Congress shall be appointed a judge of any of the said courts.

The United States in Congress assembled shall also be the last resort on appeal in all disputes and differences now subsisting or that hereafter may arise between two or more States concerning boundary, jurisdiction or any other cause whatever *** provided also that no State shall be deprived of territory for the benefit of the United States.

All controversies concerning the private right of soil claimed under different grants of two or more States, *** shall on the petition of either party to the Congress of the United States, be finally determined as near as may be in the same manner as is before prescribed for deciding disputes respecting territorial jurisdiction between different States.

The United States in Congress assembled shall also have the sole and exclusive right and power of regulating the alloy and value of coin struck by their own authority, or by that of the respective States-fixing the standard of weights and measures throughout the United States.-regulating the trade and managing all affairs with the Indians, not members of any of the States, provided that the legislative right of any state within its own limits be not infringed or violated-establishing and regulating post offices from one State to another, throughout all the United States, and exacting such postage on the papers passing through the same as may be requisite to defray the expenses of the said office-appointing all officers of the land forces, in the service of the United States, excepting regimental officers-appointing all the officers of the naval forces, and commissioning all officers whatever in the service of the United States-making rules for the government and regulation of the said land and naval forces, and directing their operations.

The United States in Congress assembled shall have authority to appoint a committee, to sit in the recess of Congress, to be denominated "A Committee of the States," and to consist of one delegate from each state; and to appoint such other committees and civil officers as may be necessary for managing the general affairs of the United States under their direction-to appoint one of their number to preside, provided that no person be allowed to serve in the office of president more than one year in any term of three years; to ascertain the necessary sums of Money to be raised for the service of the United States, and to appropriate and apply the same for defraying the public expenses-to borrow money, or emit bills on the credit of the United States, transmitting every half year to the respective States an account of the sums of money so borrowed or emitted,-to build and equip a navy-to agree upon the number of land forces, and to make requisitions from each state for its quota, in proportion to the number of white inhabitants in such state; ***.

The United States in Congress assembled shall never engage in a war, nor grant letters of marque and reprisal in time of peace, nor enter into any treaties or alliances, nor coin money, nor regulate the value thereof, nor ascertain the sums and expenses necessary for the defence and welfare of the United States, or any of them, nor emit bills, nor borrow money on the credit of the United States, nor appropriate money, nor agree upon the number of vessels of war, to be built or purchased, or the number of land or sea forces to be raised, nor appoint a commander-in-chief of the army or navy, unless nine States assent to the same: nor shall a question on any other point, except for adjourning from day to day be determined, unless by the votes of a majority of the United States in Congress assembled.

The Congress of the United States shall have power to adjourn to any time within the year, and to any place within the United States, so that no period of adjournment be for a longer duration than the space of six months, and shall publish the journal of their proceedings monthly, except such parts thereof relating to treaties, alliances or military operations as in their judgment require secrecy; and the yeas and nays of the delegates of each state on any question shall be entered on the journal, when it is desired by any delegate; and the delegates of a State, or any of them, at his or their request shall be furnished with a transcript of the said journal, except such parts as are above excepted, to lay before the legislatures of the several States.

Article X. The Committee of the States, or any nine of them, shall be authorized to execute, in the recess of Congress, such of the powers of Congress as the United States in Congress assembled, by the consent of nine States, shall from time to time think expedient to vest them with; provided that no power be delegated to the said Committee, for the exercise of which, by the Articles of Confederation, the voice of nine States in the Congress of the United States assembled is requisite.

Article XI. Canada acceding to this Confederation, and joining in the measures of the United States, shall be admitted into, and entitled to all the advantages of this Union: but no other colony shall be admitted into the same, unless such admission be agreed to by nine States.

Article XII. All bills of credit emitted, monies borrowed and debts contracted by, or under the authority of Congress, before the assembling of the United States, in pursuance of the present Confederation, shall be deemed and considered as a charge against the United States, for payment and satisfaction whereof the said United States, and the public faith are hereby solemnly pledged.

Article XIII. Every State shall abide by the determinations of the United States in Congress assembled, on all questions which by this Confederation are submitted to them. And the Articles of this Confederation shall be inviolably observed by every state, and the union shall be perpetual; nor shall any alteration at any time hereafter be made in any of them; unless such alteration be agreed to in a Congress of the United States, and be afterwards confirmed by the legislatures of every State.

And whereas it hath pleased the Great Governor of the World to incline the hearts of the legislatures we respectively represent in Congress, to approve of, and to authorize us to ratify the said Articles of Confederation and perpetual Union, KNOW YE that we the undersigned delegates, by virtue of the power and authority to us given for that purpose, do by these presents, in the name and in behalf of our respective constituents, fully and entirely ratify and confirm each and every of the said Articles of Confederation and perpetual Union, ***. And that the Articles thereof shall be inviolably observed by the States we respectively represent, and that the Union shall be perpetual. ***

Appendix B

JAMES MADISON'S SPEECH TO THE HOUSE OF REPRESENTATIVES PRESENTING THE PROPOSED BILL OF RIGHTS, JUNE 8, 1789

(from Gales & Seaton's HISTORY OF DEBATES IN CONGRESS, pp.448–459)

Mr. Madison.– [I move] that a select committee be appointed to consider and report such amendments as are proper for Congress to propose to the Legislatures of the several States, conformably to the fifth article of the constitution. *** Government by eleven of the thirteen United States, in some cases unanimously, in others by large majorities; *** the great mass of the people who opposed it, disliked it because it did not contain effectual provisions against the encroachments on particular rights, *** nor ought we to consider them safe, while a great number of our fellow-citizens think these securities necessary. *** The amendments which have occurred to me, proper to be recommended by Congress to the State Legislatures, are these:

First. That there be prefixed to the constitution a declaration, that all power is originally vested in, and consequently derived from, the people.

That Government is instituted and ought to be exercised for the benefit of the people; which consists in the enjoyment of life and liberty, with the right of acquiring and using property, and generally of pursuing and obtaining happiness and safety.

That the people have an indubitable, unalienable, and indefeasible right to reform or change their Government, whenever it be found adverse or inadequate to the purposes of its institution.

Secondly. That in article 1st, section 2, clause 3, these words be struck out, to wit: "The number of Representatives shall not exceed one for ever thirty thousand, but each State shall have at least one Representative, and until such enumeration shall be made," and that in place thereof inserted these words, to wit: "After the first actual enumeration, there shall be on Representative for every thirty thousand until the number amounts to _____, after which the proportion shall be so regulated by Congress, that the number shall never be less than, nor more than _____, but each State shall, after the first enumeration, have at least two Representatives; and prior thereto."

Thirdly. That in article 1st, section 6, clause 1, there be added to the end of the first sentence, these words, to wit: "But no law varying the compensation last ascertained shall operate before the next ensuing election of Representatives."

Fourthly. That in article 1st, section 9, between clauses 3 and 4, be inserted these clauses, to wit: The civil rights of none shall be abridged on account of religious belief or worship, nor shall any national religion be established, nor shall the full and equal rights of conscience be in any manner, or on any pretext, infringed.

The people shall not be deprived or abridged of their right to speak, to write, or to publish their sentiments; and the freedom of the press, as one of the great bulwarks of liberty, shall be inviolable.

The people shall not be restrained from peaceably assembling and consulting for their common good; nor from applying to the Legislature by petitions, or remonstrances, for redress of their grievances.

The right of the people to keep and bear arms shall not be infringed; a well armed and well regulated militia being the best security of a free country: but no person religiously scrupulous of bearing arms shall be compelled to render military service in person.

No soldier shall in time of peace be quartered in any house without the consent of the owner; nor at any time, but in a manner warranted by law.

No person shall be subject, except in cases of impeachment, to more than one punishment or one trial for the same offence; nor shall be compelled to be a witness against himself; nor be deprived of life, liberty, or property without due process of law; nor be obliged to relinquish his property, where it may be necessary for public use, without a just compensation.

Excessive bail shall not be required, nor excessive fines imposed, nor cruel and unusual punishments inflicted.

The rights of the people to be secured in their persons, their houses, their papers, and their other property, from all unreasonable searches and seizures, shall not be violated by warrants issued without probable cause, supported by oath or affirmation, or not particularly describing the places to be searched, or the persons or things to be seized.

In all criminal prosecutions, the accused shall enjoy the right to a speedy and public trial, to be informed of the cause and nature of the accusation, to be confronted with his accusers, and the witnesses against him; to have a compulsory process for obtaining witnesses in his favor; and to have the assistance of counsel for his defence.

The exceptions here or elsewhere in the constitution, made in favor of particular rights, shall not be so construed as to diminish the just importance of other rights retained by the people, or as to enlarge the powers delegated by the constitution; but either as actual limitations of such powers, or as inserted merely for greater caution.

Fifthly. That in article 1st, section 10, between clauses 1 and 2, be inserted this clause, to wit:

No State shall violate the equal rights of conscience, or the freedom of the press, or the trial by jury in criminal cases.

Sixthly. That, in article 3d, section 2, be annexed to the end of clause 2d, these words, to wit:

But no appeal to such court shall be allowed where the value in controversy shall not amount to _____ dollars; nor shall any fact triable by jury, according to the course of common law, be otherwise re-examinable than may consist with the principles of common law.

Seventhly. That in article 3d, section 2, the third clause be struck out, and in its place be inserted the clauses following, to wit:

The trial of all crimes (except in cases of impeachments, and cases arising in the land or naval forces, or the militia when on actual service, in time of war or public danger) shall be by an impartial jury of freeholders of vicinage, with the requisite of unanimity for conviction, of the right of challenge, and other accustomed requisites; and in all crimes punishable with loss of life or member, presentment or indictment by a grand jury shall be an essential preliminary, provided that in cases of crimes committed within any county which may be in possession of an enemy, or in which a general insurrection may prevail, the trial may by law be authorized in some other county of the same State, as near as may be to the seat of the offence.

In cases of crimes committed not within any county, the trial may by law be in such county as the laws shall have prescribed. In suits at common law, between man and man, the trial by jury, as one of the best securities to the rights of the people, ought to remain inviolate.

Eighthly. That immediately after article 6th, be inserted as article 7th, the clauses following, to wit:

The powers delegated by this constitution are appropriated to the departments to which they are respectively distributed: so that the legislative department shall never exercise powers vested in the executive or judicial, nor the executive exercise powers vested in the legislative or judicial, nor the judicial exercise the powers vested in the legislative or executive departments.

The powers not delegated by this constitution, nor prohibited by it to the States, are reserved to the States respectively.

Ninthly. That article 7th be numbered as article 8th. ***

The people of many States have thought it necessary to raise barriers against power in all forms and departments of Government, and I am inclined to believe, if once bills of rights are established in all the States as well as the federal constitution, we shall find, that, although some of them are rather unimportant, yet, upon the whole, they will have a salutary tendency. *** In some instances they assert those rights which are exercised by the people in forming and establishing a plan of Government. In other instances, they specify those rights which are retained when particular powers are given up to be exercised by the Legislature. In other instances, they specify positive rights, which may seem to result from the nature of the compact. *** In other instances, they lay down dogmatic maxims with respect to the construction of the government; declaring that the legislative, executive, and judicial branches shall be kept separate and distinct. Perhaps the best way of securing this in practice is to provide such checks as will prevent the encroachment of the one upon the other. *** But I confess that I do conceive, that in a Government modified like this of the United States, the great danger lies rather in the abuse of the community than in the Legislative body. The prescriptions in favor of liberty ought to be levelled against that quarter where the greatest danger lies, namely, that which possesses the highest prerogative of power. But this is not found in either the executive or legislative departments of Government, but in the body of the people, operating by the majority against the minority. ***

It has been said, that in the Federal Government they are unnecessary, because the powers are enumerated, and it follows, that all that are not granted are retained; that the constitution is a bill of powers, the great residuum being the rights of the people; and, therefore, a bill of rights cannot be so necessary as if the residuum was thrown into the hands of the Government. I admit that these arguments are not entirely without foundation; but they are not conclusive to the extent which has been supposed. It is true, the powers of the General Government are circumscribed, they are directed to particular objects; but even if Government keeps within these limits, it has certain discretionary powers with respect to the means, which may admit of abuse to a certain extent, in the same manner as the powers of the State Governments under their constitutions may to an indefinite extent; because in the constitution of the United States, there is a clause granting to Congress the power to make all laws which shall be necessary and proper for carrying into execution all the powers vest in the Government of the United States, or in any department or officer thereof; this enables them to fulfil every purpose for which the Government was established. Now, may not laws be considered necessary and proper by Congress, for it is for them to judge of the necessity and propriety to accomplish those special purposes which they may have in contemplation, which laws in themselves are neither necessary nor proper; as well as improper laws could be enacted by the State Legislatures, for fulfilling the more extended objects of those Governments? I will state an instance, which I think in point, that proves that this might be the case. The General Government has a right to pass all laws which shall be necessary to collect its revenue; the means for enforcing the collection are within the direction of the Legislature: may not general warrants be considered necessary for this purpose, as well as for some purposes which it was supposed at the framing of their constitutions the State Governments had in view? If there was reason for restraining the State Governments from exercising this power, there is like reason for restraining the Federal Government.

It may be said, indeed it has been said, that a bill of rights is not necessary, because the establishment of this Government has not repealed those declarations of rights which are added to the several State constitutions; that those rights of the people which had been established by the most solemn act, could not be annihilated by a subsequent act of that people, who meant and declared at the head of the instrument, that they ordained and established a new system, for the express purpose of securing to themselves and posterity the liberties they had gained by an arduous conflict.

I admit the force of this observation, but I do not look upon it to be conclusive. In the first place, it is too uncertain ground to leave this provision upon, if a provision is at all necessary to secure rights so important as many of those I have mentioned are conceived to be, by the public in general, as well as those in particular who opposed the adoption of this constitution. Besides, some States have no bills of rights, there are others provided with very defective ones, and there are others whose bills of rights are not only defective, but absolutely improper; instead of securing some in the full extent which republican principles would require, they limit them too much to agree with the common ideas of liberty.

It has been objected also against a bill of rights, that, by enumerating particular exceptions to the grant of power, it would disparage those rights which were not placed in that enumeration; and it might follow by implication, that those rights which were not singled out, were intended to be assigned into the hands of the General Government, and were consequently insecure. This is one of the most plausible arguments I have ever heard urged against the admission of a bill of rights into this system; but, I conceive, that it may be guarded against. I have attempted it, as gentlemen may see by turning to the last clause of the fourth resolution.

It has been said, that it is unnecessary to load the constitution with this provision, because it was not found effectual in the constitution of the particular States. It is true, there are a few particular States in which some of the most valuable articles have not, at one time or other, been violated; but it does not follow but they may have to a certain degree, a salutary effect against the abuse of power. If they are incorporated into the constitution, independent tribunals of justice will consider themselves in a peculiar manner the guardians of those rights; they will be in an impenetrable bulwark against every assumption of power in the Legislative or Executive; they will be naturally led to resist every encroachment upon rights expressly stipulated for the constitution by the declaration of rights. Besides this security, there is a great probability that such a declaration in the federal system would be enforced; because the State Legislatures will jealously and closely watch the operations of this Government, and be able to resist with more effect every assumption of power, than any other power on earth can do; and the greatest opponents to a Federal Government admit the State Legislatures to be sure guardians of the people's liberty. ***

I wish, also, in revising the constitution, we may throw into that section, which interdicts the abuse of certain powers in the State Legislatures, some other provisions of equal, if not greater importance than those already made. *** I should, therefore, wish to extend to extend this interdiction, and add, as I have stated in the 5th resolution, that no State shall violate the equal right of conscience, freedom of the press, or trial by jury in criminal cases; because it is proper that every Government should be disarmed of powers which trench upon those particular rights. ***

Appendix C

THE CONSTITUTION AND THE WAR ON TERRORISM

The War on Terrorism affords an excellent window into some central constitutional law issues. What powers does the President have in this war? What role do the courts have in cases raising civil liberties objections to government actions in the War on Terrorism? These materials shed light on the balancing of security and liberty in times of crisis.

A. PRESIDENTIAL POWER IN THE WAR ON TERRORISM

Shortly after the September 11, 2001 attacks on the World Trade Center and the Pentagon, President Bush said the United States was at war. Congress authorized the President to use military force to deal with the attackers; military force was then employed in Afghanistan to drive al Qaeda from its sanctuary, destroy its training camps, and capture its leaders. Other nations were enlisted to assist in tracking down terrorists, freezing their assets, and disrupting their plans.

Congress rather than the President has the power to "Declare War." If so, what was the legal effect of President Bush's announcement that the United States was "at war?" On September 18, 2001, Congress passed a Joint Resolution authorizing the President to use "all necessary and appropriate force against those nations, organizations, or persons he determines planned, authorized, committed, or aided the terrorist attacks" or "harbored such organizations or persons." Was this a declaration of war? If not, does the President have lesser powers than if Congress had declared war? Congress subsequently appropriated funds to conduct military actions in Afghanistan, to build a new detention facility at Guantanamo Bay, Cuba, and for other purposes.

Two months after the attacks, President Bush issued an executive order entitled "Detention, Treatment, and Trial of Certain Non-Citizens in the War Against Terrorism." To date there have been but no military tribunals or commissions. Do these detentions and possible trials fall within the scope of Congress' mandate to the President or the President's separate powers as Commander-in-Chief? President Bush's order, in pertinent part, appears below, followed by an edited version of the most relevant Supreme Court precedent concerning military tribunals and some supplemental questions concerning the constitutionality of such tribunals.

November 13, 2001
66 FR 57833

By the authority vested in me as President and as Commander in Chief of the Armed Forces of the United States by the Constitution and the laws of the United States of America *** it is hereby ordered as follows:

Section 1. Findings.

*** (e) To protect the United States and its citizens, and for the effective conduct of military operations and prevention of terrorist attacks, it is necessary for individuals subject to this order *** to be detained, and, when tried, to be tried for violations of the laws of war and other applicable laws by military tribunals. ***

Sec. 2. Definition and Policy.

(a) The term "individual subject to this order" shall mean any individual who is not a United States citizen ***

Sec. 3. Detention Authority of the Secretary of Defense.   Any individual subject to this order shall be

(a) detained at an appropriate location designated by the Secretary of Defense outside or within the United States; ***

Sec. 4. Authority of the Secretary of Defense Regarding Trials of Individuals Subject to this Order.

(a) Any individual subject to this order shall, when tried, be tried by military commission for any and all offenses triable by military commission ***

(c) [Such trials] shall at a minimum provide for-- ***

(2) a full and fair trial, with the military commission sitting as the triers of both fact and law;

(3) admission of such evidence as would *** have probative value to a reasonable person; ***

(6) conviction only upon the concurrence of two-thirds of the members of the commission ***

Sec. 7. Relationship to Other Law and Forums. ***

(b) With respect to any individual subject to this order—

(1) military tribunals shall have exclusive jurisdiction with respect to offenses by the individual; and

(2) the individual shall not be privileged to seek any remedy or maintain any proceeding, directly or indirectly, or to have any such remedy or proceeding sought on the individual's behalf, in (i) any court of the United States, or any State thereof, (ii) any court of any foreign nation, or (iii) any international tribunal.***

EX PARTE QUIRIN.
317 U.S. 1, 63 S.Ct. 2, 87 L.Ed. 3 (1942)

MR. CHIEF JUSTICE STONE delivered the opinion of the Court.

*** The question for decision is whether the detention of petitioners by respondent for trial by Military Commission, appointed by Order of the President of July 2, 1942, on charges preferred against them purporting to set out their violations of the law of war and of the Articles of War, is in conformity to the laws and Constitution of the United States. *** [W]e directed that petitioners' applications be set down for full oral argument at a special term of this Court, convened on July 29, 1942. *** On July 31, 1942, *** this Court *** denied petitioners' applications for leave to file petitions for habeas corpus. ***

All the petitioners were born in Germany; all have lived in the United States. All returned to Germany between 1933 and 1941. All except petitioner Haupt are admittedly citizens of the German Reich, with which the United States is at war. Haupt came to this country with his parents when he was five years old; it is contended that he became a citizen of the United States by virtue of the naturalization of his parents during his minority and that he has not since lost his citizenship. *** After the declaration of war between the United States and the German Reich, petitioners received training at a sabotage school near Berlin, Germany, where they were instructed in the use of explosives and in methods of secret writing. Thereafter petitioners, with a German citizen, Dasch, proceeded from Germany to a seaport in Occupied France, where petitioners *** boarded [two] German submarine[s] which proceeded across the Atlantic to Amagansett Beach on Long Island, New York [and Ponte Vedra Beach, Florida]. The[y landed on June 13 and June 17, 1942] in the hours of darkness *** carrying with them a supply of explosives, fuses and incendiary and timing devices. While landing they wore German Marine Infantry uniforms or parts of uniforms. Immediately after landing they buried their uniforms and the other articles mentioned and proceeded in civilian dress to New York City [and Jacksonville, Florida]. *** All were taken into custody in New York or Chicago by agents of the Federal Bureau of Investigation. ***

The President, as President and Commander in Chief of the Army and Navy, by Order of July 2, 1942, appointed a Military Commission and directed it to try petitioners for offenses against the law of war and the Articles of War, and prescribed regulations for the procedure on the trial and for review of the record of the trial and of any judgment or sentence of the Commission. On the same day, by Proclamation, the President declared that 'all persons who are subjects, citizens or residents of any nation at war with the United States or who give obedience to or act under the direction of any such nation, and who during time of war enter or attempt to enter the United States *** through coastal or boundary defenses, and are charged with committing or attempting or preparing to commit sabotage, espionage, hostile or warlike acts, or violations of the law of war, shall be subject to the law of war and to the jurisdiction of military tribunals'.

The Proclamation also stated in terms that all such persons were denied access to the courts.

Pursuant to direction of the Attorney General, the Federal Bureau of Investigation surrendered custody of petitioners to respondent, Provost Marshal of the Military District of Washington, who was directed by the Secretary of War to receive and keep them in custody, and who thereafter held petitioners for trial before the Commission.

On July 3, 1942, the Judge Advocate General's Department of the Army prepared and lodged with the Commission [charges alleging violation of the law of war, violation of Article 81 of the Articles of War (corresponding with or giving intelligence to, the enemy), violation of Article 82 (spying), and. conspiracy to commit these offenses]. The Commission met on July 8, 1942, and proceeded with the trial, which continued in progress while the causes were pending in this Court. On July 27th, *** all the evidence for the prosecution and the defense had been taken by the Commission and the case had been closed except for arguments of counsel. *** [T]the state and federal courts *** have been open and functioning normally. ***

Petitioners' main contention is that the President is without any statutory or constitutional authority to order the petitioners to be tried by military tribunal for offenses with which they are charged; that in consequence they are entitled to be tried in the civil courts with the safeguards, including trial by jury, which the Fifth and Sixth Amendments guarantee to all persons charged in such courts with criminal offenses [and that the President's Order conflicts with certain of the Articles of War]. The Government challenges each of these propositions *** [and] also insists that petitioners must be denied access to the courts, both because they are enemy aliens or have entered our territory as enemy belligerents, and because the President's Proclamation undertakes in terms to deny such access to the class of persons defined by the Proclamation, which aptly describes the character and conduct of petitioners. It is urged that if they are enemy aliens or if the Proclamation has force no court may afford the petitioners a hearing. But there is certainly nothing in the Proclamation to preclude access to the courts for determining its applicability to the particular case. And neither the Proclamation nor the fact that they are enemy aliens forecloses consideration by the courts of petitioners' contentions that the Constitution and laws of the United States constitutionally enacted forbid their trial by military commission. As announced in our per curiam opinion we have resolved those questions by our conclusion that the Commission has jurisdiction to try the charge preferred against petitioners. *** We pass at once to the consideration of the basis of the Commission's authority.

We are not here concerned with any question of the guilt or innocence of petitioners.[15] Constitutional safeguards for the protection of all who are

---

[15] As appears from the stipulation, a defense offered before the Military Commission was that petitioners had had no intention to obey the orders given them by the officer of the German High Command.

charged with offenses are not to be disregarded in order to inflict merited punishment on some who are guilty. But the detention and trial of petitioners--ordered by the President in the declared exercise of his powers as Commander in Chief of the Army in time of war and of grave public danger--are not to be set aside by the courts without the clear conviction that they are in conflict with the Constitution or laws of Congress constitutionally enacted.

Congress and the President, like the courts, possess no power not derived from the Constitution. But one of the objects of the Constitution, as declared by its preamble, is to 'provide for the common defence'. As a means to that end the Constitution gives to Congress [and the President various powers]. *** The Constitution thus invests the President as Commander in Chief with the power to wage war which Congress has declared, and to carry into effect all laws passed by Congress for the conduct of war and for the government and regulation of the Armed Forces, and all laws defining and punishing offences against the law of nations, including those which pertain to the conduct of war.

By the Articles of War, Congress has provided rules for the government of the Army. It has provided for the trial and punishment, by courts-martial, of violations of the Articles by members of the armed forces and by specified classes of persons associated or serving with the Army. But the Articles also recognize the 'military commission' appointed by military command as an appropriate tribunal for the trial and punishment of offenses against the law of war not ordinarily tried by court martial. Articles 38 and 46 authorize the President, with certain limitations, to prescribe the procedure for military commissions. Articles 81 and 82 authorize trial, either by court martial or military commission, of those charged with relieving, harboring or corresponding with the enemy and those charged with spying. And Article 15 declares that 'the provisions of these articles conferring jurisdiction upon courts-martial shall not be construed as depriving military commissions *** or other military tribunals of concurrent jurisdiction in respect of offenders or offenses that by statute or by the law of war may be triable by such military commissions *** or other military tribunals'. Article 2 includes among those persons subject to military law the personnel of our own military establishment. But this, as Article 12 provides, does not exclude from that class 'any other person who by the law of war is subject to trial by military tribunals' and who under Article 12 may be tried by court martial or under Article 15 by military commission.

Similarly the Espionage Act of 1917, which authorizes trial in the district courts of certain offenses that tend to interfere with the prosecution of war, provides that nothing contained in the act 'shall be deemed to limit the jurisdiction of the general courts-martial, military commissions, or naval courts-martial'.

From the very beginning of its history this Court has recognized and applied the law of war as including that part of the law of nations which prescribes, for the conduct of war, the status, rights and duties of enemy nations as well as of enemy individuals. By the Articles of War, and especially Article 15, Congress has explicitly provided, so far as it may constitutionally do so, that military tribunals shall have jurisdiction to try offenders or offenses against the law of war in appropriate cases. Congress, in addition to making rules for the government of our Armed Forces, has thus exercised its authority to define and punish offenses against the law of nations by sanctioning, within constitutional limitations, the jurisdiction of military commissions to try persons for offenses which, according to the rules and precepts of the law of nations, and more particularly the law of war, are cognizable by such tribunals. And the President, as Commander in Chief, by his Proclamation in time of war his invoked that law. By his Order creating the present Commission he has undertaken to exercise the authority conferred upon him by Congress, and also such authority as the Constitution itself gives the Commander in Chief, to direct the performance of those functions which may constitutionally be performed by the military arm of the nation in time of war.

An important incident to the conduct of war is the adoption of measures by the military command not only to repel and defeat the enemy, but to seize and subject to disciplinary measures those enemies who in their attempt to thwart or impede our military effort have violated the law of war. It is unnecessary for present purposes to determine to what extent the President as Commander in Chief has constitutional power to create military commissions without the support of Congressional legislation. For here Congress has authorized trial of offenses against the law of war before such commissions. We are concerned only with the question whether it is within the constitutional power of the national government to place petitioners upon trial before a military commission for the offenses with which they are charged. We must therefore first inquire whether any of the acts charged is an offense against the law of war cognizable before a military tribunal, and if so whether the Constitution prohibits the trial. We may assume that there are acts regarded in other countries, or by some writers on international law, as offenses against the law of war which would not be triable by military tribunal here, either because they are not recognized by our courts as violations of the law of war or because they are of that class of offenses constitutionally triable only by a jury. It was upon such grounds that the Court denied the right to proceed by military tribunal in Ex parte Milligan, supra. But as we shall show, these petitioners were charged with an offense against the law of war which the Constitution does not require to be tried by jury. ***

But petitioners insist that even if the offenses with which they are charged are offenses against the law of war, their trial is subject to the requirement of the Fifth Amendment that no person shall be held to answer for a capital or otherwise infamous crime unless on a presentment or indictment of a grand jury, and that such trials by Article III, § 2, and the Sixth Amendment must be by jury in a civil court. Before the Amendments, § 2 of Article III, the Judiciary Article, had provided: 'The Trial of all Crimes, except in Cases of Impeachment, shall be by Jury', and had directed that 'such Trial shall be held in the State where the said Crimes shall have been committed'.

Presentment by a grand jury and trial by a jury of the vicinage where the crime was committed were at the time of the adoption of the Constitution familiar parts of the machinery for criminal trials in the civil courts. But they were procedures unknown to military tribunals, which are not courts in the sense of the Judiciary Article, and which in the natural course of events are usually called upon to function under conditions precluding resort to such procedures. As this Court has often recognized, it was not the purpose or effect of § 2 of Article III, read in the light of the common law, to enlarge the then existing right to a jury trial. The object was to preserve unimpaired trial by jury in all those cases in which it had been recognized by the common law and in all cases of a like nature as they might arise in the future, but not to bring within the sweep of the guaranty those cases in which it was then well understood that a jury trial could not be demanded as of right.

The Fifth and Sixth Amendments, while guaranteeing the continuance of certain incidents of trial by jury which Article III, § 2 had left unmentioned, did not enlarge the right to jury trial as it had been established by that Article. Hence petty offenses triable at common law without a jury may be tried without a jury in the federal courts, notwithstanding Article III, § 2, and the Fifth and Sixth Amendments. ***

All these are instances of offenses committed against the United States, for which a penalty is imposed, but they are not deemed to be within Article III, § 2 or the provisions of the Fifth and Sixth Amendments relating to 'crimes' and 'criminal prosecutions'. In the light of this long- continued and consistent interpretation we must concluded that § 2 of Article III and the Fifth and Sixth Amendments cannot be taken to have extended the right to demand a jury to trials by military commission, or to have required that offenses against the law of war not triable by jury at common law be tried only in the civil courts.

The fact that 'cases arising in the land or naval forces' are excepted from the operation of the Amendments does not militate against this conclusion. Such cases are expressly excepted from the Fifth Amendment, and are deemed excepted by implication from the Sixth. It is argued that the exception, which excludes from the Amendment cases arising in the armed forces, has also by implication extended its guaranty to all other cases; that since petitioners, not being members of the Armed Forces of the United States, are not within the exception, the Amendment operates to give to them the right to a jury trial. But we think this argument misconceives both the scope of the Amendment and the purpose of the exception.

We may assume, without deciding, that a trial prosecuted before a military commission created by military authority is not one 'arising in the land *** forces', when the accused is not a member of or associated with those forces. But even so, the exception cannot be taken to affect those trials before military commissions which are neither within the exception nor within the provisions of Article III, § 2, whose guaranty the Amendments did not enlarge. No exception is necessary to exclude from the operation of these provisions cases never deemed to be within their terms. An express exception from Article III, § 2, and from the Fifth and Sixth Amendments, of trials of petty offenses and of criminal contempts has not been found necessary in order to preserve the traditional practice of trying those offenses without a jury. It is no more so in order to continue the practice of trying, before military tribunals without a jury, offenses committed by enemy belligerents against the law of war.

Section 2 of the Act of Congress of April 10, 1806, 2 Stat. 371, derived from the Resolution of the Continental Congress of August 21, 1776, imposed the death penalty on alien spies 'according to the law and usage of nations, by sentence of a general court martial'. This enactment must be regarded as a contemporary construction of both Article III, § 2, and the Amendments as not foreclosing trial by military tribunals, without a jury, of offenses against the law of war committed by enemies not in or associated with our Armed Forces. It is a construction of the Constitution which has been followed since the founding of our government, and is now continued in the 82nd Article of War. Such a construction is entitled to the greatest respect. It has not hitherto been challenged, and so far as we are advised it has never been suggested in the very extensive literature of the subject that an alien spy, in time of war, could not be tried by military tribunal without a jury. ***

The exception from the Amendments of 'cases arising in the land or naval forces' was not aimed at trials by military tribunals, without a jury, of such offenses against the law of war. Its objective was quite different--to authorize the trial by court martial of the members of our Armed Forces for all that class of crimes which under the Fifth and Sixth Amendments might otherwise have been deemed triable in the civil courts. The cases mentioned in the exception are not restricted to those involving offenses against the law of war alone, but extend to trial of all offenses, including crimes which were of the class traditionally triable by jury at common law. ***

We cannot say that Congress in preparing the Fifth and Sixth Amendments intended to extend trial by jury to the cases of alien or citizen offenders against the law of war otherwise triable by military commission, while withholding it from members of our own armed forces charged with infractions of the Articles of War punishable by death. It is equally inadmissible to construe the Amendments whose primary purpose was to continue unimpaired presentment by grand jury and trial by petit jury in all those cases in which they had been customary--as either abolishing all trials by military tribunals, save those of the personnel of our own armed forces, or what in effect comes to the same thing, as imposing on all such tribunals the necessity of proceeding against unlawful enemy belligerents only on presentment and trial by jury. We conclude that the Fifth and Sixth Amendments did not restrict whatever authority was conferred by the Constitution to try offenses against the law of war by military commission, and that petitioners, charged with such an offense not required to be tried by jury at common law, were lawfully placed on trial by the Commission without a jury. ***

We have no occasion now to define with meticulous care the ultimate boundaries of the jurisdiction of military tribunals to try persons according to the law of war. It is enough that petitioners here, upon the conceded facts, were plainly within those boundaries, and were held in good faith for trial by military commission, charged with being enemies who, with the purpose of destroying war materials and utilities, entered or after entry remained in our territory without uniform--an offense against the law of war. We hold only that those particular acts constitute an offense against the law of war which the Constitution authorizes to be tried by military commission. ***

MR. JUSTICE MURPHY took no part in the consideration or decision of these cases.

Notes

1. **Questioning *Quirin*.** The *Quirin* appeal was extraordinary. The Supreme Court heard argument two days after the military commission evidence was closed and before counsel's final arguments; the decision was issued two days later; the written opinion followed three months thereafter on October 29, 1942. Meanwhile, six of the defendants had been executed. Is anything wrong with this picture? *See* Louis Fisher, *Military Tribunals: The Quirin Precedent*, Congressional Research Service Report to Congress (March 26, 2002).

2. **Distinguishing *Milligan*.** *Quirin* distinguished a Civil War case, *Ex parte Milligan*, 71 U.S. 2 (1866), in which the Court had held that an Ohio civilian accused of aiding the enemy was found not subject to court-martial jurisdiction because he could have been tried in a civilian court. Was the Court correct to place no emphasis on the availability of civilian courts to try the *Quirin* defendants?

3. **Separation of Powers.** Does President Bush's order violate the separation of powers? Consider the relevance of the September 18, 2001 Joint Resolution (*see* App. C, p. 2) and 10 U.S.C. §821 (1994): "The provisions of this chapter conferring jurisdiction upon courts-martial do not deprive military commissions, provost courts, or other military tribunals of concurrent jurisdiction with respect to offenders or offenses that by statute or by the law of war may be tried by military commissions, provost courts, or other military tribunals." Is it constitutionally relevant that military tribunals have a substantial history in the United States?

4. **Citizens and Others.** Why does President Bush's order apply only to non-citizens? Could the President have made it applicable to citizens working on behalf of foreign-based terrorist organizations? Could an American citizen accused of terrorism be tried by a military commission <u>not</u> set up under the November 13, 2001 Executive Order? If so, what constitutional rights, if any, would such a citizen have? What is the relevance of 18 U.S.C. § 4001(a), which says "no citizen shall be imprisoned or otherwise detained except pursuant to an Act of Congress." Has there been such an Act of Congress? *Padilla v. Bush*, 233 F. Supp. 2d 564 (S.D.N.Y. 2002), accepted the President's declaration of a national emergency and the Joint Resolution as the "legal predicate" for the government's detention of an American citizen arrested at O'Hare airport. Do you agree?

5. **World War II and the War on Terrorism.** Would a person tried and convicted under President Bush's order be any differently situated from the *Quirin* petitioners? One distinction that might be made was that WWII was a declared war; another that the war on terrorism is not against a nation-state; yet another,

that this war has no probable conclusion. Do these distinctions make any difference? *Hamdi v. Rumsfeld*, 316 F. 3d 430 (4th Cir. 2003), a habeas case by an American citizen taken prisoner in Afghanistan held: "[N]either the absence of set-piece battles nor the intervals of calm between terrorist assaults suffice to nullify the war making authority entrusted to the executive and legislative branches. *** [T]he cessation of hostilities would seem no less a matter of political competence than the initiation of them." Do you agree?

6. **Equal Protection.** Below is a chart adapted from a New York Times article of June 23, 2002 (p. 16). What analytical framework would be appropriate to assess whether these individuals received "equal protection of the laws?"

	John Walker Lindh	Yasser Esam Hamdi	Jose Padilla	Zacarias Moussaqui	Richard C. Reid
American Citizen?*	Yes	Yes	Yes	No	No
Taken Into Custody	November 2001	November 2001	May 2002	August 2001	December 2001
Access To A Lawyer?	Yes	No	No	Yes	Yes
Charged With	Conspiracy to kill Americans, providing support to terrorists.	No charges. Detained in Afghanistan and held in Guantánamo Bay, Cuba.	No charges. Implicated in a plot to detonate a radioactive dirty bomb.	Conspiring with Osama bin Laden and al Qaeda in the Sept. 11 attacks.	Attempted murder and WMD use, for trying to detonate a shoe bomb on a plane.
Status	Pled guilty in federal court in Alexandria, Va.	Detained by the military in Norfolk, Va.	Detained by the military near Charleston, S.C.	Pre-trial proceedings in federal court in Alexandria, Va.	Pled guilty in federal court in Boston.

*Does taking up arms against the U.S. amount to a renunciation of U.S. citizenship? *See Schneiderman*, supra p. 10.

B. THE ROLE OF COURTS IN THE WAR ON TERRORISM

Three differences between law in war and in peace are summarized by CHIEF JUSTICE WILLIAM REHNQUIST in ALL THE LAWS BUT ONE: CIVIL LIBERTIES IN WARTIME (1998), at 224-225. First, "in time of war the government's authority to restrict civil liberty is greater than in peacetime." Second, wartime presidents may "act in ways that push their legal authority to the maximum, if not beyond." Third, the timing of judicial decisions about the exercise of wartime power is important: "If the decision is made after hostilities have ceased, it is more likely to favor civil liberty than if made while hostilities continue." In conclusion, CHIEF JUSTICE REHNQUIST states that "[i]t is neither desirable nor is it remotely likely that civil liberty will occupy as favored a position in wartime as it does in peacetime. *** The laws will thus not be silent in time of war, but they will speak with a somewhat different voice."

These observations, arguably supported by substantial case law (some of which appears in this book) does not answer some specific questions about the judiciary's role in the War on Terrorism. Can the President immunize military tribunals from judicial review, as § 7(b)(2) of President Bush's order purports to do? Does § 7(b)(2) preclude habeas corpus review concerning the legality of detention of an individual? Does it matter whether detention takes place inside or outside the United States, whether the detainee is charged with a crime or not, whether the detainee is a citizen or not? The following case casts some light on these issues.

JOHNSON v. EISENTRAGER.
339 U.S. 763, 70 S.Ct. 936, 94 L. Ed. 1255 (1950).

MR. JUSTICE JACKSON delivered the opinion of the Court.

*** Twenty-one German nationals petitioned *** for writs of habeas corpus. They alleged that, prior to May 8, 1945, they were in service of German armed forces in China. *** On May 8, 1945, the German High Command executed an act of unconditional surrender, expressly obligating all forces under German control at once to cease active hostilities. These prisoners have been convicted of violating laws of war, by engaging in, permitting or ordering continued military activity against the United States after surrender of Germany and before surrender of Japan. *** They, with six others who were acquitted, were taken into custody by the United States Army after the Japanese surrender and were tried and convicted by a Military Commission ***. The Commission sat in China, with express consent of the Chinese Government. The proceeding was conducted wholly under American auspices and involved no international participation. *** The prisoners were repatriated to Germany to serve their sentences. Their immediate custodian is Commandant of Landsberg Prison, an American Army officer. *** The petition prays an order that the prisoners be produced before the District Court, that it may inquire into their confinement and order them discharged from such offenses and confinement. It is claimed that their trial, conviction and imprisonment violate Articles I and III of the Constitution, and the Fifth Amendment thereto, and other provisions of the Constitution and laws of the United States and provisions of the Geneva Convention governing treatment of prisoners of war. ***

We are cited to no instance where a court, in this or any other country where the writ is known, has issued it on behalf of an alien enemy who, at no relevant time and in no stage of his captivity, has been within its territorial jurisdiction. Nothing in the text of the Constitution extends such a right, nor does anything in our statutes. Absence of support from legislative or juridical sources is implicit in the statement of the court below that 'The answers stem directly from fundamentals. They cannot be found by casual reference to statutes or cases.' The breadth of the court's premises and solution requires us to consider questions basic to alien enemy and kindred litigation which for some years have been beating upon our doors.

I

Modern American law has come a long way since the time when outbreak of war made every enemy national an outlaw, subject to both public and private slaughter, cruelty and plunder. But even by the most magnanimous view, our law does not abolish inherent distinctions recognized throughout the civilized world between citizens and aliens, nor between aliens of friendly and of enemy allegiance, nor between resident enemy aliens who have submitted themselves to our laws and nonresident enemy aliens who at all times have remained with, and adhered to, enemy governments.

With the citizen we are now little concerned, except to set his case apart as untouched by this decision and to take measure of the difference between his status and that of all categories of aliens. Citizenship as a head of jurisdiction and a ground of protection was old when Paul invoked it in his appeal to Caesar. The years have not destroyed nor diminished the importance of citizenship nor have they sapped the vitality of a citizen's claims upon his government for protection. If a person's claim to United States citizenship is denied by any official, Congress has directed our courts to entertain his action to declare him to be a citizen 'regardless of whether he is within the United States or abroad.' This Court long ago extended habeas corpus to one seeking admission to the country to assure fair hearing of his claims to citizenship, and has secured citizenship against forfeiture by involuntary formal acts. Because the Government's obligation of protection is correlative with the duty of loyal support inherent in the citizen's allegiance, Congress has directed the President to exert the full diplomatic and political power of the United States on behalf of any citizen, but of no other, in jeopardy abroad. When any citizen is deprived of his liberty by any foreign government, it is made the duty of the President to demand the reasons and, if the detention appears wrongful, to use means not amounting to acts of war to effectuate his release. It is neither sentimentality nor chauvinism to repeat that 'Citizenship is a high privilege.'

The alien, to whom the United States has been traditionally hospitable, has been accorded a generous and ascending scale of rights as he increases his identity with our society. Mere lawful presence in the country creates an implied assurance of safe conduct and gives him certain rights; they become more extensive and secure when he makes preliminary declaration of intention to become a citizen, and they expand to those of full citizenship upon naturalization. During his probationary residence, this Court has steadily enlarged his right against Executive deportation except upon full and fair hearing. And, at least since 1886, we have extended to the person and property of resident aliens important constitutional guaranties--such as the due process of law of the Fourteenth Amendment. *Yick Wo v. Hopkins*, 118 U.S. 356.

But, in extending constitutional protections beyond the citizenry, the

Court has been at pains to point out that it was the alien's presence within its territorial jurisdiction that gave the Judiciary power to act. In the pioneer case of *Yick Wo v. Hopkins*, the Court said of the Fourteenth Amendment, 'These provisions are universal in their application, to all persons within the territorial jurisdiction, without regard to any differences of race, of color, or of nationality; ***.' And in *The Japanese Immigrant Case*, the Court held its processes available to 'an alien who has entered the country, and has become subject in all respects to its jurisdiction, and a part of its population, although alleged to be illegally here.'

Since most cases involving aliens afford this ground of jurisdiction, and the civil and property rights of immigrants or transients of foreign nationality so nearly approach equivalence to those of citizens, courts in peace time have little occasion to inquire whether litigants before them are alien or citizen.

It is war that exposes the relative vulnerability of the alien's status. The security and protection enjoyed while the nation of his allegiance remains in amity with the United States are greatly impaired when his nation takes up arms against us. While his lot is far more humane and endurable than the experience of our citizens in some enemy lands, it is still not a happy one. But disabilities this country lays upon the alien who becomes also an enemy are imposed temporarily as an incident of war and not as an incident of alienage. Judge Cardozo commented concerning this distinction: 'Much of the obscurity which surrounds the rights of aliens has its origin in this confusion of diverse subjects.' *Techt v. Hughes*, 229 N.Y. 222, 237.

American doctrine as to effect of war upon the status of nationals of belligerents took permanent shape following our first foreign war. Chancellor Kent, after considering the leading authorities of his time, declared the law to be that '*** in war, the subjects of each country were enemies to each other, and bound to regard and treat each other as such.' If this was ever something of a fiction, it is one validated by the actualities of modern total warfare. Conscription, compulsory service and measures to mobilize every human and material resource and to utilize nationals--wherever they may be--in arms, intrigue and sabotage, attest the prophetic realism of what once may have seemed a doctrinaire and artificial principle. With confirmation of recent history, we may reiterate this Court's earlier teaching that in war 'every individual of the one nation must acknowledge every individual of the other nation as his own enemy--because the enemy of his country.' And this without regard to his individual sentiments or disposition. The alien enemy is bound by an allegiance which commits him to lose no opportunity to forward the cause of our enemy; hence the United States, assuming him to be faithful to his allegiance, regards him as part of the enemy resources. It therefore takes measures to disable him from commission of hostile acts imputed as his intention because they are a duty to his sovereign.

The United States does not invoke this enemy allegiance only for its own interest, but respects it also when to the enemy's advantage. In World War I our conscription act did not subject the alien enemy to compulsory military service. *** Thus the alien enemy status carries important immunities as well as disadvantages. The United States does not ask him to violate his allegiance or to commit treason toward his own country for the sake of ours. This also is the doctrine and the practice of other states comprising our Western Civilization.

The essential pattern for seasonable Executive constraint of enemy aliens, not on the basis of individual prepossessions for their native land but on the basis of political and legal relations to the enemy government, was laid down in the very earliest days of the Republic and has endured to this day. It was established by the Alien Enemy Act of 1798. And it is to be noted that, while the Alien and Sedition Acts of that year provoked a reaction which helped sweep the party of Mr. Jefferson into power in 1800, and though his party proceeded to undo what was regarded as the mischievous legislation of the Federalists, this enactment was never repealed.[6] Executive power over enemy aliens, undelayed and unhampered by litigation, has been deemed, throughout our history, essential to war-time security. This is in keeping with the practices of the most enlightened of nations and has resulted in treatment of alien enemies more considerate than that which has prevailed among any of our enemies and some of our allies. This statute was enacted or suffered to continue by men who helped found the Republic and formulate the Bill of Rights, and although it obviously denies enemy aliens the constitutional immunities of citizens, it seems not then to have been supposed that a nation's obligations to its foes could ever be put on a parity with those to its defenders.

The resident enemy alien is constitutionally subject to summary arrest, internment and deportation whenever a 'declared war' exists. Courts will entertain his plea for freedom from Executive custody only to ascertain the existence of a state of war and whether he is an alien enemy and so subject to the Alien Enemy Act. Once these jurisdictional elements have been determined, courts will not inquire into any other issue as to his internment.

The standing of the enemy alien to maintain any action in the courts of the United States has been often challenged and sometimes denied. *** [T]he nonresident enemy alien, especially one who has remained in the service of the enemy *** neither has comparable claims upon our institutions nor could his use of them fail to be helpful to the enemy. Our law on this subject first emerged about 1813 when the Supreme Court of the State of New York *** concluded the rule of the common law and the law of nations to

---

6 ' *** In 1798, the 5th Congress passed three acts in rapid succession. *** The first and last were the Alien and Sedition Acts, vigorously attacked in Congress and by the Virginia and Kentucky Resolutions as unconstitutional. But the members of Congress who vigorously fought the Alien Act saw no objection to the Alien Enemy Act. In fact, Albert Gallatin, who led that opposition, was emphatic in distinguishing between the two bills and in affirming the constitutional power of Congress over alien enemies as part of the power to declare war. *** It is certain that in the white light which beat about the subject in 1798, if there had been the slightest question in the minds of the authors of the Constitution or their contemporaries concerning the constitutionality of the Alien Enemy Act, it would have appeared. None did. The courts, in an unbroken line of cases *** have asserted or assumed the validity of the Act and based numerous decisions upon the assumption. The judicial view has been without dissent. ***

be that alien enemies resident in the country of the enemy could not maintain an action in its courts during the period of hostilities. ***

II

*** We are here confronted with a decision whose basic premise is that these prisoners are entitled, as a constitutional right, to sue in some court of the United States for a writ of habeas corpus. To support that assumption we must hold that a prisoner of our military authorities is constitutionally entitled to the writ, even though he (a) is an enemy alien; (b) has never been or resided in the United States; (c) was captured outside of our territory and there held in military custody as a prisoner of war; (d) was tried and convicted by a Military Commission sitting outside the United States; (e) for offenses against laws of war committed outside the United States; (f) and is at all times imprisoned outside the United States.

We have pointed out that the privilege of litigation has been extended to aliens, whether friendly or enemy, only because permitting their presence in the country implied protection. No such basis can be invoked here, for these prisoners at no relevant time were within any territory over which the United States is sovereign, and *** their offense, their capture, their trial and their punishment were all beyond the territorial jurisdiction of any court of the United States.

Another reason for a limited opening of our courts to resident aliens is that among them are many of friendly personal disposition to whom the status of enemy is only one imputed by law. But these prisoners were actual enemies, active in the hostile service of an enemy power. There is no fiction about their enmity. Yet the decision below confers upon them a right to use our courts, free even of the limitation we have imposed upon resident alien enemies, to whom we deny any use of our courts that would hamper our war effort or aid the enemy.

A basic consideration in habeas corpus practice is that the prisoner will be produced before the court. This is the crux of the statutory scheme established by the Congress; indeed, it is inherent in the very term 'habeas corpus.' And though production of the prisoner may be dispensed with where it appears on the face of the application that no cause for granting the writ exists, we have consistently adhered to and recognized the general rule. To grant the writ to these prisoners might mean that our army must transport them across the seas for hearing. This would require allocation of shipping space, guarding personnel, billeting and rations. It might also require transportation for whatever witnesses the prisoners desired to call as well as transportation for those necessary to defend legality of the sentence. The writ, since it is held to be a matter of right, would be equally available to enemies during active hostilities as in the present twilight between war and peace. Such trials would hamper the war effort and bring aid and comfort to the enemy. They would diminish the prestige of our commanders, not only with enemies but with wavering neutrals. It would be difficult to devise more effective fettering of a field commander than to allow the very enemies he is ordered to reduce to submission to call him to account in his own civil courts and divert his efforts and attention from the military offensive abroad to the legal defensive at home. Nor is it unlikely that the result of such enemy litigiousness would be a conflict between judicial and military opinion highly comforting to enemies of the United States.

Moreover, we could expect no reciprocity for placing the litigation weapon in unrestrained enemy hands. The right of judicial refuge from military action, which it is proposed to bestow on the enemy, can purchase no equivalent for benefit of our citizen soldiers. Except England, whose law appears to be in harmony with the views we have expressed, and other English-speaking peoples in whose practice nothing has been cited to the contrary, the writ of habeas corpus is generally unknown.

The prisoners rely, however, upon two decisions of this Court to get them over the threshold--*Ex parte Quirin*, 317 U.S. 1, and *In re Yamashita*, 327 U.S. 1. Reliance on the *Quirin* case is clearly mistaken. Those prisoners were in custody in the District of Columbia. One was, or claimed to be, a citizen. They were tried by a Military Commission sitting in the District of Columbia at a time when civil courts were open and functioning normally. *** None of the places where they were acting, arrested, tried or imprisoned were, it was contended, in a zone of active military operations, were not under martial law or any other military control, and no circumstances justified transferring them from civil to military jurisdiction. None of these grave grounds for challenging military jurisdiction can be urged in the case now before us.

Nor can the Court's decision in the *Yamashita* case aid the prisoners. This Court refused to receive Yamashita's petition for a writ of habeas corpus. For hearing and opinion, it was consolidated with another application for a writ of certiorari to review the refusal of habeas corpus by the Supreme Court of the Philippines over whose decisions the statute then gave this Court a right of review. By reason of our sovereignty at that time over these insular possessions, Yamashita stood much as did Quirin before American courts. Yamashita's offenses were committed on our territory, he was tried within the jurisdiction of our insular courts and he was imprisoned within territory of the United States. None of these heads of jurisdiction can be invoked by these prisoners.

Despite this, the doors of our courts have not been summarily closed upon these prisoners. Three courts have considered their application and have provided their counsel opportunity to advance every argument in their support and to show some reason in the petition why they should not be subject to the usual disabilities of non-resident enemy aliens. *** After hearing all contentions they have seen fit to advance and considering every contention we *** [conclude] that no right to the writ of habeas corpus appears.

III

The Court of Appeals dispensed with all requirement of territorial jurisdiction *** [and] gave our Constitution an extraterritorial application to embrace our enemies in arms. Right to the writ, it reasoned, is a subsidiary procedural right that follows from possession of substantive constitutional rights. These prisoners, it considered, are invested with a right of personal liberty by our Constitution and therefore must have the right to the remedial writ. ***

When we analyze the claim prisoners are asserting and the court below sustained, it amounts to a right not to be tried at all for an offense against our armed forces. If the Fifth Amendment protects them from military trial, the Sixth Amendment as clearly prohibits their trial by civil courts. The latter requires in all criminal prosecutions that 'the accused' be tried 'by an impartial jury of the State and district wherein the crime shall have been committed, which district shall have been previously ascertained by law.' And if the Fifth be held to embrace these prisoners because it uses the inclusive term 'no person,' the Sixth must, for it applies to all 'accused.' No suggestion is advanced by the court below or by prisoners of any constitutional method by which any violations of the laws of war endangering the United States forces could be reached or punished, if it were not by a Military Commission in the theatre where the offense was committed. ***

If [the Fifth] Amendment invests enemy aliens in unlawful hostile action against us with immunity from military trial, it puts them in a more protected position than our own soldiers. American citizens conscripted into the military service are thereby stripped of their Fifth Amendment rights and as members of the military establishment are subject to its discipline, including military trials for offenses against aliens or Americans. Can there be any doubt that our foes would also have been excepted, but for the assumption 'any person' would never be read to include those in arms against us? It would be a paradox indeed if what the Amendment denied to Americans it guaranteed to enemies. And, of course, it cannot be claimed that such shelter is due them as a matter of comity for any reciprocal rights conferred by enemy governments on American soldiers.

The decision below would extend coverage of our Constitution to nonresident alien enemies denied to resident alien enemies. The latter are entitled only to judicial hearing to determine what the petition of these prisoners admits: that they are really alien enemies. When that appears, those resident here may be deprived of liberty by Executive action without hearing. While this is preventive rather than punitive detention, no reason is apparent why an alien enemy charged with having committed a crime should have greater immunities from Executive action than one who it is only feared might at some future time commit a hostile act.

If the Fifth Amendment confers its rights on all the world except Americans engaged in defending it, the same must be true of the companion civil-rights Amendments, for none of them is limited by its express terms, territorially or as to persons. Such a construction would mean that during military occupation irreconcilable enemy elements, guerrilla fighters, and 'were-wolves' could require the American Judiciary to assure them freedoms of speech, press, and assembly as in the First Amendment, right to bear arms as in the Second, security against 'unreasonable' searches and seizures as in the Fourth, as well as rights to jury trial as in the Fifth and Sixth Amendments.

Such extraterritorial application of organic law would have been so significant an innovation in the practice of governments that, if intended or apprehended, it could scarcely have failed to excite contemporary comment. Not one word can be cited. No decision of this Court supports such a view. None of the learned commentators on our Constitution has ever hinted at it. The practice of every modern government is opposed to it.

We hold that the Constitution does not confer a right of personal security or an immunity from military trial and punishment upon an alien enemy engaged in the hostile service of a government at war with the United States.

IV

*** These prisoners do not assert, and could not, that anything in the Geneva Convention makes them immune from prosecution or punishment for war crimes.[14] *** We are unable to find that the petition alleges any fact showing lack of jurisdiction in the military authorities to accuse, try and condemn these prisoners or that they acted in excess of their lawful powers. ***

MR. JUSTICE BLACK, with whom MR. JUSTICE DOUGLAS and MR. JUSTICE BURTON concur, dissenting.

*** The contention that enemy alien belligerents have no standing whatever to contest conviction for war crimes by habeas corpus proceedings has twice been emphatically rejected by a unanimous Court. *** Since the Court expressly disavows conflict with the *Quirin* or *Yamashita* decisions, it must be relying not on the status of these petitioners as alien enemy belligerents but rather on the fact that they were captured, tried and imprisoned outside our territory. The Court cannot, and despite its rhetoric on the point does not, deny that if they were imprisoned in the United States our courts would clearly have jurisdiction to hear their habeas corpus complaints. Does a prisoner's right to test legality of a sentence then depend on where the Government chooses to imprison him?   Certainly the *Quirin* and *Yamashita* opinions lend no support to that conclusion, for in upholding jurisdiction they place no reliance whatever on territorial location. The Court is fashioning wholly indefensible doctrine if it permits the executive branch, by deciding where its prisoners will be tried and imprisoned, to deprive all federal courts of their power to protect against a federal executive's illegal incarcerations.

---

[14] We are not holding that these prisoners have no right which the military authorities are bound to respect. The United States, by the Geneva Convention of July 27, 1929, concluded with forty-six other countries, including the German Reich, an agreement upon the treatment to be accorded captives. These prisoners claim to be and are entitled to its protection. It is, however, the obvious scheme of the Agreement that responsibility for observance and enforcement of these rights is upon political and military authorities. Rights of alien enemies are vindicated under it only through protests and intervention of protecting powers as the rights of our citizens against foreign governments are vindicated only by Presidential intervention.

If the opinion thus means, and it apparently does, that these petitioners are deprived of the privilege of habeas corpus solely because they were convicted and imprisoned overseas, the Court is adopting a broad and dangerous principle. The range of that principle is underlined by the argument of the Government brief that habeas corpus is not even available for American citizens convicted and imprisoned in Germany by American military tribunals. While the Court wisely disclaims any such necessary effect for its holding, rejection of the Government's argument is certainly made difficult by the logic of today's opinion. Conceivably a majority may hereafter find citizenship a sufficient substitute for territorial jurisdiction and thus permit courts to protect Americans from illegal sentences. But the Court's opinion inescapably denies courts power to afford the least bit of protection for any alien who is subject to our occupation government abroad, even if he is neither enemy nor belligerent and even after peace is officially declared.

*** It would be fantastic to suggest that alien enemies could hail our military leaders into judicial tribunals to account for their day to day activities on the battlefront. Active fighting forces must be free to fight while hostilities are in progress. *** When a foreign enemy surrenders, the situation changes markedly. If our country decides to occupy conquered territory either temporarily or permanently, it assumes the problem of deciding how the subjugated people will be ruled, what laws will govern, who will promulgate them, and what governmental agency of ours will see that they are properly administered. This responsibility immediately raises questions concerning the extent to which our domestic laws, constitutional and statutory, are transplanted abroad. Probably no one would suggest, and certainly I would not, that this nation either must or should attempt to apply every constitutional provision of the Bill of Rights in controlling temporarily occupied countries. But that does not mean that the Constitution is wholly inapplicable in foreign territories that we occupy and govern.

The question here involves a far narrower issue. Springing from recognition that our government is composed of three separate and independent branches, it is whether the judiciary has power in habeas corpus proceedings to test the legality of criminal sentences imposed by the executive through military tribunals in a country which we have occupied for years. The extent of such a judicial test of legality under charges like these, as we have already held in the *Yamashita* case, is of most limited scope. We ask only whether the military tribunal was legally constituted and whether it had jurisdiction to impose punishment for the conduct charged. Such a limited habeas corpus review is the right of every citizen of the United States, civilian or soldier (unless the Court adopts the Government's argument that Americans imprisoned abroad have lost their right to habeas corpus). Any contention that a similarly limited use of habeas corpus for these prisoners would somehow give them a preferred position in the law cannot be taken seriously.

Though the scope of habeas corpus review of military tribunal sentences is narrow, I think it should not be denied to these petitioners and others like them. We control that part of Germany we occupy. These prisoners were convicted by our own military tribunals under our own Articles of War, years after hostilities had ceased. However illegal their sentences might be, they can expect no relief from German courts or any other branch of the German Government we permit to function. Only our own courts can inquire into the legality of their imprisonment. Perhaps, as some nations believe, there is merit in leaving the administration of criminal laws to executive and military agencies completely free from judicial scrutiny. Our Constitution has emphatically expressed a contrary policy. ***

Conquest by the United States, unlike conquest by many other nations, does not mean tyranny. For our people 'choose to maintain their greatness by justice rather than violence.' Our constitutional principles are such that their mandate of equal justice under law should be applied as well when we occupy lands across the sea as when our flag flew only over thirteen colonies. Our nation proclaims a belief in the dignity of human beings as such, no matter what their nationality or where they happen to live. Habeas corpus, as an instrument to protect against illegal imprisonment, is written into the Constitution. Its use by courts cannot in my judgment be constitutionally abridged by Executive or by Congress. I would hold that our courts can exercise it whenever any United States official illegally imprisons any person in any land we govern. Courts should not for any reason abdicate this, the loftiest power with which the Constitution has endowed them.

Notes

1. **Application of** *Johnson* **to Guantanamo Bay Detainees.** *Johnson v. Eisentrager* has been applied to deny habeas petitions filed by aliens held in the detention facility at the United States Naval Base at Guantanamo Bay, Cuba. In *Al Odah v. United States*, 472 F. 3d 1134 (D.C. Cir. 2003), the court said it was immaterial that the petitioners, had not been charged with any crime, that the U.S. military controls Guantanamo Bay, and that no court anywhere would have jurisdiction over their petitions. The perpetual lease of Guantanamo Bay recognizes "the ultimate sovereignty of the Republic of Cuba" over the base. A cert petition has been filed in *Al Odah*.   Should the Supreme Court grant the petition? Reverse the lower court?

2.   **International Law.** President Bush's order raises questions of the relevance of international law and treaties.   One of the Geneva Conventions prohibits interrogation of prisoners of war and establishes minimum standards for their treatment.   Does this mean that the Guantanamo Bay detainees cannot be interrogated?   The United States classifies captives in Guantanamo Bay as "unlawful combatants," a term used in *Quirin*. Does this characterization avoid the prohibition on interrogation?   Another Geneva Convention says that prisoners of war can be punished "only if the sentence has been pronounced by the same courts according to the same procedure as in the case of members of the armed forces of the Detaining Power." The military commission rules issued by Secretary of Defense Rumsfeld differ from the procedures for courts-martial under the Uniform Code for Military Justice. Does this violate international law? To what extent is international law part of the law of the United States?

Index

References are to Pages